Collins eas

Mandarin Chinese Dictionary

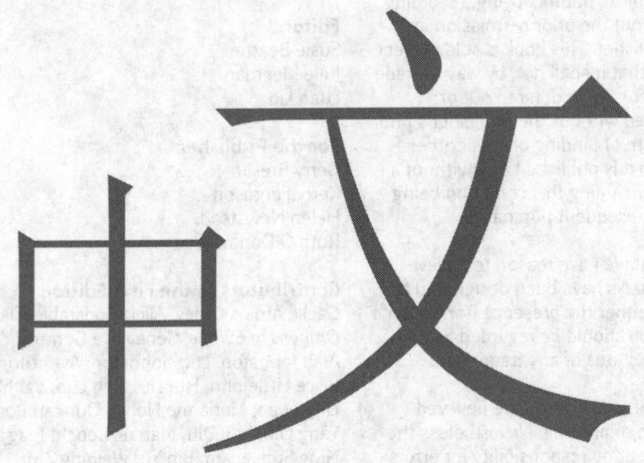

Published by Collins
An imprint of HarperCollins Publishers
Westerhill Road
Bishopbriggs
Glasgow G64 2QT

Second Edition 2015

10 9 8 7 6 5 4 3 2 1

ISBN 978-0-00-811951-5

Collins® is a registered trademark of HarperCollins Publishers Limited

www.collinsdictionary.com
www. collins.co.uk/languagesupport

Typeset by Davidson Publishing Solutions

Printed in Italy by GRAFICA VENETA S.p.A.

A catalogue record for this book is available from the British Library.

If you would like to comment on any aspect of this book, please contact us at the given address or online.
E-mail: dictionaries@harpercollins.co.uk
facebook.com/collinsdictionary
@collinsdict

Acknowledgements
We would like to thank those authors and publishers who kindly gave permission for copyright material to be used in the Collins Corpus. We would also like to thank Times Newspapers Ltd for providing valuable data.

Editors
Susie Beattie
Julie Kleeman
Luan Lin

For the Publisher
Gerry Breslin
Kerry Ferguson
Helen Newstead
Ruth O'Donovan

Contributors to the First Edition
Gaëlle Amiot-Cadey, Alicia Constable, Daphne Day, *Dragons in Europe*, Genevieve Gerrard, Yueshi Gu, Alan Johnston, Lucy Johnston, Aventurina King, Joyce Littlejohn, Hui Liu, Ting Luo, Val McNulty, Ling Miao, Marianne Noble, Duncan Poupard, Yang Qin, Jing Qiu, Marcus Reoch, Maggie Seaton, Ning Sun, Li Xin, Bin Yu, Weiqing Zhu

MIX
Paper from responsible sources
FSC C007454

FSC™ is a non-profit international organisation established to promote the responsible management of the world's forests. Products carrying the FSC label are independently certified to assure consumers that they come from forests that are managed to meet the social, economic and ecological needs of present and future generations, and other controlled sources.

Find out more about HarperCollins and the environment at
www.harpercollins.co.uk/green

Contents

Introduction

Collins Easy Learning Mandarin Chinese Dictionary is an innovative dictionary designed specifically for anyone starting to learn Chinese. We are grateful to everyone who has contributed to the development of the Easy Learning series, and acknowledge the help of the examining boards in providing us with word lists and exam papers, which we carefully studied when compiling this dictionary.

Free downloadable resources are now available for teachers and learners of Chinese at **www.collins.co.uk/languagesupport**.

Note on trademarks

Words which we have reason to believe constitute trademarks have been designated as such. However, neither the presence nor the absence of such designation should be regarded as affecting the legal status of any trademark.

Dictionary Skills

Using a dictionary is a skill you can improve with practice and by following some basic guidelines. This section gives you a detailed explanation of how to use this dictionary to ensure you get the most out of it.

Make sure you look on the right side of the dictionary

The Chinese-English side comes first: you look there to find the meaning of a Chinese word. The second part is English-Chinese. That's what you need for translating into Chinese. At the side of every page, you will see a tab with either **Chinese-English** or **English-Chinese**. The **Chinese-English** side has a blue tab, the **English-Chinese** side has a black tab, so you can see immediately if you've got the side you want.

Finding the word you want

Chinese-English side

- On the Chinese-English side words are ordered alphabetically by **Pinyin**. Pinyin is the Chinese phonetic alphabet. It was developed to help children learn to write characters, and foreigners and speakers of other Chinese dialects to pronounce Chinese correctly. It is also very useful for dictionaries, as it provides an alphabetical order by which characters can be organised. However, please be aware that Pinyin is not used much in China, and most Chinese people do not understand Pinyin as they would Chinese characters. In short, Pinyin shouldn't be regarded as a substitute for learning Chinese characters, but it is a good guide to pronunciation. (See also the section on Chinese pronunciation on pages 17–18.)

A single-character word will come first, followed by words with more than one character which begin with the same first character.

科 kē NOUN
discipline
■ 文科 wénkē humanities
科技 kējì NOUN
science and technology
科目 kēmù NOUN
subject
科学 kēxué NOUN
science
科学家 kēxuéjiā NOUN
scientist

Single-character entries are ordered by Pinyin, that is alphabetically, and then by tone. In Chinese there are four tones, each represented by a different mark above the relevant vowel. Some characters have a light tone, or no tone, and have no tone mark.

¯	first tone	(flat tone)	mā
´	second tone	(rising tone)	má
ˇ	third tone	(falling rising tone)	mǎ
`	fourth tone	(falling tone)	mà
	light or no tone		ma

Where characters have the same Pinyin and tone, they are ordered by the number of strokes in the character, with the smallest number of strokes first.

八 bā
巴 bā
芭 bā
疤 bā

For more help with strokes and stroke order see pages 13–16.

Similarly, words with more than one character which follow on from single-character words are ordered alphabetically by the Pinyin of the second character, including tone, and then by number of strokes.

蒸 zhēng VERB
1 to steam *(one way of cooking)*
2 to evaporate
蒸气 zhēngqì NOUN
vapour
蒸汽 zhēngqì NOUN
steam

If you want to look up the meaning of a Chinese character you are not familiar with and do not know the Pinyin for, you will need to use the **radical index** at the start of the Chinese-English side. Detailed guidance on using the index can be found in the introduction to that section on page 19.

At the top of each page you will find the Pinyin for the first and last single-character entries which appear on that page.

English-Chinese side

On the English-Chinese side words are ordered alphabetically. At the top of each page you will find the first and last words which appear on that page.

Make sure you look at the right entry

An entry is made up of a **word**, its translations and, often, example phrases to show you how to use the translations. If there is more than one entry for the same word, then there is a note to tell you so.

Look at the following example entries:

flat ADJECTIVE
▷ *see also* **flat** NOUN
1 平的 píng de
□ flat shoes 平底鞋 píngdǐ xié
2 气不足的 qì bùzú de *(tyre, ball)*
□ I've got a flat tyre. 我的轮胎没气了。 Wǒ de lúntāi méi qì le.
3 没电的 méidiàn de *(battery)*

flat NOUN
▷ *see also* **flat** ADJECTIVE
公寓 gōngyù [套 tào]
□ She lives in a flat. 她住在一套公寓里。 Tā zhù zài yítào gōngyù lǐ.

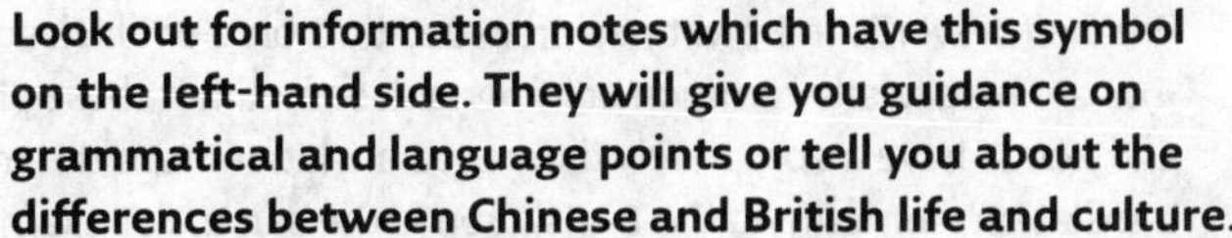

Look out for information notes which have this symbol on the left-hand side. They will give you guidance on grammatical and language points or tell you about the differences between Chinese and British life and culture.

Choosing the right translation

The main translation of a word is shown on a new line. If there is more than one translation for a word, each one is numbered. Pinyin is given for all translations on the English-Chinese side.

Often you will see phrases in light blue. These show you how the translation can be used. They also help you choose the translation you want depending on the context.

Words often have more than one meaning and more than one translation: if you don't *get* to the station on time, you don't arrive on time, but if you say 'I don't *get* it', you mean you don't understand. When you are translating from English, be careful to choose the Chinese word that has the particular meaning you want. The dictionary offers you a lot of help with this. Look at the following entry:

pool NOUN
1 水塘 shuǐtáng [个 gè] ***(pond)***
2 游泳池 yóuyǒngchí [个 gè] ***(swimming pool)***
3 美式台球 měishì táiqiú ***(game)***
□ Shall we have a game of pool? 我们玩台球吧？ Wǒmen wán táiqiú ba?

A **pool** can be a pond or a swimming pool; **pool** can also be a game. The numbers tell you that there is more than one possible translation and the words in brackets in *italics* after the translations help you choose the translation you want.

Never take the first translation you see without looking at the others.

Phrases or words in **bold type** preceded by a blue or black square ■/■ are particularly common or important. Sometimes these phrases and words have a completely different translation from the main translation; sometimes the translation is the same. For example:

指 zhǐ
I NOUN
finger
■中指 zhōngzhǐ middle finger
■无名指 wúmíngzhǐ ring finger

sponge NOUN
海绵 hǎimián
■ **a sponge bag** 一只盥洗用具袋 yìzhī guànxǐ yòngjùdài
■ **a sponge cake** 一块松糕 yíkuài sōnggāo

When you look up a word, make sure you look beyond the main translations to see if the entry includes any **bold phrases**.

Don't overuse the dictionary

It takes time to look up words so try to avoid using the dictionary unnecessarily, especially in exams. Think carefully about what you want to say and see if you can put it another way, using words you already know. To rephrase things you can:

> Use a word with a similar meaning. This is particularly easy with adjectives, as there are lots of words which mean *good*, *bad*, *big* etc and you're sure to know at least one.

> Use negatives: if the cake you made was a total disaster, you could just say it wasn't very good.

> Use particular examples instead of general terms. If you are asked to describe the sports facilities in your area, and time is short, don't look up *facilities* – say something like *'In our town there is a swimming pool and a football pitch.'*

Parts of Speech

If you look up the word **flat**, you will see that there are two entries for this word as it can be a noun or an adjective. Knowing how to recognize these different types of words helps you choose correctly between entries.

Nouns and pronouns

Nouns often appear with words like *a*, *the*, *this*, *that*, *my*, *you* and *his*. They can be either singular (abbreviated to SING in the dictionary):
*his **dog*** *her **cat*** *a **street***

or plural (abbreviated to PL in the dictionary):
*the **facts*** *these **people*** *his **shoes*** *our **holidays***

They can be the subject of a verb:
***Vegetables** are good for you.*

or the object of a verb:
*I play **tennis.***

Chinese nouns do not change according to number as they do in English. For example, in English an 's' is usually added to a noun to show that there is more than one. This is not the case in Chinese. For example, 'one girl' in Chinese would translate as 一个女孩 yī gè nǚhái, and 'two girls' would be 两个女孩 liǎng gè nǚhái; the noun doesn't change in the plural.

You will notice in the above example that a word (个 gè) is added after the number. This is a **measure word**.

On the English-Chinese side of the dictionary measure words are given in square brackets after translations of nouns which have a plural form, so there is a measure word at the translation for '*dog*' but not at the translation for '*money*'.

Measure words are not unique to Chinese as a concept – you occasionally see something similar in English:

*a **gaggle** of geese* *a **piece** of fruit* *six **pints** of milk*

They do not occur very often in English. In Chinese, however, measure words are vital. It is important to remember to put them in and also to get them right, as there are a lot of measure words in Chinese:

frog NOUN
青蛙 qīngwā [只 zhī] 一只青蛙 yī zhī qīngwā one frog

letter NOUN
1 信 xìn [封 fēng] 五封信 wǔ fēng xìn five letters

Different measure words are used for different types of things. 张 zhāng is used for flat things, such as tickets, sheets and tables. 条 tiáo is used to talk about long, thin things such as ribbons or fish. The most common measure word is 个 gè. It is a useful 'default setting' for when you cannot remember the exact measure word you need.

Chinese doesn't really have a word that corresponds to *the* or *a* so remember not to try and introduce one.

Words like *I*, *me*, *you*, *he*, *she*, *him*, *her* and *they* are pronouns. They can be used instead of nouns. You can refer to a person as *he* or *she*, and to a thing as *it*.

Adjectives

Flat can be an adjective as well as a noun. Adjectives describe nouns: your tyre can be **flat**, you can have a pair of **flat** shoes.

Chinese adjectives are often followed by 的 de when describing a noun, and this is how they appear as translations in this dictionary. 的 de is dropped in sentences where the adjective describes the subject.

ambitious ADJECTIVE
雄心勃勃的 xióngxīn bóbó de
□ She's very ambitious. 她雄心勃勃。 Tā xióngxīn bóbó.

Verbs

She's going to record the programme for me.
His time in the race was a new world record.

Record in the first sentence is a verb. In the second, it is a noun.

One way to recognize a verb is that it frequently comes with a pronoun such as **I**, **you** or **she**, or with somebody's name. Verbs can relate to the present, the past or the future. They have a number of different forms to show this: **I'm going** (present), **he will go** (future), and **Nicola went by herself** (past). Often verbs appear with **to**: **they promised to go**. This basic form of the verb is called the infinitive.

In this dictionary, on the English-Chinese side verbs are preceded by 'to', so you can identify them at a glance. No matter which of the four previous examples you want to translate, you should look up 'to **go**', not '**going**' or '**went**'. If you want to translate '**I thought**', look up 'to **think**'.

In Chinese the form of the verb doesn't change to indicate the present, future and past as it does in English. The verb itself stays as it is given in the dictionary. Instead certain words are placed before or after the verb to indicate when the action being described takes place. Some of the most common of these words are: 了 le (for completed actions, usually in the past), 过 guò (for events that have already taken place), 要 yào (for things that are going to happen) and 在 zài (for things that are in the process of happening). These are generalizations, however, and it is important not to use them indiscriminately as substitutes for English tenses.

Adverbs of time are also used to show how the times of events or actions relate to one another, such as 已经 yǐjīng (already), 曾经 céngjīng (once), or specific times or dates, eg:

明年我去中国。Míngnián wǒ qù Zhōngguó.
(literally: Next year I go China.) I'm going to China next year.

Adverbs

An adverb is a word that describes a verb or an adjective:

*Write **soon**.* *Check your work **carefully**.*
*They arrived **late**.* *The film was **very** good.*

In the sentence *'The pool is open daily'*, **daily** is an adverb describing the adjective **open**. In the phrase *'my daily routine'*, **daily** is an adjective describing the noun **routine**. We use the same word in English, but to get the right Chinese translation, it is important to know if it's being used as an adjective or an adverb. When you look up **daily** you find:

daily ADJECTIVE
▹ *see also* **daily** ADVERB
每日的 měirì de
□ It's part of my daily routine. 这是我每日事务的一部分。 Zhè shì wǒ měirì shìwù de yíbùfèn.

daily ADVERB
▹ *see also* **daily** ADJECTIVE
每天地 měitiān de
□ The pool is open daily. 这个泳池每天都开。 Zhège yǒngchí měitiān dōu kāi.

The examples show you **daily** being used as an adjective and as an adverb and will help you choose the right Chinese translation.

Prepositions

Prepositions are words like **for**, **with** and **across**, which are followed by nouns or pronouns:

*I've got a present **for** David.* *Come **with** me.* *He ran **across** the road.*

Writing Chinese

Basic strokes

Every Chinese character is made up of strokes and these are written in a set way. It is important to practise these as it will make writing any Chinese character easy and will help when looking up characters in the dictionary.

The table below shows the basic strokes and some strokes with hooks and turns.

Stroke	Direction	Examples
dot		六 主 文
horizontal		三 干 上
vertical		十 开 千
downward stroke to the left		人 为 发
downward stroke to the right		木 大 夫
rising stroke		拉 习 状
hooks		丁 买 找 心
turns		山 女 马 云

Stroke order

Each of the strokes in a Chinese character is written according to rules. These rules not only ensure that the characters look correct but also make them easier to learn. After a while writing characters will become second nature and you will write them correctly without having to think about stroke order.

The general rule for writing Chinese characters is to write **from top to bottom** and **from left to right**. This is simple with characters such as 三 sān (three) or 川 chuān (river) as shown below.

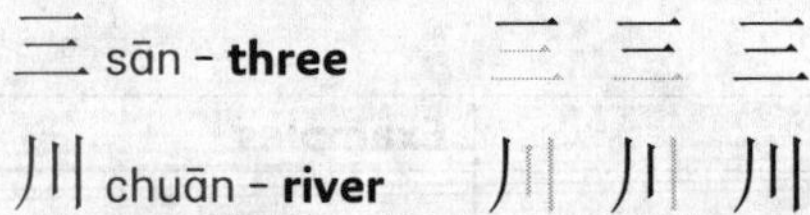

If there is more than one component to a character then each component should be completed by following the above rule.

For example the character 爸 bà (father) is made up of the top component 父 and the bottom component 巴. First of all you would write the whole of the top component 父 and then the bottom component 巴 as shown below.

爸 bà - **father**

Similarly the character 和 hé (and) is made up of the left component 禾 and the right component 口. Therefore, you would first write the whole of the left component 禾 and then write the component on the right 口.

和 hé - **and**

However, there are a number of exceptions to this rule and some of these are given below.

1 Horizontal strokes are written before vertical strokes.

十 shí - **ten**

千 qiān – **thousand**

2 Left falling strokes are written before right falling strokes.

人 rén – **person**

文 wén – **writing, language**

3 Left vertical strokes are written before top horizontal strokes.

口 kǒu – **mouth**

日 rì – **sun**

4 Bottom horizontal strokes are written last.

王 wāng – **king**

由 yóu – **cause, due to**

5 Centre strokes are written before outside strokes.

小 xiǎo – **small**

水 shuǐ – **water**

6 Crossing strokes are written last.

This can be a vertical crossing stroke as in:

中 zhōng – **centre**, **China**

or a horizontal stroke as in:

母 mǔ – **mother**

7 Minor strokes are written last.

玉 yù – **jade** 玉 玉 玉 玉 玉

发 fā – **to send** 发 发 发 发 发

8 Enclosing strokes are written before enclosed strokes.

同 tóng – **same** 同 同 同 同 同 同

月 yuè – **moon** 月 月 月 月

9 Bottom enclosing strokes are written after enclosed strokes.

这 zhè – **this** 这 这 这

凶 xiōng – **unlucky** 凶 凶 凶 凶

10 First inside, then outside and "close the door".

This refers to characters that have a box, i.e. they have strokes on all four sides. With such characters you must first write the strokes that make up three sides of the box, then fill in the contents of the box before finishing off the box with the lower horizontal stroke, or "closing the door" as it is referred to in Chinese.

国 gúo – **country** 国 国 国 国 国 国 国 国

园 yuān – **garden, park** 园 园 园 园 园 园 园

There are exceptions to these rules too so it is important to watch teachers and Chinese people closely in order to pick up the correct order for different characters. With lots of practice you can write beautiful Chinese characters too.

Chinese Pronunciation

Chinese characters often give an indication of the meaning of a word, or how to say it, but not in a reliable or consistent way. To make it easier to learn Chinese, a system of writing down the sounds was devised using the letters of the roman alphabet. This is the **Pinyin** system, which Chinese children learn along with their characters, and for which the foreign student is also very grateful.

You will notice accents over some of the letters in Pinyin. These are **tones**. There are four tones: **first tone** (high, even pitch); **second tone** (rising pitch); **third tone** (falling then rising) and **fourth tone** (falling pitch). In addition some sounds are toneless. There is no tone mark for a neutral tone.

¯	first tone	(flat tone)	mā
´	second tone	(rising tone)	má
ˇ	third tone	(falling rising tone)	mǎ
`	fourth tone	(falling tone)	mà
	light or no tone		ma

Tones are a very important part of the pronunciation. Wrong tones can cause real confusion. It may seem odd to native speakers of English to have pitch so rigidly attached to words, but the tone is as fundamental a part of any syllable as its vowels and consonants.

EXAMPLES OF DIFFERENCES IN TONES:

First tone	Second tone	Third tone	Fourth tone	Neutral tone
mā	má	mǎ	mà	ma
妈	麻	马	骂	吗
mother	hemp	horse	curse; swear	[question particle]

Some of the trickier sounds of Pinyin are listed below:

Pinyin	**Sound**	**(as in) English**
c	ts	ca**ts**
chi	chur	**char**
ci	tsur	whi**te surf**
e	er	th**ere**'s
ei	ay	m**ay**
ie	yeh	**ye**llow
iu	yo	**yo**yo
o	or	**or**
ou	oh	**oh**
q	ch	**ch**eat
ri	rur	**rur**al, child**re**n (this is not a rolled *r*)
shi	shur	**shir**t
si	sur	ab**sur**d
u	oo	s**oo**n
ü	u	like the French "r**u**e", or German "**ü**ber"
ui	way	**way**
uo	war	**war**
x	sh	who'**s she**
z	dz	be**ds**
zh	dj	**j**ar
zhi	jur	in**jur**y
zi	dzur	o**dds are**

After most letters such as **j**, **q**, **x** (common sources of confusion), **l**, **n**, **m** and most other consonants:

- **e** is pronounced "eh" (as in "yes")
- **i** is pronounced "eeee" (as in "peaches" or "green")
- **u** is pronounced "oo" like (as in "you"), *except* after **j**, **q** and **x**, when it is pronounced like the German **ü**

After the following common consonants or groups of consonants such as **zh**, **ch**, **sh**, **r**, **z**, **c**, **s**:

- **e** is pronounced "ur" (as in "shirt")
- **i** is barely pronounced at all, but the consonant is pronounced in a slightly more long-drawn-out way (think the **r** in "grrrrr")
- **u** is pronounced "oo" (as in "you")

Radical Index

There is no way of predicting the sound and meaning of an unknown Chinese character with any degree of accuracy. This does not mean, however, that there is no system behind the characters at all. All characters contain at least one of the component parts known as **radicals** or **head components**, 部首 bùshǒu, sometimes shortened to 部 bù, and almost all radicals will have an element of meaning. If you are familiar with these, not only will using a dictionary be much easier, it will also help you identify more of the building blocks you are trying to learn.

If you come across a character that you aren't familiar with, and so don't know the pronunciation of, you can look it up in the radical index, as follows:

1. Use the **Radical Index** on pages 19-20 to identify the radical according to the number of strokes. Note the number preceding it.
2. In the **Character Index** on pages 21-40, use this number to find all the characters appearing in this dictionary which contain that radical. Characters are ordered according to the number of strokes (not including the radical). The Pinyin given will lead you to the correct entry on the Chinese-English side of the dictionary.

1 stroke

1 一
2 丨
3 丿
4 丶
5 乙（乚乛）

2 strokes

6 二
7 十
8 厂
9 匚
10 刂
11 卜
12 冂
13 亻
14 八（丷）
15 人（入）
16 勹
17 几
18 儿
19 亠
20 冫
21 冖
22 讠
23 卩
24 阝 *(on the left)*
25 阝 *(on the right)*
26 凵
27 刀（⺈）
28 力
29 厶
30 又
31 廴

3 strokes

32 工
33 土
34 士
35 扌
36 艹
37 寸
38 廾 *(underneath)*
39 大
40 尢
41 小（⺌）
42 口
43 囗
44 巾
45 山
46 彳
47 彡
48 犭
49 夕
50 夂
51 饣
52 丬
53 广
54 忄
55 门
56 氵
57 宀
58 辶
59 彐（⺕）
60 尸
61 己（巳）
62 弓
63 子
64 女
65 纟
66 马
67 幺

4 strokes

68 王
69 韦
70 木（朩）
71 犬
72 歹
73 车
74 比
75 瓦
76 止
77 攴
78 日
79 曰
80 水
81 贝
82 见
83 牛
84 手
85 毛
86 气
87 攵
88 片
89 斤
90 爪（爫）
91 父
92 月
93 欠
94 风
95 文
96 方
97 火
98 斗
99 灬
100 户
101 礻
102 心
103 肀（聿）
104 戈

5 strokes

105 母
106 示
107 石
108 龙
109 业
110 目
111 田
112 罒
113 皿
114 钅
115 矢
116 禾
117 白
118 瓜
119 用
120 鸟
121 疒
122 立
123 穴
124 衤
125 疋
126 皮
127 矛

6 strokes

128 老 （耂）
129 耳
130 西 （覀）
131 页
132 虍
133 虫
134 缶
135 舌
136 竹 （⺮）
137 臼
138 自
139 血
140 舟
141 衣
142 羊 （⺶，⺷）
143 米
144 艮 （飠）
145 羽
146 糸

7 strokes

147 走
148 豆
149 酉
150 卤
151 里
152 足 （⻊）
153 身
154 采
155 豸
156 角
157 言
158 辛
159 谷

8 strokes

160 金
161 青
162 雨
163 隹
164 鱼

9 strokes

165 革
166 骨
167 鬼
168 食
169 音

10 strokes

170 髟

11 strokes

171 麻

12 strokes

172 黑

13 strokes

173 鼠

14 strokes

174 鼻

Character Index

1 一

一 yī

1 stroke

七 qī

2 strokes

三 sān
干 gān; gàn
于 yú
下 xià
丈 zhàng
与 yǔ
才 cái
万 wàn
上 shàng

3 strokes

丰 fēng
井 jǐng
开 kāi
夫 fū
天 tiān
无 wú
才 cái
专 zhuān
五 wǔ
不 bù
互 hù
牙 yá
丑 chǒu

4 strokes

末 mò
未 wèi
正 zhēng; zhèng
世 shì
可 kě
平 píng
东 dōng
册 cè
丝 sī

5 strokes

亚 yà
再 zài
百 bǎi
而 ér

6 strokes

严 yán
更 gēng; gèng
束 shù
两 liǎng
来 lái
求 qiú

7 strokes

表 biǎo
事 shì

8 strokes

甚 shèn
巷 xiàng
歪 wāi
面 miàn

9 strokes

哥 gē
恭 gōng

15 strokes

整 zhěng

2 丨

3 strokes

中 zhōng
内 nèi

4 strokes

卡 kǎ
北 běi
旧 jiù
申 shēn
由 yóu
出 chū

5 strokes

师 shī
曲 qǔ
肉 ròu

6 strokes

串 chuàn

7 strokes

非 fēi

8 strokes

临 lín

3 丿

1 stroke

九 jiǔ

2 strokes

川 chuān
及 jí
久 jiǔ

3 strokes

午 wǔ
长 cháng; zhǎng
币 bì
反 fǎn

4 strokes

生 shēng
失 shī
乐 lè; yuè

5 strokes

年 nián
丢 diū
乒 pīng
向 xiàng
后 hòu

6 strokes

我 wǒ
每 měi
龟 guī
系 jì; xì

7 strokes

乖 guāi
质 zhì
周 zhōu

8 strokes

拜 bài
重 chóng; zhòng
复 fù

9 strokes

乘 chéng

13 strokes

舞 wǔ
疑 yí

14 strokes

靠 kào

4 丶

2 strokes

义 yì
之 zhī

3 strokes

为 wèi

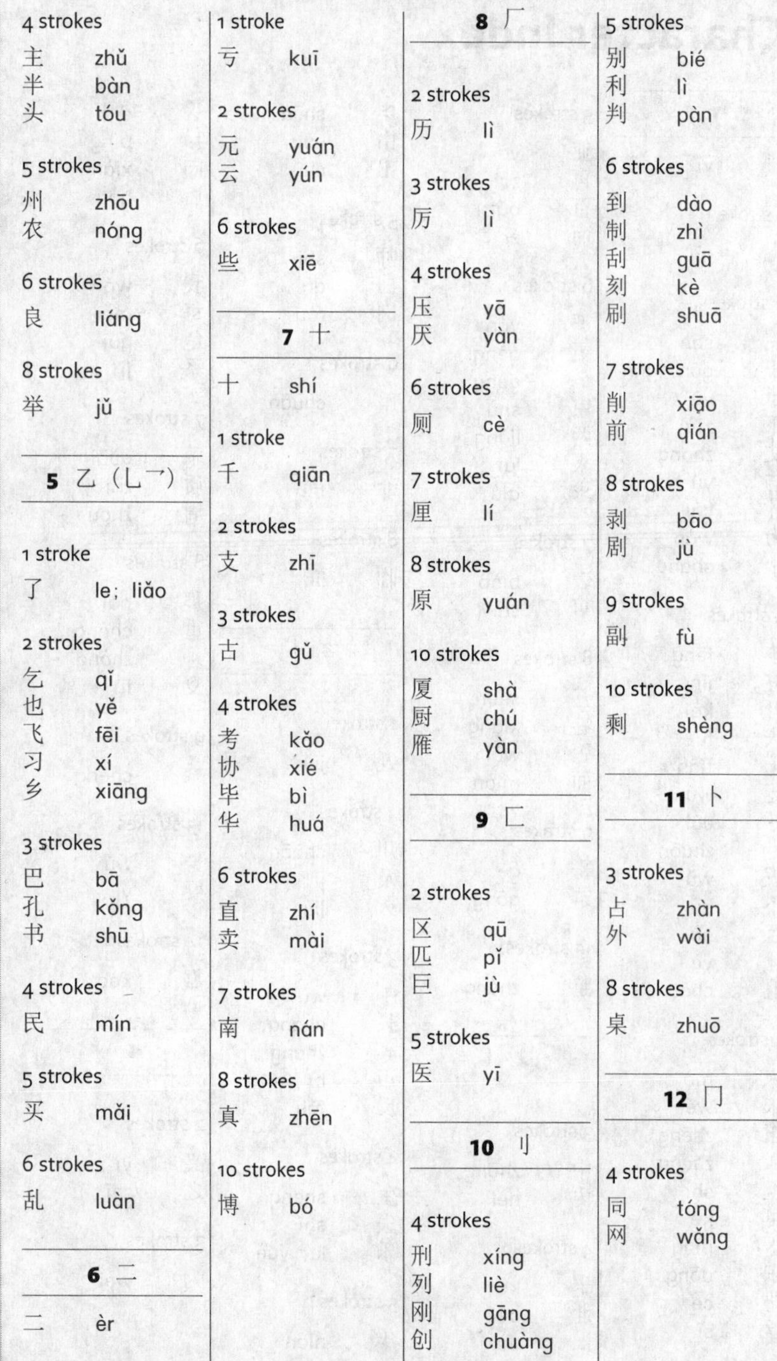

4 strokes

主 zhǔ
半 bàn
头 tóu

5 strokes

州 zhōu
农 nóng

6 strokes

良 liáng

8 strokes

举 jǔ

5 乙（乚乛）

1 stroke

了 le；liǎo

2 strokes

乞 qǐ
也 yě
飞 fēi
习 xí
乡 xiāng

3 strokes

巴 bā
孔 kǒng
书 shū

4 strokes

民 mín

5 strokes

买 mǎi

6 strokes

乱 luàn

6 二

二 èr

1 stroke

亏 kuī

2 strokes

元 yuán
云 yún

6 strokes

些 xiē

7 十

十 shí

1 stroke

千 qiān

2 strokes

支 zhī

3 strokes

古 gǔ

4 strokes

考 kǎo
协 xié
毕 bì
华 huá

6 strokes

直 zhí
卖 mài

7 strokes

南 nán

8 strokes

真 zhēn

10 strokes

博 bó

8 厂

2 strokes

历 lì

3 strokes

厉 lì

4 strokes

压 yā
厌 yàn

6 strokes

厕 cè

7 strokes

厘 lí

8 strokes

原 yuán

10 strokes

厦 shà
厨 chú
雁 yàn

9 匚

2 strokes

区 qū
匹 pǐ
巨 jù

5 strokes

医 yī

10 刂

4 strokes

刑 xíng
列 liè
刚 gāng
创 chuàng

5 strokes

别 bié
利 lì
判 pàn

6 strokes

到 dào
制 zhì
刮 guā
刻 kè
刷 shuā

7 strokes

削 xiāo
前 qián

8 strokes

剥 bāo
剧 jù

9 strokes

副 fù

10 strokes

剩 shèng

11 卜

3 strokes

占 zhàn
外 wài

8 strokes

桌 zhuō

12 冂

4 strokes

同 tóng
网 wǎng

13 亻

1 stroke

亿 yì

2 strokes

什 shén
仍 réng
仅 jǐn

3 strokes

代 dài
付 fù
仙 xiān
们 men
仪 yí
他 tā
仔 zǐ

4 strokes

伟 wěi
传 chuán
休 xiū
优 yōu
件 jiàn
任 rèn
伤 shāng
价 jià
伦 lún
份 fèn
仰 yǎng
仿 fǎng
伙 huǒ
伪 wěi

5 strokes

体 tǐ
但 dàn
伸 shēn
作 zuò
伯 bó
佣 yōng; yòng
低 dī
你 nǐ
住 zhù
位 wèi
伴 bàn
佛 fó

6 strokes

使 shǐ
佰 bǎi
例 lì
侄 zhí
侧 cè
依 yī

7 strokes

便 biàn; pián
俩 liǎ
修 xiū
保 bǎo
促 cù
俄 é
俗 sú
信 xìn
侵 qīn

8 strokes

候 hòu
借 jiè
值 zhí
倾 qīng
倒 dǎo; dào
倍 bèi
健 jiàn
俱 jù

9 strokes

做 zuò
偶 ǒu
偷 tōu
停 tíng
假 jiǎ; jià

10 strokes

傲 ào
傍 bàng

11 strokes

傻 shǎ
像 xiàng

14 八（丷）

八 bā

2 strokes

分 fēn; fèn
公 gōng

3 strokes

只 zhī; zhǐ

4 strokes

兴 xīng; xìng
共 gòng
并 bìng
关 guān

5 strokes

兵 bīng
弟 dì

6 strokes

其 qí
具 jù
典 diǎn
卷 juǎn
单 dān

7 strokes

养 yǎng
首 shǒu

8 strokes

益 yì

9 strokes

黄 huáng

10 strokes

普 pǔ
曾 céng; zēng

15 人（入）

人 rén
入 rù

1 stroke

个 gè

2 strokes

介 jiè
从 cóng
今 jīn
以 yǐ

3 strokes

令 lìng

4 strokes

全 quán
会 huì; kuài
合 hé
企 qǐ
伞 sǎn

5 strokes

余 yú
含 hán

6 strokes

舍 shè
命 mìng

8 strokes

拿 ná

9 strokes

盒 hé

10 strokes

舒 shū

16 勹

1 stroke

勺 sháo

2 strokes

勿 wù

匀 yún

3 strokes

句 jù
匆 cōng
包 bāo

9 strokes

够 gòu

---

17 几

几 jī; jǐ

---

18 儿

儿 ér

2 strokes

允 yǔn

3 strokes

兄 xiōng

4 strokes

光 guāng
先 xiān

---

19 亠

---

1 stroke

亡 wáng

2 strokes

六 liù

3 strokes

市 shì

4 strokes

交 jiāo
产 chǎn
充 chōng

6 strokes

变 biàn
京 jīng
享 xiǎng
夜 yè

7 strokes

哀 āi
亮 liàng

8 strokes

高 gāo
离 lí
旁 páng

9 strokes

商 shāng

10 strokes

就 jiù

15 strokes

赢 yíng

---

20 冫

---

4 strokes

冲 chōng
次 cì
决 jué
冰 bīng

5 strokes

冷 lěng

8 strokes

准 zhǔn
凉 liáng; liàng

9 strokes

凑 còu
减 jiǎn

10 strokes

寒 hán

---

21 冖

---

3 strokes

写 xiě

4 strokes

军 jūn

7 strokes

冠 guàn

---

22 讠

---

2 strokes

计 jì
订 dìng
认 rèn

3 strokes

讨 tǎo
让 ràng
训 xùn
议 yì
记 jì

4 strokes

讲 jiǎng
许 xǔ
论 lùn
设 shè
访 fǎng

5 strokes

证 zhèng
评 píng
译 yì
词 cí
识 shí

6 strokes

试 shì
诗 shī
诚 chéng
话 huà
询 xún
该 gāi
详 xiáng

7 strokes

语 yǔ
误 wù
诱 yòu
说 shuō

8 strokes

谁 shéi; shuí
请 qǐng
读 dú
课 kè
调 diào
谈 tán
谊 yì

9 strokes

谋 móu
谎 huǎng
谚 yàn
谜 mí

10 strokes

谢 xiè
谣 yáo
谦 qiān

---

23 卩

---

1 stroke

卫 wèi

3 strokes

印 yìn

5 strokes

却 què
即 jí

7 strokes

卸　xiè

24 阝 *(on the left)*

2 strokes

队　duì

4 strokes

阳　yáng
阶　jiē
阴　yīn
防　fáng

5 strokes

陆　liù；lù
阿　ā
阻　zǔ
附　fù

6 strokes

陌　mò
降　jiàng
限　xiàn

7 strokes

除　chú
险　xiǎn
院　yuàn

8 strokes

陷　xiàn
陪　péi

9 strokes

随　suí
隐　yǐn

11 strokes

障　zhàng

12 strokes

隧　suì

25 阝 *(on the right)*

4 strokes

邪　xié
那　nà

5 strokes

邮　yóu
邻　lín

6 strokes

耶　yē
郁　yù
郊　jiāo

8 strokes

都　dōu；dū
部　bù

26 凵

2 strokes

凶　xiōng

6 strokes

画　huà

7 strokes

幽　yōu

27 刀（⺈）

刀　dāo

2 strokes

切　qiē

3 strokes

召　zhào

4 strokes

危　wēi
负　fù
争　zhēng
色　sè

5 strokes

免　miǎn

6 strokes

兔　tù

9 strokes

象　xiàng

28 力

力　lì

2 strokes

办　bàn

3 strokes

功　gōng
务　wù
加　jiā

4 strokes

动　dòng
劣　liè

5 strokes

劳　láo
助　zhù
男　nán
努　nǔ

7 strokes

勉　miǎn
勇　yǒng

11 strokes

勤　qín

29 厶

3 strokes

去　qù
台　tái

5 strokes

县　xiàn

6 strokes

参　cān

8 strokes

能　néng

30 又

又　yòu

1 stroke

叉　chā

2 strokes

友　yǒu
劝　quàn
双　shuāng

3 strokes

发　fā；fà
圣　shèng
对　duì

4 strokes

戏　xì
观　guān
欢　huān

6 strokes

取　qǔ
叔　shū
受　shòu

7 strokes

叙　xù

8 strokes

难　nán

31 廴

4 strokes
延 yán

6 strokes
建 jiàn

32 工

工 gōng

2 strokes
巧 qiǎo
左 zuǒ

3 strokes
式 shì

4 strokes
攻 gōng

6 strokes
项 xiàng
差 chā；chà

33 土

土 tǔ

3 strokes
寺 sì
地 de；dì
场 chǎng
在 zài
至 zhì

4 strokes
坏 huài
坟 fén
块 kuài
坚 jiān
坐 zuò

5 strokes
垃 lā
幸 xìng

6 strokes
型 xíng
城 chéng

7 strokes
埋 mái；mán

8 strokes
域 yù
培 péi
基 jī
堂 táng

9 strokes
塔 tǎ

10 strokes
填 tián
塑 sù

11 strokes
墙 qiáng

12 strokes
增 zēng
墨 mò

34 士

4 strokes
声 shēng

9 strokes
喜 xǐ

10 strokes
鼓 gǔ

35 扌

2 strokes
打 dǎ
扑 pū
扔 rēng

3 strokes
扣 kòu
执 zhí
扩 kuò
扫 sǎo

4 strokes
扶 fú
技 jì
扰 rǎo
拒 jù
找 zhǎo
批 pī
抄 chāo
折 shé；zhé
抓 zhuā
抢 qiǎng
抑 yì
护 hù
把 bǎ
报 bào
扮 bàn
抛 pāo

5 strokes
拔 bá
担 dān
押 yā
抽 chōu
拐 guǎi
拖 tuō
拍 pāi
拎 līn
拥 yōng
抱 bào
拉 lā
拦 lán
拌 bàn
招 zhāo
拨 bō
抬 tái
拇 mǔ

6 strokes
挂 guà
拾 shí
挑 tiāo
指 zhǐ
挣 zhèng
拼 pīn
挖 wā
按 àn
挥 huī
挪 nuó

7 strokes
捞 lāo
捕 bǔ
振 zhèn
捉 zhuō
捌 bā
捡 jiǎn
换 huàn
挽 wǎn
挨 āi；ái

8 strokes
描 miáo
排 pái
掉 diào
推 tuī
掀 xiān
接 jiē
据 jù

9 strokes
提 tí
搭 dā
插 chā
援 yuán
搂 lǒu
握 wò

10 strokes
摆 bǎi
携 xié
搬 bān
摇 yáo

11 strokes
摘 zhāi
摔 shuāi

12 strokes
撒 sā
播 bō
撞 zhuàng

13 strokes
操 cāo
擅 shàn

36 艹

1 stroke
艺 yì

2 strokes
艾 ài
节 jié

3 strokes
芝 zhī

4 strokes
花 huā
芭 bā
苏 sū

5 strokes
茉 mò
苦 kǔ
茂 mào
苹 píng
苗 miáo
英 yīng
范 fàn
茄 qié

6 strokes
草 cǎo
茶 chá
荣 róng
荫 yìn
荔 lì
药 yào

7 strokes
莲 lián
获 huò

8 strokes
著 zhù
萝 luó
菜 cài
菠 bō
萤 yíng
营 yíng

9 strokes
葡 pú
落 là; luò
葬 zàng

10 strokes
蒜 suàn
蓝 lán
蒙 měng
蒸 zhēng

12 strokes
蔬 shū

13 strokes
薯 shǔ
薪 xīn
薄 báo

16 strokes
蘑 mó

37 寸

3 strokes
寻 xún
导 dǎo

6 strokes
封 fēng
耐 nài

9 strokes
尊 zūn

38 廾 *(underneath)*

3 strokes
异 yì

39 大

大 dà; dài

1 stroke
太 tài

3 strokes
夸 kuā
夺 duó
尖 jiān

5 strokes
奇 qí
奋 fèn

6 strokes
牵 qiān
美 měi
奖 jiǎng

7 strokes
套 tào

9 strokes
奥 ào

40 尢

1 stroke
尤 yóu

2 strokes
龙 lóng

41 小（⺌）

小 xiǎo

1 stroke
少 shǎo; shào

3 strokes
当 dāng; dàng

6 strokes
省 shěng
尝 cháng

8 strokes
常 cháng

9 strokes
掌 zhǎng

42 口

口 kǒu

2 strokes
史 shǐ
司 sī
右 yòu
叶 yè
号 hào
叫 jiào
另 lìng

3 strokes
吐 tǔ; tù
吓 xià
吃 chī
吸 xī
吗 ma
各 gè
名 míng

4 strokes
否 fǒu
呆 dāi

呕 ǒu
呀 yā
吵 chǎo
员 yuán
听 tīng
吩 fēn
吻 wěn
吹 chuī
告 gào
吝 lìn
启 qǐ
吧 ba

5 strokes

味 wèi
哎 āi
呼 hū
呢 ne
咖 gā；kā
知 zhī
和 hé

6 strokes

咸 xián
哑 yǎ
虽 suī
品 pǐn
咽 yān；yàn
咱 zán
响 xiǎng
哈 hā
咬 yǎo
咳 ké
哪 nǎ
哟 yō

7 strokes

哲 zhé
哮 xiào
哭 kū
哦 ó；ò
啊 ā

8 strokes

啦 la
唱 chàng
啤 pí

9 strokes

喷 pēn
喇 lǎ
喊 hǎn
喂 wèi
喧 xuān
喝 hē

10 strokes

嗓 sǎng

11 strokes

嘛 ma

13 strokes

嘴 zuǐ
器 qì
噪 zào

43 囗

2 strokes

四 sì

3 strokes

因 yīn
回 huí

4 strokes

园 yuán
围 wéi
困 kùn

5 strokes

国 guó
图 tú

7 strokes

圆 yuán

8 strokes

圈 quān

44 巾

2 strokes

布 bù
帅 shuài

4 strokes

帐 zhàng
希 xī

5 strokes

贴 tiē
帘 lián

6 strokes

帮 bāng
带 dài

9 strokes

幅 fú
帽 mào

45 山

山 shān

3 strokes

岁 suì

5 strokes

岸 àn
岳 yuè
岩 yán

6 strokes

峡 xiá

8 strokes

崭 zhǎn
崇 chóng

46 彳

3 strokes

行 háng；xíng

5 strokes

征 zhēng
往 wǎng
彼 bǐ

6 strokes

待 dāi；dài
律 lǜ
很 hěn

8 strokes

得 de；dé；děi

9 strokes

街 jiē
循 xún

10 strokes

微 wēi

12 strokes

德 dé

47 彡

4 strokes

形 xíng

6 strokes

须 xū

8 strokes

彩 cǎi

12 strokes

影 yǐng

48 犭

2 strokes

犯 fàn

4 strokes

犹 yóu

5 strokes

狐 hú
狗 gǒu

6 strokes

狭 xiá
狮 shī
独 dú
狱 yù

7 strokes

狼 láng

8 strokes

猪 zhū
猎 liè
猫 māo
猛 měng

9 strokes

猩 xīng
猴 hóu

10 strokes

猿 yuán

49 夕

夕 xī

3 strokes

多 duō

8 strokes

梦 mèng

50 夂

2 strokes

处 chǔ
冬 dōng

4 strokes

麦 mài
条 tiáo

5 strokes

备 bèi

7 strokes

夏 xià

51 饣

4 strokes

饭 fàn
饮 yǐn

5 strokes

饱 bǎo

6 strokes

饺 jiǎo
饼 bǐng

7 strokes

饿 è

8 strokes

馅 xiàn

11 strokes

馒 mán

52 丬

4 strokes

状 zhuàng

6 strokes

将 jiāng

53 广

广 guǎng

3 strokes

庄 zhuāng
庆 qìng

4 strokes

床 chuáng
应 yīng；yìng

5 strokes

店 diàn
庙 miào
底 dǐ
废 fèi

6 strokes

度 dù
庭 tíng

7 strokes

席 xí
座 zuò

8 strokes

廊 láng
康 kāng
鹿 lù

15 strokes

鹰 yīng

54 忄

1 stroke

忆 yì

3 strokes

忙 máng

4 strokes

怀 huái
忧 yōu
快 kuài

5 strokes

性 xìng
怕 pà
怪 guài

6 strokes

恢 huī
恰 qià
恨 hèn

7 strokes

悄 qiāo

8 strokes

情 qíng
惊 jīng
惯 guàn

9 strokes

愤 fèn
慌 huāng
愉 yú

11 strokes

慢 màn

12 strokes

懂 dǒng
懊 ào

13 strokes

懒 lǎn

55 门

门 mén

2 strokes

闪 shǎn

3 strokes

问 wèn

4 strokes

闲 xián
间 jiān
闷 mēn；mèn

5 strokes

闹 nào

6 strokes

闻 wén

7 strokes

阅 yuè

56 氵

2 strokes

汉 hàn

3 strokes

汗 hàn
污 wū
江 jiāng
汤 tāng

4 strokes

沙 shā
汽 qì
没 méi
沉 chén

5 strokes

沫 mò
浅 qiǎn
法 fǎ
泄 xiè
河 hé
泪 lèi
油 yóu
沿 yán
泡 pào
注 zhù
泳 yǒng
泥 ní
波 bō
治 zhì

6 strokes

洒 sǎ
测 cè
洗 xǐ
活 huó
派 pài
洋 yáng
浓 nóng

7 strokes

酒 jiǔ
消 xiāo
海 hǎi
浴 yù
流 liú
浪 làng

8 strokes

清 qīng
淋 lín
淹 yān
渠 qú
渔 yú
液 yè
深 shēn

9 strokes

港 gǎng
湖 hú
湿 shī
温 wēn
渴 kě
滑 huá
渡 dù
游 yóu

10 strokes

满 mǎn
源 yuán
溪 xī
溜 liū
滚 gǔn

11 strokes

漂 piāo；piào
漫 màn
演 yǎn
漏 lòu

12 strokes

澳 ào

57 宀

2 strokes

宁 níng；nìng
它 tā

3 strokes

宇 yǔ
安 ān
字 zì

4 strokes

完 wán
灾 zāi

5 strokes

宝 bǎo
宗 zōng
定 dìng
宠 chǒng
官 guān
实 shí
宜 yí

6 strokes

宣 xuān
室 shì
宫 gōng
宪 xiàn
客 kè

7 strokes

害 hài
宽 kuān
家 jiā
宵 xiāo
宴 yàn
宾 bīn
容 róng

8 strokes

寄 jì
宿 sù
密 mì

9 strokes

富 fù
寓 yù

10 strokes

塞 sāi

11 strokes

赛 sài
蜜 mì

58 辶

2 strokes

边 biān

3 strokes

达 dá
迈 mài
过 guò
迅 xùn
巡 xún

4 strokes

进 jìn
远 yuǎn
违 wéi
运 yùn
还 hái；huán
连 lián
近 jìn
返 fǎn
迎 yíng
这 zhè
迟 chí

6 strokes

送 sòng
选 xuǎn
适 shì
追 zhuī
逃 táo
迷 mí
退 tuì

7 strokes

速 sù
逗 dòu
逐 zhú
造 zào
透 tòu
逛 guàng
通 tōng

8 strokes

逻 luó

9 strokes

逼 bī
遇 yù
遗 yí
道 dào
遍 biàn

10 strokes

遥 yáo
遛 liù

11 strokes

遭 zāo

12 strokes

遵 zūn

13 strokes

邀 yāo
避 bì

59 彐（彑）

2 strokes

归 guī

4 strokes

灵 líng

5 strokes

录 lù

60 尸

3 strokes

尽 jǐn

4 strokes

层 céng
屁 pì
尾 wěi
局 jú

5 strokes

居 jū

6 strokes

屋 wū
屎 shǐ

7 strokes

展 zhǎn

9 strokes

犀 xī
属 shǔ

61 己（巳）

己 jǐ
已 yǐ

62 弓

1 stroke

引 yǐn

4 strokes

张 zhāng

5 strokes

弦 xián

6 strokes

弯 wān

7 strokes

弱 ruò

8 strokes

弹 dàn；tán

9 strokes

强 qiáng；qiǎng

63 子

子 zǐ

2 strokes

孕 yùn

3 strokes

存 cún
孙 sūn

4 strokes

孝 xiào

5 strokes

学 xué

6 strokes

孩 hái

64 女

女 nǚ

2 strokes

奶 nǎi

3 strokes

如 rú
妇 fù
她 tā
好 hǎo；hào
妈 mā

4 strokes

妙 miào
妖 yāo

5 strokes

妻 qī
妹 mèi
姑 gū
姐 jiě
姓 xìng
始 shǐ

6 strokes

要 yāo；yào
威 wēi
姿 zī
娃 wá
姥 lǎo
姨 yí

7 strokes

娱 yú

8 strokes

娶 qǔ
婴 yīng
婚 hūn

9 strokes

媒 méi
嫂 sǎo
婿 xù

10 strokes

媳 xí
嫌 xián

65 纟

2 strokes

纠 jiū

3 strokes

红 hóng
纤 xiān
级 jí
约 yuē
纪 jì

4 strokes

纯 chún
纷 fēn
纸 zhǐ
纽 niǔ

5 strokes

线 xiàn
练 liàn
组 zǔ
绅 shēn
细 xì
织 zhī
终 zhōng
绊 bàn
经 jīng

6 strokes

绑 bǎng
结 jiē; jié
给 gěi
绝 jué

7 strokes

绣 xiù
继 jì

8 strokes

绳 shéng
维 wéi
综 zōng
绿 lǜ

9 strokes

缆 lǎn
编 biān
缘 yuán

10 strokes

缝 féng; fèng

66 马

马 mǎ

3 strokes

驯 xùn

4 strokes

驴 lǘ

5 strokes

驾 jià

6 strokes

骂 mà
骄 jiāo
骆 luò

7 strokes

验 yàn

8 strokes

骑 qí

9 strokes

骗 piàn

67 幺

2 strokes

幼 yòu

68 王

王 wáng

1 stroke

玉 yù

3 strokes

玖 jiǔ

4 strokes

玩 wán
环 huán
现 xiàn
玫 méi

5 strokes

玻 bō
皇 huáng

6 strokes

班 bān

7 strokes

球 qiú
理 lǐ
望 wàng

8 strokes

琴 qín

69 韦

8 strokes

韩 hán

70 木（朩）

木 mù

1 stroke

本 běn

2 strokes

朵 duǒ
机 jī
权 quán
杀 shā
杂 zá

3 strokes

杆 gān
材 cái
村 cūn
杏 xìng
极 jí
李 lǐ

4 strokes

林 lín
枝 zhī
杯 bēi
柜 guì
板 bǎn
松 sōng
枪 qiāng
枕 zhěn
果 guǒ
采 cǎi

5 strokes

柠 níng
某 mǒu
标 biāo
查 chá
相 xiāng; xiàng
柳 liǔ
柿 shì
栏 lán
树 shù
亲 qīn
柒 qī
架 jià
柔 róu
染 rǎn

6 strokes

桥 qiáo
桃 táo
校 xiào
样 yàng
根 gēn

栗 lì
案 àn
桑 sāng

7 strokes

检 jiǎn
梳 shū
梯 tī
桶 tǒng
梨 lí

8 strokes

棒 bàng
棋 qí
椰 yē
植 zhí
森 sēn
椅 yǐ
棵 kē
棍 gùn
棉 mián
集 jí

9 strokes

楼 lóu

10 strokes

模 mó; mú
榜 bǎng

11 strokes

樱 yīng
橡 xiàng

12 strokes

橱 chú
橘 jú

71 犬

6 strokes

臭 chòu

9 strokes

献 xiàn

72 歹

2 strokes

死 sǐ

5 strokes

残 cán

73 车

车 chē

2 strokes

轨 guǐ

4 strokes

转 zhuǎn; zhuàn
轮 lún
软 ruǎn

5 strokes

轻 qīng

7 strokes

辆 liàng

9 strokes

输 shū

74 比

比 bǐ

75 瓦

6 strokes

瓶 píng

76 止

止 zhǐ

2 strokes

此 cǐ

3 strokes

步 bù

4 strokes

武 wǔ
肯 kěn

77 支

10 strokes

敲 qiāo

78 日

日 rì

2 strokes

早 zǎo

3 strokes

时 shí

4 strokes

明 míng
易 yì

5 strokes

春 chūn
是 shì
显 xiǎn
星 xīng
昨 zuó

6 strokes

晒 shài
晓 xiǎo
晕 yūn; yùn

7 strokes

晨 chén
晚 wǎn

8 strokes

暂 zàn
晴 qíng
量 liáng; liàng
景 jǐng
晾 liàng
智 zhì

9 strokes

暖 nuǎn
暗 àn

11 strokes

暴 bào

79 曰

5 strokes

冒 mào

8 strokes

最 zuì

80 水

水 shuǐ

1 strokes

永 yǒng

5 strokes

泉 quán

81 贝

贝 bèi

3 strokes

财 cái

4 strokes

责 zé
败 bài
账 zhàng

贬 biǎn
购 gòu
贫 pín

5 strokes
贵 guì
费 fèi
贺 hè

6 strokes
资 zī

8 strokes
赔 péi

10 strokes
赚 zhuàn

12 strokes
赠 zèng
赞 zàn

82 见

见 jiàn

4 strokes
规 guī

5 strokes
觉 jué

83 牛

牛 niú

4 strokes
牧 mù
物 wù

6 strokes
特 tè
牺 xī

84 手

手 shǒu

6 strokes
拳 quán

11 strokes
摩 mó

85 毛

毛 máo

8 strokes
毯 tǎn

86 气

气 qì

87 攵

2 strokes
收 shōu

3 strokes
改 gǎi

5 strokes
政 zhèng
故 gù

6 strokes
敌 dí
效 xiào

7 strokes
教 jiāo; jiào
救 jiù
敏 mǐn

8 strokes
散 sàn
敬 jìng

9 strokes
数 shǔ; shù

88 片

片 piàn

4 strokes
版 bǎn

8 strokes
牌 pái

89 斤

斤 jīn

4 strokes
欣 xīn
所 suǒ

9 strokes
新 xīn

90 爪(爫)

4 strokes
爬 pá

6 strokes
爱 ài

91 父

父 fù

2 strokes
爷 yé

4 strokes
爸 bà

92 月

月 yuè

2 strokes
有 yǒu
肋 lèi

3 strokes
肝 gān
肚 dù

4 strokes
肾 shèn
肺 fèi
服 fú
朋 péng
肮 āng
肥 féi
育 yù

5 strokes
胡 hú
背 bēi; bèi
胃 wèi
胆 dǎn
胖 pàng

6 strokes
胳 gē
脆 cuì
胸 xiōng
脏 zāng
脑 nǎo
朗 lǎng

7 strokes
脚 jiǎo
脖 bó
脸 liǎn
脱 tuō

8 strokes
期 qī
脾 pí

9 strokes
腰 yāo
腥 xīng
腺 xiàn
腿 tuǐ

11 strokes
膝 xī

13 strokes
臂 bì

93 欠

欠 qiàn

4 strokes
欧 ōu

7 strokes
欲 yù

8 strokes
欺 qī

9 strokes
歇 xiē

10 strokes
歌 gē

94 风

风 fēng

95 文

文 wén

2 strokes
齐 qí

96 方

方 fāng

4 strokes
放 fàng
房 fáng

6 strokes
旅 lǚ

7 strokes
旋 xuán; xuàn

10 strokes
旗 qí

97 火

火 huǒ

1 stroke
灭 miè

2 strokes
灰 huī
灯 dēng

4 strokes
炒 chǎo
炎 yán
炉 lú

5 strokes
炸 zhá
炮 pào
烂 làn

6 strokes
烤 kǎo
烦 fán
烧 shāo
烟 yān
烫 tàng

8 strokes
焰 yàn

9 strokes
煤 méi

10 strokes
熄 xī

11 strokes
熨 yùn

15 strokes
爆 bào

98 斗

6 strokes
料 liào

7 strokes
斜 xié

99 灬

5 strokes
点 diǎn

6 strokes
烈 liè
热 rè

8 strokes
煮 zhǔ
然 rán

9 strokes
照 zhào

10 strokes
熬 áo
熊 xióng

11 strokes
熟 shú

12 strokes
燕 yàn

100 户

户 hù

5 strokes
扁 biǎn

101 礻

1 stroke
礼 lǐ

5 strokes
祖 zǔ
祝 zhù

9 strokes
福 fú

102 心

心 xīn

1 stroke
必 bì

3 strokes
忘 wàng
忍 rěn

4 strokes
念 niàn
忽 hū
态 tài

5 strokes
怎 zěn
急 jí
总 zǒng
怒 nù

6 strokes
息 xī
恐 kǒng
恶 ě; è
恋 liàn

7 strokes
悬 xuán
悠 yōu
您 nín

8 strokes

悲 bēi

9 strokes

想 xiǎng
感 gǎn
愚 yú
意 yì

10 strokes

愿 yuàn

103 聿(⺻)

9 strokes

肆 sì

104 戈

2 strokes

成 chéng

4 strokes

或 huò

5 strokes

战 zhàn

13 strokes

戴 dài

105 母

母 mǔ

4 strokes

毒 dú

106 示

6 strokes

票 piào

107 石

石 shí

3 strokes

矿 kuàng
码 mǎ

4 strokes

研 yán
砖 zhuān
砍 kǎn

5 strokes

砸 zá
破 pò

6 strokes

硕 shuò

7 strokes

硬 yìng
确 què

8 strokes

碑 bēi
碰 pèng
碗 wǎn

9 strokes

碳 tàn

10 strokes

磅 bàng

108 龙

6 strokes

聋 lóng
袭 xí

109 业

业 yè

110 目

目 mù

3 strokes

盲 máng

4 strokes

看 kān；kàn
眉 méi

5 strokes

眠 mián

6 strokes

睁 zhēng
眼 yǎn

8 strokes

睦 mù
瞄 miáo
睡 shuì

10 strokes

瞒 mán
瞎 xiā

12 strokes

瞧 qiáo

111 田

1 stroke

电 diàn

5 strokes

留 liú
畜 xù

6 strokes

略 lüè
累 lěi；lèi

7 strokes

番 fān

112 罒

4 strokes

罚 fá

8 strokes

罪 zuì

113 皿

4 strokes

盆 pén

5 strokes

盏 zhǎn
盐 yán
盎 àng

6 strokes

盛 chéng
盘 pán
盖 gài

114 钅

2 strokes

针 zhēn

4 strokes

钟 zhōng
钙 gài
钞 chāo
钢 gāng
钥 yào
钩 gōu

5 strokes

钱 qián
钻 zuān；zuàn
铁 tiě
铃 líng
铅 qiān

6 strokes

铝 lǚ
铜 tóng
银 yín

7 strokes

铺 pū; pù
销 xiāo
锁 suǒ
锅 guō
锈 xiù
锋 fēng

8 strokes

错 cuò
锯 jù

9 strokes

锻 duàn

10 strokes

镇 zhèn
镑 bàng

11 strokes

镜 jìng

115 矢

7 strokes

短 duǎn

8 strokes

矮 ǎi

116 禾

2 strokes

秀 xiù
私 sī

3 strokes

季 jì

4 strokes

秒 miǎo
种 zhǒng; zhòng
秋 qiū
科 kē
香 xiāng

5 strokes

租 zū
积 jī
秩 zhì
称 chēng
秘 mì

6 strokes

移 yí

7 strokes

稀 xī
税 shuì

9 strokes

稳 wěn

11 strokes

穆 mù

117 白

白 bái

3 strokes

的 de; dí; dì

118 瓜

瓜 guā

14 strokes

瓣 bàn

119 用

用 yòng

120 鸟

鸟 niǎo

2 strokes

鸡 jī

5 strokes

鸭 yā
鸳 yuān

6 strokes

鸽 gē

7 strokes

鹅 é

8 strokes

鹌 ān

121 疒

4 strokes

疯 fēng
疤 bā

5 strokes

病 bìng
疼 téng

6 strokes

痒 yǎng

7 strokes

痛 tòng

9 strokes

瘦 shòu

10 strokes

瘤 liú

11 strokes

瘾 yǐn
瘸 qué

12 strokes

癌 ái

122 立

立 lì

5 strokes

站 zhàn
竞 jìng

6 strokes

章 zhāng

7 strokes

童 tóng

9 strokes

端 duān

123 穴

穴 xué

2 strokes

究 jiū
穷 qióng

3 strokes

空 kōng; kòng

4 strokes

突 tū
穿 chuān
窃 qiè

5 strokes

窄 zhǎi

7 strokes

窗 chuāng

124 衤

2 strokes
补 bǔ
初 chū

3 strokes
衬 chèn
社 shè

4 strokes
袄 ǎo

5 strokes
袜 wà
袖 xiù
被 bèi

7 strokes
裤 kù
裙 qún

8 strokes
裸 luǒ

125 疋

6 strokes
蛋 dàn

126 皮

皮 pí

127 矛

矛 máo

128 老（耂）

老 lǎo

129 耳

耳 ěr

4 strokes
耽 dān

5 strokes
职 zhí
聊 liáo

6 strokes
联 lián

9 strokes
聪 cōng

130 西（覀）

西 xī

131 页

页 yè

3 strokes
顺 shùn

4 strokes
顾 gù
顿 dùn
预 yù

5 strokes
领 lǐng

7 strokes
频 pín

8 strokes
颗 kē

9 strokes
题 tí
颜 yán
额 é

132 虍

2 strokes
虎 hǔ

5 strokes
虚 xū

133 虫

虫 chóng

3 strokes
虾 xiā
蚁 yǐ
蚂 mǎ

4 strokes
蚊 wén

5 strokes
蛇 shé

6 strokes
蛙 wā

7 strokes
蜂 fēng

8 strokes
蜡 là
蝇 yíng
蜘 zhī

9 strokes
蝴 hú
蝎 xiē
蝙 biān

11 strokes
螺 luó

13 strokes
蟹 xiè

134 缶

3 strokes
缸 gāng

4 strokes
缺 quē

17 strokes
罐 guàn

135 舌

舌 shé

5 strokes
甜 tián

7 strokes
辞 cí

8 strokes
舔 tiǎn

136 竹（⺮）

竹 zhú

4 strokes
笔 bǐ
笑 xiào
笋 sǔn

5 strokes
笨 bèn
笼 lóng
符 fú
第 dì

6 strokes
等 děng
答 dā; dá

7 strokes
签 qiān

筷　kuài
简　jiǎn

8 strokes
算　suàn
管　guǎn

9 strokes
箱　xiāng
篇　piān

10 strokes
篮　lán

137 臼

7 strokes
舅　jiù

138 自

自　zì

139 血

血　xiě; xuè

140 舟

4 strokes
航　háng

5 strokes
船　chuán

141 衣

衣　yī

5 strokes
袋　dài

6 strokes
裂　liè
装　zhuāng

142 羊（⺶，⺷）

羊　yáng

4 strokes
羞　xiū

5 strokes
着　zháo

6 strokes
羡　xiàn

7 strokes
群　qún

143 米

米　mǐ

3 strokes
类　lèi

4 strokes
粉　fěn

5 strokes
粘　zhān
粗　cū
粒　lì

7 strokes
粮　liáng

8 strokes
精　jīng
粽　zòng

9 strokes
糊　hú

10 strokes
糖　táng
糕　gāo

11 strokes
糟　zāo

144 艮（饣）

3 strokes
既　jì

145 羽

羽　yǔ

12 strokes
翻　fān

146 糸

4 strokes
素　sù
紧　jǐn

6 strokes
紫　zǐ

11 strokes
繁　fán

147 走

走　zǒu

3 strokes
赶　gǎn
起　qǐ

5 strokes
越　yuè
趋　qū
超　chāo

8 strokes
趣　qù

148 豆

豆　dòu

5 strokes
登　dēng

149 酉

4 strokes
酗　xù

7 strokes
酸　suān

8 strokes
醉　zuì

9 strokes
醒　xǐng

150 卤

卤　lǔ

151 里

里　lǐ

4 strokes
野　yě

152 足（⻊）

足　zú

4 strokes
距　jù
跃　yuè

5 strokes
跌 diē
跑 pǎo

6 strokes
跳 tiào
跪 guì
路 lù
跟 gēn

8 strokes
踢 tī

11 strokes
蹦 bèng

153 身

身 shēn

6 strokes
躲 duǒ

8 strokes
躺 tǎng

154 采

5 strokes
释 shì

155 豸

3 strokes
豹 bào

156 角

6 strokes
解 jiě

157 言

言 yán

12 strokes
警 jǐng

158 辛

辛 xīn

7 strokes
辣 là

9 strokes
辩 biàn

159 谷

谷 gǔ

160 金

金 jīn

161 青

青 qīng

6 strokes
静 jìng

162 雨

雨 yǔ

3 strokes
雪 xuě

5 strokes
雷 léi
零 líng
雾 wù
雹 báo

6 strokes
需 xū

9 strokes
霜 shuāng

13 strokes
露 lòu; lù

163 隹

4 strokes
雄 xióng

164 鱼

鱼 yú

4 strokes
鱿 yóu

6 strokes
鲜 xiān

12 strokes
鳞 lín

165 革

4 strokes
靴 xuē

6 strokes
鞋 xié
鞍 ān

9 strokes
鞭 biān

166 骨

骨 gǔ

167 鬼

鬼 guǐ

5 strokes
魅 mèi

11 strokes
魔 mó

168 食

食 shí

7 strokes
餐 cān

169 音

音 yīn

170 髟

8 strokes
鬈 quán

171 麻

麻 má

172 黑

黑 hēi

173 鼠

鼠 shǔ

174 鼻

鼻 bí

Aa

阿 ā PREFIX
■阿爸 ābà dad

阿拉伯 Ālābó NOUN
Arabia

阿拉伯数字 Ālābó shùzì NOUN
Arabic numerals *pl*

LANGUAGE TIP Arabic numerals are used in Chinese.

阿姨 āyí NOUN
auntie

啊 ā INTERJECTION
oh
啊！着火了！ Ā! Zháohuǒ le! Oh! It's caught fire!

哎 āi INTERJECTION
1 oh *(surprise, discontentment)*
哎！这么贵！ Āi! Zhème guì! Oh! That expensive!
2 hey *(as a reminder)*
哎！别踩了那朵花。Āi! Bié cǎi le nà duǒ huā. Hey! Don't tread on that flower.

哎呀 āiyā INTERJECTION
oh dear
哎呀，这条路真难走！ Āiyā, zhè tiáo lù zhēn nán zǒu! Oh dear, this road is hard going!

哀 āi ADJECTIVE
sad

哀悼 āidào VERB
to mourn

挨 āi VERB
▷ *see also* ái
to be next to
两个孩子挨着门坐。Liǎnggè háizi āi zhe mén zuò. The two children sat by the door.
■挨个儿 āigèr one by one

挨 ái VERB
▷ *see also* āi
1 to suffer
■挨饿 ái'è to suffer from hunger
■挨骂 áimà to get told off
2 to endure
这种日子很难挨。Zhèzhǒng rìzi hěn nán ái. These sort of days are hard to endure.

挨打 áidǎ VERB
to be beaten up

癌 ái NOUN
cancer
■癌症 áizhèng cancer

矮 ǎi ADJECTIVE
1 short
个子矮 gèzi ǎi short in stature
2 low
■矮墙 ǎiqiáng a low wall

艾 ài NOUN
mugwort

艾滋病 àizībìng NOUN
AIDS

爱 ài VERB
1 to love
我爱你。Wǒ ài nǐ. I love you.
2 to enjoy
爱上网 ài shàngwǎng to enjoy surfing the net
3 to tend to
她爱晕车。Tā ài yùnchē. She tends to get car sick.

爱好 àihào
I VERB
to be keen on
她爱好音乐。Tā àihào yīnyuè. She is keen on music.
II NOUN
hobby
她爱好广泛。Tā àihào guǎngfàn. She has many hobbies.

爱护 àihù VERB
to take care of

爱情 àiqíng NOUN
love

Chinese-English

a

安 ān

I ADJECTIVE

1 quiet

■不安 bù'ān anxious

2 safe

■治安 zhì'ān public order

II VERB

1 to calm

■安神 ānshén to calm the nerves

2 to fit

门上安把锁 mén shàng ān bǎ suǒ to fit a lock on the door

安保 ānbǎo NOUN

security

安定 āndìng

I ADJECTIVE

stable

II VERB

to stabilize

安定局面 āndìng júmiàn to stabilize the situation

安家 ānjiā VERB

to settle

安检 ānjiǎn NOUN

security check

安静 ānjìng ADJECTIVE

1 quiet

安静的环境 ānjìng de huánjìng a quiet environment

2 peaceful

她的内心很安静。Tā de nèixīn hěn ānjìng. Her heart is at peace.

安乐死 ānlèsǐ NOUN

euthanasia

安排 ānpái VERB

to arrange

安全 ānquán ADJECTIVE

safe

注意安全。Zhùyì ānquán. Make sure you are safe. 人身安全 rénshēn ānquán personal safety

安全套 ānquántào NOUN

condom

安慰 ānwèi

I VERB

to comfort

II ADJECTIVE

reassured

安心 ānxīn VERB

to stop worrying

安装 ānzhuāng VERB

to install

鹌 ān

▷ *see below:*

鹌鹑 ānchún NOUN

quail

鞍 ān NOUN

saddle

■马鞍 mǎ'ān saddle

岸 àn NOUN

edge

■河岸 hé'àn river bank

■海岸 hǎi'àn seashore

按 àn

I VERB

1 to press

按电钮 àn diànniǔ to press a button

按门铃 àn ménlíng to push a doorbell

2 to push... down

把人按倒 bǎ rén àndǎo to push someone down

3 to restrain

按不住心头怒火 àn búzhù xīntóu nùhuǒ to be unable to restrain one's fury

II PREPOSITION

according to

按制度办事 àn zhìdù bànshì to do things by the book

按揭 ànjiē NOUN

mortgage

按摩 ànmó VERB

to massage

按照 ànzhào PREPOSITION

according to

按照课本 ànzhào kèběn according to the text book

案 àn NOUN

case

■案子 ànzi case

案件 ànjiàn NOUN

case

暗 àn

I ADJECTIVE

dim

今晚月光很暗。Jīnwǎn yuèguāng hěn àn. Tonight the moon is very dim.

II ADVERB

secretly

■暗自 ànzì inwardly

暗号 ànhào NOUN

secret signal

暗杀 ànshā VERB

to assassinate

暗示 ànshì VERB

to hint

肮 āng

▷ *see below:*
肮脏 āngzāng ADJECTIVE
1 filthy
2 vile
肮脏的交易 āngzāng de jiāoyì vile deals

盎 àng ADJECTIVE
abundant *(formal)*
盎司 àngsī MEASURE WORD
ounce

熬 áo VERB
1 to stew
■ 熬粥 áozhōu to make porridge
2 to endure
■ 难熬 nán'áo hard to endure
熬夜 áoyè VERB
to stay up late

袄 ǎo NOUN
coat
■ 棉袄 mián'ǎo padded jacket

傲 ào ADJECTIVE
proud
傲慢 àomàn ADJECTIVE
arrogant
傲气 àoqì NOUN
arrogance

奥 ào ADJECTIVE
profound
■ 奥秘 àomì a mystery
奥林匹克运动会 Àolínpǐkè Yùndònghuì NOUN
Olympic Games *pl*

澳 ào NOUN
bay
澳大利亚 Àodàlìyà NOUN
Australia

懊 ào ADJECTIVE
1 regretful
2 annoyed
■ 懊恼 àonǎo annoyed
懊悔 àohuǐ VERB
to regret

Bb

八 bā NUMBER
eight
■ 八月 bāyuè August

巴 bā NOUN
■ 下巴 xiàbā chin
■ 尾巴 wěibā tail
■ 嘴巴 zuǐbā mouth
巴士 bāshì NOUN
bus
巴掌 bāzhang NOUN
palm
拍巴掌 pāi bāzhang to clap

芭 bā NOUN
banana
■ 芭蕉 bājiāo banana
芭蕾舞 bāléiwǔ NOUN
ballet

疤 bā NOUN
scar
他脸上有疤。Tā liǎn shàng yǒu bā.
He has a scar on his face.

捌 bā NUMBER
eight

> LANGUAGE TIP This is the complex character for eight, which is mainly used in banks, on receipts etc to prevent mistakes and forgery.

拔 bá VERB
1 to pull... up
■ 拔草 bácaǒ to weed
2 to pull... out
■ 拔牙 báyá to pull out a tooth
3 to choose
■ 选拔 xuǎnbá to select *(a candidate)*
4 to exceed
■ 海拔 hǎibá height above sea level
拔河 báhé NOUN
tug-of-war

把 bǎ
I VERB
1 to hold
把住栏杆 bǎ zhù lángān to hold onto the rails
2 to guard
把大门 bǎ dàmén to guard the gate
3 to take
别把这当回事。Bié bǎ zhè dāng huí shì.
Don't take this too seriously.
II NOUN
handle
■ 把手 bǎshǒu handle
III MEASURE WORD
handful

> LANGUAGE TIP This is a measure word used for the quantity of something that can be held in a hand.

一把米 yì bǎ mǐ a handful of rice

> LANGUAGE TIP This is a measure word used for objects with a handle.

一把刀 yì bǎ dāo a knife 一把剪子 yì bǎ jiǎnzi a pair of scissors

> LANGUAGE TIP This is a measure word used for something that can be bundled together.

两把花 liǎng bǎ huā two bunches of flowers
IV PREPOSITION

> LANGUAGE TIP 把 bǎ is used to alter the word order of a sentence, especially when the verb is a complex one. The normal word order of subject + verb + object, becomes subject + 把 + object + verb. It is very commonly used when the verb implies a change of place, or when the verb is followed by certain complements. For instance, a word-for-word translation of the sentence, 我把书放在那儿。Wǒ bǎ shū fàng zài nàr. **I put the book there** is I 把 **book put there**.

把门关好 bǎ mén guān hǎo to shut the door 把作业做完 bǎ zuòyè zuò wán to finish doing one's homework 她把书放在桌子上了。Tā bǎ shū fàng zài zhuōzi shàng le. She put the book on the table.

把手 bǎshou NOUN
handle

把握 bǎwò
I VERB
to grasp
把握时机 bǎwò shíjī to seize the opportunity
II NOUN
certainty
没把握 méi bǎwò there is no certainty

爸 bà NOUN
father

爸爸 bàba NOUN
dad

吧 ba AUXILIARY WORD
LANGUAGE TIP 吧 ba at the end of a sentence forms a suggestion.
我们回家吧。Wǒmen huíjiā ba. Let's go home. 吃吧！Chī ba! Eat!
再想想吧。Zài xiǎngxiǎng ba. Think about it again.
LANGUAGE TIP 吧 ba at the end of a sentence also forms a question.
我们走吗？Wǒmen zǒu ma? Shall we go?
他明天走吧？Tā míngtiān zǒu ba? Is he leaving tomorrow?

白 bái
I ADJECTIVE
1 white
■ 白色 báisè white
■ 白糖 báitáng white sugar
2 clear
■ 明白 míngbai clear
3 daytime
■ 白天 báitiān daytime
4 plain
■ 白开水 bái kāishuǐ plain boiled water
■ 白米饭 bái mǐfàn plain boiled rice
II VERB
■ 辩白 biànbái to argue
■ 坦白 tǎnbái to confess

白菜 báicài NOUN
Chinese cabbage

白酒 báijiǔ NOUN
Chinese liqueur
DID YOU KNOW...? This is a clear spirit usually distilled from sorghum or maize.

白人 báirén NOUN
white people *pl*
他是白人。Tā shì báirén. He's white.

百 bǎi NUMBER
hundred

百分之百 bǎi fēn zhī bǎi ADVERB
absolutely
LANGUAGE TIP 百分之百 bǎi fēn zhī bǎi literally means **100%**.
他百分之百会来。Tā bǎi fēn zhī bǎi huì lái. He will definitely come.

百科全书 bǎikē quánshū NOUN
encyclopaedia

百万 bǎiwàn NUMBER
million

佰 bǎi NUMBER
hundred
LANGUAGE TIP This is the complex character for hundred which is used in banks, on receipts, cheques etc.

摆 bǎi VERB
1 to arrange
请把桌子摆好。Qǐng bǎ zhuōzi bǎihǎo. Please lay the table.
■ 摆放 bǎifàng to place
2 to wave
■ 摆动 bǎidòng to sway 柳条迎风摆动。Liǔtiáo yíngfēng bǎidòng. The willows swayed in the breeze.
■ 摆手 bǎishǒu to beckon 她向我摆手。Tā xiàng wǒ bǎi shǒu. She waved her hand at me.

摆设 bǎishè VERB
to furnish and decorate
客厅里摆设得很讲究。Kètīng lǐ bǎishè de hěn jiǎngjiū. The living room was tastefully furnished.

败 bài VERB
to defeat
大败敌人 dàbài dírén to defeat the enemy

败坏 bàihuài
I VERB
to corrupt
败坏声誉 bàihuài shēngyù to damage somebody's reputation
II ADJECTIVE
corrupt
道德品质败坏 dàodé pǐnzhì bàihuài morally corrupt

败仗 bàizhàng NOUN
defeat
这位将军从未打过败仗。Zhèwèi jiāngjūn cóngwèi dǎguò bàizhàng. This general has never suffered defeat.

拜 bài VERB
to pay a visit
■ 拜访 bàifǎng to visit 学生家长昨天拜访了校长。Xuéshēng jiāzhǎng zuótiān bàifǎng le xiàozhǎng. The students' parents visited the headteacher yesterday.

拜年 bàinián VERB
to pay a New Year call
他每年春节都给老师拜年。Tā měinián chūnjié dōu gěi lǎoshī bàinián. He pays a New Year call to his teacher every Spring Festival.

拜托 bàituō VERB
to request ... to do ... *(polite)*
拜托您给看会儿我女儿。Bàituō nín gěi kān huìr wǒ nǚ'ér. Would you be kind enough to look after my daughter for a while?

班 bān
I NOUN
1 class
■ 班长 bānzhǎng class monitor
2 shift
■ 上班 shàngbān to go to work
■ 下班 xiàbān to finish work
■ 夜班 yèbān night shift 值夜班 zhí yèbān to be on the night shift
3 squad
■ 班长 bānzhǎng squad leader
II ADJECTIVE
scheduled
■ 班机 bānjī scheduled flight
■ 末班车 mòbānchē the last bus
III MEASURE WORD
LANGUAGE TIP This is a measure word used for scheduled transportation.
下一班船 xià yi bān chuán the next boat
错过一班飞机 cuòguò yìbān fēijī to miss a flight

班级 bānjí NOUN
classes *pl*

搬 bān VERB
1 to take... away
把这些东西搬走。Bǎ zhèxiē dōngxi bān zuǒ. Take these things away.
2 to move
■ 搬家 bānjiā to move house

板 bǎn
I NOUN
board
■ 木板 mùbǎn plank
II VERB
to put on a stern expression
板着脸 bǎn zhe liǎn to look stern

版 bǎn NOUN
edition
修订版 revised edition

办 bàn VERB
1 to handle
我们该怎么办？Wǒmen gāi zěnme bàn? What should we do?
■ 办事 bànshì to handle affairs
2 to set... up
办工厂 bàn gōngchǎng to set up a factory
3 to run
■ 办学 bànxué to run a school
4 to hold
办画展 bàn huàzhǎn to hold an art exhibition

办法 bànfǎ NOUN
way
开动脑筋想办法 kāidòng nǎojīn xiǎng bànfǎ to get your brains in gear to come up with a solution 联系办法 liánxì bànfǎ means of contact

办公 bàngōng VERB
to handle official business
办公地点 bàngōng dìdiǎn place of work

办理 bànlǐ VERB
to handle
办理入学手续 bànlǐ rùxué shǒuxù to go through school entrance procedures

半 bàn
I NUMBER
half
半价 bàn jià half price 半年 bàn nián half a year
II NOUN
middle
■ 半夜 bànyè midnight
III ADVERB
partially
半新 bàn xīn almost new

半岛 bàndǎo NOUN
peninsula

半径 bànjìng NOUN
radius

半球 bànqiú NOUN
hemisphere
南半球 nán bànqiú the Southern Hemisphere

半天 bàntiān NOUN
quite a while
他等了半天。Tā děng le bàntiān. He waited for quite a while.

扮 bàn VERB
to play
他在影片中扮坏人。Tā zài yǐngpiàn zhōng bàn huàirén. He played the villain in the film.
扮演 bànyǎn VERB
to act
她将扮演白雪公主。Tā jiāng bànyǎn Báixuě gōngzhǔ. She will play the part of Snow White.

伴 bàn NOUN
company
■ 伙伴 huǒbàn companion
■ 做伴 zuòbàn to keep company 我会和你做伴的。Wǒ huì hé nǐ zuòbàn de. I will keep you company.
伴随 bànsuí VERB
to follow
幸福未必伴随财富而来。Xìngfú wèibì bànsuí cáifù érlái. Wealth isn't necessarily followed by happiness.
伴奏 bànzòu VERB
to accompany
她用手风琴为我伴奏。Tā yòng shǒufēngqín wèi wǒ bànzòu. She accompanied me on the accordion.

拌 bàn VERB
to mix
■ 搅拌 jiǎobàn to mix
■ 凉拌菜 liángbàn cài Chinese salad
LANGUAGE TIP This is usually a cold dish consisting of vegetables and other ingredients mixed with a dressing.

绊 bàn VERB
to trip up
他下楼时绊了一跤。Tā xiàlóu shí bàn le yìjiāo. He tripped over on his way downstairs.
■ 绊倒 bàndǎo to knock down

瓣 bàn
I NOUN
petal
■ 花瓣 huābàn petal
■ 橘子瓣 júzi bàn orange segment
II MEASURE WORD
LANGUAGE TIP This is a measure word used to describe small sections such as flower petals, segments of fruit and cloves of garlic.
几瓣蒜 jǐ bàn suàn a few cloves of garlic
一瓣橘子 yí bàn júzi a segment of orange

帮 bāng VERB
to help
我帮他买票。Wǒ bāng tā mǎi piào. I helped him to buy the tickets.
我帮他修改作文。Wǒ bāng tā xiūgǎi zuòwén. I helped him to improve his composition.
帮倒忙 bāng dàománg VERB
to do... a disservice
他这么说其实是在给我帮倒忙。Tā zhème shuō qíshí shì zài gěi wǒ bāng dàománg. Actually what he said did me quite a disservice.
帮忙 bāngmáng VERB
to help
请您帮忙传个口信。Qǐng nín bāngmáng chuán gè kǒuxìn. Please can you pass on a message for me.
帮手 bāngshǒu NOUN
assistant
他是妈妈的好帮手。Tā shì māma de hǎo bāngshǒu. He's mum's helper.
帮助 bāngzhù VERB
to help
他帮助我们渡过难关。Tā bāngzhù wǒmen dùguò nánguān. He helped us through a difficult time. 水果帮助消化。Shuǐguǒ bāngzhù xiāohuà. Fruit aids digestion.

绑 bǎng VERB
to tie up
他帮我把这些书绑好。Tā bāng wǒ bǎ zhèxiē shū bǎnghǎo. He helped me to bundle up all these books.
■ 捆绑 kǔnbǎng to tie up

榜 bǎng NOUN
list of names
光荣榜 guāngróngbǎng roll of honour
榜样 bǎngyàng NOUN
model
他是全班同学的榜样。Tā shì quánbān tóngxué de bǎngyàng. He sets an example for all the students in the class.

棒 bàng
I NOUN
stick
■ 棒子 bàngzi club
■ 木棒 mùbàng wooden club
■ 棍棒 gùnbàng club
II ADJECTIVE
great *(informal)*
他英语说得很棒。Tā Yīngyǔ shuō de hěn bàng. He speaks great English.

傍 bàng VERB
to be close to

傍晚 bàngwǎn NOUN
dusk
他们常常傍晚时散步。Tāmen chángcháng bàngwǎn shí sànbù. They usually go for a walk in the evening.

磅 bàng MEASURE WORD
pound *(weight)*
这个包裹重三磅。Zhègè bāoguǒ zhòng sānbàng. This parcel weighs three pounds.

镑 bàng NOUN
pound
一镑的硬币 yíbàng de yìngbì one-pound coin
■ 英镑 Yīngbàng pound Sterling

包 bāo
I VERB
1 to wrap
把这件礼物包起来吧。Bǎ zhèjiàn lǐwù bāo qǐlái ba. Please can you wrap the present.
■ 包裹 bāoguǒ to wrap
2 to include
你的学费里不包食宿。Nǐde xuéfèi lǐ bùbāo shísù. Your tuition fee doesn't include meals or accommodation.
■ 包含 bāohán to contain
II NOUN
1 parcel
我今天收到一个大包裹。Wǒ jīntiān shōudào yígè dà bāoguǒ. I received a large parcel today.
2 bag
■ 背包 bēibāo backpack
■ 书包 shūbāo school bag
■ 钱包 qiánbāo wallet
■ 公文包 gōngwénbāo briefcase
III MEASURE WORD
bag

LANGUAGE TIP This is a measure word used to describe things that are wrapped up.

一包烟 yì bāo yān a packet of cigarettes 一包衣服 yì bāo yīfu a bag of clothes 他送给我一大包水果。Tā sòng gěi wǒ yí dàbāo shuǐguǒ. He sent me a large basket of fruit.

包括 bāokuò VERB
to include
这门课程不包括实验。Zhèmén kèchéng bù bāokuò shíyàn. There are no experiments covered in the course. 餐费包括百分之十的服务费。Cānfèi bāokuò bǎi fēn zhī shí de fúwùfèi. A ten percent service charge is included in the bill.

包围 bāowéi VERB
to surround
这座城市四周被群山包围着。Zhèzuò chéngshì sìzhōu bèi qúnshān bāowéi zhe. The city is surrounded by mountains on all sides.

包子 bāozi NOUN
steamed stuffed bun

DID YOU KNOW...?
包子 bāozi are bigger than 饺子 jiǎozi. Shaped like buns, they are usually stuffed with meat or vegetable fillings, and are steamed rather than boiled.

包装 bāozhuāng
I VERB
to package... up
请帮我把这些糖果包装起来。Qǐng bāng wǒ bǎ zhèxiē tángguǒ bāozhuāng qǐlái. Please help me to package up the sweets.
II NOUN
package
这只杯子的包装很漂亮。Zhèzhī bēizi de bāozhuāng hěn piàoliàng. The cup is beautifully packaged.
■ 包装盒 bāozhuānghé box

剥 bāo VERB
to peel
剥香蕉 bāo xiāngjiāo to peel a banana
剥豌豆 bāo wāndòu to shell peas

雹 báo NOUN
hail
■ 雹子 báozi hailstone

薄 báo ADJECTIVE
thin
冰层太薄，不能滑冰。Bīngcéng tài báo, bùnéng huábīng. The ice is too thin to go ice-skating.
■ 薄片 báopiàn thin slice
■ 薄饼 báobǐng thin pancake

宝 bǎo
I NOUN
treasure
妈妈把他当个宝。Māma bǎ tā dāng gè bǎo. He is mother's little treasure.
■ 国宝 guóbǎo national treasure
II ADJECTIVE
precious
■ 宝藏 bǎozàng precious minerals
■ 宝地 bǎodì a great place

宝贝 bǎobèi NOUN

1 treasure
他把这本书当成一件宝贝。Tā bǎ zhèbēn shū dāngchéng yíjiàn bǎobèi. He really treasures this book.
2 darling
他是爸妈的好宝贝。Tā shì bàmā de hǎo bǎobèi. He is mum and dad's darling child.

宝贵 bǎoguì ADJECTIVE
valuable
宝贵首饰 bǎoguì shǒushì valuable jewellery 宝贵意见 bǎoguì yìjiàn valuable suggestion

---

饱 bǎo ADJECTIVE
full
我吃饱了。Wǒ chī bǎo le. I am full.

保 bǎo VERB
1 to protect
■ 保卫 bǎowèi to defend
2 to keep
这盒子可以保鲜。Zhè hézi kěyǐ bǎoxiān. This box can keep food fresh.
■ 保密 bǎomì to keep... secret
■ 保鲜膜 bǎoxiān mó Clingfilm®
3 to ensure
这次他保准能赢。Zhècì tā bǎozhǔn néng yíng. This time he will ensure he wins.

保安 bǎo'ān NOUN
security guard

保镖 bǎobiāo NOUN
bodyguard

保持 bǎochí VERB
to maintain
保持良好的秩序 bǎochí liánghǎo de zhìxù to maintain good order 保持警惕 bǎochí jǐngtì to stay vigilant 保持清醒的头脑 bǎochí qīngxǐng de tóunǎo to keep a clear head

保存 bǎocún VERB
to preserve
这座老房子保存完好。Zhèzuò lǎo fángzi bǎocún wánhǎo. This old house has been preserved in good condition. 他一直保存着这张旧照片。Tā yìzhí bǎocún zhe zhèzhāng jiù zhàopiān. He's always kept this old picture.

保护 bǎohù VERB
to protect
保护环境 bǎohù huánjìng to protect the environment 保护眼睛 bǎohù yǎnjīng to protect one's eyes 保护私人资料 bǎohù sīrén zīliào data protection

保龄球 bǎolíngqiú NOUN
bowling
他非常喜欢打保龄球。Tā fēicháng xǐhuān dǎ bǎolíngqiú. He loves bowling.

保留 bǎoliú VERB
1 to preserve
这座城市还保留着500多年前的寺庙。Zhèzuò chéngshì hái bǎoliú zhe wǔbǎi duō nián qián de sìmiào. A temple more than 500 years old has been preserved in the town.
2 to hold back
你可以保留自己的意见。Nǐ kěyǐ bǎoliú zìjǐ de yìjiàn. You can keep your opinions to yourself.

保密 bǎomì VERB
to keep... secret
这个消息可要保密。Zhègè xiāoxi kě yào bǎomì. This information must be kept secret.

保姆 bǎomǔ NOUN
1 domestic help
2 nanny

保守 bǎoshǒu ADJECTIVE
conservative
他很保守。Tā hěn bǎoshǒu. He is very conservative.

保卫 bǎowèi VERB
to defend
保卫祖国 bǎowèi zǔguó to defend one's country

保险 bǎoxiǎn
I NOUN
insurance
II ADJECTIVE
safe
这样做不保险。Zhèyàng zuò bù bǎoxiǎn. This isn't a safe way of doing it.

保证 bǎozhèng VERB
to guarantee
我保证能按时到达。Wǒ bǎozhèng néng ànshí dàodá. I guarantee I will be there on time.

保重 bǎozhòng VERB
to take care of oneself
请多保重。Qǐng duō bǎozhòng. Take care of yourself.

报 bào
I VERB
to report
■ 汇报 huìbào to report
II NOUN
1 newspaper
■ 日报 rìbào daily newspaper
■ 报社 bàoshè newspaper office
2 periodical
■ 画报 huàbào glossy magazine

报仇 bàochóu VERB
to take revenge
报酬 bàochou NOUN
pay
报到 bàodào VERB
to register
新生都报到了。Xīnshēng dōu bàodào le. The new students have all registered.
报道 bàodào
I VERB
to report
电视台报道了这条新闻。Diànshì tái bàodào le zhè tiáo xīnwén. The television station reported this news story.
II NOUN
report
新闻报道 xīnwén bàodào news report
报复 bàofù VERB
to retaliate
报告 bàogào
I VERB
to report
向老师报告 xiàng lǎoshī bàogào to report to the teacher
II NOUN
report
在大会上作报告 zài dàhuì shàng zuò bàogào to give a talk at a conference
报刊 bàokān NOUN
newspapers and periodicals *pl*
报名 bàomíng VERB
to sign up
报名参加演讲比赛 bàomíng cānjiā yǎnjiǎng bǐsài to sign up for a speaking competition
报失 bàoshī VERB
to report a loss
丢了东西去哪里报失？Diū le dōngxi qù nǎlǐ bàoshī? Where do I go to report lost property?
报销 bàoxiāo VERB
to claim for
报销车费 bàoxiāo chēfèi to claim back travel expenses
报纸 bàozhǐ NOUN
newspaper

抱 bào VERB
1 to carry in one's arms
抱小孩 bào xiǎohái to hold a baby
2 to adopt
他们想抱养一个孩子。Tāmen xiǎng bàoyàng yígè háizi. They want to adopt a child.
3 to cherish
对某事抱幻想 duì mǒushì bào huànxiǎng to have illusions about something
抱歉 bàoqiàn
I ADJECTIVE
sorry
II VERB
to apologize
抱怨 bàoyuàn VERB
to complain
小男孩抱怨爸爸脾气坏。Xiǎo nánhái bàoyuàn bàba píqì huài. The little boy complained that his dad had a bad temper.

豹 bào NOUN
leopard

暴 bào ADJECTIVE
violent
■ 暴雨 bàoyǔ rainstorm
暴力 bàolì NOUN
violence

爆 bào VERB
1 to explode
气球爆了。Qìqiú bào le. The balloon burst.
■ 爆炸 bàozhà to explode
2 to break out
■ 爆发 bàofā to break out

杯 bēi
I NOUN
cup (*for drink, trophy*)
■ 玻璃杯 bōli bēi glass
■ 酒杯 jiǔbēi wine glass
■ 世界杯 Shìjièbēi World Cup
II MEASURE WORD
cup
一杯咖啡 yì bēi kāfēi a cup of coffee 两杯水 liǎng bēi shuǐ two glasses of water

---

背 bēi VERB
▷ *see also* bèi
to carry... on one's back
她背着个双肩背。Tā bēizhe ge shuāngjiānbēi. She was carrying a backpack on her back.

悲 bēi ADJECTIVE
sad
悲惨 bēicǎn ADJECTIVE
miserable
悲观 bēiguān ADJECTIVE
pessimistic
悲伤 bēishāng ADJECTIVE
sad

碑 bēi NOUN

tablet
■ 纪念碑 jìniànbēi monument

北 běi NOUN
north
■ 北边 běibiān north
■ 北方 běifāng the North
■ 北京 Běijīng Beijing

北极 běijí NOUN
the North Pole

贝 bèi NOUN
shellfish

贝壳 bèiké NOUN
shell

备 bèi VERB
1 to have
学校备有午餐。Xuéxiào bèiyǒu wǔcān. Lunch is available at school.
2 to prepare
佐料备齐了。Zuóliào bèiqí le. The seasoning is prepared.

备份 bèifèn VERB
to keep a backup copy

备用 bèiyòng ADJECTIVE
backup
备用光盘 bèiyòng guāngpán backup CD

备注 bèizhù NOUN
notes *pl*

背 bèi
I NOUN
▷ *see also* bēi
1 back *(of person, object)*
■ 背疼 bèiténg backache
■ 背面 bèimiàn reverse side
2 behind
■ 背后 bèihòu behind
II VERB
to recite
背首诗 bèi shǒu shī to recite a poem

背景 bèijǐng NOUN
background

背诵 bèisòng VERB
to recite

被 bèi
I NOUN
quilt
■ 棉被 miánbèi cotton-padded quilt
II PREPOSITION
LANGUAGE TIP 被 bèi introduces the agent in a passive sentence.
他被哥哥打了一顿。Tā bèi gēge dǎ le yí dùn. He was beaten up by his elder brother.
III AUXILIARY WORD
LANGUAGE TIP 被 bèi is also used before a notional verb to indicate that the subject is the receiver of the action.
他被跟踪了。Tā bèi gēnzōng le. He was followed.

倍 bèi NOUN
times *pl*
这本书比那本书厚三倍。Zhè běn shū bǐ nà běn shū hòu sānbèi. This book is three times thicker than that one. 物价涨了两倍。Wùjià zhǎng le liǎngbèi. Prices have doubled.

本 běn
I NOUN
1 book
■ 笔记本 bǐjìběn notebook
2 edition
■ 手抄本 shǒuchāo běn hand-written copy
II ADJECTIVE
1 one's own
■ 本人 běnrén oneself
2 this
■ 本月 běnyuè this month
III ADVERB
originally
我本想亲自去一趟。Wǒ běn xiǎng qīnzì qù yítàng. I originally wanted to go myself.
IV MEASURE WORD
LANGUAGE TIP This is a measure word used for counting books, magazines, dictionaries, etc.
几本书 jǐ běn shū a few books

本地 běndì NOUN
locality
她是本地人。Tā shì běndì rén. She is a native of this place.

本科 běnkē NOUN
undergraduate course
本科生 běnkē shēng undergraduate

本来 běnlái
I ADJECTIVE
original
本来的打算 běnlái de dǎsuàn the original plan
II ADVERB
at first
我本来以为你已经走了。Wǒ běnlái yǐwéi nǐ yǐjīng zǒu le. At first, I thought you had already left.

本领 běnlǐng NOUN
skill

本身 běnshēn NOUN
itself

本事 běnshi NOUN
ability

本质 běnzhì NOUN
essence

笨 bèn ADJECTIVE
1 stupid
他很苯。Tā hěn bèn. He is rather stupid.
2 clumsy
他嘴很笨。Tā zuǐ hěn bèn. He's very inarticulate.

蹦 bèng VERB
to leap

逼 bī VERB
1 to force
2 to press for
3 to close in on

逼近 bījìn VERB
to close in on
飓风已逼近海岸。Jùfēng yǐ bījìn hǎi'àn. The hurricane has already drawn near to the coast.

逼迫 bīpò VERB
to force
我不想逼迫你做这件事。Wǒ bùxiǎng bīpò nǐ zuò zhè jiàn shì. I don't want to force you to do this.

鼻 bí NOUN
nose

鼻涕 bíti NOUN
mucus

鼻子 bízi NOUN
nose

比 bǐ
I VERB
1 to compare
比比过去，现在的生活好多了。Bǐbǐ guòqù, xiànzài de shēnghuó hǎo duō le. Life now is much better compared to the past.
2 to compete
他们要比比谁游得快。Tāmen yào bǐbǐ shuí yóu de kuài. They are competing to see who swims the fastest.
II PREPOSITION
LANGUAGE TIP 比 bǐ is used to indicate the different scores of two competing individuals or teams.
零比零 líng bǐ líng nil-nil
LANGUAGE TIP 比 bǐ is used to express comparisons.
今年冬天比去年冷。Jīnnián dōngtiān bǐ qùnián lěng. It is colder this winter than last winter.

比方 bǐfang NOUN
analogy
比方说 bǐfang shuō for example

比分 bǐfēn NOUN
score

比基尼 bǐjīní NOUN
bikini

比较 bǐjiào
I VERB
to compare
让我们比较一下两张图片的区别。Ràng wǒmen bǐjiào yíxià liǎngzhāng túpiàn de qūbié. Let's compare the two photos and spot the differences.
II ADVERB
relatively
这里的水果比较新鲜。Zhèlǐ de shuǐguǒ bǐjiào xīnxian. The fruit here is relatively fresh.

比例 bǐlì NOUN
proportion

比率 bǐlǜ NOUN
ratio

比如 bǐrú CONJUNCTION
for instance
有些事情不能马虎，比如学习。Yǒuxiē shìqing bùnéng mǎhu, bǐrú xuéxí. Some things just can't be done in a slapdash way, like studying for example.

比赛 bǐsài NOUN
match
演讲比赛 yǎnjiǎng bǐsài public speaking competition

彼 bǐ PRONOUN
1 that
■ 彼时 bǐshí at that time
2 the other side
■ 彼岸 bǐ'àn the other shore

彼此 bǐcǐ PRONOUN
both sides
他们彼此不太了解。Tāmen bǐcǐ bú tài liǎojiě. Neither of them really understood.

笔 bǐ
I NOUN
1 pen
■ 圆珠笔 yuánzhūbǐ ball-point pen
2 brush stroke
这个字一共几笔？Zhègè zì yígòng jǐbǐ? How many strokes are there in this character?
II MEASURE WORD
LANGUAGE TIP This is a measure word used for money.

一笔钱 yì bǐ qián a sum of money

笔记 bǐjì NOUN
note
记笔记 jì bǐjì to take notes

笔记本电脑 bǐjìběn diànnǎo NOUN
laptop

笔试 bǐshì NOUN
written examination

币 bì NOUN
coin
■ 货币 huòbì currency
■ 外币 wàibì foreign currency

必 bì ADVERB
certainly
你这次必能成功。Nǐ zhècì bìnéng chénggōng. You will certainly be successful this time.
■ 必修课 bìxiūkè compulsory course

必然 bìrán
I ADJECTIVE
inevitable
必然的趋势 bìrán de qūshì an inexorable trend
II NOUN
necessity
对于很多年轻人来说，出国留学已成为必然。Duìyú hěnduō niánqīngrén lái shuō, chūguó liúxué yǐ chéngwéi bìrán. Studying abroad has already become a necessity for many young people.

必须 bìxū ADVERB
你们必须准时来上课。Nǐmen bìxū zhǔnshí lái shàngkè. You must come to class on time.

必需 bìxū VERB
to need
考试时别忘带上必需的文具用品。Kǎoshì shí bié wàng dàishàng bìxū de wénjù yòngpǐn. Don't forget to bring the writing materials you need for the exam.

必要 bìyào ADJECTIVE
essential
必要措施 bìyào cuòshī necessary measure

毕 bì VERB
to finish

毕业 bìyè VERB
to graduate
她明年高中毕业。Tā míngnián gāozhōng bìyè. She will graduate from high school next year.

避 bì VERB
1 to avoid
■ 避风 bìfēng to shelter from the wind
2 to prevent
■ 避孕 bìyùn to use contraceptives 避孕药 bìyùn yào the pill

避免 bìmiǎn VERB
to avoid
避免错误 bìmiǎn cuòwù to avoid mistakes

避难 bìnàn VERB
to take refuge

臂 bì NOUN
arm

臂膀 bìbǎng NOUN
arm

边 biān NOUN
1 side
街两边 jiē liǎngbiān both sides of the street 在床边 zài chuáng biān by the bed
2 edge
路边 lù biān roadside
3 border
国家边界 guójiā biānjiè national border

边...边... biān...biān... CONJUNCTION
while...

> LANGUAGE TIP This is used before two verbs respectively to indicate simultaneous actions.

边吃边谈 biān chī biān tán to talk while eating

边疆 biānjiāng NOUN
border area

边界 biānjiè NOUN
border

边境 biānjìng NOUN
border
边境小镇 biānjìng xiǎozhèn small border town

边缘 biānyuán NOUN
edge
他正处于考试不及格的边缘。Tā zhèng chùyú kǎoshì bù jígé de biānyuán. He was on the borderline of the exam pass mark.

编 biān VERB
1 to edit
■ 编程 biānchéng to program
2 to write
编歌词 biān gēcí to write lyrics
3 to fabricate
编谎话 biān huǎnghuà to fabricate a lie

编辑 biānjí
I VERB
to edit
编辑词典 biānjí cídiǎn to edit a dictionary

II NOUN
editor
他将来想当一名报社编辑。Tā jiānglái xiǎng dāng yìmíng bàoshè biānjí. He wants to be a newspaper editor.

蝙 biān
▷ *see below:*
蝙蝠 biānfú NOUN
bat

鞭 biān NOUN
1 whip
2 firecracker
鞭炮 biānpào NOUN
firecracker

> **DID YOU KNOW...?**
> Firecrackers are believed by the Chinese to scare off evil spirits and attract the god of good fortune to people's doorsteps, especially in the celebration of the Spring Festival and at weddings.

贬 biǎn VERB
■ 贬值 biǎnzhí to depreciate
贬义词 biǎnyìcí NOUN
derogatory expression

扁 biǎn ADJECTIVE
flat
自行车胎扁了。Zìxíngchē tāi biǎn le. The bicycle tyre is flat.

变 biàn VERB
1 to change
小城的面貌变了。Xiǎochéng de miànmào biàn le. The appearance of the town has changed.
2 to become
他变懂事了。Tā biàn dǒngshì le. He has grown up.
变化 biànhuà
I VERB
to change
事物随时都在变化。Shìwù suíshí dōu zài biànhuà. Things are always changing.
II NOUN
change
季节的变化 jìjié de biànhuà the changing of the seasons

便 biàn
▷ *see also* pián
I ADJECTIVE
1 convenient
■ 轻便 qīngbiàn portable
2 simple
■ 便饭 biànfàn simple meal
II VERB
to excrete
■ 小便 xiǎobiàn to urinate
■ 大便 dàbiàn to defecate
III ADVERB
■ 稍等片刻演出便开始。Shāoděng piànkè yǎnchū biàn kāishǐ. The performance will start in a moment.
便士 biànshì MEASURE WORD
pence
便条 biàntiáo NOUN
note
便携式 biànxiéshì ADJECTIVE
portable
便携式收音机 biànxiéshì shōuyīnjī a portable radio
便于 biànyú VERB
to be easy to
便于联系 biànyú liánxì to be easy to contact

遍 biàn
I ADVERB
all over
找了个遍 zhǎo le ge biàn searched high and low
II MEASURE WORD

> **LANGUAGE TIP** This is a measure word used for the number of times the same action takes place.

我说了两遍。Wǒ shuō le liǎng biàn. I said it twice.

> **LANGUAGE TIP** Another measure word with a similar meaning to 遍 biàn is 次 cì. The main difference between the two is that 遍 biàn stresses a course from the beginning to end and so it is applied to actions like 读 dú **read**, 写 xiě **write** and 唱 cháng **sing**.

辩 biàn VERB
to debate
■ 辩论 biànlùn to argue
■ 争辩 zhēngbiàn to contend
辨认 biànrèn VERB
to identify
他写的字很难辨认。Tā xiě de zì hěnnán biànrèn. His handwriting is really hard to read.

标 biāo
I NOUN
1 mark
2 standard

Chinese-English

b

II VERB
to mark
■ 标价 to set a price
标本 biāoběn NOUN
specimen
标点 biāodiǎn NOUN
punctuation
标记 biāojì NOUN
mark
标题 biāotí NOUN
1 title
文章标题 wénzhāng biāotí the title of the article
2 headline
标王 biāowáng NOUN
top bidder
标志 biāozhì NOUN
sign
成功的标志 chénggōng de biāozhì a mark of success
标准 biāozhǔn
I NOUN
standard
道德标准 dàodé biāozhǔn moral standard
II ADJECTIVE
standard
标准时间 biāozhǔn shíjiān standard time

表 biǎo NOUN
1 watch
■ 手表 shǒubiǎo wristwatch
2 meter
■ 电表 diànbiǎo electricity meter
3 form
火车时间表 huǒchē shíjiān biǎo train timetable 申请表 shēnqǐng biǎo application form
4 cousin
■ 表哥 biǎogē cousin

> **LANGUAGE TIP** 表哥 biǎogē refers to an elder male cousin. Similarly, 表姐 biǎojiě, 表弟 biǎodì and 表妹 biǎomèi refer to an elder female cousin, younger male cousin and younger female cousin respectively.

> **DID YOU KNOW...?**
> Due to the closeness and importance of extended family in Chinese society, it is extremely common for cousins to be addressed and referred to as simply brother or sister.

表达 biǎodá VERB
to express
表达感情 biǎodá gǎnqíng to express one's feelings
表格 biǎogé NOUN
form
表面 biǎomiàn NOUN
surface
表明 biǎomíng VERB
to make clear
表明态度 biǎomíng tàidù to make one's attitude to something clear
表情 biǎoqíng NOUN
expression
丰富的表情 fēngfù de biǎoqíng vivid expression
表示 biǎoshì
I VERB
to express
表示感谢 biǎoshì gǎnxiè to express gratitude
II NOUN
1 gesture
不友好的表示 bù yǒuhǎo de biǎoshì unfriendly gesture
2 attitude
对于孩子能否上网，他没做明确的表示。Duìyú háizi néngfǒu shàngwǎng, tā méizuò míngquè de biǎoshì. He didn't make his attitude towards children using the Internet clear.
表现 biǎoxiàn
I VERB
to show
II NOUN
performance *(behaviour, style)*
学生在校表现 xuéshēng zàixiào biǎoxiàn the students' behaviour at school
表演 biǎoyǎn
I VERB
to perform
II NOUN
performance
表扬 biǎoyáng VERB
to praise

别 bié
I ADJECTIVE
other
■ 别人 biérén other people
II AUXILIARY VERB
don't
别忘了关灯。Bié wàng le guāndēng. Don't forget to turn off the light.
别针 biézhēn NOUN
safety pin

宾 bīn NOUN
guest
宾馆 bīnguǎn NOUN
hotel

Chinese-English

b

冰 bīng
I NOUN
ice
II VERB
1 to be freezing
这水冰手。Zhè shuǐ bīng shǒu. This water is freezing.
2 to cool
冰镇啤酒 bīngzhèn píjiǔ ice-cold beer
冰淇淋 bīngqílín NOUN
ice cream
冰糖 bīngtáng NOUN
rock sugar
冰箱 bīngxiāng NOUN
fridge

兵 bīng NOUN
1 the army
当兵 dāng bīng to join the army
2 soldier

饼 bǐng NOUN
cake
■ 月饼 yuèbǐng moon cake
饼干 bǐnggān NOUN
biscuit

并 bìng
I VERB
1 to merge
■ 合并 hébìng to merge
2 to bring... together
把脚并起来。Bǎ jiǎo bìng qǐlai. Put your feet together.
II ADVERB
in fact
他今晚并不想出去。Tā jīnwǎn bìng bù xiǎng chūqù. He doesn't want to go out this evening actually.
III CONJUNCTION
and
他会说法语，并在学习西班牙语。Tā huì shuō Fǎyǔ, bìng zài xuéxí Xībānyá yǔ. He can speak French, and he is studying Spanish at the moment.
并且 bìngqiě CONJUNCTION
1 and
她聪明并且用功。Tā cōngmíng bìngqiě yònggōng. She is clever and diligent.
2 also
我们有信心，并且有实力赢得这场比赛。Wǒmen yǒu xìnxīn, bìngqiě yǒu shílì yíngde zhèchǎng bǐsài. We have the confidence and also the ability to win the match.

病 bìng
I NOUN
disease
他去看病了。Tā qù kànbìng le. He went to see a doctor.
■ 心脏病 xīnzàng bìng heart disease
II VERB
to be ill
他病得不轻。Tā bìng de bùqīng. He was seriously ill.
病毒 bìngdú NOUN
virus
病房 bìngfáng NOUN
ward
病句 bìngjù NOUN
ungrammatical sentence
病菌 bìngjūn NOUN
bacteria
病人 bìngrén NOUN
1 patient
2 invalid

波 bō NOUN
wave
波浪 bōlàng NOUN
wave

拨 bō VERB
1 to dial
拨电话号 bō diànhuà hào to dial a phone number
2 to change over to
请拨到少儿台好吗？Qǐng bōdào shào'ér tái hǎoma? Can you change over to the children's channel please?

玻 bō
▷ see below:
玻璃 bōlí NOUN
glass

菠 bō
▷ see below:
菠菜 bōcài NOUN
spinach
菠萝 bōluó NOUN
pineapple

播 bō VERB
to propagate
■ 播放 bōfàng to broadcast

伯 bó NOUN
uncle
伯伯 bóbo NOUN
uncle

LANGUAGE TIP 伯伯 bóbo is a form of address used specifically for one's father's elder brother.

脖 bó NOUN
neck
■ 脖子 bózi neck

博 bó ADJECTIVE
abundant

博物馆 bówùguǎn NOUN
museum

补 bǔ VERB
1 to mend
2 to fill
■ 补牙 bǔyá to fill a tooth
3 to add
请把邮编补上。Qǐng bǎ yóubiān bǔshàng. Please add the postcode.

补充 bǔchōng
I VERB
to add
II ADJECTIVE
supplementary
补充说明 bǔchōng shuōmíng additional explanation

补考 bǔkǎo VERB
to resit
她下学期得补考数学。Tā xià xuéqī děi bǔkǎo shùxué. She has to resit her maths exam next term.
II NOUN
resit
我下个月要参加补考。Wǒ xiàgè yuè yào cānjiā bǔkǎo. I will be taking resits next month.

补习 bǔxí VERB
to take extra lessons

补助 bǔzhù NOUN
subsidy
每月200美元的生活补助 měiyuè èrbǎi měiyuán de shēnghuó bǔzhù a monthly subsidy of 200 US dollars

捕 bǔ VERB
to catch

捕捉 bǔzhuō VERB
1 to seize
捕捉机会 bǔzhuō jīhuì to seize an opportunity
2 to hunt down
捕捉逃犯 bǔzhuō táofàn to hunt down a convict

不 bù ADVERB

LANGUAGE TIP 不 bù is fourth tone unless it is followed by another fourth tone syllable, in which case it is usually pronounced as a second tone, for example 不要 búyào. For more information on tones, see the introduction.

1 not
我不喜欢游泳。Wǒ bù xǐhuān yóuyǒng. I don't like swimming. 不诚实 bù chéngshí dishonest
2 no
你累了吧？— 不，不累。Nǐ lèi le ba? — Bù, búlèi. Are you tired? — No, I'm not.

LANGUAGE TIP 不 bù is also used in polite remarks.

不客气。Bú kèqi. Don't mention it.
不谢。Bú xiè. You're welcome.

LANGUAGE TIP To make a Chinese sentence negative, use 不 bù before the verb.

我不喝酒。Wǒ bù hējiǔ. I don't drink alcohol.

LANGUAGE TIP The only exception is the verb 有 yǒu, **to have**, for which you must use 没 méi.

不必 búbì ADVERB
■ 明天你们不必来了。Míngtiān nǐmen búbì lái le. You don't have to come tomorrow.

不错 búcuò ADJECTIVE
correct

不但 búdàn CONJUNCTION
not only
这辆车的设计不但美观，而且实用。Zhè liàng chē de shèjì búdàn měiguān, érqiě shíyòng. The design of this car is not only beautiful, it's also practical.

不得了 bùdéliǎo ADJECTIVE
extreme
这孩子淘气得不得了。Zhè háizi táoqì de bùdéliǎo. This child is terribly naughty.

不断 búduàn ADVERB
continually
不断进步 búduàn jìnbù to continually progress 沙漠不断扩大。Shāmò búduàn kuòdà. The desert is expanding all the time.

不敢 bùgǎn VERB
to not dare

不管 bùguǎn CONJUNCTION
no matter *(what, how etc)*
不管出什么事，我们都要保持镇定。Bùguǎn chū shénme shì, wǒmen dōuyào bǎochí zhèndìng. Whatever

happens, we should remain calm.

不过 búguò

I ADVERB

only

不过是点小伤。Búguò shì diǎn xiǎoshāng. It's only a slight injury.

LANGUAGE TIP When placed after an adjective 不过 búguò is used to indicate the superlative.

这是最简单不过的方法。Zhè shì zuì jiǎndān búguò de fāngfǎ. This is by far the easiest method.

II CONJUNCTION

but

他很喜欢新学校，不过离家太远了。Tā hěn xǐhuān xīn xuéxiào, búguò lí jiā tài yuǎn le. He really likes his new school, but it's a very long way from home.

不仅 bùjǐn ADVERB

1 not just

这不仅是学校的问题。Zhè bùjǐn shì xuéxiào de wèntí. This is not just the school's problem.

2 not only

这地毯不仅质量好，而且价格便宜。Zhè dìtǎn bùjǐn zhìliàng hǎo, érqiě jiàgé piányi. Not only is the carpet good quality, it's also cheap.

不久 bùjiǔ NOUN

soon

他们不久就要毕业了。Tāmen bùjiǔ jiùyào bìyè le. It's not long until they graduate.

不论 búlùn CONJUNCTION

no matter

不论是谁，都必须遵守纪律。Búlùn shì shuí, dōu bìxū zūnshǒu jìlǜ. No matter who you are, you have to abide by the rules.

不满 bùmǎn ADJECTIVE

dissatisfied

不免 bùmiǎn ADVERB

inevitably

孩子生病，妈妈不免有些担心。Háizi shēngbìng, māma bùmiǎn yǒuxiē dānxīn. The child is ill, so inevitably his mum is a bit worried.

不然 bùrán CONJUNCTION

otherwise

多谢你提醒我，不然我就忘了。Duōxiè nǐ tíxǐng wǒ, bùrán wǒ jiù wàng le. Thanks very much for reminding me, otherwise I would have forgotten about it.

不如 bùrú VERB

to not be as good as

城里太吵，不如住在郊区。Chénglǐ tài chǎo, bùrú zhùzài jiāoqū. The city is too noisy; it's better living in the suburbs.

不少 bùshǎo ADJECTIVE

a lot of

她有不少好朋友。Tā yǒu bùshǎo hǎo péngyou. She has a lot of good friends.

不舒服 bùshūfu ADJECTIVE

unwell

不同 bùtóng ADJECTIVE

different

不幸 búxìng

I ADJECTIVE

1 unhappy

2 unfortunate

II NOUN

misfortune

III ADVERB

unfortunately

不幸，他的话是真的。Búxìng, tāde huà shì zhēnde. Unfortunately, what he said is true.

不要紧 búyàojǐn ADJECTIVE

1 not serious

他的病不要紧。Tā de bìng búyàojǐn. His illness is not serious.

2 it doesn't matter

不要紧，我不会生气的。Búyàojǐn, wǒ búhuì shēngqì de. It doesn't matter, I won't get angry.

不一定 bùyídìng ADVERB

LANGUAGE TIP 不一定 bùyídìng is placed before a verb to express uncertainty about the action.

她不一定会回电话。Tā bùyídìng huì huí diànhuà. She may not return your call.

不怎么样 bùzěnmeyàng ADJECTIVE

not up to much

不止 bùzhǐ ADVERB

1 incessantly

大笑不止 dàxiào bùzhǐ to laugh incessantly

2 more than

不止一次 bùzhǐ yícì on more than one occasion

布 bù NOUN

cloth

布娃娃 bùwáwa rag doll

布丁 bùdīng NOUN

pudding

布置 bùzhì VERB

1 to decorate

布置房间 bùzhì fángjiān to decorate a room

2 to assign

布置任务 bùzhì rènwù to assign a task

步 bù NOUN

1 step

■ 步伐 bùfá pace

2 stage

■ 步骤 bùzhòu step

3 situation

到了这一步，我也没有办法。Dàole zhèyíbù, wǒ yě méiyǒu bànfǎ. In this situation, there is nothing I can do either.

II MEASURE WORD

a move

走一步棋 zǒu yíbù qí to take a move in a game of chess

步行 bùxíng VERB

to go on foot

步行去超市 bùxíng qù chāoshì to walk to the supermarket

部 bù

I NOUN

1 part

■ 局部 júbù part

■ 东部 dōng bù the eastern part

2 department

■ 总部 zǒngbù headquarters *pl* 教育部 jiàoyù bù education department

II MEASURE WORD

LANGUAGE TIP This is a measure word used for films, phones, dictionaries and literary works but not for books.

一部字典 yíbù zìdiǎn a dictionary 一部电话 yí bù diànhuà a telephone

部队 bùduì NOUN

armed forces *pl*

部分 bùfen NOUN

part

部门 bùmén NOUN

department

部位 bùwèi NOUN

place

受伤部位 shòushāng bùwèi the location of an injury

Cc

才 cái
I NOUN
1 ability
■ 有才 yǒucái to have abilities
2 talent
■ 人才 réncái talented people
II ADVERB
1 just
我才到家，电话就响了。Wǒ cái dào jiā, diànhuà jiù xiǎng le. Just as I arrived home, the phone rang.
2 not...until *(later than expected)*
我10点才到学校。Wǒ shídiǎn cái dào xuéxiào. I didn't arrive at school until 10 o'clock.
3 only...if
只有努力，才能考上好大学。Zhǐyǒu nǔlì, cái néng kǎoshàng hǎo dàxué. Only by making an effort will you get into a good university.
4 only *(small amount)*
他才喝了一杯酒。Tā cái hē le yì bēi jiǔ. He only drank one glass of wine.
5 really *(to emphasize)*
他才不想见你呢！ Tā cái bù xiǎng jiàn nǐ ne! He really doesn't want to see you!
才能 cáinéng NOUN
ability
他有领导才能。Tā yǒu lǐngdǎo cáinéng. He has leadership abilities.
才艺秀 cáiyìxiù NOUN
talent show

材 cái NOUN
material
■ 教材 jiàocái teaching materials
材料 cáiliào NOUN
1 material
这张桌子是用什么材料做的？Zhè zhāng zhuōzi shì yòng shénme cáiliào zuò de? What material is this table made from?
2 talent
我不是唱歌的材料。Wǒ búshì chànggē de cáiliào. I don't have what it takes to be a singer.

LANGUAGE TIP …不是…的材料 ...búshì ... de caíliaò is a commonly used construction in Chinese. It literally means **...is not material for...**

财 cái NOUN
wealth
■ 发财 fācái to become wealthy
财富 cáifù NOUN
wealth
国家财富 guójiā cáifù national wealth

采 cǎi VERB
1 to pick
■ 采茶 cǎi chá to pick tea leaves
2 to gather
■ 采集 cǎijí to collect
采访 cǎifǎng VERB
to interview
采取 cǎiqǔ VERB
to adopt
他们采取了不一样的解决方法。Tāmen cǎiqǔ le bùyíyàng de jiějué fāngfǎ. They adopted a different solution.

彩 cǎi NOUN
1 colour
■ 彩带 cǎidài colour stripe
■ 彩虹 cǎihóng rainbow
2 variety
丰富多彩 fēng fù duō cǎi rich and varied
彩电 cǎidiàn NOUN
colour TV
彩票 cǎipiào NOUN
lottery ticket
彩色 cǎisè NOUN
colour
彩色照片 cǎisè zhàopiàn colour pictures

菜 cài NOUN
1 vegetable
2 dish

她会做上海菜。Tā huì zuò shànghǎi cài. He can cook Shanghai cuisine.

DID YOU KNOW...? In the most formal Chinese restaurants, meals begin with a few 冷菜 léng cài **cold dishes**, followed by 热菜 rè cài **hot dishes**. Then come 主食 zhǔ shí **staples** and finally 甜点 tián diǎn **desserts**.

菜单 càidān NOUN
menu
菜单上有二十多个菜。Càidān shàng yǒu èrshí duō gè cài. There are twenty dishes on the menu.

菜谱 càipǔ NOUN
1 menu
2 recipe
3 cookbook

参 cān VERB
1 to join
■ 参军 cānjūn to enlist *(in the military)*
2 to refer to
■ 参考 cānkǎo to consult 请参考这本书。Qǐng cānkǎo zhè běn shū. Please consult this book.

参观 cānguān VERB
to tour
学生们参观了一家工厂。Xuésheng men cānguān le yìjiā gōngchǎng. The students toured a factory.

参加 cānjiā VERB
to take part in
参加足球比赛 cānjiā zúqiú bǐsài to participate in a football match

参考书 cān kǎo shū NOUN
reference book

参与 cānyù VERB
to participate in
参与课外活动 cānyù kèwài huódòng to participate in extracurricular activities

---

餐 cān NOUN
meal
■ 午餐 wǔcān lunch

LANGUAGE TIP As a foreigner in China, locals who invite you out to dinner will often ask whether you would like to eat 西餐 xī cān **western food** or 中餐 zhōng cān **Chinese food**.

餐具 cānjù NOUN
cutlery
一套餐具 yí tào cānjù a cutlery set

餐厅 cāntīng NOUN
1 canteen
2 restaurant

残 cán ADJECTIVE
incomplete
■ 残品 cánpǐn damaged goods

残疾 cánjí NOUN
disability

操 cāo
I VERB
to hold
操一把刀 cāo yì bǎ dāo to hold a knife
II NOUN
exercise
■ 早操 zǎocāo morning exercise

DID YOU KNOW...? Many Chinese elders go to the parks in the morning to run or do t'ai chi.

操场 cāochǎng NOUN
sports ground

操心 cāoxīn VERB
to worry about
父母为他的身体操心。Fùmǔ wèi tā de shēntǐ cāoxīn. His parents worried about his health.

草 cǎo
I NOUN
1 grass
■ 草地 cǎodì lawn
2 straw
■ 草鞋 cǎoxié sandals
II ADJECTIVE
illegible
他的字写得太草。Tā de zì xiě de tài cǎo. His handwriting is illegible.

DID YOU KNOW...? There is a Chinese calligraphic style named 草书 cǎo shū after the seemingly messy flow of its brushstrokes.

草稿 cǎogǎo NOUN
rough draft

草原 cǎoyuán NOUN
grasslands

册 cè
I NOUN
book
■ 手册 shǒucè handbook
■ 相册 xiàngcè photo album
II MEASURE WORD
1 copy
2 volume

厕 cè NOUN
toilet
■ 公厕 gōngcè public toilet

厕所 cèsuǒ NOUN
toilet

侧 cè
I NOUN
side
■ 两侧 liǎngcè both sides 马路的两侧 mǎlù de liǎngcè both sides of the street
II VERB
to turn... away
我侧过脸去。Wǒ cè guò liǎn qù. I turned my face away.

侧面 cèmiàn
I ADJECTIVE
1 unofficial
侧面消息 cèmiàn xiāoxi unofficial information
2 side
侧面的大楼是另外一个公司的。Cèmiàn de dàlóu shì lìngwài yí gè gōngsī de. The building to the side here belongs to another company.
II NOUN
side

测 cè VERB
to measure
■ 自测 zìcè medical self-test

测量 cèliáng
I VERB
to measure
测量土地 cèliáng tǔdì to measure an area of land
II NOUN
survey

测试 cèshì
I VERB
to test
测试学生的写作能力 cèshì xuésheng de xiězuò nénglì to test the students' writing skills
II NOUN
test

测验 cèyàn
I VERB
to test
测验分析能力 cèyàn fēnxi nénglì to test analytical skills
II NOUN
test

层 céng
I MEASURE WORD
1 floor
这座大楼有50层。Zhè zuò dàlóu yǒu wǔshí céng. This building has 50 floors.
2 layer
书上有一层灰。Shúshàng yǒu yì céng huī. There is a layer of dust on the book.
II NOUN
layer
飞机穿过云层。Fēijī chuānguò yúncéng. The plane passed through layers of cloud.

曾 céng ADVERB
▷ *see also* zēng
once
他曾当过三年厨师。Tā céng dāngguo sānnián chúshī. In the past, he worked as a chef for three years.

曾经 céngjīng ADVERB
once
我曾经想出国留学。Wǒ céngjīng xiǎng chūguó liúxué. I once wanted to study abroad.

叉 chā
I NOUN
1 fork
吃西餐要用刀和叉。Chī xīcān yàoyòng dāo hé chā. To eat Western food one must use a fork and a knife.
2 cross
II VERB
to spear

叉子 chāzi NOUN
1 cross
在纸上画叉子 zài zhǐ shàng huà chāzi to draw a cross on a piece of paper
2 fork

差 chā NOUN
▷ *see also* chà
difference
这两个数的差是多少？Zhè liǎnggè shù de chā shì duōshǎo? What's the difference between these two numbers?

差别 chābié NOUN
difference
这两个城市差别很大。Zhè liǎnggè chéngshì chābié hěn dà. The difference between these two cities is big.

差错 chācuò NOUN
mistake
他做事很马虎，经常出差错。Tā zuòshì hěn mǎhu, jīngcháng chū chācuò. He does things in a careless way and often makes mistakes.

差距 chājù NOUN
difference
姐妹俩在学习上的差距越来越大。Jiěmèi liǎ zài xuéxí shang de chājù yuèláiyuè dà.

Study-wise, the difference between the two sisters is growing larger.

插 chā VERB

1 to insert

插插销 chā chāxiāo to plug in a plug

2 to interject *(in speech)*

我能不能插一句？Wǒ néngbunéng chā yíjù? Can I interrupt just a second?

插入 chārù VERB

to insert

插图 chātú NOUN

illustration

插销 chāxiāo NOUN

1 bolt

2 electrical plug

插座 chāzuò NOUN

socket

茶 chá NOUN

tea

泡茶 pào chá to make tea

■ 红茶 hóngchá black tea

■ 茶杯 chábēi teacup

■ 茶壶 cháhú teapot

■ 茶馆 cháguǎn teahouse

DID YOU KNOW...?

Tea is an integral part of Chinese culture. Aside from being a widely consumed drink, it is considered a medicine for various ailments. The Classic of Tea, 茶经 chájīng, written by 陆羽 Lù Yǔ (733-804 AD), was the very first treatise written on tea in the world.

茶叶 cháyè NOUN

tea leaves

查 chá VERB

1 to check

我忘了查短信了。Wǒ wàng le chá duǎnxìn le. I forgot to check my text messages.

2 to look... up

查字典 chá zìdiǎn to consult the dictionary

查找 cházhǎo VERB

to look for

在网上查找老朋友 zài wǎngshang cházhǎo lǎo péngyou to look for old friends on the internet

差 chà

▷ *see also* chā

I VERB

1 to be different from

你比他差远了。Nǐ bǐ tā chà yuǎn le. You are not nearly as good as him.

2 to be short of

差3个人 chà sān gè rén to be three people short 他还差我10镑钱。Tā hái chà wǒ shí bàng qián. He still owes me ten pounds.

II ADJECTIVE

bad

质量差 zhìliàng chà bad quality 这些鞋的质量很差。Zhèxiē xié de zhìliàng hěn chà. These shoes are of poor quality.

差不多 chà bu duō

I ADJECTIVE

very similar

这两块布颜色差不多。Zhè liǎng kuài bù yánsè chà bu duō. The colour of these two pieces of material is very similar.

II ADVERB

almost

晚饭差不多快做好了。Wǎnfàn chà bu duō kuài zuò hǎo le. Dinner is almost ready.

产 chǎn VERB

1 to give birth to

2 to produce

这里产石油。Zhèlǐ chǎn shíyòu. Oil is produced here.

产品 chǎnpǐn NOUN

product

产品质量 chǎnpǐn zhìliàng product quality

产生 chǎnshēng VERB

to become

他对电脑产生了兴趣。Tā duì diànnǎo chǎnshēng le xìngqù. He became interested in computers.

长 cháng

▷ *see also* zhǎng

I ADJECTIVE

long

长发 cháng fà long hair

II NOUN

length

这张桌子有两米长。Zhè zháng zhuōzi yǒu liǎng mǐ cháng. This table is two metres in length.

长城 Chángchéng NOUN

the Great Wall

DID YOU KNOW...?

As one of the longest man-made mega structures in the world, the Great Wall of China is nearly 4,000 miles in length, reaching from the border of Xinjiang province in the west to the eastern coast just north of Beijing.

长度 chángdù NOUN

length

桌子的长度 zhuōzi de chángdù the length of the table

长江 Cháng Jiāng NOUN
the Yangtze

> **DID YOU KNOW...?**
> The Yangtze is the longest river in Asia. It divides North and South China. The Three Gorges Dam, the largest irrigation project in the world, constitutes an attempt to tame the river's frequent floods.

长久 chángjiǔ ADJECTIVE
long-term
长久的打算 chángjiǔ de dǎsuàn long-term plans

长跑 chángpǎo VERB
to go long-distance running
你参加过长跑比赛吗？Nǐ cānjiā guo chángpǎo bǐsài ma? Have you ever taken part in any long-distance running competitions?

长寿 chángshòu ADJECTIVE
long-lived
祝您长寿！ Zhù nín chángshòu! Here's to a long life!

长途 chángtú ADJECTIVE
long-distance
长途电话 chángtú diànhuà long-distance phone call 长途旅行 chángtú lǚxíng long-distance journey

---

尝 cháng VERB
to taste
你尝一下这个菜。Nǐ cháng yixià zhège cài. Taste this food.

尝试 chángshì VERB
to try

常 cháng

I ADJECTIVE
frequent
■ 常客 chángkè regular guest

II ADVERB
often
我常去看戏。Wǒ cháng qù kànxì. I often go to the theatre.

常常 chángcháng ADVERB
often
我常常去北京看朋友。Wǒ chángcháng qù Běijīng kàn péngyou. I often go to Beijing to see friends.

常识 chángshí NOUN
1 general knowledge
健康常识 jiànkāng chángshí general health knowledge
2 common sense
不懂常识 bùdǒng chángshí to not have common sense

场 chǎng

I NOUN
1 ground
■ 排球场 páiqiúchǎng volleyball court
■ 操场 cāochǎng sports ground
■ 市场 shìchǎng market
2 stage
■ 上场 shàngchǎng to go on stage

II MEASURE WORD

> **LANGUAGE TIP** This is a measure word used for games and shows.

一场足球赛 yì chǎng zúqiú sài a football match 两场音乐会 liǎng chǎng yīnyuèhuì two concerts

> **LANGUAGE TIP** This is a measure word used for illnesses.

一场重病 yì chǎng zhòngbìng a serious illness

> **LANGUAGE TIP** This is a measure word used for afflictions, wars, accidents etc.

一场火灾 yì chǎng huǒzāi a fire 一场战争 yì chǎng zhànzhēng a war

唱 chàng VERB
to sing
■ 独唱 dúchàng solo
■ 合唱 héchàng chorus

唱歌 chànggē VERB
to sing
我们一起唱歌吧。Wǒmen yìqǐ chànggē ba. Let's sing together.

抄 chāo VERB
1 to copy
2 to plagiarize
不要抄别人的作业。Búyào chāo biérén de zuòyè. Don't copy other people's homework.

钞 chāo NOUN
banknote

钞票 chāopiào NOUN
banknote

超 chāo

I VERB
to exceed
参加会议的超百人。Cānjiā huìyì de chāo bǎi rén. There were more than one hundred people participating in the conference.

II ADJECTIVE
super
■ 超短裙 chāoduǎnqún miniskirt

超级 chāojí ADJECTIVE

super
超级大国 chāojí dàguó superpower

超人 chāorén NOUN
superman

超市 chāoshì NOUN
supermarket

吵 chǎo
I VERB
1 to make a racket
他声音太大，吵得人不能睡觉。Tā shēngyīn tài dà, chǎo de rén bùnéng shuìjiào. His voice is too loud; it makes such a racket that no one can sleep.
2 to squabble
他们在一起总是吵。Tāmen zài yìqǐ zǒngshì chǎo. They always squabble when they're together.
II ADJECTIVE
noisy
这里太吵。Zhèlǐ tàichǎo. It's too noisy here.

吵架 chǎojià VERB
to quarrel
他的父母又吵架了。Tāde fùmǔ yòu chǎojià le. His parents had another argument.

炒 chǎo VERB
1 to stir-fry
炒菜 chǎocài to stir-fry
■ 炒饭 chǎofàn stir-fried rice
2 to speculate *(stocks)*
■ 炒股 chǎogǔ to speculate in stocks and shares
3 to sack
他被老板炒了。Tā bèi lǎobǎn chǎo le. He was sacked by the boss.
■ 炒鱿鱼 chǎo yóuyú to be fired

车 chē NOUN
vehicle
■ 汽车 qìchē car
■ 公共汽车 gōnggòng qìchē bus
■ 风车 fēngchē windmill

车本儿 chē běnr NOUN
driving licence

车库 chēkù NOUN
garage

车厢 chēxiāng NOUN
carriage *(in trains)*

车站 chēzhàn NOUN
1 railway station
2 bus stop

沉 chén
I VERB
1 to sink
船沉到了海底。Chuán chén dào le hǎi dǐ. The ship sank to the bottom of the sea.
2 to become grave
她沉下了脸。Tā chén xià le liǎn. Her face became grave.
II ADJECTIVE
1 heavy
这个箱子很沉。Zhège xiāngzi hěn chén. This box is very heavy.
2 deep *(sleep)*
昨晚我睡得很沉。Zuówǎn wǒ shuì de hěn chén. Last night I slept very deeply.

晨 chén NOUN
morning
■ 早晨 zǎochén early morning

衬 chèn NOUN
lining
■ 衬衫 chènshān shirt

称 chēng
I VERB
1 to call
我们都称他老王。Wǒmen dōu chēng tā lǎo Wáng. We all call him Old Wang.
2 to weigh
称重量 chēng zhòngliàng to weigh
II NOUN
name
■ 简称 jiǎnchēng abbreviation

称呼 chēnghu
I VERB
to call
请问您怎么称呼? Qǐng wèn nín zěnme chēnghu? Excuse me, what is your name?
II NOUN
form of address
不礼貌的称呼 bù lǐmào de chēnghu an impolite form of address

称赞 chēngzàn VERB
to praise
老师常常称赞她。Lǎoshī chángcháng chēngzàn tā. The teacher often praises her.

成 chéng
I VERB
1 to accomplish
那件事成了。Nà jiàn shì chéng le. The job is done.
2 to become
两个人成了好朋友。Liǎng gè rén chéng le hǎo péngyou. The two of them became good friends.

LANGUAGE TIP 成 chéng can be used in combination with other verbs to indicate a transformation through an action. 生米煮成了熟饭 shēngmǐ zhǔ chéngle shúfàn is a saying which literally means **Raw rice has turned into cooked rice** and describes a change which cannot be reversed.

II ADJECTIVE
OK
成！就这么定了。Chéng! Jiù zhème dìng le. OK! That's agreed.

成功 chénggōng
I VERB
to succeed
II ADJECTIVE
successful
运动会开得很成功。Yùndònghuì kāi de hěn chénggōng. The sports competition was very successful.

成绩 chéngjì NOUN
grade
他的学习成绩非常好。Tā de xuéxí chéngjì fēicháng hǎo. He has very good grades.

成就 chéngjiù NOUN
achievement
他在事业上很有成就。Tā zài shìyè shàng hěn yǒu chéngjiù. He has achieved much in his career.

成立 chénglì VERB
to establish
一所新学校成立了。Yì suǒ xīn xuéxiào chénglì le. A new school has been established.

成年 chéngnián VERB
1 to mature *(animals, plants)*
2 to grow up
孩子们都成年了。Hǎizi men dōu chéngnián le. All of the children have grown up.

成年人 chéngniánrén NOUN
adult

成人 chéngrén
I NOUN
adult
成人班 chéngrén bān adult class
II VERB
to grow up

成熟 chéngshú ADJECTIVE
1 ripe *(fruit, crops, opportunities)*
苹果成熟了。Píngguǒ chéngshú le. The apples are ripe.
2 mature *(mentally)*
他的想法很不成熟。Tā de xiǎngfǎ hěn bù chéngshú. His way of thinking is very immature.

成为 chéngwéi VERB
to become
她成为了一名作家。Tā chéngwéi le yì míng zuòjiā. She became an author.

成语 chéngyǔ NOUN
idiom

DID YOU KNOW...?
The Chinese language is full of four-character idioms. These sayings are often distillations of legends which succinctly and colourfully capture a particular situation. An example of a popular idiom is 骑虎难下 qí hǔ nán xià, **once you have hopped on a tiger, it is difficult to dismount**. This idiom warns that it isn't easy to disentangle oneself from difficult situations.

成员 chéngyuán NOUN
member
家庭成员 jiātíng chéngyuán family member

成长 chéngzhǎng VERB
to grow up
希望孩子们健康成长 xīwàng háizi men jiànkāng chéngzhǎng to hope children will grow in a healthy way

---

诚 chéng ADJECTIVE
honest
■诚心 chéngxīn sincere

诚恳 chéngkěn ADJECTIVE
sincere
他诚恳地向她表示了感谢。Tā chéngkěng de xiàng tā biǎoshì le gǎnxiè. He thanked her sincerely.

诚实 chéngshí ADJECTIVE
honest
每个人都应该诚实。Měigè rén dōu yīnggāi chéngshí. Everyone should be honest.

城 chéng NOUN
1 city
2 town
■进城 jìnchéng to go to town

城市 chéngshì NOUN
city

乘 chéng VERB
1 to travel by
乘火车 chéng huǒchē to travel by train
2 to multiply
8乘5等于40。Bā chéng wǔ děngyú sìshí. 8 times 5 is 40.

乘客 chéngkè NOUN
passenger

乘务员 chéngwùyuán NOUN
1 conductor *(on trains, buses)*
2 air hostess

盛 chéng VERB
1 to ladle... out
盛饭 chéng fàn to ladle out food
2 to contain
这个袋子可以盛50公斤。Zhège dàizi kěyǐ chéng wǔshí gōngjīn. This bag can hold 50 kilos.

吃 chī VERB
1 to eat
吃面条 chī miàntiáo to eat noodles
2 to take *(medicine)*
■ 吃药 chīyào to take medicine

吃醋 chīcù VERB
to be jealous
我的女友好吃醋。Wǒ de nǚyǒu hào chīcù. My girlfriend gets jealous easily.

吃饭 chīfàn VERB
to have a meal

LANGUAGE TIP To ask **How do you do?**, Chinese people will often ask 你吃饭了吗? Nǐ chī fàn le ma? which literally means **Have you eaten?**

吃惊 chījīng VERB
to surprise
他的话很让人吃惊。Tā de huà hěn ràngrén chījīng. His words really surprised us.

迟 chí ADJECTIVE
late
对不起，迟了10分钟。Duìbuqǐ, chí le shí fēnzhōng. Sorry, I'm ten minutes late.

迟到 chídào VERB
to arrive late
她上班常常迟到。Tā shàngbān chángcháng chídào. She often arrives late for work.

冲 chōng VERB
1 to rush forward
冲向终点 chōng xiàng zhōngdiǎn to rush towards the destination
2 to rinse
冲一冲碗筷 chōng yi chōng wǎn kuài to rinse the bowls and chopsticks

冲洗 chōngxǐ VERB
1 to wash
冲洗汽车 chōngxǐ qìchē to clean a car
2 to develop *(film)*

充 chōng VERB
1 to fill
■ 充值 chōngzhí to top up
2 to act as
■ 充当 chōngdāng to act as 充当助手 chōngdāng zhùshǒu to act as an assistant

充电 chōngdiàn VERB
1 to charge
给电池充电 gěi diànchí chōngdiàn to charge batteries
2 to recharge one's batteries

充分 chōngfèn
I ADJECTIVE
full
做好充分的准备 zuò hǎo chōngfèn de zhǔnbèi to make full preparations
II ADVERB
fully
充分认识自己 chōngfèn rènshi zìjǐ to fully know oneself

充满 chōngmǎn VERB
1 to fill
他的眼里充满泪水。Tā de yǎnlǐ chōngmǎn lèishuǐ. His eyes were filled with tears.
2 to brim with
他的话充满自信。Tā de huà chōngmǎn zìxìn. His speech brimmed with confidence.

虫 chóng NOUN
insect
■ 虫子 chóngzi insect

重 chóng
▷ *see also* zhòng
I VERB
to repeat
书买重了。Shū mǎi chóng le. I bought the same book twice.
II ADVERB
again
他把作文重写了一遍。Tā bǎ zuòwén chóngxiě le yíbiàn. He wrote his essay all over again.

重复 chóngfù VERB
to repeat
那句话他重复了三遍。Nà jù huà tā chóngfù le sān biàn. He repeated that sentence three times.

重新 chóngxīn ADVERB
again
重新开始 chóngxīn kāishǐ to start again

崇 chóng VERB
to think highly of
■ 推崇 tuīchóng to hold... in great esteem

崇拜 chóngbài VERB
to worship
他很崇拜那个歌星。Tā hěn chóngbài nàge gēxīng. She worships that singer.

宠 chǒng VERB
to spoil
他被妈妈宠坏了。Tā bèi māma chǒng huài le. He was spoilt by his mum.

宠爱 chǒng'ài VERB
to dote on

宠物 chǒngwù NOUN
pet
养宠物 yǎng chǒngwù to have a pet

抽 chōu VERB
1 to draw out *(from a pile)*
抽出一张纸 chōu chū yì zhāng zhǐ to pull out a piece of paper
2 to find *(time)*
抽时间 chōu shíjiān to find time
3 to draw
抽水 chōushuǐ to pump water
■抽烟 chōuyān to smoke
■抽血 chōuxiě to take blood

抽屉 chōuti NOUN
drawer

丑 chǒu ADJECTIVE
ugly
他长得不丑。Tā zhǎng de bù chǒu. He's not ugly.

臭 chòu ADJECTIVE
smelly

出 chū VERB
1 to go out

LANGUAGE TIP 出 chū can also be used either with 来 lái or 去 qù to indicate movement towards or away from the speaker respectively.

她出去了。Tā chūqù le. He went out.
他出来了。Tā chūlái le. He came out.
■出国 chūguó to go abroad
2 to appear
■出庭 chūtíng to appear in court
3 to exceed
不出三天货就到了。Bù chū sān tiān huò jiù dào le. The goods arrived within three days.
4 to produce
这个地方出苹果。Zhège dìfang chū píngguǒ. This area produces apples.
5 to occur
■出事 chūshì to have an accident
6 to come out
■出血 chūxiě to bleed
■出汗 chūhàn to sweat
7 to become
■出名 chūmíng to become famous

出差 chūchāi VERB
to go away on business
我经常去北京出差。Wǒ jīngcháng qù Běijīng chūchāi. I often go to Beijing on business.

出发 chūfā VERB
to set out
我们明天早上六点出发。Wǒmen míngtiān zǎoshang liù diǎn chūfā. We set out tomorrow morning at 6.

出口 chūkǒu
I VERB
to export
II NOUN
exit

出去 chūqù VERB
to go out
出去吃饭 chūqù chīfàn to go out and eat

出色 chūsè ADJECTIVE
outstanding
爸爸是一位出色的警察。Bàba shì yí wèi chūsè de jǐngchá. Dad is an outstanding policeman.

出生 chūshēng VERB
to be born
她出生在英国。Tā chūshēng zài Yīngguó. She was born in Great Britain.

出售 chūshòu VERB
to sell
这个商店不出售酒。Zhège shāngdiàn bù chūshòu jiǔ. This shop does not sell alcohol.

出现 chūxiàn VERB
to appear
他的名字很久没出现在报纸上了。Tā de míngzi hěnjiǔ méi chūxiàn zài bàozhǐ shàng le. His name hasn't appeared in the papers for a long time.

出租 chūzū VERB
to let
有房出租 yǒu fáng chūzū room to let

出租车 chūzūchē NOUN
taxi

初 chū ADJECTIVE
1 first
初次交往 chū cì jiāowǎng first contact
■初恋 chūliàn first love
2 primary
■初级产品 chūjí chǎnpǐn primary products

3 early
■ 初冬 chūdōng early winter

初中 chūzhōng NOUN
junior middle school
上初中 shàng chūzhōng to go to junior middle school

除 chú
I VERB
1 to get rid of
■ 开除 kāichú to dismiss
■ 去除 qùchú to remove
2 to divide *(in maths)*
16除8等于2。Shíliù chú bā děngyú èr. 16 divided by 8 is 2.
■ 除法 chúfǎ division
II PREPOSITION
1 except
除彼得外大家都来了。Chú Bǐdé wài dàjiā dōu lái le. Everyone came except Peter.
2 apart from
除了珍妮，谁还去过上海？Chúle Zhēnní, shuí hái qùguo Shànghǎi? Apart from Jenny, who else has been to Shanghai?

除非 chúfēi CONJUNCTION
unless
除非他要我去，否则我不去。Chúfēi tā yào wǒ qù, fǒuzé wǒ bú qù. I won't go unless he wants me to.

除了 chúle PREPOSITION
1 except
除了你，其他人都参加了会议。Chúle nǐ, qítā rén dōu cānjiā le huìyì. Everyone attended the meeting except you.
2 apart from
他除了学习英语，还学习日语。Tā chúle xuéxí Yīngyǔ, hái xuéxí Rìyǔ. Apart from studying English, he also studies Japanese.
3 apart from... the only...
他除了工作就是睡觉。Tā chúle gōngzuò jiùshì shuìjiào. The only thing he does apart from work is sleep.

除夕 chúxī NOUN
Chinese New Year's Eve

厨 chú NOUN
1 kitchen
■ 厨房 chúfáng kitchen
2 cook

厨师 chúshī NOUN
cook

橱 chú NOUN
cabinet

橱柜 chúguì NOUN
cupboard

处 chǔ VERB
to get along with
她俩处得像姐妹一样。Tā liǎ chǔ de xiàng jiěmèi yíyàng. The two women get along like sisters.

处分 chǔfèn
I VERB
to punish
这次一共处分了5个人。Zhè cì yígòng chǔfèn le wǔ gè rén. This time around, a total of five people were punished.
II NOUN
punishment
纪律处分 jìlǜ chǔfèn disciplinary punishment

处理 chǔlǐ VERB
1 to deal with
你来处理这件事吧。Nǐ lái chǔlǐ zhè jiàn shì ba. Come and take care of this.
2 to sell... at a reduced price
处理品 chǔlǐ pǐn goods sold at a discount
3 to treat
经过高温处理的奶粉 jīngguò gāowēn chǔlǐ de nǎifěn UHT milk powder

处于 chǔyú VERB
to be in a position
处于重要时期 chǔyú zhòngyào shíqī at an important time

川 chuān NOUN
1 river
2 plain

穿 chuān VERB
1 to wear
她喜欢穿蓝色的衣服。Tā xǐhuan chuān lánsè de yīfu. She likes to wear blue clothes.
2 to cross
穿过人群 chuān guò rénqún to pass through the crowd
3 to pierce
墙上穿了一个洞。Qiángshang chuān le yígè dòng. There is a hole in the wall.

传 chuán VERB
to hand... down
这条项链是奶奶传下来的。Zhè tiáo xiàngliàn shì nǎinai chuán xiàlái de. This necklace was handed down by grandma.

传播 chuánbō VERB
to disseminate

传播信息 chuánbō xìnxī to disseminate information

传染 chuánrǎn VERB
to infect *(virus)*
我把感冒传染给他了。Wǒ bǎ gǎnmào chuánrǎn gěi tā le. I've infected him with my cold.

传染病 chuánrǎnbìng NOUN
infectious disease

传说 chuánshuō NOUN
legend

传统 chuántǒng
I NOUN
tradition
II ADJECTIVE
1 traditional
传统节日 chuántǒng jiérì traditional holiday
2 conservative

传真 chuánzhēn NOUN
fax
给我发个传真吧。Gěi wǒ fā ge chuánzhēn ba. Send me a fax.

传真机 chuánzhēnjī NOUN
fax machine

船 chuán NOUN
1 boat
2 ship

串 chuàn
I VERB
1 to string... together
她把珍珠串了起来。Tā bǎ zhēnzhū chuàn le qǐlái. She strung the pearls together.
2 to drop by
■ 串门 chuànmén to drop by 他爱来我家串门。Tā ài lái wǒ jiā chuànmén. He likes to drop by my place.
II MEASURE WORD
bunch

> LANGUAGE TIP This is a measure word used for keys, necklaces, bracelets etc.

两串钥匙 liǎng chuàn yàoshi two bunches of keys

窗 chuāng NOUN
window
■ 窗子 chuāngzi window

窗户 chuānghu NOUN
window

床 chuáng
I NOUN
bed
单人床 dānrén chuáng single bed 双人床 shuāngrén chuáng double bed
■ 床单 chuángdān bed sheet
■ 上床 shàngchuáng to go to bed
II MEASURE WORD
一床被子 yì chuáng bèizi one quilt

创 chuàng VERB
to create
■ 独创 dúchuàng an original creation

创造 chuàngzào VERB
to create
创造财富 chuàngzào cáifù to create wealth

创作 chuàngzuò VERB
to create *(creative works)*
创作文学作品 chuàngzuò wénxué zuòpǐn to create literary works

吹 chuī VERB
1 to blow
吹蜡烛 chuī làzhú to blow out a candle
2 play *(wind instrument)*
吹口琴 chuī kǒuqín to play the harmonica
3 to boast
他老吹他有钱。Tā lǎo chūi tā yǒu qián. He always boasts about his money.
4 to fall through
我和女友吹了。Wǒ hé nǚyǒu chuī le. I broke up with my girlfriend.

吹风 chuīfēng VERB
to blow-dry

吹牛 chuīniú VERB
to brag

春 chūn NOUN
spring

春节 Chūn Jié NOUN
Chinese New Year
过春节 guò Chūn Jié to spend the Chinese New Year

> DID YOU KNOW...?
> 春节 Chūn Jié **Chinese New Year**, or **Spring Festival**, is the most important festival of the year and falls on the first day of the lunar calendar. Traditionally families gather together, children receive money in red envelopes, and in some parts of China everyone helps make and eat a festival feast. When greeting people during this festival it is traditional to wish them wealth and happiness, by saying 恭喜发财 gōngxǐ fācái.

春卷 chūnjuǎn NOUN
spring roll

春天 chūntiān NOUN
spring

纯 chún ADJECTIVE
pure

纯粹 chúncuì ADVERB
purely
这纯粹是他的错。Zhè chúncuì shì tā de cuò. This is entirely his mistake.

纯洁 chúnjié ADJECTIVE
pure
纯洁的心灵 chúnjié de xīnlíng a pure soul

纯净水 chúnjìng shuǐ NOUN
pure water

词 cí NOUN
1 word

> LANGUAGE TIP 词 cí means **word** whereas 字 zì means **character**. A 词 cí can be formed by one or more 字 zì.

2 speech
■ 闭幕词 bìmùcí closing speech

词典 cídiǎn NOUN
dictionary

词汇 cíhuì NOUN
vocabulary

词语 cíyǔ NOUN
word
请用下面的词语造句。Qǐng yòng xiàmiàn de cíyǔ zàojù. Please use the following words to make sentences.

词组 cízǔ NOUN
phrase

辞 cí VERB
1 to resign
他辞掉了工作。Tā cí diào le gōngzuò. He resigned from work.
2 to dismiss
他被经理辞了。Tā bèi jīnglǐ cí le. He was dismissed by the manager.

辞职 cízhí VERB
to resign

此 cǐ PRONOUN
this
此人不是本地人。Cǐ rén bú shì běndì rén. This person is not local.

此外 cǐwài CONJUNCTION
apart from this
她会说英语和法语，此外还对汉语感兴趣。Tā huì shuō Yīngyǔ hé Fǎyǔ, cǐwài hái duì Hànyǔ gǎn xìngqù. He can speak English and French. Apart from these, he's interested in Chinese.

次 cì
I MEASURE WORD
time
我去过中国很多次了。Wǒ qùguò Zhōngguó hěnduō cì le. I've been to China many times.
II ADJECTIVE
poor
电影拍得太次了。Diànyǐng pāi de tài cì le. The film was really badly made.

匆 cōng ADJECTIVE
hurried

匆忙 cōngmáng ADJECTIVE
hurried
匆忙的生活 cōngmáng de shēnghuó a hectic life

聪 cōng ADJECTIVE
clever

聪明 cōngming ADJECTIVE
clever

从 cóng PREPOSITION
from
从前到后 cóng qián dào hòu from front to back 飞机从我们头顶飞过。Fēijī cóng wǒmen tóudǐng fēiguò. The plane passed over our heads.

从此 cóngcǐ ADVERB
from then on
他从此再不能开车了。Tā cóngcǐ zài bù néng kāichē le. From then on, he couldn't drive.

> LANGUAGE TIP When used with the present tense, translate as **from now on**.

从来 cónglái ADVERB
never *(used in negative sentences)*
我从来没去过美国。Wǒ cónglái méi qù guo měiguó. I've never been to the States.

从来不 cóngláibù ADVERB
never

从没 cóngméi ADVERB
never
他从没见过大海。Tā cóngméi jiàn guò dàhǎi. He has never seen the ocean.

> LANGUAGE TIP When using 从没 cóngméi, 过 guò is placed after the verb.

从前 cóngqián NOUN
past
希望你比从前快乐。Xīwàng nǐ bǐ cóngqián kuàilè. I hope you are happier than you were before.

凑 còu VERB
1 to gather... together
他们经常凑在一起打牌。Tāmen jīngcháng còu zài yìqǐ dǎpái. They often gather together to play cards.
2 to approach
你凑近点儿看一看。Nǐ còu jìn diǎnr kàn yi kàn. Come closer and take a look.

凑合 còuhe VERB
to make do
这支笔你就凑合着用吧。Zhè zhī bǐ nǐ jiù còuhe zhe yòng ba. Make do with this pen.

凑巧 còuqiǎo ADJECTIVE
lucky
真不凑巧，没带钱。Zhēn bú còuqiǎo, méi dài qián. It's a shame that I didn't bring my money.

粗 cū ADJECTIVE
1 thick
这条绳子很粗。Zhè tiáo shéngzi hěn cū. This rope is very thick.
2 coarse
粗布衣服 cū bù yīfu clothes made of coarse fabric
3 gruff
粗嗓门儿 cū sǎngménr a gruff voice

粗糙 cūcāo ADJECTIVE
1 rough
这面墙很粗糙。Zhè miàn qiáng hěn cūcāo. This wall's surface is very rough.
2 crude *(drawing, object)*

粗话 cūhuà NOUN
obscene language
这个人经常讲粗话。Zhègè rén jīngcháng jiǎng cūhuà. This person often uses obscene language.

粗心 cūxīn ADJECTIVE
careless

促 cù VERB
to hurry
■ 催促 cuīcù to hurry

促进 cùjìn VERB
to promote
促进两国的合作 cùjìn liǎng guó de hézuò to promote collaboration between both countries

---

脆 cuì ADJECTIVE
1 crispy *(referring to food)*
2 crisp *(referring to voice)*

脆弱 cuìruò ADJECTIVE
fragile
性格脆弱 xìnggé cuìruò a fragile personality

村 cūn NOUN
village
■ 村子 cūnzi village

存 cún VERB
1 to save *(money)*
■ 存款 cúnkuǎn savings
2 to store
他们把行李存在了火车站。Tāmen bǎ xíngli cún zài le huǒchēzhàn. They stored their luggage in the train station. 我把车存在了存车场。Wǒ bǎ chē cún zài le cúnchēchǎng. I put the vehicle in the garage.

存心 cúnxīn ADVERB
deliberately
她存心叫我出丑。Tā cúnxīn jiào wǒ chūchǒu. She deliberately made a fool of me.

存在 cúnzài VERB
to exist

错 cuò
I ADJECTIVE
1 incorrect
这个字写错了。Zhège zì xiě cuò le. This character is written incorrectly.
2 bad
今天天气不错。Jīntiān tiānqì búcuò. Today's weather isn't bad.
II VERB
1 to miss
错过机会 cuò guo jīhuì to miss an opportunity
2 to stagger
把上课和开会时间错开。Bǎ shàngkè hé kāihuì shíjiān cuò kāi. Stagger the time between classes and meetings.
III NOUN
fault
这是我的错。Zhè shì wǒ de cuò. This is my fault.

错过 cuòguò VERB
to miss *(opportunities)*

错误 cuòwù
I ADJECTIVE
wrong
错误的决定 cuòwù de juédìng a wrong decision
II NOUN
mistake
犯了个错误 fàn le gè cuòwù to make a mistake 拼写错误 pīnxiě cuòwù a spelling mistake

Dd

搭 dā VERB
1 to put... up
搭帐篷 dā zhàngpeng to put up a tent
2 to hang
我把大衣搭在胳膊上。Wǒ bǎ dàyī dāzai gēbo shang. I hung my coat over my arm.
3 to join
■ 搭伙 dāhuǒ to join forces

搭档 dādàng
I NOUN
partner
II VERB
to team up
我们搭档一起完成这个作业吧。Wǒmen dādàng yì qǐ wánchéng zhège zuòyè ba. Let's team up and finish our homework together.

搭配 dāpèi VERB
to combine
把这两件衣服搭配在一起会很漂亮。Bǎ zhè liǎngjiàn yīfu dāpèi zai yìqǐ huì hěn piàoliang. This outfit would look great if you matched these two pieces together.

答 dā VERB
▷ *see also* dá
to answer

答理 dāli VERB
to bother

答应 dāying VERB
1 to agree
他答应了这个请求。Tā dāying le zhège qǐngqiú. He agreed to this request.
2 to promise
他答应会永远爱她。Tā dāying huì yǒngyuǎn ài tā. He promised he would love her forever.

达 dá VERB
1 to reach *(amount, target)*
2 to express
■ 表达 biǎodá to express

达到 dádào VERB
to achieve *(requirement, level, aim)*

答 dá VERB
▷ *see also* dā
1 to answer
2 to repay
■ 报答 bàodá to repay

答案 dá'àn NOUN
answer

答复 dáfù VERB
to respond

答卷 dájuàn NOUN
answer sheet

打 dǎ VERB
1 to hit
■ 打人 dǎrén to beat somebody up
2 to beat
打鼓 dǎ gǔ to beat a drum
3 to dial
打电话 dǎ diànhuà to make a phone call
4 to play
打篮球 dǎ lánqiú to play basketball
5 to open

LANGUAGE TIP 打 dǎ works as a prefix in front of certain words to indicate action.

■ 打扮 dǎbàn to put on makeup
■ 打针 dǎzhēn to have an injection

打的 dǎ dī VERB
to take a taxi

打动 dǎdòng VERB
to move *(emotionally)*
这首歌打动了我。Zhè shǒu gē dǎdòng le wǒ. This song moved me.

打赌 dǎdǔ VERB
to bet

打工 dǎgōng VERB
to temp

打架 dǎjià VERB
to have a fight

打开 dǎkāi VERB
1 to open
2 to turn... on

打雷 dǎléi VERB
to thunder

打扫 dǎsǎo VERB
to clean

打算 dǎsuan
I VERB
to plan
II NOUN
plan

打听 dǎtīng VERB
to ask about
去打听一下这份工作。Qù dǎtīng yíxià zhè fèn gōngzuò. Go and inquire about the job.

打招呼 dǎ zhāohu VERB
to greet

打折 dǎzhé VERB
to discount
这条裙子打六折。Zhé tiáo qúnzi dǎ liù zhé. This dress is 40% off.

LANGUAGE TIP 20% off an item translates as 打八折 dǎ bā zhé, literally, 80% of the price.

打针 dǎzhēn
I NOUN
injection
II VERB
to inject

大 dà ADJECTIVE
▷ *see also* dài
1 big *(amount, surface area, volume)*
■ 大街 dàjiē street
2 important
3 loud
■ 大声 dàshēng loudly
4 old
你多大了？Nǐ duōdà le? How old are you?
他比我大。Tā bǐ wǒ dà. He's older than me.
5 eldest
大姐 dà jiě eldest sister
■ 大笑 dàxiào to roar with laughter

大胆 dàdǎn ADJECTIVE
bold

大方 dàfang ADJECTIVE
1 generous
2 natural

大概 dàgài
I ADJECTIVE
approximate
大概有一百人参加了活动。Dàgài yǒu yìbǎi rén cānjiā le huódòng. There were approximately 100 people who attended the event.
II ADVERB
probably
他大概还没有到家。Tā dàgài hái méiyǒu dàojiā. He probably hasn't arrived home yet.

大家 dàjiā PRONOUN
everybody

大量 dàliàng ADJECTIVE
large amount of
大量资金 dàliàng zījīn a large investment

大陆 dàlù NOUN
1 continent
2 mainland
中国大陆 Zhōngguó dàlù mainland China

大米 dàmǐ NOUN
rice

大人 dàrén NOUN
adult

大使 dàshǐ NOUN
ambassador

大使馆 dàshǐguǎn NOUN
embassy

大事 dàshì NOUN
important event

大小 dàxiǎo NOUN
size
这件衣服大小合适。Zhèjian yīfu dàxiǎo héshì. The size of this piece of clothing is right.

大熊猫 dàxióngmāo NOUN
panda

大写 dàxiě NOUN
capital letter

大选 dàxuǎn NOUN
general election

大学 dàxué NOUN
university

大学生 dàxuéshēng NOUN
university student

大雪 dàxuě NOUN
heavy snow

大衣 dàyī NOUN
overcoat

大雨 dàyǔ NOUN
downpour

大约 dàyuē ADVERB
approximately

大众 dàzhòng NOUN
the people *pl*

大自然 dàzìrán NOUN
nature

呆 dāi
I ADJECTIVE
1 slow-witted
2 blank
■ 发呆 fādāi to stare blankly
II VERB
to stay
我在北京呆了一个星期。Wǒ zài Běijīng dāi le yígè xīngqī. I stayed in Beijing for a week.

待 dāi VERB
▷ *see also* dài
to stay

大 dài
▷ *see also* dà
▷ *see below:*
大夫 dàifu NOUN
doctor

代 dài
I VERB
1 to do... on behalf of
2 to send regards to
你见到他时，代我问好。Nǐ jiàndào tā shí, dài wǒ wènhǎo. When you see him, say hello from me.
3 to act as
代校长 dài xiàozhǎng acting headmaster
II NOUN
1 times *pl*
■ 古代 gǔdài ancient times
2 generation
3 dynasty
清代 Qīng dài Qing Dynasty
代表 dàibiǎo
I NOUN
representative
II VERB
1 to stand in for
2 to represent
代价 dàijià NOUN
cost
代理 dàilǐ VERB
1 to act on behalf of
2 to represent
代理人 dàilǐrén NOUN
agent
代替 dàitì VERB
to replace

带 dài
I NOUN
strap
■ 皮带 pídài leather belt
■ 磁带 cídài cassette
II VERB
1 to take
别忘了带钱包！ Bié wàng le dài qiánbāo! Don't forget to take your wallet!
2 to wear
面带笑容 miàn dài xiàoróng to wear a smile on one's face
3 to lead
带动 dàidòng VERB
to drive
带领 dàilǐng VERB
1 to guide
2 to lead

待 dài VERB
▷ *see also* dāi
1 to treat
■ 对待 duìdài to treat
2 to entertain
■ 招待 zhāodài to receive *(of guests)*
3 to wait for
待业 dàiyè VERB
to be unemployed
待遇 dàiyù NOUN
pay
这个工作待遇很好。Zhège gōngzuò dàiyù hěnhǎo. The pay for this work is very good.

袋 dài
I NOUN
bag
II MEASURE WORD
bag
一袋大米 yí dài dàmǐ a bag of rice

戴 dài VERB
to wear *(accessories, glasses, hats, jewellery)*

单 dān
I ADJECTIVE
1 single
■ 单身 dānshēn single
2 odd
3 solitary
4 simple
5 weak
6 thin *(clothes, trousers)*
II ADVERB
only
成功不能单凭运气。Chénggōng bùnéng dān píng yùnqi. To be successful you can't rely only on luck.
III NOUN
1 sheet
■ 床单 chuángdān bed sheet
2 list
■ 菜单 càidān menu
单程 dānchéng NOUN
single trip
单纯 dānchún ADJECTIVE
simple
单词 dāncí NOUN
word
单调 dāndiào ADJECTIVE
monotonous
单独 dāndú ADJECTIVE

1 alone
他总是单独一个人。Tā zǒngshì dāndú yígè rén. He is always alone.
2 unaided
他可以单独完成这个工作。Tā kěyǐ dāndú wánchéng zhège gōngzuò. He can finish this work on his own.

担 dān VERB
1 to carry... on one's shoulder
2 to take... on
担保 dānbǎo VERB
to guarantee
担当 dāndāng VERB
to take... on
担当责任 dāndāng zérèn to take responsibility
担任 dānrèn VERB
to hold the post of
担心 dānxīn VERB
to worry
我担心你。Wǒ dānxīn nǐ. I worry about you.

耽 dān
▷ *see below:*
耽误 dānwù VERB
to delay
耽误时间 dānwù shíjiān to waste time

胆 dǎn NOUN
courage
胆量 dǎnliàng NOUN
guts *pl*
胆子 dǎnzi NOUN
guts *pl*

但 dàn
I CONJUNCTION
but
II ADVERB
only
■ 但愿 dànyuàn wish
但是 dànshì CONJUNCTION
but
虽然下雨，但是不冷。Suīrán xiàyǔ, dànshì bù lěng. Even though it's raining, it's not cold.

蛋 dàn NOUN
egg
■ 鸡蛋 jīdàn egg
蛋糕 dàngāo NOUN
cake

弹 dàn NOUN
▷ *see also* tán
bullet
■ 原子弹 yuánzǐdàn atomic bomb

当 dāng PREPOSITION
▷ *see also* dàng
in front of
■ 当众 dāngzhòng in public
■ 当我们到时，电影已开始了。Dāng wǒmen dào shí, diànyǐng yǐ kāishǐ le. When we arrived the film had already started.
当初 dāngchū NOUN
at first
当代 dāngdài NOUN
present
■ 当代文学 dāngdài wénxué contemporary literature
当地 dāngdì NOUN
locality
当面 dāngmiàn VERB
to do... face to face
当年 dāngnián NOUN
1 at that time
2 that very year
当然 dāngrán ADVERB
of course
他当然会很高兴。Tā dāngrán huì hěn gāoxìng. Of course he will be very happy.
当时 dāngshí ADVERB
at that time
我当时高兴极了。Wǒ dāngshí gāoxìng jí le. I was ecstatic at the time.
当心 dāngxīn VERB
to be careful
当心小偷！Dāngxīn xiǎotōu! Beware of thieves.

当 dàng ADJECTIVE
▷ *see also* dāng
appropriate
■ 适当 shìdàng appropriate

刀 dāo NOUN
knife
■ 刀子 dāozi knife

导 dǎo VERB
1 to guide
2 to give guidance
3 to direct
导演 dǎoyǎn
I VERB
to direct
II NOUN
director

导游 dǎoyóu
I VERB
to guide
II NOUN
tour guide
导致 dǎozhì VERB
to lead to
粗心导致她没考好。Cūxīn dǎozhì tā méi kǎo hǎo. Because of her carelessness she failed the exam.

倒 dǎo VERB
▷ *see also* dào
1 to fall
■ 摔倒 shuāidǎo to fall down
2 to fail
■ 倒闭 dǎobì to go bankrupt
倒霉 dǎoméi ADJECTIVE
unlucky
倒塌 dǎotā VERB
to collapse

到 dào VERB
1 to arrive
火车到了。Huǒchē dào le. The train has arrived.
2 to go
我到厦门旅游。Wǒ dào Xiàmén lǚyóu. I'm going to Xiamen on a tour.
LANGUAGE TIP 到 dào can also be used as a suffix to a number of Chinese verbs to indicate receiving. For example, 看 kàn means **to look**, 看到 kàn dào means **to see**. 听 tīng means **to listen to**, 听到 tīngdào means **to hear**.
到处 dàochù NOUN
everywhere
到达 dàodá VERB
to arrive
到底 dàodǐ ADVERB
at last
他到底成功了。Tā dàodǐ chénggōng le. At last he has succeeded.
■ 坚持到底 jiānchí dàodǐ to keep going until the end
LANGUAGE TIP 到底 dàodǐ is also used for emphasis.
你到底在干什么？Nǐ dàodǐ zài gàn shénme? What on earth are you up to?

倒 dào VERB
▷ *see also* dǎo
1 upside down
■ 他把地图挂倒了。Tā bǎ dìtú guà dào le. He hung the map up upside down.
2 to reverse
■ 倒车 dàochē to reverse
3 to empty out
倒垃圾 dào lājī to empty the rubbish out
倒立 dàolì VERB
to do a handstand
倒计时 dàojìshí VERB
to count down
倒退 dàotuì VERB
to go back

道 dào
I NOUN
road
■ 近道 jìndào shortcut
II MEASURE WORD
LANGUAGE TIP This is a measure word used for things in the shape of a long strip.
一道阳光 yí dào yángguāng a beam of sunlight
LANGUAGE TIP This is a measure word used for doors, walls etc.
第二道门 dì'èr dào mén the second door
LANGUAGE TIP This is a measure word used for orders, questions, procedures etc.
三道题 sān dào tí three questions
LANGUAGE TIP This is a measure word used for dishes or meal courses.
五道菜 wǔ dào cài five dishes
道德 dàodé NOUN
morals *pl*
道理 dàolǐ NOUN
principle
道路 dàolù NOUN
path
道歉 dàoqiàn VERB
to apologize

得 dé VERB
▷ *see also* de, děi
1 to get
■ 得奖 déjiǎng to win a prize
2 to catch *(disease)*
他得了流感。Tā dé le liúgǎn. He caught the flu.
3 to equal
四减二得二。Sì jiǎn èr dé èr. Four minus two equals two.
4 to be suitable
■ 得体 détǐ appropriate
得到 dédào VERB
to get
得到帮助 dédào bāngzhù to get help
得意 déyì ADJECTIVE

pleased with oneself

得罪 dézuì VERB
to offend

德 dé NOUN
1 morality
■ 品德 pǐndé moral character
2 kindness
■ 恩德 ēndé kindness
3 Germany
■ 德国 Déguó Germany
■ 德语 Déyǔ German

德文 Déwén NOUN
German language

地 de AUXILIARY WORD
▷ *see also* dì

LANGUAGE TIP 地 de is added after an adjective to modify the following verb.

刻苦地学习 kèkǔ de xuéxí to study hard

的 de AUXILIARY WORD
▷ *see also* dí, dì

LANGUAGE TIP 的 de is used to link descriptive words, phrases and clauses to the noun they describe.

她是一个很漂亮的女人。Tā shì yíge hěn piàoliang de nǚrén. She is a very beautiful woman. 这是他昨天给我的书。Zhè shì tā zuótiān gěi wǒ de shū. This is the book which he gave me yesterday. 他的哥哥 tā de gēge his elder brother

LANGUAGE TIP 的 de is used together with a verb to make it a noun.

画画的 huàhuà de painter

得 de AUXILIARY WORD
▷ *see also* dé, děi

LANGUAGE TIP 得 de is used between a verb and its complement.

她抬得动。Tā tái de dòng. She can carry it. 我写得完。Wǒ xiě de wán. I am able to finish writing it.

LANGUAGE TIP 得 de is used after a verb or an adjective to link it to an adverbial phrase. Such statements are often evaluations or judgements, and contain the idea of **to the extent of** or **to the degree that**.

他英语学得很快。Tā Yīngyǔ xué de hěn kuài. He's learning English very quickly. 风大得很。Fēng dà de hěn. The wind's very strong.

得 děi VERB
▷ *see also* dé, de

1 must
要想成功，就得艰苦奋斗。 If you want to succeed, you must work hard. 我们得6点出发。 We have to leave at six.
2 will
再不听话，就得挨批评了。 If you don't do as you are told, you will get a telling off. 快走，电影得开始了。 Get a move on, the film's just about to start.

灯 dēng NOUN
light
■ 台灯 táidēng desk lamp
■ 红绿灯 hónglǜdēng traffic lights *pl*

登 dēng VERB
1 to go up
2 to publish
3 to get up onto

登记 dēngjì VERB
to register

登录 dēnglù VERB
to log in
登录网站 dēnglù wǎngzhàn to log in to a website

等 děng
I NOUN
level
■ 中等 zhōngděng medium
II VERB
1 to equal
2 to wait
■ 等车 děngchē to wait for a bus
III CONJUNCTION
when
等他来了，我们再讨论。Děng tā lái le, wǒmen zài tǎolùn. We'll talk about it when he comes.
IV AUXILIARY WORD
etc
他人满好：老实、善良、大方等等。Tā rén mǎnhǎo: láoshi, shànliáng, dàfang děngděng. He is a very good person: honest, nice, generous etc.

等待 děngdài VERB
to wait for

等到 děngdào CONJUNCTION
when
等到那一天，我们就成功了。Děngdào nà yìtiān, wǒmen jiù chénggōng le. When that day comes, we will be successful.

等等 děngděng AUXILIARY WORD
and so on

等号 děnghào NOUN
equal sign

等级 děngjí NOUN
grade
等于 děngyú VERB
1 to equal
2 to be equivalent to

低 dī ADJECTIVE
1 low
2 lower
■ 我比她低两届。Wǒ bǐ tā dī liǎngjiè. I am two years below her.
低级 dījí ADJECTIVE
1 inferior
2 vulgar

的 dí
▷ *see also* de, dì
▷ *see below:*
的确 díquè ADVERB
really
他的确很优秀。Tā díquè hěn yōuxiù. He really is excellent.

敌 dí NOUN
enemy
敌人 dírén NOUN
enemy

底 dǐ NOUN
1 bottom
■ 底下 dǐxia under
2 end
■ 年底 niándǐ the end of the year

地 dì NOUN
▷ *see also* de
1 the Earth
■ 地球 dìqiú the Earth
2 land
3 fields *pl*
4 location
■ 目的地 mùdìdì destination
地点 dìdiǎn NOUN
location
地方 dìfāng NOUN
1 locality
地方政府 dìfāng zhèngfǔ local government
2 place
你是哪个地方的人？Nǐ shì nǎ ge dìfang de rén? Where do you come from?
3 room
你家还有地方住吗？Nǐ jiā háiyǒu dìfang zhù ma? Does your house have a room in which to stay?
4 part
有不明白的地方吗？Yǒu bù míngbai de dìfang ma? Are there any parts that are not clear?
地面 dìmiàn NOUN
the Earth's surface
地区 dìqū NOUN
area
地毯 dìtǎn NOUN
carpet
地铁 dìtiě NOUN
underground
坐地铁 zuò dìtiě to take the underground
地图 dìtú NOUN
map
地位 dìwèi NOUN
position
平等的地位 píngděng de dìwèi equal status
地下 dìxià NOUN
underground
地下室 dìxiàshì NOUN
basement
地震 dìzhèn NOUN
earthquake
地址 dìzhǐ NOUN
address
通信地址 tōngxìn dìzhǐ postal address

弟 dì NOUN
younger brother
■ 表弟 biǎodì cousin
■ 弟弟 dìdi younger brother
弟兄 dìxiong NOUN
brothers *pl*

的 dì NOUN
▷ *see also* de, dí
target
■ 目的 mùdì goal

第 dì NOUN
第一次世界大战 dì yī cì shìjiè dàzhàn the First World War

典 diǎn NOUN
1 standard work
■ 词典 cídiǎn dictionary
2 ceremony
典礼 diǎnlǐ NOUN
ceremony
毕业典礼 bìyè diǎnlǐ graduation ceremony
典型 diǎnxíng ADJECTIVE
representative

点 diǎn
I NOUN
1 o'clock

Chinese-English

d

早上8点 zǎoshang bā diǎn eight o'clock in the morning
2 drop
■ 雨点 yǔdiǎn raindrops *pl*
3 point
■ 终点 zhōngdiǎn end point
■ 优点 yōudiǎn strong point
■ 重点 zhòngdiǎn focal point
II VERB
1 to make a dot
2 to nod
■ 点头 diǎntóu to nod one's head
3 to check
■ 点名 diǎnmíng to do roll call
4 to select
■ 点菜 diǎncài to order food
5 to light *(candle, cigarette)*
III MEASURE WORD
1 a little
有一点问题。Yǒu yì diǎn wèntí. There is a bit of a problem.
2 item
我们有4点建议。Wǒmen yǒu sì diǎn jiànyì. We have four recommendations.

点击 diǎnjī VERB
to click *(with a computer mouse)*

点心 diǎnxin NOUN
snack

点子 diǎnzi NOUN
idea

电 diàn NOUN
electricity
停电了。Tíng diàn le. There's been a power cut.

电池 diànchí NOUN
battery

电话 diànhuà NOUN
1 telephone
2 call
接电话 jiē diànhuà to answer the phone

电话号码 diànhuà hàomǎ NOUN
phone number

电脑 diànnǎo NOUN
computer
手提电脑 shǒutí diànnǎo laptop

电器 diànqì NOUN
electrical appliance

电视 diànshì NOUN
television

电影 diànyǐng NOUN
film

电影院 diànyǐngyuàn NOUN
cinema

电子 diànzǐ NOUN
electron
■ 电子图书 diànzǐ túshū e-book
■ 电子邮件 diànzǐ yóujiàn email

店 diàn NOUN
shop
■ 商店 shāngdiàn shop

调 diào
I VERB
to transfer
II NOUN
melody
■ 走调 zǒudiào to be out of tune

调查 diàochá VERB
to investigate

掉 diào VERB
1 to fall
2 to fall behind
3 to swap
■ 掉换 diàohuàn to swap
4 to reduce
■ 去掉 qùdiào to take out

跌 diē VERB
to fall down

订 dìng VERB
1 to order
■ 订票 dìngpiào to order tickets
2 to fasten... together

订单 dìngdān NOUN
order form

订购 dìnggòu VERB
to order

订婚 dìnghūn VERB
to get engaged

定 dìng
I ADJECTIVE
fixed
■ 定义 dìngyì definition
II VERB
to decide
定计划 dìng jìhuà to decide on a plan
III ADVERB
definitely
■ 一定 yídìng certainly 他一定可以实现梦想。Tā yídìng kěyǐ shíxiàn mèngxiǎng. He can certainly realize his dream.

定期 dìngqī ADVERB
regularly
领导定期来检查。Lǐngdǎo dìngqī lái jiǎnchá. The boss comes to inspect things regularly.

丢 diū VERB
to lose
丢东西 diū dōngxi to lose things

东 dōng NOUN
east
东北边 dōngběibiān NOUN
northeast
东边 dōngbiān NOUN
east side
东方 dōngfāng NOUN
the East
东西 dōngxi NOUN
thing
今天他买了不少东西。Jīntiān tā mǎi le bùshǎo dōngxi. He bought a lot of things today.

冬 dōng NOUN
winter
冬天 dōngtiān NOUN
winter

懂 dǒng VERB
to understand
■ 懂得 dǒngdé to understand

动 dòng VERB
to move *(physically, emotionally)*
不许动！Bùxǔ dòng! Don't move!
■ 动人 dòngrén moving
动机 dòngjī NOUN
motive
动静 dòngjing NOUN
1 sound
2 movement
动力 dònglì NOUN
1 power
2 strength
3 motivation
动物 dòngwù NOUN
animal
动物园 dòngwùyuán NOUN
zoo
动作 dòngzuò NOUN
movement
她的体操动作很漂亮。Tā de tǐcāo dòngzuò hěn piàoliang. Her gymnastics movements are very beautiful.

都 dōu ADVERB
▹ *see also* dū
1 all
大家都同意。Dàjiā dōu tóngyì. Everybody agrees. 都是他的错。Dōu shì tā de cuò. It's all his fault.
2 even
老师待他比亲生父母都好。Lǎoshī dài tā bǐ qīnshēng fùmǔ dōu hǎo. The teacher treated him even better than his parents.
3 already
都到冬天了！ Dōu dào dōngtiān le! It's winter already!

豆 dòu NOUN
bean
豆子 dòuzi NOUN
bean

逗 dòu VERB
to tease
不要逗我。Búyào dòu wǒ. Don't tease me.
逗号 dòuhào NOUN
comma

都 dū NOUN
▹ *see also* dōu
capital
■ 首都 shǒudū capital
都市 dūshì NOUN
metropolis

毒 dú
I NOUN
poison
II ADJECTIVE
poisonous
毒品 dúpǐn NOUN
drug

独 dú
I ADJECTIVE
only
■ 独生子 dúshēngzǐ only son
■ 独生女 dúshēngnǚ only daughter
II ADVERB
1 alone
2 only
独立 dúlì VERB
1 to declare independence *(country)*
■ 独立宣言 dúlì xuānyán declaration of independence
2 to be independent *(person)*
独特 dútè ADJECTIVE
distinctive
独自 dúzì ADVERB
alone
他总是独自行动。Tā zǒngshì dúzì xíngdòng. He always does things alone.

读 dú VERB
to read
读书 dúshū VERB

Chinese-English

d

1 to read
2 to study
你在哪个学校读书？Nǐ zài nǎgè xuéxiào dúshū? In which school are you studying?
读者 dúzhě NOUN
reader

肚 dù NOUN
belly
肚子 dùzi NOUN
stomach

度 dù
I NOUN
1 limit
2 tolerance
■ 大度 dàdù magnanimous
3 degree
■ 厚度 hòudù thickness
II MEASURE WORD
degree

LANGUAGE TIP This is a measure word used for longitude, latitude, temperature, electricity, angles etc.

III VERB
to spend *(time)*
他们要去瑞士度周末。Tāmen yào qù Ruìshì dùzhōumò. They are going to spend the weekend in Switzerland.
■ 度假 dùjià to go on holiday

渡 dù VERB
1 to ferry
渡黄河 dù huánghé to ferry across the Yellow River
2 to survive
渡难关 dù nánguān to go through difficult times

端 duān
I NOUN
1 end
2 beginning
■ 开端 kāiduān beginning
II VERB
to carry
端盘子 duānpánzi
端午节 Duānwǔjié NOUN
Dragon Boat Festival

DID YOU KNOW...? The Dragon Boat Festival is celebrated on the fifth day of the fifth month of the Chinese lunar calendar. The two main activities which take place at this time are dragon boat racing and eating 粽子 zòngzi **rice dumplings**.

端正 duānzhèng ADJECTIVE
proper
他坐姿很端正。Tā zuòzī hěn duānzhèng. He sits upright.

短 duǎn
I ADJECTIVE
short
■ 短期 duǎnqī short-term
II VERB
to owe
III NOUN
weakness
短处 duǎnchu NOUN
weakness
短裤 duǎnkù NOUN
1 pants *pl*
2 briefs *pl*
3 shorts *pl*
短缺 duǎnquē VERB
to lack
短信 duǎnxìn NOUN
text message
短暂 duǎnzàn ADJECTIVE
brief

锻 duàn VERB
to forge
锻炼 duànliàn VERB
to work out
锻炼身体 duànliàn shēntǐ to exercise the body

队 duì NOUN
1 line
2 team
■ 队长 duìzhǎng team leader
■ 队员 duìyuán team member
队伍 duìwu NOUN
1 troops *pl*
2 contingent

对 duì
I VERB
1 to face
2 to suit
对脾气 duì píqi to suit one's temperament
3 to check
对表 duì biǎo to set one's watch
II ADJECTIVE
1 opposite
2 correct
答案是对的。Dá'àn shì duìde. The response is correct.
III MEASURE WORD
pair

一对夫妻 yí duì fūqī a married couple

IV PREPOSITION

1 of

我对他的看法很好。Wǒ duì tā de kànfǎ hěn hǎo. I have a very good opinion of him.

2 to

他对我很好。Tā duì wǒ hěn hǎo. He is very nice to me.

对比 duìbǐ VERB

to contrast

■ 鲜明的对比 xiānmíng de duìbǐ marked contrast

对不起 duìbuqǐ

I VERB

to be sorry

我对不起她。Wǒ duìbuqǐ tā. I did wrong to her.

II ADJECTIVE

sorry

对不起，我迟到了。Duìbuqǐ, wǒchídào le. Sorry, I'm late.

对待 duìdài VERB

to treat

对方 duìfāng NOUN

other side

对付 duìfù VERB

1 to deal with

他是个难对付的对手。Tā shì gè nán duìfù de duìshǒu. He's a very hard opponent to deal with.

2 to make do

吃饭不要对付。Chīfán búyào duìfù. You shouldn't be careless of what you eat.

对话 duìhuà

I NOUN

dialogue

II VERB

to hold talks

对立 duìlì VERB

to counter

对面 duìmiàn NOUN

opposite

对手 duìshǒu NOUN

opponent

竞争对手 jìngzhēng duìshǒu competitor

对象 duìxiàng NOUN

1 object

2 partner

对于 duìyú PREPOSITION

regarding

对于这篇文章，大家理解不一。Duìyú zhè piān wénzhāng, dàjiā lǐjiě bù yī. Not everyone has the same understanding of this article.

> LANGUAGE TIP 对于 duìyú has a variety of meanings depending on the context. Broadly speaking, it qualifies the link between a subject and an object of a sentence. Often, it indicates a point of view or an emotion of the subject regarding the object.

你对于她的抱怨不觉得讨厌？Nǐ duìyú tā de bàoyuàn bù juéde tǎoyàn? Aren't you annoyed by her complaining?

顿 dùn

I VERB

to pause

II MEASURE WORD

> LANGUAGE TIP This is a measure word used for meals.

一顿饭 yí dùn fàn a meal

顿时 dùnshí ADVERB

immediately

教室里顿时安静。Jiàoshì lǐ dùnshí ānjìng. In the classroom, immediately there was silence.

多 duō

I ADJECTIVE

1 a lot of

很多书 hěn duō shū a lot of books

2 more

我比你大多了。Wǒ bǐ nǐ dà duō le. I'm much older than you are.

3 too many

她喝多了。Tā hē duō le. She drank too much.

4 excessive

■ 多疑 duōyí over-suspicious

II NUMBER

more than

两年多前 liǎngnián duō qián over two years ago

III ADVERB

1 how *(in questions, exclamations)*

你儿子多大了？Nǐ érzi duō dà le? How old is your son? 多美的城市！ Duō měi de chéngshì! How beautiful this town is!

2 however

给我一把尺，多长都行。Gěi wǒ yì bǎ chǐ, duō cháng dōu xíng. Give me a ruler; any length will do.

多长 duōcháng ADVERB

how long

多媒体 duōméitǐ NOUN

multimedia

多么 duōme ADVERB

1 how much

他到底有多么聪明？Tā dàodǐ yǒu duōme cōngming? How clever is he really?

2 how *(to add emphasis)*

多么蓝的天啊！ Duōme lán de tiān a! What a clear day!

3 no matter how

多么难他都不会放弃。Duōme nán tā dōu búhuì fàngqì. No matter how hard it is, he won't give up.

多少 duōshǎo

I ADVERB

somewhat

这笔买卖多少能赚点钱。Zhè bǐ mǎimai duōshǎo néng zhuàn diǎn qián. We're bound to earn some money from this deal.

II PRONOUN

LANGUAGE TIP 多少 duōshao is used for asking a question about an amount.

这台电视机多少钱？Zhè tái diànshìjī duōshao qián? How much is this television?

III NUMBER

LANGUAGE TIP When not used in a question, 多少 duōshao has the meaning of a fixed amount, a number that is unknown to the speaker, literally **however many**.

你们有多少我们要多少。Nǐmen yǒu duōshao wǒmen yào duōshao. We want as many as you have.

多数 duōshù NOUN

majority

多余 duōyú ADJECTIVE

1 surplus

2 redundant

夺 duó VERB

1 to seize

2 to compete for

夺取 duóqǔ VERB

1 to capture

2 to strive for

朵 duǒ MEASURE WORD

LANGUAGE TIP This is a measure word used for clouds and flowers.

几朵玫瑰 jǐ duǒ méigui some roses

躲 duǒ VERB

1 to hide

2 to avoid

躲避 duǒbì VERB

1 to run away from

2 to hide

躲藏 duǒcáng VERB

to hide

Ee

俄 é NOUN
Russia
■俄罗斯 Éluósī Russia
■俄国 Éguó Russia

俄语 Éyǔ NOUN
Russian language

鹅 é NOUN
goose

额 é NOUN
forehead
■额头 étóu forehead

恶 ě
▹*see also* è
▹*see below:*

恶心 ěxīn
I VERB
to feel nauseous
下车后，她一阵恶心。Xià chē hòu, tā yízhèn ěxīn. After she got out of the car, she had a nauseous spell.
II ADJECTIVE
nauseating
这个画面看起来很恶心。Zhège huàmiàn kànqǐlái hěn ěxīn. Looking at this painting is nauseating.

恶 è ADJECTIVE
▹*see also* ě
1 ferocious
2 evil

恶劣 èliè ADJECTIVE
bad *(weather)*

恶梦 èmèng NOUN
nightmare

饿 è
I ADJECTIVE
hungry
我很饿。Wǒ hěn è. I'm very hungry.
II VERB
to starve
■饥饿 jī'è starving

儿 ér NOUN
1 child
2 son
■儿子 érzi son

儿女 érnǚ NOUN
children *pl*

儿童 értóng NOUN
child

而 ér CONJUNCTION
and
他辞了职而成为了一个演员。Tā cílezhí ér chéngwěi le yíge yǎnyuán. He quit his job and became an actor.

LANGUAGE TIP 而 ér links phrases. It cannot link nouns or adjectives alone.

而且 érqiě CONJUNCTION
and what's more
他会讲英语，而且讲得好。Tā huì jiǎng Yīngyǔ, érqiě jiǎng de hǎo. He can speak English, and what's more he speaks it very well.

耳 ěr NOUN
ear
■耳朵 ěrduo ear

二 èr NUMBER
two
第二次 dì èr cì the second time
■二月 èryuè February

二十 èrshí NUMBER
twenty

Ff

发 fā VERB
▹*see also* fà
1 to send
发工资 fā gōngzī to pay wages
2 to emit
■ 发光 fāguāng to shine
3 to produce
■ 发电 fādiàn to generate electricity
4 to show feeling
发脾气 fā píqi to lose one's temper
5 to leave
■ 出发 chūfā to set out

发财 fācái VERB
to make a fortune

DID YOU KNOW...?
Number eight 八 bā sounds like 发 fā, therefore Chinese people pick mobile phone numbers with as many eights in them as possible. Mobile phone numbers with more eights are also more expensive.

发出 fāchū VERB
1 to send out
发出通知 fāchū tōngzhī to send out notification
2 to give out
星星发出光芒。Xīngxing fāchū guāngmáng. The stars emit light.

发达 fādá ADJECTIVE
developed
发达国家 fādá guójiā a developed country

发动 fādòng VERB
1 to start
发动汽车 fādòng qìchē to start a car
2 to launch

发动机 fādòngjī NOUN
engine

发抖 fādǒu VERB
to shiver

发挥 fāhuī VERB
to bring... into play
她发挥了最佳水平。Tā fāhuī le zuìjiā shuǐpíng. He exhibited the highest level of talent.

发火 fāhuǒ VERB
to lose one's temper
他发火了。Tā fāhuǒ le. He lost his temper.

发霉 fāméi VERB
to go mouldy

发明 fāmíng
I VERB
to invent
II NOUN
invention
新发明 xīn fāmíng new invention

发票 fāpiào NOUN
receipt

发烧 fāshāo VERB
to have a temperature
弟弟发高烧。Dìdi fā gāoshāo. My younger brother has a high temperature.

发生 fāshēng VERB
to happen
这事发生在昨天。Zhèshì fāshēng zài zuótiān. This happened yesterday.

发现 fāxiàn VERB
to discover
他发现了新大陆。Tā fāxiàn le xīn dàlù. He discovered the new continent.

发言 fāyán VERB
to make a speech
轮到他发言了。Lún dào tā fā yán le. It came his turn to make a speech.

发音 fāyīn
I VERB
to pronounce
II NOUN
pronunciation
你的汉语发音很好。Nǐ de Hànyǔ fāyīn hěn hǎo. Your pronunciation of Mandarin is very good.

发展 fāzhǎn VERB
to develop
社会发展了。Shèhuì fāzhǎn le. Society developed.

罚 fá VERB
to punish
■ 罚金 fájīn fine

罚款 fákuǎn
I VERB
to fine
闯红灯要罚款。Chuǎng hóngdēng yào fákuǎn. Crossing a red light has to be fined.
II NOUN
fine
他去交罚款。Tā qù jiāo fákuǎn. He went to pay his fine.

法 fǎ NOUN
1 law
2 method
■ 用法 yòngfǎ use

> **LANGUAGE TIP** 法 fǎ can also be used in the construction 没法做… měi fǎ zuò… **it is impossible to do …**

法国 Fǎguó NOUN
France
法律 fǎlǜ NOUN
law
法庭 fǎtíng NOUN
court
法语 Fǎyǔ NOUN
French

发 fà NOUN
▹ *see also* fā
hair
■ 头发 tóufa hair

番 fān
▹ *see below:*
番茄 fānqié NOUN
tomato
番茄酱 fānqié jiàng tomato sauce

> **DID YOU KNOW...?**
> A more common word for tomato in mainland China is 西红柿 xī hóng shì.

翻 fān VERB
1 to turn over
我翻了几页书。Wǒ fān le jǐ yè shū. I turned over a few pages of the book.
2 to get across
我们翻过了一座山。Wǒmen fān guò le yí zuò shān. We crossed a mountain.
翻译 fānyì
I VERB
to translate
这篇文章是他翻译的。Zhèpiān wénzhāng shì tā fānyì de. This article was translated by him.
II NOUN
translator
他是这次会议的翻译。Tā shì zhècì huìyì de fānyì. He is the translator at this conference.

烦 fán
I VERB
to trouble
烦您尽快回复。Fán nín jìnkuài huífù. Please respond as fast as possible.
II ADJECTIVE
fed up
堵车真让人烦。Dǔchē zhēn ràng rén fán. Traffic jams make me fed up.
烦恼 fánnǎo ADJECTIVE
worried

繁 fán ADJECTIVE
numerous
■ 繁多 fánduō numerous
繁华 fánhuá ADJECTIVE
bustling
上海是一个繁华的都市。Shànghǎi shì yíge fánhuá de dūshì. Shanghai is a bustling city.
繁忙 fánmáng ADJECTIVE
busy *(person, city, street, traffic, train station)*

反 fǎn
I VERB
to oppose
■ 反对 fǎnduì to oppose
II ADJECTIVE
opposite
你的帽子戴反了。Nǐ de màozi dài fǎn le. Your hat is on backwards.
反复 fǎnfù ADVERB
repeatedly
他反复地改变想法。Tā fǎnfù de gǎibiàn xiǎngfǎ. He repeatedly changed his mind.
反面 fǎnmiàn
I NOUN
other side
请看试卷的反面。Qǐng kàn shìjuàn de fǎnmiàn. Please look at the other side of the examination paper.
II ADJECTIVE
negative
反面的影响 fǎnmiàn de yǐngxiǎng negative influence
反应 fǎnyìng NOUN
response
我们问他什么他都没有反应。Wǒmen wèn tā shénme tā dōu méiyǒu fǎnyìng. We asked him and he didn't react at all.
反映 fǎnyìng VERB
1 to reflect

反映社会状况 fǎnyìng shèhuì zhuàngkuàng to reflect the social situation
2 to report
他向经理反映了这个情况。Tā xiàng jīnglǐ fǎnyìng le zhègè qíngkuàng. He reported this situation to the director.

反正 fǎnzhèng ADVERB
anyway
我们开始吧，反正他也不会来。Wǒmen kāishǐ ba, fǎnzhèng tā yě búhuì lái. Let's start, he's not going to come anyway.

返 fǎn VERB
to return

返回 fǎnhuí VERB
to come back

犯 fàn VERB
1 to commit *(mistake, crime)*
我犯了很多错误。Wǒ fàn le hěnduō cuòwù. I made a lot of mistakes.
2 to break *(law, rule)*

犯法 fànfǎ VERB
to break the law

犯规 fànguī VERB
to break the rules *(in sports)*

犯人 fànrén NOUN
prisoner

犯罪 fànzuì VERB
to commit a crime

饭 fàn NOUN
1 meal
■ 晚饭 wǎnfàn supper
2 food
■ 吃饭 chīfàn to eat food

DID YOU KNOW...?
The question 你吃饭了吗？nǐ chīfàn le ma is often used to ask **How are you?** in Chinese.

饭店 fàndiàn NOUN
1 hotel
2 restaurant

饭馆 fànguǎn NOUN
restaurant
■ 饭馆儿 fànguǎnr restaurant

饭厅 fàntīng NOUN
dining room

范 fàn NOUN
model
■ 模范 mófàn model

范围 fànwéi NOUN
limit
送货范围 sònghuò fànwéi delivery limits

方 fāng
I NOUN
1 direction
■ 南方 nánfāng the South
2 square
■ 长方形 chángfāngxíng rectangle
3 side
■ 方面 fāngmiàn aspect

LANGUAGE TIP 方面 fāng miàn is also used in the construction 一方面…另一方面… yì fāngmiàn...lìng yi fāng miàn... **on the one hand... on the other hand....**

II ADJECTIVE
square
■ 方桌 fāngzhuō square table

方便 fāngbiàn ADJECTIVE
1 convenient
公共交通很方便。Gōnggòng jiāotōng hěn fāngbiàn. Public transportation is very convenient.

DID YOU KNOW...?
A common Chinese snack is 方便面 fāngbiàn miàn or literally, **instant noodles**.

2 appropriate
什么时间对你最方便？Shénme shíjiān duì nǐ zuì fāngbiàn? What time would be most appropriate for you?

方法 fāngfǎ NOUN
method
不同的解决方法 bùtóng de jiějué fāngfǎ different solutions

方面 fāngmiàn NOUN
1 side
多方面的努力 duō fāngmiàn de nǔlì efforts on multiple sides
2 aspect
他在很多方面都很出色。Tā zài hěnduō fāngmiàn dōu hěn chūsè. He is outstanding in many different aspects.

防 fáng VERB
to defend
■ 防洪 fánghóng to prevent flooding

防止 fángzhǐ VERB
to prevent
防止病毒传播 fángzhǐ bìngdú chuánbō to prevent viral dissemination

房 fáng NOUN
1 house
■ 房子 fángzi house 我要租一栋房子。Wǒ yào zū yídòng fángzi. I want to rent a house.
2 room

■ 书房 shūfáng study
■ 卧房 wòfáng bedroom

房东 fángdōng NOUN
landlord

房屋 fángwū NOUN
building

房租 fángzū NOUN
rent

仿 fǎng VERB
to copy
■ 模仿 mófǎng to copy

仿佛 fǎngfú CONJUNCTION
as if

访 fǎng VERB
to call on
■ 拜访 bàifǎng to pay a visit to

访问 fǎngwèn VERB
to visit *(political leader, website)*
布朗首相访问了美国。Bùlǎng shǒuxiàng fǎngwèn le Měiguó. Prime Minister Brown visited the United States.

放 fàng VERB
1 to put
你把书放到书架上了吗？Nǐ bǎ shū fàng dào shūjià shang le ma? Did you put the books on the bookshelf?
2 to release
放学了。Fàngxué le. School is now over.
那个小偷被放出来了。Nàge xiǎotōu bèi fàng chūlai le. That thief was let loose.
3 to set... off *(firecrackers, fireworks)*
■ 放火 fànghuǒ to set fire to

放大 fàngdà VERB
to enlarge
放大照片 fàngdà zhàopiàn to enlarge pictures

放假 fàngjià VERB
to go on holiday
学校放假了。Xuéxiào fàngjiàle. The school went on holiday.

放弃 fàngqì VERB
to give... up

放松 fàngsōng VERB
to relax

放心 fàngxīn VERB
to set one's mind at rest
你放心，我们一定不会迟到。Nǐ fàngxīn, wǒmen yídìng búhuì chídào. Set your mind at rest, we will arrive on time for sure.

飞 fēi VERB
to fly

飞机 fēijī NOUN
airplane
■ 飞机票 fēijī piào plane ticket

非 fēi ADVERB
not
我不让他去，他非去不可。Wǒ bú ràng tā qù, tā fēi qù bù kě. I've tried to stop him, but he simply has to go.

> **LANGUAGE TIP** 非 fēi is used in the construction 非…不可 fēi... bù kě to indicate ... **must be done**.

非常 fēicháng ADVERB
very
湖区的景色非常美。Húqū de jǐngsè fēicháng měi. The landscape around the lake is very beautiful.

非典型性肺炎 fēi diǎnxíngxìng fèiyán NOUN
Severe Acute Respiratory Syndrome (SARS)

非法 fēifǎ ADJECTIVE
illegal

非洲 Fēizhōu NOUN
Africa

肥 féi ADJECTIVE
1 fat
这块肉真肥。Zhè kuài ròu zhēn féi. This piece of meat has a lot of fat in it.
2 fertile

肥胖 féipàng ADJECTIVE
fat *(person)*

肥皂 féizào NOUN
soap

肺 fèi NOUN
lung

废 fèi ADJECTIVE
1 waste
■ 废品 fèipǐn waste
2 useless
■ 废物 fèiwu rubbish

费 fèi
I NOUN
fee
公车费 gōngchē fèi bus fare
II VERB
to waste *(time)*
这太费时间了。Zhè tài fèi shíjiān le. This wastes too much time.

费用 fèiyong NOUN
expense

分 fēn
▷ *see also* fèn
I VERB

1 to divide
把瓜给分了。Bǎ guā gěi fēn le. Divide the melon.
2 to distinguish
分不出男女 fēn bu chū nán nǚ unable to distinguish men from women
3 to distribute
我们把摘下来的草莓分了些给邻居。Wǒmen bǎ zhāi xiàlai de cǎoméi fēn le xiē gěi línjū. We gave a few of the strawberries that we picked to the neighbours.
II NOUN
1 fraction
四分之三 sì fēn zhī sān three quarters
2 minute
五点过五分 wǔ diǎn guò wǔ fēn 5 minutes past 5

分别 fēnbié
I ADVERB
separately
II VERB
to part

分公司 fēn gōngsī NOUN
company branch

分开 fēnkāi VERB
to separate

分配 fēnpèi VERB
to assign

分手 fēnshǒu VERB
to break up *(couple)*

分数 fēnshù NOUN
1 fraction
2 grades

分析 fēnxī VERB
to analyze

分钟 fēnzhōng NOUN
minute *(duration)*

吩 fēn
▹ *see below:*

吩咐 fēnfu VERB
to instruct

纷 fēn ADJECTIVE
numerous

纷纷 fēnfēn ADVERB
one after another
人们纷纷去拿菜。Rénmen fēnfēn qù nácài. One after another, the people went to get their food.

坟 fén NOUN
grave

坟墓 fénmù NOUN
grave

粉 fěn
I ADJECTIVE
pink
■ 粉色 fěnsè pink
II NOUN
powder
■ 粉末 fěnmò powder
III VERB
to crumble
■ 粉碎 fěnsuì to crush

粉笔 fěnbǐ NOUN
chalk

粉红 fěnhóng ADJECTIVE
pink

粉丝 fěnsī NOUN
follower *(on social media sites)*

分 fèn NOUN
▹ *see also* fēn
1 component
■ 成分 chéngfèn component
2 limit
■ 过分 guòfèn excessive

分量 fènliàng NOUN
weight

份 fèn
I NOUN
part
■ 股份 gǔfèn share
II MEASURE WORD
1 portion
一份食物 yífèn shíwù a portion of food
2 copy
一份报纸 yífèn bàozhǐ a newspaper

奋 fèn VERB
to exert oneself
■ 勤奋 qínfèn diligent

奋斗 fèndòu VERB
to fight
他为自己的理想而奋斗。Tā wèi zìjǐ de lǐxiǎng ér fèndòu. He fought for his ideals.

愤 fèn ADJECTIVE
indignant
■ 气愤 qìfèn indignant

愤怒 fènnù ADJECTIVE
angry

丰 fēng ADJECTIVE
abundant

丰富 fēngfù ADJECTIVE
abundant
丰富的课余生活 fēngfù de kèyú shēnghuó

a rich extracurricular life

丰收 fēngshōu VERB
to have a good harvest

风 fēng
I NOUN
1 wind
2 scene
■ 风光 fēngguān scenery
II VERB
to air
■ 风干 fēnggān to air-dry

风格 fēnggé NOUN
style

风景 fēngjǐng NOUN
scenery

风险 fēngxiǎn NOUN
risk
冒风险 mào fēngxiǎn to take risks

封 fēng
I VERB
to seal
■ 封闭 fēngbì to seal up
II NOUN
envelope
■ 信封 xìnfēng envelope
III MEASURE WORD
一封信 yì fēng xìn a letter

疯 fēng ADJECTIVE
mad

疯子 fēngzi NOUN
lunatic

锋 fēng NOUN
edge *(of knives)*

锋利 fēnglì ADJECTIVE
sharp *(tools, knives)*

蜂 fēng NOUN
bee

蜂蜜 fēngmì NOUN
honey

缝 féng VERB
▷ *see also* fèng
to sew

缝 fèng NOUN
▷ *see also* féng
1 seam
2 crack

佛 fó NOUN
1 Buddhism
■ 佛教 fójiào Buddhism
2 Buddha
■ 佛像 fóxiàng figure of Buddha

否 fǒu
I VERB
to deny
■ 否认 fǒurèn to deny
II ADVERB
or not
他明天是否来参加聚会？Tā míngtiān shìfǒu lái cānjiā jùhuì? Is he coming to the party tomorrow or not?

LANGUAGE TIP 是否 shì fǒu is more formal than 是不是 shì bú shì.

否定 fǒudìng
I VERB
to negate
教授否定了他的计划。Jiàoshòu fǒudìng le tāde jìhuà. The teacher negated his plans.
II ADJECTIVE
negative
答案是否定的。Dá'àn shì fǒudìng de. The answer is negative.

否则 fǒuzé CONJUNCTION
otherwise

夫 fū NOUN
husband
■ 丈夫 zhàngfu husband

夫妇 fūfù NOUN
husband and wife

夫妻 fūqī NOUN
husband and wife

夫人 fūrén NOUN
Mrs

扶 fú VERB
to help up
扶她起床 fú tā qǐchuáng He helped her out of bed.

服 fú
I NOUN
clothes
■ 校服 xiàofú school uniform
II VERB
1 to take
■ 服药 fúyào to take medicine
2 to serve
■ 服役 fúyì to serve in the army

服从 fúcóng VERB
to obey

服务 fúwù VERB
to serve
为公众服务 wèi gōngzhòng fúwù to serve

the public
服务员 fúwùyuán NOUN
1 shop assistant
2 waiter
waitress
3 room attendant
服装 fúzhuāng NOUN
clothing

符 fú
I NOUN
mark
■ 字符 zìfú character
II VERB
to be in keeping with
■ 相符 xiāngfú to match up with
符号 fúhào NOUN
mark
符合 fúhé VERB
to match
符合实际情况 fúhé shíjì qíngkuàng to match reality

幅 fú MEASURE WORD
LANGUAGE TIP This is a measure word used for paintings, Chinese calligraphy etc.
一幅自画像 yì fú zìhuàxiàng a self-portrait

福 fú NOUN
good fortune
■ 福气 fúqì good fortune

父 fù NOUN
father
■ 父亲 fùqīn father
父母 fùmǔ NOUN
parents

付 fù VERB
to pay
■ 付费 fùfèi to pay
付账 fùzhàng VERB
to pay the bill

负 fù
I VERB
to bear *(responsibilities)*
II ADJECTIVE
negative
■ 负数 fùshù negative number
负担 fùdān
I VERB
to bear
我自己负担我的生活开支。Wǒ zìjǐ fùdān wǒde shēnghuó kāizhī. I'm responsible for paying my living costs.
II NOUN
burden
工作负担 gōngzuò fùdān work pressure
负责 fùzé
I VERB
to be responsible
他负责这个项目。Tā fùzé zhège xiàngmù. He's responsible for this project.
II ADJECTIVE
conscientious
他是个很负责的人。Tā shìge hěnfùzé de rén. He's a very conscientious person.

妇 fù NOUN
1 woman
■ 妇科 fùkē gynaecology
2 married woman
妇女 fùnǚ NOUN
women

附 fù VERB
to be close to
附件 fùjiàn NOUN
attachment *(in emails)*
附近 fùjìn ADJECTIVE
nearby
加油站就在附近。Jiāyóuzhàn jiùzài fùjìn. The gas station is nearby.

复 fù
I ADJECTIVE
duplicated
■ 复件 fùjiàn copy
II VERB
1 to reply
■ 答复 dáfù to reply
2 to recover
■ 复活 fùhuó resurrection
3 to take revenge
■ 复仇 fùchóu to revenge
复活节 Fùhuó Jié NOUN
Easter
复习 fùxí VERB
to revise
复习功课 fùxí gōngkè to revise homework
复印 fùyìn VERB
to photocopy
复印机 fùyìnjī NOUN
photocopy machine
复杂 fùzá ADJECTIVE
complex

副 fù
I ADJECTIVE
deputy

副经理 fù jīnglǐ deputy director

II NOUN
assistant
■副手 fùshǒu assistant

III MEASURE WORD
pair
一副手套 yí fù shǒutào a pair of gloves

副作用 fùzuòyòng NOUN
side effect

富 fù

I ADJECTIVE
1 rich
■富人 fùrén the rich
2 abundant

II NOUN
wealth

富有 fùyǒu

I ADJECTIVE
wealthy

II VERB
to be full of
富有同情心 fùyǒu tóngqíngxīn to be full of sympathy

富裕 fùyù ADJECTIVE
prosperous

Gg

咖 gā
▷ *see also* kā
▷ *see below:*

咖喱 gālí NOUN
curry

LANGUAGE TIP 咖喱 gālí actually comes from the English word **curry**.

该 gāi VERB
1 ought to
我们该回家了。Wǒmen gāi huíjiā le. We ought to go home.
2 to serve... right
■ 活该 huógāi to deserve to be punished
他活该受罚！ Tā huógāi shòufá! He deserves to be fined.
3 should
工作明天该完成了。Gōngzuò míngtiān gāi wánchéng le. The work should be finished by tomorrow.

LANGUAGE TIP 该 gāi is also used for emphasis.

要是他能在这儿该多好啊！Yàoshì tā néng zài zhè'r gāi duō hǎo a! It would be great if he could be here.

LANGUAGE TIP 该 gāi is also used to express assumptions.

再不吃的话，菜都该凉了。Zài bù chī de huà, cài dōu gāi liáng le. If we don't start eating, the food is going to get cold.

改 gǎi VERB
1 to change
改地址 gǎi dìzhǐ to change address
2 to correct
请把错误答案改了。Qǐng bǎ cuòwù dá'àn gǎi le. Please correct the incorrect answers.

改变 gǎibiàn VERB
to change
我改变了主意。Wǒ gǎibiàn le zhǔyì. I changed my mind.

改革 gǎigé VERB
to reform
改革开放 gǎigé kāifàng to reform and open up

DID YOU KNOW...?
改革开放 gǎigé kāifàng is a major policy of China that reformed the political and economic systems and opened up its domestic markets. It was initiated in 1978 at the 3rd Session of the 11th Meeting of the Communist Party of China.

改正 gǎizhèng VERB
to correct
你应该改正缺点。Nǐ yīnggāi gǎizhèng quēdiǎn. You should mend your ways.

钙 gài NOUN
calcium

盖 gài
I NOUN
cover
■ 盖子 gàizi lid
II VERB
1 to cover *(with blankets etc)*
2 to stamp
他在信封上盖了一个章。Tā zài xìnfēng shang gài le yíge zhāng. He stamped the envelope.
3 to build *(buildings)*

干 gān
▷ *see also* gàn
I VERB
to have to do with
这不干我事。Zhè bù gān wǒ shì. This has nothing to do with me.
II ADJECTIVE
dry
衣服干了。Yīfu gān le. The clothes are dry.

干杯 gānbēi VERB
to drink a toast
干杯！Gānbēi! Cheers!

DID YOU KNOW...?
This term literally means **dry cup** and therefore implies that you should finish your drink; however, sometimes drinking just a mouthful is acceptable.

To ensure the correct etiquette at formal occasions it is best to follow the example of your host.

干净 gānjìng ADJECTIVE
1 clean
2 complete
请把汤喝干净。Qǐng bǎ tāng hē gānjìng. Please finish your soup.

干燥 gānzào ADJECTIVE
dry

杆 gān NOUN
post

肝 gān NOUN
liver

赶 gǎn VERB
1 to catch
赶公共汽车 gǎn gōnggòng qìchē to catch a bus
2 to rush
赶着回家 gǎn zhe huíjiā to rush home
3 to drive
爷爷赶着马车。Yéye gǎn zhe mǎchē. Grandad is driving a horse and cart.
4 to drive... out *(of room, house)*
我把他赶了出去。Wǒ bǎ tā gǎn le chūqù. I drove him out.

赶紧 gǎnjǐn ADVERB
hurriedly
他们赶紧买了票。Tāmen gǎnjǐn mǎi le piào. They hurriedly bought their tickets.

赶快 gǎnkuài ADVERB
at once
我们得赶快走了！Wǒmen děi gǎnkuài zǒu le! We must go at once!

赶上 gǎnshàng VERB
to catch up with
她赶上了火车。Tā gǎnshàng le huǒchē. She caught the train in time.

感 gǎn
I VERB
to feel
II NOUN
sense
方向感 fāngxiànggǎn a sense of direction

感到 gǎndào VERB
to feel
我感到幸运。Wǒ gǎndào xìngyùn. I feel lucky.

感动 gǎndòng VERB
to move
他容易被感动。Tā róngyì bèi gǎndòng. He's very easily moved.

感恩节 Gǎn'ēn Jié NOUN
Thanksgiving

感觉 gǎnjué
I NOUN
feeling
我们的脚没有了感觉。Wǒmen de jiǎo méiyǒu le gǎnjué. We can't feel our feet.
II VERB
1 to feel
她感觉热。Tā gǎnjué rè. She felt hot.
2 to sense
他们感觉有危险。Tāmen gǎnjué yǒu wēixiǎn. They sensed it was dangerous.

感冒 gǎnmào
I NOUN
cold
得了感冒 dé le gǎnmào to catch a cold
II VERB
to have a cold
我感冒了。Wǒ gǎnmào le. I have a cold.

感情 gǎnqíng NOUN
1 emotion
他感情丰富。Tā gǎnqíng fēngfù. He is very emotional.
2 feelings *pl*
我们感情很深。Wǒmen gǎnqíng hěn shēn. Our feelings for each other are very deep.

感染 gǎnrǎn VERB
1 to contract
我同学感染上了水痘。Wǒ tóngxué gǎnrǎn shang le shuǐdòu. My classmate contracted chicken pox.
2 to infect
我的电脑感染了病毒。Wǒ de diànnǎo gǎnrǎn le bìngdú. My computer was infected by a virus.

感谢 gǎnxiè VERB
to thank
感谢您的指导。Gǎnxiè nín de zhǐdǎo. Thank you for your guidance.

感兴趣 gǎn xìngqù VERB
to be interested in
他对绘画感兴趣。Tā duì huìhuà gǎn xìngqù. He's interested in painting.

干 gàn VERB
▷ *see also* gān
1 to do
■ 干活 gànhuó to work
2 to act as
他干过队长。Tā gànguo duìzhǎng. He acted as team leader.

刚 gāng
I ADJECTIVE

strong

II ADVERB

1 just *(about, only)*

水温刚好。Shuǐwēn gāng hǎo. The temperature of the water was just right. 这儿刚够放一把椅子。Zhèr gāng gòu fàng yì bǎ yǐzi. There is just enough room for a chair.

2 only just

小宝宝刚会走路。Xiǎo bǎobao gāng huì zǒulù. The baby has only just started walking.

刚才 gāngcái ADVERB

just

你妈妈刚才来了电话。Nǐ māma gāngcái lái le diànhuà. Your mother just phoned.

刚刚 gānggāng ADVERB

just

电影刚刚完。Diànyǐng gānggāng wán. The film has just finished.

刚好 gānghǎo

I ADJECTIVE

just right

温度刚好。Wēndù gānghǎo. The temperature is just right.

II ADVERB

luckily

我刚好有零钱。Wǒ gānghǎo yǒu língqián. Luckily I had some loose change.

钢 gāng NOUN

steel

■ 钢铁 gāngtiě steel

钢笔 gāngbǐ NOUN

fountain pen

钢琴 gāngqín NOUN

piano

我妹妹在学弹钢琴。Wǒ mèimei zài xué tán gāngqín. My younger sister is learning to play the piano.

缸 gāng NOUN

vat

■ 鱼缸 yúgāng fish bowl

港 gǎng NOUN

1 harbour

2 Hong Kong

■ 香港 Xiānggǎng Hong Kong

■ 港币 gǎngbì Hong Kong dollar

港口 gǎngkǒu NOUN

port

高 gāo ADJECTIVE

1 tall

高楼 gāo lóu tall building

2 high *(degree)*

高标准 gāo biāozhǔn high standard

3 senior

■ 高中 gāozhōng senior high school

4 high *(price)*

价太高了。Jià tài gāo le. The price is too high.

高大 gāodà ADJECTIVE

huge

恐龙真的很高大吗？Kǒnglóng zhēnde hěn gāodà ma? Were dinosaurs really huge?

高档 gāodàng ADJECTIVE

high-quality

他的手表很高档。Tā de shǒubiǎo hěn gāodàng. His watch is very high-quality.

高等 gāoděng ADJECTIVE

higher

高等教育 gāoděng jiàoyù higher education

高级 gāojí ADJECTIVE

1 senior

高级工程师 gāojí gōngchéngshī senior engineer

2 high-quality

高级英语 gāojí Yīngyǔ advanced English

高级宾馆 gāojí bīnguǎn luxury hotel

高考 gāokǎo NOUN

college entrance examination

高科技 gāokējì ADJECTIVE

hi-tech

高速公路 gāosù gōnglù NOUN

motorway

高兴 gāoxìng

I ADJECTIVE

happy

II VERB

to be delighted

她为孩子恢复了健康而高兴。Tā wèi háizi huīfù le jiànkāng ér gāoxìng. She was delighted that the child had regained his health.

糕 gāo NOUN

cake

■ 蛋糕 dàngāo cake

告 gào VERB

1 to tell

2 to sue

家长们告了学校。Jiāzhǎng men gào le xuéxiào. The students' parents sued the school.

告别 gàobié VERB

to say goodbye

他向父母告了别。Tā xiàng fùmǔ gào le bié. He said goodbye to his parents.

告诉 gàosu VERB
to tell
我告诉了老师。Wǒ gàosu le lǎoshī. I told the teacher.

哥 gē NOUN
1 elder brother
2 brother
LANGUAGE TIP 哥 gē is used as an affectionate address to a close male friend.
哥哥 gēge NOUN
elder brother

胳 gē
▷ see below:
胳膊 gēbo NOUN
arm

鸽 gē NOUN
dove
■ 鸽子 gēzi dove

歌 gē
I NOUN
song
II VERB
to sing
学生们唱了首歌。Xuésheng men chàng le shǒu gē. The students sang a song.
歌剧 gējù NOUN
opera
歌曲 gēqǔ NOUN
song
歌手 gēshǒu NOUN
singer

个 gè
I NOUN
size (for a person)
■ 个儿 gèr build
II MEASURE WORD
LANGUAGE TIP This is the most useful and common measure word, and can be used as the default measure word when you are unsure. It can be used for people, objects, fruit, countries, cities, companies, dates, weeks, months and ideas.
六个桃子 liù ge táozi six peaches 两个月 liǎng ge yuè two months
LANGUAGE TIP This measure word can also refer to actions.
开个会 kāi ge huì to have a meeting 冲个澡 chōng ge zǎo to have a shower
个唱 gè chàng NOUN
solo concert
个性 gèxìng NOUN
personality
他个性很强。Tā gèxìng hěn qiáng. He has a very strong personality.
个子 gèzi NOUN
height (of person)
一个高个子女人 yígè gāo gèzi nǚrén a tall woman

各 gè PRONOUN
each
各学校 gè xuéxiào each school
各种 gèzhǒng PRONOUN
all kinds
动物园里有各种动物。Dòngwù yuán lǐ yǒu gèzhǒng dòngwù. There are all kinds of animals at the zoo.

给 gěi
I VERB
1 to give
老师给了我一本书。Lǎoshī gěi le wǒ yì běn shū. The teacher gave me a book.
2 to let
别给人骗了！Bié gěi rén piàn le! Don't let people deceive you!
II PREPOSITION
1 for
我给妻子做早餐。Wǒ gěi qīzǐ zuò zǎocān. I made breakfast for my wife.
2 to
妈妈递给我一个苹果。Māma dì gěi wǒ yíge píngguǒ. My mother gave me an apple.

根 gēn
I NOUN
root
大树的根很深。Dàshù de gēn hěn shēn. Tall trees have very deep roots.
II MEASURE WORD
LANGUAGE TIP This is a measure word used for long thin objects, body parts and plants.
一根绳子 yì gēn shéngzi a rope 一根头发 yì gēn tóufa a hair

跟 gēn
I NOUN
heel
■ 高跟鞋 gāogēnxié high-heeled shoes
II VERB
to follow
小狗跟着他。Xiǎo gǒu gēn zhe tā. The little dog was following him.

III PREPOSITION
1 with
我跟朋友去公园了。Wǒ gēn péngyou qù gōngyuán le. I went to the park with friends.
2 to
他跟我抱怨。Tā gēn wǒ bàoyuàn. He complained to me.
3 as *(in comparison)*
他头发的颜色跟我的一样。Tā tóufa de yánsè gēn wǒ de yíyàng. His hair is the same colour as mine.
IV CONJUNCTION
and
你跟我 nǐ gēn wǒ you and me

更 gēng VERB
▷ *see also* gèng
to change
■ 更正 gēngzhèng to correct
更衣室 gēngyīshì NOUN
changing room

更 gèng ADJECTIVE
▷ *see also* gēng
even more
天更黑了。Tiān gèng hēi le. It's getting even darker.
更加 gèngjiā ADVERB
even more

工 gōng NOUN
1 worker
■ 童工 tónggōng child labour
2 work
工厂 gōngchǎng NOUN
factory
工程师 gōngchéngshī NOUN
engineer
工夫 gōngfu NOUN
time
你有闲工夫吗？Nǐ yǒu xián gōngfu ma? Do you have any free time?
工具 gōngjù NOUN
tool
工人 gōngrén NOUN
worker
工艺品 gōngyìpǐn NOUN
handicraft
工资 gōngzī NOUN
salary
工作 gōngzuò NOUN
1 work
爸爸有很多工作。Bàba yǒu hěnduō gōngzuò. My father has a lot of work.
2 job
妈妈的工作是工程师。Māma de gōngzuò shì gōngchéngshī. My mother is an engineer.

公 gōng
I ADJECTIVE
1 public
■ 公物 gōngwù public property
2 fair
■ 公正 gōngzhèng just
3 male
一头公牛 yì tóu gōng niú a bull
II NOUN
1 father-in-law
■ 公公 gōnggong father-in-law
2 official business
办公地点 bàn gōng dìdiǎn work place
公安 gōng'ān NOUN
public security
公安局 gōng'ānjú NOUN
1 Public Security Bureau
2 police station
公布 gōngbù VERB
to announce
公厕 gōngcè NOUN
public toilet
公尺 gōngchǐ NOUN
metre
公费 gōngfèi NOUN
public expense
公费医疗 gōngfèi yīliáo publicly funded medical care
公分 gōngfēn NOUN
centimetre
公共 gōnggòng ADJECTIVE
public
公共图书馆 gōnggòng túshūguǎn public library
公共汽车 gōnggòng qìchē NOUN
bus
公共汽车站 gōnggòng qìchēzhàn NOUN
1 bus station
2 bus stop
公斤 gōngjīn NOUN
kilogram
公开 gōngkāi
I ADJECTIVE
public
■ 公开道歉 gōngkāi dàoqiàn to publicly apologise
II VERB
to make public
校长公开了名单。Xiàozhǎng gōngkāi le míngdān. The school principal made the name list public.
公里 gōnglǐ NOUN
kilometre

公路 gōnglù NOUN
motorway

公民 gōngmín NOUN
citizen

公平 gōngpíng ADJECTIVE
fair
太不公平了！ Tài bù gōngpíng le! That's so unfair!

公司 gōngsī NOUN
company

公用 gōngyòng ADJECTIVE
public
这台电脑是公用的。Zhè tái diànnǎo shì gōngyòng de. This computer is for public use.

公寓 gōngyù NOUN
flat

公元 gōngyuán NOUN
A.D.

公园 gōngyuán NOUN
park
■ 公园儿 gōngyuánr park

公主 gōngzhǔ NOUN
princess

功 gōng NOUN
1 skill
■ 基本功 jīběngōng basic skill
2 power *(in physics)*

功夫 gōngfu NOUN
martial arts

功课 gōngkè NOUN
homework

功劳 gōngláo NOUN
contribution

功能 gōngnéng NOUN
function
多功能电话 duōgōngnéng diànhuà multi-functional telephone

攻 gōng VERB
to attack

攻击 gōngjī VERB
to attack
人身攻击 rénshēn gōngjī personal attack

宫 gōng NOUN
palace
■ 王宫 wánggōng royal palace

恭 gōng ADJECTIVE
respectful

恭喜 gōngxǐ VERB
to congratulate
恭喜你中奖了！ Gōngxǐ nǐ zhòngjiǎng le! Congratulations on winning the lottery!

共 gòng ADVERB
altogether
■ 一共 yígòng in total 一共来了50人。Yígòng lái le wǔshí rén. Fifty people came in total.

共产党 gòngchǎndǎng NOUN
communist party

共和国 gònghéguó NOUN
republic

共同 gòngtóng
I ADJECTIVE
common
我们没有共同的爱好。Wǒmen méiyǒu gòngtóng de àihào. We don't have any interests in common.
II ADVERB
together
共同生活 gòngtóng shēnghuó to live together

钩 gōu NOUN
1 hook
挂衣钩 guà yī gōu clothes-hook
2 tick
■ 对钩 duìgōu tick
II VERB
to hook
钉子钩住了我的毛衣。Dīngzi gōu zhù le wǒde máoyī. My sweater is caught on the nail.

狗 gǒu NOUN
dog

购 gòu VERB
to buy

购买 gòumǎi VERB
to buy

购物 gòuwù VERB
to go shopping
她爱购物。Tā ài gòuwù. She likes shopping.

够 gòu ADJECTIVE
enough
五个就够了。Wǔ gè jiù gǒu le. Five is enough.

姑 gū NOUN
aunt

姑娘 gūniang NOUN
girl

姑姑 gūgu NOUN
aunt

LANGUAGE TIP 姑姑 gūgu refers specifically to a father's sister.

古 gǔ
I NOUN
ancient times *pl*
II ADJECTIVE
ancient

古代 gǔdài NOUN
antiquity

古典 gǔdiǎn ADJECTIVE
classical
古典音乐 gǔdiǎn yīnyuè classical music

古董 gǔdǒng NOUN
antique

古迹 gǔjì NOUN
historic site

古老 gǔlǎo ADJECTIVE
ancient

谷 gǔ NOUN
1 valley
2 grain

谷歌 Gǔ gē NOUN
Google®

骨 gǔ NOUN
bone

骨头 gǔtou NOUN
bone

鼓 gǔ
I NOUN
drum
II ADJECTIVE
bulging

鼓励 gǔlì VERB
to encourage
爸爸鼓励我学钢琴。Bàba gǔlì wǒ xué gāngqín. My father encouraged me to learn the piano.

鼓舞 gǔwǔ
I VERB
to inspire
II ADJECTIVE
inspiring

鼓掌 gǔzhǎng VERB
to applaud

故 gù NOUN
reason

故宫 gùgōng NOUN
the Forbidden City

DID YOU KNOW...?
As the largest collection of ancient wooden structures in the world, 故宫 gùgōng formed the imperial palaces of the Ming (1368-1644) and Qing (1644-1911) dynasties. It is located at what was once the exact centre of the old city of Beijing, just to the north of Tiananmen Square. It is now a major tourist attraction.

故事 gùshi NOUN
story

故乡 gùxiāng NOUN
birthplace

故意 gùyì ADVERB
deliberately
我不是故意的。Wǒ búshì gùyì de. I didn't do it deliberately.

故障 gùzhàng NOUN
fault

顾 gù VERB
1 to look
■ 回顾 huígù to look back
■ 环顾 huángù to look around
2 to look after
■ 照顾 zhàogù to look after

顾客 gùkè NOUN
customer

瓜 guā NOUN
melon
■ 西瓜 xīguā watermelon

刮 guā VERB
1 to shave *(facial hair)*
2 to blow *(wind)*
今天刮大风。Jīntiān guā dà fēng. It's really windy today.

挂 guà VERB
1 to hang
钥匙挂在墙上。Yàoshi guà zài qiáng shang. The key is hanging on the wall.
2 to hang up *(telephone)*

挂号 guàhào
I VERB
to register
先挂号，再看病。Xiān guàhào, zài kànbìng. Please register first, then you can see the doctor.
II ADJECTIVE
registered
挂号信 guàhào xìn registered mail

挂历 guàlì NOUN
wall calendar

乖 guāi ADJECTIVE
well-behaved *(children, pets)*

拐 guǎi
I NOUN
crutch

II VERB
to turn *(right, left)*
向左拐 xiàng zuǒ guǎi to turn left

怪 guài
I ADJECTIVE
strange
她的衣服很怪。Tā de yīfu hěn guài. Her clothes are really weird.
II VERB
to blame
出了问题，别怪我。Chū le wèntí, bié guài wǒ. If there's a problem, don't blame me.
III NOUN
monster
■ 妖怪 yāoguài monster
怪不得 guàibude CONJUNCTION
no wonder
他搬家了，怪不得没回信。Tā bān jiā le, guàibude méi huíxìn. It's no wonder that he didn't reply to my letter, he had moved house.

关 guān VERB
1 to shut *(doors, windows)*
2 to imprison *(people)*
3 to close down *(shops, companies)*
4 to turn... off *(TV, lights, computer)*
关灯 guān dēng to turn off the light
5 to concern
这不关他的事。Zhè bù guān tā de shì. It does not concern him.
关系 guānxì
I NOUN
1 relationship
我们的关系很好。Wǒmen de guānxì hěn hǎo. We have a really good relationship.
2 consequence
我明天不能来看你了。— 没有关系。Wǒ míngtiān bù néng lái kàn nǐ le. — Méiyǒu guānxì. I can't come and see you tomorrow. — Never mind, it doesn't matter.
多一个人没有关系。Duō yíge rén méiyǒu guānxì. One extra person won't make any difference.
3 relevance
这件事和他有关系。Zhè jiàn shì hé tā yǒu guānxì. This business has something to do with him.
II VERB
to impact on
这关系到孩子的健康。Zhè guānxì dào háizi de jiànkāng. This will impact on the child's health.
关心 guānxīn VERB
1 to be concerned about
她过分关心女儿的学习了。Tā guòfèn guānxīn nǚ'ér de xuéxí le. She is overly concerned about her daughter's studies.
2 to care about
你对我太不关心了！ Nǐ duì wǒ tài bù guānxīn le! You don't care about me at all!
关于 guānyú PREPOSITION
on
关于治安问题 guānyú zhì'ān wèntí on a matter of public security

观 guān VERB
to look
■ 围观 wéiguān to gather round to watch
观察 guānchá VERB
to observe
观点 guāndiǎn NOUN
point of view
观看 guānkàn VERB
to watch
观看表演 guānkàn biǎoyǎn to watch a performance
观念 guānniàn NOUN
concept
观众 guānzhòng NOUN
audience

官 guān NOUN
official
官员 guānyuán NOUN
official

管 guǎn
I NOUN
1 pipe
■ 水管 shuǐguǎn water pipe
2 tube *(metal, glass, rubber)*
II VERB
1 to be in charge of
王老师管图书馆。Wáng lǎoshī guǎn túshūguǎn. Mrs Wang is in charge of the library.
2 to discipline
好好管管这孩子！ Hǎohao guǎn guǎn zhè háizi! Make sure you discipline this child properly!
3 to interfere
这事不用你管。Zhè shì bú yòng nǐ guǎn. It's no use you interfering in this.
管理 guǎnlǐ VERB
to be in charge

冠 guàn NOUN
crown
冠军 guànjūn NOUN
champion

惯 guàn VERB
1 to be used to
我吃西餐已经惯了。Wǒ chī xīcān yǐjīng guàn le. I'm already used to Western food.
2 to spoil
惯孩子 guàn háizi to spoil the children

罐 guàn
I NOUN
1 jar
2 can
3 cylinder
■ 煤气罐 méiqìguàn gas cylinder
II MEASURE WORD
can
两罐啤酒 liǎng guàn píjiǔ two cans of beer
五罐苏打水 wǔ guàn sūdǎshuǐ five cans of soda water
罐头 guàntou NOUN
tin
■ 金枪鱼罐头 jīnqiāngyú guàntou tinned tuna fish

光 guāng
I NOUN
light
■ 月光 yuèguāng moonlight
■ 阳光 yángguāng sunlight
II ADJECTIVE
1 bare
■ 光脚 guāngjiǎo barefooted
2 used up
钱都用光了。Qián dōu yòng guāng le. All the money's used up.
光明 guāngmíng
I NOUN
light
II ADJECTIVE
bright
光盘 guāngpán NOUN
CD-ROM
光荣 guāngróng ADJECTIVE
glorious
光线 guāngxiàn NOUN
light

广 guǎng ADJECTIVE
broad
广播 guǎngbō VERB
to broadcast
广场 guǎngchǎng NOUN
square
广泛 guǎngfàn ADJECTIVE
wide-ranging
■ 广泛开展活动 guǎngfàn kāizhǎn huódòng to initiate a wide range of activities
广告 guǎnggào NOUN
advertisement
广阔 guǎngkuò ADJECTIVE
broad

逛 guàng VERB
to stroll
逛街 guàng jiē to go shopping 上周末我们去逛了商场。Shàng zhōumò wǒmen qù guàng le shāngchǎng. We went shopping at the department store last weekend.

归 guī VERB
to be under the charge of
这本书归他所有。Zhè běn shū guī tā suǒyǒu. This book belongs to him.
归还 guīhuán VERB
to return

龟 guī NOUN
tortoise
■ 乌龟 wūguī tortoise

规 guī NOUN
rule
规定 guīdìng
I VERB
to stipulate
II NOUN
regulation
规范 guīfàn NOUN
standard
■ 一定要规范市场秩序。Yídìng yào guīfàn shìchǎng zhìxù. We must standardize the market order.
规律 guīlǜ NOUN
1 law
物理规律 wùlǐ guīlǜ the law of physics
2 regular pattern
我的生物钟很有规律。Wǒ de shēngwùzhōng hěn yǒu guīlǜ. My body clock has a very regular pattern.
规模 guīmó NOUN
scale
规则 guīzé NOUN
regulation

轨 guǐ NOUN
rail
■ 轨道 guǐdào track

鬼 guǐ NOUN
ghost
■ 酒鬼 jiǔguǐ alcoholic
■ 烟鬼 yānguǐ chain-smoker

鬼混 guǐhùn VERB
to mess around

鬼脸 guǐliǎn NOUN
grimace
做鬼脸 zuò guǐliǎn to make a funny face

柜 guì NOUN
cupboard
- 衣柜 yīguì wardrobe
- 保险柜 bǎoxiǎnguì safe

柜台 guìtái NOUN
counter

贵 guì ADJECTIVE
1 expensive
太贵了！ Tài guì le! That's way too expensive!
2 honourable
- 贵宾 guìbīn honourable guest

贵宾 guìbīn NOUN
VIP

跪 guì VERB
to kneel
- 跪下 guìxià to kneel down

滚 gǔn VERB
1 to roll
- 滚动 gǔndòng to roll
2 to get lost
滚！ Gǔn! Get lost!

棍 gùn NOUN
stick
- 棍子 gùnzi stick

锅 guō NOUN
pot
- 炒菜锅 chǎocàiguō wok
- 火锅 huǒguō hotpot

国 guó NOUN
country
- 国徽 guóhuī national emblem
- 国歌 guógē national anthem
- 国旗 guóqí national flag

国画 guóhuà NOUN
traditional Chinese painting

国会 guóhuì NOUN
parliament

国籍 guójí NOUN
nationality

国际 guójì ADJECTIVE
international

国家 guójiā NOUN
nation state

国民 guómín NOUN
citizen

国内 guónèi ADJECTIVE
domestic

国庆节 Guóqìng Jié NOUN
National Day

> **DID YOU KNOW...?**
> 国庆节 Guóqìng Jié **National Day** falls on 1 October and commemorates the anniversary of the founding of the People's Republic of China in 1949. The PRC was declared by Chairman Mao Zedong in Tiananmen Square in Beijing.

国王 guówáng NOUN
king

国营 guóyíng ADJECTIVE
state-run

果 guǒ NOUN
fruit
- 果子 guǒzi fruit

果然 guǒrán ADVERB
really

果实 guǒshí NOUN
1 fruit
2 fruits *pl (achievements)*

果真 guǒzhēn ADVERB
really

过 guò
I PREPOSITION
past
现在是9点过8分。Xiànzài shì jiǔ diǎn guò bā fēn. It is now eight minutes past nine.
过10分钟再打过来。Guò shí fēnzhōng zài dǎ guòlai. Call back in ten minutes.
II VERB
1 to pass *(a bridge, crossing)*
过马路 guò mǎlù to cross the road
2 to spend
你假期怎么过的？Nǐ jiàqī zěnme guò de? How did you spend your holiday?
3 to live
我们过得很好。Wǒmen guò de hěn hǎo. We live very comfortably.
4 to celebrate
给我过生日 gěi wǒ guò shēngrì to celebrate my birthday

过程 guòchéng NOUN
process

过道 guòdào NOUN
corridor

过分 guòfèn ADJECTIVE
excessive

过奖 guòjiǎng VERB

to flatter
您过奖了。Nín guòjiǎng le. I'm flattered.

过来 guòlái VERB
to come over

过敏 guòmǐn ADJECTIVE
allergic

过年 guònián VERB
to celebrate the Chinese New Year

过期 guòqī VERB
to expire

过去 guòqù NOUN
past

过去 guòqu VERB
to pass by
他们走过去了。Tāmen zǒu guòqu le. They've already passed by.

过日子 guò rìzi VERB
to live

过时 guòshí
I ADJECTIVE
outdated
II VERB
to pass time

Hh

哈 hā INTERJECTION
ha ha
哈哈大笑 hā hā dàxiào
to roar with laughter

还 hái ADVERB
▷ *see also* huán
yet
她还没回来。Tā hái méi huílai.
She hasn't come back yet.

还是 háishì
I ADVERB
1 still
她还是很漂亮。
Tā háishì hěn piàoliang.
She is still very beautiful.
2 had better
你还是先完成作业吧。
Nǐ háishì xiān wánchéng zuòyè ba.
You'd better finish your homework first.
II CONJUNCTION
or
你是去巴黎还是去伦敦？
Nǐ shì qù Bālí háishì qù Lúndūn?
Are you going to Paris or London?

孩 hái NOUN
child
孩子 háizi NOUN
child

海 hǎi NOUN
ocean
■ 地中海 Dìzhōnghǎi
the Mediterranean Sea
海边 hǎibiān NOUN
coast
海报 hǎibào NOUN
poster
海滨 hǎibīn NOUN
seaside
海滩 hǎitān NOUN
beach
海鲜 hǎixiān NOUN
seafood
海洋 hǎiyáng NOUN
ocean

害 hài
I VERB
to harm
II NOUN
harm
■ 害处 hàichù harm
■ 灾害 zāihài disaster
害怕 hàipà VERB
to be afraid
害羞 hàixiū VERB
to be shy

含 hán VERB
to contain
含义 hányì NOUN
meaning

寒 hán ADJECTIVE
cold
■ 寒风 hánfēng chilly wind
寒假 hánjià NOUN
winter holiday
寒冷 hánlěng ADJECTIVE
cold

韩 hán NOUN
▷ *see below:*
韩国 Hánguó NOUN
South Korea

喊 hǎn VERB
to shout
■ 喊叫 hǎnjiào to cry out

汉 hàn NOUN
the Han *pl*
■ 汉人 Hànrén
the Han people *pl*
汉语 Hànyǔ NOUN
Chinese *(language)*
汉字 Hànzì NOUN
Chinese characters *pl*

DID YOU KNOW...?
There are around 47,000 Chinese characters. Studies have concluded that only about 3,000 to 4,000 characters are necessary for full literacy in Chinese.

汉族 Hànzú NOUN
the Han *pl*

汗 hàn NOUN
sweat
■ 汗水 hànshuǐ sweat

行 háng
▹ *see also* xíng
I NOUN
1 row
第一行 dìyī háng first row
2 profession
■ 同行 tóngháng people in the same profession
II MEASURE WORD
line
一行字 yì háng zì a line of words

行业 hángyè NOUN
industry

航 háng VERB
to fly

航班 hángbān NOUN
scheduled flight

好 hǎo
▹ *see also* hào
I ADJECTIVE
1 good
他脾气好。Tā píqì hǎo. He's good-natured.
2 well
你身体好吗？Nǐ shēntǐ hǎo ma? Are you feeling well?

LANGUAGE TIP 好 hǎo is used to express agreement.

好，我们现在就去！ Hǎo, wǒmen xiànzài jiù qù! OK, let's go then!

LANGUAGE TIP 好 hǎo is also used in greetings.

■ 你好！ Nǐ hǎo! Hello!
■ 大家好。Dàjiā hǎo. Hello everyone.
II ADVERB
very
我等了好久她才来。Wǒ děng le hǎo jiǔ tā cái lái. I waited for a long time before she arrived.
III NOUN
regards *pl*
请代我向你太太问好。Qǐng dài wǒ xiàng nǐ tàitai wènhǎo. Please send my regards to your wife.

好吃 hǎochī ADJECTIVE
delicious

好处 hǎochu NOUN
benefit

好久 hǎojiǔ ADVERB
for a long time

好看 hǎokàn ADJECTIVE
1 nice-looking
2 good *(object you can look at or through)*
这本书很好看。Zhè běn shū hěn hǎokàn. This book is very good.

好听 hǎotīng ADJECTIVE
lovely *(music, voice)*
这首歌很好听。Zhè shǒu gē hěn hǎotīng. This song is lovely.

好玩儿 hǎowánr ADJECTIVE
fun
这个游戏很好玩儿。Zhè gè yóuxì hěn hǎowánr. This game is a lot of fun.

好笑 hǎoxiào ADJECTIVE
funny

号 hào NOUN
1 name
■ 外号 wàihào nickname
2 date
六月一号 liùyuè yī hào the first of June
3 size
■ 大号 dàhào large-size

号码 hàomǎ NOUN
number

LANGUAGE TIP In Chinese, when you ask for a number, you don't say **What is it?** but **How much is it?** For example 你的电话号码是多少？Ní de diàn huà hào mǎ shì duō shǎo? **What is your phone number?**

好 hào VERB
▹ *see also* hǎo
to like
■ 爱好 aìhào hobby

好奇 hàoqí ADJECTIVE
curious

喝 hē VERB
to drink
■ 喝酒 hējiǔ to drink alcohol

喝醉 hēzuì VERB
to get drunk

合 hé VERB
1 to close

合起书 hé qǐ shū to close the book

2 to join

■ 合并 hébíng to merge

合唱 héchàng NOUN
chorus

合法 héfǎ ADJECTIVE
legal

合格 hégé ADJECTIVE
qualified

合理 hélǐ ADJECTIVE
rational

合身 héshēn ADJECTIVE
fitted

合适 héshì ADJECTIVE
appropriate

合作 hézuò VERB
to cooperate

和 hé

I CONJUNCTION

and

她和她姐姐都喜欢红色。
Tā hé tā jiějiě dōu xǐhuān hóngsè.
She and her older sister like red.

II PREPOSITION

with

这事和你没关系。Zhè shì hé nǐ méi guānxi. This has nothing to do with you.

和好 héhǎo VERB
to reconcile

和平 hébíng NOUN
peace

河 hé NOUN
river

盒 hé NOUN
box

盒子 hézi NOUN
box

贺 hè VERB
to congratulate

贺卡 hèkǎ NOUN
greetings card

黑 hēi ADJECTIVE

1 black

■ 黑板 hēibǎn blackboard

2 dark

黑暗 hēi'àn ADJECTIVE
dark

黑人 hēirén NOUN
black person

很 hěn ADVERB
very

■ 很少 hěnshǎo seldom

恨 hèn VERB

1 to hate

■ 痛恨 tònghèn hatred

2 to regret

■ 悔恨 huǐhèn remorse

红 hóng ADJECTIVE

1 red

■ 红酒 hóngjiǔ red wine

■ 红烧肉 hóngshāoròu braised meat in soy sauce

2 popular

■ 走红 zǒuhóng to be popular

3 successful

■ 红运 hóngyùn good fortune

DID YOU KNOW...?
Red is a lucky colour in China, worn by brides at weddings, and gifted in the form of red envelopes full of money on the Chinese New Year.

红绿灯 hónglǜdēng NOUN
traffic lights

红色 hóngsè ADJECTIVE
red

猴 hóu NOUN
monkey

猴子 hóuzi NOUN
monkey

后 hòu NOUN
back

房后有个车库。Fánghòu yǒu ge chēkù.
At the back of the house is a garage.

■ 后天 hòutiān the day after tomorrow

后代 hòudài NOUN
offspring

后果 hòuguǒ NOUN
consequence

后悔 hòuhuǐ VERB
to regret

后来 hòulái ADVERB
afterwards

我后来再也没有见过他。Wǒ hòulái zài yě méiyǒu jiànguo tā. I didn't see him again after that.

后门 hòumén NOUN
back door

后面 hòumian NOUN
back

那只狗一直跟在他的后面。Nà zhī gǒu

yìzhí gēnzai tā de hòumian. That dog is always following behind him.

后年 hòunián NOUN
the year after next

后退 hòutuì VERB
to retreat

候 hòu VERB
to wait

呼 hū VERB
1 to exhale
■ 呼气 hūqì expiration
2 to shout
■ 呼喊 hūhǎn to shout
3 to call
■ 呼叫 hūjiào to call

呼噜 hūlu NOUN
snore

呼吸 hūxī VERB
to breathe

忽 hū ADVERB
suddenly

忽然 hūrán ADVERB
suddenly

忽视 hūshì VERB
to ignore

狐 hú
▷ see below:

狐狸 húli NOUN
fox

胡 hú
I NOUN
1 moustache
2 beard
II ADVERB
recklessly

胡乱 húluàn ADVERB
carelessly
不要胡乱讲话。Búyào húluàn jiǎnghuà. You shouldn't speak carelessly.

胡闹 húnào VERB
to play around

胡说 húshuō VERB
to talk nonsense

LANGUAGE TIP 胡说 hú shuō is often used in the combination 胡说八道 hú shuō bā dào which also means **to talk nonsense**.

胡同 hútòng NOUN
lane

DID YOU KNOW...? 胡同 hú tòng also describes old quarters of Chinese cities composed of blocks of one-floor stone houses divided by small lanes.

胡子 húzi NOUN
1 moustache
2 beard

湖 hú NOUN
lake

蝴 hú
▷ see below:

蝴蝶 húdié NOUN
butterfly

糊 hú VERB
to paste

糊涂 hútu ADJECTIVE
confused
这个故事把她弄糊涂了。Zhège gùshì bǎ tā nòng hútu le. This story confused her.

LANGUAGE TIP 糊涂 hútu is often used in the combination 一塌糊涂 yí tà hútu which means **in a complete mess**.

虎 hǔ NOUN
tiger

互 hù ADVERB
mutually

互联网 hùliánwǎng NOUN
internet

互相 hùxiāng ADVERB
mutually
朋友之间应该互相帮助。Péngyǒu zhījiān yīnggāi hùxiāng bāngzhù. Friends should help each other.

户 hù NOUN
door

户口 hùkǒu NOUN
registered permanent residence

护 hù VERB
to protect

护士 hùshi NOUN
nurse

护照 hùzhào NOUN
passport

花 huā
I NOUN
flower

II ADJECTIVE
floral
■ 花篮 huālán flower basket
III VERB
to spend *(money, time)*
花费 huāfèi VERB
to spend
留学花费了他很多钱。Liǔxué huāfèi le tā hěnduō qián. He spent a lot of money on his study abroad.
花生 huāshēng NOUN
peanut
花园 huāyuán NOUN
garden

华 huá NOUN
China
华侨 huáqiáo NOUN
overseas Chinese
华人 huárén NOUN
Chinese

滑 huá
I ADJECTIVE
slippery
II VERB
to slip
滑冰 huábīng VERB
to ice skate
滑雪 huáxuě VERB
to ski

画 huà
I VERB
1 to draw
2 to paint
II NOUN
1 drawing
2 painting
■ 油画 yóuhuà oil painting
画报 huàbào NOUN
pictorial
画家 huàjiā NOUN
painter
画像 huàxiàng NOUN
portrait
画展 huàzhǎn NOUN
art exhibition

话 huà NOUN
words *pl*
■ 对话 duìhuà conversation
■ 谎话 huǎnghuà lie
话题 huàtí NOUN
subject

怀 huái VERB
1 to think of
2 to keep... in mind
怀念 huáiniàn VERB
to cherish the memory of
怀疑 huáiyí VERB
to doubt
他怀疑那些话都是谎言。Tā huáiyí nàxiē huà dōu shì huǎngyán. He suspected that all those words were lies.

坏 huài
I ADJECTIVE
bad
II VERB
to go off
空调坏了。Kōngtiáo huài le. The air-conditioning has broken down.
坏处 huàichù NOUN
disadvantage
坏蛋 huàidàn NOUN
scoundrel

欢 huān ADJECTIVE
happy
欢呼 huānhū VERB
to cheer
观众们为球队的胜利欢呼。Guānzhòng men wèi qiúduì de shènglì huānhū. The audience cheered for the team's victory.
欢快 huānkuài ADJECTIVE
cheerful
这是首欢快的乐曲。Zhè shì shǒu huānkuài de yuèqǔ. This is a cheerful piece of music.
欢乐 huānlè ADJECTIVE
joyful
欢迎 huānyíng VERB
to welcome
欢迎来中国。Huānyíng lái Zhōngguó. Welcome to China.

还 huán VERB
▷ *see also* hái
to return
还书 huán shū to return books
■ 还债 huánzhài to repay a debt

环 huán NOUN
1 ring
■ 耳环 ěrhuán earring
2 element
■ 环节 huánjié element
环保 huánbǎo NOUN
environmental protection

环境 huánjìng NOUN
environment
生活环境 shēnghuó huánjìng living conditions *pl*

环绕 huánrào VERB
to surround

换 huàn VERB
1 to exchange
■ 交换 jiāohuàn to exchange
2 to replace
他给门换了锁。Tā gěi mén huàn le suǒ. He replaced the lock in the door.

慌 huāng ADJECTIVE
nervous

慌张 huāngzhāng ADJECTIVE
nervous

皇 huáng NOUN
emperor
■ 皇帝 huángdì emperor

黄 huáng ADJECTIVE
yellow

黄瓜 huángguā NOUN
cucumber

黄河 Huánghé NOUN
Yellow River

黄昏 huánghūn NOUN
dusk

黄金 huángjīn NOUN
gold

黄色 huángsè NOUN
1 yellow
2 pornographic

黄油 huángyóu NOUN
butter

谎 huǎng NOUN
lie

谎言 huǎngyán NOUN
lie

灰 huī
I NOUN
dust
II VERB
to be disheartened

灰尘 huīchén NOUN
dust

灰色 huīsè NOUN
grey

灰心 huīxīn VERB
to lose heart

恢 huī ADJECTIVE
vast

恢复 huīfù VERB
to recover

挥 huī VERB
1 to wave
他挥了挥手。Tā huī le huī ...shǒu. He waved his hand.
2 to command
■ 指挥 zhǐhuī to command

回 huí
I VERB
1 to return
回家 huíjiā to return home
2 to turn around
■ 回头 huítóu to turn one's head
■ 回头见。Huítóujiàn. See you later.
3 to reply
■ 回信 huíxìn to reply to a letter
II MEASURE WORD
time
我去过两回。Wǒ qùguo liǎng huí. I have been there twice.

回报 huíbào VERB
to repay

回答 huídá VERB
to answer

回复 huífù VERB
to reply

回来 huílái VERB
to come back

回去 huíqù VERB
to go back

回忆 huíyì VERB
to recall

会 huì
▷ *see also* kuài
I VERB
can
我不会下象棋。Wǒ búhuì xià xiàngqí. I can't play chess.
II NOUN
1 association
■ 学生会 xuéshēnghuì student union
2 opportunity
■ 机会 jīhuì opportunity

LANGUAGE TIP 会 huì can also be used to express a possible or probable outcome.

明天会下雨。Míngtiān huì xiàyǔ. It might rain tomorrow.

会议 huìyì NOUN
meeting

会员 huìyuán NOUN
member

婚 hūn
I NOUN
marriage
II VERB
to marry
■ 结婚 jiéhūn to marry
婚礼 hūnlǐ NOUN
wedding ceremony
婚姻 hūnyīn NOUN
marriage

活 huó
I VERB
to live
II ADJECTIVE
alive
活动 huódòng
I VERB
to take exercise
年轻人应该多活动。Niánqīngrén yīnggāi duō huódòng. Young people should exercise more.
II NOUN
activity
活力 huólì NOUN
vitality
活泼 huópō ADJECTIVE
lively

火 huǒ
I NOUN
fire
II VERB
to be in a rage
■ 发火 fāhuǒ to get angry
III ADJECTIVE
flaming red
■ 火红 huǒhóng flaming red
火柴 huǒchái NOUN
match
火车 huǒchē NOUN
train
■ 火车站 huǒchēzhàn train station
火鸡 huǒjī NOUN
turkey
火腿 huǒtuǐ NOUN
ham

伙 huǒ
I NOUN
companion
II MEASURE WORD
group
一伙年轻人 yì huǒ niánqīngrén a group of young people
伙伴 huǒbàn NOUN
companion

或 huò CONJUNCTION
or
或许 huòxǔ ADVERB
perhaps
他或许不会来了。Tā huòxǔ búhuì lái le. Maybe he won't come.
或者 huòzhě CONJUNCTION
or
你可以买项链或者耳环送给她。Nǐ kěyǐ mǎi xiàngliàn huòzhě ěrhuán sòng gěi tā. You can buy a necklace or earrings to give her.

获 huò VERB
1 to obtain
2 to reap
■ 收获 shōuhuò to harvest
获得 huòdé VERB
to gain

Jj

几 jī NOUN
▹see also jǐ
small table
■ 几 chájī tea table

几乎 jīhū ADVERB
almost
那件事我几乎忘了。Nà jiàn shì wǒ jīhū wàngle. I'd almost forgotten about that.

机 jī
I NOUN
1 machine
■ 发动机 fādòngjī engine
2 aeroplane
■ 客机 kèjī airliner
3 pivot
■ 转机 zhuǎnjī turning point
II ADJECTIVE
quick-witted
■ 机智 jīzhì ingenious

机场 jīchǎng NOUN
airport

机关 jīguān NOUN
1 mechanism
2 department
政府机关 zhèngfǔ jīguān government body

机会 jīhuì NOUN
opportunity

机灵 jīling ADJECTIVE
clever

机器 jīqì NOUN
machine

机械 jīxiè
I NOUN
machinery
II ADJECTIVE
mechanical
这个动作太机械。Zhège dòngzuò tài jīxiè. The movement is very mechanical. 机械照搬他人的做法 jīxiè zhàobān tārén de zuòfǎ to copy someone else's method exactly

机遇 jīyù NOUN
opportunity

鸡 jī NOUN
chicken
■ 公鸡 gōngjī cock
■ 母鸡 mǔjī hen

鸡蛋 jīdàn NOUN
egg

积 jī VERB
to accumulate
院子里积了很多雪。Yuànzi lǐ jī le hěnduō xuě. The courtyard was full of snow.

积极 jījí ADJECTIVE
1 positive
态度积极 tàidù jījí a positive attitude
2 active
积极地工作 jījí de gōngzuò an active job

积极性 jījíxìng NOUN
enthusiasm

积累 jīlěi VERB
to accumulate
积累知识 jīlěi zhīshi to accumulate knowledge

积蓄 jīxù
I VERB
to save
积蓄力量 jīxù lìliàng to gather strength
II NOUN
savings

基 jī
I NOUN
base
II ADJECTIVE
primary
■ 基层 jīcéng grass roots

基本 jīběn
I ADJECTIVE
1 basic
基本原则 jīběn yuánzé basic principles
2 essential
基本条件 jīběn tiáojiàn basic requirements
3 elementary
基本知识 jīběn zhīshi basic knowledge
II ADVERB
basically

基础 jīchǔ
I NOUN
foundation
经济基础 jīngjì jīchǔ economic foundation
II ADJECTIVE
basic
基础课 jīchǔ kè elementary class

基督教 Jīdūjiào NOUN
Christianity

及 jí
I VERB
1 to reach
2 to be as good as
我的成绩不及她。Wǒ de chéngjì bù jí tā. My score wasn't as good as hers.
3 to be in time for
来不及做。Láibují zuò. There's not enough time to do it.
II CONJUNCTION
and

及格 jígé VERB
to pass
你考试及格了吗？Nǐ kǎoshì jígé le ma? Did you pass your exam?

及时 jíshí
I ADJECTIVE
timely
医生来得很及时。Yīshēng lái de hěn jíshí. The doctor arrived just in time.
II ADVERB
without delay

级 jí
I NOUN
1 level
八级风 bā jí fēng force 8 wind
2 year *(school, university)*
小学三年级 xiǎoxué sān niánjí third grade of primary school
II MEASURE WORD
step
一百多级台阶 yìbǎi duō jí táijiē a staircase of more than 100 steps

极 jí
I NOUN
1 extreme
2 magnetic pole
■ 南极 nánjí the South Pole
II ADJECTIVE
extreme
■ 极限 jíxiàn limit
III ADVERB
extremely

极其 jíqí ADVERB
extremely

即 jí
I VERB
to mean *(formal, in written Chinese)*
II ADJECTIVE
present
■ 即日 jírì this very day

即将 jíjiāng ADVERB
soon
演出即将开始。Yǎnchū jíjiāng kāishǐ. The performance is about to start.

即使 jíshǐ CONJUNCTION
even if
即使明天下雨，我也要去。Jíshǐ míngtiān xiàyǔ, wǒ yě yào qù. Even if it rains tomorrow, I'm still going to go.

急 jí
I ADJECTIVE
1 anxious
2 impatient
别急，我们马上就走。Biéjí, wǒmen mǎshàng jiù zǒu. Don't worry, we'll leave soon.
3 rapid
水流很急。Shuǐ liú hěn jí. There's a strong current.
4 urgent
急事 jíshì urgent matter
II VERB
to worry

急忙 jímáng ADVERB
hurriedly

集 jí
I VERB
to gather
II NOUN
1 market
■ 赶集 gǎnjí to go to market
2 anthology
■ 诗集 shījí an anthology of poems
3 part *(of book, film, TV series)*
这部电视剧一共十五集。Zhè bù diànshì jù yígòng shíwǔ jí. There are 15 episodes in this TV series.

集合 jíhé VERB
to assemble

集中 jízhōng VERB
to concentrate

几 jǐ NUMBER
▷ *see also* jī
several

几本书 jǐ běn shū several books

LANGUAGE TIP 几 jǐ is also used in questions.

昨天来了几位客人？Zuótiān lái le jǐ wèi kèrén? How many customers came yesterday?

己 jǐ NOUN
self
■ 自己 zìjǐ oneself

计 jì
I VERB
1 to calculate
■ 共计 gòngjì to total
2 to plan
II NOUN
1 strategy
2 gauge
■ 温度计 wēndùjì thermometer

计划 jìhuà
I NOUN
plan
旅行计划 lǚxíng jìhuà travel itinerary
II VERB
to plan

计算 jìsuàn VERB
1 to calculate
一共来了多少人，你计算一下吧。Yígòng lái le duōshǎo rén, nǐ jìsuàn yíxià ba. Can you calculate how many people came in total?
2 to scheme

计算机 jìsuànjī NOUN
computer

计算器 jìsuànqì NOUN
calculator

记 jì
I VERB
1 to remember
2 to record
II NOUN
1 record *(books, articles)*
■ 日记 rìjì diary
2 mark

记得 jìde VERB
to remember

记号 jìhào NOUN
mark

记录 jìlù
I VERB
to write... down
记录历史 jìlù lìshǐ to make a historical record
II NOUN
record
打破记录 dǎpò jìlù to break a record

记忆 jìyì
I VERB
to remember
II NOUN
memory

记者 jìzhě NOUN
journalist

纪 jì
I NOUN
1 age
■ 中世纪 Zhōngshìjì the Middle Ages
2 period *(geology)*
■ 侏罗纪 Zhūluójì the Jurassic period
3 discipline
II VERB
to record

纪律 jìlǜ NOUN
discipline
遵守纪律 zūnshǒu jìlǜ to observe discipline

纪念 jìniàn
I VERB
to commemorate
II NOUN
memento
■ 纪念品 jìniànpǐn souvenir

技 jì NOUN
1 skill
■ 技能 jìnéng skill
■ 技巧 jìqiǎo technique
2 ability

技术 jìshù NOUN
technology
科学技术 kēxué jìshù science and technology

系 jì VERB
▷ *see also* xì
1 to tie
2 to fasten

季 jì NOUN
season
■ 春季 chūnjì spring

季节 jìjié NOUN
season

季军 jìjūn NOUN
third place

LANGUAGE TIP Behind 亚军 yàjūn, **second place**, and 冠军 guànjūn, **first place**.

既 jì
I ADVERB
already
II CONJUNCTION
■ 她既聪明又漂亮。Tā jì cōngmíng yòu piàoliang. She is not only beautiful but also intelligent.

既然 jìrán CONJUNCTION
since
他既然来了，你就别生气了。Tā jìrán lái le, nǐ jiù bié shēngqì le. Seeing as he came, there's no need to get angry.

继 jì
I ADVERB
1 continuously
2 successively
■ 相继 xiāngjì one after another
II VERB
to continue

继续 jìxù
I VERB
to continue
请大家继续读书。Qǐng dàjiā jìxù dúshū. Please continue reading everybody.
II NOUN
continuation

寄 jì VERB
1 to post
寄信 jìxìn to post a letter
2 to depend on
寄宿 jìsù to lodge

加 jiā VERB
1 to add
2加2等于4。Èr jiā èr děngyú sì. 2 plus 2 is 4. 加糖 jiā táng to add sugar
2 to increase

加工 jiāgōng VERB
1 to process
2 to polish
这篇文章还需要加工。Zhè piān wénzhāng hái xūyào jiāgōng. This article still needs some polishing.

加拿大 Jiānádà NOUN
Canada

加强 jiāqiáng VERB
to strengthen
加强联系 jiāqiáng liánxì to strengthen relations

加油 jiāyóu VERB
1 to refuel
给汽车加油 gěi qìchē jiāyóu to fill the car up with petrol
2 to make more effort
快，加油！Kuài, jiāyóu! Be quick, come on!

家 jiā
I NOUN
1 family
2 home
3 expert
■ 专家 zhuānjiā
II ADJECTIVE
domestic
III MEASURE WORD
LANGUAGE TIP This is a measure word used for families, companies, banks, factories, restaurants, hotels etc.
一家公司 yì jiā gōngsī a company 两家人 liǎng jiā rén two families

家具 jiājù NOUN
furniture

家庭 jiātíng NOUN
family

家务 jiāwù NOUN
housework
做家务 zuò jiāwù to do the housework

家乡 jiāxiāng NOUN
hometown

家长 jiāzhǎng NOUN
1 head of the family
2 parent
家长会 jiāzhǎng huì parents' meeting

假 jiǎ
▷ *see also* jià
I ADJECTIVE
1 false
2 artificial
■ 假发 jiǎfà wig
■ 假话 jiǎhuà lie
II CONJUNCTION
if
■ 假如 jiǎrú if

假设 jiǎshè
I VERB
to suppose
II NOUN
hypothesis

假装 jiǎzhuāng VERB
to pretend
他假装不认识我。Tā jiǎzhuāng bú rènshi wǒ. He pretended he didn't know me.

价 jià NOUN
1 price
■ 物价 wùjià price
2 value

价格 jiàgé NOUN

price
提高价格 tígāo jiàgé to put prices up

价钱 jiàqian NOUN
price

价值 jiàzhí NOUN
value

驾 jià

I VERB
1 to harness
2 to drive
驾车 jià chē to drive a car

II PRONOUN
■ 劳驾 láojià excuse me

驾驶 jiàshǐ VERB
to steer
他驾驶一辆吉普车去了山区。Tā jiàshǐ yí liàng jípǔchē qù le shānqū. He drove the jeep into the mountains.

驾照 jiàzhào NOUN
driving licence

架 jià

I NOUN
1 frame
■ 书架 shūjià bookshelf
2 *(action)*
■ 吵架 chǎojià to quarrel
■ 打架 dǎjià to fight

II VERB
to support

III MEASURE WORD
LANGUAGE TIP This is a measure word used for pianos, aircraft and machines.
五架飞机 wǔ jià fēijī five planes 一架钢琴 yí jià gāngqín a piano

假 jià NOUN

▷ *see also* jiǎ
holiday
■ 暑假 shǔjià summer holiday
■ 病假 bìngjià sick leave

假期 jiàqī NOUN
holiday

假条 jiàtiáo NOUN
application for leave *(work, school, army)*
写假条 xiě jiàtiáo to write an application for leave

尖 jiān

I ADJECTIVE
1 pointed
尖刀 jiāndāo sharp knife
2 shrill
3 sensitive

II NOUN
1 tip
■ 笔尖 bǐjiān pen tip
2 the best
他是我们班的尖子。Tā shì wǒmen bān de jiānzi. He's the best in our class.

尖锐 jiānruì ADJECTIVE
1 sharp
尖锐的问题 jiānruì de wèntí an acute question
2 penetrating
3 shrill

坚 jiān

I ADJECTIVE
hard

II NOUN
stronghold

III ADVERB
firmly
■ 坚信 jiānxìn to firmly believe

坚持 jiānchí VERB
1 to persist
一定要坚持下去！Yídìng yào jiānchí xiàqù! Hold in there, you can do it!
2 to stick to
坚持自己的观点 jiānchí zìjǐ de guāndiǎn to stick to one's point of view

坚定 jiāndìng ADJECTIVE
steadfast

坚决 jiānjué ADVERB
resolutely
态度坚决 tàidù jiānjué a determined attitude

坚强 jiānqiáng ADJECTIVE
strong
坚强的性格 jiānqiáng de xìnggé strong willed

坚硬 jiānyìng ADJECTIVE
hard

间 jiān

I PREPOSITION
between
■ 课间 kèjiān between lessons
■ 晚间 wǎnjiān in the evening

II NOUN
room
■ 房间 fángjiān room
■ 洗手间 xǐshǒujiān toilet

III MEASURE WORD
LANGUAGE TIP This is a measure word used for rooms, lounges, hospital wards etc.
两间客厅 liǎng jiān kètīng two living rooms

兼职 jiānzhí
I NOUN
part-time job
他在这家公司做兼职。Tā zài zhè jiā gōngsī zuò jiānzhí. He works part-time at this company.
II ADJECTIVE
兼职汉语教师 jiānzhí Hànyǔ jiàoshī a part-time Chinese teacher

捡 jiǎn VERB
to pick... up

检 jiǎn VERB
to examine
■ 体检 tǐjiǎn medical examination
检查 jiǎnchá
I VERB
to examine
检查卫生 jiǎnchá wèishēng to inspect hygiene
II NOUN
self-criticism

减 jiǎn VERB
1 to subtract
2 to reduce
3 to decrease
■ 减退 jiǎntuì to fail
减肥 jiǎnféi VERB
to lose weight
他从上星期开始减肥。Tā cóng shàng xīngqī kāishǐ jiǎnféi. He started a diet last week.
减轻 jiǎnqīng VERB
to reduce
减轻压力 jiǎnqīng yālì to reduce pressure
减少 jiǎnshǎo VERB
to reduce
减少人数 jiǎnshǎo rénshù to reduce the population

简 jiǎn
I ADJECTIVE
simple
II VERB
to simplify
■ 简化 jiǎnhuà to simplify
简单 jiǎndān ADJECTIVE
1 simple
这道题很简单。Zhè dào tí hěn jiǎndān. This problem is very simple.
2 casual
3 easy
这孩子能说两门外语，真不简单。Zhè háizi néng shuō liǎng mén wàiyǔ, zhēn bù jiǎndān. It is quite extraordinary that this child can speak two foreign languages.
简体字 jiǎntǐzì NOUN
simplified characters

DID YOU KNOW...?
简体字 jiǎntǐzì **simplified characters** are the type of Chinese characters used today throughout mainland China, and mostly derive from the PRC government's efforts during the 1950s and 1960s to make the script more accessible and improve literacy. The alternative and older form of the script, known as complex or traditional characters, 繁体字 fántǐzì, is used predominantly in Taiwan, Hong Kong and many overseas Chinese communities. The two systems are closely related.

见 jiàn
I VERB
1 to see
见上图。Jiàn shàngtú. See the above diagram.
■ 罕见 hǎnjiàn rare
2 to come into contact with
汽油见火就着。Qìyóu jiàn huǒ jiù zháo. Petrol ignites on contact with a flame.
3 to meet
■ 接见 jiējiàn to receive
II NOUN
opinion
■ 偏见 piānjiàn prejudice
见面 jiànmiàn VERB
to meet
我们明天下午三点见面。Wǒmen míngtiān xiàwǔ sān diǎn jiànmiàn. Let's meet at 3 o'clock tomorrow afternoon.

件 jiàn
I MEASURE WORD
item
一件衣服 yí jiàn yīfu an item of clothing 两件事 liǎng jiàn shì two things
II NOUN
correspondence
急件 jíjiàn urgent letter

建 jiàn VERB
1 to build
建楼房 jiàn lóufáng to build a house
2 to found
建国 jiànguó to found a nation
3 to propose
■ 建议 jiànyì to propose

建立 jiànlì VERB
to establish

建设 jiànshè VERB
to build
建设一个新网站 jiànshè yí gè xīn wǎngzhàn to build a new website

建筑 jiànzhù
I VERB
to build
II NOUN
building

建筑师 jiànzhùshī NOUN
architect

健 jiàn
I ADJECTIVE
■ 强健 qiángjiàn strong and healthy
■ 健全 jiànquán sound
II VERB
1 to strengthen
■ 健身 jiànshēn to keep fit 健身房 jiànshēnfáng gym
2 to be good at
■ 健谈 jiàntán to be good at small-talk

健康 jiànkāng ADJECTIVE
healthy

健忘 jiànwàng ADJECTIVE
forgetful

江 jiāng NOUN
1 river
2 Yangtze

将 jiāng
I ADVERB
他将成为一名医生。Tā jiāng chéngwéi yì míng yīshēng. He is going to become a doctor.
II PREPOSITION
with
请将车停在路边。Qǐng jiāng chē tíng zài lùbiān. Please stop the car by the side of the road.

将军 jiāngjūn NOUN
general

将来 jiānglái NOUN
future

将要 jiāngyào ADVERB
她将要做妈妈了。Tā jiāngyào zuò māma le. She is going to be a mother.

讲 jiǎng VERB
1 to speak
2 to explain
3 to discuss
4 to emphasize
讲卫生 jiǎng wèishēng to pay attention to hygiene

讲话 jiǎnghuà
I VERB
1 to speak
2 to address
II NOUN
speech
他的讲话非常精彩。Tā de jiǎnghuà fēicháng jīngcǎi. His speech was really brilliant.

讲台 jiǎngtái NOUN
dais

讲座 jiǎngzuò NOUN
course of lectures
参加讲座的有八十多人。Cānjiā jiǎngzuò de yǒu bāshí duō rén. More than 80 people attended the lectures.

奖 jiǎng
I VERB
to encourage
■ 夸奖 kuājiǎng to praise
II NOUN
award
她在比赛中得了奖。Tā zài bǐsài zhōng dé le jiǎng. She won a prize in the competition.

奖金 jiǎngjīn NOUN
bonus

奖励 jiǎnglì VERB
to encourage and reward

奖品 jiǎngpǐn NOUN
trophy

奖学金 jiǎngxuéjīn NOUN
scholarship

降 jiàng VERB
1 to drop
2 to reduce
■ 降价 jiàngjià to reduce prices

降低 jiàngdī VERB
to reduce
降低房价 jiàngdī fángjià to reduce house prices

降落 jiàngluò VERB
to land
飞机安全降落了。Fēijī ānquán jiàngluò le. The plane landed safely.

交 jiāo VERB
1 to hand... in
交作业 jiāo zuòyè to hand in one's homework
2 to pay
■ 交税 jiāoshuì to pay tax
3 to associate with

■ 交友 jiāoyǒu to make friends
交换 jiāohuàn VERB
to exchange
交换意见 jiāohuàn yìjiàn to exchange views
交际 jiāojì VERB
to socialize
交流 jiāoliú VERB
to exchange
交流经验 jiāoliú jīngyàn to exchange experiences
交谈 jiāotán VERB
to talk
交通 jiāotōng NOUN
traffic
出门要注意交通安全。Chūmén yào zhùyì jiāotōng ānquán. Please pay attention to road safety.
交往 jiāowǎng VERB
to have contact with
他们已经交往了三年多。Tāmen yǐjīng jiāowǎng le sān nián duō. They have been associates for more than 3 years.
交易 jiāoyì
I VERB
to trade
II NOUN
transaction
做一笔交易 zuò yì bǐ jiāoyì to make a transaction

郊 jiāo NOUN
suburbs
■ 郊外 jiāowài outskirts
郊区 jiāoqū NOUN
suburbs

骄 jiāo ADJECTIVE
arrogant
■ 骄气 jiāoqì arrogance
骄傲 jiāo'ào
I ADJECTIVE
1 arrogant
2 proud
父母为他感到骄傲。Fùmǔ wèi tā gǎndào jiāo'ào. His parents are very proud of him.
II NOUN
pride

教 jiāo VERB
to teach
▹ *see also* jiào

饺 jiǎo NOUN
Chinese dumpling
■ 水饺 shuǐjiǎo boiled dumplings
饺子 jiǎozi NOUN
dumpling

DID YOU KNOW...?
Chinese dumplings, wrapped with a thin doughy skin, are usually filled with minced meat and mixed vegetables. They are normally steamed or boiled and served with vinegar, soy sauce and other spices.

脚 jiǎo NOUN
1 foot *(of person, animal)*
■ 脚印 jiǎoyìn footprint
2 base *(of object)*
■ 山脚 shānjiǎo foot of a mountain

叫 jiào VERB
1 to shout
2 to call
她跟我叫姐姐。Tā gēn wǒ jiào jiějie. She calls me 'big sister'.
3 to order *(dishes, taxis, people)*
咱们叫一辆出租车吧。Zánmen jiào yí liàng chūzūchē ba. Let's call a taxi. 爸爸叫他去上学。Bàba jiào tā qù shàngxué. His father ordered him to go to school.
4 to be called
叫喊 jiàohǎn VERB
to yell
叫做 jiàozuò VERB
to be called

教 jiào
▹ *see also* jiāo
I VERB
to teach
■ 教导 jiàodǎo to instruct
II NOUN
religion
佛教 Fójiào Buddhism
教材 jiàocái NOUN
teaching materials
教科书 jiàokēshū NOUN
textbook
教练 jiàoliàn NOUN
coach
教师 jiàoshī NOUN
teacher
教室 jiàoshì NOUN
classroom
教授 jiàoshòu
I NOUN
professor
II VERB
to lecture in
教学 jiàoxué NOUN

1 teaching
他做教学工作。Tā zuò jiàoxué gōngzuò. He is a teacher.
2 teaching and study
3 tuition

教训 jiàoxùn
I NOUN
lesson
历史教训 lìshǐ jiàoxùn history lesson
II VERB
to teach... a lesson

教育 jiàoyù
I NOUN
education
高等教育 gāoděng jiàoyù higher education
II VERB
to educate

阶 jiē NOUN
1 step
■ 台阶 táijiē a flight of steps
2 rank

阶段 jiēduàn NOUN
stage
初级阶段 chūjí jiēduàn primary stage *(of Socialism)*

阶级 jiējí NOUN
class
中产阶级 zhōngchǎn jiējí middle class

结 jiē VERB
▷ *see also* jié
to bear
■ 结果 jiēguǒ to bear fruit

结实 jiēshi ADJECTIVE
1 sturdy
2 strong
爷爷已经七十岁了，身体还很结实。Yéye yǐjīng qīshí suì le, shēntǐ hái hěn jiēshi. Grandpa is 70 and still going strong.

接 jiē VERB
1 to draw near
2 to connect
3 to catch
接球！ Jiē qiú! Catch the ball!
4 to receive
接电话 jiē diànhuà to answer the phone
5 to meet
我去机场接朋友。Wǒ qù jīchǎng jiē péngyou. I'm going to the airport to meet my friend.

接触 jiēchù VERB
to come into contact with
他们以前接触过。Tāmen yǐqián jiēchù guo. They've met before.

接待 jiēdài VERB
to receive
接待客人 jiēdài kèrén to receive a guest

接到 jiēdào VERB
to receive
我刚才接到一个手机短信。Wǒ gāngcái jiēdào yí gè shǒujī duǎnxìn. I just received a text message.

接见 jiējiàn VERB
1 to have an interview with
2 to receive
接见外宾 jiējiàn wàibīn to receive foreign guests

接近 jiējìn
I VERB
to approach
II ADJECTIVE
approachable

接受 jiēshòu VERB
to accept
接受邀请 jiēshòu yāoqǐng to accept an invitation

接着 jiēzhe VERB
1 to catch
2 to follow
他们一个接着一个走进大门。Tāmen yígè jiēzhe yígè zǒujìn dàmén. They went through the door one by one.

街 jiē NOUN
street

街道 jiēdào NOUN
1 street
2 neighbourhood

节 jié
I NOUN
1 joint
2 paragraph
3 festival
■ 圣诞节 Shèngdàn Jié Christmas
4 item
■ 细节 xìjié details
II VERB
to save
■ 节水 jiéshuǐ to save water
III MEASURE WORD
section

LANGUAGE TIP This is a measure word used for school classes, carriages and batteries.

一节管子 yì jié guǎnzi a length of pipe
三节课 sān jié kè three classes

节目 jiémù NOUN
programme

晚会上的节目很好看。Wǎnhuì shàng de jiémù hěn hǎokàn. The programme for the evening party was really good.

节日 jiérì NOUN
festival

结 jié
▷ *see also* jiē

I VERB
1 to tie
■ 结网 jiéwǎng to weave a net
2 to unite
3 to freeze
■ 结冰 jiébīng to ice up
4 to settle up
■ 结账 jiézhàng to settle up

II NOUN
knot

结构 jiégòu NOUN
composition
建筑结构 jiànzhù jiégòu architectural construction

结果 jiéguǒ
I NOUN
result
大选结果怎么样？Dàxuǎn jiéguǒ zěnmeyàng? What were the results of the election?
II ADVERB
in the end

结合 jiéhé VERB
1 to combine
2 to become husband and wife
他们终于结合在一起了。Tāmen zhōngyú jiéhé zài yìqǐ le. They finally became husband and wife.

结婚 jiéhūn VERB
to get married
她跟一位大学教授结婚了。Tā gēn yí wèi dàxué jiàoshòu jiéhūn le. She got married to a university professor.

结论 jiélùn NOUN
conclusion

结束 jiéshù VERB
to end

姐 jiě NOUN
elder sister

姐姐 jiějie NOUN
elder sister

姐妹 jiěmèi NOUN
sisters

解 jiě VERB
1 to divide
■ 解剖 jiěpōu to dissect
2 to untie
解扣子 jiě kòuzi to unbutton
3 to answer
■ 解题 jiětí to solve a problem
4 to understand

解答 jiědá VERB
to answer
解答问题 jiědá wèntí to answer a question

解放 jiěfàng VERB
to liberate

解雇 jiěgù VERB
to dismiss
他被解雇了。Tā bèi jiěgù le. He was fired.

解决 jiějué VERB
to resolve
问题解决了吗？Wèntí jiějué le ma? Has the issue been resolved?

解释 jiěshì VERB
to explain

介 jiè VERB
to be situated between

介绍 jièshào VERB
1 to introduce
我来介绍一下。Wǒ lái jièshào yíxià. Let me introduce you.
2 to sponsor
他介绍我到这个公司工作。Tā jièshào wǒ dào zhège gōngsī gōngzuò. He recommended me to work at this company.
3 to give an introduction to
介绍新产品 jièshào xīn chǎnpǐn to introduce a new product

借 jiè VERB
1 to borrow
从图书馆借书 cóng túshūguǎn jiè shū to borrow books from the library
2 to lend
我借给他五块钱。Wǒ jiègěi tā wǔ kuài qián. I lent him 5 yuan.
3 to use... as a means of
4 to make use of

借口 jièkǒu
I VERB
to use... as an excuse
她借口生病没来开会。Tā jièkǒu shēngbìng méi lái kāihuì. She used being ill as an excuse not to attend the meeting.
II NOUN
excuse

斤 jīn MEASURE WORD
unit of weight *(equal to 500 grams)*

今 jīn

I ADJECTIVE
1 present
2 current
II NOUN
today

今后 jīnhòu ADVERB
from now on

今年 jīnnián NOUN
this year

今天 jīntiān NOUN
today

金 jīn
I NOUN
1 gold *(chemical)*
2 metal
■ 五金 wǔjīn hardware
3 money
II ADJECTIVE
golden
■ 金发 jīnfà blonde hair

金融 jīnróng NOUN
finance

金属 jīnshǔ NOUN
metal

金子 jīnzi NOUN
gold

仅 jǐn ADVERB
only

仅仅 jǐnjǐn ADVERB
just
他学习外语不仅仅是为了工作。Tā xuéxí wàiyǔ bù jǐnjǐn shì wèile gōngzuò. He was studying a foreign language for other reasons besides for work.

尽 jǐn
I ADVERB
1 as far as possible
■ 尽快 jǐnkuài as early as possible
2 most
II VERB
1 to take no more than
2 to give priority to

尽管 jǐnguǎn
I ADVERB
without reserve
有话尽管说。Yǒu huà jǐnguǎn shuō. If there's something you'd like to say please don't hold back.
II CONJUNCTION
even though

尽量 jǐnliàng ADVERB
to the best of one's ability
我尽量少吃肉。Wǒ jǐnliàng shǎo chī ròu. I'll try my best to eat less meat.

尽早 jǐnzǎo ADVERB
as soon as possible
尽早写完作业 jǐnzǎo xiěwán zuòyè to finish one's homework as soon as possible

---

紧 jǐn
I ADJECTIVE
1 tight
2 secure
3 close
4 pressing
时间紧，我们得快点。Shíjiān jǐn, wǒmen děi kuài diǎn. We haven't got much time so we'd better be quick.
5 strict
三班的老师管得特别紧。Sān bān de lǎoshī guǎn de tèbié jǐn. The teacher of class 3 is very strict.
II VERB
to tighten

紧急 jǐnjí ADJECTIVE
urgent

紧张 jǐnzhāng ADJECTIVE
1 intense
紧张的生活开始了。Jǐnzhāng de shēnghuó kāishǐ le. Life is stressful nowadays.
2 nervous
她紧张得说不出话来。Tā jǐnzhāng de shuōbuchū huà lái. She was so nervous that she was lost for words.
3 in short supply

进 jìn VERB
1 to advance
2 to enter
■ 进球 jìnqiú to score a goal
3 to bring... in
■ 进货 jìnhuò to stock up

进步 jìnbù
I VERB
to improve
他在学习上比去年进步了。Tā zài xuéxí shàng bǐ qùnián jìnbù le. His studies have improved a lot since last year.
II ADJECTIVE
advanced

进攻 jìngōng VERB
to attack

进化 jìnhuà VERB
to evolve

进口 jìnkǒu VERB
to import
我们需要进口大量工业产品。Wǒmen xūyào jìnkǒu dàliàng gōngyè chǎnpǐn.

We need to import a large amount of industrial products.

进去 jìnqù VERB
to enter

进入 jìnrù VERB
1 to enter
不许进入这个大门！ Bùxǔ jìnrù zhège dàmén! No entry through this door!
2 to reach
3 to get inside

进行 jìnxíng VERB
to carry... out *(reforms, an investigation)*
会议正在进行。Huìyì zhèngzài jìnxíng. The meeting is in progress.

近 jìn ADJECTIVE
1 near
这两所大学离得很近。 The two universities are very near one another.
■ 近日 recently
2 close
平易近人 approachable

京 jīng NOUN
1 capital
2 Beijing
■ 北京 Běijīng Beijing

京剧 jīngjù NOUN
Beijing opera
■ 剧院 jùyuàn theatre

DID YOU KNOW...?
京剧 jīngjù is a form of Chinese traditional opera which enjoys a history of over two hundred years, and is regarded as one of the most important Chinese cultural heritages. The performances combine singing, acting, music, dialogue, dancing and acrobatics. Different roles follow different patterns of acting, which are all rather symbolic, suggestive and exaggerated.

经 jīng
I NOUN
1 scripture
2 channels *pl (in traditional Chinese medicine)*
3 longitude
II VERB
1 to run
■ 经商 jīngshāng to be in business
2 to endure
经受考验 jīngshòu kǎoyàn to endure an ordeal
3 to pass through
途经西安 tújīng Xī'ān to go via Xi'an
III ADJECTIVE
regular

经常 jīngcháng
加班对他是经常的事。Jiābān duì tā shì jīngcháng de shì. He often works overtime.
I ADJECTIVE
day-to-day
II ADVERB
often
经常迟到 jīngcháng chídào to often arrive late

经过 jīngguò
I VERB
1 to pass
经过学校 jīngguò xuéxiào past the school
2 after
经过三年的恋爱, 他们终于结婚了。Jīngguò sān nián de liàn'ài, tāmen zhōngyú jiéhūn le. Having been together for three years, they finally got married.
3 through
企业经过裁员降低了成本。Qǐyè jīngguò cáiyuán jiàngdī le chéngběn. The company lowered costs by laying off employees.
II NOUN
course
他给我们讲了事情的经过。Tā gěi wǒmen jiǎng le shìqing de jīngguò. He gave us an account of what happened.

经济 jīngjì
I NOUN
1 economy
2 financial situation
II ADJECTIVE
economical
经济舱 jīngjìcāng economy class

经理 jīnglǐ NOUN
manager

经历 jīnglì
I VERB
to experience
II NOUN
experience
个人经历 gèrén jīnglì personal experience

经验 jīngyàn NOUN
experience

惊 jīng VERB
to startle
这匹马受了惊。Zhèpī mǎ shòu le jīng. This horse has been startled.
■ 惊醒 jīngxǐng to wake with a start

惊奇 jīngqí ADJECTIVE
surprised

惊人 jīngrén ADJECTIVE
amazing

惊喜 jīngxǐ VERB
to be pleasantly surprised

惊讶 jīngyà ADJECTIVE
astonished

精 jīng

I ADJECTIVE

1 refined
■ 精兵 jīngbīng crack troops

2 excellent
■ 精美 jīngměi exquisite

3 precise
■ 精密 jīngmì precise

4 sharp
■ 精明 jīngmíng shrewd

5 skilled

II NOUN

1 essence
■ 酒精 jiǔjīng alcohol

2 energy

精彩 jīngcǎi ADJECTIVE
wonderful

精力 jīnglì NOUN
energy

精确 jīngquè ADJECTIVE
precise

精神 jīngshén NOUN
mind

精神 jīngshen

I NOUN
energy
这个孩子今天没有精神。Zhègè háizi jīntiān méiyǒu jīngshen. This child has no energy today.

II ADJECTIVE
energetic
她总是看上去很精神。Tā zǒngshì kànshàngqù hěn jīngshen. She always seems very energetic.

精通 jīngtōng VERB
to be proficient in

井 jǐng

I NOUN
well
■ 天井 tiānjǐng skylight
■ 矿井 kuàngjǐng mine shaft

景 jǐng

I NOUN

1 scenery

2 situation
■ 背景 bèijǐng background

3 scene
■ 外景 wàijǐng outdoor scene

II VERB
to admire
■ 景仰 jǐngyǎng to look up to

景点 jǐngdiǎn NOUN
scenic spot

景色 jǐngsè NOUN
scenery

警 jǐng

I ADJECTIVE
alert
■ 警惕 jǐngtì vigilant

II VERB

1 to warn
■ 警戒 jǐngjiè to warn

2 to be on the alert
■ 警卫 jǐngwèi to guard

III NOUN

1 alarm
■ 报警 bàojǐng to raise the alarm

2 police
■ 巡警 xúnjǐng an officer on the beat
■ 骑警 qíjǐng mounted police

警报 jǐngbào NOUN
alarm

警察 jǐngchá NOUN
police

警告 jǐnggào VERB
to warn

竞 jìng VERB
to compete

竞赛 jìngsài NOUN
competition

竞争 jìngzhēng VERB
to compete

敬 jìng

I VERB

1 to respect

2 to offer
敬一杯酒 jìng yībēi jiǔ to offer a toast

II ADJECTIVE
respectful
■ 恭敬 gōngjìng reverent

敬爱 jìng'ài VERB
to revere

敬礼 jìnglǐ VERB
to salute

静 jìng ADJECTIVE

1 still
■ 静止 jìngzhǐ static

2 quiet
■ 安静 ānjìng tranquil

镜 jìng NOUN
1 mirror
2 lens
■眼镜 yǎnjìng glasses
镜子 jìngzi NOUN
mirror

纠 jiū VERB
1 to entangle
■纠缠 jiūchán to be entangled
2 to assemble
■纠集 jiūjí to get together
3 to supervise
■纠察 jiūchá to maintain public order
4 to correct
■纠错 jiūcuò to correct
纠正 jiūzhèng VERB
to correct

究 jiū
I VERB
to investigate
■探究 tànjiū to make a thorough inquiry
II ADVERB
actually
究竟 jiūjìng
I NOUN
outcome
II ADVERB
actually

九 jiǔ NUMBER
nine
九月 jiǔyuè NOUN
September

久 jiǔ ADJECTIVE
long
他等了很久了。Tā děng le hěnjiǔ le. He waited for a long time. 你多久能完成这些作业？Nǐ duōjiǔ néng wánchéng zhèxiē zuòyè? How long will it take you to finish these assignments?

玖 jiǔ NUMBER
nine
LANGUAGE TIP This is the complex character for **nine**, which is mainly used in banks, on receipts etc to prevent mistakes and forgery.

酒 jiǔ NOUN
alcohol
■葡萄酒 pútaojiǔ wine
■敬酒 jìngjiǔ to propose a toast

酒吧 jiǔbā NOUN
pub

旧 jiù
I ADJECTIVE
1 old
旧房子 jiù fángzi an old house
2 used
■旧货 jiùhuò second-hand goods
II NOUN
old friend

救 jiù VERB
to save
救护车 jiùhùchē NOUN
ambulance
救命 jiùmìng VERB
to save a life
救命啊！Jiùmìng a! Help!

就 jiù
I VERB
1 to move close to
就着路灯看书 jiùzhe lùdēng kànshū to read under the streetlight
2 to take ... up
■就业 jiùyè to get a job
3 to accomplish
成就事业 chéngjiù shìyè to have a successful career
4 to take the opportunity
就着出国的热潮，他也去了英国学。Jiùzhe chūguó de rècháo, tā yě qùle Yīngguó liúxué. As going abroad became increasingly popular, he too took the opportunity to go to Britain to study.
5 to eat ... with
就着炒菜吃米饭 jiùzhe chǎocài chī mǐfàn to eat rice with a stir-fry
II ADVERB
1 shortly
我的作业马上就写完了。Wǒde zuòyè mǎshàng jiù xiě wán le. I'm nearly finished writing my assignment.
2 already
孩子早就睡了。Háizi zǎojiù shuì le. The child is already asleep.
3 as soon as
吃了就出发 chī le jiù chūfā to set off after eating
4 then
只要努力就一定能进步。Zhǐyào nǔlì jiù yídìng néng jìnbù. As long as you put the effort in, you're sure to make progress.
5 as much as

他一天就读了五十页书。Tā yìtiān jiù dú le wǔshí yè shū. He read fifty pages in one day.

6 only
他就拿了一个行李箱。Tā jiù nále yígè xínglǐxiāng. He only took one piece of luggage.

7 simply
他就是说说而已。Tā jiùshì shuōshuō éryǐ. He was only saying that.

8 exactly
这就是我要找的书。Zhè jiùshì wǒ yào zhǎo de shū. This is exactly the book I'm looking for.

III CONJUNCTION
even if
你就再忙，也要给家里打电话。Nǐ jiù zàimáng, yě yào gěi jiālǐ dǎ diànhuà. Even if you're busy, you should still call home.

IV PREPOSITION
on
就我而言 jiù wǒ ér yán as far as I'm concerned

就是 jiùshì

I ADVERB

1 exactly
这就是王老师。Zhè jiùshì Wáng lǎoshī. This is teacher Wang.

2 still
他就是不肯认错。Tā jiùshì bùkěn rèncuò. He still isn't willing to admit he was wrong.

3 really
他的字写得就是好。Tāde zì xiěde jiùshì hǎo. He is really good at calligraphy.

4 only
就是这样 jiùshì zhèyàng just like this

II AUXILIARY WORD

LANGUAGE TIP Used adverbially, 就 jiù can express emphasis, statement of fact, or immediacy.

你干就是了，没人说你。Nǐ gàn jiùshì le, méi rén shuō nǐ. Just go ahead and do it; no one will blame you!

III CONJUNCTION
even if
就是你不会，也不应该抄袭别人的。Jiùshì nǐ búhuì, yě bù yīnggāi chāoxí biérén de. Even if you can't do it, you still shouldn't copy from other people.

就算 jiùsuàn CONJUNCTION
even if
就算你不来，我们也会给你留份礼物的。Jiùsuàn nǐ búlái, wǒmen yě huì géi nǐ liú fèn lǐwù de. Even if you don't come, we'll keep a present for you.

舅 jiù NOUN

1 uncle

2 brother-in-law

舅舅 jiùjiu NOUN
uncle

居 jū

I VERB
to live

II NOUN
house
■ 故居 gùjū former residence

居住 jūzhù VERB
to live

局 jú

I NOUN

1 chessboard
■ 棋局 qíjú chessboard

2 game
■ 平局 píngjú a draw

3 situation
■ 时局 shíjú current political situation

4 gathering
■ 饭局 fànjú dinner party

5 ruse
■ 骗局 piànjú fraud

6 part
■ 局部 júbù part

7 department
■ 教育局 jiàoyùjú department of education

8 office
■ 邮电局 yóudiànjú post and telegraph office

II MEASURE WORD
set
我赢了这局棋。Wǒ yíng le zhè jú qí. I won the game of chess.

局长 júzhǎng NOUN
director

橘 jú NOUN
tangerine

橘子 júzi NOUN
orange
橘子汁 júzi zhī orange juice

举 jǔ

I VERB

1 to raise
■ 举重 jǔzhòng weightlifting

2 to mobilize
■ 举兵 jǔbīng to dispatch troops

3 to elect
■ 选举 xuǎnjǔ to elect

4 to cite

■ 举例 jǔlì to cite an example
II NOUN
act
■ 举动 jǔdòng movement
III ADJECTIVE
whole *(formal, written)*
■ 举国 jǔguó a whole nation
举办 jǔbàn VERB
to hold
举行 jǔxíng VERB
to hold

巨 jù ADJECTIVE
huge
巨大 jùdà ADJECTIVE
huge
巨人 jùrén NOUN
giant

句 jù
I NOUN
sentence
II MEASURE WORD
LANGUAGE TIP This is a measure word used for sentences and lines in a speech, song or poem.
说几句话 shuō jǐ jù huà to say a few words
写两句诗 xiě liǎng jù shī to write two lines of verse
句子 jùzi NOUN
sentence

拒 jù VERB
1 to resist
■ 抗拒 kàngjù to resist
2 to refuse
拒绝 jùjué VERB
to refuse

具 jù
I VERB
to have
II NOUN
utensil
■ 玩具 wánjù toy
具备 jùbèi VERB
to have
具体 jùtǐ ADJECTIVE
1 detailed
具体说明 jùtǐ shuōmíng detailed instructions
2 particular
具体人选 jùtǐ rénxuǎn specific candidate
具有 jùyǒu VERB
to have

俱 jù ADVERB
complete
■ 俱全 jùquán all complete
俱乐部 jùlèbù NOUN
club

剧 jù
I NOUN
drama
■ 喜剧 xǐjù comedy
II ADJECTIVE
severe
■ 剧变 jùbiàn dramatic change
剧场 jùchǎng NOUN
theatre
剧烈 jùliè ADJECTIVE
severe
剧院 jùyuàn NOUN
1 theatre
2 company
青年艺术剧院 qīngnián yìshù jùyuàn youth art theatre

据 jù
I VERB
1 to occupy
■ 盘据 pánjù to forcibly occupy
2 to rely on
■ 据点 jùdiǎn stronghold
II PREPOSITION
according to
■ 据理 jùlǐ reasonably
III NOUN
evidence
■ 收据 shōujù receipt
据说 jùshuō VERB
to be said

距 jù NOUN
distance
距离 jùlí VERB
to be at a distance from

锯 jù
I NOUN
saw
II VERB
to saw

卷 juǎn
I VERB
1 to roll ... up
2 to sweep ... up
3 to be swept up in *(figurative)*
■ 卷入 juǎnrù to be drawn into
II NOUN

roll
■ 花卷 huājuǎn steamed roll
III MEASURE WORD
roll
一卷卫生纸 yī juǎn wèishēngzhǐ a roll of toilet paper

决 jué

I VERB
1 to decide
2 to execute
■ 处决 chǔjué to execute
3 to burst
■ 决堤 juédī to burst a dike
4 to decide on a result
■ 决战 juézhàn decisive battle
II ADVERB
under any circumstances
■ 决不 juébù never
III ADJECTIVE
decisive
■ 果决 guǒjué resolute

决定 juédìng VERB
1 to decide
决定日期 juédìng rìqī to decide on a date
2 to determine
性格决定行为模式。Xìnggé juédìng xíngwéi móshì. Personality determines one's behavioural patterns.

决心 juéxīn NOUN
determination

觉 jué

I VERB
1 to feel
2 to become aware of
II NOUN
sense
■ 知觉 zhījué consciousness

觉得 juéde VERB
1 to feel
觉得冷 juéde lěng to feel cold
2 to think
你觉得怎么样？Nǐ juéde zěnmeyàng? What do you think?

觉悟 juéwù NOUN
awareness

绝 jué

I VERB
1 to cut ... off
■ 隔绝 géjué isolate
2 to exhaust
3 to have no descendants
4 to die
■ 灭绝 mièjué to die out
II ADJECTIVE
1 hopeless
■ 绝路 juélù blind alley
2 superb
■ 绝技 juéjì a special skill
III ADVERB
1 extremely
■ 绝密 juémì top secret
2 absolutely
绝不让步 juébù ràngbù never give in

绝对 juéduì
I ADJECTIVE
absolute
II ADVERB
absolutely

绝望 juéwàng VERB
to feel desperate

军 jūn

I NOUN
1 army
■ 参军 cānjūn enlist
2 regiment
3 forces
劳动大军 láodòng dàjūn labour force *pl*
II ADJECTIVE
military
■ 军费 jūnfèi military expenditure

军队 jūnduì NOUN
troops *pl*

军官 jūnguān NOUN
officer

军人 jūnrén NOUN
soldier

军事 jūnshì NOUN
military affairs *pl*

Kk

咖 kā
▷ *see also* gā
▷ *see below:*
咖啡 kāfēi NOUN
coffee
速溶咖啡 sùróng kāfēi instant coffee

卡 kǎ NOUN
card
■ 卡片 kǎpiàn card
卡车 kǎchē NOUN
lorry
卡拉OK kǎlā'ōukèi NOUN
karaoke
卡通 kǎtōng NOUN
cartoon

开 kāi VERB
1 to open
开门 kāimén to open the door
2 to bloom
花开了。Huā kāi le. The flowers are in bloom.
3 to start *(school, course, show)*
4 to turn on
开灯 kāi dēng to turn on the light
5 to hold
开会 kāihuì to have a meeting 开晚会 kāiwǎnhuì to have an evening party
6 to drive
■ 开车 kāichē to drive
开关 kāiguān NOUN
switch
开户 kāihù VERB
to open an account
开朗 kāilǎng ADJECTIVE
cheerful
他的性格很开朗。Tā de xìnggé hěn kāilǎng. He is a really cheerful person.
开始 kāishǐ
I VERB
to start
开始学汉语 kāishǐ xué Hànyǔ to start studying Chinese
II NOUN
beginning
开水 kāishuǐ NOUN
boiling water
开玩笑 kāi wánxiào VERB
to joke
别拿我开玩笑。Bié ná wǒ kāi wánxiào. Don't make fun of me.
开心 kāixīn ADJECTIVE
happy

看 kān VERB
▷ *see also* kàn
to look after
看家 kānjiā to look after the house

砍 kǎn VERB
1 to chop
2 to cut
■ 砍价 kǎnjià to bargain

看 kàn VERB
▷ *see also* kān
1 to look at
看电视 kàn diànshì to watch TV
■ 看到 kàndào to see
2 to read *(books, magazines, newspapers)*
3 to visit
有人来看你。Yǒu rén lái kàn nǐ. Someone has come to see you.
■ 看望 kànwàng to visit
4 to treat *(an illness)*
■ 看病 kànbìng to see a doctor
看不起 kànbuqǐ VERB
to look down on
看法 kànfǎ NOUN
opinion
看见 kànjiàn VERB
to see
看来 kànlái VERB
to seem
看来今天要下雨。Kànlái jīntiān yào xiàyǔ. It looks like it's going to rain today.

康 kāng ADJECTIVE
healthy

■ 康复 kāngfù to recover

考 kǎo VERB
to have an exam
考大学 kǎo dàxué to take the university entrance exams

考虑 kǎolǜ VERB
to consider

考试 kǎoshì VERB
to sit an exam

烤 kǎo VERB
to roast
■ 烤鸭 kǎoyā to roast duck

烤炉 kǎolú NOUN
oven

靠 kào VERB
to lean on
我靠着墙站着。Wǒ kào zhe qiáng zhàn zhe. I'm leaning against the wall.

科 kē NOUN
discipline
■ 文科 wénkē humanities

科技 kējì NOUN
science and technology

科目 kēmù NOUN
subject

科学 kēxué NOUN
science

科学家 kēxuéjiā NOUN
scientist

棵 kē MEASURE WORD
LANGUAGE TIP This is a measure word used for plants, trees and vegetables.
一棵水仙 yì kē shuǐxiān a narcissus

颗 kē MEASURE WORD
LANGUAGE TIP This is a measure word used for small, round objects.
一颗种子 yì kē zhǒngzi a seed

咳 ké VERB
to cough

咳嗽 késou VERB
to cough

可 kě VERB
can
■ 可能性 kěnéngxìng possibility

可爱 kě'ài ADJECTIVE
adorable

可靠 kěkào ADJECTIVE
reliable
消息可靠 xiāoxī kěkào reliable information

可乐 kělè NOUN
Coke®

可怜 kělián
I ADJECTIVE
pitiful
他很可怜。Tā hěn kělián. He is really pitiful.
II VERB
to pity
不要可怜他。Bú yào kělián tā. Don't feel sorry for him.

可怕 kěpà ADJECTIVE
frightening

可是 kěshì CONJUNCTION
but

可惜 kěxī
I ADJECTIVE
regrettable
扔掉它，很可惜。Rēng diào tā, hěn kěxī. It's such a shame to throw it away.
II ADVERB
regrettably
可惜，他没有来。Kěxī, tā méiyǒu lái. It's a shame that he didn't come.

可笑 kěxiào ADJECTIVE
1 funny
2 ridiculous

可以 kěyǐ
I VERB
LANGUAGE TIP 可以 kěyǐ is used to express being able to do something because you have been granted permission.
你可以/能借我的照相机。Nǐ kěyǐ/néng jiè wǒ de zhàoxiàngjī. You can borrow my camera.
II ADJECTIVE
not bad
这饭馆还可以。Zhè fànguǎn hái kěyǐ. This restaurant's not bad.

渴 kě ADJECTIVE
thirsty
■ 渴望 kěwàng to long for 他渴望有一辆车。Tā kěwàng yǒu yíliàng chē. He longs to have a bike.

刻 kè
I VERB
to engrave
II NOUN
quarter
■ 一刻钟 yíkèzhōng a quarter of an hour
现在三点一刻。Xiànzài sāndiǎn yíkè. It's

quarter past three.

刻苦 kèkǔ ADJECTIVE
hardworking
她学习很刻苦。Tā xuéxí hěn kèkǔ. She is really hardworking.

客 kè NOUN
1 visitor
■ 客厅 kètīng living room
2 customer
■ 客户 kèhù customer

客气 kèqi
I ADJECTIVE
polite
II VERB
to be polite

客人 kèrén NOUN
guest

课 kè NOUN
1 class
■ 上课 shàngkè to have a class
■ 下课 xiàkè to finish class
2 lesson
两节课 liǎng jié kè two lessons

课本 kèběn NOUN
textbook

课程 kèchéng NOUN
course

课程表 kèchéngbiǎo NOUN
school timetable

课堂 kètáng NOUN
classroom

课题 kètí NOUN
topic

课文 kèwén NOUN
text

肯 kěn VERB
to be willing

肯定 kěndìng VERB
to confirm
我肯定这个答案是对的。Wǒ kěndìng zhègè dá'àn shì duìde. I'm certain that this is the correct answer.

空 kōng
▷ *see also* kòng
I ADJECTIVE
empty
II NOUN
sky
■ 空中小姐 kōngzhōng xiǎojiě air stewardess

空间 kōngjiān NOUN
space

空调 kōngtiáo NOUN
air conditioning

空气 kōngqì NOUN
air

孔 kǒng NOUN
hole

孔子 Kǒngzǐ NOUN
Confucius

DID YOU KNOW...?
孔子 Kǒngzǐ Confucius (trad. 551-479 BC) was a hugely influential thinker. A posthumous compilation of his sayings, 论语 Lúnyǔ The Analects, is China's most important philosophical work and was the key text on which much of the traditional Chinese education system was based.

恐 kǒng VERB
to fear

恐怖 kǒngbù NOUN
terror
■ 恐怖份子 kǒngbù fènzi terrorist
■ 恐怖主义 kǒngbù zhǔyì terrorism

恐龙 kǒnglóng NOUN
dinosaur

恐怕 kǒngpà ADVERB
probably
恐怕要下雨。Kǒngpà yào xiàyǔ. It's probably going to rain.

空 kòng
▷ *see also* kōng
I VERB
to leave... empty
空一行 kòng yi háng to leave a blank line
II ADJECTIVE
vacant
■ 空白 kòngbái blank
■ 空缺 kòngquē vacancy
III NOUN
1 space
2 free time
有空 yǒu kòng to have free time 我今天没空。Wǒ jīntiān méi kòng. I don't have any free time today.

口 kǒu
I NOUN
1 mouth
■ 口吃 kǒuchī stammer
■ 口红 kǒuhóng lipstick
■ 出口 chūkǒu exit
■ 入口 rùkǒu entrance
2 rim

瓶口 píng kǒu the mouth of a bottle

II MEASURE WORD

LANGUAGE TIP This is a measure word used for the number of people in a family.

我家有五口人。Wǒ jiā yǒu wǔ kǒu rén. There are five people in my family.

口袋 kǒudài NOUN
1 bag
2 pocket

口试 kǒushì NOUN
oral exam

口头 kǒutóu ADJECTIVE
oral
口头作文 kǒutóu zuòwén oral presentation

口音 kǒuyīn NOUN
accent

口语 kǒuyǔ NOUN
spoken language

口渴 kǒukě ADJECTIVE
thirsty
他口渴了。Tā kǒukě le. He's thirsty.

扣 kòu NOUN
button
■ 扣子 kòuzi button

哭 kū VERB
to cry

苦 kǔ
I ADJECTIVE
1 bitter
2 hard
学小提琴很苦。Xué xiǎotíqín hěn kǔ. It's really difficult to learn to play the violin.
II ADVERB
painstakingly
■ 苦练 kǔ liàn to train hard
III NOUN
suffering
■ 吃苦 chīkǔ to bear hardships

苦恼 kǔnǎo ADJECTIVE
distressed

裤 kù NOUN
trousers *pl*
■ 裤子 kùzi trousers *pl*

夸 kuā VERB
1 to praise
2 to exaggerate

夸奖 kuājiǎng VERB
to praise
老师夸奖他。Lǎoshī kuājiǎng tā. The teacher praised him.

夸张 kuāzhāng ADJECTIVE
exaggerated
他说的太夸张了。Tā shuō de tài kuāzhāng le. He's over exaggerating.

会 kuài NOUN
▷ *see also* huì
accounting
■ 财会 cáikuài finance and accounting

会计 kuàijì NOUN
1 accounting
2 accountant

块 kuài
I NOUN
lump
II MEASURE WORD
piece
一块蛋糕 yí kuài dàngāo a piece of cake
一块方糖 yí kuài fāngtáng a lump of sugar

快 kuài ADJECTIVE
1 fast
他跑步很快。Tā pǎobù hěn kuài. He's a really fast runner.
2 quick
他脑子快。Tā nǎozi kuài. He's quick-witted.

快餐 kuàicān NOUN
fast food

快活 kuàihuo ADJECTIVE
delighted

快乐 kuàilè ADJECTIVE
happy

筷 kuài NOUN
chopsticks *pl*
■ 筷子 kuàizi chopsticks *pl*

宽 kuān
I ADJECTIVE
1 wide
2 broad
■ 宽敞 kuānchang spacious
II NOUN
width

矿 kuàng NOUN
mine

矿泉水 kuàngquánshuǐ NOUN
mineral water

亏 kuī ADVERB
luckily
亏你把我叫醒，要不我就迟到了。Kuī nǐ bǎ

wǒ jiào xǐng, yào bu wǒ jiù chídào le. It's lucky you woke me up or I would have been late.

困 kùn

I ADJECTIVE
sleepy

II VERB
to trap

困难 kùnnan ADJECTIVE
difficult
克服困难 kèfú kùnnan to overcome difficulties

扩 kuò VERB
to expand

扩大 kuòdà VERB
to expand

L

垃 lā
▹ *see below:*
垃圾 lājī NOUN
rubbish
垃圾食品 lājī shípǐn junk food

拉 lā VERB
1 to pull
把桌子向左边拉一点儿。Bǎ zhuōzi xiàng zuǒbiān lā yìdiǎnr. Pull the table a little to the left.
2 to transport
出租车司机拉我到了机场。Chūzūchē sījī lā wǒ dào le jīchǎng. The taxi driver took me to the airport.
3 to play *(string instruments)*
拉小提琴 lā xiǎotíqín to play the violin

喇 lǎ
▹ *see below:*
喇叭 lǎba NOUN
1 trumpet
2 loudspeaker

落 là VERB
▹ *see also* luò
1 to be missing
你抄写的这段文字落了两句话。Nǐ chāoxiě de zhèduàn wénzì làle liǎngjù huà. You have missed out two sentences in the text that you copied.
2 to leave
他把书包落在操场上了。Tā bǎ shūbāo làzài cāochǎng shàng le. He left his schoolbag at the sports ground.

辣 là ADJECTIVE
hot
■ **辣酱** làjiàng chilli sauce
■ **辣椒** làjiāo chillies

蜡 là NOUN
candle
■ **蜡烛** làzhú candle

啦 la AUXILIARY WORD
你回来啦！ Nǐ huílai la! Hey, you're back!

来 lái
I VERB
1 to come
家里来了几个客人。Jiā lǐ lái le jǐ gè kèrén. Some guests came to the house.
2 to happen
刚到家，麻烦来了。Gāng dào jiā, máfan lái le. As soon as I got home, the trouble started.

LANGUAGE TIP 来 lái is used to express doing something.

你累了，让我来。Nǐ lèi le, ràng wǒ lái. You're tired, let me do it.

LANGUAGE TIP 来 lái is used to express an inclination to do something.

请你来帮个忙。Qǐng nǐ lái bāng gè máng. Can you help me with this?

LANGUAGE TIP 来 lái is used to express purpose or intent.

我要想个法子来对付他。Wǒ yào xiǎng gè fǎzi lái duìfu ta. I must think of a way to deal with him.

LANGUAGE TIP 来 lái is used to express taking something somewhere.

服务员很快就把饭菜端了上来。Fúwùyuán hěnkuài jiù bǎ fàncài duān le shànglai. The waiter brought the food to the table very quickly.

II ADJECTIVE
coming
■ **来年** láinián the coming year

III AUXILIARY WORD
about *(approximate number)*
十来公斤重 shí lái gōngjīn zhòng about 10 kilos
■ **几年来** jǐ nián lái in the last few years
■ **近来** jìnlái lately

来不及 láibují VERB
to not have enough time
再不走就来不及了。Zài bùzǒu jiù láibují le. If we don't leave now, we won't have enough time.

来得及 láidejí VERB
to have enough time for
不用着急，时间还来得及。Búyòng zháojí, shíjiān hái láidejí. Don't worry, there is still enough time.
来回 láihuí
I VERB
1 to make a round trip
从住宅小区到市中心来回有多远？Cóng zhùzhái xiǎoqū dào shìzhōngxīn láihuí yǒu duō yuǎn? How far is it from the residential area to the city centre and back?
2 to move back and forth
II NOUN
round trip
我从学校到家一天跑两个来回。Wǒ cóng xuéxiào dào jiā yìtiān pǎo liǎnggè láihuí. I make the round trip from school to home twice a day.
来往 láiwǎng VERB
to have dealings with
来自 láizì VERB
to come from

拦 lán VERB
to stop

栏 lán NOUN
1 fence
■ 栏杆 lángān railing
2 column
■ 栏目 lánmù column

蓝 lán ADJECTIVE
blue
■ 蓝色 lánsè blue
■ 蓝天 lántiān blue sky

篮 lán NOUN
basket
■ 篮子 lánzi basket
篮球 lánqiú NOUN
basketball

缆 lǎn NOUN
cable
缆车 lǎnchē NOUN
cable car

懒 lǎn ADJECTIVE
1 lazy
2 lethargic
他刚起床，一副懒懒的样子。Tā gāng qǐchuáng, yífù lǎnlǎn de yàngzi. He just got out of bed and still looks half asleep.
懒得 lǎnde VERB
to not feel like
天太热，我懒得出门。Tiān tài rè, wǒ lǎn de chūmén. I don't feel like going out, it's too hot.
懒惰 lǎnduò ADJECTIVE
lazy

烂 làn
I ADJECTIVE
1 worn-out
2 messy
■ 烂摊子 làn tānzi a shambles
II VERB
to be rotten
西瓜烂了。Xīguā làn le. The watermelon has gone off.

狼 láng NOUN
wolf

廊 láng NOUN
corridor
■ 走廊 zǒuláng corridor

朗 lǎng ADJECTIVE
1 bright
■ 晴朗 qínglǎng sunny
2 clear
明朗 mínglǎng bright and clear
朗读 lǎngdú VERB
to read... aloud
朗诵 lǎngsòng VERB
to recite

浪 làng
I NOUN
wave
■ 浪潮 làngcháo tide
II ADJECTIVE
wasteful
■ 浪费 làngfèi squander
浪漫 làngmàn ADJECTIVE
romantic

捞 lāo VERB
to take
■ 捕捞 bǔlāo to fish for

劳 láo VERB
1 to work
2 to trouble
劳您帮我看下行李。Láo nín bāng wǒ kān xià xíngli. Would you mind keeping an eye on my luggage?
劳动 láodòng NOUN
labour

脑力劳动 nǎolì láodòng brain work

劳动力 láodònglì NOUN
1 labour
劳动力的价值 láodònglì de jiàzhí the value of labour
2 workforce
缺乏劳动力 quēfá láodònglì to be short of workers

劳驾 láojià VERB
excuse me

老 lǎo
I ADJECTIVE
1 old *(in age, former)*
老年人 lǎonián rén the elderly 老同学 lǎo tóngxué old school friend
2 experienced
■ 老手 lǎoshǒu veteran
3 over-done
牛肉煮老了。Niúròu zhǔ lǎo le. The beef is over-cooked.
II NOUN
old people
III ADVERB
1 always
他老是迟到。Tā lǎoshì chídào. He is always late.
2 for a long time
这是个老大难问题。Zhèshì gè lǎodànán wèntí. This is a long standing problem.
3 very
■ 老远 lǎoyuǎn very far

老百姓 lǎobǎixìng NOUN
ordinary people

DID YOU KNOW...?
The term 老百姓 lǎobǎixìng is a colloquial expression that literally means **the old hundred surnames**, referring to the hundred most common family names, and is used in Chinese to mean ordinary folk, the people or commoners.

老板 lǎobǎn NOUN
boss

老虎 lǎohǔ NOUN
tiger

老家 lǎojiā NOUN
hometown
我老家在上海。Wǒ lǎojiā zài Shànghǎi. Shanghai is my hometown.

老练 lǎoliàn ADJECTIVE
experienced

老年 lǎonián NOUN
old age

老婆 lǎopo NOUN
wife

老师 lǎoshī NOUN
teacher

老实 lǎoshi ADJECTIVE
1 honest
2 naive

老鼠 lǎoshǔ NOUN
mouse

老外 lǎowài NOUN
foreigner

DID YOU KNOW...?
The term 老外 lǎowài is one of several Chinese words for foreigner. It is the informal version of 外国人 wàigúorén and literally translates as **old foreigner**. It is a commonly used term in everyday spoken Chinese to refer to foreigners in general.

姥 lǎo
▷ *see below:*

姥姥 lǎolao NOUN
granny *(colloquial)*

LANGUAGE TIP 姥姥 lǎolao is used specifically for the granny on the mother's side.

姥爷 lǎoye NOUN
grandpa *(colloquial: maternal)*

乐 lè
▷ *see also* yuè
I ADJECTIVE
happy
II VERB
1 to take pleasure in
乐于助人 lèyú zhùrén to take pleasure in helping others
2 to laugh

乐观 lèguān ADJECTIVE
optimistic

乐趣 lèqù NOUN
delight

乐意 lèyì VERB
to be willing to
他乐意帮我们。Tā lèyì bāng wǒmen. He is happy to help us.

了 le AUXILIARY WORD
▷ *see also* liǎo

LANGUAGE TIP 了 le is used to indicate the completion of an action or a change.

他买了这本书。Tā mǎi le zhè běn shū. He bought this book.

LANGUAGE TIP 了 le is used to indicate the completion of a supposition for the future.

下个月我考完了试回家。Xià gè yuè wǒ kǎo wán le shì huíjiā. I'll go home next month once my exams are over.

LANGUAGE TIP 了 le is used at the end of a sentence to indicate the appearance of a change.

下雨了。Xiàyǔ le. It's raining.

LANGUAGE TIP 了 le is used at the end of a sentence to indicate reminding, persuasion or urgency.

该回家了。Gāi huíjiā le. It's time to go home. 别喊了！ Bié hǎn le! Stop shouting!

LANGUAGE TIP The usage of 了 le is one of the most complex parts of Chinese grammar, partly because it has two completely different functions. It can indicate completion of an action, for example 他喝了三杯啤酒。Tā hē le sān bēi píjiǔ. **He drank three glasses of beer**. When placed at the end of a clause or a sentence, it usually indicates a change of some kind, for example 天黑了。Tiān hēi le. **It's gone dark.**

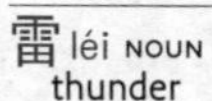

雷 léi NOUN
thunder
- 雷电 léidiàn thunder and lightning

累 lěi VERB
▹ *see also* lèi
to accumulate
- 累积 lěijī to accumulate

累计 lěiji VERB
to add up

肋 lèi NOUN
rib
- 肋骨 lèigǔ rib bone

泪 lèi NOUN
tear
- 眼泪 yǎnlèi tears *pl*
- 流泪 liúlèi to shed tears

类 lèi
I NOUN
kind
- 分类 fēnlèi classify
- 类型 lèixíng type

II VERB
to be similar to

类别 lèibié NOUN
category

类似 lèisì ADJECTIVE
similar

累 lèi
▹ *see also* lěi
I ADJECTIVE
tired
II VERB
to tire
别累着自己。Bié lèizhe zìjǐ. Don't tire yourself out.

冷 lěng ADJECTIVE
1 cold
2 frosty
- 冷淡 lěngdàn to give the cold shoulder to

冷藏 lěngcáng VERB
to refrigerate

冷冻 lěngdòng VERB
to freeze
冷冻食品 lěngdòng shípǐn frozen produce

冷静 lěngjìng ADJECTIVE
cool-headed

冷饮 lěngyǐn NOUN
cold drink

厘 lí
▹ *see below:*

厘米 límǐ MEASURE WORD
centimetre

离 lí VERB
1 to leave
- 分离 fēnlí to separate

2 to be far away from
我家离办公室不太远。Wǒ jiā lí bàngōngshì bú tài yuǎn. My home is not too far from the office.

离婚 líhūn VERB
to divorce

离开 líkāi VERB
to depart

梨 lí NOUN
pear

礼 lǐ NOUN
1 ceremony
- 礼仪 lǐyí ceremony

2 courtesy
3 present

礼拜 lǐbài NOUN
week

礼貌 lǐmào NOUN
manners *pl*

礼堂 lǐtáng NOUN
hall

礼物 lǐwù NOUN
present

李 lǐ NOUN
plum

里 lǐ
I NOUN
1 inside
衣服的丝绸里子 yīfu de sīchóu lǐzi the silk lining of the clothes
2 inner
■ 里屋 lǐwū inner room
II PREPOSITION
in
屋子里 wūzi lǐ in the room
III ADVERB
■ 这里 zhèlǐ here
■ 那里 nàlǐ there
IV MEASURE WORD
Chinese unit of length *(equal to 1/3 of a mile)*
■ 英里 yīnglǐ mile

里面 lǐmiàn ADJECTIVE
inside

理 lǐ
I NOUN
1 reason
■ 合理 hélǐ reasonable
2 natural science
■ 理科 lǐkē science
II VERB
1 to manage
■ 理财 lǐcái to manage financial matters
2 to tidy
■ 理发 lǐfà to have a hair cut
3 to acknowledge
■ 理睬 lǐcǎi to pay attention

理解 lǐjiě VERB
to understand

理论 lǐlùn NOUN
theory

理想 lǐxiǎng
I NOUN
ideal
II ADJECTIVE
ideal

理由 lǐyóu NOUN
reason

力 lì NOUN
1 force
■ 影响力 yǐngxiǎnglì power
2 strength
3 physical strength

力量 lìliang NOUN
1 power
这一拳力量很大。Zhèyìquán lìliang hěn dà. That was a very powerful punch. 团结的力量 tuánjié de lìliang the power of solidarity
2 strength
这种药的力量大。Zhèzhǒng yào de lìliang dà. This medicine is very strong.

力气 lìqi NOUN
strength

历 lì NOUN
experience

历史 lìshǐ NOUN
history

厉 lì ADJECTIVE
1 strict
■ 严厉 yánlì severe
2 stern
老师厉声批评了他。Lǎoshī lìshēng pīpíng le tā. The teacher severely criticised him.

厉害 lìhai ADJECTIVE
terrible
他口渴得厉害。Tā kǒukě de lìhai. He was terribly thirsty.

立 lì
I VERB
1 to stand
2 to stand… up
3 to establish
■ 立功 lìgōng to make a contribution
4 to set… up
■ 立法 lìfǎ to legislate
II ADJECTIVE
upright
■ 立柜 lìguì wardrobe

立方 lìfāng
I NOUN
cube
II MEASURE WORD
cubic
■ 立方米 lìfāngmǐ cubic metre

立即 lìjí ADVERB
immediately

立刻 lìkè ADVERB
immediately

利 lì
I ADJECTIVE
sharp
II NOUN
1 interest
■ 利弊 lìbì pros and cons *pl*
2 profit and interest
■ 暴利 bàolì staggering profits *pl*
III VERB
to benefit

利害 lìhai ADJECTIVE
terrible
天冷得利害。Tiān lěng de lìhai. It's terribly cold today.

利率 lìlǜ NOUN
interest rate

利润 lìrùn NOUN
profit

利息 lìxī NOUN
interest

利益 lìyì NOUN
benefit

利用 lìyòng VERB
1 to use
利用资源 lìyòng zīyuán to use resources
2 to exploit
他被利用了。Tā bèi lìyòng le. He was exploited.

例 lì NOUN
example
■ 举例 jǔlì to give an example

例如 lìrú VERB
to give an example
大商场货物齐全，例如服装、家电、食品等。Dà shāngchǎng huòwù qíquán, lìrú fúzhuāng, jiādiàn, shípǐn děng. The big shopping centre sells all kinds of things, for example, clothes, household appliances and food.

例外 lìwài VERB
to be an exception

例子 lìzi NOUN
example

荔 lì
▷ *see below:*

荔枝 lìzhī NOUN
lychee

栗 lì NOUN
chestnut
■ 栗子 lìzi chestnut

粒 lì MEASURE WORD

LANGUAGE TIP This is a measure word used for small round objects, such as sand, grain, pills etc.

一粒珍珠 yílì zhēnzhū a pearl 三粒种子 sānlì zhǒngzi three seeds

俩 liǎ NUMBER
two *(colloquial)*
我俩 wǒ liǎ the two of us

连 lián

I VERB
to connect
■ 相连 xiānglián to be joined

II ADVERB
in succession
连看了几眼 lián kàn le jǐ yǎn glance at something several times

III PREPOSITION
1 including
连他四人 lián tā sì rén four people, including him
2 even
他连最简单的问题都不会回答。Tā lián zuì jiǎndān de wèntí dōu búhuì huídá. He can't even answer the most simple question.

连接 liánjiē VERB
to connect

连忙 liánmáng ADVERB
at once

连续 liánxù VERB
to go on without stopping
他连续工作了三天，觉都没睡。Tā liánxù gōngzuò le sān tiān, jiào dōu méi shuì. He worked for three days in a row without sleeping.

帘 lián NOUN
curtain
■ 窗帘 chuānglián curtain

莲 lián NOUN
lotus
■ 莲花 liánhuā lotus flower

联 lián VERB
to unite
■ 联赛 liánsài league match

联合 liánhé

I VERB
to unite

II ADJECTIVE
joint

联合国 Liánhéguó NOUN
United Nations

联络 liánluò VERB
to contact
联络方式 liánluò fāngshì means of contact

联系 liánxì VERB
to connect
理论联系实际 lǐlùn liánxì shíjì to apply theory to practice 有事跟我联系。Yǒushì gēn wǒ liánxì. Contact me if anything happens.

脸 liǎn NOUN

1 face
■ 脸面 liǎnmiàn face
2 front
■ 门脸 ménliǎn shop front
脸谱网 Liǎnpǔ wǎng NOUN
Facebook®
脸色 liǎnsè NOUN
complexion

练 liàn
I VERB
to practise
■ 练武 liànwǔ to practise martial arts
II ADJECTIVE
experienced
■ 熟练 shúliàn skilful
练习 liànxí
I VERB
to practise
II NOUN
exercise

恋 liàn VERB
1 to love
■ 相恋 xiānglián to fall in love with each other
2 to miss
■ 恋家 liànjiā to be homesick
恋爱 liàn'ài VERB
to love
■ 谈恋爱 tán liàn'ài to be in love
恋人 liànrén NOUN
lover

良 liáng ADJECTIVE
good
良好 liánghǎo ADJECTIVE
good
良心 liángxīn NOUN
conscience

凉 liáng ADJECTIVE
▷ *see also* liàng
cool
凉快 liángkuai ADJECTIVE
cool

量 liáng VERB
▷ *see also* liàng
to measure

粮 liáng NOUN
grain
粮食 liángshi NOUN
food

两 liǎng
I NUMBER
1 two
两个小时 liǎng gè xiǎoshí two hours
2 a few
说两句 shuō liǎng jù to say a few words
II MEASURE WORD
liang *(a Chinese unit of weight, equal to 50 grams)*

LANGUAGE TIP When citing numbers, including cardinal numbers, ordinal numbers, telephone numbers and serial numbers, 二 èr is used for the number two. However, when you want to talk about two things, you must use 两 liǎng and a measure word.

两个人 liǎng gè rén two people 两杯茶 liǎng bēi chá two cups of tea

---

亮 liàng
I ADJECTIVE
bright
灯光很亮。Dēngguāng hěn liàng. The lamp is very bright.
II VERB
to shine
灯还亮着。Dēng hái liàng zhe. The lights are still on.

凉 liàng VERB
▷ *see also* liáng
to let... cool

辆 liàng MEASURE WORD

LANGUAGE TIP This is a measure word used for vehicles and bicycles.

一辆汽车 yí liàng qìchē a car 两辆自行车 liǎngliàng zìxíngchē two bicycles

---

量 liàng NOUN
▷ *see also* liáng
1 capacity
■ 酒量 jiǔliàng capacity to drink alcohol
2 quantity

晾 liàng VERB
1 to dry
2 to air

聊 liáo VERB
to chat *(colloquial)*
■ 聊天室 liáotiānshì chat room

了 liǎo VERB
▷ *see also* le

to finish

LANGUAGE TIP 了 liǎo is used following a verb indicating a possibility.

办不了 bàn bu liǎo to not be able to handle
受得了 shòu de liǎo to be able to bear

了不起 liǎobuqǐ ADJECTIVE
amazing

了解 liǎojiě VERB
1 to understand
他不了解实情。Tā bù liǎojiě shíqíng. He doesn't understand the situation.
2 to find... out
我想了解一下当地的风俗。Wǒ xiǎng liǎojiě yíxià dāngdì de fēngsú. I would like to find out something about the local customs.

料 liào NOUN
material
■ 木料 mùliào timber

列 liè
I VERB
1 to set... out
列出方程式 lièchū fāngchéngshì to set out the equation
2 to list
■ 列举 lièjǔ to list
II NOUN
1 rank
三列纵队 sānliè zòngduì lined up in three ranks
2 category
不在此列 búzài cǐ liè not in this category

列车 lièchē NOUN
train

劣 liè ADJECTIVE
bad
■ 恶劣 èliè bad

劣质 lièzhì ADJECTIVE
poor-quality

烈 liè ADJECTIVE
strong
■ 激烈 jīliè fierce
■ 烈性酒 lièxìngjiǔ strong liquor

猎 liè VERB
to hunt
■ 打猎 dǎliè to go hunting

裂 liè VERB
to split
■ 分裂 fēnliè to split
■ 破裂 pòliè to break

裂口 lièkǒu NOUN
split

拎 līn VERB
to carry
■ 拎包 līnbāo handbag

邻 lín NOUN
neighbour
■ 邻国 línguó neighbouring country

邻近 línjìn VERB
to be close to

邻居 línjū NOUN
neighbour

林 lín NOUN
1 wood
2 forestry
■ 林业 línyè forestry

临 lín VERB
1 to face
■ 临危 línwēi to face danger
2 to reach
■ 光临 guānglín presence
3 to be about to
■ 临产 línchǎn to be in labour

临近 línjìn VERB
to be close to
考试临近了。Kǎoshì línjìn le. The exams are approaching.

临时 línshí ADVERB
temporarily

淋 lín VERB
to drench

淋浴 línyù VERB
to take a shower

鳞 lín NOUN
scale

吝 lìn ADJECTIVE
stingy
■ 吝啬 lìnsè stingy

灵 líng
I ADJECTIVE
1 nimble
■ 灵敏 língmǐn agile
2 effective
这种药治感冒很灵。Zhèzhǒng yào zhì gǎnmào hěn líng. This medicine is really effective for colds.
II NOUN
1 soul

Chinese-English

l

2 deity
■ 精灵 jīnglíng spirit

灵活 línghuó ADJECTIVE
1 agile
尽管上了年纪，他的身体仍然很灵活。Jǐnguǎn shàngle niánji, tā de shēntǐ rēngrán hěn línghuó. Although he's getting on a bit, he's still very agile.
2 flexible
灵活的工作时间 línghuó de gōngzuò shíjiān Flexible working hours

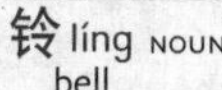

铃 líng NOUN
bell
■ 铃铛 língdang small bell
■ 哑铃 yǎlíng dumb-bell

零 líng
I NOUN
1 zero
2 odd
她年纪七十有零。Tā niánjì qīshí yǒu líng. She's seventy-odd years old.
II ADJECTIVE
1 odd
■ 零活 línghuó odd jobs *pl*
2 spare
■ 零件 língjiàn spare parts *pl*
III CONJUNCTION
两年零三个月 liǎng nián líng sān gè yuè two years and three months 五元零二分 wǔ yuán líng èr fēn five yuan and two fen

零钱 língqián NOUN
small change

零食 língshí NOUN
snack

零售 língshòu VERB
to retail

零用钱 língyòngqián NOUN
pocket money

领 lǐng
I NOUN
1 collar
2 neck
II VERB
1 to lead
■ 率领 shuàilǐng to lead
2 to possess
■ 占领 zhànlǐng to occupy

领带 lǐngdài NOUN
tie

领导 lǐngdǎo
I VERB
to lead
他领导有方。Tā lǐngdǎo yǒufāng. He's an effective leader.
II NOUN
leader

领土 lǐngtǔ NOUN
territory

领先 lǐngxiān VERB
to lead
他在比赛中遥遥领先。Tā zài bǐsài zhōng yáoyáo lǐngxiān. He took a runaway lead in the competition.

领袖 lǐngxiù NOUN
leader

领养 lǐngyǎng VERB
to adopt

另 lìng
I PRONOUN
another
II ADVERB
separately

另外 lìngwài
I PRONOUN
other
我不喜欢这些衣服，我喜欢另外那些。Wǒ bù xǐhuan zhèxiē yīfu, wǒ xǐhuan lìngwài nàxiē. I don't like these clothes; I like the others.
II ADVERB
in addition

令 lìng
I NOUN
order
II VERB
1 to order
2 to make
令人愉快 lìng rén yúkuài pleasing

溜 liū VERB
to sneak off

溜达 liūda VERB
to go for a stroll

留 liú VERB
1 to stay
她今晚留下来陪我。Tā jīnwǎn liú xià lái péi wǒ. She will stay to keep me company tonight.
2 to keep... back
■ 挽留 wǎnliú to persuade... to stay
3 to be careful
■ 留心 liúxīn to take note
4 to keep
■ 留存 liúcún to keep
5 to grow
留胡子 liú húzi to grow a beard

6 to accept
他们把这个求职者留下了。Tāmen bǎ zhègè qiúzhízhě liúxià le. They have kept this jobseeker on.
7 to leave... behind
他把这个问题留在了脑后。Tā bǎ zhègè wèntí liúzài le nǎohòu. He has put this question to the back of his mind.
8 to study abroad
留英 liú Yīng to study in Britain

留步 liúbù VERB
to stop here

留念 liúniàn VERB
to keep as a souvenir

留神 liúshén VERB
to be careful

留言 liúyán VERB
to leave a message

留意 liúyì VERB
to look... out

流 liú
I VERB
to flow
■ 漂流 piāoliú to drift
II NOUN
1 current
■ 洪流 hóngliú torrent
2 grade
■ 一流 yīliú first-class

流传 liúchuán VERB
to spread

流动 liúdòng VERB
to flow

流感 liúgǎn NOUN
flu

流利 liúlì ADJECTIVE
fluent

流氓 liúmáng NOUN
1 perversion
2 hooligan

流水 liúshuǐ NOUN
running water

流行 liúxíng VERB
to be fashionable

瘤 liú NOUN
tumour
■ 瘤子 liúzi tumour

柳 liǔ NOUN
willow
■ 柳树 liǔshù willow

六 liù NUMBER
six

六月 liùyuè NOUN
June

陆 liù NUMBER
▷ *see also* lù
six

LANGUAGE TIP This is the complex character for **six**, which is mainly used in banks, on receipts etc to prevent mistakes and forgery.

遛 liù VERB
1 to take a stroll
■ 遛弯 liùwān to take a stroll
2 to walk
■ 遛狗 liùgǒu to walk the dog

龙 lóng NOUN
dragon

龙卷风 lóngjuǎnfēng NOUN
tornado

龙头 lóngtóu NOUN
tap

聋 lóng ADJECTIVE
deaf

聋子 lóngzi NOUN
他是个聋子。Tā shì gè lóngzi. He's deaf.

笼 lóng NOUN
cage
■ 鸟笼子 niǎolóngzi birdcage

楼 lóu NOUN
1 tall building
教学楼 jiàoxué lóu teaching block
2 floor
他家住三楼。Tājiā zhù sānlóu. He lives on the third floor.

楼房 lóufáng NOUN
multi-storey building

楼梯 lóutī NOUN
stairs *pl*

搂 lǒu VERB
to embrace

漏 lòu VERB
1 to leak
水桶漏了。Shuǐtǒng lòu le. The bucket has got a leak.
2 to divulge
走漏风声 zǒulòu fēngshēng to divulge a secret
3 to leave... out
这句话漏了两个单词。Zhè jù huà lòu le

liǎnggè dāncí. There are two words missing in this sentence.

漏斗 lòudǒu NOUN
funnel

露 lòu VERB
▷ *see also* lù
to reveal

露马脚 lòumǎjiǎo VERB
to give oneself away

炉 lú NOUN
stove

炉灶 lúzào NOUN
kitchen range

卤 lǔ
I NOUN
1 bittern
2 thick gravy
II VERB
to stew... in soy sauce

陆 lù NOUN
▷ *see also* liù
land

陆地 lùdì NOUN
land

录 lù
I NOUN
record
II VERB
1 to record
■ 记录 jìlù to take notes
2 to tape-record
录磁带 lù cídài to record on tape

录取 lùqǔ VERB
to admit
她被剑桥大学录取了。Tā bèi Jiànqiáo Dàxué lùqǔ le. She was given a place at the University of Cambridge.

录像 lùxiàng VERB
to video

录音 lùyīn VERB
to record

鹿 lù NOUN
deer

路 lù NOUN
1 road
■ 路标 lùbiāo signpost
2 journey
一路平安 yí lù píng'ān to have a safe journey
3 means
■ 财路 cáilù a means of getting rich
4 sequence
■ 思路 sīlù train of thought
5 route
■ 八路车 bālù chē number 8 bus

路程 lùchéng NOUN
journey

路过 lùguò VERB
to pass through

路口 lùkǒu NOUN
crossing

路线 lùxiàn NOUN
1 route
交通路线 jiāotōng lùxiàn traffic route
2 line
思想路线 sīxiǎng lùxiàn line of thought

露 lù
▷ *see also* lòu
I NOUN
dew
II VERB
to reveal
■ 暴露 bàolù to expose

露天 lùtiān NOUN
the open air
露天剧场 lùtiān jùchǎng open-air theatre

露营 lùyíng VERB
to camp out

驴 lǘ NOUN
donkey

旅 lǚ VERB
to travel
■ 差旅费 chāilǚfèi travel expenses *pl*

旅馆 lǚguǎn NOUN
hotel

旅客 lǚkè NOUN
passenger

旅途 lǚtú NOUN
journey

旅行 lǚxíng VERB
to travel

旅游 lǚyóu NOUN
tour
旅游业 lǚyóu yè tourism 去国外旅游 qù guówài lǚyóu to travel abroad

铝 lǚ NOUN
aluminium

律 lǜ NOUN
law
■ 纪律 jìlǜ discipline

律师 lǜshī NOUN
lawyer

绿 lǜ ADJECTIVE
green
■ 绿灯 lǜdēng green light
绿化 lǜhuà VERB
to make... green
绿化荒山 lǜhuà huāngshān to plant trees on the mountains
绿卡 lǜkǎ NOUN
green card
绿洲 lǜzhōu NOUN
oasis

乱 luàn
I ADJECTIVE
1 disorderly
■ 杂乱 záluàn messy
2 disturbed
■ 烦乱 fánluàn agitated
II NOUN
chaos
■ 战乱 zhànluàn war chaos
乱哄哄 luànhōnghōng ADJECTIVE
chaotic
乱七八糟 luànqībāzāo ADJECTIVE
in a mess

略 lüè
I NOUN
1 summary
■ 简略 jiǎnlüè brief
2 plan
■ 策略 cèlüè tactic
II VERB
1 to capture
■ 侵略 qīnlüè to invade
2 to simplify
■ 省略 shěnglüè to omit

伦 lún NOUN
1 human relationships *pl*
2 ethics
伦敦 Lúndūn NOUN
London
伦理 lúnlǐ NOUN
ethics *sg*

轮 lún NOUN
1 wheel
■ 轮胎 lúntāi tyre
2 steamship
■ 班轮 bānlún passenger ship, cargo ship
轮船 lúnchuán NOUN
steamship
轮换 lúnhuàn VERB
to take turns
轮廓 lúnkuò NOUN
outline
轮流 lúnliú ADVERB
in turns
轮椅 lúnyǐ NOUN
wheelchair

论 lùn
I NOUN
1 essay
■ 议论文 yìlùnwén discursive essay
2 theory
相对论 xiāngduì lùn theory of relativity
II VERB
to discuss
■ 评论 pínglùn to comment on
论文 lùnwén NOUN
dissertation

萝 luó NOUN
trailing plant
萝卜 luóbo NOUN
turnip
■ 胡萝卜 húluóbo carrot

逻 luó VERB
to patrol
逻辑 luóji NOUN
logic

螺 luó NOUN
snail
螺钉 luódīng NOUN
screw

裸 luǒ VERB
to expose
裸体 luǒtǐ ADJECTIVE
naked

骆 luò
▷ *see below:*
骆驼 luòtuo NOUN
camel

落 luò VERB
▷ *see also* là
1 to fall
■ 坠落 zhuìluò to fall
2 to go down
■ 降落 jiàngluò to descend
3 to lower
■ 落幕 luòmù the curtain falls

4 to decline
■ 衰落 shuāiluò to wane

5 to fall behind
由于贪玩，他学习落后了。Yóuyú tānwán, tā xuéxí luòhòu le. Her studies have fallen behind because she likes to have too much fun.

6 to fall to
这张地图不能落入敌人手中。Zhèzhāng dìtú bùnéng luòrù dírén shǒuzhōng. This map cannot fall into enemy hands.

落后 luòhòu

I VERB
to fall behind
经济落后 jīngji luòhòu backward economy

II ADJECTIVE
backward
落后地区 luòhòu dìqū backward region

Mm

妈 mā NOUN
mum

妈妈 māma NOUN
mum

麻 má

I NOUN
hemp

II ADJECTIVE
numb

麻烦 máfán

I ADJECTIVE
problematic
这是个麻烦的问题。Zhè shì gè máfán de wèntí. This is a troublesome issue.

II NOUN
trouble

III VERB
to trouble
不好意思，麻烦您了。Bùhǎo yìsi, máfán nín le. Sorry to trouble you.

麻将 májiàng NOUN
mah jong

DID YOU KNOW...?
The game of mah jong is usually played by four people. 144 tiles appearing like dominoes and bearing various designs are drawn and discarded until one player has an entire hand of winning combinations. The game requires strategy as well as luck. In China, mah jong is also a popular gambling game.

马 mǎ NOUN
horse

马虎 mǎhu ADJECTIVE
careless

马马虎虎 mǎmǎhūhū ADJECTIVE
1 careless
2 just passable

马拉松 mǎlāsōng NOUN
marathon

马路 mǎlù NOUN
road

马上 mǎshàng ADVERB
right away
他马上就到。Tā mǎshàng jiù dào. He'll be here right away.

马戏 mǎxì NOUN
circus

马来西亚 mǎláixīyà NOUN
Malaysia

码 mǎ NOUN
numeral
■ 页码 yèmǎ page number

码头 mǎtóu NOUN
pier

蚂 mǎ
▹ *see below:*

蚂蚁 mǎyǐ NOUN
ant

骂 mà VERB
1 to insult
不要骂人！ Búyaò màrén! Don't call people names!
2 to tell... off
他爸爸骂他不努力。Tā bàbà mà tā bù nǔlì. His father told him off for not working hard enough.

吗 ma AUXILIARY WORD

LANGUAGE TIP 吗 ma is added to the end of any statement to turn it into a simple yes/no question.

你去银行吗？Nǐ qù yínháng ma? Are you going to the bank?

嘛 ma AUXILIARY WORD

LANGUAGE TIP 嘛 ma can be used for emphasis.

事实就是这样嘛！ Shìshí jiùshì zhèyàng ma! That's just the way things are!

LANGUAGE TIP 嘛 ma can be used to express expectation.

别不高兴嘛！ Bié bù gāoxìng ma. Please don't be unhappy.

埋 mái VERB
▷ *see also* mán
1 to bury
2 to hide

买 mǎi VERB
1 to buy
我去市场买东西。Wǒ qù shìchǎng mǎi dōngxi. I'm going shopping in the market.
2 to win... over
■ 买通 mǎitōng to buy... off 他买通了法官，没有被判罪。Tā mǎitōng le fǎguān, méiyǒu bèi pànzuì. Because he had bribed the judge, he wasn't convicted.
买单 mǎidān VERB
to pay a bill
买单！Mǎidān! The bill, please!

迈 mài VERB
to step
■ 迈步 màibù to stride

麦 mài NOUN
wheat
■ 燕麦 yànmài oats *pl*
麦克风 màikèfēng NOUN
microphone

卖 mài VERB
to sell
书都卖完了。Shū dōu mài wán le. The books are all sold out.
卖弄 màinòng VERB
to show off
她喜欢卖弄口才。Tā xǐhuan màinòng kǒucái. She likes to show off her gift of the gab.

埋 mán
▷ *see also* mái
▷ *see below:*
埋怨 mányuàn VERB
1 to blame
老板埋怨员工太懒惰。Lǎobǎn mányuàn yuángōng tài lǎnduò. The proprietor grumbled about his employees being so lazy.
2 to complain
他不停埋怨天气太热。Tā bùtíng mányuàn tiānqì tài rè. He is always complaining that the weather is too hot.

馒 mán
▷ *see below:*
馒头 mántou NOUN
steamed bun

瞒 mán VERB
to hide the truth from
别瞒着我们！Bié mán zhe wǒmen! Don't keep us in the dark!

满 mǎn
I ADJECTIVE
1 full
2 complete
II VERB
to reach
孩子刚满六岁。Háizi gāng mǎn liùsuì. The child has just turned six years old.
III ADVERB
fully
满意 mǎnyì VERB
to be satisfied
满足 mǎnzú VERB
1 to be satisfied
这样的收入，他已经很满足了。Zhèyàng de shōurù, tā yǐjīng hěn mǎnzú le. He's already very satisfied with that level of income.
2 to satisfy
他的妈妈可以满足他所有的需要。Tā de māmā kěyǐ mǎnzú tā suǒyǒu de xūyào. His mother can provide for his every need.

漫 màn VERB
to overflow
漫长 màncháng ADJECTIVE
endless
漫画 mànhuà NOUN
comic strip

慢 màn
I ADJECTIVE
slow
II VERB
to slow
钟慢了十分钟。Zhōng màn le shí fēnzhōng. The clock is ten minutes slow.

忙 máng
I ADJECTIVE
busy
我非常忙。Wǒ féicháng máng. I'm extremely busy.
II VERB
to be busy with
你这一段忙什么呢？Nǐ zhè yíduàn máng shénme ne? What's been keeping you busy recently?

盲 máng ADJECTIVE
blind

■ 文盲 wénmáng illiterate

盲目 mángmù ADJECTIVE
blind

猫 māo NOUN
cat

猫儿眼 māoryǎn NOUN
spyhole

毛 máo NOUN
1 hair
■ 羽毛 yǔmáo feather
2 fur
■ 毛皮 máopí fur
3 wool
■ 毛衣 máoyī sweater
4 mao

DID YOU KNOW...? 毛 máo is a unit of Chinese currency. Each 元 yuán is divided into ten 毛 máo.

毛笔 máobǐ NOUN
brush pen

毛病 máobìng NOUN
1 problem
电视出毛病了。Diànshì chū máobìng le. The television is faulty.
2 shortcoming
他的毛病是粗心。Tā de máobìng shì cūxīn. His shortcoming is his carelessness.
3 illness
他的心脏有毛病。Tā de xīnzàng yǒu máobìng. He has a heart problem.

毛巾 máojīn NOUN
towel

矛 máo NOUN
spear

矛盾 máodùn
I NOUN
1 conflict
2 contradiction
II ADJECTIVE
uncertain
我很矛盾，不知如何决定。Wǒ hěn máodùn, bùzhī rúhé juédìng. I'm completely at a loss about what decision to make.

茂 mào ADJECTIVE
luxuriant

茂盛 màoshèng ADJECTIVE
flourishing

冒 mào VERB
1 to risk
冒着生命危险 mào zhe shēngmìng wēixiǎn putting one's life at risk
2 to pretend to be

冒充 màochōng VERB
to pass... off as

冒牌 màopái VERB
to pirate
冒牌商品 màopái shāngpǐn pirated goods

冒险 màoxiǎn VERB
to take a risk

帽 mào NOUN
hat

帽子 màozi NOUN
hat

没 méi
I VERB
to not have
屋子里没人。Wūzi lǐ méi rén. There's no one in the room.
■ 没关系 méiguānxi it doesn't matter
II ADVERB
not
他没看过大海。Tā méi kànguò dàhǎi. He's never seen the sea before.

LANGUAGE TIP 没 méi is used to make a Chinese sentence negative with the verb 有 yǒu **to have** and in past tense sentences.

我没喝酒。Wǒ méi hējiǔ. I didn't drink alcohol. 我没有钱。Wǒ méiyǒu qián. I don't have any money.

没劲 méijìn
I VERB
to have no energy
他没劲儿了。Tā méijìnr le. He's worn out.
II ADJECTIVE
uninteresting
这个游戏真没劲。Zhègè yóuxì zhēn méijìn. This game is really boring.

没门儿 méiménr VERB
to be impossible

LANGUAGE TIP Word for word, these characters mean 'there is no door'.

没事 méishì VERB
to be free
我今晚没事。Wǒ jīnwǎn méishì. I'm free tonight.
■ 没事。Méishì. It doesn't matter.

没有 méiyǒu
I VERB
1 to not have
我没有钱。Wǒ méiyǒu qián. I don't have any money.
2 there is not

月球上没有人。Yuèqiú shàng méiyǒu rén. There's no life on the moon.

3 to be not as... as ...
他没有你努力。Tā méiyǒu nǐ nǔlì. He's not as hard-working as you.

II ADVERB
1 not yet
她还没有到。Tā hái méiyǒu dào. She hasn't arrived yet.
2 to never before
我没有吃过西餐。Wǒ méiyǒu chīguò xīcān. I have never eaten Western food before.

玫 méi
▷ *see below:*

玫瑰 méiguī NOUN
rose

眉 méi NOUN
eyebrow
■ 眉毛 méimao eyebrow

媒 méi NOUN
1 matchmaker
■ 做媒 zuòméi to be a matchmaker
2 intermediary

媒体 méitǐ NOUN
media

煤 méi NOUN
coal

煤气 méiqì NOUN
1 gas
2 carbon monoxide

每 měi
I ADJECTIVE
1 every
■ 每次 měicì every time
■ 每天 měitiān every day
2 each
II ADVERB
every time
每走一步，他的脚都很疼。Měi zǒu yí bù, tāde jiǎo dōu hěn téng. His feet ache with every step he takes.

美 měi
I ADJECTIVE
1 beautiful
2 good
我们的明天会更美。Wǒmen de míngtiān huì gèng měi. Our future will be even better.
II NOUN
1 North and South America
■ 南美 Nánměi South America
■ 北美 Běiměi North America
■ 美洲 měizhōu the Americas
2 USA

美国 Měiguó NOUN
USA
■ 美国人 Měiguórén American

美好 měihǎo ADJECTIVE
wonderful

美甲 měijiǎ VERB
to get a manicure

美丽 měilì ADJECTIVE
beautiful

美满 měimǎn ADJECTIVE
perfectly satisfactory

美容 měiróng VERB
to make oneself more beautiful
美容店 měiróng diàn beauty salon

美食 měishí NOUN
delicacy

美术 měishù NOUN
1 fine arts *pl*
2 painting

美元 měiyuán NOUN
US dollar

妹 mèi NOUN
younger sister
■ 表妹 biǎomèi cousin

妹妹 mèimei NOUN
younger sister

魅 mèi NOUN
demon

魅力 mèilì NOUN
charm

闷 mēn
▷ *see also* mèn
I ADJECTIVE
stuffy
II VERB
1 to keep silent
2 to shut oneself in
他是个很闷的人。Tā shì gè hěn mēn de rén. He's a pretty boring person.

闷热 mēnrè ADJECTIVE
muggy

门 mén
I NOUN
door
■ 门口 ménkǒu entrance
II MEASURE WORD

LANGUAGE TIP This is a measure word used for academic subjects, courses and technology.

五门课 wǔ mén kè five courses

门卫 ménwèi NOUN
guard

门诊 ménzhěn NOUN
outpatient department

闷 mèn ADJECTIVE
▷ *see also* mēn
bored

们 men SUFFIX

LANGUAGE TIP 们 men is used after singular personal pronouns to form plural forms.

- 我们 wǒmen **1** we **2** us
- 你们 nǐmen you
- 他们 tāmen **1** they **2** them

猛 měng ADJECTIVE
fierce

猛烈 měngliè ADJECTIVE
fierce

蒙 měng NOUN
Mongolia

- 蒙古 Měnggǔ Mongolia
- 蒙古人 Měnggǔrén Mongolian
- 内蒙古 Nèiměnggǔ Inner Mongolia

梦 mèng

I NOUN

1 dream

- 白日梦 báirìmèng daydream
- 做梦 zuòmèng to have a dream

2 illusion

II VERB
to dream

梦话 mènghuà NOUN
说梦话 shuō mènghuà to talk in one's sleep

梦想 mèngxiǎng VERB
to dream
他梦想成为一名科学家。Tā mèngxiǎng chéngwéi yìmíng kēxuéjiā. He dreams of becoming a scientist.

迷 mí

I VERB

1 to be lost

- 迷路 mílù to lose one's way

2 to become obsessed with

II NOUN
fan

- 球迷 qiúmí sports fan

迷你 mínǐ ADJECTIVE
mini
迷你裙 mínǐ qún mini-skirt

迷信 míxìn VERB

1 to be superstitious about

2 to have blind faith in

谜 mí NOUN

1 riddle

2 mystery

谜语 míyǔ NOUN
riddle

米 mǐ

I NOUN
rice

- 米饭 mǐfàn cooked rice

II MEASURE WORD
metre
一米长 yìmǐ cháng one metre long

秘 mì

I ADJECTIVE
secret

II VERB
to keep... secret

III NOUN
secretary

秘密 mìmì NOUN
secret
一定要保守秘密！ Yídìng yào bǎoshǒu mìmì! You must keep this a secret!

秘书 mìshū NOUN
secretary

密 mì ADJECTIVE

1 dense

2 close

- 亲密 qīnmì intimate

3 secret

- 保密 bǎomì to keep secret

密码 mìmǎ NOUN

1 password

2 code

密切 mìqiè ADJECTIVE
close

蜜 mì

I NOUN
honey

II ADJECTIVE
sweet

蜜蜂 mìfēng NOUN
bee

蜜月 mìyuè NOUN
honeymoon

眠 mián VERB
to sleep
■ 失眠 shīmián to suffer from insomnia

棉 mián NOUN
cotton
棉花 miánhuā NOUN
cotton
棉衣 miányī NOUN
cotton-padded clothing

免 miǎn VERB
1 to exempt
■ 免试 miǎnshì to be exempt from an exam
2 to not be allowed
闲人免进 xiánrén miǎnjìn staff only
免费 miǎnfèi VERB
to be free of charge
注册一个免费电子邮箱 zhùcè yígè miǎnfèi diànzǐ yǒuxiāng to register for free email

勉 miǎn VERB
1 to strive
2 to encourage
3 to force… to carry on
勉强 miǎnqiǎng
I VERB
1 to push oneself hard
做事不要太勉强。Zuòshì búyào tài miǎnqiǎng. Don't push yourself too hard.
2 to force
不要勉强孩子学钢琴。Búyào miǎnqiǎng háizi xué gāngqín. Don't force the child to study the piano.
II ADJECTIVE
1 reluctant
■ 我让他帮忙，他勉强答应了。Wǒ ràng tā bāngmáng, tā miǎnqiǎng dāyìng le. I asked him to help, and he reluctantly agreed.
2 barely enough
他挣的钱勉强够自己花。Tā zhèng de qián miǎnqiǎng gòu zìjǐ huā. The money he earned was barely enough to support himself.
3 far-fetched
这个理论有点勉强。Zhègè lǐlùn yǒudiǎn miǎnqiǎng. This theory is a bit far-fetched.

面 miàn
I NOUN
1 face
2 surface
3 aspect
■ 前面 qiánmiàn front
4 powder
■ 辣椒面 làjiāomiàn chilli powder
5 flour
■ 面粉 miànfěn flour
6 noodles *pl*
II VERB
to face
III MEASURE WORD

LANGUAGE TIP This is a measure word used for objects with a flat surface, such as walls, mirrors, drums etc.

一面墙 yí miàn qiáng a wall

LANGUAGE TIP This is a measure word used for encounters between two people.

我们见过几面。Wǒmen jiànguò jǐ miàn. We've met a few times.
面包 miànbāo NOUN
bread
■ 面包房 miànbāofáng bakery
面对 miànduì VERB
to face
面积 miànjī NOUN
area
面临 miànlín VERB
to face
面前 miànqián NOUN
in front of
在困难面前 zài kùnnan miànqián in the face of difficulties
面试 miànshì VERB
to have an interview
面条 miàntiáo NOUN
noodles *pl*
意大利面条 Yìdàlì miàntiáo spaghetti
面子 miànzi NOUN
1 face
丢面子 diū miànzi to lose face

DID YOU KNOW…?
Face is an important aspect of Chinese culture, and is associated with pride and dignity. It applies to both personal and business relationships.

2 feelings *pl*
给我点面子，你就答应吧！ Gěi wǒ diǎn miànzi, nǐ jiù dāying ba! Show some respect for my feelings and say yes!

苗 miáo NOUN
seedling
■ 树苗 shùmiáo sapling

苗条 miáotiao ADJECTIVE
slim

描 miáo VERB
1 to trace
2 to touch... up

描述 miáoshù VERB
to describe

描写 miáoxiě VERB
to describe

瞄 miáo VERB
to fix one's eyes on

瞄准 miáozhǔn VERB
to take aim

秒 miǎo MEASURE WORD
second
五秒 wǔ miǎo five seconds

妙 miào ADJECTIVE
1 wonderful
■ 美妙 měimiào wonderful
2 ingenious

庙 miào NOUN
temple

灭 miè VERB
1 to go out
2 to extinguish
■ 灭火器 mièhuǒqì fire extinguisher
3 to perish
4 to kill

灭绝 mièjué VERB
to become extinct

民 mín NOUN
1 the people *pl*
2 person
■ 网民 wǎngmín internet user
3 folk
4 civilian

民歌 míngē NOUN
folk song

民间 mínjiān NOUN
1 folk
民间传说 mínjiān chuánshuō folklore
2 non-governmental
民间组织 mínjiān zǔzhi non-governmental organization

民警 mínjǐng NOUN
civil police

民主 mínzhǔ
I NOUN
democracy
II ADJECTIVE
democratic

民族 mínzú NOUN
nationality
少数民族 shǎoshù mínzú ethnic minority

敏 mǐn ADJECTIVE
1 quick
■ 敏感 mǐngǎn sensitive
2 clever
■ 机敏 jīmǐn quick-witted

敏捷 mǐnjié ADJECTIVE
quick

名 míng
I NOUN
1 name
书名 shū míng book title
2 reputation
II ADJECTIVE
famous
■ 名著 míngzhù masterpiece *pl*
III MEASURE WORD

LANGUAGE TIP This is a measure word used for people of any profession.

5名工人 wǔ míng gōngrén five workers

名称 míngchēng NOUN
name

名次 míngcì NOUN
ranking

名单 míngdān NOUN
list of names

名额 míng'é NOUN
quota

名牌 míngpái NOUN
big brand
名牌服装 míngpái fúzhuāng designer clothing

名片 míngpiàn NOUN
business card

DID YOU KNOW...?
In formal situations, business cards should be presented and received with both hands in China.

名气 míngqì NOUN
fame

名人 míngrén NOUN
famous person

名声 míngshēng NOUN
reputation

名胜 míngshèng NOUN
tourist site

名字 míngzi NOUN
1 name *(name, full name)*
你叫什么名字？Nǐ jiào shénme míngzi? What's your name?

2 first name
她的名字是琼。Tāde míngzi shì Qióng. Her first name is Joan.

明 míng
I ADJECTIVE
1 bright
2 clear
II NOUN
sight
■ 失明 shīmíng to lose one's eyesight
III VERB
1 to understand
■ 明理 mínglǐ to be understanding
2 to show
■ 表明 biǎomíng to indicate

明白 míngbái
I ADJECTIVE
1 clear
他的解释很明白易懂。Tā de jiěshì hěn míngbái yìdǒng. His explanation was clear and easy to understand.
2 sensible
他是个明白人。Tā shì gè míngbái rén. He's a sensible person.
II VERB
to understand
我明白你的意思。Wǒ míngbái nǐde yìsī. I know what you mean.

明亮 míngliàng ADJECTIVE
1 bright
2 shining

明确 míngquè
I ADJECTIVE
clear-cut
他的立场很明确。Tāde lìchǎng hěn míngquè. His position is very clear-cut.
II VERB
to clarify
他明确了比赛的意义不是胜利，而是友谊。Tā míngquè le bǐsài de yìyì búshì shènglì, érshì yǒuyì. He realised that the purpose of a match was to develop friendships rather than to win.

明显 míngxiǎn ADJECTIVE
obvious

明星 míngxīng NOUN
star

明智 míngzhì ADJECTIVE
sensible
这是个明智的决定。Zhèshì gè míngzhì de juédìng. This is a wise decision.

明天 míngtiān NOUN
tomorrow

明信片 míngxìnpiàn NOUN
postcard

命 mìng NOUN
1 life
2 fate
3 order

命令 mìnglìng VERB
to order

命名 mìngmíng VERB
to name

命运 mìngyùn NOUN
fate

模 mó
▷ see also mú
I NOUN
model
II VERB
to imitate

模范 mófàn ADJECTIVE
model
劳动模范 láodòngmófàn model worker

模仿 mófǎng VERB
to imitate
小孩子都喜欢模仿大人。Xiǎoháizi dōu xǐhuan mófǎng dàrén. All children like to imitate adults.

模糊 móhū ADJECTIVE
blurred

模拟 mónǐ VERB
to imitate
■ 模拟考试 mónǐ kǎoshì mock exam

模特儿 mótèr NOUN
model

模型 móxíng NOUN
1 model
2 mould

摩 mó VERB
to rub... together

摩托车 mótuōchē NOUN
motorbike

蘑 mó NOUN
mushroom

蘑菇 mógu NOUN
mushroom

魔 mó
I NOUN
1 demon
2 magic
II ADJECTIVE
magic

魔法 mófǎ NOUN
magic

魔鬼 móguǐ NOUN
devil

魔术 móshù NOUN
magic
魔术师 móshùshī NOUN
magician

末 mò NOUN
end
世纪末 shìjì mò the end of the century

LANGUAGE TIP 末 is an interesting character because it is an ideogram. It modifies the pictographic character 木 mù **tree**, with a horizontal line at the top, to indicate **tip** or **end**.

末尾 mòwěi NOUN
end

沫 mò NOUN
foam
■ 泡沫 pàomò bubble

茉 mò
▹ *see below:*
茉莉 mòlì NOUN
jasmine

陌 mò NOUN
footpath
陌生 mòshēng ADJECTIVE
unfamiliar
陌生人 mòshēngrén NOUN
stranger

墨 mò
I NOUN
ink
■ 墨汁 mòzhī ink
II ADJECTIVE
dark
■ 墨镜 mòjìng sunglasses

谋 móu NOUN
plan
■ 阴谋 yīnmóu plot
谋杀 móushā VERB
to murder
谋生 móushēng VERB
to make a living
他以教书谋生。Tā yǐ jiāoshū móushēng. He makes a living as a teacher.

某 mǒu PRONOUN
■ 某人 mǒurén somebody

模 mú NOUN
▹ *see also* mó
mould
模样 múyàng NOUN
looks *pl*
她的模样很好看。Tā de múyàng hěn hǎokàn. She is very pretty.

母 mǔ
I NOUN
mother

LANGUAGE TIP 母 mǔ can be used to indicate a female of an older generation.

■ 祖母 zǔmǔ grandmother
II ADJECTIVE
female *(animal)*
■ 母牛 mǔniú cow
母亲 mǔqīn NOUN
mother

拇 mǔ
▹ *see below:*
拇指 mǔzhǐ NOUN
1 thumb
2 big toe

木 mù
I NOUN
1 tree
2 wood
II ADJECTIVE
numb
木材 mùcái NOUN
timber
木匠 mùjiang NOUN
carpenter
木偶 mù'ǒu NOUN
puppet
木头 mùtou NOUN
wood

目 mù NOUN
1 eye
2 item
目标 mùbiāo NOUN
1 target
射中目标 shèzhòng mùbiāo to hit the target
2 goal
他的目标是进入前三名。Tāde mùbiāo shì jìnrù qiánsānmíng. His goal is to get into the top three.
目的 mùdì NOUN
1 destination
目的地 mùdì dì destination
2 aim
3 intention
他的目的是打乱敌人的计划。Tāde mùdì

shì dǎluàn dírén de jìhuà. His intention was to throw the enemy's plans into disarray.

目光 mùguāng NOUN
look
他的目光很严厉。Tāde mùguāng hěn yánlì. He has a severe gaze.

目录 mùlù NOUN
1 catalogue
2 table of contents

目前 mùqián NOUN
present
我们目前的任务 wǒmen mùqián de rènwù our current tasks

牧 mù VERB
to herd

牧民 mùmín NOUN
herdsman

牧师 mùshī NOUN
priest

牧业 mùyè NOUN
animal husbandry

睦 mù VERB
to get on
■ 和睦 hémù harmonious

穆 mù ADJECTIVE
solemn

穆斯林 Mùsīlín NOUN
Muslim

Nn

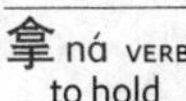

拿 ná VERB
to hold
他拿着一杯水。Tā názhe yìbēi shuǐ. He's holding a glass of water.

哪 nǎ PRONOUN
1 which
哪个人是李先生？Nǎ gè rén shì Lǐ Xiānsheng? Which one is Mr Li?
2 any
你哪天来都行。Nǐ nǎ tiān lái dōu xíng. You can come any day.

哪个 nǎgè PRONOUN
which
哪个是正确答案？Nǎgè shì zhèngquè dáàn? Which is the correct answer?

哪里 nǎlǐ PRONOUN
where
你住在哪里？Nǐ zhù zài nǎlǐ? Where do you live?
■哪里，哪里，你过奖了。Nǎli, nǎli, nǐ guòjiǎng le. No, no, it was nothing.

那 nà
I PRONOUN
that
那些人 nàxiē rén those people
II CONJUNCTION
then
你想买，那就买吧。Nǐ xiǎng mǎi, nà jiù mǎi ba. If you want to buy it, then buy it.

那边 nàbiān NOUN
that side

那个 nàge PRONOUN
that
那个人 nàgè rén that person

那里 nàli PRONOUN
there
我去过那里。Wǒ qùguo nàli. I've been there.

那么 nàme
I PRONOUN
LANGUAGE TIP 那么 nàme is used to express extent.
你不该那么相信他。Nǐ bù gāi nàme xiāngxìn tā. You shouldn't trust him so much.
LANGUAGE TIP 那么 nàme is also used to express a way of doing things.
你别那么想。Nǐ bié nàme xiǎng. Don't think in that way.
II CONJUNCTION
then
你觉得如此，那么我们这样做吧。Nǐ juédé rúcí, nàme wǒmen zhè yàng zuò ba. If you feel so inclined, then let's do it that way.

那儿 nàr
there

那些 nàxiē PRONOUN
those

那样 nàyàng ADVERB
我没有说过那样的话。Wǒ méiyǒu shuōguo nàyàng de huà. I never said anything like that.

奶 nǎi NOUN
milk
■酸奶 suānnǎi yoghurt

奶酪 nǎilào NOUN
cheese

奶奶 nǎinai NOUN
grandmother
LANGUAGE TIP 奶奶 nǎinai refers specifically to the grandmother on the father's side.

耐 nài VERB
1 to endure
■耐性 nàixìng patience
2 to be resistant
■耐用 nàiyòng enduring

耐力 nàilì NOUN
stamina

耐心 nàixīn ADJECTIVE
patient

男 nán NOUN
male

男孩子 nánháizi NOUN
boy

男朋友 nánpéngyou NOUN
boyfriend

男人 nánrén NOUN
man

南 nán NOUN
south
■ 东南 dōngnán south-east
■ 西南 xīnán south-west

南边 nánbiān NOUN
the south

南部 nánbù NOUN
southern part

南方 nánfāng NOUN
the South

南极 nánjí NOUN
South Pole

南面 nánmiàn NOUN
south

难 nán ADJECTIVE
hard

难道 nándào ADVERB
could it be that...? *(to add emphasis)*
你难道还不明白吗？Nǐ nándào hái bù míngbai ma? How can you still not understand? 难道你就不累？Nándào nǐ jiù bú lèi? Aren't you tired?

难过 nánguò
I ADJECTIVE
sad
因为失败，他很难过。Yīnwéi shībài, tā hěn nánguò. He was upset by his failure.
II VERB
to be hard to go through
那段时间很难过。Nàduàn shíjiān hěn nánguò. Those times were hard to go through.

难看 nánkàn ADJECTIVE
1 ugly
2 ashamed
他的表情很难看。Tā de biǎoqíng hěn nánkàn. He looked ashamed.

难免 nánmiǎn VERB
to be unavoidable
失误是难免的。Shīwù shì nánmiǎn de. Mistakes are unavoidable.

难受 nánshòu VERB
1 to not feel well
她生病了，很难受。Tā shēngbìng le, hěn nánshòu. She doesn't feel well.
2 to feel down
他心情不好，很难受。Tā xīnqíng bùhǎo, hěn nánshòu. He's feeling down.

脑 nǎo NOUN
1 brain
2 head
3 leader
■ 首脑 shǒunǎo head

脑袋 nǎodai NOUN
head

脑子 nǎozi NOUN
brain

闹 nào
I ADJECTIVE
noisy
II VERB
to have a row
闹别扭 nào bièniu to fall out

闹钟 nàozhōng NOUN
alarm clock

呢 ne AUXILIARY WORD
LANGUAGE TIP 呢 ne is used in questions.
我到底错在哪儿呢？Wǒ dàodǐ cuò zài nǎr ne? What did I actually do wrong?
LANGUAGE TIP 呢 ne is also used to state facts or give information.
离北京还远着呢。Lí Běijīng hái yuǎnzhe ne. Beijing is still quite far.
LANGUAGE TIP 呢 ne is used in sentences to mean **still**.
老师还在办公室呢。Lǎoshī hái zài bàngōngshì ne. The teacher is still in the office.
LANGUAGE TIP 呢 ne is added to the end of a statement to form a tentative question or to indicate that a response is expected.
你好吗？— 我很好，你呢？Nǐ hǎo ma? — Wǒ hěn hǎo, nǐ ne? How are you? — Fine, and you?

内 nèi NOUN
inside
他在一个月内完成了任务。Tā zài yí gè yuè nèi wánchéngle rènwu. He finished the task within a month.
■ 室内 shìnèi indoor
■ 内地 nèidì mainland China

内部 nèibù ADJECTIVE
internal

内行 neìháng NOUN
expert

内容 nèiróng NOUN
content

内向 nèixiàng ADJECTIVE
introverted

他性格内向。Tā xìnggé nèixiàng. He's an introvert.

能 néng
I NOUN
1 ability
2 energy
■能量 néngliàng
II ADJECTIVE capable
III VERB
to be able to

LANGUAGE TIP 能 néng is used to express physical ability.

我能跑得很快。Wǒ néng pǎo de hěn kuài. I can run very fast.

LANGUAGE TIP 能 néng can also be used to express being able to do something because you have been granted permission.

你能/可以借我的照相机。Nǐ néng/kěyǐ jiè wǒ de zhàoxiàngjī. You can borrow my camera.

能干 nénggàn ADJECTIVE
capable
能够 nénggòu VERB
to be able to
能力 nénglì NOUN
ability
能源 néngyuán NOUN
energy

泥 ní NOUN
mud
■泥土 nítǔ clay

你 nǐ PRONOUN
1 you
2 your
你家有几口人？Nǐ jiā yǒu jǐ kǒu rén? How many people are there in your family?
你们 nǐmen PRONOUN
you *pl*
你好 nǐhǎo INTERJECTION
hello

LANGUAGE TIP 你好 nǐhǎo is the most common way to say **hello** in Chinese.

年 nián
I NOUN
1 year
2 New Year
3 age
II ADJECTIVE
annual
年代 niándài NOUN
period
年级 niánjí NOUN
year
他在三年级。Tā zài sān niánjí. He is in his third year of studying.
年纪 niánjì NOUN
age
年龄 niánlíng NOUN
age
年轻 niánqīng ADJECTIVE
young

念 niàn VERB
1 to read
2 to study
念书 niànshū VERB
to study
念头 niàntou NOUN
idea
他打消了放弃的念头。Tā dǎxiāo le fàngqì de niàntou. He dispelled the idea of giving up.

鸟 niǎo NOUN
bird

您 nín PRONOUN
you *(polite form)*
您慢走！ Nín màn zǒu! Mind how you go!

宁 níng ADJECTIVE
▷ *see also* nìng
peaceful
■宁静 níngjìng tranquil

柠 níng
▷ *see below:*
柠檬 níngméng NOUN
lemon

宁 nìng ADVERB
▷ *see also* níng
■宁愿 nìngyuàn would rather

牛 niú NOUN
1 cow
■公牛 gōngniú bull
2 beef
■牛肉 niúròu beef
牛奶 niúnǎi NOUN
milk
牛仔裤 niúzǎikù NOUN
jeans *pl*

纽 niǔ NOUN
button
■纽扣 niǔkòu button

纽约 Niǔyuē NOUN
New York

农 nóng NOUN
1 agriculture
2 farmer
农场 nóngchǎng NOUN
farm
农村 nóngcūn NOUN
countryside
农历 nónglì NOUN
lunar calendar
农民 nóngmín NOUN
farmer
农业 nóngyè NOUN
agriculture

浓 nóng ADJECTIVE
1 strong *(of a flavour, smell etc)*
2 thick *(of smoke, fog etc)*
3 great
他对语言有很浓的兴趣。Tā duì yǔyán yǒu hěn nóng de xìngqù. He has a great interest in languages.

努 nǔ VERB
to make an effort
我们再努把力。Wǒmen zài nǔ bǎ lì. Let's make one last effort.
努力 nǔlì VERB
to try hard
我会尽最大努力。Wǒ huì jìn zuìdà nǔlì. I'll try my very best.

怒 nù
I ADJECTIVE
angry
■ 恼怒 nǎonù furious
II NOUN
anger
■ 发怒 fānù to lose one's temper

女 nǚ NOUN
1 woman
女演员 nǚyǎnyuán actress
2 daughter
■ 子女 zǐnǚ children *pl*
女儿 nǚ'ér NOUN
daughter
女 nǚháir NOUN
girl
女孩子 nǚháizi NOUN
girl
女朋友 nǚpéngyou NOUN
girlfriend
女人 nǚrén NOUN
woman
女士 nǚshì NOUN
1 Ms

LANGUAGE TIP In Chinese, titles such as **Mr**, **Mrs**, **Miss** and **Ms** come after the surname.

王女士 Wáng nǚshì Ms Wang
2 lady
女婿 nǚxu NOUN
son-in-law

暖 nuǎn
I ADJECTIVE
warm
II VERB
to warm up
暖和 nuǎnhuo
I ADJECTIVE
warm
II VERB
to warm up
暖气 nuǎnqì NOUN
heating

挪 nuó VERB
to move
■ 挪动 nuódòng to move

Oo

哦 ó INTERJECTION
▷ *see also* ò
oh

LANGUAGE TIP 哦 ó is used to express surprise, doubt etc.

哦，他也来了。Ó, tā yě láile. Oh, he's come too.

哦 ò INTERJECTION
▷ *see also* ó
oh

LANGUAGE TIP 哦 ò is used to express understanding.

哦，我明白了。Ò, wǒ míngbai le. Oh, now I understand.

欧 ōu NOUN
Europe
■ 欧洲 Ōuzhōu Europe

欧元 ōuyuán NOUN
euro

呕 ǒu VERB
to vomit

呕吐 ǒutù VERB
to vomit

偶 ǒu NOUN
1 image
■ 木偶 mù'ǒu puppet
2 even number
■ 偶数 ǒushù even number

偶尔 ǒu'ěr ADVERB
occasionally

偶然 ǒurán ADJECTIVE
chance

偶然一次，我遇见了她。Ǒurán yícìwǒ yùjiàn le tā. I once bumped into her by chance.

Pp

爬 pá VERB
to climb
爬山 páshān to climb a mountain

怕 pà VERB
1 to fear
她怕老鼠。Tā pà lǎoshǔ. She's scared of mice.
2 to be afraid
我怕我会迟到。Wǒ pà wǒ huì chídào. I'm afraid that I might be late.

拍 pāi VERB
1 to pat *(back, head, shoulder)*
我拍了他一下。Wǒ pāi le tā yíxià. I patted him.
2 to shoot
拍照片 pāi zhàopiàn to take a photo
3 to flatter
拍马屁 pāimǎpì to suck up to

拍子 pāizi
I NOUN
bat
网球拍子 wǎngqiú pāizi tennis racket
II VERB
to beat

排 pái MEASURE WORD
row

排毒 pái dú VERB
to detox

排队 páiduì VERB
to queue

排球 páiqiú NOUN
volleyball

牌 pái NOUN
1 card
■ 扑克牌 pūkèpái playing cards
2 board
■ 车牌 chēpái number plate
3 brand
■ 名牌 míngpái famous brand

派 pài VERB
to send
我的老板派我去法国。Wǒde lǎobǎn pài wǒ qù Fǎguó. My boss sent me to France on business.

派对 pàiduì NOUN
party

盘 pán NOUN
tray

盘子 pánzi NOUN
plate

判 pàn VERB
to judge

判断 pànduàn VERB
to judge

旁 páng NOUN
side

旁边 pángbiān NOUN
side
超市在我家的旁边。Chāoshì zài wǒ jiā de pángbiān. The supermarket is next to my house.

胖 pàng ADJECTIVE
fat

抛 pāo VERB
to throw

抛弃 pāoqì VERB
to abandon

跑 pǎo VERB
1 to run
2 to escape
小偷跑了。Xiǎotōu pǎo le. The thief ran off.

跑步 pǎobù VERB
to run

泡 pào
I NOUN
1 bubble
2 blister

LANGUAGE TIP 泡 pào can describe things in the shape of a bubble.
■ 灯泡 dēngpào light bulb

II VERB
1 to soak
泡衣服 pào yīfu to soak clothes
2 to infuse
泡茶 pào chá to make tea

炮 pào NOUN
1 cannon
2 firecracker

陪 péi VERB
to accompany
我要陪母亲去医院。Wǒ yào péi mǔqīn qù yīyuàn. I will go to the hospital with my mother.

培 péi VERB
to foster
培训 péixùn VERB
to train

赔 péi VERB
to make a loss
他的生意赔了。Tāde shēngyì péi le. His business made a loss.
赔偿 péicháng VERB
to compensate

喷 pēn VERB
to gush
喷泉 pēnquán NOUN
fountain
喷嚏 pēntì NOUN
sneeze

盆 pén NOUN
basin
■ 脸盆 liǎnpén washbasin

朋 péng NOUN
friend
朋友 péngyou NOUN
friend

碰 pèng VERB
1 to touch
他碰了我一下。Tā pèng le wǒ yíxià. He touched me.
2 to bump into
碰到了老同学 pèng dào le lǎo tóngxué to bump into an old classmate
碰见 pèngjiàn VERB
to run into *(acquaintances)*
碰巧 pèngqiǎo ADVERB
by chance

批 pī
I VERB
to criticize
■ 批评 pīpíng to criticize
II MEASURE WORD
group
一批毕业生 yì pī bìyèshēng a group of graduates

皮 pí
I NOUN
1 skin
2 leather
3 peel *(of vegetables, fruit)*
II ADJECTIVE
naughty
这孩子太皮了！Zhè háizi tài pí le! This child is really naughty!
皮包 píbāo NOUN
leather handbag
皮肤 pífū NOUN
skin

啤 pí
▷ *see below:*
啤酒 píjiǔ NOUN
beer

脾 pí NOUN
spleen
脾气 píqi NOUN
1 temper
发脾气 fā píqì to lose one's temper
2 temperament
脾气很坏 píqì hěn huài bad tempered

匹 pǐ MEASURE WORD
LANGUAGE TIP This is a measure word used for horses, camels, wolves etc.
三匹马 sān pǐ mǎ three horses

屁 pì NOUN
wind
■ 放屁 fàngpì 1 to fart 2 fart
屁股 pìgu NOUN
1 bottom
2 rear
车的屁股 chē de pìgu rear of a car

篇 piān MEASURE WORD
LANGUAGE TIP This is a measure word used for articles, essays etc.
三篇文章 sān piān wénzhāng three articles

便 pián
▷ *see also* biàn
▷ *see below:*

便宜 piányi ADJECTIVE
cheap

片 piàn MEASURE WORD

LANGUAGE TIP This is a measure word used for flat objects that are in pieces, for example paper, leaves, bread, sliced meat, snowflakes. It is also used for an expanse of land or water, and for scenery, weather and mood.

两片药 liǎng piàn yào two tablets

骗 piàn VERB
to deceive

骗子 piànzi NOUN
swindler

漂 piāo VERB
▷ *see also* piào
1 to float
2 to drift

票 piào NOUN
ticket
■ 电影票 diànyǐng piào cinema ticket

漂 piào
▷ *see also* piāo
▷ *see below:*

漂亮 piàoliang ADJECTIVE
1 good-looking
2 wonderful
工作做的漂亮！gōngzuò zuò de piàoliàng! You've done a wonderful job!

拼 pīn VERB
to spell *(words)*
你能拼一下这个词吗？Nǐ néng pīn yixià zhègè cí ma? Can you spell this word?

拼音 pīnyīn NOUN
Pinyin

LANGUAGE TIP This is the phonetic system of Mandarin Chinese used in mainland China.

贫 pín ADJECTIVE
poor

贫穷 pínqióng ADJECTIVE
poor

频 pín ADVERB
frequently

频率 pínlǜ NOUN
frequency

品 pǐn NOUN
1 article
■ 商品 shāngpǐn merchandise
2 character
■ 品德 pǐndé moral character

乒 pīng NOUN
table tennis

乒乓球 pīngpāngqiú NOUN
table tennis

平 píng ADJECTIVE
1 flat
■ 平原 píngyuán plain
2 calm
■ 平静 píngjìng calm
3 even
■ 平均 píngjūn average

平方 píngfāng NOUN
square

平方米 píngfāngmǐ NOUN
square metre

平时 píngshí ADVERB
usually
我平时不抽烟。Wǒ píngshí bù chōuyān. I don't usually smoke.

评 píng VERB
to criticize
■ 评论 pínglùn to comment on

苹 píng
▷ *see below:*

苹果 píngguǒ NOUN
apple

瓶 píng NOUN
bottle

瓶子 píngzi NOUN
bottle

破 pò ADJECTIVE
1 broken
皮破了。Pí pò le. The skin has broken.
2 worn
这件衣服很破。Zhè jiàn yīfu hěn pò. This piece of clothing is completely worn out.

破坏 pòhuài VERB
to destroy
■ 破坏环境 pòhuài huànjìng to damage the environment

扑 pū
▷ *see below:*
扑克 pūkè NOUN
poker

铺 pū VERB
▷ *see also* pù
to spread
■ 铺床 pūchuáng to make the bed

葡 pú
▷ *see below:*
葡萄 pútao NOUN
grape

普 pǔ ADJECTIVE
general
普通 pǔtōng ADJECTIVE
common
普通话 pǔtōnghuà NOUN
standard Mandarin

铺 pù NOUN
▷ *see also* pū
plank bed
■ 上铺 shàngpù upper berth

Qq

七 qī NUMBER
seven
七月 Qīyuè NOUN
July

妻 qī NOUN
wife
■ 未婚妻 wèihūnqī fiancée
妻子 qīzǐ NOUN
wife

柒 qī NUMBER
seven
LANGUAGE TIP This is the complex character for **seven**, which is mainly used in banks, on receipts etc to prevent mistakes and forgery.

期 qī
I NOUN
1 time limit
■ 到期 dàoqī to expire
2 period of time
■ 假期 jiàqī holiday
II MEASURE WORD
1 class
一期培训班 yīqī péixùnbān a training course
2 issue
一期杂志 yìqī zázhì a magazine
III VERB
to expect
期待 qīdài VERB
to await
LANGUAGE TIP 期待 qīdài can be used at the end of Chinese emails:
很期待您的回复。Hěn qīdài nín de huífù. I look forward to your response.
期间 qījiān NOUN
period of time
期望 qīwàng
I NOUN
expectations *pl*
II VERB
to expect

欺 qī VERB
1 to deceive
2 to bully
欺负 qīfu VERB
to bully
欺骗 qīpiàn VERB
to deceive

齐 qí
I ADJECTIVE
1 neat
■ 整齐 zhěngqí neat
2 joint
■ 齐声 qíshēng chorus
3 ready
■ 齐备 qíbèi ready
II VERB
1 to reach
人都到齐了。Rén dōu dào qí le. Everyone has arrived.
2 to level
把小树齐着根砍断 bǎ xiǎoshù qízhe gēn kǎnduàn to cut the small trees at their roots
III ADVERB
at the same time
■ 齐唱 qíchàng to sing in unison

其 qí PRONOUN
LANGUAGE TIP 其 qí is used in written Chinese to translate the possessive pronouns **his**, **her**, **its**, **their**.
他是演员，其父也是演员。Tā shì yǎnyuán, qí fù yě shì yǎnyuán. He's an actor, and his father is also an actor.
LANGUAGE TIP 其 qí is used in written Chinese to translate the object pronouns **him**, **her**, **it**, **them**.
劝其戒烟。Quàn qí jièyān. Urge him to give up smoking.
LANGUAGE TIP 其 qí is used in written Chinese to translate the pronoun **that**.
是否真有其事？Shìfǒu zhēn yǒu qí shì? Could that be true?

其次 qícì PRONOUN
next
其次要做的事是什么？Qícì yào zuò de shì shì shénme? What do we have to do next?
1 the second

其实 qíshí ADVERB
actually

其他 qítā PRONOUN
other
我不知道，你问其他人吧。Wǒ bù zhīdào, nǐ wèn qítā rén ba. I don't know, ask someone else. 还有其他事情没有？Háiyǒu qítā shìqing méiyǒu? Is there anything else?

其余 qíyú PRONOUN
the rest

其中 qízhōng NOUN
among which
他有六套西服，其中两套是黑色的。Tā yǒu liù tào xīfú, qízhōng liǎng tào shì hēisè de. He has six suits, of which two are black.

奇 qí
I ADJECTIVE
1 strange
■ 奇闻 qíwén fantastic story
■ 奇事 qíshì miracle
2 unexpected
■ 奇袭 qíxí surprise attack
■ 奇遇 qíyù lucky encounter
II VERB
to surprise
■ 惊奇 jīngqí to surprise
III ADVERB
unusually
■ 奇贵 qíguì unusually expensive

奇怪 qíguài ADJECTIVE
strange

奇迹 qíjì NOUN
miracle

骑 qí
I VERB
to ride

LANGUAGE TIP 骑 qí is only used in the context of horses, bicycles or other vehicles that you can ride. For cars, trains and buses use 坐 zuò or 乘 chéng.

II NOUN
cavalry

棋 qí NOUN
chess
■ 围棋 wéiqí the game of go *(board game)*

旗 qí NOUN
flag
■ 国旗 guóqí national flag

旗袍 qípáo NOUN
cheongsam *(a Chinese-style dress)*

旗子 qízi NOUN
flag

乞 qǐ VERB
to beg
■ 行乞 xíngqǐ to go begging

乞丐 qǐgài NOUN
beggar

乞求 qǐqiú VERB
to beg

企 qǐ VERB
to look forward to
■ 企盼 qǐpàn to look forward to

企图 qǐtú
I VERB
to attempt *(used in pejorative circumstances)*
她企图影响我的工作。Tā qǐtú yǐngxiǎng wǒ de gōngzuò. She tried to affect my work.
II NOUN
attempt
■ 谋杀企图 móushā qǐtú an assassination attempt

企业 qǐyè NOUN
enterprise

启 qǐ VERB
1 to open
■ 开启 kāiqǐ to open
2 to enlighten
3 to start

启发 qǐfā
I VERB
to inspire
II NOUN
inspiration

起 qǐ
I VERB
1 to rise
■ 起立 qǐlì to stand up
2 to remove
起罐头 qǐ guàntou to open the tin can
3 to form
脚上起泡 jiǎoshang qǐ pào a blister forms on one's foot
4 to become
■ 起皱 qǐzhòu to wrinkle
5 to sketch out
■ 起草 qǐcǎo to draft

II MEASURE WORD

LANGUAGE TIP This is a measure word used for accidents.

一起交通事故 yì qǐ jiāotōng shìgù a traffic accident 一起火灾 yì qǐ huǒzāi a fire

起床 qǐchuáng VERB
to get up

起点 qǐdiǎn NOUN
starting point

起飞 qǐfēi VERB
to take off
飞机准时起飞。Fēijī zhǔnshí qǐfēi. The plane took off on time.

起来 qǐlái VERB
to get up
他今天早上六点就起来了。Tā jīntiān zǎoshàng liùdiǎn jiù qǐlái le. Today he got up at 6 o'clock in the morning. 站起来 zhàn qǐlái to stand up

起源 qǐyuán NOUN
origin
■ 生命的起源 shēngmìng de qǐyuán the origin of life

气 qì

I NOUN

1 gas
■ 毒气 dúqì poison gas

2 air
这球没气了。Zhè qiú méi qì le. There's no air in the ball.

3 breath

4 mood
■ 英雄的气概 yīngxióng de qìgài spirit of a hero

5 to smell
■ 臭气 chòuqì stink

6 manner
■ 孩子气 háiziqì childishness

7 anger
■ 气愤 qìfèn anger

8 qi *(medicine)*

II VERB

1 to be angry

2 to provoke

气氛 qìfēn NOUN
atmosphere

气功 qìgōng NOUN
qigong

DID YOU KNOW...?
气功 qìgōng is an ancient Chinese system of postures, breathing exercises and meditations to improve one's 气 qì or **body's energy flow**.

气候 qìhòu NOUN
climate

气温 qìwēn NOUN
temperature

气象 qìxiàng NOUN

1 weather
观察气象 guānchá qìxiàng to observe the weather

2 meteorology
■ 气象学 qìxiàngxué meteorology

汽 qì NOUN

1 vapour

2 steam

汽车 qìchē NOUN
car
■ 公共汽车 gōnggòng qìchē bus

汽水 qìshuǐ NOUN
fizzy drink

汽油 qìyóu NOUN
petrol

器 qì NOUN

1 utensil
■ 乐器 yuèqì musical instrument
■ 瓷器 cíqì porcelain

2 organ

器官 qìguān NOUN
organ

恰 qià ADVERB

1 appropriately

2 exactly

恰当 qiàdàng ADJECTIVE
appropriate

恰好 qiàhǎo ADVERB
luckily

千 qiān

I NUMBER
thousand

II ADJECTIVE
many

千万 qiānwàn

I NUMBER
ten million

II ADVERB
no matter what
你千万别做傻事。Nǐ qiānwàn bié zuò shǎshì. No matter what, don't do anything stupid.

牵 qiān VERB

1 to pull
■ 牵牛 qiānniú to lead a cow

2 to involve
■ 牵扯 qiānchě to involve

铅 qiān NOUN
lead

铅笔 qiānbǐ NOUN
pencil

谦 qiān ADJECTIVE
modest

谦虚 qiānxū
I ADJECTIVE
modest
II VERB
to speak modestly

签 qiān
I VERB
1 to sign
2 to endorse
II NOUN
1 a lot
他抽签而赢了奖。Tā chōuqiān ér yíng le jiǎng. He won the prize draw.
2 label
■ 书签 shūqiān bookmark
3 a stick
■ 牙签 yáqiān toothpick

签名 qiānmíng VERB
to sign one's name

签证 qiānzhèng NOUN
visa

签字 qiānzì VERB
to sign one's name

前 qián
I ADJECTIVE
1 front
2 first
3 former
■ 前夫 qiánfū ex-husband
4 future
II VERB
to advance

前进 qiánjìn VERB
1 to advance
2 to make progress

前面 qiánmian
I ADVERB
in front
II NOUN
front
他衣服的前面很脏。Tā yīfu de qíanmiàn hěn zāng. There was dirt on the front of his clothes.

前年 qiánnián NOUN
the year before last

前天 qiántiān NOUN
the day before yesterday

前头 qiántóu
front

前途 qiántú NOUN
future

前夕 qiánxī NOUN
eve
■ 圣诞节前夕 Shēngdànjié Qiánxī Christmas Eve

钱 qián NOUN
money

钱包 qiánbāo NOUN
wallet

浅 qiǎn ADJECTIVE
1 shallow
水很浅。Shuǐ hěn qiǎn. The water is very shallow.
2 easy
■ 浅显 qiǎnxiǎn easy to understand
3 light
浅蓝色 qiǎnlánsè light blue
浅绿色 qiǎnlǜsè light green

欠 qiàn VERB
1 to owe
■ 欠钱 qiànqián to owe money
2 to lack
■ 欠缺 qiànquē to lack
3 to raise... slightly *(from a sitting position)*
他欠了欠身子。Tā qiànleqiàn shēnzi. He rose slightly.

枪 qiāng NOUN
1 spear
2 gun
■ 手枪 shǒuqiāng pistol

强 qiáng
▷ *see also* qiǎng
I ADJECTIVE
1 strong
■ 强壮 qiángzhuàng muscular
2 able
坚强 jiānqiáng tough
3 better
姐姐比妹妹各方面都强。Jiějie bǐ mèimei gè fāngmiàn dōu qiáng. The older sister is better than the younger sister in every respect.
4 extra
三分之一强 sān fēn zhī yī qiáng a third extra
II VERB
to force
强人所难 qiáng rén suǒ nán to force someone to do something against their will

强大 qiángdà ADJECTIVE
powerful

强盗 qiángdào NOUN
robber

强调 qiángdiào VERB
to emphasize

强度 qiángdù NOUN
intensity

强奸 qiángjiān VERB
to rape

强烈 qiángliè ADJECTIVE
intense

墙 qiáng NOUN
wall

抢 qiǎng VERB
1 to rob
抢银行 qiǎng yínháng to rob a bank
2 to grab
■ 抢夺 qiǎngduó pillage
3 to forestall
■ 抢先 qiǎngxiān to get a head start
4 to rush
■ 抢救 qiǎngjiù to save

抢劫 qiǎngjié VERB
to rob

强 qiǎng VERB
▷ *see also* qiáng
1 to make an effort
■ 勉强 miǎnqiǎng to manage to do something with difficulty
2 to force

强迫 qiǎngpò VERB
to force

悄 qiāo
▷ *see below:*

悄悄 qiāoqiāo ADVERB
1 quietly
■ 静悄悄 jìngqiāoqiāo quietly
2 stealthily
她悄悄溜走了。Tā qiāoqiāo liūzǒu le.
She stealthily slipped away.

敲 qiāo VERB
1 to knock
■ 敲门 qiāomén to knock on the door
2 to blackmail

敲诈 qiāozhà VERB
to extort

桥 qiáo NOUN
bridge

桥梁 qiáoliáng NOUN
bridge

瞧 qiáo VERB
to look

巧 qiǎo ADJECTIVE
1 nimble
■ 手巧 shǒuqiǎo dexterous
2 skilful
■ 巧计 qiǎojì scheme
3 coincidental
■ 恰巧 qiàqiǎo by coincidence

巧克力 qiǎokèlì NOUN
chocolate

巧妙 qiǎomiào ADJECTIVE
clever

切 qiē VERB
to cut

茄 qié NOUN
aubergine

茄子 qiézi NOUN
aubergine

窃 qiè
I VERB
to steal
II ADVERB
surreptitiously

窃听 qiètīng VERB
to eavesdrop

窃贼 qièzéi NOUN
thief

侵 qīn VERB
to invade

侵略 qīnlüè VERB
to invade

亲 qīn
I NOUN
1 parent
2 relative
3 marriage
■ 定亲 dìngqīn engagement
4 bride
■ 娶亲 qǔqīn to marry a bride
II ADJECTIVE
1 blood
■ 亲缘 qīnyuán consanguinity
2 intimate
她俩像亲姐妹。Tāliǎ xiàng qīn jiěmèi.
Those two are as close as sisters.
III ADVERB
personally

IV VERB
1 to kiss
2 to be close to

亲爱 qīn'ài ADJECTIVE
dear

亲爱的 qīn'ài de NOUN
darling *(an affectionate term of address)*

亲近 qīnjìn ADJECTIVE
close

亲密 qīnmì ADJECTIVE
close
亲密朋友 qīnmì péngyǒu close friend 亲密无间 qīnmì wújiàn to be on very intimate terms

亲戚 qīnqi NOUN
relative

亲切 qīnqiè ADJECTIVE
affectionate

亲热 qīnrè ADJECTIVE
affectionate

亲自 qīnzì ADVERB
personally

琴 qín NOUN
musical instrument
■ 钢琴 gāngqín piano
■ 小提琴 xiǎotíqín violin

勤 qín

I ADJECTIVE
hard-working

II ADVERB
regularly
小朋友一定要勤洗手。Xiǎopéngyǒu yídìng yào qín xǐshǒu. Kids must wash their hands regularly.

III NOUN
1 duty
■ 值勤 zhíqín to be on duty
2 attendance
■ 考勤 kǎoqín to check attendance

勤奋 qínfèn ADJECTIVE
diligent

勤劳 qínláo ADJECTIVE
hard-working

青 qīng

I ADJECTIVE
1 green
■ 青草 qīngcǎo green grass
■ 青菜 qīngcài green vegetable
2 black
他的脸上青一块，紫一块。Tāde liǎnshàng qīng yíkuài, zǐ yíkuài. His face was bruised black and purple.
3 young

II NOUN
1 grass
2 unripe crops *pl*

青年 qīngnián NOUN
youth

青少年 qīngshàonián NOUN
teenager

轻 qīng

I ADJECTIVE
1 light
这个包很轻。Zhège bāo hěn qīng. This bag is very light.
2 young
他们年纪很轻。Tāmen niánjì hěn qīng. They are quite young.
3 not important
4 relaxed
■ 轻音乐 qīngyīnyuè light music

II ADVERB
1 gently
2 rashly

III VERB
to disparage
■ 看轻 kànqīng to underestimate

轻松 qīngsōng ADJECTIVE
relaxing

轻易 qīngyì ADVERB
1 easily
轻易做到 qīngyì zuòdào easy to do
2 rashly
轻易答应 qīngyì dāying to rashly agree to

倾 qīng

I VERB
1 to lean
■ 倾斜 qīngxié tilted
2 to collapse
3 to empty out
4 to exhaust

II NOUN
tendency

倾向 qīngxiàng

I VERB
to be inclined to
他倾向于喝酒。Tā qīngxiàng yú hējuǐ. He is inclined to drink.

II NOUN
tendency

清 qīng

I ADJECTIVE
1 clear
■ 清水 qīngshuǐ clear water
2 quiet
3 distinct

■ 分清 fēnqīng distinguish

II VERB

1 to get rid of

■ 清除 qīngchú to get rid of

2 to put in order

■ 清理 qīnglǐ to put in order

清楚 qīngchu

I ADJECTIVE

clear

II VERB

to understand

清洁 qīngjié ADJECTIVE

clean

清静 qīngjìng ADJECTIVE

quiet

清明节 Qīngmíng Jié NOUN

Tomb Sweeping Festival

DID YOU KNOW...?

清明节 Qīngmíng Jié **Tomb Sweeping Festival**, sometimes translated literally as **Clear and Bright Festival**, is celebrated on the 4th, 5th or 6th of April. It is traditionally the time when Chinese families visit graves to honour their dead ancestors.

情 qíng NOUN

1 feeling

■ 热情 rèqíng warmth

2 kindness

3 love

4 condition

■ 实情 shíqíng true state of affairs

情节 qíngjié NOUN

1 plot

戏剧情节 xìjù qíngjié the plot of the play

2 circumstances *pl*

有些情节还弄不清楚。Yǒuxiē qíngjié hái nòng bù qīngchu. There are some circumstances that are still unclear.

情景 qíngjǐng NOUN

sight

情况 qíngkuàng NOUN

situation

情侣 qínglǚ NOUN

lovers *pl*

情人节 Qíngrén Jié NOUN

Valentine's Day

DID YOU KNOW...?

In China, Valentine's day is celebrated twice, once on the western-imported 14th of February and once on the 7th of July in the Chinese calendar. Chinese people call the second Valentine's day 七夕 Qī xī.

情书 qíngshū NOUN

love letter

情形 qíngxíng NOUN

situation

情绪 qíngxù NOUN

1 mood

情绪不佳 qíngxù bùjiā a bad mood

2 moodiness

他正在跟老师闹情绪。Tā zhèngzài gēn lǎoshī nào qíngxù. He is venting in front of the teacher.

晴 qíng ADJECTIVE

fine

晴朗 qínglǎng ADJECTIVE

sunny

请 qǐng VERB

1 to ask

请他进来。Qǐng tā jìnlai. Ask him to come in.

2 to invite

3 *(formal)*

请这边走。Qǐng zhèbiān zǒu. This way, please. 请大家安静一下。Qǐng dàjiā ānjìng yíxià. Everyone quiet, please.

请假 qǐngjià VERB

to ask for a leave

请教 qǐngjiào VERB

to consult

请客 qǐngkè VERB

to treat

请求 qǐngqiú VERB

to ask

请问 qǐngwèn VERB

excuse me *(generally used before a question)*

请问怎么出去？Qǐngwèn zěnme chūqù? Could you show me the way out, please?

请勿 qǐngwù VERB

please do not...

请勿吸烟。Qǐngwù xīyān. No smoking.

庆 qìng

I VERB

to celebrate

II NOUN

festival

■ 国庆 guóqìng National Day

庆贺 qìnghè VERB

to celebrate

庆祝 qìngzhù VERB

to celebrate

穷 qióng

I ADJECTIVE

poor

■ 贫穷 pínqióng poor
II NOUN
limit
III ADVERB
thoroughly
■ 穷尽 qióngjìn dearth

秋 qiū NOUN
1 autumn
2 harvest time
3 year
秋天 qiūtiān NOUN
autumn

求 qiú
I VERB
1 to request
■ 请求 qǐngqiú to request
2 to strive
■ 追求 zhuīqiú to pursue
II NOUN
demand
要求 yāoqiú a demand

球 qiú NOUN
1 sphere
2 ball
■ 雪球 xuěqiú snowball
■ 篮球 lánqiú basketball
■ 足球 zúqiú football
3 ball game
4 the Earth
■ 全球 quánqiú the whole world
球场 qiúchǎng NOUN
court
球迷 qiúmí NOUN
fan

区 qū
I VERB
to distinguish
II NOUN
1 area
2 region
■ 自治区 zìzhìqū autonomous region
区别 qūbié
I NOUN
difference
II VERB
to distinguish
区分 qūfēn VERB
to differentiate
区域 qūyù NOUN
area

趋 qū VERB
1 to hasten
2 to tend to become
趋势 qūshì NOUN
trend
趋向 qūxiàng
I VERB
to tend to
II NOUN
trend

渠 qú NOUN
ditch
渠道 qúdào NOUN
1 irrigation ditch
挖渠道 wā qúdào to dig an irrigation ditch
2 channel
销售渠道 xiāoshòu qúdào marketing channel

曲 qǔ NOUN
1 song
2 music
曲子 qǔzi NOUN
tune

取 qǔ VERB
1 to take
他明天来取书。Tā míngtiān lái qǔ shū. He will come and pick up the books tomorrow.
2 to obtain
■ 取得 qǔdé to obtain
3 to adopt
■ 采取 cǎiqǔ to adopt
4 to choose
■ 选取 xuǎnqǔ to choose
取消 qǔxiāo VERB
to cancel

娶 qǔ VERB
to marry

去 qù
I VERB
1 to go
2 to get rid of
3 to be apart
4 to send
II ADJECTIVE
past
去年 qùnián NOUN
last year
去世 qùshì VERB
to pass away

趣 qù
I NOUN

interest
■ 志趣 zhìqù interest
II ADJECTIVE
interesting
趣味 qùwèi NOUN
taste

圈 quān
I NOUN
1 circle
■ 北极圈 Běijíquān Arctic Circle
2 social circle
■ 演艺圈 yǎnyì quān entertainment circle
II VERB
to circle
圈套 quāntào NOUN
trap

权 quán
I NOUN
1 power
主动权 zhǔdòng quán initiative
控制权 kòngzhì quán control
■ 当权 dāngquán to be in power
2 right
II ADVERB
for the time being
权力 quánlì NOUN
power

全 quán
I ADJECTIVE
1 complete
2 whole
II ADVERB
entirely
III VERB
to keep... intact
全部 quánbù ADJECTIVE
whole
全面 quánmiàn ADJECTIVE
comprehensive
全体 quántǐ NOUN
everyone

泉 quán NOUN
spring
■ 温泉 wēnquán hot spring

拳 quán NOUN
fist
拳头 quántou NOUN
fist
拳击 quánjī NOUN
boxing

鬈 quán ADJECTIVE
curly

劝 quàn VERB
1 to advise
2 to encourage
劝告 quàngào VERB
to advise

缺 quē
I VERB
1 to lack
■ 缺钱 quēqián to lack money
2 to be incomplete
这张纸币缺了一角。Zhèzhāng zhǐbì quēle yìjiǎo. This bank note is missing a corner.
3 to be absent
还缺三个人没有来开会。Hái quē sānge rén méiyǒu lái kāihuì. There are still three people who are absent from the meeting.
II NOUN
vacancy
■ 补缺 bǔquē fill a vacancy
缺点 quēdiǎn NOUN
shortcoming
缺乏 quēfá VERB
to lack
缺口 quēkǒu NOUN
1 gap
2 shortfall
缺少 quēshǎo VERB
to lack
缺席 quēxí VERB
to be absent
缺陷 quēxiàn NOUN
defect

瘸 qué VERB
to be lame

却 què
I VERB
1 to step back
■ 退却 tuìquè recede
2 to drive... back
3 to decline
■ 推却 tuīquè to decline
■ 冷却 lěngquè to cool off
■ 忘却 wàngquè to forget
II ADVERB
however

确 què ADVERB
1 really
2 firmly
■ 确信 quèxìn firmly believe

确定 quèdìng

I VERB
to determine

II ADJECTIVE
definite

确实 quèshí

I ADJECTIVE
true

II ADVERB
really

裙 qún NOUN
skirt

裙子 qúnzi NOUN
skirt

群 qún

I NOUN
crowd

II MEASURE WORD

1 herd

一群奶牛 yì qún nǎiníu a herd of cows 一群绵羊 yì qún miányáng a flock of sheep 一群蜜蜂 yì qún mìfēng a swarm of bees

2 group

一群学生 yì qún xuésheng a group of students

群众 qúnzhòng NOUN
the masses *pl*

Rr

然 rán PRONOUN
so

然而 rán'ér CONJUNCTION
however

然后 ránhòu CONJUNCTION
afterwards
你先写作业，然后我们一起去吃饭。Nǐ xiān xiě zuòyè, ránhòu wǒmen yìqǐ qù chīfán. Do your homework first, and then we can go and have dinner together.

染 rǎn VERB
to dye
■ 染发 rǎn fà to dye one's hair

让 ràng VERB
1 to make allowances
姐姐要让着妹妹。Jiějiě yào ràngzhe mèimèi. She made allowances for her little sister.
2 to let
老师让我们早点下课。Laǒshī ràng wǒmen zaǒdiǎn xiàkè. Our teacher let us out of class early.
3 to make
他妈妈让他多读书。Tā māmā ràng tā duō dúshū. His mum made him study more.
4 to transfer
■ 转让 zhuǎnràng to transfer

扰 rǎo VERB
to disturb
■ 打扰 dǎrǎo to disturb

热 rè
I NOUN
1 heat
2 fever
■ 发热 fārè to have a fever
II ADJECTIVE
1 hot
今天很热。Jīntiān hěn rè. It's really hot today.
2 popular
今年这个发型很热。Jīnnián zhègè fàxíng hěn rè. This hairstyle is really popular this year.
III VERB
to heat

热爱 rè'ài VERB
to love

热狗 règǒu NOUN
hot dog

热烈 rèliè ADJECTIVE
heated
气氛很热烈。Qìfēn hěn rèliè. The atmosphere is very heated.

热闹 rènào ADJECTIVE
lively

热情 rèqíng
I NOUN
passion
II ADJECTIVE
enthusiastic

热心 rèxīn ADJECTIVE
warm-hearted

人 rén NOUN
1 human being
■ 人权 rénquán human rights *pl*
2 person
■ 军人 jūnrén soldier
■ 中国人 Zhōngguórén 1 A Chinese person 2 Chinese people
3 manpower

人才 réncái NOUN
talent

人工 réngōng ADJECTIVE
man-made

人口 rénkǒu NOUN
population

人类 rénlèi NOUN
mankind

人们 rénmen NOUN
people

人民 rénmín NOUN
the people

人民币 rénmínbì NOUN
Renminbi

LANGUAGE TIP **Renminbi**, the currency of the People's Republic of China (PRC), can be abbreviated to **RMB**.

人生 rénshēng NOUN
life
人生的意义在于永不放弃。Rénshēng de yìyì zàiyú yǒngbúfàngqì. The meaning of life is to never give up.

人体 réntǐ NOUN
the human body

人物 rénwù NOUN
1 figure
2 character

忍 rěn VERB
to endure

忍耐 rěnnài VERB
to show restraint
她一直在忍耐。Tā yìzhí zài rěnnài. She always shows restraint.

忍受 rěnshòu VERB
to endure
她忍受了很多病痛。Tā rěnshòu le hěnduō bìngtòng. She has endured many illnesses.

认 rèn VERB
1 to know
2 to admit

认得 rènde VERB
to be acquainted with

认识 rènshi
I VERB
to know
我认识她。Wǒ rènshi ta. I know her.
II NOUN
understanding
他认识了事情的重要性。Tā rènshi le shìqíng de zhòngyàoxìng. He knows how important the situation is.

认为 rènwéi VERB
to think

认真 rènzhēn
I ADJECTIVE
serious
II VERB
to take... seriously
不要对这件事情太认真。Búyào duì zhèjiàn shìqíng tài rènzhēn. Don't take this thing too seriously.

任 rèn
I VERB
to let
II NOUN
responsibility

任何 rènhé ADJECTIVE
any
任何人都不能迟到。Rènhé rén dōu bù néng chídào. No one can be late.

任务 rènwù NOUN
task

扔 rēng VERB
1 to throw
2 to throw... away

仍 réng ADVERB
still

仍然 réngrán ADVERB
still
他仍然没有回家。Tā réngrán méiyǒu huíjiā. He still hasn't come home.

日 rì NOUN
1 sun
■ 日出 rìchū sunrise
■ 日落 rìluò sunset
2 daytime
3 day
■ 明日 míngrì tomorrow
■ 生日 shēngrì birthday
4 every day
城市面貌日见改善。Chéngshì miànmào rìjiàn gǎishàn. The city looks better every day.

LANGUAGE TIP The character 日 rì represents a pictorial version of the sun and therefore carries the meaning of **sun** or **day**. This character can describe something which happens on a daily basis. It is a basic unit to describe the date.

日报 rìbào NOUN
daily paper

日本 Rìběn NOUN
Japan

日常 rìcháng ADJECTIVE
everyday

日记 rìjì NOUN
diary

日历 rìlì NOUN
calendar

日期 rìqī NOUN
date

日用品 rìyòngpǐn NOUN
daily necessities

日语 Rìyǔ NOUN
Japanese

日元 Rìyuán NOUN
Japanese yen

日子 rìzi NOUN

1 date
今天是什么日子？Jīntiān shì shénme rìzi? What is the date today?
2 day
很多个日子过去了。Hěnduō gè rìzi guòqù le. Many days have passed.
3 life
过安生日子 Guò ānshēng rìzi To live a peaceful life.

荣 róng ADJECTIVE
glorious

荣幸 róngxìng ADJECTIVE
honoured
认识您，我感到非常荣幸。Rènshi nín, wǒ gǎndào fēicháng róngxìng. I feel honoured to know you.

荣誉 róngyù NOUN
honour
他为祖国获得了荣誉。Tā wèi zǔguó huòdé le róngyù. He won honour for his country.

容 róng
I VERB
1 to fit
■ 容纳 róngnà to hold
■ 容量 róngliàng capacity
■ 容器 róngqì container
2 to tolerate
■ 容忍 róngrěn to tolerate
II NOUN
appearance
■ 容貌 róngmào features *pl*

容易 róngyì ADJECTIVE
easy

柔 róu ADJECTIVE
1 soft
2 gentle
■ 温柔 wēnróu gentle

柔软 róuruǎn ADJECTIVE
soft

肉 ròu NOUN
1 flesh *(of humans, fruit)*
果肉 guǒròu flesh *(of fruit)*
2 meat
猪肉 zhūròu pork

如 rú VERB
1 to be like
2 to be as good as
■ 不如 bùrú not as good as

如此 rúcǐ PRONOUN
so
他的态度竟如此恶劣。Tā de tàidù jìng rúcǐ èliè. His attitude was so nasty.

如果 rúguǒ CONJUNCTION
if

如何 rúhé PRONOUN
what
你今后如何打算？Nǐ jīnhòu rúhé dǎsuàn? What are your plans for the future?

入 rù VERB
1 to enter
■ 入场 rùchǎng to enter
2 to join
■ 入学 rùxué to enrol in education

入境 rùjìng VERB
to enter a country

入口 rùkǒu NOUN
entrance

软 ruǎn ADJECTIVE
1 soft
■ 软和 ruǎnhuo soft
2 gentle
3 weak
■ 软弱 ruǎnruò weak

软件 ruǎnjiàn NOUN
software

软卧 ruǎnwò NOUN
light sleeper

软饮料 ruǎnyǐnliào NOUN
soft drink

弱 ruò ADJECTIVE
weak

弱点 ruòdiǎn NOUN
weakness

Ss

撒 sā VERB
to let go
撒谎 sāhuǎng VERB
to lie

洒 sǎ VERB
to sprinkle
别把汤洒了。Bié bǎ tāng sǎ le. Don't spill the soup.

塞 sāi VERB
to stuff... into
塞车 sāichē NOUN
traffic jam
长安街上经常塞车。Cháng'ān jiēshàng jīngcháng sāichē. Roads in Chang'an are often congested.

赛 sài NOUN
match
比赛 bǐsài match

三 sān NUMBER
1 three
■ 三月 sānyuè March
2 third
■ 第三 dìsān the third
三明治 sānmíngzhì NOUN
sandwich

伞 sǎn NOUN
umbrella

散 sàn VERB
to scatter
散步 sànbù VERB
to go for a stroll
我喜欢晚饭后散步。Wǒ xǐhuan wǎnfàn hòu sànbù. I like to go for a stroll after dinner.

桑 sāng
▷ *see below:*
桑拿浴 sāngnáyù NOUN
sauna

嗓 sǎng NOUN
throat
嗓子 sǎngzi NOUN
throat

扫 sǎo VERB
to sweep

嫂 sǎo NOUN
sister-in-law
嫂子 sǎozi NOUN
sister-in-law *(colloquial)*

色 sè NOUN
colour
色盲 sèmáng NOUN
colour blindness

森 sēn ADJECTIVE
wooded
森林 sēnlín NOUN
forest

杀 shā VERB
to kill

沙 shā NOUN
sand
沙发 shāfā NOUN
sofa
沙漠 shāmò NOUN
desert
沙滩 shātān NOUN
beach

傻 shǎ ADJECTIVE
stupid
傻子 shǎzi NOUN
fool

厦 shà NOUN
tall building
■ 大厦 dàshà tall building

晒 shài VERB

1 to shine upon
他被晒黑了。Tā bèi shài hēi le. He's tanned.
2 to lie in the sun
她在沙滩上晒太阳。Tā zài shātān shàng shài tàiyáng. She was sunbathing on the beach.

山 shān NOUN
mountain

DID YOU KNOW...?
山 shān is a good example of a Chinese character that is a pictogram, a stylised drawing of the object that it represents.

闪 shǎn VERB
to flash
闪电 shǎndiàn NOUN
lightning

擅 shàn VERB
to be expert at
擅长 shàncháng VERB
to be skilled in
她很擅长跳舞。Tā hěn shàncháng tiàowǔ. He is very good at dancing.

伤 shāng
I VERB
1 to injure
他打篮球的时候伤了腿。Tā dǎ lánqiú de shíhou shāng le tuǐ. He injured his leg whilst playing basketball.
2 to hurt
II NOUN
injury
伤害 shānghài VERB
1 to hurt *(feelings)*
你的话伤害了他。Nǐ de huà shānghài le tā. What you said hurt his feelings.
2 to damage *(body)*

商 shāng
I VERB
to discuss
■ 商量 shāngliang to discuss 我们明天商量一下旅游的事情吧。Wǒmen míngtiān shāngliang yīxià lǚyóu de shìqing ba. Let's discuss our travel plans tomorrow.
II NOUN
1 commerce
2 business person
■ 商人 shāngrén business person
商场 shāngchǎng NOUN
shopping centre
商店 shāngdiàn NOUN
shop
商量 shāngliang VERB
to discuss
商品 shāngpǐn NOUN
commodity
商人 shāngrén NOUN
businessman
businesswoman
商学院 shāngxuéyuàn NOUN
business school
商业 shāngyè NOUN
commerce

上 shàng
I NOUN
upper part
■ 上星期 shàng xīngqī last week
II VERB
1 to go up
上楼 shànglóu to go upstairs
2 to go
■ 上班 shàngbān to go to work 我每天早上8点上班。Wǒ měitiān zǎoshàng bādiǎn shàngbān. I start work at 8 in the morning every day.
3 to board *(car, boat, plane)*
III PREPOSITION
1 on
椅子上 yǐzi shàng on the chair
2 in
报纸上 bàozhǐ shàng in the newspaper
上帝 Shàngdì NOUN
God
上车 shàngchē VERB
to get into a vehicle
快上车，我们要迟到了。Kuài shàngchē, wǒmen yào chídào le. Hurry up and get in the car, we're going to be late.
上海 Shànghǎi NOUN
Shanghai
上课 shàngkè VERB
to go to class
上网 shàngwǎng VERB
to go online

LANGUAGE TIP Literally, this means **on the net**.

上午 shàngwǔ NOUN
morning
上涨 shàngzhǎng VERB
to rise

烧 shāo VERB
1 to burn
2 to heat
3 to have a temperature

烧烤 shāokǎo VERB
to barbecue

勺 sháo NOUN
ladle

少 shǎo
▷ *see also* shào
I ADJECTIVE
few
屋里家具太少。Wū lǐ jiājù tài shǎo. There is very little furniture in the room.
II VERB
to lack
汤里少了葱。Tāng lǐ shǎo le cōng. There is no onion in the soup.

少数民族 shǎoshù mínzú NOUN
ethnic minorities

DID YOU KNOW...?
少数民族 shǎoshù mínzú refers to China's ethnic minorities. There are 56 distinct ethnic groups in China, of which the Han is by far the largest, accounting for over 90% of the population. The other 55 minorities are mainly located in the southwestern and northwestern provinces. Five regions have been set up as ethnic minority autonomous regions.

少 shào ADJECTIVE
▷ *see also* shǎo
young
■ 少女 shàonǚ young girl

舌 shé NOUN
tongue

舌头 shétou NOUN
tongue

折 shé VERB
▷ *see also* zhé
to break
他的腿折了。Tāde tuǐ shé le. His leg is broken.

蛇 shé NOUN
snake

设 shè VERB
to plan

设计 shèjì VERB
to design

社 shè NOUN
organization
■ 旅行社 lǚxíngshè travel agent

社会 shèhuì NOUN
society

社交 shèjiāo NOUN
social contact
他不喜欢社交，只喜欢看书。Tā bù xǐhuan shèjiāo, zhǐ xǐhuan kàn shū. He doesn't enjoy socialising, all he likes to do is read.

舍 shè NOUN
house
■ 宿舍 sùshè dormitory

谁 shéi PRONOUN
▷ *see also* shuí
who
他是谁？Tā shì sheí? Who is he?

LANGUAGE TIP 谁 has two official pronunciations, shéi and shuí. Shéi is the more colloquial pronunciation and therefore more commonly heard in native Mandarin speaking areas. Shuí is the more formal, literary pronunciation.

申 shēn VERB
to express

申请 shēnqǐng VERB
to apply

伸 shēn VERB
to stretch

伸手 shēnshǒu VERB
to hold out one's hand

身 shēn NOUN
body

身材 shēncái NOUN
figure

身份证 shēnfènzhèng NOUN
identity card

身体 shēntǐ NOUN
1 body
2 health
你身体怎么样？Nǐshēntǐ zěnmeyàng? How's your health? 你父母的身体怎么样？Nǐ fùmǔ de shēntǐ zěnmeyàng? How are your parents doing?

绅 shēn NOUN
gentry

绅士 shēnshì NOUN
gentleman

深 shēn

I ADJECTIVE
1 deep
2 difficult
3 dark
深蓝 shēnlán dark blue
II NOUN
depth

什 shén
▷ *see below:*

什么 shénme PRONOUN
1 what
你要什么？Nǐ yào shénme? What do you want?
2 something
我想吃点儿什么。Wǒ xiǎng chī diǎnr shénme. I want to eat something.
3 anything
我什么都不怕。Wǒ shénme dōu búpà. I'm not afraid of anything.
4 what
什么！他不来了？Shénme! Tā bù lái le? What! He isn't coming?

什么的 shénmede PRONOUN
and so on
桌子上放着香蕉、李子、苹果什么的。Zhuōzi shàng fàngzhe xiāngjiāo, lǐzi, píngguǒ shénme de. The table was loaded with bananas, plums, apples and so on.

神 shén NOUN
god

神经 shénjīng NOUN
nerve
他得了腰部神经错位。Tā déle yāobù shénjīng cuòwèi. He has a trapped nerve in his lower back.

神秘 shénmì ADJECTIVE
mysterious

肾 shèn NOUN
kidney

甚 shèn
I ADJECTIVE
extreme
II ADVERB
very

甚至 shènzhì ADVERB
even
他工作太多，甚至常常忘了吃饭。Tā gōngzuò tài duō, shènzhì chángcháng wàng le chīfàn. He works too much, so much so that he often forgets to eat.

生 shēng
I VERB
1 to give birth to
生孩子 shēng háizi to have a baby
2 to live
3 to get
■ 生病 shēngbìng to get ill 他今天生病了。Tā jīntiān shēngbìng le. He is sick today.
II ADJECTIVE
1 unripe
这些葡萄还是生的。Zhèxiē pútao hái shì shēng de. These grapes aren't ripe yet.
2 raw
中国人不喜欢吃生肉。Zhōngguórén bù xǐhuan chī shēngròu. Chinese people don't like eating raw meat.

生产 shēngchǎn VERB
to produce

生活 shēnghuó
I NOUN
life
II VERB
to live
他在上海生活了八年。Tā zài Shànghǎi shēnghuó le bā nián. He has lived in Shanghai for eight years.

生气 shēngqì VERB
to get angry
你生气了吗？Nǐ shēngqì le ma? Are you angry?

生日 shēngrì NOUN
birthday

生意 shēngyi NOUN
business
他在美国做生意。Tā zài Měiguó zuò shēngyi. He is doing business in America.

声 shēng NOUN
1 sound
2 reputation
■ 声誉 shēngyù fame
3 tone *(of Chinese phonetics)*

声调 shēngdiào NOUN
tone

声音 shēngyīn NOUN
1 voice
2 sound

绳 shéng NOUN
rope

绳子 shéngzi NOUN
rope

省 shěng
I VERB
to save

省钱 shěng qián to save money

II NOUN
province

省会 shěnghuì NOUN
provincial capital

圣 shèng ADJECTIVE
holy

■ 圣诞节 Shèngdàn Jié Christmas

圣诞 Shèngdàn NOUN
Christmas

圣经 Shèngjīng NOUN
the Bible

剩 shèng VERB
to be left

■ 剩下 shèngxià to remain 我吃了昨天剩下的菜。Wǒ chī le zuótiān shèngxià de cài. I ate yesterday's leftovers.

失 shī VERB
1 to lose

■ 失去 shīqù to lose 他失去了一个很好的工作机会。Tā shīqù le yígè hěnhǎo de gōngzuò jīhuì. He lost a very good work opportunity.

2 to fail

失败 shībài VERB
to fail

失望 shīwàng

I ADJECTIVE
disappointed

我不会让你失望。Wǒ búhuì ràng nǐ shīwàng. I won't let you down.

II VERB
to lose hope

失业 shīyè VERB
to be unemployed

师 shī NOUN
teacher

师傅 shīfu NOUN
master

诗 shī NOUN
poetry

诗人 shīrén NOUN
poet

狮 shī
▷ *see below:*

狮子 shīzi NOUN
lion

湿 shī ADJECTIVE
wet

十 shí NOUN
ten

■ 十月 shíyuè October
■ 十一月 shíyīyuè November
■ 十二月 shí'èryuè December

十分 shífēn ADVERB
extremely

十字路口 shízì lùkǒu NOUN
crossroads

LANGUAGE TIP Literally, this means, **ten-character crossing**, because the character 十 shows a horizontal stroke intersecting with a vertical stroke, like two roads crossing each other.

石 shí NOUN
stone

石油 shíyóu NOUN
oil

时 shí NOUN
1 hour
2 time

■ 当时 dāngshí at that time

时差 shíchā NOUN
time difference

时候 shíhou NOUN
time

你什么时候上班? Nǐ shénme shíhou shàngbān? What time do you go to work?

时间 shíjiān NOUN
time

时间到了。Shíjiān dào le. Time's up!

识 shí

I VERB
to know

II NOUN
knowledge

实 shí ADJECTIVE
true

实习 shíxí VERB
to practise

实习生 shíxíshēng NOUN
trainee

实在 shízài ADVERB
really

拾 shí

I VERB
to pick... up

II NUMBER
ten

Chinese-English

LANGUAGE TIP This is the complex character for **ten**, which is mainly used in banks, on receipts etc to prevent mistakes and forgery.

食 shí
I VERB
to eat
II NOUN
food
食堂 shítáng NOUN
canteen
食物 shíwù NOUN
food
食欲 shíyù NOUN
appetite

史 shǐ NOUN
history

使 shǐ VERB
to use
使馆 shǐguǎn NOUN
embassy
使用 shǐyòng VERB
to use
■ 使用说明 shǐyòng shuōmíng operating instructions

始 shǐ VERB
to start
始终 shǐzhōng ADVERB
all along

屎 shǐ NOUN
1 excrement
2 wax *(ear)*

世 shì NOUN
1 age
2 world
世纪 shìjì NOUN
century
世界 shìjiè NOUN
world

市 shì NOUN
1 city
2 market
市场 shìchǎng NOUN
market
市民 shìmín NOUN
city residents *pl*

式 shì NOUN
style
式样 shìyàng NOUN
style

事 shì NOUN
1 thing
2 accident
3 problem
有事吗？— 没事。Yǒushì ma? — Méishì. Are you OK? — I'm fine.
事故 shìgù NOUN
accident
事情 shìqing NOUN
matter
我今天有很多事情要做。Wǒ jīntiān yǒu hěnduō shìqing yào zuò. I have a lot of things to do today.
事实 shìshí NOUN
fact
事实上 shìshí shàng in fact

试 shì
I VERB
to try
我可以试一下这双鞋吗？Wǒ kěyǐ shì yixià zhè shuāng xié ma? Can I try on this pair of shoes?
II NOUN
examination

柿 shì
▷ *see below:*
柿子 shìzi NOUN
persimmon

是 shì
I VERB
to be
我是学生。Wǒ shì xuésheng. I am a student.

LANGUAGE TIP When **to be** is used with an adjective, 是 shì is omitted.

我很忙。Wǒ hěn máng. I am very busy.
II ADVERB
yes

适 shì ADJECTIVE
suitable
适合 shìhé ADJECTIVE
suitable
这个工作很适合我。Zhègè gōngzuò hěn shìhé wǒ. This job is very suitable for me.
适应 shìyìng VERB
to adapt
我还不适应这里的天气。Wǒ hái bú tài shìyìng zhèlǐ de tiānqì. I haven't quite got used to the weather here yet.

S

室 shì NOUN
room
■办公室 bàngōngshì office
室外 shìwài ADJECTIVE
outdoor

释 shì VERB
to explain

收 shōu VERB
1 to accept
2 to gain
■收入 shōurù income
收集 shōují VERB
to collect
收据 shōujù NOUN
receipt
收下 shōuxià VERB
to accept
我收下了他的礼物。Wǒ shōuxià le tāde lǐwù. I accepted his gift.
收音机 shōuyīnjī NOUN
radio

手 shǒu NOUN
1 hand
2 expert
■歌手 gēshǒu singer
手表 shǒubiǎo NOUN
watch
手工 shǒugōng NOUN
craft
手机 shǒujī NOUN
mobile phone
手套 shǒutào NOUN
glove
一副手套 yí fù shǒutào a pair of gloves
手提 shǒutí ADJECTIVE
portable
手纸 shǒuzhǐ NOUN
toilet paper
手指 shǒuzhǐ NOUN
finger

首 shǒu
I ADJECTIVE
first
II MEASURE WORD
LANGUAGE TIP This measure word is used for music, songs and poems.
两首歌 liǎng shǒu gē two songs
首都 shǒudū NOUN
capital
首先 shǒuxiān ADVERB
first of all

受 shòu VERB
1 to receive
2 to bear
受不了 shòu bu liǎo to be unable to bear

瘦 shòu ADJECTIVE
1 thin *(people)*
2 lean *(meat)*
3 tight *(clothes, shoes)*

书 shū NOUN
book
书店 shūdiàn NOUN
bookshop

叔 shū NOUN
uncle *(father's younger brother)*
叔叔 shūshu NOUN
uncle *(spoken: relative, man of father's generation)*
LANGUAGE TIP 叔叔 shūshu specifically refers to one's father's younger brother. However, it is also an informal form of address used by children when addressing an unrelated male of a similar age to their parents.

梳 shū
I NOUN
comb
■梳子 shūzi comb
II VERB
to comb

舒 shū VERB
to relax *(mood)*
舒服 shūfu ADJECTIVE
comfortable

输 shū VERB
1 to transport
2 to lose *(game, match, bet)*

蔬 shū NOUN
vegetable
蔬菜 shūcài NOUN
vegetable

熟 shú ADJECTIVE
1 ripe *(fruit)*
2 cooked *(food)*
3 familiar
他对北京很熟。Tā duì Běijīng hěn shú. He knows Beijing well.
4 skilled

这个软件我用得很熟。Zhègè ruǎnjiàn wǒ yòng de hěn shú. I'm very skilled at using this software.

熟练 shúliàn ADJECTIVE
skilled

熟悉 shúxī
I VERB
to know well
II ADJECTIVE
familiar
我和他不是很熟悉。Wǒ hé tā búshì hěn shúxī. I'm not very familiar with him.

属 shǔ VERB
1 to be under
2 to be born under *(zodiac sign)*
你属什么？Nǐ shǔ shénme? What sign of the Chinese zodiac are you?

属于 shǔyú VERB
to belong to
那本字典是属于我的。Nà běn zìdiǎn shì shǔyú wǒ de. That dictionary belongs to me.

鼠 shǔ NOUN
1 mouse
■ 老鼠 lǎoshǔ mouse
2 rat

鼠标 shǔbiāo NOUN
mouse

数 shǔ VERB
to count

薯 shǔ NOUN
potato
■ 红薯 hóngshǔ sweet potato

束 shù MEASURE WORD
bunch *(flowers)*
一束花 yí shù huā a bunch of flowers

树 shù NOUN
tree

树林 shùlín NOUN
wood

数 shù NOUN
number

数量 shùliàng NOUN
quantity

数学 shùxué NOUN
mathematics

刷 shuā NOUN
brush
■ 牙刷 yáshuā toothbrush

刷卡 shuākǎ VERB
to swipe a card
您要刷卡还是现金？Nín yào shuākǎ háishì xiànjīn? Do you want to pay by card or cash?

刷牙 shuāyá VERB
to brush one's teeth

刷子 shuāzi NOUN
brush

摔 shuāi VERB
1 to fall
■ 摔倒 shuāidǎo to fall over 我昨天打篮球的时候摔倒了。Wǒ zuótiān dǎ lánqiú de shíhou shuāidǎo le. I fell over yesterday whilst playing basketball.
2 to fall out
他从床上摔了下来。Tā cóng chuáng shàng shuāi le xiàlái. He fell out of bed.

帅 shuài ADJECTIVE
handsome

双 shuāng MEASURE WORD
pair
一双鞋 yì shuāng xié a pair of shoes

双胞胎 shuāngbāotāi NOUN
twins

霜 shuāng NOUN
frost

谁 shuí PRONOUN
▷ *see also* shéi
who
他是谁？Tā shì shuí? Who is he?

LANGUAGE TIP 谁 has two official pronunciations, shéi and shuí. Shéi is the more colloquial pronunciation and therefore more commonly heard in native Mandarin speaking areas. Shuí is the more formal, literary pronunciation.

水 shuǐ NOUN
1 water
2 waters *(rivers, lakes, seas)*
浙江是个有山有水的地方。Zhèjiāng shì gè yǒushānyǒushuǐ de dìfāng. Zhejiang is an area with both mountain and river scenery.
3 liquid
■ 洗发水 xǐfàshuǐ shampoo

水果 shuǐguǒ NOUN
fruit

■ 水果店 shuǐguǒdiàn fruit shop

税 shuì NOUN
tax

睡 shuì VERB
to sleep

睡觉 shuìjiào VERB
to sleep

顺 shùn PREPOSITION
1 with *(direction)*
2 along

顺利 shùnlì ADVERB
smoothly
希望你的生活和工作都顺利！Xīwàng nǐde shēnghuó hé gōngzuò dōu shùnlì! I wish you all the best in both your personal and professional life!

顺序 shùnxù NOUN
order

说 shuō VERB
1 to say
2 to tell... off

说服 shuōfú VERB
to persuade
他说服我来北京工作。Tā shuōfú wǒ lái Běijīng gōngzuò. He persuaded me to come to work in Beijing.

说话 shuōhuà VERB
1 to talk
我不想和他说话。Wǒ bù xiǎng hé tā shuōhuà. I don't want to talk to him.
2 to chat
他们上课的时候总是说话。Tāmen shàngkè de shíhou zǒngshì shuōhuà. They're always chatting during class.

硕 shuò ADJECTIVE
large

硕士 shuòshì NOUN
master's degree

司 sī VERB
to take charge of

司机 sījī NOUN
driver

丝 sī NOUN
silk

私 sī ADJECTIVE
1 private
2 selfish
■ 自私 zìsī selfish

私人 sīrén ADJECTIVE
1 private
他是我的私人教练。Tā shì wǒde sīrén jiàoliàn. He is my personal trainer.
2 personal
工作的时候不可以做私人的事情。Gōngzuò de shíhou bù kěyǐ zuò sīrén de shìqíng. You can't handle personal matters whilst you are working.

私信 sīxìn NOUN
private message

死 sǐ
I VERB
to die
II ADJECTIVE

死机 sǐjī VERB
to crash *(computer)*

四 sì NUMBER
four

四声 sìshēng NOUN
the four tones

> LANGUAGE TIP 四声 sìshēng refers to the four pitched tones of Mandarin Chinese. There is also a toneless neutral tone, which is sometimes referred to as the fifth tone, 轻声 qīngshēng, literally meaning **light tone**.

四月 sìyuè NOUN
April

寺 sì NOUN
1 temple *(Buddhist)*
2 mosque *(Muslim)*

肆 sì NOUN
four

> LANGUAGE TIP This is the complex character for **four**, which is mainly used in banks, on receipts etc to prevent mistakes and forgery.

松 sōng
I NOUN
pine tree
II VERB
to relax
■ 放松 fàngsōng to relax
III ADJECTIVE
loose
你的鞋带松了。Nǐde xiédài sōng le. Your shoelace is loose.

送 sòng VERB

1 to deliver
请把饭送到我的办公室。Qǐng bǎ fàn sòng dào wǒde bàngōngshì. Please deliver the food to my office.
2 to give *(gift)*
他送了她一本书。Tā sòng le tā yìběn shū. He gave her a book.
3 to see... off
他送女朋友回家。Tā sòng nǚpéngyǒu huí jiā. He saw his girlfriend home.

苏 sū
▷ *see below:*
苏打 sūdá NOUN
soda
苏格兰 Sūgélán NOUN
Scotland

俗 sú
popular
俗语 súyǔ NOUN
common saying

素 sù NOUN
vegetable
素食 sùshí NOUN
vegetarian food

速 sù
I NOUN
speed
II ADJECTIVE
quick
速度 sùdù NOUN
speed
速溶 sùróng VERB
to dissolve quickly
速溶咖啡 sùróng kāfēi instant coffee

宿 sù VERB
to stay
宿舍 sùshè NOUN
dormitory

塑 sù
I VERB
to model
II NOUN
mould
塑料袋 sùliàodài NOUN
plastic bag

酸 suān ADJECTIVE
sour *(taste)*
酸奶 suānnǎi NOUN
yoghurt

蒜 suàn NOUN
garlic

算 suàn VERB
1 to calculate
2 to consider
■ 算了 suàn le forget it

虽 suī CONJUNCTION
although
虽然 suīrán CONJUNCTION
although
虽然她很年轻，可是却很成熟。Suīrán tā hěn niánqīng, kěshì què hěn chéngshú. Although she is very young, she is quite mature.

随 suí VERB
to follow
随便 suíbiàn ADVERB
as one wishes
大家随便坐。Dàjiā suíbiàn zuò. Everyone can sit where they like.
随时 suíshí ADVERB
at any time
有问题的话随时给我打电话。Yǒu wèntí de huà suíshí gěi wǒ dǎ diànhuà. Call me anytime if you have any problems.

岁 suì NOUN
year
他二十岁了。Tā èrshí suì le. He's 20 years old.

隧 suì NOUN
tunnel
隧道 suìdào NOUN
tunnel

孙 sūn NOUN
grandchild
孙女 sūnnǚ NOUN
granddaughter
孙子 sūnzi NOUN
grandson

笋 sǔn NOUN
bamboo shoot

所 suǒ
I NOUN
office
■ 派出所 pàichūsuǒ local police station
II MEASURE WORD

LANGUAGE TIP This is a measure word used for buildings.

三所医院 sān suǒ yīyuàn three hospitals

所以 suǒyǐ CONJUNCTION

so

路上堵车，所以我迟到了。Lù shàng dǔchē, suǒyǐ wǒ chídào le. There was a lot of traffic, so I am late.

所有 suǒyǒu ADJECTIVE

all

所有的人都喜欢他。Suǒyǒu de rén dōu xǐhuan tā. Everybody likes him.

锁 suǒ

I NOUN

lock

II VERB

to lock

走的时候锁上门。Zǒu de shíhou suǒshàng mén. Lock the door when you leave.

Tt

他 tā PRONOUN
he
他在工作。Tā zài gōngzuò. He is working.

LANGUAGE TIP The Chinese for **he**, **she** and **it** all have different characters, but share the same pronunciation, tā, so you have to use context to differentiate between the three in spoken Chinese.

他们 tāmen PRONOUN
they
他们在一起。Tāmen zài yìqǐ. They are together.

它 tā PRONOUN
it
它只是个娃娃。Tā zhǐshì ge wáwa. It's just a baby doll.

它们 tāmen PRONOUN
they
它们是没有生命的。Tāmen shì méiyǒu shēngmìng de. They're not alive.

她 tā PRONOUN
she
她是个漂亮姑娘。Tā shì gè piàoliàng gūniáng. She's a beautiful girl.

她们 tāmen PRONOUN
they

塔 tǎ NOUN
1 pagoda
■ 宝塔 bǎotǎ pagoda
2 tower
■ 塔楼 tǎlóu tower

台 tái
I NOUN
anything shaped like a platform or stage
■ 舞台 wǔtái stage
II MEASURE WORD
一台电脑 yìtái diànnǎo a computer

台风 táifēng NOUN
typhoon

台湾 táiwān NOUN
Taiwan

台阶 táijiē NOUN
steps
三十九级台阶 sānshíjiǔjí táijiē 39 steps

台球 táiqiú NOUN
billiards

抬 tái VERB
to raise
■ 抬头 táitóu VERB to raise one's head

太 tài ADVERB
1 too
这部电影太长。Zhè bù diànyǐng tài cháng. This film is too long.
2 so
我太高兴了。Wǒ tài gāoxìng le. I am so happy.

太极拳 tàijíquán NOUN
t'ai chi

太平洋 Tàipíngyáng NOUN
the Pacific Ocean

太太 tàitai NOUN
1 wife
2 lady *(old woman)*
3 Mrs *(married woman)*

LANGUAGE TIP In Chinese, titles such as **Mr**, **Mrs**, **Miss** and **Ms** come after the surname.

张太太 Zhāng tàitai Mrs Zhang

太阳 tàiyáng NOUN
sun

态 tài NOUN
state
■ 状态 zhuàngtài state

态度 tàidù NOUN
attitude
服务态度 fúwù tàidù customer service attitude

谈 tán VERB
to talk
■ 谈话 tánhuà to talk

谈判 tánpàn VERB
to negotiate

弹 tán VERB
▷ *see also* dàn
to play *(instrument)*

弹簧 tánhuáng NOUN
spring

毯 tǎn NOUN
carpet
■ 地毯 dìtǎn carpet

碳 tàn NOUN
carbon
■ 碳水化合物 tànshuǐhuàhéwù carbohydrate

汤 tāng NOUN
soup

堂 táng
I NOUN
hall
■ 教堂 jiàotáng church
II MEASURE WORD
LANGUAGE TIP This is a measure word used for lessons.
两堂课 liǎngtáng kè two lessons

糖 táng NOUN
1 sugar
■ 白糖 báitáng sugar
2 sweet
■ 糖果 tángguǒ sweet

躺 tǎng VERB
to lie
躺在床上 tǎngzài chuángshàng to lie on the bed

烫 tàng
I ADJECTIVE
very hot
LANGUAGE TIP 烫 tàng can only be used to describe things that you can touch, such as water, food, or an oven. It cannot be used to describe the weather.
这汤真烫。Zhè tāng zhēn tàng. This soup is very hot.
II VERB
to perm
烫头发 tàng tóufa to perm one's hair

逃 táo VERB
to run away
■ 逃生 táoshēng to run for one's life

逃跑 táopǎo VERB
to escape
俘虏逃跑了。Fúlǔ táopǎo le. The slaves escaped.

桃 táo NOUN
peach
■ 桃子 táozi peach

讨 tǎo VERB
to discuss
■ 讨论 tǎolùn VERB to discuss

讨厌 tǎoyàn
I ADJECTIVE
annoying
令人讨厌 lìngrén tǎoyàn annoying
II VERB
to dislike
他讨厌数学。Tā tǎoyàn shùxué. He dislikes maths.

套 tào MEASURE WORD
set
LANGUAGE TIP This is a measure word used for suits, collections of books, tools etc.
一套西装 yítào xīzhuāng a suit

套餐 tàocān NOUN
set meal

特 tè ADJECTIVE
special
■ 特殊 tèshū ADJECTIVE special

特别 tèbié
I ADJECTIVE
peculiar
特别的礼物 tèbié de lǐwù a special gift
II ADVERB
exceptionally
他特别聪明。Tā tèbié cōngmíng. He is exceptionally clever.

特点 tèdiǎn NOUN
characteristic
这座桥很有特点。Zhèzuò qiáo hěnyǒu tèdiǎn. This is a very unique bridge.

特价 tèjià NOUN
bargain price
特价商品 tèjià shāngpǐn bargain

特色 tèsè NOUN
characteristic
特色小吃 tèsè xiǎochī snacks

疼 téng ADJECTIVE
sore
我牙疼。Wǒ yá téng. I have toothache.

梯 tī NOUN
ladder
- ■电梯 diàntī lift
- ■楼梯 lóutī stairs

踢 tī VERB
to kick
踢足球 tī zúqiú to play football

提 tí VERB
1 to carry *(in one's hand with the arm down)*
提着袋子 tízhe dàizi to carry a bag
2 to put... forward
他提了个建议。Tā tí le gè jiànyì. He put forward a proposal.
3 to mention
别再提那件事了。Bié zài tí nà jiàn shì le. Don't mention that subject again.

提高 tígāo VERB
to improve
提高水平 tígāo shuǐpíng to improve the standard

提供 tígōng VERB
to provide
提供粮食 tígōng liángshí to provide food

提醒 tíxǐng VERB
to remind
妈妈提醒我把伞带上。Māma tíxǐng wǒ bǎ sǎn dàishàng. Mum reminded me to take an umbrella.

题 tí NOUN
subject
- ■标题 biāotí title

体 tǐ NOUN
body

体温 tǐwēn NOUN
temperature

体育 tǐyù NOUN
sport
体育运动 tǐyù yùndòng athletic sports

体育场 tǐyùchǎng NOUN
stadium

体育馆 tǐyùguǎn NOUN
gym

体重 tǐzhòng NOUN
weight

天 tiān NOUN
1 sky
- ■天空 tiānkōng sky

2 day
- ■昨天 zuótiān yesterday

3 season
- ■秋天 qiūtiān autumn

4 weather
天很热。Tiān hěn rè. It's a very hot day.

天才 tiāncái NOUN
genius

天气 tiānqì NOUN
weather
天气预报 tiānqì yùbào weather forecast

天使 tiānshǐ NOUN
angel

LANGUAGE TIP Word for word, this means 'heaven's envoy'.

天堂 tiāntáng NOUN
heaven

天天 tiāntiān ADVERB
every day

甜 tián ADJECTIVE
sweet
- ■甜味 tiánwèi sweet taste

甜点 tiándiǎn NOUN
dessert

填 tián VERB
to complete
填表格 tián biǎogé to fill in a form

舔 tiǎn VERB
to lick
舔嘴唇 tiǎn zuǐchún to lick one's lips

挑 tiāo VERB
to choose
- ■挑选 tiāoxuǎn to choose

挑剔 tiāotì ADJECTIVE
picky
她对住宿条件很挑剔。Tā duì zhùsù tiáojiàn hěn tiāotì. He's very picky about the standard of accommodation.

条 tiáo MEASURE WORD

LANGUAGE TIP This is a measure word used for long thin things, news and human lives.

两条腿 liǎng tiáo tuǐ two legs

跳 tiào VERB
to jump
- ■跳高 tiàogāo high jump

跳舞 tiàowǔ VERB
to dance
他邀请我跳舞。Tā yāoqǐng wǒ tiàowǔ. He asked me to dance.

贴 tiē VERB
to stick
贴墙纸 tiē qiángzhǐ to wallpaper

铁 tiě NOUN
iron *(metal)*

听 tīng VERB
to listen to
■ 听见 tīngjiàn to hear
■ 听课 tīngkè to attend a lecture

听说 tīngshuō VERB
to hear
我听说他病了。Wǒ tīngshuō tā bìng le. I heard he is sick.

听众 tīngzhòng NOUN
audience

庭 tíng NOUN
1 hall
2 courtyard
3 law court

停 tíng VERB
1 to stop
2 to park

停车场 tíngchēchǎng NOUN
parking lot

停止 tíngzhǐ VERB
to stop
停止说话 tíngzhǐ shuōhuà to stop talking

通 tōng ADJECTIVE
through
电话打通了。Diànhuà dǎ tōng le. The call has been put through.

通常 tōngcháng
I ADJECTIVE
normal
II NOUN
normal circumstances
我通常七点起床。Wǒ tōngcháng qīdiǎn qǐchuáng. Under normal circumstances, I get up at seven o'clock.

同 tóng ADJECTIVE
same
■ 同样 tóngyàng the same

同情 tóngqíng VERB
to sympathize
表示同情 biǎoshì tóngqíng to express sympathy

同时 tóngshí NOUN
at the same time
同时发生 tóngshí fāshēng occur simultaneously

同事 tóngshì NOUN
colleague

同性恋 tóngxìngliàn NOUN
homosexuality

同学 tóngxué NOUN
1 fellow student
2 classmate

同意 tóngyì VERB
to agree
我同意你的说法。Wǒ tóngyì nǐ de shuōfǎ. I agree with you.

铜 tóng NOUN
copper

铜牌 tóngpái NOUN
bronze medal

童 tóng NOUN
child
■ 儿童 értóng child

童年 tóngnián NOUN
childhood

桶 tǒng
I NOUN
bucket
■ 水桶 shuǐtǒng bucket
II MEASURE WORD
barrel
两桶牛奶 liǎng tǒng niúnǎi two churns of milk

痛 tòng VERB
to ache
头痛 tóutòng to have a headache

痛苦 tòngkǔ ADJECTIVE
painful
痛苦的经历 tòngkǔ de jīnglì a painful experience

偷 tōu
I VERB
to steal
■ 偷窃 tōuqiè to steal
II ADVERB
stealthily
■ 偷偷 tōutōu secretly

头 tóu
I NOUN
head
II ADJECTIVE
1 first-class
■ 头等舱 tóuděng cāng first-class cabin
2 first
头几年 tóu jǐ nián first few years
III MEASURE WORD
LANGUAGE TIP This is a measure word used for animals.
三头母牛 sān tóu mǔniú three cows

头发 tóufa NOUN
hair

> LANGUAGE TIP 头发 tóufa can only be used to describe the hair on one's head, not body hair or animal hair. The two characters here mean **head hair**.

透 tòu ADJECTIVE
transparent
■ 透明 tòumíng transparent

突 tū ADVERB
suddenly

突然 tūrán

I ADJECTIVE
sudden
母亲的去世很突然。Mǔqīn de qùshì hěn tūrán. Mother's passing away was very sudden.

II ADVERB
suddenly
突然发生 tūrán fāshēng to suddenly occur

图 tú NOUN
picture
■ 图画 túhuà picture

图书馆 túshūguǎn NOUN
library

土 tǔ NOUN
1 soil
■ 土壤 tǔrǎng soil
2 land
■ 土地 tǔdì land

土豆 tǔdòu NOUN
potato

吐 tǔ VERB
▷ *see also* tù
to spit
吐口香糖 tǔ kǒuxiāngtáng to spit chewing gum

吐 tù VERB
▷ *see also* tǔ
to vomit
■ 呕吐 ǒutù to vomit

兔 tù NOUN
rabbit

推 tuī VERB
to push

推迟 tuīchí VERB
to put... off
推迟会议 tuīchí huìyì to postpone the meeting

推荐 tuījiàn VERB
to recommend
■ 推荐信 tuījiànxìn letter of recommendation

推特 Tuītè NOUN
Twitter®

腿 tuǐ NOUN
leg

退 tuì VERB
1 to cause... to withdraw
■ 退后 tuìhòu to drop back
2 to quit
■ 退队 tuìduì to quit the team

退休 tuìxiū VERB
to retire
他明年退休了。Tā míngnián tuìxiū le. He will retire next year.

拖 tuō VERB
to pull

拖鞋 tuōxié NOUN
slipper

> DID YOU KNOW...? In many Chinese homes, slippers are worn to keep both the floor and your socks clean.

脱 tuō VERB
to take... off
脱衣服 tuō yīfu to take off clothes

Ww

挖 wā VERB
to dig
■ 挖掘 wājué to excavate

蛙 wā NOUN
frog
■ 青蛙 qīngwā frog

蛙泳 wāyǒng NOUN
breaststroke

娃 wá NOUN
baby

娃娃 wáwa NOUN
1 baby
2 doll

袜 wà NOUN
sock
■ 长筒袜 chángtǒngwà stocking

袜子 wàzi NOUN
sock

歪 wāi ADJECTIVE
slanting
这行树种歪了。Zhèháng shù zhòng wāile. This tree is growing at a slant.

外 wài
I NOUN
outside
■ 外面 wàimian outside
II ADJECTIVE
foreign
■ 外语 wàiyǔ foreign language

外表 wàibiǎo NOUN
exterior
注重外表是基本的礼貌。Zhùzhòng wàibiǎo shì jīběn de lǐmào. Paying attention to one's appearance is basic manners.

外地 wàidì NOUN
other parts of the country
■ 外地人 wàidìrén person from another part of the country

DID YOU KNOW...?
The term 外地 wàidì refers literally to outsiders, for example in Beijing any person from outside of Beijing are referred to as 外地人 wàidìrén. This term is particularly important in China as it is a huge country with more than thirty different provinces and there is a large flow of population from the countryside to cities and between provinces.

外公 wàigōng NOUN
maternal grandfather

外国 wàiguó NOUN
foreign country
■ 外国人 wàiguórén foreigner

外卖 wàimài NOUN
takeaway
我们叫一份外卖吧。Wǒmen jiào yífen wàimài ba. Let's call for a takeaway.

外婆 wàipó NOUN
maternal grandmother

外套 wàitào NOUN
overcoat
别忘了你的外套。Bié wàngle nǐde wàitào. Don't forget your coat.

弯 wān
I ADJECTIVE
curved
■ 弯路 wānlù winding road
II NOUN
bend
下一个弯右拐。Xiàyígè wān yòuguǎi. Turn right at the next bend.

完 wán
I ADJECTIVE
whole
■ 完整 wánzhěng complete
II VERB
1 to complete
■ 完成 wánchéng to complete
2 to finish
■ 完结 wánjié to finish

Chinese-English

完美 wánměi ADJECTIVE
perfect
完美的人生 wánměi de rénshēng
a perfect life

完全 wánquán ADVERB
completely
他完全疯了。Tā wánquán fēngle.
He has gone completely crazy.

玩 wán VERB
1 to play
玩游戏 wán yóuxì to play a game
2 to have a good time
我去泰国玩了一个星期。Wǒ qù Tàiguó wán le yígè xīngqī. I went to Thailand for a week's holiday.
3 to visit
他这周来我们家玩。Tā zhèzhōu lái wǒmenjiā wán. He is going to visit our house this week.

玩具 wánjù NOUN
toy

玩笑 wánxiào NOUN
joke
他喜欢跟人开玩笑。Tā xǐhuān gēn rén kāi wánxiào. He likes to play jokes on people.

挽 wǎn VERB
1 to hold
手挽手 shǒu wǎn shǒu to hold hands
2 to roll... up
挽起袖子 wǎnqǐ xiùzi to roll up sleeves

晚 wǎn
I ADJECTIVE
late
我起晚了。Wǒ qǐ wǎn le. I got up late.
II NOUN
evening
■ 晚上 wǎnshàng evening

晚安 wǎn'ān ADJECTIVE
good night

晚饭 wǎnfàn NOUN
dinner

晚会 wǎnhuì NOUN
party
春节晚会 chūnjié wǎnhuì Spring Festival party

碗 wǎn NOUN
bowl

万 wàn NUMBER
ten thousand
■ 十万 shíwàn one hundred thousand

亡 wáng VERB
to die
■ 死亡 sǐwáng to die

王 wáng NOUN
king

王国 wángguó NOUN
kingdom

王子 wángzǐ NOUN
prince

网 wǎng NOUN
1 net
■ 渔网 yúwǎng fishing net
2 network
■ 互联网 Hùliánwǎng the internet

网吧 wǎngbā NOUN
internet café

DID YOU KNOW...?
Internet cafés are very common and very popular all over China. They often have blacked-out windows or are not on the ground floor. Look out for signs pointing to 网吧.

网络 wǎngluò NOUN
network
人际网络 rénjì wǎngluò a network of personal relationships

网球 wǎngqiú NOUN
tennis
■ 网球场 wǎngqiúchǎng tennis court

网页 wǎngyè NOUN
web page
刷新网页 shuāxīn wǎngyè to refresh a webpage

网站 wǎngzhàn NOUN
website
这是一个新建的网站。Zhèshì yígè xīnjiàn de wǎngzhàn. This is a new website.

网址 wǎngzhǐ NOUN
web address
请告诉我网址。Qǐng gàosù wǒ wǎngzhǐ. Please tell me the web address.

往 wǎng PREPOSITION
to
往东走。Wǎng dōng zǒu. Go East.

往往 wǎngwǎng ADVERB
often
少数人的观点往往是正确的。Shǎoshùrén de guāndiǎn wǎngwǎng shì zhèngquè de. The opinions of the minority are often correct.

忘 wàng VERB
to forget

W

■ 忘记 wàngjì to forget

望 wàng VERB
1 to look into the distance
2 to watch
■ 望风 wàngfēng to keep watch
3 to hope
望身体健康。Wàng shēntǐ jiànkāng. To wish for good health.

危 wēi
I ADJECTIVE
dangerous
■ 危楼 wēilóu a building that is in danger of falling down
II VERB
to endanger
■ 危害 wēihài to harm

危机 wēijī NOUN
crisis
金融危机 jīnróng wēijī financial crisis

危险 wēixiǎn ADJECTIVE
dangerous
跳水是一项危险的运动。Tiàoshuǐ shì yíxiàng wēixiǎn de yùndòng. Diving is a dangerous sport.

威 wēi NOUN
power
■ 威力 wēilì power 这种炸药有很强的威力。Zhèzhǒng zhàyào yǒu hěnqiáng de wēilì. This kind of explosive is very powerful.

威士忌 wēishìjì NOUN
whisky

威胁 wēixié VERB
to threaten
洪水威胁着村民的人身安全。Hóngshuǐ wēixié zhe cūnmín de rénshén ānquán. Floods threaten the safety of the people in this village.

微 wēi
I ADJECTIVE
tiny
■ 微秒 wēimiǎo microsecond
II ADVERB
slightly
■ 微颤 wēichàn slight tremor

微波炉 wēibōlú NOUN
microwave oven

微博 wēi bó NOUN
microblog

微风 wēifēng NOUN
gentle breeze

微妙 wēimiào ADJECTIVE
delicate
微妙的变化 wēimiào de biànhuà subtle change

微弱 wēiruò ADJECTIVE
faint
微弱的呼吸 wēiruò de hūxī faint breathing

微小 wēixiǎo ADJECTIVE
tiny
微小的生物 wēixiǎo de shēngwù microorganism

微笑 wēixiào VERB
to smile
她总是在微笑。Tā zǒngshì zài wēixiào. She is always smiling.

违 wéi VERB
to break
■ 违章 wéizhāng to break regulations

违法 wéifǎ ADJECTIVE
illegal
偷窃是违法的。Tōuqiè shì wéifǎ de. Stealing is against the law.

违反 wéifǎn VERB
to go against
违反规则 wéifǎn guīzé to go against the rules

围 wéi
I VERB
to surround
■ 围绕 wéirào to surround
II NOUN
1 all sides
■ 围墙 wéiqiáng surrounding wall
2 measurement
■ 胸围 xiōngwéi chest measurement

维 wéi VERB
1 to hold... together
■ 维系 wéixì to hold together
2 to maintain
■ 维修 wéixiū to maintain

维持 wéichí VERB
1 to maintain
维持现状 wéichí xiànzhuàng to maintain the current situation
2 to support
维持生计 wéichí shēngjì to support one's livelihood

维护 wéihù VERB
to safeguard
维护家人 wéihù jiārén to safeguard one's family

维生素 wéishēngsù NOUN
vitamin

伟 wěi ADJECTIVE
great
■ 伟大 wěidà great

伟人 wěirén NOUN
great man
牛顿是个伟人。Niúdùn shì gè wěirén. Newton was a great man.

伪 wěi ADJECTIVE
false
■ 伪钞 wěichāo counterfeit note

伪造 wěizào VERB
to forge
伪造证据 wěizào zhèngjù to forge evidence

伪装 wěizhuāng VERB
to disguise
特工把自己伪装成商人。Tègōng bǎ zìjǐ wěizhuāng chéng shāngrén. The secret agent disguised himself as a businessman.

尾 wěi NOUN
1 tail
■ 尾巴 wěibā tail
2 end
■ 结尾 jiéwěi end
3 remainder
■ 扫尾 sǎowěi to finish off

卫 wèi VERB
to protect
■ 卫士 wèishì bodyguard

卫生 wèishēng
I NOUN
1 hygiene
■ 卫生状况 wèishēng zhuàngkuàng hygienic conditions
2 cleaning *(of house)*
打扫卫生 dǎsǎo wèishēng to do the cleaning
II ADJECTIVE
hygienic
这个餐馆很卫生。Zhègè cānguǎn hěn wèishēng. This restaurant is very clean.

卫生间 wèishēngjiān NOUN
toilet

卫生纸 wèishēngzhǐ NOUN
toilet paper

卫星 wèixīng NOUN
satellite

为 wèi PREPOSITION
for
我真为你高兴！Wǒ zhēn wèi nǐ gāoxìng! I am really happy for you!

为了 wèile PREPOSITION
in order to
他为了家人的幸福努力工作。Tā wèile jiārén de xìngfú nǔlì gōngzuò. He works really hard for his family's welfare.

为什么 wèishénme ADVERB
why
这是为什么？Zhèshì wèishénme? Why is this?

未 wèi ADVERB
not
■ 未婚 wèihūn unmarried

未成年人 wèichéngniánrén NOUN
minor

未婚夫 wèihūnfū NOUN
fiancé *(male)*

未婚妻 wèihūnqī NOUN
fiancée *(female)*

未来 wèilái NOUN
future
美好的未来 měihǎo de wèilái a wonderful future

位 wèi
I NOUN
1 location
■ 位置 wèizhi location
2 position
■ 地位 dìwèi position
3 digit
两位数 liǎng wèi shù two-digit number
II MEASURE WORD

LANGUAGE TIP This is a measure word used for people.

两位教授 liǎng wèi jiàoshòu two professors

位置 wèizhi NOUN
location
教学楼的位置 jiàoxuélóu de wèizhi the location of the classroom

位子 wèizi NOUN
seat
请给老人让个位子。Qǐnggěi lǎorén ràng gè wèizi. Please give your seat to the elderly.

味 wèi NOUN
1 taste
■ 味觉 wèijué taste
2 smell
■ 气味 qìwèi smell

味道 wèidao NOUN
taste
草莓的味道 cǎoméi de wèidao strawberry flavour

胃 wèi NOUN
stomach

胃口 wèikǒu NOUN
appetite
他的胃口很好。Tāde wèikǒu hěnhǎo. He has a very good appetite.

喂 wèi
I VERB
to feed
■ 喂养 wèiyǎng to raise
II INTERJECTION
to say hello *(when making a phone call)*

温 wēn
I ADJECTIVE
1 warm
■ 温水 wēnshuǐ warm water
2 mild
■ 温情 wēnqíng tender feelings
II NOUN
temperature
■ 温度 wēndù temperature

温和 wēnhé ADJECTIVE
1 mild
态度温和 tàidù wēnhé gentle manner *(of person)*
2 temperate *(climate)*
气候温和湿润 qìhòu wēnhé shīrùn mild and moist climate

温暖 wēnnuǎn ADJECTIVE
warm
温暖的阳光 wēnnuǎn de yángguāng warm sunlight

温泉 wēnquán NOUN
hot spring

温柔 wēnróu ADJECTIVE
gentle
温柔的女孩 wēnróu de nǚhái a gentle girl

文 wén NOUN
1 writing
■ 文字 wénzì words
2 language
■ 中文 Zhōngwén the Chinese language
3 essay
■ 文章 wénzhāng article

文化 wénhuà NOUN
1 culture
传统文化 chuántǒng wénhuà traditional culture
2 education
文化教育 wénhuà jiàoyù cultural education

文件 wénjiàn NOUN
1 document
打印文件 dǎyìn wénjiàn to print document
2 file
删除文件 shānchú wénjiàn to delete file

文具 wénjù NOUN
stationery

文明 wénmíng
I NOUN
civilization
人类文明 rénlèi wénmíng human civilization
II ADJECTIVE
civilized
文明的社会 wénmíng de shèhuì civilised society

文凭 wénpíng NOUN
diploma
大学文凭 dàxué wénpíng university diploma

文学 wénxué NOUN
literature
文学作品 wénxué zuòpǐn literary work

闻 wén
I VERB
to smell
闻起来很香 wénqǐlái hěnxiāng to smell fragrant
II NOUN
news
■ 新闻 xīnwén news

蚊 wén NOUN
mosquito
■ 蚊子 wénzi mosquito

吻 wěn
I NOUN
kiss
II VERB
to kiss
■ 亲吻 qīnwěn to kiss

稳 wěn
I ADJECTIVE
1 steady
■ 平稳 píngwěn steady
2 composed
■ 稳重 wěnzhòng composed
3 responsible
■ 稳妥 wěntuǒ responsible
II VERB
to keep calm
稳住 wěnzhù to keep calm

稳定 wěndìng VERB
to settle
稳定情绪 wěndìng qíngxù to reassure

问 wèn
I VERB
1 to ask
■ 问答 wèndá to ask and answer
2 to send regards to
■ 问候 wènhòu to send regards to
II NOUN
question
■ 疑问 yíwèn doubt

问题 wèntí NOUN
1 question
第一道问题的答案是一。Dìyīdào wèntí de dá'àn shì yī. The answer to the first question is 1.
2 problem
这辆车有问题。Zhèliàngchē yǒu wèntí. There is a problem with this car.

我 wǒ PRONOUN
1 I
我是谁？Wǒ shì shéi? Who am I?
2 me
你叫我？Nǐ jiào wǒ? Are you calling for me?

我们 wǒmen PRONOUN
1 we
我们要去公园。Wǒmen yàoqù gōngyuán. We are going to the park.
2 us
我们走吧！Wǒmen zǒuba! Let's go!

握 wò VERB
1 to grasp
■ 握手 wòshǒu to shake hands
2 to master
■ 掌握 zhǎngwò to master

污 wū ADJECTIVE
dirty
■ 污点 wūdiǎn stain

污染 wūrǎn VERB
to pollute
污染环境 wūrǎn huánjìng to pollute the environment

屋 wū NOUN
1 house
■ 房屋 fángwū house
2 room
■ 屋子 wūzi room

屋顶 wūdǐng NOUN
roof

无 wú
I VERB
to not have
■ 无效 wúxiào invalid
■ 无形 wúxíng invisible
II ADVERB
not
■ 无论如何 wúlùn rúhé no matter what

无辜 wúgū ADJECTIVE
innocent
无辜的百姓 wúgū de bǎixìng the innocent masses

无关 wúguān VERB
to have nothing to do with
这件事与她无关。Zhèjiànshì yǔtā wúguān. This is nothing to do with her.

无情 wúqíng ADJECTIVE
heartless
■ 无情无义 wúqíngwúyì heartless

无数 wúshù ADJECTIVE
countless
无数的星星 wúshù de xīngxing countless stars

五 wǔ NOUN
five
五分之一 wǔ fēn zhī yī one fifth
■ 五月 wǔyuè May

五官 wǔguān NOUN
the five sense organs

午 wǔ NOUN
midday
■ 中午 zhōngwǔ midday

午饭 wǔfàn NOUN
lunch

午夜 wǔyè NOUN
midnight

武 wǔ ADJECTIVE
1 military
■ 武装 wǔzhuāng armed forces
2 valiant
■ 威武 wēiwǔ powerful

武力 wǔlì NOUN
1 military strength
武力对抗 wǔlì duìkàng military confrontation
2 force
武力解决不了问题。Wǔlì jiějuébùliǎo wèntí. Force cannot solve problems.

武器 wǔqì NOUN
weapon

武士 wǔshì NOUN
warrior

武术 wǔshù NOUN
martial arts circles
武术表演 wǔshù biǎoyǎn martial arts performance

舞 wǔ NOUN
dance
■ 舞蹈 wǔdǎo dance
II VERB
to dance
■ 起舞 qǐwǔ to dance

舞台 wǔtái NOUN
stage

勿 wù ADVERB
not
请勿吸烟 qǐng wù xīyān no smoking

务 wù NOUN
business
■ 任务 rènwu task

物 wù NOUN
1 thing
■ 物体 wùtǐ object
2 produce
■ 物产 wùchǎn produce
3 creature
■ 动物 dòngwù animal

物理 wùlǐ NOUN
physics

物质 wùzhì NOUN
material things
物质的构成 wùzhì de gòuchéng material structure

误 wù
I NOUN
mistake
■ 错误 cuòwù mistake
II ADJECTIVE
erroneous
■ 误会 wùhuì misunderstand
accidental
■ 误伤 wùshāng to accidentally injure
III VERB
to miss
快点儿，别误了火车！ Kuàidiǎnr, bié wù le huǒchē! Hurry up, we don't want to miss the train!

雾 wù NOUN
fog

Xx

夕 xī NOUN
1 sunset
■ 夕阳 xīyáng setting sun
2 evening
■ 除夕 chúxī New Year's Eve

西 xī NOUN
1 west
■ 西北 xīběi northwest
■ 西南 xīnán southwest
2 the West
■ 西藏 Xīzàng Tibet

西班牙 Xībānyá NOUN
Spain
西班牙人 Xībānyárén Spaniard 西班牙语 Xībānyáyǔ the Spanish language

西餐 xīcān NOUN
Western food

西方 xīfāng NOUN
the West

西服 xīfú NOUN
Western clothes

西瓜 xīguā NOUN
watermelon

西红柿 xīhóngshì NOUN
tomato

西药 xīyào NOUN
Western medicine

西医 xīyī NOUN
1 Western medicine
2 doctor trained in Western medicine

吸 xī VERB
1 to suck... in
■ 吸管 xīguǎn straw
■ 吸血鬼 xīxuèguǐ vampire
2 to inhale
■ 吸烟 xīyān to smoke cigarettes
3 to absorb
4 to attract

吸尘器 xīchénqì NOUN
vacuum cleaner

吸收 xīshōu VERB
1 to absorb
吸收水分 xīshōu shuǐfèn to absorb moisture
2 to recruit
这个部门吸收了三名新人。Zhègè bùmén xīshōu le sānmíng xīnrén. This department recruited three new people.

吸引 xīyǐn VERB
to attract

希 xī VERB
to hope

希望 xīwàng
I VERB
to hope
II NOUN
hope

牺 xī
▷ *see below:*

牺牲 xīshēng VERB
1 to sacrifice oneself
牺牲在战场上 xīshēng zài zhànchǎng shàng to sacrifice oneself on the battlefield
2 to sacrifice
牺牲休息时间 xīshēng xiūxi shíjiān to sacrifice resting time

息 xī VERB
to rest
■ 歇息 xīexi to have a rest

稀 xī ADJECTIVE
1 rare
■ 稀罕 xīhan rare
2 sparse
稀疏的头发 xīshū de tóufa thinning hair
3 watery
■ 稀饭 xīfàn rice porridge

稀少 xīshǎo ADJECTIVE
sparse

稀有 xīyǒu ADJECTIVE
rare

犀 xī NOUN
rhinoceros
■ 犀牛 xīniú rhinoceros

溪 xī NOUN
brook

熄 xī VERB
to put... out
■ 熄灯 xīdēng to put out the light

熄灭 xīmiè VERB
to put... out

膝 xī NOUN
knee
■ 膝盖 xīgài knee

习 xí
I VERB
1 to practise
■ 习武 xíwǔ to study martial arts
2 to be used to
习以为常 xí yǐ wéi cháng to become used to
II NOUN
custom
■ 习俗 xísú custom
■ 习气 xíqì bad habit

习惯 xíguàn
I VERB
to be used to
II NOUN
habit

习性 xíxìng NOUN
habits *pl*

席 xí NOUN
1 mat
■ 竹席 zhúxí bamboo mat
2 seat
■ 席位 xíwèi seat
■ 出席 chūxí to be present
■ 毛主席 Máo zhǔxí chairman Mao
3 feast
■ 酒席 jiǔxí banquet

袭 xí VERB
1 to make a surprise attack
■ 空袭 kōngxí air raid
2 to follow the pattern of
■ 抄袭 chāoxí to plagiarize

袭击 xíjī VERB
to attack

媳 xí NOUN
daughter-in-law

媳妇 xífù NOUN
1 daughter-in-law
2 wife

洗 xǐ VERB
1 to wash
■ 洗衣店 xǐyīdiàn launderette®
2 to develop
洗胶卷 xǐ jiāojuǎn to develop film
3 to wipe
把磁带的这段内容洗掉 bǎ cídài de zhèduàn nèiróng xǐdiào to wipe out the content from this piece of magnetic tape
4 to shuffle
洗扑克牌 xǐ pūkèpái to shuffle the poker cards

洗衣机 xǐyījī NOUN
washing machine

洗澡 xǐzǎo VERB
to take a shower

喜 xǐ
I ADJECTIVE
1 happy
■ 欢喜 huānxǐ joyful
2 celebratory
■ 可喜 kěxǐ gratifying
II VERB
1 to like
■ 喜好 xǐhào like
2 to suit

喜爱 xǐ'ài VERB
to like

喜欢 xǐhuān VERB
to like

喜剧 xǐjù NOUN
comedy

戏 xì
I NOUN
show
■ 京戏 jīngxì Beijing Opera
■ 马戏 mǎxì circus
II VERB
to joke
■ 戏弄 xìnòng to tease

戏法 xìfǎ NOUN
magic

戏剧 xìjù NOUN
theatre

戏曲 xìqǔ NOUN
Chinese opera

戏院 xìyuàn NOUN
theatre

系 xì
▷ *see also* jì
I NOUN
1 system
■ 太阳系 tàiyángxì the solar system

2 department
■ 英语系 yīngyǔxì English department
II VERB
to tie
系列 xìliè NOUN
series *sg*
■ 一系列问题 yí xìliè wèntí a series of problems
系统 xìtǒng NOUN
system

细 xì
I ADJECTIVE
1 thin
■ 细绳 xìshéng a string
2 fine
■ 细粮 xìliáng refined food
3 gentle
细嗓音 xì sǎngyīn a gentle voice
4 detailed
■ 细节 xìjié details *pl*
II ADVERB
minutely
■ 细想 xìxiǎng to consider carefully
细胞 xìbāo NOUN
cell
细菌 xìjūn NOUN
germ
细心 xìxīn ADJECTIVE
careful
细致 xìzhì ADVERB
meticulously

虾 xiā NOUN
shrimp
■ 龙虾 lóngxiā lobster
■ 对虾 duìxiā prawn

瞎 xiā ADJECTIVE
blind
瞎话 xiāhuà NOUN
lie

峡 xiá NOUN
gorge
■ 海峡 hǎixiá strait
峡谷 xiágǔ NOUN
canyon

狭 xiá ADJECTIVE
narrow
■ 狭窄 xiázhǎi narrow

下 xià
I VERB
1 to go down
下山 xià shān to go down the mountain
下楼 xià lóu to go downstairs
下床 xià chuáng to get out of bed
2 to fall
■ 下雪 xiàxuě to snow
■ 下雨 xiàyǔ to rain
3 to issue
下发通知 xiàfā tōngzhī to issue a notification
4 to put... in
下饺子 xià jiǎozi to put the dumplings in boiling water
5 to give
下命令 xià mìnglìng to give an order
6 to begin
■ 下笔 xiàbǐ to start to write
7 to get off of
■ 下班 xiàbān to get off of work
■ 下课 xiàkè to get out of class
8 to lay
下蛋 xià dàn to lay an egg

LANGUAGE TIP 下 xià is used following a verb to indicate separation from an object.

拧下灯泡 nǐng xià dēngpào to unscrew a light bulb

LANGUAGE TIP 下 xià is also used following a verb to indicate the completion of an action.

记录下会议内容 jìlù xià huìyì nèiróng to take the minutes at a meeting
II ADJECTIVE
1 lower *(used before a noun)*
■ 下层 xiàcéng lower level
2 next *(in time, order)*
下个星期 xià gè xīngqī next week
■ 下次 xiàcì next time
III PREPOSITION
1 beneath *(used after a noun)*
桌子下 zhuōzi xià under the table
■ 楼下 lóuxià downstairs
2 under *(scope, situation, condition)*
在压力下 zài yālì xià under pressure
■ 在朋友的帮助下 zài péngyǒu de bāngzhù xià with help from friends
IV MEASURE WORD
time
拍了几下 pāi le jǐ xià to tap a few times 拧了两下 nǐng le liǎng xià to turn a couple of times
下跌 xiàdiē VERB
to fall
物价在下跌。Wùjià zài xiàdiē. Prices are falling.
下岗 xiàgǎng VERB
1 to stand down *(from duty)*

2 to be laid off

下海 xiàhǎi VERB
to go into business

下级 xiàjí NOUN
subordinate

下来 xiàlai VERB
1 to come down
我不上去了，你下来吧。Wǒ bú shàngqu le, nǐ xiàlai ba. I won't come up, you come down.
2 to be harvested
现在葡萄还没下来。Xiànzài pútao hái méi xiàlai. Right now the grapes haven't been harvested yet.

LANGUAGE TIP 下来 xiàlai is used following a verb to indicate separation.

他把眼镜摘了下来。Tā bǎ yǎnjìng zhāi le xiàlai. He took off his glasses.

LANGUAGE TIP 下来 xiàlai is used following a verb to indicate the completion of an action.

暴乱平息下来了。Bàoluàn píngxī xiàlai le. The riot has calmed down.

LANGUAGE TIP 下来 xiàlai is also used to indicate the occurrence of a certain state.

灯光暗了下来。Dēngguāng àn le xiàlai. The light faded.

下流 xiàliú ADJECTIVE
crude

下面 xiàmiàn
I ADVERB
1 underneath
2 next
II NOUN
lower levels *pl*

下去 xiàqu VERB
to go down
月亮下去了。Yuèliang xiàqu le. The moon went down.

LANGUAGE TIP 下去 xiàqu is used following a verb to indicate a downward motion.

从楼上跳下去 cóng lóu shàng tiào xiàqu to jump down from a building

LANGUAGE TIP 下去 xiàqu is used following a verb to indicate the continuation of an action.

唱下去 chàng xiàqu to continue singing

LANGUAGE TIP 下去 xiàqu is used following a verb to indicate a decline.

高烧已经退下去了。Gāoshāo yǐjing tuì xiàqu le. His temperature has already gone down.

LANGUAGE TIP 下去 xiàqu is used following a verb to indicate a deepening of the degree.

天气有可能热下去。Tiānqì yǒu kěnéng rè xiàqu. The weather will probably go on getting hotter.

下网 xiàwǎng
to go offline

下午 xiàwǔ NOUN
afternoon

下载 xiàzǎi VERB
to download

吓 xià VERB
to frighten
■ 吓人 xiàrén scary

吓唬 xiàhu VERB
to frighten

夏 xià NOUN
summer

夏令营 xiàlìngyíng NOUN
summer camp

夏天 xiàtiān NOUN
summer

仙 xiān NOUN
immortal
■ 仙人 xiānrén immortal

先 xiān ADJECTIVE
first
■ 事先 shìxiān beforehand

先后 xiānhòu ADVERB
successively

先进 xiānjìn ADJECTIVE
advanced

先生 xiānsheng NOUN
1 Mr

LANGUAGE TIP In Chinese, titles such as **Mr**, **Mrs**, **Miss** and **Ms** come after the surname.

王先生 Wáng xiānsheng Mr Wang
2 teacher
3 husband

纤 xiān ADJECTIVE
fine

纤维 xiānwéi NOUN
fibre

掀 xiān VERB
to lift

掀起 xiānqǐ VERB
1 to lift
把锅盖掀起 bǎ guōgài xiānqǐ to lift the

pot's lid
2 to surge
暴风掀起巨浪。Bàofēng xiānqǐ jùlàng. The wind made huge waves surge.

鲜 xiān
I ADJECTIVE
1 fresh
2 delicious
II NOUN
delicacy
■ 海鲜 hǎixiān seafood
鲜艳 xiānyàn ADJECTIVE
brightly-coloured

闲 xián
I ADJECTIVE
1 idle
■ 闲逛 xiánguàng to stroll
2 quiet
■ 安闲 ānxián inactive
3 unused
■ 闲房 xiánfáng empty house
II NOUN
leisure
闲话 xiánhuà NOUN
1 gossip
2 digression
闲事 xiánshì NOUN
other people's business

弦 xián NOUN
1 string
管弦乐器 guǎnxián yuèqì string instruments
2 a spring
■ 上弦 shàngxián to wind up

咸 xián ADJECTIVE
salted
■ 咸菜 xiáncài pickled vegetables *pl*

嫌 xián VERB
to dislike
他嫌这儿吵，搬走了。Tā xián zhèr chǎo, bānzǒu le. He found it too noisy here and moved away.
嫌弃 xiánqì VERB
to cold-shoulder
嫌疑 xiányí NOUN
suspicion

显 xiǎn VERB
1 to display
2 to be apparent
显然 xiǎnrán ADVERB
obviously
显示 xiǎnshì VERB
to demonstrate
显眼 xiǎnyǎn ADJECTIVE
conspicuous
显著 xiǎnzhù ADJECTIVE
striking

险 xiǎn ADJECTIVE
1 strategic
■ 险要的地方 xiǎnyào de dìfang a strategic place
2 dangerous
■ 险境 xiǎnjìng precipice

县 xiàn NOUN
county

现 xiàn ADJECTIVE
1 present
■ 现状 xiànzhuàng present situation
2 ready
■ 现金 xiànjīn cash
现场 xiànchǎng NOUN
scene
现场报道 xiànchǎng bàodào live report
现成 xiànchéng ADJECTIVE
ready-made
现代 xiàndài
I ADJECTIVE
modern
现代舞蹈 xiàndài wǔdǎo modern dance
II NOUN
modern times *pl*
现代化 xiàndàihuà NOUN
modernization
现实 xiànshí NOUN
reality
现象 xiànxiàng NOUN
phenomenon
现在 xiànzài NOUN
now

限 xiàn
I VERB
to limit
■ 限定 xiàndìng to limit
II NOUN
limit
■ 上限 shàngxiàn upper limit
限期 xiànqī
I NOUN
time limit
II VERB
to set a deadline

限制 xiànzhì VERB
to restrict

线 xiàn NOUN
1 thread
■ 电线 diànxiàn electric wire
2 line
线索 xiànsuǒ NOUN
clue

宪 xiàn NOUN
constitution
宪法 xiànfǎ NOUN
constitution

陷 xiàn
I NOUN
1 trap *(formal)*
2 fault
■ 缺陷 quēxiàn defect
II VERB
1 to get bogged down
■ 陷入 xiànrù
2 to sink
■ 内陷 nèixiàn concave
3 to get involved
陷入一场纷争 xiànrù yìchǎng fēnzhēng to get involved in a dispute
陷害 xiànhài VERB
to cast blame on
陷阱 xiànjǐng NOUN
trap

馅 xiàn NOUN
stuffing
饺子馅 jiǎozi xiàn dumpling filling

羡 xiàn VERB
to admire
羡慕 xiànmù VERB
to admire

献 xiàn VERB
1 to give
■ 献血 xiànxiě to donate blood
2 to show
■ 献艺 xiànyì to demonstrate an art form

腺 xiàn NOUN
gland

乡 xiāng NOUN
1 countryside
2 home town
乡村 xiāngcūn NOUN
village
乡下 xiāngxià NOUN
countryside

相 xiāng ADVERB
▷ *see also* xiàng
mutually
■ 相差 xiāngchà to differ
相处 xiāngchǔ VERB
to get along
相当 xiāngdāng
I VERB
to match
双方实力相当。Shuāngfāng shílì xiāngdāng. Both sides are of equal strength.
II ADJECTIVE
appropriate
相当的人选 xiāngdāng de rénxuǎn an appropriate selection
III ADVERB
quite
相当满意 xiāngdāng mǎnyì quite satisfied
相对 xiāngduì
I VERB
to be opposite
II ADJECTIVE
1 relative
相对收入 xiāngduì shōurù relative income
2 comparative
相对而言 xiāngduì ér yán comparatively speaking
相反 xiāngfǎn
I ADJECTIVE
opposite
II CONJUNCTION
on the contrary
相关 xiāngguān VERB
to be related
相互 xiānghù
I ADJECTIVE
mutual
II ADVERB
相互理解 xiānghù lǐjiě to understand each other
相识 xiāngshí VERB
to be acquainted
相似 xiāngsì ADJECTIVE
similar
相同 xiāngtóng ADJECTIVE
identical
相像 xiāngxiàng VERB
to be alike
相信 xiāngxìn VERB
to believe

香 xiāng

I ADJECTIVE
1 fragrant
2 delicious
饭菜很香。Fàncài hěn xiāng. The food is delicious.
3 sound
睡得香 shuì de xiāng to sleep soundly
II NOUN
1 spice
2 incense

香波 xiāngbō NOUN
shampoo

香肠 xiāngcháng NOUN
sausage

香港 Xiānggǎng NOUN
Hong Kong

香蕉 xiāngjiāo NOUN
banana

香料 xiāngliào NOUN
spice

香水 xiāngshuǐ NOUN
perfume

香烟 xiāngyān NOUN
cigarette

香皂 xiāngzào NOUN
soap

箱 xiāng NOUN
box

箱子 xiāngzi NOUN
box

详 xiáng ADJECTIVE
detailed

详情 xiángqíng NOUN
details *pl*

详细 xiángxì ADJECTIVE
detailed

享 xiǎng VERB
to enjoy

享受 xiǎngshòu VERB
to enjoy

响 xiǎng
I NOUN
1 echo
2 sound
II VERB
to sound
手机响了。Shǒujī xiǎng le. The mobile phone rang.
III ADJECTIVE
loud

响亮 xiǎngliàng ADJECTIVE
loud and clear

响应 xiǎngyìng VERB
to respond

想 xiǎng VERB
1 to think
想办法 xiǎng bànfǎ to think of a way
2 to reckon
3 to want to
4 to miss

想法 xiǎngfǎ NOUN
opinion

想念 xiǎngniàn VERB
to miss

想像 xiǎngxiàng
I VERB
to imagine
II NOUN
imagination

向 xiàng
I NOUN
direction
II VERB
1 to face
■ 向阳 xiàngyáng to face the sun
2 to side with
妈妈向着妹妹。Māma xiàngzhe mèimei. Mother sided with my sister.
III PREPOSITION
to
我向他表示了感谢。Wǒ xiàng tā biǎoshì le gǎnxiè. I expressed my thanks to him.

向导 xiàngdǎo NOUN
guide

向来 xiànglái ADVERB
always

项 xiàng
I NOUN
item
■ 事项 shìxiàng item
II MEASURE WORD
item
三项要求 sān xiàng yāoqiú three requirements 二项任务 liǎng xiàng rènwu two tasks

项链 xiàngliàn NOUN
necklace

项目 xiàngmù NOUN
1 item
2 project

巷 xiàng NOUN
lane

相 xiàng NOUN

▷ *see also* xiāng

1 appearance

■ 面相 miànxiàng physiognomy

2 posture

■ 坐相 zuòxiàng seated posture

3 minister

■ 外相 wàixiàng foreign minister

4 photograph

■ 照相 zhàoxiàng to take a photograph

相貌 xiàngmào NOUN
appearance

相片 xiàngpiàn NOUN
photograph

象 xiàng NOUN

1 elephant

2 appearance

象棋 xiàngqí NOUN
Chinese chess

DID YOU KNOW...?
象棋 xiàngqí is a very popular board game in China. There are some similarities between Chinese chess and international chess.

象牙 xiàngyá NOUN
ivory

象征 xiàngzhēng VERB
to symbolize

像 xiàng

I NOUN
portrait

■ 画像 huàxiàng to paint portraits

■ 雕像 diāoxiàng statue

II VERB
to look like

他们兄弟俩长得很像。Tāmen xiōngdìliǎ zhǎngde hěnxiàng. The two brothers look alike.

III PREPOSITION
like

像他这样的好孩子，谁不喜欢呢！Xiàng tā zhèyàng de hǎo háizi, shéi bù xǐhuān ne! Who doesn't like good children like this one!

IV ADVERB
as if

像要下雪了。Xiàng yào xiàxuě le. It looks as if it might snow.

橡 xiàng NOUN

1 oak

2 rubber tree

橡胶 xiàngjiāo NOUN
rubber

橡皮 xiàngpí NOUN
rubber

削 xiāo VERB
to peel

消 xiāo VERB

1 to disappear

2 to remove

消除 xiāochú VERB
to eliminate

消防 xiāofáng NOUN
fire fighting

消费 xiāofèi VERB
to consume

消耗 xiāohào VERB
to consume

消化 xiāohuà VERB
to digest

消极 xiāojí ADJECTIVE

1 negative

2 demoralized

消灭 xiāomiè VERB

1 to die out

2 to eradicate

消失 xiāoshī VERB
to vanish

消息 xiāoxi NOUN
news *sg*

宵 xiāo NOUN
night

■ 通宵 tōngxiāo all night

销 xiāo VERB

1 to melt

2 to cancel

■ 销假 xiāojià to cancel the vacation

3 to market

■ 畅销小说 chàngxiāo xiǎoshuō bestselling novel

4 to spend

■ 开销 kāixiāo overhead

销路 xiāolù NOUN
sales *pl*

销售 xiāoshòu VERB
to sell

小 xiǎo ADJECTIVE
small

年龄小 niánlíng xiǎo young

小便 xiǎobiàn

I VERB
to urinate

II NOUN
urine

小吃 xiǎochī NOUN

1 snack

2 cold dish

Chinese-English

小丑 xiǎochǒu NOUN
clown

小儿科 xiǎo'érkē NOUN
paediatrics department

小费 xiǎofèi NOUN
tip

小伙子 xiǎohuǒzi NOUN
lad

小姐 xiǎojiě NOUN
1 Miss
■ 张小姐 Zhāng xiǎojiě Miss Zhang
2 young lady

小看 xiǎokàn VERB
to underestimate

小麦 xiǎomài NOUN
wheat

小名 xiǎomíng NOUN
pet name

小气 xiǎoqì ADJECTIVE
1 petty
2 stingy

小区 xiǎoqū NOUN
housing complex

小时 xiǎoshí NOUN
hour

LANGUAGE TIP In Chinese, 小时 xiǎoshí can be used with or without a measure word.

小说 xiǎoshuō NOUN
novel

小提琴 xiǎotíqín NOUN
violin

小偷 xiǎotōu NOUN
thief

小心 xiǎoxīn
I VERB
to be careful
II ADJECTIVE
careful

小学 xiǎoxué NOUN
primary school

小学生 xiǎoxuéshēng NOUN
primary school pupil

小组 xiǎozǔ NOUN
group

晓 xiǎo
I NOUN
dawn
II VERB
1 to know
2 to tell

晓得 xiǎode VERB
to know

孝 xiào
I VERB
to be dutiful
■ 孝子 xiàozǐ a filial son
II NOUN
filial piety

DID YOU KNOW...?
The concept of filial piety, 孝 xiào, was central to the works of the Chinese philosopher Confucius who believed that filial piety kept a society harmonious, whether in the form of devotion towards the Emperor or towards one's parents.

孝顺 xiàoshùn
I VERB
to show filial obedience
II ADJECTIVE
filial

校 xiào NOUN
school
■ 学校 xuéxiào school

校长 xiàozhǎng NOUN
principal

哮 xiào
I NOUN
wheezing
II VERB
to wheeze

哮喘 xiàochuǎn NOUN
asthma

笑 xiào VERB
1 to laugh
2 to laugh at

笑话 xiàohua
I NOUN
joke
II VERB
to laugh at

效 xiào
I NOUN
effect
II VERB
1 to imitate
■ 效仿 xiàofǎng to follow the lead of
2 to devote... to
他效力于哪家足球俱乐部？Tā xiàolì yú nǎjiā zúqiú jùlèbù? For which football club does he work?

效果 xiàoguǒ NOUN
1 effect
教学效果 jiàoxué xiàoguǒ education's effect

X

2 effects *pl*
戏剧效果 xìjù xiàoguǒ theatrical effects
效率 xiàolǜ NOUN
efficiency
效益 xiàoyì NOUN
returns *pl*

些 xiē MEASURE WORD
1 some
多吃些水果。Duō chī xiē shuǐguǒ. Eat some more fruit.
2 a little
有些累 yǒuxiē lèi a little tired

歇 xiē VERB
to rest
歇息 xiēxi VERB
1 to have a rest
2 to go to sleep

蝎 xiē NOUN
scorpion
■ 蝎子 xiēzi scorpion

协 xié
I VERB
to assist
II ADVERB
jointly
■ 妥协 tuǒxié compromise
协会 xiéhuì NOUN
association
协调 xiétiáo
I VERB
to coordinate
II ADJECTIVE
coordinated
协议 xiéyì NOUN
agreement
协助 xiézhù VERB
to help
协作 xiézuò VERB
to collaborate

邪 xié ADJECTIVE
evil
邪恶 xié'è ADJECTIVE
evil

斜 xié
I ADJECTIVE
slanting
II VERB
to slant
斜坡 xiépō NOUN
slope

携 xié VERB
1 to carry
2 to hold
携带 xiédài VERB
to carry

鞋 xié NOUN
shoe
鞋匠 xiéjiàng NOUN
cobbler

写 xiě VERB
1 to write
■ 写字 xiězì to write characters
2 to describe
■ 描写 miáoxiě to describe
3 to draw
■ 写生 xiěshēng to sketch
写作 xiězuò VERB
to write

血 xiě NOUN
▷ *see also* xuè
blood *(colloquial)*

泄 xiè VERB
to let... out
泄露 xièlòu VERB
to let... out
她泄露了消息。Tā xièlòu le xiāoxi. She divulged information.

卸 xiè VERB
1 to unload
■ 卸车 xièchē to unload a vehicle
2 to remove
■ 卸妆 xièzhuāng to remove one's makeup
3 to take apart
■ 拆卸手表 chāixiè shǒubiǎo to take apart watches
4 to be relieved of
■ 卸任 xièrèn to step down

谢 xiè VERB
1 to thank
多谢！Duōxiè! Thanks a lot!
2 to apologize
■ 谢罪 xièzuì to apologize
3 to decline
■ 谢绝 xièjué to decline
4 to wither
花谢了。Huā xiè le. The flowers have withered.
谢谢 xièxie VERB
thank you

蟹 xiè NOUN
crab
■ 螃蟹 pángxiè crab

心 xīn NOUN
1 heart
2 mind
■ 用心 yòngxīn attentively
■ 谈心 tánxīn to talk heart-to-heart
3 centre

心得 xīndé NOUN
what one has learned

心理 xīnlǐ NOUN
psychology

心灵 xīnlíng NOUN
mind

心情 xīnqíng NOUN
mood
■ 你今天心情好不好？Nǐ jīntiān xīnqíng hǎo bù hǎo? How are you feeling today?

心愿 xīnyuàn NOUN
wish

心脏 xīnzàng NOUN
heart

心脏病 xīnzàngbìng NOUN
heart disease

辛 xīn ADJECTIVE
1 hot
2 laborious
3 bitter
■ 辛酸的回忆 xīnsuān de huíyì a bitter memory

辛苦 xīnkǔ
I ADJECTIVE
laborious
II VERB
to trouble
辛苦你了！Xīnkǔ nǐ le! You took all this trouble for me!

辛勤 xīnqín ADJECTIVE
hardworking

欣 xīn ADJECTIVE
glad

欣赏 xīnshǎng VERB
1 to admire
他的上司很欣赏他。Tāde shàngsi hěn xīnshǎng tā. His boss admires him.
2 to enjoy
欣赏音乐 xīnshǎng yīnyuè to enjoy music

新 xīn
I ADJECTIVE
new
II ADVERB
newly

新潮 xīncháo
I ADJECTIVE
fashionable
II NOUN
new trend

新陈代谢 xīn chén dàixiè NOUN
metabolism

新郎 xīnláng NOUN
bridegroom

新年 xīnnián NOUN
1 New Year
2 New Year's Day

新娘 xīnniáng NOUN
bride

新闻 xīnwén NOUN
news *sg*

新鲜 xīnxiān ADJECTIVE
1 fresh
新鲜水果 xīnxiān shuǐ guǒ fresh fruit 新鲜空气 xīnxiān kōngqì fresh air 新鲜观点 xīnxiān guāndiǎn a fresh point of view
2 tender
新鲜的嫩叶 xīnxiān de nènyè tender young leaves

新颖 xīnyǐng ADJECTIVE
original

薪 xīn NOUN
salary

薪水 xīnshuǐ NOUN
salary

信 xìn
I VERB
1 to believe
■ 轻信 qīngxìn credulity
2 to believe in
■ 信教 xìnjiào to be religious
II NOUN
1 letter
■ 信箱 xìnxiāng letterbox
2 information
■ 口信 kǒuxìn verbal message
3 trust
■ 失信 shīxìn to lose trust

信贷 xìndài NOUN
credit

信封 xìnfēng NOUN
envelope

信号 xìnhào NOUN
signal
我在这儿不能说话，手机信号不好。Wǒ zài zhèr bùnéng shuōhuà, shǒujī xìnhào bùhaǒ. I can't talk here, the mobile phone signal is weak.

信件 xìnjiàn NOUN
letter
信赖 xìnlài VERB
to trust
信任 xìnrèn VERB
to trust
信息 xìnxī NOUN
information
信心 xìnxīn NOUN
confidence
信仰 xìnyǎng NOUN
belief
他没有宗教信仰。Tā méiyǒu zōngjiào xìnyǎng. He has no religious faith.
信用 xìnyòng NOUN
1 credence
他很讲信用。Tā hěn jiǎng xìnyòng. He always keeps his word.
2 credit
信用等级 xìnyòng děngjí credit rating
信用卡 xìnyòngkǎ NOUN
credit card
信誉 xìnyù NOUN
reputation

兴 xīng VERB
▹ *see also* xìng
1 to prosper
■ 兴旺 xīngwàng prosperous
2 to be popular
■ 时兴 shíxīng fashionable
3 to promote
现在兴起了一股中国风。Xiànzài xīngqǐ le yìgǔ zhōngguó fēng. China is now trendy.
兴奋 xīngfèn VERB
to be excited
兴盛 xīngshèng ADJECTIVE
prosperous

星 xīng NOUN
star *(in astrology, famous person)*
■ 星星 xīngxing star
■ 球星 qiúxīng football star
星期 xīngqī NOUN
week
明天星期几？Míngtiān xīngqī jǐ? What day is it tomorrow?
■ 星期天 xīngqītiān Sunday

LANGUAGE TIP In Chinese, except for Sunday, the days of the week are expressed by adding a number, from 1 to 6 (1 being Monday and 6 being Saturday) behind 星期 xīngqī **week**: 星期二 xīngqī èr **Tuesday**.

猩 xīng NOUN
orang-utan
■ 黑猩猩 hēixīngxing chimpanzee

腥 xīng ADJECTIVE
fishy
■ 腥气 xīngqì fishy smell

刑 xíng NOUN
punishment
■ 死刑 sǐxíng the death penalty

行 xíng
▹ *see also* háng
I VERB
1 to walk
■ 步行 bùxíng to go on foot
2 to be current
■ 发行 fāxíng to issue
3 to do
■ 行医 xíngyī to practise medicine
II ADJECTIVE
1 OK
行，我明白了。Xíng, wǒ míngbai le. OK, I get it.
2 capable
他在体育方面样样都行。Tā zài tǐyù fāngmiàn yàngyàng dōu xíng. He is good at everything sports-wise.
III NOUN
1 travel
■ 出行 chūxíng to travel
2 behaviour
■ 暴行 bàoxíng savage act
行动 xíngdòng VERB
1 to move about
行动不便 xíngdòng búbiàn moving about isn't easy
2 to take action
下一步你将采取什么行动？Xiàyíbù nǐ jiāng cǎiqǔ shénme xíngdòng? What action will you take for the next step?
行李 xíngli NOUN
luggage
行人 xíngrén NOUN
pedestrian
行驶 xíngshǐ VERB
to travel
行为 xíngwéi NOUN
behaviour
行走 xíngzǒu VERB
to walk

形 xíng NOUN
1 shape
■ 圆形 yuánxíng circular shape

2 body
■形体 xíngtǐ figure

形成 xíngchéng VERB
to form

形容 xíngróng VERB
to describe

形式 xíngshì NOUN
form

形象 xíngxiàng NOUN
image
■公司形象 gōngsī xíngxiàng company image

形状 xíngzhuàng NOUN
shape

型 xíng NOUN
type
■体型 tǐxíng build
■血型 xuèxíng blood group

型号 xínghào NOUN
model

醒 xǐng VERB
1 to come to
■苏醒 sūxǐng to regain consciousness
2 to wake up
3 to become aware
■提醒 tíxǐng to remind

兴 xìng NOUN
▷ *see also* xīng
excitement

兴趣 xìngqù NOUN
interest
他对集邮有浓厚的兴趣。Tā duì jíyóu yǒu nónghòu de xìngqù. He has a deep interest in stamp-collecting.

杏 xìng NOUN
apricot

幸 xìng
I ADJECTIVE
lucky
II ADVERB
fortunately

幸福 xìngfú
I NOUN
happiness
II ADJECTIVE
happy

幸亏 xìngkuī ADVERB
fortunately

幸运 xìngyùn
I NOUN
good luck
II ADJECTIVE
lucky

性 xìng NOUN
character
1 character
■任性 rènxìng stubborn
2 function
■酸性 suānxìng acidity
3 gender *(of person, in grammar)*
■男性 nánxìng male
■阳性 yángxìng masculine
4 sex
■性生活 xìng shēnghuó sex life

LANGUAGE TIP 性 xìng can be added at the end of an adjective to make it a noun.

■可靠性 kěkàoxìng reliability
■实用性 shíyòngxìng utility

性别 xìngbié NOUN
sex

性感 xìnggǎn ADJECTIVE
sexy

性格 xìnggé NOUN
personality

性质 xìngzhì NOUN
character

姓 xìng
I VERB
to have the surname...
我姓李。Wǒ xìng Lǐ. My surname is Li.
II NOUN
surname

姓名 xìngmíng NOUN
full name

凶 xiōng ADJECTIVE
1 unlucky
2 fierce
他很凶。Tā hěn xiōng. He is ferocious.
■凶相 xiōngxiàng fierce look

凶狠 xiōnghěn ADJECTIVE
vicious

凶手 xiōngshǒu NOUN
murderer

兄 xiōng NOUN
brother

兄弟 xiōngdì NOUN
brother

胸 xiōng NOUN
1 chest
■胸膛 xiōngtáng chest
2 heart
■心胸 xīnxiōng breadth of mind

胸脯 xiōngpú NOUN
chest

雄 xióng ADJECTIVE
1 male
■ 雄性 xióngxìng male
2 imposing
■ 雄伟 xióngwěi majestic
3 strong
■ 英雄 yīngxióng hero

熊 xióng NOUN
bear
熊猫 xióngmāo NOUN
panda

休 xiū VERB
1 to stop
2 to rest
休息 xiūxi VERB
to rest
休闲 xiūxián VERB
to be at leisure
■ 休闲服装 xiūxián fúzhuāng casual clothes

修 xiū VERB
1 to mend
2 to build
3 to trim
修改 xiūgǎi VERB
to alter
修建 xiūjiàn VERB
to build
修理 xiūlǐ VERB
to repair
修饰 xiūshì VERB
1 to decorate
修饰房间 xiūshì fángjiān to decorate a room
2 to polish
修饰文章 xiūshì wénzhāng to polish an article
修养 xiūyǎng NOUN
refinement
文化修养 wénhuà xiūyǎng refinement of character

羞 xiū ADJECTIVE
shy
■ 害羞 hàixiū to be shy

秀 xiù
I ADJECTIVE
1 elegant
2 outstanding
II NOUN
talent
■ 新秀 xīnxiù new talent
秀气 xiùqi ADJECTIVE
1 delicate
2 refined

袖 xiù NOUN
sleeve
■ 袖子 xiùzi sleeve
袖珍 xiùzhēn ADJECTIVE
pocket-sized
袖珍收音机 xiùzhēn shōuyīnjī pocket radio

绣 xiù
I VERB
to embroider
II NOUN
embroidery

锈 xiù NOUN
rust
■ 生锈 shēngxiù to go rusty

须 xū
I ADVERB
■ 必须 bìxū must
II NOUN
beard
须要 xūyào VERB
to need
我需要吃健康的菜。Wǒ xūyaò chī jiànkāng de cài. I need to eat healthy food.
须知 xūzhī NOUN
essential knowledge

虚 xū ADJECTIVE
1 empty
2 timid
3 false
4 modest
5 weak
虚构 xūgòu VERB
to fabricate
虚假 xūjiǎ ADJECTIVE
false
虚荣 xūróng NOUN
vanity
虚弱 xūruò ADJECTIVE
frail
虚伪 xūwěi ADJECTIVE
hypocritical
虚心 xūxīn ADJECTIVE
modest

需 xū

I VERB
to need
II NOUN
needs *pl*
■ 军需 jūnxū military requirements

需求 xūqiú NOUN
requirements *pl*

需要 xūyào
I VERB
to need
II NOUN
needs *pl*
日常生活需要 rìcháng shēnghuó xūyào necessities of daily life

许 xǔ VERB
1 to praise
■ 赞许 zànxǔ approval
2 to promise
■ 许诺 xǔnuò a promise
3 to allow
妈妈不许她看太多电视。Māma bùxǔ tā kàn tàiduō diànshì. Mom doesn't allow her to watch too much TV.

许多 xǔduō ADJECTIVE
many
他养了许多金鱼。Tā yǎng le xǔduō jīnyú. He kept a lot of goldfish.

叙 xù VERB
1 to chat
2 to recount

叙事 xùshì VERB
to narrate

叙述 xùshù VERB
to recount

畜 xù VERB
to raise

畜牧 xùmù VERB
to rear
畜牧业 xùmùyè livestock breeding

酗 xù
▷ *see below:*

酗酒 xùjiǔ
I VERB
to drink to excess
II NOUN
excessive drinking

婿 xù NOUN
son-in-law
■ 女婿 nǚxù son-in-law

宣 xuān VERB
to announce
■ 宣泄 xuānxiè to get... off one's chest

宣布 xuānbù VERB
to announce

宣称 xuānchēng VERB
to announce

宣传 xuānchuán NOUN
publicity
政治宣传 zhèngzhì xuānchuán political propaganda

宣告 xuāngào VERB
to proclaim

宣誓 xuānshì VERB
to take an oath

宣言 xuānyán NOUN
declaration

宣扬 xuānyáng VERB
to advocate

宣战 xuānzhàn VERB
to declare war

喧 xuān VERB
to make noise

喧哗 xuānhuá
I ADJECTIVE
riotous
II VERB
to create a disturbance

喧闹 xuānnào ADJECTIVE
noisy

悬 xuán VERB
1 to hang
2 to be concerned about
看激烈的比赛，大家的心都悬着。Kàn jīliè de bǐsài, dàjiā de xīn dōu xuánzhe. Watching the fierce competition, everyone became worried.
3 to be unresolved

悬挂 xuánguà VERB
to hang

悬念 xuánniàn NOUN
suspense

悬崖 xuányá NOUN
precipice

旋 xuán
▷ *see also* xuàn
I VERB
1 to revolve
2 to return
■ 凯旋 kǎixuán victorious return
II NOUN
spiral

旋律 xuánlǜ NOUN
melody

旋钮 xuánniǔ NOUN
knob
旋涡 xuánwō NOUN
whirlpool
旋转 xuánzhuǎn VERB
to revolve

选 xuǎn
I VERB
1 to choose
他选了三本书。Tā xuǎn le sānběn shū. He chose three books.
2 to vote
老师们选他作校长。Lǎoshī men xuǎn tā zuò xiàozhǎng. The teachers elected him schoolmaster.
II NOUN
1 selection
■ 人选 rénxuǎn selected candidate
2 collection
■ 文选 wénxuǎn collected works *pl*
选拔 xuǎnbá VERB
to select
选举 xuǎnjǔ NOUN
election
选民 xuǎnmín NOUN
electorate
选手 xuǎnshǒu NOUN
contestant
选修 xuǎnxiū VERB
to take as an elective course
选修课程 xuǎnxiū kèchéng elective course
选择 xuǎnzé VERB
to choose
别无选择 biéwú xuǎnzé to have no choice

旋 xuàn VERB
▹ *see also* xuán
to spin
旋风 xuànfēng NOUN
whirlwind

靴 xuē NOUN
boot
靴子 xuēzi NOUN
boot

穴 xué NOUN
1 den
■ 虎穴 hǔxué tiger den
2 acupuncture point
穴位 xuéwèi NOUN
acupuncture point

学 xué
I VERB
1 to study
学英语 xué Yīngyǔ to learn English
2 to imitate
学习别人的走路姿势 xué biérén de zǒulù zīshì to imitate other people's way of walking
II NOUN
1 learning
■ 博学 bóxué erudite
2 science
■ 生物学 shēngwùxué biology
■ 化学 huàxué chemistry
3 school
■ 大学 dàxué university
■ 中学 zhōngxué senior school
■ 小学 xiǎoxué primary school
学费 xuéfèi NOUN
tuition fee
学科 xuékē NOUN
subject
学历 xuélì NOUN
educational background
学生 xuéshēng NOUN
student
学士 xuéshì NOUN
bachelor's degree
学术 xuéshù NOUN
learning
学说 xuéshuō NOUN
theory
学位 xuéwèi NOUN
degree
学问 xuéwèn NOUN
learning
学院 xuéyuàn NOUN
college
学习 xuéxí VERB
to study
学校 xuéxiào NOUN
school
学业 xuéyè NOUN
studies *pl*
学者 xuézhě NOUN
scholar

雪 xuě NOUN
snow
■ 下雪 xiàxuě to snow
雪花 xuěhuā NOUN
snowflake

血 xuè NOUN
▹ *see also* xiě
blood
血统 xuètǒng NOUN
blood relation

血型 xuèxíng NOUN
blood type

血压 xuèyā NOUN
blood pressure

血液 xuèyè NOUN
blood

刚来的年轻老师为学校注入了新鲜血液。Gānglái de niánqīng lǎoshī wèi xuéxiào zhùrù le xīnxiān xuèyè. The young teacher who had just arrived injected new life into the school.

血缘 xuèyuán NOUN
blood relation

熏 xūn VERB

1 to blacken

工厂排出的浓烟把周围的建筑都熏黑了。Gōngchǎng páichū de nóngyān bǎ zhōuwéi de jiànzhù dōu xūn hēi le. The thick smoke produced by the factory blackened all the surrounding architecture.

2 to smoke

■ 熏肉 xūnròu smoked meat

寻 xún VERB
to search

寻常 xúncháng ADJECTIVE
usual

寻求 xúnqiú VERB
to seek

寻找 xúnzhǎo VERB
to look for

巡 xún VERB
to patrol

巡逻 xúnluó VERB
to patrol

询 xún VERB
to inquire

询问 xúnwèn VERB
to ask

循 xún VERB
to abide by

■ 遵循 zūnxún to abide by

循环 xúnhuán VERB
to circulate

■ 恶性循环 èxìng xúnhuán a vicious circle

训 xùn

I VERB

1 to teach

■ 训话 xùnhuà pontification

2 to train

■ 训练 xùnliàn to train

II NOUN
rule

■ 校训 xiàoxùn school motto

迅 xùn ADJECTIVE
swift

迅速 xùnsù ADJECTIVE
swift

驯 xùn

I ADJECTIVE
tame

■ 温驯 wēnxùn tame

II VERB
to tame

■ 驯兽 xùnshòu tame animals

驯服 xùnfú

I ADJECTIVE
tame

II VERB
to tame

Yy

压 yā
I VERB
1 to press
2 to suppress
II NOUN
pressure

压力 yālì NOUN
pressure
他的生活压力很大。Tā de shēnghuó yālì hěndà. He's under a lot of stress in his life.

压岁钱 yāsuìqián NOUN
New Year's money

> **DID YOU KNOW...?**
> 压岁钱 yāsuìqián **New Year's money** is a gift given to young children by parents and older relatives traditionally on New Year's Eve. The gift usually takes the form of brand new bank notes, presented in a red envelope.

压抑 yāyì VERB
to suppress
他受不了这样压抑地生活下去了。Tā shòubùliǎo zhèyàng yāyì de shēnghuó xiàqù le. He can't stand this repressed lifestyle any longer.

呀 yā INTERJECTION
oh
呀！已经12点了！Yā! Yǐjīng shí'èr diǎn le! Oh! It's 12 o'clock already!

押 yā VERB
to leave... as a security

押金 yājīn NOUN
deposit

鸭 yā NOUN
duck

牙 yá NOUN
tooth

牙齿 yáchǐ NOUN
tooth

牙膏 yágāo NOUN
toothpaste

牙签 yáqiān NOUN
toothpick

牙刷 yáshuā NOUN
toothbrush

> **LANGUAGE TIP** 牙刷 yáshuā is a reversible word. Swap the characters around and you get the verb **to brush one's teeth** 刷牙 shuāyá.

牙痛 yátòng NOUN
toothache

牙医 yáyī NOUN
dentist

哑 yǎ ADJECTIVE
1 mute
2 speechless
3 hoarse
声音沙哑 shēngyīn shāyǎ a hoarse voice

哑巴 yǎba NOUN
mute

哑语 yǎyǔ NOUN
sign language

亚 yà
I ADJECTIVE
inferior
■ 亚军 yàjūn runner-up
II NOUN
Asia

亚洲 Yàzhōu NOUN
Asia
■ 她是亚洲人。Tā shì Yàzhōurén. She's Asian.

咽 yān NOUN
▷ *see also* yàn
pharynx

咽喉 yānhóu NOUN
throat

烟 yān NOUN
1 smoke
2 tobacco
■ 香烟 xiāngyān cigarette

烟草 yāncǎo NOUN
1 tobacco plant
2 tobacco
烟花 yānhuā NOUN
firework
烟灰缸 yānhuīgāng NOUN
ashtray

淹 yān VERB
to flood
淹没 yānmò VERB
to submerge
洪水淹没了村庄。Hóngshuǐ yānmò le cūnzhuāng. The village was submerged by the flood.

延 yán VERB
1 to extend
2 to delay
延长 yáncháng VERB
to extend
延迟 yánchí VERB
to delay
开会延迟了一个小时。Kāihuì yánchí le yígè xiǎoshí. The meeting was delayed by one hour.

严 yán ADJECTIVE
1 tight
2 strict
严格 yángé ADJECTIVE
strict
严厉 yánlì ADJECTIVE
severe
严肃 yánsù ADJECTIVE
1 solemn
这是一个非常严肃的活动。Zhè shì yígè fēicháng yánsù de huódòng. This is an extremely solemn activity.
2 severe
这是一个非常严肃的问题。Zhè shì yígè fēicháng yánsù de wèntí. This is an extremely severe problem.
严重 yánzhòng ADJECTIVE
serious

言 yán
I VERB
to speak
II NOUN
1 speech
2 words *pl*
言论 yánlùn NOUN
speech
言论自由 yánlùn zìyóu freedom of speech

言情片 yánqíngpiān NOUN
romantic film
言语 yányǔ NOUN
language
这份感情不能够用言语来表达。Zhèfèn gǎnqíng bù nénggòu yòng yányǔ lái biǎodá. This feeling cannot be expressed in words.

岩 yán NOUN
rock
■ 岩石 yánshí rock

炎 yán
I ADJECTIVE
scorching
II NOUN
inflammation
炎黄子孙 Yán-Huáng zǐsūn NOUN
Chinese people

> LANGUAGE TIP This literally means **the descendants of Yan Di and Huang Di**, two legendary rulers of remote antiquity.

炎热 yánrè ADJECTIVE
scorching hot
炎症 yánzhèng NOUN
inflammation

沿 yán PREPOSITION
along
沿岸 yán'àn NOUN
bank
沿海 yánhǎi NOUN
coast

研 yán VERB
to research
■ 研究院 yánjiūyuàn research institute
■ 研究生 yánjiūshēng postgraduate student
研究 yánjiū VERB
1 to research
科学研究 kēxué yánjiū scientific research
2 to discuss
我们一起来研究一下解决办法吧。Wǒmen yìqǐ lái yánjiū yíxià jiějué bànfǎ ba. Let's work out a solution together.

盐 yán NOUN
salt

颜 yán NOUN
1 face
■ 颜面 yánmiàn 1 face 2 prestige
2 colour

颜料 yánliào NOUN
colouring

颜色 yánsè NOUN
colour

眼 yǎn NOUN
1 eye
2 small hole

眼光 yǎnguāng NOUN
1 gaze
2 vision
他看人的眼光很独到。Tā kàn rén de yǎnguāng hěn dúdào. He's got a very good eye for people.

眼红 yǎnhóng VERB
to be jealous

眼界 yǎnjiè NOUN
horizons *pl*

眼睛 yǎnjing NOUN
eye

眼镜 yǎnjìng NOUN
glasses *pl*

眼泪 yǎnlèi NOUN
tear

眼神 yǎnshén NOUN
expression
老师给学生一个鼓励的眼神。Lǎoshī gěi xuéshēng yígè gǔlì de yǎnshén. The teacher gave the students an encouraging look.

演 yǎn VERB
to perform

演出 yǎnchū VERB
to perform

演讲 yǎnjiǎng VERB
to make a speech

演示 yǎnshì VERB
to demonstrate

演说 yǎnshuō VERB
to make a speech

演员 yǎnyuán NOUN
performer

演奏 yǎnzòu VERB
to perform *(song, music)*

厌 yàn VERB
to detest

厌烦 yànfán VERB
to be sick of

厌恶 yànwù VERB
to loathe

咽 yàn VERB
▷ *see also* yān
to swallow

宴 yàn VERB
to host a dinner
■ 宴请 yànqǐng to invite... to dinner

宴会 yànhuì NOUN
banquet

验 yàn VERB
to test

验光 yànguāng VERB
to have an eye test

验血 yànxiě VERB
to have a blood test

谚 yàn NOUN
saying
■ 谚语 yànyǔ proverb

雁 yàn NOUN
wild goose

焰 yàn NOUN
flame

燕 yàn NOUN
swallow

燕麦 yànmài NOUN
oats *pl*

燕尾服 yànwěifú NOUN
tailcoat

羊 yáng NOUN
sheep
■ 山羊 shānyáng goat

羊毛 yángmáo NOUN
wool

羊绒衫 yángróngshān NOUN
cashmere

羊肉 yángròu NOUN
mutton

阳 yáng NOUN
1 Yang
2 sun
■ 阳光 yángguāng sunlight

DID YOU KNOW...?
阳 yáng **yang**, in ancient Chinese thought, is the positive, masculine principle. Together with **yin**, it is one of the two opposites that exist in all things under heaven. **Yang** represents the sun and the living world.

阳台 yángtái NOUN
balcony

阳性 yángxìng NOUN
1 positive

2 masculine

洋 yáng
I NOUN
ocean
II ADJECTIVE
foreign
洋葱 yángcōng NOUN
onion

仰 yǎng VERB
to look up
仰望 yǎngwàng VERB
to look up

养 yǎng
I VERB
1 to provide for
2 to keep
我爱养花。Wǒ ài yǎng huā. I like growing flowers.
3 to form
养成习惯 yǎng chéng xíguàn to form a habit
II ADJECTIVE
foster
■ 养母 yǎngmǔ foster mother
■ 养子 yǎngzǐ adopted son
养料 yǎngliào NOUN
nourishment
养育 yǎngyù VERB
to bring up

痒 yǎng VERB
to itch

样 yàng
I NOUN
1 style
2 sample
II MEASURE WORD
type
三样水果 sān yàng shuǐguǒ three types of fruit
样品 yàngpǐn NOUN
sample
样式 yàngshì NOUN
style
样子 yàngzi NOUN
1 appearance
2 expression

妖 yāo NOUN
evil spirit
妖精 yāojing NOUN
demon

要 yāo VERB
▷ *see also* yào
to ask
要求 yāoqiú
I VERB
to demand
老板尽量满足顾客的一切要求。Lǎobǎn jìnliàng mǎnzú gùkè de yíqiè yāoqiú. The proprietor did his best to satisfy the customer's every demand.
II NOUN
request
老师要求学生保持安静。Lǎoshī yāoqiú xuéshēng bǎochí ānjìng. The teacher asked the students to keep quiet.

腰 yāo NOUN
waist
腰带 yāodài NOUN
belt
腰果 yāoguǒ NOUN
cashew nut
腰围 yāowéi NOUN
waistline

邀 yāo VERB
to invite
邀请 yāoqǐng VERB
to invite

谣 yáo NOUN
1 folk song
■ 歌谣 gēyáo folk song
2 rumour
■ 谣言 yáoyán hearsay
谣传 yáochuán
I VERB
to be rumoured
II NOUN
rumour

摇 yáo VERB
to shake
摇动 yáodòng VERB
1 to wave
2 to shake
摇滚乐 yáogǔnyuè NOUN
rock and roll
摇晃 yáohuàng VERB
to shake
摇篮 yáolán NOUN
cradle

遥 yáo ADJECTIVE
distant
■ 遥控器 yáokòngqì remote control

遥控 yáokòng VERB
to operate by remote control

遥远 yáoyuǎn ADJECTIVE
1 distant
我们相隔遥远。Wǒmen xiānggé yáoyuǎn. A great distance lies between us.
2 far-off
离成功那一天还很遥远。Lí chénggōng nàyìtiān hái hěn yáoyuǎn. Success is still a long way off.

咬 yǎo VERB
to bite

药 yào NOUN
medicine

药材 yàocái NOUN
medicinal material

药店 yàodiàn NOUN
chemist's

药方 yàofāng NOUN
prescription

药物 yàowù NOUN
medicine

要 yào
▷ *see also* yāo

I ADJECTIVE
important

II VERB
1 to want
我女儿要一个新书包。Wǒ nǚ'ér yào yí gè xīn shūbāo. My daughter wants a new schoolbag. 我要学开车。Wǒ yào xué kāichē. I want to learn to drive.
2 to ask
老师要我们安静。Lǎoshī yào wǒmen ānjìng. The teacher asked us to be quiet.
3 should
饭前要洗手。Fàn qián yào xǐshǒu. You should wash your hands before you eat.
4 to need
我要上厕所。Wǒ yào shàng cèsuǒ. I need the toilet.
5 to be about to
我们要放暑假了。Wǒmen yào fàng shǔjià le. We're about to break for summer vacation.

LANGUAGE TIP 要 yào can be used to express something definite.

我明天要上班。Wǒ míngtiān yào shàngbān. I am going to work tomorrow.

III CONJUNCTION
if
你要碰见他，替我问声好。Nǐ yào pèngjiàn tā, tì wǒ wèn shēng hǎo. If you meet him, say hello from me.

要不 yàobù CONJUNCTION
1 otherwise
快点走，要不你要迟到了。Kuàidiǎn zǒu, yàobù nǐ yào chídào le. Go quickly, otherwise you'll be late.
2 either... or
我们要不去看电影，要不去咖啡厅，你说呢？Wǒmen yàobù qù kàn diànyǐng, yàobù qù kāfēitīng, nǐ shuō ne? We can either go to see a film or go to a coffee shop; which would you prefer?

要紧 yàojǐn ADJECTIVE
1 important
2 serious

要么 yàome CONJUNCTION
either... or
你要么学文，要么学理。Nǐ yàome xué wén, yàome xué lǐ. You either study arts or science.

要是 yàoshi CONJUNCTION
if
要是你不满意，可以随时退货。Yàoshi nǐ bù mǎnyì, kěyǐ suíshí tuìhuò. If you're not satisfied, you can return the goods at any time.

钥 yào
▷ *see below:*

钥匙 yàoshi NOUN
key

耶 yē
▷ *see below:*

耶稣 Yēsū NOUN
Jesus

椰 yē NOUN
coconut

椰子 yēzi NOUN
coconut

爷 yé NOUN
grandfather

LANGUAGE TIP 爷 yé refers specifically to the grandfather on the father's side.

爷爷 yéye NOUN
granddad

LANGUAGE TIP 爷 yé refers specifically to the granddad on the father's side.

也 yě ADVERB
1 also
他也去过中国。Tā yě qùguò Zhōngguó. He's been to China too.
2 still
即使他来了，也帮不上忙。Jíshǐ tā lái le,

yě bāng bú shàng máng. Even if he comes, it still won't be of any use.

也许 yěxǔ ADVERB
perhaps

野 yě
I NOUN
open country
■ 野餐 yěcān picnic
II ADJECTIVE
1 wild
■ 野菜 yěcài wild herbs *pl*
2 rude
■ 粗野 cūyě rough
3 unruly

野蛮 yěmán ADJECTIVE
1 uncivilized
2 brutal

野生 yěshēng ADJECTIVE
wild

野兽 yěshòu NOUN
wild animal

野外 yěwài NOUN
open country

野心 yěxīn NOUN
ambition

业 yè NOUN
1 industry
饮食业 yǐnshí yè the food and drink industry
2 job
■ 失业 shīyè to be unemployed
3 studies *pl*
■ 毕业 bìyè graduate
4 property
■ 家业 jiāyè family property

业务 yèwù NOUN
profession

业余 yèyú
I NOUN
spare time
II ADJECTIVE
amateurish

叶 yè NOUN
leaf

页 yè
I NOUN
page
II MEASURE WORD
page
一页书 yíyèshū a page of a book

页码 yèmǎ NOUN
page number

夜 yè NOUN
night

夜班 yèbān NOUN
night shift

夜生活 yèshēnghuó NOUN
nightlife

夜市 yèshì NOUN
night market

夜宵 yèxiāo NOUN
late-night snack

夜总会 yèzǒnghuì NOUN
nightclub

液 yè NOUN
liquid

液体 yètǐ NOUN
liquid

一 yī NUMBER
one
■ 一辈子 yíbèizi a lifetime
■ 一类人 yí lèi rén the same sort of people
■ 一屋子烟 yì wūzi yān full of smoke

LANGUAGE TIP The character 一 yī is originally first tone, but like 不 bù, it can change tone in certain situations. It remains first tone when used by itself, if used at the end of the sentence, and when used as a numeral or ordinal numeral such as 二十一 èrshíyī, **21**, and 第一 dìyī, **the first**. Its tone changes in the following situations: 1) Directly before the fourth tone, 一 becomes second tone. For example, 一样 yíyàng, 一次 yícì, 一下子 yíxiàzi. 2) Directly before the first, second and third tones, 一 becomes fourth tone. For example, 一年 yìnián, 一起 yìqǐ. 3) Between repeated verbs, 一 is unstressed. For example, 试一试 shìyishì, 看一看 kànyikàn. 4) Used between a verb/adjective and a measure word, 一 is usually unstressed. For example 去一趟 qùyitàng, 好一点儿 hǎoyidiǎn'er.

一般 yìbān ADJECTIVE
1 same
他们俩一般大。Tāmen liǎ yìbān dà. The two of them are the same age.
2 ordinary
这个商品质量一般。Zhègè shāngpǐn zhìliàng yìbān. This is an average quality product.

一半 yíbàn NOUN
half

一边 yìbiān

I NOUN
side
这一边人比较少。Zhè yìbiān rén bǐjiào shǎo. There are fewer people on this side.

II ADVERB
at the same time
他一边吃饭，一边看电视。Tā yìbiān chīfàn, yìbiān kàn diànshì. He ate dinner whilst watching television.

一边儿 yìbiānr CONJUNCTION

> **LANGUAGE TIP** 一边儿 yìbiānr is used to link two activities taking place at the same time.

一边儿…一边儿… yìbiānr...yìbiānr... while...

一点儿 yìdiǎnr MEASURE WORD

1 some
你行李太多，我帮你提一点儿吧。Nǐ xíngli tàiduō, wǒ bāng nǐ tí yìdiǎnr ba. You've got so much luggage, let me help you with some of it.

2 a little
这件事我一点儿都不知道。Zhè jiàn shì wǒ yìdiǎnr dōu bù zhīdào. I know nothing about this.

一定 yídìng ADVERB
definitely
放心，我一定去机场接你。Fàngxīn, wǒ yídìng qù jīchǎng jiē nǐ. Don't worry, I'll definitely pick you up at the airport.

一共 yígòng ADVERB
altogether
这套书一共多少本？Zhè tào shū yígòng duōshao běn? How many books are there in this set?

一…就… yī...jiù... ADVERB
as soon as
我一到家就给你打电话。Wǒ yí dào jiā jiù gěi nǐ dǎ diànhuà. I'll call you as soon as I get home.

一连 yìlián ADVERB
in succession
一连下了几个月的雨。Yìlián xià le jǐ gè yuè de yǔ. It's been raining for months on end.

一路 yílù NOUN

1 journey
一路顺利吗？Yílù shùnlì ma? Did you have a good journey?

2 the same way
咱俩是一路。Zán liǎ shì yílù. We're going the same way.

一面 yímiàn

I NOUN
aspect
积极的一面 jījí de yímiàn a positive aspect

II ADVERB
at the same time
她一面听音乐，一面看小说。Tā yímiàn tīng yīnyuè, yímiàn kàn xiǎoshuō. She was listening to music and reading a novel at the same time.

一齐 yìqí ADVERB
simultaneously
大家一齐唱着同一首歌。Dàjiā yìqí chàng zhe tóng yìshǒugē. Everyone sang the song together.

一起 yìqǐ ADVERB
together
我和妹妹住在一起。Wǒ hé mèimei zhù zài yìqǐ. I live with my younger sister.

一切 yíqiè PRONOUN

1 all

2 everything

一时 yìshí ADVERB
for the moment
她只是一时不开心。Tā zhǐshì yìshí bù kāixīn. She was only unhappy for a moment.

一同 yìtóng ADVERB
together
我们一同努力，一定可以的。Wǒmen yìtóng nǔlì, yídìng kěyǐ de. I'm sure we can do it if we put the effort in together.

一下 yíxià

I MEASURE WORD

> **LANGUAGE TIP** This is a measure word used after verbs to indicate one's attempts to do something.

我去问一下。Wǒ qù wèn yíxià. I'll just go and ask.

II ADVERB
at once
天一下就冷了。Tiān yíxià jiù lěng le. All at once the weather turned cold.

一向 yíxiàng ADVERB
always

一些 yìxiē MEASURE WORD

1 some

2 a few

3 a little
她感觉好一些了。Tā gǎnjué hǎo yìxiē le. She feels a little better.

一样 yíyàng ADJECTIVE
same
他俩爱好一样。Tā liǎ àihào yíyàng. They have the same hobbies.

一月 yīyuè NOUN
January

一再 yízài ADVERB
repeatedly
他一再失误，输掉了比赛。Tā yízài shīwù,

shūdiào le bǐsài. His repeated mistakes lost him the match.

一直 yìzhí ADVERB
1 straight
这条路一直走，就到了。Zhètiáolù yìzhí zǒu, jiù dào le. To get there just keep going straight down this road.
2 always
大风一直刮了两天两夜。Dàfēng yìzhí guā le liǎng tiān liǎng yè. The gale blew for two days and two nights.
3 all the way
从南一直到北 cóng nán yìzhí dào běi from the south all way to the north

一致 yízhì
I ADJECTIVE
unanimous
II ADVERB
unanimously
大家都一致同意这个决定。Dàjiā dōu yízhì tóngyì zhègè juédìng. Everyone was in unanimous agreement on the decision.

衣 yī NOUN
clothing
■ 衣裳 yīshang clothes *pl*

衣服 yīfu NOUN
clothes *pl*

衣柜 yīguì NOUN
wardrobe

医 yī
I NOUN
1 doctor
2 medicine
■ 中医 zhōngyī Chinese traditional medicine
II VERB
to treat

> **DID YOU KNOW...?**
> In China, hospitals and clinics are often categorised by the kind of medicine that is practiced. It can be 中医 zhōngyī **Chinese traditional medicine** or 西医 xīyī, **Western medicine** or indeed both.

医疗 yīliáo VERB
to treat
■ 免费医疗制度 miǎnfèi yīliáo zhìdù system of free medical care

医生 yīshēng NOUN
doctor

医术 yīshù NOUN
medical skill

医学 yīxué NOUN
medicine

医药 yīyào NOUN
medicine

医院 yīyuàn NOUN
hospital

医治 yīzhì VERB
to cure

依 yī VERB
1 to depend on
2 to comply with

依旧 yījiù ADVERB
still

依据 yījù NOUN
basis
你这样说有什么依据吗? Nǐ zhèyàng shuō yǒu shénme yījù ma? What grounds do you have for saying that?

依靠 yīkào
I VERB
to rely on
他依靠乞讨生活。Tā yīkào qǐtǎo shēnghuó. He relies on begging to survive.
II NOUN
support

依赖 yīlài VERB
to depend on

依然 yīrán ADVERB
still

依照 yīzhào PREPOSITION
according to
依照这本书，这个结论是错误的。Yīzhào zhèběnshū, zhègè jiélùn shì cuòwù de. According to this book, the conclusion is wrong.

仪 yí NOUN
1 appearance
2 ceremony
3 instrument

仪器 yíqì NOUN
instrument

仪式 yíshì NOUN
ceremony

宜 yí ADJECTIVE
suitable

姨 yí NOUN
aunt

> **LANGUAGE TIP** 姨 yí refers specifically to the sister of one's mother.

移 yí VERB
1 to move
2 to change

移动 yídòng VERB
to move
移民 yímín
I VERB
to emigrate
II NOUN
immigrant

遗 yí VERB
1 to lose
2 to leave... behind
遗产 yíchǎn NOUN
legacy
遗传 yíchuán VERB
to inherit
遗憾 yíhàn
I NOUN
regret
II VERB
to be a pity
很遗憾你没有来。Hěn yíhàn nǐ méiyǒu lái. It's such a pity that you didn't come.
遗书 yíshū NOUN
last letter *(of dying man)*
遗忘 yíwàng VERB
to forget
遗址 yízhǐ NOUN
ruins *pl*

疑 yí VERB
to doubt
疑难 yínán ADJECTIVE
knotty
疑问 yíwèn NOUN
question

已 yǐ ADVERB
already
已经 yǐjīng ADVERB
already

以 yǐ
I VERB
to use
以强凌弱 yǐ qiáng líng ruò to use one's strength to humiliate the weak
II PREPOSITION
1 according to
2 because of
■ 以内 yǐnèi within
■ 以南 yǐnán to the south
III CONJUNCTION
in order to
我们要改进技术，以提高生产效率。Wǒmen yào gǎijìn jìshù, yǐ tígāo shēngchǎn xiàolǜ. We should improve the technology in order to increase production.
以后 yǐhòu
I NOUN
future
以后我们去看电影。Yǐhòu wǒmen qù kàn diànyǐng. We'll go to the cinema sometime.
II ADVERB
later
两年以后 liǎngnián yǐhòu two years later
以及 yǐjí CONJUNCTION
as well as
工人们以及农民们都支持这个政策。Gōngrén men yǐjí nóngmín men dōu zhīchí zhègè zhèngcè. This policy is supported by both workers as well as farmers.
以来 yǐlái NOUN
入冬以来 rù dōng yǐlái since the beginning of the winter
以免 yǐmiǎn CONJUNCTION
in order to avoid
小心一点，以免失败。Xiǎoxīn yìdiǎn, yǐmiǎn shībài. In order to avoid defeat, you should be more careful.
以前 yǐqián
I NOUN
past
她以前是老师。Tā yǐqián shì lǎoshī. She used to be a teacher.
II ADVERB
before
十年以前 shí nián yǐqián ten years ago
以为 yǐwéi VERB
to think
以下 yǐxià NOUN
三十岁以下 sānshí suì yǐxià under thirty
以致 yǐzhì CONJUNCTION
so that
他多次撒谎，以致大家都不再相信他。Tā duōcì sāhuǎng, yǐzhì dàjiā dōu búzài xiāngxìn tā. He lied so much that everyone just stopped believing him.

蚁 yǐ NOUN
ant
■ 蚂蚁 mǎyǐ ant

椅 yǐ NOUN
chair
椅子 yǐzi NOUN
chair

亿 yì NUMBER
hundred million

Chinese-English

义 yì
I NOUN
1 righteousness
■正义 zhèngyì justice
2 human relationship *pl*
3 meaning
II ADJECTIVE
1 just
2 adopted
■义父 yìfù adoptive father
义卖 yìmài VERB
to sell... for charity
义气 yìqi
I NOUN
loyalty
II ADJECTIVE
loyal
义务 yìwù NOUN
duty
这是作为一名老师的义务。Zhèshì zuòwéi yìmíng lǎoshī de yìwù. This is a teacher's duty.

艺 yì NOUN
1 skill
■手艺 shǒuyì craftsmanship
2 art
艺人 yìrén NOUN
performer
艺术 yìshù
I NOUN
1 art
2 skill
管理艺术 guǎnlǐ yìshù management skills
II ADJECTIVE
artistic
艺术家 yìshùjiā NOUN
artist

忆 yì VERB
to remember
■记忆 jìyì memory

议 yì
I NOUN
opinion
■建议 jiànyì propose
II VERB
to discuss
■商议 shāngyì to discuss
议会 yìhuì NOUN
parliament
议论 yìlùn
I VERB
to discuss
II NOUN
talk

异 yì
I ADJECTIVE
1 different
■差异 chāyì difference
2 strange
3 other
■异国 yìguó foreign country
II VERB
to separate
■离异 líyì to separate
异常 yìcháng ADJECTIVE
unusual
异性 yìxìng NOUN
the opposite sex

译 yì VERB
to translate
译文 yìwén NOUN
translation

抑 yì VERB
to repress
抑郁 yìyù ADJECTIVE
depressed

易 yì ADJECTIVE
easy
易传染 yì chuánrǎn easily transmissible
易拉罐 yìlāguàn NOUN
ring-pull can

益 yì
I NOUN
benefit
II ADJECTIVE
beneficial
益处 yìchù NOUN
benefit

谊 yì NOUN
friendship
■友谊 yǒuyì friendship

意 yì NOUN
1 meaning
2 wish
■好意 hǎoyì good intention
意见 yìjiàn NOUN
1 opinion
对于这件事情，你有什么意见？Duìyú zhèjiàn shìqíng, nǐyǒu shénme yìjiàn? What do you think about this?
2 objection

y

大家都没意见，就这样做吧。Dàjiā dōu méi yìjiàn, jiù zhèyàng zuò ba. Seeing as nobody has any objections, we'll do it like this.

意识 yìshi
I NOUN
consciousness
II VERB
to realize
他还没有意识到他已经失败了。Tā háiméiyǒu yìshi dào tā yǐjīng shībài le. He's already failed, he just doesn't know it yet.

意思 yìsi NOUN
1 meaning
这个词什么意思？Zhègè cí shénme yìsi? What does this word mean?
2 interest
■ 有意思 yǒu yìsi interesting
■ 没意思 méi yìsi boring

意图 yìtú NOUN
intention

意外 yìwài
I NOUN
accident
II ADJECTIVE
unexpected

意义 yìyì NOUN
1 meaning
2 significance

因 yīn
I CONJUNCTION
because
II PREPOSITION
because of
昨天他因病缺课。Zuótiān tā yīn bìng quēkè. He missed a class yesterday because of illness.
III NOUN
cause
■ 病因 bìngyīn cause of the illness

因此 yīncǐ CONJUNCTION
therefore
她努力学习，因此通过了考试。Tā nǔlì xuéxí, yīncǐ tōngguò le kǎoshì. Because she worked hard, she passed the exam.

因而 yīn'ér CONJUNCTION
therefore

因特网 Yīntèwǎng NOUN
internet

因为 yīnwéi CONJUNCTION
because

阴 yīn
I ADJECTIVE
1 overcast
2 insidious
■ 阴谋 yīnmóu plot
3 negative
■ 阴性 yīnxìng negative
II NOUN
1 Yin *(from Yin and Yang)*
2 moon
■ 阴历 yīnlì lunar calendar
3 shade
■ 树阴 shùyīn the shade

DID YOU KNOW...?
阴 yīn **yin**, in ancient Chinese thought, is the feminine or negative principle. Together with yang, it is one of the two opposites that exist in all things under heaven. **Yin** represents the moon, shade and the nether world.

阴暗 yīn'àn ADJECTIVE
gloomy

阴凉 yīnliáng ADJECTIVE
shady and cool

音 yīn NOUN
sound

音量 yīnliàng NOUN
volume

音响 yīnxiǎng NOUN
acoustics *pl*

音像 yīnxiàng NOUN
audio and video

音乐 yīnyuè NOUN
music

音乐会 yīnyuèhuì NOUN
concert

银 yín
I NOUN
1 silver
2 money
■ 收银台 shōuyíntái cashier's desk
II ADJECTIVE
silver

银行 yínháng NOUN
bank

银河 yínhé NOUN
the Milky Way

银幕 yínmù NOUN
screen

银牌 yínpái NOUN
silver medal

引 yǐn VERB
1 to lead
■ 引路 yǐnlù to lead the way

2 to cause
3 to cite

引导 yǐndǎo VERB
1 to lead
2 to guide

引进 yǐnjìn VERB
1 to recommend
引进人才 yǐnjìn réncái to introduce qualified personnel
2 to import
引进物资 yǐnjìn wùzī to introduce goods

引力 yǐnlì NOUN
gravitation

引起 yǐnqǐ VERB
to cause
吃的太饱会引起睡意。Chīde tài bǎo huì yǐnqǐ shuìyì. A full stomach can cause drowsiness.

引用 yǐnyòng VERB
to quote

引诱 yǐnyòu VERB
1 to induce
2 to tempt

饮 yǐn
I VERB
to drink
II NOUN
drink

饮料 yǐnliào NOUN
drink

饮食 yǐnshí NOUN
food and drink

饮用水 yǐnyòngshuǐ NOUN
drinking water

隐 yǐn VERB
to conceal

隐藏 yǐncáng VERB
to conceal

隐瞒 yǐnmán VERB
to cover... up
他们在隐瞒真相。Tāmen zài yǐnmán zhēnxiàng. They're covering up the truth.

隐私 yǐnsī NOUN
private matters *pl*

瘾 yǐn NOUN
addiction
■ 上瘾 shàngyǐn to be addicted to

印 yìn
I NOUN
1 stamp
2 print
II VERB
to print

印度 yìndù NOUN
India

印刷 yìnshuā VERB
to print

印象 yìnxiàng NOUN
impression

印章 yìnzhāng NOUN
seal

荫 yìn ADJECTIVE
shady

荫凉 yìnliáng ADJECTIVE
shady and cool

应 yīng VERB
▷ *see also* yìng
1 to answer
2 to agree
3 should

应当 yīngdāng VERB
should

应该 yīnggāi VERB
should

英 yīng NOUN
1 hero
■ 精英 jīngyīng elite
2 Britain

英镑 yīngbàng NOUN
pound sterling

英格兰 Yīnggélán NOUN
England

英国 Yīngguó NOUN
Great Britain
英国的 Yīngguó de British

英国人 Yīngguórén NOUN
the British

英俊 yīngjùn ADJECTIVE
handsome

英文 yīngwén NOUN
English

> **LANGUAGE TIP** 英文 yīngwén generally refers to the written English language, whereas 英语 yīngyǔ refers to the spoken English language, although they are to some extent interchangeable. This is the same for all languages.

英雄 yīngxióng
I NOUN
hero
II ADJECTIVE
heroic

英勇 yīngyǒng ADJECTIVE
brave

英语 yīngyǔ NOUN
English

婴 yīng NOUN
baby

婴儿 yīng'ér NOUN
baby

樱 yīng NOUN
1 cherry
■ 樱桃 yīngtáo cherry
2 cherry blossom
■ 樱花 yīnghuā cherry blossom

鹰 yīng NOUN
eagle

迎 yíng VERB
1 to welcome
2 to meet

迎合 yínghé VERB
to cater to
他得迎合他的老板。Tā děi yínghé tāde lǎobǎn. He has to cater to his boss's needs.

迎接 yíngjiē VERB
to welcome
迎接新生 yíngjiē xīnshēng to welcome new students

萤 yíng NOUN
firefly
■ 萤火虫 yínghuǒchóng firefly

营 yíng
I VERB
to operate
II NOUN
camp
■ 营地 yíngdì camp

营救 yíngjiù VERB
to rescue

营养 yíngyǎng NOUN
nourishment

营业 yíngyè VERB
to do business

蝇 yíng NOUN
fly
■ 苍蝇 cāngying fly

赢 yíng VERB
1 to win
我们赢了！Wǒmen yíng le! We won!
2 to gain

赢利 yínglì NOUN
profit

影 yǐng NOUN
1 shadow
2 photograph
3 film

影片 yǐngpiàn NOUN
film

影响 yǐngxiǎng
I VERB
to affect
II NOUN
influence

影印 yǐngyìn VERB
to photocopy

应 yìng VERB
▷ *see also* yīng
1 to answer
■ 回应 huíyìng to answer
2 to respond to
3 to handle
■ 应急 yìngjí to handle an emergency

应酬 yìngchou
I VERB
to socialize with
下班后，他还要应酬客人。Xiàbān hòu, tā háiyào yìngchou kèrén. He has to socialise with guests even after leaving the office.
II NOUN
social engagement

应付 yìngfu VERB
1 to handle
2 to do half-heartedly

应用 yìngyòng
I VERB
to apply
要学会把知识应用到实践。Yào xuéhuì bǎ zhīshi yìngyòng dào shíjiàn. One should learn how to apply one's knowledge practically.
II ADJECTIVE
applied

硬 yìng
I ADJECTIVE
1 hard
2 firm
3 strong
II ADVERB
obstinately

硬币 yìngbì NOUN
coin

硬件 yìngjiàn NOUN
1 hardware
2 equipment

硬盘 yìngpán NOUN
hard disk

哟 yō INTERJECTION
oh *(surprised)*
哟，您终于到了！yō, nín zhōngyú dào le! Oh! You're here at last!

> LANGUAGE TIP 哟 yo can be added to the end of a sentence for emphasis. When used like this, the yo is unstressed.

我来了哟！Wǒ láile yo! I've arrived!

佣 yōng
▷ *see also* yòng
I VERB
to hire
II NOUN
servant
■ 佣人 yòngrén servant

拥 yōng VERB
1 to embrace
2 to gather round
3 to swarm
4 to support

拥抱 yōngbào VERB
to embrace

拥护 yōnghù VERB
to support

拥挤 yōngjǐ
I ADJECTIVE
crowded
II VERB
to crowd

拥有 yōngyǒu VERB
to have

永 yǒng
I ADJECTIVE
everlasting
II ADVERB
forever

永恒 yǒnghéng ADJECTIVE
everlasting

永久 yǒngjiǔ ADJECTIVE
eternal

永远 yǒngyuǎn ADVERB
eternally

泳 yǒng NOUN
swim

泳道 yǒngdào NOUN
lane

勇 yǒng ADJECTIVE
brave

勇敢 yǒnggǎn ADJECTIVE
brave

勇气 yǒngqì NOUN
courage

用 yòng
I VERB
1 to use
2 to consume
■ 用餐 yòngcān to have a meal
II NOUN
1 expense
■ 费用 fèiyòng expenses *pl*
2 use
■ 没用 méiyòng useless

用处 yòngchù NOUN
use

用功 yònggōng
I ADJECTIVE
hardworking
II VERB
to work hard
他学习很用功。Tā xuéxí hěn yònggōng. He's a very diligent student.

用户 yònghù NOUN
user
网络用户 wǎngluò yònghù internet user

用具 yòngjù NOUN
tool

用品 yòngpǐn NOUN
goods *pl*

用途 yòngtú NOUN
use
这个工具有很多用途。Zhègè gōngjù yǒu hěnduō yòngtú. This tool has many uses.

佣 yòng
▷ *see also* yōng
▷ *see below:*

佣金 yòngjīn NOUN
commission

优 yōu ADJECTIVE
excellent

优点 yōudiǎn NOUN
strong point

优良 yōuliáng ADJECTIVE
fine

优美 yōuměi ADJECTIVE
elegant

优势 yōushì NOUN
advantage

优先 yōuxiān VERB
to have priority

优秀 yōuxiù ADJECTIVE
outstanding

忧 yōu
I ADJECTIVE
anxious
II VERB
to worry
III NOUN
anxiety
忧伤 yōushāng ADJECTIVE
sad
忧郁 yōuyù ADJECTIVE
depressed

幽 yōu ADJECTIVE
dim
■ 幽暗 yōu'àn gloomy
幽默 yōumò ADJECTIVE
humorous

悠 yōu ADJECTIVE
1 remote
2 leisurely
悠久 yōujiǔ ADJECTIVE
long-standing
悠闲 yōuxián ADJECTIVE
leisurely

尤 yóu ADVERB
especially
尤其 yóuqí ADVERB
especially

由 yóu
I PREPOSITION
due to
由此可见… yóu cǐ kě jiàn... from this we can see...
II NOUN
cause
■ 理由 lǐyóu reason
由于 yóuyú PREPOSITION
as a result of
由于管理不善，这个公司倒闭了。Yóuyú guǎnlǐ bú shàn, zhègè gōngsī dǎobì le. As a result of mismanagement, the company has gone bankrupt.

邮 yóu
I VERB
to post
II NOUN
1 post
2 stamp
邮递 yóudì VERB
to send... by post
■ 邮递员 yóudìyuán postman
邮电 yóudiàn NOUN
post and telecommunications
邮寄 yóujì VERB
to post
邮件 yóujiàn NOUN
post
邮局 yóujú NOUN
post office
邮票 yóupiào NOUN
stamp
邮政 yóuzhèng NOUN
postal service

DID YOU KNOW...?
Postboxes in China are green, and are marked with the characters 中国邮政 Zhōngguó yóuzhèng **China Post**.

邮资 yóuzī NOUN
postage

犹 yóu ADVERB
still
犹豫 yóuyù ADJECTIVE
hesitant

油 yóu
I NOUN
oil
II ADJECTIVE
oily
油滑 yóuhuá ADJECTIVE
slippery
油腻 yóunì
I ADJECTIVE
greasy
II NOUN
greasy food
油漆 yóuqī
I NOUN
paint
II VERB
to paint

鱿 yóu NOUN
squid
鱿鱼 yóuyú NOUN
squid

游 yóu VERB
1 to swim
2 to tour
游客 yóukè NOUN
tourist
游览 yóulǎn VERB
to tour
游牧 yóumù VERB
to live a nomadic life
游戏 yóuxì

I NOUN
game
II VERB
to play

游行 yóuxíng VERB
1 to parade
2 to demonstrate

游泳 yóuyǒng
I VERB
to swim
II NOUN
swimming

游泳池 yóuyǒngchí NOUN
swimming pool

友 yǒu
I NOUN
friend
■ 男友 nányǒu boyfriend
II ADJECTIVE
friendly
■ 友好 yǒuhǎo friendly

友爱 yǒu'ài ADJECTIVE
affectionate

友情 yǒuqíng NOUN
friendship

友人 yǒurén NOUN
friend

友谊 yǒuyì NOUN
friendship

有 yǒu VERB
1 to have
2 to exist
院子里有一棵大树。Yuànzi li yǒu yì kē dàshù. There's a big tree in the courtyard.
3 to occur
我的生活有了一些变化。Wǒ de shēnghuó yǒu le yìxiē biànhuà. A few changes have occurred in my life.
■ 有时候 yǒushíhou sometimes 他有时候会过来看我。Tā yǒushíhou huì guòlái kàn wǒ. Sometimes he will come and pay me a visit.

有的 yǒude NOUN
some
展出的作品，有的来自本土，有的来自海外。Zhǎnchū de zuòpǐn, yǒude láizì běntǔ, yǒude láizì hǎiwài. Of the articles on display, some are local, others are from overseas.

有点儿 yǒudiǎnr ADVERB
somewhat

有关 yǒuguān VERB
1 to be relevant
2 to be about

有利 yǒulì ADJECTIVE
favourable

有名 yǒumíng ADJECTIVE
famous

有趣 yǒuqù ADJECTIVE
interesting

有限 yǒuxiàn ADJECTIVE
limited

有线电视 yǒuxiàn diànshì NOUN
cable TV

有幸 yǒuxìng ADJECTIVE
fortunate

有意思 yǒuyìsi ADJECTIVE
interesting
这个故事很有意思。Zhègè gùshi hěn yǒu yìsi. This is a very interesting story.

又 yòu ADVERB
1 again
他又来了。Tā yòu lái le. Here he is again.
2 at the same time
她是一个好教师，又是一个好妈妈。Tā shì yí gè hǎo jiàoshī, yòu shì yí gè hǎo māma. She's both a good teacher and a great mother.
3 another
又来了一位顾客。Yòu lái le yíwèi gùkè. Another customer arrived.
■ 又…又… yòu...yòu... both... and...

右 yòu NOUN
right
请向右转。Qǐng xiàng yòu zhuǎn. Please turn right.
■ 右边 yòubian right side
■ 右面 yòumiàn right side

幼 yòu
I ADJECTIVE
young
II NOUN
child
■ 幼儿园 yòu'éryuán nursery school

幼儿 yòu'ér NOUN
small child

幼年 yòunián NOUN
infancy

幼小 yòuxiǎo ADJECTIVE
young

幼稚 yòuzhì ADJECTIVE
1 young
2 naive

诱 yòu VERB
1 to guide
2 to entice

诱饵 yòu'ěr NOUN
bait

诱惑 yòuhuò VERB
1 to entice
2 to attract

于 yú PREPOSITION
1 in
2 than
■ 大于 dàyú bigger than

于是 yúshì CONJUNCTION
so
她完成了工作，于是就离开了。Tā wánchéng le gōngzuò, yúshì jiù líkāi le. She left after finishing her work.

余 yú NOUN
1 more than *(after numbers)*
500余人 wǔbǎi yú rén more than five hundred people
2 extra *(for time)*
■ 课余 kèyú extra-curricular

余地 yúdì NOUN
room
没有怀疑的余地。Méiyǒu huáiyí de yúdì. There's no room for doubt.

鱼 yú NOUN
fish
■ 鱼肉 yúròu fish

娱 yú
I VERB
to amuse
II NOUN
amusement

娱乐 yúlè
I VERB
to have fun
II NOUN
entertainment

渔 yú VERB
to fish
■ 渔业 yúyè fisheries

愉 yú ADJECTIVE
happy

愉快 yúkuài ADJECTIVE
happy
祝你旅行愉快！Zhù nǐ lǚxíng yúkuài! Have a pleasant journey!

愚 yú
I ADJECTIVE
foolish
■ 愚蠢 yúchǔn foolish
II VERB
to fool
■ 愚弄 yúnòng to make a fool of

愚昧 yúmèi ADJECTIVE
ignorant

与 yǔ
I PREPOSITION
with
她与一个德国人结婚了。Tā yǔ yígè Déguórén jiéhūn le. She married a German.
II CONJUNCTION
and

宇 yǔ NOUN
universe

宇航 yǔháng
I VERB
to travel through space
II NOUN
space travel

宇航员 yǔhángyuán NOUN
astronaut

宇宙 yǔzhòu NOUN
universe

羽 yǔ NOUN
feather

羽毛 yǔmáo NOUN
feather

羽毛球 yǔmáoqiú NOUN
1 badminton
2 shuttlecock

羽绒服 yǔróngfú NOUN
down coat

雨 yǔ NOUN
rain
■ 下雨 xiàyǔ to rain

雨具 yǔjù NOUN
waterproofs *pl*

雨水 yǔshuǐ NOUN
rain

语 yǔ
I NOUN
language
■ 手语 shǒuyǔ sign language
II VERB
to talk

语调 yǔdiào NOUN
tone

语法 yǔfǎ NOUN
grammar

语句 yǔjù NOUN
sentence
语气 yǔqì NOUN
tone of voice
她的语气很和善。Tāde yǔqì hěn héshàn.
She has a very genial tone of voice.
语文 yǔwén NOUN
Chinese
语言 yǔyán NOUN
language
语音 yǔyīn NOUN
pronunciation
语音信箱 yǔyīn xìnxiāng NOUN
voice mail
语种 yǔzhǒng NOUN
language

玉 yù NOUN
jade
玉米 yùmǐ NOUN
maize

郁 yù ADJECTIVE
gloomy
郁闷 yùmèn ADJECTIVE
melancholy

育 yù
I VERB
1 to give birth to
■ 生育 shēngyù to give birth to
2 to raise
■ 养育 yǎngyù to bring up
II NOUN
education
■ 教育 jiàoyù education

狱 yù NOUN
prison
■ 监狱 jiānyù prison

浴 yù VERB
to wash
浴盆 yùpén NOUN
bath
浴室 yùshì NOUN
bathroom

预 yù ADVERB
in advance
预报 yùbào VERB
to predict
■ 天气预报 tiānqì yùbào weather forecast
预备 yùbèi VERB
to prepare
预测 yùcè VERB
to predict
预防 yùfáng VERB
to prevent
预防感冒 yùfáng gǎnmào to prevent a cold
预感 yùgǎn VERB
to have a premonition
预计 yùjì VERB
to estimate
预见 yùjiàn VERB
to foresee
预科 yùkē NOUN
foundation course
预料 yùliào VERB
to predict
预习 yùxí VERB
to prepare for lessons
预言 yùyán VERB
to predict

域 yù NOUN
region
■ 领域 lǐngyù realm

欲 yù NOUN
desire
欲望 yùwàng NOUN
desire

遇 yù
I VERB
to meet
■ 遇到 yùdào to meet
II NOUN
1 treatment
■ 待遇 dàiyù 1 treatment 2 salary
2 opportunity
■ 机遇 jīyù opportunity

寓 yù
I VERB
to live
II NOUN
residence
■ 公寓 gōngyù flat
寓言 yùyán NOUN
fable

鸳 yuān NOUN
mandarin duck
鸳鸯 yuānyang NOUN
mandarin duck

元 yuán
I NOUN
1 first
2 component

■单元 dānyuán unit
II MEASURE WORD
yuan
五元钱 wǔ yuán qián five yuan
元旦 Yuándàn NOUN
New Year's Day
元件 yuánjiàn NOUN
part
元宵 yuánxiāo NOUN
glutinous rice balls
元宵节 Yuánxiāo Jié NOUN
the Lantern Festival

DID YOU KNOW...?
The Lantern Festival is celebrated on the 15th day of the first month in the lunar calendar. The festival marks the end of the Chinese New Year festivities and takes place under a full moon. The traditional food which is eaten at this festival is called 元宵 yuánxiāo or 汤圆 tāngyuán, a round dumpling made from glutinous rice flour with various, usually sweet, fillings.

园 yuán NOUN
1 garden
2 park
公园 gōngyuán park
园丁 yuándīng NOUN
gardener
园林 yuánlín NOUN
garden
园艺 yuányì NOUN
gardening

员 yuán NOUN
1 employee
■理发员 lǐfàyuán hairdresser
■服务员 fúwùyuán waiter
2 member
■成员 chéngyuán member
员工 yuángōng NOUN
staff *pl*

原 yuán ADJECTIVE
1 original
2 raw
■原油 yuányóu crude oil
原来 yuánlái
I ADJECTIVE
original
II ADVERB
1 originally
这里原来是块平地。Zhèlǐ yuánlái shì kuài píngdì. This was originally just a flat piece of land.
2 all along
原来你早就认识她啊。Yuánlái nǐ zǎo jiù rènshi tā a. So you knew her all along.
原理 yuánlǐ NOUN
principle
原谅 yuánliàng VERB
to forgive
原料 yuánliào NOUN
ingredient
原始 yuánshǐ ADJECTIVE
1 primitive
2 original
原先 yuánxiān
I ADJECTIVE
original
II ADVERB
originally
原因 yuányīn NOUN
reason
原则 yuánzé NOUN
principle
原著 yuánzhù NOUN
original

圆 yuán
I ADJECTIVE
1 round
■圆圈 yuánquān circle
2 satisfactory
II NOUN
circle *(mathematics)*
圆满 yuánmǎn ADJECTIVE
satisfactory

援 yuán VERB
to help
■支援 zhīyuán to support
援救 yuánjiù VERB
to rescue
援助 yuánzhù VERB
to help

缘 yuán NOUN
1 cause
2 fate
缘分 yuánfèn NOUN
fate
缘故 yuángù NOUN
cause

猿 yuán NOUN
ape
猿猴 yuánhóu NOUN
apes and monkeys *pl*
猿人 yuánrén NOUN
ape-man

源 yuán NOUN
source
■ 水源 shuǐyuán source

远 yuǎn ADJECTIVE
far
■ 远程 yuǎnchéng long-distance

远大 yuǎndà ADJECTIVE
far-reaching

远方 yuǎnfāng NOUN
afar

远见 yuǎnjiàn NOUN
foresight

远亲 yuǎnqīn NOUN
distant relative

远视 yuǎnshì NOUN
long sightedness

远足 yuǎnzú VERB
to hike

院 yuàn NOUN
1 courtyard
■ 院子 yuànzi yard
■ 电影院 diànyǐngyuàn cinema
2 college
■ 学院 xuéyuàn college
3 hospital
■ 医院 yīyuàn hospital

愿 yuàn
I NOUN
wish
II VERB
■ 我不愿说。Wǒ bú yuàn shuō. I'd rather not say.

愿望 yuànwàng NOUN
wish

愿意 yuànyì VERB
to be willing to
我愿意这样做。Wǒ yuànyì zhèyàng zuò. I'm willing do it this way.

约 yuē
I VERB
1 to restrict
2 to arrange
我们约好七点见面。Wǒmen yuēhǎo qīdiǎn jiànmiàn. We arranged to meet at seven o'clock.
II ADJECTIVE
brief
■ 简约 jiǎnyuē brief
III ADVERB
about
■ 大约 dàyuē about 这块布大约一米长。Zhèkuài bù dàyuē yìmǐ cháng. This piece of cloth is about a metre long.

约会 yuēhuì NOUN
date

约束 yuēshù VERB
to bind

月 yuè NOUN
1 moon
■ 满月 mǎnyuè full moon
2 month
■ 三月 sānyue March
3 monthly
■ 月薪 yuèxīn monthly salary

月饼 yuèbing NOUN
mooncake

> **DID YOU KNOW...?**
> Mooncakes, the traditional festival food for 中秋节 Zhōngqiū Jié **the Mid-Autumn Festival**, are round pastries made with a variety of sweet and savoury fillings, including bean paste, egg and peanut.

月份 yuèfèn NOUN
month

月光 yuèguāng NOUN
moonlight

月亮 yuèliang NOUN
moon

月票 yuèpiào NOUN
monthly ticket

乐 yuè NOUN
▷ *see also* lè
music

乐队 yuèduì NOUN
band

乐器 yuèqì NOUN
musical instrument

乐曲 yuèqǔ NOUN
music

乐团 yuètuán NOUN
philharmonic orchestra

岳 yuè NOUN
parents-in-law *pl*

岳父 yuèfù NOUN
father-in-law

岳母 yuèmǔ NOUN
mother-in-law

阅 yuè VERB
1 to read
2 to experience

阅读 yuèdú VERB
to read

阅览 yuèlǎn VERB

to read

阅历 yuèlì VERB
to experience

跃 yuè VERB
to leap
■ 跳跃 tiàoyuè to jump

越 yuè
I VERB
to exceed
■ 超越 chāoyuè to exceed
II ADVERB
■ 越发 yuèfā increasingly

越来越 yuèláiyuè ADVERB
more and more
天气越来越暖和了。Tiānqì yuèláiyuè nuǎnhuo le. The weather is getting warmer and warmer.

越野 yuèyě VERB
to go cross-country

越…越… yuè…yuè… ADVERB
the more… the more …
越早越好 yuè zǎo yuè hǎo the earlier the better

晕 yūn VERB
▹ *see also* yùn
1 to feel dizzy
2 to faint
她晕过去了。Tā yūn guòqu le. She passed out.

云 yún NOUN
cloud

云彩 yúncai NOUN
cloud

匀 yún ADJECTIVE
even

匀称 yúnchèn ADJECTIVE
well-proportioned
她身材匀称。Tā shēncái yúnchèn. She has a well-proportioned figure.

允 yǔn VERB
to allow

允许 yǔnxǔ VERB
to allow

孕 yùn
I VERB
to be pregnant
■ 怀孕 huáiyùn to be pregnant
II NOUN
pregnancy
■ 孕妇 yùnfù pregnant woman

运 yùn
I VERB
1 to move
2 to transport
II NOUN
luck
■ 好运 hǎoyùn good luck

运动 yùndòng NOUN
sport

运动鞋 yùndòngxié NOUN
trainer *(shoe)*

运动员 yùndòngyuán NOUN
athlete

运气 yùnqi NOUN
luck

运输 yùnshū VERB
to transport

运行 yùnxíng VERB
to move

运用 yùnyòng VERB
to make use of

运转 yùnzhuǎn VERB
to run *(machine)*

晕 yùn VERB
▹ *see also* yūn
to feel giddy
■ 晕机 yùnjī to be airsick
■ 晕车 yùnchē to be carsick
■ 晕船 yùnchuán to be seasick

熨 yùn VERB
to iron

熨斗 yùndǒu NOUN
iron

Zz

杂 zá ADJECTIVE
miscellaneous
■ 复杂 fùzá complicated

杂货 záhuò NOUN
groceries *pl*

杂技 zájì NOUN
acrobatics *pl*

杂志 zázhì NOUN
magazine

砸 zá VERB
1 to pound
2 to break
杯子砸坏了。Bēizi záhuài le. The cup was broken.

灾 zāi NOUN
1 disaster
■ 水灾 shuǐzāi flood
2 misfortune

灾害 zāihài NOUN
disaster

灾难 zāinàn NOUN
disaster

再 zài ADVERB
1 again
你再说一遍。Nǐ zài shuō yí biàn. Say that again.
2 more
请把音量放得再大些。Qǐng bǎ yīnliàng fàngde zài dàxiē. Please turn the volume up a bit.
3 continue
我不能再等了。Wǒ bùnéng zài děng le. I can't wait any longer.
4 then
你做完功课再看小说。Nǐ zuòwán gōngkè zài kàn xiǎoshuō. You can read your book when you've finished your homework.
■ 再说 zàishuō besides

再见 zàijiàn VERB
to say goodbye
再见！Zàijiàn! Goodbye!

在 zài
I VERB
1 to be
我父母在纽约。Wǒ fùmǔ zài Niǔyuē. My parents are in New York.
2 to rest with
II ADVERB
情况在改变。Qíngkuàng zài gǎibiàn. Things are changing. 他们在看电视。Tāmen zài kàn diànshì. They're watching TV.
III PREPOSITION
at
在机场等候 zài jīchǎng děnghòu to wait at the airport

在乎 zàihu VERB
to care

在于 zàiyú VERB
to depend on
是否成功在于你的努力程度。Shìfǒu chénggōng zàiyú nǐde nǔlì chéngdù. Whether or not you succeed depends on how hard you work.

咱 zán PRONOUN
we
咱是最聪明的！Zán shì zuì cōngmíng de! We're the smartest!

咱们 zánmen PRONOUN
we

暂 zàn
I ADJECTIVE
brief
II ADVERB
temporarily

暂时 zànshí NOUN
■ 暂时的需要 zànshí de xūyào temporary need

赞 zàn VERB
1 to assist
■ 赞助 zànzhù assistance
2 to commend
■ 赞赏 zànshǎng to admire

赞成 zànchéng VERB
to approve
赞美 zànměi VERB
to praise
赞同 zàntóng VERB
to approve of
赞扬 zànyáng VERB
to pay tribute to

脏 zāng ADJECTIVE
dirty

葬 zàng VERB
to bury
葬礼 zànglǐ NOUN
funeral

遭 zāo VERB
to meet with
遭到 zāodào VERB
to encounter
他们在路上遭到敌人的袭击。Tāmen zài lùshàng zāodào dírén de xíjī. Whilst making their journey they were set upon by the enemy.
遭受 zāoshòu VERB
to suffer
他的公司今年遭受了巨大的损失。Tā de gōngsī jīnnián zāoshòu le jùdà de sǔnshī. His company suffered enormous losses this year.

糟 zāo
I NOUN
dregs *pl*
II VERB
to waste
■ 糟蹋 zāota to spoil
糟糕 zāogāo ADJECTIVE
terrible
真糟糕，我的钥匙丢了。Zhēn zāogāo, wǒ de yàoshi diū le! Oh no, I've lost my key!

早 zǎo
I NOUN
morning
II ADVERB
a long time ago
III ADJECTIVE
early
早安 zǎo'ān NOUN
■ 早安！Zǎo'ān! Good morning!
早餐 zǎocān NOUN
breakfast
早晨 zǎochén NOUN
morning
早饭 zǎofàn NOUN
breakfast
早晚 zǎowǎn
I NOUN
morning and evening
II ADVERB
sooner or later
他早晚会后悔的。Tā zǎowǎn huì hòuhuǐ de. He'll regret it sooner or later.
早上 zǎoshang NOUN
morning

造 zào VERB
1 to make
■ 制造 zhìzào to manufacture
2 to concoct
■ 造谣 zàoyáo to start a rumour
造成 zàochéng VERB
to cause
造反 zàofǎn VERB
to rebel
造型 zàoxíng NOUN
model

噪 zào VERB
to clamour
■ 噪音 zàoyīn noise

责 zé
I NOUN
responsibility
■ 负责 fùzé to be responsible for
II VERB
to blame
■ 指责 zhǐzé to censure
责备 zébèi VERB
to blame
责任 zérèn NOUN
responsibility

怎 zěn PRONOUN
how
你怎能相信他的话？Nǐ zěn néng xiāngxìn tā de huà? How can you believe him?
怎么 zěnme
I PRONOUN
你看这事我该怎么办？Nǐ kàn zhè shì wǒ gāi zěnme bàn? What do you think I should do about this?
II ADVERB *(the way of doing things)*
我是怎么想就怎么说。Wǒ shì zěnme xiǎng jiù zěnme shuō. I say whatever I think. 他最近怎么样？Tā zuìjìn zěnme yàng? How has he been doing recently?

怎样 zěnyàng ADVERB
how

曾 zēng NOUN
▹ *see also* céng
曾祖父母 great-grandparents
曾孙 zēngsūn NOUN
great-grandson
曾祖 zēngzǔ NOUN
great-grandfather

增 zēng VERB
to increase
增加 zēngjiā VERB
to increase
增长 zēngzhǎng VERB
to increase

赠 zèng VERB
to present
■ 捐赠 juānzèng to donate
赠品 zèngpǐn NOUN
gift

炸 zhá VERB
▹ *see also* zhà
to fry

炸 zhà VERB
▹ *see also* zhá
1 to blow... up
2 to explode
炸弹 zhàdàn NOUN
bomb
炸药 zhàyào NOUN
explosive

摘 zhāi VERB
1 to pick
2 to select

窄 zhǎi ADJECTIVE
1 narrow
2 narrow-minded
他心胸很狭窄。Tā xīnxiōng hěn xiázhǎi.
He's very narrow-minded.

粘 zhān VERB
to stick

盏 zhǎn
I NOUN
small cup
II MEASURE WORD
LANGUAGE TIP This is a measure word used for lamps and lights.
一盏灯 yì zhǎn dēng a lamp

DID YOU KNOW...?
In ancient China, people would use the expression 一盏茶时分 yìzhǎnchá shífèn, literally **the time of a cup of tea**, to express a unit of time, roughly approximate to 15 minutes, about the time it takes to drink a cup of tea.

展 zhǎn
I VERB
to develop
II NOUN
exhibition
展出 zhǎnchū VERB
to exhibit
展开 zhǎnkāi VERB
1 to spread
它展开了翅膀。Tā zhǎnkāi le chìbǎng.
It spread its wings.
2 to develop
校园里展开了各种各样的活动。Xiàoyuánlǐ zhǎnkāi le gèzhǒnggèyàng de huódòng.
All kinds of events were in full swing across the campus.
展览 zhǎnlǎn NOUN
exhibition
展品 zhǎnpǐn NOUN
exhibit

崭 zhǎn
▹ *see below:*
崭新 zhǎnxīn ADJECTIVE
brand-new

占 zhàn VERB
to occupy

战 zhàn
I NOUN
war
II VERB
1 to fight
2 to shiver
战斗 zhàndòu VERB
to fight
战胜 zhànshèng VERB
to overcome
战士 zhànshì NOUN
soldier
战争 zhànzhēng NOUN
war

站 zhàn
I VERB

to stand
站在那里的那个人就是他。Zhàn zài nàlǐ de nàgèrén jiù shì tā. He's the one standing over there.

II NOUN
stop
公共汽车站 gōnggòngqìchē zhàn bus stop

张 zhāng
I VERB
1 to extend
■ 扩张 kuòzhāng to stretch
2 to exaggerate
■ 夸张 kuāzhāng to exaggerate
3 to look
■ 张望 zhāngwàng to look around
4 to open for business
■ 开张 kāizhāng to open for business

II MEASURE WORD
LANGUAGE TIP This is a measure word used for flat objects such as newspapers, maps, paintings, cards, tickets and pancakes and furniture such as beds, desks and sofas.
一张海报 yì zhāng hǎibào a poster 一张书桌 yì zhāng shūzhuō a desk
LANGUAGE TIP This is also a measure word used for mouths and faces.
一张大嘴 yì zhāng dà zuǐ a big mouth 一张脸 yì zhāng liǎn a face
DID YOU KNOW...?
张 zhāng is one of the "big three" most common surnames in China. About 78 million people have this surname, more than the entire population of the UK.

章 zhāng NOUN
1 article
■ 文章 wénzhāng article
2 chapter
3 regulation
■ 宪章 xiànzhāng charter
4 seal

长 zhǎng
▷ *see also* cháng
I ADJECTIVE
1 older
他年长我三岁。Tā niánzhǎng wǒ sān suì. He's three years older than me.
2 oldest
■ 长兄 zhǎngxiōng oldest brother
II NOUN
1 *(someone elder)*
■ 兄长 xiōngzhǎng elder brother
2 head
■ 校长 xiàozhǎng head teacher
III VERB
to grow
■ 长大 zhǎngdà to grow up

掌 zhǎng
I NOUN
1 palm
2 sole
3 foot
■ 仙人掌 xiānrénzhǎng cactus
II VERB
to be in charge of

掌握 zhǎngwò VERB
to control

丈 zhàng NOUN
Chinese unit of length *(equal to 3.3 metres)*

丈夫 zhàngfu NOUN
husband

帐 zhàng NOUN
curtain
■ 蚊帐 wénzhàng mosquito net

帐篷 zhàngpeng NOUN
tent

账 zhàng NOUN
1 accounts *pl*
2 ledger
3 credit

账单 zhàngdān NOUN
bill

账号 zhànghào NOUN
account number

障 zhàng NOUN
barrier

障碍 zhàng'ài NOUN
obstacle

招 zhāo
I VERB
1 to beckon
2 to recruit
3 to attract
4 to provoke
5 to confess
II NOUN
1 trick
2 move

招待 zhāodài VERB
to entertain
招待会 zhāodàihuì reception

招呼 zhāohu VERB
to greet
等下，我去和朋友打个招呼。Děngxià, wǒ qù hé péngyǒu dà gè zhāohu. Wait a minute, I'm just going to go and say hello to a friend.

着 zháo VERB
1 to touch
2 to be affected by
3 to be lit
■ 着火 zháohuǒ to catch fire
4 to fall asleep
■ 睡着 shuìzháo to fall asleep

着急 zháojí ADJECTIVE
worried

找 zhǎo VERB
1 to look for
2 to give change
■ 找钱 zhǎoqián to give change
3 to call on

召 zhào VERB
to summon

召开 zhàokāi VERB
to hold *(meeting)*

照 zhào
I VERB
1 to light up
2 to take a photograph
3 to look after
4 to refer to
■ 参照 cānzhào to consult
II NOUN
1 photograph
2 licence

照常 zhàocháng ADVERB
as usual

照顾 zhàogù VERB
1 to look after
2 to consider
你要照顾他的感受。Nǐ yào zhàogù tāde gǎnshòu. You should take his feelings into consideration.

照看 zhàokàn VERB
to look after

照料 zhàoliào VERB
to take care of

照片 zhàopiàn NOUN
photograph

照相 zhàoxiàng VERB
to take a picture

照相机 zhàoxiàngjī NOUN
camera

折 zhé
▷ *see also* shé
I VERB
1 to break
2 to wind
3 to turn back
4 to fold
II NOUN
1 notebook
■ 存折 cúnzhé deposit book
2 to discount

折叠 zhédié VERB
to fold

折扣 zhékòu NOUN
discount

LANGUAGE TIP 20% off an item translates as 打八折 dǎ bā zhé, literally, 80% of the price.

折磨 zhémó VERB
to torment

哲 zhé
I ADJECTIVE
wise
II NOUN
sage

哲学 zhéxué NOUN
philosophy

这 zhè PRONOUN
this

这边 zhèbiān ADVERB
here

这个 zhègè PRONOUN
this
这个可比那个好多了。Zhègè kě bǐ nàgè hǎo duō le. This one is much better than that one.

这么 zhème PRONOUN
1 so
今天这么热。Jīntiān zhème rè. It's so hot today.
2 such
我看就应该这么做。Wǒ kàn jiù yīnggāi zhème zuò. I think it should be done this way.

这儿 zhèr ADVERB
here
我们这儿风景很美。Wǒmen zhèr fēngjǐng hěnměi. The scenery we have here is wonderful.

这些 zhèxiē PRONOUN
these *pl*

这样 zhèyàng PRONOUN
1 so
乡村的风景这样美。Xiāngcūn de fēngjǐng zhèyàng měi. The scenery in the

countryside is so beautiful.

2 such

再这样下去可不行。Zài zhèyàng xiàqù kě bùxíng. It really won't do to carry on like this.

针 zhēn NOUN

1 needle

■ 表针 biǎozhēn hand *(on watch)*

■ 别针 biézhēn safety pin

2 injection

针对 zhēnduì VERB

to be aimed at

我这样说不是针对你。Wǒ zhèyàng shuō búshì zhēnduì nǐ. What I'm saying isn't aimed at you.

真 zhēn

I ADJECTIVE

true

■ 真话 zhēnhuà truth

■ 真品 zhēnpǐn genuine product

II ADVERB

really

他真勇敢。Tā zhēn yǒnggǎn. He is really brave.

真的 zhēnde ADVERB

really

真理 zhēnlǐ NOUN

truth

真实 zhēnshí ADJECTIVE

true

真正 zhēnzhèng ADJECTIVE

true

枕 zhěn NOUN

pillow

枕头 zhěntou NOUN

pillow

振 zhèn VERB

1 to vibrate

2 to boost

振动 zhèndòng VERB

to vibrate

镇 zhèn

I NOUN

town

II ADJECTIVE

calm

■ 镇静 zhènjìng calm

镇定 zhèndìng ADJECTIVE

calm

正 zhēng

▷ *see also* zhèng

▷ *see below:*

正月 zhēngyuè NOUN

first month of the lunar year

争 zhēng VERB

1 to contend

2 to argue

争论 zhēnglùn VERB

to argue

争取 zhēngqǔ VERB

to strive for

征 zhēng NOUN

1 journey

■ 长征 chángzhēng the Long March

2 sign

■ 特征 tèzhēng feature

征服 zhēngfú VERB

to conquer

征求 zhēngqiú VERB

to solicit

征兆 zhēngzhào NOUN

sign

睁 zhēng VERB

to open

睁开眼睛 zhēngkāi yǎnjing to open one's eyes

蒸 zhēng VERB

1 to steam *(one way of cooking)*

2 to evaporate

蒸气 zhēngqì NOUN

vapour

蒸汽 zhēngqì NOUN

steam

整 zhěng

I ADJECTIVE

1 whole

2 tidy

II VERB

1 to sort... out

2 to repair

整个 zhěnggè ADJECTIVE

whole

整理 zhěnglǐ VERB

to sort... out

整齐 zhěngqí ADJECTIVE

1 orderly

2 even

正 zhèng

▷ *see also* zhēng

I ADJECTIVE

1 straight
正前方 zhèng qiánfāng directly ahead 这照片挂得不正。Zhè zhàopiàn guà de bú zhèng. This photograph is not hung straight.
2 upright
■ 公正 gōngzhèng just
3 right
■ 正轨 zhèngguǐ the right track
4 pure
这道菜的味儿不正。Zhè dào cài de wèir bú zhèng. This dish does not taste authentic.
5 principal
■ 正餐 zhèngcān main meal
6 positive
■ 正数 zhèngshù positive number
II VERB
1 to straighten
2 to put... right
III ADVERB
1 just
■ 正好 zhènghǎo just
2 right now
天正刮着风。Tiān zhèng guā zhe fēng. It's windy right now.

正常 zhèngcháng ADJECTIVE
normal

正当 zhèngdāng ADJECTIVE
legitimate

正确 zhèngquè ADJECTIVE
correct

正式 zhèngshì ADJECTIVE
official

正在 zhèngzài ADVERB
right now

证 zhèng
I VERB
to prove
II NOUN
1 evidence
■ 物证 wùzhèng material evidence
2 licence
■ 身份证 shēnfènzhèng identity card

证明 zhèngmíng
I VERB
to prove
我可以证明他是清白的。Wǒ kěyǐ zhèngmíng tā shì qīngbái de. I can prove that he is innocent.
II NOUN
certificate

政 zhèng NOUN
politics *sg*

政策 zhèngcè NOUN
policy

政党 zhèngdǎng NOUN
political party

政府 zhèngfǔ NOUN
government

政权 zhèngquán NOUN
political power

政治 zhèngzhì NOUN
politics *sg*

挣 zhèng VERB
1 to earn
■ 挣钱 zhèngqián to earn money
2 to break free
挣开绳索 zhèngkāi shéngsuǒ to break free from one's bonds

之 zhī AUXILIARY WORD
■ 父母之爱 fùmǔ zhī ài parental love

之后 zhīhòu PREPOSITION
after

之间 zhījiān PREPOSITION
1 between
他们两个之间有秘密。Tāmen liǎnggè zhījiān yǒu mìmì. There's a secret between those two.
2 among

之前 zhīqián PREPOSITION
before

之上 zhīshàng PREPOSITION
above

之下 zhīxià PREPOSITION
below

之一 zhīyī PRONOUN
one of

之中 zhīzhōng PREPOSITION
amid

支 zhī
I VERB
1 to prop... up
2 to pay... out
II MEASURE WORD

> **LANGUAGE TIP** This is a measure word used for songs, troops and stick-like objects.

一支钢琴曲 yì zhī gāngqín qǔ a piano tune 一支钢笔 yì zhī gāngbǐ a pen 一支部队 yì zhī bùduì an army unit

支持 zhīchí VERB
1 to support
2 to hold out

支付 zhīfù VERB
to pay

支票 zhīpiào NOUN
cheque

支援 zhīyuán VERB
to help

只 zhī MEASURE WORD
▹ *see also* zhǐ
LANGUAGE TIP This is a measure word used for one of a pair such as gloves, eyes and feet.
一只拖鞋 yì zhī tuōxié a slipper
LANGUAGE TIP It is also a measure word for animals, insects, birds and boats.
两只小船 liǎng zhī xiǎochuán two boats
三只小鸟 sān zhī xiǎo niǎo three birds

芝 zhī
▹ *see below:*
芝麻 zhīma NOUN
sesame

枝 zhī NOUN
branch
■ 树枝 shùzhī branch

知 zhī
I VERB
1 to know
2 to inform
■ 通知 tōngzhī to notify
II NOUN
knowledge
知道 zhīdaò VERB
to know
这事我可不知道。Zhè shì wǒ kě bù zhīdaò. I really know nothing about this.
知识 zhīshi NOUN
knowledge

织 zhī VERB
to knit

蜘 zhī
▹ *see below:*
蜘蛛 zhīzhū NOUN
spider

执 zhí VERB
1 to stick to
■ 执迷不悟 zhímíbúwù to stick to one's bad old ways
2 to carry out
执行 zhíxíng VERB
to carry out
执照 zhízhào NOUN
licence

直 zhí
I ADJECTIVE
1 straight
2 vertical
3 upstanding
他为人正直。Tā wéi rén zhèng zhí. He's an upstanding person.
4 candid
II VERB
to straighten
III ADVERB
1 straight
2 continuously
他一直都来这里吃饭。Tā yìzhí dōu lái zhèlǐ chīfàn. He always comes here to eat.
直到 zhídào PREPOSITION
until
直接 zhíjiē ADJECTIVE
direct
直升机 zhíshēngjī NOUN
helicopter

侄 zhí NOUN
nephew
侄女 zhínǔ NOUN
niece
侄子 zhízi NOUN
nephew

值 zhí
I NOUN
1 value
II VERB
1 to be worth
2 to be on duty
值班 zhíbān VERB
to be on duty
值得 zhíde VERB
to be worth
这书值得买。Zhè shū zhíde mǎi. This book is worth buying.

职 zhí NOUN
1 position
2 duty
职工 zhígōng NOUN
1 staff
2 blue-collar worker
职业 zhíyè NOUN
occupation
职员 zhíyuán NOUN
member of staff

植 zhí VERB
1 to plant

2 to establish

植物 zhíwù NOUN
plant

止 zhǐ VERB
1 to stop
2 to end
到此为止 dào cǐ wéi zhǐ to be the end of

只 zhǐ ADVERB
▷ *see also* zhī
only
我只在周末有时间。Wǒ zhǐ zài zhōumò yǒu shíjiān. I only have time at the weekend.

只好 zhǐhǎo ADVERB
have to

只是 zhǐshì
I ADVERB
merely
你看到的只是一部分。Nǐ kàndào de zhǐshì yí bùfèn. You've only seen a part of it.
II CONJUNCTION
but

只要 zhǐyào CONJUNCTION
so long as

只有 zhǐyǒu ADVERB
only

纸 zhǐ NOUN
paper

纸币 zhǐbì NOUN
banknote

指 zhǐ
I NOUN
finger
■ 中指 zhōngzhǐ middle finger
■ 无名指 wúmíngzhǐ ring finger
II VERB
1 to point to
2 to point... out
3 to refer to
4 to rely on

指出 zhǐchū VERB
to point... out

指导 zhǐdǎo VERB
to instruct

指挥 zhǐhuī
I VERB
to command
II NOUN
conductor

指南针 zhǐnánzhēn NOUN
compass

DID YOU KNOW...?
This is one of China's 四大发明 sì dà fāmíng **the Four Great Inventions of ancient China**: the compass, gunpowder, paper and the art of printing.

指示 zhǐshì VERB
to instruct

指责 zhǐzé VERB
to criticize

至 zhì
I VERB
to arrive
II PREPOSITION
to
从东至西 cóng dōng zhì xī from east to west
III ADVERB
extremely
■ 至于 zhìyú as to 至于冬天，我现在还没有计划。Zhìyú dōngtiān, wǒ xiànzài hái méiyǒu jìhuà. As for winter, I haven't made any plans yet.

至今 zhìjīn ADVERB
so far

至少 zhìshǎo ADVERB
at least

至于 zhìyú PREPOSITION
as to

制 zhì
I VERB
1 to make
2 to work... out
3 to restrict
II NOUN
system

制订 zhìdìng VERB
to work... out

制定 zhìdìng VERB
to draw... up *(law, plan)*

制度 zhìdù NOUN
system

制造 zhìzào VERB
1 to manufacture *(products)*
2 to create *(atmosphere, situation)*

制作 zhìzuò VERB
to make
制作网页 zhìzuò wǎngyè to create a web page
■ 制作商 zhìzuòshāng manufacturer

质 zhì
I NOUN
1 nature

■ 本质 běnzhì nature
2 quality
3 matter
4 pledge
■ 人质 rénzhì hostage
II VERB
to question
■ 质疑 zhìyí to cast doubt on

质量 zhìliàng NOUN
quality

治 zhì VERB
1 to control
2 to cure
3 to punish

治安 zhì'ān NOUN
security
■ 社会治安 shèhuì zhì'ān public order

治疗 zhìliáo VERB
to cure

秩 zhì NOUN
order

秩序 zhìxù NOUN
sequence

智 zhì
I ADJECTIVE
wise
II NOUN
wisdom

智慧 zhìhuì NOUN
intelligence

智力 zhìlì NOUN
intelligence

智商 zhìshāng NOUN
IQ

中 zhōng
I NOUN
1 centre
■ 中央 zhōngyāng central
2 China
■ 中餐 zhōngcān Chinese food
3 middle
■ 中层 zhōngcéng mid-level
4 impartial
■ 适中 shìzhōng moderate
II VERB
to be suitable for

中国 Zhōngguó NOUN
China

中国人 Zhōngguórén NOUN
Chinese person

中华人民共和国 Zhōnghuá Rénmín Gònghéguó NOUN
People's Republic of China

> **DID YOU KNOW...?**
> The **People's Republic of China** was declared in Tiananmen Square on October 1st 1949 by Chairman Mao Zedong.

中华 Zhōnghuá NOUN
China

中间 zhōngjiān NOUN
middle *(position in a group)*
我站在他俩中间。Wǒ zhàn zài tā liǎ zhōngjiān. I was standing in between the two of them.

中介 zhōngjiè NOUN
agency
房产中介 fángchǎn zhōngjiè estate agent

中年 zhōngnián NOUN
middle age

中秋节 Zhōngqiū Jié NOUN
Mid-Autumn Festival

> **DID YOU KNOW...?**
> 中秋节 Zhōngqiū Jié **the Mid-Autumn Festival** is celebrated on the 15th day of the 8th month of the Chinese lunar calendar. Traditionally families gather to observe the moon and eat 月饼 yuèbing **mooncakes**. The roundness of both the full moon and the cakes symbolizes the unity of the family.

中文 Zhōngwén NOUN
Chinese

中午 zhōngwǔ NOUN
noon

中心 zhōngxīn NOUN
centre

中学 zhōngxué NOUN
secondary school

中旬 zhōngxún NOUN
middle ten days of a month

中央 zhōngyāng NOUN
1 centre
2 central government

中药 zhōngyào NOUN
Chinese medicine

中医 zhōngyī NOUN
1 traditional Chinese medicine
2 doctor of traditional Chinese medicine

终 zhōng
I VERB
to die
II ADVERB
in the end
III ADJECTIVE
all

■ 终身 zhōngshēn all one's life

终点 zhōngdiǎn NOUN
1 terminus
2 finish *(in sports)*

终于 zhōngyú ADVERB
finally

终止 zhōngzhǐ VERB
to stop

钟 zhōng NOUN
1 bell
2 clock

LANGUAGE TIP 钟 zhōng is also used to express time.

五点钟 wǔ diǎnzhōng five o'clock

钟表 zhōngbiǎo NOUN
clocks and watches

钟头 zhōngtóu NOUN
hour

种 zhǒng
▷ *see also* zhòng

I NOUN
1 species *sg*
2 race
3 seed

II MEASURE WORD
kind

各种商品 gè zhǒng shāngpǐn all kinds of commodities 三种选择 sān zhǒng xuǎnzé three choices

种子 zhǒngzi NOUN
seed

种族 zhǒngzú NOUN
race

种 zhòng VERB
▷ *see also* zhǒng
to sow

■ 种田 zhòngtián to farm

重 zhòng
▷ *see also* chóng

I NOUN
weight

II ADJECTIVE
1 heavy
2 important

■ 重任 zhòngrèn important task

3 serious

■ 稳重 wěnzhòng staid

III VERB
to stress

■ 注重 zhùzhòng to pay attention to

重大 zhòngdà ADJECTIVE
major

重点 zhòngdiǎn NOUN
key point

重量 zhòngliàng NOUN
weight

重视 zhòngshì VERB
to attach importance to

重要 zhòngyào ADJECTIVE
important

州 zhōu NOUN
1 autonomous prefecture
2 state

周 zhōu

I NOUN
1 circle
2 week

II VERB
to circle

III ADJECTIVE
thorough

周到 zhōudào ADJECTIVE
thorough

周到的服务 zhōudào de fúwù thoughtful service

周末 zhōumò NOUN
weekend

周围 zhōuwéi NOUN
vicinity

猪 zhū NOUN
pig

猪肉 zhūròu NOUN
pork

竹 zhú NOUN
bamboo

竹子 zhúzi NOUN
bamboo

DID YOU KNOW...? Bamboo is highly valued in China for its versatility and aesthetic qualities, and is a symbol of Chinese culture.

逐 zhú

I VERB
1 to chase
2 to drive... away

II ADVERB
one after another

逐步 zhúbù ADVERB
step by step

逐渐 zhújiàn ADVERB
gradually

主 zhǔ
I NOUN
1 host
■ 东道主 dōngdàozhǔ host
2 owner
■ 房主 fángzhǔ home-owner
3 idea
4 God
II ADJECTIVE
main
III VERB
1 to take charge
■ 主办 zhǔbàn to take charge of
2 to look at... subjectively
■ 主观 zhǔguān subjective

主动 zhǔdòng ADJECTIVE
voluntary

主人 zhǔrén NOUN
1 host
2 owner

主席 zhǔxí NOUN
1 chairman
2 chairwoman

主要 zhǔyào ADJECTIVE
major

主义 zhǔyì NOUN
doctrine
■ 社会主义 shèhuì zhǔyì socialism
■ 浪漫主义 làngmàn zhǔyì romanticism

主意 zhǔyi NOUN
idea

主张 zhǔzhāng
I VERB
to advocate
II NOUN
standpoint

煮 zhǔ VERB
to boil

煮饭 zhǔfàn VERB
to cook

助 zhù VERB
to help

助手 zhùshǒu NOUN
assistant

住 zhù VERB
1 to live
2 to stop

住宿 zhùsù VERB
to stay

住院 zhùyuàn VERB
to be hospitalized

住宅 zhùzhái NOUN
house

住址 zhùzhǐ NOUN
address

注 zhù
I VERB
1 to pour
■ 注射 zhùshè to inject
2 to concentrate
3 to explain
II NOUN
1 note
■ 脚注 jiǎozhù footnote
2 stake
■ 赌注 dǔzhù stake

注意 zhùyì VERB
to be careful

祝 zhù VERB
to wish
祝你生日快乐！ Zhù nǐ shēngrì kuàilè!
Happy birthday!

祝贺 zhùhè VERB
to congratulate

著 zhù
I ADJECTIVE
marked
II VERB
to write

著名 zhùmíng ADJECTIVE
famous

著作 zhùzuò NOUN
writings *pl*

抓 zhuā VERB
1 to grab
2 to catch
警察抓住了凶手。Jǐngchá zhuāzhù le xiōngshǒu. The police caught the murderer.
3 to take control of
4 to seize

抓紧 zhuājǐn VERB
to make the most of

专 zhuān VERB
1 to concentrate
2 to dominate
■ 专卖 zhuānmài monopoly

专家 zhuānjiā NOUN
expert

专门 zhuānmén
I ADJECTIVE
specialized
II ADVERB
especially

专心 zhuānxīn ADJECTIVE
single-minded

专业 zhuānyè NOUN
special field of study

砖 zhuān NOUN
brick

转 zhuǎn VERB
▹ *see also* zhuàn
1 to turn
■ 转弯 zhuǎnwān to turn a corner
■ 转学 zhuǎnxué to change schools
2 to pass... on
■ 转送 zhuǎnsòng to deliver

转变 zhuǎnbiàn VERB
to transform

转告 zhuǎngào VERB
to pass on
请转告他我一切都好。Qǐng zhuǎngào tā wǒ yíqiè dōu hǎo. Please let him know that I am doing fine.

转 zhuàn VERB
▹ *see also* zhuǎn
to turn
■ 转动 zhuàndòng to turn

赚 zhuàn VERB
1 to make a profit
2 to earn

庄 zhuāng NOUN
1 village
2 manor
■ 庄园 zhuāngyuán manor
3 *(shops, restaurants)*
■ 茶庄 cházhuāng teahouse
■ 饭庄 fànzhuāng restaurant

庄稼 zhuāngjia NOUN
crops *pl*

庄严 zhuāngyán ADJECTIVE
solemn

装 zhuāng
I VERB
1 to dress up
■ 装饰 zhuāngshì to decorate
2 to pretend
不要装作不知道！Búyào zhuāngzuò bùzhīdào! Don't pretend that you don't know!
3 to load
II NOUN
clothing
■ 套装 tàozhuāng matching outfit

状 zhuàng NOUN
1 shape
2 state
■ 症状 zhèngzhuàng symptom
3 complaint
■ 告状 gàozhuàng to bring a case
4 certificate
■ 奖状 jiǎngzhuàng certificate

状况 zhuàngkuàng NOUN
condition

状态 zhuàngtài NOUN
condition

撞 zhuàng VERB
1 to collide
2 to bump into
我在路上撞见了那个男生。Wǒ zài lùshang zhuàngjiàn le nàgè nánshēng. I bumped into that boy on the road.

撞车 zhuàngchē VERB
to collide

追 zhuī VERB
1 to chase
2 to investigate
3 to seek

追捕 zhuībǔ VERB
to pursue and capture

追求 zhuīqiú VERB
1 to seek
2 to chase after

准 zhǔn
I VERB
to allow
■ 批准 pīzhǔn to ratify
II NOUN
standard
III ADJECTIVE
accurate
■ 准时 zhǔnshí punctual

准备 zhǔnbèi VERB
1 to prepare
2 to plan

准确 zhǔnquè ADJECTIVE
accurate

准时 zhǔnshí ADJECTIVE
punctual

捉 zhuō VERB
to catch
警察们捉住了凶手。Jǐngchá men zhuō zhù le xiōngshǒu. The policemen caught the murderer.

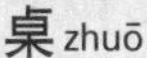 zhuō

I NOUN
table
■ 书桌 shūzhuō desk
II MEASURE WORD
table
一桌菜 yì zhuō cài a table covered in dishes
桌子 zhuōzi NOUN
table

姿 zī NOUN
1 looks *pl*
2 posture
姿势 zīshì NOUN
posture

资 zī
I NOUN
1 money
■ 外资 wàizī foreign capital
2 ability
■ 天资 tiānzī natural ability
3 qualifications *pl*
■ 资历 zīlì record of service
II VERB
to aid... financially
资本 zīběn NOUN
capital *(advantages)*
资格 zīgé NOUN
1 qualifications *pl*
2 seniority
资料 zīliào NOUN
material
资源 zīyuán NOUN
resources *pl*

子 zǐ
I NOUN
1 son
■ 母子 mǔzǐ mother and son
2 person
■ 男子 nánzǐ man
3 seed
■ 瓜子 guāzǐ melon seed
4 *(something shaped like grain)*
■ 棋子 qízǐ chess piece
II ADJECTIVE
1 young
2 affiliated
子女 zǐnǚ NOUN
children

仔 zǐ ADJECTIVE
young
仔细 zǐxì ADJECTIVE
1 thorough
2 careful

紫 zǐ ADJECTIVE
purple

自 zì
I PRONOUN
oneself
II ADVERB
certainly
III PREPOSITION
from
自从 zìcóng PREPOSITION
since
自动 zìdòng ADJECTIVE
1 voluntary
2 automatic
自动取款机 zìdòng qǔkuǎnjī NOUN
cashpoint
自费 zìfèi ADJECTIVE
self-funded
自己 zìjǐ
I PRONOUN
oneself
II ADJECTIVE
own
自觉 zìjué
I VERB
to be aware of
II ADJECTIVE
conscientious
自来水 zìláishuǐ NOUN
tap water
自拍 zìpāi VERB
to take a selfie
自然 zìrán
I NOUN
nature
II ADJECTIVE
natural
III ADVERB
naturally
自杀 zìshā VERB
to commit suicide
自私 zìsī ADJECTIVE
selfish
自我 zìwǒ PRONOUN
self
自信 zìxìn ADJECTIVE
self-confident
自行车 zìxíngchē NOUN
bicycle
自学 zìxué VERB
to teach oneself
自由 zìyóu
I NOUN
freedom

II ADJECTIVE
free

自愿 zìyuàn VERB
to volunteer

自助餐 zìzhùcān NOUN
self-service buffet

字 zì NOUN
1 character
2 calligraphy
■ 字画 zìhuà painting and calligraphy
3 script

字典 zìdiǎn NOUN
dictionary

字母 zìmǔ NOUN
letter

宗 zōng NOUN
1 ancestor
2 clan
3 school
■ 正宗 zhèngzōng orthodox school
4 purpose

宗教 zōngjiào NOUN
religion

综 zōng VERB
to summarize
■ 综述 zōngshù to sum… up

综合 zōnghé
I VERB
to synthesize
II ADJECTIVE
comprehensive

总 zǒng
I VERB
to gather
■ 总括 zǒngkuò to sum… up
II ADJECTIVE
1 total
■ 总数 zòngshù total
2 chief
■ 总部 zǒngbù headquarters *pl*
III ADVERB
1 always
他总在忙。Tā zǒng zài máng. He's always busy.
2 after all

总理 zǒnglǐ NOUN
premier

总是 zǒngshì ADVERB
always

总算 zǒngsuàn ADVERB
finally

总统 zǒngtǒng NOUN
president

粽 zòng
▷ *see below:*

粽子 zòngzi NOUN
glutinous rice dumplings

> **DID YOU KNOW...?**
> The traditional festival food for the Dragon Boat Festival is large pyramid-shaped glutinous rice dumplings wrapped in reed or bamboo leaves, often with sweet or savoury fillings.

走 zǒu VERB
1 to walk
出去走走 chūqù zǒuzǒu to go out for a walk
■ 走路 zǒulù to walk
2 to leave
我先走。Wǒ xiān zǒu. I'll be off.
3 to visit
4 to die
他奶奶走了。Tā nǎinai zǒu le. His paternal grandma passed away.

走动 zǒudòng VERB
1 to walk about
2 to visit each other

走后门 zǒu hòumén VERB
to use one's connections for personal advantage

> **LANGUAGE TIP** Word for word, this means 'walk through the back door'.

走廊 zǒuláng NOUN
corridor

租 zū
I VERB
1 to rent *(house, car)*
2 to rent out
II NOUN
rent
■ 房租 fángzū rent

足 zú
I NOUN
foot
■ 足迹 zújì footprint
II ADJECTIVE
ample
■ 充足 chōngzú adequate
III ADVERB
1 as much as
2 enough

足够 zúgòu VERB
to be enough

足球 zúqiú NOUN
football

阻 zǔ VERB
to block

阻止 zǔzhǐ VERB
to stop

组 zǔ
I VERB
to form
II NOUN
group

组成 zǔchéng VERB
to form

组织 zǔzhī
I VERB
to organize
II NOUN
organization

祖 zǔ NOUN
1 grandparent
2 ancestor
3 founder

祖父 zǔfù NOUN
paternal grandfather

祖国 zǔguó NOUN
motherland

祖母 zǔmǔ NOUN
paternal grandmother

祖先 zǔxiān NOUN
ancestors *pl*

钻 zuān VERB
▷ *see also* zuàn
1 to go through
它钻进山洞里。Tā zuānjìn shāndòng lǐ. It burrowed into the cave.
2 to bury one's head in

钻研 zuānyán VERB
to study... intensively

钻 zuàn NOUN
▷ *see also* zuān
1 drill
2 diamond

钻石 zuànshí NOUN
1 diamond
2 jewel

嘴 zuǐ NOUN
1 mouth

LANGUAGE TIP 嘴 zuǐ can also describe something that has the shape or function of a mouth.

茶壶嘴 cháhú zuǐ spout of a teapot
2 words *pl*
■ 插嘴 chāzuǐ to interrupt

最 zuì ADVERB
most
这家饭店服务最好。Zhè jiā fàndiàn fúwù zuì hǎo. The service at this restaurant is the best.

最初 zuìchū
I ADJECTIVE
initial
II ADVERB
at first

最好 zuìhǎo
I ADJECTIVE
best
II ADVERB
had better
你最好放弃吧。Nǐ zuìhǎo fàngqì ba. You'd better give up.

最后 zuìhòu
I ADJECTIVE
final
II ADVERB
at last

最近 zuìjìn ADJECTIVE
recent

罪 zuì NOUN
1 crime
■ 犯罪 fànzuì to commit a crime
2 hardship
3 punishment
■ 死罪 sǐzuì death sentence

罪犯 zuìfàn NOUN
criminal

醉 zuì
I ADJECTIVE
1 drunk
■ 醉鬼 zuìguǐ the drunk
2 steeped in wine
II VERB
to drink too much

尊 zūn
I ADJECTIVE
senior
II VERB
to respect

尊敬 zūnjìng VERB
to respect

尊重 zūnzhòng
I VERB
to respect

II ADJECTIVE
serious
放尊重些！Fàng zūnzhòng xiē! Behave yourself!

遵 zūn VERB
to follow

遵守 zūnshǒu VERB
to observe

昨 zuó NOUN
1 yesterday
■ 昨日 zuórì yesterday
2 the past

昨天 zuótiān NOUN
yesterday

左 zuǒ NOUN
left
■ 左边 zuǒbiān the left
■ 左面 zuǒmiàn left side

左右 zuǒyòu
I NOUN
left and right
■ 他身高一点七五米左右。Tā shēngāo yìdiǎn qīwǔ mǐ zuǒyòu. He is about 1.75 metres tall.
II VERB
to control
你不要左右他的决定。Nǐ búyào zuǒyòu tā de juédìng. You shouldn't influence his decision.

作 zuò
I VERB
1 to write
■ 作家 zuòjiā writer
■ 作曲 zuòqǔ to compose music
2 to pretend
3 to take… as
■ 作废 zuòfèi to become invalid
II NOUN
work
■ 杰作 jiézuò masterpiece

作家 zuòjiā NOUN
writer

作品 zuòpǐn NOUN
work

作为 zuòwéi
I NOUN
action
II VERB
to regard… as

作文 zuòwén
I VERB
to write an essay
II NOUN
composition

作业 zuòyè NOUN
work

作用 zuòyòng
I VERB
to affect
II NOUN
effect

作者 zuòzhě NOUN
author

坐 zuò VERB
1 to sit
坐在窗口 zuò zài chuāngkǒu to sit by the window
2 to travel by
坐飞机 zuò fēijī to travel by plane

座 zuò
I NOUN
1 seat
■ 座号 zuòhào seat number
2 stand
3 constellation
双子座 Shuāngzǐ Zuò Gemini
II MEASURE WORD

> LANGUAGE TIP This is a measure word used for mountains, buildings, bridges etc.

一座山 yí zuò shān a mountain 三座桥 sān zuò qiáo three bridges 五座办公楼 wǔ zuò bàngōnglóu five office buildings

座位 zuòwèi NOUN
seat

做 zuò VERB
1 to make
2 to do
做生意 zuò shēngyì to do business
3 to be
做大会主席 zuò dàhuì zhǔxí to chair a meeting
4 to be used as
5 to become
做朋友 zuò péngyǒu to be friends

做法 zuòfǎ NOUN
method

做饭 zuòfàn VERB
to cook

做客 zuòkè VERB
to be a guest

做梦 zuòmèng VERB
to dream

Chinese in Action

Map of China

Map of China

- China has a total area of nearly 9,596,960 square kilometres and has a total of 22,117 kilometres of land boundaries with 14 other nations.
- China has the largest population in the world, currently estimated at 1.7 billion.
- The Yangtze is the longest river in China and the third longest in the world, at about 6,385 km long (3,915 miles). It flows into the East China Sea at Shanghai.
- China has five main mountain ranges and seven of its mountain peaks are higher than 8,000 metres above sea level. Mountains cover 33% of China's land mass.

Relationships and feelings

Some useful phrases

这是我的男朋友。
Zhè shì wǒ de nánpéngyǒu.
This is my boyfriend.

这是我的妻子。
Zhè shì wǒ de qīzǐ.
This is my wife.

我有两个小孩。
Wǒ yǒu liǎnggè xiǎohaí.
I have two children.

我女儿十岁了。
Wǒ nǚ'ér shí suì le.
My daughter is ten years old.

我的孩子都成年了。
Wǒ de háizi dōu chéngnián le.
My children are grown up.

我有两个孙子。
Wǒ yǒu liǎnggè sūnzi.
I have two grandchildren.

我离婚了。
Wǒ líhūn le.
I'm divorced.

我和丈夫分居了。
Wǒ hé zhàngfu fēnjū le.
I'm separated.

这是我的岳母。
Zhè shì wǒ de yuèmǔ.
This is my mother-in-law.

这是我的岳父。
Zhè shì wǒ de yuèfù.
This is my father-in-law.

他是我的女婿。
Tā shì wǒ de nǚxu.
He is my son-in-law.

她是我的媳妇。
Tā shì wǒ de xífu.
She is my daughter-in-law.

关系 Guānxì — Relationships

我们相处得很融洽。
Wǒmen xiāngchǔ dé hěn róngqià.
We get on very well.

我们总是争吵不断。
Wǒmen zǒngshì zhēngchǎo búduàn.
We are always quarrelling.

我有很多朋友。
Wǒ yǒu hěnduō péngyǒu.
I have a lot of friends.

我们和朋友正一块儿度假。
Wǒmen hé péngyǒu zhèng yíkuài'er dùjià.
We are on holiday with friends.

我和爸爸关系融洽。
Wǒ hé bàba guānxì róngqià.
I get on well with my dad.

我都在周末见我爸爸。
Wǒ dōu zài zhōumò jiàn wǒ bàba.
I see my dad at weekends.

我和约翰分手了。
Wǒ hé Yuēhàn fēnshǒu le.
John and I have split up.

她人非常好。
Tā rén fēicháng hǎo.
She's really nice.

我很喜欢刘新。
Wǒ hěn xǐhuān Liú Xīn.
I really like Liu Xin.

我实在受不了她！
Wǒ shízài shòubuliǎo tā!
I can't stand her!

家庭成员 Jiātíngchéngyuán — Members of the family

我的父亲 wǒ de fùqin	my father
我的爸爸 wǒ de bàba	my dad
我的母亲 wǒ de mǔqin	my mother
我的妈妈 wǒ de māma	my mum
我的哥哥 wǒ de gēge	my older brother
我的弟弟 wǒ de dìdi	my younger brother
我的姐姐 wǒ de jiějie	my older sister
我的妹妹 wǒ de mèimei	my younger sister
我的兄弟姐妹 wǒ de xiōngdìjiěmèi	my brothers and sisters

In Chinese, there are two words to translate, for example, **grandfather**, depending on whether you mean your father's father or your mother's father. For other family members, for example, **cousin**, it becomes more complex. Look at the dictionary entries for translations.

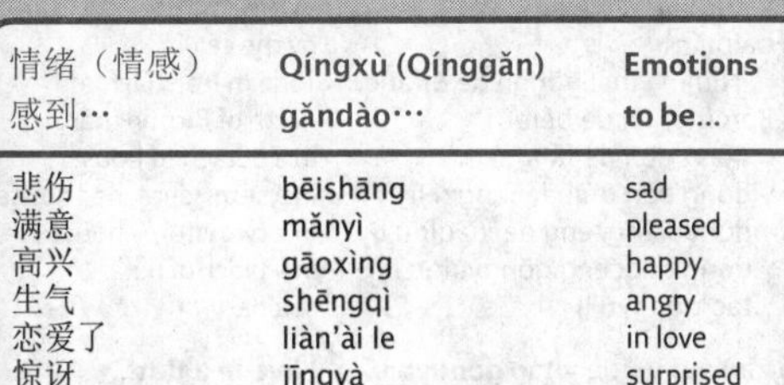

情绪（情感） 感到…	Qíngxù (Qínggǎn) gǎndào…	Emotions to be...
悲伤	bēishāng	sad
满意	mǎnyì	pleased
高兴	gāoxìng	happy
生气	shēngqì	angry
恋爱了	liàn'ài le	in love
惊讶	jīngyà	surprised

我和陈旬相爱了。	Wǒ hé Chén Xún xiāng'ài le.	I'm in love with Chen Xun.
我很高兴你要来。	Wǒ hěn gāoxìng nǐ yào lái.	I'm pleased you're coming.
我好难过。	Wǒ hǎo nánguò.	I'm so sad!
你为什么生气啊？	Nǐ wèishénme shēngqì a?	Why are you angry?
但愿你不要气坏了。	Dànyuàn nǐ búyào qìhuài le.	I hope you're not too angry.

At home

At home

从家到市中心 / Cóng jiā dào shìzhōngxīn / From home into town

我家离市中心挺远的。
Wǒ jiā lí shìzhōngxīn tǐng yuǎn de.
The town centre is quite a long way from my house.

我家离市中心只有5分钟车程。
Wǒ jiā lí shìzhōngxīn zhǐyǒu wǔ fēnzhōng chēchéng.
I live five minutes' from the centre of town.

我进城得搭公车。
Wǒ jìnchéng děi dā gōngchē.
I have to catch a bus into town.

在城中心找停车位非常难。
Zài chéngzhōngxīn zhǎo tíngchēwèi fēicháng nán.
It is very difficult to park in town.

我通常都是步行去城里。
Wǒ tōngcháng dōushì bùxíng qù chénglǐ.
I usually walk into town.

Some useful phrases

我的房子很小。
Wǒ de fángzi hěnxiǎo.
My house is very small.

那儿有一座花园。
Nà'r yǒu yízuò huāyuán.
There is a garden.

家里没有车库。
Jiālǐ méiyǒu chēkù.
We don't have a garage.

我居住的地段很安静。
Wǒ jūzhù de dìduàn hěn ānjìng.
I live in a quiet area.

我家附近有一个运动中心。
Wǒ jiā fùjìn yǒu yígè yùndòng zhōngxīn.
There's a sports centre near to my house.

我们下个月搬家。
Wǒmen xià gè yuè bānjiā.
We're moving next month.

在家 / Zaìjiā / At home

在家	Zaìjiā	At home
一楼有…	**Yìlóu yǒu…**	**On the ground floor there is...**
厨房	chúfáng	the kitchen
客厅	kètīng	the living room
饭厅	fàntīng	the dining room
休闲厅	xiūxiántīng	the lounge
楼上有…	**Lóushàng yǒu…**	**Upstairs there is...**
我的卧室	wǒ de wòshì	my bedroom
我儿子的房间	wǒ érzi de fángjiān	my son's bedroom
我女儿的房间	wǒ nǚ'ér de fángjiān	my daughter's bedroom
客房	kèfáng	the spare bedroom
浴室	yùshì	the bathroom
书房	shūfáng	a study

你家住哪里? / Nǐ jiā zhù nǎlǐ? / Where do you live?

你家住哪里?	Nǐ jiā zhù nǎlǐ?	Where do you live?
我住…	**Wǒ zhù…**	**I live...**
在一个小村子里	zài yígè xiǎo cūnzi lǐ	in a village
在一个小镇上	zài yígè xiǎozhèn shàng	in a small town
在市中心	zài shìzhōngxīn	in the town centre
在伦敦的郊区	zài Lúndūn de jiāoqū	on the outskirts of London
在乡下	zài xiāngxià	in the country
在海边	zài hǎibiān	by the sea
在距牛津100公里的地方	zài jù Niújīn yìbǎi gōnglǐ de dìfāng	100 km from Oxford
在伯明翰的北部	zài Bómínghàn de běibù	north of Birmingham
在一栋独立的房子里	zài yídòng dúlì de fángzi lǐ	in a detached house
在一栋半独立的房子里	zài yídòng bàn dúlì de fángzi lǐ	in a semi-detached house
在一栋两层的小楼里	zài yídòng liǎngcéng de xiǎolóu lǐ	in a two-storey house
在一栋高层公寓楼里	zài yídòng gāocéng gōngyùlóu lǐ	in a block of flats
在一套公寓里	zài yítào gōngyù lǐ	in a flat
我住在…的一套公寓里	**Wǒ zhù zài … de yítào gōngyù lǐ**	**I live in a flat...**
一楼	yīlóu	on the ground floor
二楼	èrlóu	on the first floor
三楼	sānlóu	on the second floor
顶楼	dǐnglóu	on the top floor
一栋新建的楼房里	yídòng xīnjiàn de lóufáng lǐ	in a new building
一栋漂亮的老楼里	yídòng piàoliàng de lǎolóu lǐ	in a beautiful old building

在当地的	Zài dāngdì de	In the local area
一家电影院	yìjiā diànyǐngyuàn	a cinema
一个剧场	yígè jùchǎng	a theatre
一座博物馆	yízuò bówùguǎn	a museum
一个公园	yígè gōngyuán	park
一台取款机	yìtái qǔkuǎnjī	a cash machine/ATM
旅游咨询处	lǚyóu zīxúnchù	the tourist office
一座大教堂	yízuò dàjiàotáng	a cathedral
一座教堂	yízuò jiàotáng	a church
一座清真寺	yízuò qīngzhēnsì	a mosque
一个步行区	yígè bùxíngqū	a pedestrian area
一家银行	yìjiā yínháng	a bank
一个游泳池	yígè yóuyǒngchí	a swimming pool
一个足球场	yígè zúqiúchǎng	a football pitch
一个网球场	yígè wǎngqiúchǎng	tennis court
一个溜冰场	yígè liūbīngchǎng	an ice rink
一个图书馆	yígè túshūguǎn	a library
市政厅	shìzhèngtīng	the town hall
一个市场	yígè shìchǎng	a market

方向（方位）	Fāngxiàng (Fāngwèi)	Directions
对面的	duìmiàn de	opposite
隔壁的	gébì de	next to
附近的	fùjìn de	near
在…和…之间的	zài … hé … zhījiān de	between ... and ...
请问汽车站在哪儿？	Qǐngwěn qìchēzhàn zài nǎ'r?	Where's the bus station?
我在找旅游咨询处。	Wǒ zài zhǎo lǚyóu zīxúnchù.	I'm looking for the tourist office.
你径直走到这条街的尽头。	Nǐ jìngzhí zǒudào zhètiáo jiē de jìntóu.	Go right to the end of the street.
向右转。	Xiàngyòu zhuǎn.	Turn right.
过桥。	Guòqiáo.	Cross the bridge.
走到第一个街口左转。	Zòudào dìyīgè jiēkǒu zuǒzhuǎn.	Take the first street on the left.
它就在你的右手边。	Tā jiù zài nǐ de yòushǒubiān.	It's on your right.
它就在电影院的对面。	Tā jiù zài diànyǐngyuàn de duìmiàn.	It's opposite the cinema.
它就在邮政局的隔壁。	Tā jiù zài yóuzhèngjú de gébì.	It's next to the post office.

What I do

工作	Gōngzuò	Work
我是学…的	**Wǒ shì xué … de**	**I studied...**
医学	yīxué	medicine
工程学	gōngchéngxué	engineering
法律	fǎlǜ	law
社会学	shèhuìxué	sociology
心理学	xīnlǐxué	psychology
语言	yǔyán	languages
建筑学	jiànzhùxué	architecture
我是…	**Wǒ shì…**	**I'm...**
一名教师	yìmíng jiàoshī	a teacher
一名牙医	yìmíng yáyī	a dentist
一名医生	yìmíng yīshēng	a doctor
一位歌手	yíwèi gēshǒu	a singer
一位发型师	yíwèi fàxíngshī	a hairdresser
一名记者	yìmíng jìzhě	a journalist
一个演员	yígè yǎnyuán	an actor
一位律师	yíwèi lǜshī	a solicitor
一名学生	yìmíng xuésheng	a student
我想…	**Wǒ xiǎng…**	**I'd like to...**
挣很多的钱	zhèng hěnduō de qián	earn lots of money
到东南亚旅行	dào dōngnányà lǚxíng	travel in South East Asia
在电视媒体工作	zài diànshìméitǐ gōngzuò	work in television
写一本书	xiě yìběn shū	write a book
做和孩子有关的工作	zuò hé háizi yǒuguān de gōngzuò	work with children
我觉得它是…	**Wǒ juédé tā shì…**	**I think it's...**
有趣的	yǒuqù de	interesting
乏味的	fáwèi de	boring
令人疲劳的	lìng rén píláo de	tiring
值得做的	zhídé zuò de	rewarding
紧张的	jǐnzhāng de	stressful
容易的	róngyì de	easy
太难了	tài nán le	too difficult

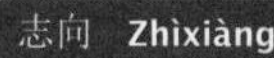

志向 Zhìxiàng — Ambitions

我希望能找到一个更好的工作
Wǒ xīwàng néng zhǎodào yígè gènghǎo de gōngzuò.
I'd like to get a better job.

我们退休后想去乡下生活。
Wǒmen tuìxiū hòu xiǎng qù xiāngxià shēnghuó.
We'd like to retire to the country.

我想在北京工作。
Wǒ xiǎng zài Běijīng gōngzuò.
I want to get a job in Beijing.

他想成为宇航员。
Tā xiǎng chéngwéi yǔhángyuán.
He'd like to become an astronaut.

她希望成为名人。
Tā xīwàng chéngwéi míngrén.
She wants to be famous.

工作	Gōngzuò	Work
一份简历	yífèn jiǎnlì	a CV
一条招聘信息	yìtiáo zhāopìn xìnxī	a job advert
一张申请表	yìzhāng shēnqǐngbiǎo	an application form
一次面试	yícì miànshì	an interview
几封推荐信	jǐfēng tuījiànxìn	references
一份假期工	yífèn jiàqīgōng	a holiday job
一份长期工作	yífèn chángqī gōngzuò	a permanent job
一份临时工作	yífèn línshí gōngzuò	a temporary job
我做全职。	Wǒ zuò quánzhí.	I work full-time.
我正在寻找一份兼职。	Wǒ zhèngzài xúnzhǎo yífèn jiānzhí.	I'm looking for a part-time job.

运动	Yùndòng	Sports
我打…	**Wǒ dá…**	**I play…**
篮球	lánqiú	basketball
高尔夫	gāo'ěrfū	golf
英式橄榄球	yīngshì gǎnlǎnqiú	rugby
网球	wǎngqiú	tennis
羽毛球	yǔmáoqiú	badminton
乒乓球	pīngpāngqiú	table tennis
我踢足球	Wǒ tī zúqiú.	I play football.
我滑雪。	Wǒ huáxuě.	I ski.
我划独木舟。	Wǒ huá dúmùzhōu.	I canoe.
我骑山地车。	Wǒ qí shāndìchē.	I go mountain-biking.
我游泳。	Wǒ yóuyǒng.	I swim.
我骑马。	Wǒ qímǎ.	I go horse riding.
我驾船出游。	Wǒ jiàchuán chūyóu.	I go sailing.
这个夏天我要参加一个学习驾船的课程。	Zhègè xiàtiān wǒ yào cānjiā yígè xuéxí jiàchuán de kèchéng.	I'm going to do a sailing course this summer.
我从没滑过雪。	Wǒ cóng méi huá guò xuě.	I've never been skiing.
我打算去学习划独木舟。	Wǒ dǎsuàn qù xuéxí huá dúmùzhōu.	I'm going to learn how to canoe.

乐器	Yuèqì	Musical instruments
我…	**Wǒ…**	**I…**
拉小提琴	lā xiǎotíqín	play the violin
弹钢琴	tán gāngqín	play the piano
弹吉他	tán jíta	play the guitar
吹长笛	chuī chángdí	play the flute

我在学校里学过弹钢琴。
Wǒ zài xuéxiào lǐ xué guò tán gāngqín.
I learnt to play the piano at school.

你会什么乐器么？
Nǐ huì shénme yuèqì me?
Do you play any instruments?

我是乐队成员。
Wǒ shì yuèduì chéngyuán.
I play in a band.

我女儿是管弦乐队队员。
Wǒ nǚ'ér shì guǎnxián yuèduì duìyuán.
My daughter plays in an orchestra.

在家做饭 Zàijiā zuòfàn — Cooking at home

我喜欢烹饪。
Wǒ xǐhuan pēngrèn.
I like cooking.

我不会做饭。
Wǒ búhuì zuòfàn.
I can't cook.

来我家吃晚饭吧！
Lái wǒ jiā chī wǎnfàn ba!
Come and have dinner at ours.

休闲娱乐 Xiūxián yúlè — Leisure

我丈夫特别喜欢驾船出游。
Wǒ zhàngfu tèbié xǐhuan jiàchuán chūyóu.
My husband loves sailing.

我喜爱听音乐。
Wǒ xǐ'ài tīng yīnyuè.
I love listening to music.

我喜爱和朋友去购物。
Wǒ xǐ'ài hé péngyǒu qù gòuwù.
I love shopping with my friends.

我花很多时间在我的花园里。
Wǒ huā hěnduō shíjiān zài wǒ de huāyuán lǐ.
I spend a lot of time in my garden.

我不喜欢电子游戏。
Wǒ bù xǐhuān diànzǐ yóuxì.
I hate video games.

Describing someone

Describing someone

性格	Xìnggé	Personality
他/她是…	**Tā shì…**	**He/She is...**
有趣的	yǒuqù de	funny
友好的	yǒuhǎo de	nice
害羞的	hàixiū de	shy
安静的	ānjìng de	quiet
讨厌的	tǎoyàn de	annoying
大方的	dàfang de	generous
健谈的	jiàntán de	talkative
聪明的	cōngmíng de	intelligent
愚蠢的	yúchǔn de	stupid
小气的	xiǎoqì de	stingy
奇怪的	qíguài de	strange

颜色	Yánsè	Colours
黄色的	huángsè de	yellow
橙色的	chéngsè de	orange
红色的	hóngsè de	red
粉红色的	fěnhóngsè de	pink
紫色的	zǐsè de	purple
蓝色的	lánsè de	blue
绿色的	lǜsè de	green
棕色的	zōngsè de	brown
灰色的	huīsè de	grey
黑色的	hēisè de	black
白色的	báisè de	white
栗色的	lìsè de	maroon
藏青色的	zàngqīngsè de	navy blue
青绿色的	qīnglǜsè de	turquoise
灰棕色的	huìzōngsè de	beige
乳白色的	rǔbáisè de	cream
眼睛	**Yǎnjīng**	**Eyes**
淡褐色的	dàn hèsè de	hazel
深色的	shēnsè de	dark
头发	**Tóufa**	**Hair**
赤褐色的	chìhèsè de	auburn
金色的	jīnsè de	blonde
棕色的	zōngsè de	brown
浅棕色的	qiǎn zōngsè de	light brown
深棕色的	shēn zōngsè de	dark brown
直的	zhí de	straight
红色的	hóngsè de	red

我的眼睛是淡褐色的。
Wǒ de yǎnjīng shì dàn hèsè de. — I've got hazel eyes.

他的头发是棕色的。
Tā de tóufa shì zōngsè de. — He's got brown hair.

她留了一头灰色短发。
Tā liú le yìtóu huīsè duǎnfà. — She's got short grey hair.

他秃顶了。
Tā tūdǐng le. — He's bald.

她有一头金色的长发。
Tā yǒu yìtóu jīnsè de chángfà. — She's got long curly blonde hair.

Describing someone

特征	Tèzhēng	Characteristics
他/她…	**Tā…**	**He/She is...**
个子高	gèzi gāo	tall
个子矮	gèzi ǎi	short
身材矮小	shēncái ǎixiǎo	small
苗条	miáotiao	slim
胖	pàng	fat
长得标致	zhǎng dé biāozhì	good-looking
年轻	niánqīng	young
老	lǎo	old
他大概三十岁左右。	Tā dàgài sānshi suì zuǒyòu.	He's about thirty.
她很瘦小，头发是金色的。	Tā hěn shòuxiǎo, tóufa shì jīnsè de.	She is small, thin and blonde.

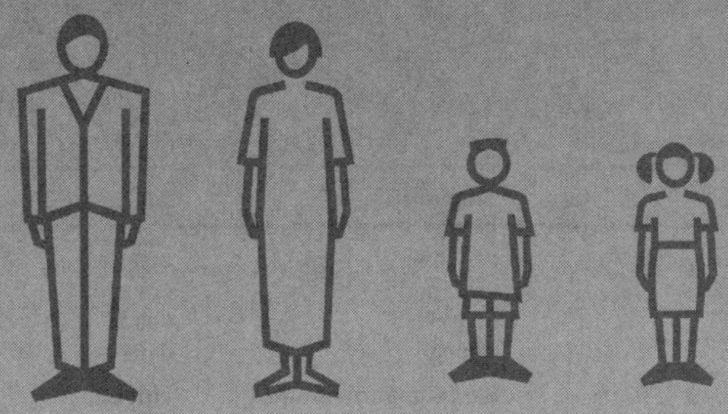

穿着	Chuānzhuó	Clothes
一件毛衣	yíjiàn máoyī	a jumper
裤子	kùzi	trousers
一件女式衬衫	yíjiàn nǚshì chènshān	a blouse
一件体恤	yíjiàn tīxù	a T-shirt
一件外套	yíjiàn wàitào	a coat
一件夹克	yíjiàn jiákè	a jacket
一件开襟毛衣	yíjiàn kāijīn máoyī	a cardigan
一条连衣裙	yìtiáo liányīqún	a dress
一条短裙	yìtiáo duǎnqún	a skirt
一条领带	yìtiáo lǐngdài	a tie
一件衬衫	yíjiàn chènshān	a shirt
鞋子	xiézi	shoes
运动鞋	yùndòngxié	trainers
靴子	xuēzi	boots

她穿了一件浅蓝色的体恤。
Tā chuān le yíjiàn qiǎnlánsè de tīxù.
She's wearing a light blue T-shirt.

他穿着一身深灰色的西装。
Tā chuānzhe yìshēn shēnhuīsè de xīzhuāng.
He's wearing a dark grey suit.

他里面穿着白衬衫，外面套着藏青色的西服，配上红灰条纹的领带，灰色的袜子和黑色皮鞋。
Tā lǐmiàn chuānzhe bái chènshān, wàimiàn tàozhe zàngqīngsè de xīfú, pèi shàng hónghuī tiáowén de lǐngdài, huīsè de wàzi hé hēisè píxié.
He is wearing a navy blue suit, a white shirt, a tie with red and grey stripes, grey socks and black shoes.

Keeping fit and healthy

身体不适	Shēntǐ búshì	Ailments
我的…疼	**Wǒ de … téng.**	**I have a sore …**
胃	wèi	stomach
背	bèi	back
膝盖	xīgài	knee
脚	jiǎo	foot
脖子	bózi	neck
头	tóu	head
喉咙	hóulóng	throat
腿	tuǐ	leg
我牙疼。	Wǒ yá téng.	I've got toothache.
我耳朵疼。	Wǒ ěrduō téng.	I've got earache.
我眼睛疼。	Wǒ yǎnjīng téng.	My eyes are sore.
我感冒了。	Wǒ gǎnmào le.	I've got a cold.
我患上了流感。	Wǒ huànshàng le liúgǎn.	I've got flu.
我不太舒服。	Wǒ bú tài shūfu.	I feel sick.
我累了。	Wǒ lèi le.	I'm tired.
我病了。	Wǒ bìng le.	I'm ill.
冷	lěng	to be cold
热	rè	to be hot
口渴	kǒukě	to be thirsty
饿	è	to be hungry

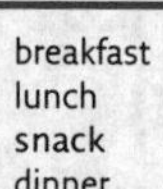

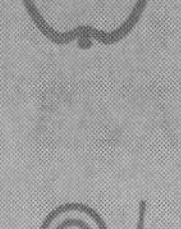

膳食	Shànshí	Meals
早餐	zǎocān	breakfast
午餐	wǔcān	lunch
点心	diǎnxīn	snack
晚餐	wǎncān	dinner
我非常喜欢…	**Wǒ fēicháng xǐhuan…**	**I love...**
意大利面食	Yìdàlì miànshí	pasta
沙拉	shālā	salad
鱼	yú	fish
米饭	mǐfàn	rice
我喜欢…	**Wǒ xǐhuan…**	**I like...**
草莓	cǎoméi	strawberries
巧克力	qiǎokelì	chocolate
我讨厌…	**Wǒ tǎoyàn…**	**I don't like...**
橙汁	chéngzhī	orange juice
汽水	qìshǔi	sparkling water
香蕉	xiāngjiāo	bananas
我不吃猪肉。	Wǒ bù chī zhūròu.	I don't eat pork.
我喜欢吃水果。	Wǒ xǐhuān chī shǔiguǒ.	I eat a lot of fruit.
我不许我的孩子吃垃圾食品。	Wǒ bùxǔ wǒ de háizi chī lājī shípǐn.	I don't let my children eat junk food.
我是素食者。	Wǒ shì sùshízhě.	I'm a vegetarian.
他对花生过敏。	Tā duì huāshēng guòmǐn.	He's allergic to peanuts.

保持健康	Bǎochí jiànkāng	Keeping fit
我经常运动。	Wǒ jīngcháng yùndòng.	I do a lot of sport.
我不吸烟。	Wǒ bù xīyān.	I don't smoke.
我晚上睡得早。	Wǒ wǎnshang shuì dé zǎo.	I go to bed early.
我走路去上班。	Wǒ zǒulù qù shàngbān.	I walk to work.
它对你的健康有益。	Tā duì nǐ de jiànkāng yǒuyì.	It's good for your health.
酒有害健康。	Jiǔ yǒuhài jiànkāng.	Alcohol is bad for your health.

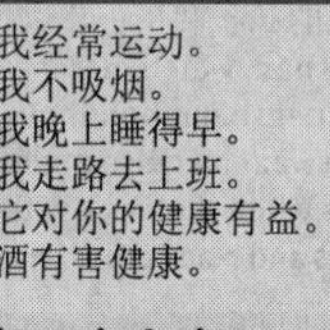

When your number answers

喂，你好！请问李新在吗？ Wèi, nǐhǎo! Qǐngwèn Lǐxīn zài ma?	Hello! Could I speak to Lixin, please?
麻烦你叫他/她给我打电话，行吗？ Máfán nǐ jiào tā gěi wǒ dǎdiànhuà,xíng ma?	Would you ask him/her to call me back, please?
我半小时后再打过来。 Wǒ bàn xiǎoshí hòu zài dǎ guò lái.	I'll call back in half an hour.

Answering the telephone

你好，我是简。	Nǐhǎo, wǒ shì Jiǎn.	Hello! It's Jane speaking.
请讲。	Qǐng jiǎng.	Speaking.
请问您是哪位？	Qǐngwèn nín shì nǎ wèi?	Who's speaking?

When the switchboard answers

请问您贵姓？	Qǐngwèn nín guìxìng?	Who shall I say is calling?
正在为您接通。	Zhèngzài wèi nín jiētōng.	I'm putting you through.
请稍等。	Qǐng shāoděng.	Please hold.
请问您要留言吗？	Qǐngwèn nín yào liúyán ma?	Would you like to leave a message?

Difficulties

我拨不通电话。
Wǒ bō bù tōng diànhuà.
I can't get through.

不好意思，我拨错号码了。
Bù hǎo yìsi, wǒ bō cuò hàomǎ le.
I'm sorry, I dialled the wrong number.

我的手机没信号。
Wǒ de shǒujī méi xìnhào.
I can't get a signal.

他们的手机关机了。
Tāmen de shǒujī guānjī le.
Their mobile is switched off.

我不太听得清楚你在讲什么。
Wǒ bú tài tīng de qīngchǔ nǐ zài jiǎng shénme.
I can't hear you very well.

我的手机欠费了。
Wǒ de shǒujī qiànfèi le.
I've no credit left on my mobile phone.

Letter

Writing a personal letter

Note the use of a colon after the name.

婷婷：

好久没给你写信了。近来还好吗？最近工作忙吗？你是否还在上夜校？

我工作还很忙，天天加班。但老板对我很好，晚上经常开车顺路送我回家。过两天公司放假，准备和同事一起去旅游。

先写到这儿吧，有空给你打电话。

祝
万事如意！

毛毛
2009年2月4日

Writing an envelope
In Chinese you should start in the upper left-hand corner with the addressee's postcode.

The address is written in the middle of the envelope in the following order:
province, city
street, house number
addressee's name

The sender's address and name, followed by their postcode, should be written in the lower right-hand corner of the envelope.

310000

浙江 杭州
定安路99号3幢1单元201室
张鹏收

北京长安路37号 王露
100018

Starting a personal letter

感谢你的来信。	Gǎnxiè nǐ de láixìn.	Thank you for your letter.
真高兴收到你的信。	Zhēn gāoxìng shōudào nǐ de xìn.	It was lovely to hear from you.
对不起，没能及时给你回信。	Duìbuqǐ, méi néng jíshí gěi nǐ huíxìn.	I'm sorry I didn't write sooner.

Ending a personal letter

期待你的回信！	Qīdài nǐ de huíxìn!	Write soon!
请代我问候婷婷。	Qǐng dài wǒ wènhòu Tíngting.	Give my love to Ting ting.
保罗让我替他问候你。	Bǎoluó ràng wǒ tì tā wènhòu nǐ.	Paul sends his best wishes.

Alternative endings for a personal letter

保重	bǎozhòng	Take care
万事如意	wànshì rúyì	All the best
保持联系	bǎochí liánxì	Keep in touch

Writing an email

回复　　转发　　写信　　收件箱　　收信

收件人：　lili@cmail.com.cn

主题：　拓展产品系列讨论会

王经理：

根据近期的市场调研，我公司的彩电产品系列目前有些滞后于市场的发展需要，为提高企业竞争力，建议召开一次讨论会，共同商讨，制定相应措施。

会议时间暂定为2007年6月2日星期三下午2:00，地点在公司二楼小会议室，请通知相关人员准时参加。

如有问题，请尽早回复。
此致
敬礼！

张力

Chinese		English
短信	duǎnxìn	text message
发短信	fā duǎnxìn	to send a text message
微博	wēibó	microblog (Weibo, China's Twitter)
发微博	fā wēibó	to tweet (on Weibo)
微信	Wēixìn	WeChat
发微信	fā Wēixìn	to send a WeChat message
移动设备	yídòng shèbèi	mobile device
智能手机	zhìnéng shǒujī	smartphone
应用程序/软件	yìngyòng chéngxù/ruǎnjiàn	app

Chinese		English
新信息	xīn xìnxī	new message
收件人	shōujiànrén	to
发件人	fājiànrén	from
主题	zhǔtí	subject
日期	rìqī	date
抄送	chāosòng	cc (carbon copy)
密件抄送	mìjiàn chāosòng	bcc (blind carbon copy)
附件	fùjiàn	attachment
发送	fāsòng	send
文件	wénjiàn	file
编辑	biānji	edit
浏览	liúlǎn	view
编写	biānxiě	compose
帮助	bāngzhù	help
回复发信人	huífù fāxìnrén	reply to sender
回复所有联系人	huífù suǒyǒu liánxìrén	reply to all
转发	zhuǎnfā	forward
发送	fāsòng	send
@	quān ēi	@, at

Dates, festivals and holidays

Dates, festivals & holidays

月份	Yuèfèn	Months of the year
一月	yīyuè	January
二月	èryuè	February
三月	sānyuè	March
四月	sìyuè	April
五月	wǔyuè	May
六月	liùyuè	June
七月	qīyuè	July
八月	bāyuè	August
九月	jiǔyuè	September
十月	shíyuè	October
十一月	shíyīyuè	November
十二月	shí'èryuè	December

一周七天	Yìzhōu qītiān	Days of the week
星期一	xīngqīyī	Monday
星期二	xīngqī'èr	Tuesday
星期三	xīngqīsān	Wednesday
星期四	xīngqīsì	Thursday
星期五	xīngqīwǔ	Friday
星期六	xīngqīliù	Saturday
星期天	xīngqītiān	Sunday
在星期一	zài xīngqīyī	on Monday
上星期一	shàng xīngqīyī	last Monday
下星期一	xià xīngqīyī	next Monday
昨天	zuótiān	yesterday
今天	jīntiān	today
明天	míngtiān	tomorrow

今天几号？	Jīntiān jǐ hào?	What date is it today?
六月十六号。	Liùyuè shíliù hào.	It's 16 June.
你的生日是哪天？	Nǐ de shēngrì shì nǎ tiān?	What date is your birthday?
五月二十二号。	Wǔyuè èrshí'èr hào.	It's 22 May.

节假日	Jiéjiàrì	Festivals
圣诞节	Shèngdàn Jié	Christmas Day
元旦	Yuándàn	New Year's Day
愚人节	Yúrén Jié	April Fool's Day
复活节	Fùhuó Jié	Easter
春节	Chūn Jié	Spring Festival
端午节	Duānwǔ Jié	Dragon Boat Festival
中秋节	Zhōngqiū Jié	Mid-Autumn Festival
母亲节	Mǔqīn Jié	Mother's Day
父亲节	Fùqīn Jié	Father's Day
万圣节	Wànshèng Jié	Halloween
清明节	QīngmíngJié	Chinese Halloween
斋月	Zhāiyuè	Ramadan
生日快乐！	Shēngrì kuàilè!	Happy Birthday!
圣诞快乐！	Shèngdàn kuàilè!	Happy Christmas!
愚人节快乐！	Yúrén Jié kuàilè!	April fool!
复活节时	Fùhuó Jié shí	at Easter
你生日那天打算做什么？	Nǐ shēngrì nàtiān dǎsuàn zuò shénme?	What are you doing for your birthday?
你要办派对吗？	Nǐ yào bàn pàiduì ma?	Are you having a party?
我们去爷爷家过年。	Wǒmen qù yéye jiā guònián.	We go to our friends' for New Year.

假期	jiàqī	Holidays
暑假	shǔjià	the summer holidays
圣诞假期	Shèngdàn jiàqī	the Christmas holidays
复活节假期	Fùhuó Jié jiàqī	the Easter holidays
寒暑假	hánshǔjià	the school holidays
长周末	cháng zhōumò	a long weekend

你假期有什么计划？
Nǐ jiàqī yǒu shénme jìhuà?
What are you going to do in the holidays?

我要去和我阿姨待一个礼拜。
Wǒ yào qù hé wǒ āiyí dāi yígè lǐbài.
I'm going to stay with my aunt for a week.

我们经常在二月去滑雪。
Wǒmen jīngcháng zài èryuè qù huáxuě.
We always go skiing in February.

去年夏天我去了美国。
Qùnián xiàtiān wǒ qù le Měiguó.
Last summer I went to the United States.

几点了？ Jǐ diǎn le? What time is it?

一点
yì diǎn

四点十分
sì diǎn shí fēn

四点一刻
sì diǎn yíkè

四点半
sì diǎn bàn

四点四十分
sìdiǎn sìshí fēn

四点四十五分
sìdiǎn sìshíwǔ fēn

什么时候？ Shénme shíhòu? At what time?

午夜十二点
wǔyè shí'èr diǎn

中午十二点
zhōngwǔ shí'èr diǎn

下午一点
xiàwǔ yì diǎn

晚上十一点
wǎnshàng shíyī diǎn

24

Numbers

Numbers

Numbers		
0	零	líng
1	一	yī
2	二	èr
3	三	sān
4	四	sì
5	五	wǔ
6	六	liù
7	七	qī
8	八	bā
9	九	jiǔ
10	十	shí
11	十一	shíyī
12	十二	shí'èr
13	十三	shísān
14	十四	shísì
15	十五	shíwǔ
16	十六	shíliù
17	十七	shíqī
18	十八	shíbā
19	十九	shíjiǔ
20	二十	èrshí
21	二十一	èrshíyī
22	二十二	érshí'èr
30	三十	sānshí
40	四十	sìshí
50	五十	wǔshí
60	六十	liùshí
70	七十	qīshí
80	八十	bāshí
90	九十	jiǔshí
100	一百	yìbǎi
101	一百零一	yìbǎi líng yī
300	三百	sānbǎi
301	三百零一	sānbǎi líng yī
1000	一千	yìqiān
2000	两千	liǎngqiān
1, 000, 000	一百万	yìbǎiwàn

Examples

在第十九页上 — on page nineteen
zài dì shíjiǔ yè shàng

在第七章里 — in chapter seven
zài dì qī zhāng lǐ

Fractions etc		
1/2	二分之一	èr fēn zhī yī
1/3	三分之一	sān fēn zhī yī
2/3	三分之二	sān fēn zhī èr
1/4	四分之一	sì fēn zhī yī
1/5	五分之一	wǔ fēn zhī yī
0.5	零点五	líng diǎn wǔ
3.4	三点四	sān diǎn sì
10%	百分之十	bǎi fēn zhī shí
100%	百分之百	bǎi fēn zhī bǎi
1st	第一	dìyī
2nd	第二	dìèr
3rd	第三	dìsān
4th	第四	dìsì
5th	第五	dìwǔ
6th	第六	dìliù
7th	第七	dìqī
8th	第八	dìbā
9th	第九	dìjiǔ
10th	第十	dìshí
11th	第十一	dìshíyī
12th	第十二	dìshí'èr
13th	第十三	dìshísān
14th	第十四	dìshísì
15th	第十五	dìshíwǔ
16th	第十六	dìshíliù
17th	第十七	dìshíqī
18th	第十八	dìshíbā
19th	第十九	dìshíjiǔ
20th	第二十	dìèrshí
21st	第二十一	dìèrshíyī
22nd	第二十二	dìèrshí'èr
30th	第三十	dìsānshí
100th	第一百	dìyìbǎi
101st	第一百零一	dìyìbǎi líng yī
1000th	第一千	dìyìqiān

Examples

他住在五楼。 — He lives on the fifth floor.
Tā zhùzài wǔlóu.

他第三个进来。 — He came in third.
Tā dìsān gè jìnlái.

Aa

a ARTICLE

LANGUAGE TIP There is no indefinite article in Chinese. The indefinite determiner 一 yī **one** + measure word is the closest to an indefinite article. For more information on measure words, see the relevant section at the beginning of the dictionary.

□ a man 一个男人 yígè nánrén □ a girl 一个女孩 yígè nǚhái □ an elephant 一只大象 yìzhī dàxiàng □ She's a doctor. 他们没有一台电视。Tāmen méiyǒu yìtái diànshì.

■ **They haven't got a television.** 他们没有电视。Tāmen méiyǒu diànshì.

■ **a year ago** 一年前 yìnián qián

■ **a hundred pounds** 一百磅 yìbǎibàng

■ **once a week** 每周一次 měizhōu yícì

■ **100 km an hour** 每小时一百公里 měi xiǎoshí yìbǎi gōnglǐ

■ **30 pence a kilo** 三十便士一公斤 sānshí biànshì yìgōngjīn

AA NOUN *(= Automobile Association)*
汽车协会 Qìchē xiéhuì [家 jiā]

A & E NOUN *(= accident and emergency)*
急诊室 jízhěnshì

aback ADVERB
吃惊 chījīng
□ I was taken aback by his reaction. 他的反应让我大吃一惊。Tāde fǎnyìng ràngwǒ dàchīyìjīng.

to **abandon** VERB
放弃 fàngqì

abbey NOUN
大修道院 dà xiūdàoyuàn [座 zuò]

abbreviation NOUN
缩写 suōxiě [个 gè]

ability NOUN
■ **to have the ability to do something** 有能力做某事 yǒunénglì zuòmǒushì

able ADJECTIVE
■ **to be able to do something** **1** *(have skill, ability)* 能够做某事 nénggòu zuò mǒushì **2** *(have opportunity)* 可以做某事 kěyǐ zuò mǒushì

to **abolish** VERB
废止 fèizhǐ

abortion NOUN
流产 liúchǎn [次 cì]
□ She had an abortion. 她做了一次流产。Tā zuòle yícì liúchǎn.

about PREPOSITION, ADVERB

1 关于 guānyú
□ a book about London 关于伦敦的一本书 guānyú Lúndūn de yìběn shū □ What's it about? 这是关于什么的？Zhèshì guānyú shénme de? □ I'm phoning you about tomorrow's meeting. 我给你打电话是关于明天开会的事。Wǒ gěi nǐ dǎ diànhuà shì guānyú míngtiān kāihuìdeshì.
■ **We talked about it.** 我们谈到了这事。Wǒmen tándào le zhèshì.
■ **to be sorry about something** 对某事感到抱歉 duì mǒushì gǎndào bàoqiàn
■ **to be pleased about something** 对某事感到开心 duì mǒushì gǎndào kāixīn

2 大约 dàyuē *(approximately)*
□ It takes about 10 hours. 这大约要花十个小时。Zhè dàyuē yàohuā shígè xiǎoshí. □ about a hundred people 大约一百人 dàyuē yìbǎi rén □ at about 11 o'clock 大约十一点时 dàyuē shíyīdiǎn shí

3 四处 sìchù *(around)*
□ to walk about the town 在城镇四处散步 zàichéngzhèn sìchù sànbù
■ **to be about to do something** 正要做某事 zhèng yào zuò mǒushì □ I was about to go out. 我正要出去。Wǒ zhèngyào chūqù.
■ **How about eating out?** 出去吃怎么样？Chūqù chī zěnmeyàng?

above PREPOSITION, ADVERB

1 在...上方 zài...shàngfāng
□ He put his hands above his head. 他把手放在头上方。Tā bǎshǒu fàngzài tóu shàngfāng. □ There was a picture above the fireplace. 壁炉上方有一幅画。Bìlú shàngfāng yǒu yìfú huà.
■ **the flat above** 楼上的公寓 lóushàngde gōngyù
■ **above all** 首先 shǒuxiān

2 以上 yǐshàng *(more than)*
□ above 40 degrees 四十度以上 sìshídù yǐshàng

abroad ADVERB
■ **to live abroad** 在国外生活 zài guówài shēnghuó
■ **to go abroad** 出国 chūguó

abrupt ADJECTIVE
无礼的 wúlǐde
□ He was a bit abrupt with me. 他对我有点无礼。Tā duìwǒ yǒudiǎn wúlǐ.

abruptly ADVERB
突然 tūrán
□ He got up abruptly. 他突然起身。Tā tūrán qǐshēn.

absence NOUN
1 缺席 quēxí [次 cì] *(of person)*
2 缺乏 quēfá *(of thing)*

absent ADJECTIVE
缺席的 quēxí de
■ **to be absent** 不在 búzài

absent-minded ADJECTIVE
心不在焉的 xīnbúzàiyān de
LANGUAGE TIP Word for word, this means 'the mind is not present'.
□ She's a bit absent-minded. 她有点心不在焉。Tā yǒudiǎn xīnbúzàiyān.

absolutely ADVERB
1 绝对地 juéduì de *(completely)*
□ David's absolutely right. 大卫绝对是对的。Dàwèi juéduì shì duìde.
2 当然 dāngrán
□ Do you think it's a good idea? — Absolutely! 你认为这是个好主意吗？ — 当然！Nǐrènwéi zhèshìge hǎozhǔyìma? — Dāngrán!

absorbed ADJECTIVE
■ **to be absorbed in something** 全神贯注于某物 quánshén guànzhùyú mǒuwù

absurd ADJECTIVE
荒唐 huāngtáng
□ That's absurd! 真荒唐！Zhēn huāngtáng!

abuse NOUN
▷ *see also* **abuse** VERB
1 滥用 lànyòng [种 zhǒng] *(misuse)*
2 虐待 nüèdài *(physical)*
3 猥亵 wěixiè *(sexual)*
■ **to shout abuse at somebody** 冲某人骂脏话 chòngmǒurén màzānghuà
■ **the problem of drug abuse** 药物滥用问题 yàowù lànyòng wèntí

to **abuse** VERB
▷ *see also* **abuse** NOUN
1 虐待 nüèdài *(physically)*
2 猥亵 wěixiè *(sexually)*
3 侮辱 wǔrǔ *(insult)*
■ **to abuse drugs** 滥用药物 lànyòng yàowù

abusive ADJECTIVE
1 骂人的 màrénde *(language)*
2 说人坏话的 shuōrén huàihuàde *(person)*

academic ADJECTIVE
学术的 xuéshù de
□ the academic year 学年 xuénián

academy NOUN
1 学会 xuéhuì [个 gè] *(a society of scholars, scientists, artists)*
□ The American Academy of Ophthalmology 美国眼科医师学会 Měiguóyǎnkēyīshīxuéhuì
2 学院 xuéyuàn [个 gè] *(school, college)*
□ a military academy 军事学院 jūnshìxuéyuàn

to **accelerate** VERB
加速 jiāsù *(in car)*

accelerator NOUN
加速器 jiāsùqì [个 gè]

accent NOUN
口音 kǒuyīn [种 zhǒng]
□ He's got an Irish accent. 他有爱尔兰口音。Tā yǒu Aìěrlán kǒuyīn.

to **accept** VERB
接受 jiēshòu

acceptable ADJECTIVE
可以接受的 kěyǐ jiēshòude

access NOUN
1 进入 jìnrù
□ You can't get access to the computing room without a card. 没有卡，你不能进入计算机房。Méiyǒu kǎ, nǐ bùnéng jìnrù jìsuànjīfáng.
2 接触 jiēchù
□ He has access to confidential information. 他可以接触机密信息。Tā kěyǐ jiēchù jīmì xìnxī.
3 接近 jiējìn
□ He is not allowed access to the children. 他是不允许接近儿童的。Tāshì bù yǔnxǔ jiējín értóng de.

accessible ADJECTIVE
可以获得的 kěyǐ huòdéde

accessory NOUN
配件 pèijiàn [个 gè]
□ fashion accessories 时尚配件 shíshàng pèijiàn

accident NOUN
1 事故 shìgù [起 qǐ] *(involving vehicle)*
□ You're bound to have an accident if you drive so fast down the motorway. 你在公路上要是开这么快肯定会出事故。Nǐ zàigōnglùshàng yàoshì kāi zhème kuài

kěndìng huì chūshìgù.

2 意外 yìwài [次 cì] *(mishap)*
□ He had an accident when he was hunting in the desert. 他在沙漠里打猎时出了意外。Tā zài shāmòlǐ dǎlièshí chūle yìwài.
■ **by accident** 1 *(by mistake)* 因失误 yīnshīwù □ The burglar killed him by accident. 那个入室窃贼因失误错杀了他。Nàgè rùshìqièzéi yīnshīwù cuòshā le tā.
2 *(by chance)* 偶然 ǒurán □ She met him by accident. 她偶然遇见了他。Tā ǒurán yùjiànle tā.

accidental ADJECTIVE
意外的 yìwài de

accident and emergency NOUN
急诊室 jízhěnshì [个 gè]

to **accommodate** VERB
供...住宿 gòng...zhùsù
□ The hotel can accommodate 50 people. 那家酒店可供五十人住宿。Nàjiājiǔdiàn kěgòng wǔshírén zhùsù.

accommodation NOUN
住处 zhùchù

to **accompany** VERB
1 陪伴 péibàn *(escort)*
2 为...伴奏 wèi...bànzòu *(on a musical instrument)*

accord NOUN
■ **of his own accord** 自愿地 zìyuànde
□ He left of his own accord. 他自愿地离开了。Tā zìyuànde líkāi le.

according to PREPOSITION
1 据...所说 jù...suǒshuō
□ According to him, everyone had gone. 据他所说，每个人都走了。Jùtāsuǒshuō, měigèrén dōuzǒule.
2 根据 gēnjù
□ According to their records, she never existed. 根据他们的记录，她从来没有存在过。Gēnjù tāmen de jìlù, tā cóngláiméiyǒu cúnzàiguò.

accordingly ADVERB
因此 yīncǐ

accordion NOUN
手风琴 shǒufēngqín [架 jià]

account NOUN
1 账户 zhànghù [个 gè]
□ a bank account 一个银行帐户 yígè yínháng zhànghù
■ **to do the accounts** 算帐 suànzhàng
2 描述 miáoshù [番 fān] *(report)*
□ He gave a detailed account of what happened. 他对发生的事做了一番详细描述。Tā duì fāshēng de shì zuòle yìfān xiángxìmiáoshù.
■ **to take something into account** 考虑到某事 kǎolǜ dào mǒushì
■ **on account of** 由于 yóuyú □ We couldn't go out on account of the bad weather. 由于天气不好，我们没有出去。Yóuyú tiānqì bùhǎo, wǒmen méiyǒu chūqù.

to **account for** VERB
说明 shuōmíng
□ She had to account for her absence. 她得说明为什么缺席。Tā děi shuōmíng wèishénme quēxí.

accountable ADJECTIVE
负有责任的 fùyǒu zérènde
■ **to be accountable to someone for something** 为某事对某人负责 wèi mǒushì duì mǒurén fùzé

accountancy NOUN
会计学 kuàijìxué

accountant NOUN
会计师 kuàijìshī [位 wèi]
□ She's an accountant. 她是一位会计师。Tāshì yíwèi kuàijìshī.

accuracy NOUN
1 准确 zhǔnquè *(of information, measurements)*
2 精确 jīngquè *(of person, device)*

accurate ADJECTIVE
1 精确的 jīngquè de *(information, measurement)*
2 准确的 zhǔnquè de *(description, person)*

accurately ADVERB
精确地 jīngquède

accusation NOUN
指控 zhǐkòng [项 xiàng]

to **accuse** VERB
■ **to accuse somebody of something** 指控某人做某事 zhǐkòng mǒurén zuò mǒushì
□ The police are accusing her of murder. 警方指控她谋杀。Jǐngfāng zhǐkòng tā móushā.

ace NOUN
么点 yāodiǎn
□ the ace of hearts 红桃么 hóngtáo yāo

to **ache** VERB
▷ *see also* **ache** NOUN
痛 tòng
□ My leg's aching. 我腿痛。Wǒ tuǐtòng.

ache NOUN
▷ *see also* **ache** VERB
疼痛 téngtòng [种 zhǒng]
■ **I've got stomach ache.** 我胃痛。Wǒ wèi tòng.

LANGUAGE TIP Both 疼 téng and 痛 tòng mean **ache** or **pain**, and can be used interchangeably.

to **achieve** VERB
取得 qǔdé *(success, result)*

achievement NOUN
成就 chéngjiù [项 xiàng]
□ That was quite an achievement. 这是相当大的一项成就。Zhè shì xiāngdāngdà de yíxiàng chéngjiù.

acid NOUN
酸 suān [种 zhǒng]

acid rain NOUN
酸雨 suānyǔ [场 chǎng]

acne NOUN
粉刺 fěncì [颗 kē]

acre NOUN
英亩 yīngmù

acrobat NOUN
杂技演员 zájìyǎnyuán [位 wèi]
□ He's an acrobat. 他是一位杂技演员。Tā shì yíwèi zájìyǎnyuán.

across PREPOSITION, ADVERB
1 穿过 chuānguò
□ an expedition across the Sahara 穿越撒哈拉的探险 chuānyuè Sāhālā de tànxiǎn
2 在...对面 zài...duìmiàn
□ the shop across the road 路对面那家商店 lù duìmiàn nàjiā shāngdiàn
■ **to walk across the road** 走到路对面 zǒudào lùduìmiàn
■ **to run across the road** 跑到路对面 pǎodào lùduìmiàn
■ **across from** *(opposite)* 在…对面 zài...duìmiàn □ He sat down across from her. 他在她对面坐了下来。Tā zàitā duìmiàn zuòlexiàlái.

to **act** VERB
▷ *see also* **act** NOUN
1 行动 xíngdòng *(take action)*
□ The police acted quickly. 警方迅速行动。Jǐngfāng xùnsù xíngdòng.
2 举止 jǔzhǐ *(behave)*
□ They were acting suspiciously. 他们举止可疑。Tāmen jǔzhǐ kěyí.
3 演戏 yǎnxì *(in play, film)*
□ He acts really well. 他演戏真好。Tā yǎnxì zhēnhǎo.
■ **She acts as his interpreter.** 她担任他的翻译。Tā dānrèn tāde fānyì.

act NOUN
▷ *see also* **act** VERB
幕 mù *(in play)*
□ in the first act 在第一幕中 zài dìyīmù zhōng

action NOUN
1 动作 dòngzuò
□ The film was full of action. 那部影片中充满动作场面。Nàbù yǐngpiān chōngmǎn dòngzuò chǎngmiàn.
2 行动 xíngdòng *(steps, measures)*
□ to take firm action against 对…采取坚决行动 duì...cǎiqǔ jiānjué xíngdòng

active ADJECTIVE
活跃的 huóyuè de
□ He's a very active person. 他是个很活跃的人。Tā shìge hěnhuóyuède rén.
■ **an active volcano** 活火山 huóhuǒshān

activity NOUN
活动 huódòng [项 xiàng]
□ outdoor activities 户外活动 hùwài huódòng

actor NOUN
演员 yǎnyuán [个 gè]
□ Brad Pitt is a well-known actor. 布拉德·皮特是著名演员。Bùlādé Pítè shì zhùmíng yǎnyuán.

actress NOUN
女演员 nǚ yǎnyuán [个 gè]
□ Julia Roberts is a well-known actress. 朱丽娅·罗伯茨是著名女演员。Zhūlìyà Luóbócí shì zhùmíng nǚyǎnyuán.

actual ADJECTIVE
真实的 zhēnshí de
□ The film is based on actual events. 那部电影是以真实事件为题材的。Nàbù diànyǐng shì yǐ zhēnshíshìjiàn wéi tícáide.
■ **What's the actual amount?** 实际金额是多少？ Shíjì jīn'é shì duōshǎo?

actually ADVERB
1 实际地 shíjì de
□ Did it actually happen? 这事实际发生了吗？ Zhèshì shíjì fāshēngle ma?
2 事实上 shìshíshang *(in fact)*
□ Actually, I don't know him at all. 事实上，我根本不认识他。Shìshíshàng, wǒ gēnběn bú rènshi tā.

acupuncture NOUN
针刺疗法 zhēncìliáofǎ [次 cì]

AD ABBREVIATION *(= Anno Domini)*
公元 gōngyuán
□ in 800 AD 公元八零零年 gōngyuán bālínglíngnián

ad NOUN
广告 guǎnggào *(advertisement)*

to **adapt** VERB
使适合 shǐ shìhé
□ His novel was adapted for television. 他的小说为拍电视进行了改编。Tāde xiǎoshuō wèipāi diànshì jìnxíngle gǎibiān.
■ **to adapt to something** *(get used to)* 适应某物 shìyìng mǒuwù □ He adapted to his new school very quickly. 他很快适应了新学校。Tā hěnkuài shìyìngle xīnxuéxiào.

adaptor NOUN
转接器 zhuǎnjiēqì [个 gè]

to **add** VERB
加入 jiārù
□ Add two eggs to the mixture. 在混合物中加入两个鸡蛋。Zài hǔnhéwùzhōng jiārù liǎnggèjīdàn.

to **add up** VERB
加起来 jiāqǐlái
□ Add the figures up. 把那些数字加起来。Bǎ nàxiēshùzì jiāqǐlái.

addict NOUN
■ **a drug addict** 吸毒成瘾的人 xīdú chéngyǐn de rén
■ **Peter's a football addict.** 彼得是个足球迷。Bǐdé shìgè zúqiúmí.

addicted ADJECTIVE
■ **to be addicted to something** *(drug)* 对某种药物上瘾 duì mǒuzhǒngyàowù shàngyǐn □ She's addicted to heroin. 她对海洛因上瘾。Tā duì hǎiluòyīn shàngyǐn.
■ **She's addicted to soap operas.** 她看肥皂剧上瘾。Tā kàn féizàojù shàngyǐn.

addition NOUN
加法 jiāfǎ *(maths)*
■ **in addition** 另外 lìngwài □ He's broken his leg and, in addition, he's caught a cold. 他折断了腿，另外还得了感冒。Tā zhéduànle tuǐ, lìngwài háidéle gǎnmào.
■ **in addition to** 除…之外 chú...zhīwài □ There's a postage fee in addition to the repair charge. 除修理费之外还有邮费。Chú xiūlǐfèi zhīwài háiyǒu yóufèi.

address NOUN
地址 dìzhǐ [个 gè]
□ What's your address? 你的地址是哪里？Nǐde dìzhǐ shì nǎlǐ?

adjective NOUN
形容词 xíngróngcí [个 gè]

to **adjust** VERB
调整 tiáozhěng
□ You can adjust the height of the chair. 你可以调整椅子的高度。Nǐ kěyǐ tiáozhěng yǐzi de gāodù.
■ **to adjust to something** *(get used to)* 适应某事 shìyìng mǒushì □ He adjusted to his new school very quickly. 他很快适应了新学校。Tā hěnkuài shìyìng le xīnxuéxiào.

adjustable ADJECTIVE
可调节的 kě tiáojié de

administration NOUN
行政管理 xíngzhèng guǎnlǐ

admiral NOUN
海军上将 hǎijūn shàngjiàng [位 wèi]

to **admire** VERB
钦佩 qīnpèi

admission NOUN
允许进入 yúnxǔ jìnrù
■ **'admission free'** "免费入场" 'miǎnfèi rùchǎng'

to **admit** VERB
承认 chéngrèn
□ He admitted that he'd done it. 他承认那是他干的。Tā chéngrèn nàshì tā gànde.
□ I must admit that... 我必须承认… Wǒ bìxū chéngrèn...
■ **to be admitted to hospital** 住进医院 zhùjìn yīyuàn

admittance NOUN
■ **'no admittance'** "禁制入内" 'jìnzhǐ rùnèi'

adolescence NOUN
青春期 qīngchūnqī

adolescent NOUN
青少年 qīngshàonián [个 gè]

to **adopt** VERB
收养 shōuyǎng
□ Phil was adopted. 菲尔是收养的。Fēi'ěr shì shōuyǎngde.

adopted ADJECTIVE
被收养的 bèi shōuyǎng de
■ **an adopted son** 一个养子 yígè yǎngzǐ

adoption NOUN
收养 shōuyǎng

to **adore** VERB
喜爱 xǐ'ài

Adriatic Sea NOUN
亚德里亚海 Yàdélǐyàhǎi

adult NOUN
成年人 chéngniánrén [个 gè]
■ **adult education** 成人教育 chéngrén jiàoyù

to **advance** VERB
▷ *see also* **advance** NOUN
1 前进 qiánjìn *(move forward)*
□ The troops are advancing. 部队在前进。Bùduì zài qiánjìn.
2 进步 jìnbù *(progress)*
□ Technology has advanced a lot. 技术已经进步了很多。Jìshù yǐjīng jìnbule hěnduō.

advance NOUN
▷ *see also* **advance** VERB
■ **in advance** 提前 tíqián □ They bought the tickets in advance. 他们提前买了票。Tāmen tíqián mǎile piào.

advance booking NOUN
■ **Advance booking is essential.** 预订是非常重要的。Yùdìng shì fēicháng zhòngyàode.

advanced ADJECTIVE
1 先进的 xiānjìn de *(highly developed)*
2 高等的 gāoděng de *(student)*

advantage NOUN
好处 hǎochù [种 zhǒng]

□ Going to university has many advantages. 上大学有许多好处。Shàngdàxué yǒu xǔduō hǎochù.

■ **to take advantage of something** 利用某物 lìyòng mǒuwù □ He took advantage of the good weather to go for a walk. 他利用好天气去散步。Tā lìyòng hǎotiānqì qùsànbù.

■ **to take advantage of somebody** 利用某人 lìyòng mǒurén □ The company was taking advantage of its employees. 那家公司在利用员工。Nàjiā gōngsī zài lìyòng yuángōng.

adventure NOUN
冒险活动 màoxiǎn huódòng [次 cì]

adverb NOUN
副词 fùcí [个 gè]

advert NOUN
广告 guǎnggào [则 zé]

to **advertise** VERB
1 为...做广告 wèi...zuò guǎnggào
□ They're advertising the new model. 他们正在为那个新款做广告。Tāmen zhèngzài wèinàge xīnkuǎn zuòguǎnggào.
2 刊登 kāndēng
□ Jobs are advertised in the paper. 职位刊登在报纸上。Zhíwèi kāndēng zài bàozhǐshàng.

advertisement NOUN
广告 guǎnggào [则 zé]

advertising NOUN
广告业 guǎnggàoyè

advice NOUN
忠告 zhōnggào
■ **to give somebody advice** 给某人忠告 gěimǒurén zhōnggào
■ **a piece of advice** 一条忠告 yìtiáo zhōnggào □ He gave me a good piece of advice. 他给了我一条好忠告。Tā gěilewǒ yìtiáo hǎo zhōnggào.

to **advise** VERB
■ **to advise somebody to do something** 劝某人做某事 quàn mǒurén zuò mǒushì □ He advised me to wait. 他劝我等待。Tā quànwǒ děngdài.

aerial NOUN
天线 tiānxiàn [根 gēn]

aerobics NOUN
有氧健身操 yǒuyǎng jiànshēncāo
□ I'm going to aerobics tonight. 我今晚要去做有氧健身操。Wǒ jīnwǎn yàoqùzuò yǒuyǎng jiànshēncāo.

aeroplane NOUN
飞机 fēijī [架 jià]

aerosol NOUN
烟雾剂 yānwùjì

affair NOUN
1 事情 shìqing
□ The government has mishandled the affair. 政府错误地处理了那件事情。Zhèngfǔ cuòwùde chǔlǐle nàjiàn shìqing.
2 风流韵事 fēngliú yùnshì [桩 zhuāng]
■ **to have an affair with somebody** 和某人有了风流韵事 hé mǒurén yǒule fēngliú yùnshì

to **affect** VERB
影响 yǐngxiǎng

affectionate ADJECTIVE
充满深情的 chōngmǎn shēnqíngde

to **afford** VERB
买得起 mǎideqǐ
□ I can't afford a new pair of jeans. 我买不起一条新牛仔裤。Wǒ mǎibùqǐ yìtiáo xīnniúzǎikù.

afraid ADJECTIVE
害怕的 hàipà de *(frightened)*
■ **to be afraid of something** 害怕某物 hàipà mǒuwù □ I'm afraid of spiders. 我怕蜘蛛。Wǒ hàipà zhīzhū.
■ **I'm afraid I can't come.** 我恐怕不能来。Wǒ kǒngpà bùnénglái.
■ **I'm afraid so.** 恐怕是这样。Kǒngpà shìzhèyàng.
■ **I'm afraid not.** 恐怕不是。Kǒngpà búshì.

Africa NOUN
非洲 Fēizhōu

African ADJECTIVE
▷ *see also* **African** NOUN
非洲的 Fēizhōu de

African NOUN
▷ *see also* **African** ADJECTIVE
非洲人 Fēizhōurén [个 gè]

after PREPOSITION, CONJUNCTION, ADVERB
1 在...以后 zài...yǐhòu *(in time)*
■ **after dinner** 饭后 fànhòu
■ **the day after tomorrow** 后天 hòutiān
2 在...后面 zài...hòumiàn *(in place, order)*
□ He ran after me. 他在我后面跑。Tā zàiwǒhòumiàn pǎo.
3 以后 yǐhòu
□ soon after 不久以后 bùjiǔ yǐhòu
■ **after doing something** 做完某事后 zuòwán mǒushì hòu □ After watching television I went to bed. 我看完电视以后上床睡觉了。Wǒ kànwán diànshì yǐhòu shàngchuáng shuìjiàole.
■ **after all** 毕竟 bìjìng □ After all, nobody can make us go. 毕竟，没人能让我们走。Bìjìng, méirén néngràng wǒmenzǒu.

afternoon NOUN
下午 xiàwǔ [个 gè]
□ 3 o'clock in the afternoon 下午三点 xiàwǔ sāndiǎn □ this afternoon 今天下午 jīntiān xiàwǔ □ on Saturday afternoon 在星期六下午 zài xīngqīliù xiàwǔ
■ **Good afternoon!** 下午好！Xiàwǔ hǎo!

afters NOUN
正餐后的甜食 zhèngcānhòude tiánshí

aftershave NOUN
须后水 xūhòu shuǐ

afterwards ADVERB
以后 yǐhòu
□ She left not long afterwards. 她不久以后就走了。Tā bùjiǔyǐhòu jiùzǒule.

again ADVERB
1 再次 zàicì *(one more time)*
□ They're friends again. 他们再次成为朋友。Tāmen zàicì chéngwéi péngyǒu. □ I won't go there again. 我再也不去那儿了。Wǒ zàiyě búqùnàerle.
2 重新地 chóngxīn de *(from the beginning)*
□ Can you tell me again? 你能重新告诉我一遍吗？Nǐ néng chóngxīn gàosù wǒ yíbiàn ma?

against PREPOSITION
1 紧靠在 jǐnkào zài
□ He leant against the wall. 他紧靠在墙上。Tā jǐnkaòzài qiángshàng.
2 反对 fǎnduì
□ I'm against nuclear testing. 我反对核试验。Wǒ fǎnduì héshìyàn.
3 同...对抗 tóng...duìkàng
□ They'll be playing against Australia. 他们将在比赛中同澳大利亚队对抗。Tāmen jiāng zài bǐsài zhōng tóng Àodàlìyà duì duìkàng.
■ **against the law** 违反法律 wéifǎn fǎlǜ

age NOUN
年龄 niánlíng
□ What age is he? 他多大年龄了？Tā duōdà niánlíng le?
■ **at the age of 20** 二十岁时 èrshí suì shí
■ **I haven't been to the cinema for ages.** 我很久没去看电影了。Wǒ hěnjiǔ méiqù kàndiànyǐngle.
■ **an age limit** 一个年龄限制 yígè niánlíng xiànzhì

aged ADJECTIVE
■ **aged 10** 十岁 shí suì

agenda NOUN
议程 yìchéng
□ on the agenda 在议程上 zàiyìchéngshàng

agent NOUN
1 代理人 dàilǐrén [个 gè]
□ a travel agent 旅行代理人 lǚxíng dàilǐrén
2 经纪人 jīngjìrén
□ an estate agent 房地产经纪人 fángdìchǎn jīngjìrén

aggressive ADJECTIVE
好斗的 hàodòu de

ago ADVERB
■ **two days ago** 两天前 liǎngtiān qián
■ **long ago** 很久以前 hěnjiǔ yǐqián
■ **not long ago** 不久以前 bùjiǔyǐqián
■ **How long ago did it happen?** 那是多久以前发生的？Nàshì duōjiǔ yǐqián fāshēngde?

agony NOUN
痛苦 tòngkǔ [种 zhǒng]
□ He is in agony. 他很痛苦。Tā hěn tòngkǔ.

to **agree** VERB
同意 tóngyì *(have same opinion)*
□ I don't agree! 我不同意！Wǒ bùtóngyì!
■ **to agree with...** 同意…的意见 tóngyì... de yìjiàn □ I agree with Carol. 我同意卡罗尔的意见。Wǒ tóngyì Kǎluó'ěr de yìjiàn.
■ **to agree to do something** 允诺做某事 yǔnnuò zuò mǒushì □ He agreed to go and pick her up. 他允诺去接她。Tā yǔnnuò qù jiētā.
■ **to agree that...** 承认… chéngrèn...
□ I agree that it's difficult. 我承认那是困难的。Wǒ chéngrèn nàshì kùnnánde.
■ **Garlic doesn't agree with me.** 我不适宜吃大蒜。Wǒ búshìyí chī dàsuàn.

agreed ADJECTIVE
约定的 yuēdìngde
□ at the agreed time 在约定的时间 zài yuēdìng de shíjiān

agreement NOUN
一致 yízhì
■ **to be in agreement** 同意…的意见 tóngyì...deyìjiàn □ Everybody was in agreement with Ray. 每个人都同意雷的观点。Měigèrén dōu tóngyì Léide guāndiǎn.

agricultural ADJECTIVE
农业的 nóngyè de

agriculture NOUN
农业 nóngyè

ahead ADVERB
向前地 xiàngqián de *(in front)*
□ She looked straight ahead. 她一直向前看。Tā yìzhí xiàngqiánkàn.
■ **ahead of time** 提前 tíqián
■ **The Chinese team are 5 points ahead.** 中国队领先五分。Zhōngguóduì lǐngxiān wǔfēn.
■ **the months ahead** 今后几个月 jīnhòu jǐgè yuè

■ **to plan ahead** 提前做计划 tíqián zuò jìhuà
■ **Go ahead!** 干吧！Gànba!

aid NOUN
援助 yuánzhù
■ **in aid of charity** 作为援助慈善之用 zuòwéi yuánzhù císhàn zhīyòng

AIDS NOUN
艾滋病 àizībìng

to **aim** VERB
▷ *see also* **aim** NOUN
■ **to aim at** 瞄准 miáozhǔn □ He aimed a gun at me. 他拿枪瞄准我。Tā náqiāng miáozhǔn wǒ.
■ **The film is aimed at children.** 这部电影是针对儿童的。Zhèbù diànyǐng shì zhēnduì értóngde.
■ **to aim to do something** 打算做某事 dǎsuàn zuò mǒushì □ Janice aimed to leave at 5 o'clock. 珍妮斯打算五点钟离开。Zhēnnísī dǎsuàn wǔdiǎnzhōng líkāi.

aim NOUN
▷ *see also* **aim** VERB
目标 mùbiāo [个 gè]
□ The aim of the festival is to raise money. 会演的目的是筹款。Huìyǎn de mùdì shì chóukuǎn.

air NOUN
空气 kōngqì
□ to get some fresh air 呼吸些新鲜空气 hūxīxiē xīnxian kōngqì
■ **by air** 乘飞机 chéng fēijī □ I prefer to travel by air. 我更喜欢乘飞机旅游。Wǒ gèngxǐhuān chéngfēijī lǚyóu.

air-conditioned ADJECTIVE
装有空调的 zhuāngyǒu kōngtiáo de

air conditioning NOUN
空气调节 kōngqì tiáojié

Air Force NOUN
空军 kōngjūn [支 zhī]

air hostess NOUN
空中小姐 kōngzhōng xiǎojiě [位 wèi]
□ She's an air hostess. 她是一位空中小姐。Tā shì yíwèi kōngzhōng xiǎojiě.

airline NOUN
航空公司 hángkōng gōngsī [家 jiā]

airmail NOUN
■ **by airmail** 航空邮寄 hángkōng yóujì

airplane NOUN (US)
飞机 fēijī [架 jià]

airport NOUN
飞机场 fēijīchǎng [个 gè]

aisle NOUN
过道 guòdào [条 tiáo]
■ **aisle seat** *(on plane)* 靠过道的座位 kào guòdào de zuòwèi

alarm NOUN
1 警报 jǐngbào [个 gè] *(warning device)*
■ **a fire alarm** 一起火警 yìqǐ huǒjǐng
2 闹钟 nàozhōng [个 gè] *(on clock)*

alarm clock NOUN
闹钟 nàozhōng [个 gè]

Albania NOUN
阿尔巴尼亚 Ā'ěrbāníyà

album NOUN
1 册子 cèzi [本 běn] *(book, also for photos)*
2 唱片 chàngpiàn [张 zhāng] *(music)*

alcohol NOUN
酒 jiǔ

alcoholic NOUN
▷ *see also* **alcoholic** ADJECTIVE
酒鬼 jiǔguǐ [个 gè]
LANGUAGE TIP Word for word, this means 'alcohol demon'.
□ He's an alcoholic. 他是个酒鬼。Tā shìge jiǔguǐ.

alcoholic ADJECTIVE
▷ *see also* **alcoholic** NOUN
含酒精的 hán jiǔjīng de
□ alcoholic drinks 酒精饮料 jiǔjīng yǐnliào

alert ADJECTIVE
1 机灵的 jīlíngde *(bright)*
□ a very alert baby 一个非常机灵的宝宝 yígè fēicháng jīlíng de bǎobǎo
2 警惕的 jǐngtìde *(paying attention)*
□ We must stay alert. 我们必须保持警惕。Wǒmen bìxū bǎochí jǐngtì.

A levels PL NOUN
中学中高级考试 zhōngxué zhōnggāojíkǎoshì

Algeria NOUN
阿尔及利亚 Ā'ěrjílìyà

alien NOUN
外星人 wàixīngrén [个 gè] *(from outer space)*

alike ADVERB
■ **to look alike** 看起来很像的 kànqǐlái xiāngsì de □ The two sisters look alike. 两姐妹看起来很像。Liǎngjiěmèi kànqǐlái hěnxiàng.

alive ADJECTIVE
■ **to be alive** 活着的 huózhe de

all ADJECTIVE, PRONOUN, ADVERB
所有的 suǒyǒu de
□ all big cities 所有的大城市 suǒyǒu de dàchéngshì
■ **all day** 整日 zhěngrì
■ **all the time** 始终 shǐzhōng
■ **I ate all of it.** 我把它全都吃了。Wǒ bǎ tā quán dōu chīle.
■ **all of us** 我们中的所有人 wǒmen zhōng de suǒyǒu rén

■ **We all sat down.** 我们都坐下了。Wǒmen dōu zuòxià le.
■ **Is that all?** 那就是全部吗？Nà jiùshì quánbù ma?
■ **after all** 毕竟 bìjìng ◻ After all, nobody can make us go. 毕竟，没人能让我们走。Bìjìng, méirén néngràng wǒmenzǒu.
■ **best of all** 最好不过的是 zuìhǎo búguò de shì
■ **not at all** 根本不 gēnběnbù ◻ I'm not tired at all. 我根本不累。Wǒ gēnběn búlèi.
■ **all by oneself** 完全靠自己 wánquán kào zìjǐ ◻ He was doing it all by himself. 他完全是靠自己做的。Tā wánquán shì kào zìjǐ zuò de.
■ **all alone** 孤零零的 gūlínglíng de ◻ She's all alone. 她孤零零的。Tā gūlínglíng de.
■ **The score is 2 all.** 比分二比二平。Bǐfēn èr bǐ èr píng.

allergic ADJECTIVE
过敏的 guòmǐn de*(reaction)*
■ **to be allergic to something** 对某物过敏 duì mǒuwù guòmǐn ◻ I'm allergic to cat hair. 我对猫毛过敏。Wǒ duì māomáo guòmǐn.

alley NOUN
小巷 xiǎoxiàng [条 tiáo]

DID YOU KNOW...?
Beijing is famous for its network of narrow streets and alleys, known as 胡同 hútòng, which are formed by lines of traditional courtyard residences.

to **allow** VERB
允许 yǔnxǔ
■ **to allow somebody to do something** 允许某人做某事 yǔnxǔ mǒurén zuò mǒushì ◻ His mum allowed him to go out. 他妈妈允许他出去。Tāmāma yǔnxǔ tā chūqù.
■ **to be allowed to do something** 获准做某事 huòzhǔn zuòmǒushì ◻ He's not allowed to go out at night. 不准他晚上出去。Bùzhǔntā wǎnshàng chūqù.

all right ADVERB, ADJECTIVE
1 顺利地 shùnlì de
◻ Everything turned out all right. 一切顺利。Yíqiè shùnlì.
■ **Are you all right?** 你没事吧？Nǐ méishìba?
2 不错 búcuò*(not bad)*
◻ The film was all right. 那部电影不错。Nàbù diànyǐng búcuò.
3 好 hǎo*(when agreeing)*
◻ We'll talk about it later. — All right. 我们一会儿再谈这个。— 好。Wǒmen yíhuǐr zàitán zhège. — Hǎo.
■ **Is that all right with you?** 你觉得合适吗？Nǐ juédé héshìma?

almond NOUN
杏仁 xìngrén [颗 kē]

almost ADVERB
差不多 chàbuduō
◻ I've almost finished. 我已经差不多完成了。Wǒ yǐjīng chàbuduō wánchéngle.

alone ADJECTIVE, ADVERB
独自的 dúzì de
◻ She lives alone. 她独自生活。Tā dúzì shēnghuó.
■ **to leave somebody alone** 不打扰某人 bù dǎrǎo mǒurén ◻ Leave her alone! 别打扰她！Biédǎrǎotā.
■ **to leave something alone** 不动某物 búdòng mǒuwù ◻ Leave my things alone! 别动我的东西！Biédòng wǒde dōngxi!

along PREPOSITION, ADVERB
沿着 yánzhe
◻ Chris was walking along the beach. 克里斯正沿着海滩走。Kèlìsī zhèng yánzhe hǎitān zǒu.
■ **all along** 一直 yìzhí ◻ He was lying to me all along. 他一直在对我说谎。Tā yìzhí zài duìwǒ shuōhuǎng.

aloud ADVERB
大声地 dàshēngde
◻ He read the poem aloud. 他大声朗读那首诗。Tā dàshēng lǎngdú nàshǒushī.

alphabet NOUN
■ **the alphabet** 字母表 zìmǔbiǎo

Alps PL NOUN
阿尔卑斯山 Āěrbēisīshān

already ADVERB
已经 yǐjīng
◻ I have already started making dinner. 我已经开始做晚餐了。Wǒ yǐjīng kāishǐ zuò wǎncān le. ◻ Is it five o'clock already? 已经到五点了吗？Yǐjīng dào wǔdiǎn le ma?

also ADVERB
也 yě*(too)*

altar NOUN
祭坛 jìtán [座 zuò]

to **alter** VERB
改变 gǎibiàn

alternate ADJECTIVE
1 间隔的 jiāngé de
■ **on alternate days** 隔天 gétiān
2 供替代的 gōng tìdài de(US: *alternative*)
◻ an alternate route 一条替代路线 yìtiáo tìdàilùxiàn

alternative ADJECTIVE
▷ *see also* **alternative** NOUN
另外的 lìngwài de
◻ They made alternative plans. 他们制定了

English-Chinese

a

另外的计划。Tāmen zhìdìngle lìngwàide jìhuà.
■ **an alternative solution** 一套替代性的解决方案 yítào tìdàixìngde jiějué fāng'àn
■ **alternative medicine** 替代性医学 tìdàixìng yīxué

alternative NOUN
▷ *see also* **alternative** ADJECTIVE
选择 xuǎnzé
□ You have no alternative. 你别无选择。Nǐ biéwú xuǎnzé. □ There are several alternatives. 有几种选择。Yǒu jǐzhǒng xuǎnzé.
■ **Fruit is a healthy alternative to chocolate.** 水果是健康的巧克力替代品。Shǔiguǒ shì jiànkāng de qiǎokèlì tìdàipǐn.

alternatively ADVERB
或者 huòzhě
□ Alternatively, we could just stay at home. 或者，我们可以就待在家里。Huòzhě, wǒmen kěyǐ jiù dāizài jiālǐ.

although CONJUNCTION
尽管 jǐnguǎn
□ Although she was tired, she stayed up late. 尽管她累了，但还是很晚才睡。Jǐnguǎn tālèile, dàn háishì hěnwǎn cáishuì.

altogether ADVERB
1 总共 zǒnggòng *(in total)*
□ How much is that altogether? 总共多少钱？Zǒnggòng duōshǎo qián?
2 完全 wánquán *(completely)*
□ I'm not altogether happy with your work. 我对你的工作不完全满意。Wǒ duì nǐde gōngzuò bù wánquán mǎnyì.

aluminium NOUN
铝 lǚ

always ADVERB
总是 zǒngshì
□ He's always late. 他总是迟到。Tā zǒngshì chídào.

am VERB ▷ *see* **be**

a.m. ABBREVIATION
上午 shàngwǔ
□ at 4 a.m. 上午四点 shàngwǔ sìdiǎn

amateur NOUN
业余爱好者 yèyú àihàozhě [个 gè]

amazed ADJECTIVE
惊讶的 jīngyàde
□ I was amazed that I managed to do it. 我很惊讶自己做到了。Wǒ hěnjīngyà zìjǐ zuòdàole.

amazing ADJECTIVE
1 令人惊讶的 lìng rén jīngyà de
□ That's amazing news! 那是个令人惊讶的消息！Nàshìge lìngrén jīngyà de xiāoxī!
2 令人惊叹的 lìngrén jīngtànde *(excellent)*
□ Vivian's an amazing cook. 维维安是一位令人惊叹的厨师。Wéiwéiān shìyíwèi lìngrénjīngtànde chúshī.

ambassador NOUN
大使 dàshǐ [位 wèi]

amber ADJECTIVE
■ **an amber light** 一盏黄色信号灯 yìzhǎn huángsè xìnhàodēng

ambition NOUN
1 雄心 xióngxīn *(desire to be successful)*
2 抱负 bàofu *(for fame, career)*
■ **to achieve one's ambition** 实现自己的抱负 shíxiàn zìjǐ de bàofu

ambitious ADJECTIVE
雄心勃勃的 xióngxīn bóbó de
□ She's very ambitious. 她雄心勃勃。Tā xióngxīn bóbó.

ambulance NOUN
救护车 jiùhùchē [辆 liàng]

amenities PL NOUN
令人愉快的事物 lìngrén yúkuàide shìwù
■ **The hotel has very good amenities.** 那家酒店设施极好。Nàjiā jiǔdiàn shèshī jíhǎo.

America NOUN
美洲 Měizhōu

American ADJECTIVE
▷ *see also* **American** NOUN
美国的 Měiguó de
□ an American film 一部美国电影 yíbù Měiguó diànyǐng □ He's American. 他是美国人。Tāshì Měiguórén.

American NOUN
▷ *see also* **American** ADJECTIVE
美国人 Měiguórén [个 gè]
■ **the Americans** 美国人 Měiguórén

among PREPOSITION
在…当中 zài…dāngzhōng
□ There were six children among them. 他们当中有六名儿童。Tāmen dāngzhōng yǒu liùmíng értóng.
■ **We were among friends.** 我们和朋友在一起。Wǒmen hé péngyǒu zàiyìqǐ.
■ **among other things** 除了别的以外 chúle biéde yǐwài

amount NOUN
数量 shùliàng *(quantity)*
□ a huge amount of rice 数量巨大的大米 shùliàng jùdà de dàmǐ
■ **a large amount of money** 一大笔钱 yí dàbǐqián

amp NOUN
安培 ānpéi

amplifier NOUN
扬声器 yángshēngqì [个 gè]

to **amuse** VERB
■ **to be amused by something** 被某事逗乐 bèi mǒushì dòulè □ He was most amused by the story. 那个故事逗得他特开心。Nàge gùshì dòude tā tè kāixīn.

amusement arcade NOUN
游乐场 yóulèchǎng [个 gè]

an ARTICLE ▷ *see* **a**

anaesthetic (US **anesthetic**) NOUN
麻醉剂 mázuìjì [种 zhǒng]
■ **local anaesthetic** 局部麻醉 júbù mázuì
■ **general anaesthetic** 全身麻醉 quánshēn mázuì

to **analyse** VERB
分析 fēnxī

analysis NOUN
分析 fēnxī [种 zhǒng]

to **analyze** VERB (US)
分析 fēnxī

ancestor NOUN
祖先 zǔxiān [位 wèi]

anchor NOUN
锚 máo [具 jù]

ancient ADJECTIVE
1 古代的 gǔdài de *(civilization)*
□ ancient Greece 古希腊 gǔ Xīlà
2 古老的 gǔlǎo de *(very old)*
□ an ancient custom 一项古老的风俗 yíxiàng gǔlǎodē fēngsú

and CONJUNCTION
和 hé
□ men and women 男人和女人 nánrén hé nǚrén □ 2 and 2 are 4 2加2等于4 èr jiā èr děngyúsì
■ **Please try and come!** 请尽量来！Qǐngjìnliànglái!
■ **He talked and talked.** 他说啊说。Tā shuōashuō.
■ **better and better** 越来越好 yuè lái yuè hǎo

anesthetic NOUN (US)
麻醉剂 mázuìjì [种 zhǒng]

angel NOUN
天使 tiānshǐ [个 gè]

anger NOUN
生气 shēngqì

angle NOUN
角度 jiǎodù [个 gè]

angler NOUN
钓鱼者 diàoyúzhě [个 gè]

angling NOUN
钓鱼 diàoyú

angry ADJECTIVE
生气的 shēngqì de
□ Dad looks very angry. 爸爸看起来非常生气。Bàba kànqǐlái fēicháng shēngqì.
■ **to be angry with somebody** 生某人的气 shēngmǒuréndeqì □ Mum's really angry with you. 妈妈真生你的气了。Māma zhēn shēngnǐde qìle.
■ **to get angry** 生气 shēngqì
■ **to make somebody angry** 使某人生气 shǐ mǒurén shēngqì

animal NOUN
动物 dòngwù [只 zhī]

ankle NOUN
踝 huái [个 gè]

anniversary NOUN
周年纪念 zhōunián jìniàn [个 gè]
□ It's their wedding anniversary. 那是他们的结婚周年纪念日。Nàshì tāmende jiéhūn zhōunián jìniànrì.

to **announce** VERB
宣布 xuānbù
■ **The government has announced that...** 政府宣称… Zhèngfǔ xuānchēng...

announcement NOUN
1 宣布 xuānbù
2 通告 tōnggào [个 gè] *(at airport or station)*
■ **to make an announcement** 发表声明 fābiǎo shēngmíng

to **annoy** VERB
使烦恼 shǐ fánnǎo
■ **to get annoyed** 苦恼 kǔnǎo □ Don't get so annoyed! 别这么苦恼！Bié zhème kǔnǎo!

annoying ADJECTIVE
讨厌的 tǎoyàn de
□ It's really annoying. 真讨厌。Zhēntǎoyàn.

annual ADJECTIVE
1 每年的 měinián de *(meeting, report)*
2 年度的 niándù de *(sales, income)*

anorak NOUN
连帽防风夹克 liánmào fángfēng jiákè [件 jiàn]

anorexic ADJECTIVE
厌食的 yànshíde

another ADJECTIVE
1 再一 zàiyī *(one more)*
□ another book 另一本书 lìng yì běn shū
□ Would you like another piece of cake? 你想再要一块蛋糕吗？Nǐ xiǎng zàiyào yíkuài dàngāo ma?
■ **another 5 years** 再有五年 zài yǒu wǔ nián
2 别的 bié de *(a different one)*
□ Have you got another skirt? 你还有别的裙子吗？Nǐ háiyǒu biéde qúnzi ma?

answer NOUN
▷ *see also* **answer** VERB
1 答案 dá'àn [个 gè] *(to question)*

English-Chinese

a

2 解答 jiědá [个 gè] *(to problem)*

to **answer** VERB

▷ *see also* **answer** NOUN

回答 huídá

□ Can you answer my question? 你能回答我的问题吗？Nǐ néng huídá wǒde wèntí ma?

■ **to answer the phone** 接听电话 jiētīng diànhuà

■ **to answer the door** 应门 yīngmén

□ Can you answer the door please? 你去应门好吗？Nǐqù yīngmén hǎoma?

answering machine NOUN

电话答录机 diànhuà dálùjī [台 tái]

ant NOUN

蚂蚁 mǎyǐ [只 zhī]

to **antagonize** VERB

让…讨厌 ràng...tǎoyàn

□ He didn't want to antagonize her. 他不想让她讨厌。Tā bùxiǎng ràngtā tǎoyàn.

Antarctic NOUN

■ **the Antarctic** 南极 Nánjí

anthem NOUN

■ **the national anthem** 赞美诗 zànměishī

antibiotic NOUN

抗生素 kàngshēngsù [种 zhǒng]

antidepressant NOUN

抗抑郁剂 kàng yìyùjì

antique NOUN

古董 gǔdǒng [件 jiàn]

antique shop NOUN

古董店 gǔdǒngdiàn [家 jiā]

antiseptic NOUN

杀菌剂 shājūnjì [种 zhǒng]

anxious ADJECTIVE

忧虑的 yōulǜ de

any ADJECTIVE

▷ *see also* **any** PRONOUN, ADVERB

LANGUAGE TIP You use 一些的 yìxiē de in questions.

□ Have you got any chocolate? 你有一些巧克力吗？Nǐ yǒu yìxiē qiǎokèlì ma?

LANGUAGE TIP **any** is not translated in negative sentences.

□ I haven't got any chocolate. 我没有巧克力了。Wǒ méiyǒu qiǎokèlì le. □ There was hardly any food. 几乎没有食物了。Jīhū méiyǒu shíwù le.

LANGUAGE TIP You use 任何的 rènhé de in **if** clauses, and when **any** means **no matter which**.

□ If there are any tickets left... 如果有任何票剩下的话… rúguǒ yǒu rènhé piào shèngxia de huà... □ Take any card you like. 拿你喜欢的任何一张卡。Ná nǐ xǐhuan de rènyì yì zhāng kǎ.

any PRONOUN

▷ *see also* **any** ADJECTIVE, ADVERB

LANGUAGE TIP **any** is not translated in negative sentences.

□ I didn't eat any of it. 这个我一点也没吃。Zhège wǒ yìdiǎn yěméichī. □ I haven't got any. 我一个也没有。Wǒ yígè yě méiyǒu.

LANGUAGE TIP **any** used in a question is translated by 一些 yìxiē or can be omitted.

□ Have you found any? 你找到一些了吗？Nǐ zhǎo dào yìxiē le ma? □ Have you got any? 你有吗？Nǐ yǒu ma?

LANGUAGE TIP When **any** is used in **if** clauses, or when it means **no matter which**, it is translated by 任何 rènhé.

□ If any of you would like to take part... 如果你们中任何人想参加的话，… Rúguǒ nǐmen zhōng rènhé rén xiǎng cānjiā de huà... □ I don't like any of the books here. 我不喜欢这里的任何一本书。Wǒ bù xǐhuan zhèlǐ de rènhé yìběn shū.

any ADVERB

▷ *see also* **any** ADJECTIVE, PRONOUN

1 丝毫 sīháo *(with a negative)*

□ The situation isn't getting any better. 情况没有丝毫的好转。Qíngkuàng méi yǒu sīháo de hǎozhuǎn.

2 ...一点 ...yìdiǎn *(in questions)*

□ Do you want any more soup? 你还想再要一点汤吗？Nǐ hái xiǎng zài yào yìdiǎn tāng ma?

■ **Are you feeling any better?** 你觉得好一点吗？Nǐ juédé hǎoyìdiǎn ma?

anybody PRONOUN

任何人 rènhé rén

□ I can't see anybody. 我见不到任何人。Wǒ jiànbúdào rènhé rén. □ Anybody could do it. 任何人都能做到。Rènhé rén dōunéng zuòdào. □ Did anybody see you? 有任何人看到你吗？Yǒu rènhérén kàndào nǐ ma?

anyhow ADVERB

反正 fǎnzhèng

□ He doesn't want to go out and anyhow he's not allowed. 他不想出去，反正也不许他出去。Tā bùxiǎng chūqù, fǎnzhèng yě bùxǔ tāchūqù.

anyone PRONOUN

任何人 rènhé rén

□ I can't see anyone. 我见不到任何人。Wǒ jiànbúdào rènhé rén. □ Anyone could do it. 任何人都能做到。Rènhé rén dōunéng zuòdào. □ Did anyone see you? 有任何人看到你吗？Yǒu rènhérén kàndào nǐ ma?

anything PRONOUN
1 任何东西 rènhé dōngxi
□ hardly anything 几乎没有任何东西 jīhū méiyǒu rènhé dōngxi

LANGUAGE TIP **anything** in negative sentences and questions is translated by 什么 shénme.

□ I can't see anything. 我什么也看不见。Wǒ shénme yě kànbújiàn. □ Did you find anything? 你找到些什么吗？Nǐ zhǎodào xiē shénme ma?
2 任何事情 rènhéshìqing
□ Anything could happen. 任何事情都可能发生。Rènhéshìqing dōu yǒukěnéng fāshēng.
■ **If anything happens to me...** 如果任何事情发生在我身上… Rúguǒ rènhé shìqing fāshēng zài wǒ shēnshàng...
■ **You can say anything you like.** 你什么都可以说。Nǐ shénme dōu kěyǐ shuō.

anyway ADVERB
1 反正 fǎnzhèng
□ He doesn't want to go out and anyway he's not allowed. 他不想出去，反正也不许他出去。Tā bùxiǎng chūqù, fǎnzhèng yě bùxǔ tāchūqù.
2 无论如何 wúlùnrúhé
□ I shall go anyway. 无论如何我要走了。Wúlùn rúhé wǒ yào zǒu le.

anywhere ADVERB
1 任何地方 rènhé dìfāng
□ I can't find him anywhere. 我任何地方都找不到他。Wǒ rènhé difang dōu zhǎobúdào tā.
2 在哪儿 zàinǎr
□ Have you seen my coat anywhere? 你在哪儿看到我的外衣了吗？Nǐ zàinǎr kàndào wǒde wàiyīlema?

apart ADVERB
1 分开 fēnkāi *(couple, family)*
□ It was the first time we had been apart. 那是我们第一次分开。Nàshì wǒmen dìyīcì fēnkāi.
2 相距 xiāngjù
□ The two towns are 10 kilometres apart. 两座城镇相距十公里。Liǎngzuò chéngzhèn xiāngjù shígōnglǐ.
■ **to take something apart** 拆卸某物 chāixiè mǒuwù
■ **apart from** 除去 chúqù □ Apart from that, everything's fine. 除去那一点什么都好。Chúqù nàyìdiǎn shénme dōuhǎo.

apartment NOUN
公寓 gōngyù [处 chù]

to **apologize** VERB
道歉 dàoqiàn
□ He apologized for being late. 他为迟到而道歉。Tā wèi chídào ér dàoqiàn. □ I apologize! 我道歉！Wǒ dàoqiàn!

apology NOUN
道歉 dàoqiàn [个 gè]

apostrophe NOUN
撇号 piěhào [个 gè]

apparently ADVERB
表面看来 biǎomiàn kànlái

to **appeal** VERB
▷ *see also* **appeal** NOUN
请求 qǐngqiú
□ They appealed for help. 他们请求帮助。Tāmen qǐngqiú bāngzhù.
■ **Greece doesn't appeal to me.** 希腊对我没有吸引力。Xīlà duìwǒ méiyǒu xīyǐnlì.
■ **Does that appeal to you?** 那对你有吸引力吗 Nàduìnǐ yǒu xīyǐnlì ma?

appeal NOUN
▷ *see also* **appeal** VERB
上诉 shàngsù [项 xiàng]
□ They have launched an appeal. 他们已经提起上诉。Tāmen yǐjīng tíqǐ shàngsù.

to **appear** VERB
1 看起来 kànqǐlái *(seem)*
□ She appeared to be unwell. 她看起来不舒服。Tā kànqǐlái bù shūfu.
2 出现 chūxiàn *(come into view)*
□ The bus appeared around the corner. 公共汽车出现在拐角处。Gōnggòngqìchē chūxiànzài guǎijiǎochù.
■ **to appear on TV** 上电视 shàngdiànshì

appendicitis NOUN
阑尾炎 lánwěiyán

appetite NOUN
食欲 shíyù

to **applaud** VERB
鼓掌喝彩 gǔzhǎng hècǎi

applause NOUN
掌声 zhǎngshēng

apple NOUN
苹果 píngguǒ [个 gè]
■ **an apple tree** 一棵苹果树 yìkē píngguǒshù

appliance NOUN
器具 qìjù [件 jiàn]

applicant NOUN
申请人 shēnqǐngrén [个 gè]
□ There were a hundred applicants for the job. 有一百个申请人申请那个职位。Yǒu yìbǎigè shēngqǐngrén shēnqǐng nàgè zhíwèi.

application NOUN
申请 shēnqǐng [份 fèn]
□ a job application 一份职位申请 yífèn zhíwèi shēnqǐng

application form NOUN
申请表格 shēnqǐng biǎogé [份 fèn]
to **apply** VERB
■ **to apply for a job** 申请一份工作 shēnqǐng yífèn gōngzuò
■ **to apply to** *(be relevant)* 适用于 shìyòngyú □ This rule doesn't apply to us. 这项规则不适用于我们。Zhèxiàng guīzé búshìyòng yú wǒmen.
appointment NOUN
预约 yùyuē [个 gè]
□ I've got a dental appointment. 我有个牙医预约。Wǒ yǒugè yáyī yùyuē.
■ **to make an appointment with somebody** 和某人预约 hé mǒurén yùyuē
to **appreciate** VERB
感谢 gǎnxiè
□ I really appreciate your help. 我十分感谢你的帮助。Wǒ shífēn gǎnxiè nǐde bāngzhù.
apprentice NOUN
学徒 xuétú [名 míng]
to **approach** VERB
1 向...靠近 xiàng...kàojìn *(get nearer to)*
□ He approached the house. 他向那座房子靠近。Tā xiàng nàzuò fángzi kàojìn.
2 处理 chǔlǐ *(tackle)*
□ to approach a problem 处理一个问题 chǔlǐ yígè wèntí
appropriate ADJECTIVE
适合 shìhé
□ That dress isn't very appropriate for an interview. 那身服装不适合面试穿。Nàshēn fúzhuāng búshìhé miànshìchuān.
approval NOUN
批准 pīzhǔn
to **approve** VERB
赞成 zànchéng
■ **to approve of** 赞成 zànchéng □ I don't approve of his choice. 我不赞成他的选择。Wǒ búzànchéng tāde xuǎnzé.
■ **They didn't approve of his girlfriend.** 他们对他的女友不满意。Tāmen duì tāde nǚyǒu bùmǎnyì.
approximate ADJECTIVE
近似的 jìnsì de
apricot NOUN
杏子 xìngzi [个 gè]
April NOUN
四月 sìyuè
□ in April 在四月 zài sìyuè □ the first of April 四月一日 sìyuè yīrì □ at the beginning of April 在四月初 zài sìyuè chū □ at the end of April 在四月末 zài sìyuè mò □ every April 每年四月 měinián sìyuè
■ **April Fool's Day** 愚人节 yúrénjié

apron NOUN
围裙 wéiqún [条 tiáo]
Aquarius NOUN
宝瓶座 Bǎopíng Zuò gè
□ I'm Aquarius. 我是宝瓶座的。Wǒ shì Bǎopíngzuòde.
Arab ADJECTIVE
▷ *see also* **Arab** NOUN
阿拉伯的 Ālābó de
□ the Arab countries 阿拉伯国家 Ālābó guójiā
Arab NOUN
▷ *see also* **Arab** ADJECTIVE
阿拉伯人 Ālābórén [个 gè]
Arabic NOUN
阿拉伯语 Ālābóyǔ
arch NOUN
拱 gǒng [个 gè]
archaeologist NOUN
考古学家 kǎogǔxuéjiā [位 wèi]
archaeology NOUN
考古学 kǎogǔxué
archbishop NOUN
大主教 dàzhǔjiào [位 wèi]
archeologist NOUN (US)
考古学家 kǎogǔxuéjiā [位 wèi]
archeology NOUN (US)
考古学 kǎogǔxué
architect NOUN
建筑师 jiànzhùshī [位 wèi]
□ She's an architect. 她是一位建筑师。Tā shì yíwèi jiànzhùshī.
architecture NOUN
建筑学 jiànzhùxué
Arctic NOUN
北极 Běijí
are VERB ▷ *see* **be**
area NOUN
1 地区 dìqū [个 gè]
□ She lives in the London area. 她住在在伦敦周边地区。Tā zhùzài Lúndūn zhōubiān dìqū.
2 部分 bùfen [个 gè]
□ My favourite area of London is Chelsea. 伦敦我最喜欢的部分是切尔西。Lúndūn wǒ zuì xǐhuān de bùfen shì Qièěrxī.
3 面积 miànjī [个 gè]
□ The field has an area of 1500m². 那块场地面积一千五百平方米。Nàkuài chǎngdì miànjī yìqiānwǔbǎi píngfāngmǐ.
Argentina NOUN
阿根廷 Āgēntíng
Argentinian ADJECTIVE
阿根廷的 Āgēntíngde
to **argue** VERB
争论 zhēnglùn

□ They never stop arguing. 他们争论不休。Tāmen zhēnglùn bùxiū.

argument NOUN
争吵 zhēngchǎo [阵 zhèn] *(quarrel)*
■ to have an argument 吵架 chǎojià
□ They had an argument. 他们吵了一架。Tāmen chǎole yíjià.

Aries NOUN
白羊座 Báiyáng Zuò
□ I'm Aries. 我是白羊座的。Wǒ shì Báiyángzuòde.

arm NOUN
胳膊 gēbo [条 tiáo]

armchair NOUN
扶手椅 fúshǒuyǐ [把 bǎ]

armour (US **armor**) NOUN
盔甲 kuījiǎ [副 fù]

army NOUN
军队 jūnduì [支 zhī]

around PREPOSITION, ADVERB
1 围绕 wéirào
□ They are sitting around a table. 他们围绕着桌子坐着。Tāmen wéirào zhe zhuōzi zuò zhe.
2 大约 dàyuē *(approximately)*
□ It costs around £100. 那大约值一百镑。Nà dàyuē zhí yìbǎibàng. □ Let's meet at around 8 p.m. 我们大约八点钟见。Wǒmen dàyuē bādiǎnzhōngjiàn.
3 到处 dàochù
□ I've been walking around the town. 我们在镇上到处走走。Wǒmen zài zhènshàng dàochù zǒuzǒu.
■ around here *(nearby)* 这附近 zhèfùjìn
□ Is there a chemist's around here? 这附近有药店吗？Zhèfùjìn yǒu yàodiàn ma?

to **arrange** VERB
1 安排 ānpái
□ She arranged the trip. 她安排了那次旅程。Tā ānpáile nàcì lǚchéng.
■ to arrange to do something 安排做某事 ānpái zuò mǒushì □ They arranged to go out together on Friday. 他们安排周五一起出去。Tāmen ānpái zhōuwǔ yìqǐ chūqù.
2 排列 páiliè
□ The chairs were arranged in a circle. 椅子排成一圈。Yǐzi páichéng yìquān.

arrangement NOUN
1 约定 yuēdìng [个 gè] *(agreement)*
□ We have an arrangement. 我们有个约定。Wǒmen yǒugè yuēdìng.
2 安排 ānpái *(plan)*
□ They made arrangements to go out on Friday night. 他们安排周五晚上出去。Tāmen ānpái zhōuwǔ wǎnshàng chūqù.

to **arrest** VERB
▷ *see also* **arrest** NOUN
逮捕 dàibǔ
□ The police have arrested 5 people. 警方逮捕了五个人。Jǐngfāng dàibǔle wǔgèrén.

arrest NOUN
▷ *see also* **arrest** VERB
逮捕 dàibǔ
■ to be under arrest 被逮捕 bèi dàibǔ
□ You're under arrest! 你被逮捕了！Nǐ bèidàibǔle!

arrival NOUN
到达 dàodá

to **arrive** VERB
到 dào
□ I arrived at 5 o'clock. 我五点钟到的。Wǒ wǔdiǎnzhōng dàode.

arrow NOUN
1 箭 jiàn [支 zhī] *(weapon)*
2 箭头标志 jiàntóu biāozhì [个 gè] *(sign)*

art NOUN
1 艺术 yìshù
2 美术 měishù *(activity of drawing, painting etc)*
■ art school 美术学校 měishù xuéxiào

art gallery NOUN
美术馆 měishùguǎn [个 gè]

article NOUN
文章 wénzhāng [篇 piān]
□ a newspaper article 一篇报纸文章 yìpiān bàozhǐ wénzhāng

artificial ADJECTIVE
人造的 rénzào de

artist NOUN
画家 huàjiā [位 wèi]

artistic ADJECTIVE
艺术的 yìshùde

as CONJUNCTION, ADVERB, PREPOSITION
1 当…时 dāng…shí *(referring to time)*
□ He came in as I was leaving. 当我离开时，他进来了。Dāng wǒ líkāi shí, tā jìnlái le.
2 因为 yīnwèi *(since)*
□ As you can't come, I'll go on my own. 既然你不能来，我就自己去。Jìrán nǐ bùnéng lái, wǒ jiù zìjǐ qù.
■ as you can see 如你所见到的 rú nǐ suǒ jiàndào de
■ It's on the left as you go in. 在你进入时的左侧。Zài nǐ jìnrù shí de zuǒcè.
■ as ... as 同…一样 tóng...yíyàng
□ Helen's as tall as David. 海伦同大卫一样高。Hǎilún tóng Dàwèi yíyàng gāo.
■ twice as ... as 同…一样 tóng...yíyàng
□ Her coat cost twice as much as mine. 她的衣服同我的一样贵。Tāde yīfù tóng

wǒdè yíyàng guì.
■ **as much ... as** 同…一样多 tóng... yíyàngduō □ I haven't got as much money as you. 我没有同你一样多的钱。Wǒ méiyǒu tóng nǐ yíyàng duōdè qiǎn.
■ **as soon as possible** 尽快 jìnkuài □ I'll do it as soon as possible. 我会尽快做。Wǒhuì jìnkuài zuò.
■ **as from tomorrow** 从明天开始 cóng míngtiān kāishǐ □ As from tomorrow, the shop will be closed on Sundays. 从明天开始, 商店星期天关门。Cóng míngtiān kāishǐ,shāngdiàn xīngqītiān guānmén.
■ **as though** 好像 hǎoxiàng □ She acted as though she hadn't seen me. 她好像没开见我一样。Tā hǎoxiàng měi kànjiàn wǒ yíyàng.
■ **as if** 好像 hǎoxiàng
■ **He works as a salesman.** 他做推销员的工作。Tā zuò tuīxiāoyuán de gōngzuò.
■ **He was very energetic as a child.** 他小时候精力很旺盛。Tā xiǎoshíhou jīnglì hěn wàngshèng.

asap ABBREVIATION *(= as soon as possible)*
尽快 jìnkuài

ash NOUN
灰末 huīmò

ashamed ADJECTIVE
■ **to be ashamed** 感到羞愧 gǎndào xiūkuì □ You should be ashamed of yourself! 你应该感到羞愧！Nǐ yīnggāi gǎndào xiūkuì!

ashtray NOUN
烟灰缸 yānhuīgāng [个 gè]

Asia NOUN
亚洲 Yàzhōu

Asian ADJECTIVE
▷ *see also* **Asian** NOUN
亚洲的 Yàzhōu de

Asian NOUN
▷ *see also* **Asian** ADJECTIVE
亚洲人 Yàzhōurén [个 gè]

to **ask** VERB
1 问 wèn
□ 'Have you finished?' she asked. 她问：“你做完了吗？” Tāwèn: “nízuòwánle ma?”
■ **to ask somebody something** 问某人某事 wèn mǒurén mǒushì □ I asked him his name. 我问他叫什么。Wǒ wèn tā jiào shénme.
■ **to ask for something** 要…东西 yào... dōngxi □ He asked for a cup of tea. 他要了一杯茶。Tā yàole yìbēichá.
■ **to ask somebody to do something** 请求某人做某事 qǐngqiú mǒurén zuò mǒushì □ She asked him to do the shopping. 她请求他去买东西。Tā qǐngqiú tā qùmǎi dōngxi.
■ **to ask about something** 询问 xúnwèn □ I asked about train times to Leeds. 我询问了去利兹的火车时间。Wǒ xúnwènle qù Lìzī de huǒchē shíjiān.
■ **to ask somebody a question** 问某人一个问题 wèn mǒurén yígè wèntí
■ **to ask somebody the time** 向某人询问时间 xiàng mǒurén xúnwèn shíjiān
2 邀请 yāoqǐng
□ Have you asked Matthew to the party? 你邀请马修来聚会了吗？Nǐ yāoqǐng Mǎxiū láijùhuì le ma?
■ **He asked her out.** *(on a date)* 他请她出去约会. Tā qǐng tā chūqù yuēhuì.

asleep ADJECTIVE
睡着的 shuìzháo de
■ **to be asleep** 睡着了 shuìzháo le □ He's asleep. 他睡着了。Tā shuìzháo le.
■ **to fall asleep** 睡着了 shuìzháo le □ I fell asleep in front of the TV. 我在电视前睡着了。Wǒ zài diànshìqián shuìzháo le.

asparagus NOUN
芦笋 lúsǔn [棵 kē]

aspirin NOUN
阿司匹林药片 āsīpīlín yàopiàn [片 piàn] *(tablet)*

asset NOUN
财富 cáifù
□ Her experience will be an asset to the firm. 她的经验会成为公司的财富。Tādè jīngyàn huìchéngwéi gōngsīdè cáifù.

assignment NOUN
作业 zuòyè [个 gè] *(for student)*

assistance NOUN
帮助 bāngzhù

assistant NOUN
1 营业员 yíngyèyuán [个 gè] *(in shop)*
2 助手 zhùshǒu [个 gè] *(helper)*

association NOUN
协会 xiéhuì [家 jiā]

assortment NOUN
■ **an assortment of something** 各种各样的某物 gèzhǒng gèyàng de mǒuwù [件 jiàn]

to **assume** VERB
猜想 cāixiǎng
□ I assume she won't be coming. 我猜想她不会来了。Wǒ cāixiǎng tā búhuì lái le.

to **assure** VERB
保证 bǎozhèng
□ He assured me he was coming. 他向我保证他会来。Tā xiàng wǒ bǎozhèng tā huìlái.

asterisk NOUN
星号 xīnghào [个 gè]

asthma NOUN
哮喘 xiàochuǎn
▫ I've got asthma. 我得了哮喘。Wǒ délè xiàochuǎn.

astonishing ADJECTIVE
惊人的 jīngrén de

astrology NOUN
占星术 zhānxīngshù

DID YOU KNOW...?
The Chinese Zodiac is a 12 year cycle, and each year is governed by one of 12 animals, representing 12 different personality types: the rat, ox, tiger, rabbit, dragon, snake, horse, sheep, monkey, rooster, dog and pig.

astronaut NOUN
宇航员 yǔhángyuán [位 wèi]

LANGUAGE TIP In English, Chinese space travellers are sometimes called **taikonauts**, a combination of the Chinese word 太空 tàikōng, meaning **space**, and the Greek naut, meaning **traveller**.

astronomy NOUN
天文学 tiānwénxué

asylum seeker NOUN
寻求避难的人 xúnqiú bìnànde rén [位 wèi]

at PREPOSITION
▹ *see also* **at** NOUN
1 在 zài
▫ We had dinner at a restaurant. 我们在一家饭店吃了饭。Wǒmen zài yìjiā fàndiàn chī le fàn. ▫ at home 在家 zàijiā ▫ at work 在工作 zài gōngzuò ▫ at school 在学校 zàixuéxiào
▪ **at night** 在晚上 zàiwǎnshàng
▪ **What are you doing at the weekend?** 你周末做什么？Nǐ zhōumò zuò shénmò?
▪ **to be sitting at a desk** 坐在书桌边 zuòzài shūzhuōbiān
▪ **There's someone at the door.** 门口有人。Ménkǒu yǒurén.
2 以 yǐ
▫ at 50 km/h 以每小时五十公里的速度 yǐ měi xiǎoshí wǔshí gōnglǐ de sùdù
▫ apples at £2 a kilo 苹果每公斤两镑 píngguǒ měi gōngjīn liǎngbàng
▪ **two at a time** 一次两个 yícìliǎnggè
▪ **to throw something at somebody** 向某人扔某物 xiàng mǒurén rēng mǒuwù

at NOUN
▹ *see also* **at** PREPOSITION
A 圈 A quān *(@ symbol)*

LANGUAGE TIP Word for word, this means **curly A**.

ate VERB ▹ *see* **eat**

athlete NOUN
运动员 yùndòngyuán [名 míng]

athletic ADJECTIVE
运动的 yùndòngde

athletics NOUN
田径运动 tiánjìng yùndòng

Atlantic NOUN
大西洋 Dàxīyáng

atlas NOUN
地图册 dìtúcè [本 běn]

atmosphere NOUN
1 大气层 dàqìcéng [个 gè] *(of planet)*
2 气氛 qìfēn *(of place)*

atomic ADJECTIVE
原子的 yuánzǐde

to **attach** VERB
附上 fùshàng
▫ He attached some photos to the email. 他在邮件里附上了一些照片。Tā zài yóujiàn lǐ fùshàng le yìxiē zhàopiān.
▪ **Please find attached...** 请见附上的文件… Qǐngjiàn fùshàngde wénjiàn...

attached ADJECTIVE
▪ **to be attached to** 依恋 yīliàn ▫ He's very attached to his family. 他很依恋他的家庭。Tā hěn yīliàn tādè jiātíng.

attachment NOUN
附件 fùjiàn [个 gè] *(of tool, computer file)*

to **attack** VERB
▹ *see also* **attack** NOUN
1 袭击 xíjī
▫ The dog attacked her. 狗袭击了她。Gǒu xíjīle tā.
2 攻击 gōngjī
▫ The soldiers attacked under the cover of darkness. 士兵们趁黑攻击。Shìbīngmen chènhēi gōngjī.

attack NOUN
▹ *see also* **attack** VERB
1 袭击 xíjī [次 cì] *(on person)*
2 攻击 gōngjī [次 cì] *(military assault)*
3 发作 fāzuò [阵 zhèn] *(of illness)*

attempt NOUN
▹ *see also* **attempt** VERB
尝试 chángshì [个 gè]
▫ She gave up after several attempts. 尝试几次后她放弃了。Chángshì jǐcìhòu tā fàngqì le.

to **attempt** VERB
▹ *see also* **attempt** NOUN
▪ **to attempt to do something** 试图做某事 shìtú zuò mǒushì ▫ I attempted to write a song. 我试图写歌。Wǒ shìtú xiěgē.

to **attend** VERB
1 参加 cānjiā
▫ to attend a meeting 参加会议 cānjiāhuìyì

English-Chinese

a

2 上 shàng *(regularly)*
□ She attends church weekly. 她每周上教堂。Tā měizhōu shàng jiàotáng.

attention NOUN
■ **to pay attention** 关注 guānzhù □ He didn't pay attention to what I was saying. 他没关注我所说的。Tā méiguānzhù wǒ suǒshuōde.

attic NOUN
阁楼 gélóu [间 jiān]

attitude NOUN
态度 tàidù
□ I really don't like your attitude! 我很不喜欢你的态度！Wǒ hěnbùxǐhuān nǐdè tàidù!

attorney NOUN (US)
律师 lǜshī [位 wèi]

to **attract** VERB
吸引 xīyǐn
□ The Lake District attracts lots of tourists. 湖区吸引很多游客。Húqū xīyǐn hěnduō yóukè.

attractive ADJECTIVE
1 有魅力的 yǒu mèilì de *(man, woman)*
□ He was very attractive to women. 他对女人很有吸引力。Tā duì nǚrén hěnyǒu xīyǐnlì.
2 吸引人的 xīyǐn rén de *(thing, place)*

aubergine NOUN
茄子 qiézi [个 gè]

auction NOUN
拍卖 pāimài [次 cì]

audience NOUN
1 观众 guānzhòng [位 wèi] *(in theatre)*
2 听众 tīngzhòng [位 wèi] *(for radio, TV)*

audition NOUN
试演 shìyǎn [次 cì]

August NOUN
八月 bāyuè
□ in August 在八月 zài bāyuè □ the first of August 八月一日 bāyuè yīrì □ at the beginning of August 在八月初 zài bāyuè chū □ at the end of August 在八月末 zài bāyuè mò □ every August 每年八月 měinián bāyuè

aunt, aunty NOUN
1 姑母 gūmǔ [位 wèi] *(father's sister)*
2 伯母 bómǔ [位 wèi] *(father's older brother's wife)*
3 婶母 shěnmǔ [位 wèi] *(father's younger brother's wife)*
4 姨母 yímǔ [位 wèi] *(mother's sister)*
5 舅母 jiùmǔ [位 wèi] *(mother's brother's wife)*

Australia NOUN
澳大利亚 Àodàlìyà

Australian ADJECTIVE
▷ *see also* **Australian** NOUN
澳大利亚的 Àodàlìyà de

Australian NOUN
▷ *see also* **Australian** ADJECTIVE
澳大利亚人 Àodàlìyàrén [个 gè]
■ **the Australians** 澳大利亚人 Àodàlìyàrén

Austria NOUN
奥地利 Àodìlì

Austrian NOUN
▷ *see also* **Austrian** ADJECTIVE
奥地利人 Àodìlì [个 gè]
■ **the Austrians** 奥地利人 Àodìlì

Austrian ADJECTIVE
▷ *see also* **Austrian** NOUN
奥地利的 Àodìlìdè

author NOUN
作家 zuòjiā [位 wèi] *(of novel)*

autobiography NOUN
自传 zìzhuàn [部 bù]

autograph NOUN
签名 qiānmíng [个 gè]

automatic ADJECTIVE
自动的 zìdòng de

automatically ADVERB
自动地 zìdòng de
□ The door opened automatically. 门自动打开了。Mén zìdòng dǎkāi le.

automobile NOUN (US)
汽车 qìchē [辆 liàng]

autumn NOUN
秋季 qiūjì [个 gè]
■ **in autumn** 在秋季 zài qiūjì

available ADJECTIVE
1 备有 bèiyǒu
□ Free brochures are available on request. 备有免费宣传册。Bèiyǒu miǎnfèi xuānchuáncè.
2 有空的 yǒukòng de *(person)*
□ Is Mr Cooke available today? 库克先生今天有空吗？Kùkèxiānshēng jīntiān yǒukòngma?

avalanche NOUN
雪崩 xuěbēng [次 cì]

average NOUN
▷ *see also* **average** ADJECTIVE
平均数 píngjūnshù [个 gè]
■ **on average** 平均 píngjūn

average ADJECTIVE
▷ *see also* **average** NOUN
平均的 píngjūn de
□ the average price 平均价 píngjūnjià

avocado NOUN
牛油果 niúyóuguǒ [个 gè]

to **avoid** VERB
1 避免 bìmiǎn *(person, obstacle)*
2 防止 fángzhǐ *(trouble, danger)*

■ **to avoid doing something** 避免做某事 bìmiǎn zuò mǒushì □ Avoid going out on your own at night. 晚上避免一个人外出。Wǎnshàng bìmiǎn yígèrén wàichū.

awake ADJECTIVE

■ **to be awake** 醒着的 xǐngzhe de □ Is she awake? 她醒着吗？Ta xǐngzhe ma?

award NOUN

奖 jiǎng [个 gè]
□ He's won an award. 他赢了一个奖。Tā yíngle yígè jiǎng.

aware ADJECTIVE

■ **to be aware of something** *(know about)* 意识到某事 yìshi dào móushì □ We are aware of what is happening. 我们意识到正在发生的一切。Wǒmén yìshídào zhèngzài fāshēngde yíqiè.

■ **to be aware that...** 知道… zhīdào...

away ADVERB, ADJECTIVE

不在 búzài*(not here)*
□ Violette's away today. 维奥莱特今天不在。Wéiàoláitè jīntiān búzài. □ He's away for a week. 他一周不在。Tā yìzhōu búzài.

■ **The town's 2 kilometres away.** 市中心离这里两公里远。Shìzhōngxīn lí zhèlǐ liǎnggōnglǐ yuǎn.

■ **The coast is 2 hours away by car.** 海岸离这两个小时的车程。Hǎiàn lízhè liǎnggè xiǎoshíde chēchéng.

■ **Go away!** 走开！Zǒukāi.

■ **to put something away** 把某物放到某处 bǎ mǒuwù fàngdào mǒuchù □ He put the books away in the cupboard. 他把书放到柜子里。Tā bǎ shū fàngdào guìzilǐ.

away match NOUN

客场 kèchǎng [次 cì]

awful ADJECTIVE

1 糟糕的 zāogāo de
□ The weather's awful. 天气糟糕。Tiānqì zāogāo.

2 可怕的 kěpà de*(shock, crime)*
□ That's awful! 那很可怕！Nà hěnkěpà!

■ **I feel awful.** 我感觉很糟糕。Wǒ gǎnjué hěn zāogāo.

■ **an awful lot of work** 特别多的工作 tèbiéduōde gōngzuò

awkward ADJECTIVE

1 困难的 kùnnánde
□ It was awkward to carry. 很难拿。Hěnnán ná.

2 尴尬的 gāngàde*(embarrassing)*
□ an awkward question 尴尬的问题 gāngàdewèntí

■ **It's a bit awkward for me to come and see you.** 我很尴尬来见你。Wǒ hěngāngà lǎi jiàn nǐ.

■ **Mike is being awkward about letting me have the car.** 麦克不太情愿把车给我。Màikè bútài qíngyuàn bǎ chē gěi wǒ.

axe (US **ax**) NOUN

斧 fǔ [把 bǎ]

English-Chinese

a

Bb

BA NOUN
文科学士 wénkē xuéshì
■ **a BA in French** 一个法语专业的文科学士 yígè fǎyǔ zhuānyè de wénkē xuéshì

baby NOUN
婴儿 yīng'ér [个 gè]

> LANGUAGE TIP A more colloquial word for **baby** in Chinese is 宝贝 bǎobèi. Word for word, these characters mean **valuable conch shell** — conch shells were used as currency in ancient China.

■ **to have a baby** 生孩子 shēng háizi

baby carriage NOUN (US)
婴儿车 yīng'ér chē [辆 liàng]

to **babysit** VERB
代人照看孩子 dài rén zhàokàn háizi

babysitter NOUN
代人照看孩子的人 dài rén zhàokàn háizi de rén [个 gè]

babysitting NOUN
代人看孩子 dàirén kān háizi [次 cì]

bachelor NOUN
单身汉 dānshēnhàn [个 gè]
□ He's a bachelor. 他是一个单身汉。Tā shì yígè dānshēnhàn.

back NOUN
▷ *see also* **back** ADJECTIVE, ADVERB, VERB
1 背部 bèibù [个 gè] *(of person)*
2 背面 bèimiàn [个 gè] *(of hand, neck)*
3 后面 hòumiàn [个 gè] *(of house, door, book)*
4 后部 hòubù [个 gè] *(of car)*
□ in the back 在车的后部 zài chē de hòubù
5 封底 fēngdǐ [页 yè] *(of page)*
6 最里面 zuì lǐmiàn *(of room, garden)*

back ADJECTIVE
▷ *see also* **back** NOUN, ADVERB, VERB
后面的 hòumiàn de
□ the back seat 后面的座位 hòumiàn de zuòwèi □ the back wheel of my bike 我自行车的后轮 wǒ zìxíngchē de hòulún
■ **the back door** 后门 hòumén [扇 shàn]

back ADVERB
▷ *see also* **back** NOUN, ADJECTIVE, VERB
回 huí *(returned)*
■ **to be back** 回来 huílai □ He's not back yet. 他还没回来。Tā hái méi huílái.
■ **We went there by bus and walked back.** 我们乘车去然后走回来的。Wǒmen chéngchē qù ránhòu zǒu huílái de.
■ **can I have it back?** 我能要回它吗？Wǒ néng yàohuí tā ma?
■ **to get back** 返回 fǎnhuí □ What time did you get back? 你什么时候返回的？Nǐ shénme shíhòu fǎnhuí de?
■ **to call somebody back** 回某人电话 huí mǒurén diànhuà □ I'll call you back later. 我待会儿回你电话。Wǒ dāihuì'ér huí nǐ diànhuà.

to **back** VERB
▷ *see also* **back** ADJECTIVE, ADVERB, NOUN
支持 zhīchí *(support)*
■ **to back a horse** 下一个赌注 xià yígè dǔzhù

to **back down** VERB
做出让步 zuòchū ràngbù

to **back out** VERB
退出 tuìchū
□ They backed out at the last minute. 他们在最后时刻退出了。Tāmen zài zuìhòu shíkè tuìchū le.

to **back up** VERB
1 证实 zhèngshí
□ There's no evidence to back up his theory. 没有依据来证实他的理论。Méiyǒu yījù lái zhèngshí tā de lǐlùn.
■ **to back somebody up** 支持某人 zhīchí mǒurén
2 备份 bèifèn *(on computer)*

backache NOUN
背痛 bèitòng [阵 zhèn]
□ to have backache 背痛 bèitòng

backbone NOUN
脊椎 jízhuī [条 tiáo]

to **backfire** VERB
事与愿违 shìyǔyuànwéi *(go wrong)*

background NOUN
1 背景 bèijǐng [个 gè] *(of picture, scene, events)*
■ **in the background** 在背后 zài bèihòu

2 出身 chūshēn [种 zhǒng]
□ his family background 他的家庭出身 tāde jiātíng chūshēn
■ **background noise** 背景噪音 bèijǐng zàoyīn

backhand NOUN
反手击球 fǎnshǒu jīqiú [次 cì]

backing NOUN
1 支持 zhīchí *(support)*
2 资助 zīzhù *(financial)*

backpack NOUN
双肩背包 shuāngjiān bēibāo [个 gè]

backpacker NOUN
背包旅行者 bēibāo lǚxíngzhě [名 míng]

backpacking NOUN
■ **to go backpacking** 去背包旅行 qù bēibāo lǚxíng

back pain NOUN
背痛 bèitòng [阵 zhèn]
□ to have back pain 背痛 bèitòng

backside NOUN
臀部 túnbù [个 gè]

backstroke NOUN
仰泳 yǎngyǒng

backup ADJECTIVE
▷ *see also* **backup** NOUN
备份的 bèifèn de
■ **a backup file** 一个备份文件 yígè bèifèn wénjiàn

backup NOUN
▷ *see also* **backup** ADJECTIVE
支持 zhīchí *(support)*

backwards ADVERB
向后地 xiàng hòu de
□ to take a step backwards 向后退一步 xiànghòu tuì yíbù
■ **to fall backwards** 向后倒 xiànghòudǎo

back yard NOUN
后院 hòuyuàn [个 gè]

bacon NOUN
腌猪肉 yān zhūròu [块 kuài]

bad ADJECTIVE
1 差的 chà de *(weather, health, temper)*
□ a bad film 一部差的电影 yíbù chà de diànyǐng □ to be in a bad mood 心情差 xīnqíng chà
2 不胜任的 bú shèngrèn de *(actor, driver)*
3 不良的 bùliáng de *(behaviour, habit)*
4 不听话的 bù tīnghuà de *(naughty)*
□ You bad boy! 你这个不听话的男孩！Nǐ zhègè bùtīnghuà de nánhái!
5 严重的 yánzhòng de *(serious)*
□ a bad accident 一场严重的事故 yìchǎng yánzhòng de shìgù
■ **to be bad for somebody** 对某人有害 duì mǒurén yǒuhài □ Smoking is bad for you. 吸烟对你有害。Xīyān duì nǐ yǒuhài.
■ **to go bad** *(food)* 变质 biànzhì
■ **I feel bad about it.** 对此我感觉不好。Duìcǐ wǒ gǎnjué bùhǎo.
■ **not bad** 不错 búcuò □ That's not bad at all. 那很不错。Nà hěn búcuò.
■ **to be bad at something** 在某方面差劲 zài mǒufāngmiàn chājìn □ I'm really bad at maths. 我数学非常差劲。Wǒ shùxué fēicháng chājìn.

badge NOUN
徽章 huīzhāng [个 gè]

badly ADVERB
1 不令人满意地 bú lìng rén mǎnyì de
□ badly paid 不令人满意的薪水 bú lìngrén mǎnyì de xīnshuǐ
2 严重地 yánzhòng de
□ badly wounded 严重受伤的 yánzhòng shòushāng de
■ **He badly needs a rest.** 他迫切地需要休息。Tā pòqiè de xūyào xiūxi.

badminton NOUN
羽毛球 yǔmáoqiú
□ to play badminton 打羽毛球 dǎ yǔmáoqiú

bad-tempered ADJECTIVE
脾气坏的 píqi huài de
■ **to be bad-tempered** **1** *(by nature)* 脾气坏的 píqi huài de □ He's a really bad-tempered person. 他真是一个脾气坏的人。Tā zhēnshì yígè píqi huài de rén.
2 *(temporarily)* 心情不好的 xīnqíng bùhǎo de □ He was really bad-tempered yesterday. 他昨天心情实在是不好。Tā zuótiān xīnqíng shízàishì bùhǎo.

bag NOUN
1 包 bāo [个 gè] *(school bag)*
2 手袋 shǒudài [个 gè] *(handbag)*
3 行李箱 xínglǐxiāng [个 gè] *(suitcase)*
■ **to pack one's bags** 准备离开 zhǔnbèi líkāi

baggage NOUN
行李 xíngli

baggage reclaim NOUN
行李领取 xíngli lǐngqǔ

baggy ADJECTIVE
宽松的 kuānsōng de

bagpipes PL NOUN
风笛 fēngdí [支 zhī]

to **bake** VERB
烤 kǎo
■ **to bake a cake** 烤一个蛋糕 kǎo yígè dàngāo

baked ADJECTIVE
烤的 kǎode

□ baked potatoes 烤的土豆 kǎode tǔdòu
■ **baked beans** 烤豆 kǎodòu

baker NOUN
1 面包师 miànbāoshī [位 wèi]*(person)*
2 面包店 miànbāodiàn [家 jiā]*(shop)*

bakery NOUN
面包房 miànbāofáng [个 gè]

balance NOUN
1 平衡 pínghéng
■ **to lose one's balance** 失去某人的平衡 shīqù mǒurén de pínghéng
2 余额 yú'é [笔 bǐ]*(in bank account)*
3 余欠之数 yúqiàn zhī shù*(remainder to be paid)*

balanced ADJECTIVE
平衡的 pínghéng de

balcony NOUN
露台 lùtái [个 gè]

bald ADJECTIVE
秃的 tū de
■ **to go bald** 变秃 biàntū

ball NOUN
球 qiú [个 gè]

ballet NOUN
芭蕾舞 bāléiwǔ

ballet dancer NOUN
芭蕾舞演员 bāléiwǔ yǎnyuán [位 wèi]

ballet shoes PL NOUN
芭蕾舞鞋 bāléi wǔxié [双 shuāng]

balloon NOUN
气球 qìqiú [只 zhī]
■ **a hot-air balloon** 一只热气球 yìzhī rè qìqiú

ballpoint pen NOUN
圆珠笔 yuánzhūbǐ [支 zhī]

ban NOUN
▷ *see also* **ban** VERB
禁止 jìnzhǐ [种 zhǒng]

to **ban** VERB
▷ *see also* **ban** NOUN
禁止 jìnzhǐ

banana NOUN
香蕉 xiāngjiāo [只 zhī]

band NOUN
乐队 yuèduì [个 gè]
□ He plays the guitar in a band. 他在乐队里弹吉他。Tā zài yuèduì lǐ tán jíta.

bandage NOUN
▷ *see also* **bandage** VERB
绷带 bēngdài [条 tiáo]

to **bandage** VERB
▷ *see also* **bandage** NOUN
用绷带包扎 yòng bēngdài bāozhā
□ The nurse bandaged his arm. 护士用绷带包扎了他的手臂。Hùshi yòng bēngdài bāozhā le tā de shǒubì.

Band-Aid® NOUN (US)
邦迪创可贴 Bāngdí chuàngkětiē [贴 tiē]

bang NOUN
▷ *see also* **bang** VERB
1 砰的一声 pēng de yìshēng
□ I heard a loud bang. 我听到很响的砰的一声。Wǒ tīngdào hěnxiǎng de pēng de yìshēng.
2 撞击 zhuàngjī [下 xià]
□ a bang on the head 撞了一下头 zhuàngle yíxià tóu
■ **Bang!** 砰！Pēng!

to **bang** VERB
▷ *see also* **bang** NOUN
撞 zhuàng*(part of body)*
□ I banged my head. 我撞到了我的头。Wǒ zhuàngdàole wǒde tóu.
■ **to bang on the door** 使劲敲门 shǐjìn qiāomén
■ **to bang into something** 猛撞某物 měngzhuàng mǒuwù

Bangladesh NOUN
孟加拉国 Mèngjiālāguó

bangs PL NOUN
刘海 liúhǎi [束 shù]*(US: fringe)*

bank NOUN
1 银行 yínháng [家 jiā]*(financial)*
2 岸 àn [个 gè]*(of river, lake)*

bank account NOUN
银行账户 yínháng zhànghù [个 gè]

bank card NOUN
银行卡 yínhángkǎ [张 zhāng]*(for cash machine)*

banker NOUN
银行家 yínhángjiā [位 wèi]

bank holiday NOUN
法定假期 fǎdìng jiàqī [个 gè]

banknote NOUN
纸币 zhǐbì [张 zhāng]

banned ADJECTIVE
禁止的 jìnzhǐ de

bar NOUN
1 酒吧 jiǔbā [个 gè]*(pub)*
2 吧台 bātái [个 gè]*(counter)*
■ **a bar of chocolate** 一块巧克力 yíkuài qiǎokèlì
■ **a bar of soap** 一块肥皂 yíkuài féizào

barbecue NOUN
烧烤聚会 shāokǎo jùhuì [次 cì]

barefoot ADVERB
赤脚地 chìjiǎo de
□ The children go around barefoot. 孩子们赤脚地到处跑。Háizimen chìjiǎo de dàochù pǎo.

barely ADVERB
几乎不 jīhū bù

□ I could barely hear what she was saying. 我几乎不能听到她在说什么。Wǒ jīhū bùnéng tīngdào tā zài shuō shénme.

bargain NOUN
物美价廉的东西 wùměijiàlián de dōngxi [件 jiàn]*(good buy)*
□ It was a bargain! 那是一件物美价廉的东西！Nà shì yíjiàn wùměijiàlián de dōngxi!

barge NOUN
平底货船 píngdǐ huòchuán [艘 sōu]

to **bark** VERB
叫 jiào

barmaid NOUN
酒吧女侍 jiǔbā nǚshì [个 gè]

barman NOUN
酒吧男侍 jiǔbā nánshì [个 gè]

barn NOUN
谷仓 gǔcāng [座 zuò]

barrel NOUN
桶 tǒng [个 gè]

barrier NOUN
关口 guānkǒu [个 gè]

bartender NOUN (US)
酒吧侍者 jiǔbā shìzhě [个 gè]

base NOUN
▷ *see also* **base** VERB
1 底部 dǐbù [个 gè]*(bottom)*
2 基地 jīdì [个 gè]*(military)*

to **base** VERB
▷ *see also* **base** NOUN
■ **to be based on something** 以某物为根据 yǐ mǒuwù wéi gēnjù □ The film is based on a play by Shakespeare. 这部电影是以莎士比亚的一部戏剧为根据的。Zhèbù diànyǐng shì yǐ Shāshìbǐyà de yíbù xìjù wéi gēnjù de.
■ **I'm based in London.** 我长驻伦敦。Wǒ chángzhù Lúndūn.

baseball NOUN
棒球 bàngqiú
■ **a baseball cap** 一顶棒球帽 yìdǐng bàngqiúmào

basement NOUN
地下室 dìxiàshì [间 jiān]

basic ADJECTIVE
基本的 jīběn de
□ It's a basic model. 这是个基本的模型。Zhè shì gè jīběn de móxíng.

basically ADVERB
简而言之 jiǎnéryánzhī
□ Basically, I just don't like him. 简而言之，我就是不喜欢他。Jiǎnéyánzhī, wǒ jiùshì bù xǐhuān tā.

basics PL NOUN
■ **the basics** 基本点 jīběndiǎn

basil NOUN
罗勒 luólè [株 zhū]

basin NOUN
1 盆 pén [个 gè]*(bowl)*
2 洗脸盆 xǐliǎnpén [个 gè]*(washbasin)*

basis NOUN
基础 jīchǔ
■ **on a daily basis** 在每日基础上 zài měirì jīchǔ shàng
■ **on a regular basis** 在一个规律的基础上 zài yígè guīlǜ de jīchǔ shàng

basket NOUN
筐 kuāng [个 gè]

basketball NOUN
篮球 lánqiú

bass NOUN
1 贝斯 bèisī [把 bǎ]*(guitar, singer)*
□ He plays the bass. 他会弹贝斯。Tā huì tánbèisī.
2 男低音 nán dīyīn
□ He's a bass. 他是位男低音。Tā shì wèi nán dīyīn.
■ **a bass guitar** 一把低音吉他 yìbǎ dīyīn jítā
■ **a double bass** 一把低音提琴 yìbǎ dīyīn tíqín

bat NOUN
1 蝙蝠 biānfú [只 zhī]*(animal)*
2 球板 qiúbǎn [个 gè]*(for cricket)*
3 球棒 qiúbàng [支 zhī]*(for baseball)*
4 球拍 qiúpāi [只 zhī]*(for table tennis)*

bath NOUN
1 洗澡 xǐzǎo [次 cì]
□ a hot bath 一个热水澡 yígè rèshuǐzǎo
■ **to have a bath** 泡澡 pàozǎo
2 浴缸 yùgāng [个 gè]*(bathtub)*
□ There's a spider in the bath. 浴缸里有一只蜘蛛。Yùgāng lǐ yǒu yìzhī zhīzhū.

to **bathe** VERB
戏水 xìshuǐ*(swim)*

bathing suit NOUN (US)
紧身泳衣 jǐnshēn yǒngyī [件 jiàn]

bathroom NOUN
1 卫生间 wèishēngjiān [个 gè]
■ **to go to the bathroom** 去卫生间 qù wèishēngjiān
2 厕所 cèsuǒ [处 chù](US: *toilet*)

bath towel NOUN
浴巾 yùjīn [条 tiáo]

bathtub NOUN (US)
浴缸 yùgāng [个 gè]

batter NOUN
击球手 jīqiúshǒu [名 míng]

battery NOUN
1 电池 diànchí [块 kuài]*(for torch, toy)*
2 电瓶 diànpíng [个 gè]*(in car)*

battle NOUN
1 战役 zhànyì [场 chǎng]
□ the Battle of Hastings 黑斯廷斯战役 Hēisītíngsī zhànyì
2 斗争 dòuzhēng [场 chǎng] *(struggle)*
□ It was a battle, but we managed in the end. 那是一场斗争，不过我们最后还是做到了。Nà shì yìchǎng dòuzhēng, búguò wǒmen zuìhòu háishì zuòdào le.

battleship NOUN
战列舰 zhànlièjiàn [艘 sōu]

bay NOUN
湾 wān [个 gè]

BC ABBREVIATION *(= before Christ)*
公元前 gōngyuán qián
□ in 200 BC 公元前两百年 gōngyuán qián liǎngbǎi nián

to **be** VERB
1 是 shì
□ He's a doctor. 他是一位医生。Tā shì yíwèi yīshēng. □ This is my mother. 这是我的妈妈。Zhèshì wǒde māma. □ Who is it? 是谁啊？Shì sheí a? □ It's 5 o'clock. 现在是五点钟。Xiànzài shì wǔdiǎnzhōng. □ The problem is that... 问题是… Wèntí shì... □ I'm English. 我是英格兰人。Wǒ shì Yīnggélánrén.

LANGUAGE TIP 是 shì is not usually used when linking a noun with an adjective.

□ I'm hot. 我好热。Wǒ hǎo rè. □ She's tall. 她长得高。Tā zhǎngde gāo. □ It's hot. 天好热。Tiān hǎo rè. □ It's too cold. 天太冷了。Tiān tàilěng le.
■ **How are you?** 你好吗？Nǐ hǎo mā?

LANGUAGE TIP When saying how old somebody is, **to be** is usually not translated.

□ I'm fourteen. 我十四岁。Wǒ shísì suì. □ How old are you? 你多大了？Nǐ duōdà le?

LANGUAGE TIP When talking about the location of a place or person, the location marker 在 zài **at** is used and there is no need to translate the verb **to be**.

□ Madrid is in Spain. 马德里在西班牙。Mǎdélǐ zài Xībānyá. □ I won't be here tomorrow. 我明天不在这儿。Wǒ míngtiān búzài zhè'er. □ We've been here for ages. 我们已经在这里好久了。Wǒmen yǐjīng zài zhèlǐ hǎojiǔ le. □ The meeting will be in the canteen. 会议将在食堂举行。Huìyì jiāng zài shítáng jǔxíng.

LANGUAGE TIP When talking about exact distances, use the verb 有 yǒu **to have**.

□ It's 10 km to the village. 这儿离村庄有十公里远。Zhè'er lí cūnzhuāng yǒu shí gōnglǐ yuǎn.
2 花 huā
□ How much was the meal? 这顿饭花了多少钱？Zhèdùn fàn huāle duōshǎo qián?

LANGUAGE TIP When **to be** is used as part of an imperative, it is not translated and the adjective alone is used.

□ Be careful! 当心！Dāngxīn! □ Be quiet! 安静！Ānjìng!

LANGUAGE TIP Progressive sentences are formed with the progressive aspect marker 在 zài + verb.

□ What are you doing? 你在干什么？Nǐ zài gàn shénme? □ I'm running. 我在跑步。Wǒ zài pǎobù.

LANGUAGE TIP Passive sentences are formed using 被 bèi.

□ I was bitten by a dog. 我被狗咬了一口。Wǒ bèi gǒu yǎole yìkǒu. □ He was expelled. 他被开除了。Tā bèi kāichúle. □ He was killed in a car crash. 他在一场车祸中被夺走了生命。Tā zài yìchǎng chēhuò zhōng bèi duózǒu le shēngmìng.

LANGUAGE TIP A statement can be turned into a question by the addition of the verb + negative particle 不 bù + verb question form, which is tagged onto the end of the statement.

□ It was fun, wasn't it? 有意思，是不是？Yǒu yìsi, shì bú shì? □ He's good-looking, isn't he? 他长得不错，是不是？Tā zhǎngde búcuò, shìbúshì?

beach NOUN
海滩 hǎitān [片 piàn]

beads PL NOUN
项链 xiàngliàn [条 tiáo] *(necklace)*

beak NOUN
鸟喙 niǎohuì [个 gè]

beam NOUN
1 光线 guāngxiàn [束 shù] *(of light)*
2 梁 liáng [根 gēn] *(of wood)*

bean NOUN
豆 dòu [粒 lì]
■ **coffee beans** 咖啡豆 kāfēi dòu
■ **baked beans** 烤豆 kǎodòu
■ **broad beans** 蚕豆 cándòu
■ **green beans** 青豆 qīngdòu
■ **kidney beans** 四季豆 sìjìdòu

bear NOUN
▷ *see also* **bear** VERB
熊 xióng [头 tóu]

to **bear** VERB
▷ *see also* **bear** NOUN

容忍 róngrěn *(tolerate)*
□ I can't bear it! 我不能容忍它！Wǒ bùnéng róngrěn tā！

beard NOUN
胡须 húxū [根 gēn]

to **beat** VERB
▷ *see also* **beat** NOUN
击败 jībài
□ We beat them 3-0. 我们以三比零击败了他们。Wǒmen yǐ sānbǐlíng jībài le tāmen.
■ **Beat it!** *(informal)* 走开！Zǒukāi！
■ **to beat somebody up** *(informal)* 暴打某人 bàodǎ mǒurén

beat NOUN
▷ *see also* **beat** VERB
拍子 pāizi [个 gè]

beautiful ADJECTIVE
1 美丽的 měilì de *(for views)*
2 漂亮的 piàoliàng de *(for persons)*

beautifully ADVERB
极好地 jíhǎo de

beauty NOUN
美 měi

became VERB ▷ *see* **become**

because CONJUNCTION
因为 yīnwéi
□ I did it because... 我那样做了是因为… Wǒ nàyàng zuòle shì yīnwéi...
■ **because of** 因为 yīnwéi □ because of the weather 因为天气 yīnwéi tiānqì

to **become** VERB
1 成为 chéngwéi *(with noun)*
□ He became a famous writer. 他成为了一位著名的作家。Tā chéngwéi le yíwèi zhùmíng de zuòjiā.
2 变 biàn *(with adjective)*
□ It became increasingly difficult to cover costs. 要应付花销变得越来越难了。Yào yìngfù huāxiāo biàndé yuèláiyuè nán le.

bed NOUN
床 chuáng [张 zhāng]
□ in bed 在床上 zài chuángshàng
■ **to go to bed** 去睡觉 qù shuìjiào
■ **to go to bed with somebody** 与某人睡觉 yǔ mǒurén shuìjiào

bed and breakfast NOUN
包早餐的旅馆 bāo zǎocān de lǚguǎn [家 jiā]
□ We stayed in a bed and breakfast. 我们住在一家包早餐的旅馆里。Wǒmen zhùzài yìjiā bāo zǎocān de lǚguǎn lǐ.

bedding NOUN
床上用品 chuángshang yòngpǐn [套 tào]

bedroom NOUN
卧室 wòshì [间 jiān]

bedsit NOUN
卧室兼起居室 wòshì jiān qǐjūshì [间 jiān]

bedspread NOUN
床罩 chuángzhào [张 zhāng]

bedtime NOUN
就寝时间 jiùqǐn shíjiān
□ Ten o'clock is my usual bedtime. 十点是我通常的就寝时间。Shídiǎn shì wǒ tōngcháng de jiùqǐn shíjiān.
■ **Bedtime!** 该就寝啦！Gāi jiùqǐn la！

bee NOUN
蜜蜂 mìfēng [只 zhī]

beef NOUN
牛肉 niúròu
■ **roast beef** 烤牛肉 kǎo niúròu

beefburger NOUN
牛肉汉堡包 niúròu hànbǎobāo [个 gè]

been VERB ▷ *see* **be**

beer NOUN
啤酒 píjiǔ
■ **would you like a beer?** 你想喝一瓶啤酒吗？Nǐ xiǎng hē yìpíng píjiǔ ma?

beetle NOUN
甲虫 jiǎchóng [只 zhī]

beetroot NOUN
甜菜根 tiáncàigēn [根 gēn]

before PREPOSITION, CONJUNCTION, ADVERB
1 之前 zhīqián
□ before Tuesday 星期二之前 xīngqī'èr zhīqián
2 在...之前 zài...zhīqián *(used with a verb)*
□ before going 在去之前 zài qù zhīqián
□ I'll call her before she leaves. 在她离开之前我会给她打电话。Zài tā líkāi zhīqián wǒ huì gěi tā dǎ diànhuà.
3 以前 yǐqián *(already)*
□ I've seen this film before. 我以前已经看过这部电影了。Wǒ yǐqián yǐjīng kànguò zhèbù diànyǐng le. □ Have you been to Scotland before? 你以前去过苏格兰吗？Nǐ yǐqián qùguò Sūgélán mā?
■ **the day before** …的前一天 ...de qián yìtiān
■ **the week before** …的前一周 ... de qián yìzhōu

beforehand ADVERB
事先 shìxiān

to **beg** VERB
1 乞讨 qǐtǎo *(for money, food)*
2 乞求 qǐqiú
□ He begged me to stop. 他乞求我停下。Tā qǐqiú wǒ tíngxià.
■ **I beg your pardon 1** *(apologizing)* 对不起。Duìbuqǐ. **2** *(not hearing)* 请再说一遍。Qǐng zàishuō yíbiàn.

began VERB ▷ *see* **begin**

beggar NOUN
乞丐 qǐgài [个 gè]

to **begin** VERB
开始 kāishǐ
□ The match began at 2 p.m. 比赛下午两点开始的。Bǐsài xiàwǔ liǎngdiǎn kāishǐ de.
■ **to begin doing something** 开始做某事 kāishǐ zuò mǒushì

beginner NOUN
初学者 chūxuézhě [位 wèi]
□ I'm just a beginner. 我只是个初学者。Wǒ zhǐshì gè chūxuézhě.

beginning NOUN
开始 kāishǐ [个 gè]
■ **at the beginning** 开始时 kāishǐ shí

begun VERB ▷ *see* **begin**

behalf NOUN
代表 dàibiǎo
■ **on behalf of somebody** 代表某人 dàibiǎo mǒurén

to **behave** VERB
表现 biǎoxiàn
□ He behaved like an idiot. 他表现得像个傻子。Tā biǎoxiàn dé xiàng gè shǎzi.
■ **to behave oneself** 遵守规矩 zūnshǒu guījù □ Did the children behave themselves? 这些孩子遵守规矩了吗？Zhèxiē háizi zūnshǒu guījù le mā?
■ **Behave!** 守规矩点！Shǒu guījù diǎn!

behaviour (US **behavior**) NOUN
举止 jǔzhǐ

behind PREPOSITION, ADVERB
▷ *see also* **behind** NOUN
在…后面 zài…hòumian
□ behind the television 在电视后面 zài diànshì hòumiàn
■ **to be behind** *(late)* 落后于 zhìhòu yú
□ I'm behind with my revision. 我落后于我的复习进度。Wǒ luòhòu yú wǒde fùxí jìndù.
■ **to leave something behind** *(forget)* 落下某物 làxià mǒuwù

behind NOUN
▷ *see also* **behind** PREPOSITION, ADVERB
臀部 túnbù

beige ADJECTIVE
灰棕色的 huīzōngsè de

Beijing NOUN
北京 Běijīng

> **DID YOU KNOW...?**
> Word for word, this means 'northern capital'.

Belgian ADJECTIVE
▷ *see also* **Belgian** NOUN
比利时的 Bǐlìshí de

Belgian NOUN
▷ *see also* **Belgian** ADJECTIVE
比利时人 Bǐlìshírén [个 gè] *(person)*

Belgium NOUN
比利时 Bǐlìshí

to **believe** VERB
相信 xiāngxìn
□ I don't believe you. 我不相信你。Wǒ bù xiāngxìn nǐ.
■ **to believe in something** 相信某事 xiāngxìn mǒushì □ Do you believe in ghosts? 你相信鬼吗？Nǐ xiāngxìn guǐ mā?
■ **to believe in God** 信仰上帝 xìnyǎng Shàngdì
■ **to believe that...** 认为… rènwéi...

bell NOUN
门铃 ménlíng [个 gè] *(on door)*
■ **to ring the bell** 按门铃 àn ménlíng

belly NOUN
肚子 dùzi

to **belong** VERB
■ **to belong to somebody** 属于某人 shǔyú mǒurén □ Who does it belong to? 它属于谁？Tā shǔyú shéi? □ That belongs to me. 它属于我。Tā shǔyú wǒ.
■ **Do you belong to any clubs?** 你是哪个俱乐部的成员吗？Nǐ shì nǎgè jùlèbù de chéngyuán mā?
■ **Where does this belong?** 这属于哪儿？Zhè shǔyú nǎ'er?

belongings PL NOUN
所有物 suǒyǒuwù

below PREPOSITION, ADVERB
1 在…之下 zài…zhīxià
□ below the castle 在城堡之下 zài chéngbǎo zhīxià
2 下面地 xiàmiàn de
□ on the floor below 在下面一层 zài xiàmiàn yìcéng
■ **10 degrees below freezing** 冰点以下十度 bīngdiǎn yǐxià shídù

belt NOUN
腰带 yāodài [条 tiáo]

beltway NOUN (US)
环型公路 huánxíng gōnglù [条 tiáo]

bench NOUN
长椅 chángyǐ [条 tiáo]

bend NOUN
▷ *see also* **bend** VERB
弯 wān [个 gè] *(in road, river)*

to **bend** VERB
▷ *see also* **bend** NOUN
使弯曲 shǐ wānqū
□ I can't bend my arm. 我不能弯手臂。Wǒ bùnéng wān shǒubì. □ It bends easily. 它很容易弯曲。Tā hěn róngyì wānqū.

■ **'do not bend'** "不要折叠" "búyào zhédié"

to **bend down** VERB
弯腰 wānyāo

beneath PREPOSITION
在...之下 zài...zhīxià

benefit NOUN
▷ *see also* **benefit** VERB
好处 hǎochù [个 gè]
■ **unemployment benefit** 失业救济 shīyè jiùjì

to **benefit** VERB
▷ *see also* **benefit** NOUN
■ **to benefit from something** 从某事中获益 cóng mǒushì zhōng huòyì □ He'll benefit from the change. 他会从这种改变中获益的。Tā huì cóng zhèzhǒng gǎibiàn zhōng huòyì de.

bent VERB ▷ *see* **bend**

bent ADJECTIVE
弯曲的 wānqū de
□ a bent fork 一把弯曲的叉子 yìbǎ wānqū de chāzi

beret NOUN
贝雷帽 bèiléimào [顶 dǐng]

berth NOUN
卧铺 wòpù [张 zhāng] *(on boat, train)*

beside PREPOSITION
在...旁边 zài...pángbiān
□ beside the television 在电视机旁边 zài diànshìjī pángbiān
■ **He was beside himself.** 他发狂了。Tā fākuáng le.
■ **That's beside the point.** 它离题了。Tā lítí le.

besides ADVERB
另外 lìngwài
□ Besides, it's too expensive. 另外，它太贵了。Lìngwài, tā tài guì le.

best ADJECTIVE, ADVERB
1 最好的 zuìhǎo de
□ He's the best player in the team. 他是队里最好的队员。Tā shì duìlǐ zuìhǎo de duìyuán.
2 最好地 zuìhǎo de
□ Emma sings best. 艾玛唱得最好。Àimǎ chàngdé zuìhǎo. □ That's the best I can do. 那是我能做到的最好的。Nà shì wǒ néng zuòdào de zuìhǎo de.
■ **to do one's best** 尽某人最大的努力 jìn mǒurén zuìdà de nǔlì □ It's not perfect, but I did my best. 它并不完美，但我已经尽了最大的努力了。Tā bìng bù wánměi, dàn wǒ yǐjīng jìnle zuìdà de nǔlì le.
■ **to make the best of it** 充分利用它 chōngfēn lìyòng tā □ We'll have to make the best of it. 我们得充分利用它。Wǒmen děi chōngfēn lìyòng tā.

best man NOUN
伴郎 bànláng [个 gè]

bet NOUN
▷ *see also* **bet** VERB
赌注 dǔzhù [个 gè]
□ to make a bet 下个赌注 xià gè dǔzhù

to **bet** VERB
▷ *see also* **bet** NOUN
打赌 dǎdǔ
□ I bet you he won't come. 我和你打赌他不会来了。Wǒ hé nǐ dǎdǔ tā búhuì lái le. □ I bet he forgot. 我打赌他忘了。Wǒ dǎdǔ tā wàngle.
■ **to bet somebody 100 pounds that...** 就…和某人赌一百英镑 jiù...hé mǒurén dǔ yībǎi yīngbàng
■ **to bet on a horse** 下赌注一匹马 xià dǔzhù yìpǐ mǎ

to **betray** VERB
背叛 bèipàn

better ADJECTIVE, ADVERB
1 更好的 gènghǎo de
□ This one's better than that one. 这个比那个更好。Zhègè bǐ nàgè gènghǎo. □ a better way to do it 完成它的一种更好的方式 wánchéng tā de yìzhǒng gènghǎo de fāngshì
2 好转的 hǎozhuǎn de
□ Are you feeling better now? 你现在有没有好转？Nǐ xiànzài yǒuméiyǒu hǎozhuǎn?
■ **That's better!** 好多了！Hǎo duō le!
■ **the sooner the better** 越快越好 yuèkuàiyuèhǎo □ Phone her, the sooner the better. 打电话给她，越快越好。Dǎ diànhuà gěi tā, yuèkuàiyuèhǎo.
■ **to get better 1** *(improve)* 变好 biànhǎo □ I hope the weather gets better soon. 我希望天气会很快变好。Wǒ xīwàng tiānqì huì hěnkuài biànhǎo. □ My Chinese is getting better. 我的中文水平正在变好。Wǒde zhōngwén shuǐpíng zhèngzài biànhǎo. **2** *(from illness)* 康复 kāngfù □ I hope you get better soon. 我祝你早日康复。Wǒ zhù nǐ zǎorì kāngfù.
■ **You'd better do it straight away.** 你最好立刻就去做。Nǐ zuìhǎo lìkè jiù qù zuò.
■ **I'd better go home.** 我还是回家好了。Wǒ háishì huíjiā hǎole.

between PREPOSITION
1 在...中间 zài...zhōngjiān *(in space)*
□ Stroud is between Oxford and Bristol. 斯特劳德位于牛津和布里斯托中间。Sītèláodé wèiyú Niújīn hé Bùlǐsītuō zhōngjiān.

2 介于…之间 jièyú…zhījiān *(in time, amount)*
□ between 15 and 20 minutes 介于十五到二十分钟之间 jièyú shíwǔ dào èrshí fēnzhōng zhījiān

beyond PREPOSITION
在…的另一边 zài…de lìng yìbiān
□ There was a lake beyond the mountain. 在这座山的另一边有一个湖。Zài zhèzuò shān de lìng yìbiān yǒu yígè hú.
■ **beyond belief** 难以置信地 nányǐzhìxìn de
■ **beyond repair** 无法修理地 wúfǎ xiūlǐ de

Bible NOUN
■ **the Bible** 圣经 Shèngjīng [部 bù]

bicycle NOUN
自行车 zìxíngchē [辆 liàng]
LANGUAGE TIP Word for word, this means 'self-propelled vehicle'.
■ **to ride a bicycle** 骑自行车 qí zìxíngchē

big ADJECTIVE
大的 dà de
□ a big house 一个大房子 yígè dà fángzi
■ **He's a big guy.** 他是一个大人了。Tā shì yígè dàrén le.
■ **my big brother** 我的哥哥 wǒde gēge
■ **her big sister** 她的姐姐 tāde jiějie
■ **It's no big deal.** 没什么大不了的。Méishénme dàbuliǎo de.

bike NOUN
自行车 zìxíngchē [辆 liàng]
□ by bike 骑自行车 qí zìxíngchē

bikini NOUN
比基尼 bǐjīní [套 tào]

bilingual ADJECTIVE
双语的 shuāngyǔ de

bill NOUN
1 账单 zhàngdān [张 zhāng]
□ Can we have the bill, please? 请给我们账单好吗？Qǐng gěi wǒmen zhàngdān hǎo mā？ □ the gas bill 煤气账单 méiqì zhàngdān
2 钞票 chāopiào [张 zhāng] (US)
□ a five-dollar bill 一张五美元的钞票 yìzhāng wǔ měiyuán de chāopiào

billfold NOUN (US)
钱夹 qiánjiā [个 gè]

billiards NOUN
桌球 zhuōqiú [局 jú]
□ to play billiards 打桌球 dǎ zhuōqiú

billion NOUN
十亿 shíyì

bin NOUN
垃圾箱 lājīxiāng [个 gè]

bingo NOUN
宾戈游戏 bīnxì yóuxì

binoculars PL NOUN
双筒望远镜 shuāngtǒng wàngyuǎnjìng
■ **a pair of binoculars** 一副双筒望远镜 yífù shuāngtǒng wàngyuǎnjìng

biography NOUN
传记 zhuànjì [部 bù]

biology NOUN
生物学 shēngwùxué

bird NOUN
鸟 niǎo [只 zhī]

Biro® NOUN
圆珠笔 yuánzhūbǐ [支 zhī]

birth NOUN
出生 chūshēng
■ **date of birth** 出生日期 chūshēng rìqī

birth certificate NOUN
出生证明 chūshēng zhèngmíng [个 gè]

birth control NOUN
节育 jiéyù

birthday NOUN
生日 shēngrì [个 gè]
□ When's your birthday? 你的生日是什么时候？Nǐde shēngrì shì shénme shíhòu？
■ **a birthday cake** 一个生日蛋糕 yígè shēngrì dàngāo
■ **a birthday card** 一张生日卡 yìzhāng shēngrìkǎ

biscuit NOUN
饼干 bǐnggān [片 piàn]

bishop NOUN
主教 zhǔjiào [位 wèi]

bit VERB ▷ *see* **bite**

bit NOUN
少许 shǎoxǔ
□ Would you like another bit? 你还想要少许吗？Nǐ hái xiǎng yào shǎoxǔ mā？
■ **a bit of 1** *(piece of)* 一小块 yìxiǎokuài □ a bit of cake 一小块蛋糕 yìxiǎokuài dàngāo **2** *(a little)* 一点儿 yìdiǎn'ér □ a bit of music 一点儿音乐 yìdiǎn'ér yīnyuè
■ **It's a bit of a nuisance.** 那有点讨厌。Nà yǒudiǎn tǎoyàn.
■ **a bit** 有点 yǒudiǎn □ He's a bit mad. 他有点疯狂。Tā yǒudiǎn fēngkuáng. □ a bit too hot 有点太热 yǒudiǎn tàirè □ Wait a bit! 等一下！Děng yíxià！ □ Do you play football? — A bit. 你会踢足球吗？— 会一点。Nǐ huì tī zúqiú mā？— Huì yìdiǎn.
■ **to fall to bits** 摔得粉碎 shuāidé fěnsuì
■ **to take something to bits** 把某物拆卸开 bǎ mǒuwù chāixièkāi
■ **bit by bit** 逐渐地 zhújiàn de

bitch NOUN
母狗 mǔgǒu [只 zhī] *(female dog)*

to **bite** VERB
▷ *see also* **bite** NOUN
咬 yǎo

□ The dog bit him. 那只狗咬了他。Nà zhī gǒu yǎo le tā. □ I got bitten by mosquitoes. 我被蚊子咬了。Wǒ bèi wénzi yǎo le.

■ **to bite one's nails** 咬指甲 yǎo zhǐjia

bite NOUN

▷ *see also* **bite** VERB

1 咬伤 yǎoshāng [处 chù]

□ a dog bite 一个被狗咬的伤口 yígè bèi gǒu yǎode shāngkǒu

2 咬痕 yǎohén [个 gè]

□ lots of mosquito bites 很多蚊子叮的包 hěnduō wénzi dīng de bāo

■ **to have a bite to eat** 随便吃点东西 suíbiàn chī diǎn dōngxi

bitten VERB ▷ *see* **bite**

bitter ADJECTIVE

▷ *see also* **bitter** NOUN

1 苦的 kǔ de

□ It tastes bitter. 它尝起来是苦的。Tā chángqǐlái shì kǔde.

2 天冷的 tiānlěng de

□ It's bitter today. 今天天冷。Jīntiān tiānlěng.

bitter NOUN

▷ *see also* **bitter** ADJECTIVE

苦啤酒 kǔ píjiǔ

black ADJECTIVE

1 黑色的 hēisè de

□ a black jacket 一件黑色的夹克 yíjiàn hēisè de jiákè

■ **black coffee** 苦咖啡 kǔ kāfēi

2 黑人的 hēirén de *(person)*

□ She's black. 她是黑人。Tā shì hēirén.

to **black out** VERB

暂时失去知觉 zànshí shīqù zhījué *(faint)*

blackberry NOUN

黑莓 hēiméi [粒 lì]

blackbird NOUN

画眉鸟 huàméiniǎo [只 zhī]

blackboard NOUN

黑板 hēibǎn [个 gè]

blackcurrant NOUN

黑醋栗 hēicùlì [颗 kē]

blackmail NOUN

▷ *see also* **blackmail** VERB

敲诈 qiāozhà

to **blackmail** VERB

▷ *see also* **blackmail** NOUN

敲诈 qiāozhà

□ He blackmailed her. 他敲诈了她。Tā qiāozhà le tā.

blackout NOUN

停电 tíngdiàn [次 cì] *(power cut)*

■ **to have a blackout** *(faint)* 暂时失去知觉 zànshí shīqù zhījué

blade NOUN

刃 rèn

to **blame** VERB

责备 zébèi

□ Don't blame me! 不要责备我！Búyào zébèi wǒ！ □ I blame the police. 我责备警方。Wǒ zébèi jǐngfāng.

■ **He blamed it on my sister.** 他把错归咎于我妹妹。Tā bǎ cuò guījiūyú wǒ mèimei.

blank ADJECTIVE

▷ *see also* **blank** NOUN

空白的 kòngbái de

□ My mind went blank. 我的脑子变得一片空白。Wǒde nǎozi biàndé yípiàn kòngbái.

blank NOUN

▷ *see also* **blank** ADJECTIVE

空白处 kòngbáichù [个 gè]

□ Fill in the blanks. 填在空白处。Tián zài kòngbáichù.

blanket NOUN

毛毯 máotǎn [床 chuáng]

blast NOUN

爆炸 bàozhà [次 cì]

□ a bomb blast 一次炸弹爆炸 yícì zhàdàn bàozhà

blaze NOUN

大火 dàhuǒ [场 chǎng]

blazer NOUN

上装 shàngzhuāng [件 jiàn]

bleach NOUN

漂白剂 piǎobáijì [克 kè]

bleached ADJECTIVE

漂白的 piǎobái de

□ bleached hair 漂白的头发 piǎobái de tóufa

to **bleed** VERB

流血 liúxuě

■ **My nose is bleeding.** 我鼻子流血了。Wǒ bízi liúxuě le.

blender NOUN

搅拌器 jiǎobànqì [个 gè]

to **bless** VERB

赐福 cìfú

> **DID YOU KNOW...?**
> The Chinese do not traditionally say **bless you** or any equivalent after somebody sneezes and so may find it quite strange should you do so.

blew VERB ▷ *see* **blow**

blind ADJECTIVE

▷ *see also* **blind** NOUN

失明的 shīmíng de

blind NOUN

▷ *see also* **blind** ADJECTIVE

向上卷的帘子 xiàng shàng juǎn de liánzi *(for window)*

blindfold NOUN
▷ *see also* **blindfold** VERB
眼罩 yǎnzhào [个 gè]

to **blindfold** VERB
▷ *see also* **blindfold** NOUN
蒙骗 méngpiàn
■ **to blindfold somebody** 蒙骗某人 méngpiàn mǒurén

to **blink** VERB
眨眼睛 zhǎ yǎnjīng

bliss NOUN
天赐的福 tiān cì de fú [个 gè]
■ **It was bliss!** 那真是天赐的福！Nà zhēnshì tiān cì de fú!

blister NOUN
水泡 shuǐpào [个 gè]

blizzard NOUN
暴风雪 bàofēngxuě [场 chǎng]

block NOUN
▷ *see also* **block** VERB
1 单元 dānyuán [个 gè]
□ He lives in our block. 他住在我们这个单元里。Tā zhùzài wǒmen zhègè dānyuán lǐ.
■ **a block of flats** 公寓楼 gōngyùlóu
2 块 kuài *(of stone, ice)*

to **block** VERB
▷ *see also* **block** NOUN
堵塞 dǔsè *(entrance, road)*

blockage NOUN
封锁 fēngsuǒ [次 cì]

bloke NOUN
家伙 jiāhuo [个 gè]

blonde ADJECTIVE
金色的 jīnsè de
□ She's got blonde hair. 她的头发是金色的。Tā de tóufa shì jīnsè de.

blood NOUN
血液 xuèyè

blood pressure NOUN
血压 xuèyā
■ **to have high blood pressure** 有高血压 yǒu gāo xuèyā
■ **to take somebody's blood pressure** 量某人的血压 liáng mǒurén de xuèyā

blood test NOUN
验血 yànxuè [次 cì]
■ **to have a blood test** 验血 yànxuè

bloody ADJECTIVE
非常的 fēicháng de *(informal)*
■ **It's bloody difficult.** 非常难。Fēicháng nán.
■ **Bloody hell!** 该死的！Gāisǐ de!

blouse NOUN
女士衬衫 nǚshì chènshān [件 jiàn]

blow NOUN
▷ *see also* **blow** VERB
1 拳打 quándǎ [顿 dùn] *(punch)*
2 打击 dǎjī [个 gè] *(setback)*

to **blow** VERB
▷ *see also* **blow** NOUN
吹 chuī *(wind, person)*
■ **to blow one's nose** 擤鼻子 xǐng bízi
■ **to blow a whistle** 吹一声口哨 chuī yìshēng kǒushào
■ **to blow out a candle** 吹灭一支蜡烛 chuīmiè yìzhī làzhú

to **blow up** VERB
1 炸毁 zhàhuǐ
□ The terrorists blew up a police station. 恐怖份子炸毁了一个警察局。Kǒngbù fènzi zhàhuǐ le yígè jǐngchájú.
2 使充气 shǐ chōngqì *(a balloon)*
3 爆炸 bàozhà
□ The house blew up. 房子爆炸了。Fángzi bàozhà le.

blow-dry NOUN
吹干定型 chuīgān dìngxíng [次 cì]
■ **A cut and blow-dry, please.** 请修剪一下再吹干定型。Qǐng xiūjiǎn yíxià zài chuīgān dìngxíng.

blown VERB ▷ *see* **blow**

blue ADJECTIVE
蓝色的 lánsè de
□ a blue dress 一条蓝色的裙子 yìtiáo lánsè de qúnzi
■ **navy blue** 海军蓝 hǎijūnlán
■ **It came out of the blue.** 它出乎意料地发生了。Tā chūhūyìliào de fāshēng le.

blues PL NOUN
■ **the blues** *(music)* 蓝调 lándiào

blunder NOUN
重大失误 zhòngdà shīwù [次 cì]

blunt ADJECTIVE
1 钝的 dùn de *(knife)*
2 直率的 zhíshuài de *(person, remark)*

to **blush** VERB
脸红 liǎnhóng

board NOUN
▷ *see also* **board** VERB
1 木板 mùbǎn [块 kuài] *(piece of wood)*
2 公告板 gōnggàobǎn [块 kuài] *(noticeboard)*
3 黑板 hēibǎn [个 gè] *(blackboard)*
4 盘 pán *(for chess)*
■ **on board 1** *(ship)* 在船上 zài chuán shàng **2** *(train)* 在火车上 zài huǒchē shàng **3** *(plane)* 在飞机上 zài fēijī shàng
■ **full board** 食住全包 shízhù quánbāo

to **board** VERB
▷ *see also* **board** NOUN
上 shàng *(ship, train, plane)*

board game NOUN
棋盘游戏 qípán yóuxì [种 zhǒng]

boarding card NOUN
登机卡 dēngjīkǎ [张 zhāng]

boarding school NOUN
寄宿学校 jìsù xuéxiào [个 gè]
■ **I go to boarding school.** 我上的是寄宿学校。Wǒ shàng de shì jìsù xuéxiào.

to **boast** VERB
说大话 shuō dàhuà
□ Stop boasting! 不要再说大话了！Búyào zài shuō dàhuà le!
■ **to boast about something** 说关于某事的吹牛 shuō guānyú mǒushì de chuīniú

boat NOUN
船 chuán [艘 sōu]
■ **to go by boat** 乘船去 chéngchuán qù

body NOUN
1 身体 shēntǐ [个 gè]
□ the human body 人类身体 rénlèi shēntǐ
2 尸体 shītǐ [具 jù] *(corpse)*

bodybuilding NOUN
健身 jiànshēn [次 cì]

bodyguard NOUN
保镖 bǎobiāo [个 gè]

to **boil** VERB
▷ *see also* **boil** NOUN
1 烧开 shāokāi
□ to boil some water 烧些水 shāo xiē shuǐ
2 煮 zhǔ
■ **to boil an egg** 煮一个蛋 zhǔ yígè dàn
3 沸腾 fèiténg
□ The water's boiling. 水正在沸腾。Shuǐ zhèngzài fèiténg.

boil NOUN
▷ *see also* **boil** VERB
疖子 jiēzi [个 gè]

boiled ADJECTIVE
煮熟的 zhǔshóu de
□ boiled potatoes 煮熟的土豆 zhǔshóu de tǔdòu
■ **a boiled egg** 一个煮熟的蛋 yígè zhǔshóu de dàn

boiler NOUN
锅炉 guōlú [个 gè]

bolt NOUN
1 插销 chāxiāo [个 gè] *(to lock door)*
2 螺钉 luódīng [颗 kē] *(used with nut)*

bomb NOUN
▷ *see also* **bomb** VERB
炸弹 zhàdàn [颗 kē]

to **bomb** VERB
▷ *see also* **bomb** NOUN
轰炸 hōngzhà

bomber NOUN
1 轰炸机 hōngzhàjī [架 jià] *(plane)*
2 投放炸弹的人 tóufàng zhàdàn de rén [个 gè] *(terrorist)*

bombing NOUN
轰炸 hōngzhà [阵 zhèn]

bone NOUN
1 骨头 gǔtou [根 gēn] *(of human, animal)*
2 刺 cì [根 gēn] *(in fish)*

bonfire NOUN
1 篝火 gōuhuǒ [堆 duī] *(as part of a celebration)*
2 火堆 huǒduī [个 gè] *(to burn rubbish)*

bonnet NOUN
引擎罩 yǐnqíngzhào [个 gè] *(of car)*

bonus NOUN
1 红利 hónglì [份 fèn] *(extra payment)*
2 额外收获 éwài shōuhuò [份 fèn] *(additional benefit)*

book NOUN
▷ *see also* **book** VERB
1 书 shū [本 běn] *(novel)*
2 册 cè *(of stamps, tickets)*

to **book** VERB
▷ *see also* **book** NOUN
预订 yùdìng *(ticket, table, room)*
□ We haven't booked. 我们还没预订。Wǒmen hái méi yùdìng.
■ **fully booked** 预订一空 yùdìng yìkōng

bookcase NOUN
书橱 shūchú [个 gè]

booklet NOUN
小册子 xiǎocèzi [本 běn]

bookshelf NOUN
书架 shūjià [个 gè]

bookshop NOUN
书店 shūdiàn [家 jiā]

to **boost** VERB
促进 cùjìn
□ to boost the economy 促进经济 cùjìn jīngjì □ The win boosted the team's morale. 那次胜利促进了这支队的士气。Nàcì shènglì cùjìn le zhè zhī duì de shìqì.

boot NOUN
1 车尾箱 chēwěixiāng [个 gè] *(of car)*
2 靴子 xuēzi [双 shuāng] *(for winter)*
3 鞋 xié [双 shuāng] *(for football, walking)*

border NOUN
边界 biānjiè [条 tiáo]

bore VERB ▷ *see* **bear**

bored ADJECTIVE
■ **to be bored** 觉得无聊 juéde wúliáo □ I was bored. 我觉得无聊。Wǒ juéde wúliáo.

LANGUAGE TIP Be careful though. 我很无聊。Wǒhěn wúliáo. does not mean **I am very bored.** as you may expect. It actually means **I am very boring.**

boredom NOUN
无聊 wúliáo

boring ADJECTIVE
乏味的 fáwèi de

born ADJECTIVE
■ **to be born** 出生 chūshēng □ I was born in 1990. 我出生于1990年。Wǒ chūshēngyú yījiǔjiǔlíng nián.

to **borrow** VERB
借 jiè
□ Can I borrow your pen? 我能借你的笔吗？Wǒ néng jiè nǐde bǐ mā？
■ **to borrow something from somebody** 向某人借某物 xiàng mǒurén jiè mǒuwù
□ I borrowed some money from a friend. 我向一个朋友借了些钱。Wǒ xiàng yígè péngyǒu jièle xiē qián.

Bosnia NOUN
波斯尼亚 Bōsīníyà

Bosnian ADJECTIVE
波斯尼亚的 Bōsīníyà de

boss NOUN
老板 lǎobǎn [个 gè]

to **boss around** VERB
■ **to boss somebody around** 指挥某人 zhǐhuī mǒurén

bossy ADJECTIVE
霸道的 bàdào de

both ADJECTIVE, PRONOUN, ADVERB
1 两个都 liǎnggè dōu
□ We both went. 我们两个都去了。Wǒmen liǎnggè dōu qù le. □ Emma and Jane both went. 艾玛和简都去了。Àimǎ hé Jiǎn dōu qù le.
2 两个 liǎnggè *(things)*
□ Both of your answers are wrong. 你的两个答案都是错的。Nǐde liǎnggè dá'àn dōushì cuò de.
3 两个 liǎnggè *(people)*
□ Both of us went. 我们两个都去了。Wǒmen liǎnggè dōuqù le. □ Both Maggie and John are against it. 玛吉和约翰都反对它。Mǎjí hé Yuēhàn dōu fǎnduì tā.
■ **He speaks both German and Italian.** 他既能讲德语又能讲意大利语。Tā jì néng jiǎng Déyǔ yòu néng jiǎng Yìdàliyǔ.

to **bother** VERB
1 烦扰 fánrǎo
□ What's bothering you? 有什么事烦扰你？Yǒu shénme shì fánrǎo nǐ？
2 打扰 dǎrǎo
□ I'm sorry to bother you. 对不起，打扰你了。Duìbuqǐ, dǎrǎo nǐ le.
■ **Don't bother!** 不用了！Búyòng le！
■ **to bother to do something** 费神做某事 fèishén qù zuò mǒushì □ He didn't bother to tell me about it. 他不觉得费神告诉我那事。Tā bù juéde fèishén gàosù wǒ nà shì.

bottle NOUN
瓶子 píngzi [个 gè]
■ **a bottle of wine** 一瓶葡萄酒 yìpíng pútáojiǔ

bottle bank NOUN
玻璃瓶回收站 bōlípíng huíshōuzhàn [个 gè]

bottle-opener NOUN
开瓶器 kāipíngqì [个 gè]

bottom NOUN
▷ *see also* **bottom** ADJECTIVE
1 底部 dǐbù [个 gè] *(of container, sea)*
■ **at the bottom of** 在…的底部 zài...de dǐbù
2 下端 xiàduān [个 gè] *(of page, list)*
□ at the bottom of the page 在这页的下端 zài zhèyè de xiàduān
3 最后一名 zuìhòu yìmíng *(of class, league)*
□ He was always bottom of the class. 他总是班里的最后一名。Tā zǒngshì bānlǐ de zuìhòu yìmíng.
4 最底部 zuìdǐbù [个 gè] *(of hill, tree, stairs)*
□ She found it at the bottom of the stairs. 她在楼梯的最底部找到了它。Tā zài lóutī de zuìdǐbù zhǎodào le tā.
5 臀部 túnbù [个 gè] *(buttocks)*

bottom ADJECTIVE
▷ *see also* **bottom** NOUN
最下面的 zuì xiàmian de
□ the bottom shelf 最下面的架子 zuìxiàmiàn de jiàzi

bought VERB ▷ *see* **buy**

bound ADJECTIVE [必然的 bìrán de]
■ **He's bound to fail.** 他必然会失败。Tā bìrán huì shībài.

boundary NOUN
边界 biānjiè [个 gè]

bow NOUN
▷ *see also* **bow** VERB
1 蝴蝶结 húdiéjié [个 gè] *(knot)*
□ to tie a bow 打一个蝴蝶结 dǎ yígè húdiéjié
2 弓 gōng [把 bǎ]
□ a bow and arrows 一副弓箭 yífù gōngjiàn

to **bow** VERB
▷ *see also* **bow** NOUN
鞠躬 jūgōng

bowels PL NOUN
内脏 nèizàng

bowl NOUN
碗 wǎn [个 gè]

bowling NOUN
保龄球 bǎolíngqiú
■ **to go bowling** 打保龄球 dǎ bǎolíngqiú
■ **a bowling alley** 一条保龄球道 yìtiáo bǎolíngqiú dào

bowls PL NOUN
保龄球 bǎolíngqiú
□ to play bowls 打保龄球 dǎ bǎolíngqiú

bow tie NOUN
蝶形领结 diéxíng lǐngjié [个 gè]

box NOUN
1 盒子 hézi [个 gè]
□ a box of matches 一盒火柴 yìhé huǒchái
2 箱 xiāng *(crate)*
■ **a cardboard box** 一个纸板箱 yígè zhǐbǎnxiāng

boxer NOUN
拳击运动员 quánjī yùndòngyuán [位 wèi]

boxer shorts, boxers PL NOUN
平角裤 píngjiǎokù

boxing NOUN
拳击 quánjī

Boxing Day NOUN
圣诞节后的第一天 Shèngdànjié hòu de dìyītiān

boy NOUN
1 男孩 nánhái [个 gè] *(male child)*
□ a boy of seven 一个七岁的男孩 yígè qīsuì de nánhái □ She has two boys and a girl. 她有两个儿子和一个女儿。Tā yǒu liǎnggè érzi hé yígè nǚ'ér.
2 男青年 nán qīngnián [个 gè] *(young man)*
□ a boy of fifteen 一个十五岁的男青年 yígè shíwǔsuì de nánqīngnián

boyfriend NOUN
男朋友 nánpéngyou [个 gè]
□ Have you got a boyfriend? 你有男朋友吗？Nǐ yǒu nánpéngyǒu ma？

bra NOUN
胸罩 xiōngzhào [件 jiàn]

brace NOUN
牙箍 yágū [副 fù] *(on teeth)*
□ She wears a brace. 她戴了一副牙箍。Tā dàile yífù yágū.

bracelet NOUN
手镯 shǒuzhuó [只 zhī]

braces PL NOUN
牙箍 yágū *(on teeth)*
□ She wears braces. 她戴了牙箍。Tā dàile yágū.

brackets PL NOUN
括号 kuòhào [组 zǔ]
■ **in brackets** 在括号内 zài kuòhào nèi

brain NOUN
脑 nǎo [个 gè]

brainy ADJECTIVE
聪明的 cōngming de *(informal)*

brake NOUN
▷ *see also* **brake** VERB
刹车 shāchē [个 gè] *(in car)*

to **brake** VERB
▷ *see also* **brake** NOUN
刹车 shāchē

branch NOUN
1 树枝 shùzhī [条 tiáo] *(of tree)*
2 分店 fēndiàn [家 jiā] *(of shop)*
3 分支机构 fēnzhī jīgòu [个 gè] *(of bank, company)*

brand NOUN
牌子 páizi [块 kuài]
□ a well-known brand of coffee 一种知名牌子的咖啡 yìzhǒng zhīmíng páizi de kāfēi

brand-new ADJECTIVE
全新的 quánxīn de

brandy NOUN
白兰地酒 báilándìjiǔ [瓶 píng]

brass NOUN
铜管乐器 tóngguǎn yuèqì
■ **the brass section** 铜管乐组 tóngguǎn yuèzǔ

brass band NOUN
铜管乐队 tóngguǎn yuèduì [支 zhī]

brat NOUN
小子 xiǎozi [个 gè]
□ He's a spoiled brat. 他是个被宠坏了的小子。Tā shì gè bèi chǒnghuàile de xiǎozi.

brave ADJECTIVE
勇敢的 yǒnggǎn de

Brazil NOUN
巴西 Bāxī

bread NOUN
面包 miànbāo [个 gè]
□ brown bread 杂粮面包 záliáng miànbāo
□ white bread 白面包 bái miànbāo
■ **bread and butter** 生活资源 shēnghuó zīyuán

break NOUN
▷ *see also* **break** VERB
1 休息 xiūxi [次 cì] *(rest)*
■ **to take a break** *(for a few minutes)* 休息一下 xiūxi yíxià
2 课间休息 kèjiān xiūxi [段 duàn] *(at school)*
□ during morning break 在早晨课间休息期间 zài zǎochén kèjiān xiūxi qījiān
■ **the Christmas break** 圣诞假期 Shèngdàn jiàqī
■ **Give me a break!** 饶了我吧！Ráole wǒ ba！

to **break** VERB
▷ *see also* **break** NOUN
1 打碎 dǎsuì
□ Careful, you'll break something! 当心点，你会打碎什么的！Dāngxīndiǎn, nǐ huì dǎsuì shénme de！
2 破碎 pòsuì *(get broken)*
□ Careful, it'll break! 当心点，它会碎的！Dāngxīndiǎn, tā huì suì de！

■ **to break one's leg** 弄折某人的腿骨 nòngshé mǒurén de tuǐgǔ □ I broke my leg. 我弄折了我的腿骨。Wǒ nòngshé le wǒde tuǐgǔ.

■ **to break a promise** 违背一个诺言 wéibèi yígè nuòyán

■ **to break the law** 违反法律 wéifǎn fǎlǜ

■ **to break a record** 打破一项纪录 dǎpò yíxiàng jìlù

to **break down** VERB

坏掉 huàidiào

□ The car broke down. 车坏掉了。Chē huàidiào le.

to **break in** VERB

破门而入 pòmén ér rù *(burglar)*

to **break into** VERB

强行进入 qiángxíng jìnrù *(house)*

to **break off** VERB

1 掰下 bāixià

□ He broke off a piece of chocolate. 他掰下一块巧克力。Tā bāixià yíkuài qiǎokèlì.

2 折断 zhéduàn

□ The branch broke off in the storm. 树枝在风暴中折断了。Shùzhī zài fēngbào zhōng zhéduàn le.

to **break open** VERB

砸开 zákāi *(door, cupboard)*

to **break out** VERB

1 突发 tūfā *(fire)*

2 爆发 bàofā *(war)*

3 逃脱 táotuō *(prisoner)*

■ **to break out in a rash** 突发皮疹 tūfā pízhěn

to **break up** VERB

1 分手 fēnshǒu

□ David and Susan have broken up. 戴维和苏珊已经分手了。Dàiwéi hé Sūshān yǐjīng fēnshǒu le.

■ **to break up with somebody** 同某人分手 tóng mǒurén fēnshǒu

2 驱散 qūsàn

□ Police broke up the demonstration. 警方驱散了示威人群。Jǐngfāng qūsànle shìwēi rénqún.

3 解散 jiěsàn

□ The crowd broke up. 人群解散了。Rénqún jiěsàn le.

■ **to break up a fight** 制止一场打斗 zhìzhǐ yìchǎng dǎdòu

■ **We break up next Wednesday.** 我们下周三休假。Wǒmen xià zhōusān xiūjià.

■ **You're breaking up!** 你快要跨了！Nǐ kuài yào kuǎ le!

breakdown NOUN

1 故障 gùzhàng [个 gè] *(in vehicle)*

□ to have a breakdown 发生一个故障 fāshēng yígè gùzhàng

2 精神崩溃 jīngshén bēngkuì [阵 zhèn] *(mental)*

□ He had a breakdown because of the stress. 他因为压力大曾经精神崩溃过。Tā yīnwéi yālì dà céngjīng bēngkuì guò.

breakfast NOUN

早餐 zǎocān [顿 dùn]

□ What would you like for breakfast? 你早餐想吃什么？Nǐ zǎocān xiǎng chī shénme?

break-in NOUN

闯入 chuǎngrù

breast NOUN

乳房 rǔfáng [个 gè] *(of woman)*

■ **a chicken breast** 一块鸡胸肉 yíkuài jīxiōngròu

to **breast-feed** VERB

母乳喂养 mǔrǔ wèiyǎng

breaststroke NOUN

蛙泳 wāyǒng

breath NOUN

1 呼吸 hūxī [下 xià]

□ Take a deep breath. 深呼吸一下。Shēn hūxī yíxià.

2 口气 kǒuqì

□ bad breath 口臭 kǒuchòu

■ **to be out of breath** 上气不接下气 shàngqì bùjiē xiàqì

■ **to get one's breath back** 恢复正常呼吸 huīfù zhèngcháng hūxī

■ **to hold one's breath** 屏住呼吸 bǐngzhù hūxī

to **breathe** VERB

呼吸 hūxī

LANGUAGE TIP Word for word, this means 'exhale inhale'.

to **breathe in** VERB

吸入 xīrù

to **breathe out** VERB

呼出 hūchū

to **breed** VERB

▷ *see also* **breed** NOUN

繁殖 fánzhí *(reproduce)*

□ They rarely breed in captivity. 他们很少在圈养环境下繁殖。Tāmen hěnshǎo zài juànyǎng huánjìng xià fánzhí.

■ **to breed dogs** 繁殖小狗 fánzhí xiǎogǒu

breed NOUN

▷ *see also* **breed** VERB

品种 pǐnzhǒng [个 gè]

breeze NOUN

微风 wēifēng [阵 zhèn]

brewery NOUN

啤酒厂 píjiǔchǎng [家 jiā]

bribe NOUN

▷ *see also* **bribe** VERB

贿赂 huìlù [种 zhǒng]

to **bribe** VERB

▷ *see also* **bribe** NOUN

贿赂 huìlù

■ **to bribe somebody to do something** 贿赂某人去做某事 huìlù mǒurén qù zuò mǒushì

brick NOUN

砖 zhuān [块 kuài]

bricklayer NOUN

泥瓦匠 níwǎjiàng [名 míng]

bride NOUN

新娘 xīnniáng [个 gè]

bridegroom NOUN

新郎 xīnláng [个 gè]

bridesmaid NOUN

伴娘 bànniáng [个 gè]

bridge NOUN

1 桥 qiáo [座 zuò]

□ a suspension bridge 一座吊桥 yízuò diàoqiáo

2 桥牌 qiáopái *(card game)*

□ to play bridge 打桥牌 dǎ qiáopái

brief ADJECTIVE

1 短暂的 duǎnzàn de *(life)*

2 简短的 jiǎnduǎn de *(description, speech)*

briefcase NOUN

公事包 gōngshìbāo [个 gè]

briefly ADVERB

简短地 jiǎnduǎn de

briefs PL NOUN

1 男式三角内裤 nánshì sānjiǎo nèikù *(for men)*

2 女式三角内裤 nǚshì sānjiǎo nèikù *(for women)*

bright ADJECTIVE

1 鲜亮的 xiānliàng de

□ a bright colour 一种鲜亮的颜色 yìzhǒng xiānliàng de yánsè

■ **bright blue** 蔚蓝色 wèilánsè

2 亮的 liàng de *(light)*

3 聪明的 cōngming de

□ He's not very bright. 他不是很聪明。Tā búshì hěn cōngmíng.

brilliant ADJECTIVE

1 出色的 chūsè de

□ He's a brilliant actor. 他是位出色的演员。Tā shì wèi chūsè de yǎnyuán.

2 非常棒的 fēicháng bàng de

□ We had a brilliant time! 我们度过了一段非常棒的时光！Wǒmen dùguò le yíduàn fēicháng bàng de shíguāng!

■ **Brilliant!** 太棒了！Tài bàng le!

3 非常聪明的 fēicháng cōngmíng de *(clever)*

□ a brilliant scientist 一位非常聪明的科学家 yíwèi fēicháng cōngmíng de kēxuéjiā

to **bring** VERB

1 带来 dàilái *(with you)*

□ Bring warm clothes. 带些厚衣服来。Dàixiē hòu yīfu lái. □ Can I bring a friend? 我能带个朋友来吗？Wǒ néng dài gè péngyǒu lái mā?

2 拿来 nálái *(to somebody)*

□ Could you bring me my trainers? 你能把我的运动鞋拿来吗？Nǐ néng bǎ wǒde xùnliànxié nálái mā?

to **bring along** VERB

随身携带 suíshēn xiédài

to **bring back** VERB

带回来 dài huílái *(return)*

to **bring forward** VERB

提前 tíqián

□ The meeting was brought forward. 会议提前了。Huìyì tíqián le.

to **bring round** VERB

使苏醒 shǐ sūxǐng *(unconscious person)*

to **bring up** VERB

抚养 fǔyǎng

□ She brought up 5 children on her own. 她独自抚养了五个孩子。Tā dúzì fǔyǎng le wǔgè háizi.

Britain NOUN

英国 Yīngguó

■ **in Britain** 在英国 zài Yīngguó

■ **to Britain** 去英国 qù Yīngguó

■ **I'm from Britain.** 我来自英国。Wǒ láizì Yīngguó.

British ADJECTIVE

英国的 Yīngguó de

■ **the British** 英国人 Yīngguórén

■ **the British Isles** 不列颠群岛 Búlièdiān qúndǎo

broad ADJECTIVE

宽的 kuān de

■ **in broad daylight** 光天化日之下 guāngtiānhuàrì zhīxià

broadband NOUN

宽带 kuāndài *(internet)*

□ Do you have broadband? 你安宽带了吗？Nǐ ān kuāndài le ma?

broad bean NOUN

蚕豆 cándòu [个 gè]

broadcast NOUN

▷ *see also* **broadcast** VERB

广播 guǎngbō [段 duàn]

to **broadcast** VERB

▷ *see also* **broadcast** NOUN

播送 bōsòng

□ The interview was broadcast yesterday. 那段采访昨天就播送了。Nàduàn cǎifǎng zuótiān jiù bōsòng le.

■ **to broadcast live** 现场直播 xiànchǎngzhíbō

broad-minded ADJECTIVE
度量大的 dùliàngdà de

broccoli NOUN
花椰菜 huāyēcài

brochure NOUN
小册子 xiǎocèzi [本 běn]

to **broil** VERB (US)
烤 kǎo
■ **to broil something** 烤某物 kǎo mǒuwù

broke VERB ▷ *see* **break**

broke ADJECTIVE
身无分文的 shēn wú fēnwén de *(informal: penniless)*

broken ADJECTIVE
1 破碎的 pòsuì de
□ a broken glass 一块破碎的玻璃 yíkuài pòsuì de bōli
2 坏的 huàide *(machine)*
□ It's broken. 它是坏的。Tā shì huàide.
■ **He's got a broken leg.** 他折断了腿。Tā zhéduàn le tuǐ.

bronchitis NOUN
支气管炎 zhīqìguǎnyán

bronze NOUN
铜 tóng
□ the bronze medal 铜牌 tóngpái

brooch NOUN
胸针 xiōngzhēn [枚 méi]

broom NOUN
扫帚 sàozhou [把 bǎ]

brother NOUN
1 兄弟 xiōngdì [个 gè]
□ Do you have any brothers? 你有兄弟吗？Nǐ yǒu xiōngdì mā?
2 哥哥 gēge [个 gè] *(elder)*
□ my big brother 我的哥哥 wǒde gēge
3 弟弟 dìdi [个 gè] *(younger)*
□ my little brother 我的弟弟 wǒde dìdi

brother-in-law NOUN
1 姐夫 jiěfu [个 gè] *(older sister's husband)*
2 妹夫 mèifu [个 gè] *(younger sister's husband)*
3 大伯子 dàbǎizi [个 gè] *(husband's older brother)*
4 小叔子 xiǎoshūzi [个 gè] *(husband's younger brother)*
5 内兄 nèixiōng [个 gè] *(wife's older brother)*
6 内弟 nèidì [个 gè] *(wife's younger brother)*

brought VERB ▷ *see* **bring**

brown ADJECTIVE
1 褐色的 hèsè de *(clothes)*
2 棕色的 zōngsè de *(hair, eyes)*
3 晒黑的 shàiheī de *(tanned)*

■ **brown bread** 杂粮面包 záliáng miànbāo [个 gè]

to **browse** VERB
浏览 liúlǎn *(on the internet)*

browser NOUN
浏览器 liúlǎnqì [种 zhǒng] *(for internet)*

bruise NOUN
青瘀 qīngyū [块 kuài]

brush NOUN
▷ *see also* **brush** VERB
1 扫帚 sàozhǒu [把 bǎ] *(for cleaning)*
2 发刷 fàshuā [把 bǎ] *(for hair)*
3 画笔 huàbǐ [支 zhī] *(for painting)*

to **brush** VERB
▷ *see also* **brush** NOUN
刷 shuā
■ **to brush one's hair** 刷头发 shuā tóufa
■ **to brush one's teeth** 刷牙 shuāyá

Brussels sprout NOUN
芽甘蓝 yágānlán [个 gè]

brutal ADJECTIVE
野蛮的 yěmán de

BSc NOUN *(= Bachelor of Science)*
理科学士 Lǐkē xuéshì
■ **a BSc in Mathematics** 一位数学专业的理科学士 yíwèi shùxué zhuānyè de lǐkē xuéshì

bubble NOUN
泡 pào [个 gè]

bubble gum NOUN
泡泡糖 pàopàotáng [个 gè]

bucket NOUN
桶 tǒng [个 gè]

buckle NOUN
扣环 kòuhuán [个 gè] *(on belt, shoe)*

Buddhism NOUN
佛教 Fójiào

Buddhist ADJECTIVE
佛教的 Fójiào de

buddy NOUN (US)
伙计 huǒjì [个 gè]

budget NOUN
预算 yùsuàn [笔 bǐ]

budgie NOUN
虎皮鹦鹉 hǔpí yīngwǔ [只 zhī]

buffet NOUN
自助餐 zìzhùcān [顿 dùn]

LANGUAGE TIP Word for word, this means 'self help meal'.

buffet car NOUN
餐车 cānchē [节 jié]

bug NOUN
1 虫子 chóngzi [只 zhī] *(insect)*
2 病毒 bìngdú [种 zhǒng] *(in computer)*
3 病菌 bìngjūn [种 zhǒng] *(virus)*
□ There's a bug going round. 有一种病菌到

处流传。Yǒu yìzhǒng bìngjūn dàochù liúchuán.

■ **a stomach bug** 一种肠胃病菌 yìzhǒng chángwèi bìngjūn

bugged ADJECTIVE
被窃听的 bèi qiètīng de
□ The room was bugged. 这间房曾被窃听过。Zhèjiān fáng céng bèi qiètīng guò.

to **build** VERB
建造 jiànzào
□ He's building a garage. 他在建造一个车库。Tā zài jiànzào yígè chēkù.

to **build up** VERB
1 收集 shōují
□ He has built up a huge collection of stamps. 他收集了很多邮票。Tā shōují le hěnduō yóupiào.
2 累积 lěijī
□ Her debts are building up. 她的负债正在累积。Tāde fùzhài zhèngzài lěijī.

builder NOUN
1 建造商 jiànzàoshāng [名 míng] *(owner of building firm)*
2 建筑工人 jiànzhù gōngrén [位 wèi] *(worker)*

building NOUN
建筑物 jiànzhùwù [座 zuò]
■ **a building site** 一个建筑工地 yígè jiànzhù gōngdì

built VERB ▷ *see* **build**

bulb NOUN
1 电灯泡 diàndēngpào [个 gè] *(electric)*
2 球茎 qiújīng [个 gè] *(of flower)*

Bulgaria NOUN
保加利亚 Bǎojiālìyà

bull NOUN
公牛 gōngniú [头 tóu]

bullet NOUN
子弹 zǐdàn [发 fā]

bulletin board NOUN
1 公共留言板 gōnggòng liúyánbǎn *(on computer)*
2 布告栏 bùgàolán (us: *noticeboard)*

bully NOUN
▷ *see also* **bully** VERB
恃强凌弱者 shìqiáng língruò zhě [个 gè]
□ He's a big bully. 他是个恃强凌弱者。Tā shì gè shìqiáng língruò zhě.

to **bully** VERB
▷ *see also* **bully** NOUN
欺侮 qīwǔ

bum NOUN
1 屁股 pìgu [个 gè] *(informal: backside)*
2 流浪汉 liúlànghàn [个 gè] (us: *tramp)*

bump NOUN
▷ *see also* **bump** VERB
1 肿包 zhǒngbāo [个 gè] *(on head)*
2 隆起物 lóngqǐwù [个 gè] *(on road)*
3 颠簸 diānbǒ [阵 zhèn] *(minor accident)*
□ We had a bump. 我们颠簸了一阵。Wǒmen diānbǒ le yízhèn.

to **bump** VERB
▷ *see also* **bump** NOUN
碰 pèng *(strike)*

to **bump into** VERB
■ **to bump into something** 撞到某物 zhuàngdào mǒuwù □ I bumped into the table in the dark. 我在黑暗中撞到了桌子。Wǒ zài hēi'àn zhōng zhuàngdào le zhuōzi.
■ **to bump into somebody 1** *(literally)* 撞上某人 zhuàngshàng mǒurén □ He stopped suddenly and I bumped into him. 他突然停住所以我撞上了他。Tā tūrán tíngzhù suǒyǐ wǒ zhuàngshàng le tā. **2** *(meet by chance)* 碰见某人 pèngjiàn mǒurén □ I bumped into Jane in the supermarket. 我在超市碰见了简。Wǒ zài chāoshì pèngjiàn le Jiǎn.

bumper NOUN
缓冲器 huǎnchōngqì [个 gè]

bumpy ADJECTIVE
崎岖不平的 qíqū bùpíng de

bun NOUN
圆面包 yuán miànbāo [个 gè]

bunch NOUN
■ **a bunch of flowers** 一束花 yíshù huā
■ **a bunch of grapes** 一串葡萄 yíchuàn pútao
■ **a bunch of keys** 一串钥匙 yíchuàn yàoshi

bunches PL NOUN
发束 fàshù
□ She has her hair in bunches. 她把头发扎成了发束。Tā bǎ tóufa zhāchéng le fàshù.

bungalow NOUN
平房 píngfáng [间 jiān]

bunk NOUN
铺位 pùwèi [个 gè]
■ **bunk beds** 双层床 shuāngcéngchuáng

burger NOUN
汉堡包 hànbǎobāo [个 gè]

burglar NOUN
窃贼 qièzéi [个 gè]

burglary NOUN
盗窃 dàoqiè [次 cì] *(act)*

to **burgle** VERB
盗窃 dàoqiè
□ Her house was burgled. 她的房子被盗窃了。Tāde fángzi bèi dàoqiè le.

burn NOUN
▷ *see also* **burn** VERB

English-Chinese
b

烧伤 shāoshāng [次 cì]

to **burn** VERB

▷ *see also* **burn** NOUN

1 烧毁 shāohuǐ *(rubbish, documents)*

2 烤糊 kǎohú

□ I burned the cake. 我把蛋糕烤糊了。Wǒ bǎ dàngāo kǎohú le.

3 刻录 kèlù *(CD, DVD)*

■ **to burn oneself** 烫伤自己 tàngshāng zìjǐ

□ I burned myself on the oven door. 我在烤箱门上把自己烫伤了。Wǒ zài kǎoxiāngmén shàng bǎ zìjǐ tàngshāng le.

■ **I've burned my hand.** 我烫到了我的手。Wǒ tàngdào le wǒde shǒu.

to **burn down** VERB

烧毁 shāohuǐ

□ The factory burned down. 那家工厂被烧毁了。Nà jiā gōngchǎng bèi shāohuǐ le.

to **burst** VERB

爆裂 bàoliè

□ The balloon burst. 气球爆裂了。Qìqiú bàoliè le.

■ **to burst into flames** 突然着火 tūrán zháohuǒ

■ **to burst into tears** 突然大哭起来 tūrán dàkū qǐlái

■ **to burst out laughing** 突然大笑起来 tūrán dàxiào qǐlái

to **bury** VERB

1 掩埋 yǎnmái *(gold)*

2 埋葬 máizàng *(dead person)*

bus NOUN

公共汽车 gōnggòng qìchē [辆 liàng]

□ a bus stop 一个公共汽车站 yígè gōnggòng qìchē zhàn

■ **the school bus** 一辆校车 yíliǎng xiàochē

■ **a bus pass** 一张公共汽车月票 yìzhāng gōnggòng qìchē yuèpiào

■ **a bus station** 一个公共汽车车站 yígè gōnggòng qìchē chēzhàn

■ **a bus ticket** 一张公共汽车票 yìzhāng gōnggòng qìchē piào

bus driver NOUN

公共汽车司机 gōnggòng qìchē sījī [位 wèi]

bush NOUN

灌木 guànmù [丛 cóng]

business NOUN

1 公司 gōngsī [家 jiā]

□ He's got his own business. 他有自己的公司。Tā yǒu zìjǐ de gōngsī.

2 商业 shāngyè *(occupation)*

3 生意 shēngyì

□ to do business with somebody 和某人做生意 hé mǒurén zuò shēngyì

■ **to be away on business** 出差 chūchāi

■ **a business trip** 一次商务旅行 yícì shāngwù lǚxíng

■ **It's none of my business.** 这不关我的事。Zhè bùguān wǒde shì.

businessman NOUN

商人 shāngrén [个 gè]

businesswoman NOUN

女商人 nǚ shāngrén [个 gè]

bust NOUN

胸部 xiōngbù

busy ADJECTIVE

1 忙的 máng de

■ **I'm busy.** 我正忙呢。Wǒ zhèng máng ne.

2 繁忙的 fánmáng de *(shop, street)*

3 忙碌的 mánglù de *(schedule, day)*

4 占线的 zhànxiàn de *(phone line)*

busy signal NOUN (US)

忙音 mángyīn [阵 zhèn]

but CONJUNCTION

但是 dànshì

□ I'd love to come, but I'm busy. 我想来，但是我有事。Wǒ xiǎnglái, dànshì wǒ yǒushì.

butcher NOUN

屠夫 túfū [个 gè]

□ He's a butcher. 他是个屠夫。Tā shì gè túfū.

butcher's NOUN

肉铺 ròupù [个 gè]

butter NOUN

黄油 huángyóu

butterfly NOUN

蝴蝶 húdié [只 zhī]

buttocks PL NOUN

屁股 pìgǔ [个 gè]

button NOUN

1 钮扣 niǔkòu [颗 kē] *(on clothes)*

2 按钮 ànniǔ [个 gè] *(on machine)*

3 徽章 huīzhāng [个 gè] *(US: badge)*

to **buy** VERB

▷ *see also* **buy** NOUN

买 mǎi

□ I bought him an ice cream. 我给他买了个冰激凌。Wǒ gěi tā mǎile gè bīngjīlíng.

■ **to buy something from somebody** 从某人处购买某物 cóng mǒurén chù gòumǎi mǒuwù □ I bought a watch from him. 我从他那儿买了一块表。Wǒ cóng tā nà'er mǎile yíkuài biǎo.

buy NOUN

▷ *see also* **buy** VERB

所买之物 suǒ mǎi zhī wù [件 jiàn]

□ It was a good buy. 那是一件买得好的东西。Nà shì yíjiàn mǎidéhǎo de dōngxi.

to **buzz** VERB
发出嗡嗡声 fāchū wēngwēngshēng *(insect, machine)*

by PREPOSITION

1 由 yóu *(referring to cause, agent)*
□ The thieves were caught by the police. 这些贼是由警察抓住的。Zhèxiē zéi shì yóu jǐngchá zhuāzhù de.
■ **a painting by Picasso** 一幅由毕加索作的画 yìfú yóu Bìjiāsuǒ zuò de huà

2 乘 chéng *(referring to method, manner, means)*
□ by car 乘汽车 chéng qìchē □ by train 乘火车 chéng huǒchē □ by bus 乘巴士 chéng bāshì
■ **to pay by cheque** 以支票支付 yǐ zhīpiào zhīfù
■ **by moonlight** 借助月光 jièzhù yuèguāng

3 经由 jīngyóu *(via, through)*
□ He came in by the back door. 他经由后门进来的。Tā jīngyóu hòumén jìnlai de.

4 靠近 kào jìn *(close to, beside)*
■ **He was standing by the door.** 他在靠近门的地方站着。Tā zài kàojìn mén de dìfāng zhànzhe.
■ **the house by the river** 靠近河的房子 kàojìn hé de fángzi

5 之前 zhīqián *(not later than)*
■ **by 4 o'clock** 四点之前 sìdiǎn zhīqián
■ **by April 7** 四月七号之前 sì yuè qī hào zhīqián
■ **by the time...** 到…的时候 dào...de shíhòu □ By the time I got there it was too late. 到我到那儿的时候已经太晚了。Dào wǒ dào nà'r de shíhòu yǐjīng tài wǎn le.
■ **That's fine by me.** 对我来说没问题。Duì wǒ láishuō méi wèntí.
■ **all by himself** 全靠他自己 quánkào tā zìjǐ
■ **I did it all by myself.** 我全靠自己做成的。Wǒ quán kào zìjǐ zuòchéng de.
■ **by the way** 顺便说一下 shùnbiàn shuō yíxià

bye, bye-bye EXCLAMATION
再见 zàijiàn

> LANGUAGE TIP 拜拜 bābā meaning '88' is often used in informal speech and emails because it sounds like the English **bye-bye**.

bypass NOUN
旁道 pángdào [条 tiáo] *(road)*

Cc

cab NOUN
出租车 chūzūchē [辆 liàng]
cabbage NOUN
卷心菜 juǎnxīncài [颗 kē]
cabin NOUN
船舱 chuáncāng [个 gè] *(on ship)*
cabinet NOUN
柜子 guìzi
■ **a bathroom cabinet** 一个浴室柜子 yígè yùshì guìzi
■ **a drinks cabinet** 一个酒柜 yígè jiǔguì
cable NOUN
电缆 diànlǎn [根 gēn] *(electric)*
cable car NOUN
缆车 lǎnchē [台 tái]
cable television NOUN
有线电视 yǒuxiàn diànshì
cactus NOUN
仙人掌 xiānrénzhǎng [棵 kē]
café NOUN
咖啡馆 kāfēiguǎn [家 jiā]
cafeteria NOUN
自助餐厅 zìzhù cāntīng [个 gè]
cage NOUN
笼子 lóngzi [个 gè]
cagoule NOUN
连帽防雨长夹克衫 liánmào fángyǔ cháng jiákèshān [件 jiàn]
cake NOUN
蛋糕 dàngāo [块 kuài]
to **calculate** VERB
计算 jìsuàn
calculator NOUN
计算器 jìsuànqì [个 gè]
calendar NOUN
日历 rìlì [本 běn]
calf NOUN
1 小牛 xiǎoniú [头 tóu] *(of cow)*
2 腿肚 tuǐdù [个 gè] *(of leg)*
call NOUN
▹ *see also* **call** VERB
电话 diànhuà [次 cì] *(by phone)*
▫ Thanks for your call. 谢谢你的来电。Xièxie nǐde láidiàn.
■ **to make a phone call** 打电话 dǎ diànhuà
■ **to give somebody a call** 打电话给某人 dǎ diànhuà gěi mǒurén
■ **to be on call** *(doctor)* 候诊的 hòuzhěnde
▫ He's on call this evening. 他今天晚上候诊。Tā jīntiān wǎnshàng hòuzhěn.
to **call** VERB
▹ *see also* **call** NOUN
1 打电话 dǎ diànhuà *(by phone)*
▫ I'll tell him you called. 我会转告他你打过电话。Wǒ huì zhuǎngào tā nǐ dǎ guò diànhuà. ▫ This is the number to call. 这是要打的电话号码。Zhè shì yào dǎ de diànhuà hàomǎ.
2 召唤 zhāohuàn *(summon)*
▫ We called the police. 我们报了警。Wǒmen bàole jǐng.
■ **to be called** 被叫作 bèi jiào zuò ▫ He's called Paul. 他被叫作保罗。Tā bèi jiào zuò Bǎoluó. ▫ What's she called? 她被叫作什么？Tā bèi jiào zuò shénme?
■ **Everyone calls him Jimmy.** 大家叫他杰米。Dàjiā jiào tā Jiémi.
■ **to call somebody names** 骂某人 mà mǒurén
■ **He called me an idiot.** 他骂我白痴。Tā mà wǒ báichī.
to **call back** VERB
回电 huídiàn
▫ I'll call back at 6 o'clock. 我会在六点钟回电。Wǒ huì zài liùdiǎnzhōng huídiàn.
▫ Can I call you back? 我能给你回电吗？Wǒ néng gěi nǐ huídiàn ma?
to **call for** VERB
接 jiē
▫ I'll call for you at 2.30. 我会在两点半去接你。Wǒ huì zài liǎngdiǎnbàn qù jiē nǐ.
to **call off** VERB
取消 qǔxiāo
▫ The match was called off. 比赛被取消了。Bǐsài bèi qǔxiāo le.
call box NOUN
电话亭 diànhuàtíng [个 gè]
call centre (US **call center**) NOUN
电话中心 diànhuà zhōngxīn [个 gè]

calm ADJECTIVE
1 冷静的 lěngjìng de *(person)*
2 平静的 píngjìng de *(sea)*
to **calm down** VERB
冷静 lěngjìng
□ Calm down! 冷静！Lěngjìng!
calorie NOUN
卡路里 kǎlùlǐ
calves PL NOUN ▷ *see* **calf**
Cambodia NOUN
柬埔寨 Jiǎnpǔzhài
camcorder NOUN
摄像放像机 shèxiàng fàngxiàng jī [部 bù]
came VERB ▷ *see* **come**
camel NOUN
骆驼 luòtuo [头 tóu]
camera NOUN
1 照相机 zhàoxiàngjī [架 jià] *(for photos)*
2 摄影机 shèyǐngjī [部 bù] *(for filming, TV)*
cameraman NOUN
摄影师 shèyǐngshī [位 wèi]
camera phone NOUN
多媒体手机 duō méitǐ shǒujī [台 tái]
camp NOUN
▷ *see also* **camp** VERB
营地 yíngdì [个 gè]
□ a summer camp 一个夏令营 yígè xiàlìngyíng □ a refugee camp 一个难民营 yígè nànmínyíng
to **camp** VERB
▷ *see also* **camp** NOUN
扎营 zhāyíng
campaign NOUN
运动 yùndòng [场 chǎng]
camper NOUN
1 露营者 lùyíngzhě [个 gè] *(person)*
2 露营车 lùyíngchē [辆 liàng] *(van)*
camping NOUN
露营 lùyíng
■ **to go camping** 外出露营 wàichū lùyíng
□ We went camping in Cornwall. 我们去了康沃尔露营。Wǒmen qùle Kāngwò'ěr lùyíng.
camping gas® NOUN
露营煤气 lùyíng méiqì [罐 guàn]
campsite NOUN
营地 yíngdì [个 gè]
campus NOUN
校园 xiàoyuán [个 gè]
can NOUN
▷ *see also* **can** VERB
1 罐头 guàntou [个 gè] *(for food, drinks)*
□ a can of sweet corn 一个玉米罐头 yígè yùmǐ guàntóu □ a can of beer 一罐啤酒 yíguàn píjiǔ
2 罐 guàn [个 gè] *(for petrol, oil)*
□ a can of petrol 一罐汽油 yíguàn qìyóu
can VERB
▷ *see also* **can** NOUN
1 能 néng *(be able to)*
□ I can't come. 我不能来。Wǒ bùnéng lái.
□ You can do it if you try. 如果试试的话你是能行的。Rúguǒ shìshì de huà nǐ shì néng xíng de. □ You could hire a bike. 你能租一辆自行车。Nǐ néng zū yíliàng zìxíngchē.
□ I couldn't sleep because of the noise. 因为噪音我不能入睡。Yīnwèi zàoyīn wǒ bùnéng rùshuì.
LANGUAGE TIP **can** is sometimes not translated.
□ I can't hear anything. 我什么也听不见。Wǒ shénme yě tīng bújiàn. □ I can't remember. 我记不起来了。Wǒ jì bù qǐlái le.
2 会 huì *(know how to)*
□ I can swim. 我会游泳。Wǒ huì yóuyǒng.
□ Can you speak English? 你会讲英文吗？Nǐ huì jiǎng Yīngwén mā?
3 可以 kěyǐ *(asking permission, requests)*
□ Can I use your phone? 我可以用你的电话吗？Wǒ kěyǐ yòng nǐde diànhuà ma?
□ Can you help me? 你可以帮我一下吗？Nǐ kěyǐ bāng wǒ yíxià ma?
■ **Can I help you? 1** *(in shop)* 您要买点儿什么？Nín yào mǎidiǎn'r shénme? **2** *(in general)* 我能帮你吗？Wǒ néng bāngnǐ ma?
■ **You could be right.** 你可能是对的。Nǐ kěnéng shì duì de.
Canada NOUN
加拿大 Jiānádà
Canadian ADJECTIVE
▷ *see also* **Canadian** NOUN
加拿大的 Jiānádà de
Canadian NOUN
▷ *see also* **Canadian** ADJECTIVE
加拿大人 Jiānádàrén [个 gè]
canal NOUN
运河 yùnhé [条 tiáo]
to **cancel** VERB
取消 qǔxiāo
□ The match was cancelled. 比赛被取消了。Bǐsài bèi qǔxiāo le.
cancellation NOUN
取消 qǔxiāo
cancer NOUN
1 癌症 áizhèng [种 zhǒng]
□ He's got cancer. 他得了癌症。Tā déle áizhèng.
2 巨蟹座 Jùxiè Zuò *(sign)*
□ I'm Cancer. 我是巨蟹座的。Wǒ shì Jùxiè Zuò de.

candidate NOUN
候选人 hòuxuǎnrén [位 wèi] *(for job)*
candle NOUN
蜡烛 làzhú [根 gēn]
candy NOUN (US)
糖果 tángguǒ [块 kuài]
■ **a candy** 一块糖果 yíkuài tángguǒ
candyfloss NOUN
棉花糖 miánhuātáng [朵 duǒ]
LANGUAGE TIP Word for word, this means 'cotton sugar'.
cannabis NOUN
大麻 dàmá [克 kè]
canned ADJECTIVE
罐装的 guànzhuāng de
cannot = **can not**
canoe NOUN
独木船 dúmùchuán [艘 sōu]
canoeing NOUN
划独木船 huá dúmùchuán
■ **to go canoeing** 去划独木船 qù huá dúmùchuán
can-opener NOUN
开罐器 kāi guànqì [个 gè]
can't = **can not**
canteen NOUN
食堂 shítáng [个 gè]
to **canter** VERB
慢跑 mànpǎo
canvas NOUN
帆布 fānbū
cap NOUN
帽 mào [顶 dǐng]
capable ADJECTIVE
有能力的 yǒu nénglì de
■ **to be capable of doing something** 有能力做某事 yǒu nénglì zuò mǒushì
capacity NOUN
1 容量 róngliàng
□ The tank has a 40-litre capacity. 这个容器有四十升的容量。Zhègè róngqì yǒu sìshí shēng de róngliàng.
2 能力 nénglì
□ He has a capacity for hard work. 他有勤奋工作的能力。Tā yǒu qínfèn gōngzuò de nénglì.
capital NOUN
1 首都 shǒudū [个 gè]
□ Cardiff is the capital of Wales. 卡迪夫是威尔士的首都。Kǎdífū shì Wēi'ěrshì de shǒudū.
2 大写字母 dàxiě zìmù [个 gè] *(letter)*
□ Write your address in capitals. 用大写字母写下你的地址。Yòng dàxiě zìmǔ xiěxià nǐde dìzhǐ.
capitalism NOUN
资本主义 zīběn zhǔyì
capital punishment NOUN
死刑 sǐxíng
Capricorn NOUN
摩羯座 Mójié Zuò
□ I'm Capricorn. 我是摩羯座的。Wǒ shì Mójié Zuò de.
captain NOUN
1 队长 duìzhǎng [个 gè] *(of team)*
2 船长 chuánzhǎng [位 wèi] *(of ship)*
to **capture** VERB
1 捕获 bǔhuò *(animal)*
2 俘虏 fúlǔ *(person)*
car NOUN
汽车 qìchē [辆 liàng]
■ **to go by car** 坐汽车去 zuò qìchē qù
□ We went by car. 我们坐汽车去的。Wǒmen zuò qìchē qù de.
■ **a car crash** 一场车祸 yìchǎng chēhuò
caramel NOUN
焦糖 jiāotáng
caravan NOUN
房车 fángchē [辆 liàng]
□ a caravan site 一个房车营地 yígè fángchē yíngdì
carbohydrate NOUN
碳水化合物 tànshuǐhuàhéwù
card NOUN
1 卡片 kǎpiàn [张 zhāng]
□ I got lots of cards on my birthday. 我在生日的时候收到了很多卡片。Wǒ zài shēngrì de shíhòu shōudào le hěnduō kǎpiàn.
2 扑克牌 pūkèpái [张 zhāng]
■ **a card game** 一种扑克游戏 yìzhǒng pūkè yóuxì
■ **to play cards** 打牌 dǎpái
3 名片 míngpiàn [张 zhāng] *(business card)*
DID YOU KNOW...? Business cards should be received and presented with both hands in China.
4 银行卡 yínhángkǎ [张 zhāng] *(debit or credit card)*
cardboard NOUN
纸板 zhǐbǎn [张 zhāng]
■ **a cardboard box** 一个纸板盒子 yígè zhǐbǎn hézi
cardigan NOUN
开襟毛衣 kāijīn máoyī [件 jiàn]
care NOUN
▷ *see also* **care** VERB
照顾 zhàogù
■ **with care** 小心 xiǎoxīn
■ **to take care of** 照顾 zhàogù □ I take care of the children on Saturdays. 星期六都是我来照顾孩子们。Xīngqīliù dōushì wǒ

lái zhàogù háizimen.

■ **Take care!** 1 *(Be careful!)* 小心点！Xiǎoxīn diǎn！ 2 *(Look after yourself!)* 保重！Bǎozhòng！

to **care** VERB

▷ *see also* **care** NOUN

■ **to care about** 在乎 zàihu □ They don't really care about their image. 他们并不在乎他们的形象。Tāmen bìng bú zàihu tāmen de xíngxiàng. □ She doesn't care. 她不在乎。Tā bú zàihu.

■ **to care for somebody** *(patients, old people)* 照料某人 zhàoliào mǒurén

career NOUN

1 事业 shìyè [项 xiàng] *(job, profession)*

□ She had a successful career in journalism. 她有过一项成功的事业作为记者。Tā yǒuguò yíxiàng chénggōng de shìyè zuòwéi jìzhě.

2 职业生涯 zhíyè shēngyá [个 gè] *(working life)*

□ Throughout his career he'd remained committed to helping others. 在整个职业生涯中，他始终乐于助人。Zài zhěnggè zhíyè shēngyá zhōng, tā shǐzhōng lèyúzhùrén.

careful ADJECTIVE

小心的 xiǎoxīn de

■ **Be careful!** 小心！Xiǎoxīn!

carefully ADVERB

谨慎地 jǐnshèn de *(safely)*

□ Drive carefully! 谨慎驾驶！Jǐnshèn jiàshǐ!

■ **Think carefully!** 谨慎考虑！Jǐnshèn kǎolǜ！ □ She carefully avoided talking about it. 她谨慎地避免谈及它。Tā jǐnshèn de bìmiǎn tánjí tā.

careless ADJECTIVE

1 粗心的 cūxīn de

□ She's very careless. 她很粗心。Tā hěn cūxīn. □ It was careless of him to let the dog out. 他真粗心，把狗放了出去。Tā zhēn cūxīn, bǎ gǒu fàng le chūqù. □ a careless driver 一个粗心的司机 yígè cūxīn de sījī

2 疏忽的 shūhu de

■ **a careless mistake** 一个疏忽的错误 yígè shūhū de cuòwù

caretaker NOUN

看门人 kānménrén [个 gè]

car ferry NOUN

汽车渡轮 qìchē dùlún [艘 sōu]

cargo NOUN

货物 huòwù [批 pī]

car hire NOUN

汽车出租 qìchē chūzū

Caribbean NOUN

▷ *see also* **Caribbean** ADJECTIVE

1 加勒比群岛 Jiālèbǐ qúndǎo *(islands)*

□ We're going to the Caribbean. 我们要去加勒比群岛。Wǒmen yào qù Jiālèbǐ qúndǎo.

■ **He's from the Caribbean.** 他来自加勒比群岛。Tā láizì Jiālèbǐ qúndǎo.

2 加勒比海 Jiālèbǐ hǎi *(sea)*

Caribbean ADJECTIVE

▷ *see also* **Caribbean** NOUN

加勒比的 Jiālèbǐ

□ Caribbean food 加勒比的食物 Jiālèbǐ de shíwù

caring ADJECTIVE

关心人的 guānxīn rén de

■ **She's a very caring teacher.** 她是位非常关心人的老师。Tā shì wèi fēicháng guānxīn rén de lǎoshī.

carnival NOUN

狂欢节 kuánghuānjié [个 gè] *(festival)*

carol NOUN

颂歌 sònggē [首 shǒu]

■ **a Christmas carol** 一首圣诞颂歌 yìshǒu Shèngdàn sònggē

car park NOUN

停车场 tíngchēchǎng [处 chù]

carpenter NOUN

木匠 mùjiàng [个 gè]

□ He's a carpenter. 他是个木匠。Tā shì gè mùjiàng.

carpet NOUN

1 地毯 dìtǎn [条 tiáo] *(fitted)*

2 小地毯 xiǎo dìtǎn [块 kuài] *(rug)*

□ a Persian carpet 一块波斯小地毯 yíkuài Bōsī xiǎo dìtǎn

car phone NOUN

车载电话 chēzǎi diànhuà [台 tái]

car rental NOUN (US)

汽车租赁 qìchē zūlìn

carriage NOUN

车厢 chēxiāng [节 jié]

carrier bag NOUN

购物袋 gòuwùdài [个 gè]

carrot NOUN

胡萝卜 húluóbo [根 gēn]

to **carry** VERB

1 抱 bào *(person)*

□ He carried his young son in his arms. 他怀里抱着他的小儿子。Tā huáilǐ bàozhe tāde xiǎo érzi.

2 提 tí *(by hand)*

□ I'll carry your bag. 我会提着你的包。Wǒ huì tízhe nǐde bāo.

3 背 bēi *(on one's back)*

□ She was carrying a rucksack. 她背着一个背包。Tā bēizhe yígè bēibāo.

4 运载 yùnzài *(transport)*
□ a plane carrying 100 passengers 一架运载一百名乘客的飞机 yíjià yùnzài yìbǎi míng chéngkè de fēijī

to **carry on** VERB
继续 jìxù
□ Carry on! 继续！Jìxù！ □ She carried on talking. 她继续讲。Tā jìxù jiǎng.

to **carry out** VERB
执行 zhíxíng *(order, instruction)*

cart NOUN
大车 dàchē [辆 liàng]

carton NOUN
纸盒 zhǐhé [个 gè] *(of milk, juice, yoghurt)*

cartoon NOUN
1 卡通片 kǎtōngpiàn [部 bù] *(film)*
2 漫画 mànhuà [幅 fú] *(in newspaper)*
3 连环画 liánhuán huà [本 běn] *(comic strip)*

cartridge NOUN
1 弹壳 dànké [个 gè] *(for gun)*
2 墨盒 mòhé [个 gè] *(for printer)*

to **carve** VERB
切 qiē *(meat)*

case NOUN
1 行李箱 xínglixiāng [个 gè]
□ I've packed my case. 我已经整理好了行李箱。Wǒ yǐjīng zhěnglǐ hǎo le xínglixiāng.
2 情况 qíngkuàng [种 zhǒng] *(instance)*
□ in some cases 在某些情况下 zài mǒuxiē qíngkuàng xià
■ **in that case** 既然那样 jìrán nàyàng
□ I don't want it. — In that case, I'll take it. 我不想要。— 既然那样，我就要了。Wǒ bùxiǎng yào. — Jìrán nàyàng，wǒ jiù yào le.
■ **in case** 万一 wànyī □ in case it rains 万一下雨 wànyī xiàyǔ
■ **just in case** 以防万一 yǐfáng wànyī
□ Take some money, just in case. 带些钱，以防万一。Dài xiē qián, yǐfáng wànyī.

cash NOUN
▷ *see also* **cash** VERB
现款 xiànkuǎn
□ I'm a bit short of cash. 我有点缺现款。Wǒ yǒudiǎn quē xiànkuǎn.
■ **in cash** 现金 xiànjīn □ £2000 in cash 两千镑现金 liǎngqiān bàng xiànjīn
■ **to pay cash** 付现金 fù xiànjīn
■ **the cash desk** 收银台 shōuyíntái
■ **a cash dispenser** 一台自动提款机 yìtái zìdòng tíkuǎnjī
■ **a cash register** 一台收银机 yìtái shōuyínjī

to **cash** VERB
▷ *see also* **cash** NOUN
兑现 duìxiàn

cashew NOUN
腰果 yāoguǒ [颗 kē]

cashier NOUN
收银员 shōuyínyuán [个 gè]

cashmere NOUN
羊绒 yángróng
□ a cashmere sweater 一件羊绒毛衣 yíjiàn yángróng máoyī

casino NOUN
赌场 dǔchǎng [个 gè]

casserole NOUN
焙盘菜 bèipáncài [份 fèn]
□ I'm going to make a casserole. 我去做一份焙盘菜。Wǒ qù zuò yífèn bèipáncài.
■ **a casserole dish** 一个焙盘 yígè bèipán

cassette NOUN
磁带 cídài [盘 pán]
■ **a cassette player** 一台磁带播放器 yìtái cídài bōfàngqì
■ **a cassette recorder** 一台磁带录音机 yìtái cídài lùyīnjī

cast NOUN
演员表 yǎnyuánbiǎo [份 fèn]
□ the cast of Ugly Betty 丑女贝蒂的演员表 Chǒunǔ Bèidì de yǎnyuánbiǎo

castle NOUN
城堡 chéngbǎo [座 zuò]

casual ADJECTIVE
1 休闲的 xiūxián de
□ casual clothes 休闲服饰 xiūxián fúshì
2 漫不经心的 màn bù jīngxīn de
□ a casual attitude 一种漫不经心的态度 yìzhǒng màn bù jīngxīn de tàidù
3 非正式的 fēizhèngshì de
□ It was just a casual remark. 那只是一个非正式的评论。Nà zhǐshì yígè fēizhèngshì de pínglùn.

casually ADVERB
■ **to dress casually** 穿着休闲 chuānzhuó xiūxián

casualty NOUN
1 急诊室 jízhěnshì [个 gè] *(hospital department)*
2 伤员 shāngyuán [个 gè] *(injured person)*
□ There were no casualties. 那儿没有伤员。Nà'r méiyǒu shāngyuán.
3 伤亡人员 shāngwáng rényuán [批 pī] *(person killed)*
□ The casualties include a young boy. 伤亡人员中包括一个小男孩。Shāngwáng rényuán zhōng bāokuò yígè xiǎo nánhái.

cat NOUN
猫 māo [只 zhī]

catalogue (US **catalog**) NOUN
目录 mùlù [个 gè]

catastrophe NOUN
大灾难 dàzāinàn [场 chǎng]
to **catch** VERB
1 抓获 zhuāhuò
□ They caught the thief. 他们抓获了小偷。Tāmen zhuāhuò le xiǎotōu.
2 捕捉 bǔzhuō
□ My cat catches birds. 我的猫会捕捉鸟。Wǒde māo huì bǔzhuō niǎo.
3 接 jiē
□ She caught the ball easily. 她轻松地接住了球。Tā qīngsōng de jiēzhù le qiú.
4 赶上 gǎnshàng *(bus, train, plane)*
□ We caught the last bus. 我们赶上了末班车。Wǒmen gǎnshàng le mòbānchē.
5 听清 tīngqīng *(hear)*
□ I didn't catch his name. 我没有听清他的名字。Wǒ méiyǒu tīngqīng tāde míngzi.
■ **to catch somebody doing something** 撞见某人做某事 zhuàngjiàn mǒurén zuò mǒushì □ If they catch you smoking... 如果他们撞见你在吸烟… Rúguǒ tāmen zhuàngjiàn nǐ zài xīyān...
■ **to catch a cold** 染上感冒 rǎnshàng gǎnmào
to **catch up** VERB
赶上 gǎn shàng
□ I've got to catch up on my work. 我得赶上我的工作进度。Wǒ děi gǎnshàng wǒde gōngzuò.
category NOUN
种类 zhǒnglèi [个 gè]
catering NOUN
饮食业 yǐnshíyè
cathedral NOUN
大教堂 dàjiàotáng [座 zuò]
Catholic ADJECTIVE
▷ *see also* **Catholic** NOUN
天主教的 Tiānzhǔjiào de
Catholic NOUN
▷ *see also* **Catholic** ADJECTIVE
天主教徒 Tiānzhǔjiào tú [个 gè]
□ I'm a Catholic. 我是个天主教徒。Wǒ shì gè Tiānzhǔjiào tú.
cattle PL NOUN
家畜 jiāchù
caught VERB ▷ *see* **catch**
cauliflower NOUN
菜花 càihuā [头 tóu]
cause NOUN
▷ *see also* **cause** VERB
起因 qǐyīn [个 gè]
to **cause** VERB
▷ *see also* **cause** NOUN
引发 yǐnfā
□ to cause an accident 引发一场事故 yǐnfā yìchǎng shìgù
cautious ADJECTIVE
谨慎的 jǐnshèn de
cave NOUN
山洞 shāndòng [个 gè]
CCTV NOUN *(= closed-circuit television)*
闭路电视 bìlù diànshì [个 gè]
CD NOUN *(= compact disc)*
激光唱片 jīguāng chàngpiàn [张 zhāng]
CD burner NOUN
激光光盘刻录机 jīguāng guāngpán kèlùjī [台 tái]
CD player NOUN
激光唱机 jīguāng chàngjī [部 bù]
CD-ROM NOUN *(= compact disc read-only memory)*
光盘只读存储器 guāngpán zhǐdú cúnchǔ qì [部 bù]
■ **on CD-ROM** 光盘版 guāngpán bǎn
ceasefire NOUN
停火 tínghuǒ [次 cì]
ceiling NOUN
天花板 tiānhuābǎn [块 kuài]
to **celebrate** VERB
庆祝 qìngzhù
celebrity NOUN
名人 míngrén [位 wèi]
celery NOUN
芹菜 qíncài [株 zhū]
cell NOUN
1 牢房 láofáng [间 jiān] *(in prison)*
2 细胞 xìbāo [个 gè] *(in biology)*
cellar NOUN
1 地下室 dìxiàshì [间 jiān]
2 酒窖 jiǔjiào [个 gè] *(for wine)*
cello NOUN
大提琴 dàtíqín [把 bǎ]
□ I play the cello. 我会拉大提琴。Wǒ huì lā dàtíqín.
cellphone NOUN (US)
手机 shǒujī [部 bù]
LANGUAGE TIP Word for word, this means 'hand machine'.
cement NOUN
水泥 shuǐní
cemetery NOUN
墓地 mùdì [块 kuài]
cent NOUN
分 fēn
□ twenty cents 二十分 èrshí fēn
centenary NOUN
一个世纪 yígè shìjì
center NOUN (US)
中心 zhōngxīn [个 gè]
centigrade ADJECTIVE
摄氏的 shèshì de

□ 20 degrees centigrade 二十摄氏度 èrshí shèshìdù

centimetre (US **centimeter**) NOUN
厘米 límǐ

central ADJECTIVE
中心的 zhōngxīn de

central heating NOUN
中央供暖系统 zhōngyāng gōngnuǎn xìtǒng [个 gè]

centre (US **center**) NOUN
中心 zhōngxīn [个 gè]
□ a sports centre 一个运动中心 yígè yùndòng zhōngxīn □ the city centre 市中心 shì zhōngxīn

century NOUN
世纪 shìjì [个 gè]
□ the 20th century 二十世纪 èrshí shìjì
□ in the 21st century 在二十一世纪 zài èrshíyī shìjì

cereal NOUN
谷类食品 gǔlèi shípǐn [种 zhǒng]
□ I have cereal for breakfast. 我吃谷类食品作为早餐。Wǒ chī gǔlèi shípǐn zuòwéi zǎocān.

> **DID YOU KNOW...?**
> Eating cereal, especially with milk, is unusual in China, where people traditionally eat rice porridge, eggs, dumplings or dough sticks for breakfast.

ceremony NOUN
典礼 diǎnlǐ [个 gè]

certain ADJECTIVE
1 肯定的 kěndìng de *(sure)*
□ I'm absolutely certain it was him. 我非常肯定是他。Wǒ fēicháng kěndìng shì tā.
■ **I don't know for certain.** 我不肯定。Wǒ bù kěndìng.
■ **to make certain** 确定 quèdìng □ I made certain the door was locked. 我确定门关好了。Wǒ quèdìng mén guān hǎo le.
2 某 mǒu *(particular)*
□ a certain person 某人 mǒu rén

certainly ADVERB
当然地 dāngrán de
□ I shall certainly be there. 我当然会去的。Wǒ dāngrán huì qù de.
■ **Certainly not!** 当然不行！Dāngrán bùxíng!
■ **So it was a surprise? — It certainly was!** 那么，是个惊喜了？— 当然是！Nàme, shì gè jīngxǐ le?— Dāngrán shì!

certificate NOUN
1 证 zhèng [张 zhāng] *(of birth, marriage)*
2 结业证书 jiéyè zhèngshū [个 gè] *(diploma)*

CFCs PL NOUN
氟利昂 fúlì'áng

chain NOUN
链子 liànzi [条 tiáo]
□ a gold chain 一条金链子 yìtiáo jīn liànzi

chair NOUN
1 椅子 yǐzi [把 bǎ]
□ a table and 4 chairs 一张桌子和四把椅子 yìzhāng zhuōzi hé sìbǎ yǐzi
2 扶手椅 fúshǒuyǐ [把 bǎ] *(armchair)*

chairlift NOUN
升降缆椅 shēngjiàng lǎnyǐ [台 tái]

chairman NOUN
主席 zhǔxí [位 wèi]

chalk NOUN
粉笔 fěnbǐ [支 zhī]

challenge NOUN
▷ *see also* **challenge** VERB
挑战 tiǎozhàn [个 gè]

to **challenge** VERB
▷ *see also* **challenge** NOUN
■ **She challenged me to a race.** 她向我挑战赛跑。Tā xiàng wǒ tiǎozhàn sàipǎo.

challenging ADJECTIVE
有挑战性的 yǒu tiǎozhànxìng de
□ a challenging job 一份有挑战性的工作 yífèn yǒu tiǎozhànxìng de gōngzuò

champagne NOUN
香槟酒 xiāngbīn jiǔ [瓶 píng]

champion NOUN
冠军 guànjūn [位 wèi]

championship NOUN
锦标赛 jǐnbiāo sài [届 jiè]

chance NOUN
1 机会 jīhuì [个 gè]
□ Do you think I've got any chance? 你认为我有机会吗？Nǐ rènwéi wǒ yǒu jīhuì mā?
□ He hasn't much chance of winning. 他赢的机会不大。Tā yíng de jīhuì búdà.
■ **No chance!** 没有机会！Méiyǒu jīhuì!
2 时间 shíjiān
□ I'd like to have a chance to travel. 我希望有时间去旅行。Wǒ xīwàng yǒu shíjiān qù lǚxíng. □ I'll write when I get the chance. 我有时间就会写的。Wǒ yǒu shíjiān jiù huì xiě de.
■ **by chance** 偶然地 ǒurán de □ We met by chance. 我们偶然遇到了。Wǒmen ǒurán yùdào le.
■ **to take a chance** 抓住机会 zhuāzhù jīhuì □ I'm taking no chances! 我不冒险！Wǒ bú màoxiǎn!

to **change** VERB
▷ *see also* **change** NOUN
1 变化 biànhuà
□ The town has changed a lot. 这个小城变化很大。Zhègè xiǎochéng biànhuà hěndà.

2 改变 gǎibiàn

■ **to change one's mind** 改变主意 gǎibiàn zhǔyì □ I've changed my mind. 我改变了主意。Wǒ gǎibiàn le zhǔyì.

3 更换 gēnghuàn *(job, address)*

□ He wants to change his job. 他想更换工作。Tā xiǎng gēnghuàn gōngzuò.

4 换 huàn

□ Can I change this sweater? It's too small. 我能换这件毛衣吗？它太小了。Wǒ néng huàn zhèjiàn máoyī mā? Tā tài xiǎo le.

□ You have to change trains in Paris. 你得在巴黎换乘火车。Nǐ děi zài Bālí huànchéng huǒchē. □ to change gear 换档 huàndǎng

□ to change a nappy 换尿布 huàn niàobù

□ I'm going to change my shoes. 我要去换双鞋。Wǒ yào qù huàn shuāng xié.

5 换衣服 huàn yīfu *(change clothes)*

□ She changed to go to the party. 她换了衣服去参加派对。Tā huàn le yīfu qù cānjiā pàiduì.

■ **to get changed** 换衣服 huàn yīfu □ I'm going to get changed. 我去换衣服。Wǒ qù huàn yīfu.

6 兑换 duìhuàn *(money)*

□ I'd like to change £50. 我想兑换五十镑。Wǒ xiǎng duìhuàn wǔshí bàng.

change NOUN

▷ *see also* **change** VERB

1 变动 biàndòng [种 zhǒng]

□ There's been a change of plan. 计划有所变动。Jìhuà yǒusuǒ biàndòng.

2 替换物 tìhuànwù

■ **for a change** 替换一下 tìhuànyixià

□ Let's play tennis for a change. 我们打网球吧，换一下。Wǒmen dǎ wǎngqiú ba, huànyixià.

■ **a change of clothes** 一套替换的衣服 yítào tìhuàn de yīfu

3 零钱 língqián *(coins)*

□ I haven't got any change. 我没有一点零钱。Wǒ méiyǒu yìdiǎn língqián.

■ **to give somebody change of 10 pounds** 给某人十英镑的零钱 gěi mǒurén shí yīngbàng de língqián

4 找零 zhǎolíng *(money returned)*

■ **Keep the change!** 不用找零了！Búyòng zhǎolíng le!

changing room NOUN

1 试衣室 shìyīshì [间 jiān] *(in shop)*

2 更衣室 gēngyīshì [间 jiān] *(for sport)*

channel NOUN

频道 píndào [个 gè] *(TV)*

□ There's football on the other channel. 在另外一个频道有足球赛。Zài lìngwài yígè píndào yǒu zúqiúsài.

■ **the Channel** 英吉利海峡 Yīngjílì hǎixiá

■ **the Channel Tunnel** 英吉利海峡隧道 Yīngjílì hǎixiá suìdào

chaos NOUN

混乱 hùnluàn [阵 zhèn]

chap NOUN

小伙子 xiǎohuǒzi [个 gè] *(informal)*

□ He's a nice chap. 他是个好小伙子。Tā shì gè hǎo xiǎohuǒzi.

chapel NOUN

礼拜堂 lǐbàitáng [个 gè] *(part of church)*

chapter NOUN

章 zhāng

character NOUN

1 性格 xìnggé [种 zhǒng]

□ Can you give me some idea of his character? 你能说说他性格怎样吗？Nǐ néng shuōshuo tā xìnggé zěnyàng ma?

2 角色 juésè [个 gè] *(in novel, film)*

□ the character played by Depardieu 由德帕迪约扮演的角色 yóu Dépàdíyuē bànyǎn de juésè

3 字 zì [个 gè] *(letter, symbol)*

□ Chinese characters 汉字 Hànzì

■ **She's quite a character.** 她是个怪人。Tā shì gè guàirén.

characteristic NOUN

特征 tèzhēng [种 zhǒng]

■ **to be characteristic of somebody** 反映某人的特性 fǎnyìng mǒurén de tèxìng

charcoal NOUN

木炭 mùtàn [块 kuài]

charge NOUN

▷ *see also* **charge** VERB

费用 fèiyòng [笔 bǐ]

□ Is there a charge for delivery? 投递需要费用吗？Tóudì xūyào fèiyòng mā?

■ **an extra charge** 一笔额外费用 yìbǐ éwài fèiyòng

■ **free of charge** 免费 miǎnfèi

■ **to reverse the charges** 让接电话方付款 ràng jiē diànhuà fāng fùkuǎn □ I'd like to reverse the charges. 我想让接电话方付款。Wǒ xiǎng ràng jiē diànhuà fāng fùkuǎn.

■ **to be in charge** 负责 fùzé □ Mrs Jones was in charge of the group. 琼斯太太曾负责这个团体。Qióngsī tàitai céng fùzé zhègè tuántǐ.

to **charge** VERB

▷ *see also* **charge** NOUN

1 要价 yàojià

□ How much did he charge you? 他问你要价多少？Tā wèn nǐ yàojià duōshǎo?

□ How much do you charge? 你要价多少？Nǐ yàojiàduōshǎo? □ They charge £10 an hour. 他们要价十镑每小时。Tāmen yàojià shí bàng měixiǎoshí.

2 收费 shōufèi *(customer, client)*

□ They will charge you for home delivery. 他们会收你送货费。Tāmen huì shōu nǐ sònghuòfèi.

3 控告 kònggào *(with crime)*

□ The police have charged him with murder. 警方控告他谋杀。Jǐngfāng kònggào tā móushā.

4 使充电 shǐ chōngdiàn *(battery)*

charity NOUN

慈善机构 císhàn jīgòu [个 gè] *(organization)*

□ He gave the money to charity. 他把钱捐给了慈善机构。Tā bǎ qián juāngěi le císhàn jīgòu.

charm NOUN

1 魅力 mèilì [种 zhǒng] *(of person)*

2 吸引力 xīyǐnlì [种 zhǒng] *(of place, thing)*

charming ADJECTIVE

1 有魅力的 yǒu mèilì de *(person)*

2 有吸引力的 yǒu xīyǐnlì de *(place, custom)*

chart NOUN

图表 túbiǎo [个 gè]

□ The chart shows the rise of unemployment. 图表显示失业率的上升。Túbiǎo xiǎnshì shīyèlǜ de shàngshēng.

■ **the charts** 排行榜 páihángbǎng

□ This album is number one in the charts. 这张专辑现在是排行榜的第位。Zhèzhāng zhuānjí xiànzài shì páihángbǎng de dìyīwèi.

charter flight NOUN

包机 bāojī [架 jià]

to **chase** VERB

追赶 zhuīgǎn

chat NOUN

▷ *see also* **chat** VERB

聊天 liáotiān [次 cì]

■ **to have a chat** 聊一下天 liáoyixià tiān

to **chat** VERB

▷ *see also* **chat** NOUN

聊天 liáotiān

■ **to chat somebody up** *(informal)* 与某人闲聊 yǔ mǒurén xiánliáo

□ He likes to chat up the girls. 他喜欢和女孩们闲聊。Tā xǐhuan hé nǚháimen xiánliáo.

■ **She likes chatting online.** 她喜欢在网上聊天。Tā xǐhuān zài wǎngshàng liáotiān.

chatroom NOUN

聊天室 liáotiānshì [个 gè]

chat show NOUN

访谈节目 fǎngtán jiémù [个 gè]

chauvinist NOUN

■ **a male chauvinist** 一个大男子主义者 yígè dànánzǐzhǔyìzhě

cheap ADJECTIVE

便宜的 piányi de

□ a cheap T-shirt 一件便宜的体恤 yíjiàn piányì de tīxu

cheaper ADJECTIVE

更便宜 gèng piányì

□ It's cheaper to go by bus. 坐公车去更便宜。Zuò gōngchē qù gèng piányì.

to **cheat** VERB

▷ *see also* **cheat** NOUN

作弊 zuòbì

□ You're cheating! 你是在作弊！Nǐ shì zài zuòbì!

cheat NOUN

▷ *see also* **cheat** VERB

作弊者 zuòbìzhě [个 gè] *(in games, exams)*

check NOUN

▷ *see also* **check** VERB

1 检查 jiǎnchá [次 cì]

□ a security check 一次安全检查 yícì ānquán jiǎnchá

2 支票 zhīpiào [张 zhāng] (US)

□ to write a check 开一张支票 kāiyizhāng zhīpiào

3 账单 zhàngdān [张 zhāng] *(US: in restaurant)*

□ Can we have the check, please? 有劳，能给我们账单吗？Yǒuláo, néng gěi wǒmen zhàngdān mā?

to **check** VERB

▷ *see also* **check** NOUN

1 核对 héduì

□ I'll check the time of the train. 我会核对火车的时刻。Wǒ huì héduì huǒchē de shíkè.

2 检查 jiǎnchá *(passport, ticket)*

■ **to check with somebody** 向某人求证 xiàng mǒurén qiúzhèng □ I'll check with Ian what time the bus leaves. 我会向伊安求证巴士开车的时间。Wǒ huì xiàng Yī'ān qiúzhèng bāshì kāichē de shíjiān.

to **check in** VERB

1 入住登记 rùzhù dēngjì *(at hotel)*

■ **I'd like to check in.** 我想办理入住登记。Wǒ xiǎng bànlǐ rùzhù dēngjì.

2 办理登机 bànlǐ dēngjī *(at airport)*

□ Where do we check in? 我们在哪儿办理登机？Wǒmen zài nǎ'r bànlǐ dēngjī?

to **check out** VERB

结账 jiézhàng *(of hotel)*

□ Can I check out, please? 我能结账吗？Wǒ néng jiézhàng ma?

checkers PL NOUN (US)

西洋跳棋 xīyáng tiàoqí
□ to play checkers 玩西洋跳棋 wán xīyáng tiàoqí

check-in NOUN
登记 dēngjì [次 cì]

checking account NOUN (US)
支票账户 zhīpiào zhànghù [个 gè]

checkout NOUN
结账 jiézhàng [次 cì]

check-up NOUN
1 体检 tǐjiǎn [次 cì] *(by doctor)*
2 牙科检查 yákē jiǎnchá [次 cì] *(by dentist)*

cheek NOUN
脸颊 liǎnjiá [个 gè]
□ He kissed her on the cheek. 他在脸颊上吻了她。Tā zài liǎnjiá shàng wěn le tā.
■ **What a cheek!** 真厚颜无耻！Zhēn hòuyánwúchǐ!

cheeky ADJECTIVE
恬不知耻的 tiánbùzhīchǐ de
□ Don't be cheeky! 不要恬不知耻！Búyào tiánbùzhīchǐ
■ **a cheeky smile** 一个坏笑 yígè huàixiào

to **cheer** VERB
▷ *see also* **cheer** NOUN
欢呼 huānhū
■ **to cheer somebody up** 让某人高兴起来 ràng mǒurén gāoxìng qǐlái □ I was trying to cheer him up. 我曾试图让他高兴起来。Wǒ céng shìtú ràng tā gāoxìng qǐlái.
■ **Cheer up!** 高兴起来！Gāoxìng qǐlái!

cheer NOUN
▷ *see also* **cheer** VERB
欢呼 huānhū [阵 zhèn]
■ **to give a cheer** 欢呼一下 huānhū yixià
■ **Cheers! 1** *(good health)* 干杯！Gānbēi!
2 *(thanks)* 谢谢！Xièxie!

cheerful ADJECTIVE
兴高采烈的 xìnggāocǎiliè de

cheerio EXCLAMATION
再见！Zàijiàn!

cheese NOUN
干酪 gānlào [块 kuài]

chef NOUN
厨师 chúshī [位 wèi]

chemical NOUN
化学剂 huàxué jì [种 zhǒng]

chemist NOUN
1 药店 yàoshāng [个 gè] *(shop)*
□ You get it from the chemist. 你在药店可以买到。Nǐ zài yàodiàn kěyǐ mǎidào.
2 化学家 huàxuéjiā [位 wèi] *(scientist)*

chemistry NOUN
化学 huàxué
□ the chemistry lab 化学实验室 huàxué shíyànshì

cheque (US **check**) NOUN
支票 zhīpiào [张 zhāng]
□ to write a cheque 开一张支票 kāiyizhāng zhīpiào □ to pay by cheque 用支票付款 yòng zhīpiào fùkuǎn

chequebook (US **checkbook**) NOUN
支票簿 zhīpiào bù [本 běn]

cherry NOUN
樱桃 yīngtáo [颗 kē]

chess NOUN
1 象棋 xiàngqí *(Chinese chess)*
□ to play chess 下象棋 xià xiàngqí
2 国际象棋 guójì xiàngqí *(international chess)*

chest NOUN
胸部 xiōngbù
□ I've got a pain in my chest. 我的胸部痛。Wǒde xiōngbù tòng.
■ **a chest of drawers** 一个五斗橱 yígè wǔdǒuchú

chestnut NOUN
栗子 lìzi [颗 kē]

to **chew** VERB
嚼 jiáo

chewing gum NOUN
口香糖 kǒuxiāngtáng

chick NOUN
小鸡 xiǎojī [只 zhī]
□ a hen and her chicks 一只母鸡和她的小鸡们 yìzhī mǔjī hé tāde xiǎojīmen

chicken NOUN
1 鸡 jī [只 zhī] *(bird)*
2 鸡肉 jīròu [块 kuài] *(meat)*

chickenpox NOUN
水痘 shuǐdòu [颗 kē]

chickpeas PL NOUN
鹰嘴豆 yīngzuǐdòu [粒 lì]

chief NOUN
▷ *see also* **chief** ADJECTIVE
长官 zhǎngguān [个 gè]
□ the chief of security 安全长官 ānquán zhǎngguān

chief ADJECTIVE
▷ *see also* **chief** NOUN
首要的 shǒuyào de
□ His chief reason for resigning was stress. 他辞职的首要原因是压力。Tā cízhí de shǒuyào yuányīn shì yālì.

child NOUN
1 儿童 értóng [个 gè]
□ a child of six 一个六岁的儿童 yígè liùsuì de értóng
2 孩子 háizi [个 gè] *(son, daughter)*
□ She's just had her second child. 她刚生了第二个孩子。Tā gāng shēng le dì'èr gè háizi. □ They've got three children. 他们有三个孩子。Tāmen yǒu sāngè háizi.

English-Chinese

C

childish ADJECTIVE
幼稚的 yòuzhì de
child minder NOUN
保姆 bǎomǔ [个 gè]
children PL NOUN ▹*see* **child**
Chile NOUN
智利 Zhìlì
to **chill** VERB
使冷藏 shǐ lěngcáng
□ Put the wine in the fridge to chill. 把酒放进冰箱冷藏。Bǎ jiǔ fàngjìn bīngxiāng lěngcáng.
chilli (US **chili**) NOUN
辣椒 làjiāo [个 gè]
chilly ADJECTIVE
相当冷的 xiāngdāng lěng de
chimney NOUN
烟囱 yāncōng [节 jié]
chin NOUN
下巴 xiàba [个 gè]
China NOUN
中国 Zhōngguó
LANGUAGE TIP Word for word, this means 'middle kingdom'.
■ **in China** 在中国 zài Zhōngguó
china NOUN
陶瓷 táocí
□ a china plate 一个陶瓷盘子 yígè táocí pánzi
Chinese ADJECTIVE
▹*see also* **Chinese** NOUN
中国的 Zhōngguó de
□ a Chinese restaurant 一家中国餐馆 yìjiā Zhōngguó cānguǎn
■ **a Chinese man** 一个中国男人 yígè Zhōngguó nánrén
■ **a Chinese woman** 一个中国女人 yígè Zhōngguó nǚrén
Chinese NOUN
▹*see also* **Chinese** ADJECTIVE
1 中国人 Zhōngguórén [个 gè] *(person)*
■ **the Chinese** *(people)* 中国人 Zhōngguórén
2 汉语 Hànyǔ *(language)*
chip NOUN
1 薯条 shǔtiáo [根 gēn]
□ We ordered steak and chips. 我们点了牛排和薯条。Wǒmén diǎnle niúpái hé shǔtiáo.
2 薯片 shǔpiàn [片 piàn] (US: *crisp*)
3 集成电路片 jíchéng diànlù piàn [块 kuài] *(in computer)*
chiropodist NOUN
足医 zúyī [位 wèi]
□ He's a chiropodist. 他是位足医。Tā shì wèi zúyī.

chives PL NOUN
细葱 xìcōng
chocolate NOUN
1 巧克力 qiǎokèlì
□ a chocolate cake 一块巧克力蛋糕 yíkuài qiǎokèlì dàngāo □ a bar of chocolate 一板巧克力 yìbǎn qiǎokèlì □ a piece of chocolate 一块巧克力 yíkuài qiǎokèlì
■ **a cup of hot chocolate** 一杯热巧克力 yìbēi rè qiǎokèlì
2 巧克力糖 qiǎokèlì táng [颗 kē]
□ a box of chocolates 一盒巧克力糖 yìhé qiǎokèlì táng
choice NOUN
选择 xuǎnzé [个 gè]
□ I had no choice. 我没得选择。Wǒ méi de xuǎnzé.
choir NOUN
合唱团 héchàngtuán [个 gè]
to **choke** VERB
噎住 yēzhù
□ She choked on a fishbone. 她被一根鱼骨噎住了。Tā bèi yìgēn yúgǔ yēzhù le.
to **choose** VERB
选择 xuǎnzé
□ It's difficult to choose. 难以选择。Nányǐ xuǎnzé.
chop NOUN
▹*see also* **chop** VERB
排骨 páigǔ [根 gēn]
□ a pork chop 一匹猪排 yìpí zhūpái
to **chop** VERB
▹*see also* **chop** NOUN
切 qiē
□ Chop the onions. 切洋葱。Qiē yángcōng.
to **chop down** VERB
砍倒 kǎndǎo *(tree)*
to **chop up** VERB
切 qiē
chopsticks PL NOUN
筷子 kuàizi
chose, chosen VERB ▹*see* **choose**
Christ NOUN
耶稣 Yēsū
christening NOUN
洗礼 xǐlǐ [次 cì]
Christian ADJECTIVE
▹*see also* **Christian** NOUN
基督教的 Jīdūjiào de
Christian NOUN
▹*see also* **Christian** ADJECTIVE
基督徒 Jīdūtú [个 gè]
Christian name NOUN
教名 jiàomíng [个 gè]
Christmas NOUN

圣诞节 Shèngdàn Jié [个 gè]
■ **Happy Christmas!** 圣诞快乐！Shèngdàn Kuàilè!
■ **at Christmas** 在圣诞节 zài Shèngdànjié
■ **for Christmas** 为了圣诞节 wèile Shèngdànjié
■ **Christmas Day** 圣诞节 Shèngdànjié
■ **Christmas Eve** 圣诞夜 Shèngdàn Yè
■ **a Christmas tree** 一棵圣诞树 yìkē Shèngdànshù
■ **a Christmas card** 一张圣诞卡 yìzhāng Shèngdànkǎ
■ **Christmas dinner** 圣诞晚餐 Shèngdàn wǎncān

chunk NOUN
块 kuài
□ Cut the meat into chunks. 把肉切成块。Bǎ ròu qiē chéng kuài.

church NOUN
教堂 jiàotáng [座 zuò]
□ I don't go to church every Sunday. 我不是每周日都去教堂。Wǒ búshì měi zhōurì dōu qù jiàotáng.
■ **the Church of England** 英格兰国教 Yīnggélán guójiào

cider NOUN
苹果酒 píngguǒ jiǔ [瓶 píng]

cigar NOUN
雪茄烟 xuějiā yān [支 zhī]

cigarette NOUN
香烟 xiāngyān [支 zhī]

cigarette lighter NOUN
打火机 dǎhuǒjī [个 gè]

cinema NOUN
电影院 diànyǐng yuàn [个 gè]

cinnamon NOUN
肉桂 ròuguì [片 piàn]

circle NOUN
圆圈 yuánquān [个 gè]

circular ADJECTIVE
圆形的 yuánxíng de

circulation NOUN
1 循环 xúnhuán *(of blood)*
2 发行 fāxíng *(of newspaper)*

circumstances PL NOUN
情况 qíngkuàng
□ in the circumstances 在这种情况下 zài zhèzhǒng qíngkuàng xià □ under no circumstances 决不 juébù

circus NOUN
马戏团 mǎxì tuán [个 gè]

citizen NOUN
公民 gōngmín [个 gè]
□ a British citizen 一个英国公民 yígè Yīngguó gōngmín

citizenship NOUN
公民身份 gōngmín shēnfèn [种 zhǒng]

City NOUN
■ **the City** 伦敦商业区 Lúndūn shāngyèqū

city NOUN
城市 chéngshì [座 zuò]
■ **the city centre** 市中心 shì zhōngxīn
□ It's in the city centre. 在市中心。Zài shì zhōngxīn.

civilization NOUN
文明 wénmíng [种 zhǒng]

civilized ADJECTIVE
文明的 wénmíng de *(society, people)*

civil servant NOUN
公务员 gōngwùyuán [名 míng]

civil war NOUN
内战 nèizhàn [场 chǎng]

to **claim** VERB
▷ *see also* **claim** NOUN
1 声称 shēngchēng
□ He claims to have found the money. 他声称找到了那些钱。Tā shēngchēng zhǎodào le nàxiē qián.
2 索取 suǒqǔ *(compensation, benefit)*
□ She's claiming unemployment benefit. 她正在索取失业救济。Tā zhèngzài suǒqǔ shīyè jiùjì.
3 要求 yāoqiú *(expenses, inheritance)*
□ She was able to claim expenses for her trip. 她可以要求差旅费。Tā kěyǐ yāoqiú chāilǚ fèi.
■ **to claim on one's insurance** 提出保险索赔的要求 tíchū bǎoxiǎn suǒpéi de yāoqiú
□ We claimed on our insurance. 我们提出了保险索赔的要求。Wǒmen tíchū le bǎoxiǎn suǒpéi de yāoqiú.

claim NOUN
▷ *see also* **claim** VERB
索赔 suǒpéi [项 xiàng]
□ an insurance claim 一项保险索赔 yíxiàng bǎoxiǎn suǒpéi
■ **to make a claim** 提出要求 tíchū yāoqiú

to **clap** VERB
鼓掌 gǔzhǎng
□ Everybody clapped. 每个人都鼓掌了。Měigèrén dōu gǔzhǎng le.
■ **to clap one's hands** 拍手 pāishǒu □ My dog sits when I clap my hands. 当我拍手的时候我的狗就会坐下。Dāng wǒ pāishǒu de shíhòu wǒde gǒu jiù huì zuòxià.

clarinet NOUN
单簧管 dānhuángguǎn [根 gēn]

to **clash** VERB
1 相抵触 xiāng dǐchù *(colours)*
□ These two colours clash. 这两种颜色相抵触。Zhè liǎngzhǒng yánsè xiāng dǐchù.
2 相冲突 xiāng chōngtū *(events)*

□ The concert clashes with Ann's party. 音乐会和安的派对相冲突了。Yīnyuèhuì hé Ān de pàiduì xiāng chōngtū le.

class NOUN

1 班级 bānjí [个 gè]
□ We're in the same class. 我们在同一个班级。Wǒmen zài tóngyígè bānjí.

2 课 kè [堂 táng]
□ I go to dancing classes. 我在上舞蹈课。Wǒ zài shàng wǔdǎokè.

classic NOUN
▷ *see also* **classic** ADJECTIVE
经典 jīngdiǎn [种 zhǒng]

classic ADJECTIVE
▷ *see also* **classic** NOUN
经典的 jīngdiǎn de
□ a classic example 一个经典的例子 yígè jīngdiǎn de lìzi

classical ADJECTIVE
古典的 gǔdiǎn de
□ classical music 古典音乐 gǔdiǎn yīnyuè

classmate NOUN
同学 tóngxué [位 wèi]

classroom NOUN
教室 jiàoshì [间 jiān]

claw NOUN
爪子 zhuǎzi [只 zhī]

clay NOUN
黏土 niántǔ

clean ADJECTIVE
▷ *see also* **clean** VERB

1 干净的 gānjìng de
□ a clean shirt 一件干净的衬衫 yíjiàn gānjìng de chènshān

2 洁净的 jié jìng de
□ clean water 洁净的水 jiéjìng de shuǐ

to **clean** VERB
▷ *see also* **clean** ADJECTIVE

1 弄干净 nòng gānjìng *(car, cooker)*

2 打扫 dǎsǎo *(room)*
■ **to clean one's teeth** 刷牙 shuāyá

cleaner NOUN
清洁工 qīngjié gōng [位 wèi] *(person)*

cleaner's NOUN
洗衣店 xǐyīdiàn [家 jiā]
□ He took his coat to the cleaner's. 他把外套拿去了洗衣店。Tā bǎ wàitào náqù le xǐyīdiàn.

clear ADJECTIVE
▷ *see also* **clear** VERB

1 清楚的 qīngchǔ de
□ a clear explanation 一个清楚的解释 yígè qīngchǔ de jiěshì
■ **Have I made myself clear?** 我表达清楚了吗？Wǒ biǎodá qīngchǔ le mā？

2 清晰的 qīngxī de
□ a clear view 一个清晰的视野 yígè qīngxī de shìyě

3 明显的 míngxiǎn de
□ It's clear you don't believe me. 很明显你不信任我。Hěn míngxiǎn nǐ bú xìnrèn wǒ.

4 透明的 tòumíng de
□ It comes in a clear bottle. 它是用一个透明的瓶子装的。Tā shì yòng yígè tòumíng de píngzi zhuāng de.

5 畅通的 chàngtōng de
□ The road's clear now. 道路现在畅通了。Dàolù xiànzài chàngtōng le.

to **clear** VERB
▷ *see also* **clear** ADJECTIVE

1 清空 qīngkōng
□ The police are clearing the road after the accident. 事故后，警方在清空道路。Shìgù hòu，jǐngfāng zài qīngkōng dàolù.

2 放晴 fàngqíng *(weather, sky)*
□ The sky has cleared. 天空放晴了。Tiānkōng fàngqíng le.
■ **to be cleared of a crime** 宣告罪名不成立 xuāngào zuìmíng bù chénglì □ She was cleared of murder. 她被宣告谋杀罪不成立。Tā bèi xuāngào móushāzuì bù chénglì.
■ **to clear the table** 收拾饭桌 shōushi fànzhuō □ I'll clear the table. 我来收拾饭桌。Wǒ lái shōushi fànzhuō.

to **clear off** VERB
走开 zǒukāi *(informal)*
□ Clear off and leave me alone! 走开，让我单独待一会儿！Zǒukāi, ràng wǒ dāndú dāi yihui'r！

to **clear up** VERB

1 清理 qīnglǐ
□ Who's going to clear all this up? 谁去把所有这些都清理了？Shéi qù bǎ suǒyǒu zhèxiē dōu qīnglǐ le？

2 处理 chùlǐ
□ I'm sure we can clear up this problem right away. 我确信我们可以马上把这个问题处理了。Wǒ quèxìn wǒmen kěyǐ mǎshàng bǎ zhègè wèntí chùlǐ le.
■ **I think it's going to clear up.** *(weather)* 我猜就要天晴了。Wǒ cāi jiù yào tiānqíng le.

clearly ADVERB

1 有条理地 yǒutiáolǐ de
□ She explained it very clearly. 她解释得非常有条理。Tā jiěshì de fēicháng yǒutiáolǐ.

2 清楚地 qīngchǔ de
□ You could clearly make out the coastline. 你能够清楚地辨认出海岸线。Nǐ nénggòu qīngchǔ de biànrèn chū hǎi'ànxiàn.

3 清晰地 qīngxī de

◻ to speak clearly 清晰地讲话 qīngxī de jiǎnghuà
4 显然地 xiǎnrán de
◻ Clearly this project will cost money. 显然地，这个项目会费钱。Xiǎnrán de, zhègè xiàngmù huì fèiqián.

clever ADJECTIVE
1 聪明的 cōngmíng de
◻ She's very clever. 她非常聪明。Tā fēicháng cōngmíng.
2 巧妙的 qiǎomiào de *(ingenious)*
◻ What a clever idea! 好一个巧妙的想法！Hǎo yígè qiǎomiào de xiǎngfǎ!

click NOUN
▷ *see also* **click** VERB
滴答声 dīdāsheng [下 xià] *(of door, camera)*

to **click** VERB
▷ *see also* **click** NOUN
点击 diǎnjī *(with mouse)*
◻ to click on an icon 点击一个图标 diǎnjī yígè túbiāo

client NOUN
1 委托人 wěituōrén [个 gè] *(of lawyer)*
2 顾客 gùkè [位 wèi] *(of company, shop)*

cliff NOUN
悬崖 xuányá [个 gè]

climate NOUN
气候 qìhòu [种 zhǒng]

to **climb** VERB
1 攀登 pāndēng
◻ Her ambition is to climb Mount Everest. 她的梦想是攀登珠穆郎玛峰。Tāde mèngxiǎng shì pāndēng Zhūmùlángmǎ fēng.
2 爬上 páshàng
◻ They climbed a tree. 他们爬上了一棵树。Tāmen páshàng le yìkē shù. ◻ He climbed the ladder carefully. 他小心地爬上梯子。Tā xiǎoxīn de páshàng tīzi. ◻ We had to climb three flights of stairs. 我们得爬上三段楼梯。Wǒmen děi páshàng sānduàn lóutī.

climber NOUN
登山者 dēngshānzhě [个 gè]

climbing NOUN
登山 dēngshān
■ **to go climbing** 去登山 qù dēngshān
◻ We're going climbing in Scotland. 我们要去苏格兰登山。Wǒmen yào qù Sūgélán dēngshān.

Clingfilm® NOUN
保鲜膜 bǎoxiānmó [卷 juǎn]

clinic NOUN
诊所 zhěnsuǒ [家 jiā]

clip NOUN
1 发卡 fàqiǎ [个 gè] *(for hair)*
2 片段 piànduàn [个 gè] *(film)*
◻ some clips from Disney's latest film 迪斯尼最新电影里的一些片段 Dísīní zuìxīn diànyǐng lǐ de yìxiē piànduàn

clippers PL NOUN
■ **nail clippers** 指甲刀 zhǐjiadāo [个 gè]

cloakroom NOUN
1 衣帽间 yīmàojiān [个 gè] *(for coats)*
2 厕所 cèsuǒ [处 chù] *(toilet)*

clock NOUN
钟 zhōng [个 gè]

to **clock in** VERB
打卡上班 dǎkǎ shàngbān

to **clock off** VERB
打卡下班 dǎkǎ xiàbān

clockwork NOUN
发条 fātiáo [个 gè]
■ **Everything went like clockwork.** 一切进行得像发条一样顺利。Yíqiè jìnxíng dé xiàng fātiáo yíyàng shùnlì.

clone NOUN
▷ *see also* **clone** VERB
克隆 kèlóng [个 gè] *(animal, plant)*

to **clone** VERB
▷ *see also* **clone** NOUN
克隆 kèlóng
◻ a cloned sheep 一只克隆羊 yìzhī kèlóng yáng

close ADJECTIVE, ADVERB
▷ *see also* **close** VERB
1 近的 jìn de
◻ The shops are very close. 商店离得很近。Shāngdiàn lí de hěn jìn.
■ **close to** 近 jìn ◻ The youth hostel is close to the station. 这家青年旅社离车站近。Zhèjiā qīngnián lǚshè lí chēzhàn jìn.
■ **Come closer.** 靠近点。Kào jìn diǎn.
2 有血缘关系的 yǒu xuěyuánguānxì de *(relative)*
◻ We're just inviting close relations. 我们只邀请一些有血缘关系的亲戚。Wǒmen zhǐ yāoqǐng yìxiē yǒu xuěyuánguānxì de qīnqì.
3 亲密的 qīnmì de *(friend)*
◻ She's a close friend of mine. 她是我的一个亲密朋友。Tā shì wǒde yígè qīnmì péngyǒu. ◻ I'm very close to my sister. 我和我姐姐很亲密。Wǒ hé wǒ jiějie hěn qīnmì.
4 势均力敌的 shìjūnlìdí de *(contest)*
◻ It's going to be very close. 它将会是势均力敌的。Tā jiāng huì shì shìjūnlìdí de.
5 闷的 mēn de *(weather)*
◻ It's close this afternoon. 今天下午天气很闷。Jīntiān xiàwǔ tiānqì hěn mēn.

to **close** VERB

▷ *see also* **close** ADJECTIVE, ADVERB

1 关上 guānshàng
□ Please close the door. 请关上门。Qǐng guānshàng mén. □ The doors close automatically. 这些门会自动关上。Zhèxiē mén huì zìdòng guānshàng.

2 关闭 guānbì
□ What time does the library close? 图书馆什么时候关闭？Túshūguǎn shénme shíhòu guānbì?

to **close down** VERB
关闭 guānbì *(factory, business)*

closed ADJECTIVE
1 关着的 guānzhe de *(door, window)*
2 关着门的 guānzhe mén de *(shop, library)*
3 封锁着的 fēngsuǒzhe de *(road)*

closely ADVERB
仔细地 zǐxì de *(examine, watch)*

closet NOUN (US)
壁橱 bìchú [个 gè]

cloth NOUN
布料 bùliào [块 kuài] *(fabric)*
■ **a cloth** 一块布 yíkuài bù □ Wipe it with a damp cloth. 用一块湿布把它擦干净。Yòng yíkuài shībù bǎ tā cā gānjìng.

clothes PL NOUN
衣服 yīfu
□ new clothes 新衣服 xīn yīfu
■ **to take one's clothes off** 脱衣服 tuō yīfu
■ **a clothes line** 一根晾衣绳 yìgēn liàngyīshéng
■ **a clothes peg** 一个晾衣夹 yígè liàngyījiá

cloud NOUN
云 yún [片 piàn]

cloudy ADJECTIVE
多云的 duōyún de
■ **It's cloudy.** 天空多云。Tiānkōng duōyún.

clove NOUN
丁香 dīngxiāng
■ **a clove of garlic** 一瓣蒜 yíbàn suàn

clown NOUN
小丑 xiǎochǒu [个 gè]

club NOUN
1 俱乐部 jùlèbù [个 gè]
□ a youth club 一家青年俱乐部 yìjiā qīngnián jùlèbù □ a golf club 一家高尔夫俱乐部 yìjiā gāo'ěrfū jùlèbù
2 夜总会 yèzǒnghuì [家 jiā] *(nightclub)*
■ **clubs** *(in cards)* 梅花 méihuā □ the ace of clubs 梅花尖 méihuā jiān

clubbing NOUN
■ **to go clubbing** 去俱乐部玩 qù jùlèbù wán

clue NOUN
1 线索 xiànsuǒ [条 tiáo] *(in investigation)*
2 提示 tíshì [个 gè] *(in crossword, game)*
■ **I haven't a clue.** 我一无所知。Wǒ yìwúsuǒzhī.

clumsy ADJECTIVE
笨拙的 bènzhuó de

clutch NOUN
离合器 líhéqì [个 gè] *(of car)*

coach NOUN
1 长途汽车 chángtú qìchē [辆 liàng]
□ We went there by coach. 我们乘长途汽车去那儿的。Wǒmen chéng chángtú qìchē qù nà'r de.
■ **the coach station** 长途汽车站 chángtú qìchē zhàn
■ **a coach trip** 一次长途旅行 yícì chángtú lǚxíng
2 教练 jiàoliàn [位 wèi] *(trainer)*
□ the French coach 法国教练 Fǎguó jiàoliàn

coal NOUN
煤 méi
■ **a coal mine** 一个煤矿 yígè méikuàng
■ **a coal miner** 一个煤矿工人 yígè méikuàng gōngrén

coarse ADJECTIVE
1 粗糙的 cūcāo de *(surface, fabric)*
□ The bag was made of coarse cloth. 这个包是用粗糙的布料做的。Zhègè bāo shì yòng cūcāo de bùliào zuò de.
2 粗俗的 cūsú de *(vulgar)*
□ coarse language 粗俗的语言 cūsú de yǔyán

coast NOUN
海岸 hǎi'àn [个 gè]
□ It's on the west coast of Scotland. 在苏格兰的西海岸上。Zài Sūgélán de xī hǎi'àn shàng.

coastguard NOUN
海岸警卫 hǎi'àn jǐngwèi [名 míng]

coat NOUN
外套 wàitào [件 jiàn]
□ a warm coat 一件暖和的外套 yíjiàn nuǎnhuo de wàitào
■ **a coat of paint** 一层油漆 yìcéng yóuqī

coat hanger NOUN
衣架 yījià [个 gè]

cobweb NOUN
蜘蛛网 zhīzhūwǎng [个 gè]

cocaine NOUN
可卡因 kěkǎyīn [克 kè]

cock NOUN
公鸡 gōngjī [只 zhī] *(cockerel)*

cockerel NOUN
公鸡 gōngjī [只 zhī]

cocoa NOUN
可可 kěkě

□ a cup of cocoa 一杯可可 yìbēi kěkě

coconut NOUN

椰子 yēzi [个 gè]

cod NOUN

鳕鱼 xuěyú [条 tiáo]

code NOUN

1 代码 dàimǎ [个 gè]

□ It's written in code. 它是用代码写的。Tā shì yòng dàimǎ xiě de.

2 区号 qūhào [个 gè] *(for telephone)*

□ What is the code for London? 伦敦的区号是多少？Lúndūn de qūhào shì duōshǎo?

coffee NOUN

咖啡 kāfēi [杯 bēi]

□ A cup of coffee, please. 请来一杯咖啡。Qǐng láii yìbēi kāfēi.

■ **a black coffee** 一杯黑咖啡 yìbēi hēi kāfēi

■ **a white coffee** 一杯加奶咖啡 yìbēi jiānǎi kāfēi

LANGUAGE TIP The word 咖啡 kāfēi comes from the English **coffee**.

coffee table NOUN

咖啡桌 kāfēizhuō [张 zhāng]

coffin NOUN

棺材 guāncai [口 kǒu]

coin NOUN

硬币 yìngbì [枚 méi]

■ **a £2 pound coin** 一枚两镑的硬币 yìméi liǎng bàng de yìngbì

DID YOU KNOW...?
The largest coin in circulation in China has a value of one yuan, 一元 yìyuán.

coincidence NOUN

巧合 qiǎohé [种 zhǒng]

Coke® NOUN

可口可乐 Kěkǒu Kělè

□ a can of Coke 一罐可口可乐 yíguàn Kěkǒu Kělè

colander NOUN

滤器 lǜqì [个 gè]

cold ADJECTIVE

▷ *see also* **cold** NOUN

1 冷的 lěng de

□ It's cold today. 今天天冷。Jīntiān tiān lěng.

2 冷淡的 lěngdàn de

□ a cold nature 一种冷淡的性格 yìzhǒng lěngdàn de xìnggé

■ **to be cold** *(person)* 感到冷 gǎndào lěng

□ I'm cold. 我感到冷。Wǒ gǎndào lěng.

□ Are you cold? 你感到冷吗？Nǐ gǎndào lěng mā?

cold NOUN

▷ *see also* **cold** ADJECTIVE

1 寒冷天气 hánlěng tiānqì

□ I can't stand the cold. 我不能忍受寒冷天气。Wǒ bùnéng rěnshòu hánlěng tiānqì.

2 感冒 gǎnmào [次 cì]

■ **to have a cold** 患感冒 huàn gǎnmào

□ I've got a bad cold. 我患上了重感冒。Wǒ huànshàng le zhòng gǎnmào.

■ **a cold sore** 一个唇疱疹 yígè chún pāozhěn

coleslaw NOUN

凉拌卷心菜 liángbàn juǎnxīncài [份 fèn]

to **collapse** VERB

1 倒塌 dǎotā

□ The bridge collapsed last year. 那座桥去年倒塌了。Nà zuò qiáo qùnián dǎotā le.

2 倒下 dǎoxià

□ He collapsed while playing tennis. 他在打网球的时候倒下了。Tā zài dǎ wǎngqiú de shíhòu dǎoxià le.

collar NOUN

领子 lǐngzi [个 gè]

collarbone NOUN

锁骨 suǒgǔ [根 gēn]

colleague NOUN

同事 tóngshì [个 gè]

to **collect** VERB

1 收 shōu

□ The teacher collected the exercise books. 老师收了练习册。Lǎoshī shōu le liànxícè.

□ They collect the rubbish on Fridays. 他们每周五收垃圾。Tāmen měi zhōuwǔ shōu lājī.

2 收集 shōují

□ I collect stamps. 我收集邮票。Wǒ shōují yóupiào.

3 接 jiē

□ Their mother collects them from school. 他们的妈妈来学校接他们。Tāmen de māma lái xuéxiào jiē tāmen.

4 募捐 mùjuān

□ They're collecting money for charity. 他们在为慈善募捐。Tāmen zài wèi císhàn mùjuān.

collect call NOUN (US)

对方付费电话 duìfāng fùfèi diànhuà [个 gè]

■ **to make a collect call** 打对方付款的电话 dǎ duìfāng fùkuǎn de diànhuà

collection NOUN

1 收藏 shōucáng [件 jiàn]

□ my DVD collection 我的DVD 收藏 wǒde DVD shōucáng

2 募捐 mùjuān [次 cì]

□ a collection for charity 一次慈善募捐 yícì císhàn mùjuān

collector NOUN

收藏家 shōucáng jiā [位 wèi]

college NOUN
学院 xuéyuàn [个 gè]
■ **to go to college** 上大学 shàng dàxué

to **collide** VERB
碰撞 pèngzhuàng
■ **to collide with something** 与某物碰撞 yǔ mǒuwù pèngzhuàng

collision NOUN
碰撞 pèngzhuàng [下 xià] *(of vehicles)*

colon NOUN
冒号 màohào [个 gè] *(punctuation mark :)*

colonel NOUN
上校 shàngxiào [位 wèi]

colour (US **color**) NOUN
颜色 yánsè [种 zhǒng]
□ What colour is it? 什么颜色？Shénme yánsè?
■ **a colour film** *(for camera)* 一卷彩色胶片 yìjuǎn cǎisè jiāopiàn

colourful (US **colorful**) ADJECTIVE
色泽鲜艳的 sèzé xiānyàn de

colouring (US **coloring**) NOUN
食用色素 shíyòng sèsù [种 zhǒng] *(for food)*

comb NOUN
▷ *see also* **comb** VERB
梳子 shūzi [把 bǎ]

to **comb** VERB
▷ *see also* **comb** NOUN
梳理 shūlǐ
■ **to comb one's hair** 梳理某人的头发 shūlǐ mǒurén de tóufa □ You haven't combed your hair. 你还没梳理头发呢。Nǐ hái méi shūlǐ tóufa ne.

combination NOUN
混合 hùnhé [种 zhǒng]

to **combine** VERB
1 使结合 shǐ jiéhé
□ The film combines humour with suspense. 这部电影使幽默与悬疑相结合。Zhèbù diànyǐng shǐ yōumò yǔ xuányí xiāng jiéhé.
2 两者兼顾 liǎngzhě jiāngù
□ It's difficult to combine a career with a family. 家庭和事业，难以两者兼顾。Jiātíng hé shìyè, nányǐ liǎngzhějiāngù.

to **come** VERB
1 来 lái
□ Come here! 到这儿来！Dào zhè'r lái! □ Can I come too? 我也能来吗？Wǒ yě néng lái ma? □ Come with me. 跟我来。Gēn wǒ lái. □ He's come here to work. 他是来这里工作的。Tā shì laí zhèlǐ góngzuò de. □ I'm coming! 我来啦！Wǒ lái lā!
2 到 dào *(arrive)*
□ They came late. 他们到得晚。Tāmen dàodádewǎn. □ The letter came this morning. 信今天早上到的。Xìn jīntiān zǎoshàng dào de.
■ **to come first** *(in competition, race)* 位居第一 wèijū dìyī
■ **Where do you come from?** 你是哪里人？Nǐ shì nǎlǐ rén?
■ **I come from London.** 我来自伦敦。Wǒ láizì Lúndūn.
■ **Come on! 1** *(giving encouragement)* 加油！Jiāyóu! **2** *(hurry up)* 快一点！Kuàiyidiǎn!
■ **to come to a decision** 做出决定 zuòchū juédìng
■ **The bill came to £40.** 账单共计四十英镑。Zhàngdān gòngjì sìshí yīngbàng.

to **come back** VERB
回来 huílái
□ Come back! 回来！Huílái!

to **come down** VERB
1 降下 jiàngxià *(descend)*
2 降低 jiàngdī *(price)*

to **come in** VERB
进入 jìnrù
□ Come in! 进来！Jìnlái!

to **come off** VERB
脱落 tuōluò *(button, handle)*

to **come out** VERB
1 出来 chūlái
□ I tripped as we came out of the cinema. 当我们从电影院出来的时候我摔倒了。Dāng wǒmen cóng diànyǐngyuàn chūlái de shíhòu wǒ shuāidǎo le.
2 出现 chūxiàn
□ The sun came out just in time for our picnic. 对于我们的野餐，太阳出现得正是时候。Duìyú wǒmen de yěcān, tàiyáng chūxiàn dé zhèngshì shíhòu.
3 出版 chūbǎn
□ Her book comes out in May. 她的书五月出版。Tāde shū wǔyuè chūbǎn.
4 发行 fāxíng
□ It's just come out on DVD. 它刚刚在DVD上发行。Tā gānggāng zài DVD shàng fāxíng.
5 出来 chūlái
□ None of my photos came out. 我的照片都还没出来。Wǒde zhàopiàn dōu hái méi chūlái.

to **come round** VERB
苏醒 sūxǐng *(after faint, operation)*

to **come up** VERB
突然出现 tūrán chūxiàn
□ Something's come up so I'll be late home. 突然有事出现，所以我会晚到家。Tūrán

yǒushì chūxiàn, suǒyǐ wǒ huì wǎn dàojiā.

■ **to come up to somebody** **1** 走近某人 zǒujìn mǒurén □ She came up to me and kissed me. 她走近我然后亲了我。Tā zǒujìn wǒ ránhòu qīn le wǒ. **2** *(to speak to them)* 走上前来对某人说 zǒu shàngqián lái duì mǒurén shuō □ A man came up to me and said... 一个男人走上前来对我说… Yígè nánrén zǒu shàngqián lái duì wǒ shuō...

comedian NOUN
喜剧演员 xǐjù yǎnyuán [个 gè]

comedy NOUN
1 幽默 yōumò *(humour)*
2 喜剧 xǐjù [部 bù] *(play, film)*

comfortable ADJECTIVE
1 舒服的 shūfu de *(person)*
□ I'm very comfortable, thanks. 我觉得很舒服，谢谢。Wǒ juédé hěn shūfu, xièxie.
2 令人舒适的 lìngrén shūshì de *(furniture, room, clothes)*
■ **to make oneself comfortable** 自在点 zìzài diǎn

comic NOUN
漫画 mànhuà [本 běn] *(magazine)*

comic strip NOUN
连环画 liánhuánhuà [幅 fú]

coming ADJECTIVE
接下来的 jiēxiàlái de
□ in the coming months 在接下来的几个月里 zài jiēxiàlái de jǐgè yuè lǐ

comma NOUN
逗号 dòuhào [个 gè]

command NOUN
命令 mìnglìng [项 xiàng] *(order)*

comment NOUN
▷ *see also* **comment** VERB
评论 pínglùn [种 zhǒng]
□ He made no comment. 他没有作出评论。Tā méiyǒu zuòchū pínglùn.
■ **No comment!** 无可奉告！Wú kě fèng gào!

to **comment** VERB
▷ *see also* **comment** NOUN
■ **to comment on something** 对某事发表意见 duì mǒushì fābiǎo yìjiàn

commentary NOUN
实况解说 shíkuàng jiěshuō [段 duàn] *(on TV, radio)*

commentator NOUN
解说员 jiěshuōyuán [位 wèi]

commercial NOUN
广告 guǎnggào [则 zé]

commission NOUN
佣金 yōngjīn [笔 bǐ]
□ Salesmen work on commission. 销售人员赚取佣金。Xiāoshòu rényuán zuànqǔ yōngjīn.

to **commit** VERB
犯 fàn
■ **to commit a crime** 犯罪 fànzuì
■ **to commit oneself** 使作出承诺 shǐ zuòchū chéngnuò □ I don't want to commit myself. 我不想作出承诺。Wǒ bùxiǎng zuòchū chéngnuò.
■ **to commit suicide** 自杀 zìshā □ He committed suicide. 他自杀了。Tā zìshā le.

committee NOUN
委员会 wěiyuánhuì [个 gè]

common ADJECTIVE
▷ *see also* **common** NOUN
常见的 chángjiàn de
□ 'Smith' is a very common surname. "史密斯"是个非常常见的姓。"Shǐmìsī" shì gè fēicháng chángjiàn de xìng.
■ **to have something in common with somebody** 与某人有某共同点 yǔ mǒurén yǒu mǒu gòngtóngdiǎn

common NOUN
▷ *see also* **common** ADJECTIVE
公用空地 gōngyòng kòngdì [块 kuài]
□ The boys play football on the common. 男孩子们在公用空地上踢球。Nánháizimen zài gōngyòng kòngdì shàng tīqiú.

common sense NOUN
常识 chángshí
□ Use your common sense! 用用你的常识！Yòngyong nǐde chángshí!

to **communicate** VERB
联络 liánluò

communication NOUN
交流 jiāoliú

communion NOUN
圣餐礼 Shèngcānlǐ [次 cì]
□ my First Communion 我的第一次圣餐礼 wǒde dìyīcì Shèngcānlǐ

communism NOUN
共产主义 gòngchǎnzhǔyì

communist NOUN
▷ *see also* **communist** ADJECTIVE
共产主义者 gòngchǎnzhǔyìzhě [个 gè]

communist ADJECTIVE
▷ *see also* **communist** NOUN
共产主义的 gòngchǎnzhǔyì de
■ **the Communist Party** 共产党 Gòngchǎndǎng

community NOUN
社区 shèqū [个 gè]

to **commute** VERB
定期乘车往返 dìngqī chéngchē wǎngfǎn
□ She commutes between Oxford and

London. 她定期乘车往返于牛津和伦敦之间。Tā dìngqī chéngchē wǎngfǎn yú Niújīn hé Lúndūn zhījiān.

compact disc NOUN
激光唱片 jīguāng chàngpiàn [张 zhāng]
■ **a compact disc player** 一个激光唱片播放器 yígè jīguāng chàngpiàn bōfàngqì

company NOUN
公司 gōngsī [家 jiā]
□ He works for a big company. 他为一家大公司工作。Tā wèi yìjiā dà gōngsī gōngzuò.
■ **a theatre company** 一家剧团 yìjiā jùtuán
■ **to keep somebody company** 陪伴某人 péibàn mǒurén □ I'll keep you company. 我会陪伴着你。Wǒ huì péibàn zhe nǐ.

comparatively ADVERB
相对地 xiāngduì de

to **compare** VERB
比较 bǐjiào
□ They compared his work to that of Joyce. 他们比较了他和乔伊斯的作品。Tāmen bǐjiào le tā hé Qiáoyīsī de zuòpǐn.
□ People always compare him with his brother. 人们总是比较他和他哥哥。Rénmen zǒngshì bǐjiào tā hé tā gēge.
■ **compared with** 与…相比 yǔ...xiāngbǐ □ Oxford is small compared with London. 与伦敦相比，牛津很小。Yǔ Lúndūn xiāngbǐ, Niújīn hěn xiǎo.

comparison NOUN
比较 bǐjiào [种 zhǒng]

compartment NOUN
隔间 géjiàn [个 gè] *(on train)*

compass NOUN
指南针 zhǐnánzhēn [个 gè]

compensation NOUN
赔偿金 péicháng jīn [笔 bǐ]
□ They got £2000 compensation. 他们拿到了两千镑的赔偿金。Tāmen nádào le liǎngqiān bàng de péichángjīn.

to **compete** VERB
1 竞争 jìngzhēng
□ There were 5 companies competing for the contract. 有五家公司在竞争这个合同。Yǒu wǔjiā gōngsī zài jìngzhēng zhègè hétong.
2 比赛 bǐsài
□ I'm competing in the marathon. 我在比赛马拉松。Wǒ zài bǐsài mǎlāsōng.
■ **to compete for something** 争夺某物 zhēngduó mǒuwù □ There are 50 students competing for 6 places. 有五十名学生在争夺六个名额。Yǒu wǔshí míng xuéshēng zài zhēngduó liùgè míng'é.

competent ADJECTIVE
能胜任的 néng shèngrèn de

competition NOUN
1 比赛 bǐsài [项 xiàng]
□ a singing competition 一项唱歌比赛 yíxiàng chànggē bǐsài
2 竞争 jìngzhēng
□ Competition is fierce. 竞争激烈。Jìngzhēng jīliè.

competitive ADJECTIVE
有竞争力的 yǒu jìngzhēnglì de
□ a very competitive price 一个非常有竞争力的价格 yígè yǒu jìngzhēnglì de jiàgé
■ **to be competitive** *(person)* 好竞争的 hào jìngzhēng de □ He's a very competitive person. 他是一个非常好竞争的人。Tā shì yígè fēicháng hào jìngzhēng de rén.

competitor NOUN
1 竞争对手 jìngzhēng duìshǒu [个 gè] *(in business)*
2 参赛者 cānsàizhě [个 gè] *(participant)*

to **complain** VERB
1 投诉 tóusù
□ I'm going to complain to the manager. 我去向经理投诉。Wǒ qù xiàng jīnglǐ tóusù.
2 抱怨 bàoyuàn *(grumble)*
□ She's always complaining about her husband. 她总是抱怨她的丈夫。Tā zǒngshì bàoyuàn tāde zhàngfu.

complaint NOUN
抱怨 bàoyuàn [个 gè]
□ There were lots of complaints about the food. 关于这些食物有很多抱怨。Guānyú zhèxiē shíwù yǒu hěnduō bàoyuàn.
■ **to make a complaint** 投诉 tóusù □ I'd like to make a complaint. 我想投诉。Wǒ xiǎng tóusù.

complete ADJECTIVE
▷ *see also* **complete** VERB
1 完全的 wánquán de
□ The party was a complete disaster. 那个派对完全是场噩梦。Nàgè pàiduì wánquán shì chǎng èmèng.
2 完成的 wánchéng de
□ She had to make sure her homework was complete before she went out. 她得确保在她出门之前完成了家庭作业。Tā děi quèbǎo zài tā chūmén zhīqián wánchéng le jiātíng zuòyè.

to **complete** VERB
▷ *see also* **complete** ADJECTIVE
完成 wánchéng
□ They completed the assignment on time. 他们准时完成了任务。Tāmen zhǔnshí wánchēng le rènwù.

completely ADVERB

完全地 wánquán de *(totally)*
□ The rumours were completely untrue. 那些谣言完全是假的。Nàxiē yáoyán wánquán shì jiǎ de.

complexion NOUN
面色 miànsè [种 zhǒng]

complicated ADJECTIVE
复杂的 fùzá de

compliment NOUN
▷ *see also* **compliment** VERB
赞美 zànměi [种 zhǒng]
■ **to pay somebody a compliment** 赞美某人 zànměi mǒurén □ He's always paying her compliments. 他总是赞美她。Tā zǒngshì zànměi tā.

to **compliment** VERB
▷ *see also* **compliment** NOUN
称赞 chēngzàn
■ **to compliment somebody on something** 为某事称赞某人 wèi mǒushì chēngzàn mǒurén □ They complimented me on my French. 他们称赞了我的法语。Tāmen chēngzàn le wǒde Fǎyǔ.

complimentary ADJECTIVE
赠送的 zèngsòng de *(free)*
□ I've got two complimentary tickets for tonight. 我有两张今晚的赠票。Wǒ yǒu liǎngzhāng jīnwǎn de zèngpiào.

composer NOUN
作曲家 zuòqǔjiā [位 wèi]

comprehension NOUN
1 理解 lǐjiě *(understanding)*
2 理解力练习 lǐjiělì liànxí [项 xiàng] *(school exercise)*

comprehensive ADJECTIVE
1 全面的 quánmiàn de
□ a comprehensive guide 一本全面的指南 yìběn quánmiàn de zhǐnán
2 综合的 zōnghé de *(of insurance)*

comprehensive school NOUN
综合性中学 zōnghéxìng zhōngxué [所 suǒ]

compromise NOUN
▷ *see also* **compromise** VERB
折衷办法 zhézhōng bànfǎ [个 gè]
□ We reached a compromise. 我们最后找到一个折衷办法。Wǒmen zuìhòu zhǎodào yígè zhézhōng bànfǎ.

to **compromise** VERB
▷ *see also* **compromise** NOUN
妥协 tuǒxié
■ **Let's compromise.** 让我们妥协吧。Ràng wǒmen tuǒxié ba.

compulsory ADJECTIVE
必须的 bìxū de

computer NOUN
计算机 jìsuànjī [台 tái]

computer program NOUN
电脑程序 diànnǎo chéngxù [个 gè]

computer game NOUN
电脑游戏 diànnǎo yóuxì [局 jú]

computer programmer NOUN
电脑编程员 diànnǎo biānchéngyuán [位 wèi]
□ She's a computer programmer. 她是一位电脑编程员。Tā shì yíwèi diànnǎo biānchéngyuán.

computer room NOUN
机房 jīfáng [间 jiān]

computer science NOUN
计算机科学 jìsuànjī kēxué

computing NOUN
计算机学 jìsuànjīxué *(computing studies)*

computing course NOUN
电脑课程 diànnǎo kèchéng [门 mén]

to **concentrate** VERB
集中精力 jízhōng jīnglì
□ I couldn't concentrate. 我不能集中精力。Wǒ bùnéng jízhōng jīnglì.

concentration NOUN
专心 zhuānxīn

concern NOUN
担忧 dānyōu [份 fèn]
□ They expressed concern about her health. 他们表达了对她健康的担忧。Tāmen biǎodá le duì tā jiànkāng de dānyōu.

concerned ADJECTIVE
担心的 dānxīn de
□ His mother is concerned about him. 他的母亲担心他。Tāde mǔqīn dānxīn tā.
■ **as far as I'm concerned** 据我看来 jù wǒ kànlái

concerning PREPOSITION
关于 guānyú
□ For further information concerning the job, contact... 关于这个工作的更多信息，请联系… Guānyú zhègè gōngzuò de gèngduō xìnxī, qǐng liánxì...

concert NOUN
音乐会 yīnyuèhuì [个 gè]

concert hall NOUN
音乐厅 yīnyuètīng [个 gè]

concrete NOUN
混凝土 hùnníngtǔ

to **condemn** VERB
谴责 qiǎnzé
□ The government has condemned the decision. 政府谴责了这个决定。Zhèngfǔ qiǎnzé le zhègè juédìng.

condition NOUN
1 状况 zhuàngkuàng [种 zhǒng]
□ in bad condition 状况不好 zhuàngkuàng

bùhǎo □ in good condition 状况良好 zhuàngkuàng liánghǎo
2 条件 tiáojiàn [个 gè]
□ I'll do it, on one condition... 我来做，但有一个条件… Wǒ lái zuò, dàn yǒu yígè tiáojiàn...

conditional NOUN
■ **the conditional** *(tense)* 条件从句 tiáojiàn cóngjù

conditioner NOUN
护发素 hùfàsù [种 zhǒng]

condom NOUN
安全套 ānquán tào [只 zhī]

to **conduct** VERB
指挥 zhǐhuī *(orchestra)*

conductor NOUN
指挥家 zhǐhuījiā [位 wèi] *(of orchestra)*

cone NOUN
1 锥形蛋卷 zhuīxíng dànjuǎn [个 gè]
□ an ice-cream cone 一个锥形蛋卷冰淇淋 yígè zhuīxíng dànjuǎn bīngqílín
2 圆锥体 yuánzhuītǐ [个 gè] *(shape)*
■ **a traffic cone** 一个锥型路标 yígè zhuīxíng lùbiāo

conference NOUN
会议 huìyì [次 cì]

to **confess** VERB
坦白 tǎnbái
□ He finally confessed. 他最终坦白了。Tā zuìzhōng tǎnbái le.
■ **to confess to something** 承认某事 chéngrèn mǒushì □ He confessed to the murder. 他承认了杀人。Tā chéngrèn le shārén.

confession NOUN
坦白 tǎnbái [种 zhǒng]
■ **to make a confession** 坦白 tǎnbái

confidence NOUN
1 信心 xìnxīn
□ I've got confidence in you. 我对你有信心。Wǒ duì nǐ yǒu xìnxīn.
2 自信 zìxìn
□ She lacks confidence. 她缺乏自信。Tā quēfá zìxìn. □ I told you that story in confidence. 我私下告诉了你那个故事。Wǒ sīxià gàosù le nǐ nàgè gùshì.

confident ADJECTIVE
自信的 zìxìn de
□ She's seems quite confident. 她看起来蛮自信的。Tā kànqǐlái mán zìxìn de.
■ **to be confident that...** 坚信… jiānxìn...
□ I'm confident that everything will be okay. 我坚信一切都会顺利。Wǒ jiānxìn yíqiè dōu huì shùnlì.

confidential ADJECTIVE
机密的 jīmì de

to **confirm** VERB
1 肯定 kěndìng
2 确认 quèrèn *(appointment, date)*

confirmation NOUN
确认 quèrèn

to **confiscate** VERB
没收 mòshōu
■ **to confiscate something from somebody** 没收某人的某物 mòshōu mǒurén de mǒuwù

to **confuse** VERB
■ **to confuse somebody** 使某人困惑 shǐ mǒurén kùnhuò □ Don't confuse me! 不要使我困惑！Búyào shǐ wǒ kùnhuò !

confused ADJECTIVE
困惑的 kùnhuò de

confusing ADJECTIVE
含混不清的 hánhùn bùqīng de
■ **The traffic signs are confusing.** 交通标识含混不清。Jiāotōng biāoshí hánhùn bùqīng.

confusion NOUN
1 困惑 kùnhuò [种 zhǒng] *(uncertainty)*
2 混淆 hùnxiáo *(mix-up)*

to **congratulate** VERB
祝贺 zhùhè
□ My aunt congratulated me on my test results. 阿姨祝贺我的考试结果。Āyí zhùhè wǒde kǎoshì jiēguǒ.

congratulations PL NOUN
祝贺 zhùhè [份 fèn]
■ **Congratulations on your engagement!** 祝贺你订婚了！Zhùhè nǐ dìnghūn le!

Congress NOUN (US)
国会 guóhuì

congressman NOUN (US)
国会议员 guóhuì yìyuán [位 wèi]

congresswoman NOUN (US)
女国会议员 nǚ guóhuì yìyuán [位 wèi]

conjunction NOUN
连词 liáncí [个 gè]

connection NOUN
1 联系 liánxì [种 zhǒng]
□ What is the connection between them? 他们之间有什么联系？Tāmen zhījiān yǒu shénme liánxì?
2 接头 jiētóu [个 gè] *(electrical)*
□ There's a loose connection. 这儿有个不牢固的接头。Zhè'r yǒu gè bù láogù de jiētóu.
3 联运 liányùn [种 zhǒng] *(of trains, planes)*
□ We missed our connection. 我们错过了联运。Wǒmen cuòguò le liányùn.

to **conquer** VERB
征服 zhēngfú

conscience NOUN

良心 liángxīn [种 zhǒng]
■ to have a guilty conscience 有愧于良心 yǒukuì yú liángxīn

conscientious ADJECTIVE
认真的 rènzhēn de

conscious ADJECTIVE
1 清醒的 qīngxǐng de
□ He was still conscious when the doctor arrived. 医生到的时候他还是清醒的。Yīshēng dào de shíhòu tā háishì qīngxǐng de.
2 有意的 yǒuyì de
□ He made a conscious decision to tell nobody. 他有意不告诉其他人。Tā yǒuyì bú gàosù qítārén.
■ to be conscious of something 清楚某事 qīngchǔ mǒushì □ She was conscious of Max looking at her. 她清楚马克斯在看她。Tā qīngchǔ Mǎkèsī zài kàn tā.

consciousness NOUN
知觉 zhījué
■ to lose consciousness 失去知觉 shīqù zhījué □ I lost consciousness. 我失去了知觉。Wǒ shīqù le zhījué.

consequence NOUN
后果 hòuguǒ [种 zhǒng]
LANGUAGE TIP Word for word, this means 'after result'.
□ What are the consequences for the environment? 对于环境的后果是什么？Duìyú huánjìng de hòuguǒ shì shénme?
■ as a consequence 因此 yīncǐ

consequently ADVERB
所以 suǒyǐ

conservation NOUN
1 保护 bǎohù *(of environment)*
2 节约 jiéyuē *(of energy)*

conservative ADJECTIVE
保守的 bǎoshǒu de
■ the Conservative Party 保守党 Bǎoshǒudǎng

Conservative NOUN
保守党党员 Bǎoshǒudǎng dǎngyuán [名 míng]
■ to vote Conservative 选举保守党党员 xuǎnjǔ Bǎoshǒudǎng dǎngyuán
■ the Conservatives 保守派 Bǎoshǒupài

conservatory NOUN
暖房 nuǎnfáng [间 jiān]

to **consider** VERB
1 考虑 kǎolǜ *(think about)*
□ We considered cancelling our holiday. 我们考虑过取消我们的假期。Wǒmen kǎolǜ guò qǔxiāo wǒmen de jiàqī.
■ I'm considering the idea. 我正在考虑这个构思。Wǒ zhèngzài kǎolǜ zhègè gòusī.
2 考虑到 kǎolǜ dào *(take into account)*
□ They hadn't fully considered how much money it would cost. 他们没有全面考虑到会花掉多少钱。Tāmen méiyǒu wánquán kǎolǜdào huì huādiào duōshǎo qián.
3 认为 rènwéi
□ He considers it a waste of time. 他认为这是浪费时间。Tā rènwéi zhè shì làngfèi shíjiān.

considerate ADJECTIVE
体贴的 tǐtiē de

considering PREPOSITION
1 考虑到 kǎolǜ dào
□ Considering we were there for a month... 考虑到我们在那儿已经一个月了… Kǎolǜ dào wǒmen zài nà'r yǐjīng yígè yuè le...
2 总的来说 zǒngde láishuō
□ I got a good mark, considering. 总的来说，我拿到了一个好分数。Zǒngde láishuō, wǒ nádào le yígè hǎo fēnshù.

to **consist** VERB
■ to consist of 由…组成 yóu...zǔchéng
□ The band consists of a singer and a guitarist. 这个乐队由一个歌手和一个吉他手组成。Zhègè yuèduì yóu yígè gēshǒu hé yígè jítāshǒu zǔchéng.

consonant NOUN
辅音 fǔyīn [个 gè]

constant ADJECTIVE
1 不断的 búduàn de *(threat, pain, reminder)*
2 重复的 chóngfù de *(interruptions, demands)*
3 恒定的 héngdìng de *(temperature, speed)*

constantly ADVERB
1 反复地 fǎnfù de *(repeatedly)*
2 不断地 búduàn de *(uninterruptedly)*

constipated ADJECTIVE
便秘的 biànmì de

to **construct** VERB
建造 jiànzào

construction NOUN
建造 jiànzào *(of building, road, machine)*

to **consult** VERB
1 咨询 zīxún *(doctor, lawyer, friend)*
2 查阅 cháyuè *(book, map)*

consumer NOUN
消费者 xiāofèizhě [个 gè] *(of goods, services)*

contact NOUN
▷ *see also* **contact** VERB
联络 liánluò [种 zhǒng]
□ I'm in contact with her. 我在与她联络。Wǒ zài yǔ tā liánluò.

to **contact** VERB
▷ *see also* **contact** NOUN
联系 liánxì

□ Where can we contact you? 你的联系地址是什么？Nǐde liánxì dìzhǐ shì shénme?

contact lenses PL NOUN
隐形眼镜 yǐnxíng yǎnjìng [副 fù]

to **contain** VERB
1 装有 zhuāngyǒu *(objects)*
2 含有 hányǒu *(component, ingredient)*

container NOUN
容器 róngqì [个 gè] *(box, jar etc)*

contempt NOUN
藐视 miǎoshì

content NOUN
▷ *see also* **content** ADJECTIVE
内容 nèiróng [项 xiàng]

content ADJECTIVE
▷ *see also* **content** NOUN
满足的 mǎnzú de

contents PL NOUN
所含之物 suǒhán zhī wù *(of bottle, packet)*

contest NOUN
比赛 bǐsài [项 xiàng]

contestant NOUN
参赛者 cānsàizhě [位 wèi]

context NOUN
上下文 shàngxiàwén [个 gè] *(of word, phrase)*

LANGUAGE TIP Word for word, this means 'the writing that comes above and below'.

continent NOUN
大陆 dàlù [个 gè]
■ **the Continent** 欧洲大陆 Ōuzhōu dàlù

continental breakfast NOUN
欧洲大陆式早餐 Ōuzhōu dàlù shì zǎocān [顿 dùn]

to **continue** VERB
继续 jìxù
□ She continued talking to her friend. 她继续和她的朋友聊天。Tā jìxù hé tāde péngyǒu liáotiān.

continuous ADJECTIVE
连续不停的 liánxù bù tíng de
■ **continuous assessment** 连续评估 liánxù pínggū

contraception NOUN
避孕 bìyùn

contract NOUN
合同 hétong [份 fèn]

to **contradict** VERB
驳斥 bóchì

contrary NOUN
■ **the contrary** 相反 xiāngfǎn
■ **on the contrary** 正相反 zhèng xiāngfǎn

contrast NOUN
明显的差异 míngxiǎn de chāyì [种 zhǒng]

to **contribute** VERB
1 作出贡献 zuòchū gòngxiàn
□ The treaty will contribute to world peace. 这份条约将对世界和平作出贡献。Zhèfèn tiáoyuē jiāng duì shìjiè hépíng zuòchū gòngxiàn.
2 分享 fēnxiǎng *(share in)*
□ He didn't contribute to the discussion. 他没有在讨论中分享他的想法。Tā méiyǒu zài tǎolùn zhōng fēnxiǎng tāde xiǎngfǎ.
3 捐赠 juānzèng *(give)*
□ She contributed £10. 她捐赠了十镑。Tā juānzèng le shíbàng.

contribution NOUN
捐献 juānxiàn [次 cì]

to **control** VERB
▷ *see also* **control** NOUN
1 统治 tǒngzhì *(country, organization)*
2 控制 kòngzhì *(person, emotion, fire)*
■ **to control oneself** 克制自己 kèzhì zìjǐ

control NOUN
▷ *see also* **control** VERB
统治权 tǒngzhìquán *(of country, organization)*
■ **to lose control** *(of vehicle)* 失去控制 shīqù kòngzhì □ He lost control of the car. 他失去了对汽车的控制。Tā shīqù le duì qìchē de kòngzhì.
■ **the controls** *(of machine)* 操纵装置 cāozòng zhuāngzhì
■ **to be in control** 控制 kòngzhì
■ **to keep control** *(of people)* 管理 guǎnlǐ
□ He can't keep control of the class. 他不能管理这个班级。Tā bùnéng guǎnlǐ zhègè bānjí.
■ **out of control** *(child, class)* 不受控制 búshòu kòngzhì

controversial ADJECTIVE
1 有争议的 yǒu zhēngyì de
□ Euthanasia is a controversial issue. 安乐死是一个有争议的话题。Ānlèsǐ shì yígè yǒu zhēngyì de huàtí.
2 引起争论的 yǐnqǐ zhēnglùn de
□ a controversial book 一本引起争论的书 yìběn yǐnqǐ zhēnglùn de shū

convenient ADJECTIVE
1 方便的 fāngbiàn de *(method, system, time)*
□ It's not a convenient time for me. 对我来说不是一个方便的时间。Duì wǒ lái shuō búshì yígè fāngbiàn de shíjiān.
2 近便的 jìnbiàn de *(place)*
□ The hotel's convenient for the airport. 这家宾馆去机场很近便。Zhèjiā bīnguǎn qù jīchǎng hěn jìnbiàn.

conventional ADJECTIVE
1 习俗性的 xísúxìng de *(custom)*

2 符合常规的 fǔhéchángguī de *(method, product)*

conversation NOUN
交谈 jiāotán [次 cì]
□ We had a long conversation. 我们交谈了很长时间。Wǒmen jiāotán le hěncháng shíjiān.

to **convert** VERB
改建 gǎijiàn *(building)*
□ We've converted the loft into a spare room. 我们已经将这个阁楼改建成了一个客房。Wǒmen yǐjīng jiāng zhègè fángjiān gǎijiàn chéng le yígè kèfáng.

to **convict** VERB
宣告罪名成立 xuāngào zuìmíng chénglì
□ He was convicted of the murder. 他被宣告了谋杀罪名成立。Tā bèi xuāngào le móushā zuìmíng chénglì.

to **convince** VERB
1 使信服 shǐ xìnfú
□ I'm not convinced he's right. 我还没信服他是对的。Wǒ hái méi xìnfú tā shì duì de.
2 说服 shuōfú
□ He convinced me to go with him. 他说服了我和他一起去。Tā shuōfú le wǒ hé tā yìqǐ qù.

to **cook** VERB
▷ *see also* **cook** NOUN
1 煮 zhǔ *(food)*
□ Cook the rice for 10 minutes. 将米煮十分钟。Jiāng mǐ zhǔ shí fēnzhōng.
■ **to be cooked** 煮着 zhǔzhe □ When the potatoes are cooked... 当土豆煮着的时候… Dāng tǔdòu zhǔzhe de shíhòu...
2 做 zuò *(meal)*
□ She's cooking lunch. 她在做午饭。Tā zài zuò wǔfàn.
3 烹饪 pēngrèn *(person)*
□ I can't cook. 我不会烹饪。Wǒ búhuì pēngrèn.

cook NOUN
▷ *see also* **cook** VERB
厨师 chúshī [位 wèi]
■ **a good cook** 一个好厨师 yígè hǎo chúshī

cookbook NOUN
烹饪书 pēngrènshū [本 běn]

cooker NOUN
厨灶 chúzào [个 gè]
□ a gas cooker 一个燃气灶 yígè ránqì zào

cookie NOUN (US)
小甜饼 xiǎotiánbǐng [块 kuài]

cooking NOUN
烹饪 pēngrèn
□ I like cooking. 我喜欢烹饪。Wǒ xǐhuan pēngrèn.

cool ADJECTIVE
1 阴凉的 yīnliáng de
□ Put the wine in a cool place. 把酒放在一个阴凉的地方。Bǎ jiǔ fàngzài yígè yīnliáng de dìfang.
2 冷静的 lěngjìng de
□ He stayed cool throughout the crisis. 整个危机期间他始终保持冷静。Zhěnggè wēijī qījiān tā shǐzhōng bǎochí lěngjìng.
3 刺激的 cìjī de
□ They think it's cool to do drugs. 他们觉得嗑药很刺激。Tāmen juédé kēyào hěn cìjī.
4 酷的 kù de
□ a cool top 一件酷的上衣 yíjiàn kù de shàngyī

to **cool down** VERB
变凉 biànliáng

to **cooperate** VERB
合作 hézuò
■ **to cooperate with someone** 与某人合作 yǔ mǒurén hézuò

cooperation NOUN
合作 hézuò [次 cì]

cop NOUN
警察 jǐngchá [名 míng] *(informal)*

to **cope** VERB
应付 yìngfu
□ It was hard, but we coped. 尽管难，我们还是应付了。Jǐnguǎn nán, wǒmen háishì yìngfu le.
■ **to cope with** 处理 chǔlǐ □ She's got a lot of problems to cope with. 她有很多事要处理。Tā yǒu hěnduō shì yào chǔlǐ.

copper NOUN
1 铜 tóng
□ a copper bracelet 一个铜手镯 yígè tóng shǒuzhuó
2 警察 jǐngchá [名 míng] *(informal: policeman)*

copy NOUN
▷ *see also* **copy** VERB
1 复制品 fùzhìpǐn [件 jiàn]
■ **to make a copy of something** 复制某物 fùzhì mǒuwù
2 份 fèn *(newspaper)*

to **copy** VERB
▷ *see also* **copy** NOUN
1 抄袭 chāoxí
□ The teacher accused him of copying. 老师责备他抄袭。Lǎoshī zébèi tā chāoxí.
2 复制 fùzhì
■ **to copy and paste** 复制再粘贴 fùzhì zài zhāntiē

core NOUN
果核 guǒhé [粒 lì] *(of fruit)*

cork NOUN
瓶塞 píngsāi [个 gè]

corkscrew NOUN
瓶塞钻 píngsāizuàn [个 gè]

corn NOUN
1 谷物 gǔwù *(wheat)*
2 玉米 yùmǐ [根 gēn] *(sweet corn)*
■ **corn on the cob** 玉米棒子 yùmǐ bàngzi

corner NOUN
1 角落 jiǎoluò [个 gè]
□ in a corner of the room 在房间的一个角落 zài fángjiān de yígè jiǎoluò
2 街角 jiējiǎo [个 gè]
■ **the shop on the corner** 街角的商店 jiējiǎo de shāngdiàn □ He lives just round the corner. 他就住在街角处。Tā jiù zhùzài jiējiǎo chù.
3 角球 jiǎoqiú [个 gè] *(in football)*

cornet NOUN
1 短号 duǎnhào [把 bǎ]
□ He plays the cornet. 他会吹短号。Tā huì chuī duǎnhào.
2 锥形蛋卷 zhuīxíng dànjuǎn [个 gè] *(ice cream)*

cornflakes PL NOUN
脆玉米片 cuì yùmǐpiàn

Cornwall NOUN
康沃尔 Kāngwò'ěr
■ **in Cornwall** 在康沃尔 zài Kāngwò'ěr

corporal punishment NOUN
体罚 tǐfá [种 zhǒng]

corpse NOUN
死尸 sǐshī [具 jù]

correct ADJECTIVE
▷ *see also* **correct** VERB
正确的 zhèngquè de
□ That's correct. 是正确的。Shì zhèngquè de.
■ **the correct choice** 正确的选择 zhèngquè de xuǎnzé
■ **the correct answer** 正确的答案 zhèngquè de dá'àn

to **correct** VERB
▷ *see also* **correct** ADJECTIVE
1 纠正 jiūzhèng *(mistake, fault, person)*
2 修改 xiūgǎi *(essays)*

correction NOUN
修改 xiūgǎi [次 cì]

correctly ADVERB
正确地 zhèngquè de

corridor NOUN
走廊 zǒuláng [条 tiáo] *(in house, building)*

corruption NOUN
腐败 fǔbài

cosmetics PL NOUN
化妆品 huàzhuāng pǐn *(beauty products)*

cosmetic surgery NOUN
整容手术 zhěngróng shǒushù [次 cì]

cost NOUN
▷ *see also* **cost** VERB
价格 jiàgé [种 zhǒng]
■ **the cost of living** 生活费用 shēnghuó fèiyòng
■ **at all costs** 无论如何 wúlùn rúhé

to **cost** VERB
▷ *see also* **cost** NOUN
花费 huāfèi
□ The meal cost thirty pounds. 那顿饭花费了三十镑。Nà dùn fàn huāfèi le sānshí bàng. □ How much does it cost? 这多少钱？Zhè duōshǎo qián? □ It costs too much. 花费太高。Huāfèi tàigāo.

costume NOUN
戏装 xìzhuāng [套 tào]

cot NOUN
1 幼儿床 yòu'ér chuáng [张 zhāng] *(for baby)*
2 帆布床 fānbù chuáng [张 zhāng] *(US: bed)*

cottage NOUN
小屋 xiǎowū [个 gè]

cotton NOUN
棉布 miánbù
□ a cotton shirt 一件棉布衬衫 yíjiàn miánbù chènshān
■ **cotton wool** 脱脂棉 tuōzhī mián

couch NOUN
长沙发 cháng shāfā [个 gè]

to **cough** VERB
▷ *see also* **cough** NOUN
咳嗽 késòu

cough NOUN
▷ *see also* **cough** VERB
咳嗽 késòu [阵 zhèn]
□ I've got a cough. 我咳嗽了。Wǒ késòu le.
■ **cough mixture** 止咳剂 zhǐkéjì

could VERB
LANGUAGE TIP In the past tense, **could** is translated by 没能 méinéng.
□ We couldn't go to the party. 我们没能去参加派对。Wǒmen méi néng qù cānjiā pàiduì. □ I couldn't do it. 我没能做的。Wǒ méinéng zuòde.
■ **He couldn't read or write.** 他不会读也不会写。Tā búhuì dú yě búhuì xiě.
LANGUAGE TIP When talking about a possibility, **could** is translated by 可能 kěnéng.
□ He could be in the library. 他可能在图书馆。Tā kěnéng zài túshūguǎn. □ You could have been killed! 可能你连命都没了！Kěnéng nǐ lián mìng dōu méile!
■ **If we had more time, I could finish this.** 如果有更多时间，我能够完成的。Rúguǒ yǒu gèngduō shíjiān, wǒ nénggòu wánchéng de.

LANGUAGE TIP In offers, suggestions and requests, **could** is translated by 可以 kěyǐ.

□ I could call a doctor. 我可以叫个医生。Wǒ kěyǐ jiào gè yīshēng. □ Could I borrow the car? 我可以借一下车吗？Wǒ kěyǐ jiè yīxià chē mā? □ He asked if he could make a phone call. 他问是否可以打个电话。Tā wèn shìfǒu kěyǐ dǎgè diànhuà.

council NOUN
议会 yìhuì [个 gè]
□ He's on the council. 他在议会工作。Tā zài yìhuì gōngzuò.
■ **a council estate** 一处地方政府所属房产 yíchù dìfāng zhèngfǔ suǒshǔ fángchǎn
■ **a council house** 一栋政府房 yídòng zhèngfǔ fáng

councillor NOUN
议员 yìyuán [名 míng]
■ **She's a local councillor.** 她是一名地方议员。Tā shì yìmíng dìfāng yìyuán.

to **count** VERB
数 shǔ

to **count on** VERB
依靠 yīkào
□ You can count on me. 你可以依靠我。Nǐ kěyǐ yīkào wǒ.

counter NOUN
柜台 guìtái [个 gè]

country NOUN
1 国家 guójiā [个 gè]
□ the border between the two countries 两个国家间的界线 liǎnggè guójiā jiān de jièxiàn
2 乡下 xiāngxià [个 gè]
□ I live in the country. 我住在乡下。Wǒ zhùzài xiāngxià.
■ **country dancing** 乡间舞 xiāngjiānwǔ

countryside NOUN
农村 nóngcūn [个 gè]

couple NOUN
1 夫妻 fūqī [对 duì] *(married)*
□ the couple who live next door 住在隔壁的夫妻 zhùzài gébì de fūqī
2 情侣 qínglǚ [对 duì] *(unmarried)*
■ **a couple** 几个 jǐgè □ a couple of hours 几个小时 jǐgè xiǎoshí
■ **Could you wait a couple of minutes?** 你能等几分钟吗？Nǐ néng děng jǐ fēnzhōng mā?

courage NOUN
勇气 yǒngqì

courgette NOUN
西葫芦 xīhúlu [根 gēn]

courier NOUN
1 导游 dǎoyóu [个 gè] *(for tourists)*
2 信使 xìnshǐ [个 gè] *(delivery service)*
□ They sent it by courier. 他们差信使送的。Tāmen chāi xìnshǐ sòng de.

course NOUN
1 课程 kèchéng [门 mén]
□ a French course 一门法语课程 yìmén Fǎyǔ kèchéng □ to go on a course 继续学一门课程 jìxù xué yìmén kèchéng
2 菜 cài [道 dào] *(of meal)*
□ the main course 主菜 zhǔ cài □ the first course 首道菜 shǒudào cài
3 场地 chǎngdì [个 gè]
□ a golf course 一个高尔夫场地 yígè gāo'ěrfū chǎngdì
■ **of course** 当然 dāngrán □ Do you love me? — Of course I do! 你爱我吗？— 当然啦！Nǐ ài wǒ mā? — Dāngrán lā!

court NOUN
1 法庭 fǎtíng [个 gè]
□ He was in court yesterday. 他昨天在法庭上。Tā zuótiān zài fǎtíng shàng.
2 球场 qiúchǎng [个 gè]
□ There are tennis and squash courts. 有网球和壁球球场。Yǒu wǎngqiú hé bìqiú qiúchǎng.

courthouse NOUN (US)
法院 fǎyuàn [个 gè]

courtyard NOUN
庭院 tíngyuàn [个 gè]

cousin NOUN
1 堂兄 tángxiōng [个 gè] *(older male on father's side)*
2 堂弟 tángdì [个 gè] *(younger male on father's side)*
3 堂姐 tángjiě [个 gè] *(older female on father's side)*
4 堂妹 tángmèi [个 gè] *(younger female on father's side)*
5 表兄 biǎoxiōng [个 gè] *(older male on mother's side)*
6 表弟 biǎodì [个 gè] *(younger male on mother's side)*
7 表姐 biǎojiě [个 gè] *(older female on mother's side)*
8 表妹 biǎomèi [个 gè] *(younger female on mother's side)*

to **cover** VERB
▷ *see also* **cover** NOUN
1 遮住 zhēzhù
□ I covered my face. 我遮住了我的脸。Wǒ zhēzhù le wǒde liǎn.
2 覆盖 fùgài
□ My legs were covered with mosquito bites. 我的腿上覆盖了好多蚊子叮的包。Wǒde tuǐshàng fùgài le hǎoduō wénzi dīng de bāo.

3 涵盖 hángài
□ Our insurance didn't cover it. 我们的保险没有涵盖它。Wǒmen de bǎoxiǎn méiyǒu hángài tā.
■ **to cover up a scandal** 掩盖一个丑闻 yǎngài yígè chǒuwén

cover NOUN
▷ *see also* **cover** VERB
1 盖子 gàizi [个 gè] *(of a container)*
2 封面 fēngmiàn [个 gè] *(of book, magazine)*

covers PL NOUN
铺盖 pūgai *(on bed)*

cow NOUN
奶牛 nǎiniú [头 tóu]

coward NOUN
胆小鬼 dǎnxiǎoguǐ [个 gè]
□ She's a coward. 她是个胆小鬼。Tā shì gè dǎnxiǎoguǐ.

cowardly ADJECTIVE
胆怯地 dǎnqiè de

cowboy NOUN
牛仔 niúzǎi [个 gè]

crab NOUN
1 螃蟹 pángxiè [只 zhī] *(creature)*
2 蟹肉 xièròu *(meat)*

DID YOU KNOW...?
Crab is a favourite dish across China, but it is generally served whole.

crack NOUN
▷ *see also* **crack** VERB
1 裂缝 lièfèng [条 tiáo]
2 快克可卡因 kuàikè kěkǎyīn *(drug)*
■ **I'll have a crack at it.** 我会试一试。Wǒ huì shìyishì.

to **crack** VERB
▷ *see also* **crack** NOUN
使破裂 shǐ pòliè *(nut, egg)*
■ **to crack a joke** 开玩笑 kāi wánxiào

to **crack down on** VERB
对...严惩不贷 duì...yánchěng búdài
□ The police are cracking down on drink-drivers. 警方对酒后驾车者严惩不贷。Jǐngfāng duì jiǔhòu jiàchēzhě yánchěng búdài.

cracked ADJECTIVE
破裂的 pòliè de

cracker NOUN
薄脆饼干 báocuì bǐnggān [块 kuài] *(biscuit)*
■ **a Christmas cracker** 一个圣诞爆竹 yígè Shèngdàn bàozhú

cradle NOUN
摇篮 yáolán [个 gè]

craft NOUN
手工艺 shǒugōngyì [门 mén] *(weaving, pottery etc)*
■ **a craft shop** 一家手工艺店 yìjiā shǒugōngyì diàn

craftsman NOUN
手工艺者 shǒugōngyì zhě [名 míng]

to **cram** VERB
1 填塞 tiánsāi
□ We crammed our stuff into the boot. 我们把东西填塞进了后备箱里。Wǒmen bǎ dōngxi tiánsāi jìn le hòubèixiāng lǐ.
2 抱佛脚 bào fójiǎo *(for exams)*

LANGUAGE TIP Word for word, this means 'to embrace Buddha's feet' – to profess devotion only when in trouble. This has come to mean making a hasty, last-ditch attempt, that is, cramming for an exam.

crammed ADJECTIVE
■ **crammed with** 塞满的 sāimǎn de
□ Her bag was crammed with books. 她的包被书塞满了。Tāde bāo bèi shū sāimǎn le.

cramp NOUN
抽筋 chōujīn [阵 zhèn]

crane NOUN
起重机 qǐzhòngjī [部 bù]

crash NOUN
▷ *see also* **crash** VERB
1 车祸 chēhuò [场 chǎng] *(of car)*
2 坠机 zhuìjī [次 cì] *(of plane)*
3 哗啦声 huālā shēng [声 shēng] *(noise)*
■ **a crash helmet** 一个头盔 yígè tóukuī
■ **a crash course** 一个速成班 yígè sùchéngbān

to **crash** VERB
▷ *see also* **crash** NOUN
1 坠毁 zhuìhuǐ *(plane)*
□ The plane crashed. 飞机坠毁了。Fēijī zhuìhuǐ le.
2 撞毁 zhuàngjī *(car)*
□ He went round the bend too fast and crashed his car. 他在转弯处开得太快了，撞毁了他的车。Tā zài zhuǎnwānchù kāide tàikuài le, zhuànghuǐ le tāde chē.
■ **to crash into something** 猛地撞上某物 měngde zhuàngshàng mǒuwù
3 死机 sǐjī *(computer)*

to **crawl** VERB
▷ *see also* **crawl** NOUN
爬 pá

crawl NOUN
▷ *see also* **crawl** VERB
自由泳 zìyóuyǒng
□ to do the crawl 游自由泳 yóu zìyóuyǒng

crazy ADJECTIVE
发疯的 fāfēng de *(informal)*
■ **to go crazy** 发疯 fāfēng

cream NOUN
▷ *see also* **cream** ADJECTIVE
1 奶油 nǎiyóu
□ strawberries and cream 草莓和奶油 cǎoméi hé nǎiyóu
■ **a cream cake** 一个奶油蛋糕 yígè nǎiyóu dàngāo
■ **cream cheese** 奶油干酪 nǎiyóu gānlào
2 乳霜 rǔshuāng [瓶 píng] *(for skin)*
□ sun cream 防晒霜 fángshàishuāng

cream ADJECTIVE
▷ *see also* **cream** NOUN
乳白色的 rǔbáisè de *(colour)*

crease NOUN
折痕 zhéhén [道 dào] *(in cloth, paper)*

creased ADJECTIVE
褶皱的 zhézhòu de

to **create** VERB
创造 chuàngzào

creation NOUN
创造 chuàngzào [个 gè]

creative ADJECTIVE
有创造力的 yǒu chuàngzàolì de

creature NOUN
动物 dòngwù [种 zhǒng]

crèche NOUN
儿所 tuō'érsuǒ [个 gè]

credit NOUN
贷款 dàikuǎn *(financial)*
■ **on credit** 赊账 shēzhàng
■ **I've no credit left on my phone.** 我的手机没有余额了。Wǒde shǒujī méiyǒu yú'é le.

credit card NOUN
信用卡 xìnyòng kǎ [张 zhāng]

creeps PL NOUN
■ **It gives me the creeps.** 它给我毛骨悚然的感觉。Tā gěi wǒ máogǔsǒngrán de gǎnjué.

to **creep up** VERB
■ **to creep up on somebody** 悄悄靠近某人 qiāoqiāo kàojìn mǒurén

crept VERB ▷ *see* **creep up**

cress NOUN
水芹 shuǐqín [簇 cù]

crew NOUN
1 全体人员 quántǐ rényuán
□ a flight crew 一个飞行机组 yígè fēixíng jīzǔ
2 组 zǔ [个 gè]
□ a film crew 一个电影剧组 yígè diànyǐng jùzǔ

crib NOUN (US)
婴儿床 yīng'érchuáng [张 zhāng]

cricket NOUN
1 板球 bǎnqiú
□ I play cricket. 我会打板球。Wǒ huì dǎ bǎnqiú.
■ **a cricket bat** 一个板球球拍 yígè bǎnqiú qiúpāi
2 蟋蟀 xīshuài [只 zhī] *(insect)*

crime NOUN
1 罪行 zuìxíng [种 zhǒng]
□ Murder is a crime. 谋杀是一种罪行。Móushā shì yìzhǒng zuìxíng.
2 违法行为 wéifǎ xíngwéi *(lawlessness)*
□ Crime is rising. 违法行为日渐猖獗。Wéifǎ xíngwéi rìjiàn chāngjué.

criminal NOUN
▷ *see also* **criminal** ADJECTIVE
罪犯 zuìfàn [个 gè]

criminal ADJECTIVE
▷ *see also* **criminal** NOUN
违法的 wéifǎ de
□ It's criminal! 这是违法的！Zhèshì wéifǎ de!
■ **It's a criminal offence.** 这是违法犯罪。Zhè shì wéifǎ fànzuì.

crisis NOUN
危机 wēijī [个 gè]

crisp NOUN
▷ *see also* **crisp** ADJECTIVE
薯片 shǔpiàn [片 piàn]
□ a bag of crisps 一袋薯片 yídài shǔpiàn

crisp ADJECTIVE
▷ *see also* **crisp** NOUN
脆的 cuì de *(food)*

criterion NOUN
标准 biāozhǔn [个 gè]
□ the selection criteria 挑选标准 tiāoxuǎn biāozhǔn □ Only one candidate met all the criteria. 只有一个候选人符合所有的标准。Zhǐyǒu yígè hòuxuǎnrén fúhé suǒyǒu de biāozhǔn.

critic NOUN
评论员 pínglùnyuán [位 wèi]

critical ADJECTIVE
1 批评性的 pīpíngxìng de *(negative)*
■ **a critical remark** 一个批评性的评论 yígè pīpíngxìng de pínglùn
2 危急的 wēijí de *(serious)*
□ He's in a critical condition in hospital. 他现在在医院里情况很危急。Tā xiànzài zài yīyuàn lǐ qíngkuàng hěn wēijí.

to **criticize** VERB
批评 pīpíng

Croatia NOUN
克罗地亚 Kèluódìyà

crocodile NOUN
鳄鱼 èyú [只 zhī]

crook NOUN
骗子 piànzi [个 gè] *(criminal)*

crooked ADJECTIVE
歪的 wāi de

LANGUAGE TIP This character is composed of two different characters, 不 bù **not** and 正 zhèng **straight**.

crop NOUN
收成 shōuchéng [次 cì] *(amount produced)*
□ a good crop of apples 苹果的一次好收成 píngguǒ de yícì hǎo shōuchéng

cross NOUN
▷ *see also* **cross** ADJECTIVE, VERB
1 交叉符号 jiāochā fúhào [个 gè] *(x shape)*
2 十字 shízì [个 gè] *(crucifix shape)*
3 十字架 shízìjià [个 gè] *(religious)*

cross ADJECTIVE
▷ *see also* **cross** NOUN, VERB
生气的 shēngqì de
□ to be cross about something 对某事感到生气 duì mǒushì gǎndào shēngqì

to **cross** VERB
▷ *see also* **cross** ADJECTIVE, NOUN
横穿 héngchuān *(street, room)*
□ He crossed the road at the traffic lights. 他在交通灯处横穿了马路。Tā zài jiāotōngdēng chù héngchuān le mǎlù.

to **cross out** VERB
取消 qǔxiāo

to **cross over** VERB
过马路 guò mǎlù

cross-country NOUN
越野赛 yuèyěsài [次 cì] *(race)*
■ **cross-country skiing** 越野滑雪 yuèyě huáxuě

crossing NOUN
1 横渡 héngdù [次 cì]
□ a 10-hour crossing 一次十小时的横渡 yícì shí xiǎoshí de héngdù
2 人行横道 rénxíng héngdào [个 gè] *(for pedestrians)*

crossroads NOUN
十字路口 shízì lùkǒu [个 gè]

crosswalk NOUN (US)
人行横道 rénxíng héngdào [个 gè]

crossword NOUN
填字游戏 tánzì yóuxì [个 gè]
□ I like doing crosswords. 我喜欢做填字游戏。Wǒ xǐhuan zuò tiánzì yóuxì.

crow NOUN
乌鸦 wūyā [只 zhī]

crowd NOUN
人群 rénqún [个 gè]
■ **crowds of people** 大批人群 dàpī rénqún
■ **the crowd** *(at sports match)* 观众 guānzhòng

crowded ADJECTIVE
拥挤的 yōngjǐ de

crown NOUN
皇冠 huángguān [个 gè]

crude ADJECTIVE
粗暴的 cūbào de *(vulgar)*

cruel ADJECTIVE
残忍的 cánrěn de *(treatment, behaviour)*
■ **to be cruel to somebody** 残酷地对待某人 cánkù de duìdài mǒurén

cruelty NOUN
残忍 cánrěn

cruise NOUN
游船 yóuchuán [艘 sōu]
■ **to go on a cruise** 乘游船旅行 chéng yóuchuán lǚxíng

crumb NOUN
碎屑 suìxiè [搓 cuō]

to **crush** VERB
1 使挤在一起 shǐ jǐzài yìqǐ *(person)*
2 压碎 yāsuì *(garlic)*

crutch NOUN
拐杖 guǎizhàng [支 zhī]

to **cry** VERB
▷ *see also* **cry** NOUN
哭 kū
■ **What are you crying about?** 你哭什么？Nǐ kū shénme?
■ **She had a good cry!** 她大哭了一场！Tā dàkū le yichǎng!

cry NOUN
▷ *see also* **cry** VERB
叫喊 jiàohǎn [声 shēng]
□ He gave a cry of surprise. 他惊讶的叫喊了一声。Tā jīngyà de jiàohǎn le yìshēng.

crystal NOUN
水晶 shuǐjīng [块 kuài]

cub NOUN
1 幼兽 yòushòu [只 zhī] *(animal)*
2 幼童军 yòutóngjūn [名 míng] *(scout)*

cube NOUN
立方体 lìfāngtǐ [个 gè]

cubic ADJECTIVE
立方的 lìfāng de
■ **a cubic metre** 一立方米 yí lìfāngmǐ

cucumber NOUN
黄瓜 huángguā [根 gēn]

to **cuddle** VERB
▷ *see also* **cuddle** NOUN
搂抱 lǒubào
□ Emma cuddled her teddy bear. 艾玛搂抱着她的泰迪熊。Àimǎ lǒubào zhe tāde tàidíxióng.

cuddle NOUN
▷ *see also* **cuddle** VERB
拥抱 yōngbào [个 gè]
□ Come and give me a cuddle. 来给我一个拥抱。Lái gěi wǒ yígè yōngbào.

cultural ADJECTIVE
文化的 wénhuà de
culture NOUN
文化 wénhuà [种 zhǒng]
cunning ADJECTIVE
狡猾的 jiǎohuá de
cup NOUN
1 杯子 bēizi [个 gè]
□ a china cup 一个陶瓷杯 yígè táocíbēi
■ **a cup of tea** 一杯茶 yìbēi chá
2 奖杯 jiǎngbēi [个 gè] *(trophy)*
cupboard NOUN
柜子 guìzi [个 gè]
curb NOUN (US)
路缘 lùyuán [个 gè]
to **cure** VERB
▷ *see also* **cure** NOUN
1 治疗 zhìliáo *(disease)*
2 治愈 zhìyù *(patient)*
cure NOUN
▷ *see also* **cure** VERB
疗法 liáofǎ [种 zhǒng]
curious ADJECTIVE
好奇的 hàoqí de
■ **to be curious about something** 对某物感到好奇 duì mǒuwu gǎndào hàoqí
curl NOUN
卷发 juǎnfà [头 tóu]
curly ADJECTIVE
卷曲的 juǎnqū de
currant NOUN
无子葡萄干 wúzǐ pútao gān [粒 lì]
currency NOUN
货币 huòbì [种 zhǒng]
■ **foreign currency** 外汇 wàihuì [种 zhǒng]
current NOUN
▷ *see also* **current** ADJECTIVE
1 电流 diànliú [股 gǔ] *(electricity)*
2 流 liú [股 gǔ] *(of air, water)*
current ADJECTIVE
▷ *see also* **current** NOUN
目前的 mùqián de
□ the current situation 目前的形势 mùqián de xíngshì
current account NOUN
活期账户 huóqī zhànghù [个 gè]
current affairs PL NOUN
时事 shíshì
curriculum NOUN
1 全部课程 quánbù kèchéng
2 课程 kèchéng [门 mén] *(for particular subject)*
curriculum vitae NOUN
简历 jiǎnlì [份 fèn]
curry NOUN
咖哩 gālí [种 zhǒng]
LANGUAGE TIP gālí actually comes from the English word **curry**.
curtain NOUN
窗帘 chuānglián [幅 fù]
cushion NOUN
靠垫 kàodiàn [个 gè]
custard NOUN
软冻 ruǎndòng [个 gè] *(for pouring)*
custody NOUN
监护 jiānhù *(of child)*
custom NOUN
习俗 xísú [个 gè]
□ It's an old custom. 这是个旧习俗。Zhè shì gè jiù xísú.
customer NOUN
顾客 gùkè [位 wèi]
customs PL NOUN
海关 hǎiguān
■ **to go through customs** 过海关 guò hǎiguān
customs officer NOUN
海关官员 hǎiguān guānyuán [位 wèi]
cut NOUN
▷ *see also* **cut** VERB
1 伤口 shāngkǒu [个 gè]
□ He's got a cut on his forehead. 他的额头上有一个伤口。Tāde étou shàng yǒu yígè shāngkǒu.
2 剪发 jiǎnfà [次 cì] *(haircut)*
□ a cut and blow-dry 剪发吹干 jiǎnfà chuīgān
3 削减 xuējiǎn [次 cì] *(reduction)*
to **cut** VERB
▷ *see also* **cut** NOUN
1 切 qiē
□ I'll cut some bread. 我去切些面包。Wǒ qù qiē xiē miànbāo.
■ **to cut something in half** 将某物切成两半 jiāng mǒuwù qiēchéng liǎngbàn
■ **to cut oneself** 割破自己 gēpò zìjǐ
□ I cut my foot on a piece of glass. 我的脚被一片玻璃割破了。Wǒde jiǎo bèi yípiàn bōli gēpò le.
2 削减 xiāojiǎn *(price, spending)*
3 修剪 xiūjiǎn *(grass, hair, nails with scissors)*
■ **to get one's hair cut** 剪发 jiǎnfà
to **cut down** VERB
1 砍倒 kǎndǎo *(tree)*
2 减少 jiǎnshǎo *(reduce)*
□ I'm cutting down on coffee and cigarettes. 我正在减少喝咖啡和吸烟。Wǒ zhèngzài jiǎnshǎo hē kāfēi hé xīyān.
to **cut off** VERB
1 切掉 qiēdiào
□ Cut off the ends of the carrots. 切掉胡萝

卜的根部。Qiēdiào húluóbo de gēnbù.
2 切断 qiēduàn
▫ The electricity was cut off. 电被切断了。 Diàn bèi qiēduàn le.

to **cut up** VERB
切碎 qiēsuì

cutback NOUN
减少 jiǎnshǎo [次 cì]
▫ staff cutbacks 裁员 cáiyuán

cute ADJECTIVE
可爱的 kě'ài de

cutlery NOUN
餐具 cānjù [套 tào]

CV NOUN
简历 jiǎnlì [份 fèn]

cyberbullying NOUN
网络暴力 wǎngluò bàolì

cybercafé NOUN
网吧 wǎngbā

cycle NOUN
▹ *see also* **cycle** VERB
自行车 zìxíngchē [辆 liàng]
▫ a cycle ride 一次自行车骑行 yícì zìxíngchē qíxíng
▪ **a cycle lane** 一条自行车道 yìtiáo zìxíngchēdào

to **cycle** VERB
▹ *see also* **cycle** NOUN
骑自行车 qí zìxíngchē
▫ I like cycling. 我喜欢骑自行车。Wǒ xǐhuan qí zìxíngchē. ▫ I cycle to school. 我骑自行车去学校。Wǒ qí zìxíngchē qù xuéxiào.

cycling NOUN
骑自行车 qí zìxíngchē

cyclist NOUN
骑自行车的人 qí zìxíngchē de rén [个 gè]

cylinder NOUN
罐 guàn [个 gè] *(of gas)*

cynical ADJECTIVE
愤世嫉俗的 fènshìjísú de

Cyprus NOUN
塞浦路斯 Sàipǔlùsī

Czech NOUN
▹ *see also* **Czech** ADJECTIVE
1 捷克人 Jiékèrén [个 gè] *(person)*
2 捷克语 Jiékèyǔ *(language)*

Czech ADJECTIVE
▹ *see also* **Czech** NOUN
捷克的 Jiékè de
▪ **the Czech Republic** 捷克共和国 Jiékègònghéguó

Dd

dad NOUN
爸 bà [个 gè]
□ my dad 我爸 wǒ bà □ Dad! 爸！Bà!

daddy NOUN
爸爸 bàba [个 gè]
□ Say hello to your daddy! 跟爸爸打招呼！Gēn bàba dǎ zhāohu!

daffodil NOUN
黄水仙 huángshuǐxiān [支 zhī]

daft ADJECTIVE
笨的 bèn de

daily ADJECTIVE
▷ *see also* **daily** ADVERB
每日的 měirì de
□ It's part of my daily routine. 这是我每日事务的一部分。Zhè shì wǒ měirì shìwù de yíbùfèn.

daily ADVERB
▷ *see also* **daily** ADJECTIVE
每天地 měitiān de
□ The pool is open daily. 这个泳池每天都开。Zhège yǒngchí měitiān dōu kāi.

dairy products PL NOUN
乳制品 rǔzhìpǐn [种 zhǒng]

daisy NOUN
雏菊 chújú [朵 duǒ]

dam NOUN
水坝 shuǐbà [个 gè]

damage NOUN
▷ *see also* **damage** VERB
1 损坏 sǔnhuài
□ The storm did a lot of damage. 风暴造成严重的损坏。Fēngbào zàochéng yánzhòng de sǔnhuài.
2 损伤 sǔnshāng *(dents, scratches)*

to **damage** VERB
▷ *see also* **damage** NOUN
毁坏 huǐhuài

damn ADJECTIVE, ADVERB
■ **It's a damn nuisance!** *(informal)* 真是该死地讨厌！Zhēnshì gāisǐ de tǎoyàn!
■ **Damn!** *(informal)* 该死！Gāisǐ!

damp ADJECTIVE
潮湿的 cháoshī de

dance NOUN
▷ *see also* **dance** VERB
1 舞蹈 wǔdǎo [曲 qǔ]
□ The last dance was a waltz. 最后的舞蹈是一支华尔兹。Zuìhòu de wǔdǎo shì yìzhī huá'ěrzī.
2 舞会 wǔhuì [个 gè] *(social event)*
□ Are you going to the dance tonight? 你去今晚的舞会吗？Nǐ qù jīnwǎn de wǔhuì ma?

to **dance** VERB
▷ *see also* **dance** VERB
跳舞 tiàowǔ
■ **to go dancing** 去跳舞 qù tiàowǔ □ Let's go dancing! 我们去跳舞吧！Wǒmen qù tiàowǔ ba!

dancer NOUN
舞蹈演员 wǔdǎo yǎnyuán [位 wèi]

dancing NOUN
跳舞 tiàowǔ

dandruff NOUN
头皮屑 tóupíxiè

Dane NOUN
丹麦人 Dānmàirén [个 gè]

danger NOUN
危险 wēixiǎn [种 zhǒng]
□ There is a danger that... 有…的危险 Yǒu...de wēixiǎn
■ **in danger** 有危险 yǒu wēixiǎn □ His life is in danger. 他有生命危险。Tā yǒu shēngmìng wēixiǎn.
■ **to be in danger of doing something** 有某事的危险 yǒu mǒushì de wēixiǎn □ We were in danger of missing the plane. 我们有赶不上飞机的危险。Wǒmen yǒu gǎnbushàng fēijī de wēixiǎn.

dangerous ADJECTIVE
危险的 wēixiǎn de
□ It's dangerous to... …是危险的 ...shì wēixiǎn de

Danish ADJECTIVE
▷ *see also* **Danish** NOUN
丹麦的 Dānmài de

Danish NOUN
▷ *see also* **Danish** ADJECTIVE
丹麦语 Dānmàiyǔ *(language)*

to **dare** VERB
■ **to dare to do something** 敢做某事 gǎn zuò mǒushì □ I didn't dare to tell my parents. 我不敢告诉我父母。Wǒ bùgǎn gàosù wǒ fùmǔ. □ I daren't tell him. 我不敢告诉他。Wǒ bùgǎn gàosù tā.
■ **to dare somebody to do something** *(challenge)* 激某人做某事 jī mǒurén zuò mǒushì
■ **I dare say** *(I suppose)* 我相信 wǒ xiāngxìn □ I dare say it'll be okay. 我相信会没事的。Wǒ xiāngxìn huì méishì de.
■ **How dare you!** 你竟敢！Nǐ jìnggǎn!

daring ADJECTIVE
勇敢的 yǒnggǎn de

dark ADJECTIVE
▷ *see also* **dark** NOUN
1 黑暗的 hēi'àn de *(room, night)*
2 黑色的 hēisè de *(eyes, hair, skin)*
□ She's got dark hair. 她头发是黑色的。Ta tóufà shì hēisè de.
3 深色的 shēnsè de *(suit, fabric)*
■ **dark green** 深绿色 shēnlǜsè □ a dark green sweater 一件深绿色的毛衣 yíjiàn shēnlǜsè de máoyī
■ **It's dark.** 天黑了。Tiān hēile. □ It's dark outside. 外面天黑了。Wàimiàn tiān hēile. □ It's getting dark. 天要黑了。Tiān yào hēile.

dark NOUN
▷ *see also* **dark** ADJECTIVE
■ **the dark** 黑暗 hēi'àn □ I'm afraid of the dark. 我怕黑。Wǒ pà hēi.
■ **after dark** 天黑以后 tiānhēi yǐhòu

darkness NOUN
黑暗 hēi'àn
□ The room was in darkness. 房间里一片黑暗。Fángjiān lǐ yípiàn hēi'àn.

darling NOUN
亲爱的 qīn'àide
□ Thank you, darling! 谢谢你，亲爱的！Xièxie nǐ, qīn'àide!

dart NOUN
飞镖 fēibiāo [支 zhī]
■ **darts** 飞镖游戏 fēibiāo yóuxì □ to play darts 玩飞镖游戏 wán fēibiāo yóuxì

to **dash** VERB
▷ *see also* **dash** NOUN
冲 chōng
□ Everyone dashed to the window. 每个人都冲到窗户前。Měigèrén dōu chōng dào chuānghu qián.
■ **I must dash!** 我得赶紧走了！Wǒ děi gǎnjǐn zǒu le!

dash NOUN
▷ *see also* **dash** VERB
破折号 pòzhéhào [个 gè] *(punctuation mark)*

data PL NOUN
数据 shùjù

database NOUN
数据库 shùjùkù [个 gè]

date NOUN
▷ *see also* **date** VERB
1 日期 rìqī [个 gè]
□ date of birth 出生日期 chūshēng rìqī
■ **What's the date today?** 今天几号？Jīntiān jǐhào?
■ **to be out of date** 1 *(old-fashioned)* 落伍 luòwǔ 2 *(expired)* 过期 guòqī
■ **to be up to date** *(modern)* 时新 shíxīn
2 约会 yuēhuì [个 gè]
■ **to have a date with somebody** 和某人约会 hé mǒurén yuēhuì □ She's got a date with Ian tonight. 她今晚和伊安有约会。Tā jīnwǎn hé Yī'ān yǒu yuēhuì.
3 海枣 hǎizǎo [颗 kē] *(fruit)*

to **date** VERB
▷ *see also* **date** NOUN
给...注明日期 gěi...zhùmíng rìqī *(letter, cheque)*

daughter NOUN
女儿 nǚ'ér [个 gè]

daughter-in-law NOUN
儿媳妇 érxífu [个 gè]

dawn NOUN
黎明 límíng [个 gè]
■ **at dawn** 拂晓 fúxiǎo

day NOUN
1 天 tiān
□ We stayed in Shanghai for three days. 我们在上海待了三天。Wǒmen zài Shànghǎi dāile sāntiān.
2 白天 báitiān [个 gè] *(daylight hours)*
□ during the day 在白天 zài báitiān □ by day 在白天 zài báitiān
■ **the day before** 前一天 qián yìtiān □ the day before my birthday 我生日前一天 wǒ shēngrì qián yìtiān
■ **the day after tomorrow** 后天 hòutiān □ We're leaving the day after tomorrow. 我们后天动身。Wǒmen hòutiān dòngshēn.
■ **the day before yesterday** 前天 qiántiān □ He arrived the day before yesterday. 他是前天到的。Tā shì qiántiān dào de.
■ **these days** *(nowadays)* 现今 xiànjīn
■ **the following day** 第二天 dì'èrtiān
■ **one of these days** 有一天 yǒu yìtiān
■ **every day** 每天 měitiān
■ **all day** 终日 zhōngrì □ I stayed at home all day. 他终日待在家里。Tā zhōngrì dāi zài jiālǐ.

■ **to work an 8 hour day** 每天工作八小时 měitiān gōngzuò bā xiǎoshí

daylight NOUN
白昼 báizhòu

dead ADJECTIVE, ADVERB
1 死的 sǐ de
□ He was already dead when the doctor came. 医生来的时候他已经死了。Yīshēng lái de shíhòu tā yǐjīng sǐ le.
■ **He was shot dead.** 他中枪身亡。Tā zhòngqiāng shēnwáng.
■ **Over my dead body!** *(informal)* 绝对不行！Juéduì bùxíng!
2 不能再用的 bùnéng zài yòng de *(battery)*
3 十分 shífēn *(informal: totally)*
□ You're dead right! 你说的十分对！Nǐ shuōde shífēn duì!
■ **dead on time** 准时 zhǔnshí □ The train arrived dead on time. 火车准时到达。Huǒchē zhǔnshí dàodá.

deadline NOUN
截止日期 jiézhǐ rìqī [个 gè]
□ The deadline for entries is May 2nd. 参赛截止日期是五月二号。Cānsài jiézhǐ rìqī shì wǔyuè èrhào.
■ **to meet a deadline** 如期 rúqī

deaf ADJECTIVE
1 聋的 lóng de
2 耳背的 ěrbèi de *(partially)*

deafening ADJECTIVE
震耳欲聋的 zhèn ěr yù lóng de *(noise)*

LANGUAGE TIP Word for word, this means 'shaking one's ears to the point of causing deafness'.

deal NOUN
▷ *see also* **deal** VERB
交易 jiāoyì [个 gè]
■ **to make a deal with somebody** 和某人做买卖 hé mǒurén zuò mǎimài
■ **It's a deal!** 成交！Chéngjiāo!
■ **a great deal** 很多 hěnduō □ a great deal of money 很多钱 hěnduō qián

to **deal** VERB
▷ *see also* **deal** NOUN
发牌 fāpái *(cards)*
□ It's your turn to deal. 该你发牌了。Gāi nǐ fāpái le.
■ **to deal with something** 处理某事 chùlǐ mǒushì □ He promised to deal with it immediately. 他承诺会立即处理。Tā chéngnuò huì lìjí chùlǐ.

dealer NOUN
1 商人 shāngrén [个 gè] *(in goods)*
2 毒品贩子 dúpǐn fànzi [个 gè] *(in drugs)*

dealt VERB ▷ *see* **deal**

dear ADJECTIVE
▷ *see also* **dear** NOUN, EXCLAMATION
1 亲爱的 qīn'ài de
■ **Dear Sir** 亲爱的先生 Qīn'ài de xiānshēng
■ **Dear Jane** 亲爱的简 Qīn'ài de Jiǎn
■ **Dear Sir/Madam** 尊敬的先生/女士 Zūnjìng de xiānshēng/nǚshì
2 昂贵的 ángguì de *(expensive)*

dear NOUN, EXCLAMATION
▷ *see also* **dear** ADJECTIVE
■ **my dear** 亲爱的 qīn'ài de
■ **Oh dear!** 哎呀！Āiyā!

death NOUN
死亡 sǐwáng [个 gè]
□ after his death 在他死后 zài tā sǐhòu
■ **a matter of life and death** 生死攸关的事情 shēngsǐ yōuguān de shìqing
■ **to bore somebody to death** 使某人感到无聊之极 shǐ mǒurén gǎndào wúliáo zhī jí
□ I was bored to death. 我真是无聊极了。Wǒ zhēnshì wúliáo jíle.

death penalty NOUN
■ **the death penalty** 死刑 sǐxíng

debate NOUN
▷ *see also* **debate** VERB
讨论 tǎolùn [次 cì]

to **debate** VERB
▷ *see also* **debate** NOUN
辩论 biànlùn

debt NOUN
1 债务 zhàiwù [笔 bǐ] *(money owed)*
□ He's got a lot of debts. 他欠了很多债。Tā qiànle hěnduō zhài.
2 欠债 qiànzhài *(indebtedness)*
■ **to be in debt** 负债 fùzhài

decade NOUN
十年 shínián [个 gè]

decaffeinated ADJECTIVE
不含咖啡因的 bù hán kāfēiyīn de

to **decay** VERB
衰败 shuāibài *(building)*
□ a decaying mansion 一栋破败的大楼 yídòng pòbài de dàlóu

to **deceive** VERB
欺骗 qīpiàn

December NOUN
十二月 shí'èryuè
□ in December 在十二月 zài shí'èryuè □ at the beginning of December 在十二末 zài shí'èryuè mò □ at the end of December 每年十二月 měinián shí'èryuè □ every December

decent ADJECTIVE
体面的 shòu zūnzhòng de *(person)*
■ **a decent education** 体面的教育 tǐmiàn de jiàoyù

English-Chinese

d

to **decide** VERB
1 解决 jiějué *(question, argument)*
2 决定 juédìng *(make up one's mind)*
□ I can't decide. 我做不了决定。Wǒ zuòbuliǎo juédìng. □ Haven't you decided yet? 你还没决定吗？Nǐ háiméi juédìng ma? □ I can't decide whether... 我无法决定是否… Wǒ wúfǎ juédìng shìfǒu...
■ **to decide to do something** 决定做某事 juédìng zuò mǒushì □ I decided to write to her. 我决定给她写信。Wǒ juédìng gěi tā xiěxìn. □ I decided not to go. 我决定不去了。Wǒ juédìng búqùle.
■ **to decide on something** 定下某事 dìng xià mǒushì □ They haven't decided on a name yet. 他们还没定下起什么名字。Tāmen hái méi dìng xià qǐ shénme míngzì.

decimal ADJECTIVE
▷ *see also* **decimal** NOUN
十进位的 shíjìnwèi de *(system, currency)*
□ the decimal system 十进制 shíjìnzhì

decimal NOUN
▷ *see also* **decimal** ADJECTIVE
小数 xiǎoshù [个 gè]

decision NOUN
决定 juédìng [个 gè]
■ **to make a decision** 作出决定 zuòchū juédìng

decisive ADJECTIVE
果断的 guǒduàn de *(person)*

deck NOUN
1 甲板 jiǎbǎn [个 gè]
■ **on deck** 在甲板上 zài jiǎbǎn shàng
2 一付纸牌 yífù zhǐpái *(of cards)*

deckchair NOUN
折叠式躺椅 zhédiéshì tǎngyǐ [把 bǎ]

to **declare** VERB
1 宣布 xuānbù *(intention, attitude)*
2 表明 biǎomíng *(support)*
3 报关 bàoguān *(at customs)*
■ **to declare war on** 对…宣战 duì... xuānzhàn

to **decorate** VERB
1 装饰 zhuāngshì
□ I decorated the cake with glacé cherries. 我用糖衣樱桃装饰了蛋糕。Wǒ yòng tángyī yīngtáo zhuāngshì le dàngāo.
2 装潢 zhuānghuáng *(paint, wallpaper)*

decoration NOUN
装饰 zhuāngshì [种 zhǒng]

decrease NOUN
▷ *see also* **decrease** VERB
■ **decrease in something** 某物减少 mǒuwù jiǎnshǎo □ a decrease in the number of unemployed 失业人员人数的减少 shīyè rényuán rénshù de jiǎnshǎo

to **decrease** VERB
▷ *see also* **decrease** NOUN
减少 jiǎnshǎo

dedicated ADJECTIVE
献身的 xiànshēn de
□ a very dedicated teacher 一位很有献身精神的老师 yíwèi hěn yǒu xiànshēn jīngshénde lǎoshī
■ **dedicated to 1** 专用于某事的 zhuānyòng yú mǒushì de □ a museum dedicated to science 一座专用于科学展览的博物馆 yízuò zhuānyòng yú kēxué zhǎnlǎn de bówùguǎn **2** 献给 xiàngěi
□ The book is dedicated to Emma. 此书献给艾玛。Cǐ shū xiàngěi Àimǎ.

dedication NOUN
1 献身 xiànshēn *(commitment)*
2 题辞 tící *(in book, on radio)*

to **deduct** VERB
■ **to deduct something from something** 从某物中减去某物 cóng mǒuwùzhōng jiǎnqù mǒuwù

deep ADJECTIVE
1 深的 shēn de
□ Is it deep? 这个深吗？Zhège shēn ma?
□ How deep is the lake? 这湖有多深？Zhè hú yǒu duō shēn? □ The snow was really deep. 积雪很深。Jīxuě hěnshēn.
2 深 shēn *(in depth)*
□ It is 1 m deep. 它有一米深。Tā yǒu yìmǐ shēn.
3 低沉的 dīchén de *(voice, sound)*
□ He's got a deep voice. 他嗓音低沉。Tā sǎngyīn dīchén.
4 酣睡的 hānshuì de *(sleep)*
■ **to take a deep breath** 深呼吸 shēn hūxī

deeply ADVERB
1 深深地 shēnshēn de *(breathe, sigh)*
2 沉沉地 chénchén de *(sleep)*

deer NOUN
鹿 lù [头 tóu]

defeat NOUN
▷ *see also* **defeat** VERB
1 战败 zhànbài [次 cì] *(of army)*
2 击败 jībài [次 cì] *(of team)*

to **defeat** VERB
▷ *see also* **defeat** NOUN
1 战胜 zhànshèng *(enemy, opposition)*
2 击败 jībài *(team)*

defect NOUN
缺点 quēdiǎn [个 gè]

defence (US **defense**) NOUN
1 防御 fángyù *(protection)*
2 国防措施 guófáng cuòshī *(military)*
■ **the Ministry of Defence** 国防部

Guófángbù

to **defend** VERB
防御 fángyù
■ **to defend oneself** 自卫 zìwèi

defender NOUN
防守队员 fángshǒu duìyuán [个 gè] *(in team)*

defense NOUN (US)
1 防御 fángyù *(protection)*
2 国防措施 guófáng cuòshī *(military)*

to **define** VERB
下定义 xiàdìngyì

definite ADJECTIVE
1 明确的 míngquè de *(plan, answer, views)*
□ I haven't got any definite plans. 我没有什么明确的计划。Wǒ méiyǒu shénme míngquè de jìhuà.
2 肯定的 kěndìng de *(possibility, advantage)*
□ It's a definite improvement. 这肯定是种进步。Zhè kěndìng shì zhǒng jìnbù. □ Is that definite? 肯定吗？Kěndìng ma? □ We might go to Spain, but it's not definite. 我们有可能去西班牙，但还不肯定。Wǒmen yǒu kěnéng qù Xībānyá, dàn hái bù kěndìng. □ He was definite about it. 他对此很肯定。Tā duì cǐ hěn kěndìng.

definitely ADVERB
绝对地 juéduì de
□ He's definitely the best player. 他绝对是最棒的选手。Tā juéduì shì zuìbàng de xuǎnshǒu. □ I definitely think he'll come. 我认为他绝对会来。Wǒ rènwéi tā juéduì huì lái.

definition NOUN
定义 dìngyì [个 gè]

to **defy** VERB
蔑视 miǎoshì *(law, ban)*

degree NOUN
1 度 dù *(measure of temperature, angle, latitude)*
□ a temperature of 30 degrees 三十度的气温 sānshídù de qìwēn □ 10 degrees below zero 零下十度 língxià shídù
2 学位 xuéwèi [个 gè] *(at university)*
□ a degree in maths 数学学位 shùxué xuéwèi
■ **to some degree** 就一定程度上来说 jiù yídìng chéngdù shàng lái shuō

to **delay** VERB
▷ *see also* **delay** NOUN
1 延迟 yánchí *(decision, event)*
□ We decided to delay our departure. 我们决定延迟离开。Wǒmen juédìng yánchí líkāi.
2 耽搁 dānge *(person)*
3 延误 yánwù *(plane, train)*
■ **to be delayed** *(person, flight, departure)* 晚点 wǎndiǎn □ Our flight was delayed. 我们的飞机晚点了。Wǒmen de fēijī wǎndiǎn le.
4 拖延 tuōyán *(be slow)*
□ Don't delay! 别拖延了！Bié tuōyán le!

delay NOUN
▷ *see also* **delay** VERB
延误 yánwù [个 gè]
□ There will be delays to trains on the London-Brighton line. 伦敦、布莱顿方向的列车会出现延误。Lúndūn–Bùláidùn fāngxiàng de lièchē huì chūxiàn yánwù.
■ **without delay** 立即 lìjí

to **delete** VERB
删除 shānchú

deliberate ADJECTIVE
故意的 gùyì de
□ It wasn't deliberate. 那不是故意的。Nà búshì gùyì de.

deliberately ADVERB
故意地 gùyì de
□ She did it deliberately. 她是故意这么做的。Tā shì gùyì zhème zuò de.

delicate ADJECTIVE
1 易碎的 yìsuì de *(fragile)*
2 微妙的 wēimiào de *(problem, situation, issue)*
3 清淡的 qīngdàn de *(colour, flavour, smell)*

delicious ADJECTIVE
美味的 měiwèi de

delight NOUN
快乐 kuàilè
■ **to her delight** 让她高兴的是 ràng tā gāoxìng de shì

delighted ADJECTIVE
■ **to be delighted to do something** 乐意做某事 lèyì zuò mǒushì □ He'll be delighted to see you. 他会很乐意见到你。Tā huì hěn lèyì jiàndào nǐ.
■ **delighted with something** 喜欢某物 xǐhuan mǒuwù

delightful ADJECTIVE
愉快的 yúkuàide *(meal, evening)*

to **deliver** VERB
1 传送 chuánsòng *(letter, parcel)*
□ I deliver newspapers. 我送报纸。Wǒ sòng bàozhǐ.
2 接生 jiēshēng *(baby)*

delivery NOUN
1 递送服务 dìsòng fúwù *(service)*
2 递送的货物 dìsòng de huòwù [件 jiàn] *(consignment)*

to **demand** VERB
▷ *see also* **demand** NOUN
要求 yāoqiú *(apology, explanation, pay rise)*

demand NOUN
▷ *see also* **demand** VERB
1 要求 yāoqiú [个 gè] *(request)*
2 需求 xūqiú *(for product)*
■ **to make demands on somebody** 对某人提出要求 duì mǒurén tíchū yāoqiú
■ **to be in demand** 销路好 xiāolù hǎo

demanding ADJECTIVE
要求高的 yāoqiú gāo de
□ It's a very demanding job. 这是一份要求很高的工作。Zhè shì yífèn yāoqiú hěn gāo de gōngzuò.

demo NOUN
示威 shìwēi *(protest)*

democracy NOUN
1 民主 mínzhǔ *(system)*
2 民主国家 mínzhǔ guójiā [个 gè] *(country)*

democratic ADJECTIVE
民主的 mínzhǔ de

to **demolish** VERB
拆毁 chāihuǐ

to **demonstrate** VERB
1 演示 yǎnshì *(skill, appliance)*
□ She demonstrated the technique. 她演示这种技术。Tā yǎnshì zhèzhǒng jìshù.
■ **to demonstrate how to do something** 演示如何做某事 yǎnshì rúhé zuò mǒushì
2 示威 shìwēi *(protest)*
□ to demonstrate against something 示威反对某事 shìwēi fǎnduì mǒushì

demonstration NOUN
1 示威 shìwēi [次 cì] *(protest)*
2 演示 yǎnshì [个 gè] *(of appliance, cooking)*

demonstrator NOUN
示威者 shìwēizhě [个 gè] *(protester)*

denim NOUN
斜纹粗棉布 xiéwén cū miánbù
□ a denim jacket 一件斜纹粗棉布夹克 yíjiàn xiéwén cū miánbù jiákè

denims PL NOUN
牛仔裤 niúzǎikù *(jeans)*

Denmark NOUN
丹麦 Dānmài

dense ADJECTIVE
浓密的 nóngmì de *(crowd, fog, smoke)*

dent NOUN
▷ *see also* **dent** VERB
凹痕 āohén [个 gè]

to **dent** VERB
▷ *see also* **dent** NOUN
使凹下 shǐ āo xià

dental ADJECTIVE
牙齿的 yáchǐ de
■ **dental floss** 牙线 yáxiàn

dentist NOUN
牙医 yáyī [位 wèi]

LANGUAGE TIP Word for word, this means 'tooth doctor'.

■ **the dentist's** 牙医诊所 yáyī zhěnsuǒ [家 jiā]

to **deny** VERB
否认 fǒurèn
□ She denied everything. 她否认了一切。Tā fǒurèn le yíqiè.

deodorant NOUN
除臭剂 chúchòujì [种 zhǒng]

to **depart** VERB
■ **to depart from somewhere** 从某地出发 cóng mǒudì chūfā

department NOUN
1 部 bù [个 gè] *(in shop)*
□ the children's shoe department 商场童鞋部门 shāngchǎng tóngxié bùmén
2 系 xì [个 gè] *(in university, school)*
□ the English department 英语系 yīngyǔxì

department store NOUN
百货商店 bǎihuò shāngdiàn [家 jiā]

departure NOUN
出发 chūfā

departure lounge NOUN
候机厅 hòujītīng [个 gè]

to **depend** VERB
■ **to depend on 1** *(be affected by)* 依而定 yī érdìng □ The price depends on the quality. 价格依品质而定。Jiàgé yī pǐnzhì érdìng. □ depending on the weather 依天气而定 yī tiānqì érdìng **2** *(rely on, trust)* 仰赖 yǎnglài □ You can depend on him. 你可以仰赖他。Nǐ kěyǐ yǎnglài tā.
■ **It all depends.** 要看情况而定。Yào kàn qíngkuàng érdìng.

to **deport** VERB
把...驱逐出境 bǎ...qūzhúchūjìng

deposit NOUN
1 存款 cúnkuǎn [笔 bǐ] *(in account)*
2 押金 yājīn [份 fèn] *(on house, hired article)*
□ You get the deposit back when you return the bike. 你归还自行车时可以拿回押金。Nǐ guīhuán zìxíngchē shí kěyǐ náhuí yājīn.
■ **to put down a deposit of 50 pounds** 支付五十英镑的保证金 zhīfù wǔshí yīngbàng de bǎozhèngjīn

depressed ADJECTIVE
沮丧的 jǔsàng de
□ I'm feeling depressed. 我感到沮丧。Wǒ gǎndào jǔsàng.

depressing ADJECTIVE
令人沮丧的 lìng rén jǔsàng de

to **deprive** VERB
■ **to deprive somebody of something** 剥夺某人某物 bōduó mǒurén mǒuwù

depth NOUN
深 shēn
■ **to a depth of 3 metres** 深达三米 shēndá sānmǐ
■ **to study something in depth** 深入研究某事 shēnrù yánjiū mǒushì

deputy head NOUN
副校长 fùxiàozhǎng [个 gè]

to **descend** VERB
下来 xiàlái
■ **to be descended from** 是…的后裔 shì... de hòuyì

to **describe** VERB
描述 miáoshù

description NOUN
描述 miáoshù [种 zhǒng]

desert NOUN
1 沙漠 shāmò [片 piàn]*(sand)*
2 荒地 huāngdì [片 piàn]*(wasteland)*

desert island NOUN
荒岛 huāngdǎo [座 zuò]

to **deserve** VERB
应受 yīng shòu
■ **to deserve to do something** 应受某物 yīngshòu mǒuwù

design NOUN
▷ *see also* **design** VERB
1 设计 shèjì*(art, process, layout, shape)*
■ **fashion design** 时尚设计 shíshàng shèjì
2 图案 tú'àn [种 zhǒng]*(pattern)*
□ a geometric design 一种几何图案 yìzhǒng jǐhé tú'àn

to **design** VERB
▷ *see also* **design** NOUN
设计 shèjì
■ **to be designed to do something** 专门为某事设计的 zhuānmén wèi mǒushì shèjì de

designer NOUN
▷ *see also* **designer** ADJECTIVE
设计师 shèjìshī [位 wèi]*(person)*

designer ADJECTIVE
▷ *see also* **designer** NOUN
名师设计的 míngshī shèjì de*(clothes, label, jeans)*

desire NOUN
▷ *see also* **desire** VERB
欲望 yùwàng [种 zhǒng]

to **desire** VERB
▷ *see also* **desire** NOUN
渴望 kěwàng

desk NOUN
1 办公桌 bàngōngzhuō [张 zhāng]*(in office)*
2 课桌 kèzhuō [张 zhāng]*(for pupil)*
3 服务台 fúwùtái [个 gè]*(in hotel, at airport, hospital)*

desk clerk NOUN (US)
接待员 jiēdàiyuán [位 wèi]

desktop NOUN
桌面 zhuōmiàn*(computer)*

despair NOUN
绝望 juéwàng
■ **in despair** 绝望地 juéwàng de □ I was in despair. 我很绝望。Wǒ hěn juéwàng.

desperate ADJECTIVE
1 绝望的 juéwàng de*(person)*
■ **to get desperate** 变得绝望 biàn de juéwàng □ I was getting desperate. 我变得绝望了。Wǒ biàn de juéwàng le.
2 不顾一切的 búgù yíqiè de*(attempt, effort)*
3 无可救药的 wúkějiùyào de*(situation)*

desperately ADVERB
1 拼命地 pīnmìng de*(try, struggle)*
□ He was desperately trying to persuade her. 他拼命地试着劝服她。Tā pīnmìng de shìzhe quànfú tā.
2 极度地 jídù de*(extremely)*
□ We're desperately worried. 我们极度地担心。Wǒmen jídùde dānxīn.

to **despise** VERB
鄙视 bǐshì

despite PREPOSITION
尽管 jǐnguǎn

dessert NOUN
饭后甜点 fànhòu tiándiǎn [份 fèn]
□ for dessert 作为饭后甜点 zuòwéi fànhòu tiándiǎn

> **DID YOU KNOW...?**
> Sweet desserts are not traditionally popular in China, where meals often finish with a serving of fruit.

destination NOUN
目的地 mùdìdì [个 gè]

to **destroy** VERB
破坏 pòhuài

destruction NOUN
破坏 pòhuài

detached house NOUN
独立式房屋 dúlì shì fángwū [栋 dòng]

detail NOUN
细节 xìjié [个 gè]
■ **in detail** 详细 xiángxì
■ **details** *(information)* 详情 xiángqíng

detailed ADJECTIVE
详细的 xiángxì de

detective NOUN
侦探 zhēntàn [个 gè]
■ **a private detective** 一个私家侦探 yíge sījiā zhēntàn

detective story NOUN
侦探小说 zhēntàn xiǎoshuō [部 bù]

detention NOUN
扣留 kòuliú [次 cì]
■ **to get a detention** 被课后留校 bèi kèhòu liúxiào

detergent NOUN
清洁剂 qīngjiéjì [种 zhǒng]

determined ADJECTIVE
坚定的 jiāndìng de
■ **to be determined to do something** 决心做某事 juéxīn zuò mǒushì □ She's determined to succeed. 她决心要成功。Tā juéxīn yào chénggōng.

detour NOUN
■ **to make a detour** 1 绕道 ràodào
2 (US: *on road*) 绕行道路 ràoxíng dàolù

devaluation NOUN
贬值 biǎnzhí

devastated ADJECTIVE
受到巨大打击的 shòu dào jùdà dǎjī de
□ I was devastated. 我收到巨大的打击。Wǒ shòu dào jùdà de dǎjī.

devastating ADJECTIVE
1 破坏性的 pòhuàixìng de *(upsetting)*
2 毁灭性的 hǔimièxìng de *(flood, storm)*

to **develop** VERB
1 发展 fāzhǎn *(business, idea, relationship)*
2 开发 kāifā *(land, resource, product, weapon)*
3 冲洗 chōngxǐ *(film)*
□ to get a film developed 冲洗照片 chōngxǐ zhàopiàn
4 发育 fāyù *(person)*
□ Girls develop faster than boys. 女孩发育比男孩早。Nǚhái fāyù bǐ nánhái zǎo.
5 发展壮大 fāzhǎn zhuàngdà *(become stronger, more complex)*
□ a developing country 发展中国家 fāzhǎnzhōng guójiā
■ **to develop into** 发展成 fāzhǎnchéng
□ The argument developed into a fight. 争论发展成了争斗。Zhēnglùn fāzhǎn chéngle zhēngdòu.

development NOUN
1 成长 chéngzhǎng *(growth)*
2 发展 fāzhǎn *(political, economic)*
3 进展 jìnzhǎn [种 zhǒng] *(event)*
□ the latest developments 最新的进展 zuìxīn de jìnzhǎn

devil NOUN
■ **the Devil** 魔王 mówáng [个 gè]

to **devise** VERB
发明 fāmíng

devoted ADJECTIVE
忠实的 zhōngshí de
□ He's completely devoted to her. 他对她十分忠实。Tā duì tā shífēn zhōngshí.
■ **devoted to something** *(specialising in)* 致力于某事的 zhìlì yú mǒushì de

diabetes NOUN
糖尿病 tángniàobìng

diabetic NOUN
糖尿病患者 tángniàobìng huànzhě [个 gè]
□ I'm a diabetic. 我是个糖尿病患者。Wǒ shìge tángniàobìng huànzhě.

diagonal ADJECTIVE
斜的 xié de

diagram NOUN
图解 tújiě [个 gè]

dial NOUN
▷ *see also* **dial** VERB
标度盘 biāodùpán [个 gè] *(on clock or meter)*

to **dial** VERB
▷ *see also* **dial** NOUN
1 拨 bō *(number)*
2 拨号 bōhào
□ Check the number and dial again. 检查下号码再拨打一次。Jiǎnchá xià hàomǎ zài bōdǎ yícì.

dialling code NOUN
电话区号 diànhuà qūhào [个 gè]

dialling tone NOUN
拨号音 bōhàoyīn [声 shēng]

dialogue (US **dialog**) NOUN
对话 duìhuà [次 cì] *(conversation)*

diamond NOUN
钻石 zuànshí [颗 kē]
□ a diamond ring 一枚钻石戒指 yìméi zuànshí jièzhǐ
■ **diamonds** *(cards)* 方块 fāngkuài □ the ace of diamonds 方块A fāngkuài A

diaper NOUN (US)
尿布 niàobù [块 kuài]

diarrhoea (US **diarrhea**) NOUN
腹泻 fùxiè [次 cì]
■ **to have diarrhoea** 腹泻 fùxiè □ I've got diarrhoea. 我腹泻了。Wǒ fùxiè le.

diary NOUN
1 日记簿 rìjìbù [本 běn]
□ I've got her phone number in my diary. 我日记簿里有她的电话号码。Wǒ rìjìbù lǐ yǒu tā de diànhuà hàomǎ.
2 日记 rìjì [篇 piān] *(daily account)*
□ I keep a diary. 我记日记。Wǒ jì rìjì.

dice NOUN
骰子 shǎizi [个 gè]

dictation NOUN
听写 tīngxiě [次 cì] *(at school, college)*

dictionary NOUN
词典 cídiǎn [本 běn]

did VERB ▷ *see* **do**

to **die** VERB
死 sǐ

▫ He died last year. 他去年死了。Tā qùnián sǐ le.

■ **to die of something** 死于某事 sǐyú mǒushì

■ **to be dying** 奄奄一息 yǎn yǎn yì xī

■ **to be dying to do something** 极想做某事 jíxiǎng zuò mǒushì ▫ I'm dying to see you. 我极想见你。Wǒ jí xiǎng jiàn nǐ.

to **die out** VERB

1 消灭 xiāomiè *(custom, way of life)*

2 灭绝 mièjué *(species)*

diesel NOUN

1 柴油 cháiyóu

▫ 30 litres of diesel 三十公升的柴油 sānshí gōngshēng de cháiyóu

2 柴油机驱动的车辆 cháiyóujī qūdòng de chēliàng [辆 liàng] *(car)*

▫ My car's a diesel. 我的车是柴油驱动的。Wǒ de chē shì cháiyóu qūdòng de.

diet NOUN

▹ *see also* **diet** VERB

1 饮食 yǐnshí [种 zhǒng]

▫ a healthy diet 一种健康的饮食 yìzhǒng jiànkāng de yǐnshí

2 减肥饮食 jiǎnféi yǐnshí [份 fèn] *(slimming)*

■ **to be on a diet** 实行减肥节食 shíxíng jiǎnféi jiéshí ▫ I'm on a diet. 我在减肥节食。Wǒ zài jiǎnféi jiéshí.

to **diet** VERB

▹ *see also* **diet** NOUN

节食 jiéshí

▫ I've been dieting for two months. 我已经节食两个月了。Wǒ yǐjīng jiéshí liǎng ge yuè le.

difference NOUN

差异 chāyì [种 zhǒng]

▫ the difference in size 尺寸上的差异 chǐcùn shàng de chāyì ▫ There's not much difference in age between us. 我们两个年龄相差不大。Wǒmen liǎngge niánlíng xiāngchà bú dà.

■ **to make a difference** 使…有区别 shǐ... yǒu qūbié ▫ It makes no difference. 这没什么区别。Zhè méi shénme qūbié.

different ADJECTIVE

不同的 bùtóng de

▫ We are very different. 我们很不相同。Wǒmen hěn bù xiāngtóng. ▫ Beijing is different from London. 北京不同于伦敦。Běijīng bùtóng yú Lúndūn.

difficult ADJECTIVE

1 困难的 kùnnán de

▫ It's difficult to choose. 这很难选择。Zhè hěn nán xuǎnzé. ▫ It is difficult for us to understand her. 我们很难理解她。Wǒmen hěnnán lǐjiě tā.

2 执拗的 zhí'ào de *(person, child)*

difficulty NOUN

困难 kùnnán [个 gè]

■ **to have difficulty doing something** 做某事有困难 zuòmǒushì yǒu kùnnán

▫ without difficulty 轻易 qīngyì

to **dig** VERB

1 挖掘 wājué *(use spade)*

2 挖 wā *(hole)*

3 掘土 juétǔ *(garden)*

to **dig up** VERB

挖出 wāchū *(plant, body)*

digestion NOUN

消化 xiāohuà

digger NOUN

挖掘器 wājuéqì [台 tái] *(machine)*

digital ADJECTIVE

1 数字的 shùzì de *(clock, watch)*

2 数码的 shùmǎ de *(recording, technology)*

digital camera NOUN

数码相机 shùmǎ xiàngjī [台 tái]

digital radio NOUN

数码收音机 shùmǎ shōuyīnjī [台 tái]

digital television NOUN

数字电视 shùzì diànshì

dim ADJECTIVE

1 暗淡的 àndàn de *(light)*

2 迟钝的 chídùn de *(stupid)*

dime NOUN (US)

一角银币 yìjiǎo yínbì [枚 méi]

dimension NOUN

维 wéi [个 gè] *(aspect)*

■ **dimensions** *(measurements)* 面积 miànjī

to **diminish** VERB

减少 jiǎnshǎo

to **dine** VERB

吃饭 chīfàn

diner NOUN

廉价餐馆 liánjià cānguǎn [家 jiā] *(US: restaurant)*

dinghy NOUN

小船 xiǎochuán [艘 sōu]

▫ a rubber dinghy 一艘小橡皮船 yì sōu xiǎoxiàngpíchuán

■ **a sailing dinghy** 一艘小帆船 yì sōu xiǎofānchuán

dining car NOUN

餐车 cānchē [节 jié]

dining room NOUN

1 饭厅 fàntīng [个 gè] *(in house)*

2 餐厅 cāntīng [个 gè] *(in hotel)*

dinner NOUN

1 晚餐 wǎncān [顿 dùn]

2 宴会 yánhuì [次 cì] *(formal meal)*

dinner lady NOUN

食堂阿姨 shítáng āyí [位 wèi]

dinner party NOUN
宴会 yànhuì [个 gè]
dinner time NOUN
晚饭时间 wǎnfàn shíjiān [段 duàn]
dinosaur NOUN
恐龙 kǒnglóng [只 zhī]
to **dip** VERB
▷ *see also* **dip** NOUN
蘸 zhàn
□ He dipped a biscuit into his tea. 他把一块饼干放到茶里蘸了蘸。Tā bǎ yíkuài bǐnggān fàng dào chá lǐ zhàn le zhàn.
dip NOUN
▷ *see also* **dip** VERB
■ **to go for a dip** 去游泳 qù yóuyǒng
diploma NOUN
文凭 wénpíng [张 zhāng]
□ a diploma in social work 一张社会工作专业的文凭 yìzhāng shèhuì gōngzuò zhuānyè de wénpíng
diplomat NOUN
外交官 wàijiāoguān
diplomatic ADJECTIVE
外交的 wàijiāo de
direct ADJECTIVE
▷ *see also* **direct** ADVERB
直达的 zhídá de
□ the most direct route 直达路线 zhídá lùxiàn
to **direct** VERB
1 给…指路 gěi...zhǐlù *(show)*
2 管理 guānlǐ *(manage)*
3 导演 dǎoyǎn *(play, film, programme)*
direct ADVERB
▷ *see also* **direct** ADJECTIVE
直接地 zhíjiē de *(go, write, fly)*
□ You can't fly to Beijing direct from Liverpool. 你不能从利物浦直飞北京。Nǐ bùnéng cóng Lìwùpǔ zhífēi Běijīng.
direction NOUN
方向 fāngxiàng [个 gè]
□ We're going in the wrong direction. 我们走错方向了。Wǒmen zǒucuò fāngxiàng le.
■ **in the direction of** 朝 cháo
■ **to ask somebody for directions** 向某人问路 xiàng mǒurén wènlù
■ **directions for use** 使用说明 shǐyòng shuōmíng
director NOUN
1 经理 jīnglǐ [位 wèi] *(of company)*
2 主任 zhǔrèn [位 wèi] *(of organization, public authority)*
3 导演 dǎoyǎn [位 wèi] *(of play, film)*
directory NOUN
1 电话号码簿 diànhuà hàomǎbù [个 gè] *(phone book)*
2 文件目录 wénjiàn mùlù [个 gè] *(on computer)*
dirt NOUN
污物 wūwù
dirty ADJECTIVE
脏的 zāng de
■ **to get dirty** 弄脏 nòng zàng
■ **to get something dirty** 把某物弄脏 bǎ mǒuwù nòng zāng
disabled ADJECTIVE
残疾的 cánjí de
■ **the disabled** 残疾人 cánjí rén
disadvantage NOUN
不利 búlì [种 zhǒng] *(drawback)*
to **disagree** VERB
不同意 bù tóngyì
□ We always disagree. 我们总是意见不同。Wǒmen zǒngshì yìjiàn bùtóng. □ I disagree! 我不同意！Wǒ bùtóngyì!
■ **to disagree with somebody** 不同意某人的观点 bù tóngyì mǒurén de guāndiǎn
□ He disagrees with me. 他不同意我的观点。Tā bùtóngyì wǒ de guāndiǎn.
■ **to disagree with something** *(action, proposal)* 不赞成某事 bú zànchéng mǒushì
disagreement NOUN
争执 zhēngzhí [个 gè] *(argument)*
to **disappear** VERB
1 消失 xiāoshī *(from view)*
2 失踪 shīzōng *(go missing)*
3 绝迹 juéjì *(cease to exist)*
disappearance NOUN
失踪 shīzōng [次 cì] *(of person)*
to **disappoint** VERB
使失望 shǐ shīwàng *(person)*
disappointed ADJECTIVE
失望的 shīwàng de
disappointing ADJECTIVE
令人失望的 lìng rén shīwàng de
disappointment NOUN
1 失望 shīwàng *(emotion)*
2 令人失望的人 lìng rén shīwàng de rén [个 gè] *(cause, person)*
3 令人失望的事 lìng rén shīwàng de shì [件 jiàn] *(cause, thing)*
to **disapprove** VERB
■ **to disapprove of something** 不同意某事 bù tóngyì mǒushì
disaster NOUN
1 灾难 zāinàn [次 cì] *(earthquake, flood)*
2 事故 shìgù [场 chǎng] *(accident, crash)*
3 惨败 cǎnbài [次 cì] *(fiasco)*
4 灾难 zāinàn [个 gè] *(serious situation)*
disastrous ADJECTIVE
1 灾难性的 zāinànxìng de *(catastrophic)*
2 惨败的 cǎnbài de *(unsuccessful)*

disc NOUN
圆盘 yuánpán [个 gè]
discipline NOUN
纪律 jìlǜ
disc jockey NOUN
音乐主持人 yīnyuè zhǔchírén
disco NOUN
迪斯科 dísīkē *(event)*
to **disconnect** VERB
1 拆开 chāikāi *(pipe, tap, hose)*
2 断开 duànkāi *(computer, cooker, TV)*
discount NOUN
折扣 zhékòu [个 gè]
□ a discount for students 给学生的折扣 gěi xuéshēng de zhékòu
to **discourage** VERB
使泄气 shǐ xièqì
■ **to get discouraged** 泄气 xièqì □ Don't get discouraged! 别泄气！Bié xièqì!
to **discover** VERB
发现 fāxiàn
discovery NOUN
1 发现 fāxiàn *(of treasure, cure)*
2 被发现的事物 bèi fāxiàn de shìwù [个 gè] *(thing found)*
discrimination NOUN
歧视 qíshì
■ **racial discrimination** 种族歧视 zhǒngzú qíshì
to **discuss** VERB
讨论 tǎolùn
□ I'll discuss it with my parents. 我会和父母讨论下。Wǒ huì hé fùmǔ tǎolùn xià. □ We discussed the problem of pollution. 我们讨论了污染的问题。Wǒmen tǎolùn le wūrǎn de wèntí.
discussion NOUN
讨论 tǎolùn [次 cì]
disease NOUN
病 bìng [场 chǎng] *(illness)*
disgraceful ADJECTIVE
可耻的 kěchǐ de
disguise NOUN
▷ *see also* **disguise** VERB
伪装 wěizhuāng [个 gè]
■ **in disguise** 乔装的 qiáozhuāng de
to **disguise** VERB
▷ *see also* **disguise** NOUN
■ **to be disguised as something** 假扮成某物 jiǎbànchéng mǒuwù □ He was disguised as a policeman. 他假扮成一名警察。Tā jiǎbàn chéng yìmíng jǐngchá.
disgusted ADJECTIVE
感到厌恶的 gǎndào yànwù de
□ I was absolutely disgusted. 我感到非常厌恶。Wǒ gǎndào fēicháng yànwù.
disgusting ADJECTIVE
1 恶心的 ěxīn de *(food, habit)*
□ It looks disgusting. 这看上去真恶心。Zhè kànshàngqù zhēn ěxīn.
2 讨厌的 tǎoyàn de *(behaviour, situation)*
□ That's disgusting! 那真是讨厌！Nà zhēnshi tǎoyàn!
dish NOUN
1 盘 pán [个 gè] *(for serving)*
□ a plastic dish 一个塑料盘子 yíge sùliào pánzi
2 碟 dié [个 gè] *(for eating)*
3 菜 cài [道 dào] *(recipe, food)*
□ a vegetarian dish 一道素食菜 yídào sùshícài
4 卫星接收器 wèixīng jiēshōu qì [个 gè] *(satellite dish)*
■ **to do the dishes** 洗碗 xǐwǎn □ He never does the dishes. 他从来不洗碗。Tā cónglái bù xǐwǎn.
dishonest ADJECTIVE
1 不诚实的 bù chéngshí de *(person)*
2 不正直的 bú zhèngzhí de *(behaviour)*
dish towel NOUN (US)
洗碗毛巾 xǐwǎn máojīn [条 tiáo]
dishwasher NOUN
洗碗机 xǐwǎnjī [台 tái]
dishwashing liquid NOUN (US)
洗洁剂 xǐjiéjì [瓶 píng]
disinfectant NOUN
消毒剂 xiāodújì [种 zhǒng]
disk NOUN
1 硬盘 yìngpán [个 gè] *(hard)*
□ the hard disk 硬盘 yìngpán
2 软盘 ruǎnpán [张 zhāng] *(floppy)*
to **dislike** VERB
▷ *see also* **dislike** NOUN
不喜欢 bù xǐhuan
□ I really dislike him. 我真不喜欢他。Wǒ zhēn bù xǐhuan tā.
dislike NOUN
▷ *see also* **dislike** VERB
■ **one's likes and dislikes** 某人的爱好和厌恶 mǒurén de àihào hé yànwù
dismal ADJECTIVE
阴沉的 yīnchén de
to **dismiss** VERB
解雇 jiěgù
disobedient ADJECTIVE
不服从的 bù fúcóng de
to **disobey** VERB
1 不顺从 bú shùncóng *(person)*
2 不服从 bù fúcóng *(order)*
display NOUN
▷ *see also* **display** VERB
1 陈列 chénliè [种 zhǒng] *(in shop, at exhibition)*

□ There was a lovely display of fruit in the window. 橱窗里陈列着好看的水果。Chúchuāng lǐ chénliè zhe hǎokàn de shuǐguǒ.

2 显示 xiǎnshì [个 gè] *(information on screen)*

3 显示屏 xiǎnshìpíng [个 gè] *(screen)*

■ **to be on display** 展览 zhǎnlǎn □ Her best paintings were on display. 她最好的画作正在展览中。Tā zuìhǎo de huàzuò zhèngzài zhǎnlǎn zhōng.

■ **a firework display** 焰火大会 yānhuǒ dàhuì

to **display** VERB

▷ *see also* **display** NOUN

1 陈列 chénliè *(exhibits)*

2 展示 zhǎnshì *(results, information)*

□ She proudly displayed her medal. 她自豪地展示自己的奖牌。Tā zìháo de zhǎnshì zìjǐ de jiǎngpái.

3 陈列 chénliè *(in shop window)*

disposable ADJECTIVE

一次性的 yícìxìng de

dispute NOUN

争端 zhēngduān *(industrial)*

to **disqualify** VERB

使...失去资格 shǐ...shīqù zīgé

■ **to be disqualified** 失去资格 shīqù zīgé □ He was disqualified. 他失去了资格。Tā shīqù le zīgé.

to **disrupt** VERB

1 扰乱 rǎoluàn *(conversation, meeting)*

□ Protesters disrupted the meeting. 抗议者扰乱了会议的进行。Kàngyìzhě rǎoluàn le huìyì de jìnxíng.

2 中断 zhōngduàn *(plan, process)*

□ Train services are being disrupted by the strike. 铁道服务因罢工而中断。Tiědào fúwù yīn bàgōng ér zhōngduàn.

dissatisfied ADJECTIVE

■ **We were dissatisfied with the service.** 我们对服务不满意。Wǒmen duì fúwù bùmǎnyì.

to **dissolve** VERB

溶解 róngjiě *(in liquid)*

distance NOUN

距离 jùlí [个 gè]

□ a distance of 40 kilometres 四十公里的距离。sìshí gōnglǐ de jùlí.

■ **within walking distance** 步行可到 bùxíng kě dào

distant ADJECTIVE

遥远的 yáoyuǎn de

□ in the distant future 在遥远的将来 zài yáoyuǎn de jiānglái

distillery NOUN

酒厂 jiúchǎng [个 gè]

□ a whisky distillery 一个威士忌酒厂 yígè wēishìjì jiǔchǎng

distinct ADJECTIVE

明显的 míngxiǎn de *(advantage, change)*

distinction NOUN

1 区分 qūfén

□ to make a distinction between... 区分…两者 qūfēn...liǎngzhě

2 优秀 yōuxiù

□ I got a distinction in my piano exam. 我在钢琴考试中得了优秀。Wǒ zài gāngqín kǎoshì zhōng dé le yōuxiù.

distinctive ADJECTIVE

独特的 dútède

to **distinguish** VERB

■ **to distinguish one thing from another** 将一事物与另一事物区别开来 jiāng yíshìwù yǔ lìngyí shìwù qūbié kāilái

to **distract** VERB

使分心 shǐ fēnxīn *(person)*

■ **to distract somebody's attention** 分散某人的注意力 fēnsàn mǒurén de zhùyìlì

to **distribute** VERB

1 分发 fēnfā *(hand out)*

2 分配 fēnpèi *(share out)*

district NOUN

地区 dìqū [个 gè]

to **disturb** VERB

打扰 dǎrǎo

□ I'm sorry to disturb you. 很抱歉打扰你。Hěn bàoqiàn dǎrǎo nǐ.

disturbing ADJECTIVE

令人不安的 lìng rén bù'ān de

ditch NOUN

▷ *see also* **ditch** VERB

沟 gōu [条 tiáo]

to **ditch** VERB

▷ *see also* **ditch** NOUN

甩 shuǎi *(informal)*

□ She's just ditched her boyfriend. 她刚把男朋友甩了。Tā gāng bǎ nánpéngyǒu shuǎi le.

to **dive** VERB

1 跳水 tiàoshuǐ *(into water)*

2 潜水 qiánshuǐ *(under water)*

diver NOUN

潜水员 qiánshuǐyuán [位 wèi]

diversion NOUN

临时改道 línshí gǎidào [次 cì]

to **divide** VERB

1 划分 huàfēn *(into groups, areas, categories)*

2 除 chú *(in maths)*

□ 40 divided by 5 四十除以五 sìshí chúyǐ wǔ

■ **to divide something in half** 将某物一分为二 jiāng mǒuwù yì fēn wéi èr □ Divide the pastry in half. 将糕点一分为二。Jiāng gāodiān yì fēn wéi èr.

■ **to divide something between two people** *(share)* 在两人之间分配某物 zài liǎng rén zhījiān fēnpèi mǒuwù

3 分开 fēnkāi *(into groups)*

□ We divided into two groups. 我们被分成两组。Wǒmen bèi fēnchéng liǎngzǔ.

diving NOUN

1 潜水 qiánshuǐ *(underwater)*

2 跳水 tiàoshuǐ *(from board)*

■ **a diving board** 一个跳水板 yígè tiàoshuǐbǎn

division NOUN

1 除法 chúfǎ *(mathematical)*

2 分配 fēnpèi *(sharing out)*

divorce NOUN

▷ *see also* **divorce** VERB

离婚 líhūn [次 cì]

to **divorce** VERB

▷ *see also* **divorce** NOUN

1 离婚 líhūn *(get divorced)*

2 与…离婚 yǔ…líhūn *(husband, wife)*

divorced ADJECTIVE

离异的 líyì de

□ My parents are divorced. 我双亲离异。Wǒ shuāngqīn líyì.

■ **to get divorced** 离婚 líhūn

DIY NOUN *(= do-it-yourself)*

自己动手的活计 zìjǐ dòngshǒu de huójì

■ **to do DIY** 自己动手做 zìjǐ dòngshǒu zuò

□ a DIY shop 一家自己动手商店 yì jiā zìjǐ dòngshǒu shāngdiàn

dizzy ADJECTIVE

■ **to feel dizzy** 感到头晕 gǎndào tóuyūn

□ I feel dizzy. 我感到头晕。Wǒ gǎn dào tóuyūn.

DJ NOUN *(= disc jockey)*

音乐主持人 yīnyuè zhǔchírén

to **do** VERB

1 做 zuò

□ What are you doing? 你在做什么呢？Nǐ zài zuò shénme ne? □ What are you doing this evening? 你今晚打算做什么？Nǐ jīnwǎn dǎsuàn zuò shénme? □ I haven't done my homework. 我还没做家庭作业。Wǒ hái méi zuò jiātíngzuòyè. □ Do as I tell you. 按我告诉你的做。Àn wǒ gàosù nǐ de zuò.

■ **Are you doing anything tomorrow evening?** 你明晚有什么打算？Nǐ míngwǎn yǒu shénme dǎsuàn?

■ **What did you do with the money?** 你怎么用这笔钱的？Nǐ zěnme yòng zhèbǐ qián de?

■ **What are you going to do about this?** 你打算对此怎么办？Nǐ dǎsuàn duìcǐ zěnmebàn?

■ **What do you do?** *(for a living)* 你做什么工作？Nǐ zuò shénme gōngzuò?

LANGUAGE TIP Sometimes a more specific verb is used in Chinese.

□ I do a lot of cycling. 我经常骑自行车。Wǒ jīngcháng qí zìxíngchē. □ The car was doing 100. 汽车以一百英里的时速行进。Qìchē yǐ yìbǎi yīnglǐ de shísù xíngjìn. □ The explosion did a lot of damage. 爆炸造成了很大损失。Bàozhà zàochéng le hěndà sǔnshī.

■ **to do somebody good** 对某人有好处 duì mòurén yǒu hǎochù □ A holiday will do you good. 休次假会对你有好处。Xiū cì jià huì duì nǐ yǒu hǎochù.

2 进展 jìnzhǎn *(get on)*

□ The firm is doing well. 公司进展良好。Gōngsī jìnzhǎn liánghǎo.

■ **How do you do?** 你好！Nǐhǎo！

3 行 xíng *(be suitable)*

□ Will it do? 这行吗？Zhè xíngma? □ It's not very good, but it'll do. 不是很好，但还行。Búshì hěnhǎo, dàn hái xíng.

4 足够 zúgòu *(be sufficient)*

■ **That'll do, thanks.** 够了，谢谢。Gòu le, xièxie.

LANGUAGE TIP **do** is often not translated.

□ I don't understand. 我不懂。Wǒ bùdǒng. □ She doesn't want it. 她不想要这个。Tā bùxiǎng yào zhège. □ Don't be silly! 别傻了！Bié shǎ le!

LANGUAGE TIP In questions, **do** is not translated and the interrogative particle 吗 ma is often used in its place.

□ Do you like jazz? 你喜欢爵士乐吗？Nǐ xǐhuan juéshìyuè ma? □ Where does he live? 他住在哪里？Tā zhù zài nǎlǐ? □ What do you think? 你怎么想？Nǐ zěnme xiǎng? □ Why didn't you come? 你为什么没来？Nǐ wèishénme méilái?

LANGUAGE TIP When used for emphasis in polite expressions, **do** is translated by 请 qǐng, which means **please**.

□ Do sit down. 请坐。Qǐng zuò.

LANGUAGE TIP When **do** is used to avoid repeating a verb, it is not translated and the verb is generally repeated in Chinese.

□ They say they don't care, but they do. 他们说不在乎，但实际是在乎的。Tāmen shuō bú zàihu, dàn shíjì shì zàihu de.

□ Who made this mess? — I did. 是谁弄得乱七八糟的？ 一是我。Shì shuí nòngde luàn qī bā zāo de? — Shì wǒ.

■ **so do I** 我也是 wǒ yěshì

■ **neither did we** 我们也不 wǒmen yěbù

■ **I don't know him, do I?** 我不认识他，是吗？Wǒ bú rènshi tā, shìma?

■ **She lives in London, doesn't she?** 她住在伦敦，不是吗？Tā zhùzài Lúndūn, búshì ma?

to **do up** VERB

1 系好 jìhǎo *(laces)*

□ Do up your shoes! 系好你的鞋带！Jìhǎo nǐde xiédài!

2 拉上 lā shàng *(dress, coat, buttons)*

□ Do up your zip! 拉好你的拉链！Lāhǎo nǐ de lāliàn!

3 整修 zhěngxiū *(renovate)*

□ They're doing up an old cottage. 他们正在整修一栋老旧的农舍。Tāmen zhèngzài zhěngxiū yídòng lǎojiù de nóngshè.

to **do with** VERB

■ **I could do with some help.** *(need)* 我需要帮助。Wǒ xūyào bāngzhù.

■ **to have to do with** *(be connected)* 与…有关 yǔ…yǒuguān

■ **What has it got to do with you?** 这跟你有什么关系？Zhè gēn nǐ yǒu shénme guānxi?

to **do without** VERB

没有…也行 méiyǒu…yě xíng

□ I couldn't do without my computer. 我不能没有我的电脑。Wǒ bùnéng méiyǒu wǒde diànnǎo.

dock NOUN

船坞 chuánwù [个 gè] *(for ships)*

doctor NOUN

医生 yīshēng [位 wèi]

□ I'd like to be a doctor. 我想当一位医生。Wǒ xiǎng dāng yí wèi yīshēng.

■ **the doctor's** 诊所 zhěnsuǒ [家 jiā]

document NOUN

1 文件 wénjiàn [份 fèn]

2 文档 wéndàng [个 gè] *(electronic)*

documentary NOUN

纪录片 jìlùpiàn [部 bù]

to **dodge** VERB

躲避 duǒbì *(attacker)*

does VERB ▷ *see* **do**

doesn't = **does not**

dog NOUN

1 狗 gǒu [只 zhī]

□ Have you got a dog? 你有养狗吗？Nǐ yǒu yǎng gǒu ma?

2 雄兽 xióngshòu [头 tóu] *(male)*

do-it-yourself NOUN

▷ *see also* **do-it-yourself** ADJECTIVE

自己动手的活计 zìjǐ dòngshǒu de huójì

do-it-yourself ADJECTIVE

▷ *see also* **do-it-yourself** NOUN

出售供购买者自行装配物品的 chūshòu gòng gòumǎizhě zìxíng zhuāngpèi wùpǐn de *(store)*

dole NOUN

■ **the dole** *(payment)* 失业救济金 shīyè jiùjìjīn

■ **to be on the dole** 靠失业救济金生活 kào shīyè jiùjìjīn shēnghuó □ A lot of people are on the dole. 很多人靠失业救济金生活。Hěn duō rén kào shīyè jiùjìjīn shēnghuó.

■ **to go on the dole** 领失业救济金 lǐng shīyè jiùjìjīn

doll NOUN

娃娃 wáwa [个 gè]

dollar NOUN

元 yuán

dolphin NOUN

海豚 hǎitún [只 zhī]

domestic ADJECTIVE

国内的 guónèi de

■ **a domestic flight** 一架国内航班 yíjià guónèi hángbān

dominoes PL NOUN

多米诺骨牌 duōmǐnuò gǔpái

■ **to have a game of dominoes** 玩多米诺骨牌 wán duōmǐnuò gǔpái

to **donate** VERB

捐献 juānxiàn *(blood, organs)*

■ **to donate something to somebody** *(money, clothes)* 捐赠某物给某人 juānzèng mǒuwù gěi mǒurén

done VERB ▷ *see* **do**

donkey NOUN

驴 lǘ [头 tóu]

donor NOUN

捐赠者 juānzèngzhě [名 míng]

don't = **do not**

donut NOUN (US)

甜甜圈 tiántiánquān [个 gè]

door NOUN

门 mén [扇 shàn]

□ the first door on the right 右边第一扇门 yòubiān dìyīshàn mén

■ **to answer the door** 应门 yìngmén

doorbell NOUN

门铃 ménlíng [个 gè]

□ Suddenly the doorbell rang. 突然门铃响了。Tūrán ménlíng xiǎng le.

■ **to ring the doorbell** 按门铃 àn ménlíng

doorman NOUN

门房 ménfáng

doorstep NOUN
门阶 ménjiē

dormitory NOUN
1 宿舍 sùshè [间 jiān] *(room)*
2 宿舍楼 sùshèlóu [座 zuò] *(US: building)*

dose NOUN
剂量 jìliàng

dot NOUN
圆点 yuándiǎn [个 gè]
■ **on the dot** *(punctually)* 准时地 zhǔnshí de □ He arrived at 9 o'clock on the dot. 他九点整准时到达。Tā jiǔdiǎnzhěng zhǔnshí dàodá.

dot-com NOUN
网络公司 wǎngluò gōngsī [家 jiā]

double ADJECTIVE, ADVERB
▷ *see also* **double** VERB
双份的 shuāngfèn de
□ a double helping 双份饭 shuāngfèn fàn
□ It's spelt with a double "M". 它的拼写中有两个 "M"。Tāde pīnxiě zhōng yǒu liǎnggè "M".
■ **double the size of something** 是某物大小的两倍 shì mǒuwù dàxiǎo de liǎngbèi
■ **to cost double** 花双倍的钱 huā shūangbèi de qián □ First-class tickets cost double. 买头等票要花双倍的钱。Mǎi tóuděngpiào yào huā shuāngbèi de qián.
■ **a double bed** 双人床 shuāngrénchuáng

to **double** VERB
▷ *see also* **double** ADJECTIVE, ADVERB
加倍 jiābèi *(population, size)*
□ The number of attacks has doubled. 袭击案件的数量增加了一倍。Xíjī ànjiàn de shùliàng zēngjiā le yí bèi.

double bass NOUN
低音提琴 dīyīn tíqín [把 bǎ]

to **double-click** VERB
双击 shuāngjī
□ to double-click on an icon 双击一个图标 shuāngjī yígè túbiāo

double-decker NOUN
双层公共汽车 shuāngcéng gōnggòng qìchē [辆 liàng] *(bus)*

double glazing NOUN
双层玻璃 shuāngcéng bōlí

double room NOUN
双人房 shuāngrénfáng

doubles PL NOUN
双打 shuāngdǎ *(in tennis)*
□ to play mixed doubles 打混合双打 dǎ hùnhé shuāngdǎ

doubt NOUN
▷ *see also* **doubt** VERB
疑问 yíwèn [种 zhǒng]
□ I have my doubts. 我有疑问。Wǒ yǒu yíwèn.

to **doubt** VERB
▷ *see also* **doubt** NOUN
不信 bùxìn *(person's word)*
■ **to doubt whether...** 拿不准是否… nábùzhǔn shìfǒu...
■ **to doubt that...** 怀疑… huáiyí... □ I doubt he'll agree. 我怀疑他会同意。Wǒ huáiyí tā huì tóngyì.
■ **I doubt it.** 我很怀疑。Wǒ hěn huáiyí.

doubtful ADJECTIVE
拿不准的 nábùzhǔn de *(uncertain)*
□ It's doubtful. 这还拿不准。Zhè hái nábùzhǔn. □ You sound doubtful. 你听上去有点拿不准。Nǐ tīngshàngqù yǒudiǎn nábùzhǔn.
■ **It is doubtful whether...** *(questionable)* 不能确定…/是否… bùnéng quèdìng.../shìfǒu...
■ **to be doubtful whether...** *(unconvinced)* 怀疑…/是否… huáiyí.../shìfǒu...
■ **to be doubtful about something** 对某事不确定 duì mǒushì búquèdìng □ I'm doubtful about going by myself. 我不确定是否该独自去。Wǒ búquèdìng shìfǒu gāi dúzì qù.

dough NOUN
生面团 shēngmiàntuán

doughnut (US **donut**) NOUN
甜甜圈 tiántiánquān [个 gè]
□ a jam doughnut 一个果酱甜甜圈 yíge guǒjiàng tiántiánquān

down ADVERB
▷ *see also* **down** PREPOSITION, ADJECTIVE
1 向下 xiàngxià *(downwards)*
□ She looked down. 她向下看。Tā xiàngxià kàn. □ Come down here! 下来这里！Xiàlai zhèlǐ!
2 在下面 zài xiàmian *(in a lower place)*
□ His office is down on the first floor. 他的办公室在下面一楼。Tā de bàngōngshì zài xiàmiàn yìlóu.
3 丢在地上 diū zài dìshàng *(to the ground)*
□ He threw down his racket. 他把他的球拍丢在地上。Tā bǎ tā de qiúpāi diū zài dìshàng.
■ **down there** 在那儿 zài nàr □ It's down there. 在那儿。Zài nàr.
■ **England are two goals down.** *(behind)* 英格兰落后两球。Yīnggélán luòhòu liǎngqiú.

down PREPOSITION
▷ *see also* **down** ADVERB, ADJECTIVE
1 沿着…往下 yánzhe...wǎng xià *(towards lower level)*

2 在下面 zài xiàmian *(at lower part of)*
3 沿着 yánzhe *(along)*
□ He walked down the road. 他沿街走去。Tā yánjiē zǒuqù.
■ **They live just down the road.** 他们就住在马路那头。Tāmen jiù zhùzài mǎlù nàtóu.

down ADJECTIVE
▷ *see also* **down** PREPOSITION, ADVERB
沮丧 jǔsàng
■ **to feel down** 感到沮丧 gǎndào jǔsàng
□ I'm feeling a bit down. 我感到有点沮丧。Wǒ gǎndào yǒudiǎn jǔsàng.
■ **The computer's down.** 电脑出故障了。Diànnǎo chū gùzhàng le.

to **download** VERB
▷ *see also* **download** NOUN
下载 xiàzǎi
□ to download a file 下载一个文件 xiàzǎi yíge wénjiàn

download NOUN
▷ *see also* **download** VERB
下载的文件 xiàzǎi de wénjiàn
□ a free download 一个免费下载的文件 yíge miǎnfèi xiàzǎi de wénjiàn

downpour NOUN
倾盆大雨 qīngpéndàyǔ
□ a sudden downpour 一场突如其来的倾盆大雨 yìchǎng tūrúqílái de qīngpéndàyǔ

downstairs ADVERB
▷ *see also* **downstairs** ADJECTIVE
1 楼下 lóuxià *(on or to floor below)*
□ the people downstairs 楼下的人们 lóuxià de rénmen
2 底楼 dǐlóu *(on or to ground level)*
□ The bathroom's downstairs. 卫生间在底楼。Wèishēngjiān zài dǐlóu.

downstairs ADJECTIVE
▷ *see also* **downstairs** ADVERB
楼下的 lóuxià de
□ the downstairs bathroom 楼下的卫生间 lóuxià de wèishēngjiān

downtown ADVERB (US)
▷ *see also* **downtown** ADJECTIVE
1 在市中心 zài shì zhōngxīn *(be, work)*
2 去市中心 qù shì zhōngxīn *(go)*

downtown ADJECTIVE
▷ *see also* **downtown** ADVERB
■ **downtown Chicago** 芝加哥的市中心 Zhījiāgē de shì zhōngxīn

dozen NOUN
一打 yìdá
□ two dozen eggs 两打鸡蛋 liǎngdá jīdàn
■ **dozens of** 很多 hěnduō □ I've told you that dozens of times. 我跟你说过很多次了。Wǒ gēn nǐ shuō guò hěnduō cì le.

to **doze off** VERB
打盹 dǎdǔn

draft NOUN
1 草稿 cǎogǎo [份 fèn] *(first version)*
2 气流 qìliú [股 gǔ] *(US: draught)*

to **drag** VERB
拖 tuō *(pull: large object, body)*
■ **drag and drop** 拖放 tuōfàng

dragon NOUN
龙 lóng [条 tiáo]

drain NOUN
▷ *see also* **drain** VERB
下水道 xiàshuǐdào [个 gè]
□ The drains are blocked. 下水道被堵住了。Xiàshuǐdào bèi dǔzhù le.

to **drain** VERB
▷ *see also* **drain** NOUN
1 排去水 páiqù shuǐ *(vegetables)*
2 流干 liúgān *(liquid: drain away)*

drainpipe NOUN
排水管 páishuǐguǎn [条 tiáo]

drama NOUN
1 戏剧 xìjù *(theatre)*
2 一出戏剧 yìchū xìjù [出 chū] *(play)*
3 戏剧性 xìjùxìng [种 zhǒng] *(excitement)*
4 戏剧 xìjù *(school subject)*
□ Drama is my favourite subject. 戏剧是我最喜欢的学科。Xìjù shì wǒ zuìxǐhuan de xuékē.
■ **drama school** 戏剧学校 xìjù xuéxiào
□ I'd like to go to drama school. 我想去读戏剧学校。Wǒ xiǎng qù dú xìjù xuéxiào.

dramatic ADJECTIVE
1 戏剧性的 xìjùxìng de *(marked, sudden)*
□ a dramatic improvement 一个戏剧性的改进 yígè xìjùxìng de gǎijìn
2 激动人心的 jīdòng rénxīn de *(exciting, impressive)*
□ It was really dramatic! 真是太激动人心了！Zhēnshì tài jīdòng rénxīn le!
□ dramatic news 激动人心的消息 jīdòng rénxīn de xiāoxi
3 戏剧的 xìjù de *(theatrical)*

drank VERB ▷ *see* **drink**

drapes PL NOUN (US)
窗帘 chuānglián

drastic ADJECTIVE
激烈的 jīliè de *(change)*
■ **to take drastic action** 采取激烈的行动 cǎiqǔ jīliè de xíngdòng

draught (US **draft**) NOUN
气流 qìliú [股 gǔ]

draughts NOUN
西洋跳棋 xīyáng tiàoqí
□ to play draughts 玩西洋跳棋 wán xīyáng tiàoqí

draw NOUN
▹ *see also* **draw** VERB
1 平局 píngjú [个 gè]
▫ The game ended in a draw. 比赛以平局结束。Bǐsài yǐ píngjú jiéshù.
2 抽奖 chōujiǎng [次 cì] *(in lottery)*
▫ The draw takes place on Saturday. 抽奖于星期六举行。Chōu jiǎng yú xīngqīliù jǔxíng.

to **draw** VERB
▹ *see also* **draw** NOUN
1 画 huà
▫ to draw a picture 画一幅画 huà yì fú huà
▫ to draw a picture of somebody 画一副某人的肖像 huà yí fù mǒurén de xiāoxiàng
▫ to draw a line 画一条线 huà yì tiáo xiàn
2 拉上 lāshang *(close curtains)*
3 拉开 lākāi *(open curtains)*
4 打成平局 dǎ chéng píngjú
▫ We drew 2-2. 我们打成二比二平。Wǒmen dǎ chéng ér bǐ ér píng.

to **draw up** VERB
草拟 cǎonǐ *(document, plan)*

drawback NOUN
不足之处 bùzúzhīchù [个 gè]

drawer NOUN
抽屉 chōuti [个 gè]

drawing NOUN
1 素描 sùmiáo [幅 fú] *(picture)*
2 绘画 huìhuà *(skill, discipline)*
▫ He's good at drawing. 他擅长绘画。Tā shàncháng huìhuà.

drawing pin NOUN
图钉 túdīng [枚 méi]

drawn VERB ▹ *see* **draw**

to **dread** VERB
惧怕 jùpà *(fear)*

dreadful ADJECTIVE
糟透的 zāotòu de
▫ a dreadful mistake 一个糟透了的错误 yígè zāotòu le de cuòwù

dream NOUN
▹ *see also* **dream** VERB
1 梦 mèng [场 chǎng]
▫ It was just a dream. 这只是一场梦。Zhè zhǐshì yìchǎng mèng.
■ **a bad dream** 一个噩梦 yíge èmèng
2 梦想 mèngxiǎng [个 gè] *(ambition)*

to **dream** VERB
▹ *see also* **dream** NOUN
■ **to dream that** 梦想 mèng xiǎng ▫ I dreamed I was in the jungle. 我梦想自己是在丛林里。Wǒ mèngxiǎng zìjǐ shì zài cónglín lǐ.
■ **to dream about** 梦到 mèngdào

dreamt VERB ▹ *see* **dream**

to **drench** VERB
使湿透 shǐ shītòu *(soak)*
■ **to get drenched** 淋湿了 línshī le ▫ We got drenched. 我们都淋湿了。Wǒmen dōu línshī le.

dress NOUN
▹ *see also* **dress** VERB
连衣裙 liányīqún [条 tiáo]

to **dress** VERB
▹ *see also* **dress** NOUN
1 穿衣 chuān yī *(oneself)*
▫ I got up, dressed, and went downstairs. 我起床穿衣下了楼。Wǒ qǐchuáng chuānyī xià le lóu.
2 给...穿衣 gěi...chuān yī *(somebody)*
▫ She dressed the children. 她给孩子们穿好衣服。Tā gěi háizimen chuānhǎo yīfu.
■ **to get dressed** 穿好衣服 chuānhǎo yīfu
▫ I got dressed quickly. 我迅速穿好衣服。Wǒ xùnsù chuānhǎo yīfu.
3 拌 bàn *(salad)*

to **dress up** VERB
穿上盛装 chuānshang shèngzhuāng *(wear best clothes)*
■ **to dress up as** 化装成 huàzhuāng chéng
▫ I dressed up as a ghost. 我化装成个幽灵。Wǒ huàzhuāng chéng ge yōulíng.

dressed ADJECTIVE
穿着衣服的 chuānzhe yīfú de
▫ I'm not dressed yet. 我还没穿衣服。Wǒ hái méi chuān yīfu. ▫ How was she dressed? 她穿得什么样？Tā chuān de shénmeyàng? ▫ She was dressed in a green sweater and jeans. 她穿了件绿色的毛衣和牛仔裤。Tā chuān le jiàn lǜsè de máoyī hé niúzǎikù.

dresser NOUN
1 碗橱 wǎnchú [个 gè] *(cupboard)*
2 梳妆台 shūzhuāngtái [个 gè] (US: *chest of drawers)*

dressing gown NOUN
晨衣 chényī [套 tào]

dressing table NOUN
梳妆台 shūzhuāngtái [个 gè]

drew VERB ▹ *see* **draw**

dried ADJECTIVE
1 干的 gān de *(fruit, herbs, flowers)*
2 粉状的 fěnzhuàng de *(eggs, milk)*

dried VERB ▹ *see* **dry**

drier NOUN
1 干衣机 gānyījī [台 tái] *(tumble drier, spin-drier)*
2 吹风机 chuīfēngjī [个 gè] *(hair drier)*

to **drift** VERB
1 漂流 piāoliú *(boat)*
2 雪堆 xuěduī *(snow)*

English-Chinese

d

drill NOUN
▷ *see also* **drill** VERB
1 钻子 zuànzi [个 gè] *(for DIY)*
2 牙钻 yázuàn [个 gè] *(of dentist)*

to **drill** VERB
▷ *see also* **drill** NOUN
在…上钻孔 zài...shàng zuānkǒng

drink NOUN
▷ *see also* **drink** VERB
1 饮料 yǐnliào [种 zhǒng] *(tea, water)*
□ a cold drink 一杯冰镇饮料 yìbēi bīngzhèn yǐnliào □ a hot drink 一杯热饮料 yìbēi rè yǐnliào
2 酒 jiǔ [瓶 píng] *(alcoholic)*
□ They've gone out for a drink. 他们出去喝酒了。Tāmen chūqù hējiǔ le.
■ **to have a drink 1** *(non-alcoholic)* 喝一杯 hē yìbēi **2** *(alcoholic)* 喝酒 hējiǔ

to **drink** VERB
▷ *see also* **drink** NOUN
1 喝 hē
□ What would you like to drink? 请问您想喝点什么？Qǐngwèn nín xiǎng hē diǎn shénme? □ She drank three cups of tea. 她喝了三杯茶。Tā hē le sān bēi chá.
2 喝酒 hējiǔ *(drink alcohol)*
□ He'd been drinking. 他有喝酒。Tā yǒu hējiǔ. □ I don't drink. 我不喝酒。Wǒ bù hējiǔ.

drinking water NOUN
饮用水 yǐnyòngshuǐ [种 zhǒng]

drive NOUN
▷ *see also* **drive** VERB
1 车程 chēchéng [段 duàn] *(journey)*
□ It's a 3-hour drive from London. 到伦敦要三个小时的车程。Dào Lúndūn yào sāngè xiǎoshí de chēchéng.
■ **to go for a drive** 开车兜风 kāichē dōufēng □ We went for a drive in the country. 我们去乡下开车兜风。Wǒmen qù xiāngxià kāichē dōufēng.
2 私家车道 sījiā chēdào [条 tiáo] *(driveway)*
□ He parked his car in the drive. 他把车停在私家车道上。Tā bǎ chē tíng zài sījiā chēdào shàng.
3 驱动器 qūdòngqì [个 gè] *(CD-ROM drive)*

to **drive** VERB
▷ *see also* **drive** NOUN
1 驾驶 jiàshǐ *(vehicle)*
■ **to drive somebody to the station** 驾车送某人去车站 jiàchē sòng mǒurén qù chēzhàn
■ **to drive somebody home** 开车送某人回家 kāichē sòng mǒurén huíjiā.
□ He offered to drive me home. 他提出要开车送我回家。Tā tíchū yào kāichē sòng wǒ huíjiā.
2 开车 kāichē *(person driving)*
□ She's learning to drive. 她在学开车。Tā zài xué kāichē. □ Can you drive? 你会开车吗？Nǐ huì kāichē ma?
■ **to drive at 50 km an hour** 以每小时五十公里的速度驾车 yǐ měi xiǎoshí wǔshí gōnglǐ de sùdù jiàchē
■ **to drive somebody mad** 逼得某人发疯 bīde mǒurén fāfēng □ He drives her mad. 他要把她逼疯了。Tā yào bǎ tā bī fēng le.

driver NOUN
1 驾车人 jiàchērén [位 wèi] *(of own car)*
2 司机 sījī [位 wèi] *(of taxi, bus, lorry, train)*
□ He's a bus driver. 他是位公交车司机。Tā shì wèi gōngjiāochē sījī.

driver's license NOUN (US)
驾驶执照 jiàshǐ zhízhào [个 gè]

driveway NOUN
车道 chēdào [条 tiáo]

driving instructor NOUN
驾驶教练 jiàshǐ jiàoliàn [位 wèi]

driving lesson NOUN
驾驶课 jiàshǐkè [堂 táng]

driving licence NOUN
驾驶执照 jiàshǐ zhízhào [个 gè]

driving test NOUN
驾驶执照考试 jiàshǐ zhízhào kǎoshì [次 cì]
□ She's just passed her driving test. 她刚通过驾驶执照考试。Tā gāng tōngguò jiàshǐ zhízhào kǎoshì.
■ **to take one's driving test** 考驾驶执照 kǎo jiàshǐzhízhào □ He's taking his driving test tomorrow. 他明天要考驾驶执照。Tā míngtiān yào kǎo jiàshǐzhízhào.

drop NOUN
▷ *see also* **drop** VERB
滴 dī
□ a drop of water 一滴水 yì dī shuǐ
■ **a drop in something** *(reduction)* 某物的下降 mǒuwù de xiàjiàng

to **drop** VERB
▷ *see also* **drop** NOUN
1 失手落下 shīshǒu luòxià
□ I dropped the glass and it broke. 我失手落下杯子，打碎了。Wǒ shīshǒu luòxià bēizi, dǎsuìle.
2 放 fàng *(deliberately)*
□ Drop your weapons! 放下武器！Fàng xià wǔqì!
3 放弃 fàngqì *(subject, activity)*
□ I'm going to drop chemistry. 我准备放弃化学了。Wǒ zhǔnbèi fàngqì huàxué le.
4 让…下车 ràng...xiàchē *(passenger)*
□ Could you drop me at the station? 你能在车站那里让我下车吗？Nǐ néng zài

chēzhàn nàlǐ ràng wǒ xiàchē ma?
5 下降 xiàjiàng *(fall: amount, level)*
6 落下 luòxià *(fall: object)*
to **drop in** VERB
■ **to drop in on somebody** 顺便拜访某人 shùnbiàn bàifǎng mǒurén
to **drop off** VERB
睡着 shuìzháo *(fall asleep)*
to **drop out** VERB
辍学 chuòxué *(of college, university)*
drought NOUN
旱灾 hànzāi [场 chǎng]
drove VERB ▷ *see* **drive**
to **drown** VERB
淹死 yānsǐ
□ A boy drowned here yesterday. 一个男孩昨天在这里淹死了。Yíge nánhái zuótiān zài zhèlǐ yānsǐ le.
■ **to be drowned** 被淹死 bèi yānsǐ
drug NOUN
1 药 yào [片 piàn] *(prescribed)*
□ They need food and drugs. 他们需要食物和药品。Tāmen xūyào shíwù hé yàopǐn.
2 毒品 dúpǐn [种 zhǒng] *(recreational)*
■ **to take drugs** 吸毒 xīdú
3 吸毒 xīdú
■ **hard drugs** 硬毒品 yìng dúpǐn
■ **a drug smuggler** 毒品走私犯 dúpǐn zǒusīfàn
■ **the drugs squad** 缉毒队 jídúduì
drug addict NOUN
瘾君子 yǐnjūnzǐ [个 gè]
□ She's a drug addict. 她是个瘾君子。Tā shìge yǐnjūnzǐ.
drug dealer NOUN
毒品贩子 dúpǐn fànzi [个 gè]
druggist NOUN (US)
药剂师 yàojìshī [位 wèi] *(person)*
■ **druggist's** 药店 yàodiàn [家 jiā] *(shop)*
drugstore NOUN (US)
药房 yàofáng [家 jiā]
drum NOUN
鼓 gǔ [面 miàn]
□ an African drum 一面非洲鼓 yímiàn Fēizhōu gǔ
■ **a drum kit** 一套架子鼓 yítào jiàzigǔ
■ **drums** 鼓 gǔ □ I play drums. 我打鼓。Wǒ dǎ gǔ.
drummer NOUN
鼓手 gǔshǒu [位 wèi]
drunk VERB ▷ *see* **drink**
drunk ADJECTIVE
▷ *see also* **drunk** NOUN
醉了的 zuì le de
□ He was drunk. 他喝醉了。Tā hēzuì le.
■ **to get drunk** 喝醉了 hēzuì le
drunk NOUN
▷ *see also* **drunk** ADJECTIVE
醉鬼 zuìguǐ
□ The streets were full of drunks. 街道上满是醉鬼。Jiēdào shàng mǎn shì zuìguǐ.
dry ADJECTIVE
▷ *see also* **dry** VERB
1 干的 gān de
□ The paint isn't dry yet. 油漆还未干。Yóuqī hái wèi gān.
2 干燥的 gānzào de *(climate, weather, day)*
□ a long dry period 一段漫长的干燥期 yíduàn mànchāng de gānzàoqī
to **dry** VERB
▷ *see also* **dry** ADJECTIVE
1 变干 biàn gān *(paint, washing)*
□ The washing will dry quickly in the sun. 洗好的衣服在阳光下很快就会变干的。Xǐhǎo de yīfú zài yángguāng xià hěn kuài jiù huì biàn gān de.
2 把…弄干 bǎ…nòng gān *(to dry something)*
□ There's nowhere to dry clothes here. 这里没有地方弄干衣服。Zhèlǐ méiyǒu dìfāng nòng gān yīfu.
■ **to dry one's hair** 弄干头发 nònggān tóufa □ I haven't dried my hair yet. 我还没把头发弄干。Wǒ hái méi bǎ tóufa nòng gān.
■ **to dry the dishes** 弄干盘子 nòng gān pánzi
dry-cleaner's NOUN
干洗店 gānxǐdiàn [家 jiā]
dryer NOUN
1 干衣机 gānyījī [台 tái] *(tumble dryer, spin-dryer)*
2 吹风机 chuīfēngjī [个 gè] *(hair dryer)*
dubbed ADJECTIVE
配音的 pèiyīn de
□ The film was dubbed into Chinese. 这部电影是中文配音的。Zhè bù diànyǐng shì zhōngwén pèiyīn de.
dubious ADJECTIVE
怀疑的 huáiyí de
□ My parents were a bit dubious about it. 我父母对此有点怀疑。Wǒ fùmǔ duìcǐ yǒudiǎn huáiyí.
duck NOUN
1 鸭 yā [只 zhī] *(bird)*
2 鸭肉 yāròu *(as food)*
due ADJECTIVE
▷ *see also* **due** ADVERB
■ **to be due 1** *(person, train, bus)* 应到 yīng dào □ The plane's due in half an hour. 飞机应在半小时后到。Fēijī yīng zài bànxiǎoshí hòu dào. **2** *(baby)* 预计的 yùjì de □ When's the baby due? 她的宝宝

English-Chinese

d

预计什么时候出生？Tā de bǎobao yùjì shénme shíhòu chūshēng? **3** *(rent, payment)* 到期 dàoqī

■ **to be due to do something** 预订做某事 yùdìng zuò mǒushì □ He's due to arrive tomorrow. 他预订明天到。Tā yùdìng míngtiān dào.

■ **due to...** *(because of)* 由于… yóuyú... □ The trip was cancelled due to bad weather. 旅行由于天气不好而取消了。Lǚxíng yóuyú tiānqì bùhǎo ér qǔxiāo le.

due ADVERB

▷ *see also* **due** ADJECTIVE

■ **due south** 正南方 zhèng nánfāng

dug VERB ▷ *see* **dig**

dull ADJECTIVE

1 阴沉的 yīnchén de *(weather, day)*

2 单调乏味的 dāndiào fáwèi de *(boring)* □ He's nice, but a bit dull. 他人很好，但是有点乏味。Tā rén hěnhǎo, dànshì yǒudiǎn fáwèi.

dumb ADJECTIVE

1 哑的 yǎ de □ She's deaf and dumb. 她又聋又哑。Tā yòu lóng yòu yǎ.

2 愚蠢的 yúchǔn de *(stupid)* □ That was a really dumb thing I did! 那真是我干的一件蠢事！Nà zhēn shì wǒ gàn de yíjiàn chǔnshì!

dummy NOUN

橡皮奶嘴 xiàngpí nǎizuǐ *(for baby)*

dump NOUN

▷ *see also* **dump** VERB

垃圾场 lājīchǎng [个 gè] *(for rubbish)*

■ **a rubbish dump** 破陋的地方 pòlòu de dìfang

■ **It's a real dump!** *(unattractive place)* 这真是个破地方！Zhè zhēn shìge pò dìfang!

to **dump** VERB

▷ *see also* **dump** NOUN

1 倾倒 qīngdào *(get rid of)* □ 'no dumping' "严禁倾倒垃圾" "Yánjìn qīngdào lājī"

2 转储 zhuǎn chǔ *(computer data)*

3 甩 shuǎi □ He's just dumped his girlfriend. 他刚甩了他的女朋友。Tā gāng shuǎi le tā de nǚpéngyǒu.

Dumpster® NOUN (US)

废料箱 fèiliàoxiāng [个 gè]

dungarees PL NOUN

背带裤 bēidàikù [条 tiáo]

duration NOUN

持续 chíxù

during PREPOSITION

1 在...期间 zài...qījiān □ during the meeting 在会议期间 zài huìyì qījiān

2 在...时候 zài...shíhou *(at some point in)* □ during the day 在白天的时候 zài báitiān de shíhòu

dusk NOUN

黄昏 huánghūn [个 gè]

■ **at dusk** 黄昏时刻 huánghūn shíkè

dust NOUN

▷ *see also* **dust** VERB

1 尘土 chéntǔ *(outdoors)*

2 灰尘 huīchén *(indoors)*

to **dust** VERB

▷ *see also* **dust** NOUN

掸去灰尘 dǎnqù huīchén □ I dusted the shelves. 我掸去了架子上的灰尘。Wǒ dǎn qù le jiàzi shàng de huīchén. □ I hate dusting! 我讨厌掸灰！Wǒ tǎoyàn dǎnhuī!

dustbin NOUN

垃圾箱 lājīxiāng [个 gè]

dustman NOUN

清洁工 qīngjiégōng [位 wèi]

dusty ADJECTIVE

满是尘土的 mǎn shì chéntǔ de

Dutch ADJECTIVE

▷ *see also* **Dutch** NOUN

荷兰的 Hélán de □ She's Dutch. 她是荷兰人。Tā shì Hélánrén.

Dutch NOUN

▷ *see also* **Dutch** ADJECTIVE

荷兰语 Hélányǔ *(language)*

■ **the Dutch** *(people)* 荷兰人 Hélánrén

Dutchman NOUN

荷兰男人 Hélán nánrén [个 gè]

Dutchwoman NOUN

荷兰女人 Hélán nǚrén [个 gè]

duty NOUN

1 责任 zérèn [个 gè] *(responsibility)* □ It was his duty to tell the police. 告诉警察是他的责任。Gàosù jǐngchá shì tā de zérèn.

2 税 shuì [种 zhǒng] *(tax)*

■ **to be on duty** *(policeman, doctor, nurse)* 当值的 dāngzhí de

■ **duties** *(tasks)* 任务 rènwù

duty-free ADJECTIVE

免税的 miǎnshuì de *(drink, cigarettes)*

■ **duty-free shop** 免税商店 miǎnshuì shāngdiàn

duvet NOUN

被褥 bèirù [床 chuáng]

DVD NOUN

光碟 guāngdié [张 zhāng]

□ I've got that film on DVD. 我有那部电影的光碟。Wǒ yǒu nàbù diànyǐng de guāngdié.

DVD player NOUN
DVD播放器 DVD bōfàngqì [台 tái]

dwarf NOUN
矮人 ǎirén [个 gè]

dye NOUN
▷ *see also* **dye** VERB
染料 rǎnliào [种 zhǒng]

to **dye** VERB
▷ *see also* **dye** NOUN
染色 rǎnsè

dying VERB ▷ *see* **die**

dynamic ADJECTIVE
有活力的 yǒu huólì de

dyslexia NOUN
诵读困难 sòngdú kùnnan

dyslexic ADJECTIVE
诵读有困难的 sòngdú yǒu kùnnan de

Ee

each ADJECTIVE
▷ *see also* **each** PRONOUN
每 měi
□ Each house in our street has its own garden. 我们那条街上每户人家都有自己的花园。Wǒmen nàtiáo jiēshàng měihù rénjiā dōuyǒu zìjǐ de huāyuán.
■ **each day** 每一天 měiyìtiān
■ **each one of them** 他们中的每一个 tāmen zhōngde měiyígè

each PRONOUN
▷ *see also* **each** ADJECTIVE
每个 měigè *(each one)*
□ They cost five pounds each. 每个售价五镑。Měigè shòujià wǔbàng. □ They have two books each. 他们每人有两本书。Tāmen měirén yǒu liǎngběnshū. □ The girls each have their own bedroom. 这些女孩每人都有自己独立的卧室。Zhèxiē nǚhái měirén dōuyǒu zìjǐ de wòshì. □ He gave each of us £10. 他给了我们每人十镑。Tā gěile wǒmen měirén shíbàng.
■ **each other** 互相 hùxiāng □ They hate each other. 他们互相仇视。Tāmen hùxiāng chóushì.

eager ADJECTIVE
■ **to be eager to do something** 热切想做某事 rèqiè xiǎng zuò mǒushì

ear NOUN
耳朵 ěrduo [只 zhī]

earache NOUN
耳朵痛 ěrduo tòng [阵 zhèn]
■ **to have earache** 耳朵痛 ěrduo tòng

earlier ADJECTIVE
▷ *see also* **earlier** ADVERB
较早的 jiàozǎo de

earlier ADVERB
▷ *see also* **earlier** ADJECTIVE
较早地 jiàozǎo de
□ I saw him earlier. 我早些时候见过他。Wǒ zǎoxiē shíhòu jiànguò tā.
■ **earlier this year** 今年早些时候 jīnnián zǎoxiē shíhou

early ADVERB
▷ *see also* **early** ADJECTIVE
1 早地 zǎo de *(in day, month)*
■ **early in the morning** 清早 qīngzǎo
■ **early this morning** 今天一大早 jīntiān yídàzǎo
2 早 zǎo *(before usual time)*
□ I usually get up early. 我通常早起。Wǒ tōngcháng zǎoqǐ.
3 提早地 tízǎode *(ahead of time)*
□ I came early to get a good seat. 我提早去好占个好位置。Wǒ tízáo qù hǎozhànge hǎowèizhì.

early ADJECTIVE
▷ *see also* **early** ADVERB
早期的 zǎoqī de *(stage, career)*
■ **You're early!** 你怎么这么早！Nǐ zěnme zhème zǎo!
■ **to have an early night** 早早睡觉 zǎozǎoshuìjiào

to **earn** VERB
挣得 zhèngdé
□ She earns £6 an hour. 她一小时挣六镑。Tā yìxiǎoshí zhèng liùbàng.
■ **to earn one's living** 谋生 móushēng

earnings PL NOUN
收入 shōurù [笔 bǐ]

earphones PL NOUN
耳机 ěrjī [副 fù]

earring NOUN
耳环 ěrhuán [只 zhī]

earth NOUN
1 地球 dìqiú *(the Earth)*
2 陆地 lùdì [块 kuài] *(land surface)*
3 泥土 nítǔ [块 kuài] *(soil)*

earthquake NOUN
地震 dìzhèn [次 cì]

easily ADVERB
轻易地 qīngyì de

east NOUN
▷ *see also* **east** ADJECTIVE, ADVERB
东方 dōngfāng
□ the east of Spain 西班牙东部 Xībānyá dōngbù □ to the east 以东 yǐdōng □ in the east 在东部 zàidōngbù
■ **the East** *(the Orient)* 东方国家 dōngfāng guójiā

east ADJECTIVE
▷ *see also* **east** NOUN, ADVERB
东部的 dōngbù de
■ **the east coast** 东海岸 dōnghǎiàn
■ **an east wind** 一阵东风 yízhèn dōngfēng [阵 zhèn]

east ADVERB
▷ *see also* **east** NOUN, ADJECTIVE
向东方 xiàng dōngfāng
□ We were travelling east. 我们向东旅行。Wǒmen xiàngdōng lǚxíng.
■ **east of...** …以东 ...yǐdōng □ It's east of London. 那是在伦敦东面。Nàshì zài Lúndūn dōngmiàn.

eastbound ADJECTIVE
东行的 dōngxíng de
□ Eastbound traffic is moving very slowly. 东行的交通非常拥堵。Dōngxíng de jiāotōng fēicháng yōngdǔ. □ The car was eastbound on the M25. 汽车在M25公路上向东行驶。Qìchē zài M25 gōnglùshàng xiàngdōng xíngshǐ.

Easter NOUN
复活节 Fùhuó Jié
■ **at Easter** 复活节期间 Fùhuó Jié qījiān
■ **the Easter holidays** 复活节假期 Fùhuó Jié jiàqī

DID YOU KNOW...?
Easter is not traditionally celebrated in China.

Easter egg NOUN
复活节彩蛋 Fùhuó Jié Cǎidàn [个 gè]

eastern ADJECTIVE
东部的 dōngbù de
■ **the eastern part of the island** 这座岛的东部 zhè zuò dǎo de dōngbù
■ **Eastern** *(oriental)* 东方的 Dōngfāng de
■ **Eastern Europe** 东欧 Dōngōu

easy ADJECTIVE
1 容易的 róngyì de
□ It's easy to train dogs. 驯狗是容易的。Xùngǒu shì róngyì de.
2 安逸的 ānyì de *(life, time)*

easy-going ADJECTIVE
随和的 suíhéde
□ She's very easy-going. 她非常随和。Tā fēicháng suíhé.

to **eat** VERB
1 吃 chī *(consume)*
□ Would you like something to eat? 您想吃点什么吗？Nín xiǎng chī diǎn shénme ma?
2 吃饭 chīfàn *(have a meal)*

DID YOU KNOW...?
In China, 你吃饭了吗？Nǐ chīfàn le ma? **Have you eaten?** is used as a common greeting and is not actually an invitation to dinner.

eaten VERB ▷ *see* **eat**

e-card NOUN
电子卡片 diànzǐ kǎpiàn

eccentric ADJECTIVE
古怪的 gǔguài de

echo NOUN
回音 huíyīn [声 shēng]

e-cigarette NOUN
电子香烟 diànzǐ xiāngyān

eco-friendly ADJECTIVE
环保的 huánbǎo de

ecological ADJECTIVE
生态的 shēngtài de

ecology NOUN
1 生态 shēngtài *(environment)*
2 生态学 shēngtàixué *(subject)*

e-commerce NOUN
电子商务 diànzǐshāngwù

economic ADJECTIVE
1 经济的 jīngjì de *(growth, development, policy)*
2 有利可图的 yǒulì kětú de *(profitable)*

economical ADJECTIVE
节约的 jiéyuē de

economics NOUN
经济学 jīngjìxué
□ He's studying economics. 他在读经济学。Tā zài dú jīngjìxué.

to **economize** VERB
节约 jiéyuē
■ **to economize on something** 更经济地使用某物 gèng jīngjì de shǐyòng mǒuwù

economy NOUN
1 经济 jīngjì [种 zhǒng] *(of country)*
2 节约 jiéyuē *(thrift)*

eczema NOUN
湿疹 shīzhěn

edge NOUN
1 边缘 biānyuán [个 gè] *(of road, town)*
2 棱 léng [条 tiáo] *(of table, chair)*

Edinburgh NOUN
爱丁堡 Àidīngbǎo

editor NOUN
编辑 biānjí [个 gè]

to **educate** VERB
教育 jiàoyù

educated ADJECTIVE
有教养的 yǒujiàoyǎng de

education NOUN
1 教育 jiàoyù
□ There should be more investment in education. 应该增加在教育上的投资。Yīnggāi zēngjiā zài jiàoyù shàng de tóuzī.
2 教学 jiàoxué *(teaching)*

□ She works in education. 她从事教学工作。Tā cóngshì jiàoxué gōngzuò.

educational ADJECTIVE
有教育意义的 yǒujiàoyùyìyì de *(experience, toy)*
□ It was very educational. 这很有教育意义。Zhè hěn yǒujiàoyùyìyì.

effect NOUN
效果 xiàoguǒ [个 gè]
■ **to take effect** *(drug)* 见效 jiànxiào
■ **to have an effect on something** 对某物产生影响 duì mǒuwù chǎnshēng yǐngxiǎng
■ **special effects** 特效 tèxiào

effective ADJECTIVE
有效的 yǒuxiào de

effectively ADVERB
有效地 yǒuxiào de

efficiency NOUN
效率 xiàolǜ

efficient ADJECTIVE
有效率的 yǒu xiàolǜ de

effort NOUN
1 努力 nǔlì *(hard work)*
2 尝试 chángshì [次 cì] *(attempt)*
■ **to make an effort to do something** 努力做某事 nǔlì zuò mǒushì

e.g. ABBREVIATION *(= exempli gratia)*
例如 lìrú *(for example)*

egg NOUN
蛋 dàn [个 gè]
□ a hard-boiled egg 一个煮熟的蛋 yígè zhǔshú de dàn □ a soft-boiled egg 一个煮得半熟的蛋 yígè zhǔdebànshú de dàn □ a fried egg 一个煎鸡蛋 yígè jiānjīdàn
□ scrambled eggs 炒蛋 chǎodàn

egg cup NOUN
鸡蛋杯 jīdànbēi [个 gè]

eggplant NOUN (US)
茄子 qiézi [个 gè]

Egypt NOUN
埃及 Āijí
□ in Egypt 在埃及 zài Āijí

eight NUMBER
八 bā
□ She's eight. 她八岁。Ta bā suì.

eighteen NUMBER
十八 shíbā
□ She's eighteen. 她十八岁。Tā shíbā suì.

eighteenth ADJECTIVE
第十八 dì shíbā
□ her eighteenth birthday 她的十八岁生日 tā de shíbāsuì shēngrì □ the eighteenth of August 八月十八号 bāyuèshíbāhào

eighth ADJECTIVE, NOUN
1 第八 dì bā
□ the eighth of August 八月八号 bāyuèbāhào
2 八分之一 bā fēn zhī yī *(fraction)*

eighty NUMBER
八十 bāshí

Eire NOUN
爱尔兰共和国 Ài'ěrlán Gònghéguó

either ADJECTIVE
▷ *see also* **either** PRONOUN, ADVERB, CONJUNCTION
1 两者任一的 liǎngzhě rènyī de *(one or the other)*
2 两者中每一方的 liǎngzhě zhōng měiyìfāng de *(both, each)*
■ **on either side** 在两边 zài liǎngbiān

either PRONOUN
▷ *see also* **either** ADJECTIVE, ADVERB, CONJUNCTION
两者之中任何一个 liǎngzhě zhī zhōng rènhé yígè *(after negative, interrogative)*
□ I don't like either of them. 两个我都不喜欢。Liǎnggè wǒ dōu bù xǐhuan. □ Which do you want? — Either. 你要哪个？— 哪个都不要。Nǐ yào nǎgè? — Nǎgè dōu búyào.

either ADVERB, CONJUNCTION
▷ *see also* **either** ADJECTIVE, PRONOUN
也 yě *(in negative statements)*
□ No, I don't either. 不，我也不。Bù, wǒ yě bù. □ I've never been to Spain. — I haven't either. 我从没去过西班牙。— 我也没去过。Wǒ cóngméi qùguò Xībānyá. — Wǒ yě méi qùguò.
■ **either... or...** 要么…要么… yàome... yàome... □ You can have either ice cream or yoghurt. 你要么吃冰激淋，要么酸奶。Nǐ yàome chī bīngjīlín, yàome suānnǎi.

elastic NOUN
橡皮 xiàngpí [块 kuài]

elastic band NOUN
橡皮筋 xiàngpíjīn [根 gēn]

elbow NOUN
肘 zhǒu [个 gè]

elder ADJECTIVE
年龄较大的 niánlíng jiào dà de
■ **my elder sister** 我的姐姐 wǒde jiějie

elderly ADJECTIVE
年长的 niánzhǎng de
■ **the elderly** 老年人 lǎoniánrén

eldest ADJECTIVE
▷ *see also* **eldest** NOUN
年龄最大的 niánlíng zuìdà de
□ my eldest sister 我的大姐 wǒde dàjiě

eldest NOUN
▷ *see also* **eldest** ADJECTIVE
年龄最大的孩子 niánlíng zuìdà de háizi
□ He's the eldest. 他是老大。Tā shì lǎodà.

to **elect** VERB
选举 xuǎnjǔ

election NOUN
选举 xuǎnjǔ [次 cì]
■ **to hold an election** 举行选举 jǔxíng xuǎnjǔ

electric ADJECTIVE
1 电动的 diàndòng de
□ an electric blanket 一条电热毯 yìtiáo diànrè tǎn □ an electric fire 一台电子壁炉 yìtái diànzǐ bìlú
2 电的 diàn de *(current, charge, socket)*

electrical ADJECTIVE
电气的 diàndòng de
■ **an electrical engineer** 一名电气工程师 yìmíng diànqì gōngchéngshī

electric guitar NOUN
电吉他 diànjítā [把 bǎ]

electrician NOUN
电工 diàngōng [个 gè]

electricity NOUN
1 电 diàn *(energy)*
2 供电 gòngdiàn *(supply)*

electric shock NOUN
触电 chùdiàn [次 cì]

electronic ADJECTIVE
电子的 diànzǐ de

electronics NOUN
电子学 diànzǐxué

elegant ADJECTIVE
优雅的 yōuyǎ de

elementary school NOUN (US)
小学 xiǎoxué [所 suǒ]

elephant NOUN
大象 dàxiàng [头 tóu]

elevator NOUN (US)
电梯 diàntī [部 bù]

LANGUAGE TIP Word for word, this means 'electric stairs'.

eleven NUMBER
十一 shíyī
□ She's eleven. 她十一岁。Ta shíyī suì.

eleventh ADJECTIVE
第十一 dì shíyī
□ the eleventh of August 八月十一号 bāyuè shíyīhào

to **eliminate** VERB
1 消除 xiāochú *(poverty)*
2 淘汰 táotài *(team, contestant, candidate)*

else ADVERB
■ **something else** 其他东西 qítā dōngxi
■ **anything else** 任何其他东西 rènhé qítā dōngxi □ Would you like anything else? 您还需要别的吗？Nín háixūyào biéde ma?
□ I don't want anything else. 我不需要别的了。Wǒ bù xūyào biéde le.
■ **What else?** 还有什么？Háiyǒu shénme?
■ **or else** 1 *(otherwise)* 否则 fǒuzé
2 *(threatening)* 要不然 yàobùrán □ Don't talk to me like that again, or else! 别这么跟我说话，要不够你受的！Bié zhème gēn wǒ shuōhuà, yàobú gòu nǐ shòu de!
■ **everywhere else** 其他任何地方 qítā rènhé dìfāng
■ **somewhere else** 其他地方 qítā dìfāng
■ **anywhere else** 其他任何地方 qítā rènhé dìfāng
■ **everyone else** 其他人 qítā rén
■ **nobody else** 没有其他人 méiyǒu qítā rén

elsewhere ADVERB
1 在别处 zài biéchù *(be)*
2 到别处 dào biéchù *(go)*

email NOUN
▷ *see also* **email** VERB
电子邮件 diànzǐ yóujiàn [封 fēng]

to **email** VERB
▷ *see also* **email** NOUN
1 给...发电子邮件 gěi...fā diànzǐ yóujiàn *(person)*
2 用电子邮件寄 yòng diànzǐ yóujiàn jì *(file, document)*

email account NOUN
电子邮件账号 diànzǐ yóujiàn zhànghào [个 gè]

email address NOUN
电子邮件地址 diànzǐ yóujiàn dìzhǐ [个 gè]
□ My email address is... 我的电子邮件地址是… Wǒ de diànzǐ yóujiàn dìzhǐ shì...

embarrassed ADJECTIVE
■ **to be embarrassed** 尴尬的 gāngà de □ I was really embarrassed. 我真的很尴尬。Wǒ zhēnde hěn gāngà.

embarrassing ADJECTIVE
令人尴尬的 lìng rén gāngà de
□ It was so embarrassing. 这真是太令人尴尬了。Zhè zhēnshì tài lìngrén gāngà le.

embassy NOUN
大使馆 dàshǐguǎn [个 gè]
□ the Chinese Embassy 中国大使馆 Zhōngguódàshǐguǎn

to **embroider** VERB
绣 xiù

embroidery NOUN
刺绣 cìxiù

emergency NOUN
紧急情况 jǐnjí qíngkuàng [个 gè] *(crisis)*
□ This is an emergency! 这是紧急情况！Zhèshì jǐnjí qíngkuàng!
■ **in an emergency** 在紧急情况下 zài jǐnjí qíngkuàng xià
■ **an emergency exit** 一个紧急出口 yígè jǐnjí chūkǒu

■ **an emergency landing** 一次紧急迫降 yícì jǐnjí pòjiàng
■ **the emergency services** 急救服务 jíjiù fúwù

DID YOU KNOW...?
In China, the police can be contacted by dialling 110, an ambulance can be called by dialling 112 and the fire brigade by dialling 119.

emergency room NOUN (US)
急诊室 jízhěnshì [个 gè]

to **emigrate** VERB
移居外国 yíjū wàiguó

emotion NOUN
感情 gǎnqíng [种 zhǒng]

emotional ADJECTIVE
易动感情的 yì dòng gǎnqíng de

emperor NOUN
皇帝 huángdì [个 gè]

to **emphasize** VERB
强调 qiángdiào

empire NOUN
帝国 dìguó [个 gè]

to **employ** VERB
雇用 gùyòng
□ The factory employs 600 people. 这个工厂雇用了六百名员工。Zhègè gōngchǎng gùyòng le liùbǎi míng yuángōng. □ He was employed as a technician. 他受雇做技师。Tā shòugù zuò jìshī.

employee NOUN
雇员 gùyuán [个 gè]

employer NOUN
雇主 gùzhǔ [个 gè]

employment NOUN
工作 gōngzuò [份 fèn]

empty ADJECTIVE
▷ *see also* **empty** VERB
空的 kōng de

to **empty** VERB
▷ *see also* **empty** ADJECTIVE
倒空 dào kōng
■ **to empty something out** 把某物彻底清空 bǎ mǒuwù chèdǐ qīng kōng

to **encourage** VERB
1 鼓励 gǔlì *(person)*
2 支持 zhīchí *(activity, attitude)*
3 助长 zhùzhǎng *(growth, industry)*
■ **to encourage somebody to do something** 鼓励某人去做某事 gǔlì mǒurén qùzuò mǒushì

encouragement NOUN
鼓励 gǔlì [次 cì]

encyclopedia NOUN
百科全书 bǎikē quánshū [本 běn]

end NOUN
▷ *see also* **end** VERB
1 末 mòqī *(of period, event)*
□ the end of the holidays 假期末 jiàqīmò
□ at the end of August 在八月末 zài bāyuè mò
2 结局 jiéjú [个 gè] *(of film, book)*
□ the end of the film 电影结局 diànyǐng jiéjú
3 尽头 jìntóu [个 gè] *(of queue, rope)*
□ at the end of the street 在街道的尽头 zài jiēdào de jìntóu □ at the other end of the table 在桌子的另一头 zài zhuōzi de lìngyìtóu
4 端 duān *(of town)*
■ **to come to an end** 完结 wánjié
■ **in the end** 最终 zuìzhōng □ In the end I decided to stay at home. 最终我决定呆在家里。Zuìzhōng wǒ juédìng dāi zài jiālǐ.
■ **for hours on end** 很长时间 hěncháng shíjiān

to **end** VERB
▷ *see also* **end** NOUN
1 结束 jiéshù *(come to an end)*
□ What time does the film end? 电影什么时候结束？Diànyǐng shénme shíhòu jiéshù?
2 终止 zhōngzhǐ *(put to and end)*

to **end up** VERB
■ **to end up in** *(place)* 最终到了 zuìzhōng dào le
■ **to end up doing something** 最终还是做某事 zuìzhōng háishì zuò mǒushì □ I ended up walking home. 我最终还是走路回家了。Wǒ zuìzhōng háishì zǒulù huíjiā le.

ending NOUN
结局 jiéjú [个 gè]
□ It was an exciting film, especially the ending. 这电影真令人兴奋，特别是结局。Zhè diànyǐng zhēn lìngrén xīngfèn, tèbié shì jiéjú.
■ **a happy ending** 一个美满结局 yígè měimǎn jiéjú [个 gè]

endless ADJECTIVE
无尽的 wújìn de
□ The journey seemed endless. 旅程似乎是无尽的。Lǚchéng sìhū shì wújìn de.

enemy NOUN
敌人 dírén [个 gè]

energetic ADJECTIVE
1 精力充沛的 jīnglì chōngpèi de *(person)*
2 生机勃勃的 shēngjī bóbó de *(activity)*

energy NOUN
能源 néngyuán [种 zhǒng]

energy drink NOUN
能量饮料 néngliàng yǐnliào

engaged ADJECTIVE
1 已订婚的 yǐ dìnghūn de *(to be married)*
□ She's engaged to Brian. 她和布莱恩订婚了。Tā hé Bùlái'ēn dìnghūn le.

■ **to get engaged** 订婚 dìnghūn
2 占线的 zhànxiàn de *(busy: phone)*
□ I phoned, but it was engaged. 我打了，但是电话占线。Wǒ dǎ le, dànshì diànhuà zhànxiàn.
3 被占用的 bèi zhànyòng de *(occupied: toilet)*

engagement NOUN
婚约 hūnyuē [个 gè] *(to marry)*

engagement ring NOUN
订婚戒指 dìnghūn jièzhǐ [枚 méi]

engine NOUN
1 发动机 fādòngjī [台 tái] *(of car)*
2 机车 jīchē [部 bù] *(locomotive)*

engineer NOUN
1 工程师 gōngchéngshī [位 wèi] *(who designs machines, bridges)*
□ He's an engineer. 他是一位工程师。Tā shì yíwèi gōngchéngshī.
2 技师 jìshī [位 wèi] *(who repairs machines, phones)*

engineering NOUN
1 工程 gōngchéng [项 xiàng] *(of roads, bridges, machinery)*
2 工程学 gōngchéngxué *(science)*

England NOUN
英格兰 Yīnggélán
□ in England 在英格兰 zài Yīnggélán

English ADJECTIVE
▷ *see also* **English** NOUN
英国人 Yīngguórén [个 gè]
□ I'm English. 我是英国人。Wǒ shì Yīngguórén.
■ **English people** 英国人 Yīngguórén

English NOUN
▷ *see also* **English** ADJECTIVE
英语 Yīngyǔ *(language)*
□ Do you speak English? 你说英语吗？Nǐ shuō Yīngyǔ ma?
■ **an English speaker** 一个讲英语的人 yígè jiǎng Yīngyǔ de rén
■ **the English** *(people)* 英国人 Yīngguórén

Englishman NOUN
英格兰男人 Yīnggélán nánrén [个 gè]

Englishwoman NOUN
英格兰女人 Yīnggélán nǚrén [个 gè]

to **enjoy** VERB
喜欢 xǐhuan
□ Did you enjoy the film? 你喜欢那电影吗？Nǐ xǐhuan nà diànyǐng ma?
■ **Enjoy your meal!** 吃好！Chīhǎo!
■ **to enjoy doing something** 喜欢做某事 xǐhuan zuò mǒushì
■ **to enjoy oneself** 过得快乐 guòde kuàilè
□ I really enjoyed myself. 我真的很快乐。Wǒ zhēnde hěn kuàilè.

enjoyable ADJECTIVE
有乐趣的 yǒu lèqù de

enlargement NOUN
放大 fàngdà *(of photo)*

enormous ADJECTIVE
1 庞大的 pángdà de *(very big)*
2 巨大的 jùdà de *(pleasure, success, disappointment)*

enough ADJECTIVE
▷ *see also* **enough** PRONOUN, ADVERB
足够的 zúgòu de
□ enough time to do something 有足够的时间去做某事 yǒu zúgòu de shíjiān qùzuò mǒushì □ I didn't have enough money. 我没有足够的钱。Wǒ méiyǒu zúgòu de qián.
□ Will 5 be enough? 五个够吗？Wǔgè gòuma?
■ **That's enough, thanks.** 够了，谢谢。Gòule, xièxiè.

enough PRONOUN
▷ *see also* **enough** ADJECTIVE, ADVERB
足够的东西 zúgòu de dōngxi *(sufficient)*
□ enough to eat 够吃 gòuchī □ Have you got enough? 你的够吗？Nǐde gòuma?
■ **I've had enough!** 我受够了！Wǒ shòugòu le!

enough ADVERB
▷ *see also* **enough** ADJECTIVE, PRONOUN
■ **big enough** 足够大 zúgòu dà

to **enquire** VERB
■ **to enquire about something** 询问某事 xúnwèn mǒushì □ I am going to enquire about train times. 我打算问下列车时刻。Wǒ dǎsuàn wènxià lièchēshíkè.

enquiry NOUN
■ **to make enquiries** 询问 xúnwèn

to **enrol** VERB
注册 zhùcè *(at school, university, on course, in club)*
■ **to enrol somebody** *(at school, on course)* 招某人入学 zhāo mǒurén rùxué

en suite ADJECTIVE
带浴室的 dài yùshì de *(bathroom)*

to **ensure** VERB
保证 bǎozhèng

to **enter** VERB
1 进入 jìnrù *(room, building)*
2 参加 cānjiā *(race, competition)*
3 输入 shūrù *(data)*
4 进来 jìnlái *(come or go in)*
■ **'Do not enter'** "禁止入内" "Jìnzhǐrùnèi"

to **entertain** VERB
1 娱乐 yúlè *(amuse)*
2 招待 zhāodài *(invite a guest)*

entertainer NOUN
演艺者 yǎnyìzhě [个 gè]

entertaining ADJECTIVE
有趣的 yǒuqùde

entertainment NOUN
娱乐活动 yúlè huódòng [种 zhǒng]

enthusiasm NOUN
热情 rèqíng
■ **enthusiasm for something** 对某事的热情 duì mǒushì de rèqíng

enthusiast NOUN
爱好者 àihàozhě [位 wèi]
□ a railway enthusiast 一位铁路爱好者 yíwèi tiělù àihàozhě □ She's a DIY enthusiast. 她是自己动手的爱好者。Tā shì zìjǐdòngshǒu de àihàozhě.

enthusiastic ADJECTIVE
1 极感兴趣的 jí gǎn xìngqù de *(person)*
2 热情的 rèqíng de *(response, reception)*
■ **to be enthusiastic about something** 对某事满怀热情 duì mǒushì mǎnhuái rèqíng

entire ADJECTIVE
整个的 zhěnggè de
□ the entire world 整个世界 zhěnggè shìjiè

entirely ADVERB
完全地 wánquán de

entrance NOUN
入口 rùkǒu [个 gè]
□ the entrance to something 某处的入口 mǒuchù de rùkǒu
■ **an entrance fee** 一笔入场费 yìbǐ rùchǎngfèi

entry NOUN
1 入口 rùkǒu [个 gè] *(way in)*
2 参赛作品 cānsài zuòpǐn [份 fèn] *(in competition)*
3 输入项 shūrù xiàng [项 xiàng] *(in computing)*
■ **'no entry' 1** *(to land, room)* "禁止入内" "jìnzhǐ rùnèi" **2** *(on road sign)* "禁止通行" "jìnzhǐ tōngxíng"
■ **an entry form** 一张报名表 yìzhāng bàomíngbiǎo

entry phone NOUN
门铃话机 ménlínghuàjī [个 gè]

envelope NOUN
信封 xìnfēng [个 gè]

DID YOU KNOW...?
Red envelopes called 红包 hóngbāo containing money are given to children during certain festivals or to newly-married couples on their wedding day.

envious ADJECTIVE
忌妒的 jìdùde

environment NOUN
环境 huánjìng [个 gè]
■ **the environment** *(natural world)* 自然环境 zìrán huánjìng

environmental ADJECTIVE
环境的 huánjìng de

environmentally-friendly ADJECTIVE
环保的 huánbǎo de

envy NOUN
▷ *see also* **envy** VERB
羡慕 xiànmù

to **envy** VERB
▷ *see also* **envy** NOUN
忌妒 jìdù *(be jealous of)*
□ I don't envy you! 我可不忌妒你！Wǒ kě bú jìdù nǐ!
■ **to envy somebody something** 羡慕某人的某物 xiànmù mǒurénde mǒuwù

epilepsy NOUN
癫痫 diānxián [场 chǎng]

epileptic NOUN
癫痫病人 diānxián bìngrén [个 gè]

episode NOUN
集 jí

equal ADJECTIVE
▷ *see also* **equal** VERB
1 一样的 yíyàng de *(of same size)*
□ They are roughly equal in size. 它们大小几乎一样。Tāmen dàxiǎo jīhū yíyàng.
■ **to be equal to** *(the same as)* 与…相同 yǔ...xiāngtóng
2 同样的 tóngyàng de *(intensity, importance)*

to **equal** VERB
▷ *see also* **equal** ADJECTIVE
1 等于 děngyú *(number, amount)*
□ 79 minus 14 equals 65. 七十九减十四等于六十五。Qīshíjiǔ jiǎn shísì děngyú liùshíwǔ.
2 比得上 bǐdeshàng *(match, rival)*

equality NOUN
平等 píngděng

to **equalize** VERB
追平比分 zhuīpíng bǐfēn *(in sport)*

equally ADVERB
1 平等地 píngděng de *(share, divide)*
2 同样地 tóngyàng de *(good, important)*

equator NOUN
■ **the equator** 赤道 chìdào

equipment NOUN
设备 shèbèi [套 tào]
□ skiing equipment 滑雪设备 huáxuě shèbèi

equipped ADJECTIVE
■ **equipped with** 装备着 zhuāngbèizhe
■ **to be well equipped** 装备精良 zhuāngbèi jīngliáng

equivalent ADJECTIVE
▷ *see also* **equivalent** NOUN
相同的 xiāngtóng de

■ **equivalent to** 与…相同 yǔ...xiāngtóng

equivalent NOUN
▷ *see also* **equivalent** ADJECTIVE
同等物 tóngděngwù [个 gè] *(amount, value, qualities, purpose)*

ER NOUN (US) *(= emergency room)*
急诊室 jízhěnshì [间 jiān]

eraser NOUN
橡皮 xiàngpí [块 kuài]

error NOUN
错误 cuòwù [个 gè]
■ **to make an error** 犯错误 fàn cuòwù

escalator NOUN
自动扶梯 zìdòng fútī [部 bù]

to **escape** VERB
▷ *see also* **escape** NOUN
1 逃走 táozǒu *(get away)*
□ A lion has escaped. 一只狮子逃跑了。Yìzhī shīzi táopǎo le.
■ **to escape from** 1 *(place)* 从…逃跑 cóng...táopǎo 2 *(person)* 避开 bìkāi
2 逃跑 táopǎo *(from jail)*
3 避免 bìmiǎn *(injury)*
■ **to escape unhurt** *(from accident)* 安然逃脱 ānrán táotuō

escape NOUN
▷ *see also* **escape** VERB
越狱 yuèyù [次 cì] *(from prison)*

escort NOUN
护送 hùsòng [次 cì]
□ a police escort 一次警察护送 yícì jǐngchá hùsòng

especially ADVERB
尤其 yóuqí
□ It's very hot there, especially in the summer. 这里很热，尤其是夏天。Zhèlǐ hěnrè, yóuqí shì xiàtiān.

essay NOUN
论文 lùnwén [篇 piān]
□ a history essay 一篇历史论文 yìpiān lìshǐ lùnwén

essential ADJECTIVE
1 必要的 bìyào de *(necessary, vital)*
■ **it is essential to...** 必须… bìxū... □ It's essential to bring warm clothes. 必须带上厚衣服。Bìxū dàishàng hòuyīfú.
2 基本的 jīběn de *(basic)*
■ **essentials** *(necessities)* 必需品 bìxūpǐn

estate NOUN
1 庄园 zhuāngyuán [个 gè] *(land)*
2 住宅区 zhùzháiqū [片 piàn] *(housing estate)*
□ I live on an estate. 我住的地方是片住宅区。Wǒ zhù de dìfāng shì piàn zhùzháiqū.

estate agent NOUN
房地产经纪人 fángdìchǎn jīngjìrén [个 gè]

estate car NOUN
加长型轿车 jiāchángxíng jiàochē [辆 liàng]

estimate NOUN
▷ *see also* **estimate** VERB
估计 gūjì [种 zhǒng]

to **estimate** VERB
▷ *see also* **estimate** NOUN
估计 gūjì *(reckon, calculate)*
□ The damage was estimated at 300 million pounds. 估计损失为三亿英镑。Gūjì sǔnshī wéi sānyì yīngbàng. □ They estimated it would take three weeks. 他们估计这要用三周时间。Tāmen gūjì zhè yào yòng sān zhōu shíjiān.

etc (US **etc.**) ABBREVIATION *(= et cetera)*
等等 děngděng

Ethiopia NOUN
埃塞俄比亚 Āisài'ébǐyà

ethnic ADJECTIVE
1 种族的 zhǒngzú de
□ an ethnic minority 一个少数民族 yígè shǎoshù mínzú
2 民族的 mínzú de *(clothes, music)*

e-ticket NOUN
电子客票 diànzǐ kèpiào [张 zhāng]

EU NOUN *(= European Union)*
■ **the EU** 欧洲联盟 Ōuzhōu Liánméng [个 gè]

euro NOUN
欧元 Ōuyuán
□ 50 euros 五十欧元 wǔshí Ōuyuán

Europe NOUN
欧洲 Ōuzhōu
□ in Europe 在欧洲 zài Ōuzhōu □ to Europe 去欧洲 qù Ōuzhōu

European ADJECTIVE
▷ *see also* **European** NOUN
欧洲的 Ōuzhōu de

European NOUN
▷ *see also* **European** ADJECTIVE
欧洲人 Ōuzhōurén [个 gè] *(person)*

European Union NOUN
■ **the European Union** 欧洲联盟 Ōuzhōu Liánméng

to **evacuate** VERB
1 疏散 shūsàn *(people)*
2 撤离 chèlí *(place)*

to **evaluate** VERB
评估 pínggū

eve NOUN
前夕 qiánxī
■ **Christmas Eve** 圣诞节前夜 Shèngdànjié qiányè
■ **New Year's Eve** 除夕 Chúxī

even ADVERB
▷ *see also* **even** ADJECTIVE

甚至 shènzhì
□ I like all animals, even snakes. 我喜欢所有的动物，甚至蛇。Wǒ xǐhuan suǒyǒu de dòngwù, shènzhì shé. □ He didn't even hear what I said. 他甚至根本没听见我的话。Tā shènzhì gēnběn méi tīngjiàn wǒ de huà.
■ **even on Sundays** 甚至星期天 shènzhì xīngqītiān
■ **even more** 甚至更多 shènzhì gèngduō
□ I liked Shanghai even more than Beijing. 我喜欢上海甚至多过喜欢北京。Wǒ xǐhuan Shànghǎi shènzhì duōguò xǐhuān Běijīng.
■ **even if** 即使 jíshǐ □ I'd never do that, even if you asked me. 即使你要求我，我也不会那么做。Jíshǐ nǐ yāoqiú wǒ, wǒ yě búhuì nàme zuò.
■ **even though** 尽管 jǐnguǎn □ He wants to go out, even though it's raining. 尽管天在下雨，他还是想出门。Jǐnguǎn tiān zài xiàyǔ, tā háishì xiǎng chūmén.
■ **not even** 连…也不 lián...yěbù □ He never stops working, not even at the weekend. 他连周末也不停止工作。Tā lián zhōumò yě bù tíngzhǐ gōngzuò

even ADJECTIVE
▷ *see also* **even** ADVERB
1 平坦的 píngtǎn de *(flat)*
□ an even layer of snow 一层平坦的积雪 yìcéng píngtǎn de jīxuě
2 偶数的 ǒushù de *(number)*
■ **an even number** 一个偶数 yígè ǒushù
■ **to get even with somebody** 报复某人 bàofù mǒurén □ He wanted to get even with her. 他想报复她。Tā xiǎng baòfù tā.

evening NOUN
1 傍晚 bàngwǎn [个 gè] *(early)*
2 晚上 wǎnshang [个 gè] *(late, whole period, event)*
■ **in the evening** 在晚上 zài wǎnshang
■ **all evening** 整晚 zhěngwǎn
■ **this evening** 今晚 jīnwǎn
■ **tomorrow evening** 明晚 míngwǎn
■ **yesterday evening** 昨晚 zuówǎn
■ **Good evening!** 晚上好！ Wǎnshàng hǎo!

evening class NOUN
夜校 yèxiào [个 gè]

event NOUN
事件 shìjiàn [个 gè]
■ **a sporting event** 一次体育赛事 yícì tǐyù sàishì

eventful ADJECTIVE
事件多的 shìjiàn duō de

eventually ADVERB
1 终于 zhōngyú *(finally)*
2 最终 zuìzhōng *(ultimately)*

ever ADVERB
从来 cónglái
□ Have you ever been there? 你曾去过那儿吗？Nǐ céng qùguò nà'er ma?
■ **ever since 1** *(since then)* 从…以来 cóng... yǐlái □ We have been friends ever since. 我们从那时以来一直是朋友。Wǒmen cóng nàshí yǐlái yìzhí shì péngyǒu. **2** *(since the time that)* 自从 zìcóng □ Jack has loved trains ever since he was a boy. 杰克从小就喜爱火车。Jiékè cóngxiǎo jiù xǐ'ài huǒchē.
■ **ever since then** 从那以后 cóng nà yǐhòu
■ **the best ever** 迄今最佳 qìjīn zuìjiā □ the best I've ever seen 这是我迄今看过最棒的 zhè shì wǒ qìjīn kànguò zuìbàng de
■ **hardly ever** 几乎从不 jīhū cóngbù
■ **for the first time ever** 第一次 dìyīcì

every ADJECTIVE
1 每个 měigè *(each)*
□ every pupil 每个学生 měigè xuéshēng
□ Every village should have a post office. 每个村庄都应该有一个邮局。Měigè cūnzhuāng dōu yīnggāi yǒu yígè yóujú.
2 所有的 suǒyǒu de *(all possible)*
□ recipes for every occasion 所有场合均适用的菜谱 suǒyǒu chǎnghé jūn shìyòng de càipǔ
3 每 měi *(with time words)*
□ every day 每天 měitiān □ every week 每周 měizhōu □ every Sunday 每个星期天 měigè xīngqītiān
■ **every now and then** 不时地 bùshí de
■ **every time** 每次 měicì □ Every time I see him he's depressed. 我每次见到他他都很沮丧。Wǒ měicì jiàn dào tā dōu hěn jǔsàng.

everybody PRONOUN
人人 rénrén
LANGUAGE TIP Word for word, this means 'person person'.
□ Everybody knows about it. 人人都知道这个。Rénrén dōu zhīdào zhègè.
□ Everybody makes mistakes. 是人都会犯错。Shì rén dōu huì fàn cuò.
■ **everybody else** 其他所有人 qítā suǒyǒurén

everyone PRONOUN
每人 měirén
□ Everyone opened their presents. 每人都打开了礼物。Měirén dōu dǎkāile lǐwù.
□ Everyone should have a hobby. 每人都该有个爱好。Měirén dōu gāi yǒu gè àihào.
■ **everyone else** 其他所有人 qítā suǒyǒurén

everything PRONOUN

一切 yíqiè
□ Everything is ready. 一切准备就绪。Yíqiè zhǔnbèi jiùxù. □ You've thought of everything! 你把一切都考虑到了！Nǐ bǎ yíqiè dōu kǎolǜ dào le! □ Is everything OK? 一切都还好吧？Yíqiè dōu hái hǎo ba?
□ He did everything possible. 他做了一切能做的。Tā zuòle yíqiè néng zuò de.
□ Money isn't everything. 钱不是一切。Qián búshì yíqiè.

everywhere ADVERB
到处 dàochù
□ I looked everywhere, but I couldn't find it. 我到处都找了，就是找不到。Wǒ dàochù dōu zhǎo le, jiù shì zhǎo búdào. □ There's rubbish everywhere. 到处都是垃圾。Dàochù dōushì lājī.
■ **everywhere you go** 无论你去哪里 wúlùn nǐ qù nǎlǐ

evidence NOUN
迹象 jìxiàng [种 zhǒng] *(signs, indications)*

evil ADJECTIVE
邪恶的 xié'è de

ex- PREFIX
前 qián *(husband, president)*
■ **my ex-wife** 我的前妻 wǒde qiánqī

exact ADJECTIVE
确切的 quèqiè de

exactly ADVERB
1 恰好地 qiàhǎo de *(precisely)*
□ exactly the same 恰好一致 qiàhǎo yízhì
□ at 5 o'clock exactly 恰好五点整时 qiàhǎo wǔdiǎnzhěng shí
2 一点不错 yìdiǎn búcuò *(indicating agreement)*
■ **not exactly** 不完全是 bú wánquán shì

to **exaggerate** VERB
夸大 kuādà
□ You're exaggerating! 你是在夸大！Nǐ shì zài kuādà!
■ **to exaggerate something** 夸大某事 kuādà mǒushì

exaggeration NOUN
夸张 kuāzhāng [种 zhǒng]

exam NOUN
考试 kǎoshì [次 cì]
□ a Chinese exam 一次汉语考试 yícì Hànyǔ kǎoshì □ the exam results 考试结果 kǎoshì jiéguǒ

examination NOUN
1 考试 kǎoshì [次 cì] *(for student)*
2 体检 tǐjiǎn [次 cì] *(medical)*

to **examine** VERB
1 检查 jiǎnchá *(inspect)*
□ He examined her passport. 他检查了她的护照。Tā jiǎnchá le tā de hùzhào.
2 对...进行测验 duì...jìnxíng cèyàn *(student)*
3 检查 jiǎnchá *(medical)*
□ The doctor examined him. 医生给他做了检查。Yīshēng gěi tā zuò le jiǎnchá.

examiner NOUN
考官 kǎoguān [个 gè]

example NOUN
例子 lìzi [个 gè]
□ an example of something 某物的例子 mǒuwù de lìzi
■ **for example** 例如 lìrú

excellence NOUN
卓越 zhuōyuè

excellent ADJECTIVE
极好的 jíhǎo de
□ Her results were excellent. 她的成绩好极了。Tā de chéngjì hǎo jí le. □ It was excellent fun. 那个有趣极了。Nà gè yǒuqù jí le.
■ **Excellent!** 太好了！Tài hǎo le!

except PREPOSITION
除了 chúle
□ everyone except me 除了我以外每个人 chúle wǒ yǐwài měigèrén
■ **except that** 只是 zhǐshì □ The holiday was great, except that it rained. 假期好极了，只是有下雨。Jiàqī hǎojí le, zhǐshì yǒu xiàyǔ.
■ **except for** 除了…外 chúle...wài
■ **except when** …时例外 ...shí lìwài

exception NOUN
例外 lìwài [个 gè]
■ **to make an exception** 破例 pòlì

exceptional ADJECTIVE
格外的 géwài de

excess baggage NOUN
超重行李 chāozhòng xínglǐ

to **exchange** VERB
▷ *see also* **exchange** NOUN
交换 jiāohuàn *(gifts, addresses)*
■ **to exchange something for something** 用某物交换某物 yòng mǒuwù jiāohuàn mǒuwù □ I exchanged the book for a DVD. 我拿这本书换了张DVD。Wǒ ná zhèběn shū huàn le zhāng DVD.

exchange NOUN
▷ *see also* **exchange** VERB
交流 jiāoliú [次 cì] *(of students, sportspeople)*
■ **in exchange for** 换 huàn

exchange rate NOUN
汇率 huìlǜ [个 gè]

excited ADJECTIVE
兴奋的 xīngfèn de
■ **to be excited about something** 对某事感到激动 duì mǒushì gǎndào jīdòng
■ **to get excited** 激动起来 jīdòng qǐlái

English-Chinese

e

excitement NOUN
兴奋 xīngfèn
exciting ADJECTIVE
令人兴奋的 lìng rén xīngfèn de
exclamation mark (US **exclamation point**) NOUN
感叹号 gǎntànhào [个 gè]
excluding PREPOSITION
不包括 bù bāokuò
excuse NOUN
▷ *see also* **excuse** VERB
借口 jièkǒu [个 gè]
■ **to make an excuse** 找借口 zhǎo jièkǒu
to **excuse** VERB
▷ *see also* **excuse** NOUN
1 为…辩解 wèi…biànjiě *(justify)*
2 原谅 yuánliàng *(forgive)*
■ **Excuse me! 1** *(attracting attention)* 劳驾！Láojià! **2** *(as apology)* 对不起！Duìbuqǐ!
■ **Excuse me, please.** *(please let me pass)* 劳驾让一下。Láojià ràngyíxià.
■ **Excuse me?** (US: *what did you say?*) 对不起，你说什么？Duìbuqǐ, nǐ shuō shénme?
ex-directory ADJECTIVE
■ **to be ex-directory** 电话号码不入册的 diànhuà hàomǎ bú rùcè de
■ **to go ex-directory** 不把电话号码入册 bù bǎ diànhuà hàomǎ rùcè
to **execute** VERB
执行 zhíxíng
execution NOUN
执行 zhíxíng [次 cì]
exercise NOUN
▷ *see also* **exercise** VERB
1 运动 yùndòng [种 zhǒng] *(physical exertion)*
□ to take exercise 做健身活动 zuò jiànshēn huódòng
2 练习 liànxí [个 gè] *(series of movements, also for learner)*
■ **to do exercises** 锻炼身体 duànliàn shēntǐ
■ **an exercise bike** 一台自行车健身器 yìtái zìxíngchē jiànshēnqì
■ **an exercise book** 一本练习册 yìběn liànxícè
to **exercise** VERB
▷ *see also* **exercise** NOUN
锻炼 duànliàn *(take exercise)*
exhaust NOUN
1 排气管 páiqìguǎn [根 gēn] *(exhaust pipe)*
2 废气 fèiqì *(fumes)*
exhausted ADJECTIVE
精疲力竭的 jīngpílìjié de
exhibition NOUN
展览会 zhǎnlǎnhuì [个 gè]

ex-husband NOUN
前夫 qiánfū [个 gè]
to **exist** VERB
1 存在 cúnzài *(be present)*
2 生存 shēngcún *(live, subsist)*
exit NOUN
▷ *see also* **exit** VERB
出口 chūkǒu [个 gè]
to **exit** VERB
▷ *see also* **exit** NOUN
退出 tuìchū *(from program, system)*
■ **to exit from something** *(room, motorway)* 离开某处 líkāi mǒuchù
exotic ADJECTIVE
异国情调的 yìguó qíngdiào de
to **expect** VERB
1 预期 yùqī *(anticipate)*
□ I was expecting the worst. 我做了最坏的预期。Wǒ zuòle zuìhuài de yùqī.
■ **to expect something to happen** 预期某事将发生 yùqī mǒushì jiāng fāshēng
2 期待 qīdài *(await)*
□ I'm expecting him for dinner. 我期待着他来赴宴。Wǒ qīdàizhe tā lái fùyàn.
3 怀孕 huáiyùn *(baby)*
□ She's expecting a baby. 她怀孕了。Tā huáiyùn le.
■ **to be expecting** *(be pregnant)* 怀孕 huáiyùn
4 料想 liàoxiǎng *(suppose)*
□ I expect it's a mistake. 我想这是个错误。Wo xiǎng zhè shìgè cuòwù.
■ **I expect so.** 我想会的。Wǒ xiǎng huìde.
expedition NOUN
远征 yuǎnzhēng [次 cì]
to **expel** VERB
开除 kāichú
■ **to get expelled** *(from school)* 被开除 bèi kāichú
expense NOUN
费用 fèiyòng [笔 bǐ]
■ **expenses** *(money spent)* 花销 huāxiāo
expensive ADJECTIVE
1 昂贵的 ángguì de *(purchase)*
2 代价高的 dàijià gāo de *(mistake)*
experience NOUN
▷ *see also* **experience** VERB
1 经验 jīngyàn [种 zhǒng] *(in job)*
2 阅历 yuèlì *(of life)*
3 经历 jīnglì [个 gè] *(individual event)*
to **experience** VERB
▷ *see also* **experience** NOUN
体验 tǐyàn *(feeling, problem)*
experienced ADJECTIVE
有经验的 yǒu jīngyàn de
experiment NOUN

▷ *see also* **experiment** VERB
1 实验 shíyàn [个 gè] *(scientific)*
■ **to carry out an experiment** 做实验 zuò shíyàn
2 尝试 chángshì [次 cì] *(trial)*
to **experiment** VERB
▷ *see also* **experiment** NOUN
试验 shìyàn
expert NOUN
▷ *see also* **expert** ADJECTIVE
专家 zhuānjiā [位 wèi]
□ He's a computer expert. 他是位计算机专家。Tā shì wèi jìsuànjī zhuānjiā.
■ **an expert on something** 某方面的专家 mǒufāngmiàn de zhuānjiā
expert ADJECTIVE
▷ *see also* **expert** NOUN
专家的 zhuānjiā de *(opinion, help, advice)*
□ He's an expert cook. 他是烹饪专家。Tā shì pēngrèn zhuānjiā.
expertise NOUN
专门知识 zhuānmén zhīshi
to **expire** VERB
过期 guòqī *(passport, licence)*
to **explain** VERB
1 解释 jiěshì *(situation, contract)*
2 阐明 chǎnmíng *(decision, actions)*
■ **to explain how** 解释 jiěshì
■ **to explain something to somebody** 向某人解释某事 xiàng mǒurén jiěshì mǒushì
explanation NOUN
1 说明 shuōmíng [个 gè]
□ She gave a full explanation of the decision. 她对采取这个决定做出了详尽的说明。Tā duì cǎiqǔ zhègè juédìng zuòchūle xiángjìnde shuōmíng.
2 解释 jiěshì [个 gè] *(reason)*
□ There was no obvious explanation for the crash. 对于这起车祸没有明确的解释。Duìyú zhèqǐ chēhuò méiyǒu míngquè de jiěshì.
to **explode** VERB
1 爆炸 bàozhà *(go off)*
2 使爆炸 shǐ bàozhà *(set off)*
to **exploit** VERB
1 开发 kāifā *(resources)*
2 剥削 bōxuē *(person, idea)*
exploitation NOUN
剥削 bōxuē [种 zhǒng]
to **explore** VERB
1 探索 tànsuō *(area, country)*
2 探险 tànxiǎn *(go exploring)*
explorer NOUN
探险者 tànxiǎnzhě [名 míng]
explosion NOUN
1 爆炸 bàozhà [次 cì] *(of bomb)*
2 激增 jīzēng [个 gè] *(of population)*
explosive ADJECTIVE
▷ *see also* **explosive** NOUN
爆炸性的 bàozhàxìng de
explosive NOUN
▷ *see also* **explosive** ADJECTIVE
易爆炸物 yìbàozhàwù [个 gè]
to **export** VERB
▷ *see also* **export** NOUN
输出 shūchū
export NOUN
▷ *see also* **export** VERB
1 出口 chūkǒu [项 xiàng] *(process)*
2 出口物 chūkǒuwù [宗 zōng] *(product)*
express ADJECTIVE
▷ *see also* **express** VERB
特快的 tèkuài de *(service, mail)*
to **express** VERB
▷ *see also* **express** ADJECTIVE
表达 biǎodá
■ **to express oneself** 表达自己的意思 biǎodá zìjǐ de yìsi □ It's hard to express oneself in Chinese. 用汉语表达自己的意思很难。Yòng Hànyǔ biǎodá zìjǐ de yìsi hěnnán.
expression NOUN
1 措辞 cuòcí [种 zhǒng] *(word, phrase)*
□ It's an English expression. 这是一种英语措辞。Zhè shì yìzhǒng Yīngyǔ cuòcí.
2 表情 biǎoqíng [种 zhǒng] *(on face)*
expressway NOUN (US)
高速公路 gāosù gōnglù [条 tiáo]
extension NOUN
1 扩建部分 kuòjiàn bùfen [个 gè] *(of building)*
2 延期 yánqī [次 cì] *(of contract, visa)*
3 分机 fēnjī [部 bù] *(phone number)*
□ extension 3718 三七一八分机 sān qī yī bā fēnjī
extent NOUN
程度 chéngdù *(of problem, damage)*
■ **to some extent** 在一定程度上 zài yídìng chéngdù shàng
exterior ADJECTIVE
外部的 wàibù de
extinct ADJECTIVE
灭绝的 mièjué de *(animal, plant)*
■ **to become extinct** 绝种 juézhǒng
■ **to be extinct** 灭绝 mièjué □ The species is almost extinct. 这一物种几乎灭绝了。Zhè yí wùzhǒng jīhū mièjué le.
extinguisher NOUN
灭火器 mièhuǒqì [个 gè] *(fire extinguisher)*
extortionate ADJECTIVE
价格过高的 jiàgé guò gāo de
extra ADJECTIVE, PRONOUN

▷ *see also* **extra** ADVERB, NOUN

1 附加的 fùjiā de
□ an extra blanket 一条备用的毯子 yìtiáo bèiyòng de tǎnzi □ Breakfast is extra. 早餐是附加的。Zǎocān shì fùjiā de.

2 另外收钱的 lìngwài shōuqián de *(cost, pay)*
□ Wine will cost extra. 酒另外收钱。Jiǔ lìngwài shōuqián.

extra ADVERB
▷ *see also* **extra** ADJECTIVE, PRONOUN, NOUN
额外地 éwài de *(in addition)*
□ 10% extra 额外地百分之十 éwài de bǎifēnzhīshí

extra NOUN
▷ *see also* **extra** ADJECTIVE, PRONOUN, ADVERB
1 特级品 tèjípǐn [个 gè] *(luxury)*
2 附加费 fùjiāfèi [项 xiàng] *(surcharge)*

extraordinary ADJECTIVE
非凡的 fēifán de

extravagant ADJECTIVE
铺张的 pūzhāng de *(person)*

extreme ADJECTIVE
1 极度的 jídù de *(very great in degree)*
2 极端的 jíduān de *(opinions, methods)*

extremely ADVERB
非常 fēicháng

extremist NOUN
过激分子 guòjī fènzǐ [个 gè]

eye NOUN
眼睛 yǎnjing [只 zhī]
□ I've got green eyes. 我眼睛是绿色的。Wǒ yǎnjīng shì lǜsè de.
■ **to keep an eye on something** 密切注意某事 mìqiè zhùyì mǒushì

eyebrow NOUN
眉毛 méimao [根 gēn]

eyelash NOUN
眼睫毛 yǎnjiémáo [根 gēn]

eyelid NOUN
眼皮 yǎnpí [个 gè]

eyeliner NOUN
眼线笔 yǎnxiànbǐ [支 zhī]

eye shadow NOUN
眼影 yǎnyǐng [盒 hé]

eyesight NOUN
视力 shìlì

Ff

fabric NOUN
纺织品 fǎngzhīpǐn [件 jiàn]
fabulous ADJECTIVE
极好的 jíhǎo de
□ The show was fabulous. 演出好极了。Yǎnchū hǎojí le.
face NOUN
▷ *see also* **face** VERB
1 脸 liǎn [张 zhāng] *(of person)*
2 表情 biǎoqíng [个 gè] *(expression)*
■ **on the face of it** 表面上看来 biǎomiànshang kànlái
■ **in the face of these difficulties** 面对这些困难 miànduì zhèxiē kùnnán
■ **to come face to face with somebody** 与某人面对面 yǔ mǒurén miàn duì miàn
to **face** VERB
▷ *see also* **face** NOUN
1 面向 miànxiàng *(direction)*
2 面对 miànduì *(unpleasant situation)*
■ **I can't face it.** 我应付不了。Wǒ yìngfù bùliǎo.
■ **to face up to something** 1 *(truth, facts)* 面对某事 miànduì mǒushì
2 *(responsibilities, duties)* 承担某事 chéngdān mǒushì □ You must face up to your responsibilities. 你必须承担起你的责任。Nǐ bìxū chéngdānqǐ nǐde zérèn.
Facebook® NOUN
脸谱网 Liǎnpǔ wǎng
face cloth NOUN
洗脸毛巾 xǐliǎn máojīn [条 tiáo]
FaceTime® NOUN
视频通话 shìpín tōnghuà
facilities PL NOUN
设施 shèshī [种 zhǒng]
fact NOUN
真相 zhēnxiàng [个 gè]
■ **in fact** 实际上 shíjì shàng
■ **facts and figures** 精确的资料 jīngquè de zīliào
factory NOUN
工厂 gōngchǎng [家 jiā]
to **fade** VERB
1 褪色 tuìsè *(colour)*
□ The colour has faded in the sun. 颜色在暴晒下褪色了。Yánsè zài bàoshài xià tuìsè le.
2 渐渐消失 jiànjiàn xiāoshī *(light, noise)*
□ The light was fading fast. 灯光很快渐渐消失了。Dēngguāng hěnkuài jiànjiàn xiāoshī le. □ The noise gradually faded. 声音渐渐地消失了。Shēngyīn jiànjiàn de xiāoshī le.
to **fail** VERB
▷ *see also* **fail** NOUN
1 没有通过 méiyǒu tōngguò
□ I failed the history exam. 我没有通过历史考试。Wǒ méiyǒu tōngguò lìshǐ kǎoshì.
2 没通过 méi tōngguò *(candidate)*
□ In our class, no one failed. 我们班里没有人没通过。Wǒmen bānlǐ méiyǒurén méi tōngguò.
3 失败 shībài *(attempt, plan, remedy)*
■ **to fail to do something** 未能做某事 wèinéng zuò mǒushì □ She failed to return her library books. 她没能归还从图书馆借的书。Tā méinéng guīhuán cóng túshūguǎn jiè de shū.
fail NOUN
▷ *see also* **fail** VERB
■ **without fail** 必定 bìdìng
failure NOUN
1 失败 shībài [次 cì]
2 故障 gùzhàng [次 cì]
□ a mechanical failure 一次机械故障 yícì jīxiè gùzhàng
3 失败者 shībàizhě [个 gè] *(person)*
faint ADJECTIVE
▷ *see also* **faint** VERB
1 微弱的 wēiruò de *(sound, light, smell, hope)*
□ His voice was very faint. 他的声音非常微弱。Tā de shēngyīn fēicháng wēiruò.
2 隐约的 yǐnyuē de *(mark, trace)*
■ **to feel faint** 感到眩晕 gǎndào xuànyūn
to **faint** VERB
▷ *see also* **faint** ADJECTIVE
晕倒 yūndǎo
□ All of a sudden she fainted. 突然间她晕倒了。Tūránjiān tā yūndǎo le.

English-Chinese

fair ADJECTIVE
▷ *see also* **fair** NOUN
1 公平的 gōngpíng de *(just)*
■ **It's not fair!** 这不公平！Zhè bù gōngpíng!
2 相当的 xiāngdāng de *(sizeable)*
□ That's a fair distance. 那可是相当远。Nà kě shì xiāngdāng yuǎn.
3 大体的 dàtǐ de *(quite good)*
4 白皙的 báixī de *(skin)*
□ people with fair skin 肤色白皙的人 fūsè báixī de rén
5 金色的 jīnsè de *(hair)*
□ He's got fair hair. 他有一头金发。Tā yǒu yìtóu jīnfà.

fair NOUN
▷ *see also* **fair** ADJECTIVE
1 交易会 jiāoyìhuì [届 jiè] *(trade fair)*
2 游乐场 yóulèchǎng [座 zuò] *(funfair)*
□ They went to the fair. 他们去了游乐场。Tāmen qù le yóulèchǎng.

fairground NOUN
游乐场 yóulèchǎng [座 zuò]

fairly ADVERB
1 公平地 gōngpíng de *(justly)*
□ She treats her children fairly. 她公平地对待孩子们。Tā gōngpíng de duìdài háizimen.
2 相当 xiāngdāng *(quite)*
□ That's fairly good. 那挺好的。Nà tǐnghǎo de.

fairy NOUN
小精灵 xiǎo jīngling [个 gè]

> **DID YOU KNOW...?**
> In Chinese tradition, there are no fairies as we would imagine them. Instead there are celestial beings, 仙人 xiānrén, benevolent spirits from Taoist mythology, and more malicious 妖怪 yāoguài, monsters and devils that harbour ill will against humanity.

faith NOUN
1 信任 xìnrèn [份 fèn] *(trust)*
□ People have lost faith in the government. 人们对政府失去了信任。Rénmen duì zhèngfǔ shīqù le xìnrèn.
2 信仰 xìnyǎng [份 fèn]
□ the Catholic faith 天主教信仰 Tiānzhǔjiào xìnyǎng
■ **to have faith in something** 相信某事 xiāngxìn mǒushì

faithful ADJECTIVE
忠实的 zhōngshí de

faithfully ADVERB
■ **Yours faithfully...** *(in letter)* 您忠实的… Nín zhōngshí de...

fake NOUN
▷ *see also* **fake** ADJECTIVE
赝品 yànpǐn [件 jiàn]
□ The painting was a fake. 这幅画是件赝品。Zhè fú huà shì jiàn yànpǐn.

fake ADJECTIVE
▷ *see also* **fake** NOUN
假的 jiǎ de
□ She wore fake fur. 她穿着假毛皮。Tā chuānzhe jiǎ máopí.

fall NOUN
▷ *see also* **fall** VERB
1 摔倒 shuāidǎo [次 cì]
□ She had a nasty fall. 她摔得很重。Tā shuāi de hěnzhòng.
2 下降 xiàjiàng [次 cì] *(in price, temperature)*
3 秋天 qiūtiān [个 gè] (US: *autumn*)
■ **the Niagara Falls** 尼亚加拉大瀑布 Níyǎjiālā Dà Pùbù

to **fall** VERB
▷ *see also* **fall** NOUN
1 摔倒 shuāidǎo
□ He tripped and fell. 他被绊了下摔倒了。Tā bèi bànlexia shuāidǎo le.
2 下 xià *(snow, rain)*
3 下跌 xiàdiē
□ Prices are falling. 价格下跌了。Jiàgé xiàdiē le.
■ **to fall in love with somebody** 爱上某人 àishàng mǒurén

to **fall down** VERB
1 摔倒 shuāidǎo
□ She's fallen down. 她摔倒了。Tā shuāidǎo le.
2 倒塌 dǎotā
□ The house is slowly falling down. 这房子正缓缓倒塌。Zhè fángzi zhèng huǎnhuǎn dǎotā.

to **fall for** VERB
1 上了当 shàng le dàng *(prank)*
□ They fell for it. 他们上了当。Tāmen shàngledàng.
2 爱上 àishang *(love)*
□ She's falling for him. 她爱上了他。Tā àishang le tā.

to **fall off** VERB
掉下 diàoxià
□ The book fell off the shelf. 书从架子上掉下来。Shū cóng jiàzishang diàoxiàlái.

to **fall out** VERB
■ **to fall out with somebody** 与某人争吵 yǔ mǒurén zhēngchǎo □ Sarah's fallen out with her boyfriend. 莎拉和她的男友争吵了。Shālā hé tāde nányǒu zhēngchǎo le.

to **fall over** VERB
跌倒 diēdǎo

f

to **fall through** VERB
落空 luòkōng
□ Our plans have fallen through. 我们的计划落空了。Wǒmen de jìhuà luòkōng le.

fallen VERB ▷ *see* **fall**

false ADJECTIVE
假的 jiǎ de
■ **a false alarm** 一次误报 yícì wùbào
■ **false teeth** 假牙 jiǎyá

fame NOUN
声誉 shēngyù

familiar ADJECTIVE
熟悉的 shúxī de
□ a familiar face 一张熟悉的面孔 yìzhāng shúxī de miànkǒng
■ **to be familiar with something** 对某物熟悉 duì mǒuwù shúxī □ I'm familiar with his work. 我对他的作品很熟悉。Wǒ duì tā de zuòpǐn hěn shúxī.

family
1 家庭 jiātíng [个 gè] *(relations)*
■ **the Cooke family** 库克一家 Kùkè yìjiā
2 孩子 háizi [个 gè] *(children)*

famine NOUN
饥荒 jīhuāng [阵 zhèn]

famous ADJECTIVE
著名的 zhùmíng de

fan NOUN
1 扇子 shànzi [把 bǎ] *(handheld)*
2 电风扇 diànfēngshàn [台 tái] *(electric)*
3 迷 mí [个 gè] *(of person, band)*
□ I'm a fan of Coldplay. 我是酷玩乐队的歌迷。Wǒ shì Kùwán yuèduì de gēmí.
4 球迷 qiúmí [个 gè] *(of sport)*
□ football fans 足球球迷 zúqiú qiúmí

to **fancy** VERB
■ **to fancy something** 想要某物 xiǎngyào mǒuwù □ I fancy an ice cream. 我想吃冰激凌。Wǒ xiǎngchī bīngjīlíng.
■ **He fancies her.** 他喜欢她。Tā xǐhuan tā.
■ **to fancy doing something** 想要做某事 xiǎngyào zuò mǒushì

fanatic NOUN
狂热者 kuángrè zhě [名 míng]

fancy-dress party NOUN
化装舞会 huàzhuāng wǔhuì [个 gè]

fantastic ADJECTIVE
1 极好的 jíhǎo de
2 巨大的 jùdà de *(sum, amount, profit)*

FAQ NOUN *(= frequently asked question)*
常见问题 chángjiàn wèntí

far ADVERB
▷ *see also* **far** ADJECTIVE
远 yuǎn *(in space)*
□ Is it far? 那儿远吗？Nàr yuǎn ma?
■ **It's not far from Beijing.** 那儿离北京不远。Nàr lí Běijīng bùyuǎn.
■ **How far is it?** 这有多远？Zhè yǒu duōyuǎn?
■ **far away** 遥远 yáoyuǎn
■ **as far as I know** 据我所知 jùwǒ suǒzhī
■ **so far** 迄今为止 qìjīn wéizhǐ
■ **far better** 好得多 hǎodeduō

far ADJECTIVE
▷ *see also* **far** ADVERB
远的 yuǎn de
■ **the far end** 尽头的 jìntóu de □ at the far end of the room 在房间的尽头 zài fángjiān de jìntóu

fare NOUN
1 票价 piàojià [种 zhǒng] *(on trains, buses)*
2 车费 chēfèi [笔 bǐ] *(in taxi)*
■ **half fare** 半价 bànjià
■ **full fare** 全价 quánjià

Far East NOUN
■ **the Far East** 远东 Yuǎndōng

farm NOUN
农场 nóngchǎng [个 gè]

farmer NOUN
农民 nóngmín [个 gè]
□ He's a farmer. 他是个农民。Tā shìge nóngmín.
■ **a farmers' market** 一个农民市场 yígè nóngmín shìchǎng

farming NOUN
农业 nóngyè

fascinating ADJECTIVE
迷人的 mírén de

fashion NOUN
时尚 shíshàng
□ a fashion show 一次时装表演 yícì shízhuāng biǎoyǎn
■ **in fashion** 流行 liúxíng

fashionable ADJECTIVE
时尚的 shíshàng de
□ Jane wears very fashionable clothes. 简衣着时尚。Jiǎn yīzhuó shíshàng. □ a fashionable restaurant 一家时尚餐厅 yìjiā shíshàng cāntīng

fast ADJECTIVE
▷ *see also* **fast** ADVERB
快的 kuài de
□ a fast car 一辆很快的车 yíliàng hěnkuài de chē □ That clock's fast. 那个钟有点快。Nàgè zhōng yǒudiǎn kuài.

fast ADVERB
▷ *see also* **fast** ADJECTIVE
快 kuài
□ He can run fast. 他能跑很快。Tā néng pǎo hěnkuài. □ He's fast asleep. 他在酣睡。Tā zài hānshuì.

to **fasten** VERB
系 jì
fast food NOUN
快餐 kuàicān
fat ADJECTIVE
▷ *see also* **fat** NOUN
1 肥胖的 féipàng de
2 肥的 féi de *(animal)*
fat NOUN
▷ *see also* **fat** ADJECTIVE
1 脂肪 zhīfáng *(on person, animal, meat)*
□ It's very high in fat. 这个脂肪含量很高。Zhègè zhīfáng hánliàng hěn gāo.
2 脂肪 shíyòng yóu *(for cooking)*
fatal ADJECTIVE
1 致命的 zhìmìng de
□ a fatal accident 一次致命的事故 yícì zhìmìng de shìgù
2 严重的 yánzhòng de
□ He made a fatal mistake. 他犯了个严重的错误。Tā fànlegè yánzhòng de cuòwù.
father NOUN
父亲 fùqin [位 wèi]
□ my father 我的父亲 wǒ de fùqin
Father Christmas NOUN
圣诞老人 Shèngdàn Lǎorén
father-in-law NOUN
1 公公 gōnggong [位 wèi] *(of woman)*
2 岳父 yuèfù [位 wèi] *(of man)*
faucet NOUN (US)
水龙头 shuǐlóngtou [个 gè]
fault NOUN
1 错误 cuòwù
■ **It's my fault.** 这是我的错。Zhè shì wǒde cuò.
2 缺点 quēdiǎn [个 gè] *(defect: in person)*
3 故障 gùzhàng [个 gè] *(in machine)*
■ **a mechanical fault** 一次机器故障 yícì jīqì gùzhàng
fava bean NOUN (US)
蚕豆 cándòu [颗 kē]
favour (US **favor**) NOUN
恩惠 ēnhuì [种 zhōng]
■ **to do somebody a favour** 帮某人的忙 bāng mǒurén de máng □ Could you do me a favour? 你能帮我个忙吗？Nǐ néng bāng wǒ ge máng ma?
■ **to be in favour of something** 赞成某事 zànchéng mǒushì □ I'm in favour of nuclear disarmament. 我赞成核裁军。Wǒ zànchéng hécáijūn.
favourite (US **favorite**) ADJECTIVE
▷ *see also* **favourite** NOUN
最喜欢的 zuì xǐhuan de
□ Blue's my favourite colour. 蓝色是我最喜欢的颜色。Lánsè shì wǒ zuì xǐhuan de yánsè.
favourite (US **favorite**) NOUN
▷ *see also* **favourite** ADJECTIVE
获胜的可能 huòshèng de kěnéng [种 zhǒng]
□ Liverpool are favourites to win the Cup. 利物浦最有可能赢得杯赛。Lìwùpǔ zuì yǒu kěnéng yíngdé bēisài.
fax NOUN
▷ *see also* **fax** VERB
传真 chuánzhēn [份 fèn]
■ **a fax machine** 一个传真机 yígè chuánzhēnjī
to **fax** VERB
▷ *see also* **fax** NOUN *(document)*
用传真发送 yòng chuánzhēn fāsòng
fear NOUN
▷ *see also* **fear** VERB
1 害怕 hàipà [种 zhǒng] *(terror)*
2 焦虑 jiāolǜ [种 zhǒng] *(anxiety)*
to **fear** VERB
▷ *see also* **fear** NOUN
害怕 hàipà
□ You have nothing to fear. 你没什么可害怕的。Nǐ méishénme kě hàipà de.
feather NOUN
羽毛 yǔmáo [根 gēn]
feature NOUN
特点 tèdiǎn [个 gè]
□ an important feature 一个重要的特点 yígè zhòngyào de tèdiǎn
February NOUN
二月 èryuè
□ in February 在二月 zài èryuè □ the first of February 二月一日 èryuè yīrì □ at the beginning of February 在二月初 zài èryuè chū □ at the end of February 在二月末 zài èryuè mò □ every February 每年二月 měinián èryuè
fed VERB ▷ *see* **feed**
fed up ADJECTIVE *(informal)*
■ **to be fed up of something** 厌倦某事 yànjuàn mǒushì □ I'm fed up of waiting for him. 我厌倦了等他。Wǒ yànjuàn le děng tā.
fee NOUN
1 费用 fèiyòng [项 xiàng]
2 费 fèi [种 zhǒng] *(of doctor, lawyer)*
feeble ADJECTIVE
1 虚弱的 xūruò de
2 无力的 wúlì de *(attempt, excuse, argument)*
to **feed** VERB
喂 wèi
□ Have you fed the cat? 你喂过猫了吗？Nǐ wèi guò māo le ma? □ He worked hard to

feed his family. 他为了养家辛勤工作。Tā wèile yǎngjiā xīnqín gōngzuò.

to **feel** VERB
1 摸 mō *(object, face)*
□ The doctor felt his forehead. 医生摸了摸他的额头。Yīshēng mōlemō tā de étóu.
2 感到 gǎndào *(pain)*
□ I didn't feel much pain. 我没感到有多痛。Wǒ méi gǎndào yǒu duō tòng.
3 认为 rènwéi *(think, believe)*
4 觉得 juéde *(experience)*
■ **to feel hungry** 觉得饿 juéde è □ I was feeling hungry. 我觉得很饿。Wǒ juéde hěn è.
■ **to feel cold** 觉得冷 juéde lěng □ I was feeling cold, so I went inside. 我觉得很冷，就回屋里了。Wǒ juéde hěn lěng, jiù huí wūlǐ le.
■ **I don't feel well.** 我觉得身体不适。Wǒ juéde shēntǐ búshì.
■ **to feel better** 感觉好多了 gǎnjué hǎo duō le
■ **to feel lonely** 感到孤独 gǎndào gūdú
■ **to feel sorry for somebody** 同情某人 tóngqíng mǒurén
■ **I feel like...** 想要… xiǎng yào... □ Do you feel like an ice cream? 你想要个冰激淋吗？Nǐ xiǎngyào gè bīngjīlín ma?

feeling NOUN
1 感受 gǎnshòu [种 zhǒng] *(emotion)*
2 感觉 gǎnjué [种 zhǒng] *(physical sensation, impression)*
■ **I have a feeling that...** 我有种感觉… wǒ yǒuzhǒng gǎnjué...
■ **feelings** 1 *(attitude)* 感情 gǎnqíng 2 *(emotions)* 情感 qínggǎn
■ **to hurt somebody's feelings** 伤害某人的感情 shānghài mǒurén de gǎnqíng

feet PL NOUN ▷ *see* **foot**

fell VERB ▷ *see* **fall**

felt VERB ▷ *see* **feel**

felt-tip pen NOUN
毡头墨水笔 zhāntóu mòshuǐbǐ [支 zhī]

female NOUN
▷ *see also* **female** ADJECTIVE
1 雌兽 císhòu [头 tóu] *(animal)*
2 女性 nǚxìng [位 wèi] *(woman)*

female ADJECTIVE
▷ *see also* **female** NOUN
1 雌性的 cíxìng de *(animal)*
2 妇女的 fùnǚ de *(woman)*
□ male and female students 男女学生 nánnǚ xuéshēng

feminine ADJECTIVE
1 女性的 nǚxìng de
2 阴性的 yīnxìng de *(in grammar)*

feminist NOUN
女权主义者 nǚquán zhǔyìzhě [位 wèi]

fence NOUN
篱笆 líba [道 dào]

fencing NOUN
击剑 jījiàn *(sport)*

ferry NOUN
渡船 dùchuán [艘 sōu]
■ **a ferryboat** 一艘渡船 yìsōu dùchuán

festival NOUN
1 节日 jiérì [个 gè] *(religious)*
2 艺术节 yìshù jié [届 jiè]
□ a jazz festival 一届爵士音乐节 yíjiè juéshì yīnyuè jié

to **fetch** VERB
1 去拿来 qù nálái
□ Fetch the bucket. 去把桶拿来。Qù bǎ tǒng nálái.
■ **to fetch something for somebody** 去给某人拿来某物 qù gěi mǒurén nálái mǒuwù
2 卖得 mài dé *(sell for)*
□ His painting fetched £5000. 他的画作卖得了五千英镑。Tā de huàzuò màidé le wǔqiān yīngbàng.

fever NOUN
发烧 fāshāo [次 cì]

few ADJECTIVE, PRONOUN
少数的 shǎoshù de *(not many)*
□ few books 很少的书 hěnshǎo de shū
■ **a few** *(some)* 几个 jǐgè □ a few hours 几个小时 jǐgè xiǎoshí □ How many apples do you want? — A few. 你要多少苹果？— 几个。Nǐ yào duōshǎo píngguǒ? — Jǐgè.
□ quite a few people 很多人 hěnduō rén
■ **in the next few days** 在接下来的几天里 zài jiēxiàlái de jǐtiān lǐ
■ **in the past few days** 在过去的几天里 zài guòqù de jǐtiān lǐ

fewer ADJECTIVE
较少的 jiàoshǎo de
□ There are fewer people than there were yesterday. 今天这里的人比昨天的少。Jīntiān zhèlǐ de rén bǐ zuótiān de shǎo.
□ There are fewer pupils in this class. 这个班里的学生更少。Zhègè bānlǐ de xuéshēng gèng shǎo.

fiancé NOUN
未婚夫 wèihūnfū [个 gè]
LANGUAGE TIP Word for word, this means 'not yet married husband'.
□ He's my fiancé. 他是我的未婚夫。Tā shì wǒde wèihūnfū.

fiancée NOUN
未婚妻 wèihūnqī [个 gè]
LANGUAGE TIP Word for word, this means 'not yet married wife'.

English-Chinese

□ She's my fiancée. 她是我的未婚妻。Tā shì wǒde wèihūnqī.

fiction NOUN
小说 xiǎoshuō

field NOUN
1 草地 cǎodì [块 kuài] *(grassland)*
2 田地 tiándì [片 piàn] *(cultivated)*
□ a field of wheat 一片小麦田 yípiàn xiǎomài tián
3 场地 chǎngdì [个 gè] *(sport)*
□ a football field 一个足球场 yígè zúqiúchǎng
4 领域 lǐngyù [个 gè] *(subject)*
□ He's an expert in his field. 他是他领域内的专家。Tā shì tā lǐngyù nèi de zhuānjiā.

fierce ADJECTIVE
1 凶猛的 xiōngměng de
□ The dog looked very fierce. 这狗看起来非常凶猛。Zhè gǒu kànqǐlái fēicháng xiōngměng.
2 强烈的 qiángliè de *(loyalty, competition)*
□ a fierce attack 一次强烈的攻击 yícì qiángliè de gōngjī

fifteen NUMBER
十五 shíwǔ
■ **She's fifteen.** 她十五岁了。Tā shíwǔ suì le.

fifteenth NUMBER
第十五 dì shíwǔ
□ the fifteenth floor 第十五楼 dì shíwǔ lóu
□ the fifteenth of August 八月十五日 bāyuè shíwǔ rì

fifth NUMBER
1 第五 dìwǔ *(in series)*
□ the fifth floor 第五楼 dì wǔ lóu □ the fifth of August 八月五日 bāyuè wǔ rì
2 五分之一 wǔfēnzhīyī *(fraction)*

fifty NUMBER
五十 wǔshí
■ **He's in his fifties.** 他五十几岁。Tā wǔshí jǐsuì.

fight NOUN
▷ *see also* **fight** VERB
1 打架 dǎjià [场 chǎng]
□ There was a fight in the pub. 酒吧里有人打了一架。Jiǔbā lǐ yǒu rén dǎle yí jià.
2 斗争 dòuzhēng [场 chǎng] *(against disease, etc)*
□ the fight against cancer 与癌症做斗争 yǔ áizhèng zuò dòuzhēng

to **fight** VERB
▷ *see also* **fight** NOUN
1 战斗 zhàndòu
□ They were fighting. 他们在战斗。Tāmen zài zhàndòu.
2 斗争 dòuzhēng *(struggle)*
□ He fought against the urge to smoke. 他与想要抽烟的冲动做斗争。Tā yǔ xiǎngyào chōuyān de chōngdòng zuò dòuzhēng.

figure NOUN
▷ *see also* **figure** VERB
1 统计数字 tǒngjì shùzì [个 gè] *(number)*
□ Can you give me the exact figures? 你能给我确切的数字吗？Nǐ néng gěi wǒ quèqiè de shùzì ma?
2 数字 shùzì [个 gè] *(digit)*
3 身材 shēncái [个 gè] *(body, shape)*
□ Yueshi saw the figure of a man on the bridge. 月石看见桥上有个男人的身影。Yuéshì kànjiàn qiáoshàng yǒu gè nánrén de shēnyǐng.
■ **She's got a good figure.** 她有个好身材。Tā yǒu gè hǎo shēncái.
■ **I have to watch my figure.** 我得注意我的身材。Wǒ děi zhùyì wǒ de shēncái.

to **figure** VERB
▷ *see also* **figure** NOUN
估计 gūjì *(US: reckon)*
■ **that figures** *(informal)* 那不足为怪 nà bùzú wéiguài

to **figure out** VERB
1 计算 jìsuàn *(calculate)*
□ I'll try to figure out how much it'll cost. 我会试着计算下这要花多少钱。Wǒ huì shìzhe jìsuàn xià zhè yào huā duōshǎo qián.
2 明白 míngbái *(understand)*
□ I couldn't figure out what it meant. 我不明白这是什么意思。Wǒ bù míngbái zhè shì shénme yìsi.

file NOUN
▷ *see also* **file** VERB
1 档案 dàng'àn [份 fèn] *(dossier)*
□ Have we got a file on the suspect? 我们有嫌疑人的档案吗？Wǒmen yǒu xiányírén de dǎng'àn ma?
2 文件夹 wénjiànjiā [个 gè] *(folder)*
□ She keeps all her letters in a cardboard file. 她把她所有的信件都保存在一个纸板文件夹里。Tā bǎ tā suǒyǒu de xìnjiàn dōu bǎocún zài yígè zhǐbǎn wénjiànjiá lǐ.
3 文件 wénjiàn [份 fèn] *(computer)*

to **file** VERB
▷ *see also* **file** NOUN
1 把...归档 bǎ...guīdàng *(papers)*
2 把...锉平 bǎ...cuòpíng *(nails, metal)*
■ **to file one's nails** 锉指甲 cuó zhǐjia

to **fill** VERB
1 装满 zhuāngmǎn *(container)*
□ She filled the glass with water. 她把玻璃杯里装满水。Tā bǎ bōlí bēi lǐ zhuāngmǎn shuǐ.

f

2 占满 zhànmǎn *(space, area)*
3 补 bǔ *(tooth)*
■ **to fill something with something** 用某物填满某物 yòng mǒuwù tiánmǎn mǒuwù

to **fill in** VERB
填写 tiánxiě *(form, name)*
□ Can you fill this form in please? 你能填写这张表吗？Nǐ néng tiánxiě zhè zhāng biǎo ma?

to **fill out** VERB
填写 tiánxiě *(form)*

to **fill up** VERB
装满 zhuāngmǎn
□ He filled the cup up to the brim. 他把茶杯装满到杯口。Tā bǎ chábēi zhuāngmǎn dào bēikǒu. □ Fill it up, please. 请加满。Qǐng jiāmǎn.

filling NOUN
填补物 tiánbǔ wù [种 zhǒng] *(in tooth)*

film NOUN
▹ *see also* **film** VERB
1 影片 yǐngpiàn [部 bù] *(movie)*
2 胶卷 jiāojuǎn [卷 juǎn] *(for camera)*

to **film** VERB
▹ *see also* **film** NOUN
■ **to film something** 把某事拍成影片 bǎ mǒushì pāichéng yǐngpiàn

film star NOUN
影星 yǐngxīng [位 wèi]

filthy ADJECTIVE
污秽的 wūhuì de

final ADJECTIVE
▹ *see also* **final** NOUN
1 最后的 zuìhòu de
□ our final farewells 我们最后的道别 wǒmen zuìhòu de dàobié
2 最终的 zuìzhōng de *(decision, offer)*
□ a final decision 一个最终的决定 yígè zuìzhōng de juédìng □ I'm not going and that's final. 我不去，就这样定了。Wǒ búqù, jiù zhèyàng dìng le.

final NOUN
▹ *see also* **final** ADJECTIVE
决赛 juésài [场 chǎng] *(sport)*
□ Andy Murray is in the final. 安迪·穆瑞进入了决赛。Āndí Mùruì jìnrù le juésài.

finally ADVERB
1 终于 zhōngyú *(eventually)*
□ She finally chose the red shoes. 她终于选了红色的鞋子。Tā zhōngyú xuǎn le hóngsè de xiézi.
2 最后 zuìhòu *(lastly)*
3 最后 zuìhòu *(in conclusion)*
□ Finally, I would like to say... 最后，我想要说… Zuìhòu, wǒ xiǎngyào shuō...

to **find** VERB
1 找到 zhǎodào *(person, object, exit)*
□ I can't find the exit. 我找不到出口。Wǒ zhǎobúdào chūkǒu.
2 找到 zhǎodào *(lost object)*
□ Did you find your pen? 你找到你的笔了吗？Nǐ zhǎodào nǐ de bǐ le ma?
3 找到 zhǎodào *(work, job)*
4 找 zhǎo *(time)*
□ I need to find time for myself. 我得给自己找时间。Wǒ děi gěi zìjǐ zhǎo shíjiān.
■ **to find somebody guilty** 判决某人有罪 pànjué mǒurén yǒuzuì
■ **to find one's way** 认得路 rènde lù

to **find out** VERB
查明 chámíng *(fact, truth)*
■ **to find out about something**
1 *(deliberately)* 找出 zhǎochū □ Try to find out about the cost of a hotel. 试着出一家旅馆的开销。Shìzhe zhǎochū yìjiā lǚguǎn de kāixiāo. **2** *(by chance)* 发现某事 fāxiàn mǒushì □ I found out about their affair. 我发现了他们的奸情。Wǒ fāxiàn le tāmen de jiānqíng.

fine ADJECTIVE
▹ *see also* **fine** NOUN, VERB
1 好的 hǎode *(satisfactory)*
■ **to be fine** 很好 hěnhǎo □ How are you? — I'm fine. 你怎么样？— 我很好。Nǐ zěnme yàng? — Wǒ hěnhǎo.
■ **I feel fine.** 我感觉很好。Wǒ gǎnjué hěnhǎo.
■ **The weather is fine today.** 今天天气很好。Jīntiān tiānqì hěnhǎo.
2 优秀的 yōuxiù *(excellent)*
□ He's a fine musician. 他是个优秀的音乐家。Tā shìgè yōuxiù de yīnyuèjiā.
3 好的 hǎo de *(in texture)*
□ She's got very fine hair. 她的头发很好。Tā de tóufà hěnhǎo.

fine NOUN
▹ *see also* **fine** ADJECTIVE, VERB
罚款 fákuǎn [笔 bǐ] *(law)*
□ She got a £50 fine. 她被罚款五十英镑。Tā bèi fákuǎn wǔshí yīngbàng.

to **fine** VERB
▹ *see also* **fine** NOUN, ADJECTIVE
处...以罚金 chǔ...yǐ fájīn *(law)*

finger NOUN
手指 shǒuzhǐ [根 gēn]
■ **my little finger** 我的小指 wǒ de xiǎo zhǐ

to **finish** VERB
▹ *see also* **finish** NOUN
1 结束 jiéshù *(work)*
2 完成 wánchéng *(task, report)*
□ I've finished the book. 我看完了这本书。Wǒ kàn wán le zhè běn shū.

3 结束 jiéshù *(course, event)*
□ The film has finished. 电影结束了。Diànyǐng jiéshù le.
4 完成 wánchéng *(person)*
□ I've finished! 我完成了！Wǒ wánchéng le!
■ **to finish doing something** 做完某事 zuòwán mǒushì

finish NOUN
▷ *see also* **finish** VERB
终点 zhōngdiǎn [个 gè] *(sport)*
□ We saw the finish of the London Marathon. 我们看见了伦敦马拉松比赛的终点。Wǒmen kànjiàn le Lúndūn Mǎlāsōng bǐsài de zhōngdiǎn.

Finland NOUN
芬兰 Fēnlán

fir NOUN [棵 kē]
■ **a fir tree** 一棵冷杉 yì kē lěngshān

fire NOUN
▷ *see also* **fire** VERB
1 火 huǒ *(flames)*
□ He made a fire in the woods. 他在树林里生起火。Tā zài shùlín lǐ shēng qǐ huǒ.
■ **on fire** 起火 qǐhuǒ
■ **to catch fire** 着火 zháohuǒ
2 炉火 lúhuǒ [团 tuán] *(in a fireplace)*
3 火灾 huǒzāi [场 chǎng] *(accidental)*

to **fire** VERB
▷ *see also* **fire** NOUN
1 射出 shèchū *(shoot)*
2 解雇 jiěgù *(informal: dismiss)*

fire alarm NOUN
火警警报 huǒjǐng jǐngbào [个 gè]

fire brigade NOUN
消防队 xiāofáng duì [支 zhī]

fire engine NOUN
救火车 jiùhuǒchē [辆 liàng]

firefighter NOUN
消防队员 xiāofáng duìyuán [位 wèi]

fireman NOUN
消防队员 xiāofáng duìyuán [位 wèi]

fire station NOUN
消防站 xiāofángzhàn [个 gè]

fire truck NOUN (US)
救火车 jiùhuǒchē [辆 liàng]

firework NOUN
烟火 yānhuǒ [团 tuán]
■ **fireworks** *(display)* 烟火表演 yānhuǒ biǎoyǎn [次 cì]

DID YOU KNOW...?
Fireworks, being a Chinese invention, are an important part of Chinese culture, and are set off during many religious, national or family celebrations.

firm ADJECTIVE
▷ *see also* **firm** NOUN
1 硬实的 yìngshi de *(mattress, ground)*
2 坚定的 jiāndìng de *(person)*

firm NOUN
▷ *see also* **firm** ADJECTIVE
公司 gōngsī [家 jiā]

first ADJECTIVE
▷ *see also* **first** ADVERB
1 第一的 dìyī de *(in series)*
2 最初的 zuìchū de *(reaction, impression)*
3 头等的 tóuděng de *(prize, division)*
■ **the first of January** 一月一号 yīyuè yīhào

first ADVERB
▷ *see also* **first** ADJECTIVE
1 第一个 dìyīgè *(before anyone else)*
□ She spoke first. 她第一个发言。Tā dìyīgè fāyán.
2 首先 shǒuxiān *(before other things)*
□ Finish your homework first. 先完成你的家庭作业。Xiān wánchéng nǐ de jiātíng zuòyè.
3 第一 dìyī *(when listing reasons)*
4 第一次 dìyīcì *(for the first time)*
5 第一名 dìyīmíng *(in race, competition: come, finish)*
■ **at first** 起先 qǐxiān

first aid NOUN
急救 jíjiù

first-class ADJECTIVE
▷ *see also* **first-class** ADVERB
1 第一流的 dìyīliú de *(excellent)*
2 头等的 tōuděng de *(carriage, ticket, stamp)*

first-class ADVERB
▷ *see also* **first-class** ADJECTIVE
头等地 tóuděng de *(travel, send)*

firstly ADVERB
首先 shǒuxiān

first name NOUN
名 míng [个 gè]

DID YOU KNOW...?
In Chinese, first names come after surnames.

fish NOUN
▷ *see also* **fish** VERB
1 鱼 yú [条 tiáo]
2 鱼肉 yúròu *(food)*

to **fish** VERB
▷ *see also* **fish** NOUN
1 捕鱼 bǔyú *(commercially)*
2 钓鱼 diàoyú *(as sport, hobby)*
■ **to go fishing** 去钓鱼 qù diàoyú

fisherman NOUN
渔民 yúmín [位 wèi]

fishing NOUN

钓鱼 diàoyú

fishing boat NOUN

渔船 yúchuán [条 tiáo]

fist NOUN

拳头 quántou [个 gè]

fit ADJECTIVE

▷ *see also* **fit** VERB, NOUN

健康的 jiànkāng de *(healthy)*

■ **to keep fit** 保持身材 bǎochí shēncái

fit NOUN

▷ *see also* **fit** ADJECTIVE, VERB

■ **to have a fit** 癫痫病发作 diānxiánbìng fāzuò

■ **to be a good fit** 很合身 hěn héshēn

to **fit** VERB

▷ *see also* **fit** ADJECTIVE, NOUN

1 合身 héshēn *(clothes, shoes)*

□ Does it fit? 这合身吗？Zhè héshēn ma?

2 配合 pèihé *(in space, gap)*

to **fit in** VERB

定时间于 dìng shíjiān yú *(appointment, visitor)*

fitness NOUN

健康 jiànkāng

five NUMBER

五 wǔ

■ **That will be five pounds, please.** 请付五镑。Qǐng fù wǔbàng.

■ **She's five years old.** 她五岁了。Tā wǔsuì le.

■ **It's five o'clock.** 五点了。Wǔdiǎn le.

to **fix** VERB

1 确定 quèdìng *(date, price, meeting)*

□ Let's fix a date for the party. 我们给聚会定个日子吧。Wǒmen gěi jùhuì dìng ge rìzi ba.

2 修理 xiūlǐ *(mend)*

□ Can you fix my bike? 你能修下我的自行车吗？Nǐ néng xiū xià wǒ de zìxíngchē ma?

3 解决 jiějué *(problem)*

fizzy ADJECTIVE

带汽的 dàiqì de

□ I don't like fizzy drinks. 我不喜欢喝汽水。Wǒ bù xǐhuan hē qìshuǐ.

flag NOUN

旗 qí [面 miàn]

flame NOUN

火焰 huǒyàn [团 tuán]

■ **in flames** 燃烧着 ránshāo zhe

to **flash** VERB

▷ *see also* **flash** NOUN

闪光 shǎnguāng *(lightning, light)*

■ **to flash one's headlights** 亮起车头灯 liàngqǐ chētóudēng

flash NOUN

▷ *see also* **flash** VERB

1 闪光 shǎnguāng [阵 zhèn]

2 闪光灯 shǎnguāngdēng [个 gè]

□ Has your camera got a flash? 你的照相机带闪光灯吗？Nǐ de zhàoxiàngjī dài shǎnguāngdēng ma?

flashlight NOUN (US)

手电筒 shǒudiàn tǒng [个 gè]

flask NOUN

保温瓶 bǎowēnpíng [个 gè] *(vacuum flask)*

flat ADJECTIVE

▷ *see also* **flat** NOUN

1 平的 píng de

□ flat shoes 平底鞋 píngdǐ xié

2 气不足的 qì bùzú de *(tyre, ball)*

□ I've got a flat tyre. 我的轮胎没气了。Wǒ de lúntāi méi qì le.

3 没电的 méidiàn de *(battery)*

flat NOUN

▷ *see also* **flat** ADJECTIVE

公寓 gōngyù [套 tào]

□ She lives in a flat. 她住在一套公寓里。Tā zhù zài yítào gōngyù lǐ.

to **flatter** VERB

奉承 fèngchéng

flavour (US **flavor**) NOUN

口味 kǒuwèi [种 zhǒng]

□ Which flavour of ice-cream would you like? 你喜欢哪种口味的冰激淋？Nǐ xǐhuan nǎzhǒng kǒuwèi de bīngjīlín?

flea NOUN

跳蚤 tiàozao [只 zhī]

flew VERB ▷ *see* **fly**

flexible ADJECTIVE

灵活的 línghuó de

□ flexible working hours 灵活的工作时间 línghuó de gōngzuò shíjiān

flight NOUN

航班 hángbān [个 gè]

□ What time is the flight to Beijing? 到北京的航班是什么时候？Dào Běijīng de hángbān shì shénme shíhòu?

■ **a flight of stairs** 一段楼梯 yíduàn lóutī

flight attendant NOUN

1 男空服人员 nán kōngfú rényuán [位 wèi] *(man)*

2 空姐 kōngjiě [位 wèi] *(woman)*

to **float** VERB

1 漂浮 piāofú

□ A leaf was floating on the water. 一片树叶漂浮在水面。Yí piàn shùyè piāofú zài shuǐmiàn.

2 浮着 fúzhe *(stay afloat)*

flock NOUN

群 qún

■ **a flock of sheep** 一群绵羊 yìqún miányáng

■ **a flock of birds** 一群鸟 yìqún niǎo

flood NOUN
洪水 hóngshuǐ [次 cì]
□ The rain has caused many floods. 降雨造成了多次洪水。Jiàngyǔ zàochéng le duōcì hóngshuǐ.

floor NOUN
1 地板 dìbǎn [块 kuài]
□ a tiled floor 一块镶瓷砖的地板 yíkuài xiāng cízhuān de dìbǎn
■ **on the floor** 在地板上 zài dìbǎn shàng
2 楼层 lóucéng [个 gè] *(storey)*
■ **the ground floor** 一楼 yīlóu
■ **the first floor 1** 二楼 èr lóu **2** (US) 一楼 yī lóu

LANGUAGE TIP The ground floor doesn't exist in Chinese. They start counting with **the first floor** 一楼 yī lóu.

floppy NOUN
■ **floppy disk** 软盘 ruǎnpán [张 zhāng]

florist NOUN
花商 huāshāng [个 gè]
■ **the florist's** 花店 huādiàn

flour NOUN
面粉 miànfěn

to **flow** VERB
▷ *see also* **flow** NOUN
流动 liúdòng

flow NOUN
▷ *see also* **flow** VERB
1 流动 liúdòng
2 川流不息 chuānliú bùxī *(of traffic)*

flower NOUN
▷ *see also* **flower** VERB
花 huā [朵 duǒ]

to **flower** VERB
▷ *see also* **flower** NOUN
开花 kāihuā

flown VERB ▷ *see* **fly**

flu NOUN
流感 liúgǎn
□ She's got flu. 她得了流感。Tā dé le liúgǎn.

fluent ADJECTIVE
流利的 liúlì de *(speech, reading, writing)*
■ **to speak fluent French** 讲流利的法语 jiǎng liúlì de Fǎyǔ □ Duncan speaks fluent Chinese. 邓肯的中文很流利。Dèngkěn de zhōngwěn hěn liúlì.

to **flush** VERB
■ **to flush the toilet** 冲厕所 chōng cèsuǒ

flute NOUN
长笛 chángdí [支 zhī]

fly NOUN
▷ *see also* **fly** VERB
苍蝇 cāngying [只 zhī] *(insect)*

to **fly** VERB
▷ *see also* **fly** NOUN
1 飞 fēi
□ The plane flew through the night. 飞机连夜飞行。Fēijī liányè fēixíng.
2 乘飞机 chéng fēijī
□ He flew from Paris to New York. 他从巴黎飞往纽约。Tā cóng Bālí fēiwǎng Niǔyuē.

to **fly away** VERB
飞走 fēizǒu
□ The bird flew away. 鸟飞走了。Niǎo fēi zǒu le.

focus NOUN
▷ *see also* **focus** VERB
聚焦 jùjiāo *(photo)*
■ **in focus** 焦点对准 jiāodiǎn duìzhǔn
■ **out of focus** 焦点没对准 jiāodiǎn méi duìzhǔn
■ **to be the focus of attention** 成为关注的焦点 chéngwéi guānzhù de jiāodiǎn

to **focus** VERB
▷ *see also* **focus** NOUN
■ **to focus on 1** *(with a camera)* 聚焦于 jùjiāo yú □ The cameraman focused on the bird. 摄影师聚焦在小鸟身上。Shèyǐngshī jùjiāo zài xiǎoniǎo shēnshàng.
2 *(concentrate on)* 集中注意力于 jízhōng zhùyìlì yú □ Let's focus on this problem. 让我们集中注意力在这个问题上。Ràng wǒmen jízhōng zhùyìlǐ zài zhège wèntí shàng.

fog NOUN
雾 wù [场 chǎng]

foggy ADJECTIVE
有雾的 yǒuwù de
■ **It's foggy.** 今天有雾。Jīntiān yǒu wù.

foil NOUN
锡纸 xīzhǐ *(kitchen foil)*
□ She wrapped the meat in foil. 她把肉用锡纸包起来。Tā bǎ ròu yòng xīzhǐ bāo qǐlái.

to **fold** VERB
折叠 zhédié
□ He folded the newspaper in half. 他把报纸对半一折。Tā bǎ bàozhǐ duìbàn yì zhé.
■ **to fold something up** 把某物折起来 bǎ mǒuwù zhéqǐlái
■ **to fold one's arms** 两臂交叉抱拢 liǎngbì jiāochā bàolǒng □ She folded her arms. 她两臂交叉抱拢。Tā liǎngbì jiāochā bàolǒng.

folder NOUN
文件夹 wénjiàn jiā [个 gè]

folding ADJECTIVE
折叠的 zhédié de
■ **a folding chair** 一个折叠椅 yígè zhédiéyǐ

to **follow** VERB
1 跟随 gēnsuí
□ She followed him. 她跟随了他。Tā gēnsuí le tā. □ You go first and I'll follow. 你先走，我跟在后面。Nǐ xiān zǒu, wǒ gēn zài hòumian.
■ **to follow somebody on Twitter** 在推特上关注某人 zài Tuītè shàng guānzhù mǒurén
2 遵循 zūnxún *(example, advice, instructions)*
3 沿着...行进 yánzhe...xíngjìn *(route, path)*
■ **I don't quite follow you.** 我不太理解你的意思。Wǒ bùtài lǐjiě nǐde yìsi.
■ **as follows 1** *(when listing)* 如下 rúxià **2** *(in this way)* 按如下方式 àn rúxià fāngshì
■ **followed by** 接着是 jiēzhe shì

follower NOUN
粉丝 fěnsī *(on Twitter)*
□ How do I get more followers on Twitter? 我怎样在推特上获得更多的粉丝？Wǒ zěnyàng zài Tuītè shàng huòdé gèngduō de fěnsī?
■ **cat food** 猫粮 māo liáng
■ **dog food** 狗粮 gǒu liáng

following PREPOSITION
▷ *see also* **following** ADJECTIVE
在...之后 zài...zhīhòu *(after)*

following ADJECTIVE
▷ *see also* **following** PREPOSITION
1 接着的 jiēzhe de *(day, week)*
□ the following day 第二天 dì èr tiān
2 下述的 xiàshù de *(next-mentioned)*

fond ADJECTIVE
■ **to be fond of 1** *(person)* 喜爱 xǐ'ài
□ I'm very fond of her. 我非常喜欢她。Wǒ fēicháng xǐhuan tā. **2** *(food, walking)* 喜欢 xǐhuan

food NOUN
食物 shíwù [种 zhǒng]
■ **cat food** 猫粮 māo liáng
■ **dog food** 狗粮 gǒu liáng

food processor NOUN
食品处理机 shípǐn chùlǐjī [台 tái]

fool NOUN
▷ *see also* **fool** VERB
白痴 báichī [个 gè]

to **fool** VERB
▷ *see also* **fool** NOUN
欺骗 qīpiàn *(deceive)*

foot NOUN
1 脚 jiǎo [只 zhī]
■ **on foot** 步行 bùxíng
2 英尺 yīngchǐ *(12 inches)*
■ **Dave is 6 foot tall.** 戴夫有六英尺高。Dàifū yǒu liù yīngchǐ gāo.

DID YOU KNOW...?
In China, measurements are in metres and centimetres, rather than feet and inches. A foot is about 30 centimetres.

football NOUN
1 足球 zúqiú [只 zhī] *(ball)*
2 足球 zúqiú *(sport)*
□ I like playing football. 我喜欢踢足球。Wǒ xǐhuan tī zúqiú.
3 美式足球 měishì zúqiú (US: *sport*)

footballer NOUN
足球运动员 zúqiú yùndòngyuán [位 wèi]

footpath NOUN
人行小径 rénxíng xiǎojìng [条 tiáo]

footprint NOUN
脚印 jiǎoyìn [个 gè]

for PREPOSITION
1 为 wèi
□ Is this for me? 这是为我准备的吗？Zhèshì wèi wǒ zhǔnbèi de ma? □ He works for a local firm. 他为一家当地公司工作。Tā wèi yìjiā dāngdì gōngsī gōngzuò. □ I'll do it for you. 我会为你做的。Wǒ huì wèi nǐ zuò de.
■ **a table for two** 供两人用的桌子 gòng liǎngrén yòng de zhuōzi
2 为了 wèile *(purpose)*
□ He's saving up for a new car. 他为了买辆新车正在存钱。Tā wèi le mǎi liàng xīn chē zhèngzài cúnqián.
■ **What's it for?** 它有什么用途？Tā yǒu shénme yòngtú?
■ **It's time for lunch.** 该吃午饭了。Gāi chī wǔfàn le.
■ **What for?** 为什么？Wèi shénme? □ Give me some money! — What for? 给我点钱！— 为什么？Gěi wǒ diǎn qián! — Wèishénme?
■ **a knife for chopping vegetables** 用于切菜的刀 yòngyú qiēcài de dāo
3 有... yǒu... *(time)*
□ It hasn't rained for three weeks. 已经有三周没下雨了。Yǐjīng yǒu sānzhōu méi xiàyǔ le. □ He's been learning Chinese for three years. 他学中文已经有三年了。Tā xué zhōngwén yǐjīng yǒu sānnián le. □ He was away for two years. 他离开有两年了。Tā líkāi yǒu liǎngnián le. □ The trip is scheduled for June 5. 旅行安排在六月五日。Lǚxíng ānpái zài liùyuè wǔrì.
4 以... yǐ *(in exchange for)*
□ I sold it for £50. 我以五十镑的价格卖掉了它。Wǒ yǐ wǔshí bàng de jiàgé màidiào le tā.
■ **to pay 50 pence for a ticket** 花五十便士买张票 huā wǔshí biànshì mǎi zhāng piào
5 达 dá *(referring to distance)*
□ There are roadworks for 50 km. 长跑练习长达五十公里。Chángpǎo liànxí chángdá

wǔshí gōnglǐ.
6 因为 yīnwèi *(reason)*
7 赞成 zànchéng *(in favour of)*
□ Are you for or against the idea? 你是赞成还是反对这个主意？Nǐ shì zànchéng háshì fǎnduì zhège zhǔyi?
8 前往 qiánwǎng *(destination)*
■ **He left for Rome.** 他动身前往罗马。Tā dòngshēn qiánwǎng Luómǎ.
■ **G for George** George中的G George zhōng de G
■ **What's the Chinese for 'lion'?** "Lion"用中文怎么说？"Lion" yòng zhōngwén zěnme shuō?

to **forbid** VERB
禁止 jìnzhǐ
■ **to forbid somebody to do something** 禁止某人做某事 jìnzhǐ mǒurén zuò mǒushì
□ I forbid you to go out tonight! 我禁止你今晚出去！Wǒ jìnzhǐ nǐ jīnwǎn chūqù!

forbidden ADJECTIVE
禁止的 jìnzhǐ de
□ Smoking is strictly forbidden. 吸烟是被严格禁止的。Xīyān shì bèi yángé jìnzhǐ de.

force NOUN
▷ *see also* **force** VERB
1 武力 wǔlì *(violence)*
2 力量 lìliàng *(strength)*

to **force** VERB
▷ *see also* **force** NOUN
强迫 qiángpò
■ **to force somebody to do something** 强迫某人做某事 qiángpò mǒurén zuò mǒushì □ They forced him to open the safe. 他们强迫他打开保险柜。Tāmen qiángpò tā dǎkāi bǎoxiǎnguì.

forces PL NOUN
部队 bùduì [支 zhī] *(military)*

forecast NOUN
▷ *see also* **forecast** VERB
预报 yùbào [个 gè]
■ **the weather forecast** 天气预报 tiānqì yùbào

to **forecast** VERB
▷ *see also* **forecast** NOUN
预测 yùcè *(predict)*

forehead NOUN
额头 étóu [个 gè]

foreign ADJECTIVE
外国的 wàiguó de

foreigner NOUN
外国人 wàiguórén [个 gè]

forest NOUN
森林 sēnlín [片 piàn]

forever ADVERB
永远 yǒngyuǎn
□ He's gone forever. 他永远地离开了。Tā yǒngyuǎn de líkāi le.

forgave VERB ▷ *see* **forgive**

to **forge** VERB
伪造 wěizào *(signature, banknote)*

to **forget** VERB
1 忘记 wàngjì
□ I'm sorry, I completely forgot! 对不起，我彻底忘记了！Duìbuqǐ, wǒ chèdǐ wàngjì le!
□ I've forgotten his name. 我忘记了他的名字。Wǒ wàngjì le tā de míngzi.
2 忘带 wàng dài *(leave behind: object)*

to **forgive** VERB
原谅 yuánliàng
□ I forgive you. 我原谅你。Wǒ yuánliàng nǐ.
■ **to forgive somebody for something** 原谅某人某事 yuánliàng mǒurén mǒushì
□ She forgave him for forgetting her birthday. 她原谅他忘记了她的生日。Tā yuánliàng le tā wàngjì le tā de shēngrì.

forgot VERB ▷ *see* **forget**

forgotten VERB ▷ *see* **forget**

fork NOUN
1 餐叉 cānchā [把 bǎ]
2 岔路 chàlù [条 tiáo] *(in road, river, railway)*

form NOUN
▷ *see also* **form** VERB
1 类型 lèixíng [种 zhǒng] *(type)*
□ I'm against hunting in any form. 我反对任何类型的狩猎。Wǒ fǎnduì rènhé lèixíng de shòuliè.
2 年级 niánjí [个 gè] *(class)*
3 表格 biǎogé [张 zhāng] *(document)*
■ **to fill in a form** 填一张表 tián yìzhāng biǎo

to **form** VERB
▷ *see also* **form** NOUN
1 组成 zǔchéng *(make)*
2 成立 chénglì *(create: group, organization, company)*
■ **in the form of** 通过…方式 tōngguò... fāngshì

formal ADJECTIVE
正式的 zhèngshì de
□ a formal dinner 一次正式的宴会 yícì zhèngshì de yànhuì
■ **formal clothes** 正装 zhèng zhuāng

former ADJECTIVE
以前的 yǐqián de
□ a former pupil 一名以前的学生 yìmíng yǐqián de xuéshēng
■ **in former years** 往年 wǎngnián

forth ADVERB
■ **to go back and forth** 反反复复 fǎnfǎnfùfù

fortnight NOUN
两星期 liǎng xīngqī
□ I'm going on holiday for a fortnight. 我要去度假两星期。Wǒ yào qù dùjià liǎngxīngqī.

fortunate ADJECTIVE
幸运的 xìngyùn de

fortunately ADVERB
幸运的是 xìngyùn de shì
□ Fortunately, it didn't rain. 幸运的是，天没有下雨。Xìngyùn de shì, tiān méiyǒu xiàyǔ.

fortune NOUN
财富 cáifù [笔 bǐ]
■ **to make a fortune** 发财 fācái □ Kate earns a fortune! 凯特赚很多钱！Kǎitè zhuàn hěnduō qián!

forty NUMBER
四十 sìshí
□ He's forty. 他四十岁了。Tā sìshí suì le.

forward ADVERB
▷ *see also* **forward** VERB
向前 xiàngqián
■ **to move forward** 向前进 xiàng qián jìn

to **forward** VERB
▷ *see also* **forward** ADVERB
转发 zhuǎnfā
□ He forwarded all Violette's letters. 他把所有维奥莉特的信都转发了。Tā bǎ suǒyǒu Wéi'aòlìtè de xìn dōu zhuǎnfā le.

forwards ADVERB
向前 xiàngqián

forward slash NOUN
斜杠符号 xiégàng fúhào

fought VERB ▷ *see* **fight**

found VERB ▷ *see* **find**

to **found** VERB
创办 chuàngbàn *(organization, company)*

fountain NOUN
喷泉 pēnquán [个 gè]

four NUMBER
四 sì
□ She's four. 她四岁了。Tā sì suì le.

fourteen NUMBER
十四 shísì
□ I'm fourteen. 我十四岁。Wǒ shísì suì.

fourteenth ADJECTIVE
第十四 dì shísì
□ the fourteenth floor 第十四楼 dì shísì lóu
■ **the fourteenth of August** 八月十四日 bāyuè shísì rì

fourth ADJECTIVE
第四 dìsì
□ the fourth floor 第四楼 dì sì lóu
■ **the fourth of July** 七月四日 qīyuè sì rì

fox NOUN
狐狸 húli [只 zhī]

fragile ADJECTIVE
易损的 yìsǔn de

frame NOUN
框 kuàng [个 gè]
■ **frames** *(of spectacles)* 眼镜架 yǎnjìngjià

France NOUN
法国 Fǎguó

fraud NOUN
1 诈骗 zhàpiàn [种 zhǒng]
□ He was jailed for fraud. 他因诈骗而入狱。Tā yīn zhàpiàn ér rùyù.
2 骗子 piànzi [个 gè] *(person)*
□ He's not a real doctor, he's a fraud. 他不是真的医生，他是个骗子。Tā búshì zhēnde yīshēng, tā shìge piànzi.

freckle NOUN
雀斑 quèbān [个 gè]

free ADJECTIVE
1 免费的 miǎnfèi de *(costing nothing)*
□ a free brochure 一本免费小册子 yìběn miǎnfèi xiǎocèzi
■ **free of charge** 免费 miǎnfèi
2 有空的 yǒukòng de *(person)*
□ Are you free after school? 你放学后有空吗？Nǐ fàngxué hòu yǒukòng ma?
3 空闲的 kòngxián de *(time)*
4 空余的 kòngyú de *(seat, table)*
□ Is this seat free? 这个座位是空的吗？Zhège zuòwèi shì kòng de ma?

freedom NOUN
自由 zìyóu

freeway NOUN (US)
高速公路 gāosù gōnglù [条 tiáo]

to **freeze** VERB
1 结冰 jiébīng *(liquid, weather)*
□ The water had frozen. 水结冰了。Shuǐ jiébīng le.
2 冻住 dòngzhù *(pipe)*
3 冷冻 lěngdòng *(food)*
□ She froze the rest of the raspberries. 她把剩下的覆盆子冷冻起来。Tā bǎ shèngxiade fùpénzǐ lěngdòng qǐlái.

freezer NOUN
冰柜 bīngguì [个 gè]

freezing ADJECTIVE
1 极冷的 jílěng de *(day, weather)*
■ **It's freezing!** 今天冷极了！Jīntiān lěngjí le.
2 冰凉的 bīngliáng de *(person, hands)*
■ **I'm freezing!** 冻死我了！Dòngsǐ wǒ le!

French ADJECTIVE
▷ *see also* **French** NOUN
法国的 Fǎguó de

French NOUN
▷ *see also* **French** ADJECTIVE

法语 Fǎyǔ *(language)*
□ Do you speak French? 你会说法语吗？Nǐ huì shuō Fǎyǔ ma?
■ **the French** *(people)* 法国人 Fǎguórén

French beans PL NOUN
扁豆 biǎndòu

French fries PL NOUN (US)
炸薯条 zhá shǔtiáo

Frenchman NOUN
法国男人 Fǎguó nánrén [个 gè]

Frenchwoman NOUN
法国女人 Fǎguó nǚrén [个 gè]

frequent ADJECTIVE
频繁的 pínfán de
□ There are frequent buses to the town centre. 去市中心的公交车车次频繁。Qù shìzhōngxīn de gōngjiāochē chēcì pínfán.

fresh ADJECTIVE
1 新鲜的 xīnxiān de
■ **fresh air** 新鲜空气 xīnxiān kōngqì □ I need some fresh air. 我需要新鲜空气。Wǒ xūyào xīnxiān kōngqì.
2 新颖的 xīnyǐng de *(approach, way)*

Friday NOUN
星期五 xīngqīwǔ [个 gè]
□ on Friday 在星期五 zài xīngqīwǔ □ on Fridays 在每个星期五 zài měige xīngqīwǔ □ every Friday 每个星期五 měige xīngqīwǔ □ last Friday 上个星期五 shàngge xīngqīwǔ □ next Friday 下个星期五 xiàge xīngqīwǔ

fridge NOUN
冰箱 bīngxiāng [台 tái]

fried ADJECTIVE
炒的 chǎo de *(food)*
□ fried vegetables 炒蔬菜 chǎo shūcài
■ **a fried egg** 一个炒蛋 yígè chǎodàn

friend NOUN
朋友 péngyou [个 gè]
■ **to make friends with somebody** 与某人交朋友 yǔ mǒurén jiāo péngyou

friendly ADJECTIVE
友善的 yǒushàn de
□ She's really friendly. 她真的很友善。Tā zhēnde hěn yǒushàn.
■ **to be friendly with** 跟…友好 gēn... yǒuhǎo

friendship NOUN
友情 yǒuqíng [种 zhǒng]

fright NOUN
惊吓 jīngxià [个 gè]
■ **to give somebody a fright** 吓唬某人一下 xiàhu mǒurén yíxià

to **frighten** VERB
使惊恐 shǐ jīngkǒng
□ Horror films frighten him. 恐怖电影会使他惊恐。Kǒngbù diànyǐng huì shǐ tā jīngkǒng.

frightened ADJECTIVE
■ **to be frightened** 被吓倒 bèi xiàdǎo
□ I'm frightened! 我被吓倒了！Wǒ bèi xiàdào le!
■ **to be frightened of something** 害怕某事 hàipà mǒushì □ Anna's frightened of spiders. 安娜害怕蜘蛛。Ānnà hàipà zhīzhū.

frightening ADJECTIVE
令人恐惧的 lìngrén kǒngjù de

fringe NOUN
刘海 liúhǎi [束 shù] *(of hair)*
□ She's got a fringe. 她有刘海。Tā yǒu liúhǎi.

frog NOUN
青蛙 qīngwā [只 zhī]

from PREPOSITION
来自 láizì
□ Where are you from? 你来自哪里？Nǐ láizì nǎlǐ? □ a present from somebody 来自某人的礼物 láizì mǒurén de lǐwù

LANGUAGE TIP 从 cóng is used with time, distance, price, numbers.

□ from one o'clock until two 从一点直到两点 cóng yìdiǎn zhídào liǎngdiǎn □ It's 1 km from the beach. 从海滩到这儿有一公里。Cóng hǎitān dào zhèr yǒu yì gōnglǐ. □ from London to Glasgow 从伦敦到格拉斯哥 cóng Lúndūn dào Gélāsīgē

front NOUN
▷ *see also* **front** ADJECTIVE
1 正面 zhèngmiàn *(of house, dress)*
□ the front of the house 房子正面 fángzi zhèngmiàn
2 前面 qiánmiàn [个 gè] *(of coach, train, car)*
□ I was sitting in the front. 我坐在前面。Wǒ zuò zài qiánmiàn.

front ADJECTIVE
▷ *see also* **front** NOUN
前面的 qiánmiàn de
□ the front row 前排 qiánpái
■ **in front** 在前面 zài qiánmiàn
■ **in front of 1** *(facing)* 在…前面 zài... qiánmiàn □ in front of the house 在房子前面 zài fángzi qiánmiàn **2** *(in the presence of)* 在…面前 zài...miànqián

front door NOUN
前门 qiánmén [个 gè]

frontier NOUN
国界 guójiè [个 gè]

front page NOUN
头版 tóubǎn [个 gè]

frost NOUN
霜 shuāng [层 céng]

frosty ADJECTIVE
有霜冻的 yǒu shuāngdòng de
■ **It's frosty today.** 今天下霜了。Jīntiān xià shuāng le.

to **frown** VERB
皱眉 zhòuméi
□ He frowned. 他皱起了眉。Tā zhòuqǐ le méi.

froze VERB ▷ *see* **freeze**

frozen ADJECTIVE
1 冷冻的 lěngdòng de *(food)*
□ frozen chips 冷冻薯条 lěngdòng shǔtiáo
2 结冰的 jiébīng de *(ground, lake)*
3 冰冷的 bīnglěng de *(person, fingers)*

fruit NOUN
水果 shuǐguǒ [种 zhǒng]
■ **fruit juice** 果汁 guǒzhī
■ **a fruit salad** 一份水果沙拉 yífèn shuǐguǒ shālā

frustrated ADJECTIVE
沮丧的 jǔsàng de

to **fry** VERB
油煎 yóujiān
□ Fry the onions for 5 minutes. 将洋葱用油煎五分钟。Jiāng yángcōng yòng yóu jiān wǔfēnzhōng.

frying pan NOUN
平底煎锅 píngdǐ jiānguō [个 gè]

fuel NOUN
燃料 ránliào [种 zhǒng]
■ **to run out of fuel** 燃料用尽 ránliào yòngjìn

to **fulfil** VERB
实现 shíxiàn
□ Robert fulfilled his dream to visit China. 罗伯特终于实现了造访中国的梦想。Luóbótè zhōngyú shíxiàn le zàofǎng Zhōngguō de mèngxiǎng.

full ADJECTIVE
1 满的 mǎn de *(container, cinema, restaurant)*
□ The tank's full. 罐子是满的。Guànzi shì mǎn de.
2 全部的 quánbù de *(details)*
□ He asked for full details about the job. 他想知道关于这份工作的全部细节。Tā xiǎng zhīdào guānyú zhè fèn gōngzuò de quánbù xìjié.
3 完全的 wánquán de *(information, name)*
□ My full name is Ian John Marr. 我的全名是伊安・约翰・玛尔。Wǒ de quánmíng shì Yī'ān Yuēhàn Mǎ'ěr.
■ **I'm full up.** 我吃饱了。Wǒ chībǎo le.

full stop NOUN
句号 jù hào [个 gè]

full-time ADJECTIVE
▷ *see also* **full-time** ADVERB
1 全职的 quánzhí de *(work, study)*
□ She's got a full-time job. 她有一份全职的工作。Tā yǒu yífèn quánzhí de gōngzuò.
2 全日制的 quánrìzhì de *(student, staff)*

full-time ADVERB
▷ *see also* **full-time** ADJECTIVE
全日地 quánrì de *(work, study)*
□ She works full-time. 她的工作是全职的。Tā de gōngzuò shì quánzhí de.

fully ADVERB
完全地 wánquán de
□ He hasn't fully recovered from his illness. 他还没痊愈。Tā hái méi quányù.

fumes PL NOUN
浓烈刺鼻的气体 nóngliè cìbí de qìtǐ [种 zhǒng]
■ **exhaust fumes** 废气 fèiqì

fun NOUN
▷ *see also* **fun** ADJECTIVE
乐趣 lèqù [种 zhǒng]
■ **to have fun** 玩得开心 wánde kāixīn
■ **to do something for fun** 为找乐而做某事 wèi zhǎolè ěr zuò mǒushì □ He entered the competition just for fun. 他参加这个竞赛只是为了玩玩。Tā cānjiā zhège jìngsài zhǐshì wèile wánwan.
■ **to make fun of somebody** 取笑某人 qǔxiào mǒurén □ They made fun of him. 他们取笑他。Tāmen qǔxiào tā.
■ **It's fun!** 这很好玩！Zhè hěn hǎowán!
■ **Have fun!** 玩得开心！Wǎn de kāixīn!

fun ADJECTIVE
▷ *see also* **fun** NOUN
有趣的 yǒuqù de
□ She's a fun person. 她是个有趣的人。Tā shìge yǒuqù de rén.

fund NOUN
基金 jījīn [项 xiàng]

funds PL NOUN
资金 zījīn *(money)*

funeral NOUN
葬礼 zànglǐ [个 gè]

funfair NOUN
露天游乐场 lùtiān yóulèchǎng [个 gè]

funny ADJECTIVE
1 好笑的 hǎoxiào de *(amusing)*
□ It was really funny. 这真是好笑。Zhè zhēnshì hǎoxiào.
2 奇怪的 qíguài de *(strange)*
□ There's something funny about him. 他这人有点奇怪。Tā zhèrén yǒudiǎn qíguài.

fur NOUN
皮毛 máo [种 zhǒng]
□ the dog's fur 狗的皮毛 gǒu de pímáo
■ **a fur coat** 一件毛皮大衣 yíjiàn máopí dàyī

furious ADJECTIVE
大发雷霆的 dà fā léitíng de
□ Dad was furious with me. 爸爸对我大发雷霆。Bàba duì wǒ dà fā léitíng.

furniture NOUN
家具 jiājù
■ **a piece of furniture** 一件家具 yíjiàn jiājù

further ADVERB
▹ *see also* **further** ADJECTIVE
更远地 gèngyuǎn de *(in distance, time)*
□ It's further along this road. 是在沿着这条路更远的地方。Shì zài yánzhe zhè tiáo lù gèng yuǎn de dìfāng. □ London is further from Manchester than Leeds is. 伦敦离曼彻斯特比利兹远。Lúndūn lí Mànchèsītè bǐ Lìzī yuǎn.
■ **How much further is it?** 还有多远？Háiyǒu duōyuǎn?

further ADJECTIVE
▹ *see also* **further** ADVERB
更进一步的 gèng jìn yíbù de *(additional)*
□ They need further evidence. 他们需要更进一步的证据。Tāmen xūyào gèng jìn yíbù de zhèngjù.

further education NOUN
继续教育 jìxù jiàoyù

fuse (US **fuze**) NOUN
保险丝 bǎoxiǎnsī [根 gēn]
■ **A fuse has blown.** 一根保险丝烧断了。Yì gēn bǎoxiǎnsī shāoduàn le.

fuss NOUN
大惊小怪 dàjīng xiǎoguài
■ **to make a fuss about something** 对某事小题大做 duì mǒushì xiǎo tí dà zuò
□ He's always making a fuss about nothing. 他是在无事小题大做。Tā shì zài wúshì xiǎotí dàzuò.

fussy ADJECTIVE
挑剔的 tiāotì de
□ She is very fussy about her food. 她对食物非常挑剔。Tā duì shíwù fēicháng tiāotì.

future ADJECTIVE
▹ *see also* **future** NOUN
将来的 jiānglái de

future NOUN
▹ *see also* **future** ADJECTIVE
■ **the future** **1** *(in time)* 将来 jiānglái
□ What are your plans for the future? 你将来有什么计划？Nǐ jiānglái yǒu shénme jìhuà? **2** *(in grammar)* 将来时 jiāngláishí
■ **in future** *(from now on)* 今后 jīnhòu
□ Be more careful in future. 今后要更加小心了。Jīnhòu yào gèngjiā xiǎoxīn le.
■ **in the near future** 在不久的将来 zài bùjiǔ de jiānglái

Gg

to **gain** VERB
增加 zēngjiā
■ **to gain weight** 增加重量 zēngjiā zhòngliàng
■ **to gain speed** 增加速度 zēngjiā sùdù

gallery NOUN
美术馆 měishùguǎn [个 gè] *(art gallery)*

to **gamble** VERB
▷ *see also* **gamble** NOUN
1 赌博 dǔbó *(bet)*
□ He gambled £100 at the casino. 他在赌场花了一百英镑赌博。Tā zài dǔchǎng huāle yìbǎi yīngbàng dǔbó.
2 投机 tóujī *(risk)*
■ **to gamble on something** 1 *(horse, market)* 对某事打赌 duì mǒushì dǎdǔ 2 *(success, outcome)* 对某事冒险 duì mǒushì màoxiǎn

gamble NOUN
▷ *see also* **gamble** VERB
冒险 màoxiǎn [次 cì] *(risk)*

gambler NOUN
赌徒 dǔtú [个 gè]

gambling NOUN
赌博 dǔbó [次 cì]
□ He likes gambling. 他喜欢赌博。Tā xǐhuan dǔbó.

game NOUN
1 运动 yùndòng [项 xiàng] *(sport)*
2 游戏 yóuxì [项 xiàng] *(children's)*
□ The children were playing a game. 孩子们刚才在做游戏。Háizimen gāngcái zài zuò yóuxì.
■ **a board game** 一项棋盘游戏 yíxiàng qípán yóuxì
■ **a computer game** 一个电脑游戏 yígè diànnǎo yóuxì
3 比赛 bǐsài [场 chǎng] *(match)*
■ **a game of football** 一场足球比赛 yìchǎng zúqiú bǐsài
■ **a game of tennis** 一场网球比赛 yìchǎng wǎngqiú bǐsài

gamer NOUN
游戏玩家 yóuxì wánjiā *(on computer)*

gaming NOUN
游戏 yóuxì *(on computer)*

gang NOUN
帮派 bāngpài

gangster NOUN
歹徒 dǎitú [个 gè]

gap NOUN
缝隙 fèngxì [个 gè]
□ There's a gap in the hedge. 树篱上有一个缝隙。Shùlí shàng yǒu yígè fèngxì. □ a gap of four years 四年之隔 sìnián zhī gé

gap year NOUN
休学期 xiūxuéqī

garage NOUN
1 车库 chēkù [个 gè] *(of house)*
2 汽车修理厂 qìchē xiūlǐchǎng [个 gè] *(for car repairs)*
3 加油站 jiāyóuzhàn [个 gè] *(petrol station)*

garbage NOUN
1 垃圾 lājī *(US: rubbish)*
2 废话 fèihuà *(nonsense)*

garbage can NOUN (US)
垃圾箱 lājìxiāng [个 gè]

garbage man NOUN (US)
清洁工 qīngjiégōng [位 wèi]

garden NOUN
花园 huāyuán [个 gè]

gardener NOUN
1 园丁 yuándīng [位 wèi] *(professional)*
□ He's a gardener. 他是位园丁。Tā shì wèi yuándīng.
2 园艺爱好者 yuányì àihàozhě [个 gè] *(amateur)*

gardening NOUN
园艺 yuányì

gardens PL NOUN
公园 gōngyuán [座 zuò]

garlic NOUN
大蒜 dàsuàn [头 tóu]

garment NOUN
衣服 yīfu [件 jiàn]

gas NOUN
1 煤气 méiqì *(for cooking, heating)*
■ **a gas cooker** 一个煤气灶 yígè méiqì zào
■ **a gas cylinder** 一个煤气罐 yígè méiqì guàn
■ **a gas fire** 一个煤气取暖器 yígè méiqì qǔnuǎnqì

■ **a gas leak** 一次煤气泄露 yícì méiqì xièlòu
2 汽油 qìyóu *(us: petrol)*

gasoline NOUN (US)
汽油 qìyóu

gas station NOUN (US)
加油站 jiāyóuzhàn [个 gè]

gate NOUN
1 门 mén [个 gè]
■ **a garden gate** 一个花园门 yígè huāyuán mén
2 大门 dàmén [个 gè] *(of building)*
3 登机口 dēngjīkǒu [个 gè] *(at airport)*

to **gather** VERB
聚集 jùjí *(assemble)*
□ People gathered in front of Buckingham Palace. 人们在白金汉宫前面聚集。Rénmen zài Báijīnhàngōng qiánmiàn jùjí.
■ **to gather (that)...** *(understand)* 获悉… huòxī... □ I gather you used to live in Singapore. 我获悉你以前住在新加坡。Wǒ huòxī nǐ yǐqián zhùzài Xīnjiāpō.
■ **to gather speed** 提速 tísù □ The train gathered speed. 火车提速了。Huǒchē tísù le.

gave VERB ▷ *see* **give**

gay ADJECTIVE
▷ *see also* **gay** NOUN
同性恋的 tóngxìngliàn de

gay NOUN
▷ *see also* **gay** ADJECTIVE
同性恋 tóngxìngliàn [个 gè]

GCSE NOUN (= *General Certificate of Secondary Education)*
普通中等教育证书 Pǔtōng Zhōngděng Jiàoyù Zhèngshū

gear NOUN
1 排挡 páidǎng [个 gè] *(of car, bicycle)*
□ in first gear 在一档 zài yī dǎng
■ **to change gear** 换挡 huàndǎng
2 装备 zhuāngbèi [套 tào] *(equipment)*
□ camping gear 露营装备 lùyíng zhuāngbèi
3 服装 fúzhuāng *(clothing)* [件 jiàn]
□ Have you got your sports gear? 你带上运动服装了吗？Nǐ dàishàng yùndòng fúzhuāng le ma?

gear lever NOUN
变速杆 biànsùgǎn [个 gè]

gearshift NOUN (US)
变速杆 biànsùgǎn [个 gè]

geese PL NOUN
鹅 é [群 qún] ▷ *see* **goose**

gel NOUN
啫理 zhělí [瓶 píng]
■ **bath gel** 沐浴液 mùyùyè
■ **shower gel** 淋浴液 línyùyè
■ **hair gel** 发型啫理 fàxíng zhělí

gem NOUN
宝石 bǎoshí [颗 kē]

Gemini NOUN *(star sign)*
双子座 Shuāngzǐ Zuò
□ I'm Gemini. 我是双子座的。Wǒ shì Shuāngzǐ Zuò de.

gender NOUN
1 性别 xìngbié [种 zhǒng] *(of person)*
2 名词的性 míngcí de xìng [种 zhǒng] *(of noun)*

gene NOUN
基因 jīyīn [组 zǔ]

general ADJECTIVE
▷ *see also* **general** NOUN
1 总的 zǒng de
□ the general situation at home 国内的总形势 guónèi de zǒng xíngshì
2 普遍的 pǔbiàn de
□ the general decline in educational standards 教育水准的普遍下降 jiàoyù shuǐzhǔn de pǔbiàn xiàjiàng
3 笼统的 lǒngtǒng de
□ Can you give me a general idea of what your job is? 你能给我一个关于你的工作的笼统介绍吗？Nǐ néng gěi wǒ yígè guānyú nǐde gōngzuò de lǒngtǒng jièshào mā?
■ **in general** 通常地 tōngcháng de □ In general, I don't go to parties. 通常地，我不参加派对。Tōngcháng de, wǒ bù cānjiā pàiduì.

general NOUN
▷ *see also* **general** ADJECTIVE *(military)*
将军 jiāngjūn [位 wèi]

general election NOUN
大选 dàxuǎn [届 jiè] *(in Britain, United States)*

general knowledge
常识 chángshí
□ How's your general knowledge? 你的常识怎么样？Nǐde chángshí zěnmeyàng?

generally ADVERB
1 大体上 dàtǐshàng *(on the whole)*
□ Generally, people in this job have a degree. 大体上讲，做这个工作的人都有大学学位。Dàtǐshàng jiǎng, zuò zhègè gōngzuò de rén dōu yǒu dàxué xuéwèi.
2 通常地 tōngcháng de *(usually)*
□ I generally go shopping on Saturday. 我通常在周六去购物。Wǒ tōngcháng zài zhōuliù qù gòuwù.

generation NOUN
一代人 yídàirén
□ the younger generation 年轻一代 niánqīng yídài

generator NOUN
发电机 fādiànjī [台 tái]

generous ADJECTIVE
大方的 dàfāng de
□ That's very generous of you. 你真是太大方了。Nǐ zhēnshi tài dàfāng le.

genetic ADJECTIVE
基因的 jīyīn de

genetically-modified ADJECTIVE
转基因的 zhuǎn jīyīn de
□ genetically-modified crops 转基因作物 zhuǎn jīyīn zuòwù

genetics NOUN
遗传学 yíchuánxué

LANGUAGE TIP Word for word, these characters mean 'the study of that which is passed down'.

Geneva NOUN
日内瓦 Rìnèiwǎ

genius NOUN
天才 tiāncái [个 gè]
□ She's a genius! 她是个天才！Tā shì gè tiāncái!

gentle ADJECTIVE
温和的 wēnhé de

gentleman NOUN
先生 xiānsheng [位 wèi]
□ Good morning, gentlemen. 早上好，先生们。Zǎoshàng hǎo, xiānshengmen.

gently ADVERB
轻轻地 qīngqīng de
□ He touched me gently on the arm. 他轻轻地触碰我的手臂。Tā qīngqīng de chùpèng wǒde shǒubì.

gents NOUN
■ **the gents** *(men's toilet)* 男厕 náncè [个 gè]
□ Can you tell me where the gents is, please? 请问，你能告诉我男厕在哪儿吗？Qǐngwèn, nǐ néng gàosù wǒ náncè zài nǎ'r ma?

genuine ADJECTIVE
1 真正的 zhēnzhèng de *(real)*
□ These are genuine diamonds. 这些是真正的钻石。Zhèxiē shì zhēnzhèng de zuànshí.
2 真诚的 zhēnchéng de *(sincere)*
□ She's a very genuine person. 她是个非常真诚的人。Tā shì gè fēicháng zhēnchéng de rén.

geography NOUN
1 地理 dìlǐ
2 地理学 dìlǐxué *(school subject)*
□ a geography student 一个地理学专业的学生 yígè dìlǐxué zhuānyè de xuésheng

gerbil NOUN
沙鼠 shāshǔ [只 zhī]

germ NOUN
细菌 xìjūn [种 zhǒng]

German ADJECTIVE
▷ *see also* **German** NOUN
德国的 Déguó de
□ German visitors 德国游客 Déguó yóukè

German NOUN
▷ *see also* **German** ADJECTIVE
1 德国人 Déguórén [个 gè] *(person)*
2 德语 Déyǔ *(language)*
□ Do you speak German? 你会讲德语吗？Nǐ huì jiǎng Déyǔ ma?

German measles *(medicine)*
德国麻疹 Déguó mázhěn [次 cì]

Germany NOUN
德国 Déguó
■ **in Germany** 在德国 zài Déguó
■ **to Germany** 去德国 qù Déguó

gesture NOUN
1 手势 shǒushì [个 gè] *(hand movement)*
□ a rude gesture 一个没礼貌的手势 yígè méilǐmào de shǒushì
2 举动 jǔdòng [项 xiàng] *(action)*
□ a political gesture 一项政治举动 yíxiàng zhèngzhì jǔdòng

to **get** VERB
1 得到 dédào *(have, receive)*
□ What did you get for your birthday? 你生日时得到了什么礼物？Nǐ shēngrìshí dédào le shénme lǐwù? □ He got first prize. 他得到了一等奖。Tā dédào le yīděngjiǎng. □ He got good exam results. 他得到了好的考试成绩。Tā dédào le hǎode kǎoshì chéngji. □ How many have you got? 你得到了多少？Nǐ dédào le duōshǎo?
2 去拿 qùná *(fetch)*
□ Quick, get help! 快，去叫人来帮忙！Kuài, qù jiàorén lái bāngmáng!
■ **to get something for somebody** 为某人去拿某物 wèi mǒurén qù ná mǒuwù
□ Can I get you a coffee? 要我给你拿杯咖啡吗？Yào wǒ gěi nǐ ná bēi kāfēi ma?
■ **I'll come and get you.** 我会来接你的。Wǒ huì lái jiē nǐ de.
3 乘坐 chéngzuò *(train, bus)*
□ I'll get the bus. 我会乘坐公共汽车。Wǒ huì chéngzuò gōnggòng qìchē.
4 获得 huòdé *(permission, money)*
5 得到 dédào *(job, flat)*
□ He got a job in London. 他在伦敦得到一份工作。Tā zài Lúndūn dédào yífèn gōngzuò.
6 买 mǎi *(buy)*
□ I'll get some milk from the supermarket. 我要去超市买牛奶。Wǒ yào qù chāoshì mǎi niúnǎi.

7 变得 biàn de *(become)*
■ **to get old** 变老 biànlǎo
■ **to get tired** 变得疲倦 biànde píjuàn
■ **to get cold** 变冷 biànlěng
■ **to get drunk** 喝醉 hēzuì

8 到达 dàodá *(arrive)*
□ He didn't get home till 10pm. 他晚上十点才回到家。Tā wǎnshàng shídiǎn cái huídào jiā.

9 到 dào *(go, travel)*
□ How did you get here? 你是怎么到这儿的? Nǐ shì zěnme dào zhèr de? □ How long does it take to get from London to Paris? 从伦敦到巴黎需要多久? Cóng Lúndūn dào Bālí xūyào duōjiǔ?
■ **to get to work** 到办公室 dào bàngōngshì
■ **to get to Beijing** 到北京 dào Běijīng

10 理解 lǐjiě *(understand)*
□ I don't get what you're saying. 我不理解你现在在说什么。Wǒ bù lǐjiě nǐ xiànzài zài shuō shénme.
■ **to get something done** **1** *(do oneself)* 做某事 zuò mǒushì **2** *(have done)* 完成某事 wánchéng mǒushì
■ **to get one's hair cut** 理发 lǐfà
■ **to have got to do something** 必须得做某事 bìxū děi zuò mǒushì □ I've got to tell him. 我必须得告诉他。Wǒ bìxū děi gàosù tā.

to **get away** VERB
逃跑 táopǎo
□ One of the burglars got away. 其中一个盗贼逃跑了。Qízhōng yígè dàozéi táopǎo le.

to **get back** VERB
1 回来 huílái *(return)*
□ What time did you get back? 你什么时候回来的? Nǐ shénme shíhòu huílái de?
2 收回 shōuhuí *(reclaim)*
□ He got his money back. 他收回了自己的钱。Tā shōuhuí le zìjǐ de qián.
■ **get back to sleep** 接着睡 jiēzhe shuì

to **get back to** VERB
1 回到 huídào *(activity, work)*
□ I can't wait to get back to work. 我迫切地想回到工作岗位上。Wǒ pòqiè de xiǎng huídào gōngzuò gǎngwèi shàng.
2 重新回到 chóngxīn huídào *(point of discussion)*
□ Could you please get back to the point? 你能重新回到讨论重点上来吗? Nǐ néng chóngxīn huídào tǎolùn zhòngdiǎn shàng lái mā?

to **get in** VERB
1 抵达 dǐdá *(arrive)*
□ When does his plane get in? 他乘坐的飞机什么时候抵达? Tā chéngzuò de fēijī shénme shíhòu dǐdá?
2 到家 dàojiā *(arrive home)*
□ What time did you get in last night? 你昨晚什么时候到家的? Nǐ zuówǎn shénme shíhòu dàojiā de?

to **get into** VERB
坐进 zuòjìn *(vehicle)*
□ Sharon got into the car. 莎朗坐进了轿车里。Shālǎng zuòjìn le jiàochē lǐ.

to **get off** VERB
1 下车 xiàchē *(bus, train)*
□ Isobel got off the train. 伊泽贝尔下了火车。Yīzébèi'ěr xià le huǒchē.
2 放假 fàngjià *(as holiday)*
■ **We get three days off at Christmas.** 我们圣诞节放了三天假。Wǒmen Shèngdànjié fàngle sāntiānjià.

to **get on** VERB
1 和睦相处 hémù xiāngchǔ *(be friends)*
□ He doesn't get on with his parents. 他不能和父母和睦相处。Tā bùnéng hé fùmǔ hémù xiāngchǔ.
■ **to get on well with somebody** 与某人相处融洽 yǔ mǒurén xiāngchǔ róngqià
2 进展 jìnzhǎn *(progress)*
■ **How are you getting on?** 你过得怎么样? Nǐ guòde zěnmeyàng?
3 上车 shàngchē *(vehicle)*
□ Yueshi got on the bus. 越施上了巴士。Yuèshī shàng le bāshì.

to **get on with** VERB
继续做 jìxù zuò *(continue, start)*
□ I can't get on with my work when you are talking. 在你讲话的时候我没法继续我的工作。Zài nǐ jiǎnghuà de shíhòu wǒ méifǎ jìxù wǒde gōngzuò.

to **get out** VERB
下车 xiàchē
□ Helen got out the car. 海伦下了轿车。Hǎilún xià le jiàochē. □ Get out! 出去! Chūqù!
■ **to get something out** 拿出某物 náchū mǒuwù □ She got the map out. 她拿出了地图。Tā náchū le dìtú.

to **get out of** VERB
从...下来 cóng...xiàlái
□ I got out of the bus at the terminal. 我在终点站下了巴士。Wǒ zài zhōngdiǎnzhàn xià le bāshì.

to **get over** VERB
从...中恢复过来 cóng...zhōng huīfù guòlái
□ I'm not over the flu yet. 我的流感还没好。Wǒde liúgǎn hái méi hǎo. □ She never got over his death. 她一直没从他的死中恢

复过来。Tā yìzhí méi cóng tāde sǐ zhōng huīfù guòlái.

to **get through** VERB

1 接通 jiētōng *(telephone)*
□ I tried phoning but I couldn't get through. 我试过打电话，但一直接不通。Wǒ shìguò dǎ diànhuà, dàn yìzhí jiēbutōng.

2 完成 wánchéng *(work, book)*
□ I'm still trying to get through his first novel. 我仍在试着读完他的第一部小说。Wǒ réng zài shìzhe dúwán tāde dìyībù xiǎoshuō.

to **get together** VERB

聚在一起 jùzài yìqǐ
□ Could we get together this evening? 我们今天傍晚能聚在一起吗？Wǒmen jīntiān bàngwǎn néng jùzài yìqǐ mā?

to **get up** VERB

1 站起来 zhànqǐlái *(from chair)*

2 起床 qǐchuáng *(out of bed)*
□ What time do you get up for work? 你什么时候起床去上班？Nǐ shénme shíhòu qǐchuáng qù shàngbān?

ghost NOUN

鬼 guǐ [个 gè]

giant NOUN

▷ *see also* **giant** ADJECTIVE
巨人 jùrén [个 gè]

giant ADJECTIVE

▷ *see also* **giant** NOUN
巨大的 jùdà de
□ They ate a giant meal. 他们吃了一顿大餐。Tāmen chīle yídùn dàcān.

gift NOUN

1 礼物 lǐwù [件 jiàn]
□ a wedding gift 一件结婚礼物 yíjiàn jiēhūn lǐwù

2 天赋 tiānfù [种 zhǒng]
□ Dave has a gift for painting. 戴夫有绘画的天赋。Dàifū yǒu huìhuà de tiānfù.

gifted ADJECTIVE

有天赋的 yǒu tiānfù de
□ a gifted musician 一位有天赋的音乐家 yíwèi yǒu tiānfù de yīnyuèjiā

gift shop NOUN

礼品店 lǐpǐndiàn [家 jiā]

gigantic ADJECTIVE

巨大的 jùdà de
□ a gigantic birthday cake 一个巨大的生日蛋糕 yígè jùdà de shēngrì dàngāo

gin NOUN

杜松子酒 dùsōngzǐjiǔ [瓶 píng]

ginger NOUN

▷ *see also* **ginger** ADJECTIVE
姜 jiāng [块 kuài]
□ Add a teaspoon of ginger. 加一茶匙的姜。Jiā yìchāchí de jiāng.

ginger ADJECTIVE

▷ *see also* **ginger** NOUN
姜色的 jiāngsè de
□ ginger hair 姜色的头发 jiāngsè de tóufa

giraffe NOUN

长颈鹿 chángjǐnglù [只 zhī]

girl NOUN

1 女孩 nǚhái [个 gè] *(child)*
□ a seven-year-old girl 一个七岁的女孩 yígè qīsuì de nǚhái

2 姑娘 gūniang [个 gè] *(young woman, woman)*
□ an evening with the girls 一个与姑娘们共处的夜晚 yígè yǔ gūniáng men gòngchǔ de yèwǎn

3 女儿 nǚ'ér [个 gè] *(daughter)*
□ I have a girl and a boy. 我有一个女儿和一个儿子。Wǒ yǒu yígè nǚ'ér hé yígè érzi.

girlfriend NOUN

1 女朋友 nǚ péngyǒu [个 gè] *(lover)*
□ Tell me about Ian's girlfriend. 跟我说说伊恩的女朋友。Gēn wǒ shuōshuō Yī'ēn de nǚ péngyǒu.

2 女性朋友 nǚxìng péngyǒu [个 gè] *(female friend)*
□ I'm having lunch with my girlfriends. 我在和我的女性朋友们吃午饭。Wǒ zài hé wǒde nǚxìng péngyǒumen chī wǔfàn.

to **give** VERB

1 送给某人某物 sònggěi mǒurén mǒuwù *(as gift)*
■ **to give something to somebody** 给某人某物 gěi mǒurén mǒuwù □ He gave me £10. 他给了我十英镑。Tā gěi le wǒ shí yīngbàng.

2 提供 tígōng *(advice, information)*
■ **to give a speech** 做演讲 zuò yǎnjiǎng
■ **to give a lecture** 做讲座 zuò jiǎngzuò
■ **to give a party** 做东办一个聚会 zuòdōng bàn yígè jùhuì

to **give back** VERB

交还 jiāohuán
■ **to give something back to somebody** 把某物交还给某人 bǎ mǒuwù jiāohuán gěi mǒurén □ I gave the book back to him. 我把书交还给了他。Wǒ bǎ shū jiāohuán gěi le tā.

to **give in** VERB

屈服 qūfú
□ His Mum gave in and let him go out. 他妈妈最后屈服，让他出去了。Tā māma zuìhòu qūfú, ràng tā chūqù le.

to **give out** VERB

分发 fēnfā
□ The teacher gave out the exam papers.

老师分发考试试卷。Lǎoshī fēnfā kǎoshì shìjuàn.

to **give up** VERB
放弃 fàngqì
□ I couldn't do it so I gave up. 我做不了，所以放弃了。Wǒ zuòbuliǎo, suǒyǐ fàngqì le.
■ **to give up smoking** 戒烟 jièyān □ I am trying to give up smoking. 我正在尝试着戒烟。Wǒ zhèngzài chángshìzhe jièyān.
■ **to give oneself up** 自首 zìshǒu □ The thief gave himself up. 这贼自首了。Zhè zéi zìshǒu le.

glad ADJECTIVE
高兴的 gāoxìng de
■ **I'd be glad to help you.** 我很高兴帮助你。Wǒ hěn gāoxìng bāngzhù nǐ.

glamorous ADJECTIVE
1 富有魅力的 fùyǒu mèilì de
□ She's very glamorous. 她非常富有魅力。Tā fēicháng fùyǒu mèilì.
2 有吸引力的 yǒu xīyǐnlì de *(of job, life)*
□ Her job sounds glamorous, doesn't it? 她的工作听起来很有吸引力，是吧？Tāde gōngzuò tīngqǐlái hěn yǒu xīyǐnlì, shìba?

to **glance** VERB
▷ *see also* **glance** NOUN
■ **to glance at something** 瞟一眼某物 piǎo yìyǎn mǒuwù □ Peter glanced at his watch. 彼得瞟了一眼手表。Bǐdé piǎo le yìyǎn shǒubiǎo.

glance NOUN
▷ *see also* **glance** VERB
匆匆一看 cōngcōng yíkàn
■ **at first glance** 乍一看就 zhà yíkàn jiù

to **glare** VERB
瞪 dèng
□ He glared at me. 他瞪着我。Tā dèngzhe wǒ.

glaring ADJECTIVE
明显的 míngxiǎn de *(mistake)*
□ a page full of glaring errors 全是明显错误的一页 quánshì míngxiǎn cuòwù de yíyè

glass NOUN
1 玻璃杯 bōlibēi [个 gè]
□ a wine glass 一个酒杯 yígè jiǔbēi
2 一杯 yì bēi
□ a glass of milk 一杯奶 yìbēi nǎi
3 玻璃 bōlí
□ It's made of glass. 它是玻璃做的。Tā shì bōli zuò de.

glasses PL NOUN
眼镜 yǎnjing
□ I hate wearing glasses. 我讨厌戴眼镜。Wǒ tǎoyàn dài yǎnjìng.
■ **a pair of glasses** 一副眼镜 yífù yǎnjìng

glider NOUN
滑翔机 huáxiángjī [架 jià]

gliding NOUN
驾滑翔机 jià huáxiángjī [架 jià]
□ My hobby is gliding. 我的爱好是驾滑翔机。Wǒde àihào shì jià huáxiángjī.

global ADJECTIVE
全球的 quánqiú de
□ on a global scale 在全球范围上 zài quánqiú fànwéi shàng

global warming NOUN
全球变暖 quánqiú biànnuǎn

globe NOUN
地球仪 dìqiúyí [个 gè]

gloomy ADJECTIVE
1 沮丧的 jǔsàng de *(of person)*
□ She looked gloomy when she heard the bad news. 当听到那个坏消息后，她看起来很沮丧。Dāng tīngdào nàgè huài xiāoxi hòu, tā kàn qǐlái hěn jǔsàng.
2 阴暗的 yīn'àn de *(of place)*
□ He lives in a small gloomy flat. 他住在一个小而阴暗的公寓里。Tā zhùzài yígè xiǎo ér yīn'àn de gōngyù lǐ.

glorious ADJECTIVE
壮丽的 zhuànglì de
□ a glorious view 一个壮丽的风景 yígè zhuànglì de fēngjǐng

glove NOUN
手套 shǒutào [副 fù]
■ **a pair of gloves** 一副手套 yífù shǒutào

glove compartment NOUN
汽车仪表板上的小柜 qìchē yíbiǎobǎn shàng de xiǎoguì [个 gè]

glue NOUN
▷ *see also* **glue** VERB
胶 jiāo [种 zhǒng]

to **glue** VERB
▷ *see also* **glue** NOUN
粘贴 zhāntiē
□ Glue the material in place. 把材料粘贴到位在适当的位置上粘贴材料。Bǎ cáiliào zhāntiē dàowèi.

GM ADJECTIVE *(= genetically modified)*
转基因的 zhuǎn jīyīn de
■ **GM foods** 转基因食品 zhuǎn jīyīn shípǐn
■ **GM-free** 非转基因的 fēi zhuǎn jīyīn de

GMO ABBREVIATION *(= genetically-modified organism)*
转基因生物 zhuǎn jīyīn shēngwù

go NOUN
▷ *see also* **go** VERB
1 尝试 chángshì [次 cì] *(try)*
■ **to have a go at doing something** 尝试做某事 chángshì zuò mǒushì □ He had a go at making a cake. 他尝试着做了一次蛋

糕。Tā chángshìzhe zuò le yícì dàngāo.
2 轮流 lúnliú [次 cì] *(turn)*
■ **Whose go is it?** 轮到谁了？Lúndào shuí le?

to **go** VERB
▷ *see also* **go** NOUN
1 去 qù
■ **He's going to New York.** 他要去纽约。Tā yào qù Niǔyuē.
■ **Where's he gone?** 他去哪儿了？Tā qù nǎr le?
■ **Shall we go by car or train?** 我们开车去还是坐火车去？Wǒmen kāichē qù háishì zuò huǒchē qù?
2 离开 líkāi *(depart)*
■ **Let's go.** 我们走吧。Wǒmen zǒuba.
■ **I must be going.** 我必须得走了。Wǒ bìxū děi zōu le.
■ **Our plane goes at 11pm.** 我们的飞机晚上十一点起飞。Wǒmen de fēijī wǎnshàng shíyīdiǎn qǐfēi.
3 通向 tōngxiàng *(lead)*
□ Where does that road go? 那条路通向哪里？Nà tiáo lù tōngxiàng nǎlǐ?
4 消失 xiāoshī *(disappear)*
■ **all her jewellery had gone** 她所有的珠宝首饰都不见了。Tā suǒyǒu de zhūbǎo shǒushì dōu bújiàn le.
■ **to go to school** *(attend)* 上学 shàngxué
■ **to go to university** 上大学 shàng dàxué
■ **to go for a walk** 去散步 qù sànbù
■ **to go on a trip** 去旅行 qù lǚxíng
■ **to go pale** 变得苍白 biànde cāngbái
■ **to go bald** 变得秃顶 biànde tūdǐng
■ **Are you going to come?** 你要来吗？Nǐ yào lái ma?
■ **I think it's going to rain.** 我想天要下雨了。Wǒxiǎng tiān yào xiàyǔ le.
■ **How did it go?** 这事进展如何？Zhèshì jìnzhǎn rúhé?

to **go after** VERB
追赶 zhuīgǎn
□ Quick, go after them! 快点，追赶他们！Kuàidiǎn, zhuīgǎn tāmen!

to **go ahead** VERB
发生 fāshēng
□ The concert went ahead in spite of the rain. 尽管下雨，音乐会还是开始了。Jìnguǎn xiàyǔ, yīnyuèhuì háishì kāishǐ le.
■ **to go ahead with something** 着手做某事 zhuóshǒu zuò mǒushì □ I have decided to go ahead and start my own business. 我决定着手开始我自己的生意。Wǒ juédìng zhuóshǒu kāishǐ zìjǐ de shēngyì.
■ **Go ahead!** 干吧！Gànba!

to **go around** VERB
1 传播 chuánbō *(of rumour)*
2 转动 zhuàndòng *(revolve)*

to **go away** VERB
1 走开 zǒukāi
□ I wish she would just go away. 我希望她会走开。Wǒ xīwàng tā huì zǒukāi.
2 外出 wàichū
□ Are you going away this summer? 这个夏天你会外出吗？Zhègè xiàtiān nǐ huì wàichū mā?

to **go back** VERB
返回 fǎnhuí
□ I think it's time to go back. 我想是时候返回了。Wǒ xiǎng shì shíhòu fǎnhuí le.

to **go back to** VERB
接着做 jiēzhe zuò
□ When he left I went back to reading my book. 他走后我又接着看书。Tā zǒu hòu wǒ yòu jiēzhe kànshū.

to **go by** VERB
顺便来访 shùnbiàn láifǎng
□ Two policemen went by. 两个警察顺便来访过。Liǎnggè jǐngchá shùnbiàn láifǎng guò.

to **go down** VERB
1 下降 xiàjiàng *(decrease)*
□ House prices have gone down this year. 今年房价下降了。Jīnnián fángjià xiàjiàng le.
2 泄气 xièqì *(deflate)*
□ The tyre has gone down. 轮胎泄气了。Lúntāi xièqì le.
3 从...下来 cóng...xiàlái *(descend)*
□ He went down the stairs. 他从楼梯上下来。Tā cóng lóutī shàng xiàlái.
4 死机 sǐjī *(of computer)*
□ I can't read my emails because my computer has gone down. 我看不了电子邮件，因为我的电脑死机了。Wǒ kànbuliǎo diànzǐ yóujiàn, yīnwéi wǒde diànnǎo sǐjī le.
5 落下 luòxià *(of sun)*
■ **to go down with an illness** 病倒 bìngdǎo □ My brother has gone down with flu. 我的兄弟患流感病倒了。Wǒde xiōngdì huàn liúgǎn bìngdǎo le.

to **go for** VERB
1 去取 qùqǔ *(fetch)*
□ I need to go for milk. 我得去取牛奶。Wǒ děi qùqǔ niúnǎi.
2 攻击 gōngjī *(attack)*
□ Suddenly the dog went for me. 那条狗突然来攻击我。Nà tiáo gǒu tūrán lái gōngjī wǒ.
■ **Go for it!** *(encouragement)* 努力争取吧！Nǔlì zhēngqǔ ba!

to **go in** VERB
进去 jìnqù
□ He knocked on the door and went in. 他敲了敲门然后进去了。Tā qiāo le qiāo mén ránhòu jìnqù le.

to **go into** VERB
进入 jìnrù
□ I'm going to go into this shop here. 我要进这家店里去。Wǒ yào jìn zhèjiā diàn lǐ qù.

to **go off** VERB
1 爆炸 bàozhà *(of bomb)*
□ A bomb went off in the centre of town. 一颗炸弹在城中心爆炸了。Yìkē zhàdàn zài chéngzhōngxīn bàozhà le.
2 离去 líqù *(leave)*
□ He's gone off to work. 他已经离去上班了。Tā yǐjīng líqù shàngbān le.
3 响起 xiǎngqǐ *(of alarm)*
□ We all got a fright when the fire alarm went off. 当火警响起时我们都吓了一跳。Dāng huǒjǐng xiǎngqǐ shí wǒmen dōu xià le yítiào.
4 熄灭 xīmiè
□ The light's gone off again! 灯又熄灭了！Dēng yòu xīmiè le!
5 变质 biànzhì *(of food)*
□ That milk's gone off. 那瓶牛奶已经变质了。Nàpíng niúnǎi yǐjīng biànzhì le.

to **go on** VERB
1 发生 fāshēng *(happen)*
□ What's going on here? 这里发生什么事了？Zhèlǐ fāshēng shénme shì le?
2 继续 jìxù *(continue)*
■ **to go on doing something** 继续做某事 jìxù zuò mǒushì
■ **Go on!** 继续说！Jìxù shuō！□ Go on, tell me what you were whispering about! 继续说啊，你们刚才在小声说着什么！Jìxù shuō ā, nǐmen gāngcái zài xiǎoshēng shuōzhe shénme!

to **go out** VERB
1 离开 líkāi
□ Are you going out tonight? 你今晚出去吗？Nǐ jīnwǎn chūqù ma?
■ **to go out with somebody** 和某人交往 hé mǒurén jiāowǎng □ Are you going out with him? 你在和他交往吗？Nǐ zài hé tā jiāowǎng mā?
2 熄灭 xīmiè *(of light, fire)*
□ The lights went out and somebody screamed. 灯熄灭了，紧接着有人尖叫。Dēng xīmiè le, jǐnjiēzhe yǒurén jiānjiào.

to **go over** VERB
过去 guòqù

to **go round** VERB
■ **to go round a corner** 绕过一个拐角 ràoguò yígè guǎijiǎo
■ **to go round to somebody's house** 顺道拜访某人 shùndào bàifǎng mǒurén
■ **to go round a museum** 游览博物馆 yóulǎn bówùguǎn
■ **to go round the shops** 逛商店 guàng shāngdiàn
■ **to be going round** *(of illness)* 流传 liúchuán □ There's a bug going round. 最近这个病毒流传很广 Zuìjìn zhège bìngdú liúchuán de guǎngfàn.

to **go through** VERB
路过 lùguò

to **go up** VERB
1 上涨 shàngzhǎng *(increase)*
□ The price of oil keeps going up. 油价一直在上涨。Yóujià yìzhí zài shàngzhǎng.
2 上楼 shànglóu *(climb)*
□ to go up the stairs 上楼 shànglóu
■ **to go up in flames** 化为灰烬 huàwéi huījìn □ The whole factory went up in flames. 整个工厂化为灰烬了。Zhěnggè gōngchǎng huàwéi huījìn le.

to **go with** VERB
与...相处 yǔ...xiāngchǔ
□ Can you go with him? 你能和他相处吗？Nǐ néng hé tā xiāngchǔ mā?

to **go without** VERB
离得了 lídéliǎo...
□ I'm finding it hard to go without chocolate. 我发现我很难离得了巧克力。Wǒ fāxiàn wǒ hěnnán lídéliǎo qiǎokèlì.

goal NOUN
1 进球得分 jìnqiú défēn [次 cì] *(sport)*
□ a great goal 一个好球 yígè hǎoqiú
■ **to score a goal** 进一球 jìn yìqiú
2 目标 mùbiāo [个 gè] *(aim)*
□ His goal is to become world champion. 他的目标是当世界冠军。Tāde mùbiāo shì dāng shìjiè guànjūn.

goalkeeper NOUN
守门员 shǒuményuán [个 gè]

goat NOUN
山羊 shānyáng [只 zhī]
■ **goat's cheese** 山羊乳酪 shānyáng rǔlào

god NOUN
神 shén [位 wèi]

God NOUN
上帝 Shàngdì
□ I believe in God. 我信上帝。Wǒ xìn Shàngdì.

goddaughter NOUN
干女儿 gān nǚ'ér [个 gè]

godfather NOUN
干爹 gāndiē [位 wèi]

godmother NOUN
干妈 gānmā [位 wèi]

godson NOUN
干儿子 gān érzi [个 gè]

goggles PL NOUN
护目镜 hùmùjìng *(of mechanic, swimmer)*

gold NOUN
▷ *see also* **gold** ADJECTIVE
黄金 huángjīn
□ a ring made of gold 一枚黄金做的戒指 yìméi huángjīn zuòde jièzhi

gold ADJECTIVE
▷ *see also* **gold** NOUN
金的 jīn de
□ a gold necklace 一条金项链 yìtiáo jīn xiàngliàn

goldfish NOUN
金鱼 jīnyú [尾 wěi]

gold-plated ADJECTIVE
镀金的 dùjīn de
□ gold-plated taps 镀金的水龙头 dùjīn de shuǐlóngtóu [个 gè]

golf NOUN
高尔夫球 gāo'ěrfūqiú
■ **to play golf** 打高尔夫球 dǎ gāo'ěrfūqiú
□ My dad plays golf. 我爸爸打高尔夫球。Wǒ bàba dǎ gāo'ěrfūqiú.
■ **a golf club 1** *(stick)* 一支高尔夫球棍 yìzhī gāo'ěrfū qiúgùn **2** *(place)* 一个高尔夫俱乐部 yígè gāo'ěrfū jùlèbù

golf course NOUN
高尔夫球场 gāo'ěrfūqiúchǎng [个 gè]

gone VERB
▷ *see also* **gone** ADJECTIVE ▷ *see* **go**

gone ADJECTIVE
▷ *see also* **gone** VERB
没有了 méiyǒu le
□ The food's all gone. 食物都没有了。Shíwù dōu méiyǒu le.

good ADJECTIVE
▷ *see also* **good** NOUN
1 令人愉快的 lìng rén yúkuài de *(pleasant)*
□ It's a very good film. 这是部令人愉快的电影。Zhè shì bù lìng rén yúkuài de diànyǐng.
2 好的 hǎo de *(of food, school, job)*
□ I'd like to get a good job. 我想找份好工作。Wǒ xiǎng zhǎo fèn hǎo gōngzuò.
3 乖的 guāi de *(well-behaved)*
□ Be good! 乖点！Guāi diǎn!
4 好的 hǎo de *(of news, luck)*
□ I've had some good news. 我有一些好消息。Wǒ yǒu yìxiē hǎo xiāoxi.
5 友好的 yǒuhǎo de *(kind)*
□ Your family have been very good to me. 你家人对我非常友好。Nǐ jiārén duì wǒ fēicháng yǒuhǎo.
■ **Good morning!** 早上好！Zǎoshàng hǎo!
■ **Good afternoon!** 下午好！Xiàwǔ hǎo!
■ **Good evening!** 晚上好！Wǎnshang hǎo!
■ **Good night!** *(before going home)* 晚安！Wǎn'ān!
■ **Good night!** *(before going to bed)* 晚安！Wǎn'ān!
■ **to be good at something** 擅长某事 shàncháng mǒushì □ Jane's very good at maths. 简非常擅长数学。Jiǎn fēicháng shàncháng shùxué.
■ **it's no good doing...** 做…没有用 zuò... méiyǒu yòng □ It's no good complaining. 抱怨没有用。Bàoyuàn méiyǒu yòng.
■ **It's good for you!** 对你有益！Duì nǐ yǒuyì! □ Vegetables are good for you. 蔬菜对你有益。Shūcài duì nǐ yǒuyì.
■ **It's good to see you.** 很高兴见到你。Hěn gāoxìng jiàndào nǐ.

good NOUN
▷ *see also* **good** ADJECTIVE
善 shàn *(right)*
■ **Good!** 好！Hǎo!
■ **for good** *(forever)* 永久地 yǒngjiǔ de
□ He's left for good. 他永久地离开了。Tā yǒngjiǔ de líkāi le.

goodbye EXCLAMATION
再见 zàijiàn
■ **to say goodbye** 告别 gàobié

Good Friday NOUN
耶稣受难日 Yēsū shòunànrì

good-looking ADJECTIVE
好看的 hǎokàn de

good-natured ADJECTIVE
脾气好的 píqìhǎo de

goods PL NOUN
货物 huòwù
■ **a goods train** 货车 huòchē

to **Google®** VERB
用谷歌搜索 yòng Gǔgē sōusuǒ

> **DID YOU KNOW...?**
> While Google is used in China, 百度 Bǎidù is a more popular search engine.

goose NOUN
鹅 é [只 zhī]

gooseberry NOUN
鹅莓 éméi [个 gè]

gorgeous ADJECTIVE
1 宜人的 yírén de *(of weather, day)*
□ a gorgeous spring day 一个宜人的春日 yígè yírén de chūnrì
2 好看的 hǎokàn de *(of person)*
□ That gorgeous man over there. 那边那个好看的男人。Nàbiān nàgè hǎokàn de nánrén.

English-Chinese

gorilla NOUN
大猩猩 dàxīngxing [只 zhī]

gospel NOUN
福音音乐 fúyīn yīnyuè [首 shǒu] *(type of music)*

gossip NOUN
▷ *see also* **gossip** VERB
1 流言蜚语 liúyán fēiyǔ [些 xiē] *(news)*
□ Tell me all the gossip from the office! 告诉我办公室里的所有流言蜚语！Gàosù wǒ bàngōngshì lǐ de suǒyǒu liúyán fēiyǔ!
2 爱说三道四的人 àishuōsāndàosì derén [个 gè] *(person)*
□ He's the biggest gossip I know. 他是我认识的最爱说三道四的人。Tā shì wǒ rènshí de zuì àishuōsāndàosì derén.

to **gossip** VERB
▷ *see also* **gossip** NOUN
闲聊 xiánliáo
□ Stop gossiping and get on with your work! 不要再闲聊了，继续干你们的工作。Búyào zài xiánliáo le, jìxù gàn nǐmen de gōngzuo.
■ **to gossip about somebody** 讲某人的闲话 jiǎng mǒurén de xiánhuà □ Who are you gossiping about now? 你们在讲谁的闲话？Nǐmen zài jiǎng shéi de xiánhuà?

got VERB ▷ *see* **get**

gotten VERB (US) ▷ *see* **get**

government NOUN
政府 zhèngfǔ [届 jiè]
□ the Chinese government 中国政府 Zhōngguó zhèngfǔ

GP NOUN *(= general practitioner)*
家庭医生 jiātíng yīshēng [位 wèi]

GPS NOUN *(= global positioning system)*
全球定位系统 quánqiú dìngwèi xìtǒng [个 gè]

to **grab** VERB
抓住 zhuāzhù
□ She grabbed my arm and pulled me away. 她抓住我的手臂，然后把我推开。Tā zhuāzhù wǒde shǒubì, ránhòu bǎ wǒ tuīkāi.

graceful ADJECTIVE
优美的 yōuměi de

grade NOUN
1 分数 fēnshù [个 gè] *(school mark)*
□ She got good grades in her exams. 她考试拿了高分。Tā kǎoshì ná le gāofēn.
2 年级 niánjí [个 gè] *(US: school class)*
□ My daughter teaches first grade. 我女儿教一年级。Wǒ nǚ'ér jiāo yīniánjí.

grade school NOUN (US)
小学 xiǎoxué [所 suǒ]

gradual ADJECTIVE
逐渐的 zhújiàn de

gradually ADVERB
逐渐地 zhújiàn de
□ We gradually got used to it. 我们逐渐地习惯了。Wǒmen zhújiàn de xíguàn le.

graduate NOUN
▷ *see also* **graduate** VERB
1 大学毕业生 dàxué bìyèshēng [个 gè] *(from university)*
2 高中毕业生 gāozhōng bìyèshēng [个 gè] *(from US high school)*

to **graduate** VERB
▷ *see also* **graduate** NOUN
1 大学毕业 dàxué bìyè *(from university)*
2 高中毕业 gāozhōng bìyè *(from US high school)*

graffiti PL NOUN
涂鸦 túyā

grain NOUN
谷粒 gǔlì [颗 kē]

gram NOUN
克 kè

grammar NOUN
语法 yǔfǎ

grammar school NOUN
语法学校 yǔfǎ xuéxiào [所 suǒ]

grammatical ADJECTIVE
语法的 yǔfǎ de

gramme NOUN
克 kè
□ 500 grammes of cheese 五百克的干酪 wǔbǎi kè de gānlào

grand ADJECTIVE
豪华的 háohuá de
□ They live in a very grand house. 他们住在一个非常豪华的房子里。Tāmen zhù zài yígè fēicháng háohuá de fángzi lǐ.

grandchild NOUN
1 孙子 sūnzi [个 gè] *(male on father's side)*
2 孙女 sūnnǚ [个 gè] *(female on father's side)*
3 外孙 wàisūn [个 gè] *(male on mother's side)*
4 外孙女 wàisūnnǚ [个 gè] *(female on mother's side)*

granddad NOUN
1 爷爷 yéye [位 wèi] *(on father's side)*
2 外公 wàigōng [位 wèi] *(on mother's side)*
□ my granddad 我的爷爷 wǒde yéye

granddaughter NOUN
1 孙女 sūnnǚ [个 gè] *(on father's side)*
2 外孙女 wài sūnnǚ [个 gè] *(on mother's side)*

grandfather NOUN
1 外公 wàigōng [位 wèi] *(on mother's side)*
2 爷爷 yéye [位 wèi] *(on father's side)*

grandma NOUN
1 奶奶 nǎinai [位 wèi] *(on father's side)*
2 外婆 wàipó [位 wèi] *(on mother's side)*

grandmother NOUN
1 外祖母 wàizǔmǔ [位 wèi] *(on mother's side)*
2 祖母 zǔmǔ [位 wèi] *(on father's side)*
grandpa NOUN
1 爷爷 yéye [位 wèi] *(on father's side)*
2 外公 wàigōng [位 wèi] *(on mother's side)*
grandparents PL NOUN
1 祖父母 zǔ fùmǔ [位 wèi] *(on father's side)*
2 外祖父母 wài zǔ fùmǔ [位 wèi] *(on mother's side)*
grandson NOUN
1 孙子 sūnzi [个 gè] *(on father's side)*
2 外孙 wàisūn [个 gè] *(on mother's side)*
granny NOUN
1 奶奶 nǎinai [位 wèi] *(on father's side)*
2 外婆 wàipó [位 wèi] *(on mother's side)*
grant NOUN
拨款 bōkuǎn [笔 bǐ]
□ We got a grant to fund our research. 我们拿到了一笔拨款作为研究经费。Wǒmen nádào le yībǐ bōkuǎn zuòwéi yánjiū jīngfèi.
grape NOUN
葡萄 pútáo [颗 kē]
■ **a bunch of grapes** 一串葡萄 yíchuàn pútáo
grapefruit NOUN
葡萄柚 pútáo yòu [个 gè]
graph NOUN
图表 túbiǎo [幅 fú]
graphics PL NOUN
1 图像 túxiàng [组 zǔ] *(images)*
□ The graphics in this computer game are amazing. 这个电脑游戏的图像太棒了。Zhègè diànnǎo yóuxì de túxiàng tài bàng le.
2 制图学 zhìtúxué *(design)*
□ He is going to study graphics at college. 他将在大学里学习制图学。Tā jiāng zài dàxué lǐ xuéxí zhìtúxué.
to **grasp** VERB
1 抓住 zhuāzhù *(seize)*
□ She grasped both my hands. 她抓住我的两手。Tā zhuāzhù wǒde liǎngshǒu.
2 领悟 lǐngwù *(understand)*
□ I don't think you grasp the seriousness of this situation. 我觉得你还没领悟到这个形势的严峻性。Wǒ juédé nǐ hái méi lǐngwù dào zhègè xíngshì de yánjùnxìng.
grass NOUN
草 cǎo [株 zhū] *(plant)*
■ **the grass** 草坪 cǎopíng □ I'm going out to cut the grass. 我要出去剪草坪。Wǒ yào chūqù jiǎn cǎopíng.
grasshopper NOUN
蝗虫 huángchóng [只 zhī]
to **grate** VERB
磨碎 mósuì
□ Grate some cheese, will you? 你能去磨些干酪吗？Nǐ néng qù móxiē gānlào mā?
grateful ADJECTIVE
感激的 gǎnjī de
■ **to be grateful to somebody for something** 为某事感激某人 wèi mǒushì gǎnjī mǒurén
grave NOUN
坟墓 fénmù [座 zuò]
□ I visit my father's grave every week. 我每周都去我父亲的坟墓。Wǒ měizhōu dōu qù wǒ fùqīn de fénmù.
gravel NOUN
砂砾 shālì [堆 duī]
graveyard NOUN
墓地 mùdì [块 kuài]
gravy NOUN
肉汁 ròuzhī [锅 guō]
gray ADJECTIVE (US)
▷ *see also* **gray** NOUN
1 灰色的 huīsè de
□ a gray dress 一条灰色的裙子 yìtiáo huīsè de qúnzi
2 灰白的 huībái de *(hair)*
3 阴沉的 yīnchén de *(weather, day)*
gray NOUN (US)
▷ *see also* **gray** ADJECTIVE
灰色 huīsè [种 zhǒng]
grease NOUN
油脂 yóuzhī [克 kè]
greasy ADJECTIVE
1 油腻的 yóunì de *(of food)*
2 多油脂的 duō yóuzhīde *(of hair, skin)*
great ADJECTIVE
1 棒极了的 bàngjíle de *(idea)*
□ I've had a great idea. 我有个棒极了的主意。Wǒ yǒu gè bàngjíle de zhǔyì.
2 好极了的 hǎojíle de *(terrific)*
□ He's a great guy. 他是个好极了的人。Tā shì gè hǎojíle de rén.
■ **That's great!** 好极了！Hǎojíle!
■ **We had a great time.** 我们玩得很快活。Wǒmen wánde hěn kuàihuo.
3 巨大的 jùdà de *(large)*
■ **a great mansion** 一栋大厦 yídòng dàshà
4 重大的 zhòngdà de *(considerable)*
□ She's had great success in her career. 她刚在其职业生涯中取得了一个重大的成功。Tā gāng zài qí zhíyè shēngyá zhōng qǔdé le yígè zhòngdà de chénggōng.
Great Britain NOUN
英国 Yīngguó

English-Chinese
g

great-grandfather NOUN
曾祖父 zēng zǔfù
great-grandmother NOUN
曾祖母 zēng zǔmǔ
Greece NOUN
希腊 Xīlà
greedy ADJECTIVE
贪心的 tānxīn de
Greek ADJECTIVE
▷ *see also* **Greek** NOUN
希腊的 Xīlà de
□ a Greek diplomat 一位希腊外交官 yíwèi Xīlà wàijiāoguān
Greek NOUN
▷ *see also* **Greek** ADJECTIVE
1 希腊人 Xīlàrén [个 gè] *(person)*
□ Greeks living in Australia 住在澳大利亚的希腊人 zhù zài Àodàlìyà de Xīlàrén
2 希腊语 Xīlàyǔ *(language)*
□ I don't speak any Greek. 我一点都不会讲希腊语。Wǒ yìdiǎn dōu búhuì jiǎng Xīlàyǔ.
green ADJECTIVE
▷ *see also* **green** NOUN
1 绿色的 lǜsè de
□ a green coat 一件绿色的外套 yíjiàn lǜsè de wàitào
■ **green beans** 绿豆 lǜdòu
2 环保的 huánbǎo de *(environmental)*
□ green policies 环保政策 huánbǎo zhèngcè
green NOUN
▷ *see also* **green** ADJECTIVE
绿色 lǜsè [抹 mǒ]
□ the woman over there in green 那边穿绿色衣服的妇女 nàbiān chuān lǜsè yīfú de fùnǚ
■ **greens** 绿色蔬菜 lǜsè shūcài [种 zhǒng]
□ Eat your greens. 把你的绿色蔬菜吃了。Bǎ nǐde lǜsè shūcài chī le.
■ **the Greens** 绿党 lǜdǎng [个 gè]
greengrocer's NOUN
果蔬店 guǒshūdiàn [家 jiā]
greenhouse NOUN
▷ *see also* **greenhouse** ADJECTIVE
暖房 nuǎnfáng [间 jiān]
greenhouse ADJECTIVE
▷ *see also* **greenhouse** NOUN
温室效应的 wēnshì xiàoyìng de
□ a greenhouse gas 一种会导致温室效应的气体 yìzhǒng huì dǎozhì wēnshì xiàoyìng de qìtǐ
Greenland NOUN
格陵兰岛 Gélínglán dǎo
to **greet** VERB
问候 wènhòu
□ He greeted me with a kiss. 他吻了我一下以示问候。Tā wěn le wǒ yíxià yǐshì wènhòu.
greeting NOUN
问候 wènhòu [次 cì]
■ **Greetings from Bangkok!** 来自曼谷的问候！Láizì Màngǔ de wènhòu!
■ **Season's greetings.** 恭贺圣诞。Gōnghè Shèngdàn.
greetings card NOUN
贺卡 hèkǎ [张 zhāng]
grew VERB ▷ *see* **grow**
grey (US **gray**) ADJECTIVE
▷ *see also* **grey** NOUN
1 灰色的 huīsè de
□ a grey dress 一条灰色的裙子 yìtiáo huīsè de qúnzi
2 灰白的 huībái de *(hair)*
3 阴沉的 yīnchén de *(weather, day)*
grey (US **gray**) NOUN
▷ *see also* **grey** ADJECTIVE
灰色 huīsè [种 zhǒng]
□ the gentleman in grey 穿灰色衣服的先生 chuān huīsè yīfú de xiānsheng
grey-haired ADJECTIVE
灰白头发的 huībái tóufa de
grid NOUN
1 格子 gézi [个 gè] *(on map, on paper)*
2 电网 diànwǎng [个 gè] *(of electricity)*
grief NOUN
悲痛 bēitòng
grill NOUN
▷ *see also* **grill** VERB
烤架 kǎojià [份 fèn]
to **grill** VERB
▷ *see also* **grill** NOUN
烤 kǎo
□ Grill the steaks until they are cooked. 把牛排烤到熟为止。Bǎ niúpái kǎo dào shú wéizhǐ.
grim ADJECTIVE
无吸引力的 wú xīyǐnlì de *(of news)*
□ a grim picture of life in Britain 一张无吸引力的英国生活照 yìzhāng wú xīyǐnlì de Yīngguó shēnghuózhào.
to **grin** VERB
▷ *see also* **grin** NOUN
露齿而笑 lùchǐ ér xiào
LANGUAGE TIP Word for word, this means 'smile with teeth revealed'.
□ Dave grinned at me. 戴夫对着我露齿而笑。Dàifū duìzhe wǒ lùchǐ ér xiào.
grin NOUN
▷ *see also* **grin** VERB
露齿笑 lùchǐxiào [次 cì]
□ I saw the grin on his face. 我看见他露齿

笑了。Wǒ kànjiàn tā lùchǐ xiào le.

to **grind** VERB
磨 mósuì
□ Grind the pepper as you need it. 你需要多少胡椒就磨多少。Nǐ xūyào duōshǎo hújiāo jiù mó duōshǎo.

to **grip** VERB
紧握 jǐnwò
□ She gripped the rope. 她紧握住了绳子。Tā jǐnwò zhù le shéngzi.

gripping ADJECTIVE
吸引人的 xīyǐn rén de
□ a gripping story 一个吸引人的故事 yígè xīyǐn rén de gùshì

grit NOUN
沙粒 shālì [颗 kē]

to **groan** VERB
呻吟 shēnyín

grocer NOUN
食品杂货商 shípǐn záhuòshāng [个 gè] *(person)*

groceries PL NOUN
食品杂货 shípǐn záhuò [袋 dài]

grocer's NOUN
食品杂货店 shípǐn záhuòdiàn [家 jiā] *(shop)*

grocery store NOUN
食品杂货店 shípǐn záhuòdiàn [家 jiā]

groom NOUN
新郎 xīnláng [位 wèi]

to **grope** VERB
■ **to grope for something** 摸索某物 mōsuǒ mǒuwù □ He groped for the light switch. 他摸索着灯的开关。Tā mōsuǒ zhe dēng de kāiguān.

ground VERB ▷ *see* **grind**
■ **ground coffee** 磨碎的咖啡 mósuì de kāfēi

ground NOUN
1 地面 dìmiàn *(floor)*
□ The bottle fell to the ground and smashed. 瓶子掉在地面上，摔碎了。Píngzi diào zài dìmiàn shàng, shuāi suì le.
■ **on the ground** 在地面上 zài dìmiàn shàng □ We sat on the ground. 我们坐在地面上。Wǒmen zuò zài dìmiàn shàng.
2 地 dì [块 kuài] *(earth, soil, land)*
□ The ground was wet so I didn't sit down. 那块地是湿的，所以我没坐下。Nà kuài dì shì shī de, suǒyǐ wǒ méi zuòxià.
3 场 chǎng [个 gè] *(sport stadium)*
4 理由 lǐyóu [个 gè] *(reason)*
□ We have got grounds for complaint. 我们有理由投诉。Wǒmen yǒu lǐyóu tóusù.

ground floor NOUN
一楼 yīlóu

LANGUAGE TIP The ground floor doesn't exist in Chinese. They start counting with **the first floor** 一楼 yīlóu.

■ **on the ground floor** 在一楼 zài yīlóu

group NOUN
1 组 zǔ [个 gè]
2 组合 zǔhé [个 gè] *(of pop musicians)*
■ **in groups** 成组地 chéngzǔ de

to **grow** VERB
1 生长 shēngzhǎng *(of plant, tree)*
□ Grass grows quickly. 草生长得快。Cǎo shēngzhǎng dé kuài.
2 长大 zhǎngdà *(of person, animal)*
□ Haven't you grown! 你长这么大了！Nǐ zhǎng zhème dà le!
■ **to grow a beard** 留胡子 liú húzi
3 扩大 kuòdà *(increase)*
□ The number of unemployed people has grown. 失业人数扩大了。Shīyè rénshù kuòdà le.
■ **to grow by 10%** 增长百分之十 zēngzhǎng bǎi fēn zhī shí
4 栽种 zāizhòng *(cultivate)*
□ I'm growing vegetables in my garden. 我在我的花园里栽种些蔬菜。Wǒ zài wǒde huāyuán lǐ zāizhòng xiē shūcài.

to **grow up** VERB
1 长大 zhǎngdà *(be brought up)*
□ I grew up in India. 我在印度长大。Wǒ zài Yìndù zhǎngdà.
2 成熟 chéngshú *(be mature)*
□ Oh, grow up! 噢，成熟些吧！Ō, chéngshú xiē ba!

to **growl** VERB
咆哮 páoxiào

grown VERB ▷ *see* **grow**

grown-up NOUN
成年人 chéngniánrén [个 gè]

growth NOUN
1 发展 fāzhǎn *(of economy)*
■ **a growth in something** 某方面的发展 mǒu fāngmiàn de fāzhǎn
2 生长 shēngzhǎng *(of child, animal, plant)*

grub NOUN *(informal)*
食物 shíwù

grudge NOUN
怨恨 yuànhèn
■ **to bear a grudge against somebody** 怨恨某人 yuànhèn mǒurén

gruesome ADJECTIVE
令人发指的 lìngrénfāzhǐ de
□ a gruesome crime 一个令人发指的罪行 yígè lìngrénfāzhǐ de zuìxíng

to **grumble** VERB
抱怨 bàoyuàn *(complain)*

□ He's always grumbling about something. 他总是在抱怨着什么。Tā zǒngshì zài bàoyuànzhe shénme.

guarantee NOUN
▷ *see also* **guarantee** VERB
质保承诺 zhìbǎo chéngnuò [个 gè]
□ a five-year guarantee 一个五年的质保承诺 yígè wǔnián de zhìbǎo chéngnuò

to **guarantee** VERB
▷ *see also* **guarantee** NOUN
保证 bǎozhèng
□ I can't guarantee that he'll come. 我不能保证他会来。Wǒ bùnéng bǎozhèng tā huì lái.

guard NOUN
▷ *see also* **guard** VERB
警卫 jǐngwèi [个 gè] *(sentry)*
■ **a guard dog** 一条警卫犬 yìtiáo jǐngwèiquǎn
■ **to be on one's guard (against)** 提防 dīfáng

to **guard** VERB
▷ *see also* **guard** NOUN
1 守卫 shǒuwèi *(building, entrance, door)*
□ They guarded the palace. 他们守卫着这座宫殿。Tāmen shǒuwèizhe zhèzuò gōngdiàn.
2 保护 bǎohù *(person)*
□ Those men are guarding the prime minister. 那些男子正保护着首相。Nàxiē nánzǐ zhèng bǎohùzhe shǒuxiàng.

to **guess** VERB
▷ *see also* **guess** NOUN
猜测 cāicè
■ **to guess wrong** 猜错 cāicuò
■ **I guess so** 我想是吧 wǒxiǎng shìba

guess NOUN
▷ *see also* **guess** VERB
猜测 cāicè [种 zhǒng]
□ It's just a guess. 这仅仅是个猜测。Zhè jǐnjǐn shì gè cāicè.
■ **Have a guess!** 你猜测一下！Nǐ cāicè yixià！

guest NOUN
1 客人 kèrén [位 wèi] *(at home)*
□ We have guests staying with us. 我家有客人。Wǒjiā yǒu kèrén.
2 宾客 bīnkè [位 wèi] *(at special event)*
□ There were 100 guests at the wedding. 有一百名宾客出席了婚礼。Yǒu yìbǎi míng bīnkè chūxí le hūnlǐ.
3 房客 fángkè [位 wèi] *(in hotel)*
□ Guests cannot smoke in their rooms. 客人们不能在房内吸烟。Kèrén men bùnéng zài fángnèi xīyān.

guesthouse NOUN
宾馆 bīnguǎn [家 jiā]

guide NOUN
▷ *see also* **guide** VERB
1 导游 dǎoyóu [位 wèi] *(of tour)*
□ The guide told us the bus was leaving at four. 导游告诉我们巴士四点出发。Dǎoyóu gàosù wǒmen bāshì sìdiǎn chūfā. *(local guide)*
2 向导 xiàngdǎo [位 wèi] *(book)*
3 指南 zhǐnán [本 běn]
□ a guide to Beijing 北京指南 Běijīng zhǐnán

to **guide** VERB
▷ *see also* **guide** NOUN
1 给...导游 gěi...dǎoyóu *(round city, museum)*
2 给...领路 gěi...lǐnglù *(lead)*
□ I guided her to a seat in the shade. 我领着她去了阴凉处的一个座位那儿。Wǒ lǐngzhe tā qù le yīnliángchù de yígè zuòwèi nà'ér.

guidebook NOUN
旅游指南 lǚyóu zhǐnán [本 běn]

guide dog NOUN
导盲犬 dǎomángquǎn [只 zhī]

guided tour NOUN
有导游的游览 yǒu dǎoyóu de yóulǎn [次 cì]

guilty ADJECTIVE
1 内疚的 nèijiù de *(person, feelings)*
□ I feel guilty about lying to him. 我为对他撒了谎而感到内疚。Wǒ wèi duì tā sā le huǎng ér gǎndào nèijiū.
2 自知有过错的 zìzhī yǒu guòcuò de *(secret, conscience)*
3 有过失的 yǒu guòshī de *(responsible)*
■ **to be found guilty** 被发现有罪的 bèi fāxiàn yǒuzuì de
■ **guilty of murder** 谋杀 móushā

guinea pig NOUN
豚鼠 túnshǔ [只 zhī]

guitar NOUN
吉他 jítā [把 bǎ]
□ I play the guitar. 我会弹吉他。Wǒ huì tán jíta.

gum NOUN
1 牙床 yáchuáng [个 gè] *(of mouth)*
2 口香糖 kǒuxiāngtáng [粒 lì] *(chewing gum)*
3 泡泡糖 pàopaotáng [粒 lì] *(bubble gum)*

gun NOUN
1 枪 qiāng [支 zhī] *(small, medium-sized)*
2 炮 pào [架 jià] *(large)*

gust NOUN
一阵 yízhèn
■ **a gust of wind** 一阵风 yízhèn fēng

guy NOUN
家伙 jiāhuo [个 gè] *(man)*
□ He's a nice guy. 他是个好人。Tā shì gè

hǎorén. □ Who's that guy? 那个家伙是谁？Nàgè jiāhuǒ shì shéi？

■ **(you) guys** 伙计们 huǒjìmen

gym NOUN

1 健身房 jiànshēnfáng [个 gè]

□ I go to the gym every day. 我每天都去健身房。Wǒ měitiān dōu qù jiànshēnfáng.

2 体操课 tǐcāo kè [节 jié] *(class)*

□ Mary missed gym because she was sick. 玛丽错过了体操课，因为她病了。Mǎlì cuòguò le tǐcāokè, yīnwèi tā bìng le.

gymnast NOUN

体操运动员 tǐcāo yùndòngyuán [位 wèi]

□ Chinese gymnasts 中国体操运动员 Zhōngguó tǐcāo yùndòngyuán

gymnastics NOUN

体操 tǐcāo

□ My daughter would like to do gymnastics. 我的女儿想练体操。Wǒde nǚ'ér xiǎng liàn tǐcāo.

gypsy NOUN

吉卜赛人 Jípǔsàirén [个 gè]

Hh

habit NOUN
习惯 xíguàn [个 gè]
■ **to be in the habit of doing something** 有做某事的习惯 yǒu zuò mǒushì de xíguàn
■ **a bad habit** 坏习惯 huài xíguàn

hacker NOUN
黑客 hēikè *(into computer)*

had VERB ▷ *see* **have**

haddock NOUN
鳕鱼 xuěyú [条 tiáo]

hadn't = **had not**

hail NOUN
▷ *see also* **hail** VERB
冰雹 bīngbáo [场 chǎng]

to **hail** VERB
▷ *see also* **hail** NOUN
下雹 xiàbáo
□ It's hailing. 正在下雹。Zhèngzài xiàbáo.

hair NOUN
1 头发 tóufa
□ She's got long hair. 她有一头长发。Tā yǒu yìtóu chángfà. □ He's losing his hair. 他正在掉头发。Tā zhèngzài diào tóufa.
■ **to get one's hair cut** 剪头发 jiǎn tóufa
□ I've just had my hair cut. 我刚刚剪了头发。Wǒ gānggāng jiǎnle tóufa.
■ **to wash one's hair** 洗头发 xǐ tóufa □ I need to wash my hair. 我得洗头发。Wǒ děi xǐ tóufa.
2 毛发 máofà [根 gēn] *(single strand)*
3 皮毛 pímáo *(fur of animal)*

hairbrush NOUN
发刷 fàshuā [把 bǎ]

haircut NOUN
1 理发 lǐfà [次 cì]
2 发型 fàxíng [种 zhǒng] *(hairstyle)*
■ **to have a haircut** 剪头发 jiǎn tóufa
□ I've just had a haircut. 我刚刚剪了头发。Wǒ gānggāng jiǎnle tóufa.

hairdresser NOUN
美发师 měifàshī [位 wèi]
■ **hairdresser's** 发廊 fàláng [个 gè]

hairdryer NOUN
吹风机 chuīfēngjī [个 gè]

hair gel NOUN
发胶 fàjiāo [瓶 píng]

hairspray NOUN
喷发定型剂 pēnfà dìngxíngjì [瓶 píng]

hairstyle NOUN
发型 fàxíng [种 zhǒng]

hairy ADJECTIVE
多毛的 duōmáo de
□ He's got hairy legs. 他的腿很多毛。Tāde tuǐ hěn duōmáo.

half NOUN, PRONOUN
▷ *see also* **half** ADJECTIVE, ADVERB
1 一半 yíbàn
□ half of the cake 一半蛋糕 yíbàn dàngāo
■ **two and a half** 二点五 èr diǎn wǔ
■ **a day and a half** 一天半 yìtiān bàn
■ **half an hour** 半个小时 bàngè xiǎoshí
■ **half past ten** 十点半 shídiǎn bàn
■ **half a kilo** 半公斤 bàn gōngjīn
■ **to cut something in half** 把某物切成两半 bǎ mǒuwù qiē chéng liǎngbàn
2 半票 bànpiào [张 zhāng] *(child's ticket)*
□ A half to York, please. 一张去约克的半票。Yìzhāng qù Yuēkè de bànpiào.

half ADJECTIVE
▷ *see also* **half** NOUN, PRONOUN, ADVERB
一半的 yíbàn de *(bottle)*
■ **a half chicken** 半只鸡 bàn zhī jī

half ADVERB
▷ *see also* **half** NOUN, PRONOUN, ADJECTIVE
半 bàn *(empty, closed, open, asleep)*
□ He was half asleep. 他半醒半睡着。Tā bànxǐng bànshuì zhe.

half-brother NOUN
1 同母异父兄弟 tóngmǔ yìfù xiōngdì [个 gè] *(on the mother's side)*
2 同父异母兄弟 tóngfù yìmǔ xiōngdì [个 gè] *(on the father's side)*

half-hour NOUN
半小时 bàn xiǎoshí [个 gè]

half-price ADJECTIVE, ADVERB
半价的 bànjià de

half-sister NOUN
1 同母异父姐妹 tóngmǔ yìfù jiěmèi [个 gè] *(on mother's side)*

2 同父异母姐妹 tóngfù yìmǔ jiěmèi [个 gè] *(on father's side)*

half-term NOUN
期中假 qīzhōng jià [段 duàn]*(school holiday)*
□ at half-term 期中假时 qīzhōng jià shí

half-time NOUN
半场 bànchǎng*(in sport)*
□ at half-time 半场时 bànchǎng shí

halfway ADVERB
在途中 zài túzhōng*(between two points)*
□ halfway between Oxford and London 在牛津和伦敦途中 zài Niújīn hé Lúndūn túzhōng
■ **halfway through something** 在某事的中间 zài mǒushì de zhōngjiān □ halfway through the chapter 在这个章节的中间 zài zhègè zhāngjié de zhōngjiān

hall NOUN
1 门厅 méntīng [个 gè]*(entrance)*
2 礼堂 lǐtáng [个 gè]*(room)*

Hallowe'en NOUN
万圣节前夕 Wànshèngjié qiánxī

hallway NOUN
玄关 xuánguān [个 gè]

ham NOUN
火腿 huǒtuǐ
□ a ham sandwich 一个火腿三明治 yígè huǒtuǐ sānmíngzhì

hamburger NOUN
汉堡包 hànbǎobāo [个 gè]

hammer NOUN
锤子 chuízi [把 bǎ]

hamster NOUN
仓鼠 cāngshǔ [只 zhī]

hand NOUN
▷ *see also* **hand** VERB
1 手 shǒu [双 shuāng]
■ **to give somebody a hand** 帮某人 bāng mǒurén □ Can you give me a hand? 你能帮我吗？Nǐ néng bāng wǒ ma？
■ **to do something by hand** 手工制作某物 shǒugōng zhìzuò mǒwù
■ **on the one hand..., on the other hand...** 一方面…，另一方面… yìfāngmiàn..., lìng yìfāngmiàn...
2 指针 zhǐzhēn [个 gè]*(of clock)*

to **hand** VERB
▷ *see also* **hand** NOUN
递 dì
□ He handed me the book. 他递给我书。Tā dì gěi wǒ shū.

to **hand in** VERB
上交 shàngjiāo
□ He handed his exam paper in. 他上交了试卷。Tā shàngjiāo le shìjuàn.

to **hand out** VERB
分发 fēnpèi
□ The teacher handed out the books. 老师分发了书。Lǎoshī fēnfā le shū.

to **hand over** VERB
交给 jiāogěi
□ She handed the keys over to me. 她把钥匙交给了我。Tā bǎ yàoshi jiāogěi le wǒ.

handbag NOUN
手包 shǒubāo [个 gè]

handball NOUN
手球 shǒuqiú*(game)*
■ **to play handball** 打手球 dǎ shǒuqiú

handbook NOUN
手册 shǒucè [本 běn]

handcuffs PL NOUN
手铐 shǒukào [副 fù]
■ **in handcuffs** 带手铐 dài shǒukào

handkerchief NOUN
手帕 shǒupà [条 tiáo]

handle NOUN
▷ *see also* **handle** VERB
1 拉手 lāshǒu [个 gè]*(of door, window)*
2 把手 bǎshǒu [个 gè]*(of bag)*
3 柄 bǐng [个 gè]*(of cup, knife, paintbrush, broom, spade)*

to **handle** VERB
▷ *see also* **handle** NOUN
处理 chǔlǐ*(problem, job, responsibility)*
■ **He handled it well.** 他处理得很好。Tā chǔlǐ dé hěnhǎo. □ Kath handled the travel arrangements. 凯西处理了行程安排。Kǎixī chǔlǐ le xíngchéng ānpái. □ She's good at handling children. 她照顾孩子很拿手。Tā zhàogù háizi hěn náshǒu.

handlebars PL NOUN
把手 bǎshǒu

handmade ADJECTIVE
手工制作的 shǒugōng zhìzuò de

hands-free kit NOUN
免提设备 miǎntí shèbèi [个 gè]*(on phone)*

handsome ADJECTIVE
英俊的 yīngjùn de
□ He's handsome. 他很英俊。Tā hěn yīngjùn.

handwriting NOUN
笔迹 bǐjì [种 zhǒng]

handy ADJECTIVE
1 方便的 fāngbiàn de*(useful)*
□ This knife's very handy. 这把刀很方便。Zhè bǎ dāo hěn fāngbiàn.
2 手边的 shǒubiān de*(close at hand)*
□ Have you got a pen handy? 你手边有笔吗？Nǐ shǒubiān yǒu bǐ mā？

to **hang** VERB
1 挂 guà

□ Mike hung the painting on the wall. 迈克把画挂在了墙上。Màikè bǎ huà guà zài le qiángshàng.

2 挂起 guàqǐ *(coat, hat, clothes)*

3 吊起 xuánguà

□ They hanged the criminal. 他们吊起了罪犯。Tāmen diàoqǐ le zuìfàn.

to **hang around** VERB

闲逛 xiánguàng *(informal)*

□ On Saturdays we hang around in the park. 我们经常在星期六去公园闲逛。Wǒmen jīngcháng zài xīngqīliù qù gōngyuán xiánguàng.

to **hang on** VERB

稍等 shāoděng *(wait)*

□ Hang on a minute please. 请稍等一会儿。Qǐng shāoděng yíhuìr.

to **hang up** VERB

1 挂断电话 guàduàn diànhuà *(phone)*

□ Don't hang up! 请不要挂断电话！Qǐng búyào guàduàn diànhuà!

■ **to hang up on someone** 挂断某人的电话 guàduàn mǒurénde diànhuà □ He always hangs up on me. 他经常挂断我的电话。Tā jīngcháng guàduàn wǒde diànhuà.

2 把…挂起 bǎ ...guàqǐ

□ Hang your jacket up on the hook. 把你的夹克挂在挂钩上。Bǎ nǐde jiákè guà zài guàgōu shàng.

hanger NOUN

■ **coat hanger** 衣架 yījià [个 gè]

hangover NOUN

宿醉 sùzuì [次 cì]

□ I've got a terrible hangover. 我刚经历了一次严重的宿醉。Wǒ gāng jīnglì le yícì yánzhòng de sùzuì.

to **happen** VERB

发生 fāshēng

□ Tell me what happened. 告诉我发生了什么事。Gàosù wǒ fāshēng le shénme shì.

□ What's happened? 发生了什么事？Fāshēng le shénme shì?

■ **What will happen if...?** 如果…会怎么样？Rúguǒ...huì zěnmeyàng?

happily ADVERB

高兴地 gāoxìng de

□ 'Don't worry!' he said happily. "不要担心！"他高兴地说。"Búyào dānxīn!" tā gāoxìng de shuō.

happiness NOUN

幸福 xìngfú

happy ADJECTIVE

1 高兴的 gāoxìng de

□ Eve looks happy. 伊娃看起来很高兴。Yīwá kànqǐlái hěn gāoxìng.

2 美满的 měimǎn de *(life, childhood, marriage, place)*

■ **to be happy with something** *(satisfied)* 对某事满意 duì mǒushì mǎnyì

□ I'm very happy with your work. 我对你的工作很满意。Wǒ duì nǐde gōngzuò hěn mǎnyì.

■ **to be happy to do something** *(willing)* 乐意做某事 lèyì zuò mǒushì

■ **Happy birthday!** 生日快乐！Shēngrì kuàilè!

■ **Happy Christmas!** 圣诞快乐！Shèngdàn kuàilè!

harassment NOUN

骚扰 sāorǎo

harbour (US **harbor**) NOUN

港口 gǎngkǒu [个 gè]

hard ADJECTIVE

▷ *see also* **hard** ADVERB

1 硬的 yìng de *(surface, object)*

□ This cheese is very hard. 这块乳酪很硬。Zhè kuài rǔlào hěn yìng.

2 困难的 kùnnan de *(question, problem)*

□ This question's too hard for me. 这个问题对我来说很困难。Zhègè wèntí duì wǒ láishuō hěn kùnnan.

3 费力的 fèilì de *(work)*

□ It's hard work serving in a shop. 在商店工作很费力。Zài shāngdiàn gōngzuò hěn fèilì.

4 用力的 yònglì de *(push, punch, kick)*

hard ADVERB

▷ *see also* **hard** ADJECTIVE

1 努力地 nǔlì de *(work, try, think)*

□ He's worked very hard. 他工作很努力。Tā gōngzuò hěn nǔlì.

2 用力地 yònglì de *(hit, punch, kick)*

■ **It's hard to tell.** 很难讲。Hěnnán jiǎng.

■ **Such events are hard to understand.** 这种事很难理解。Zhèzhǒng shì hěnnán lǐjiě.

hard disk NOUN

硬盘 yìngpán [个 gè]

hardly ADVERB

几乎不 jīhū bù *(scarcely)*

□ I've hardly got any money. 我几乎没有钱。Wǒ jīhū méiyǒu qián. □ I hardly know you. 我几乎不认识你。Wǒ jīhū bú rènshi nǐ.

■ **He had hardly sat down when the door burst open.** 他几乎还没坐下门就被猛地打开了。Tā jīhū hái méi zuòxià mén jiù bèi měng de dǎkāi le.

■ **hardly anyone** 几乎没有任何人 jīhū méiyǒu rènhé rén

■ **hardly ever** 几乎从不 jīhū cóngbù

■ **I can hardly believe it.** 我简直不能相信。Wǒ jiǎnzhí bùnéng xiāngxìn.

hardware NOUN
硬件 yìngjiàn *(computing)*

hardworking ADJECTIVE
勤奋的 qínfèn de

hare NOUN
野兔 yětù [只 zhī]

to **harm** VERB
1 伤害 shānghài *(injure)*
□ I didn't mean to harm you. 我并非有意伤害你。Wǒ bìngfēi yǒuyì shānghài nǐ.
2 损坏 sǔnhuài *(damage)*
□ Chemicals harm the environment. 化学制品损坏环境。Huàxué zhìpǐn sǔnhuài huánjìng.

harmful ADJECTIVE
有害的 yǒuhài de
□ harmful chemicals 有害化学物质 yǒuhài huàxué wùzhì

harmless ADJECTIVE
无害的 wúhài de

harp NOUN
竖琴 shùqín [架 jià]

harvest NOUN
1 收获 shōuhuò [种 zhǒng] *(harvest time)*
2 收成 shōucheng [个 gè] *(crop)*

has VERB ▷ *see* **have**

hashtag NOUN
主题标签 zhǔtí biāoqiān

hasn't = **has not**

hat NOUN
帽子 màozi [顶 dǐng]

to **hate** VERB
1 恨 hèn *(person)*
2 讨厌 tǎoyàn *(food, activity, sensation)*
□ I hate maths. 我讨厌数学。Wǒ tǎoyàn shùxué.
■ **to hate doing something** 不喜欢做某事 bù xǐhuan zuò mǒushì

hatred NOUN
仇恨 chóuhèn [份 fèn]

haunted ADJECTIVE
闹鬼的 nàoguǐ de
□ a haunted house 一栋闹鬼的房子 yídòng nàoguǐ de fángzi

to **have** VERB
1 有 yǒu
□ Have you got a sister? 你有姐妹吗？Nǐ yǒu jiěmèi ma？ □ Do you have a car? 你有车吗？ Nǐ yǒu chē ma？ □ I've got a cold. 我患有了感冒。Wǒ huànyǒu le gǎnmào.
■ **to have something to do** 有必须得做的事 yǒu bìxū děi zuò de shì
■ **to have to do something** *(be obliged)* 不得不做某事 bùdébù zuò mǒushì □ She's got to do it. 她不得不这么做。Tā bùdébù zhème zuò.
2 长着 zhǎngzhe *(features)*
■ **He's got blue eyes.** 他长着蓝眼睛。Tā zhǎngzhe lán yǎnjīng.
■ **He's got dark hair.** 他长着黑头发。Tā zhǎngzhe hēi tóufa.
■ **She had her eyes closed.** 她闭上了眼睛。Tā bìshàng le yǎnjīng.
■ **to have breakfast** 吃早饭 chī zǎofàn
■ **to have a drink** 喝一杯 hē yìbēi
■ **to have a bath** 洗澡 xǐzǎo
■ **to have a swim** 游泳 yóuyǒng
■ **to have a meeting** 开会 kāihuì
■ **to have a party** 开派对 kāi pàiduì
3 得到 dédào *(receive, obtain)*
□ You can have it for £5. 付五英磅你就能得到它了。Fù wǔ yīngbàng nǐ jiù néng dédào tā le.
■ **Can I have your address?** 能告诉我你的地址吗？Néng gàosù wǒ nǐde dìzhǐ ma?
■ **to have a baby** 生孩子 shēng háizi
■ **to have one's hair cut** 理发 lǐfà
■ **to have a headache** 头痛 tóutòng
■ **to have an operation** 动手术 dòng shǒushù
4 已经 yǐjīng

LANGUAGE TIP 已经 yǐjīng can be used to indicate past tense in Chinese, but it is usually accompanied by past tense particles such as 了 le or 过 guò.

□ Has he told you? 他已经告诉你了吗？Tā yǐjīng gàosù nǐ le mā? □ I haven't seen him for ages. 我已经很久没见过他了。Wǒ yǐjīng hěnjiǔ méi jiànguò tā le. □ I've finished the task. 我已经完成了任务。Wǒ yǐjīng wánchéng le rènwù.
■ **You've done it, haven't you?** 你已经做了，是不是？Nǐ yǐjīng zuò le, shì búshì?
■ **to have arrived** 已到了 yǐ dàole

LANGUAGE TIP In tag questions, **have** is translated by 是不是 shìbúshì.

□ You've done it, haven't you? 你已经做了，是不是？Nǐ yǐjīng zuò le, shì búshì?

LANGUAGE TIP In short answers and questions, **have** is usually not translated.

□ Yes, I have. 是的，我已做了。Shìde, wǒ yǐzuò le. □ No I haven't! 不，我还没做呢！Bù, wǒ hái méizuò ne! □ So have I! 我也一样！Wǒ yě yíyàng! □ neither have I 我也没有 wǒ yě méiyǒu □ I've finished, have you? 我已经完成了，你呢？Wǒ yǐjīng wánchéng le, nǐne?

to **have on** VERB
穿着 chuānzhe *(clothes)*
□ He didn't have anything on. 他什么都没穿。Tā shénme dōu méi chuān.

haven't = **have not**

hay NOUN
干草 gāncǎo

hay fever NOUN
花粉病 huāfěnbìng
□ Do you get hay fever? 你有花粉病么？Nǐ yǒu huāfěnbìng me?

hazel ADJECTIVE
淡褐色的 dàn hèsè de *(eyes)*

hazelnut NOUN
榛实 zhēnshí [个 gè]

he PRONOUN
他 tā
□ He loves dogs. 他喜爱狗。Tā xǐ'ài gǒu.

head NOUN
▷ *see also* **head** VERB
1 头 tóu [个 gè]
□ The wine went to my head. 我喝酒上头了。Wǒ héjiǔ shàngtóu le.
■ **from head to toe** 从头到脚 cóng tóu dào jiǎo
■ **10 pounds per head** 每人十英镑 měirén shí yīngbàng
■ **to have a head for figures** 有数学头脑 yǒu shùxué tóunǎo
■ **Heads or tails? — Heads.** 正面还是反面？— 正面。Zhèngmiàn háishi fǎnmiàn? — Zhèngmiàn.
2 领导人 lǐngdǎorén [位 wèi] *(of company, organization, department)*
□ a head of state 一位国家领导人 yíwèi guójiā lǐngdǎorén
3 校长 xiàozhǎng [位 wèi] *(head teacher)*

to **head** VERB
▷ *see also* **head** NOUN
1 以…打头 yǐ...dǎtóu *(list, group)*
2 用头顶 yòng tóu dǐng *(football)*
■ **to head for somewhere** 前往某地 qiánwǎng mǒudì □ They headed for the church. 他们前往教堂了。Tāmen qiánwǎng jiàotáng le.

headache NOUN
头痛 tóutòng [阵 zhèn]
□ I've got a headache. 我头痛。Wǒ tóutòng.

headlight NOUN
前灯 qiándēng [个 gè]

headline NOUN
新闻标题 xīnwén biāotí [个 gè]
■ **the headlines** 1 *(in newspaper)* 头条新闻 tóutiáo xīnwén 2 *(on television, radio)* 新闻内容提要 nèiróng tíyào

headmaster NOUN
校长 xiàozhǎng [位 wèi]

headmistress NOUN
女校长 nǚ xiàozhǎng [位 wèi]

head office NOUN
总部 zǒngbù [个 gè] *(of company)*

headphones PL NOUN
耳机 ěrjī [副 fù]

headquarters PL NOUN
总部 zǒngbù

headteacher NOUN
校长 xiàozhǎng [位 wèi]

to **heal** VERB
痊愈 quányù
□ The wound soon healed. 伤口很快就痊愈了。Shāngkǒu hěnkuài jiù quányù le.

health NOUN
健康 jiànkāng
■ **to be bad for one's health** 对某人的健康不利 duì mǒurén de jiànkāng búlì
■ **to drink to somebody's health** 举杯祝某人健康 jǔbēi zhù mǒurén jiànkāng

healthy ADJECTIVE
1 健康的 jiànkāng de
□ Duncan's a healthy person. 邓肯是个健康的人。Dèngkěn shì gè jiànkāngde rén.
2 有益健康的 duì yǒuyì jiànkāng de *(diet, lifestyle)*
□ a healthy diet 一种有益健康的饮食 yìzhǒng yǒuyì jiànkāng de yǐnshí

heap NOUN
堆 duī [个 gè]

to **hear** VERB
1 听见 tīngjiàn
□ He heard the dog bark. 他听见了狗叫。Tā tīngjiàn le gǒujiào. □ She can't hear very well. 她听不太清楚。Tā tīng bú tài qīngchǔ.
■ **to hear somebody doing something** 听见某人做某事 tīngjiàn mǒurén zuò mǒushì
2 听 tīng *(news, lecture, concert)*
□ Did you hear the good news? 你听到好消息了吗？Nǐ tīngdào hǎo xiāoxi le ma?
■ **to hear that...** 听说… tīngshuō... □ I heard that she was ill. 我听说她病了。Wǒ tīngshuō tā bìng le.
■ **to hear about something** 听说某事 tīngshuō mǒushì
■ **I've never heard of him.** 我从来没听说过他。Wǒ cónglái méi tīngshuō guò tā.
■ **to hear from somebody** 得到某人的消息 dédào mǒurén de xiāoxi □ I haven't heard from him recently. 我最近都没有得到他的消息。Wǒ zuìjìn dōu méiyǒu dédào tāde xiāoxi.

heart NOUN
1 心脏 xīnzàng [颗 kē]
□ My heart's beating very fast. 我的心跳得很厉害。Wǒde xīn tiàode hěn lìhài.
2 感情 gǎnqíng [种 zhǒng] *(emotions)*
3 心形物 xīnxíng wù [个 gè] *(shape)*
■ **the ace of hearts** 红心A hóngxīn A
■ **to learn something by heart** 牢记某事 láojì mǒushì
■ **to break somebody's heart** 使某人伤心 shǐ mǒurén shāngxīn

heart attack NOUN
心脏病发作 xīnzàngbìng fāzuò [阵 zhèn]
■ **to have a heart attack** 心脏病发作 xīnzàngbìng fāzuò

heartbroken ADJECTIVE
极其伤心的 jíqí shāngxīn de
■ **to be heartbroken** 伤心至极 shāngxīnzhìjí

heat NOUN
▷ *see also* **heat** VERB
1 热度 rèdù *(temperature)*
□ I find the heat unbearable. 我实在受不了这种热度。Wǒ shízài shòubùliǎo zhèzhǒng rèdù.
2 激动的情绪 jīdòng de qíngxù *(intense feeling)*
■ **in the heat of the argument** 在争论的激动情绪中 zài zhēnglùn de jīdòng qíngxù zhōng
■ **a qualifying heat** *(sport)* 预赛 yùsài [场 chǎng]

to **heat** VERB
▷ *see also* **heat** NOUN
1 加热 jiārè *(water, food)*
□ Heat gently for 5 minutes. 小火加热五分钟。Xiǎohuǒ jiārè wǔ fēnzhōng.
2 取暖 qǔnuǎn *(room, house)*

to **heat up** VERB
1 加热 jiārè *(food)*
□ He heated the soup up. 他把汤加热了。Tā bǎ tāng jiārè le.
2 变热 biàn rè *(water, oven)*
□ The water is heating up. 水在变热。Shuǐ zài biàn rè.

heater NOUN
1 供暖装置 gōngnuǎn zhuāngzhì [个 gè] *(electric, gas heater)*
2 暖气设备 nuǎnqì shèbèi [套 tào] *(in car)*

heating NOUN
暖气 nuǎnqì *(system)*

heatwave NOUN
酷暑时期 kùshǔ shíqī [段 duàn]

heaven NOUN
天堂 tiāntáng

heavily ADVERB
1 重地 zhòng de
□ The car was heavily loaded. 这辆车装载得很重。Zhé liàng chē zhuāngzài de hěn zhòng.
2 过度地 guòdù de
■ **He drinks heavily.** 他过度地饮酒。Tā guòdù de yǐnjiǔ.

heavy ADJECTIVE
1 重的 zhòng de *(weight, fine, sentence)*
□ This bag's very heavy. 这个包很重。Zhègè bāo hěn zhòng. □ How heavy are you? 你多重？Nǐ duōzhòng?
2 拥挤的 yōngjǐ de *(traffic)*
3 繁忙的 fánmáng de *(busy)*
□ I've got a very heavy week ahead. 非常繁忙的一周正等着我。Fēicháng fánmáng de yìzhōu zhèng děngzhe wǒ.
4 过度的 guòdù de *(drinking, smoking, gambling)*
5 大的 dà de *(rain, snow)*
■ **heavy rain** 大雨 dàyǔ

he'd = **he would, he had**

hedge NOUN
树篱 shùlí [道 dào]

hedgehog NOUN
刺猬 cìwèi [只 zhī]

heel NOUN
1 脚后跟 jiǎohòugēn [个 gè] *(of foot)*
2 鞋跟 xiégēn [个 gè] *(of shoe)*

height NOUN
1 高度 gāodù [个 gè]
■ **of average height** 平均高度的 píngjūn gāodù de
2 高处 gāochù *(altitude)*

heir NOUN
继承人 jìchéngrén [位 wèi]

heiress NOUN
女继承人 nǚ jìchéngrén [位 wèi]

held VERB ▷ *see* **hold**

helicopter NOUN
直升飞机 zhíshēng fēijī [架 jià]

hell NOUN
▷ *see also* **hell** EXCLAMATION
地狱 dìyù

hell EXCLAMATION
▷ *see also* **hell** NOUN
天啊 tiān a *(informal)*
■ **It was hell.** 糟糕极了。Zāogāo jíle.

he'll = **he will, he shall**

hello EXCLAMATION
1 你好 nǐhǎo *(as greeting)*
2 喂 wèi *(on the telephone)*
3 劳驾 láojià *(to attract attention)*

helmet NOUN
1 头盔 tóukuī [个 gè]
2 钢盔 gāngkuī [个 gè] *(of soldier, policeman, fireman)*

English-Chinese

h

help NOUN
▷ *see also* **help** VERB
帮助 bāngzhù
□ Do you need any help? 你需要帮助吗？ Nǐ xūyào bāngzhù mā? □ Thanks, you've been a great help. 谢谢，你帮了很大忙。 Xièxie, nǐ bāngle hěndà máng.

to **help** VERB
▷ *see also* **help** VERB
1 帮助 bāngzhù *(person)*
□ I helped him fix his car. 我帮助他修了他的车。Wǒ bāngzhù tā xiūle tāde chē.
□ Can you help me? 你能帮助我吗？ Nǐ néng bāngzhù wǒ mā?
■ **Can I help you?** *(in shop)* 我能为您效劳吗？ Wǒ néng wèi nín xiàoláo mā?
■ **Help yourself!** 请自便！ Qǐng zìbiàn!
2 帮忙 bāngmáng *(assist)*
3 有用 yǒuyòng *(be useful)*
■ **Help!** 救命！ Jiùmìng!
■ **He can't help it.** 他情不自禁。Tā qíngbùzìjīn.
■ **I can't help feeling sorry for him.** 我情不自禁地同情他。Wǒ qíngbùzìjīn de tóngqíng tā.
■ **It can't be helped.** 没办法。Méi bànfǎ.

helpful ADJECTIVE
1 有帮助的 yǒubāngzhù de
□ He was very helpful. 他非常有帮助。 Tā fēicháng yǒu bāngzhù.
2 有建设性的 yǒu jiànshèxìng de *(advice, suggestion)*

helping NOUN
一份 yífèn *(of food)*

helpless ADJECTIVE
无依无靠的 wúyīwúkào de

hen NOUN
母鸡 mǔjī [只 zhī]

her PRONOUN
▷ *see also* **her** ADJECTIVE
她 tā
□ I haven't seen her. 我还没见到她。Wǒ hái méi jiàndào tā. □ They gave her the job. 他们给了她那份工作。Tāmen gěile tā nàfèn gōngzuò. □ Look at her! 看着她！ Kànzhe tā!

her ADJECTIVE
▷ *see also* **her** PRONOUN
她的 tā de
□ Her face was very red. 她的脸很红。 Tāde liǎn hěnhóng. □ her father 她的父亲 tāde fùqīn □ her mother 她的母亲 tāde mǔqīn

herb NOUN
草本植物 cǎoběn zhíwù [株 zhū]
■ **herbs** 香料 xiāngliào □ What herbs do you use in this sauce? 你在酱汁里放了什么香料？ Nǐ zài jiàngzhī lǐ fàngle shénme xiāngliào?

herd NOUN
牧群 mùqún [群 qún]

here ADVERB
1 在这里 zài zhèlǐ *(in or to this place)*
□ I live here. 我住在这里。Wǒ zhù zài zhèlǐ.
2 到这里 dào zhèlǐ *(near me)*
■ **Here's my phone number.** 这是我的电话号码。Zhèshì wǒde diànhuà hàomǎ.
■ **here is ...** 这是… zhèshì ... □ Here's Helen. 这是海伦。Zhèshì Hǎilún.
■ **Here he is!** 他到了！ Tā dào le!
■ **Here you are.** *(take this)* 给你。Gěi nǐ.
■ **here and there** 到处 dàochù

hero NOUN
1 男主人公 nán zhǔréngōng [个 gè] *(in novels)*
2 英雄 yīngxióng [位 wèi] *(of battle, struggle)*
□ He's a real hero! 他是个真正的英雄！ Tā shì gè zhēnzhèng de yīngxióng!

heroin NOUN
海洛因 hǎiluòyīn
■ **a heroin addict** 一个海洛因瘾君子 yígè hǎiluòyīn yǐnjūnzǐ

heroine NOUN
1 女主人公 nǚ zhǔréngōng [个 gè]
□ the heroine of the novel 小说的女主人公 xiǎoshuō de nǚ zhǔréngōng
2 女英雄 nǚ yīngxióng [位 wèi] *(of battle, struggle)*

hers PRONOUN
她的 tā de
□ This is hers. 这是她的。Zhèshì tāde. □ a friend of hers 她的一个朋友 tāde yígè péngyou □ my parents and hers 我的父母和她的父母 wǒde fùmǔ hé tāde fùmǔ □ Is this her coat? — No, hers is black. 这是她的外套吗？ — 不，她的是黑色的。Zhè shì tāde wàitào mā? — Bù, tāde shì hēisè de.

herself PRONOUN
1 她自己 tā zìjǐ
□ She made the dress herself. 她自己做的这件连衣裙。Tā zìjǐ zuòde zhèjiàn liányīqún. □ She hurt herself. 她伤了自己。Tā shāngle zìjǐ. □ She lives by herself. 她自己一人住。Tā zìjǐ yìrén zhù.
2 她本人 tā běnrén *(emphatic)*

he's = **he is, he has**

to **hesitate** VERB
犹豫 yóuyù
□ He did not hesitate to take action. 他毫不犹豫地采取了行动。Tā háobùyóuyù de cǎiqǔ le xíngdòng. □ Don't hesitate to contact me. 请务必和我联系。Qǐng wùbì

héwǒ liánxì.

heterosexual NOUN
▷ *see also* **heterosexual** ADJECTIVE
异性恋者 yìxìngliànzhě [个 gè]

heterosexual ADJECTIVE
▷ *see also* **heterosexual** NOUN
异性恋的 yìxìngliàn de

hi EXCLAMATION
1 嗨 hāi *(as greeting)*
2 你好 nǐhǎo *(in email)*

hiccups PL NOUN
■ **to have hiccups** 打嗝 dǎgé

hidden VERB ▷ *see* **hide**

to **hide** VERB
1 躲藏 duǒcáng *(person, something)*
□ He hid behind a bush. 他躲藏在灌木丛后了。Tā duǒcáng zài guànmùcóng hòu le. □ The dog hid under the table. 小狗躲藏在了桌下。Xiǎogǒu duǒcàng zài le zhuōxià.
■ **to hide from somebody** 躲着某人 duǒzhe mǒurén
2 藏 cáng
□ Paula hid the present. 波拉藏了礼物。Bōlā cángle lǐwù.
3 隐瞒 yǐnmán *(feeling, information)*

hide-and-seek NOUN
■ **to play hide-and-seek** 玩捉迷藏 wán zhuōmícáng

hideous ADJECTIVE
可怕的 kěpà de

hi-fi NOUN
高保真音响设备 gāobǎozhēn yīnxiǎng shèbèi [套 tào]

high ADJECTIVE
▷ *see also* **high** ADVERB
高的 gāo de
□ It's too high. 太高了。Tài gāo le.
■ **How high is the wall?** 这墙高多少？ Zhè qiáng gāo duōshǎo?
■ **The wall's 2 metres high.** 这墙有两米高。Zhè qiáng yǒu liǎngmǐ gāo. □ Safety has always been our highest priority. 安全一直是我们高度重视的问题。Ānquán yìzhí shì wǒmen gāodù zhòngshì de wèntí. □ a high price 高价 gāojià □ a high temperature 高温 gāowēn
■ **at high speed** 高速 gāosù □ It's very high in fat. 脂肪含量很高。zhǐfáng hánliàng hěn gāo
■ **She's got a very high voice.** 她的嗓音很高。Tāde sǎngyīn hěn gāo.
■ **to be high** *(on drugs: informal)* 亢奋的 kàngfèn de

high ADVERB
▷ *see also* **high** ADJECTIVE
1 高高地 gāogāo de *(reach, throw)*
2 高 gāo *(fly, climb)*
□ It is 20 m high. 有二十米高。Yǒu èrshímǐ gāo.
■ **high up** 离地面高的 lí dìmiàn gāo de

higher education NOUN
高等教育 gāoděng jiàoyù

to **highlight** VERB
1 勾画 gōuhuà *(underline)*
2 使醒目 shǐ xǐngmù *(with highlighter pen)*

highlighter NOUN
记号笔 jìhàobǐ [支 zhī]

high-rise ADJECTIVE
▷ *see also* **high-rise** NOUN
高层的 gāocéng de

high-rise NOUN
▷ *see also* **high-rise** ADJECTIVE
高楼 gāolóu [栋 dòng]
□ I live in a high-rise. 我住在一栋高楼里。Wǒ zhùzài yídòng gāolóu lǐ.

high school NOUN
中学 zhōngxué [所 suǒ]

> **DID YOU KNOW...?**
> Chinese high school is divided into two different periods of study, both lasting three years - 初中 chūzhōng **junior high school** and 高中 gāozhōng **senior high school**.

to **hijack** VERB
劫持 jiéchí

hijacker NOUN
劫持者 jiéchízhě [个 gè]

to **hike** VERB
▷ *see also* **hike** NOUN
步行 bùxíng

hike NOUN
▷ *see also* **hike** VERB
徒步旅行 túbù lǚxíng [次 cì] *(walk)*

hiking NOUN
步行 bùxíng
■ **to go hiking** 做徒步旅行 zuò túbù lǚxíng

hilarious ADJECTIVE
非常有趣的 fēicháng yǒuqù de
□ It was hilarious! 非常有趣！Fēicháng yǒuqù!

hill NOUN
1 小山 xiǎoshān [座 zuò]
□ She walked up the hill. 她爬上了那座小山。Tā páshàng le nàzuò xiǎoshān.
2 坡 pō [个 gè] *(slope)*

him PRONOUN
他 tā
□ I haven't seen him. 我还没看见他。Wǒ hái méi kànjiàn tā. □ They gave him the job. 他们给了他那份工作。Tāmen gěile tā nàfèn gōngzuò. □ Look at him! 看着他！Kànzhe tā!

himself PRONOUN
1 他自己 tā zìjǐ
□ He prepared the supper himself. 他自己准备了晚餐。Tā zìjǐ zhǔnbèi le wǎncān. □ He hurt himself. 他伤了自己。Tā shāngle zìjǐ. □ He lives by himself. 他独自一人住。Tā dúzì yìrén zhù.
2 他本人 tā běnrén *(emphatic)*

Hindu NOUN
▷ *see also* **Hindu** ADJECTIVE
印度教信徒 Yìndùjiào xìntú [位 wèi]

Hindu ADJECTIVE
▷ *see also* **Hindu** NOUN
与印度教有关的 yǔ Yìndùjiào yǒuguān de
□ a Hindu temple 一座印度教寺庙 yízuò Yìndùjiào sìmiào

hint NOUN
▷ *see also* **hint** VERB
暗示 ànshì [个 gè]
■ **to drop a hint** 给个暗示 gěi gè ànshì

to **hint** VERB
▷ *see also* **hint** NOUN
暗示 ànshì
□ He hinted that something was going on. 他暗示有什么事正在发生。Tā ànshì yǒu shénme shì zhèngzài fāshēng.
■ **What are you hinting at?** 你在暗示什么？Nǐ zài ànshì shénme?

hip NOUN
髋部 kuānbù [个 gè]

hippie NOUN
嬉皮士 xīpíshì [个 gè]

hippo NOUN
河马 hémǎ [只 zhī]
LANGUAGE TIP Literally, this means 'river horse'.

to **hire** VERB
▷ *see also* **hire** NOUN
1 租用 zūyòng
■ **to hire a car** 租用一辆车 zūyòng yíliàng chē
2 雇用 gùyòng *(worker)*
□ They hired a cleaner. 他们雇佣了一个清洁工。Tāmen gùyōng le yígè qīngjiégōng.

hire NOUN
▷ *see also* **hire** VERB
租赁 zūlìn
■ **car hire** 汽车租赁 qìchē zūlìn
■ **'for hire'** "出租" "chūzū"

hire car NOUN
租的车 zū de chē [辆 liàng]

his ADJECTIVE
▷ *see also* **his** PRONOUN
他的 tā de
□ His face was very red. 他的脸很红。Tāde liǎn hěnhóng. □ his father 他的父亲 tāde fùqīn □ his mother 他的母亲 tāde mǔqin

his PRONOUN
▷ *see also* **his** ADJECTIVE
他的 tā de
□ These are his. 这些是他的。Zhèxiē shì tāde. □ a friend of his 他的一个朋友 tāde yígè péngyǒu □ my parents and his 我的父母和他的父母 wǒde fùmǔ hé tāde fùmǔ
□ Is this his coat? — No, his is black. 这是他的外套吗？— 不，他的是黑色的。Zhè shì tāde wàitào ma? — Bù, tāde shì hēisè de.

history NOUN
历史 lìshǐ

to **hit** VERB
▷ *see also* **hit** NOUN
1 打 dǎ *(strike)*
□ Andrew hit him. 安德鲁打了他。Āndélǔ dǎle tā.
2 碰撞 pèngzhuàng *(collide with)*
□ He was hit by a car. 他被一辆小车撞了。Tā bèi yíliàng xiǎochē zhuàng le.
3 击中 jīzhòng *(target)*
□ The arrow hit the target. 箭击中了靶子。Jiàn jīzhòng le bǎzi.

hit NOUN
▷ *see also* **hit** VERB
1 点击 diǎnjī [次 cì] *(on website)*
2 流行曲 liúxíngqǔ [首 shǒu] *(hit song)*
□ Madonna's latest hit 麦当娜最新流行曲 Màidāngnà zuìxīn liúxíngqǔ
3 成功 chénggōng *(success)*
□ The film was a massive hit. 这部电影是个巨大的成功。Zhèbù diànyǐng shì gè jùdà de chénggōng.

to **hitchhike** VERB
搭便车旅行 dā biànchē lǚxíng

hitchhiker NOUN
搭便车旅行者 dā biànchē lǚxíngzhě [个 gè]

hitchhiking NOUN
搭便车 dā biànchē
□ Hitchhiking can be dangerous. 搭便车可能会有危险。Dā biànchē kěnéng huì yǒu wēixiǎn.

hit man NOUN
职业杀手 zhíyè shāshǒu [个 gè]

HIV NOUN (= *human immunodeficiency virus)*
艾滋病病毒 àizībìng bìngdú

HIV-negative ADJECTIVE
HIV呈阴性 HIV chéng yīnxìng

HIV-positive ADJECTIVE
HIV呈阳性 HIV chéng yángxìng

hoarse ADJECTIVE
嘶哑的 sīyǎ de

hobby NOUN
爱好 àihào [种 zhǒng]

□ What are your hobbies? 你有什么爱好？Nǐ yǒu shénme àihào?

hockey NOUN
1 曲棍球 qūgùnqiú
2 冰球 bīngqiú *(US: on ice)*

to **hold** VERB
1 抱 bào
□ She held the baby. 她抱着宝宝。Tā bàozhe bǎobao.
2 容纳 róngnà *(contain)*
□ This bottle holds one litre. 这个瓶子能容纳一升。Zhègè píngzi néng róngnà yìshēng.
■ **to hold a meeting** 开会 kāihuì
■ **Hold the line!** *(on telephone)* 别挂线！Bié guàxiàn!
■ **Hold it!** *(wait)* 等一会儿！Děng yíhuìr!
■ **to hold somebody hostage** 扣留某人作为人质 kòuliú mǒurén zuòwéi rénzhì
■ **to get hold of something** *(obtain)* 掌握某物 zhǎngwò mǒuwù □ I couldn't get hold of it. 我掌握不了它。Wǒ zhǎngwò bùliǎo tā.

to **hold on** VERB
1 抓牢 zhuāláo *(keep hold)*
■ **to hold on to something** 抓牢某物 zhuāláo mǒuwù □ He held on to the chair. 他抓牢了椅子。Tā zhuāláo le yǐzi.
2 等一会儿 děng yíhuìr *(wait)*
□ Hold on, I'm coming! 等一会儿，我就来！Děng yíhuìr, wǒ jiù lái!
■ **Hold on!** *(on telephone)* 别挂线！Bié guàxiàn!

to **hold up** VERB
1 举起 jǔqǐ *(lift up)*
■ **to hold up one's hand** 举起某人的手 jǔqǐ mǒurén de shǒu □ Ting held up her hand. 婷举起了她的手。Tíng jǔqǐ le tāde shǒu.
2 耽搁 dāngē *(delay)*
□ I was held up at the office. 我在办公室耽搁了。Wǒ zài bàngōngshì dāngē le.
■ **to hold up a bank** *(rob)* 抢劫银行 qiǎngjié yínháng

hold-up NOUN
1 持械抢劫 chíxiè qiǎngjié [次 cì] *(robbery)*
2 耽搁 dānggē [次 cì] *(delay)*
3 交通阻塞 jiāotōng zǔsè [阵 zhèn] *(in traffic)*

hole NOUN
1 洞 dòng [个 gè] *(space, gap)*
2 破洞 pòdòng [个 gè] *(tear in fabric)*

holiday NOUN
假期 jiàqī [个 gè]
□ Did you have a good holiday? 你的假期过得好吗？Nǐde jiàqī guòdé hǎo ma?
■ **public holiday** 公共假期 gōnggòng jiàqī
■ **the school holidays** 学校假期 xuéxiào jiàqī
■ **the summer holidays** 暑假 shǔjià
■ **to be on holiday** 在度假 zài dùjià □ We are on holiday. 我们在度假。Wǒmen zài dùjià. □ to go on holiday 去度假 qù dùjià
■ **a holiday camp** 一个假期野营地 yígè jiàqī yěyíngdì

holiday home NOUN
度假时的住处 dùjià shí de zhùchù [个 gè]

Holland NOUN
荷兰 Hélán

hollow ADJECTIVE
空的 kōng de *(not solid)*

holy ADJECTIVE
神圣的 shénshèng de

home NOUN
▷ *see also* **home** ADVERB
1 家 jiā [个 gè] *(house)*
■ **at home** 在家 zàijiā
■ **Make yourself at home.** 请像在自己家一样随便。Qǐng xiàng zài zìjǐ jiā yíyàng suíbiàn. □ My aunt's at home from 5 p.m. 我的阿姨下午五点以后就在家了。Wǒde āyí xiàwǔ wǔdiǎn yǐhòu jiù zàijiā le.
2 家乡 jiāxiāng [个 gè] *(country, area)*
3 收容院 shōuróngyuàn [个 gè] *(institution)*

home ADVERB
▷ *see also* **home** NOUN
在家 zàijiā
□ I'll be home at 5 o'clock. 我五点就回家。Wǒ wǔdiǎn jiù huíjiā.
■ **to get home** 到家 dàojiā □ What time did he get home? 他什么时候到家的？Tā shénme shíhòu dàojiā de?

home address NOUN
家庭住址 jiātíng zhùzhǐ [个 gè]
□ What's your home address? 你的家庭住址是什么？Nǐde jiātíng zhùzhǐ shì shénme?

homeland NOUN
祖国 zǔguó

homeless ADJECTIVE
无家可归的 wújiā kěguī de
■ **the homeless** 无家可归的人 wújiā kěguī de rén

home match NOUN
主场比赛 zhǔchǎng bǐsài [场 chǎng]

homepage NOUN
主页 zhǔyè [个 gè]

homesick ADJECTIVE
想家的 xiǎngjiā de
■ **to be homesick** 想家的 xiǎngjiā de

homework NOUN
家庭作业 jiātíng zuòyè
□ Have you done your homework? 你完成

家庭作业了吗？ Nǐ wánchéng jiātíng zuòyè le ma? □ my geography homework 我的地理家庭作业 wǒde dìlǐ jiātíng zuòyè

homosexual ADJECTIVE
▷ *see also* **homosexual** NOUN
同性恋的 tóngxìngliàn de

homosexual NOUN
▷ *see also* **homosexual** ADJECTIVE
同性恋者 tóngxìngliànzhě [个 gè]

honest ADJECTIVE
诚实的 chéngshí de
□ She's a very honest person. 她是个非常诚实的人。Tā shì gè fēicháng chéngshí de rén.
■ **To be honest, ...** 说实话，··· Shuō shíhuà, ...

honestly ADVERB
的的确确地 dídíquèquè de
□ I honestly don't know. 我的的确确不知道。Wǒ dídíquèquè bùzhīdào.

honesty NOUN
诚实 chéngshí

honey NOUN
蜂蜜 fēngmì

honeymoon NOUN
蜜月 mìyuè [个 gè]

Hong Kong NOUN
香港 Xiānggǎng

honour (US **honor**) NOUN
荣誉 róngyù

hood NOUN
1 兜帽 dōumào [个 gè] *(on clothes)*
2 发动机罩 fādòngjī zhào [个 gè] *(US: of car)*

hoof NOUN
蹄 tí

hook NOUN
钩 gōu [个 gè]
■ **to take the phone off the hook** 不把电话听筒挂上 bùbǎ diànhuà tīngtǒng guàshàng

hooray EXCLAMATION
万岁 wànsuì

Hoover® NOUN
吸尘器 xīchénqì [台 tái]

to **hoover** VERB
吸尘 xīchén
□ to hoover the lounge 给客厅吸尘 gěi kètīng xīchén

hooves PL NOUN ▷ *see* **hoof**

to **hop** VERB
单脚跳 dānjiǎo tiào

to **hope** VERB
希望 xīwàng
□ I hope he comes. 我希望他来。Wǒ xīwàng tā lái. □ I'm hoping for good results. 我希望有好的结果。Wǒ xīwàng yǒu hǎo de jiēguǒ.
■ **to hope that...** 希望··· xīwàng...
■ **to hope to do something** 希望能做某事 xīwàng néng zuò mǒushì
■ **I hope so.** 我希望如此。Wǒ xīwàng rúcǐ.
■ **I hope not.** 我希望不会。Wǒ xīwàng búhuì.

hope NOUN
希望 xīwàng
■ **to give up hope** 放弃希望 fàngqì xīwàng □ Don't give up hope! 不要放弃希望！ Búyào fàngqì xīwàng!

hopefully ADVERB
■ **hopefully,...** 如果运气好，··· rúguǒ yùnqì hǎo,...

hopeless ADJECTIVE
1 糟糕的 zāogāo de *(situation, position)*
2 无能为力的 wúnéngwéilì de *(informal: useless)*
□ I'm hopeless at maths. 我在数学方面无能为力。Wǒ zài shùxué fāngmiàn wúnéngwéilì.

horizon NOUN
■ **the horizon** 地平线 dìpíngxiàn

horizontal ADJECTIVE
水平的 shuǐpíng de

horn NOUN
1 角 jiǎo [个 gè] *(of animal)*
2 喇叭 lǎbā [个 gè] *(of car)*
□ He sounded his horn. 他按响了喇叭。Tā ànxiǎng le lǎbā.

horoscope NOUN
占星术 zhānxīngshù [种 zhǒng]

horrible ADJECTIVE
1 糟透的 zāotòu de *(colour, food, mess)*
□ What a horrible dress! 一条糟透了的裙子！ Yìtiáo zāotòu le de qúnzi!
2 可怕的 kěpà de *(accident, crime)*
3 令人恐惧的 lìng rén kǒngjù de *(experience, situation, dream)*

horror NOUN
恐怖 kǒngbù

horror film NOUN
恐怖片 kǒngbùpiān [部 bù]

horse NOUN
马 mǎ [匹 pǐ]

horse racing NOUN
赛马 sàimǎ

hose NOUN
输水软管 shūshuǐ ruǎnguǎn [根 gēn]
□ a garden hose 一根花园输水软管 yìgēn huāyuán shūshuǐ ruǎnguǎn

hosepipe NOUN
输水软管 shūshuǐ ruǎnguǎn [根 gēn]

hospital NOUN
医院 yīyuàn [家 jiā]

□ Take me to the hospital! 带我去医院！Dài wǒ qù yīyuàn！

■ **to be in hospital** 住院 zhùyuàn

hospitality NOUN
好客 hàokè

host NOUN
主人 zhǔrén [位 wèi]

hostage NOUN
人质 rénzhì [个 gè]

■ **to be taken hostage** 被扣押做人质 bèi kòuyā zuò rénzhì

hostel NOUN
旅社 lǚshè [家 jiā]

■ **a youth hostel** 一家青年旅社 yìjiā qīngnián lǚshè

hostess NOUN
女主人 nǚ zhǔrén [位 wèi]

hot ADJECTIVE
1 烫的 tàng de *(object)*
2 热的 rè de
□ a hot bath 一个热水澡 yígè rèshuǐzǎo
3 炎热的 yánrè de *(weather, person)*
□ a hot country 一个炎热的国家 yígè yánrè de guójiā □ I'm hot. 我有点热。Wǒ yǒudiǎn rè. □ I'm too hot. 我太热了。Wǒ tài rè le. □ It's hot. 天气炎热。Tiānqì yánrè.
4 辣的 là de *(spicy)*
□ a very hot curry 一种很辣的咖喱 yìzhǒng hěn là de gālí
5 性感的 xìnggǎn de
□ She is hot. 她很性感。Tā hěn xìnggǎn.

hot dog NOUN
热狗 règǒu [根 gēn]

hotel NOUN
旅馆 lǚguǎn [个 gè]

■ **to stay at a hotel** 住旅馆 zhù lǚguǎn

hour NOUN
小时 xiǎoshí [个 gè]
□ for three hours 三个小时 sāngè xiǎoshí

■ **a quarter of an hour** 一刻 yíkè

■ **half an hour** 半小时 bàn xiǎoshí

■ **two and a half hours** 两个半小时 liǎng gè bàn xiǎoshí

■ **60 miles per hour** 每小时六十英里 měi xiǎoshí liùshí yīnglǐ

■ **to pay somebody by the hour** 按小时付费给某人 àn xiǎoshí fùfèi gěi mǒurén

■ **lunch hour** 午餐时间 wǔcān shíjiān

■ **hours** *(ages)* 很长时间 hěncháng shíjiān
□ She always takes hours to get ready. 她总是花很长时间作准备。Tā zǒngshì huā hěncháng shíjiān zuò zhǔnbèi.

hourly ADJECTIVE, ADVERB
按小时的 àn xiǎoshí de
□ There are hourly buses. 有按小时发车的巴士。Yǒu àn xiǎoshí fāchē de bāshì.

■ **to be paid hourly** 按小时付薪 àn xiǎoshí fùxīn

house NOUN
家 jiā [个 gè]
□ Our house is at the end of the road. 我们家在路的尽头。Wǒmen jiā zài lù de jìntóu.

■ **at my house** 在我家 zài wǒjiā □ We stayed at their house. 我们暂住在他们家里。Wǒmen zànzhù zài tāmen jiālǐ.

■ **to my house** 到我家 dào wǒjiā

housewife NOUN
家庭主妇 jiātíng zhǔfù [个 gè]

housework NOUN
家务劳动 jiāwù láodòng

■ **to do the housework** 做家务劳动 zuò jiāwù láodòng

housing estate NOUN
住宅区 zhùzhái qū [个 gè]

hovercraft NOUN
气垫船 qìdiàn chuán [艘 sōu]

how ADVERB
▷ *see also* **how** CONJUNCTION
1 怎样 zěnyàng *(in questions)*

■ **How did you do it?** 你是怎样做的？Nǐ shì zěnyàng zuòde?

■ **How are you?** 你近来怎样？Nǐ jìnlái zěnyàng?

■ **How long have you lived here?** 你在这儿住了多久了？Nǐ zài zhèr zhùle duōjiǔ le?

■ **How many?** 多少？Duōshǎo? □ How many pupils are there in the class? 班里有多少小学生？Bānlǐ yǒu duōshǎo xiǎoxuéshēng?

■ **How much?** 多少钱？Duōshǎo qián? □ How much sugar do you want? 你要多少糖？Nǐ yào duōshǎo táng?

■ **How old are you?** 你多大了？Nǐ duōdà le?

■ **How tall is he?** 他有多高？Tā yǒu duō gāo?

■ **How far is it to Edinburgh?** 去爱丁堡有多远？Qù Àidīngbǎo yǒu duō yuǎn?

■ **How do you say 'apple' in Chinese?** 你用中文怎样说 'apple'？Nǐ yòng Zhōngwén zěnyàng shuō 'apple'?
2 怎么样 zěnmeyàng *(in suggestions)*
□ How about a cup of tea? 来杯茶怎么样？Lái bēi chá zěnmeyàng?

how CONJUNCTION
▷ *see also* **how** ADVERB
怎样 zěnyàng

■ **I know how you did it.** 我知道你怎样做的。Wǒ zhīdào nǐ zěnyàng zuòde.

■ **to know how to do something** 知道怎样做某事 zhīdào zěnyàng zuò mǒushì

however ADVERB
▷ *see also* **however** CONJUNCTION
1 但是 dànshì *(but)*
2 不管如何 bùguǎn rúhé *(with an adjective, an adverb)*
3 究竟怎样 jiūjìng zěnyàng *(in questions)*

however CONJUNCTION
▷ *see also* **however** ADVERB
然而 rán'ér
□ This, however, isn't true. 然而，这并不是真的。Rán'ér, zhè bìng búshì zhēnde.

to **hug** VERB
▷ *see also* **hug** NOUN
拥抱 yōngbào *(person)*

hug NOUN
▷ *see also* **hug** VERB
拥抱 yōngbào [个 gè]
■ **to give somebody a hug** 拥抱某人 yōngbào mǒurén

huge ADJECTIVE
1 巨大的 jùdà de
2 巨额的 jù'é de *(amount, profit, debt)*
3 庞大的 pángdà de *(task)*

human ADJECTIVE
▷ *see also* **human** NOUN
人的 rén de
□ the human body 人体 réntǐ

human NOUN
▷ *see also* **human** ADJECTIVE
人 rén [个 gè]
■ **the human race** 人类 rénlèi
■ **human nature** 人性 rénxìng

human being NOUN
人 rén [个 gè]

humour (US **humor**) NOUN
幽默 yōumò
■ **to have a sense of humour** 有幽默感 yǒu yōumògǎn

hundred NUMBER
百 bǎi
■ **a hundred** 一百 yìbǎi □ a hundred euros 一百欧元 yìbǎi ōuyuán
■ **five hundred** 五百 wǔbǎi
■ **five hundred and one** 五百零一 wǔbǎi líng yī
■ **hundreds** 几百 jǐbǎi □ hundreds of people 百号人 bǎihào rén

hung VERB ▷ *see* **hang**

Hungarian NOUN
▷ *see also* **Hungarian** ADJECTIVE
1 匈牙利人 Xiōngyálì rén *(person)*
2 匈牙利语 Xiōngyálì yǔ *(language)*

Hungarian ADJECTIVE
▷ *see also* **Hungarian** NOUN
匈牙利人的 Xiōngyálì rén de
□ She's Hungarian. 她是匈牙利人。Tā shì Xiōngyálì rén.

Hungary NOUN
匈牙利 Xiōngyálì

hunger NOUN
饥饿 jī'è

hungry ADJECTIVE
饥饿的 jī'è de
■ **to be hungry** 饿了 è le □ I'm hungry. 我饿了。Wǒ è le.

to **hunt** VERB
▷ *see also* **hunt** NOUN
1 狩猎 shòuliè *(for food, sport)*
2 追捕 zhuībǔ *(criminal)*
□ The police are hunting the killer. 警察正在追捕杀人犯。Jǐngchá zhèngzài zhuībǔ shārénfàn.
■ **to hunt for something** *(search)* 搜寻某物 sōuxún mǒwù □ I hunted everywhere for that book. 我到处搜寻那本书。Wǒ dàochù sōuxún nà běn shū.

hunt NOUN
▷ *see also* **hunt** VERB
1 狩猎 shòuliè [次 cì] *(for food, sport)*
2 搜寻 sōuxún [次 cì] *(for missing person)*
3 追捕 zhuībǔ [次 cì] *(for criminal)*

hunting NOUN
狩猎 shòuliè *(for food, sport)*
□ I'm against hunting. 我反对狩猎。Wǒ fǎnduì shòuliè.
■ **job hunting** 找工作 zhǎo gōngzuò
■ **house hunting** 找住房 zhǎo zhùfáng

hurricane NOUN
飓风 jùfēng [场 chǎng]

hurry NOUN
▷ *see also* **hurry** VERB
■ **to be in a hurry** 匆忙 cōngmáng
■ **to do something in a hurry** 匆忙地做某事 cōngmáng de zuò mǒushì
■ **There's no hurry.** 不必匆忙。Búbì cōngmáng.

to **hurry** VERB
▷ *see also* **hurry** NOUN
匆忙赶路 cōngmáng gǎnlù
□ Sharon hurried back home. 莎朗匆忙赶路回了家。Shālǎng cōngmáng gǎnlù huíle jiā.

to **hurry up** VERB
赶快 gǎnkuài

to **hurt** VERB
▷ *see also* **hurt** VERB
1 弄痛 nòngtòng *(cause pain to)*
□ You're hurting me! 你弄痛我了！Nǐ nòngtòng wǒ le !
2 使受伤 shǐ shòushāng *(injure)*
3 使伤心 shǐ shāngxīn *(emotionally)*
□ His remarks really hurt me. 他的评价实在

使我伤心了。Tāde píngjià shízài shǐ wǒ shāngxīn le.

4 痛 tòng *(be painful)*

□That hurts. 那儿痛。Nà'r tòng. □My leg hurts. 我的腿痛。Wǒde tuǐ tòng.

■ **to hurt oneself** 伤了自己 shāngle zìjǐ □I fell over and hurt myself. 我摔了一跤，伤了自己。Wǒ shuāile yìjiāo, shāngle zìjǐ.

hurt ADJECTIVE

▷ *see also* **hurt** VERB

1 受伤的 shòushāng de *(injured)*

□Is he badly hurt? 他受伤严重吗？Tā shòushāng yánzhòng ma?

2 被伤害的 bèi shānghài de *(emotionally)*

□I was hurt by what he said. 我被他的话伤害了。Wǒ bèi tāde huà shānghài le.

husband NOUN

丈夫 zhàngfu [个 gè]

hut NOUN

木棚 mùpéng [个 gè] *(shed)*

hyphen NOUN

连字符 liánzìfú [个 gè]

English-Chinese

h

Ii

I PRONOUN
我 wǒ
□ I speak Chinese. 我讲中文。Wǒ jiǎng Zhōngwén. □ Ann and I 我和安 wǒ hé Ān

ice NOUN
1 冰 bīng
□ There was ice on the lake. 湖面上有冰。Húmiàn shàng yǒu bīng.
2 冰块 bīngkuài *(for drink)*

iceberg NOUN
冰山 bīngshān [座 zuò]
■ **the tip of the iceberg** 冰山一角 bīngshān yìjiǎo

icebox NOUN (US)
冷藏柜 lěngcángguì [个 gè]

ice cream NOUN
冰淇淋 bīngqílín [个 gè]
□ vanilla ice cream 香草冰淇淋 xiāngcǎo bīngqílín

ice cube NOUN
冰块 bīngkuài [个 gè]

ice hockey NOUN
冰球 bīngqiú

Iceland NOUN
冰岛 Bīngdǎo

ice lolly NOUN
冰棍 bīnggùn [支 zhī]

ice rink NOUN
溜冰场 liūbīngchǎng [个 gè]

ice-skating NOUN
溜冰 liūbīng
■ **to go ice-skating** 去溜冰 qù liūbīng

icing NOUN
糖霜 tángshuāng *(on cake)*

icon NOUN
图标 túbiāo [个 gè] *(on computer)*

ICT NOUN *(= information and communication technology)*
通信技术 tōngxìn jìshù

icy ADJECTIVE
寒冷刺骨的 hánlěng cìgǔ de
□ There was an icy wind. 一阵寒冷刺骨的风。Yízhèn hánlěng cìgǔ de fēng.

ID NOUN *(= identification)*
身份证明 shēnfèn zhèngmíng
■ **Do you have any ID?** 你有任何身份证明吗？Nǐ yǒu rènhé shēnfèn zhèngmíng ma?

I'd = **I would, I had**

idea NOUN
1 主意 zhǔyì [个 gè] *(scheme)*
■ **Good idea!** 好主意！Hǎo zhǔyì!
2 看法 kànfǎ [种 zhǒng] *(opinion, theory)*
■ **I haven't the slightest idea.** 我没有任何看法。Wǒ méiyǒu rènhé kànfǎ.
3 概念 gàiniàn [个 gè] *(notion)*

ideal ADJECTIVE
理想的 lǐxiǎng de

identical ADJECTIVE
完全相同的 wánquán xiāngtóng de
■ **identical to...** 和…完全相同 hé... wánquán xiāngtóng

identification NOUN
身份证明 shēnfèn zhèngmíng *(proof of identity)*

to **identify** VERB
识别 shíbié *(recognize)*

identity card NOUN
身份证 shēnfènzhèng [张 zhāng]

> **DID YOU KNOW...?**
> As the majority of Chinese people do not have passports, the identity card 身份证 shēnfēnzhèng is the primary form of identification in China.

idiot NOUN
傻子 shǎzi [个 gè]

idle ADJECTIVE
懒惰的 lǎnduò de *(lazy)*

i.e. ABBREVIATION *(= id est)*
也就是 yě jiùshì

if CONJUNCTION
1 如果 rúguǒ
□ I'll go if you come with me. 如果你和我一起的话我就去。Rúguǒ nǐ hé wǒ yīqǐde huà wǒ jiù qù. □ If I were you... 如果我是你的话… Rúguǒ wǒ shì nǐ de huà...
■ **if so** 如果是这样的话 rúguǒ shì zhèyàng de huà
■ **if not** 如果不的话 rúguǒ bù de huà
□ Are you coming? If not, I'll go with Mark.

你要去么？如果不的话，我就和马克去。Nǐ yào qù me? Rúguǒ bù de hua, wǒ jiù hé Mǎkè qù.
■ **if necessary** 如有必要 rúyǒu bìyào
■ **if only** 要是…多好 yàoshì... duōhǎo
□ If only I had more money! 要是我有更多的钱多好！Yàoshi wǒ yǒu gèngduō de qián duōhǎo!
2 只要 zhǐyào *(whenever)*
□ If we are in Hong Kong, we always go to see her. 只要我们在香港，都会去看她。Zhǐyào wǒmen zài Xiānggǎng, dōuhuì qù kàn tā.
3 是否 shìfǒu *(whether)*
□ Ask him if he can come. 问他是否能来。Wèn tā shìfǒu néngláí.

ignorant ADJECTIVE
无知的 wúzhī de

to **ignore** VERB
1 不理 bùlǐ *(person)*
□ She saw me, but she ignored me. 她看见了我，但是不理我。Tā kànjiàn le wǒ, dànshì bùlǐ wǒ.
■ **Just ignore him!** 不理他！Bùlǐ tā!
2 不顾 búgù *(advice, event)*
□ She ignored my advice. 她不顾我的建议。Tā búgù wǒde jiànyì.

I'll = **I will, I shall**

ill ADJECTIVE
有病的 yǒubìng de
■ **to fall ill** 生病 shēngbìng □ She was taken ill while on holiday. 她在休假期间生病了。Tā zài xiūjià qījiān shēngbìng le.
■ **the mentally ill** 精神病人 jīngshén bìngrén
■ **the terminally ill** 晚期病人 wǎnqī bìngrén

illegal ADJECTIVE
非法的 fēifǎde

illness NOUN
病 bìng [场 chǎng]

illusion NOUN
幻想 huànxiǎng [个 gè]

illustration NOUN
插图 chātú [幅 fú]

image NOUN
形象 xíngxiàng
□ The company has changed its image. 这家公司改变了它的形象。Zhèjiā gōngsī gǎibiàn le tāde xíngxiàng.

imagination NOUN
1 想象力 xiǎngxiànglì [种 zhǒng]
2 想象 xiǎngxiàng [个 gè] *(mind's eye)*

to **imagine** VERB
1 想象 xiǎngxiàng
□ You can imagine how I felt! 你可以想象我的感受！Nǐ kěyǐ xiǎngxiàng wǒde gǎnshòu!
2 猜想 cāixiǎng
□ Is he angry? — I imagine so. 他生气了？— 我猜想是的。Tā shēngqì le? — Wǒ cāixiǎng shì de.

to **imitate** VERB
1 效仿 xiàofǎng *(copy)*
2 模仿 mófǎng *(person, sound, gesture)*

imitation NOUN
▷ *see also* **imitation** ADJECTIVE
仿制品 fǎngzhìpǐn [件 jiàn]

imitation ADJECTIVE
▷ *see also* **imitation** NOUN
仿制的 fǎngzhì de

immediate ADJECTIVE
立即的 lìjí de

immediately ADVERB
▷ *see also* **immediately** CONJUNCTION
立即地 lìjí de *(at once)*
□ I'll do it immediately. 我立即去做。Wǒ lìjí qù zuò.

immediately CONJUNCTION
▷ *see also* **immediately** ADVERB
■ **Immediately he had said it, he regretted it.** 他刚一说完马上就后悔了。Tā gāng yì shuōwán mǎshàng jiù hòuhuǐ le.
■ **immediately before** 紧接着…之前 jǐnjiēzhe...zhīqián
■ **immediately after** 紧接着…后 jǐnjiēzhe...hòu

immigrant NOUN
移民 yímín [个 gè]

immigration NOUN
移民 yímín *(process)*
■ **immigration control** 移民管理 yímín guǎnlǐ

impatient ADJECTIVE
急躁的 jízào de
■ **to get impatient** 变得急噪 biàndé jízào
□ People are getting impatient. 人们变得急噪起来。Rénmen biàndé jízào qǐlái.
■ **to get impatient with something** 对某事不耐烦 duì mǒushì bú nàifán

to **import** VERB
进口 jìnkǒu

importance NOUN
1 重要性 zhòngyàoxìng *(significance)*
2 影响 yǐngxiǎng *(influence)*

important ADJECTIVE
1 重要的 zhòngyào de
■ **It's not important.** 不重要。Bú zhòngyào.
2 有影响的 yǒu yǐngxiǎng de *(influential)*

impossible ADJECTIVE
不可能的 bù kěnéng de

English-Chinese

i

■ **It is impossible to understand what's going on.** 不可能了解事情的进展情况。Bù kěnéng liǎojiě shìqíng de jìnzhǎn qíngkuàng.

to **impress** VERB

给…留下深刻印象 gěi...liúxià shēnkè yìnxiàng *(person)*

□ She's trying to impress you. 她试图给你留下深刻印象。Tā shìtú gěi nǐ liúxià shēnkè yìnxiàng.

■ **to be impressed by somebody** 对某人印象深刻 duì mǒurén yìnxiàng shēnkè

impressed ADJECTIVE

被打动的 bèi dǎdòng de

□ I'm very impressed! 我被深深打动了！Wǒ bèi shēnshēn dǎdòng le!

impression NOUN

印象 yìnxiàng [个 gè]

□ I was under the impression that... 我给人的印象是… Wǒ gěi rén de yìnxiàng shì...

■ **to make a good impression** 留下好印象 liúxià hǎo yìnxiàng

■ **to make a bad impression** 留下坏印象 liúxià huài yìnxiàng

impressive ADJECTIVE

给人深刻印象的 gěi rén shēnkè yìnxiàng de

to **improve** VERB

1 改进 gǎijìn

□ They have improved the service. 他们改进了服务。Tāmen gǎijìn le fúwù.

2 转好 zhuǎnhǎo *(weather, situation)*

□ The weather is improving. 天气正在转好。Tiānqì zhèngzài zhuǎnhǎo.

3 进步 jìnbù *(pupil, performance)*

□ My Chinese has improved. 我的中文进步了。Wǒde Zhōngwén jìnbù le.

improvement NOUN

进步 jìnbù

□ It's a great improvement. 这是一个大的进步。Zhèshì yígè dàde jìnbù. □ There's been an improvement in his Chinese. 他的中文有了进步。Tāde Zhōngwén yǒule jìnbù.

in PREPOSITION

▷ *see also* **in** ADVERB

1 在…里 zài...lǐ

LANGUAGE TIP 里 lǐ comes after the noun.

□ in school 在学校里 zài xuéxiào lǐ □ in hospital 在医院里 zài yīyuàn lǐ □ in town 在城里 zài chéng lǐ □ in prison 在监狱里 zài jiānyù lǐ

□ It's in the house. 它在房子里。Tā zài fángzi lǐ.

2 在 zài *(with place names)*

□ in London 在伦敦 zài Lúndūn □ in England 在英格兰 zài Yīnggélán

■ **in here** 在这儿 zài zhè'r

■ **in there** 在那儿 zài nà'r

LANGUAGE TIP 在 zài is also used to translate **in** in phrases expressing time and duration.

□ in May 在5月 zài wǔyuè □ I did it in 3 hours. 我在三小时期间完成的。Wǒ zài sānxiǎoshí qījiān wánchéng de.

■ **in the morning** 在上午 zài shàngwǔ

□ at 6 in the morning 在早上六点 zài zǎoshàng liùdiǎn

■ **in the afternoon** 在下午 zài xiàwǔ

□ at 4 o'clock in the afternoon 在下午四点 zài xiàwǔ sìdiǎn

■ **in the sun** 在阳光下 zài yángguāng xià

■ **in the rain** 在雨中 zài yǔzhōng

3 后 hòu

□ I'll see you in two weeks' time. 我们两周后见。Wǒmen liǎngzhōu hòu jiàn.

4 在…期间 zài...qījiān

□ in the sixties 在六十年代期间 zài liùshí niándài qījiān

5 用 yòng

LANGUAGE TIP To indicate manner, style etc, use 用 yòng.

□ It was written in pencil. 用铅笔写的。Yòng qiānbǐ xiě de.

LANGUAGE TIP 用 yòng is also used to translate **in** when talking about languages.

□ in Chinese 用中文 yòng zhōngwén

6 穿着 chuānzhe *(dress, colour)*

□ the boy in the blue shirt 穿着蓝衬衫的男孩 chuānzhe lán chènshān de nánhái

7 之中的 zhīzhōng de *(with ratios, numbers)*

□ one in ten people 十个人之中的一个 shígè rén zhīzhōng de yígè

8 中 zhōng *(amongst a group)*

□ the best athlete in the team 队伍中最好的运动员 duìwu zhōng zuìhǎo de yùndòngyuán □ the tallest person in the family 家族中最高的人 jiāzú zhōng zuìgāo de rén

■ **in time** 及时 jíshí □ We arrived in time for dinner. 我们及时赶上了晚饭。Wǒmen jíshí gǎnshàng le wǎnfàn.

in ADVERB

▷ *see also* **in** PREPOSITION

■ **to be in** *(at home, work)* 在 zài □ He wasn't in. 他不在。Tā bú zài.

■ **to ask somebody in** 把某人请到家中 bǎ mǒurén qǐngdào jiāzhōng

inaccurate ADJECTIVE
不准确的 bù zhǔnquè de

inadequate ADJECTIVE
不充分的 bù chōngfēn de *(measures, resources)*
■ **I felt completely inadequate.** 我觉得相当不充分。Wǒ juédé xiāngdāng bù chōngfēn.

inbox NOUN
收件箱 shōujiànxiāng [个 gè] *(of email)*

inch NOUN
英寸 yīngcùn
□ 6 inches 六英寸 liù yīngcùn

incident NOUN
事件 shìjiàn [个 gè]

inclined ADJECTIVE
■ **to be inclined to do something** 倾向于做某事 qīngxiàngyú zuò mǒushì □ He's inclined to arrive late. 他倾向于晚点到。Tā qīngxiàngyú wǎndiǎn dào.

to **include** VERB
包括 bāokuò
□ Service is not included. 服务不包括在内。Fúwù bù bāokuò zài nèi.

including PREPOSITION
包括 bāokuò
■ **Nine people were injured, including two Britons.** 九个人受了伤，包括两个英国人。Jiǔgè rén shòule shāng, bāokuò liǎnggè Yīngguórén. □ It will be 200 yuan, including tax. 一共二百元，包括税。Yígòng èrbǎi Yuán, bāokuò shuì.

inclusive ADJECTIVE
一切包括在内的 yíqiè bāokuò zài nèi de
□ The inclusive price is 200 yuan. 一切包括在内的价格是二百元。Yíqiè bāokuò zài nèi de jiàgé shì èrbǎi Yuán.
■ **inclusive of tax** 含税的 hánshuì de

income NOUN
收入 shōurù [笔 bǐ]

income tax NOUN
所得税 suǒdéshuì

incompetent ADJECTIVE
不能胜任的 bùnéng shèngrèn de

incomplete ADJECTIVE
不完整的 bù wánzhěng de

inconsistent ADJECTIVE
不一致的 bù yízhì de

inconvenience NOUN
不便 búbiàn
■ **I don't want to cause any inconvenience.** 我不希望引起任何不便。Wǒ bù xīwàng yǐnqǐ rènhé búbiàn.

inconvenient ADJECTIVE
不便的 búbiàn de *(time, moment)*
■ **That's very inconvenient for me.** 对我来说非常不便。Duì wǒ láishuō fēicháng búbiàn.

incorrect ADJECTIVE
错误的 cuòwù de

increase NOUN
▷ *see also* **increase** VERB
增长 zēngzhǎng [成 chéng]
□ an increase in road accidents 公路交通事故增长 gōnglù jiāotōng shìgù de zēngzhǎng □ a 5% increase 百分之五的增长 bǎi fēn zhī wǔ de zēngzhǎng

to **increase** VERB
▷ *see also* **increase** NOUN
1 加剧 jiājù
□ Pollution has increased dramatically. 污染快速加剧。Wūrǎn kuàisù jiājù.
2 升高 shēnggāo *(price, number, level)*

incredible ADJECTIVE
不可思议的 bùkě sīyì de *(amazing, wonderful)*

indeed ADVERB
1 是的 shì de *(as a reply)*
□ Know what I mean? — Indeed I do. 明白我的意思了么？— 是的，我明白。Míngbai wǒde yìsi le me?— Shìde, wǒ míngbai.
■ **Yes indeed!** 的确如此！Díquè rúcǐ!
2 确实 quèshí
□ Thank you very much indeed! 确实很感谢你！Quèshí hěn gǎnxiè nǐ! □ It's very hard indeed. 确实很难。Quèshí hěn nán.

independence NOUN
独立 dúlì

independent ADJECTIVE
独立的 dúlì de
■ **an independent school** 一所私立学校 yìsuǒ sīlì xuéxiào

index NOUN
索引 suǒyǐn [条 tiáo]

index finger NOUN
食指 shízhǐ [只 zhī]

India NOUN
印度 Yìndù

Indian ADJECTIVE
▷ *see also* **Indian** NOUN
印度的 Yìndù de

Indian NOUN
▷ *see also* **Indian** ADJECTIVE
印度人 Yìndùrén [个 gè] *(person from India)*
■ **an American Indian** 一个美国裔印度人 yígè Měiguóyì Yìndùrén

to **indicate** VERB
1 表明 biǎomíng *(show)*
2 指向 zhǐxiàng *(point to)*

indicator NOUN
转向灯 zhuǎnxiàngdēng [个 gè] *(on car)*

English-Chinese

i

◻ Put your indicators on. 打开你的转向灯。Dǎkāi nǐde zhuǎnxiàngdēng.

indifferent ADJECTIVE
1 漠不关心的 mòbù guānxīn de
2 平庸的 píngyōng de *(mediocre)*

indigestion NOUN
消化不良 xiāohuà bù liáng
■ **I've got indigestion.** 我消化不良。Wǒ xiāohuà bù liáng.

individual NOUN
▷ *see also* **individual** ADJECTIVE
个人 gèrén

individual ADJECTIVE
▷ *see also* **individual** NOUN
个人的 gèrén de *(personal)*

indoor ADJECTIVE
室内的 shìnèi de
■ **an indoor swimming pool** 一个室内泳池 yígè shìnèi yǒngchí

indoors ADVERB
在室内 zài shì nèi
◻ They're indoors. 他们在室内。Tāmen zài shìnèi.
■ **to go indoors** 到室内去 dào shìnèi qù
◻ We'd better go indoors. 我们最好到室内去。Wǒmen zuìhǎo dào shìnèi qù.

industrial ADJECTIVE
1 工业的 gōngyè de
2 因工的 yīngōng de *(accident)*

industrial estate NOUN
工业区 gōngyè qū [个 gè]

industrial park NOUN (US)
工业区 gōngyè qū [个 gè]

industry NOUN
1 工业 gōngyè *(manufacturing)*
◻ the oil industry 石油工业 shíyóu gōngyè
◻ I'd like to work in industry. 我想在工业界工作。Wǒ xiǎng zài gōngyè jiè gōngzuò.
2 行业 hángyè [种 zhǒng] *(business)*
◻ the tourist industry 旅游行业 lǚyóu hángyè

inefficient ADJECTIVE
效率低的 xiàolǜ dī de

inevitable ADJECTIVE
不可避免的 bùkě bìmiǎn de

inexpensive ADJECTIVE
廉价的 liánjià de
◻ an inexpensive hotel 一家廉价的宾馆 yìjiā liánjià de bīnguǎn ◻ inexpensive holidays 廉价的假期 liánjià de jiàqī

LANGUAGE TIP 廉价 liánjià means cheap, but also of poor quality.

inexperienced ADJECTIVE
经验不足的 jīngyàn bùzú de

infant school NOUN
幼儿学校 yòuér xuéxiào [所 suǒ]
◻ He's just started at infant school. 他刚开始上幼儿学校。Tā gāng kāishǐ shàng yòuér xuéxiào.

infection NOUN
感染 gǎnrǎn [处 chù]
■ **to have an ear infection** 耳朵感染 ěrduo gǎnrǎn
■ **to have a throat infection** 咽喉感染 yānhóu gǎnrǎn

infectious ADJECTIVE
传染的 chuánrǎn de
◻ It's not infectious. 不传染的。Bù chuánrǎn de.

infinitive NOUN
不定词 búdìngcí [个 gè]

infirmary NOUN
医院 yīyuàn [所 suǒ]

inflatable ADJECTIVE
可充气的 kě chōngqì de *(mattress, dinghy)*

inflation NOUN
通货膨胀 tōnghuò péngzhàng

influence NOUN
▷ *see also* **influence** VERB
1 权势 quánshì [种 zhǒng] *(power)*
2 影响 yǐngxiǎng [个 gè] *(effect)*
◻ He's a bad influence on her. 他对她产生了不好的影响。Tā duì tā chǎnshēng le bùhǎo de yǐngxiǎng.

to **influence** VERB
▷ *see also* **influence** NOUN
影响 yǐngxiǎng

to **inform** VERB
告诉 gàosù
■ **to inform somebody that...** 告诉某人… gàosù mǒurén...
■ **to inform somebody of something** 告诉某人某事 gàosù mǒurén mǒushi
◻ Nobody informed me of the new plan. 没人告诉我新的计划。Méirén gàosù wǒ xīnde jìhuà.

informal ADJECTIVE
1 非正式的 fēi zhèngshì de *(relaxed meeting, discussions, agreement)*
◻ an informal visit 一次非正式的访问 yícì fēi zhèngshì de fǎngwèn
2 随便的 suíbiàn de *(clothes, party)*
■ **informal dress** 便装 biànzhuāng
3 通俗的 tōngsú de *(colloquial)*
◻ informal language 通俗用语 tōngsú yòngyǔ

information NOUN
信息 xìnxī
◻ important information 重要信息 zhòngyào xìnxī ◻ Could you give me some information about trains to Tianjin? 你能告诉我一些关于开往天津的火车的信息

吗？Nǐ néng gàosù wǒ yìxiē guānyú kāiwǎng Tiānjīn de huǒchē de xìnxī ma?

■ **a piece of information** 一条信息 yìtiáo xìnxī

information office NOUN
咨询处 zīxún chù [个 gè]

information technology NOUN
信息技术 xìnxī jìshù

ingredient NOUN
配料 pèiliào [种 zhǒng]

inhabitant NOUN
居民 jūmín [个 gè]

inhaler NOUN
哮喘喷剂 xiàochuǎn pēnjì [个 gè]
□ I mustn't forget my inhaler. 我不能忘了我的哮喘喷剂。Wǒ bùnéng wàngle wǒde xiàochuǎn pēnjì.

to **inherit** VERB
继承 jìchéng
□ She inherited her father's house. 她继承了她父亲的房子。Tā jìchéng le tā fùqin de fángzi.

initial NOUN
首字母 shǒuzìmǔ [个 gè] *(letter)*

initials PL NOUN
姓名首字母 xìngmíng shǒuzìmǔ *(of name)*
□ Her initials are LC. 她的姓名首字母是LC。Tāde xìngmíng shǒuzìmǔ shì LC.

initiative NOUN
开端 kāiduān [个 gè]

to **inject** VERB
注射 zhùshè *(drug)*

injection NOUN
注射 zhùshè
■ **to give somebody an injection** 给某人注射 gěi mǒurén zhùshè

to **injure** VERB
伤害 shānghài *(person)*
□ He was badly injured in the attack. 他在袭击中受了重伤。Tā zài xíjī zhōng shòule zhòngshāng.

injured ADJECTIVE
受伤的 shòushāng de

injury NOUN
伤害 shānghài [个 gè] *(wound)*
■ **to escape without injury** 安然脱险 ānrán tuōxiǎn

injury time NOUN
伤停补时 shāngtíng bǔshí

injustice NOUN
不公平 bù gōngping

ink NOUN
墨水 mòshuǐ [瓶 píng]

in-laws PL NOUN
姻亲 yīnqīn

inn NOUN
小旅馆 xiǎo lǚguǎn [家 jiā]

inner ADJECTIVE
中心的 zhōngxīn de
■ **the inner city** 中心城区 zhōngxīn chéngqū

innocent ADJECTIVE
无辜的 wúgū de

insane ADJECTIVE
疯狂的 fēngkuáng de

inscription NOUN
题字 tízì [个 gè]

insect NOUN
昆虫 kūnchóng [只 zhī]

insect repellent NOUN
杀虫剂 shāchóngjì [瓶 píng]

insensitive ADJECTIVE
麻木不仁 chídùn de
□ That was a bit insensitive of you. 你有点麻木不仁。Nǐ yǒudiǎn mámùbùrén.

inside NOUN
▷ *see also* **inside** ADJECTIVE, ADVERB, PREPOSITION
内部 nèibù

inside ADJECTIVE
▷ *see also* **inside** NOUN, ADVERB, PREPOSITION
内部的 nèibù de *(wall, surface)*

inside ADVERB
▷ *see also* **inside** NOUN, ADJECTIVE, PREPOSITION
1 里面 lǐmiàn *(go)*
■ **to go inside** 到里面去 dào lǐmiàn qù
■ **Come inside!** 到里面来！Dào lǐmiàn lái!
2 在里面 zài lǐmiàn *(be)*
□ They're inside. 他们在里面。Tāmen zài lǐmiàn.

inside PREPOSITION
▷ *see also* **inside** NOUN, ADJECTIVE, ADVERB
在...的里面 zài...de lǐmiàn *(place, container)*
□ inside the house 在房子里面 zài fángzi lǐmiàn

insincere ADJECTIVE
无诚意的 wú chéngyì de

to **insist** VERB
坚持 jiānchí
□ I didn't want to, but he insisted. 我不想，但他坚持。Wǒ bùxiǎng, dàn tā jiānchí.
■ **He insisted he was innocent.** 他坚持他是无辜的。Tā jiānchí tā shì wúgū de.
■ **to insist on doing something** 坚持做某事 jiānchí zuò mǒushì □ She insisted on paying. 她坚持要付款。Tā jiānchí yào fùkuǎn.

inspector NOUN
警督 jǐngdū [位 wèi] *(official)*
□ Inspector Jill Brown 吉尔・布朗警督 Jí'ěr Bùlǎng jǐngdū
■ **ticket inspector** *(on buses)* 查票员

chápiàoyuán [位 wèi]

to **install** (US **instal**) VERB
安装 ānzhuāng

instalment (US **installment**) NOUN
分期付款 fēnqī fùkuǎn [期 qī]
■ **to pay in instalments** 分期付款 fēnqī fùkuǎn

instance NOUN
例子 lìzi [个 gè] *(example)*
■ **for instance** 例如 lìrú

instant NOUN
▷ *see also* **instant** ADJECTIVE
瞬息 shùnxī [个 gè] *(moment)*
■ **for an instant** 一瞬间 yī shùnjiān

instant ADJECTIVE
▷ *see also* **instant** NOUN
1 即时的 jíshí de *(reaction, success)*
□ It was an instant success. 那是个即时的胜利。Nà shì gè jíshí de shènglì.
2 速食的 sùshí de *(coffee, soup, noodles)*
■ **instant coffee** 速溶咖啡 sùróng kāfēi

instantly ADVERB
立即 lìjí

instead ADVERB
作为代替 zuòwéi dàitì
□ The pool was closed, so we played tennis instead. 泳池关闭了，所以我们打网球作为代替。Yǒngchí guānbì le, suǒyǐ wǒmen dǎ wǎngqiú zuòwéi dàitì.
■ **instead of** 取代 qǔdài □ He went instead of Peter. 他取代彼德去了。Tā qǔdài Bǐdé qù le. □ We played tennis instead of going swimming. 我们打了网球，取代了游泳。Wǒmen dǎ le wǎngqiú, qǔdài le yóuyǒng.

instinct NOUN
本能 běnnéng [种 zhǒng]

institute NOUN
学会 xuéhuì [个 gè]

institution NOUN
机构 jīgòu [个 gè]

to **instruct** VERB
■ **to instruct somebody to do something** 示意某人做某事 shìyì mǒurén zuò mǒushì
□ She instructed us to wait outside. 她示意我们在外面等。Tā shìyì wǒmen zài wàimiàn děng.

instructions PL NOUN
1 说明 shuōmíng *(on label, in manual)*
□ Follow the instructions carefully. 谨慎遵照说明。Jǐnshèn zūnzhào shuōmíng.
2 说明书 shuōmíngshū *(booklet)*
□ Where are the instructions? 说明书在哪？Shuōmíngshū zài nǎ?

instructor NOUN
教员 jiàoyuán [位 wèi]
□ a skiing instructor 一位滑雪教员 yíwèi huáxuě jiàoyuán □ a driving instructor 一位驾驶教员 yíwèi jiàshǐ jiàoyuán

instrument NOUN
1 乐器 yuèqì [件 jiàn] *(music)*
□ Do you play an instrument? 你会弹奏乐器吗？Nǐ huì tánzòu yuèqì mā?
2 器械 qìxiè [件 jiàn] *(tool)*

insufficient ADJECTIVE
不足的 bùzú de

insulin NOUN
胰岛素 yídǎosù

insult NOUN
▷ *see also* **insult** VERB
侮辱 wǔrǔ [个 gè]

to **insult** VERB
▷ *see also* **insult** NOUN
侮辱 wǔrǔ

insurance NOUN
保险 bǎoxiǎn
□ his car insurance 他的汽车保险 tāde qìchē bǎoxiǎn
■ **life insurance** 人寿保险 rénshòu bǎoxiǎn
■ **health insurance** 健康险 jiànkāng xiǎn
■ **an insurance policy** 一项保险政策 yíxiàng bǎoxiǎn zhèngcè

to **insure** VERB
给...保险 gěi...bǎoxiǎn *(house, car)*

intelligent ADJECTIVE
聪明的 cōngmíng de

to **intend** VERB
■ **to intend to do something** 打算做某事 dǎsuàn zuò mǒushì □ I intend to do Chinese at university. 我打算在大学学习中文。Wǒ dǎsuàn zài dàxué xuéxí Zhōngwén.

intense ADJECTIVE
1 剧烈的 jùliè de *(heat, pain)*
2 激烈的 jīliè de *(competition)*

intensive ADJECTIVE
强化的 qiánghuà de

intensive care NOUN
■ **to be in intensive care** 接受强化护理 jiēshòu qiánghuà hùlǐ

intention NOUN
打算 dǎsuàn [个 gè]

intercom NOUN
内部通信系统 nèibù tōngxìn xìtǒng [个 gè]

interest NOUN
▷ *see also* **interest** VERB
1 兴趣 xìngqù *(in subject, idea, person)*
■ **to take an interest in something** 对某事感兴趣 duì mǒushì gǎn xìngqù
2 爱好 àihào [个 gè] *(pastime, hobby)*
■ **What interests do you have?** 你有什么爱好？Nǐ yǒu shénme àihào?

■ **My main interest is music.** 我的主要爱好是音乐。Wǒde zhǔyào àihào shì yīnyuè.
3 利息 lìxī *(on loan, savings)*

to **interest** VERB
▷ *see also* **interest** NOUN
吸引 xīyǐn
□ It doesn't interest me. 它并不吸引我。Tā bìng bù xīyǐn wǒ.

interested ADJECTIVE
■ **to be interested in something** 对某事感兴趣 duì mǒushì gǎn xìngqù □ I'm not interested in politics. 我对政治不感兴趣。Wǒ duì zhèngzhì bùgǎn xìngqù.

interesting ADJECTIVE
有趣的 yǒuqù de

to **interfere** VERB
干涉 gānshè *(meddle)*
■ **to interfere with something** *(plans, career, duty)* 妨碍某事 fáng'ài mǒushì

interior NOUN
内部 nèibù

interior designer NOUN
室内装饰设计师 shìnèi zhuāngshì shèjìshī [位 wèi]

intermediate ADJECTIVE
中级的 zhōngjí de *(course, level)*

intermission NOUN
休息时间 xiūxi shíjiān [段 duàn] *(in film)*

internal ADJECTIVE
内部的 nèibù de

international ADJECTIVE
国际的 guójì de

internet NOUN
■ **the internet** 因特网 Yīntèwǎng □ I read it on the internet. 我在因特网上看到的。Wǒ zài Yīntèwǎng shàng kàndào de.

DID YOU KNOW...?
China has more internet users than anywhere else in the world.

internet café NOUN
吧 wǎngbā [个 gè]

internet user NOUN
网民 wǎngmín [个 gè]

LANGUAGE TIP Word for word, this means 'person of the network'.

to **interpret** VERB
口译 kǒuyì
□ Steve interpreted into English for his friend. 史蒂夫帮他朋友做英文口译。Shǐdìfū bāng tā péngyǒu zuò yīngwén kǒuyì.

interpreter NOUN
口译者 kǒuyìzhě [位 wèi]

to **interrupt** VERB
1 打断 dǎduàn *(person)*
2 中断 zhōngduàn *(activity)*
3 打岔 dǎchà *(in conversation)*
□ Stop interrupting! 不要打岔！Búyào dǎchà!

interruption NOUN
打扰 dǎrǎo [种 zhǒng]

interval NOUN
1 间隔 jiàngé [个 gè] *(break, pause)*
2 幕间休息 mùjiān xiūxi [个 gè] *(theatre, music, sport)*

interview NOUN
▷ *see also* **interview** VERB
1 面试 miànshì [次 cì] *(for job)*
2 采访 cǎifǎng [次 cì] *(on television, radio)*

to **interview** VERB
▷ *see also* **interview** NOUN
1 面试 miànshì *(for job)*
■ **to go for an interview** 参加面试 cānjiā miànshì
2 采访 cǎifǎng *(on television, radio)*
□ I was interviewed on the radio. 我在广播中被采访了。Wǒ zài guǎngbō zhōng bèi cǎifǎng le.

interviewer NOUN
采访者 cǎifǎngzhě [位 wèi]

intimate ADJECTIVE
亲密的 qīnmì de

to **intimidate** VERB
恐吓 kǒnghè

into PREPOSITION
到...里 dào...lǐ
■ **Come into the house.** 走进房子里。Zǒujìn fángzi lǐ.
■ **Get into the car.** 进入车子里。Jìnrù chēzi lǐ.
■ **Let's go into town.** 我们去城里吧。Wǒmen qù chénglǐ ba.
■ **to translate Chinese into French** 把中文翻译成法语 bǎ Zhōngwén fānyì chéng Fǎyǔ
■ **research into cancer** 对癌症的深入研究 duì áizhèng de shēnrù yánjiū
■ **I'd like to change some dollars into euros.** 我想把一些美元换成欧元。Wǒ xiǎng bǎ yìxiē měiyuán huànchéng ōuyuán.

to **introduce** VERB
引进 yǐnjìn *(new idea, measure, technology)*
■ **to introduce somebody to somebody** 把某人介绍给某人 bǎ mǒurén jièshào gěi mǒurén □ He introduced me to his parents. 他把我介绍给他的父母。Tā bǎ wǒ jièshào gěi tāde fùmǔ.
■ **May I introduce you to...?** 让我介绍你认识…好吗？Ràng wǒ jièshaò nǐ ... hǎo ma?
□ I'd like to introduce Michelle Davies. 我想

向你们介绍米歇尔·戴维斯。Wǒ xiǎng xiàng nǐmen jièshào Mǐxiē'ěr Dàiwéisī.

introduction NOUN
1 引进 yǐnjìn *(of new idea, measure, technology)*
2 介绍 jièshào [个 gè] *(of person)*
3 引言 yǐnyán [个 gè] *(of book, talk)*

intruder NOUN
侵入者 qīnrùzhě [个 gè]

intuition NOUN
直觉 zhíjué

to **invade** VERB
侵略 qīnlüè

invalid NOUN
病弱者 bìngruòzhě [个 gè]

to **invent** VERB
发明 fāmíng

invention NOUN
发明 fāmíng [项 xiàng]

inventor NOUN
发明人 fāmíngrén [位 wèi]

to **investigate** VERB
调查 diàochá

investigation NOUN
调查 diàochá [项 xiàng]

investment NOUN
投资 tóuzī [项 xiàng]

invigilator NOUN
监考员 jiānkǎoyuán [位 wèi]

invisible ADJECTIVE
看不见的 kànbùjiàn de

invitation NOUN
1 邀请 yāoqǐng [个 gè]
2 请柬 qǐngjiǎn [封 fēng] *(card)*

to **invite** VERB
邀请 yāoqǐng
□ He's not invited. 他没有被邀请。Tā méiyǒu bèi yāoqǐng.
■ **to invite somebody to do something** 邀请某人做某事 yāoqǐng mǒurén zuò mǒushì
■ **to invite somebody to dinner** 请某人赴宴 qǐng mǒurén fùyàn
■ **to invite somebody to a party** 邀请某人去聚会 yāoqǐng mǒurén qù jùhuì

to **involve** VERB
1 涉及 shèjí *(entail)*
□ His job involves a lot of travelling. 他的工作涉及到经常出差。Tāde gōngzuò shèjí dào jīngcháng chūchāi.
2 使卷入 shǐ juǎnrù *(concern, affect)*
■ **to involve somebody in something** 使某人参与某事 shǐ mǒurén cānyù mǒushì
■ **to be involved in something** *(crime, drugs)* 牵扯到某事 qiānchě dào mǒushì
■ **to be involved with somebody** *(in relationship)* 与某人有关 yǔ mǒurén yǒuguān

iPad®
苹果平板电脑 Píngguǒ píngbǎn diànnǎo

iPhone®
苹果手机 Píngguǒ shǒujī

iPod®
数码随身听 shùmǎ suíshēntīng [个 gè]

IQ NOUN *(= intelligence quotient)*
智商 zhìshāng

Iran NOUN
伊朗 Yīlǎng

Iranian NOUN
▷ *see also* **Iranian** ADJECTIVE
伊朗人 Yīlǎngrén
■ **the Iranians** 伊朗人 Yīlǎngrén

Iranian ADJECTIVE
▷ *see also* **Iranian** NOUN
伊朗的 Yīlǎng de

Iraq NOUN
伊拉克 Yīlākè

Iraqi ADJECTIVE
▷ *see also* **Iraqi** NOUN
伊拉克的 Yīlākè de
□ the Iraqi government 伊拉克政府 Yīlákè zhèngfǔ

Iraqi NOUN
▷ *see also* **Iraqi** ADJECTIVE
伊拉克人 Yīlākèrén [名 míng] *(person)*
■ **the Iraqis** 伊拉克人 Yīlākèrén

Ireland NOUN
爱尔兰 Ài'ěrlán
■ **the Republic of Ireland** 爱尔兰共和国 Ài'ěrlán Gònghéguó
■ **I'm from Ireland.** 我来自爱尔兰。Wǒ láizì Ài'ěrlán.

Irish ADJECTIVE
▷ *see also* **Irish** NOUN
爱尔兰的 Ài'ěrlán de
□ Irish music 爱尔兰音乐 Ài'ěrlán yīnyuè

Irish NOUN
▷ *see also* **Irish** ADJECTIVE
爱尔兰语 Ài'ěrlányǔ *(language)*
■ **the Irish** *(people)* 爱尔兰人 Ài'ěrlánrén

Irishman NOUN
爱尔兰男人 Ài'ěrlán nánrén [个 gè]

Irishwoman NOUN
爱尔兰女人 Ài'ěrlán nǚrén [个 gè]

iron NOUN
▷ *see also* **iron** ADJECTIVE, VERB
1 铁 tiě *(metal)*
2 熨斗 yùndǒu [个 gè] *(for clothes)*

iron ADJECTIVE
▷ *see also* **iron** NOUN, VERB
铁的 tiě de *(bar, railings)*

to **iron** VERB
▷ *see also* **iron** ADJECTIVE, NOUN

熨 yùn *(clothes)*

ironic ADJECTIVE
讽刺的 fěngcì de

ironing NOUN
熨衣服 yùnyīfu
□ to do the ironing 熨衣服 yùnyīfu

ironing board NOUN
熨衣板 yùnyībǎn [块 kuài]

ironmonger's NOUN
五金店 wǔjīndiàn [家 jiā]

ironmonger's shop NOUN
五金店 wǔjīndiàn [家 jiā]

irrelevant ADJECTIVE
无关的 wúguān de
□ That's irrelevant. 那是无关的。Nà shì wúguān de.

irresponsible ADJECTIVE
1 无责任感的 wú zérèngǎn de *(person, driver)*
2 不负责任的 bù fù zérèn de *(attitude, behaviour)*
□ That was irresponsible of him. 他那样是不责任的。Tā màyàng shì búfùzérèn de.

irritating ADJECTIVE
烦人的 fánrén de

is VERB ▷ *see* **be**

Islam NOUN
伊斯兰教 Yīsīlánjiào

Islamic ADJECTIVE
1 伊斯兰教的 Yīsīlánjiào de *(law, faith)*
□ Islamic law 伊斯兰教法 Yīsīlánjiào jiàofǎ
2 伊斯兰的 Yīsīlán de *(country)*
■ **Islamic fundamentalists** 伊斯兰正统派教徒 Yīsīlán zhèongtǒngpài jiàotú

island NOUN
岛 dǎo [个 gè]

isle NOUN
■ **the Isle of Man** 曼岛 Màn dǎo
■ **the Isle of Wight** 怀特岛 Huáitè dǎo

isolated ADJECTIVE
1 孤零零的 gūlínglíng de *(place)*
2 孤立的 gūlì de *(person)*
3 个别的 gèbié de *(incident, case, example)*

ISP NOUN *(= internet service provider)*
网络服务供应商 Wǎngluò fúwù gōongyìngshāng [家 jiā]

Israel NOUN
以色列 Yǐsèliè

Israeli ADJECTIVE
▷ *see also* **Israeli** NOUN
以色列的 Yǐsèliè de

Israeli NOUN
▷ *see also* **Israeli** ADJECTIVE
以色列人 Yǐsèlièrén [名 míng] *(person)*

issue NOUN
▷ *see also* **issue** VERB
1 问题 wèntí [个 gè] *(problem, subject)*
□ a controversial issue 一个引争议的问题 yígè yǐn zhēngyì de wèntí
2 期 qī *(of magazine)*

to **issue** VERB
▷ *see also* **issue** NOUN
配给 pèijǐ *(equipment, supplies)*

IT NOUN *(= Information Technology)*
信息技术 xìnxī jìshù

it PRONOUN
1 它 tā *(object or animal)*
2 她 tā *(referring to a female baby)*
3 他 tā *(referring to a male baby)*

LANGUAGE TIP When **it** refers to the weather, a date or a time, it is often not translated.

□ It's raining. 正在下雨。Zhèngzài xiàyǔ.
□ It's 6 o'clock. 现在六点钟。Xiànzài liù diǎn zhōng. □ It's Friday tomorrow. 明天是星期五。Míngtiān shì Xīngqīwǔ.

LANGUAGE TIP When **it** is used as an impersonal pronoun, it is usually not translated.

□ It doesn't matter. 没关系。Méiguānxi.
□ I can't find it. 我找不到。Wǒ zhǎo bù dào. □ Where's my book? — It's on the table. 我的书在哪？— 在桌上。Wǒde shū zài nǎ? — Zài zhuōshàng. □ He's got a new car. — Yes, I saw it. 他有了一辆新车。— 嗯，我看到了。Tā yǒule yíliàng xīnchē. — En, wǒ kàndào le.
■ **What is it?** **1** *(thing)* 是什么东西？Shì shénme dōngxi? **2** *(what's the matter)* 怎么了？Zěnme le?
■ **Who is it? — It's me.** 是谁？— 是我。Shì shuí? — Shìwǒ.

Italian ADJECTIVE
▷ *see also* **Italian** NOUN
意大利的 Yìdàlì de

Italian NOUN
▷ *see also* **Italian** ADJECTIVE
1 意大利人 Yìdàlìrén [名 míng] *(person)*
2 意大利语 Yìdàlìyǔ *(language)*

Italy NOUN
意大利 Yìdàlì

to **itch** VERB
痒 yǎng
■ **It itches.** 这儿痒。Zhè'r yǎng.
■ **My head's itching.** 我的头痒。Wǒde tóu yǎng.

itchy ADJECTIVE
痒的 yǎng de
■ **My arm is itchy.** 我的胳膊痒。Wǒde gēbo yǎng.

it'd = **it would, it had**

item NOUN
1 项目 xiàngmù [个 gè]

■ **items of clothing** 几件衣服 jǐjiàn yīfu
2 物品 wùpǐn *(on bill)*

itinerary NOUN
旅程 lǔchéng [份 fèn]

it'll = **it will**

its ADJECTIVE
1 它的 tā de *(of animal)*
□ The dog is biting its foot. 这只狗正在咬它的脚。Zhè zhī gǒu zhèngzài yǎo tāde jiǎo.
2 她的 tāde *(of female baby)*
3 他的 tāde *(of male baby)*
□ What's its name? 他的名字叫什么？Tāde míngzì jiào shénme？
■ **Everything is in its place.** 每件东西都在原位。Měijiàn dōngxi dōu zài yuánwèi.

it's = **it is, it has**

itself PRONOUN
自己 zìjǐ
□ It switches itself on automatically. 它会自动打开。Tā huì zìdòng dǎkāi.
■ **by itself** *(alone)* 单独地 dāndú de

I've = **I have**

Jj

jab NOUN
注射 zhùshè [次 cì] *(injection)*
jack NOUN
千斤顶 qiānjīndǐng [个 gè]
jacket NOUN
夹克 jiākè [件 jiàn]
■ **jacket potatoes** 带皮烤的土豆 dàipí kǎo de tǔdòu
jackpot NOUN
■ **to win the jackpot** 赢头奖 yíng tóujiǎng
jail NOUN
▷ *see also* **jail** VERB
监狱 jiānyù [个 gè]
■ **to go to jail** 蹲监狱 dūn jiānyù
to **jail** VERB
▷ *see also* **jail** NOUN
监禁 jiānjìn
jam NOUN
果酱 guǒjiàng [瓶 píng] *(preserve)*
□ strawberry jam 草莓果酱 cǎoméi guǒjiàng
■ **a traffic jam** 交通堵塞 jiāotōng dǔsè
jammed ADJECTIVE
□ The window's jammed. 窗户给卡住了。Chuānghu gěi qiǎzhù le.
jam-packed ADJECTIVE
□ The room was jam-packed. 房间给挤满了。Fángjiān gěi jǐmǎn le.
janitor NOUN
大楼管理员 dàlóu guǎnlǐyuán [个 gè]
□ He's a janitor. 他是一个大楼管理员。Tā shì yígè dàlóu guǎnlǐyuán.
January NOUN
一月 yīyuè
□ in January 在一月 zài yīyuè □ the first of January 一月一日 yīyuè yīrì □ at the beginning of January 在一月初 zài yīyuè chū □ at the end of January 在一月末 zài yīyuè mò □ every January 每年一月 měinián yīyuè
Japan NOUN
日本 Rìběn
□ in Japan 在日本 zài Rìběn □ from Japan 从日本来 cóng Rìběn lái
Japanese ADJECTIVE
▷ *see also* **Japanese** NOUN
日本的 Rìběn de
Japanese NOUN
▷ *see also* **Japanese** ADJECTIVE
1 日本人 Rìběnrén [个 gè] *(person)*
■ **the Japanese** 日本人 Rìběnrén
2 日语 Rìyǔ *(language)*
□ She speaks Japanese. 她会说日语。Tā huì shuō Rìyǔ.
jar NOUN
罐子 guànzi [个 gè]
□ a jar of honey 一罐蜂蜜 yí guàn fēngmì
jaundice NOUN
黄疸病 huángdǎnbìng [场 chǎng]
jaw NOUN
下巴 xiàba [个 gè]
■ **jaws** 嘴 zuǐ
jazz NOUN
爵士乐 juéshìyuè
jealous ADJECTIVE
1 爱妒忌的 ài dùjì de
□ her jealous husband 她爱妒忌的丈夫 tā ài dùjì de zhàngfu
2 妒忌的 dùjì de *(envious)*
■ **I'm jealous!** 我很羡慕！Wǒ hěn xiànmù!
jeans PL NOUN
牛仔裤 niúzǎikù
■ **a pair of jeans** 一条牛仔裤 yìtiáo niúzǎikù
Jehovah's Witness NOUN
耶和华见证人 Yéhéhuá Jiànzhèngrén
□ She's a Jehovah's Witness. 她是一位耶和华见证人信徒。Tā shì yíwei Yéhéhuá Jiànzhèngrén xìntú.
Jello® NOUN (US)
果冻 guǒdòng [个 gè]
jelly NOUN
果冻 guǒdòng [个 gè]
jellyfish NOUN
水母 shuǐmǔ [只 zhī]
jersey NOUN *(pullover)*
针织毛衫 zhēnzhī máoshān [件 jiàn]
Jesus NOUN
耶稣 Yēsū
■ **Jesus Christ** 耶稣基督 Yēsū Jīdū

jet NOUN
喷气式飞机 pēnqìshì fēijī [架 jià] *(aeroplane)*

jet lag NOUN
时差反应 shíchā fǎnyìng

jetty NOUN
防波堤 fángbōdī [道 dào]

Jew NOUN
犹太人 Yóutàirén [个 gè]

jewel NOUN
宝石 bǎoshí [块 kuài]

jeweller NOUN
宝石商 bǎoshíshāng [个 gè]

jeweller's shop NOUN
宝石商店 bǎoshí shāngdiàn [家 jiā]

jewellery (US **jewelry**) NOUN
首饰 shǒushì

Jewish ADJECTIVE
犹太的 Yóutài de

jigsaw NOUN
拼图玩具 pīntú wánjù [套 tào]

job NOUN
1 工作 gōngzuò [份 fèn] *(position)*
□ He's lost his job. 他丢了他的工作。Tā diūle tāde gōngzuò. □ Gladys got a job as a secretary. 格拉迪斯找到了一份秘书工作。Gélādīsí zhǎodào le yífèn mìshū gōngzuò. □ I've got a Saturday job. 我有一份星期六上班的工作。Wǒ yǒu yīfèn xīngqīliù shàngbān de gōngzuò.
2 任务 rènwù [项 xiàng] *(task)*
□ That was a difficult job. 那是一项困难的任务。Nāshì yíxiàng kùnnán de rènwù.
■ **a part-time job** 一份兼职工作 yífèn jiānzhí gōngzuò
■ **a full-time job** 一份全职工作 yífèn quánzhí gōngzuò

job centre NOUN
就业中心 jiùyè zhōngxīn [个 gè]

jobless ADJECTIVE
失业的 shīyè de

jockey NOUN
赛马骑师 sàimǎ qíshī [位 wèi]

to **jog** VERB
慢跑 mànpǎo

jogging NOUN
慢跑 mànpǎo
■ **to go jogging** 去慢跑 qù mànpǎo

to **join** VERB
1 加入 jiārù
□ I'm going to join the ski club. 我将加入该滑雪俱乐部。Wǒ jiāng jiārù gāi huáxuě jùlèbù.
2 会面 huìmiàn
□ Do you mind if I join you? 你会介意我加入吗？Nǐ huì jièyì wǒ jiārù ma? □ Will you join us for dinner? 你想不想和我们一起吃晚饭？Nǐ xiǎngbuxiǎng hé wǒmen yìqǐ chīwǎnfàn?

to **join in** VERB
参与 cānyù

joiner NOUN
细木工人 xìmù gōngrén [个 gè]
□ He's a joiner. 他是一个细木工人。Tā shì yígè xìmù gōngrén.

joint NOUN
1 关节 guānjié [个 gè] *(in body)*
2 大块肉 dàkuàiròu [块 kuài] *(meat)*

joke NOUN
▷ *see also* **joke** VERB
笑话 xiàohua [个 gè]
■ **to tell a joke** 说一个笑话 shuō yígè xiàohua

to **joke** VERB
▷ *see also* **joke** NOUN
开玩笑 kāi wánxiào
□ I'm only joking. 我只是开玩笑。Wǒ zhǐshì kāi wánxiào. □ You must be joking! 你一定在开玩笑吧！Nǐ yídìng zài kāi wánxiào ba!

jolly ADJECTIVE
快活的 kuàihuo de

Jordan NOUN
约旦 Yuēdàn
□ in Jordan 在约旦 zài Yuēdàn

jotter NOUN
笔记本 bǐjìběn [本 běn]

journalism NOUN
新闻业 xīnwényè

journalist NOUN
新闻工作者 xīnwén gōngzuòzhě [位 wèi]
□ She's a journalist. 她是一位新闻工作者。Tā shì yíwei xīnwén gōngzuòzhě.

journey NOUN
旅程 lǚchéng [段 duàn]
□ I don't like long journeys. 我不喜欢长途旅程。Wǒ bù xǐhuan chángtú lǚchéng.
□ The journey to school takes about half an hour. 到学校的路程大概要半个小时。Dào xuéxiào de lùchéng dàgài yào bàngèxiǎoshí. □ a 5-hour journey 五个小时的路程 wǔgè xiǎoshí de lùchéng □ a bus journey 公共汽车旅程 gōnggòng qìchē lǚchéng
■ **to go on a journey** 去旅行 qù lǚxíng

joy NOUN
快乐 kuàilè

joystick NOUN
操纵杆 cāozònggǎn [根 gēn]

judge NOUN
▷ *see also* **judge** VERB
1 法官 fǎguān [位 wèi]

□ She's a judge. 她是一位法官。Tā shì yíwèi fǎguān.

2 裁判 cáipàn [个 gè] *(of competition)*

to **judge** VERB
▷ *see also* **judge** NOUN
评定 píngdìng

judo NOUN
柔道 róudào
□ My hobby is judo. 我的爱好是柔道。Wǒde àihào shì róudào.

jug NOUN
壶 hú [把 bǎ]

juggler NOUN
玩杂耍的人 wǎn záshuǎ de rén [个 gè]

juice NOUN
汁 zhī [杯 bēi]
□ orange juice 橙汁 chénzhī

July NOUN
七月 qīyuè
□ in July 在七月 zài qīyuè □ the first of July 七月一日 qīyuè yīrì □ at the beginning of July 在七月初 zài qīyuè chū □ at the end of July 在七月末 zài qīyuè mò □ every July 每年七月 měinián qīyuè

jumble sale NOUN
废旧杂货大拍卖 fèijiù záhuò dàpāimài [次 cì]

to **jump** VERB
▷ *see also* **jump** NOUN
跳 tiào
■ **to jump over something** 跳过某物 tiàoguò mǒuwù
■ **to jump out of a window** 从窗户跳下 cóng chuānghu tiàoxià
■ **to jump on something** 跳上某物 tiàoshàng mǒuwù
■ **to jump off something** 跳下某物 tiàoxià mǒuwù
■ **to jump the queue** 加塞儿 jiāsāi'r

jump NOUN
▷ *see also* **jump** VERB
跳 tiào

jumper NOUN
毛衣 máoyī [件 jiàn]

junction NOUN
交叉点 jiāochādiǎn [个 gè]

June NOUN
六月 liùyuè
□ in June 在六月 zài liùyuè □ the first of June 六月一日 liùyuè yīrì □ at the beginning of June 在六月初 zài liùyuè chū □ at the end of June 在六月末 zài liùyuè mò □ every June 每年六月 měinián liùyuè

jungle NOUN
丛林 cónglín [片 piàn]

junior ADJECTIVE
▷ *see also* **junior** NOUN
较年幼的 jiào niányòu de
■ **George Bush Junior** (US) 小乔治・布什 xiǎo Qiáozhì·Bùshí

junior NOUN
▷ *see also* **junior** ADJECTIVE
小学生 xiǎo xuésheng
■ **the juniors** *(in school)* 小学生们 xiǎo xuéshengmen

junior high NOUN (US)
初中 chūzhōng [所 suǒ]

junior school NOUN
小学 xiǎoxué [所 suǒ]

junk NOUN
废旧杂物 fèijiù záwù
□ The attic's full of junk. 屋顶室塞满废旧杂物。Wūdǐngshì sāimǎn fèijiù záwù.
■ **to eat junk food** 吃垃圾食品 chī lājī shípǐn
■ **a junk shop** 一家废品旧货店 yìjia fèipǐn jiùhuò diàn

jury NOUN
1 陪审团 péishěntuán [个 gè] *(at trial)*
2 评审团 píngshěn tuán [个 gè] *(in competition)*

just ADVERB
▷ *see also* **just** ADJECTIVE
1 合适 héshì
□ It's just right. 正合适。Zhèng héshì.
2 仅仅 jǐnjǐn
□ It's just a suggestion. 它仅仅是个建议而已。Tā jǐnjǐn shì gè jiànyì éryǐ.

LANGUAGE TIP A sentence using the word **just**, as in **only** or **merely**, can be emphasised by adding the phrase 而已 éryǐ to the end, which means **that's all**.

3 刚好 gānghǎo
□ We had just enough money. 我们刚好有足够的钱。Wǒmén gānghǎo yǒu zúgòu de qián. □ We were just going. 我们刚好正要走。Wǒmen gānghǎo zhèngyào zǒu. □ I'm just finishing this. 我刚好要做完了。Wǒ gānghǎo yào zuòwán le.
■ **just in time** 刚好赶上 gānghǎo gǎnshàng
■ **just here** 正是这里 zhèngshì zhèlǐ
■ **just before...** 就在…以前 jiùzài...yǐqián
■ **just after...** 就在…以后 jiùzài...yǐhòu
4 只是 zhǐshì *(in instructions, requests)*
■ **just a minute** **1** *(asking someone to wait)* 等一下 děng yixià **2** *(interrupting)* 慢着 mànzhe
■ **to have just done something** 刚刚做完某事 gānggāng zuòwán mǒushì □ He's just arrived. 他刚刚到了。Tā gānggāng dào le.

■ **just now** **1** *(a moment ago)* 刚才 gāngcái ▫ I did it just now. 我就刚才做了。Wǒ jiù gāngcái zuò le. **2** *(at the present time)* 现在 xiànzài ▫ I'm rather busy just now. 我现在相当忙。Wǒ xiànzài xiāngdāng máng.
■ **just about everything** 差不多所有东西 chàbuduō suǒyǒu dōngxi
■ **just about everyone** 差不多所有所有人 chàbuduō suǒyǒu rén
■ **just enough time** 仅仅够时间 jǐnjǐn gòu shíjiān
■ **just enough money** 仅仅够钱 jǐnjǐn gòu qián

just ADJECTIVE
▷ *see also* **just** ADVERB
1 公平的 gōngpíng de *(reward)*
2 公正的 gōngzhèng de *(society, cause)*

justice NOUN
1 司法 sīfǎ *(system)*
2 正义 zhèngyì *(fairness)*

to **justify** VERB
证明…有理 zhèngmíng…yǒulǐ

Kk

K ABBREVIATION
1 千 qiān *(thousands)*
2 千字节 qiānzìjié *(kilobytes)*

kangaroo NOUN
袋鼠 dàishǔ [只 zhī]

karaoke NOUN
卡拉OK kǎlā ōukèi

karate NOUN
空手道 kōngshǒudào

kebab NOUN
烤肉串 kǎoròu chuàn

keen ADJECTIVE
热衷的 rèzhōng de
▫ He doesn't seem very keen. 他好像不是很热衷。Tā hǎoxiàng búshì hěn rèzhōng.
■ **to be keen on something** 喜爱某事 xǐài mǒushì ▫ I'm keen on maths. 我喜爱数学。Wǒ xǐ'ài shùxué. ▫ I'm not very keen on geography. 我不是很喜爱地理科。Wǒ búshì hěn xǐ'ài dìlǐkē.
■ **to be keen to do something** 渴望做某事 kěwàng zuò mǒushì
■ **to be keen on doing something** 热衷于做某事 rèzhōng yú zuò mǒushì ▫ I'm not very keen on going. 我不是很热衷要去。Wǒ búshì hěn rèzhōng yào qù.
■ **to be keen on somebody** 对某人着迷 dùi mǒurén zháomí ▫ He's keen on her. 他对她着迷。Tā dùi tā zháomí.

to **keep** VERB
1 保留 bǎoliú
▫ You can keep it. 你可以保留它。Nǐ kěyǐ bǎoliú tā.
2 保存 bǎocún *(store)*
3 留 liú *(detain)*
■ **to keep still** 保持不动 bǎochí búdòng
■ **to keep quiet** 保持安静 bǎochí ānjìng
■ **to keep doing something** 1 *(repeatedly)* 总是做某事 zǒngshì zuò mǒushì ▫ I keep forgetting my keys. 我总是忘记我的钥匙。Wǒ zǒngshì wàngjì wǒde yàoshi.
2 *(continuously)* 不停做某事 bùtíng zuò mǒushì ▫ Keep stirring. 不停拨动。Bùtíng bōdòng.
■ **to keep somebody waiting** 让某人等着 ràng mǒurén děngzhe
■ **to keep the room tidy** 保持房间整洁 bǎochí fángjiān zhěngjié
■ **to keep a promise** 履行诺言 lǚxíng nuòyán
■ **to keep a secret** 保守秘密 bǎoshǒu mìmì ▫ Can you keep a secret? 你能保守秘密吗？Nǐ néng bǎoshǒu mìmì ma?
■ **to keep a record of something** 记录某事 jìlù mǒushì
■ **How are you keeping?** 你还好吗？Nǐ hái hǎo ma?

to **keep away** VERB
■ **to keep away from something** 不接近某处 bù jiējìn mǒuchù

to **keep off** VERB
■ **Keep off the grass!** 请勿进入草坪！Qǐng wù jìnrù cǎopíng!

to **keep on** VERB
■ **to keep on doing something** *(continue)* 继续做某事 jìxù zuò mǒushì ▫ He kept on reading. 他继续阅读。Tā jìxù yuèdú.
▫ The car keeps on breaking down. 汽车继续出毛病。Qìchē jìxù chū máobìng.

to **keep out** VERB
■ **'keep out'** "严禁入内" "yánjìn rùnèi"

to **keep up** VERB
跟上 gēnshang
▫ Matthew walks so fast I can't keep up. 马修走得那么快以致我跟不上。Mǎxiū zǒu de nàme kuài yǐzhì wǒ gēnbushang. ▫ I can't keep up with the rest of the class. 我跟不上班上其他人。Wǒ gēnbushang bānshàng qítārén.

keep-fit NOUN
健身 jiànshēn
▫ I go to keep-fit classes. 我去健身班。Wǒ qù jiànshēn bān.

kennel NOUN
狗房 gǒufáng [个 gè]

kept VERB ▷ *see* **keep**

kerb (US **curb**) NOUN
路缘 lùyuán [个 gè]

kerosene NOUN
煤油 méiyóu [罐 guàn]

ketchup NOUN
番茄酱 fānqiéjiàng

kettle NOUN
水壶 shuǐhú [把 bǎ]

key NOUN
1 钥匙 yàoshi [把 bǎ]
□ Here's your key. 这是你的钥匙。Zhèshì nǐde yàoshi.
2 键 jiàn [个 gè] *(on keyboard)*

keyboard NOUN
键盘 jiànpán [个 gè]
□ He played keyboard in high school. 他高中时演奏过键盘乐器。Tā gāozhōng shí yǎnzòu guò jiànpán yuèqì.

keyhole NOUN
钥匙孔 yàoshikǒng [个 gè]

keyring NOUN
钥匙圈 yàoshiquān [个 gè]

to **kick** VERB
▷ *see also* **kick** NOUN
踢 tī
□ He kicked me. 他踢了我。Tā tī le wǒ.
□ He kicked the ball hard. 他猛踢了那个球。Tā měng tī le nàge qiú.
■ **to kick off** *(in football)* 开赛 kāisài

kick NOUN
▷ *see also* **kick** VERB
踢 tī [顿 dùn]

kick-off NOUN
开场时间 kāichǎng shíjiān
□ The kick-off is at 10 o'clock. 开场时间是十点。Kāichǎng shíjiān shì shídiǎn.

kid NOUN
▷ *see also* **kid** VERB
1 小孩 xiǎohái [个 gè]
□ a little kid 一个小孩 yígè xiǎohái
2 年轻人 niánqīngrén [个 gè]
□ teenage kids 十几岁的少年 shíjǐ suì de shàonián

to **kid** VERB
▷ *see also* **kid** NOUN
开玩笑 kāi wánxiào
□ You're kidding! 你一定是在开玩笑吧！Nǐ yídìng shì zài kāi wánxiào ba!

to **kidnap** VERB
绑架 bǎngjià

kidney NOUN
1 肾脏 shènzàng [个 gè]
□ He's got kidney trouble. 他有肾病。Tā yǒu shènbìng.
2 腰子 yāozi [个 gè]
□ I don't like kidneys. 我不喜欢吃腰子。Wǒ bù xǐhuan chī yāozi.
■ **kidney beans** 菜豆 càidòu

to **kill** VERB
1 使...丧生 shǐ...sàngshēng
□ He was killed in a car accident. 他是在汽车意外事故中丧生的。Tā shì zài qìchē yìwài shìgù zhōng sàngshēng de.
□ Luckily, nobody was killed. 幸好没有人丧生。Xìnghǎo méiyou rén sàngshēng.
□ Six people were killed in the accident. 六个人在意外事故中丧生。Liùge rén zài yìwài shìgù zhōng sàngsheng.
■ **My back's killing me.** 我的背疼死了。Wǒde bèi téngsǐ le.
■ **to kill oneself** 自杀 zìshā □ He killed himself. 他自杀了。Tā zìshā le.
2 谋杀 móushā *(murder)*

killer NOUN
凶手 xiōngshǒu [个 gè]
□ The police are searching for the killer. 警察在搜索凶手。Jǐngchá zài sōusuǒ xiōngshǒu. □ a hired killer 受雇的杀手 shòugù de shāshǒu □ Meningitis can be a killer. 脑膜炎可以致命。Nǎomóyán kěyǐ zhìmìng.

kilo NOUN
公斤 gōngjīn
□ 10 euros a kilo 十欧元一公斤 shíōuyuán yì gōngjīn

> **DID YOU KNOW...?**
> The standard unit of weight, especially when buying food in a market is 斤 jīn, which is **half a kilo.**

kilometre (US **kilometer**) NOUN
公里 gōnglǐ

kilt NOUN
苏格兰褶子短裙 sūgélán zhězi duǎnqún [条 tiáo]

kind ADJECTIVE
▷ *see also* **kind** NOUN
友好的 yǒuhǎo de
□ Thank you for being so kind. 感谢你那么友好。Gǎn xiè nǐ nàme yǒuhǎo. □ It was kind of them to help. 他们来帮忙真是太好了。Tāmen lái bāngmáng zhēnshì tàihǎo le.
■ **to be kind to somebody** 对某人和蔼 duì mǒurén hé'ǎi

kind NOUN
▷ *see also* **kind** ADJECTIVE
种类 zhǒnglèi
□ It's a kind of sausage. 那是一类香肠。Nàshi yìzhǒng xiāngcháng. □ an opportunity to meet all kinds of people 与各种各样的人见面的机会 yǔ gèzhǒng gèyàng de rén jiànmiàn de jīhuì

kindergarten NOUN
幼儿园 yòuéryuán [所 suǒ]

kindly ADVERB
和蔼地 héǎi de

□ 'Don't worry,' she said kindly. "不要担心，" 她和蔼地说。"Búyào dānxin," tā hé'ǎi de shuō. □ Kindly refrain from smoking. 请不要吸烟。Qǐng búyào xīyān.

kindness NOUN
仁慈 réncí

king NOUN
国王 guówáng [位 wèi]

kingdom NOUN
王国 wángguó [个 gè]

kiosk NOUN
亭子 tíngzi [个 gè]

kipper NOUN
熏制的鱼 xūnzhì de yú [条 tiáo]

kiss NOUN
▷ *see also* **kiss** VERB
吻 wěn [个 gè]
□ a passionate kiss 一个热情的吻 yígè rèqíng de wěn
■ **to give somebody a kiss** 给某人一个吻 gěi mǒurén yígè wěn

to **kiss** VERB
▷ *see also* **kiss** NOUN
吻 wěn
□ He kissed her passionately. 他热烈地吻了她。Tā rèliè de wěn le tā. □ They kissed. 他们接吻了。Tāmen jiēwěn le.
■ **to kiss somebody goodbye** 与某人吻别 yǔ mǒurén wěnbié
■ **to kiss somebody goodnight** 吻某人一下，道晚安 wěn mǒurén yíxià, dào wǎn'ān

kit NOUN
1 成套用品 chéngtào yòngpǐn
□ a tool kit 工具包 gōngjùbāo □ a first aid kit 急救包 jíjiùbāo □ a puncture repair kit 穿孔修理工具包 chuānkǒng xiūlǐ gōngjùbāo □ a sewing kit 针线包 zhēnxiànbāo
2 服装 fúzhuāng
□ I've forgotten my gym kit. 我忘记了我的健身运动套装。Wǒ wàngjì le wǒde jiànshēn yùndòng tàozhuāng.
■ **a drum kit** 一套鼓乐器 yítào gǔyuèqì

kitchen NOUN
厨房 chúfáng [个 gè]
□ a fitted kitchen 按尺寸做的厨房 àn chǐcùn zuò de chúfáng
■ **the kitchen units** 厨房组合家具 chúfáng zǔhé jiājù
■ **a kitchen knife** 厨刀 chúdāo

kite NOUN
风筝 fēngzhēng [个 gè]

kitten NOUN
小猫 xiǎomāo [只 zhī]

knee NOUN
膝盖 xīgài [个 gè]
□ He was on his knees. 他跪着。Tā guìzhe.

to **kneel** VERB
跪下 guìxià

to **kneel down** VERB
跪下 guìxià

knew VERB ▷ *see* **know**

knickers PL NOUN
女式内裤 nǚshì nèikù
■ **a pair of knickers** 一条女式内裤 yìtiáo nǚshì nèikù

knife NOUN
刀 dāo [把 bǎ]
□ knife and fork 刀叉 dāochā

to **knit** VERB
织 zhī

knitting NOUN
编织 biānzhī [种 zhǒng]
□ I like knitting. 我喜欢编织。Wǒ xǐhuan biānzhī.

knives PL NOUN ▷ *see* **knife**

knob NOUN
球形把手 qiúxíng bǎshǒu [个 gè]

knock NOUN
▷ *see also* **knock** VERB
1 碰撞 pèngzhuàng [下 xià]
□ a knock on the head 在头上的一击 zài tóu shàng de yìjī
2 敲门声 qiāoménshēng [声 shēng]
■ **a knock at the door** 门上的一声敲门声 ménshàng de yìshēng qiāoménshēng

to **knock** VERB
▷ *see also* **knock** NOUN
1 碰撞 pèngzhuàng *(strike)*
■ **to knock somebody unconscious** 把某人打昏 bǎ mǒurén dǎhūn
2 敲 qiāo
□ Someone's knocking at the door. 有人在敲门。Yǒurén zài qiāo mén.

to **knock down** VERB
1 撞倒 zhuàngdǎo
□ She was knocked down by a car. 她给汽车撞倒了。Tā gěi qìchē zhuàngdǎo le.
2 拆除 chāichú
□ They're knocking down the old cinema. 他们在拆掉那个老电影院。Tāmen zài chāidiào nàge lǎo diànyǐngyuàn.

to **knock out** VERB
1 打昏 dǎhūn
□ They knocked out the security guard. 他们打昏了那个保安员。Tāmen dǎhūn le nàge bǎo'ānyuán.
2 击昏 jīhūn *(in boxing ring)*
3 淘汰 táotài
□ They were knocked out early in the tournament. 他们在比赛初期已经被淘汰了。Tāmen zài bǐsài chūqī yǐjīng bèi

táotài le.

to **knock over** VERB

撞倒 zhuàngdǎo

knot NOUN

结 jié [个 gè]

■ **to tie a knot in something** 在某物上打个结 zài mǒuwù shàng dǎ gè jié

to **know** VERB

1 知道 zhīdào

□ I don't know. 我不知道。Wǒ bù zhīdào.

□ It's a long way. — Yes, I know. 很远呢。— 对，的确如此。Hěn yuǎn ne. — Duì, díquè rúcǐ.

■ **to know where** 知道何处… zhīdào héchù...

■ **to know when** 知道何时… zhīdào héshí...

■ **to know that...** 知道… zhīdào...

□ I know that you like chocolate. 我知道你喜欢巧克力。Wǒ zhīdào nǐ xǐhuan qiǎokèlì. □ I didn't know that your Dad was a policeman. 我不知道你爸以前是警察。Wǒ bù zhīdào nǐbà yǐqián shì jǐngchá.

■ **you know** 你得知道 nǐ děi zhīdào

□ It's a long way, you know. 很远呢，你得知道。Hěnyuǎn ne, nǐ děi zhīdào.

■ **How should I know?** 我怎么会知道呢？Wǒ zěnme huì zhīdào ne?

2 懂 dǒng

□ I don't know any Japanese. 我一点不懂日语。Wǒ yìdiǎn bù dǒng Rìyǔ.

3 认识 rènshi

□ I know her. 我认识她。Wǒ rènshi tā.

■ **to get to know somebody** 逐渐开始了解某人 zhújiàn kāishǐ liǎojiě mǒurén

■ **to know about something** 1 听说过某事 tīngshuō guò mǒushì □ Do you know about the meeting this afternoon? 你听说过下午的会议吗？Nǐ tīngshuō guò xiàwǔ de huìyì ma? 2 了解某事 liǎojiě mǒushì □ He knows a lot about cars. 他对汽车很了解。Tā duì qìchē hěn liǎojiě. □ I don't know much about computers. 我对电脑了解不多。Wǒduì diànnǎo liǎojiě bùduō.

■ **You never know!** 很难讲！Hěn nánjiǎng!

know-all NOUN

自以为无所不知的人 zì yǐwéi wú suǒ bù zhī de rén

□ He's such a know-all! 他是一个如此自以为无所不知的人！Tā shì yígè rúcǐ zì yǐwéi wú suǒ bù zhī de rén!

know-how NOUN

技术 jìshù

knowledge NOUN

知识 zhīshi

■ **to the best of my knowledge** 据我所知 jù wǒ suǒzhī

knowledgeable ADJECTIVE

知识渊博的 zhīshi yuānbó de

■ **to be knowledgeable about something** 对某事很在行 duì mǒushì hěn zài háng

□ She's very knowledgeable about computers. 她非常懂得电脑。Tā fēicháng dǒngde diànnǎo.

known VERB ▷ *see* **know**

Koran NOUN

■ **the Koran** 《古兰经》 Gǔlánjīng

Korea NOUN

朝鲜半岛 Cháoxiǎn bàndǎo

□ in Korea 在韩国 zài hánguó

Korean ADJECTIVE

▷ *see also* **Korean** NOUN

朝鲜的 Cháoxiǎn de

Korean NOUN

▷ *see also* **Korean** ADJECTIVE

1 朝鲜人 Cháoxiǎnrén *(person)*

■ **the Koreans** 朝鲜族 Cháoxiǎnzú

2 朝鲜语 Cháoxiǎnyǔ *(language)*

□ She speaks Korean. 她会说朝鲜语。Tā huì shuō Cháoxiǎnyǔ.

LANGUAGE TIP People also commonly use the word 韩语 hányǔ when they want to say **Korean**, but be careful of the tones, otherwise you may end up saying 汉语 hànyǔ, which means **Chinese**.

kosher ADJECTIVE

按犹太教规制成的 àn Yóutài jiàoguī zhìchéng de

Ll

lab NOUN
研究室 yánjiūshì [个 gè]
■ **a lab technician** 一个研究室技术员 yígè yánjiūshì jìshùyuán

label NOUN
▷ *see also* **label** VERB
标签 biāoqiān [个 gè]

to **label** VERB
▷ *see also* **label** NOUN
用标签标明 yòng biāoqiān biāomíng

labor NOUN (US)
劳动力 láodònglì *(manpower)*
■ **the labor market** 劳动市场 láodòng shìchǎng
■ **to be in labor** 处于阵痛期 chǔyú zhèntòng qī

laboratory NOUN
研究室 yánjiūshì [个 gè]

labor union NOUN (US)
工会 gōnghuì [个 gè]

Labour NOUN
工党 Gōngdǎng
□ My parents vote Labour. 我父母投工党的票。Wǒ fùmǔ tóu Gōngdǎng.
■ **the Labour Party** 工党 Gōngdǎng

labour NOUN
劳动力 láodònglì *(manpower)*
■ **to be in labour** 处于阵痛期 chǔyú zhèntòng qī

labourer NOUN
工人 gōngrén [个 gè]
■ **a farm labourer** 农场工人 nóngchǎng gōngrén

lace NOUN
1 花边 huābiān
□ a lace collar 花边衣领 huābiān yīlǐng
2 系带 jìdài [根 gēn] *(of shoe)*

lack NOUN
▷ *see also* **lack** VERB
缺乏 quēfá
□ He got the job despite his lack of experience. 他尽管缺乏经验但还是得到了那份工作。Tā jǐnguǎn quēfá jīngyàn dàn háishì dédào le nà fèn gōngzuò. □ There was no lack of volunteers. 没缺过志愿者。Méi quē guō zhìyuànzhě.

to **lack** VERB
▷ *see also* **lack** NOUN
缺乏 quēfá
□ They lack experience. 他们缺乏经验。Tāmen quēfá jīngyàn.

lacquer NOUN
漆 qī [层 céng]

lad NOUN
小伙子 xiǎohuǒzi [个 gè]

ladder NOUN
梯子 tīzi [个 gè]

lady NOUN
女士 nǚshì [位 wèi]
■ **a young lady** 年轻女子 niánqīng nǚzǐ
■ **Ladies and gentlemen...** 女士们，先生们… nǚshìmen, xiānshēngmen...
■ **the ladies'** 女厕所 nǚ cèsuǒ

ladybird NOUN
瓢虫 piáochóng [只 zhī]

to **lag behind** VERB
滞后 zhìhòu

lager NOUN
淡啤酒 dànpíjiǔ [瓶 píng]

laid VERB ▷ *see* **lay**

laid-back ADJECTIVE
悠闲的 yōuxián de

lain VERB ▷ *see* **lie**

lake NOUN
湖 hú [个 gè]
■ **Lake Dongting** 洞庭湖 Dòngtínghú

lamb NOUN
1 羔羊 gāoyáng [只 zhī]
□ two lambs 两只羔羊 liǎngzhī gāoyáng
2 羔羊肉 gāoyángròu
■ **a lamb chop** 一块羊排 yíkuài yángpái

lame ADJECTIVE
跛的 bǒde
□ My pony is lame. 我的小马是跛的。Wǒde xiǎomǎ shì bǒ de.

lamp NOUN
灯 dēng [盏 zhǎn]

lamppost NOUN
路灯柱 lùdēngzhù [个 gè]

lampshade NOUN

灯罩 dēngzhào [个 gè]

land NOUN

▷ *see also* **land** VERB

1 土地 tǔdì

□ a piece of land 一块土地 yíkuài tǔdì

2 陆地 lùdì *(not sea)*

to **land** VERB

▷ *see also* **land** NOUN

1 降落 jiàngluò

□ The plane has landed. 飞机已经降落。Fēijī yǐjīng jiàngluò.

2 登陆 dēnglù *(from ship)*

landing NOUN

降落 jiàngluò [次 cì] *(of plane)*

landlady NOUN

女房东 nǚfángdōng [位 wèi]

landlord NOUN

男房东 nánfángdōng [位 wèi]

landmark NOUN

地标 dìbiāo [个 gè]

□ Big Ben is one of London's most famous landmarks. 大本钟是伦敦最著名的地标之一。Dàběnzhōng shì Lúndūn zuì zhùmíng de dìbiāo zhī yī.

landowner NOUN

地主 dìzhǔ [个 gè]

landscape NOUN

风景 fēngjǐng [道 dào]

lane NOUN

1 小路 xiǎolù [条 tiáo]

□ a country lane 一条乡间小路 yìtiáo xiāngjiān xiǎolù

2 车道 chēdào [条 tiáo]

□ the fast lane 快车道 kuài chēdào

language NOUN

1 语言 yǔyán [种 zhǒng]

□ English isn't a difficult language. 英语不是一种艰深的语言。Yīngyǔ búshì yìzhǒng jiānshēn de yǔyán.

■ **to use bad language** 用粗言秽语 yòng cūyán huìyǔ

2 语言表达能力 yǔyán biǎodá nénglì *(speech)*

language laboratory NOUN

语言实验室 yǔyán shíyànshì [个 gè]

lanky ADJECTIVE

过分瘦长的 guòfèn shòucháng de

□ a lanky boy 一个瘦瘦高高的男孩 yígè shòushou gāogāo de nánhái

lap NOUN

1 大腿的上方 dàtuǐ de shàngfāng

□ on my lap 在我大腿上 zài wǒ dàtuǐ shàng

2 圈 quān

□ I ran ten laps. 我跑了十圈。Wǒ pǎo le shíquān.

laptop NOUN

笔记本电脑 bǐjìběn diànnǎo [个 gè]

larder NOUN

食物储藏处 shíwù chǔcángchù [个 gè]

large ADJECTIVE

1 大的 dà de

□ a large house 大房子 dà fángzi □ a large dog 大狗 dà gǒu

2 大量的 dàliàng de

□ a large amount 大量的 dàliàng de

largely ADVERB

大部分 dà bùfen

□ It's largely the fault of the government. 这大部分是政府的过错。Zhè dàbùfen shì zhèngfǔ de guòcuò.

laser NOUN

1 激光 jīguāng [束 shù]

□ laser technology 激光技术 jīguāng jìshù

2 激光器 jīguāngqì [台 tái] *(machine)*

lass NOUN

小姑娘 xiǎogūniáng [个 gè]

last ADJECTIVE, ADVERB, PRONOUN

▷ *see also* **last** VERB

1 最近的 zuìjìn de

2 上一个 shàng yígè

□ last Friday 上星期五 shàng xīngqīwǔ

□ last week 上一个星期 shàng yige xīngqī

□ last summer 上一个夏天 shàng yige xiàtiān

3 最后的 zuìhòu de

□ the last programme in the series 这个系列里最后的节目 zhège xìliè lǐ zuìhòu de jiémù

4 最近 zuìjìn

□ I've lost my bag. — When did you see it last? 我丢了我的手提包。— 你最近什么时候见到过它？Wǒ diūle wǒde shǒutíbāo. — Nǐ zuìjìn shénme shíhòu jiàndào guò tā?

5 最后 zuìhòu *(at the end)*

□ He arrived last. 他最后到达。Tā zuìhòu dàodá.

■ **the last time** *(the most recent time)* 最后一次 zuìhòu yícì □ the last time I saw her 我最后一次看见她 wǒ zuìhòu yícì kànjiàn tā □ That's the last time I take your advice! 那是我最后一次采纳你的意见！Nà shì wǒ zuìhòuyícì cǎinà nǐde yìjiàn!

■ **last night** **1** *(yesterday evening)* 昨晚 zuówǎn □ I got home at midnight last night. 我昨晚半夜到家。Wǒ zuówǎn bànyè dàojiā. **2** *(during the night)* 昨天夜里 zuótiān yèli □ I couldn't sleep last night. 我昨天夜里睡不着觉。Wǒ zuótiān yèlǐ shuìbuzháojiào.

6 最后一个 zuìhòu yí gè

□ This one should be the last. 这个应该是最后一个了。Zhège yīnggāishì zuìhòuyígè le.

■ **Our house is the last but one.** 我们的房子是倒数第二个。Wǒmen de fángzi shì dàoshǔ dì'èrgè.

■ **at last** 终于 zhōngyú

■ **at long last** 终于 zhōngyú

to **last** VERB

▷ *see also* **last** ADJECTIVE, ADVERB, PRONOUN

持续 chíxù

□ The marriage lasted only a year. 这段婚姻只持续了一年。Zhèduàn hūnyīn zhǐ chíxùle yìnián. □ It lasts for 2 hours. 持续了两个小时。Chíxù le liǎnggè xiǎoshí.

lastly ADVERB

最后 zuìhòu

late ADJECTIVE, ADVERB

1 迟到的 chídào de

□ Hurry up or you'll be late! 赶快，不然你会迟到的。Gǎnkuài, bùrán nǐhuì chídàode. □ I'm often late for school. 我上学经常迟到。Wǒ shàngxué jīngcháng chídào. □ We're late. 我们迟到了。Wǒmen chídào le. □ Sorry I'm late. 对不起，我迟到了。Duìbuqǐ, wǒ chídào le.

■ **to be ten minutes late** 迟到十分钟 chídào shí fēnzhōng

2 稍晚的 shāowǎn de

□ We had a late lunch. 我们午饭吃得稍晚。Wǒmen wǔfàn chīde shāowǎn.

3 迟 chí

□ She arrived late. 她迟到了。Tā chídàole.

4 晚 wǎn

□ I went to bed late. 我上床晚了。Wǒ shàngchuáng wǎnle.

■ **in the late afternoon** 在傍晚 zài bàngwǎn

■ **in late May** 五月下旬 wǔyuè xiàxún

lately ADVERB

最近 zuìjìn

□ I haven't seen him lately. 我最近没见到他。Wǒ zuìjìn méijiàndào tā.

later ADVERB

一会儿 yì huǐr

□ I'll do it later. 我一会儿做这件事。Wǒ yìhuǐr zuò zhèjiànshì. □ See you later! 一会儿见！Yìhuǐr jiàn!

■ **some time later** 一段时间以后 yíduàn shíjiān yǐhòu

■ **some years later** 几年以后 jǐniányǐhòu

■ **later on** 以后 yǐhòu

latest ADJECTIVE

1 最新的 zuìxīn de

□ their latest album 他们的最新专辑 tāmende zuìxīn zhuānjí

2 最新式的 zuì xīnshì de

□ the latest technology 最新技术 zuìxīn jìshù

■ **at the latest** 最迟 zuìchí □ by 10 o'clock at the latest 最迟到10点 zuìchí dàoshídiǎn

Latin NOUN

拉丁语 Lādīngyǔ

□ I do Latin. 我攻读拉丁语。Wǒ gōngdú lādīngyǔ.

Latin America NOUN

拉丁美洲 Lādīngměizhōu

□ in Latin America 在拉丁美洲 zài Lādīngměizhōu

Latin American ADJECTIVE

▷ *see also* **Latin American** NOUN

拉丁美洲的 Lādīngměizhōu de

Latin American NOUN

▷ *see also* **Latin American** ADJECTIVE

拉丁美洲人 Lādīngměizhōurén [个 gè]

■ **Latin Americans** 拉丁美洲人 lādīngměizhōurén

latter NOUN

■ **the latter** 后者 hòuzhě □ The latter is the more expensive of the two systems. 两个系统中后者更贵。Liǎnggè xìtǒngzhōng hòuzhě gèng guì.

■ **the former..., the latter...** 前者…，后者… qiánzhě..., hòuzhě... □ The former lives in the US, the latter in Australia. 前者生活在美国，后者生活在澳大利亚。Qiánzhě shēnghuózài měiguó, hòuzhě shēnghuózài àodàlìyà.

laugh NOUN

▷ *see also* **laugh** VERB

笑 xiào [阵 zhèn]

□ It was a good laugh. 那很可笑。Nà hěnkěxiào.

to **laugh** VERB

▷ *see also* **laugh** NOUN

笑 xiào

to **laugh at** VERB

嘲笑... cháoxiào...

□ They laughed at her. 他们嘲笑了她。Tāmen cháoxiào le tā.

to **launch** VERB

1 发射 fāshè *(rocket)*

2 推出 tuīchū

□ They're going to launch a new model. 他们要推出一个新款。Tāmen yào tuīchū yígèxīnkuǎn.

Launderette® NOUN

自助洗衣店 zìzhù xǐyīdiàn [家 jiā]

Laundromat® NOUN

自助洗衣店 zìzhù xǐyīdiàn [家 jiā]

laundry NOUN

1 待洗的衣物 dàixǐ de yīwù [件 jiàn] *(to be washed)*

2 洗好的衣物 xǐhǎo de yīwù *(clean washing)*

laundry detergent NOUN (US)
洗衣粉 xǐyīfěn [袋 dài]

lavatory NOUN
卫生间 wèishēngjiān [个 gè]

DID YOU KNOW...?
In rural China, some lavatories are marked only with the respective characters for **male**, 男 nán, and **female**, 女 nǚ. It is therefore important to be able to distinguish these two characters.

lavender NOUN
薰衣草 xūnyīcǎo [棵 kē]

law NOUN
1 法律 fǎlǜ [项 xiàng]
□ British law 英国法律 yīngguó fǎlǜ
2 法规 fǎguī [条 tiáo]
□ The laws are very strict. 那些法规非常严厉。Nàxiē fǎguī fēicháng yánlì.
■ **against the law** 违法 wéifǎ
■ **to break the law** 违法 wéifǎ
■ **by law** 依照法律 yīzhào fǎlǜ
■ **to study law** 学习法律 xuéxí fǎlǜ □ My elder sister's studying law. 我姐姐在学习法律。Wǒ jiějie zài xuéxí fǎlǜ.

lawn NOUN
草坪 cǎopíng [片 piàn]

lawnmower NOUN
割草机 gēcǎojī [部 bù]

law school NOUN
法学院 fǎxuéyuàn [所 suǒ]

lawyer NOUN
律师 lǜshī [位 wèi]
□ My mother's a lawyer. 我母亲是一位律师。Wǒ mǔqīn shì yíwèi lǜshī.

to **lay** VERB
放 fàng
□ She laid the baby in her cot. 她把婴儿放在她的折叠床上。Tā bǎ yīngér fàngzài tāde zhédiéchuángshàng.
■ **to lay the table** 摆放餐具 bǎifàng cānjù
■ **to lay something on 1** 提供某物 tígòng mǒuwù □ They laid on extra buses. 他们提供了加开的公共汽车。Tāmen tígòng le jiākāi de gōnggòngqìchē. **2** 置办某物 zhìbàn mǒuwù □ They laid on a special meal. 他们特别置办了一顿饭。Tāmen tèbié zhìbàn le yídùnfàn.

to **lay down** VERB *(put down)*
放下 fàngxià

to **lay off** VERB
解雇 jiěgù
□ My father's been laid off. 我父亲被解雇了。Wǒfùqin bèi jiěgùle.

lay-by NOUN
紧急停车带 jǐnjí tíngchēdài. [段 duàn]

layer NOUN
层 céng
□ the ozone layer 臭氧层 chòuyǎngcéng

layout NOUN
布局 bùjú [个 gè]
□ No one likes the new office layout. 没人喜欢新的办公室布局。Méirén xǐhuān xīnde bàngōngshì bùjú.

lazy ADJECTIVE
懒惰的 lǎnduò de

lead NOUN
▷ *see also* **lead** VERB
1 皮带 pídài [条 tiáo] *(for dog)*
2 导线 dǎoxiàn [根 gēn] *(cable)*
■ **to be in the lead** 领先 lǐngxiān □ Our team is in the lead. 我们队领先。Wǒmenduì lǐngxiān.
3 铅 qiān *(metal)*

to **lead** VERB
▷ *see also* **lead** NOUN
1 带领 dàilǐng
□ She led me to the office. 她带领我来到办公室。Tā dàilǐng wǒ láidào bàngōngshì.
2 领导 lǐngdǎo *(be a leader)*
□ He led the party for many years. 他领导那个政党多年。Tā lǐngdǎo nàge zhèngdǎng duōnián.
3 位于前列 wèiyúqiánliè
□ She led the procession. 她走在队伍的前列。Tā zǒuzài duìwude qiánliè.
4 领先 lǐngxiān *(in race, competition)*
■ **to lead the way 1** *(to a place)* 引路 yǐnlù **2** *(be a leader)* 领导 lǐngdǎo

to **lead away** VERB
带走 dàizǒu
■ **to lead somebody away** 带走某人 dàizǒumǒurén □ The police led the man away. 警察把那个人带走了。Jǐngchá bǎ nàgèrén dàizǒule.

to **lead to** VERB
1 导致 dǎozhì
□ It will lead to trouble. 这会导致问题。Zhèhuì dǎozhì wèntí.
2 通向 tōngxiàng
□ the street that leads to the station 通向车站的街道 tōngxiàng chēzhànde jiēdào

leaded ADJECTIVE
加铅的 jiāqiānde
■ **leaded petrol** 加铅汽油 jiāqiān qìyóu

leader NOUN
领导人 lǐngdǎorén [位 wèi]

lead singer NOUN
主唱歌手 zhǔchàng gēshǒu [位 wèi]

leaf NOUN
叶子 yèzi [片 piàn]

leaflet NOUN
1 小册子 xiǎocèzi [本 běn] *(booklet)*
2 传单 chuándān [份 fèn] *(single sheet)*

league NOUN
联赛 liánsài [季 jì]
□ They are at the top of the league. 他们在联赛中排名首位。Tāmen zài liánsàizhōng páimíng shǒuwèi.
■ **the Premier League** 英超联赛 yīngchāoliánsài

DID YOU KNOW...?
The top Chinese football league is known as the 中超联赛 zhōngchāo liánsài.

leak NOUN
▷ *see also* **leak** VERB
1 裂隙 lièxì [条 tiáo]
□ the leak in the dike 堤防上的裂隙 dīfáng shàngde lièxì
2 泄漏 xièlòu [次 cì]
□ a gas leak 一次煤气泄漏 yícì méiqì xièlòu

to **leak** VERB
▷ *see also* **leak** NOUN
漏 lòu
□ The pipe is leaking. 管道漏了。Guǎndào lòule.

lean ADJECTIVE
▷ *see also* **lean** VERB
瘦的 shòu de
□ lean meat 瘦肉 shòuròu

to **lean** VERB
▷ *see also* **lean** ADJECTIVE
■ **to lean something against something** 把某物靠在某物上 bǎ mǒuwù kàozài mǒuwù shang □ He leant his bike against the wall. 他把自行车靠在墙上。Tā bǎ zìxíngchē kàozài qiángshàng.
■ **to lean against** 靠在…上 kàozài... shàng □ The ladder was leaning against the wall. 梯子正靠在墙上。Tīzi zhèng kàozài qiángshàng.
■ **to lean forward** 向前倾 xiàngqiánqīng
■ **to lean back** 向后倾 xiànghòuqīng

to **lean on** VERB
倚 yǐ
■ **to lean on something** 倚在某物上 yǐzài mǒuwùshàng □ He leant on the wall. 他倚在墙上。Tā yǐzài qiángshàng
■ **to lean something on something** 把某物靠在某物上 bǎ mǒuwù kàozài mǒuwù shàng □ He leant his head on his hand. 他把头靠在手上。Tā bǎtóu kàozài shǒushàng.

to **lean out** VERB
探身出去 tànshēn chūqù
■ **She leant out of the window.** 她从窗口探身出去。Tā cóngchuāngkǒu tànshēnchūqù.

to **lean over** VERB
探身 tànshēn
□ Don't lean over too far. 身子别探得太远。Shēnzi bié tànde tàiyuǎn.

to **leap** VERB
跳 tiào
□ They leapt over the stream. 他们跳过那条溪流。Tāmen tiàoguò nàtiáoxīliú. □ He leapt out of his chair when his team scored. 他的球队得分时，他从椅子上跳了起来。Tāde qiúduì défēnshí, tā cóngyǐzishàng tàoleqǐlái.

leap year NOUN
闰年 rùnnián [个 gè]

to **learn** VERB
1 学 xué
□ I'm learning fast. 我学得快。Wǒ xuédekuài.
■ **to learn to do something** 学做某事 xuézuòmǒushì □ I'm learning to ski. 我在学滑雪。Wǒzài xuéhuáxuě.
■ **to learn about something** 学到某事 xuédào mǒushì
2 背 bèi *(poem, song)*

learner NOUN
学习者 xuéxízhě [个 gè]
■ **She's a quick learner.** 她学东西快。Tā xuédōngxikuài.

learner driver NOUN
学习司机 xuéxí sījī [名 míng]

learnt VERB ▷ *see* **learn**

least ADJECTIVE, ADVERB, PRONOUN
最少的 zuìshǎo de
□ It takes the least time. 这花的时间最少。Zhè huādeshíjiān zuìshǎo.
■ **the least** 1 *(following verb)* 最不 zuìbù □ Maths is the subject I like the least. 数学是我最不喜欢的科目。Shùxué shì wǒzuìbùxǐhuande kēmù. 2 *(the minimum)* 最少 zuìshǎo □ It's the least I can do. 这是我至少能做的。Zhè shì wǒ zhìshǎo néngzuòde.
■ **the least expensive** 最便宜的 zuì piányi de □ the least expensive hotel 最便宜的宾馆 zuì piányi de bīnguǎn □ the least attractive design 最没有魅力的设计 zuì méiyǒu mèilì de shèjì □ the least interesting subject 最没意思的科目 zuì méiyìsi de kēmù
■ **at least** *(with amount)* 至少 zhìshǎo □ It'll cost at least £200. 这至少要花二百英镑。Zhè zhìshǎo yàohuā èrbǎi yīngbàng. □ ...but at least nobody was hurt. …但是至

English-Chinese

l

少没人受伤。...dànshì zhìshǎo méirén shòushāng. □ It's totally unfair. At least, that's my opinion. 这根本不公平。至少我这么认为。Zhè gēnběn bùgōngpíng. Zhìshǎo wǒ zhème rènwéi.

leather NOUN
皮 pí [种 zhǒng]
□ real leather 真皮 zhēnpí □ a black leather jacket 一件黑色皮夹克 yíjiàn hēisè píjiákè

leave NOUN
▷ *see also* **leave** VERB
1 休假 xiūjià
□ My brother is on leave for a week. 我哥哥在休假一星期。Wǒ gēge zài xiūjià yìxīngqī.
2 假期 jiàqī *(soldier)*

to **leave** VERB
▷ *see also* **leave** NOUN
1 离开 líkāi
□ She's just left. 她刚刚离开。Tā gānggāng líkāi. □ We leave London at six o'clock. 我们六点钟离开伦敦。Wǒmen liùdiǎnzhōng líkāi lúndūn. □ My sister left home last year. 我姐姐去年离开了家。Wǒjiějie qùnián líkāile jiā.
■ **to leave for** *(destination)* 前往 qiánwǎng
□ I'm leaving for Shanghai tomorrow. 我明天要前往上海。Wǒ míngtiān yào qiánwǎng shànghǎi.
2 出发 chūfā
□ The bus leaves at 8. 公共汽车八点出发。Gōnggòngqìchē bādiǎn chūfā.
3 辍学 chuòxué *(school)*
□ He left school when he was sixteen. 他十六岁时辍学。Tā shíliùsuìshí chuòxué.
□ He left without getting any qualifications. 他没拿到任何证书就辍学了。Tā méinádào rènhé zhèngshū jiù chuòxuéle.
4 辞职 cízhí *(work)*
□ The pay was so bad I left. 报酬太差，我辞职了。Bàochóu tàichà, wǒ cízhíle.
5 留下 liúxià *(deliberately)*
□ I'll leave my car at the station. 我会把车留在车站。Wǒ huì bǎ chē líuzài chēzhàn.
6 落 là *(accidentally)*
□ I've left my book at home. 我把书落家里了。Wǒ bǎshū là jiālǐ le.
7 留 liú *(message)*
□ Do you want to leave a message? 你要留言吗？Nǐ yào liúyán ma?
■ **to leave something to somebody** 把某物留给某人 bǎ mǒuwù liúgěi mǒurén
□ My grandmother left me some money. 我祖母留给我一些钱。Wǒ zǔmǔ liúgěiwǒ yìxiēqián.
■ **to leave something alone** 不动某物 bú dòng mǒuwù □ Leave that alone! 别动那个！Biédòng nàge!
■ **to leave somebody alone** 不打扰某人 bù dǎrǎo mǒurén □ Leave me alone! 别打扰我！Bié dǎrǎo wǒ!

to **leave behind** VERB
忘带 wàngdài
□ Make sure you haven't left anything behind. 千万别忘带东西。Qiānwàn biéwàng dài dōngxi.

to **leave on** VERB
开着 kāizhe *(light)*

to **leave out** VERB
冷落 lěngluò
□ As the new girl, I felt really left out. 我这个新来的女孩真觉得受冷落。Wǒzhège xīnlái de nǚhái zhēnjuéde shòulěngluò.

leaves PL NOUN ▷ *see* **leaf**

Lebanon NOUN
黎巴嫩 Líbānèn

lecture NOUN
▷ *see also* **lecture** VERB
讲座 jiǎngzuò [个 gè]
■ **to give a lecture on something** 作某方面的讲座 zuò mǒufāngmiànde jiǎngzuò

lecture VERB
▷ *see also* **lecture** NOUN
■ **She lectures at the technical college.** 她在那所工学院讲课。Tā zài nàsuǒ gōngxuéyuàn jiǎngkè.
■ **He's always lecturing us.** 他总是教训我们。Tā zǒngshì jiàoxùn wǒmen.

lecturer NOUN
讲师 jiǎngshī [位 wèi]
□ She's a lecturer. 她是一位讲师。Tā shì yíwèi jiǎngshī.

led VERB ▷ *see* **lead**

left ADJECTIVE, ADVERB
▷ *see also* **left** NOUN
1 左的 zuǒ de
□ my left hand 我的左手 wǒde zuǒshǒu
□ on the left side of the road 在路左侧 zài lùzuǒcè
2 向左 xiàngzuǒ
□ Turn left at the traffic lights. 在交通灯处向左转。Zài jiāotōngdēng chù xiànzuǒzhuǎn.
3 剩下的 shèngxiàde *(remaining)*
□ There's one left. 还剩下一个。Hái shènxià yígè. □ I haven't got any money left. 我什么钱也没剩下。Wǒ shénme qián yě méishèngxià.
■ **to be left over** 剩下 shèngxià

left NOUN
▷ *see also* **left** ADJECTIVE, ADVERB
■ **the left** 左侧 zuǒcè

English-Chinese

l

■ **on the left** 在左边 zài zuǒbiān
□ Remember to drive on the left. 记住在左边开车。Jìzhù zài zuǒbiān kāichē.
■ **to the left** 靠左边 kào zuǒbiān

left-hand ADJECTIVE
左侧的 zuǒcè de
■ **the left-hand side** 左侧 zuǒcè □ It's on the left-hand side. 它在左侧。Tā zài zuǒcè.

left-handed ADJECTIVE
左撇子的 zuǒpiězi de

left-luggage locker NOUN
行李寄存柜 xíngli jìcún guì [个 gè]

left-luggage office NOUN
行李暂存处 xíngli zàncúnchù [个 gè]

leg NOUN
1 腿 tuǐ [条 tiáo]
□ She's broken her leg. 她折断了腿。Tā zhéduànle tuǐ.
2 腿 tuǐ [根 gēn]
□ a chicken leg 一根鸡腿 yìgēnjītuǐ □ a leg of lamb 一根羊腿 yìgēn yángtuǐ

legal ADJECTIVE
1 法律的 fǎlǜ de
□ It's a legal requirement. 这是法律规定。Zhèshì fǎlǜ guīdìng.
2 合法的 héfǎ de
■ **to take legal action** 提起诉讼 tíqǐ sùsòng

legal holiday NOUN (US)
法定假期 fǎdìng jiàqī [个 gè]

leggings PL NOUN
绑腿 bǎngtuǐ [副 fù]

leisure NOUN
闲暇 xiánxiá
□ What do you do in your leisure time? 你闲暇时做什么？Nǐ xiánxiáshí zuòshénme?

leisure centre NOUN
娱乐中心 yúlè zhōngxīn [个 gè]

lemon NOUN
柠檬 níngméng [个 gè]

lemonade NOUN
柠檬汽水 níngméng qìshuǐ [瓶 píng]

to **lend** VERB
■ **to lend something to somebody** 把某物借给某人 bǎ mǒuwù jiègěi mǒurén □ I can lend you some money. 我可以借给你一些钱。Wǒ kěyǐ jiègěinǐ yìxiēqián.
贷 dài *(bank)*

length NOUN
1 长度 chángdù [个 gè]
□ It's about a metre in length. 它长度大约一米。Tā chángdù dàyuē yìmǐ.
2 篇幅 piānfú [个 gè] *(of sentence, article)*
3 时间长短 shíjiān chángduǎn
□ the length of the performance 演出的时间长短 yǎnchū de shíjiān chángduǎn

lens NOUN
1 镜片 jìngpiàn [片 piàn] *(of spectacles)*
2 镜头 jìngtóu [个 gè] *(of telescope, camera)*

Lent NOUN
大斋节 Dàzhāijié

lent VERB ▷ *see* **lend**

lentil NOUN
小扁豆 xiǎobiǎndòu [颗 kē]

Leo NOUN
狮子座 Shīzi Zuò
□ I'm Leo. 我是狮子座的。Wǒ shì shīzizuòde.

leopard NOUN
豹 bào [只 zhī]

leotard NOUN
紧身衣 jǐnshēnyī [件 jiàn]

lesbian ADJECTIVE
▷ *see also* **lesbian** NOUN
女同性恋的 nǚ tóngxìngliàn de

lesbian NOUN
▷ *see also* **lesbian** ADJECTIVE
女同性恋者 nǚ tóngxìngliànzhě [个 gè]

less ADJECTIVE, ADVERB, PRONOUN, PREPOSITION
1 更少的 gèng shǎo de
□ I've got less time for hobbies now. 我现在用于业余爱好的时间更少了。Wǒ xiànzài yòngyú yèyú aìhào de shíjiān gèngshǎole.
2 不如 bùrú
□ He's less intelligent than her. 他不如她聪明。Tā bùrú tā cōngmíng.
3 较少 jiàoshǎo
□ Try to eat less. 试着少吃。Shìzhe shǎochī.
4 较少的东西 jiàoshǎo de dōngxi
□ A bit less, please. 请少一点。Qǐng shǎoyìdiǎn.
■ **less tax** 去掉税 qùdiào shuì
■ **less 10% discount** 10%的折扣 bǎifēnzhīshí de zhékòu
■ **less than 1** *(with amounts)* 不到 búdào □ It's less than a kilometre from here. 那离这里不到一公里。Nà lízhèlǐ búdào yìgōnglǐ. □ It costs less than 100 euros. 花费不到一百欧元。Huāfèi búdào yìbǎi ōuyuán. □ less than half 不到一半 búdào yíbàn **2** *(in comparisons)* 比…少 □ He spent less than me. 他花得比我少。Tā huāde bǐwǒshǎo. □ I've got less than you. 我得到的比你少。Wǒ dédàode bǐnǐshǎo. □ It cost less than we thought. 花费比我们想象的少。Huāfèi bǐ wǒmen xiǎngxiàng de shǎo.

lesson NOUN
课 kè [堂 táng]

□ a Chinese lesson 一堂中文课 yìtáng zhōngwénkè □ 'Lesson Sixteen' "第十六课" "dì shíliùkè" □ Each lesson lasts forty minutes. 每堂课四十分钟。Měitángkè sìshífēnzhōng.

to **let** VERB

■ **to let somebody do something** 让某人做某事 ràng mǒurén zuò mǒushì □ Let me have a look. 让我看看。Ràngwǒkànkàn. □ My parents won't let me stay out that late. 我父母不让我在外面待到那么晚。Wǒfùmǔ búràngwǒ zàiwàimiàn dāidào nàmewǎn.

■ **to let something happen** 让某事发生 ràng mǒushì fāshēng □ Don't let it get cold. 别让它凉了。Bié ràngtā liángle.

■ **to let somebody know** 告诉某人 ràng mǒurén zhīdào □ I'll let you know as soon as possible. 我会尽快告诉你。Wǒ huì jìnkuài gàosù nǐ.

■ **to let somebody know that...** 告诉某人… gàosù mǒurén...

■ **to let somebody out** 让某人进去/出去 ràng mǒurén jìnqù/chūqù

■ **let's** 让我们… ràng wǒmen... □ Let's go to the cinema! 我们去看电影吧！Wǒmen qù kàndiànyǐngba! □ Let's go! 我们走吧！Wǒmen zǒuba！ □ Let's eat! 我们吃吧！Wǒmen chība!

■ **to let go of something** 放开 fàngkāi □ The dog wouldn't let go of the ball. 那只狗不肯放开那个球。Nàzhīgǒu bùkěn fàngkaī nàgèqiú.

■ **to let somebody go** 放开某人 fàngkāi mǒurén □ Let me go! 放开我！Fàngkāiwǒ!

■ **to let something go** 放走某物 fàngzǒu mǒuwù □ Let it go! 随它去！Suítāqù!

■ **'to let'** "现房待租" "xiànfáng dàizū"

to **let down** VERB

令...失望 lìng...shīwàng

□ I won't let you down. 我不会令你失望。Wǒ búhuì lìngnǐ shīwàng.

to **let in** VERB

1 允许进来 yǔnxǔ jìnlái

□ My shoes let in water. 我的鞋里进水了。Wǒ de xiélǐ jìnshuǐle.

2 让...进门 ràng...jìnmén

□ They wouldn't let me in because I was under 18. 他们不让我进门，因为我不满十八岁。Tāmen búràng wǒ jìnmén, yīnwéiwǒ bùmǎn shíbāsuì.

letter NOUN

1 信 xìn [封 fēng]

□ Write her a letter. 给她写一封信。Gěi tā xiě yìfēngxìn.

2 字母 zìmǔ [个 gè] *(of alphabet)*

letterbox NOUN

信箱 xìnxiāng [个 gè]

lettuce NOUN

生菜 shēngcài [棵 kē]

level ADJECTIVE

▷ *see also* **level** NOUN

平的 píng de

□ A snooker table must be perfectly level. 斯诺克球桌必须很平。Sīnuòkèqiúzhuō bìxū hěnpíng.

level NOUN

▷ *see also* **level** ADJECTIVE

1 水平 shuǐpíng [种 zhǒng]

□ a high level of efficiency 一种高效能水平 yìzhǒng gāoxiàonéngshuǐpíng

2 水位 shuǐwèi [个 gè]

□ The level of the river is rising. 那条河的水位在上涨。Nàtiáohéde shuǐwèi zài shàngzhǎng.

■ **A levels** 高等水平考试 gāoděng shǔipíng kǎoshì

level crossing NOUN

平交道口 píngjiāodàokǒu [个 gè]

lever NOUN

杆 gǎn [根 gēn]

liable ADJECTIVE

容易...的 róngyì...de

□ He's liable to lose his temper. 他容易发脾气。Tā róngyì fāpíqì.

liar NOUN

说谎者 shuōhuǎngzhě [个 gè]

liberal ADJECTIVE

▷ *see also* **liberal** NOUN

开明的 kāimíng de

□ She has liberal views. 她有开明的观点。Tā yǒu kāimíng de guāndiǎn.

■ **the Liberal Democrats** 自由民主党 zìyóumínzhǔdǎng

liberal NOUN

▷ *see also* **liberal** ADJECTIVE

■ **the Liberals** 自由党党员 Zìyóudǎng dǎngyuán [名 míng]

liberation NOUN

解放 jiěfàng [次 cì]

Libra NOUN

天秤座 Tiānchèng Zuò

□ I'm Libra. 我是天秤座的。Wǒ shì tiānpíngzuò de.

librarian NOUN

图书管理员 túshū guǎnlǐyuán [位 wèi]

□ She's a librarian. 她是一位图书管理员。Tā shì yíwèi túshū guǎnlǐyuán.

library NOUN

图书馆 túshūguǎn [个 gè]

Libya NOUN

利比亚 Lìbǐyà

licence (US **license**) NOUN
1 驾驶执照 jiàshǐ zhízhào [本 běn]
□ If you drink and drive you could lose your licence. 要是你酒后驾车就会丢了驾驶执照。Yàoshinǐ jiǔhòujiàchē jiùhuì diūle jiàshǐzhízhào.
■ **a driving licence** 驾照 jiàzhào
2 许可证 xǔkězhèng [张 zhāng] *(permit)*

license plate NOUN (US)
车牌照 chēpáizhào [个 gè]

to **lick** VERB
舔 tiǎn

lid NOUN
1 盖 gài [个 gè] *(of box, pan)*
2 眼睑 yǎnjiǎn [个 gè] *(eyelid)*

lie NOUN
▷ *see also* **lie** VERB
谎言 huǎngyán [个 gè]
□ That's a lie! 那是一个谎言！Nàshì yígèhuǎngyán!
■ **to tell lies** 说谎 shuōhuǎng

to **lie** VERB
▷ *see also* **lie** NOUN
1 说谎 shuōhuǎng *(tell lies)*
□ I know she's lying. 我知道她在说谎。Wǒ zhīdào tāzài shuōhuǎng.
2 躺 tǎng
□ I was lying on the beach. 我正躺在海滩上。Wǒ zhèngtǎngzài hǎitānshàng.

to **lie about** VERB
乱放 luànfàng

to **lie around** VERB
乱放 luànfàng

to **lie down** VERB *(person)*
躺下 tǎngxià
■ **to be lying down** 平躺 píngtǎng □ He was lying down on the sofa. 他平躺在沙发上。Tā píngtǎngzài shāfāshàng.

lie-in NOUN
懒觉 lǎnjiào [个 gè]
■ **to have a lie-in** 睡个懒觉 shuì gè lǎnjiào
□ I have a lie-in on Sundays. 我周日睡懒觉。Wǒ zhōurì shuì lǎnjiào.

lieutenant NOUN
中尉 zhōngwèi [名 míng]

life NOUN
1 生命 shēngmìng [个 gè]
■ **to lose one's life** 失去生命 shīqù shēngmìng
2 一生 yìshēng [个 gè]
□ all his life 他的一生 tāde yìshēng
■ **his personal life** 他的个人生活 tāde gèrén shēnghuó
■ **his working life** 他的工作生活 tāde gōngzuò shēnghuó

lifebelt NOUN
救生圈 jiùshēngquān [个 gè]

lifeboat NOUN
救生船 jiùshēngchuán [艘 sōu]

lifeguard NOUN
救生员 jiùshēngyuán [位 wèi]

life jacket NOUN
救生衣 jiùshēngyī [件 jiàn]

life preserver NOUN (US)
1 救生用具 jiùshēng yòngjù [件 jiàn] *(lifebelt)*
2 救生衣 jiùshēngyī [件 jiàn] *(life jacket)*

lifestyle NOUN
生活方式 shēnghuó fāngshì [种 zhǒng]

lift NOUN
▷ *see also* **lift** VERB
电梯 diàntī [部 bù]
□ The lift isn't working. 电梯没开动。Diàntī méi kāidòng.
■ **to give somebody a lift** 让某人搭便车 ràng mǒurén dā biànchē □ He gave me a lift to the cinema. 他让我搭他的便车去电影院。Tāràngwǒ dātāde biànchē qùdiànyǐngyuàn. □ Would you like a lift? 你要搭便车吗？Nǐ yàodābiànchēma?

to **lift** VERB
▷ *see also* **lift** NOUN
举起 jǔqǐ
□ It's too heavy, I can't lift it. 它太重了，我举不起。Tā tàizhòngle, wǒ jǔbuqǐ.

to **lift up** VERB
举起 jǔqǐ

light NOUN
▷ *see also* **light** VERB, ADJECTIVE
1 光 guāng [束 shù]
□ bright light 亮光 liàngguāng
2 灯 dēng [盏 zhǎn]
□ There's a light by my bed. 我床头有一盏灯。Wǒ chuángtoú yǒu yìzhǎn dēng.
■ **to switch on the light** 开灯 kāidēng
■ **to switch off the light** 关灯 guān dēng
3 火源 huǒyuán [处 chù]
□ Have you got a light, please? 能借个火吗？Néng jiègehuǒ ma?
■ **lights** 交通指示灯 jiāotōng zhǐshìdēng
□ Turn right at the lights. 在交通灯那里右转。Zài jiāotōngdēng nàlǐ yòuzhuǎn.

to **light** VERB
▷ *see also* **light** NOUN, ADJECTIVE
点燃 diǎnrán
□ Light the gas. 点燃煤气。Diǎnrán méiqì.

light ADJECTIVE
▷ *see also* **light** NOUN, VERB
1 淡的 dàn de
□ a light blue sweater 一件淡蓝色毛线衣 yíjiàn dànlánsè máoxiànyī
2 轻的 qīng de

□ light industry 轻工业 qīnggōngyè □ a light jacket 一件薄夹克衫 yíjiàn bójiákèshān □ a light meal 清淡的一顿饭 qīngdànde yídùnfàn

light bulb NOUN
灯泡 dēngpào [个 gè]

lighter NOUN
打火机 dǎhuǒjī [个 gè]

lighthouse NOUN
灯塔 dēngtǎ [座 zuò]

lightning NOUN
闪电 shǎndiàn [道 dào]
□ a flash of lightning 一道闪电 yídào shǎndiàn

like PREPOSITION
▷ *see also* **like** VERB
1 像 xiàng
■ **like that** 像那样 xiàng nàyàng □ It's fine like that. 像那样就好。Xiàng nàyàng jiùhǎo.
■ **like this** 像这样 xiàng zhèyàng □ Do it like this. 像这样做。Xiàng zhèyàngzuò.
■ **to be like somebody** 像某人 xiàng mǒurén
■ **to be like something** 像某物 xiàng mǒuwù □ It's a bit like salmon. 这有点像三文鱼。Zhè yǒudiǎnxiàng sānwényú.
■ **What's he like?** 他怎么样？Tā zěnmeyàng?
■ **to look like somebody** 长得像某人 zhǎngde xiàng mǒurén □ You look like my older brother. 你长得像我哥哥。Nǐ zhǎngde xiàng wǒ gēge.
■ **to look like something** 看起来像某物 kànqǐlái xiàng mǒuwù
2 像…一样 xiàng...yíyàng
□ eyes like stars 眼睛像星星一样 yǎnjīng xiàng xīngxing yíyàng
3 如 rú *(such as)*
□ a house like ours 如我们这样的房子 rú wǒmen jíyàng de fángzi □ a city like Paris 像巴黎这样的一个城市 xiàng bālí zhèyàng de yígè chéngshì
■ **What's the weather like?** 天气怎么样？Tiānqì zěnmeyàng?
■ **what does it look like?** 看起来怎么样？Kànqǐlái zěnmeyàng?
■ **what does it sound like?** 听起来怎么样？Tīngqǐlái zěnmeyàng?
■ **what does it taste like?** 尝起来怎么样？Chángqǐlái zěnmeyàng?

to **like** VERB
▷ *see also* **like** PREPOSITION
喜欢 xǐhuan
□ I don't like mustard. 我不喜欢芥末。Wǒ bùxǐhuān jièmo. □ I like riding. 我喜欢骑马。Wǒ xǐhuān qímǎ. □ I like Paul, but I don't want to go out with him. 我喜欢保罗，可是我不想跟他出去。Wǒ xǐhuān bǎoluó, kěshì wǒ bùxiǎng gēntā chūqù.
■ **to like doing something** 喜欢做某事 xǐhuān zuò mǒushì
■ **I'd like...** 我想… Wǒxiǎng... □ I'd like an orange juice, please. 我想要一杯橙汁。Wǒxiǎng yào yìbēi chéngzhī. □ I would like an ice-cream. 我想吃个冰激凌。Wǒxiǎng chīgè bīngjilíng. □ Would you like a coffee? 你想不想来杯咖啡？Nǐ xiǎngbuxiǎng láibēi kāfēi?
■ **I'd like to...** 我想… wǒxiǎng... □ I'd like to go to Russia one day. 我想有一天到俄罗斯去。Wǒxiǎng yǒuyìtiān dào Éluósīqù. □ I'd like to wash my hands. 我想洗洗手。Wǒxiǎng xǐxǐshǒu. □ Would you like to go for a walk? 你想去散散步吗？Nǐ xiǎng qù sànsànbù mā?
■ **if you like** 如果你愿意的话 rúguǒ nǐ yuànyì de huà

likely ADJECTIVE
很可能的 hěn kěnéng de
□ That's not very likely. 那不太可能。Nà bútàikěnéng.
■ **to be likely to do something** 很有可能做某事 hěnyǒu kěnéng zuò mǒushì □ She's likely to come. 她很有可能来。Tā hěnyǒu kěnéng lái. □ She's not likely to come. 她不太可能来。Tā bútàikěnéng lái.
■ **It is likely that...** 有可能… yǒu kěnéng...

lily of the valley NOUN
铃兰 línglán [株 zhū]

lime NOUN
酸橙 suānchéng [个 gè] *(fruit)*

limit NOUN
1 限度 xiàndù [个 gè]
□ within limits 有限度地 yǒuxiàndùde
2 限定 xiàndìng [种 zhǒng]
□ The speed limit is 70 mph. 限速为每小时七十英里。Xiànsù wéi měixiǎoshí qīshí yīnglǐ.

limousine NOUN
豪华轿车 háohuájiàochē [辆 liàng]

to **limp** VERB
跛行 bǒxíng

line NOUN
1 线 xiàn [条 tiáo]
□ a straight line 一条直线 yìtiáo zhíxiàn □ Draw a line under each answer. 在每个答案下面划一条线。Zài měigè dá'àn xiàmiàn huà yìtiáo xiàn.
2 排 pái
■ **to stand in line** 排队等候 páiduì děnghòu

3 行 háng
□ Read the next line. 读下一行。Dú xiàyiháng.
4 线路 xiànlù [条 tiáo]
□ a bad line 一条坏线路 yìtiáo huài xiànlù
■ **Hold the line please!** 请稍等！Qǐng shāoděng!
5 铁路线路 tiělù xiànlù [条 tiáo] *(railway track)*
■ **on the right lines** 大体正确 dàtǐ zhèngquè

linen NOUN
1 亚麻布 yàmábù
□ pure linen 纯亚麻布 chún yàmábù
2 亚麻制品 yàmá zhìpǐn *(tablecloths, sheets)*
3 亚麻料 yàmáliào
□ a linen jacket 亚麻夹克 yàmá jiákè

liner NOUN
班轮 bānlún [架 jià]

linguist NOUN
语言学家 yǔyánxuéjiā [位 wèi]
■ **to be a good linguist** 有语言天赋 yǒu yǔyán tiānfù

lining NOUN
衬里 chènlǐ [个 gè]

link NOUN
▷ *see also* **link** VERB
1 联系 liánxì [种 zhǒng]
□ a close link 一种紧密联系 yìzhǒng jǐnmì liánxì
2 超链接 chāoliànjiē [个 gè] *(hyperlink)*

to **link** VERB
▷ *see also* **link** NOUN
1 连接 liánjiē *(places, objects)*
2 联系 liánxì *(people, situations)*
□ the link between smoking and cancer 吸烟与癌症的联系 xīyān yǔ áizhèng de liánxì

lion NOUN
狮子 shīzi [头 tóu]

lioness NOUN
雌狮 císhī [头 tóu]

lip NOUN
唇 chún [片 piàn]

to **lip-read** VERB
唇读 chúndú

lip salve NOUN
润唇膏 rùnchúngāo [支 zhī]

lipstick NOUN
口红 kǒuhóng [支 zhī]

liqueur NOUN
利口酒 lìkǒujiǔ [瓶 píng]

liquid NOUN
液体 yètǐ [种 zhǒng]

liquidizer NOUN
榨汁机 zhàzhījī [个 gè]

liquor NOUN (US)
酒 jiǔ [种 zhǒng]

list NOUN
▷ *see also* **list** VERB
单子 dānzi [张 zhāng]

to **list** VERB
▷ *see also* **list** NOUN
列出 lièchū
□ List your hobbies! 列出你的业余爱好！Lièchū nǐde yèyú àihào!

to **listen** VERB
1 听 tīng
□ Listen to this! 听这个！Tīng zhège!
2 听…说 tīng…shuō
□ Go on, I'm listening. 继续，我在听。Jìxù, wǒzàitīng.
3 听从 tīngcóng *(follow advice)*
■ **to listen to somebody** **1** *(pay attention to)* 留神听某人说话 liúshén tīng mǒurén shuōhuà □ Listen to me! 听我说！Tīng wǒ shuō! **2** *(follow advice of)* 听从某人 tīngcóng mǒurén □ I warned him but he didn't listen to me. 我警告过他，可是他不听我的。Wǒ jǐnggàoguòtā, kěshì tā bùtīng wǒde.
■ **to listen to something** 听某事 tīng mǒushì

listener NOUN
听众 tīngzhòng [位 wèi]

lit VERB ▷ *see* **light**

liter NOUN (US)
升 shēng

literally ADVERB
完全 wánquán
□ It was literally impossible to find a seat. 完全不可能找到座位。Wánquán bùkěnéng zhǎodào zuòwèi.
■ **to translate literally** 逐字翻译 zhúzìfānyì

literature NOUN
文学 wénxué
□ I'm studying English Literature. 我在学习英国文学。Wǒzàixuéxí yīngguó wénxué.

litre NOUN
升 shēng

litter NOUN
垃圾 lājī

litter bin NOUN
垃圾箱 lājīxiāng [个 gè]

little ADJECTIVE, ADVERB
1 小的 xiǎo de
□ a little girl 一个小女孩 yígè xiǎonǚhái.
□ When I was little... 我小时候… wǒ xiǎoshíhòu... □ a little boy of 8 一个八岁的小男孩 yígè bāsuì de xiǎo nánhái
■ **little brother** 弟弟 dìdi

English-Chinese

l

■ **little sister** 妹妹 mèimei

2 少 shǎo

■ **to have little time** 时间少 shíjiānshǎo
□ We've got very little time. 我们时间很少。Wǒmen shíjiān hěnshǎo. □ We've got very little money. 我们钱很少。Wǒmen qián hěnshǎo.

■ **a little** 一点 yìdiǎn □ How much would you like? — Just a little. 你要多少？— 只要一点。Nǐyàoduōshǎo? — Zhǐyào yìdiǎn.
□ a little care 在意一点 zàiyì yìdiǎn

■ **a little bit** 有点 yǒudiǎn □ a little bit better 有点好转 yǒudiàn hǎozhuǎn

■ **little by little** 逐渐地 zhújiàn de

LANGUAGE TIP It's very important to remember the difference in Chinese between **little (in size)** 小 xiǎo and **little (in amount)**, 少 shǎo. It doesn't help matters that the pronunciation of these two words is very similar.

live ADJECTIVE
▷ *see also* **live** VERB

1 活的 huó de
□ live animals 活的动物 huóde dòngwu

2 实况地 shíkuàng de
□ live broadcast 实况广播 shíkuàng guǎngbō

to **live** VERB
▷ *see also* **live** ADJECTIVE

1 住 zhù
□ I live with my grandmother. 我和祖母住在一起。Wǒ hé zǔmǔ zhùzài yìqǐ. □ Where do you live? 你住在那儿？Nǐ zhùzài nǎ'ěr
□ I live in Edinburgh. 我住在爱丁堡。Wǒ zhùzài Àidīngbǎo.

2 活 huó
□ He lived a long time. 他活了很久。Tā huóle hěnjiǔ.

3 过 guò

■ **to live one's life** 过活 guòhuó

to **live on** VERB
靠…维持生活 kào…wéichí shēnghuó

■ **to live on something** 靠某物维持生活 kào mǒuwù wéichí shēnghuó □ He lives on benefit. 他靠救济金维持生活。Tā kào jiùjìjīn wéichíshēnghuó.

to **live together** VERB
同居 tóngjū
□ They're not married, they're living together. 他们没结婚，他们在同居。Tāmen méi jiéhūn, tāmen zài tóngjū.
□ My parents aren't living together any more. 我父母分居了。Wǒ fùmǔ fēnjūle.

to **live with** VERB
和…一起住 hé…yìqǐzhù
□ She's living with two Greek students. 她现在和两个希腊学生一起住。Tā xiànzài hé liǎnggè xīlàxuéshēng yìqǐzhù.*(share accommodation)*

lively ADJECTIVE

1 活泼的 huópo de*(person)*
□ She's got a lively personality. 她性格活泼。Tā xìnggé huópō.

2 活跃的 huóyuè de
□ It was a lively party. 那是一次活跃的聚会。Nà shì yícì huóyuè de jùhuì.

liver NOUN

1 肝脏 gānzàng [个 gè]
□ liver disease 肝病 gānbìng

2 肝 gān [个 gè]
□ chicken livers 鸡肝 jīgān

lives PL NOUN ▷ *see* **life**

living NOUN *(life)*
生活 shēnghuó
□ What does she do for a living? 她以什么为生？Tā yǐ shénme wéishēng?

■ **to make a living** 谋生 móushēng

living room NOUN
起居室 qǐjūshì [间 jiān]

lizard NOUN
蜥蜴 xīyì [只 zhī]

load NOUN
▷ *see also* **load** VERB
装载量 zhuāngzàiliàng [车 chē]

■ **loads of** *(informal)* 很多 hěnduō □ loads of people 很多人 hěnduōrén □ loads of money 很多钱 hěnduōqián

■ **a load of** 很多 hěnduō □ You're talking a load of rubbish! 你在说很多废话！Nǐ zài shuō hěnduō fèihuà!

to **load** VERB
▷ *see also* **load** NOUN

1 装 zhuāng
□ a trolley loaded with luggage 装着行李的手推车 zhuāngzhe xínglǐ de shǒutuīchē

2 装入 zhuāng rù*(program, data)*

loaf NOUN

■ **a loaf of bread** 一条面包 yìtiáo miànbāo

loan NOUN
▷ *see also* **loan** VERB
贷款 dàikuǎn [笔 bǐ]

to **loan** VERB
▷ *see also* **loan** NOUN

■ **to loan something to somebody** 把某物借给某人 bǎ mǒuwù jiègěi mǒurén

loaves PL NOUN ▷ *see* **loaf**

lobster NOUN
龙虾 lóngxiā [只 zhī]

local ADJECTIVE

1 当地的 dāngdì de
□ the local paper 当地的报纸 dāngdìde bàozhǐ

2 本地的 běndì de
□ local people 本地人 běndìrén

location NOUN
地点 dìdiǎn [个 gè]
□ a hotel set in a beautiful location 一家座落地点景色优美的酒店 yìjiā zuòluòdìdiǎn jǐngsè yōuměi de jiǔdiàn

loch NOUN
湖 hú [片 piàn]

lock NOUN
▷ *see also* **lock** VERB
锁 suǒ [把 bǎ]

to **lock** VERB
▷ *see also* **lock** NOUN
锁 suǒ
□ Make sure you lock your door. 一定锁好门。Yídìng suǒhǎomén. □ I've locked my screen. 我已经锁定了显示屏。Wǒ yǐjing suǒdìng le xiǎnshìpíng.

to **lock out** VERB
把...锁在外面 bǎ...suǒ zài wàimian
□ She locked him out. 她把他锁在了外面。Tā bǎtā suǒzàile wàimiàn. □ The door slammed and I was locked out. 门砰地关上了，我被锁在了外面。Mén pēngde guānshàngle, wǒ bèi sǔozàile wàimiàn.
■ **to lock oneself out** 把自己锁在外面 bǎ zìjǐ suǒ zài wàimian

to **lock up** VERB
锁好 suǒhǎo

locker NOUN
小柜 xiǎoguì [个 gè]
■ **the locker room** 衣帽间 yīmàojiān
■ **the left-luggage lockers** 行李寄存箱 xínglǐ jìcúnxiāng

lodger NOUN
房客 fángkè [个 gè]

loft NOUN
阁楼 gélóu [座 zuò] *(attic)*

log NOUN
木柴 mùchái [根 gēn] *(wood)*

to **log in** VERB
登录 dēnglù
■ **to log into an account** 登录一个帐户 dēnglù yígè zhànghù

to **log off** VERB
退出系统 tuìchū xìtǒng

to **log on** VERB
登录 dēnglù

to **log out** VERB
退出系统 tuìchū xìtǒng

logical ADJECTIVE
1 逻辑的 luójì de
□ a logical argument 一个合乎逻辑的论点 yígè héhū luójì de lùndiǎn
2 合逻辑的 hé luójì de
□ That's the logical conclusion. 那是合逻辑的结论。Nà shì hé luójì de jiélùn.
3 合乎情理的 héhū qínglǐ de
□ That's the logical thing to do. 做那件事合乎情理。Zuò nàjiànshì héhūqínglǐ.

lollipop NOUN
棒棒糖 bàngbàngtáng [支 zhī]

lolly NOUN
棒棒糖 bàngbàngtáng [支 zhī]

London NOUN
伦敦 Lúndūn
□ in London 在伦敦 zài Lúndūn □ to London 到伦敦 daò Lúndūn □ I'm from London. 我来自伦敦。Wǒ láizì Lúndūn.

Londoner NOUN
伦敦人 Lúndūnrén [个 gè]

loneliness NOUN
孤独 gūdú

lonely ADJECTIVE *(person)*
1 孤独的 gūdú de
■ **to feel lonely** 感到孤独 gǎndào gūdú
□ She feels a bit lonely. 她感到有点孤独。Tā gǎndào yǒudiǎn gūdú.
2 人迹罕至的 rénjì hǎn zhì de
□ a lonely place 人迹罕至的地方 rénjì hǎn zhì de dìfāng

lonesome ADJECTIVE
寂寞的 jìmòde
■ **to feel lonesome** 感到寂寞 gǎndào jìmò.

long ADJECTIVE
▷ *see also* **long** VERB
长的 cháng de
□ She's got long hair. 她留着长头发。Tā liúzhe cháng tóufà.
■ **6 metres long** 六米长 liùmǐ cháng
□ The room is 6 metres long. 那间屋子长六米。Nàjiān wūzi cháng liùmǐ.
■ **how long?** 多长时间？ duōcháng shíjiān？ □ How long did you stay there? 你在那儿呆了多长时间？ Nǐ zàinà'er dāi le duōcháng shíjiān？ □ How long have you been here? 你到这儿多长时间了？ Nǐ dàozhè'er duōcháng shíjiān le? □ How long is the flight? 飞行多长时间？Fēixíng duōcháng shíjiān? □ How long is the lesson? 这节课多长时间？Zhèjiékè duōcháng shíjiān?
■ **a long time** 很长一段时间 hěncháng yíduàn shíjiān □ I've been waiting a long time. 我已经等了很长一段时间。Wǒ yǐjìng děngle hěncháng yíduàn shíjiān. □ It takes a long time. 这要花很长时间。Zhè yào huā hěncháng shíjiān.
■ **It won't take long.** 这不需花很多时间。Zhè bù xūyào huā hěnduō shíjiān.

■ **as long as** 只要 zhǐyào □ I'll come as long as it's not too expensive. 只要不太贵我就来。Zhǐyào bú tàiguì wǒ jiùlái.

■ **long ago** 很久以前 hěnjiǔ yǐqián

■ **a long way** 很远 hěnyuǎn

to **long** VERB

▷ *see also* **long** ADJECTIVE

渴望 kěwàng

□ I'm longing to see my boyfriend again. 我渴望再见到我的男友。Wǒ kěwàng zàijiàn dào wǒde nányǒu.

long-distance ADJECTIVE

长途的 chángtúde

■ **a long-distance call** 长途电话 chángtú diànhuà

longer ADVERB

更久的 gèng jiǔ de

■ **They're no longer going out together.** 他们不再一起出去了。Tāmen búzài yìqǐ chūqù le.

■ **I can't stand it any longer.** 我再也受不了了。Wǒ zàiyě shòubuliǎo le.

loo NOUN

厕所 cèsuǒ [个 gè]

□ Where's the loo? 厕所在哪儿？Cèsuǒ zài nǎ'er?

look NOUN

▷ *see also* **look** VERB

表情 biǎoqíng [副 fù] *(expression)*

□ She gave him a look of surprise. 她吃惊地看了他一眼。Tā chījīng de kàn le tā yìyǎn.

■ **to have a look at** 看一看 kànyikàn

□ Have a look at this! 看看这个！Kànkan zhège!

to **look** VERB

▷ *see also* **look** NOUN

1 看 kàn

■ **to look at something** 看某物 kàn mǒuwù □ Look at the picture. 看那张画。Kàn nàzhāng huà.

■ **to look out of the window** 望向窗外 wàngxiàng chuāngwài

■ **look out!** 当心！Dāngxīn!

2 找 zhǎo

□ I've looked everywhere for my keys. 我到处找我的钥匙。Wǒ dàochù zhǎo wǒde yàoshi.

3 看起来 kànqǐlái

□ She looks surprised. 她看起来很惊讶。Tā kànqǐlái hěn jīngyà. □ That cake looks nice. 那个蛋糕看起来很好。Nàge dàngao kànqǐlái hěnhǎo. □ It looks fine. 这看起来很好。Zhè kànqǐlái hěnhǎo.

■ **to look like somebody** 长得像某人 zhǎngde xiàng mǒurén □ He looks like his younger brother. 他长得像他弟弟。Tā zhǎngde xiàng tā dìdi.

■ **it looks as if...** 看来… kànlái...

to **look after** VERB

照顾 zhàogù

□ I look after my little sister. 我照顾妹妹。Wǒ zhàogù mèimei.

to **look for** VERB

寻找 xúnzhǎo

□ I'm looking for my passport. 我在找我的护照。Wǒ zài zhǎo wǒde hùzhào.

to **look forward to** VERB

盼望 pànwàng

■ **to look forward to something** 盼望某物 pànwàng mǒuwù □ I'm looking forward to the holidays. 我盼望着假期。Wǒ pànwàngzhe jiàqī.

■ **to look forward to doing something** 盼望做某事 pànwàng zuò mǒushì □ Looking forward to hearing from you. 盼望着收到你的来信。Pànwàngzhe shōudào nǐde láixìn. □ We look forward to hearing from you. 我们盼望收到你的回音。Wǒmen pànwàng shōudào nǐde huíyīn.

to **look into** VERB *(investigate)*

调查 diàochá

to **look round** VERB

1 环顾 huángù

□ I shouted and he looked round. 我高声喊叫，他环顾四周。Wǒ gāoshēng hǎnjiào, tā huángùsìzhōu.

2 看看 kànkan *(in building)*

□ I'm just looking round. 我只是看看。Wǒ zhǐshì kànkan.

■ **to look round somewhere** 逛某地 guàng mǒudì □ I like looking round the shops. 我喜欢逛商店。Wǒ xǐhuān gùngshāngdiàn.

to **look through** VERB

翻阅 fānyuè *(book, magazine)*

to **look up** VERB

查 chá

□ Look the word up in the dictionary. 拿词典查出这个词。Ná cídiǎn cháchū zhège cí.

loose ADJECTIVE

1 松动的 sōngdòng de

□ a loose tooth 一颗松动的牙齿 yìkē sōngdòng de yáchǐ

2 散开的 sǎnkāi de

□ Her hair was loose. 她头发散开着。Tā tóufà sǎnkāi zhe.

3 宽松的 kuānsōng de

□ a loose jacket 一件宽松的夹克 yíjiàn kuānsōng de jiákè

■ **loose change** 零钱 língqián

lord NOUN

贵族 guìzú [位 wèi]

■ **the House of Lords** 上议院 shàngyìyuàn
■ **Good Lord!** 老天啊！Lǎotiāna!

lorry NOUN
卡车 kǎchē [辆 liàng]

lorry driver NOUN
卡车司机 kǎchē sījī [位 wèi]

to **lose** VERB
1 丢失 diūshī
□ I've lost my purse. 我丢了钱包。Wǒ diūle qiánbāo.
2 输 shū
□ Our team is sure to lose. 我们队肯定会输。Wǒmen duì kěndìng huì shū. □ We've lost three matches in a row. 我们已经连输了三场比赛。Wǒmen yǐjīng liánshūle sānchǎng bǐsài.
3 失去 shīqù
□ He lost his wife last year. 他去年失去了妻子。Tā qùnián shīqùle qīzi.
■ **to lose weight** 减重 jiǎnzhòng

loser NOUN
输家 shūjiā
■ **to be a bad loser** 是个输不起的人 shìge shūbuqǐ derén □ He's such a loser! 他真是个失败者！Tā zhēnshì gè shībàizhě!

loss NOUN
丧失 sàngshī [种 zhǒng]

lost VERB ▷ *see* **lose**

lost ADJECTIVE
1 丢失的 diūshī de *(object)*
2 走失的 zǒushī de *(person, animal)*
■ **to get lost** 迷路 mílù □ I was afraid of getting lost. 我怕迷路。Wǒ pà mílù.

lost and found NOUN (US)
失物招领处 shīwù zhāolǐngchù [个 gè]

lost property NOUN
1 招领的失物 zhāolǐng de shīwù [件 jiàn] *(things)*
2 失物招领处 shīwù zhāolǐngchù [个 gè] *(office)*

lost property office NOUN
失物招领处 shīwù zhāolǐngchù

lot NOUN
很多 hěnduō
□ A hundred pounds! That's a lot! 一百磅！那很多了！Yìbǎibàng! Nà hěnduōle! □ He reads a lot. 他书读得很多。Tā shū dúde hěnduō.
■ **a lot of** 许多 xǔduō □ We saw a lot of interesting things. 我们看到许多有趣的事。Wǒmen kàndào xǔduō yǒuqùde shì.
■ **lots of** 许多 xǔduō □ She's got lots of money. 她有许多钱。Tā yǒu xǔduō qián. □ He's got lots of friends. 他有许多朋友。Tā yǒu xǔduō péngyǒu.
■ **not a lot** 没有什么 méiyǒu shénme □ What did you do at the weekend? — Not a lot. 你周末干什么了？— 没干什么。Nǐ zhōumò gànshénme le? — Méi gàn shénme.
■ **That's the lot.** *(informal)* 就这些。Jiù zhèxiē.

lottery NOUN
彩票 cǎipiào [张 zhāng]
■ **to win the lottery** 彩票重奖 cǎipiào zhòngjiǎng

loud ADJECTIVE
1 响亮的 xiǎngliàng de
□ The television is too loud. 电视太响了。Diànshì tài xiǎngle.
2 大声地 dàshēng de
□ He has the television on very loud. 他把电视开得很大声。Tā bǎ diànshì kāide hěndàshēng.

loudly ADVERB
大声地 dàshēng de

loudspeaker NOUN
扬声器 yángshēngqì [个 gè]

lounge NOUN
1 休息室 xiūxishì [间 jiān] *(in hotel)*
2 等候室 děnghòushì [间 jiān] *(in airport)*
3 起居室 qǐjūshì [间 jiān] *(in house)*

lousy ADJECTIVE
恶心 ěxīn
□ The food in the canteen is lousy. 食堂的食物很差。Shítáng de shíwù hěnchà.
■ **to feel lousy** 身体不舒服 shēntǐ bù shūfu

love NOUN
▷ *see also* **love** VERB
1 爱情 àiqíng *(for partner, sweetheart)*
2 爱 ài *(for child, pet)*
■ **to be in love with somebody** 与某人恋爱 yǔ mǒurén liàn'ài □ She's in love with Paul. 她在与保罗恋爱。Tā zàiyǔ bǎoluó liàn'ài.
■ **to fall in love with somebody** 爱上某人 àishàng mǒurén
■ **to make love** 做爱 zuò'ài
■ **love from Anne** 爱你的，安妮 àinǐde, Ānní
■ **Love, Rosemary.** 爱你的，罗斯玛丽。Àinǐde,luósīmǎlì.
■ **Give Gary my love.** 替我向加里致意。Tì wǒ xiàng jiālǐ zhìyì.

to **love** VERB
▷ *see also* **love** NOUN
1 爱 ài
□ I love you. 我爱你。Wǒ ài nǐ.
□ Everybody loves her. 每个人都喜爱她。Měigèrén dōu xǐài tā.
2 热爱 rè'ài

□ I love chocolate. 我热爱巧克力。Wǒ rè'ài qiǎokèlì.

■ **to love doing something** 喜爱做某事 xǐ'ài zuò mǒushì □ I love skiing. 我喜爱滑雪。Wǒ xǐ'ài huáxuě.

■ **I'd love to** 我非常想 Wǒ fēicháng xiǎng □ I'd love to come. 我非常想来。Wǒ fēicháng xiǎng lái.

lovely ADJECTIVE

1 漂亮的 piàoliang de
□ They've got a lovely house. 他们有一幢漂亮的房子。Tāmen yǒu yízhuàng piàoliàng de fángzi.

2 令人愉快的 lìng rén yúkuài de
□ What a lovely surprise! 多么令人愉快的意外！Duōme lìngrén yúkuàide yìwài!
□ Is your meal OK? — Yes, it's lovely. 你的饭菜还可以吗？ — 是的，很好吃。Nǐde fàncài hái kěyǐma? — Shìde, hěnhǎo chī.
□ Have a lovely time! 过一段愉快的时光！Guòyíduàn yúkuàide shíguāng! □ It's a lovely day. 这是美好的一天。Zhè shì měihǎode yìtiān.

3 可爱的 kě'ài de
□ She's a lovely person. 她是个可爱的人。Tā shìge kěa'àide rén.

lover NOUN

爱好者 àihàozhě [个 gè]
□ She is a lover of good food. 她是个美食爱好者。Tā shì ge měishí àih.
■ **an art lover** 钟爱艺术的人 zhōng'ài yìshù de rén

low ADJECTIVE, ADVERB

1 矮的 ǎi de
□ a low table 一张矮桌 yìzhāng aǐzhuō

2 低的 dī de
□ a very low temperature 非常低的温度 fēichángdī de wēndù □ That plane is flying very low. 那架飞机飞得很低。Nàjià fēijī fēide hěndī.

3 低劣的 dīliè de
□ a low standard 一项低标准 yíxiàng dī biāozhǔn
■ **low in calories** 低卡路里 dī kǎlùlǐ
■ **the low season** 淡季 dànjì □ in the low season 在淡季 zàidànjì

to **lower** VERB

▷ *see also* **lower** ADJECTIVE
降低 jiàngdī

lower ADJECTIVE

▷ *see also* **lower** VERB
下面的 xiàmiànde
□ on the lower floor 在下层 zài xiàcéng

lower sixth NOUN

中学低六年级 zhōngxué dīliùniánjí
□ He's in the lower sixth. 他在上中学低六年级。Tā zàishàng zhōngxué dī liùniánjí.

low-fat ADJECTIVE

低脂肪的 dī zhīfángde
□ a low-fat yoghurt 低脂肪酸奶 dī zhīfáng suānnǎi

loyal ADJECTIVE

忠实的 zhōngshí de

loyalty NOUN

忠诚 zhōngchéng [片 piàn]

loyalty card NOUN

会员卡 huìyuánkǎ [张 zhāng]

L-plates PL NOUN

学习车牌照 xuéxíchīpáizhào [块 kuài]

luck NOUN

1 运气 yùnqi
□ It's a matter of luck. 这是运气问题。Zhè shì yùnqi wèntí.

2 幸运 xìngyùn
□ She hasn't had much luck. 她不怎么幸运。Tā bùzěnme xìngyùn.
■ **good luck** 好运 hǎoyùn
■ **Good luck!** 祝你好运！Zhùnǐ hǎoyùn!
■ **Bad luck!** 真倒霉！Zhēn daǒmeǐ!

luckily ADVERB

幸运的是 xìngyùn de shì

lucky ADJECTIVE

幸运的 xìngyùn de
□ Lucky you! 你真幸运！Nǐ zhēnxìngyùn!
■ **to be lucky 1** *(fortunate)* 走运 zǒuyùn
□ He's lucky, he's got a job. 他走运找到了一份工作。Tā zǒuyùn zhǎodàole yífèn gōngzuò. □ He wasn't hurt. — That was lucky! 他没受伤。— 真走运！Tā méishòushāng. — Zhēnzǒuyùn! □ It is lucky that... 侥幸的是… jiǎoxìng de shì...
2 吉利的 jílìde □ Black cats are lucky in Britain. 黑猫在英国是吉利的。Hēimāo zài Yīngguó shì jílìde.
■ **a lucky horseshoe** 一块幸运马蹄铁 yíkuài xìngyùn mǎtítiě
■ **to have a lucky escape** 侥幸逃脱 jiǎoxìng táotuō

> **DID YOU KNOW...?**
> In China, the number **eight** 八 is traditionally seen as very lucky, because its pronunciation bā is very similar to the Chinese word 发 fā which is short for 发财 fācái **prosper** or **wealth**. **Four** 四 sì is considered unlucky because it sounds like 死 sǐ **death**. Thirteen is not an unlucky number in China.

luggage NOUN

行李 xíngli
■ **piece of luggage** 一件行李 yíjiàn xíngli

lump NOUN
肿块 zhǒngkuài [个 gè]
▫ a lump of butter 一块黄油 yíkuàihuángyóu ▫ He's got a lump on his forehead. 他额头上起了个肿块。Tā étóushàng qǐlegè zhǒngkuài.

lunatic NOUN
疯子 fēngzi [个 gè]
▫ He drives like a lunatic. 他开车像个疯子。Tā kāichē xiànggè fēngzi.

lunch NOUN
1 午餐 wǔcān [顿 dùn]
■ **to have lunch** 吃午餐 chī wǔcān ▫ We have lunch at 12.30. 我们十二点三十分吃午餐。Wǒmen shíèrdiǎn sānshífēn chīwǔcān.
■ **to have lunch with somebody** 与某人共进午餐 yǔ mǒurén gòngjìn wǔcān
2 午餐时间 wǔcān shíjiān
▫ We met after lunch. 我们午餐以后见了面。Wǒmēn wǔcān yǐhòu jiànlemiàn.

lung NOUN
肺 fèi [片 piàn]
▫ lung cancer 肺癌 fèiái

Luxembourg NOUN
卢森堡 Lúsēnbǎo
▫ in Luxembourg 在卢森堡 zài Lúsēnbǎo
▫ to Luxembourg 到卢森堡 dào Lúsēnbǎo

luxurious ADJECTIVE
豪华的 háohuá de

luxury NOUN
奢华 shēhuá
▫ It was luxury! 那真豪华！Nà zhēn háohuá!
■ **a luxury hotel** 一家豪华酒店 yìjiā háohuá jiǔdiàn

lying VERB ▷ *see* **lie**

lyrics PL NOUN
词句 cíjù [段 duàn]

Mm

mac NOUN
雨衣 yǔyī [件 jiàn]

macaroni NOUN
管状通心粉 guǎnzhuàng tōngxīnfěn [份 fèn]

machine NOUN
机器 jīqì [台 tái]

machine gun NOUN
机关枪 jīguānqiāng [架 jià]

machinery NOUN
机器 jīqì [套 tào]

mackerel NOUN
鲐鱼 táiyú [条 tiáo]

mad ADJECTIVE
1 疯的 fēng de *(insane)*
□ You're mad! 你疯了！ Nǐ fēng le!
2 生气的 shēngqì de *(informal: angry)*
□ She'll be mad when she finds out. 她知道了的话，会生气的。Tā zhīdào le de huà, huì shēngqì de.
■ **to go mad** 1 *(go insane)* 发疯 fāfēng 2 *(get angry)* 发火 fāhuǒ
■ **to be mad about** 1 *(sport, activity)* 狂热地爱好 kuángrè de àihào □ He's mad about football. 他狂热地爱好足球。Tā kuángrè de aìhào zúqiú. 2 *(person, animal)* 狂热地喜爱 kuángrè de xǐ'aì □ She's mad about horses. 她狂热地喜爱马。Tā kuángrè de xǐ'aì mǎ.

madam NOUN
女士 nǚshì [位 wèi]
□ Would you like to order, Madam? 女士，您要点餐吗？. Nǚshì, nín yào diǎncān mā?
■ **Dear Madam** 尊敬的女士 zūnjìng de nǚshì

made VERB ▷ *see* **make**

madly ADVERB
疯狂地 fēngkuáng de
■ **They're madly in love.** 他们在疯狂地恋爱中。Tāmen zài fēngkuáng de liàn'aì zhōng.

madman NOUN
疯子 fēngzi [个 gè]

madness NOUN
1 疯狂 fēngkuáng *(insanity)*
2 愚蠢 yúchǔn *(foolishness)*
□ It's absolute madness. 这实在太愚蠢了。Zhè shízaì taì yúchǔn le.

magazine NOUN
杂志 zázhì [份 fèn]

maggot NOUN
蛆 qū [只 zhī]

magic NOUN
▷ *see also* **magic** ADJECTIVE
魔术 móshù
□ a magic trick 一个魔术 yígè móshù
□ My hobby is magic. 我的业余爱好是魔术。Wǒde yèyú àihào shì móshù.

magic ADJECTIVE
▷ *see also* **magic** NOUN
1 神奇的 shénqí de *(formula, solution, cure)*
2 魔法的 mófǎ de *(magical)*
□ a magic wand 一根魔术棒 yìgēn móshùbàng
3 棒的 bàng de *(brilliant)*
□ It was magic! 太棒了！ Tài bàng le!

magician NOUN
魔术师 móshùshī [位 wèi] *(conjurer)*

magnet NOUN
磁铁 cítiě [块 kuài]

magnificent ADJECTIVE
1 壮丽的 zhuànglì de *(beautiful)*
□ a magnificent view 一处壮丽的风景 yíchù zhuànglì de fēngjǐng
2 了不起的 liǎobuqǐ de *(outstanding)*
□ It was a magnificent achievement. 那是个了不起的成就。Nà shì gè liǎobuqǐ de chéngjiù.

magnifying glass NOUN
放大镜 fàngdàjìng [个 gè]

maid NOUN
女仆 nǚpú [个 gè] *(servant)*
■ **an old maid** *(spinster)* 未婚妇女 wèihūn fùnǚ

maiden name NOUN
娘家姓 niángjiā xìng [个 gè]

DID YOU KNOW...?
In China, women do not change their family names when they marry.

mail NOUN
▷ *see also* **mail** VERB
1 邮件 yóujiàn [封 fēng] *(letters)*
□ Here's your mail. 这是你的邮件。Zhè shì nǐ de yóujiàn.
■ **the mail** 邮政 yóuzhèng
■ **by mail** 以邮寄方式 yǐ yóujì fāngshì
2 电子邮件 diànzǐ yóujiàn *(email)*
□ Can I check my mail on your PC? 我能在你的电脑上查我的电子邮件么？Wǒ néng zài nǐ de diànnǎo shàng chá wǒde diànzǐ yóujiàn me?

to **mail** VERB
▷ *see also* **mail** NOUN
1 寄 jì *(post)*
2 伊妹儿 yīmei'er *(email)*
□ I'll mail you my address. 我会把我的地址伊妹儿给你。Wǒ huì bǎ wǒde dìzhǐ yīmei'er gěi nǐ.

mailbox NOUN
1 信箱 xìnxiāng [个 gè] (US: *to collect mail)*
2 邮筒 yóutǒng [个 gè] *(for delivered mail)*
3 电子信箱 diànzǐ xìnxiāng [个 gè] *(on computer)*

mailing list NOUN
联系地址清单 liánxì dìzhǐ qīngdān [个 gè]

mailman NOUN (US)
邮递员 yóudìyuán [位 wèi]

mailwoman NOUN (US)
女邮递员 nǚ yóudìyuán [位 wèi]

main ADJECTIVE
主要的 zhǔyào de
□ the main problem 主要问题 zhǔyào wèntí □ The main thing is to... 主要任务是… Zhǔyào rènwù shì...

main course NOUN
主菜 zhǔcài [道 dào]

mainly ADVERB
主要地 zhǔyào de

main road NOUN
主干道 zhǔ gàndào [条 tiáo]
□ I don't like cycling on main roads. 我不喜欢在主干道上骑车。Wǒ bù xǐhuān zài zhǔgàndào shàng qíchē.

to **maintain** VERB
维修 wéixiū *(machine, building)*

maintenance NOUN
维护 wéihù [次 cì] *(of machine, building)*

maize NOUN
玉米 yùmǐ [个 gè]

majesty NOUN
■ **Your Majesty** 陛下 bìxià

major ADJECTIVE
▷ *see also* **major** NOUN
重要的 zhòngyào de
□ a major problem 一个重要问题 yígè zhòngyào wèntí
■ **in C major** 在C大调上 zài C dàdiào shàng

major NOUN
▷ *see also* **major** ADJECTIVE
1 少校 shàoxiào [位 wèi] *(officer)*
2 专业 zhuānyè [个 gè] (US: *main subject)*

Majorca NOUN
马胶尔卡岛 Mǎjiāoěrkǎ dǎo
□ We went to Majorca in August. 我们八月去了马胶尔卡岛。Wǒmen bāyuè qù le Mǎjiāoěrkǎ dǎo.

majority NOUN
大多数 dàduōshù

make NOUN
▷ *see also* **make** VERB
牌子 páizi [个 gè] *(brand)*
□ What make is that car? 那辆车是啥牌子的？Nà liǎng chē shì shá páizi de?

to **make** VERB
▷ *see also* **make** NOUN
1 做 zuò *(object, clothes, cake)*
□ I'm going to make a cake. 我要去做一个蛋糕。Wǒ yào qù zuò yígè dàngāo. □ He made it himself. 他靠自己做到了。Tā kào zìjǐ zuòdào le. □ It's made of glass. 它是玻璃做的。Tā shì bōli zuò de.
2 制造 zhìzào *(noise)*
3 犯 fàn *(mistake)*
4 等于 děngyú *(equal)*
□ 2 and 2 make 4. 2加2等于4。Èr jiā èr děngyú sì.
5 生产 shēngchǎn *(manufacture)*
□ made in China 在中国生产的 zài zhōngguó shēngchǎn de
6 挣 zhèng *(earn)*
□ He makes a lot of money. 他挣很多钱。Tāzhèng hěnduō qián.
■ **to make somebody sad** 使某人难过 shǐ mǒurén nánguò
■ **to make somebody do something** 让某人做某事 ràng mǒurén zuò mǒushì □ My mother makes me do my homework. 妈妈让我做家庭作业。Māma ràng wǒ zuò jiātíngzuòyè.
■ **to make lunch** 做午饭 zuò wǔfàn
□ She's making lunch. 她在做午饭。Tā zài zuò wǔfàn.
■ **to make one's bed** 整理床铺 zhěnglǐ chuángpù □ I make my bed every morning. 我每天早上都整理床铺。Wǒ měitiān zǎoshàng dōu zhěnglǐ chuángpù.
■ **to make a phone call** 打电话 dǎ diànhuà □ I'd like to make a phone call. 我想打个电话。Wǒ xiǎng dǎ gè diànhuà.
■ **to make fun of somebody** 取笑某人

qǔxiào mǒurén □ They made fun of him. 他们曾取笑他。Tāmen céng qǔxiào tā.
■ **to make a profit** 赢利 yínglì
■ **to make a loss** 亏损 kuìsǔn
■ **What time do you make it?** 你表几点了？ Nǐ biǎo jǐdiǎn le?

to **make out** VERB
1 识别 shíbié *(read)*
□ I can't make out the address on the label. 我识别不了标签上的地址。Wǒ shíbié bù liǎo biāoqiān shàng de dìzhǐ.
2 理解 lǐjiě *(understand)*
□ I can't make her out at all. 我完全理解不了她。Wǒ wánquán lǐjiě bù liǎo tā.
3 伪称 wěichēng *(claim, pretend)*
□ They're making out it was my fault. 他们伪称那是我的过错。Tāmen wěichēng nà shì wǒde guòcuo.
■ **to make a cheque out to somebody** 开出支票给某人 kāichū zhīpiào gěi mǒurén

makeover NOUN
形象改造 xíngxiàng gǎizào [次 cì]
□ She had a complete makeover. 她经过了一次全方位的形象改造。Tā jīngguò le yícì quánfāngwèi de xíngxiàng gǎizào.

maker NOUN
制造者 zhìzàozhě [个 gè]
□ Europe's biggest car maker 欧洲最大的汽车制造者 Ōuzhōu zuìdà de qìchē zhìzàozhě
■ **a film maker** 一个电影制作人 yígè diànyǐng zhìzuò rén

to **make up** VERB
1 捏造 niēzào *(story, excuse)*
□ He made up the whole story. 整个故事都是他捏造出来的。Zhěnggè gùshì dōushì tā niēzào chūlái de.
2 和好 héhǎo *(after argument)*
□ They had a quarrel, but soon made up. 他们吵完架没多久就和好了。Tāmen chǎowán jià méi duōjiǔ jiù héhǎo le.
3 化妆 huàzhuāng *(with cosmetics)*
■ **to make oneself up** 化妆 huàzhuāng
□ She spends hours making herself up. 她花了几小时来化妆。Tā huāle jǐ xiǎoshí lái huàzhuāng.
■ **to make up one's mind** 下定决心 xià dìng juéxīn

make-up NOUN
化妆品 huàzhuāngpǐn [件 jiàn] *(cosmetics)*

Malaysia NOUN
马来西亚 Mǎláixīyà
□ in Malaysia 在马来西亚 zài Mǎláixīyà

male ADJECTIVE
1 男的 nán de *(person)*
□ Most football players are male. 大多数的足球运动员都是男的。Dàduōshù de zúqiú yùndòngyuán dōushì nán de. □ a male nurse 一个男护士 yígè nánhùshi
2 雄性的 xióngxìng de *(animal, insect, plant, tree)*
□ a male kitten 一只雄性小猫 yìzhī xióngxìng xiǎomāo
3 男性 nánxìng *(person, on official forms)*
□ Sex: male 性别：男性 xìngbié: nánxìng
■ **a male chauvinist** 一个大男子主义者 yígè dànánzizhǔyì zhě

malicious ADJECTIVE
恶毒的 èdú de
□ a malicious rumour 一个恶毒的谣言 yígè èdú de yáoyán

mall NOUN
大型购物中心 dàxíng gòuwù zhōngxīn [个 gè]

Malta NOUN
马耳他 Mǎ'ěrtā
□ in Malta 在马耳他 zài Mǎ'ěrtā □ to Malta 到马耳他 dào Mǎ'ěrtā

mammal NOUN
哺乳动物 bǔrǔ dòngwù [种 zhǒng]

mammoth NOUN
▷ *see also* **mammoth** ADJECTIVE
长毛象 chángmáoxiàng [只 zhī]

mammoth ADJECTIVE
▷ *see also* **mammoth** NOUN
浩大的 hàodà de
□ a mammoth task 一个浩大的工程 yígè hàodà de gōngchéng

man NOUN
1 男人 nánrén [个 gè] *(person)*
□ an old man 一个老男人 yígè lǎonánrén
2 人类 rénlèi *(mankind)*

to **manage** VERB
1 管理 guǎnlǐ *(business, shop, time, money)*
□ She manages a big store. 她管理一家大商店。Tā guǎnlǐ yìjiā dàshāngdiàn. □ He manages our football team. 他管理我们的足球队。Tā guǎnlǐ wǒmen de zúqiúduì.
2 过得去 guòdéqù *(get by)*
□ We haven't got much money, but we manage. 我们不是很富有，但还过得去。Wǒmen búshì hěn fùyǒu, dàn hái guòdequ.
3 应付 yìngfù *(cope)*
□ It's okay, I can manage. 没问题的，我能应付。Méiwèntí de, wǒ néng yìngfu.
□ Can you manage okay? 你能应付吗？ Nǐ néng yìngfu mā?
■ **to manage to do something** 成功做到某事 chénggōng zuòdào mǒushì □ Luckily I managed to pass the exam. 很幸运地，我成功通过了考试。Hěn xìngyùn de, wǒ

chénggōng tōngguò le kǎoshì.
■ **I can't manage all that.** *(eat)* 我吃不下所有的。Wǒ chī bú xià suǒyǒu de.

manageable ADJECTIVE
可实现的 kě shíxiàn de *(task)*

management NOUN
1 管理 guǎnlǐ *(managing)*
□ He's responsible for the management of the company. 他负责公司的管理。Tā fùzé gōngsī de guǎnlǐ.
2 管理人员 guǎnlǐ rényuán *(managers)*
■ **under new management** 在新管理层的领导下 zài xīn guǎnlǐcéng de lǐngdǎo xià

manager NOUN
1 经理 jīnglǐ [位 wèi] *(of company)*
2 球队经理 qiúduì jīnglǐ [位 wèi] *(of team)*

manageress NOUN
女经理 nǚ jīnglǐ [位 wèi] *(of shop)*

Mandarin NOUN
普通话 pǔtōnghuà

LANGUAGE TIP 普通话 pǔtōnghuà, which refers to standard Mandarin Chinese, literally means **common speech**.

mandarin NOUN
柑橘 gānjú [个 gè] *(fruit)*

mango NOUN
芒果 mángguǒ [个 gè]

mania NOUN
躁狂 zàokuáng

maniac NOUN
疯子 fēngzi [个 gè]
□ He drives like a maniac. 他驾驶起来像个疯子似的。Tā jiàshǐ qǐlái xiàng ge fēngzi sìde. □ a religious maniac 一个宗教狂热份子 yígè zōngjiào kuángrè fènzi

to **manipulate** VERB
操作 cāozuò

mankind NOUN
人类 rénlèi

man-made ADJECTIVE
人造的 rénzào de *(fibre)*

manner NOUN
方式 fāngshì [种 zhǒng] *(way)*
□ She behaves in an odd manner. 她行为举止怪异。Tā xíngwéi jǔzhǐ guàiyì. □ He has a confident manner. 他表现得很自信。Tā biǎoxiàndé hěn zìxìn.

manners PL NOUN
礼貌 lǐmào *(good manners)*
□ It's good manners to arrive on time. 准时是有礼貌的表现。Zhǔnshí shì yǒu lǐmào de biǎoxiàn. □ It's bad manners to speak with your mouth full. 口中有食物时讲话是不礼貌的。Kǒuzhōng yǒu shíwù shí jiǎnghuà shì bù lǐmào de. □ Her manners are appalling. 她的行为举止太让人吃惊了。Tā de xíngwéi jǔzhǐ tài ràng rén chījīng le.

manpower NOUN
人力 rénlì

mansion NOUN
大公寓楼 dà gōngyùlóu [栋 dòng]

mantelpiece NOUN
壁炉架 bìlújià [个 gè]

manual NOUN
手册 shǒu cè [本 běn] *(handbook)*

to **manufacture** VERB
生产 shēngchǎn

manufacturer NOUN
制造商 zhìzàoshāng [个 gè]

manure NOUN
肥料 féiliào [袋 dài]

manuscript NOUN
手稿 shǒugǎo [份 fèn]

many ADJECTIVE, PRONOUN
很多的 hěnduō de *(a lot of)*
□ The film has many special effects. 这部电影用了很多特效。Zhè bù diànyǐng yòng le hěnduō tèxiào. □ He hasn't got many friends. 他没有很多朋友。Tā méiyǒu hěnduō péngyǒu. □ Were there many people at the concert? 去音乐会的人很多么？Qù yīnyuèhuì de rén hěnduō me?
■ **very many** 非常多的 fēicháng duō de
□ I haven't got very many CDs. 我的CD不是非常多。Wǒde CD búshì fēicháng duō.
■ **not many** 不多 bùduō
■ **How many?** 多少？Duōshǎo? □ How many do you want? 你要多少？Nǐ yào duōshǎo?
■ **how many...?** 多少的 duōshǎo de
□ How many euros do you get for £100? 多少欧元才能换100英镑？Duōshǎo ōuyuán cáinéng huàn yìbǎi yīngbàng?
■ **too many** 过多的 guòduō de □ That's too many. 过多了。Guòduō le.
■ **too many...** 太多的 tàiduō de □ She makes too many mistakes. 她总是犯太多的错误。Tā zǒngshì fàn tàiduō de cuòwù.
■ **so many** 如此多 rúcǐ duō □ I didn't know there would be so many. 我之前并不知道会有如此多。Wǒ zhīqián bìng bùzhīdào huì yǒu rúcǐ duō.
■ **so many...** 这么多的 zhème duō de
□ I've never seen so many policemen. 我从来没见过这么多的警察。Wǒ cónglái méi jiànguò zhème duō de jǐngchá.
■ **twice as many as** (是…的)两倍 (shì... de) liǎngbèi

map NOUN
地图 dìtú [张 zhāng]

marathon NOUN
马拉松 mǎlāsōng [次 cì] *(race)*
□ the London marathon 伦敦马拉松 Lúndūn mǎlāsōng

marble NOUN
大理石 dàlǐshí [块 kuài]
□ a marble statue 一尊大理石雕像 yìzūn dàlǐshí diāoxiàng

marbles PL NOUN
弹子游戏 dànzǐ yóuxì [次 cì] *(game)*
■ **to play marbles** 玩弹子游戏 wán dànzi yóuxì

March NOUN
三月 sānyuè
□ in March 在三月 zài sānyuè □ the first of March 三月一日 sānyuè yīrì □ at the beginning of March 在三月初 zài sānyuè chū □ at the end of March 在三月末 zài sānyuè mò □ every March 每年三月 měinián sānyuè

DID YOU KNOW...?
8 March, known as 三八节 sānbājié, is International Women's Day. All government organisations and some private employers give their female employees an afternoon off on this day, and sometimes fund them to go on picnics and other treats.

to **march** VERB
▷ *see also* **march** NOUN
行军 xíngjūn

march NOUN
▷ *see also* **march** VERB
示威游行 shìwēi yóuxíng [次 cì] *(demonstration)*

mare NOUN
母马 mǔmǎ [匹 pǐ]

margarine NOUN
人造黄油 rénzào huángyóu [盒 hé]

margin NOUN
空白 kòngbái [个 gè]
□ Write notes in the margin. 在空白处记笔记。Zài kòngbái chù jì bǐjì.

marijuana NOUN
大麻 dàmá [克 kè]

marina NOUN
码头 mǎtóu [座 zuò]

marital status NOUN
婚姻状况 hūnyīn zhuàngkuàng [种 zhǒng]

mark NOUN
▷ *see also* **mark** VERB
1 记号 jìhao [个 gè] *(cross, tick)*
2 污点 wūdiǎn [个 gè] *(stain)*
□ You've got a mark on your skirt. 你的裙子上沾了个污点。Nǐde qúnzi shàng zhān le gè wūdiǎn.
3 分数 fēnshù [个 gè] *(grade, score)*
□ I get good marks for French. 我的法语经常拿高分。Wǒde fǎyǔ jīngcháng ná gāofēn.
4 （德国货币）马克 (déguó huòbì) mǎkè *(former German currency)*

to **mark** VERB
▷ *see also* **mark** NOUN
1 标示 biāoshì *(indicate)*
2 评分 píngfēn *(assess)*
□ The teacher hasn't marked my homework yet. 老师还没给我的家庭作业评分。Lǎoshī hái méi gěi wǒde jiātíng zuòyè píngfēn.

market NOUN
集市 jíshì [个 gè]

marketing NOUN
市场营销 shìchǎng yíngxiāo

marketplace NOUN
市场 shìchǎng [个 gè]

marmalade NOUN
果酱 guǒjiàng [瓶 píng]

maroon ADJECTIVE
栗色的 lìsè de *(colour)*

marriage NOUN
1 婚姻 hūnyīn [个 gè] *(relationship, institution)*
2 婚礼 hūnlǐ [场 chǎng] *(wedding)*

married ADJECTIVE
已婚的 yǐhūn de
□ a married couple 一对已婚夫妇 yíduì yǐhūn fūfù □ They are not married. 他们还没结婚。Tāmen hái méi jiéhūn. □ They have been married for 15 years. 他们结婚已经15年了。Tāmen jiéhūn yǐjīng shíwǔ nián le.
■ **to be married to somebody** 和某人结婚 hé mǒurén jiéhūn

marrow NOUN
南瓜 nánguā [个 gè] *(vegetable)*
■ **bone marrow** 骨髓 gǔsuí

to **marry** VERB
和...结婚 hé...jiéhūn
□ He wants to marry her. 他想和她结婚。Tā xiǎng hé tā jiéhūn.
■ **to get married** 结婚 jiéhūn □ My sister's getting married in June. 我姐姐六月就要结婚了。Wǒ jiějie liùyuè jiù yào jiéhūn le.

marvellous (US **marvelous**) ADJECTIVE
极好的 jíhǎo de
□ She's a marvellous cook. 她是一个极好的厨师。Tā shì yígè jíhǎo de chúshī. □ The weather was marvellous. 天气极好。Tiānqì jíhǎo.

marzipan NOUN
杏仁蛋软糖 xìngrén dàn ruǎntáng [块 kuài]

mascara NOUN
睫毛膏 jiémáogāo [支 zhī]
masculine ADJECTIVE
1 男性的 nánxìng de *(characteristic, value)*
2 阳性的 yángxìng de *(pronoun)*
mashed potatoes PL NOUN
土豆泥 tǔdòuní [份 fèn]
□ sausages and mashed potatoes 香肠和土豆泥 xiāngcháng hé tǔdòuní
mask NOUN
1 面具 miànjù [个 gè] *(disguise)*
2 口罩 kǒuzhào [个 gè] *(protection)*
masked ADJECTIVE
隐藏的 yǐncáng de
mass NOUN
1 大量 dàliàng *(large amount, number)*
□ a mass of books and papers 大量书和纸 dàliàng shū hé zhǐ
■ **masses of** 大量的 dàliàng de
2 弥撒 mísà *(in church)*
□ We go to mass on Sunday. 我们经常周日去做弥撒。Wǒmen jīngcháng zhōurì qù zuò mísà.
■ **the mass media** 大众传媒 dàzhòng chuánméi
massage NOUN
按摩 ànmó [次 cì]
massive ADJECTIVE
1 巨大的 jùdà de *(amount, increase)*
2 大规模的 dà guīmó de *(explosion)*
to **master** VERB
掌握 zhǎngwò *(skill, language)*
masterpiece NOUN
杰作 jiézuò [部 bù]
mat NOUN
1 席 xí [张 zhāng] *(large)*
■ **a beach mat** 一张沙滩席 yìzhāng shātān xí
2 垫 diàn [张 zhāng] *(small)*
■ **a table mat** 一张碗碟垫 yìzhāng wǎndiédiàn
match NOUN
▷ *see also* **match** VERB
1 比赛 bǐsài [场 chǎng] *(game)*
□ a football match 一场足球比赛 yìchǎng zúqiúbǐsài
2 火柴 huǒchái [根 gēn]
□ a box of matches 一盒火柴 yìhé huǒchái
to **match** VERB
▷ *see also* **match** NOUN
配 pèi *(go together)*
□ The jacket matches the trousers. 这件夹克配这条裤子。Zhéjiàn jiákè pèi zhètiáo kùzi. □ These colours don't match. 这些颜色不配。Zhèxiē yánsè bù pèi.
matching ADJECTIVE
匹配的 pǐpèi de
□ My bedroom has matching wallpaper and curtains. 我卧室里的壁纸和窗帘很匹配。Wǒ wòshì lǐ de bìzhǐ hé chuānglián hěn pǐpèi.
mate NOUN
1 配偶 pèi'ǒu [个 gè] *(animal)*
2 朋友 péngyǒu [个 gè] *(informal: friend)*
□ On Friday night I go out with my mates. 我通常周五晚上和朋友出去玩。Wǒ tōngcháng zhōuwǔ wǎnshàng hé péngyǒu chūqù wán.
material NOUN
1 衣料 yīliào [块 kuài] *(cloth)*
2 资料 zīliào [份 fèn] *(information, data)*
□ I'm collecting material for my project. 我正在为我的课题搜集资料。Wǒ zhèngzài wèi wǒde kètí sōují zīliào.
materials PL NOUN
素材 sùcái [种 zhǒng]
■ **raw materials** 原材料 yuáncáiliào [种 zhǒng]
math NOUN (US)
数学 shùxué
mathematics NOUN
数学 shùxué
maths NOUN
数学 shùxué
matron NOUN
护士长 hùshìzhǎng [位 wèi] *(in hospital)*
matter NOUN
▷ *see also* **matter** VERB
事情 shìqing [件 jiàn]
□ It's a matter of life and death. 这是一件生死攸关的事情。Zhè shì yíjiàn shēngsǐyōuguān de shìqing.
■ **What's the matter?** 怎么了？ Zěnme le? □ What's the matter with him? 他怎么了？ Tā zěnme le?
■ **as a matter of fact** 事实上 shìshí shàng
to **matter** VERB
▷ *see also* **matter** NOUN
要紧 yàojǐn *(be important)*
□ It matters a lot to me. 它对我来说很要紧。Tā duì wǒ lái shuō hěn yàojǐn.
■ **it doesn't matter 1** *(it's not a problem)* 没关系 méi guānxi □ I can't give you the money today. — It doesn't matter. 我不能今天把钱给你了。— 没关系。Wǒ bùnéng jīntiān bǎ qián gěi nǐ le. — Méi guānxi.
2 *(it makes no difference)* 无关紧要 wúguān jǐnyào □ It doesn't matter if you're late. 你迟到的话也无关紧要。Nǐ chídào de huà yě wúguān jǐnyào.
mattress NOUN
床垫 chuángdiàn [个 gè]

English-Chinese

mature ADJECTIVE
成熟的 chéngshú de
□ She's quite mature for her age. 她比她的实际年龄显得成熟。Tā bǐ tāde shíjì niánlíng xiǎndé chéngshú.

maximum ADJECTIVE
▷ *see also* **maximum** NOUN
1 最高的 zuìgāo de *(speed, height)*
□ The maximum speed is 100 km/h. 最高时速为一百公里。Zuìgāo shísù wéi yìbǎi gōnglǐ.
2 最重的 zuìzhòng de *(weight)*
□ the maximum amount 最大额 zuìdà'é

maximum NOUN
▷ *see also* **maximum** ADJECTIVE
最大量 zuìdàliàng

May NOUN
五月 wǔyuè
□ in May 在五月 zài wǔyuè □ the first of May 五月一日 wǔyuè yīrì □ at the beginning of May 在五月初 zài wǔyuè chū □ at the end of May 在五月末 zài wǔyuè mò □ every May 每年五月 měinián wǔyuè
■ **May Day** 五一节 wǔyī jié

may VERB
1 可能 kěnéng
■ **It may rain later.** 等会儿可能要下雨。Děnghuì'r kěnéng yào xiàyǔ.
■ **We may not be able to come.** 我们可能来不了。Wǒmen kěnéng láibuliǎo.
■ **He may have hurt himself.** 他可能伤了自己。Tā kěnéng shāngle zìjǐ.
2 可以 kěyǐ
■ **May I come in?** 我可以进来吗？Wǒ kěyǐ jìnlái ma?

maybe ADVERB
1 可能地 kěnéng de *(perhaps)*
□ maybe not 可能不是 kěnéng búshì □ a bit boring, maybe 可能有点无聊吧 kěnéng yǒudiǎn wúliáo ba □ Maybe she's at home. 她可能在家。Tā kěnéng zàijiā. □ Maybe he'll change his mind. 他可能会改变主意。Tā kěnéng huì gǎibiàn zhǔyì.
2 也许 yěxǔ *(making suggestions)*
3 大概 dàgài *(estimating)*

mayonnaise NOUN
蛋黄酱 dànhuángjiàng [瓶 píng]

mayor NOUN
市长 shìzhǎng [位 wèi]

maze NOUN
迷宫 mígōng

me PRONOUN
我 wǒ
□ It's me. 是我。Shì wǒ. □ Could you lend me your pen? 能借我你的笔么？Néng jiè wǒ nǐde bǐ me? □ Can you tell me the way to the station? 你能告诉我怎么去车站吗？Nǐ néng gàosù wǒ zěnme qù chēzhàn mā? □ Can you help me? 你能帮帮我吗？Nǐ néng bāngbāng wǒ mā? □ He heard me. 他听到我的话了。Tā tīngdào wǒde huà le. □ Me too! 我也是！Wǒ yěshì! □ Excuse me! 打扰一下！Dǎrǎo yixià! □ Look at me! 看着我！Kànzhe wǒ! □ Wait for me! 等等我！Děngděng wǒ! □ Come with me! 跟我来！Gēn wò lái! □ You're after me. 你在我的后面。Nǐ zài wǒde hòumiàn. □ Is it for me? 这是给我的吗？Zhè shì gěi wǒ de mā? □ She's older than me. 她比我大。Tā bǐ wǒ dà.

meal NOUN
1 一餐 yìcān [顿 dùn] *(occasion)*
2 膳食 shànshí [顿 dùn] *(food)*
■ **to go out for a meal** 出去吃饭 chūqù chīfàn

mealtime NOUN
■ **at mealtimes** 进餐时间 jìncān shíjiān [次 cì]

to **mean** VERB
▷ *see also* **mean** ADJECTIVE
1 表示…意思 biǎoshì…yìsī *(signify)*
□ What does "imperialism" mean? "Imperialism" 是什么意思？"Imperialism" shì shénme yìsi? □ I don't know what it means. 我不知道它的意思。Wǒ bùzhīdào tāde yìsī. □ What do you mean? 你什么意思？Nǐ shénme yìsi? □ That's not what I meant. 我不是那个意思。Wǒ búshì nàgè yìsi.
2 指 zhǐ *(refer to)*
□ Which one do you mean? 你指哪一个？Nǐ zhǐ nǎyigè?
■ **Do you really mean it?** 你是认真的吗？Nǐ shì rènzhēn de mā?
■ **to mean to do something** 有意做某事 yǒuyì zuò mǒushì □ I didn't mean to offend you. 我不是有意冒犯你。Wǒ búshì yǒuyì màofàn nǐ.

mean ADJECTIVE
▷ *see also* **mean** VERB
1 小气的 xiǎoqì de *(stingy)*
□ He's too mean to buy Christmas presents. 他太小气了，连圣诞礼物都舍不得买。Tā tài xiǎoqì le, lián shèngdàn lǐwù dōu shěbudé mǎi.
2 刻薄的 kèbó de *(unkind)*
□ You're being mean to me. 你对我太刻薄了。Nǐ duì wǒ tài kèbó le. □ That's a really mean thing to say! 太难以启齿了！Tài nányǐqǐchǐ le!

meaning NOUN
1 意思 yìsi [层 céng] *(of word, expression)*

m

2 含义 hányì [个 gè] *(of symbol, dream, gesture)*

means NOUN

方法 fāngfǎ [个 gè] *(method)*

□ He'll do it by any possible means. 他将采取任何可行的方法。Tā jiāng cǎiqǔ rènhé kěxíng de fāngfǎ. □ a means of transport 一种交通方式 yìzhǒng jiāotōng fāngshì

■ **by means of** 凭借 píngjiè □ He got in by means of a stolen key. 他凭借一把偷来的钥匙进了屋。Tā píngjiè yìbǎ tōu lái de yàoshi jìn le wū.

■ **by all means** 当然 dāngrán □ Can I come? — By all means! 我能来吗？— 当然可以！ Wǒ néng lái mā? — Dāngrán kěyǐ!

meant VERB ▷ *see* **mean**

meanwhile ADVERB

同时 tóngshí

measles NOUN

麻疹 mázhěn

to **measure** VERB

1 测量 cèliáng

□ I measured the page. 我测量了这页的大小。Wǒ cèliáng le zhèyè de dàxiǎo.

2 尺寸是 chǐcùn shì

□ The room measures 3 metres by 4. 这间房尺寸是四米长，三米宽。Zhèjiān fáng chǐcùn shì sìmǐ cháng, sānmǐ kuān.

measurement NOUN

尺寸 chǐcùn

□ my waist measurement 我腰的尺寸 wǒde yāo de chǐcùn □ What's your neck measurement? 你颈项的尺寸是多少？ Nǐ jǐngxiàng de chǐcùn shì duōshǎo?

measurements PL NOUN

1 三围 sānwéi *(of person)*

□ What are your measurements? 你的三围多大？ Nǐde sānwéi duō dà?

2 大小 dàxiǎo

□ What are the measurements of the room? 这间房的大小是多少？ Zhèjiān fáng de dàxiǎo shì duōshǎo?

meat NOUN

肉 ròu [块 kuài]

□ I don't eat meat. 我不吃肉。Wǒ bù chī ròu.

Mecca NOUN

麦加 Màijiā

mechanic NOUN

机械工 jīxiègōng [位 wèi]

□ He's a mechanic. 他是位机械工。Tā shì wèi jīxiègōng.

mechanical ADJECTIVE

机械的 jīxiè de

medal NOUN

奖章 jiǎngzhāng [枚 méi]

□ the gold medal 金牌 jīnpái

medallion NOUN

大奖牌 dàjiǎngpái [枚 méi]

media PL NOUN

■ **the media** 媒体 méitǐ [种 zhǒng]

median strip NOUN (US)

路中间的安全岛 lù zhōngjiān de ānquándǎo [个 gè]

medical ADJECTIVE

▷ *see also* **medical** NOUN

1 医疗的 yīliáo de

□ medical treatment 治疗 zhìliáo [次 cì]

□ medical insurance 医疗保险 yīliáo bǎoxiǎn [份 fèn]

2 医学的 yīxué de

□ She's a medical student. 她是个医科学生。Tā shì ge yīkē xuéshēng.

■ **to have medical problems** 出现健康问题 chūxiàn jiànkāng wèntí

medical NOUN

▷ *see also* **medical** ADJECTIVE

体检 tǐjiǎn [次 cì] *(examination)*

■ **to have a medical** 接受体检 jiēshòu tǐjiǎn

medicine NOUN

1 医学 yīxué *(science)*

□ I want to study medicine. 我想学医。Wǒ xiǎng xuéyī.

2 药 yào [种 zhǒng] *(medication)*

□ I need some medicine. 我需要一些药。Wǒ xūyào yìxiē yào.

■ **alternative medicine** 非常规新药 fēi chángguī xīnyào

DID YOU KNOW...?

When you are talking about medicine in China, you may run into the words 西药 xīyào **Western medicine** and 中药 zhōngyào **Chinese medicine.** These refer not only to medication but also to Western and Chinese styles of treatment.

Mediterranean NOUN

▷ *see also* **Mediterranean** ADJECTIVE

■ **the Mediterranean** **1** *(sea)* 地中海 Dìzhōnghǎi **2** *(region)* 地中海沿岸地区 Dìzhōnghǎi yán'àn dìqū

Mediterranean ADJECTIVE

▷ *see also* **Mediterranean** NOUN

地中海的 dìzhōnghǎi de

medium ADJECTIVE

1 中等的 zhōngděng de

□ a man of medium height 一个中等身材的男人 yígè zhōngděng shēncáide nánrén

2 中号的 zhōnghào de *(clothing size)*

medium-sized ADJECTIVE

中等大小的 zhōngděng dàxiǎo de

□ a medium-sized town 一个中型城镇 yígè zhōngxíng chéngzhèn

to **meet** VERB

1 遇见 yùjiàn *(accidentally)*

□ I met Paul in the street. 我在街上遇见了保罗。Wǒ zài jiēshàng yùjiàn le Bǎoluó.

□ We met by chance in the shopping centre. 我们在购物中心偶然遇见了。Wǒmen zài gòuwùzhōngxīn ǒurán yùjiàn le.

2 见面 jiànmiàn *(by arrangement)*

□ I'm going to meet my friends. 我要去和我朋友见面。Wǒ yào qù hé wǒ péngyǒu jiànmiàn. □ Let's meet in front of the tourist office. 我们在旅游咨询处外见面吧。Wǒmen zài lǚyóu zīxúnchù wài jiànmiàn ba.

3 认识 rènshi *(for the first time)*

□ I like meeting new people. 我喜欢认识新朋友。Wǒ xǐhuān rènshi xīn péngyǒu.

□ Have you met him before? 你以前认识他吗？ Nǐ yǐqián rènshi tā mā?

■ **Pleased to meet you.** 很高兴认识你。Hěn gāoxìng rènshi nǐ.

4 接 jiē *(at station, airport)*

□ I'll meet you at the station. 我去车站接你。Wǒ qù chēzhàn jiē nǐ.

to **meet up** VERB

碰面 pèngmiàn

□ What time shall we meet up? 我们什么时候碰面呢？ Wǒmen shénme shíhòu pèngmiàn ne?

meeting NOUN

1 会议 huìyì [次 cì] *(of club, committee)*

2 会面 huìmiàn [次 cì]

□ a business meeting 一次商务会谈 yícì shāngwù huìtán □ their first meeting 他们的第一次会面 tāmen de dìyīcì huìmiàn

mega ADVERB

非常地 fēicháng de *(informal)*

■ **He's mega rich.** 他非常地有钱。Tā fēicháng de yǒuqián.

megabyte NOUN

兆字节 zhàozìjié [个 gè]

melody NOUN

旋律 xuánlǜ [支 zhī]

melon NOUN

瓜 guā [个 gè]

to **melt** VERB

1 融化 rónghuà *(snow)*

□ The snow is melting. 雪正在融化。Xuě zhèngzài rónghuà.

2 使融化 shǐ rónghuà *(cause to melt: plastic, ice, snow, butter, chocolate)*

member NOUN

成员 chéngyuán [个 gè] *(of club, party)*

■ **a Member of Parliament** 一位下院议员 yíwèi xiàyuàn yìyuán

membership NOUN

会员 huìyuán [个 gè] *(of party, union)*

□ to apply for membership 申请成为会员 shēnqǐng chéngwéi huìyuán

membership card NOUN

会员卡 huìyuánkǎ [张 zhāng]

memento NOUN

回忆 huíyì [个 gè]

memorial NOUN

纪念碑 jìniànbēi [座 zuò]

□ a war memorial 一座战争纪念碑 yízuò zhànzhēng jìniànbēi

to **memorize** VERB

记住 jìzhù

memory NOUN

1 记忆力 jìyìlì [种 zhǒng] *(ability to remember)*

□ I haven't got a good memory. 我的记忆力不好。Wǒde jìyìlì bùhǎo.

■ **to have a good memory for something** (对某事) 记忆力好 (duì mǒushì) jìyìlì hǎo

2 回忆 huíyì [个 gè] *(thing remembered)*

□ to bring back memories 勾起回忆 gōuqǐ huíyì

3 存储器 cúnchǔqì [个 gè] *(of computer)*

men PL NOUN ▷ *see* **man**

to **mend** VERB

修理 xiūlǐ

meningitis NOUN

脑膜炎 nǎomóyán

mental ADJECTIVE

1 精神的 jīngshén de *(illness, health)*

□ a mental illness 一种精神疾病 yìzhǒng jīngshén jíbìng

2 发疯的 fāfēng de *(mad)*

□ You're mental! 你发疯了！ Nǐ fāfēng le!

mental hospital NOUN

精神病院 jīngshénbìngyuàn [个 gè]

mentality NOUN

智力 zhìlì

to **mention** VERB

提到 tídào

■ **Thank you! — Don't mention it!** 谢谢！— 不客气！ Xièxiè! — Bú kèqi!

menu NOUN

1 菜单 càidān [个 gè]

□ Could I have the menu please? 我能看看菜单吗？ Wǒ néng kànkan càidān mā?

2 选择菜单 xuǎnzé càidān [个 gè] *(of computer)*

merchant NOUN

商人 shāngrén [个 gè]

□ a wine merchant 一个酒商 yígè jiǔshāng

mercy NOUN

怜悯 liánmǐn

mere ADJECTIVE
1 略微的 lüèwēi de
■ **a mere five per cent** 微不足道的百分之五 wēibùzúdào de bǎifēnzhī wǔ
■ **the merest hint of criticism** 略有批评之意 lüèyǒu pīpíng zhīyì
2 仅仅的 jǐnjǐn de
■ **It's a mere formality.** 这仅仅是个礼节问题。Zhè jǐnjǐn shì gè lǐjié wèntí.

meringue NOUN
蛋白与糖的混合物 dànbái yǔ táng de hùnhéwù

merry ADJECTIVE
快乐的 kuàilè de
■ **Merry Christmas!** 圣诞快乐! Shèngdàn Kuàilè!

merry-go-round NOUN
旋转木马 xuánzhuǎn mùmǎ [座 zuò]

mess NOUN
1 凌乱 língluàn *(untidiness)*
□ My bedroom's usually in a mess. 我的卧室经常都很凌乱。Wǒde wòshì jīngcháng dōu hěn língluàn.
2 混乱的局面 hùnluàn de júmiàn *(chaotic situation)*

to **mess about** VERB
混日子 hùn rìzi
■ **to mess about with something** *(interfere with)* 胡乱摆弄某物 húluànbǎinòng mǒuwù □ Stop messing about with my computer! 不要再胡乱摆弄我的电脑了! Búyào zài húluànbǎinòng wǒde diànnǎo le! □ Don't mess about with my things! 别碰我的东西! Bié pèng wǒde dōngxi!

to **mess up** VERB
■ **to mess something up** 把某物弄的乱七八糟 bǎ mǒuwù nòngde luànqībāzāo
□ My little brother has messed up my DVDs. 我弟弟把我的DVD弄得乱七八糟。Wǒ dìdi bǎ wǒde DVD nòng dé luànqībāzāo.

message NOUN
▷ *see also* **message** VERB
消息 xiāoxi [条 tiáo]
■ **to leave somebody a message** 给某人留条消息 gěi mǒurén liú tiáo xiāoxi

to **message** VERB
▷ *see also* **message** NOUN
发消息 fā xiāoxi □ She messaged me on Facebook. 她在脸谱上给我发了消息。Tā zài Liǎnpǔ shàng gěi wǒ fā le xiāoxi.

messenger NOUN
信使 xìnshǐ [个 gè]

messy ADJECTIVE
1 肮脏的 āngzāng de *(dirty)*
□ a messy job 一个脏活 yígè zānghuó
2 凌乱的 língluàn de *(untidy)*
3 不整洁的 bù zhěngjié de *(person)*

met VERB ▷ *see* **meet**

metal NOUN
金属 jīnshǔ [种 zhǒng]

meter NOUN
1 仪表 yíbiǎo [个 gè] *(for gas, water, electricity)*
2 停车计时器 tíngchē jìshíqì [个 gè] *(parking meter)*
3 米 mǐ *(US: unit of measurement)*

method NOUN
方法 fāngfǎ [种 zhǒng]

Methodist NOUN
卫理公会派教徒 wèilǐgōnghuì pài jiàotú [个 gè]
□ I'm a Methodist. 我是个卫理公会派教徒。Wǒ shì ge wèilǐgōnghuì pài jiàotú.

metre NOUN
米 mǐ *(unit)*

metric ADJECTIVE
公制的 gōngzhì de

Mexico NOUN
墨西哥 Mòxīgē

to **miaow** VERB
猫叫 māojiào

mice PL NOUN ▷ *see* **mouse**

microblog NOUN
微博 wēibó

microchip NOUN
集成电路块 jíchéng diànlù kuài [个 gè]

microphone NOUN
话筒 huàtǒng [个 gè]

microscope NOUN
显微镜 xiǎnwēijìng [台 tái]

microwave NOUN
微波炉 wēibōlú [个 gè]

mid ADJECTIVE
中旬的 zhōngxún de
■ **in mid May** 在五月中旬 zài wǔyuè zhōngxún

midday NOUN
正午 zhèngwǔ [个 gè]
□ at midday 在正午 zài zhèngwǔ

middle NOUN
▷ *see also* **middle** ADJECTIVE
1 中央 zhōngyāng [个 gè] *(centre)*
□ in the middle of the road 在路中央 zài lù zhōngyāng
2 中 zhōng *(of month, event)*
□ in the middle of the night 在半夜 zài bànyè

middle ADJECTIVE
▷ *see also* **middle** NOUN
中间的 zhōngjiān de
□ the middle seat 中间的位子 zhōngjiān de wèizi

English-Chinese

m

middle-aged ADJECTIVE
中年的 zhōngnián de
□ a middle-aged man 一个中年男子 yígè zhōngnián nánzǐ
■ **to be middle-aged** 中年的 zhōngnián de □ She's middle-aged. 她是个中年妇女。Tā shì gè zhōngnián fùnǚ.

Middle Ages PL NOUN
■ **the Middle Ages** 中世纪 zhōngshìjì

middle-class ADJECTIVE
中产的 zhōngchǎn de
□ a middle-class family 一个中产家庭 yígè zhōngchǎn jiātíng

Middle East NOUN
■ **the Middle East** 中东 Zhōngdōng □ in the Middle East 在中东 zài zhōngdōng

middle name NOUN
中间名字 zhōngjiān míngzi [个 gè]

midge NOUN
蚊虫 wénchóng [只 zhī]

midnight NOUN
半夜 bànyè [个 gè]
□ at midnight 在半夜 zài bànyè

midwife NOUN
助产士 zhùchǎnshì [位 wèi]
□ She's a midwife. 她是助产士。Tā shì zhùchǎnshì.

might VERB
可能 kěnéng
□ I might get home late. 我可能会晚回家。Wǒ kěnéng huì wǎn huíjiā. □ It might have been an accident. 可能是个事故 Kěnéng shì gè shìgù.

migraine NOUN
偏头痛 piāntóutòng [阵 zhèn]
□ I've got a migraine. 我有偏头痛。Wǒ yǒu piāntóutòng.

mike NOUN
话筒 huàtǒng [支 zhī]

mild ADJECTIVE
1 轻微的 qīngwēi de *(infection, illness)*
2 温暖的 wēnnuǎn de *(climate, weather)*
□ The winters are quite mild. 冬天蛮温暖的。Dōngtiān mán wēnnuǎn de.

mile NOUN
英里 yīnglǐ
□ It's 5 miles from here. 距这儿5英里。Jù zhè'r wǔ yīnglǐ.
■ **70 miles an hour** 每小时70英里 měi xiǎoshí qīshí yīnglǐ
■ **miles** *(a long way)* 很远的距离 hěnyuǎn de jùlí □ We walked miles! 我们走了很远的距离！ Wǒmen zǒule hěnyuǎn de jùlí!

military ADJECTIVE
军事的 jūnshì de

milk NOUN
▷ *see also* **milk** VERB
奶 nǎi [杯 bēi]
□ tea with milk 奶茶 nǎichá

to **milk** VERB
▷ *see also* **milk** NOUN
榨取 zhàqǔ

milk chocolate NOUN
牛奶巧克力 niúnǎi qiǎokèlì [块 kuài]

milkman NOUN
送奶人 sòngnǎi rén [位 wèi]
■ **He's a milkman.** 他是个送奶人。Tā shì gè sòngnǎi rén.

milk shake NOUN
奶昔 nǎixī [杯 bēi]

mill NOUN
磨坊 mòfǎng [个 gè] *(for grain)*

millennium NOUN
千年 qiānnián [个 gè]
□ the third millennium 第三个千年 dìsāngè qiānnián
■ **the millennium** 公元2000年 gōngyuán liǎngqiānnián

millimeter NOUN (US)
毫米 háomǐ

millimetre NOUN
毫米 háomǐ

million NOUN
百万 bǎiwàn
□ a million dollars 一百万美元 yìbǎiwàn měiyuán □ two million 两百万 liǎngbǎiwàn
■ **millions** *(informal: a huge number)* 无数 wúshù

millionaire NOUN
百万富翁 bǎiwàn fùwēng [个 gè]

to **mimic** VERB
模仿 mófǎng

mince NOUN
切碎的馅儿 qiēsuì de xiànr [种 zhǒng]

mince pie NOUN
百果馅饼 bǎiguǒxiànbǐng [个 gè]

mind NOUN
▷ *see also* **mind** VERB
智力 zhìlì [种 zhǒng]
■ **to make up one's mind** 下定决心 xiàdìng juéxīn □ I haven't made up my mind yet. 我还没下定决心。Wǒ hái méi xià dìng juéxīn.
■ **to change one's mind** 改变主意 gǎibiàn zhǔyì □ He's changed his mind. 他改变了主意。Tā gǎibiàn le zhǔyì.
■ **Are you out of your mind?** 你疯了吗？ Nǐ fēngle mā?

to **mind** VERB
▷ *see also* **mind** NOUN

1 照看 zhàokàn *(look after)*
□ Could you mind the baby this afternoon? 今天下午你能照看一下孩子吗？Jīntiān xiàwǔ nǐ néng zhàokàn yixià háizi mā?
2 留意 liúyì *(keep an eye on)*
□ Could you mind my bags for a few minutes? 你能帮忙留意几分钟我的包吗？Nǐ néng bāngmáng liúyì jǐ fēnzhōng wǒde bāo mā?
3 当心 dāngxīn *(be careful of)*
□ Mind that bike! 当心那辆自行车！Dāngxīn nàliǎng zìxíngchē!
■ **Mind the step!** 当心脚下！Dāngxīn jiǎoxià!
4 介意 jièyì
■ **Do you mind?** 你介意吗？Nǐ jièyì mā?
□ Do you mind if I open the window? 你介意我开窗吗？Nǐ jièyì wǒ kāichuāng mā?
■ **I don't mind.** 我不介意。Wǒ bú jièyì.
□ I don't mind the noise. 我不介意有噪音。Wǒ bú jièyì yǒu zàoyīn.
■ **Never mind!** 没关系！Méi guānxì!
■ **I wouldn't mind a coffee.** 我挺想喝杯咖啡的。Wǒ tǐngxiǎng hē bēi kāfēi de.

mine PRONOUN
▷ *see also* **mine** NOUN
我的 wǒ de
□ This book is mine. 这是我的书。Zhèshì wǒde shū. □ These are mine. 这些是我的。Zhèxiē shì wǒde. □ Whose is this? — It's mine. 这是谁的？— 是我的。Zhè shì shéi de? — Shì wǒ de. □ Is this your coat? — No, mine's black. 这件外套是你的吗？— 不是，我的是黑色的。Zhèjiàn wàitào shì nǐde mā? — Búshì, wǒde shì hēisè de. □ her parents and mine 她的父母和我的父母 tāde fùmǔ hé wǒde fùmǔ

mine NOUN
▷ *see also* **mine** PRONOUN
矿 kuàng [座 zuò]
□ a coal mine 一座煤矿 yízuò méikuàng
□ a land mine 一个地雷 yígè dìléi

miner NOUN
矿工 kuànggōng [个 gè]

mineral water NOUN
矿泉水 kuàngquánshuǐ [瓶 píng]

miniature ADJECTIVE
▷ *see also* **miniature** NOUN
缩小的 suōxiǎo de
□ a miniature version 一个缩小版 yígè suōxiǎobǎn

miniature NOUN
▷ *see also* **miniature** ADJECTIVE
原件的缩小版 yuánjiàn de suōxiǎobǎn [个 gè]

minibus NOUN
小公共汽车 xiǎo gōnggòng qìchē [辆 liàng]

minicab NOUN
小型出租车 xiǎoxíng chūzūchē [辆 liàng]

Minidisc® NOUN
迷你光碟 mínǐ guāngdié [张 zhāng]

minimum ADJECTIVE
▷ *see also* **minimum** NOUN
最低的 zuìdī de
□ The minimum age for driving is 17. 合法驾驶的最低年龄为17岁。Héfǎ jiàshǐ de zuìdī niánlíng wéi shíqī suì. □ the minimum amount 最小额 zuìxiǎo'é

minimum NOUN
▷ *see also* **minimum** ADJECTIVE
最少量 zuìshǎoliàng

miniskirt NOUN
超短裙 chāoduǎnqún [条 tiáo]

minister NOUN
1 部长 bùzhǎng [位 wèi] *(politician)*
2 牧师 mùshī [位 wèi] *(of church)*

ministry NOUN
部门 bùmén [个 gè] *(in government)*
□ The Ministry of Culture 文化部 wénhuàbù

mink NOUN
水貂 shuǐdiāo [只 zhī]
□ a mink coat 一件貂皮大衣 yíjiàn diāopí dàyī

minor ADJECTIVE
1 次要的 cìyào de *(repairs, changes)*
□ a minor problem 一个次要的问题 yígè cìyào de wènti
2 不严重的 bù yánzhòng de *(injuries)*
■ **a minor operation** 一个小手术 yígè xiǎoshǒushù
■ **in D minor** 在D小调上 zài dì xiǎodiào shàng

minority NOUN
1 少数 shǎoshù *(of group, society)*
2 少数民族 shǎoshù mínzú [个 gè] *(ethnic, cultural, religious)*

mint NOUN
1 薄荷 bòhe [株 zhū] *(plant)*
□ mint sauce 薄荷酱 bòhejiàng
2 薄荷糖 bòhe táng [块 kuài] *(sweet)*

minus PREPOSITION
没有 méiyǒu *(informal: without)*
□ 12 minus 3 is 9 12减3等于9 shí'èr jiǎn sān děngyú jiǔ □ minus 24 *(temperature)* 零下24度 língxià èrshísì dù
■ **B minus** *(grade)* B减 bī jiǎn

minute NOUN
▷ *see also* **minute** ADJECTIVE
1 分钟 fēnzhōng *(unit)*
2 一会儿 yìhuìr *(short time)*

□ Wait a minute! 等一会儿！ Děng yìhuì'r!

minute ADJECTIVE

▷ *see also* **minute** NOUN

很小的 hěnxiǎo de

□ Her flat is minute. 她的公寓很小。Tāde gōngyù hěnxiǎo.

miracle NOUN

1 超自然的事物 chāo zìrán de shìwù [种 zhǒng] *(supernatural)*

2 奇迹 qíjì [个 gè] *(marvel)*

mirror NOUN

1 镜子 jìngzi [面 miàn]

2 后视镜 hòushìjìng [个 gè] *(in car)*

to **misbehave** VERB

行为无礼 xíngwéi wúlǐ

miscellaneous ADJECTIVE

形形色色的 xíngxíng sèsè de

mischief NOUN

恶作剧 èzuòjù [个 gè]

□ My little sister's always up to mischief. 我妹妹总喜欢搞恶作剧。Wǒ mèimei zǒng xǐhuān gǎo èzuòjù.

mischievous ADJECTIVE

淘气的 táoqì de

miserable ADJECTIVE

1 痛苦的 tòngkǔ de *(person)*

□ You're looking miserable. 你看起来好痛苦。Nǐ kànqǐlái hǎo tòngkǔ.

■ **to feel miserable** 觉得难受 juéde nánshòu □ I'm feeling miserable. 我现在很难受。Wǒ xiànzài hěn nánshòu.

2 恶劣的 èliè de *(weather, day)*

□ The weather was miserable. 天气恶劣。Tiānqì èliè.

misery NOUN

1 不幸 búxìng [个 gè] *(unhappiness)*

□ All that money brought nothing but misery. 那笔钱除了不幸什么都没带来。Nà bǐ qián chúle búxìng shénme dōu méi dàilái.

2 多愁善感的人 duōchóushàngǎn de rén [个 gè] *(unhappy person)*

□ She's a real misery. 她是个多愁善感的人。Tā shì gè duōchóushàngǎn de rén.

misfortune NOUN

不幸 búxìng [个 gè]

mishap NOUN

不幸的事 búxìng de shì [件 jiàn]

to **misjudge** VERB

判断错 pànduàncuò *(person)*

□ I've misjudged her. 我错看她了。Wǒ cuòkàn tā le. □ He misjudged the bend. 他判断错了那个弯道。Tā pànduàn cuò le nàgè wāndào.

to **mislay** VERB

误放 wùfàng

□ I've mislaid my passport. 我误放了我的护照。Wǒ wùfàng le wǒde hùzhào.

misleading ADJECTIVE

令人误解的 lìngrénwùjiě de

Miss NOUN

小姐 xiǎojiě

□ Dear Miss Smith 亲爱的史密斯小姐 qīnài de Shǐmìsī Xiǎojiě

DID YOU KNOW...?

In China, 小姐 xiǎojiě is the appropriate form of address for a young, unmarried woman. Once used to address waitresses in restaurants, 小姐 xiǎojiě is now often seen as impolite, so 服务员 fúwùyuán is a better choice.

to **miss** VERB

1 未击中 wèi jīzhòng *(fail to hit)*

□ He missed the target. 他未击中目标。Tā wèi jīzhòng mùbiāo.

2 错过 cuòguò *(train, bus, plane)*

□ Hurry or you'll miss the bus. 快点，要不你就会错过公车了。Kuàidiǎn, yàobu nǐ jiù huì cuòguò gōngchē le.

3 错过 cuòguò *(chance, opportunity)*

□ to miss an opportunity 错过一个机会 cuòguò yígè jīhuì

■ **You can't miss it.** 你不会错过它的。Nǐ búhuì cuòguò tā de.

■ **I miss you.** 我想念你。Wǒ xiǎngniàn nǐ.

□ I'm missing my family. 我想念我的家人。Wǒ xiǎngniàn wǒde jiārén.

missing ADJECTIVE

1 失踪的 shīzōng de *(person)*

2 遗漏的 yílòu de *(object)*

□ the missing part 遗漏的部分 yílòu de bùfen

■ **to be missing** 失踪 shīzōng □ My rucksack is missing. 我的帆布背包丢了。Wǒde fánbǔ bēibāo diū le. □ Two members of the group are missing. 两名成员失踪。Liǎngmíng chéngyuán shīzōng.

missionary NOUN

传教士 chuánjiàoshì [个 gè]

mist NOUN

薄雾 bówù [场 chǎng]

mistake NOUN

▷ *see also* **mistake** VERB

1 错误 cuòwù [个 gè] *(error)*

□ a spelling mistake 一个拼写错误 yígè pīnxiě cuòwù

■ **to make a mistake** 1 *(in writing)* 笔误 bǐwù 2 *(in speaking)* 口误 kǒuwù 3 *(get mixed up)* 犯错 fàncuò □ I'm sorry, I made a mistake. 对不起，我犯了个错误。Duìbuqǐ, wǒ fàn le ge cuòwù.

2 错误的决定 cuòwù de juédìng [个 gè] *(wrong decision)*
□ It was a mistake to come. 来是个错误。Lái shì gè cuòwù.
■ **by mistake** 错误地 cuòwù de □ I took his bag by mistake. 我错拿了他的包。Wǒ cuò ná le tā de bāo.

to **mistake** VERB
▷ *see also* **mistake** NOUN
把…误认为 bǎ...wùrèn wéi
■ **He mistook me for my sister.** 他把我误认为我姊妹了。Tā bǎ wǒ wùrèn wéi wǒ zǐmèi le.

mistaken VERB ▷ *see* **mistake**

mistaken ADJECTIVE
■ **to be mistaken** 搞错 gǎocuò □ If you think I'm coming with you, you're mistaken. 如果你认为我会跟你去，那么你搞错了。Rúguǒ nǐ rènwéi wǒ huì gēn nǐ qù, nàme nǐ gǎocuòle.

mistakenly ADVERB
错误地 cuòwù de

mistletoe NOUN
槲寄生 hújìshēng [棵 kē]

mistook VERB ▷ *see* **mistake**

mistress NOUN
1 女教师 nǚ jiàoshī [位 wèi] *(teacher)*
□ our French mistress 我们的女法语老师 wǒmen de nǚ fǎyǔ lǎoshī
2 女情人 nǚ qíngrén [个 gè] *(lover)*
□ He's got a mistress. 他有个情人。Tā yǒu gè qíngrén.

misty ADJECTIVE
有雾的 yǒuwù de
□ a misty morning 一个有雾的早晨 yígè yǒuwù de zǎochén

to **misunderstand** VERB
误解 wùjiě
□ Sorry, I misunderstood you. 对不起，我误解你了。Duìbuqǐ,wǒ wùjiě nǐ le.

misunderstanding NOUN
误会 wùhuì [个 gè]

misunderstood VERB ▷ *see* **misunderstand**

mix NOUN
▷ *see also* **mix** VERB
混合 hùnhé [种 zhǒng]
□ It's a mix of science fiction and comedy. 它是科幻和喜剧的混合。Tā shì kēhuàn hé xǐjù de hùnhé.
■ **a cake mix** 一种做糕点用的现成材料 yìzhǒng zuò gāodiǎn yòng de xiànchéng cáiliào

to **mix** VERB
▷ *see also* **mix** NOUN
混合 hùnhé
□ Mix the flour with the sugar. 把面粉和糖混合。Bǎ miànfěn hé táng hùnhé.

to **mix up** VERB
1 分不清 fēn bu qīng *(people)*
□ He always mixes me up with my sister. 他老是分不清我和我姊妹。Tā lǎoshì fēn bu qīng wǒ hé wǒ jiějie(mèimei).
2 混淆 hùnxiǎo *(things)*
□ The travel agent mixed up the bookings. 旅行社把旅客的预订都弄混淆了。Lǚxíngshè bǎ lǚkè de yùdìng dōu nòng hǔnxiǎo le.
■ **I'm getting mixed up.** 我开始犯迷糊了。Wǒ kāishì fànmíhu le.

mixed ADJECTIVE
1 什锦的 shíjǐn de *(group, community)*
2 男女混合的 nánnǚ hùnhé de *(school, education)*
■ **a mixed salad** 一份什锦沙拉 yífèn shíjǐn shālà
■ **a mixed school** 一所男女混合学校 yìsuǒ nánnǚ hùnhé xuéxiào
■ **a mixed grill** 一道烤杂排 yídào kǎo zápái

mixer NOUN
搅拌器 jiǎobànqì [个 gè] *(for food)*
■ **She's a good mixer.** 她是个善交际的人。Tā shì gè shànjiāoji de rén.

mixture NOUN
混合物 hùnhéwù [种 zhǒng]
□ a mixture of spices 混合香料 hùnhé xiāngliào [种 zhǒng]
■ **cough mixture** 止咳剂 zhǐkéjì [瓶 píng]

mix-up NOUN
混乱 hùnluàn [场 chǎng]

MMS NOUN
彩信 cǎixìn [条 tiáo]

to **moan** VERB
抱怨 bàoyuàn *(complain)*
□ She's always moaning. 她总是抱怨。Tā zǒngshì bàoyuàn.

mobile NOUN
手机 shǒujī [部 bù] *(phone)*

mobile home NOUN
可移动的房子 kěyídòng de fángzi [座 zuò]

mobile phone NOUN
手机 shǒujī [部 bù]

to **mock** VERB
▷ *see also* **mock** ADJECTIVE
戏弄 xìnòng

mock ADJECTIVE
▷ *see also* **mock** VERB
■ **a mock exam** 一次模拟考试 yícì mónǐ kǎoshì

mod cons PL NOUN
■ **all mod cons** 现代便捷化设备 xiàndài

biànjié huà shèbèi [套 tào]

model NOUN

▷ *see also* **model** ADJECTIVE, VERB

1 模型 móxíng [个 gè] *(of boat, building)*

□ a model of the castle 这个城堡的模型 zhègè chéngbǎo de móxíng

2 产品 chǎnpǐn [个 gè] *(product)*

□ His car is the latest model. 他的车是最新产品。Tā de chē shì zuìxīn chǎnpǐn.

3 时装模特 shízhuāng mótè [位 wèi] *(fashion model)*

□ She's a famous model. 她是位有名的时装模特。Tā shì wèi yǒumíng de shízhuāngmótè.

model ADJECTIVE

▷ *see also* **model** NOUN, VERB

■ **a model plane** 一架模型飞机 yíjià móxíng fēijī

■ **a model railway** 一个铁路模型 yígè tiělù móxíng

■ **He's a model pupil.** 他是个模范生。Tā shì gè mófànshēng.

to **model** VERB

▷ *see also* **major** NOUN, ADJECTIVE

展示 zhǎnshì *(clothes)*

□ She was modelling a Lorna Bailey outfit. 她刚才展示了一套洛娜・贝利牌的衣服。Tā gāngcái zhǎnshì le yítào Luònà Bèilì pái de yīfu.

modem NOUN

调制解调器 tiáozhì jiětiáo qì [个 gè]

moderate ADJECTIVE

中庸的 zhōngyōng de

□ His views are quite moderate. 他的观点很中庸。Tāde guāndiǎn hěn zhōngyōng.

■ **a moderate amount of** 适量的 shìliàng de

■ **a moderate price** 一个合适的价格 yígè héshì de jiàgé

modern ADJECTIVE

1 现代的 xiàndài de *(world, times, society)*

2 新式的 xīnshì de *(technology, design)*

to **modernize** VERB

使现代化 shǐ xiàndàihuà

modern languages PL NOUN

现代语言 xiàndài yǔyán [种 zhǒng]

modest ADJECTIVE

谦虚的 qiānxū de

DID YOU KNOW...?

In China, modesty is seen as an important positive trait and it is considered boastful to agree with a compliment. If you react politely when someone says something nice about you, you are likely to be further complimented for being 谦虚 qiānxū.

to **modify** VERB

修改 xiūgǎi

moist ADJECTIVE

湿润的 shīrùn de *(skin, soil)*

□ Make sure the soil is moist. 确保土壤是湿润的。Quèbǎo tǔrǎng shì shīrùn de.

moisture NOUN

湿气 shīqì [股 gǔ]

moisturizer NOUN

保湿霜 bǎoshīshuāng [瓶 píng]

moldy ADJECTIVE (US)

发霉的 fāméi de

mole NOUN

1 鼹鼠 yǎnshǔ [只 zhī] *(animal)*

2 痣 zhì [颗 kē] *(on skin)*

moment NOUN

1 片刻 piànkè *(period of time)*

□ Could you wait a moment? 你能稍等一下吗？Nǐ néng shāoděng yixià mā? □ in a moment 即刻 jíkè □ Just a moment! 稍等！Shāoděng!

2 瞬间 shùnjiān *(point in time)*

■ **at the moment** 此刻 cǐkè

■ **at the last moment** 在最后一刻 zài zuìhòu yíkè

■ **any moment now** 很快 hěnkuài

□ They'll be arriving any moment now. 他们很快就要到了。Tāmen hěnkuài jiù yào dào le.

momentous ADJECTIVE

重大的 zhòngdà de *(event)*

monarch NOUN

君主 jūnzhǔ [位 wèi]

monarchy NOUN

君主制 jūnzhǔzhì

monastery NOUN

修道院 xiūdàoyuàn [座 zuò]

Monday NOUN

星期一 xīngqīyī [个 gè]

□ on Monday 在星期一 zài xīngqīyī □ on Mondays 在所有星期一 zài suǒyǒu xīngqīyī □ every Monday 每个星期一 měigè xīngqīyī □ last Monday 上星期一 shàng xīngqīyī □ next Monday 下星期一 xià xīngqīyī

money NOUN

1 钱 qián *(cash)*

2 存款 cúnkuǎn *(savings)*

□ I need to change some money. 我需要换些钱。Wǒ xūyào huàn xiē qián.

3 货币 huòbì [种 zhǒng] *(currency)*

■ **to make money** *(person, business)* 赚钱 zhuànqián

mongrel NOUN

杂种 zázhǒng [个 gè]

□ My dog's a mongrel. 我的狗是个杂种

狗。Wǒ de gǒu shì gè zázhǒng gǒu.

monitor NOUN
显示屏 xiǎnshìpíng [个 gè]

monk NOUN
僧侣 sēnglǚ [个 gè]

monkey NOUN
猴 hóu [只 zhī]

monotonous ADJECTIVE
单调的 dāndiào de *(life, job, voice)*

monster NOUN
怪物 guàiwù [只 zhī]

month NOUN
月 yuè [个 gè]
□ this month 这个月 zhègè yuè □ next month 下个月 xiàgè yuè □ last month 上个月 shànggè yuè □ every month 每个月 měigè yuè □ at the end of the month 在月底 zài yuèdǐ

monthly ADJECTIVE
▷ *see also* **monthly** ADVERB
每月的 měiyuè de

monthly ADVERB
▷ *see also* **monthly** ADJECTIVE
按月 ànyuè *(every month)*

monument NOUN
纪念碑 jìniànbēi [座 zuò]

mood NOUN
心情 xīnqíng [种 zhǒng]
■ **to be in a bad mood** 心情差 xīnqíng chà
■ **to be in a good mood** 心情好 xīnqíng hǎo

moody ADJECTIVE
1 喜怒无常的 xǐnùwúcháng de *(temperamental)*
2 不快的 búkuài de *(in a bad mood)*

moon NOUN
月亮 yuèliàng [轮 lún]
■ **the moon** 月球 yuèqiú □ There's a full moon tonight. 今晚是满月。Jīnwǎn shì mǎnyuè.
■ **to be over the moon** *(happy)* 高兴极了 gāoxìng jíle

moonlight NOUN
月光 yuèguāng [片 piàn]

moor NOUN
▷ *see also* **moor** VERB
荒野 huāngyě [片 piàn]

to **moor** VERB
▷ *see also* **moor** NOUN
停泊 tíngbó *(boat)*

mop NOUN
拖把 tuōba [个 gè] *(for floor)*

moped NOUN
机动自行车 jīdòng zìxíngchē [辆 liàng]

moral ADJECTIVE
▷ *see also* **moral** NOUN
1 道德的 dàodé de *(issues, values)*
2 品行端正的 pǐnxíng duānzhèng de *(behaviour, person)*

moral NOUN
▷ *see also* **moral** ADJECTIVE
寓意 yùyì [种 zhǒng]
□ the moral of the story 这个故事的寓意 zhègè gùshì de yùyì
■ **morals** 道德伦理 dàodélúnlǐ

morale NOUN
士气 shìqì
□ Their morale is very low. 他们的士气很低。Tāmen de shìqì hěndī.

more ADJECTIVE
▷ *see also* **more** PRONOUN, ADVERB
1 更多的 gèngduō de
□ There are more girls in the class. 班里的女生比男生多。Bānlǐ de nǚshēng bǐ nánshēng duō. □ I get more money than you do. 我比你有更多的钱。Wǒ bǐ nǐ yǒu gèngduōde qián. □ More girls than boys do French. 学法语的女生比男生多。Xué fǎyǔ de nǚshēng bǐ nánshēng duō.
2 再一些的 zài yìxiē de *(additional)*
□ Would you like some more tea? 你要再来点茶吗？Nǐ yào zài lái diǎn chá mā? □ Is there any more wine? 还有酒吗？Háiyǒu jiǔ ma?
■ **a few more weeks** 再几个星期 zài jǐgè xīngqī

more PRONOUN
▷ *see also* **more** ADJECTIVE, ADVERB
1 更多的量 gèngduō de liàng *(in comparisons)*
□ There's more than I thought. 比我想得更多。Bǐ wǒ xiǎngde gèngduō. □ more than 20 大于20 dàyú èrshí □ She's got more than me. 她比我得到的多。Tā bǐ wǒ dédào de duō.
2 额外的量 éwài de liàng *(further, additional)*
■ **Is there any more?** 还有多的吗？Háiyǒu duōde ma? □ Would you like some more? 你还要些吗？Nǐ hái yào xiē mā? □ Have you got any more of them? 你还有吗？Nǐ háiyǒu ma? □ much more 多得多 duō dé duō □ a bit more 多一点 duō yìdiǎn

more ADVERB
▷ *see also* **more** ADJECTIVE, PRONOUN
更 gèng *(to form comparative)*
□ Beer is more expensive in Britain. 啤酒在英国卖得更贵些。Píjiǔ zài yīngguó mài dé gèng guì xiē. □ Could you speak more slowly? 你能不能讲得更慢点？Nǐ néngbunéng jiǎngdé gèng màndiǎn?
■ **more... than** 比…更… bǐ...gèng...

English-Chinese

m

□ He's more intelligent than me. 他比我更聪明。Tā bǐ wǒ gèng cōngming. □ She practises more than I do. 她练得比我更多。Tā liàndé bǐ wǒ gèng duō.
■ **more and more** 越来越 yuèláiyuè
■ **more or less** 差不多 chàbuduō
■ **more than ever** 空前的多 kōngqián de duō
■ **once more** 再一次 zài yícì

moreover ADVERB
此外 cǐwài

morning NOUN
1 早晨 zǎochén [个 gè] *(early)*
■ **Good morning!** 早上好！ Zǎoshàng hǎo! □ at 7 o'clock in the morning 早上7点 zǎoshàng qīdiǎn
■ **a morning paper** 一份晨报 yífèn chénbào
2 上午 shàngwǔ [个 gè] *(later)*
□ this morning 今天上午 jīntiān shàngwǔ
■ **on Monday morning** 星期一上午 xīngqīyī shàngwǔ □ tomorrow morning 明天上午 míngtiān shàngwǔ □ every morning 每个上午 měigè shàngwǔ □ in the morning 在上午 zài shàngwǔ

Morocco NOUN
摩洛哥 Móluògē
□ in Morocco 在摩洛哥 zài Móluògē

mortgage NOUN
抵押贷款 dǐyā dàikuǎn [笔 bǐ]

Moscow NOUN
莫斯科 Mòsīkē
□ in Moscow 在莫斯科 zài Mòsīkē

Moslem NOUN
穆斯林 mùsīlín [个 gè]
□ He's a Moslem. 他是个穆斯林。Tā shì gè mùsīlín.

mosque NOUN
清真寺 qīngzhēnsì [座 zuò]

mosquito NOUN
蚊 wén [只 zhī]
■ **a mosquito bite** 一个蚊子的咬痕 yíge wénzi de yǎohén

most ADJECTIVE
▷ *see also* **most** PRONOUN, ADVERB
大部分的 dàbùfen de *(almost all)*
□ most people 大部分的人 dàbùfen de rén
■ **the most** *(in comparisons)* 最 zuì □ Who won the most money? 谁赢了最多的钱？ Sheí yíngle zuìduō de qián?

most PRONOUN
▷ *see also* **most** ADJECTIVE, ADVERB
1 大部分 dàbùfen
□ most of it 它的大部分 tāde dà bùfen □ I paid the most. 我付了大部分钱。Wǒ fùle dà bùfen qián.
2 大多数 dàduōshù *(plural)*
□ most of my friends 我的大多数朋友 wǒde dàduōshù péngyǒu □ most of the class 班上大多数人 bānshàng dàduōshù rén
■ **to make the most of something** 充分利用某物 chōngfēn lìyòng mǒuwù
■ **at the most** 顶多 dǐngduō □ Two hours at the most. 顶多两小时。Dǐngduō liǎngxiǎoshí.
■ **most of the time** 大多数时间 dàduōshù shíjiān

most ADVERB
▷ *see also* **most** ADJECTIVE, PRONOUN
■ **the most** *(with verb)* 最 zuì □ what I miss the most 我最想念的是… wǒ zuì xiǎngniàn de shì... □ the most comfortable sofa in the shop 店里最舒服的沙发 diǎnlǐ zùi shūfu de shāfā □ most efficiently 最有效率地 zuì yǒuxiàolǜ de
■ **most of all** 最起码的 zuì qǐmǎ de

mostly ADVERB
■ **The teachers are mostly quite nice.** 老师们大部分人都很好。Lǎoshīmen dàbùfèn rén dōu hěnhǎo.

MOT NOUN
旧车性能年检 jiùchē xìngnéng niánjiǎn [次 cì]
□ Her car failed its MOT. 他的车没能通过旧车性能年检。Tā de chē méi néng tōngguò jiùchē xìngnéng niánjiǎn.

motel NOUN
汽车旅馆 qìchē lǚguǎn [个 gè]

moth NOUN
蛾子 ézi [只 zhī]

mother NOUN
母亲 mǔqīn [位 wèi]
□ my mother 我的母亲 wǒde mǔqīn
■ **mother tongue** 母语 mǔyǔ [种 zhǒng]

mother-in-law NOUN
1 婆婆 pópo [位 wèi] *(of woman)*
2 岳母 yuèmǔ [位 wèi] *(of man)*

Mother's Day NOUN
母亲节 Mǔqīn Jié [个 gè]

motionless ADJECTIVE
静止的 jìngzhǐ de

motivated ADJECTIVE
士气高涨的 shìqì gāozhàng de
□ He is highly motivated. 他很士气高涨。Tā hěn shìqì gāozhàng.

motivation NOUN
动机 dòngjī [个 gè]

motive NOUN
动机 dòngjī [个 gè]
□ the motive for the killing 这个杀人动机 zhège shārén dòngjī

motor NOUN
发动机 fādòngjī [台 tái]
□ The boat has a motor. 这艘船有一个发动机。Zhè sōu chuán yǒu yígè fādòngjī.

motorbike NOUN
摩托车 mótuōchē [辆 liàng]

motorboat NOUN
摩托艇 mótuōtǐng [艘 sōu]

motorcycle NOUN
摩托车 mótuōchē [辆 liàng]

motorcyclist NOUN
摩托车手 mótuōchēshǒu [位 wèi]

motorist NOUN
汽车驾驶员 qìchē jiàshǐyuán [个 gè]

motor mechanic NOUN
机械师 jīxièshī [个 gè]

motor racing NOUN
赛车 sàichē [场 chǎng]

motorway NOUN
高速公路 gāosù gōnglù [条 tiáo]
□ on the motorway 在高速公路上 zài gāosù gōnglù shàng

mouldy ADJECTIVE
发霉的 fāméi de

mountain NOUN
山 shān [座 zuò]

mountain bike NOUN
山地自行车 shāndì zìxíngchē [辆 liàng]

mountaineer NOUN
登山者 dēngshānzhě [个 gè]

mountaineering NOUN
登山 dēngshān [次 cì]
□ I go mountaineering. 我去登山。Wǒ qù dēngshān.

mountainous ADJECTIVE
多山的 duōshān de

mouse NOUN
1 鼠 shǔ [只 zhī]
□ white mice 白鼠 báishǔ
2 鼠标 shǔbiāo [个 gè] *(of computer)*

mouse mat NOUN
鼠标垫 shǔbiāo diàn [个 gè]

mousse NOUN
1 慕斯 mùsī [杯 bēi] *(food)*
□ chocolate mousse 巧克力慕斯 qiǎokèlì mùsī
2 摩丝 mósī [瓶 píng] *(for hair)*

moustache NOUN
小胡子 xiǎo húzi [搓 cuō]
□ He's got a moustache. 他留了一搓小胡子。Tā liúle yìcuō xiǎohúzi. □ a man with a moustache 一个长着一搓小胡子的男人 yígè zhǎngzhe yìcuō xiǎohúzi de nánrén

mouth NOUN
1 嘴 zuǐ [张 zhāng] *(of a person)*
2 河口 hékǒu [个 gè] *(of river)*

mouthful NOUN
一口 yìkǒu

mouth organ NOUN
口琴 kǒuqín [支 zhī]
□ I play the mouth organ. 我会吹口琴。Wǒ huì chuī kǒuqín.

mouthwash NOUN
漱口水 shùkǒushuǐ [瓶 píng]

move NOUN
▷ *see also* **move** VERB
1 搬家 bānjiā [次 cì] *(from house)*
□ our move from Oxford to Luton 我们从牛津搬到卢顿 wǒmen cóng Niújīn bāndào Lúdùn
2 一步 yíbù *(in game)*
□ It's your move. 轮到你了。Lúndào nǐ le.
■ **to get a move on** 快点 kuàidiǎn □ Get a move on! 快点！ Kuàidiǎn!

to **move** VERB
▷ *see also* **move** NOUN
1 行进 xíngjìn *(vehicle)*
□ The car was moving very slowly. 那车行进得好慢。Nà chē xíngjìn dé hǎomàn.
2 动 dòng *(person, object)*
□ Don't move! 不要动！ Búyào dòng!
3 搬家 bānjiā *(relocate)*
□ We're moving in July. 我们将在7月搬家。Wǒmen jiāng zài qīyuè bānjiā.
■ **to move house** 搬家 bānjiā
■ **to move offices** 更换办公地点 gēnghuàn bàngōng dìdiǎn
4 改换 gǎihuàn *(from activity)*
5 挪走 nuózǒu *(put in another place, position)*
□ Could you move your stuff please? 能把你的东西挪走吗？ Néng bǎ nǐ de dōngxi nuózǒu mā?
6 感动 gǎndòng *(affect emotionally)*
□ I was very moved by the film. 我被这部电影深深感动了。Wǒ bèi zhèbù diànyǐng shēnshēn gǎndòng le.

to **move away** VERB
1 离开 líkāi *(from town, area)*
2 走开 zǒukāi *(from window, door)*

to **move back** VERB
1 回来 huílái *(return)*
2 后退 hòutuì *(backwards)*

to **move forward** VERB
向前移动 xiàngqián yídòng *(person, troops, vehicle)*

to **move in** VERB
搬入 bānrù *(into house)*
□ They're moving in next week. 他们下周搬入。Tāmen xiàzhōu bānrù.

to **move into** VERB
搬进 bānjìn *(house, area)*

movement NOUN

1 运动 yùndòng [次 cì] *(group of people)*
2 动作 dòngzuò [个 gè] *(gesture)*
to **move out** VERB
搬出去 bān chūqù *(of house)*
to **move over** VERB
让开 ràngkāi *(to make room)*
□ Could you move over a bit? 你能让开一些吗？ Nǐ néng ràngkāi yìxiē mā?
movie NOUN (US)
电影 diànyǐng [部 bù]
■ **the movies** 电影 diànyǐng □ Let's go to the movies! 我们去看电影吧！ Wǒmen qù kàn diànyǐng ba!
movie theater NOUN (US)
电影院 diànyǐngyuàn [个 gè]
moving ADJECTIVE
1 感人的 gǎnrén de *(touching)*
□ a moving story 一个感人的故事 yígè gǎnrén de gùshì
2 行驶的 xíngshǐde *(not static)*
□ a moving bus 一辆正在行驶的巴士 yíliǎng zhèngzài xíngshǐ de bāshì
to **mow** VERB
割 gē
■ **to mow the lawn** 剪草坪 jiǎn cǎopíng
mower NOUN
割草机 gēcǎojī [台 tái]
mown VERB ▷ *see* **mow**
MP3 player NOUN
MP3 播放器 M P sān bōfàngqì [个 gè]
□ I need a new MP3 player. 我需要一个新MP3播放器。 Wǒ xūyào yígè xīn M P sān bōfàngqì.
MP NOUN *(= Member of Parliament)*
下院议员 Xiàyuàn Yìyuán [位 wèi]
□ She's an MP. 她是位下院议员。 Tā shì wèi Xiàyuàn Yìyuán.
MP3 NOUN *(format)*
1 MP3格式 M P sān géshì *(file)*
2 MP3文件 M P sān wénjiàn [个 gè]
mph ABBREVIATION *(= miles per hour)*
英里每小时 yīnglǐ měi xiǎoshí
□ to drive at 50 mph 以每小时50英里的速度驾驶 yǐ měi xiǎoshí wǔshí yīnglǐ de sùdù jiàshǐ
Mr NOUN
先生 xiāsheng
□ Mr Smith 史密斯先生 Shǐmìsī xiānsheng
Mrs NOUN
太太 tàitai
□ Mrs Smith 史密斯太太 Shǐmìsī tàitai

DID YOU KNOW...?
In China, 太太 tàitai is the polite form of address for a married woman.

MS NOUN *(= multiple sclerosis)*
多发性硬化症 duōfāxìng yìnghuà zhèng
□ She's got MS. 她得了多发性硬化症。 Tā déle duōfāxìng yìnghuà zhèng.
Ms NOUN
女士 nǚshì
□ Ms Smith 史密斯女士 Shǐmìsī nǚshì

DID YOU KNOW...?
In China, 女士 nǚshì is a formal way to address a woman regardless of her marital status.

much ADJECTIVE
▷ *see also* **much** PRONOUN, ADVERB
很多的 hěnduō de
□ We haven't got much time. 我们没有很多时间。 Wǒmen méiyǒu hěnduōshíjiān.
□ I haven't got much money. 我没有很多的钱。 Wǒ méiyǒu hěnduō de qián.
■ **very much** 非常多的 fēichángduō de
□ I haven't got very much money. 我没有非常多的钱。 Wǒ méiyǒu fēichángduō de qián.
■ **how much** 多少 duōshǎo □ How much time have you got? 你有多少时间？ Nǐ yǒu duōshǎo shíjiān?
■ **too much** 过多的 guòduō de □ They give us too much homework. 他们给我们布置了过多的家庭作业。 Tāmen gěi wǒmen bùzhì le guòduō de jiātíngzuòyè.
■ **so much** 如此多的 rúcǐduō de □ I've never seen so much traffic. 我从没见过如此多的车。 Wǒ cóng méi jiànguò rúcǐ duō de chē.
much PRONOUN
▷ *see also* **much** ADJECTIVE, ADVERB
大量 dàliàng
□ There isn't much left. 剩下的不多了。 Shèngxià de bùduō le. □ He doesn't do much at the weekends. 周末他不做太多事。 Zhōumò tā búzuò tàiduō shì.
■ **not much** 1 不多 bùduō □ Have you got a lot of luggage? — No, not much. 你的行李多吗？ — 不，不多。 Nǐde xínglǐ duō mā? — Bù, bùduō. 2 一般 yìbān □ What did you think of it? — Not much. 你觉得怎么样？ — 一般。 Nǐ juédé zěnmeyàng? — Yìbān.
■ **How much?** 多少？ Duōshǎo? □ How much is it? 这多少钱？ Zhè duōshǎo qián? □ How much do you want? 你想要多少？ Nǐ xiǎngyào duōshǎo?
■ **too much** 过量 guòliàng □ That's too much! 太多了！ Tàiduō le! □ It costs too much. 太贵了。 Tàiguì le.
■ **I didn't think it would cost so much.** 我没有想到竟这么贵。 Wǒ méiyǒu xiǎngdào jìng zhème guì.
much ADVERB

▹ see also **much** ADJECTIVE, PRONOUN
1 很多 hěnduō *(a great deal)*
□ He hasn't changed much. 他没变很多。Tā méi biàn hěnduō.
■ **I don't like sport much.** 我不太喜欢运动。Wǒ bútài xǐhuān yùndòng.
■ **I'm much better now.** 我感觉好多了。Wǒ gǎnjué hǎoduō le.
2 经常 jīngcháng *(often)*
□ Do you go out much? 你经常出去吗？Nǐ jīngcháng chūqù ma?
■ **very much** 非常地 fēicháng de □ I enjoyed the film very much. 我非常喜欢看这部电影。Wǒ fēicháng xǐhuān kàn zhèbù diànyǐng. □ Thank you very much. 非常感谢你。Fēicháng gǎnxiè nǐ.

mud NOUN
泥 ní [摊 tān]

muddle NOUN
1 混乱状态 hùnluàn zhuàngtài [个 gè] *(of papers, figures, things)*
2 糟糕局面 zāogāo júmiàn [个 gè] *(situation)*
■ **to be in a muddle** 一片混乱 yípiàn hùnluàn □ The photos are in a muddle. 这些照片一片混乱。Zhèxiē zhàopiān yípiàn hùnluàn.

to **muddle up** VERB
混淆 hùnxiǎo *(people)*
□ He muddles me up with my sister. 他总是混淆我和我姐姐。Tā zǒngshì hùnxiǎo wǒ hé wǒjiějie.
■ **to get muddled up** 犯迷糊 fàn míhu □ I'm getting muddled up. 我正在犯迷糊。Wǒ zhèngzài fàn míhu.

muddy ADJECTIVE
沾满泥的 zhānmǎn ní de

muesli NOUN
加入干水果的燕麦早餐 jiārù gān shuǐguǒ de yànmài zǎocān [份 fèn]

muffler NOUN
围巾 wéijīn [条 tiáo] *(item of clothing)*

mug NOUN
▹ see also **mug** VERB
有柄大杯 yǒu bǐng dà beī [个 gè]
□ Do you want a cup or a mug? 你想要个小杯子还是大杯子？Nǐ xiǎng yào gè xiǎo bēizi háishì dà bēizi?

to **mug** VERB
▹ see also **mug** NOUN
抢劫 qiǎngjié *(rob)*
□ He was mugged in the city centre. 他在市中心被抢劫了。Tā zài shìzhōngxīn bèi qiǎngjié le.

mugger NOUN
抢劫犯 qiǎngjiéfàn [个 gè]

mugging NOUN
行凶抢劫 xíngxiōng qiǎngjié [次 cì]

muggy ADJECTIVE
闷热的 mēnrè de
□ It's muggy today. 今天天气闷热。Jīntiān tiānqì mēnrè.

multiple choice test NOUN
选择题测试 xuǎnzétí cèshì [个 gè]

multiple sclerosis NOUN
多发性硬化症 duōfāxìng yìnghuà zhèng
□ She's got multiple sclerosis. 她得了多发性硬化症。Tā déle duōfāxìng yìnghuà zhèng.

multiplication NOUN
乘法 chéngfǎ

to **multiply** VERB
□ to multiply 6 by 3 6乘以3 liù chéngyǐ sān
增加 zēngjiā *(increase in number)*

multi-storey car park NOUN
多层停车场 duōcéng tíngchēchǎng [个 gè]

mum NOUN
妈妈 māma [位 wèi]
□ my mum 我的妈妈 wǒ de māma □ her mum 她的妈妈 tā de māma □ Mum! 妈妈！Māma! □ I'll ask Mum. 我去问妈妈。Wǒ qù wèn māma.

mummy NOUN
1 妈妈 māma [位 wèi] *(informal: mother)*
□ Mummy says I can go. 妈妈说我可以走了。Māma shuō wǒ kěyǐ zoǔ le.
2 木乃伊 mùnǎiyī [个 gè] *(Egyptian)*

mumps NOUN
腮腺炎 sāixiànyán

murder NOUN
▹ see also **murder** VERB
谋杀 móushā [个 gè]

to **murder** VERB
▹ see also **murder** NOUN
谋杀 móushā
□ He was murdered. 他被谋杀了。Tā bèi móushā le.

murderer NOUN
凶手 xiōngshǒu [个 gè]

muscle NOUN
肌肉 jīròu [块 kuài]

muscular ADJECTIVE
肌肉发达的 jīròu fādá de

museum NOUN
博物馆 bówùguǎn [个 gè]

mushroom NOUN
蘑菇 mógu [个 gè]
□ mushroom omelette 蘑菇煎蛋 mógu jiāndàn [个 gè]

music NOUN
1 音乐 yīnyuè
2 音乐课 yīnyuè kè [节 jié] *(school subject)*

musical ADJECTIVE
▷ *see also* **musical** NOUN
1 音乐的 yīnyuè de *(related to music)*
2 有音乐天赋的 yǒu yīnyuè tiānfù de *(musically gifted)*
□ I'm not musical. 我没有音乐天赋。Wǒ méiyǒu yīnyuè tiānfù.

musical NOUN
▷ *see also* **musical** ADJECTIVE
音乐剧 yīnyuèjù [场 chǎng]

musical instrument NOUN
乐器 yuèqì [件 jiàn]

music centre NOUN
组合音响 zǔhé yīnxiǎng [套 tào]

musician NOUN
音乐家 yīnyuèjiā [位 wèi]

Muslim NOUN
▷ *see also* **Muslim** ADJECTIVE
穆斯林 Mùsīlín [个 gè]
□ He's a Muslim. 他是一个穆斯林。Tā shì yígè mùsīlín.

Muslim ADJECTIVE
▷ *see also* **Muslim** NOUN
穆斯林的 Mùsīlín de

mussel NOUN
贻贝 yíbèi [个 gè]

must VERB
1 必须 bìxū *(expressing importance or necessity)*
■ **You must remember to send her a card.** 你必须记得给她寄卡片。Nǐ bìxū jìdé gěi tā jì kǎpiàn.
■ **The doctor must allow the patient to decide.** 医生必须让病人来决定。Yīshēng bìxū ràng bìngrén lái juédìng.
2 得 děi *(expressing intention)*
□ I must buy some presents. 我得去买些礼物。Wǒ děi qù mǎi xiē lǐwù. □ I really must be getting back. 我真的得回去了。Wǒ zhēnde děi huíqù le.
3 一定 yídìng *(I suppose)*
□ You must be tired. 我猜你一定是累了。Wǒ cāi nǐ yídìng shì lèile. □ You must be joking. 你一定是在开玩笑。Nǐ yídìng shì zài kāi wánxiào.
■ **You must come and see us.** *(invitation)* 你一定得来看我们。Nǐ yídìng děi lái kàn wǒmen.

mustache NOUN (US)
小胡子 xiǎo húzi [撮 cuō]

mustard NOUN
芥末 jièmo [瓶 píng]

mustn't = **must not**

to **mutter** VERB
喃喃自语 nánnánzìyǔ

mutton NOUN
羊肉 yángròu [斤 jīn]

my ADJECTIVE
我的 wǒ de
□ my father 我的父亲 wǒde fùqin
■ **I want to wash my hair.** 我想洗头发。Wǒ xiǎng xǐ tóufà.
■ **I'm going to clean my teeth.** 我去刷牙。Wǒ qù shuāyá.
■ **I've hurt my foot.** 我伤了脚。Wǒ shāngle jiǎo.

myself PRONOUN
1 我自己 wǒ zìjǐ
□ I hurt myself. 我伤了自己。Wǒ shāngle zìjǐ. □ I really enjoyed myself. 我自己过得很愉快。Wǒ zìjǐ guòdé hěn yúkuaì.
2 自己 zìjǐ *(me)*
□ I don't like talking about myself. 我不喜欢谈论自己。Wǒ bù xǐhuān tánlùn zìjǐ.
■ **by myself 1** *(unaided)* 我独立地 wǒ dúlì de **2** *(alone)* 我独自 wǒ dúzì
□ I don't like travelling by myself. 我讨厌独自旅行。Wǒ tǎoyàn dúzì lǚxíng.
3 独立地 dúlì de *(personally)*
□ I made it myself. 我独立地完成了。Wǒ dúlì de wánchéng le.

mysterious ADJECTIVE
神秘的 shénmì de

mystery NOUN
1 谜 mí [个 gè] *(puzzle)*
2 推理作品 tuīlǐ zuòpǐn [部 bù] *(story)*
■ **a murder mystery** *(novel)* 一个谋杀迷团 yígè móushā mítuán

myth NOUN
1 神话 shénhuà [个 gè] *(legend, story)*
□ a Greek myth 一个希腊神话 yígè xīlà shénhuà
2 谬论 miùlùn [个 gè] *(fallacy)*
□ That's a myth. 那是一个谬论。Nà shì yígè miùlùn.

mythology NOUN
神话学 shénhuàxué

Nn

to nag VERB
唠叨 lāodāo *(scold)*
□ She's always nagging me. 她总是向我唠叨。Tā zǒngshì xiàng wǒ lāodāo.

nail NOUN
1 指甲 zhǐjia [个 gè] *(of finger, toe)*
□ Don't bite your nails! 不要咬你的指甲！Búyào yǎo nǐde zhǐjia!
2 钉子 dīngzi [个 gè] *(made of metal)*

nailbrush NOUN
指甲刷 zhǐjiashuā [个 gè]

nailfile NOUN
指甲锉 zhǐjiacuò [个 gè]

nail polish NOUN
指甲油 zhǐjiayóu [瓶 píng]

nail scissors PL NOUN
指甲刀 zhǐjiadāo [个 gè]

nail varnish NOUN
指甲油 zhǐjiayóu [瓶 píng]

naked ADJECTIVE
裸体的 luǒtǐ de

name NOUN
1 名字 míngzi [个 gè] *(first name, full name)*
□ What's your name? 你叫什么名字？Nǐ jiào shénme míngzi? □ My name is Peter. 我的名字叫彼得。Wǒde míngzi jiào Bǐdé.
2 姓 xìng [个 gè] *(surname)*
□ My name is Wang. 我姓王。Wǒ xìng Wáng.
■ **to give one's name and address** 留下姓名和地址 liúxià xìngmíng hé dìzhǐ

DID YOU KNOW...?
In China and countries heavily influenced by Chinese culture, the surname comes first and given name second.

nanny NOUN
保姆 bǎomǔ [个 gè]

nap NOUN
小睡 xiǎoshuì
■ **to have a nap** 小睡一下 xiǎoshuì yīxià

napkin NOUN
餐巾 cānjīn [张 zhāng]

nappy NOUN
尿布 niàobù [块 kuài]

narrow ADJECTIVE
窄的 zhǎi de

narrow-minded ADJECTIVE
小心眼的 xiǎoxīnyǎn de

nasty ADJECTIVE
1 恶心的 ěxīn de *(taste, smell)*
□ a nasty smell 一阵恶心的气味 yízhèn ěxīn de qìwèi
2 严重的 yánzhòng de *(injury, accident, disease)*
□ a nasty cold 严重的感冒 yánzhòng de gǎnmào
3 面露凶相的 miàn lù xiōngxiàng de *(unfriendly)*
□ He gave me a nasty look. 他对我面露凶相。Tā duì wǒ miàn lù xiōngxiàng.

nation NOUN
国家 guójiā [个 gè]

national ADJECTIVE
▷ *see also* **national** NOUN
全国的 quánguó de
□ He's the national champion. 他是全国冠军。Tā shì quánguó guànjūn. □ the national elections 全国选举 quánguó xuǎnjǔ

national NOUN
▷ *see also* **national** ADJECTIVE
公民 gōngmín [位 wèi]

national anthem NOUN
国歌 guógē [首 shǒu]

national holiday NOUN (US)
法定假期 fǎdìng jiàqī [个 gè]

nationalism NOUN
国家主义 guójiā zhǔyì

nationalist NOUN
国家主义者 guójiā zhǔyìzhě [个 gè]

nationality NOUN
国籍 guójí [个 gè]

national park NOUN
国家公园 guójiā gōngyuán [个 gè]

native ADJECTIVE
1 出生的 chūshēng de *(country)*
□ my native country 我出生的国家 wǒ chūshēng de guójiā
2 天生的 tiānshēng de *(language, tongue)*

□ English is not their native language. 英语不是他们天生的语言。Yīngyǔ búshì tāmen tiānshēng de yǔyán.

natural ADJECTIVE
1 正常的 zhèngcháng de *(normal)*
2 天然的 tiānrán de *(material, product, food)*

naturally ADVERB
1 自然地 zìrán de *(unsurprisingly)*
□ Naturally, we were very disappointed. 自然地，我们非常地失望。Zìrán de, wǒmen fēicháng de shīwàng.
2 自然而然地 zìrán ér rán de *(occur, happen)*

nature NOUN
自然界 zìránjiè

naughty ADJECTIVE
淘气的 táoqì de
□ Naughty girl! 淘气的女孩！Táoqì de nǚhái！ □ Don't be naughty! 不要淘气！Búyào táoqì！

navy NOUN
▷ *see also* **navy** ADJECTIVE
藏青色 zàngqīngsè *(navy-blue)*
■ **the navy** *(service)* 海军 hǎijūn □ He's in the navy. 他在海军服役。Tā zài hǎijūn fúyì.

navy ADJECTIVE
▷ *see also* **navy** NOUN
藏青色的 zàngqīngsè de *(colour)*

navy-blue ADJECTIVE
藏青色 zàngqīngsè

Nazi NOUN
纳粹分子 Nàcuìfènzǐ [个 gè]
□ the Nazis 纳粹党 Nàcuìdǎng

near ADJECTIVE
▷ *see also* **near** ADVERB, PREPOSITION
近的 jìn de
□ It's fairly near. 相当近。Xiāngdāng jìn.
□ It's near enough to walk. 近得可以走过去。Jìndé kěyǐ zǒuguòqù.
■ **the nearest** 最近的 zuìjìn de □ Where's the nearest service station? 最近的服务站在哪儿？Zuìjìn de fúwùzhàn zài nǎr？
□ The nearest shops are five kilometres away. 最近的商店离这里有5公里远。Zuìjìn de shāngdiàn lí zhèlǐ yǒu wǔ gōnglǐ yuǎn.
■ **in the near future** 在不远的将来 zài bùyuǎn de jiānglái

near ADVERB
▷ *see also* **near** ADJECTIVE, PREPOSITION
近 jìn *(close)*
■ **near to** 离得近 lídéjìn □ It's very near to the school. 离学校非常近。Lí xuéxiào fēicháng jìn.

near PREPOSITION
▷ *see also* **near** ADJECTIVE, ADVERB
1 在...附近 zài...fùjìn *(physically)*
□ I live near Liverpool. 我住在利物浦附近。Wǒ zhùzài Lìwùpǔ fùjìn. □ near my house 在我的房子附近 zài wǒde fángzi fùjìn
2 临近 línjìn *(in time)*
■ **near here** 这附近 zhè fùjìn □ Is there a bank near here? 这附近有银行吗？Zhè fùjìn yǒu yínháng ma？

nearby ADJECTIVE
▷ *see also* **nearby** ADVERB
附近的 fùjìn de
□ a nearby garage 附近的一个车库 fùjìn de yígè chēkù

nearby ADVERB
▷ *see also* **nearby** ADJECTIVE
在附近 zài fùjìn
□ There's a supermarket nearby. 在附近有一家超市。Zài fùjìn yǒu yìjiā chāoshì.

nearly ADVERB
差不多 chà bù duō
□ You're nearly as tall as I am. 你跟我差不多高了。Nǐ gēn wǒ chàbùduō gāole.
■ **I'm nearly 15.** 我快要十五岁了。Wǒ kuàiyào shíwǔ suì le.
■ **I nearly missed the train.** 我差一点就错过了火车。Wǒ chàyīdiǎn jiù cuòguò le huǒchē.
■ **nearly always** 几乎总是 jīhū zǒngshì

near-sighted ADJECTIVE (US)
近视的 jìnshì de *(short-sighted)*

neat ADJECTIVE
1 整洁的 zhěngjié de
2 工整的 gōngzhěng de *(handwriting)*
□ She has very neat writing. 她的书写很工整。Tāde shūxiě hěn gōngzhěng.
3 绝妙的 juémiào de (US: *great*)

neatly ADVERB
整齐地 zhěngqí de
□ neatly folded 整齐折叠着 zhěngqí zhédiézhe □ neatly dressed 整齐穿戴着 zhěngqí chuāndài zhe

necessarily ADVERB
必然地 bìrán de
■ **not necessarily** 未必 wèibì

necessary ADJECTIVE
必要的 bìyào de
■ **if necessary** 如有必要 rú yǒu bìyào

necessity NOUN
必需品 bìxūpǐn [个 gè]
□ A car is a necessity, not a luxury. 汽车是必需品，而不是奢侈品。Qìchē shì bìxūpǐn, ér búshì shēchípǐn.

neck NOUN
1 颈 jǐng [个 gè]
□ a stiff neck 脖颈僵硬 bójǐng jiāngyìng

2 领子 lǐngzi [个 gè] *(of garment)*
□ a V-neck sweater 一件V字领毛衣 yíjiàn Vzìlǐng máoyī

necklace NOUN
项链 xiàngliàn [条 tiáo]

necktie NOUN (US)
领带 lǐngdài [条 tiáo]

to **need** VERB
▷ *see also* **need** NOUN
1 需要 xūyào *(require)*
□ I need a bigger size. 我需要稍大码的。Wǒ xūyào shāo dà mǎ de. □ The car needs servicing. 这辆车需要维修。Zhèliàng chē xūyào wéixiū.
■ **to need to do something** 必须做某事 bìxū zuò mǒushì □ I need to change some money. 我必须换些钱。Wǒ bìxū huàn xiē qián.
2 想要 xiǎngyào *(drink, holiday, cigarette)*
3 得 děi *(a haircut, a bath, a wash)*

need NOUN
▷ *see also* **need** VERB
必要 bìyào
■ **There's no need to book.** 没有必要预定。Méiyǒu bìyào yùdìng.

needle NOUN
1 针 zhēn [根 gēn] *(for sewing)*
2 注射针 zhùshèzhēn [只 zhī] *(for injections)*

negative ADJECTIVE
▷ *see also* **negative** NOUN
1 阴性的 yīnxìng de *(test, result)*
2 消极的 xiāojí de *(person, attitude, view)*
□ He's got a very negative attitude. 他的态度很消极。Tā de tàidù hěn xiāojí.
3 否定的 fǒudìng de *(answer, response)*

negative NOUN
▷ *see also* **negative** ADJECTIVE
否定词 fǒudìngcí [个 gè] *(linguistic)*

neglected ADJECTIVE
被荒废的 bèi huāngfèi de *(untidy)*
□ The garden is neglected. 花园被荒废了。Huāyuán bèi huāngfèi le.

negligee NOUN
女式长睡衣 nǚshì cháng shuìyī [件 jiàn]

to **negotiate** VERB
商讨 shāngtǎo

negotiations PL NOUN
谈判 tánpàn

neighbour (US **neighbor**) NOUN
邻居 línjū [个 gè]
□ the neighbours' garden 邻居们的花园 línjūmen de huāyuán

neighbourhood (US **neighborhood**) NOUN
临近的地区 línjìn de dìqū [个 gè]

neither PRONOUN
▷ *see also* **neither** CONJUNCTION, ADVERB
1 两人都不 liǎngrén dōu bù *(person)*
□ Neither of them is coming. 他们两人都不来了。Tāmen liǎngrén dōu bù lái le.
2 两者都不 liǎngzhě dōu bù *(thing)*
□ Carrots or peas? — Neither, thanks. 胡萝卜还是豌豆？ — 都不要了，谢谢。Húluóbo háishì wāndòu? — Dōu búyào le, xièxie.

neither CONJUNCTION, ADVERB
▷ *see also* **neither** PRONOUN

> LANGUAGE TIP When saying **neither do I** in Chinese, the negative particle 不 bù or 没 méi must agree with the negative particle used in the previous remark.

□ I didn't go. — Neither did I. 我没去。— 我也没。Wǒ méi qù. — Wǒ yě měi.
□ I don't like him. — Neither do I! 我不喜欢他。— 我也不！ Wǒ bù xǐhuan tā. — Wǒ yě bù!
■ **I didn't move and neither did John.** 我没动，约翰也没动。Wǒ méi dòng, Yuēhàn yě méi dòng.
■ **neither have I** 我也没有 wǒ yě méiyǒu
□ I don't have a watch on me. — Neither have I. 我没有表。 — 我也没有。Wǒ méiyǒu biǎo. — Wǒ yě méiyǒu.
■ **neither... nor...** …和…都不 ...hé...dōu bù □ Neither Sarah nor Tom is coming to the party. 莎拉和汤姆都不来参加派对了。Shālā hé Tāngmǔ dōu bùlái cānjiā pàiduì le.

neon NOUN
氖 nǎi
■ **a neon light** 一盏霓虹灯 yīzhǎn níhóngdēng

nephew NOUN
1 侄子 zhízi [个 gè] *(brother's son)*
2 外甥 wàisheng [个 gè] *(sister's son)*

nerve NOUN
1 神经 shénjīng [根 gēn] *(in body)*
2 胆量 dǎnliàng *(cheek)*
□ He's got a nerve! 他很有胆量！ Tā hěn yǒu dǎnliàng!
■ **to get on somebody's nerves** 使某人心烦 shǐ mǒurén xīnfán □ She sometimes gets on my nerves. 她有时候会使我心烦。Tā yǒushíhòu huì shǐ wǒ xīnfán.

nerve-racking ADJECTIVE
伤脑筋的 shāng nǎojīn de

nervous ADJECTIVE
紧张的 jǐnzhāng de
□ I bite my nails when I'm nervous. 我紧张的时候就会咬指甲。Wǒ jǐnzhāng de shíhòu jiù huì yǎo zhǐjia.
■ **to be nervous about something** 对某事

感到紧张不安 duì mǒushì gǎndào jǐnzhāng bù'ān □ I'm a bit nervous about flying to China by myself. 我对独自乘飞机去中国感到有点紧张不安。Wǒ duì dúzì chéng fēijī qù Zhōngguó gǎndào yǒudiǎn jǐnzhāng bù'ān.

nest NOUN
巢 cháo [个 gè]

Net NOUN
■ **the Net** 网络 wǎngluò [个 gè]
■ **to surf the Net** 上网 shàngwǎng

net NOUN
网 wǎng [张 zhāng]
□ a fishing net 一张渔网 yìzhāng yúwǎng

netball NOUN
投球 tóuqiú
□ Netball is a bit like basketball. 投球是一种类似篮球的运动。Tóuqiú shì yīzhǒng lèisì lánqiú de yùndòng.

Netherlands PL NOUN
■ **the Netherlands** 荷兰 Hélán

network NOUN
1 网状系统 wǎngzhuàng xìtǒng [个 gè]
2 网络 wǎngluò [个 gè] *(for mobile phone)*
□ Which network are you on? 你用的是哪个网络？Nǐ yòng de shì nǎgè wǎngluò?

neurotic ADJECTIVE
神经的 shénjīng de

never ADVERB
1 从未 cóngwèi
□ Have you ever been to Germany? — No, never. 你去过德国吗？ — 没有，从未去过。Nǐ qùguò Déguó mā? — Méiyǒu, cóngwèi qùguò. □ I never write letters. 我从未写过信。Wǒ cóngwèi xiě guò xìn. □ I have never been camping. 我从未露过营。Wǒ cóngwèi lù guò yíng.
2 决不要 jué búyào
□ Never leave valuables in your car. 决不要在汽车里留贵重物品。Jué búyào zài qìchē lǐ liú guìzhòng wùpǐn.
■ **We never saw him again.** 我们再没见过他。Wǒmen zài méi jiànguò tā.
■ **Never again!** 不要再有下次！Búyào zài yǒu xiàcì!
■ **Never mind.** 没关系。Méi guānxì.

new ADJECTIVE
1 崭新的 zhǎnxīn de
□ They've got a new car. 他们有了一辆崭新的车。Tāmen yǒule yìliǎng zhǎnxīn de chē.
2 新式的 xīnshì de *(product, system, method)*
3 新的 xīn de *(job, address, boss, president)*
□ her new boyfriend 她的新男朋友 tāde xīn nánpéngyǒu

newborn ADJECTIVE
新生的 xīnshēng de
□ a newborn baby 一个新生的婴儿 yígè xīnshēng de yīng'ér

newcomer NOUN
新来者 xīnláizhě [个 gè]

news NOUN
1 消息 xiāoxi
□ It was nice to have your news. 听到你的消息真好。Tīngdào nǐde xiāoxi zhēnhǎo.
2 一条消息 yìtiáo xiāoxi *(single piece of news)*
□ That's wonderful news! 那是条好极了的消息！Nà shì tiáo hǎojíle de xiāoxi!
■ **good news** 好消息 hǎo xiāoxi
■ **bad news** 坏消息 huài xiāoxi □ I've had some bad news. 我有一些坏消息。Wǒ yǒu yìxiē huài xiāoxi.
■ **the news** *(on TV, radio)* 新闻 xīnwén
□ I watch the news every evening. 我每天傍晚都看新闻。Wǒ měitiān bàngwǎn dōu kàn xīnwén.

newsagent NOUN
报刊店 bàokāndiàn [家 jiā]

newsdealer NOUN (US)
报刊经销者 bàokān jīngxiāozhě [个 gè]

newspaper NOUN
报纸 bàozhǐ [份 fèn]

newsreader NOUN
新闻播报员 xīnwén bōbàoyuán [个 gè]

New Year NOUN
新年 Xīnnián
□ to celebrate New Year 庆祝新年 qìngzhù Xīnnián
■ **in the New Year** 在新的一年中 zài xīnde yīnián zhōng
■ **Happy New Year!** 新年快乐！Xīnnián Kuàilè!

> **DID YOU KNOW...?**
> New Year in China generally refers to the new year of the lunar calendar, which normally occurs in late January or early February, and is celebrated during the Spring Festival.

New Year's Day (US **New Year's**) NOUN
元旦 Yuándàn

New Year's Eve (US **New Year's**) NOUN
元旦前夜 Yuándàn qiányè

New Zealand NOUN
▷ *see also* **New Zealand** ADJECTIVE
新西兰 Xīnxīlán

New Zealand ADJECTIVE
▷ *see also* **New Zealand** NOUN
新西兰的 Xīnxīlán de

New Zealander NOUN
新西兰人 Xīnxīlánrén [个 gè]

next ADJECTIVE
▷ *see also* **next** ADVERB, PREPOSITION

1 下一个的 xiàyígè de
□ next Saturday 下个星期六 xiàgè xīngqīliù □ next year 下一年 xià yìnián □ next summer 下个夏天 xiàgè xiàtiān □ the next flight 下一次航班 xià yícì hángbān
2 隔壁的 gébì de *(house, street, room)*
□ the next room 隔壁房间 gébì fángjiān
■ **the next day** 第二天 dì'èrtiān □ The next day we visited the Temple of Heaven. 第二天我们去了天坛。Dì'èrtiān wǒmen qùle Tiāntán.
■ **the next time** 下次 xiàcì □ the next time you see her 你下次见到她的时候 nǐ xiàcì jiàndào tā de shíhòu □ Next time, be a bit more careful. 下次要更谨慎些。Xiàcì yào gèng jǐnshèn xiē.
■ **Who's next?** 下一位是谁？Xià yíwèi shì shuí?
■ **Next please!** 下一位有请！Xià yíwèi yǒuqǐng!
■ **the week after next** 下下周 xià xiàzhōu

next ADVERB, PREPOSITION
▷ *see also* **next** ADJECTIVE
接下来地 jiēxiàlái de *(afterwards)*
□ What shall I do next? 我接下来应该做什么？Wǒ jiēxiàlái yīnggāi zuò shénme? □ What happened next? 接下来发生了什么？Jiēxiàlái fāshēng le shénme?
■ **next to** *(beside)* 旁边 pángbiān □ next to the bank 银行旁边 yínháng pángbiān

next door ADVERB
隔壁 gébì
□ They live next door. 他们住在隔壁。Tāmen zhùzài gébì. □ the people next door 隔壁邻居 gébì línju

NHS NOUN *(= National Health Service)*
■ **the NHS** 英国国民医疗服务 Yīngguó guómín yīliáo fúwù

nice ADJECTIVE
1 漂亮的 piàoliàng de *(pretty)*
□ That's a nice dress! 那是条漂亮的裙子！Nàshì tiáo piàoliàng de qúnzi!
2 美味的 měiwèi de *(food)*
□ It's very nice. 非常美味。Fēicháng měiwèi. □ a nice cup of coffee 一杯美味的咖啡 yìbēi měiwèi de kāfēi
3 可爱的 kě'ài de *(person: likeable)*
□ Your parents are very nice. 你的父母好可爱啊。Nǐde fùmǔ hǎo kě'ài a.
4 好 hǎo *(good)*
□ nice weather 好天气 hǎo tiānqì
□ It's a nice day. 今天天气很好。Jīntiān tiānqì hěnhǎo. □ It was nice of you to remember my birthday. 你真好，能记得我的生日。Nǐ zhēnhǎo, néng jìdé wǒde shēngrì.
■ **to look nice** 看上去不错 kànshàngqù búcuò
■ **It's nice to see you.** 很高兴见到你。Hěn gāoxìng jiàndào nǐ.
■ **to be nice to somebody** 对某人好 duì mǒurén hǎo
■ **Have a nice time!** 祝你玩得愉快！Zhù nǐ wándé yúkuài!

nickname NOUN
绰号 chuòhào [个 gè]

niece NOUN
1 侄女 zhínǚ [个 gè] *(brother's daughter)*
2 甥女 shēngnǚ [个 gè] *(sister's daughter)*

Nigeria NOUN
尼日利亚 Nírìlìyà

night NOUN
1 黑夜 hēiyè [个 gè]
□ I want a single room for two nights. 我想要一间单人房住两晚。Wǒ xiǎng yào yìjiān dānrénfáng zhù liǎngwǎn.
■ **My mother works nights.** 我母亲是上夜班的。Wǒ mǔqīn shì shàng yèbān de.
■ **at night** 夜间 yèjiān
■ **in the night** 夜里 yèlǐ
2 晚上 wǎnshang [个 gè] *(evening)*
□ last night 昨天晚上 zuótiān wǎnshàng

night club NOUN
夜总会 yèzǒnghuì [家 jiā]

nightdress NOUN
女式睡衣 nǚshì shuìyī [件 jiàn]

nightie NOUN
睡衣 shuìyī [件 jiàn]

nightmare NOUN
恶梦 èmèng [场 chǎng]
■ **to have a nightmare** 做噩梦 zuò èmèng
■ **It was a real nightmare!** 那真是一场噩梦！Nà zhēnshì yìchǎng èmèng!

nil NOUN
零 líng
□ They lost two nil to Italy. 他们以零比二输给了意大利队。Tāmen yǐ líng bǐ èr shūgěi le Yìdàlìduì. □ Their chances of survival are nil. 他们幸存的可能为零。Tāmen xìngcún de kěnéng wéi líng.

nine NUMBER
九 jiǔ
□ She's nine. 她九岁。Tā jiǔsuì.

nineteen NUMBER
十九 shíjiǔ
□ She's nineteen. 她十九岁。Tā shíjiǔsuì.

nineteenth ADJECTIVE
第十九 dì shíjiǔ
□ her nineteenth birthday 她的第十九个生日 tāde dì shíjiǔ gè shēngrì □ the nineteenth floor 第十九层 dì shíjiǔ céng

■ **the nineteenth of August** 八月十九号 bāyuè shíjiǔ hào

ninety NUMBER
九十 jiǔshí

ninth ADJECTIVE
第九 dìjiǔ
□ the ninth floor 第九层 dìjiǔ céng
■ **the ninth of August** 八月九号 bāyuè jiǔ hào

no ADVERB
▷ *see also* **no** ADJECTIVE
没有 méiyǒu
□ Did you see it? — No. 你看见了吗？— 没有。Nǐ kànjiàn le mǎ? — Méiyǒu.
■ **no thanks** 不用了，谢谢 búyòng le, xièxie □ Would you like some more? — No thanks. 你还要么？— 不用了，谢谢。Nǐ hái yào me? — Búyòng le, xièxie.

no ADJECTIVE
▷ *see also* **no** ADVERB
没有 méiyǒu *(not any)*
□ There's no hot water. 没有热水。Méiyǒu rèshuǐ. □ I have no books. 我没有书。Wǒ méiyǒu shū. □ I've got no idea. 我没有主意。Wǒ méiyǒu zhǔyì. □ No problem. 没有问题。Méiyǒu wèntí.
■ **'no smoking'** "严禁吸烟" "yánjìn xīyān"
■ **No way!** 没门儿！ Méiménr!

nobody PRONOUN
没有人 méiyǒurén
□ Who's going with you? — Nobody. 谁和你一起去？— 没有人。Shéi hé nǐ yìqǐ qù? — Méiyǒurén. □ Nobody likes him. 没有人喜欢他。Méiyǒurén xǐhuan tā.

to **nod** VERB
点头同意 diǎntóu tóngyì *(in agreement)*
■ **to nod at somebody** *(as greeting)* 向某人点头问好 xiàng mǒurén diǎntóu wèn hǎo

noise NOUN
1 响声 xiǎngshēng [阵 zhèn] *(sound)*
2 噪音 zàoyīn *(din)*
□ Please make less noise. 请少制造些噪音。Qǐng shǎo zhìzào xiē zàoyīn.

noisy ADJECTIVE
1 嘈杂的 cáozá de *(place)*
2 喧闹的 xuānnào de *(people)*

to **nominate** VERB
1 任命 rènmìng *(appoint)*
□ She was nominated as director. 她被任命为主管。Tā bèi rènmìng wéi zhǔguǎn.
2 提名 tímíng *(propose)*
□ I nominate Ian Alexander as president of the society. 我提名伊恩·亚历山大当这个团体的负责人。Wǒ tímíng Yī'ēn Yàlìshāndà dāng zhègè tuántǐ de fùzérén.
■ **He was nominated for an Oscar.** 他被提名角逐奥斯卡。Tā bèi tímíng juézhú Àosíkǎ.

none PRONOUN
1 一个也没有 yígè yě méiyǒu *(not one)*
□ How many sisters have you got? — None. 你有几个姐妹？— 一个也没有。Nǐ yǒu jǐgè jiěmèi? — Yígè yě méiyǒu. □ What sports do you do? — None. 你都做些什么运动？— 一个也没有。Nǐ dōu zuò xiē shénme yùndòng? — Yígè yě méiyǒu.
■ **none of us** 我们谁都不 wǒmen shéi dōubù
■ **None of my friends wanted to come.** 我的朋友们谁都不想来。Wǒde péngyǒumen shéi dōu bùxiǎng lái.
2 没有一点儿 méiyǒu yìdiǎn'r *(not any)*
□ There's none left. 一点也没剩。Yìdiǎn yě méi shèng. □ Matches? There are none left. 要火柴吗？一根也没有了。Yào huǒchái ma? Yìgēn yě méiyǒu le.

nonsense NOUN
废话 fèihuà
□ She talks a lot of nonsense. 她讲很多废话。Tā jiǎng hěnduō fèihuà. □ Nonsense! 废话！ Fèihuà!

non-smoker NOUN
不吸烟的人 bù xīyān de rén [个 gè]
□ He's a non-smoker. 他是个不吸烟的人。Tā shì gè bù xīyān de rén.

non-smoking ADJECTIVE
禁烟的 jìn yān de
□ a non-smoking carriage 一节禁烟的车厢 yìjié jìnyān de chēxiāng

non-stop ADVERB
▷ *see also* **non-stop** ADJECTIVE
1 不停地 bùtíng de *(ceaselessly)*
□ He talks non-stop. 他不停地讲话。Tā bùtíng de jiǎnghuà.
2 直航地 zhíháng de *(fly)*
□ We flew non-stop. 我们直航地飞行。Wǒmen zhíháng de fēixíng.

non-stop ADJECTIVE
▷ *see also* **non-stop** ADVERB
不停的 bùtíng de
□ a non-stop flight 一架直航的航班 yījià zhíháng de hángbān

noodles PL NOUN
面条 miàntiáo [碗 wǎn]

noon NOUN
中午 zhōngwǔ
□ before noon 中午之前 zhōngwǔ zhīqián
■ **at noon** 中午 zhōngwǔ

no one PRONOUN
没有人 méiyǒurén
□ Who's going with you? — No one. 谁和你

一起去？— 没有人。Shéi hé nǐ yìqǐ qù? — Méiyǒurén. □ No one likes him. 没有人喜欢他。Méiyǒurén xǐhuan tā.

nor CONJUNCTION
也不 yěbù
■ **Nor do I.** 我也不。Wǒ yě bù. □ I didn't like the film. — Nor did I. 我不喜欢这部电影。— 我也不喜欢. Wǒ bù xǐhuan zhèbù diànyǐng. — Wǒ yě bù xǐhuan.
■ **Nor have I.** 我也没有。Wǒ yě méiyǒu. □ I haven't seen him. — Nor have I. 我没见过他。— 我也没有。Wǒ méi jiànguò tā. — Wǒ yě méiyǒu.
■ **neither... nor** 既不… 也不 jìbù...yěbù □ I want to go to neither the cinema nor the swimming pool. 我既不想去电影院也不想去游泳。Wǒ jì bùxiǎng qù diànyǐngyuàn yěbù xiǎng qù yóuyǒng.

normal ADJECTIVE
1 正常的 zhèngcháng de
□ at the normal time 在正常的时间 zài zhèngcháng de shíjiān
■ **drier than normal** 比正常偏干 bǐ zhèngcháng piāngān
2 标准的 biāozhǔn de *(standard)*
□ a normal car 一辆标准的车 yīliǎng biāozhǔn de chē

normally ADVERB
1 通常地 tōngcháng de *(usually)*
□ I normally arrive at nine o'clock. 我通常会在九点到达。Wǒ tōngcháng huì zài jiǔdiǎn dàodá.
2 正常地 zhèngcháng de *(as normal)*
□ In spite of the strike, the airports are working normally. 尽管有罢工，机场仍在正常运转。Jìnguǎn yǒu bàgōng, jīchǎng rēng zài zhèngcháng yùnzhuǎn.

north NOUN
▷ *see also* **north** ADJECTIVE, ADVERB
北方 běifāng
■ **to the north** 以北 yǐběi

north ADJECTIVE
▷ *see also* **north** NOUN, ADVERB
北部的 běibù de
□ the north coast 北部海岸 běibù hǎi'àn
□ a north wind 一阵北风 yízhèn běifēng

north ADVERB
▷ *see also* **north** NOUN, ADJECTIVE
向北方 xiàng běifāng
□ We were travelling north. 我们那时正在向北方行驶。Wǒmen nàshí zhèngzài xiàng béifāng xíngshǐ.
■ **north of...** …以北 ...yǐběi □ It's north of London. 伦敦以北。Lúndūn yǐběi.

North America NOUN
北美 Běiměi

northbound ADJECTIVE
向北行驶的 xiàngběi xíngshǐ de
□ The truck was northbound on the M5. 卡车沿着M5道向北行驶。Kǎchē yánzhe Mwǔ dào xiàngběi xíngshǐ. □ Northbound traffic is moving very slowly. 向北的车辆现在行驶非常缓慢。Xiàngběi de chēliàng xiànzài xíngshǐ fēicháng huǎnmàn.

northeast NOUN
▷ *see also* **northeast** ADJECTIVE, ADVERB
东北 dōngběi

northeast ADJECTIVE
▷ *see also* **northeast** NOUN, ADVERB
东北的 dōngběi de

northeast ADVERB
▷ *see also* **northeast** NOUN, ADJECTIVE
向东北 xiàng dōngběi

northern ADJECTIVE
北方的 běifāng de
□ the northern part of the island 岛的北部 dǎo de běibù
■ **Northern Europe** 欧洲北部 ōuzhōu běibù
■ **the northern hemisphere** 北半球 běibànqiú

Northern Ireland NOUN
北爱尔兰 Běi'ài'ěrlán

North Korea NOUN
朝鲜 Cháoxiǎn

North Pole NOUN
■ **the North Pole** 北极 Běijí

North Sea NOUN
北海 Běihǎi

northwest NOUN
▷ *see also* **northwest** ADJECTIVE, ADVERB
西北 xīběi

northwest ADJECTIVE
▷ *see also* **northwest** NOUN, ADVERB
西北的 xīběi de

northwest ADVERB
▷ *see also* **northwest** NOUN, ADJECTIVE
向西北 xiàng xīběi

Norway NOUN
挪威 Nuówēi

Norwegian NOUN
▷ *see also* **Norwegian** ADJECTIVE
1 挪威人 Nuówēirén *(person)*
2 挪威语 Nuówēiyǔ *(language)*

Norwegian ADJECTIVE
▷ *see also* **Norwegian** NOUN
挪威的 Nuówēi de

nose NOUN
鼻子 bízi [个 gè]

nosebleed NOUN
■ **to have a nosebleed** 流鼻血 liú bíxiě
□ I often get nosebleeds. 我经常流鼻

血。Wǒ jīngcháng liú bíxiě.

nosy ADJECTIVE
爱管闲事的 ài guǎn xiánshì de

not ADVERB
不 bù
□ He is not here. 他不在这儿。Tā búzài zhè'er. □ I'm not sure. 我不确定。Wǒ búquèdìng. □ You shouldn't do that. 你不应该那样做。Nǐ bù yīnggāi nàyàng zuò. □ It's too late, isn't it? 现在太晚了，不是吗？ Xiànzài tàiwǎn le, bùshì ma? □ He asked me not to do it. 他叫我不要做。Tā jiào wǒ bùyào zuò. □ I hope not. 我希望不是。Wǒ xīwàng búshì. □ Can you lend me £10? — I'm afraid not. 你能借给我十镑吗？— 恐怕不行。Nǐ néng jiè gěi wǒ shíbàng mā? — Kǒngpà bùxíng.
■ **Are you coming or not?** 你来不来？ Nǐ láibùlái?
■ **not at all** *(in answer to thanks)* 不客气 bú kèqi
■ **not yet** 还没 háiméi □ Have you finished? — Not yet. 你完成了吗？— 还没。Nǐ wánchéng le ma? — Háiméi.
■ **not really** 并不是的 bìng bùshì de

note NOUN
▷ *see also* **note** VERB
1 便条 biàntiáo [张 zhāng] *(message)*
□ I'll write her a note. 我会留张便条给她。Wǒ huì liú zhāng biàntiáo gěi tā.
■ **to make a note of something** 记下某事 jìxià mǒushì
2 纸币 zhǐbì [张 zhāng] *(banknote)*
□ a £5 note 一张五英镑纸币 yìzhāng wǔ yīngbàng zhǐbì

to **note** VERB
▷ *see also* **note** NOUN
留意 liúyì *(observe)*

to **note down** VERB
记下 jìxià

notebook NOUN
笔记本 bǐjìběn [个 gè]

notepad NOUN
1 记事本 jìshìběn [个 gè] *(pad of paper)*
2 记事簿 jìshìbù [个 gè] *(on computer)*

notepaper NOUN
便签纸 biànqiānzhǐ [张 zhāng]

notes PL NOUN
笔记 bǐjì *(from or for lecture)*
■ **to take notes** 记笔记 jì bǐjì

nothing NOUN
没什么 méishénme
□ What's wrong? — Nothing. 有什么不对劲吗？— 没什么。Yǒu shénme búduìjìn ma? — Méishénme. □ nothing special 没什么特别的 méishénme tèbié de □ nothing to worry about 没什么值得担忧的 méishénme zhídé dānyōu de □ He does nothing. 他什么都不做。Tā shénme dōu bú zuò. □ He ate nothing for breakfast. 他早餐什么都没吃。Tā zǎocān shénme dōu méi chī. □ Nothing is open on Sundays. 星期天什么都不开门。Xīngqītiān shénme dōu bù kāimén.
■ **nothing else** 没有别的 méiyǒu biéde
■ **for nothing** 免费 miǎnfèi
■ **nothing at all** 什么也没有 shénme yě méiyǒu

to **notice** VERB
▷ *see also* **notice** NOUN
注意到 zhùyì dào

notice NOUN
▷ *see also* **notice** VERB
通告 tōnggào [个 gè]
□ to put up a notice 贴出一份通告 tiēchū yífèn tōnggào
■ **a warning notice** 一个警告 yígè jǐnggào
■ **to take no notice of somebody** 不理某人 bùlǐ mǒurén □ Don't take any notice of him! 不要理他！ Búyào lǐ tā!
■ **without notice** 不事先通知 bù shìxiān tōngzhī

notice board NOUN
布告栏 bùgàolán [个 gè]

nought NOUN
零 líng

noun NOUN
名词 míngcí [个 gè]

novel NOUN
小说 xiǎoshuō [部 bù]

> **DID YOU KNOW...?**
> 网络小说 wǎngluò xiǎoshuō, **internet novels**, are increasingly popular in China. They are usually published in chapters as they are written and posted online on various blogs or internet forums.

novelist NOUN
小说家 xiǎoshuōjiā [位 wèi]

November NOUN
十一月 shíyīyuè [个 gè]
□ in November 在十一月 zài shíyīyuè □ the first of November 十一月一日 shíyīyuè yīrì □ at the beginning of November 在十一月初 zài shíyīyuè chū □ at the end of November 在十一月末 zài shíyīyuè mò □ every November 每年十一月 měinián shíyīyuè

now ADVERB
▷ *see also* **now** CONJUNCTION
1 现在 xiànzài
□ What are you doing now? 你现在在做什

么？ Nǐ xiànzài zài zuò shénme?

2 如今 rújīn *(these days)*

■ **right now** 这时 zhèshí

■ **by now** 到现在 dào xiànzài □ It should be ready by now. 到现在它应该都准备好了。Dào xiànzài tā yīnggāi dōu zhǔnbèi hǎo le.

■ **just now** **1** *(at the moment)* 眼下 yǎnxià □ I'm rather busy just now. 我眼下正忙。Wǒ yǎnxià zhèngmáng. **2** *(a short time ago)* 刚才 gāngcái □ I did it just now. 我刚才做的。Wǒ gāngcái zuò de.

■ **now and then** 偶尔 ǒu'ěr

■ **from now on** 从现在起 cóng xiànzài qǐ

■ **That's all for now.** 就到这里。Jiùdào zhèli.

now CONJUNCTION

▷ *see also* **now** ADVERB

■ **now that** 既然 jìrán

nowhere ADVERB

无处 wúchù

■ **nowhere else** 没有其它地方 méiyǒu qítā dìfāng

nuclear ADJECTIVE

核的 hé de

□ nuclear power 核能 hénéng □ a nuclear power station 一座核能站 yízuò hénéng zhàn

nude ADJECTIVE

▷ *see also* **nude** NOUN

赤裸的 chìluǒ de

■ **to sunbathe nude** 裸体日光浴 luǒtǐ rìguāngyù

nude NOUN

▷ *see also* **nude** ADJECTIVE

裸体 luǒtǐ

■ **in the nude** 裸体地 chìluǒ de

nuisance NOUN

■ **to be a nuisance** *(thing)* 麻烦事 máfánshì □ It's a nuisance. 这是个麻烦事。Zhè shì gè máfánshì.

■ **Sorry to be a nuisance.** 给人添麻烦感到抱歉。Gěirén tiān máfán gǎndào bàoqiàn.

numb ADJECTIVE

麻木的 mámù de

□ My leg's gone numb. 我的腿麻了。Wǒde tuǐ má le.

■ **numb with cold** 冻僵的 dòngjiāng de

number NOUN

▷ *see also* **number** VERB

1 数字 shùzì [个 gè] *(figure, digit)*

□ I can't read the second number. 我看不清第二个数字。Wǒ kànbùqīng dì'èr gè shùzì.

2 电话号码 diànhuà hàomǎ [个 gè] *(telephone number)*

□ What's your number? 你的电话号码是多少？ Nǐde diànhuà hàomǎ shì duōshǎo?

□ You've got the wrong number. 你拨错电话号码了。Nǐ bōcuò diànhuà hàomǎ le.

3 号 hào [个 gè] *(of house, bank account, bus)*

□ They live at number 5. 他们住在五号。Tāmen zhùzài wǔhào.

4 数量 shùliàng *(quantity)*

■ **a number of** *(several)* 几个 jǐgè

■ **a small number of** 少数的 shǎoshù de

■ **a large number of people** 很多人 hěnduōrén

to **number** VERB

▷ *see also* **number** NOUN

给...标号码 gěi...biāo hàomǎ *(pages)*

number plate NOUN

车号牌 chēhàopái [个 gè]

nun NOUN

修女 xiūnǚ [名 míng]

nurse NOUN

护士 hùshi [位 wèi]

nursery NOUN

幼儿园 yòu'éryuán [家 jiā]

nursery school NOUN

幼儿园 yòu'éryuán [家 jiā]

nut NOUN

1 坚果 jiānguǒ [枚 méi] *(from tree)*

2 螺母 luómǔ [个 gè] *(metal)*

nutmeg NOUN

肉豆蔻 ròudòukòu [棵 kē]

nutritious ADJECTIVE

有营养的 yǒuyíngyǎng de

nylon NOUN

尼龙 nílóng

Oo

oak NOUN
1 橡树 xiàngshù [棵 kē] *(tree)*
2 橡木 xiàngmù *(wood)*
□ an oak table 橡木桌子 xiàngmù zhuōzi
oar NOUN
桨 jiǎng [只 zhī]
oats NOUN
燕麦 yànmài
obedient ADJECTIVE
顺从的 shùncóng de
to **obey** VERB
1 听从 tīngcóng *(person, orders)*
2 服从 fúcóng *(law, regulations)*
■ **to obey the rules** 服从规则 fúcóng guīzé
object NOUN
▷ *see also* **object** VERB
1 物体 wùtǐ [个 gè] *(thing)*
□ a familiar object 一个熟悉的物体 yígè shúxīde wùtǐ
2 宾语 bīnyǔ [个 gè] *(grammatical)*
to **object** VERB
▷ *see also* **object** NOUN
反对 fǎnduì
objection NOUN
异议 yìyì [个 gè]
objective NOUN
目标 mùbiāo
obscene ADJECTIVE
淫秽的 yínhuìde
observant ADJECTIVE
奉行者 fèngxíngzhě
to **observe** VERB
观察 guānchá
to **obsess** VERB
使着迷 shǐ zháomí
obsessed ADJECTIVE
迷住 mízhù
□ He's obsessed with trains. 他被火车迷住了。Tā bèi huǒchē mízhùle.
obsession NOUN
着迷 zháomí [种 zhǒng]
□ It's getting to be an obsession with you. 你开始对它着迷了。Nǐ kāishǐ duì tā zháomíle. □ Football's an obsession of mine. 足球很让我着迷。Zúqiú hěn ràng wǒ zháomí.
obsolete ADJECTIVE
废弃的 fèiqìde
obstacle NOUN
障碍 zhàng'ài
to **obstruct** VERB
阻塞 zǔsāi
□ A lorry was obstructing the traffic. 一辆货车阻塞了交通。Yíliàng huòchē zǔsèle jiāotōng.
to **obtain** VERB
获得 huòdé
obvious ADJECTIVE
明显的 míngxiǎn de
obviously ADVERB
1 显然地 xiǎnrán de *(of course)*
□ Do you want to pass the exam? — Obviously! 你想通过考试吗？— 显然地！Nǐ xiǎng tōngguò kǎoshì ma? — Xiǎnránde!
■ **Obviously not!** 显然不对！ Xiǎnrán búduì!
2 显然地 xiǎnránde *(visibly)*
□ She was obviously exhausted. 她显然筋疲力尽了。Tā xiǎnrán jīnpílìjìnle.
occasion NOUN
1 时刻 shíkè [个 gè] *(moment)*
■ **on several occasions** 几个时刻 jǐgè shíkè
2 场合 chǎnghé [种 zhǒng] *(event, celebration)*
□ a special occasion 一种特殊场合 yìzhǒng tèshū chǎnghé
occasionally ADVERB
偶尔地 ǒu'ěr de
occupation NOUN
职业 zhíyè [种 zhǒng]
to **occupy** VERB
1 占用 zhànyòng *(house, office)*
■ **to be occupied** *(seat, place)* 被占用 bèi zhànyòng □ That seat is occupied. 那个座位被占用了。Nàgè zuòwèi bèi zhànyòngle.
2 占用 zhànyòng *(fill: time)*

to **occur** VERB
发生 fāshēng
□ The accident occurred yesterday. 意外是昨天发生的。Yìwài shi zuótiān fāshēngde.
■ **to occur to somebody** 某人想到 mǒurén xiǎngdào
■ **It suddenly occurred to me that...** 我突然想到 Wǒ tūrán xiǎngdào

ocean NOUN
海洋 hǎiyáng [片 piàn]

o'clock ADVERB
■ **six o'clock** 六点钟 liùdiǎnzhōng
□ at four o'clock 在四点钟 zài sìdiǎnzhōng
□ It's five o'clock. 现在是五点钟。Xiànzài shì wǔdiǎnzhōng.

October NOUN
十月 shíyuè
□ in October 在十月 zài shíyuè □ the first of October 十月一日 shíyuè yīrì □ at the beginning of October 在十月初 zài shíyuè chū □ at the end of October 在十月末 zài shíyuè mò □ every October 每年十月 měinián shíyuè

octopus NOUN
章鱼 zhāngyú [只 zhī]

odd ADJECTIVE
1 奇怪的 qíguài de *(strange)*
□ That's odd! 那很奇怪的! Nà hěn qíguàide!
2 奇数的 jīshù de *(number)*
□ an odd number 一个奇数 yígè jīshù

odour (US **odor**) NOUN
气味 qìwèi [种 zhǒng]

of PREPOSITION
的 de
□ at the end of the street 在街的尽头 zài jiēde jìntóu □ the end of the film 电影的结局 diànyǐngde jiéjú □ the history of China 中国的历史 Zhōngguóde lìshǐ □ some photos of my holiday
■ **a kilo of flour** 一公斤面粉 yì gōngjīn miànfěn
■ **a cup of tea** 一杯茶 yìbēi chá
■ **a boy of ten** 一个十岁的男孩 yígè shísuìde nánhái
■ **There were three of them.** 他们有三个。Tāmen yǒu sāngè.
■ **the 5th of July** 七月五日 qīyuè wǔrì
■ **at five of three** (US) 三点差五分 sāndiǎn chà wǔfēn
■ **a friend of mine** 我的一个朋友 wǒde yígè péngyǒu
■ **That's very kind of you.** 你真的很好。Nǐ zhēnde hěnhǎo.
■ **It's made of wood.** 它是木制的。Tā shì mùzhìde.

off ADJECTIVE
▷ *see also* **off** ADVERB, PREPOSITION
1 关着的 guānzhe de
□ All the lights are off. 灯都是关着的。Dēng dōushì guānzhede. □ Are you sure the tap is off? 你确定水龙头是关着的吗? Nǐ quèdìng shuǐlóngtóu shì guānzhedema?
2 取消的 qǔxiāo de *(cancelled)*
□ The match is off. 比赛取消了。Bǐsài qǔxiāole.

off ADVERB
▷ *see also* **off** ADJECTIVE, PREPOSITION
LANGUAGE TIP For other expressions with **off**, see the verbs **get**, **take**, **turn** etc.
■ **I must be off.** *(away)* 我必须得走了。Wǒ bìxū děi zǒu le.
■ **Where are you off to?** 你上哪儿去? Nǐ shàng nǎ'r qù?
■ **to have a day off 1** *(as holiday)* 休假一天 xiūjià yìtiān **2** *(because ill)* 休病假一天 xiūbìngjià yìtiān
■ **to be off sick** 休病假 xiūbìngjià
■ **10% off** 10%的折扣 bǎifēn zhī shí de zhékòu

off PREPOSITION
▷ *see also* **off** ADJECTIVE, ADVERB
■ **to take a picture off the wall** 把画像从墙上取下来 bǎ huàxiàng cóng qiáng shang qǔ xiàlái
■ **to take a day off work** 休假一天 xiūjià yìtiān
■ **She's off school today.** 她今天休假没上学。Tā jīntiān xiūjià méishàngxué.

offence (US **offense**) NOUN
罪行 zuìxíng [种 zhǒng] *(crime)*

to **offend** VERB
得罪 dézuì *(upset)*

offense NOUN (US)
罪行 zuìxíng [种 zhǒng] *(crime)*

offensive ADJECTIVE
无礼的 wúlǐde

to **offer** VERB
▷ *see also* **offer** NOUN
1 提出 tíchū
□ He offered to help me. 他提出帮我。Tā tíchū bāngwǒ. □ I offered to go with them. 我提出同他们一起去。Wǒ tíchū tóng tāmén yìqǐqù.
2 出价 chūjià *(bid)*

offer NOUN
▷ *see also* **offer** VERB
1 提议 tíyì [项 xiàng]
□ a good offer 一项好的提议 yíxiàng hǎode tíyì

2 特价 tèjià [个 gè] *(special deal)*
■ **'on special offer'** "在打特价" "zài dǎtèjià"

office NOUN
1 办公室 bàngōngshì [间 jiān]
□ She works in an office. 她在办公室工作。Tā zài bàngōngshì gōngzuò.
2 部门 bùmén [个 gè] *(department)*
3 诊所 zhěnsuǒ [家 jiā] *(us: of doctor, dentist)*

office block NOUN
办公大楼 bàngōng dàlóu [座 zuò]

officer NOUN
1 军官 jūnguān [位 wèi] *(military)*
2 警官 jǐngguān [位 wèi] *(police officer)*

office worker NOUN
职员 zhíyuán [个 gè]

official ADJECTIVE
官方的 guānfāng de

off-licence NOUN
卖酒商店 màijiǔ shāngdiàn

off-peak ADVERB
非高峰的 fēigāofēngde *(off-season)*
□ It's cheaper to go on holiday off-peak. 在非高峰的时候去度假更便宜。Zài fēigāofēngde shíhòu qù dùjià gèng piányì.
■ **to phone off-peak** 在非高峰的时候打电话 zài fēigāofēngde shíhòu dǎdiànhuà

often ADVERB
经常 jīngcháng *(frequently)*
□ It often rains. 经常下雨。Jīngcháng xiàyǔ. □ I'd like to go skiing more often. 我想更经常去滑雪。Wǒ xiǎng gèngjīngcháng qùhuáxué.
■ **How often do you wash the car?** 你多久洗一次车? Nǐ duōjiǔ xǐ yícì chē?

oil NOUN
▹ *see also* **oil** VERB
1 油 yóu [桶 tǒng]
■ **an oil painting** 一幅油画 yìfú yóuhuà
2 原油 yuányóu *(crude oil)*
□ North Sea oil 北海油 běihǎiyóu

to **oil** VERB
▹ *see also* **oil** NOUN
给...加油 gěi...jiāyóu *(engine, machine)*

oil rig NOUN
1 石油钻塔 shíyóu zuàntǎ [个 gè] *(on land)*
2 钻井平台 zuànjǐng píngtái [个 gè] *(at sea)*

oil slick NOUN
浮油 fúyóu

oil well NOUN
油井 yóujǐng [个 gè]

okay ADJECTIVE
▹ *see also* **okay** ADVERB, EXCLAMATION
1 可以的 kěyǐ de *(acceptable)*
□ Is that okay? 可以吗? Kěyǐma?
■ **It's okay by me.** 这对我没问题。Zhè duìwǒ méi wèntí. □ I'll do it tomorrow, if that's okay by you. 如果你可以的话，我明天做。Rúguǒ nǐ kěyǐdehuà, wǒ míngtiān zuò.
2 好的 hǎo de *(safe and well)*
□ Are you okay? 你还好吗? Nǐ hái hǎoma?
3 不错 búcuò *(not bad)*
□ How was your holiday? — It was okay. 你的假期怎么样? — 还不错。Nǐde jiàqī zěnmèyàng? — Háibúcuò.

okay ADVERB
▹ *see also* **okay** ADJECTIVE, EXCLAMATION
不错 búcuò *(acceptably)*

okay EXCLAMATION
▹ *see also* **okay** ADJECTIVE, ADVERB
1 行 xíng *(expressing agreement)*
□ Could you call back later? — Okay! 你晚一点打回来可以吗? — 行! Nǐ wǎnyidiǎn dǎhuílái kěyǐma? — Xíng!
2 好吗 hǎo ma *(in questions)*
□ I'll meet you at six o'clock, okay? 我六点钟去见你，好吗? Wǒ liùdiǎnzhōng qùjiànnǐ, hǎoma?

old ADJECTIVE
1 年老的 niánlǎo de *(person, animal)*
□ an old man 一位年老的男人 yíwèi niánlǎode nánrén
2 古老的 gǔlǎo de *(not new, not recent)*
□ an old house 一座古老的房子 yízuò gǔlǎode fángzi
3 破旧的 pòjiù de *(worn out)*
4 以前的 yǐqián de *(former)*
□ my old English teacher 我以前的英文教师 Wǒ yǐqiánde yīngwén jiàoshī
5 老的 lǎo de *(friend, enemy, rival)*
■ **How old are you?** 你多大了? Nǐ duōdà le?
■ **He's 10 years old.** 他十岁了。Tā shísuì le.
■ **older brother** 哥哥 gēge
■ **older sister** 姐姐 jiějie
■ **She's two years older than me.** 她比我大两岁。Tā bǐ wǒ dà liǎngsuì.
■ **I'm the oldest in the family.** 我在家里是最大的。Wǒ zàijiālǐ shì zuìdàde.

old age pensioner NOUN
拿退休金的人 ná tuìxiūjīn de rén [位 wèi]

old-fashioned ADJECTIVE
1 老式的 lǎoshì de *(object, custom, idea)*
□ She wears old-fashioned clothes. 她穿老式的衣服。Tā chuān lǎoshìde yīfu.
2 守旧的 shǒujiù de *(person)*
□ My parents are rather old-fashioned. 我的父母很守旧的。Wǒde fùmǔ hěn shǒujiùde.

olive NOUN
橄榄 gǎnlǎn [棵 kē]

olive oil NOUN
橄榄油 gǎnlǎnyóu

olive tree NOUN
橄榄树 gǎnlǎnshù [棵 kē]

Olympic ADJECTIVE
奥林匹克的 Àolínpǐkè de

the Olympics PL NOUN
奥林匹克运动会 Àolínpǐkè Yùndònghuì

omelette (US **omelet**) NOUN
煎蛋饼 jiāndànbǐng [个 gè]

on PREPOSITION
▷ *see also* **on** ADVERB, ADJECTIVE

1 在...上 zài...shang *(indicating position)*
□ It's on the table. 它在桌上。tā zài zhuōshàng. □ on an island 在一个岛上 zài yígè dǎoshàng □ on the left 在左边 zài zuǒbiān □ on the right 在右边 zài yòubiān □ on the top floor 在顶楼 zài dǐnglóu
■ **on foot** 步行 bùxíng
■ **I go to school on my bike.** 我骑自行车上学。Wǒ qízìxíngchē shàngxué.
■ **on the bus** 1 *(be, sit)* 公共汽车上 gōnggòng qìchē shàng 2 *(travel, go)* 乘坐 chéngzuò
■ **on television** 在电视上 zài diànshì shàng □ What's on TV? 电视上演什么？Diànshìshàng yǎn shénme?
■ **on the radio** 广播中 guǎngbō zhōng
□ I heard it on the radio. 我从广播中听说的。Wǒ cóng guǎngbozhōng tīngshuōde.
■ **on the internet** 在因特网上 zài Yīntèwǎng shàng
■ **to be on antibiotics** 定期服用抗生素 dìngqī fúyòng kàngshēngsù

2 在 zài *(referring to time)*
□ on Friday 在星期五 zài xīngqīwǔ □ on my birthday 在我的生日 zài wǒde shēngrì
■ **on holiday** 在度假 zàidùjià □ They're on holiday. 他们在度假。Tāmén zàidùjià.
■ **on strike** 在罢工 zài bàgōng

on ADVERB
▷ *see also* **on** PREPOSITION, ADJECTIVE

LANGUAGE TIP For other expressions with **on**, see the verbs **go**, **put**, **turn** etc.

开着 kāizhe
□ I think I left the light on. 我想我走时开着灯。Wǒxiǎng wǒzǒushí kāizhedēng.
□ Leave the tap on. 开着水龙头。Kāizhe shuǐlóngtóu.
■ **to have one's coat on** 穿着外套 chuānzhe wàitào
■ **What's she got on?** 她穿着什么？Tā chuānzhe shénme?
■ **Screw the lid on tightly.** 把盖子旋紧。Bǎ gàizi xuánjǐn.

on ADJECTIVE
▷ *see also* **on** PREPOSITION, ADVERB

打开的 dǎkāi de *(turned on)*
□ Is the dishwasher on? 洗碗机是打开的吗？Xǐwǎnji shì dǎkāidema?
■ **Is the meeting still on?** 会议还在进行吗？Huìyì háizài jìnxíng ma?
■ **There's a good film on at the cinema.** 电影院正在上映一部好电影。Diànyǐngyuàn zhèngzài shàngyìng yíbù hǎo diànyǐng.
■ **What's on at the cinema?** 电影院里上映什么？Diànyǐngyuànlǐ shàngyìng shénme?

once ADVERB
▷ *see also* **once** CONJUNCTION

1 一次 yícì *(one time only)*
□ once a month 每月一次 měiyuè yícì
□ once more 再多一次 zài duōyícì
■ **once or twice** *(a few times)* 一两次 yíliǎng cì

2 曾经 céngjīng *(at one time)*
■ **once upon a time** *(in stories)* 很久以前 hěnjiǔ yǐqián

3 有一次 yǒu yícì *(on one occasion)*
□ I've been to China once before. 我有一次去过中国。Wǒ yǒuyícì qùguò zhōngguó.
■ **at once** *(immediately)* 立刻 lìkè
■ **once in a while** 偶尔 ǒu'ěr

once CONJUNCTION
▷ *see also* **once** ADVERB

一旦 yídàn *(as soon as)*

one ADJECTIVE, NUMBER
▷ *see also* **one** PRONOUN, NOUN

1 一 yī *(number)*
□ It's one o'clock. 现在1点。Xiànzài yīdiǎn. □ one minute 一分钟 yìfēnzhōng
□ I've got one brother and one sister. 我有一个哥哥和一个姐姐。Wǒyǒu yígè gēge hé yígè jiějie. □ one hundred children 一百个孩子 yìbǎi gè háizi

2 同一的 tóngyī de *(same)*
□ Shall I put it all on the one plate? 要我把它都放在同一个盘子里吗？Yào wǒ bǎ tā dōu fàngzài tóngyígè pánzi lǐ ma?

one PRONOUN
▷ *see also* **one** ADJECTIVE, NUMBER, NOUN

1 一 yī *(number)*
□ I've already got one. 我已经有一个了。Wǒ yǐjīng yǒu yígè le.
■ **one of them** 他们中的一个 tāmen zhōng de yígè
■ **one by one** 一个一个地 yígè yígè de

2 一个 yígè *(with adjective)*

□ I've already got a red one. 我已经有一个红的了。Wǒ yǐjīng yǒu yígè hóngde le.

3 人 rén *(in generalizations)*
□ What can one do? 一个人能做什么呢？Yígèrén néng zuò shénme ne? □ One never knows. 没人能知道。Méirén néng zhīdào.
■ **this one** 这个 zhègè □ Which is the best photo? — This one. 哪一张最好？— 这个。Nǎ yìzhāng zuìhǎo? — Zhègè.
■ **that one** 那个 nàgè □ Which bag is yours? — That one. 哪个包是你的？— 那个。Nǎgèbāo shì nǐde? — Nàgè.

one NOUN
▷ *see also* **one** ADJECTIVE, NUMBER, PRONOUN
— yī *(numeral)*

oneself PRONOUN
1 自己 zìjǐ
■ **to hurt oneself** 伤了自己 shāngle zìjǐ
2 亲自 qīnzì *(personally)*
□ It's quicker to do it oneself. 亲自做会更快。Qīnzì zuò huì gèngkuài.
■ **by oneself** **1** *(unaided)* 独力地 dúlì de **2** *(alone)* 独自 dúzì

one-way ADJECTIVE
1 单行的 dānxíng de *(street, traffic)*
□ a one-way street 单行道 dānxíngdào
2 单程的 dānchéng de *(ticket, trip)*

onion NOUN
洋葱 yángcōng [颗 kē]
□ onion soup 洋葱汤 yángcōngtāng

online ADVERB
网上 wǎngshang *(on the internet)*
□ They like to chat online. 他们喜欢网上聊天。Tāmén xǐhuan wǎngshàng liáotiān.

only ADVERB
▷ *see also* **only** ADJECTIVE, CONJUNCTION
1 仅仅 jǐnjǐn
■ **not only... but...** 不但…而且… búdàn...érqiě...
2 只 zhǐ *(emphasizing insignificance)*
■ **I was only joking.** 我只是在开玩笑。Wǒ zhǐshì zài kāi wánxiào. □ We only want to stay for one night. 我们只是想住一晚。Wǒmén zhǐshì xiǎngzhù yìwǎn. □ These books are only 3 euros. 这些书只花三欧元。Zhèxiēshū zhǐhuā sānōuyuán.

only ADJECTIVE
▷ *see also* **only** ADVERB, CONJUNCTION
唯一的 wéiyī de *(sole)*
□ Monday is the only day I'm free. 唯一星期一我有空。Wéiyī xīngqīyī wǒ yǒukòng.
■ **an only child** 独生子女 dúshēng zǐnǚ

only CONJUNCTION
▷ *see also* **only** ADVERB, ADJECTIVE
可是 kěshì *(but)*
□ I'd like the same sweater, only in black. 我喜欢同样的羊毛衫，可是颜色应该是黑色的。Wǒ xǐhuan tóngyàngde yángmáoshān, kěshì yánsè yīnggāishì hēisède.

onto, on to PREPOSITION
到...上 dào...shàng

onwards ADVERB
从...开始 cóng...kāishǐ
□ from July onwards 从七月开始 cóngqīyuè kāishǐ

open ADJECTIVE
▷ *see also* **open** VERB
1 开着的 kāizhe de *(door, window)*
2 张着的 zhāngzhe de *(mouth, eyes)*
3 营业的 yíngyè de *(shop)*
■ **in the open air** 在户外 zài hùwài

to **open** VERB
▷ *see also* **open** ADJECTIVE
1 打开 dǎkāi
□ Can I open the window? 我可以打开窗户吗？Wǒ kěyǐ dǎkāi chuānghu ma?
2 开 kāi *(door, lid, book, mouth)*
3 开门 kāimén *(public building, shop)*
□ What time do the shops open? 商店什么时候开门？Shāngdiàn shénme shíhòu kāimén?

DID YOU KNOW...?
Shops are often open late into the evening in China, usually to around 8 or 9pm, so evening shopping is quite a popular pastime in many towns and cities.

4 拆开 chāikāi *(letter)*

opening hours PL NOUN
营业时间 yíngyè shíjiān

open-minded ADJECTIVE
开明的 kāimíng de

opera NOUN
歌剧 gējù [部 bù]

to **operate** VERB
1 运作 yùnzuò *(function: company, organization)*
2 工作 gōngzuò *(work: machine, vehicle, system)*
□ The lights operate on a timer. 灯按着计时器工作。Dēng ànzhè jìshíqì gōngzuò.
3 操作 cāozuò *(make work: machine, vehicle, system)*
□ How do you operate the camcorder? 你的摄像机怎么操作？Nǐde shèxiàngjī zěnmè cāozuò?
4 动手术 dòngshǒushù *(perform surgery)*
■ **to operate on somebody** 给某人动手术 gěi mǒurén dòng shǒushù

operation NOUN

1 实施步骤 shíshī bùzhòu [个 gè] *(procedure)*
2 手术 shǒushù [次 cì] *(surgery)*
■ **to have an operation** 接受手术 jiēshòu shǒushù □ I have never had an operation. 我从没动过手术。Wǒ cóngméi dòngguò shǒushù.

operator NOUN
接线员 jiēxiànyuán [位 wèi]

opinion NOUN
观点 guāndiǎn [个 gè]
□ He asked me my opinion. 他问了我的观点。Tā wènle wǒde guāndiǎn.
■ **What's your opinion?** 你的观点是什么？Nǐde guāndiǎn shì shénme?
■ **in my opinion** 按我的意见 àn wǒde yìjiàn

opinion poll NOUN
民意测验 mínyì cèyàn [次 cì]

opponent NOUN
对手 duìshǒu [个 gè]

opportunity NOUN
机会 jīhuì [个 gè]
■ **to take the opportunity to do something** 趁机会做某事 chèn jīhuì zuò mǒushì
■ **to have the opportunity to do something** 有机会做某事 yǒu jīhuì zuò mǒushì

to **oppose** VERB
反对 fǎnduì *(person, idea)*
■ **to be opposed to something** 反对某事 fǎnduì mǒushì

opposed ADJECTIVE
反对 fǎnduì
■ **I've always been opposed to violence.** 我一直反对暴力。Wǒ yìzhí fǎnduì bàolì.
■ **as opposed to** 同某事形成对比 tóngmǒushi xíngchéng duìbǐ

opposing ADJECTIVE
对立的 duìlìde *(team)*

opposite ADJECTIVE
▷ *see also* **opposite** ADVERB, PREPOSITION, NOUN
1 对面的 duìmiàn de *(side, house)*
2 最远的 zuìyuǎn de *(end, corner)*
3 相反的 xiāngfǎn de *(meaning, direction)*
□ It's in the opposite direction. 是相反的方向。Shì xiāngfǎnde fāngxiàng.
■ **the opposite sex** 异性 yìxìng

opposite ADVERB
▷ *see also* **opposite** ADJECTIVE, PREPOSITION, NOUN
在对面 zài duìmiàn *(live, work, sit)*
□ They live opposite. 他们住在对面。Tāmén zhùzài duìmiàn.

opposite PREPOSITION
▷ *see also* **opposite** ADJECTIVE, ADVERB, NOUN
在...的对面 zài...de duìmiàn
□ the girl sitting opposite me 这个女孩坐在我对面。zhègè nǚhái zuòzài wǒduìmiàn

opposite NOUN
▷ *see also* **opposite** ADJECTIVE, ADVERB, PREPOSITION
■ **the opposite** 对立面 duìlìmiàn

opposition NOUN
反对 fǎnduì

optician NOUN
1 眼镜商 yǎnjìngshāng [个 gè]
2 眼镜店 yǎnjìngdiàn [家 jiā] *(optician's shop)*

optimist NOUN
乐观主义者 lèguān zhǔyì zhě [个 gè]

optimistic ADJECTIVE
乐观的 lèguān de

option NOUN
1 选择 xuǎnzé [种 zhǒng] *(choice)*
□ I've got no option. 我没有选择。Wǒ méiyǒu xuǎnzé.
2 选修课 xuǎnxiūkè [门 mén] *(optional subject)*
□ I'm doing geology as my option. 我的选修课是地质学。Wǒde xuǎnxiūkè shì dìzhìxué.

optional ADJECTIVE
可选择的 kěxuǎnzéde

or CONJUNCTION
1 还是 háishì
□ Would you like tea or coffee? 你喜欢茶还是咖啡？Nǐ xǐhuan chá háishì kāfēi?
2 否则 fǒuzé *(otherwise)*
□ Hurry up or you'll miss the bus. 赶快，否则你会错过公共汽车。Gǎnkuài, fǒuzé nǐhuì cuòguò gōnggòngqìchē.
■ **Give me the money, or else!** 把钱还给我，否则不行！Bǎqián huángěiwǒ, fǒuzé bùxíng!

oral ADJECTIVE
▷ *see also* **oral** NOUN
口头的 kǒutóu de *(test, report)*
■ **an oral exam** 一次口试 yícì kǒushì

oral NOUN
▷ *see also* **oral** ADJECTIVE
口试 kǒushì [次 cì]
□ I've got my English oral soon. 我很快要英语口试了。Wǒ hěnkuài yào yīngyǔ kǒushìle.

orange NOUN
▷ *see also* **orange** ADJECTIVE
柑橘 gānjú [只 zhī] *(fruit)*

orange ADJECTIVE
▷ *see also* **orange** NOUN
橙色的 chéngsè de *(in colour)*

orange juice NOUN
橘子汁 júzizhī

orchard NOUN
果园 guǒyuán [个 gè]

orchestra NOUN
管弦乐队 guǎnxián yuèduì [支 zhī]
□ I play in the school orchestra. 我在管弦乐队演奏。Wǒ zài guǎnxián yuèduì yǎnzòu.

order NOUN
▹ *see also* **order** VERB
1 命令 mìnglìng [个 gè] *(command)*
2 点菜 diǎncài [份 fèn] *(in restaurant)*
□ The waiter took our order. 我们向服务员点了菜。Wǒmén xiàng fúwùyuán diǎnle cài.
3 次序 cìxù *(sequence)*
□ in alphabetical order 按字母顺序 àn zìmǔ shùnxù
■ **in order to do something** 为了做某事 wèile zuò mǒushì □ He does it in order to earn money. 他为了赚钱作了那件事。Tā wèile zhuànqián zuòle nàjiànshì.
■ **out of order** *(not working)* 已坏停用 yǐhuài tíngyòng

to **order** VERB
▹ *see also* **order** NOUN
1 命令 mìnglìng *(command)*
■ **to order somebody to do something** 命令某人做某事 mìnglìng mǒurén zuò mǒushì
■ **to order somebody about** 把某人呼来唤去 bǎmǒurén hūláihuànqù □ She liked to order him about. 她喜欢把他呼来唤去。Tā xǐhuan bǎmǒurén hūláihuànqù.
2 定购 dìnggòu *(from shop, company)*
3 点菜 diǎncài *(in restaurant)*
□ We ordered steak and chips. 我们点了牛排和薯条。Wǒmén diǎnle niúpái hé shǔtiáo. □ Are you ready to order? 你可以点菜了吗？Nǐ kěyǐ diǎncàile ma?

ordinary ADJECTIVE
普通的 pǔtōng de
□ an ordinary day 普通的一天 pǔtōngde yìtiān

organ NOUN
1 器官 qìguān [个 gè] *(in body)*
2 管风琴 guǎnfēngqín [架 jià] *(instrument)*

organic ADJECTIVE
1 有机的 yǒujī de *(food, farming)*
2 有机物的 yǒujīwù de *(substance)*

organization NOUN
组织 zǔzhī [个 gè]

to **organize** VERB
组织 zǔzhī

origin NOUN
起源 qǐyuán

original ADJECTIVE
1 最初的 zuìchū de *(first, earliest)*
□ Our original plan was to go camping. 我们最初的计划是去野营。Wǒmén zuìchūde jìhuà shì qù yěyíng.
2 独创的 dúchuàng de *(imaginative)*
□ It's a very original idea. 那是一个独创的观点。Nàshì yígè dúchuàngde guāndiǎn.

originally ADVERB
起初 qǐchū

Orkney NOUN
奥克尼郡 àokèníjùn
□ in Orkney 在奥克尼郡 zài àokèníjùn

ornament NOUN
装饰物 zhuāngshìwù [件 jiàn]

orphan NOUN
孤儿 gū'ér [个 gè]

ostrich NOUN
鸵鸟 tuóniǎn [只 zhī]

other ADJECTIVE
▹ *see also* **other** PRONOUN
1 另外的 lìngwài de *(additional)*
□ on the other side of the street 在街的另外一边 zài jiēde lìngwài yìbiān
2 其他的 qítā de *(not this one)*
□ Have you got these jeans in other colours? 这种牛仔裤还有其他的颜色吗？Zhèzhǒng niúzǎikù háiyǒu qítāde yánsèma?
■ **the other...** *(when there are two)* 另一… lìngyī...
3 其他的 qítā de *(apart from oneself)*
■ **the other day** *(recently)* 几天前 jǐtiān qián

other PRONOUN
▹ *see also* **other** ADJECTIVE
其他 qítā *(additional one, different one)*
■ **the other** *(of two things or people)* 另一个 lìng yígè
■ **the others** 其他的 qítāde □ The others are going but I'm not. 其他的人会去，但我不去。Qítāderén huìqù, dàn wǒ búqù.

otherwise ADVERB, CONJUNCTION
1 否则 fǒuzé *(if not)*
□ Note down the number, otherwise you'll forget it. 写下数字，否则你会忘记的。Xiěxià shùzì, fǒuzé nǐ huì wàngjìde.
2 除此以外 chúcǐ yǐwài *(apart from that)*
□ I'm tired, but otherwise I'm fine. 我很累，但除此以外我很好。Wǒ hěnlèi, dàn chúcǐyǐwài wǒ hěnhǎo.

ought VERB
■ **You ought to see a doctor.** *(indicating advisability)* 你应该去看医生。Nǐ yīnggāi qù kàn yīshēng.
■ **You ought not to do that.** 你不应该做那件事。Nǐ bùyīnggāi zuò nàjiànshì.
■ **He ought to be there now.** *(indicating likelihood)* 他现在应该到那儿了。Tā xiànzài yīnggāi dào nàr le.

ounce NOUN
盎司 ángsī
□ 8 ounces of cheese 八盎司的奶酪 bāángsīde nǎilào

our ADJECTIVE
我们的 wǒmen de
□ Our house is quite big. 我们的房子相当大。Wǒmende fángzi xiāngdāng dà.

ours PRONOUN
我们的 wǒmen de
□ Your school is very different from ours. 你们的学校同我们的不一样。Nǐmende xuéxiào tóng wǒmende bùyíyàng. □ Our teachers are strict. — Ours are too. 我们的老师很严格。— 我们的也是。Wǒmende lǎoshī hěnyángé. — Wǒmende yěshì.

ourselves PRONOUN
我们自己 wǒmen zìjǐ
□ We didn't hurt ourselves. 我们没伤到自己。wǒmen méi shāngdào zìjǐ.
■ **by ourselves** 1 *(unaided)* 我们独力地 wǒmen dúlì de 2 *(alone)* 我们单独地 Wǒmen dāndú de

out ADVERB
▷ *see also* **out** ADJECTIVE

LANGUAGE TIP For other expressions with **out**, see the verbs **go**, **put**, **turn** etc.

1 在外面 zài wàimiàn *(outside)*
□ It's cold out. 在外面冷。Zài wàimiàn lěng.
■ **out there** 那儿外面 nà'r wàimiàn □ It's windy out there. 那儿外面风大。Nà'r wàimiàn fēngdà.
2 不在 bú zài *(absent, not in)*
□ Mr Green is out at the moment. 格林先生这会儿不在。Gélín xiānsheng zhèhuì'r búzài.
■ **to go out** 出去 chūqù □ I'm going out tonight. 我今天晚上出去。Wǒ jīntiān wǎnshàng chūqù.
■ **to go out with somebody** 和某人交往 hé mǒurén jiāowǎng □ I've been going out with him for two months. 我和他交往了两个月。Wǒ hé tā jiāowǎngle liǎnggèyuè.
■ **to have a night out** 外出玩一晚 wàichū wán yìwǎn
■ **The ball was out.** 球出界了。Qiú chūjiè le.
■ **out of** 1 从某物 cóngmǒuwù □ to drink out of a glass 从玻璃杯里喝 cóng bōlíbēilǐ hē 2 *(from among)* …中的 ...zhōng de □ in 9 cases out of 10 十次中的九次 shícìzhōngde jiǔcì □ one out of every three smokers 每三个烟民中的一个 měi sāngè yānmín zhōng de yígè
■ **3 km out of town** 市中心三公里以外 shìzhōngxīn sāngōnglǐ yǐwài
■ **to be out of petrol** *(without)* 汽油用完了 qìyóu yòng wán le
■ **out of curiosity** 出于好奇 chūyú hàoqí
■ **out of work** 不工作 bùgōngzuò
■ **That is out of the question.** 那是不可能的。Nà shì bùkěnéngde.
■ **'way out'** "出口" "chūkǒu"

out ADJECTIVE
▷ *see also* **out** ADVERB
■ **to be out** 1 *(out of game)* 出局的 chūjú de □ You're out! 你出局了！Nǐ chūjúle! 2 *(fire, light, gas)* 熄灭的 xīmiè de □ All the lights are out. 所有的灯都熄灭了。Suǒyǒudedēng dōu xīmièle.

outbreak NOUN
爆发 bàofā [次 cì] *(of disease)*
□ a salmonella outbreak 一次沙门氏菌的爆发 yícì shāménshìjūnde bàofā

outcome NOUN
结果 jiéguǒ
□ What was the outcome of the negotiations? 谈判的结果是什么？Tánpànde jiéguǒ shì shénme?

outdoor ADJECTIVE
1 户外的 hùwài de *(activity)*
□ outdoor activities 户外的活动 hùwàide huódòng
2 露天的 lùtiān de *(swimming pool)*
□ an outdoor swimming pool 一个露天游泳池 yígè lùtiān yóuyǒngchí

outdoors ADVERB
在户外 zài hùwài

outfit NOUN
衣服 yīfú
□ She bought a new outfit for the wedding. 她为婚礼买了一套新衣服。Tā wèi hūnlǐ mǎile yítào xīnyīfú.
■ **a cowboy outfit** 牛仔服 niúzǎifú

outgoing ADJECTIVE
开朗的 kāilǎngde
□ She's very outgoing. 她很开朗。Tā hěn kāilǎng.

outing NOUN
出游 chūyóu [次 cì]
□ to go on an outing 去出游 qù chūyóu

outlet NOUN
1 排放口 páifàngkǒu [个 gè] *(hole, pipe)*
2 电源插座 diànyuán chāzuò [个 gè] *(US: socket)*

outline NOUN
1 轮廓 lúnkuò [个 gè] *(shape)*
□ We could see the outline of the mountain in the mist. 我们在雾中可以看到山的轮廓。Wǒmén zàiwùzhōng kěyǐ kàndào

shānde lúnkuò.

2 概要 gàiyào [篇 piān] *(brief explanation)*
□ This is an outline of the plan. 这是计划的概要。Zhèshì jìhuàde gàiyào.

outlook NOUN

1 态度 tàidù *(attitude)*
□ my outlook on life 我对生活的态度 Wǒ duì shēnghuóde tàidù

2 前景 qiánjǐng *(prospects)*
□ the economic outlook 经济前景 jīngjì qiánjǐng □ The outlook is poor. 前景很差。Qiánjǐng hěnchà.

outrageous ADJECTIVE

1 令人不可容忍的 lìngrén bùkěróngrěnde *(behaviour)*

2 无耻的 wúchǐde *(price)*

outset NOUN

开始 kāishǐ
□ at the outset 在开始 zài kāishǐ

outside NOUN

▷ *see also* **outside** ADJECTIVE, ADVERB, PREPOSITION

1 外面 wàimiàn [个 gè] *(of container)*

2 外表 wàibiǎo [个 gè] *(of building)*

outside ADJECTIVE

▷ *see also* **outside** NOUN, ADVERB, PREPOSITION

外部的 wàibù de *(exterior)*
□ the outside walls 外部的墙 wàibùde qiáng

outside ADVERB

▷ *see also* **outside** NOUN, ADJECTIVE, PREPOSITION

1 在外面 zài wàimiàn *(be, wait)*
□ It's very cold outside. 外面很冷。Wàimiàn hěnlěng.

2 向外面 xiàng wàimiàn *(go)*

outside PREPOSITION

▷ *see also* **outside** NOUN, ADJECTIVE, ADVERB

1 在...外 zài...wài *(place)*
□ outside the school 在学校外 zàixuéxiàowài

2 在...以外 zài...yǐwài *(organization)*

3 在...附近 zài...fùjìn *(larger place)*
□ outside London 在伦敦附近 zài Lúndūn fùjìn

4 以外 yǐwài *(time)*
□ outside school hours 上学外的时间 shàngxuéwàide shíjiān

outsize ADJECTIVE

特大的 tèdàde

outskirts PL NOUN

■ **the outskirts** 郊区 jiāoqū
■ **on the outskirts of...** 在…的郊区 zài...de jiāoqū

outstanding ADJECTIVE

杰出的 jiéchū de

oval ADJECTIVE

椭圆形的 tuǒyuánxíng de

oven NOUN

烤箱 kǎoxiāng [个 gè]

DID YOU KNOW...?
Though not a traditional feature of a Chinese kitchen, ovens are being increasingly adopted in more cosmopolitan areas such as Shanghai.

over ADJECTIVE

▷ *see also* **over** PREPOSITION, ADVERB

结束的 jiéshù de *(finished)*
□ I'll be happy when the exams are over. 考试结束后我会很高兴。Kǎoshì jiéshùhòu wǒ huì hěn gāoxìng.

over PREPOSITION

▷ *see also* **over** ADJECTIVE, ADVERB

1 超过 chāoguò *(more than)*
□ The temperature was over thirty degrees. 温度超过了三十度。Wēndù chāoguòle sānshídù. □ Over 200 people came. 超过二百人来了。Chāoguò èrbǎirén láile.

2 在...上 zài...shang *(above, on top of)*
□ There's a mirror over the washbasin. 脸盆上有一块镜子。Liǎnpénshàng yǒu yíkuài jìngzi.

3 横跨 héngkuà *(spanning)*
□ a bridge over the river 横跨河流的一座桥 héngkuà héliú de yízuò qiáo

4 越过 yuèguò *(across)*
□ The ball went over the wall. 球越过了墙。Qiú yuèguòle qiáng.

5 在...对面 zài...duìmiàn *(on the other side of)*
□ The baker's is over the road. 面包店在路对面。Miànbāodiàn zài lùduìmiàn.

6 在...期间 zài...qījiān *(during)*
□ over the holidays 在假期 zàijiàqī □ We talked about it over dinner. 我们边吃晚饭边讨论。Wǒmen biān chī wǎnfàn biān tǎolùn.

7 康复 kāngfù *(illness, shock, trauma)*
□ I'm glad that you're over the flu. 我很高兴你流感康复了。Wǒ hěn gāoxìng nǐ liúgǎn kāngfùle.
■ **all over the floor** 满地 mǎndì □ all over Scotland 全苏格兰 quán sūgélán
■ **I spilled coffee over my shirt.** 我把咖啡撒了满衬衫都是。Wǒ bǎ kāfēi sǎle mǎnchènshān dōushì.
■ **over here** 在这里 zài zhèlǐ
■ **over there** 那里 nàlǐ

over ADVERB

▷ *see also* **over** ADJECTIVE, PREPOSITION

1 过 guò *(walk, jump, fly)*

2 超过 chāoguò *(more, above)*
■ **people aged 65 and over** 65岁及以上年

龄的人 liùshíwǔ suì jí yǐshàng niánlíng de rén

3 再 zài *(US: again)*

■ **all over** *(everywhere)* 到处 dàochù

overall ADVERB

整体 zhěngtǐ *(generally)*

□ My results were quite good overall. 我的结果整体很好。Wǒde jiéguǒ zhěngtǐ hěnhǎo.

overcast ADJECTIVE

多云的 duōyún de

□ The sky was overcast. 天空多云。Tiānkōng duōyún.

to **overcharge** VERB

讨价过高 tǎojià guògāo

■ **They overcharged us for the meal.** 这顿饭他们向我们讨价过高。Zhèdùnfàn tāmén xiàng wǒmén tǎojià guògāo.

overcoat NOUN

外套大衣 wàitàodàyī

overdone ADJECTIVE

煮得过久的 zhǔde guòjiǔde *(food)*

overdose NOUN

用药过量 yòngyào guòliàng [剂 jì]

□ to take an overdose 过量用药 guòliàng yòngyào

overdraft NOUN

透支 tòuzhī

■ **to have an overdraft** 有透支 yǒu tòuzhī

to **overestimate** VERB

估计过高 gūjì guògāo

overhead projector NOUN

投影仪 tóuyǐngyí

to **overlook** VERB

1 眺望 tiàowàng *(have view of)*

□ The hotel overlooked the beach. 酒店可以眺望海滩。Jiǔdiàn kěyǐ tiàowàng hǎitān.

2 忽略 hūlüè *(forget about)*

□ He had overlooked one important problem. 他忽略了一个重要的问题。Tā hūlüèle yígè zhòngyàode wèntí.

overseas ADVERB

向海外 xiàng hǎiwài

□ I'd like to work overseas. 我想在海外工作。Wǒ xiǎngzài hǎiwài gōngzuò.

to **oversleep** VERB

睡过头了 shuìguòtóule

□ I overslept this morning. 今天早上我睡过头了。Jīntiān zǎoshàng wǒ shuìguòtóule.

to **overtake** VERB

1 超过 chāoguò *(with vehicle as object)*

2 超车 chāochē *(with driver, vehicle as subject)*

overtime NOUN

加班时间 jiābān shíjiān

■ **to work overtime** 加班工作 jiābān gōngzuò

overtook VERB ▷ *see* **overtake**

overweight ADJECTIVE

超重的 chāozhòng de

to **owe** VERB

欠 qiàn *(money)*

■ **to owe somebody something** 欠某人某物 qiàn mǒurén mǒuwù □ I owe you 50 euros. 我欠你五十欧元。Wǒ qiàn nǐ wǔshí ōuyuán.

owing to PREPOSITION

因为 yīnwèi *(because of)*

□ owing to bad weather 因为天气不好 yīnwéi tiānqì bùhǎo

owl NOUN

猫头鹰 māotóuyīng [只 zhī]

own ADJECTIVE

▷ *see also* **own** VERB

自己的 zìjǐ de

□ I've got my own bathroom. 我有自己的洗手间。Wǒ yǒu zìjǐde xǐshǒujiān.

■ **a room of my own** 我自己的房间 wǒ zìjǐ de fángjiān

■ **on one's own** **1** *(alone)* 独自地 dúzì de **2** *(without help)* 独立地 dúlì de

to **own** VERB

▷ *see also* **own** ADJECTIVE

拥有 yōngyǒu *(house, land, car)*

to **own up** VERB

坦白 tǎnbái *(confess)*

■ **to own up to something** 对某事坦白 duìmǒushì tǎnbái

owner NOUN

物主 wùzhǔ [位 wèi]

oxygen NOUN

氧气 yǎngqì

oyster NOUN

牡蛎 mǔlì [个 gè]

ozone layer NOUN

臭氧层 chòuyǎngcéng [层 céng]

Pp

PA NOUN
私人助理 sīrénzhùlǐ *(personal assistant)*
□ She's a PA. 她是位私人助理。Tā shì wèi sīrénzhùlǐ.
■ **the PA system** *(public address)* 有线广播系统 yǒuxiànguǎngbō xìtǒng

pace NOUN
速度 sùdù *(speed)*
□ He was walking at a brisk pace. 他以轻快的速度走着。Tā yǐ qīngkuàide sùdù zǒuzhe.

Pacific NOUN
■ **the Pacific** 太平洋 Tàipíngyáng

pacifier NOUN (US)
抚慰者 fǔwèizhě [个 gè]

pack NOUN
▹ *see also* **pack** VERB
1 包 bāo *(of cigarettes)*
2 盒 hé *(of yoghurts, cans)*
3 副 fù *(of cards)*

to **pack** VERB
▹ *see also* **pack** NOUN
1 把...打包 bǎ...dǎbāo *(clothes)*
2 把...装箱 bǎ...zhuāngxiāng *(suitcase, bag)*
□ I've already packed my case. 我已经把行李装箱了。Wǒ yǐjīng bǎ xíngli zhuāngxiāng le.
3 打点行装 dǎdiǎn xíngzhuāng *(do one's packing)*
□ I'll help you pack. 我会帮你打点行装。Wǒ huì bāngnǐ dǎdiǎn xíngzhuāng.

to **pack up** VERB
打点行装 dǎdiǎn xíngzhuāng

package NOUN
1 包裹 bāoguǒ [个 gè] *(parcel)*
2 跟团旅游 gēntuán lǚyóu [个 gè] *(computer package)*
■ **a package holiday** 跟团度假 gēntuándùjià

packed ADJECTIVE
拥挤的 yōngjǐ de
□ The cinema was packed. 电影院很拥挤。Diànyǐngyuàn hěn yōngjǐ.

packed lunch NOUN
盒装午餐 hézhuāng wǔcān
□ I take a packed lunch to school. 我带盒装午餐到学校。Wǒ dài hézhuāng wǔcān dào xuéxiào.

packet NOUN
1 盒 hé *(of cigarettes, biscuits)*
2 袋 dài *(of crisps, sweets, seeds)*

pad NOUN
便笺簿 biànjiānbù [个 gè]

paddle NOUN
▹ *see also* **paddle** VERB
1 短桨 duǎnjiǎng [个 gè] *(for canoe)*
2 球拍 qiúpāi [只 zhī] *(US: for table tennis)*
■ **to go for a paddle** 去游泳 qù yóuyǒng

to **paddle** VERB
▹ *see also* **paddle** NOUN
1 划桨 huájiǎng *(canoe)*
2 戏水 xìshuǐ *(in water)*

padlock NOUN
挂锁 guàsuǒ [个 gè]

paedophile NOUN
恋童癖者 liàntóngpìzhě [个 gè]

page NOUN
▹ *see also* **page** VERB
页 yè

to **page** VERB
▹ *see also* **page** NOUN
■ **to page somebody** 传呼某人 chuánhūmǒurén

pager NOUN
传呼机 chuánhūjī [个 gè]

paid VERB ▹ *see* **pay**

paid ADJECTIVE
带薪的 dàixīnde *(work)*
□ 3 weeks' paid holiday 三周带薪假期 sānzhōu dàixīnjiàqī

pain NOUN
疼痛 téngtòng [阵 zhèn]
□ a terrible pain 一阵强烈的疼痛 yízhèn qiángliède téngtòng
■ **to have a pain in one's chest** 胸部疼痛 xiōngbù téngtòng
■ **to be in pain** 痛苦 tòngkǔ □ She's in a lot of pain. 她很痛苦。Tā hěn tòngkǔ.
■ **He's a real pain.** 他很讨厌。Tā hěn tǎoyàn.

painful ADJECTIVE
疼痛的 téngtòng de *(back, joint, swelling)*
□ Is it painful? 很疼吗？ Hěn téng ma?
painkiller NOUN
止痛药 zhǐtòngyào [片 piàn]
paint NOUN
▷ *see also* **paint** VERB
1 油漆 yóuqī [桶 tǒng] *(decorator's)*
2 颜料 yánliào [罐 guàn] *(artist's)*
□ a tin of paint 一罐颜料 yīguàn yánliào
to **paint** VERB
▷ *see also* **paint** NOUN
1 粉刷 fěnshuā *(wall, door, house)*
■ **to paint something white** 把某物粉刷成白色 bǎ mǒuwù fěnshuāchéng báisè
2 描绘 miáohuì *(person, object)*
3 用颜料画 yòng yánliào huà *(picture, portrait)*
4 绘画 huìhuà *(be an artist)*

DID YOU KNOW...?
Today, painting in the traditional Chinese style is known as 国画 guóhuà, literally **national painting**.

paintbrush NOUN
1 漆刷 qīshuā [个 gè] *(decorator's)*
2 画笔 huàbǐ [支 zhī] *(artist's)*
painter NOUN
1 画家 huàjiā [位 wèi] *(artist)*
2 油漆工 yóuqīgōng [个 gè] *(decorator)*
painting NOUN
1 绘画 huìhuà *(artistic)*
□ My hobby is painting. 我的爱好是绘画。 Wǒde àihào shì huìhuà.
2 上油漆 shàng yóuqī *(decorating walls, doors)*
3 画 huà [幅 fú] *(picture)*
□ a painting by Picasso 毕加索的一幅画 bìjiāsuǒde yífùhuà
pair NOUN
1 双 shuāng *(of shoes, gloves, socks)*
2 对 duì *(two people)*
■ **in pairs** 成对 chéngduì □ We work in pairs. 我们成对地工作。 Wǒmen chéngduìde gōngzuò.
3 条 tiáo *(of trousers, jeans)*
4 把 bǎ *(of scissors)*
pajamas PL NOUN (US)
睡衣裤 shuìyīkù
■ **a pair of pajamas** 一套睡衣裤 yìtiáo shuìyīkù
■ **a pajama top** 一件睡衣 yíjiàn shuìyī
Pakistan NOUN
巴基斯坦 Bājīsītǎn
□ He's from Pakistan. 他来自巴基斯坦。 Tā láizì Bājīsītǎn.
Pakistani ADJECTIVE
▷ *see also* **Pakistani** NOUN
巴基斯坦的 Bājīsītǎn de
Pakistani NOUN
▷ *see also* **Pakistani** ADJECTIVE
巴基斯坦人 Bājīsītǎn rén [个 gè]
pal NOUN
朋友 péngyǒu [个 gè]
palace NOUN
宫殿 gōngdiàn [座 zuò]
pale ADJECTIVE
1 淡的 dàn de *(colour)*
□ pale blue 淡蓝色 dànlánsè □ a pale blue shirt 一件淡蓝色的衬衫 yíjiàn dànlánsè de chènshān
2 白皙的 báixī de *(skin, complexion)*
3 苍白的 cāngbái de *(from sickness, fear)*
Palestine NOUN
巴勒斯坦 Bālèsītǎn
Palestinian ADJECTIVE
▷ *see also* **Palestinian** NOUN
巴勒斯坦的 Bālèsītǎn de
Palestinian NOUN
▷ *see also* **Palestinian** ADJECTIVE
巴勒斯坦人 Bālèsītǎn rén [个 gè]
palm NOUN
手掌 shǒuzhǎng *(of hand)*
■ **a palm tree** 一棵棕榈树 yìkē zōnglǘshù
pan NOUN
炖锅 dùnguō [口 kǒu] *(saucepan)*
pancake NOUN
薄煎饼 báo jiānbing [张 zhāng]
■ **Pancake Day** 煎饼节 jiānbǐngjié
panda NOUN
熊猫 xióngmāo [只 zhī]
panic NOUN
▷ *see also* **panic** VERB
惊恐 jīngkǒng
to **panic** VERB
▷ *see also* **panic** NOUN
惊慌 jīnghuāng
□ Don't panic! 不要惊慌！ Búyào jīnghuāng!
panther NOUN
黑豹 hēibào [只 zhī]
panties PL NOUN
短衬裤 duǎnchènkù
pants PL NOUN
1 一条内裤 yìtiáo nèikù *(underwear)*
2 一条裤子 yìtiáo kùzi (US: *trousers*)
■ **a pair of pants 1** *(underwear)* 一条内裤 yìtiáo nèikù **2** (US: *trousers*) 一条裤子 yìtiáo kùzi
pantyhose PL NOUN (US)
连裤袜 liánkùwà
■ **a pair of pantyhose** 一条连裤袜 yìtiáo liánkùwà

paper NOUN
1 纸 zhǐ
□ a piece of paper 一张纸 yìzhāng zhǐ
■ **a paper towel** 一张纸巾 yìzhāng zhǐjīn
2 报纸 bàozhǐ [份 fèn] *(newspaper)*
□ I saw an advert in the paper. 我看到报纸上的一个广告。Wǒ kàndào bàozhǐshàngde yígè guǎnggào.
■ **an exam paper** 一份试卷 yífèn shìjuàn

paperback NOUN
平装书 píngzhuāng shū [本 běn]

paper boy NOUN
送报男孩 sòngbào nánhái [个 gè]

paper clip NOUN
回形针 huíxíngzhēn [枚 méi]

paper girl NOUN
送报女孩 sòngbào nǚhái [个 gè]

paperwork NOUN
文书工作 wénshūgōngzuò
□ He had a lot of paperwork to do. 他有很多文书工作要做。Tā yǒu hěnduō wénshūgōngzuò yàozuò.

parachute NOUN
降落伞 jiàngluòsǎn [个 gè]

parade NOUN
游行 yóuxíng [次 cì]

paradise NOUN
1 天堂 tiāntáng *(heaven)*
2 乐园 lèyuán [个 gè] *(lovely place)*

paragraph NOUN
段落 duànluò [个 gè]

parallel ADJECTIVE
1 平行的 píngxíng de *(line)*
2 并行的 bìngxíng de *(processing)*

paralysed (US **paralyzed**) ADJECTIVE
瘫痪的 tānhuàn de

paramedic NOUN
护理人员 hùlǐ rényuán [位 wèi]

parcel NOUN
包裹 bāoguǒ [个 gè]

pardon NOUN
■ **Pardon me?** (US) 请问您刚才说什么？Qǐngwèn nín gāngcái shuō shénme?
■ **Pardon?** 能再说一遍吗？Néng zài shuō yíbiàn ma?

parent NOUN
1 父亲 fùqīn [位 wèi] *(father)*
2 母亲 mǔqīn [位 wèi] *(mother)*

parents PL NOUN
父母 fùmǔ
■ **my parents** 我的父母 wǒde fùmǔ

Paris NOUN
巴黎 Bālí

park NOUN
▷ *see also* **park** VERB
公园 gōngyuán [个 gè]
■ **a national park** 一个国家公园 yígè guójiā gōngyuán
■ **a theme park** 一个主题公园 yígè zhǔtí gōngyuán
■ **a car park** 一个停车场 yígè tíngchē chǎng

to **park** VERB
▷ *see also* **park** NOUN
1 停放 tíngfàng
□ Where can I park my car? 我能在哪儿停放我的车？Wǒ néng zài nǎr tíngfàng wǒde chē?
2 停车 tíngchē
□ We couldn't find anywhere to park. 我们找不到地方停车。Wǒmen zhǎobúdào dìfāng tíngchē.

parking NOUN
停车 tíngchē
■ **'no parking'** “严禁停车” “yánjìn tíngchē”

parking lot NOUN (US)
停车场 tíngchēchǎng [个 gè]

parking meter NOUN
停车计时器 tíngchē jìshíqì [个 gè]

parking ticket NOUN
违章停车罚款单 wéizhāng tíngchē fákuǎndān [张 zhāng]

parliament NOUN
议会 yìhuì [个 gè]

parrot NOUN
鹦鹉 yīngwǔ [只 zhī]

parsley NOUN
欧芹 ōuqín

part NOUN
1 部分 bùfen [个 gè] *(section, division)*
□ The first part of the film was boring. 电影的第一部分很无聊。Diànyǐngde dìyī bùfèn hěn wúliáo.
2 部件 bùjiàn [个 gè] *(component)*
□ spare parts 备用部件 bèiyòngbùjiàn
3 角色 juésè [个 gè] *(in play, film)*
■ **to take part in** *(participate in)* 参加 cānjiā □ A lot of people took part in the demonstration. 很多人参加示威。Hěn duō rén cānjiā shìwēi.

to **part with** VERB
1 放弃 fàngqì *(possessions)*
2 花 huā *(money, cash)*

to **participate** VERB
参与 cānyù
■ **to participate in something** *(activity, discussion)* 参与某事 cānyù mǒushì

particular ADJECTIVE
特别的 tèbié de
□ Are you looking for anything particular? 你要找什么特别的东西吗？Nǐ yàozhǎo

shénme tèbiéde dōngxi ma?

■ **nothing in particular** 没什么特别的 méishénme tèbiéde

particularly ADVERB
特别地 tèbié de

parting NOUN
分缝 fēnfèng *(in hair)*

partly ADVERB
部分地 bùfe de

partner NOUN
1 伴侣 bànlǚ [个 gè] *(wife, husband, girlfriend, boyfriend)*
2 合伙人 héhuǒrén [个 gè] *(in firm)*
3 搭档 dādàng [个 gè] *(in sport)*
4 对家 duìjiā [个 gè] *(for cards, games)*
5 舞伴 wǔbàn [个 gè] *(at dance)*

part-time ADJECTIVE
▷ *see also* **part-time** ADVERB
兼职的 jiānzhí de
□ a part-time job 一份兼职的工作 yífèn jiānzhí de gōngzuò

part-time ADVERB
▷ *see also* **part-time** ADJECTIVE
兼职地 jiānzhí de *(work, study)*
□ She works part-time. 她兼职地工作。Tā jiānzhí de gōngzuò.

party NOUN
1 党 dǎng [个 gè] *(political)*
□ the Conservative Party 保守党 bǎoshǒudǎng
2 聚会 jùhuì [次 cì] *(social event)*
□ a birthday party 生日聚会 shēngrì jùhuì
□ a Christmas party 圣诞聚会 shèngdàn jùhuì □ a New Year party 新年聚会 xīnnián jùhuì
3 群 qún *(group)*
□ a party of tourists 一群游客 yìqún yóukè

pass NOUN
▷ *see also* **pass** VERB
传球 chuánqiú *(in football)*
■ **a bus pass** 公共汽车月票 gōnggòngqìchē yuèpiào

to **pass** VERB
▷ *see also* **pass** NOUN
1 经过 jīngguò *(go past)*
□ I pass his house on my way to school. 在上学的路上我经过他家。Zài shàngxuéde lùshàng wǒ jīngguò tājiā.
2 通过 tōngguò *(exam, test)*
□ I hope I'll pass the exam. 我希望可以通过考试。Wǒ xīwàng kěyǐ tōngguò kǎoshì.
3 及格 jígé *(be successful in exam)*
□ Did you pass? 你及格了吗？Nǐ jígé le ma?
4 过去 guòqù *(go by)*
□ The time has passed quickly. 时间过得很快。Shíjiān guòde hěnkuài.
■ **to pass somebody something** *(hand)* 把某物递给某人 bǎ mǒuwù dìgěi mǒurén
□ Could you pass me the salt, please? 请你把盐递给我好吗？Qǐng nǐ bǎ yán dìgěi wǒ hǎoma?

to **pass away** VERB
去世 qùshì *(die)*

to **pass out** VERB
昏倒 hūndǎo *(faint)*

passage NOUN
1 走廊 zǒuláng [条 tiáo] *(corridor)*
2 段落 duànluò [个 gè]
□ Read the passage carefully. 仔细阅读这个段落。Zǐxì yuèdú zhègè duànluò.

passenger NOUN
乘客 chéngkè [位 wèi]

passion NOUN
热情 rèqíng

passive NOUN
▷ *see also* **passive** ADJECTIVE
■ **the passive** 被动语态 bèidòng yǔtài

passive ADJECTIVE
▷ *see also* **passive** NOUN
被动的 bèidòngde
■ **passive smoking** 被动吸烟 bèidòngxīyān

Passover NOUN
逾越节 yúyuèjié

passport NOUN
护照 hùzhào [本 běn]
□ passport control 护照管制 hùzhào guǎnzhì

password NOUN
密码 mìmǎ [个 gè]

past PREPOSITION
▷ *see also* **past** ADVERB, ADJECTIVE, NOUN
过 guò *(in front of, beyond, later than)*
□ It's on the right, just past the station. 它在右边，刚过火车站。Tā zàiyòubiān, gāngguò huǒchēzhàn.
■ **to go past something** 经过某物 jīngguò mǒuwù □ The bus goes past our house. 公共汽车经过我们家。Gōnggòngqìchē jīngguò wǒmenjiā.
■ **ten past eight** 八点十分 bādiǎnshífēn
■ **quarter past eight** 八点十五分 bādiǎnshíwǔfēn
■ **It's half past ten.** 现在十点半。Xiànzài shídiǎnbàn.
■ **It's past midnight.** 过了午夜。Guòle wǔyè.

past ADVERB
▷ *see also* **past** PREPOSITION, ADJECTIVE, NOUN
■ **to go past** 经过 jīngguò □ The bus went past without stopping. 公共汽车经过没

停。Gōnggòngqìchē jīngguò méitíng.

past ADJECTIVE

▷ *see also* **past** PREPOSITION, ADVERB, NOUN

刚过去的 gāng guòqù de *(week, month, year)*

□ for the past few days 刚过去的几天 gāng guòqù de jǐtiān

■ **the past tense** 过去时 guòqù shí

past NOUN

▷ *see also* **past** PREPOSITION, ADVERB, ADJECTIVE

■ **the past** **1** 过去 guòqù □ She lives in the past. 她生活在过去。Tā shēnghuózài guòqù. **2** *(tense)* 过去时 guòqùshí

■ **in the past** *(previously)* 在过去 zài guòqù

□ This was common in the past. 这在过去很常见。Zhè zàiguòqù hěnchángjiàn.

pasta NOUN

意大利面 Yìdàlìmiàn

□ Pasta is easy to cook. 意大利面很容易做。Yìdàlìmiàn hěn róngyì zuò.

paste NOUN

浆糊 jiànghú *(glue)*

pasteurized ADJECTIVE

灭菌的 mièjūnde

pastime NOUN

消遣方式 xiāoqiǎnfāngshì

□ Her favourite pastime is knitting. 她最喜欢的消遣方式是织毛衣。Tā zuì xǐhuān de xiāoqiǎn fāngshì shì zhīmáoyī.

pastry NOUN

1 油酥面团 yóusū miàntuán [块 kuài] *(dough)*

2 酥皮糕点 sūpí gāodiǎn [块 kuài] *(cake)*

■ **pastries** 酥皮糕点 sūpígāodiǎn

patch NOUN

1 补丁 bǔdīng [个 gè] *(piece of material)*

□ a patch of material 一个补丁 yígè bǔdīng

2 斑片 bānpiàn [块 kuài] *(area)*

pâté NOUN

浆泥 jiāngní

path NOUN

1 小路 xiǎolù [条 tiáo] *(track)*

2 小径 xiǎojìng [条 tiáo] *(in garden)*

pathetic ADJECTIVE

可悲的 kěbēi de *(excuse, effort, attempt)*

□ Our team was pathetic. 我们队很可悲。Wǒmen duì hěn kěbēi.

patience NOUN

耐心 nàixīn

□ He hasn't got much patience. 他没有很多耐心。Tā méiyǒu hěnduō nàixīn.

patient NOUN

▷ *see also* **patient** ADJECTIVE

病人 bìngrén [个 gè] *(invalid)*

patient ADJECTIVE

▷ *see also* **patient** NOUN

耐心的 nàixīn de

patio NOUN

院子 yuànzi [个 gè]

patriotic ADJECTIVE

爱国的 àiguó de

to **patrol** VERB

▷ *see also* **patrol** NOUN

在...巡逻 zài...xúnluó

patrol NOUN

▷ *see also* **patrol** VERB

巡逻 xúnluó

■ **to be on patrol** 在巡逻中 zài xúnluó zhōng

patrol car NOUN

巡逻车 xúnluóchē [辆 liàng]

pattern NOUN

1 图案 tú'àn [种 zhǒng] *(on material, carpet)*

□ a geometric pattern 一种几何图案 yìzhǒng jǐhé tú'àn

2 样式 yàngshì [种 zhǒng] *(for sewing, knitting)*

■ **a sewing pattern** 缝纫样式 féngrèn yàngshì

to **pause** VERB

▷ *see also* **pause** NOUN

1 停顿 tíngdùn *(when speaking)*

2 暂停 zàntíng *(when doing something)*

pause NOUN

▷ *see also* **pause** VERB

停顿 tíngdùn

pavement NOUN

人行道 rénxíngdào [条 tiáo]

paw NOUN

爪子 zhuǎzi [只 zhī]

pay NOUN

▷ *see also* **pay** VERB

工资 gōngzī [笔 bǐ]

to **pay** VERB

▷ *see also* **pay** NOUN

付 fù *(debt, bill, tax)*

■ **to get paid** *(person)* 领工资 lǐng gōngzī

■ **to pay somebody something** *(as wage, salary, for goods, services)* 付给某人某物 fùgěi mǒurén mǒuwù □ They pay me more on Sundays. 星期天他们付给我的钱更多。Xīngqītiān tāmén fùgěi wǒdeqián gèngduō.

■ **to pay by credit card** 用信用卡付钱 yòng xìnyòngkǎ fùqián

■ **to pay for something** 买某物 mǎi mǒuwù □ I paid for my ticket. 我的票是我买的。Wǒde piào shì wǒmǎide. □ How much did you pay for it? 你买那个花了多少钱? Nǐ mǎi nàgè huāle duōshǎo qián? □ I paid 50 pounds for it. 我买那个花了五十镑。Wǒ mǎi nàgè huāle wǔshíbàng.

■ **to pay extra for something** 另外付钱买某物 lìngwài fùqián mǎi mǒuwù ◻ You have to pay extra for breakfast. 你得另外付钱买早餐。Nǐ děi lìngwài fùqián mǎi zǎocān.

■ **to pay attention** 注意 zhùyì ◻ Don't pay any attention to him! 不要理他！ Búyào lǐ tā.

■ **to pay somebody a visit** 拜访某人 bàifǎng mǒurén ◻ Paul paid us a visit last night. 保罗昨晚来拜访我们。Bǎoluó zuówǎn lái bàifǎng wǒmen.

to **pay back** VERB

1 偿还 chánghuán *(money, loan)*

2 报复 bàofù *(person)*

◻ I'll pay you back tomorrow. 明天我会报复你的。Míngtiān wǒ huì bàofù nǐ de.

payment NOUN

付款额 fùkuǎn é [笔 bǐ]

payphone NOUN

公用电话 gōngyòng diànhuà [部 bù]

PC NOUN *(= personal computer)*

个人电脑 gèrén diànnǎo [台 tái]

◻ She typed the report on her PC. 她用个人电脑写的这份报告。Tā yòng gèrén diànnǎo xiěde zhèfèn bàogào.

■ **a PC game** 电脑游戏 diànnǎo yóuxì

PDA NOUN *(= personal digital assistant)*

掌上电脑 zhǎngshàng diànnǎo [台 tái]

PE NOUN *(= physical education)*

体育课 tǐyùkè [节 jié]

◻ We do PE twice a week. 我们一周上两次体育课。Wǒmén yìzhōu shàng liǎngcì tǐyùkè.

pea NOUN

豌豆 wāndòu [粒 lì]

peace NOUN

1 和平 hépíng *(not war)*

2 宁静 níngjìng *(of place, surroundings)*

peaceful ADJECTIVE

1 安静的 ānjìng de

◻ a peaceful afternoon 一个安静的下午 yígè ānjìngde xiàwǔ

2 和平的 hépíng de *(not violent)*

◻ a peaceful protest 一次和平抗议 yícì hépíng kàngyì

peach NOUN

桃 táo [个 gè]

> **DID YOU KNOW...?**
> In Chinese culture the peach is symbolic of long life.

peacock NOUN

孔雀 kǒngquè [只 zhī]

peak NOUN

▷ *see also* **peak** ADJECTIVE

山顶 shāndǐng [个 gè]

peak ADJECTIVE

▷ *see also* **peak** NOUN

最高 zuìgāo de *(level, times)*

■ **the peak rate** 最高价格 zuìgāo jiàgé

◻ You pay the peak rate for calls at this time of day. 在这个时间打电话要付最高价格。Zài zhège shíjiān dǎdiànhuà yàofù zuìgāo jiàgé.

■ **in peak season** 旺季 wàngjì

peanut NOUN

花生 huāshēng [粒 lì]

◻ a packet of peanuts 一包花生 yìbāo huāshēng

peanut butter NOUN

花生酱 huāshēngjiàng [瓶 píng]

◻ a peanut-butter sandwich 一个花生酱三明治 yígè huāshēngjiàng sānmíngzhì

pear NOUN

梨 lí [个 gè]

pearl NOUN

珍珠 zhēnzhū [颗 kē]

pebble NOUN

卵石 luǎnshí [块 kuài]

◻ a pebble beach 一片卵石海滩 yípiàn luǎnshí hǎitān

peculiar ADJECTIVE

奇怪的 qíguài de

◻ He's a peculiar person. 他是个奇怪的人。Tā shì gè qíguàide rén.

pedal NOUN

1 脚蹬子 jiǎodēngzi [个 gè] *(on bicycle)*

2 踏板 tàbǎn [个 gè] *(in car, on piano)*

pedestrian NOUN

行人 xíngrén [个 gè]

pedestrian crossing NOUN

人行横道 rénxíng héngdào [条 tiáo]

pedigree ADJECTIVE

纯种的 chúnzhǒng de *(animal)*

◻ a pedigree dog 一只纯种狗 yìzhī chúnzhǒng gǒu

pedophile NOUN (US)

恋童癖者 liàntóngpìzhě [个 gè]

to **pee** VERB

撒尿 sāniào

peek NOUN

■ **to have a peek at something** 偷看 tōukàn

■ **No peeking!** 不许偷看！ Bùxǔ tōukàn!

peel NOUN

▷ *see also* **peel** VERB

皮 pí

to **peel** VERB

▷ *see also* **peel** NOUN

1 削 xiāo *(vegetables, fruit)*

◻ Shall I peel the potatoes? 要我削土豆吗？ Yào wǒ xiāo tǔdòu ma?

2 蜕皮 tuìpí
□ My nose is peeling. 我鼻子在蜕皮。Wǒ bízi zài tuìpí.

peg NOUN
1 挂钉 guàdīng [枚 méi] *(for coat, hat, bag)*
2 衣夹 yījiā [个 gè] *(clothes peg)*

Pekinese NOUN
北京人 Běijīngrén

pelvis NOUN
骨盆 gǔpén

pen NOUN
1 笔 bǐ [支 zhī]
2 自来水笔 zìláishuǐbǐ [支 zhī] *(fountain pen)*
3 圆珠笔 yuánzhūbǐ [支 zhī] *(ballpoint pen)*

penalty NOUN
1 处罚 chǔfá [次 cì]
■ **the death penalty** 死刑处罚 sǐxíng chǔfá
2 罚球 fáqiú [个 gè] *(in football, rugby)*
■ **penalty shoot-out** 罚点球决胜 fádiǎnqiú juéshèng

pence PL NOUN
便士 biànshì

pencil NOUN
铅笔 qiānbǐ [支 zhī]
□ in pencil 用铅笔 yòngqiānbǐ

pencil case NOUN
铅笔盒 qiānbǐhé [个 gè]

pencil sharpener NOUN
铅笔刀 qiānbǐdāo [把 bǎ]

pendant NOUN
垂饰 chuíshì

penfriend NOUN
笔友 bǐyǒu [个 gè]

penguin NOUN
企鹅 qǐ'é [只 zhī]

penicillin NOUN
青霉素 qīngméisù

penis NOUN
阴茎 yīnjīng

penitentiary NOUN (US)
教养所 jiàoyǎngsuǒ [个 gè]

penknife NOUN
小刀 xiǎodāo [把 bǎ]

penny NOUN
便士 biànshì [枚 méi]

pension NOUN
1 养老金 yǎnglǎojīn [笔 bǐ] *(from state)*
2 退休金 tuìxiūjīn [笔 bǐ] *(from employer)*

pensioner NOUN
领养老金的人 lǐng yǎnglǎojīn de rén [个 gè]

people PL NOUN
1 人 rén
□ The people were nice. 这些人很友善。Zhèxiērén hěn yǒushàn. □ a lot of people 许多人 xǔduō rén □ six people 六个人 liùgè rén □ several people 几个人 jǐgè rén
□ How many people are there in your family? 你家里有几口人？ Nǐ jiālǐ yǒu jǐkǒu rén?
2 人们 rénmen *(generalizing)*
■ **People say that...** 有人说… yǒurén shuō...
■ **old people** 老人 lǎorén
■ **Chinese people** 中国人 Zhōngguórén
■ **black people** 黑人 hēirén

pepper NOUN
1 胡椒 hújiāo *(spice)*
□ Pass the pepper, please. 请把胡椒递给我。Qǐngbǎ hújiāo dìgěi wǒ.
2 青椒 qīngjiāo [个 gè] *(vegetable)*
□ a green pepper 绿青椒 lǜqīngjiāo

peppermill NOUN
胡椒磨 hújiāo mò [个 gè]

peppermint NOUN
薄荷糖 bòhe táng [块 kuài]
■ **peppermint chewing gum** 薄荷味的口香糖 bòhewèide kǒuxiāngtáng

per PREPOSITION
每 měi
□ per day 每天 měitiān □ per person 每人 měirén □ per annum 每年 měinián □ 30 miles per hour 每小时三十英里 měixiǎoshí sānshíyīnglǐ

per cent NOUN
百分之... bǎifēnzhī...
□ by 15 per cent 以百分之十五 yǐ bǎifēnzhī shíwǔ

percentage NOUN
百分比 bǎifēnbǐ

percussion NOUN
打击乐器 dǎjīyuèqì
□ I play percussion. 我玩打击乐器。Wǒ wán dǎjīyuèqì.

perfect ADJECTIVE
▷ *see also* **perfect** NOUN
1 完美的 wánměi de *(weather, behaviour)*
□ Weiqing speaks perfect English. 魏庆可以讲完美的英语。Wèiqīng kěyǐjiǎng wánměide Yīngyǔ.
2 无瑕的 wúxiá de *(sauce, skin, teeth)*
3 理想的 lǐxiǎng de *(crime, solution, example)*

perfect NOUN
▷ *see also* **perfect** ADJECTIVE
■ **the perfect** *(tense)* 完成时 wánchéngshí

perfectly ADVERB
1 非常好地 fēicháng hǎode
2 绝对地 juéduìde *(honest, reasonable, clear)*

to **perform** VERB
1 表演 biǎoyǎn *(role, music)*
2 演出 yǎnchū *(give performance)*

performance NOUN
1 表演 biǎoyǎn [次 cì] *(by actor, musician, singer, dancer)*
□ his performance as Hamlet 他饰演哈姆雷特的表演 tā shìyǎn Hāmǔléitè de biǎoyǎn
2 演出 yǎnchū [场 chǎng] *(of play, show)*
□ The performance lasts two hours. 这场演出持续两个小时。Zhèchǎng yǎnchū chíxù liǎnggè xiǎoshí.
3 表现 biǎoxiàn *(results)*
□ the team's poor performance 团队的糟糕表现 tuánduìde zāogāo biǎoxiàn

perfume NOUN
1 香水 xiāngshuǐ [瓶 píng] *(cosmetic)*
2 芳香 fāngxiāng [种 zhǒng] *(smell)*

perhaps ADVERB
可能 kěnéng
□ a bit boring, perhaps 可能有点无聊 kěnéng yǒudiǎn wúliáo □ Perhaps he's ill. 可能他病了。Kěnéng tābìngle.
■ **perhaps not** 未必 wèibì

period NOUN
1 周期 zhōuqī [个 gè] *(interval, stretch)*
2 时期 shíqī [段 duàn] *(time)*
□ for a limited period 有限的一段时期 yǒuxiànde yíduàn shíqī
3 时代 shídài [个 gè] *(era)*
□ the Victorian period 维多利亚时代 Wéiduōlìyà shídài
4 句号 jùhào [个 gè] (US: *punctuation mark)*
5 例假 lìjià [次 cì] *(menstruation)*
■ **to have one's period** 来例假 lái lìjià
□ I'm having my period. 我来例假了。Wǒ lái lìjià le.
6 课时 kèshí *(lesson time)*
□ Each period lasts forty minutes. 每个课时持续四十分钟。Měigè kèshí chíxù sìshí fēnzhōng.

perm NOUN
烫发 tàngfà
□ She's got a perm. 她烫发了。Tā tàngfà le.

permanent ADJECTIVE
1 持久的 chíjiǔ de
2 永久的 yǒngjiǔ de *(damage)*
3 长期的 chángqī de *(state, job, position)*

permission NOUN
1 许可 xǔkě *(consent)*
□ Could I have permission to leave early? 我能获得许可早退吗？Wǒ néng huòdé xǔkě zǎotuì ma?
2 批准 pīzhǔn *(official authorization)*

permit NOUN
许可证 xǔkězhèng [个 gè] *(authorization)*
□ a fishing permit 一个捕鱼许可证 yígè bǔyú xǔkězhèng

> **DID YOU KNOW...?**
> Most small family restaurants and food stalls in China will have their 卫生许可证 wèishēng xǔkězhèng **hygiene permit** hanging where the customer can see it.

to **persecute** VERB
迫害 pòhài

persistent ADJECTIVE
坚持的 jiānchíde *(person)*

person NOUN
人 rén [个 gè]
□ She's a very nice person. 她是个很好的人。Tā shì gè hěnhǎode rén.
■ **in person** 亲自 qīnzì
■ **first person** 第一人称 dìyī rénchēng

personal ADJECTIVE
1 私人的 sīrén de *(life, matter, phone number)*
■ **personal column** 私人广告栏 sīrén guǎnggàolán
2 个人的 gèrén de *(opinion, habits, appearance)*
3 亲自的 qīnzì de *(care, contact)*

personality NOUN
个性 gèxìng [种 zhǒng]

personally ADVERB
本人 běnrén
□ I don't know him personally. 我不认识他本人。Wǒ búrènshí tā běnrén.
□ Personally I don't agree. 我本人不同意。Wǒ běnrén bùtóngyì.

personal stereo NOUN
随身听 suíshēntīng [个 gè]

personnel NOUN
人事 rénshì

perspiration NOUN
汗 hàn

to **persuade** VERB
■ **to persuade somebody to do something** 劝说某人做某事 quànshuō mǒurén zuò mǒushì □ She persuaded me to go with her. 她劝说我跟她一起去。Tā quànshuō wǒ gēntā yìqǐ qù.

pessimist NOUN
悲观者 bēiguānzhě [个 gè]
□ I'm a pessimist. 我是个悲观者。Wǒ shìgè bēiguānzhě.

pessimistic ADJECTIVE
悲观的 bēiguān de

pest NOUN
害虫 hàichóng [只 zhī] *(insect)*
■ **to be a pest** *(person)* 当个害虫 dāng gè hàichóng □ He's a real pest! 他真是个害虫。Tā zhēn shì gè hàichóng.

to **pester** VERB
烦扰 fánrǎo

pet NOUN
宠物 chǒngwù [只 zhī]
□ Have you got a pet? 你有宠物吗？ Nǐ yǒu chǒngwù ma?
■ **She's the teacher's pet.** 她是老师的宠儿。Tā shì lǎoshīde chǒng'ér.

petition NOUN
请愿 qǐngyuàn

petrol NOUN
汽油 qìyóu [桶 tǒng]
□ unleaded petrol 无铅汽油 wúqiānqìyóu

petrol station NOUN
加油站 jiāyóuzhàn [个 gè]

petrol tank NOUN
油箱 yóuxiāng [个 gè]

phantom NOUN
幽灵 yōulíng [个 gè]

pharmacy NOUN
1 药店 yàodiàn [家 jiā] *(shop)*
2 药学 yàoxué *(science)*

pheasant NOUN
1 野鸡 yějī [只 zhī]

philosophy NOUN
哲学 zhéxué *(subject)*

phobia NOUN
恐惧症 kǒngjùzhèng

phone NOUN
▷ *see also* **phone** VERB
电话 diànhuà [部 bù]
□ Can I use the phone, please? 我可以用电话吗？ Wǒ kěyǐ yòng diànhuà ma?
■ **by phone** 通过电话 tōngguò diànhuà
■ **to be on the phone** 在通话 zài tōnghuà

to **phone** VERB
▷ *see also* **phone** NOUN
1 打电话给 dǎ diànhuà gěi *(person, place)*
□ I'll phone the station. 我会给火车站打电话。Wǒ huìgěi huǒchēzhàn dǎdiànhuà.
2 打电话 dǎ diànhuà *(make phone call)*

to **phone back** VERB
给...回电话 gěi...huí diànhuà

phone bill NOUN
话费单 huàfèi dān [张 zhāng]

phone book NOUN
电话簿 diànhuà bù [本 běn]

phone booth NOUN (US)
电话亭 diànhuà tíng [个 gè]

phone box NOUN
电话亭 diànhuà tíng [个 gè]

phone call NOUN
电话 diànhuà [个 gè]
□ There's a phone call for you. 有你的电话。Yǒu nǐde diànhuà.
■ **to make a phone call** 打电话 dǎ diànhuà □ Can I make a phone call? 我可以打电话吗？ Wǒ kěyǐ dǎdiànhuà ma?

phonecard NOUN
电话卡 diànhuà kǎ [张 zhāng]

phone number NOUN
电话号码 diànhuà hàomǎ [个 gè]

photo NOUN
照片 zhàopiàn [张 zhāng]
■ **to take a photo of somebody** 给某人拍照片 gěi mǒurén pāi zhàopiān

to **photobomb** VERB
意外被拍进照片 yìwài bèi pāi jìn zhàopiàn

photocopier NOUN
影印机 yǐngyìnjī [台 tái]

photocopy NOUN
▷ *see also* **photocopy** VERB
影印本 yǐngyìnběn [个 gè]

to **photocopy** VERB
▷ *see also* **photocopy** NOUN
影印 yǐngyìn *(document, picture)*

photograph NOUN
▷ *see also* **photograph** VERB
照片 zhàopiān [张 zhāng]
■ **to take a photograph** 照张照片 zhàozhāng zhàopiān
■ **to take a photograph of somebody** 给某人照照片 gěimǒurén zhàozhàopiān

to **photograph** VERB
▷ *see also* **photograph** NOUN
照像 zhàoxiàng

photographer NOUN
摄影师 shèyǐngshī [位 wèi]

photography NOUN
摄影 shèyǐng

Photoshop® NOUN
▷ *see also* **Photoshop** VERB
Photoshop图像处理软件 Photoshop túxiàng chǔlǐ ruǎnjiàn

to **Photoshop®** VERB
▷ *see also* **Photoshop** NOUN
用Photoshop进行图像处理 yòng Photoshop jìnxíng túxiàng chǔlǐ

phrase NOUN
1 习语 xíyǔ [个 gè] *(expression)*
2 短语 duǎnyǔ [个 gè] *(in phrase book, dictionary)*

phrase book NOUN
常用词手册 chángyòngcí shǒucè [本 běn]

physical ADJECTIVE
▷ *see also* **physical** NOUN
生理的 shēnglǐ de

physical NOUN (US)
▷ *see also* **physical** ADJECTIVE
体检 tǐjiǎn

physician NOUN (US)
医生 yīshēng [位 wèi]

physicist NOUN
物理学家 wùlǐxué jiā [位 wèi]

physics NOUN
物理学 wùlǐxué

□ She teaches physics. 她教物理。Tā jiāo wùlǐ.

physiotherapist NOUN
理疗师 lǐliáoshī [位 wèi]

physiotherapy NOUN
物理疗法 wùlǐ liáofǎ

pianist NOUN
1 钢琴家 gāngqínjiā [位 wèi] *(professional)*
2 钢琴演奏者 gāngqín yǎnzòuzhě [位 wèi] *(amateur)*

piano NOUN
钢琴 gāngqín [架 jià]
□ I play the piano. 我弹钢琴。Wǒ tán gāngqín. □ I have piano lessons. 我上钢琴课。Wǒ shàng gāngqínkè.

pick NOUN
▷ *see also* **pick** VERB
■ **Take your pick!** 随意挑选！ Suíyì tiāoxuǎn!

to **pick** VERB
▷ *see also* **pick** NOUN
1 选择 xuǎnzé *(choose)*
□ I picked the biggest piece. 我选了最大的一块。Wǒ xuǎnle zuìdàde yíkuài.
□ I've been picked for the team. 我被选进了队里。Wǒ bèi xuǎnjìnle duìlǐ.
2 采摘 cǎizhāi *(fruit, flowers)*

to **pick on** VERB
捉弄 zhuōnòng
□ She's always picking on me. 她总是捉弄我。Tā zǒngshì zhuōnòng wǒ.

to **pick out** VERB
挑中 tiāozhòng *(select: person, thing)*
□ I like them all. It's difficult to pick one out. 我都很喜欢。很难挑中一个。Wǒ dōu hěn xǐhuan. Hěn nán tiāozhòng yígè.

to **pick up** VERB
1 拿起 náqǐ *(take hold of: object)*
2 捡起 jiǎnqǐ *(from floor, ground)*
□ Could you help me pick up the toys? 你能帮我把玩具捡起来吗？ Nǐ néng bāngwǒ bǎ wánjù jiǎnqǐlái ma?
3 接 jiē *(collect: person, parcel)*
□ We'll come to the airport to pick you up. 我们会到机场接你。Wǒmen huìdào jīchǎng jiēnǐ.
4 学 xué *(learn)*
□ I picked up some Chinese during my holiday. 度假时我学了点中文。Dùjiàshí wǒ xuéle diǎn Zhōngwén.

pickpocket NOUN
扒手 páshǒu [个 gè]

picnic NOUN
野餐 yěcān [顿 dùn] *(meal)*
■ **to have a picnic** 野餐 yěcān □ We had a picnic on the beach. 我们在海滩上野餐了。Wǒmen zài hǎitānshàng yěcānle.

picture NOUN
1 画 huà [幅 fú] *(painting, drawing, print)*
□ Children's books have lots of pictures. 儿童书有很多画。Értóngshū yǒu hěnduō huà. □ a famous picture 一幅著名的画 yífù zhùmíngde huà
■ **to paint a picture of something** 画某物 huà mǒuwù
2 照片 zhàopiān [张 zhāng] *(photograph)*
□ My picture was in the paper. 我的照片上了报纸。Wǒde zhàopiān shàngle bàozhǐ.
3 电影 diànyǐng [部 bù] *(film, movie)*
■ **the pictures** *(cinema)* 电影院 diànyǐngyuàn □ Shall we go to the pictures? 我们去看电影吧？ Wǒmen qù kàn diànyǐng ba?

picture messaging NOUN
彩信 cǎixìn

pie NOUN
馅饼 xiànbǐng [个 gè]
□ an apple pie 苹果馅饼 píngguǒ xiànbǐng

piece NOUN
1 碎片 suìpiàn *(fragment)*
2 段 duàn *(of string, ribbon, sticky tape)*
3 块 kuài *(of cake, bread, chocolate)*
□ A small piece, please. 请来一小块。Qǐnglái yíxiǎokuài.
■ **a piece of paper** 一张纸 yìzhāng zhǐ
■ **a 10p piece** 一枚十便士硬币 yìméi shí biànshì yìngbì
■ **a piece of furniture** 一件家具 yíjiàn jiājù
■ **a piece of advice** 一条建议 yìtiáo jiànyì

pierced ADJECTIVE
穿洞的 chuāndòng de *(ears, nose, lip)*
□ I've got pierced ears. 我穿了耳洞。Wǒ chuānle ěrdòng.

piercing NOUN
人体穿孔 réntǐ chuānkǒng [个 gè]
□ She has several piercings. 她有几个人体穿孔。Tā yǒu jǐgè réntǐ chuānkǒng.

pig NOUN
猪 zhū [头 tóu]

pigeon NOUN
鸽子 gēzi [只 zhī]

piggyback NOUN
■ **to give somebody a piggyback** 背某人 bēimǒurén

piggy bank NOUN
猪形储蓄罐 zhūxíng chǔxùguàn [个 gè]

pigtail NOUN
辫子 biànzi [条 tiáo]

pile NOUN
▷ *see also* **pile** VERB
堆 duī
■ **piles of something** 一大堆某物 yídàduī mǒuwù

to **pile** VERB
▷ *see also* **pile** NOUN
堆起 duīqǐ

pill NOUN
药丸 yàowán [粒 lì]
■ **the pill** *(contraceptive pill)* 避孕药 bìyùnyào
■ **to be on the pill** 服避孕药 fú bìyùnyào

pillow NOUN
枕头 zhěntou [个 gè]

pilot NOUN
飞行员 fēixíngyuán [个 gè]
□ He's a pilot. 他是个飞行员。Tā shìge fēixíngyuán.

pimple NOUN
粉刺 fěncì [颗 kē]

PIN NOUN *(= personal identification number)*
密码 mìmǎ [个 gè]
■ **chip and PIN** 芯片和密码 xīnpiàn hé mìmǎ

pin NOUN
▷ *see also* **pin** VERB
1 大头针 dàtóuzhēn [枚 méi] *(used in sewing)*
2 饰针 shìzhēn [枚 méi] *(badge)*
■ **pins and needles** 发麻 fāmá

to **pin** VERB
▷ *see also* **pin** NOUN
钉住 dìngzhù *(on wall, door, board)*

pinball NOUN
弹球戏 tánqiúxì [一台 yìtái]
□ to play pinball 玩弹球戏 wántánqiúxì
■ **a pinball machine** 弹球机 tánqiújī

to **pinch** VERB
1 捏 niē *(person)*
□ He pinched me! 他捏了我。Tā niēle wǒ.
2 偷 tōu *(informal: steal)*
□ Who's pinched my pen? 谁偷了我的笔？Shuí tōule wǒde bǐ?

pine NOUN
1 松树 sōngshù [棵 kē] *(tree)*
2 松木 sōngmù *(wood)*
□ a pine table 松木桌 sōngmùzhuō

DID YOU KNOW...?
Pine trees symbolise longevity in China.

pineapple NOUN
菠萝 bōluó [个 gè]

pink ADJECTIVE
▷ *see also* **pink** NOUN
粉红色的 fěnhóngsè de

pink NOUN
▷ *see also* **pink** ADJECTIVE
粉红色 fěnhóngsè [种 zhǒng]

pint NOUN
品脱 pǐntuō
■ **a pint of milk** 一品脱牛奶 yìpǐntuō niúnǎi
■ **to have a pint** 喝啤酒 hē píjiǔ □ He's gone out for a pint. 他去喝啤酒了。Tā qù hē píjiǔ le.

pipe NOUN
1 管子 guǎnzi [根 gēn] *(for water, gas)*
□ The pipes froze. 管子冻了。Guǎnzi dòngle.
2 烟斗 yāndǒu [个 gè] *(for smoking)*
□ He smokes a pipe. 他吸烟斗。Tā xī yāndǒu.
■ **the pipes** *(bagpipes)* 风笛 fēngdí

pirate NOUN
海盗 hǎidào [个 gè]

pirated ADJECTIVE
盗版的 dàobǎn de
□ a pirated DVD 盗版影碟 dàobǎn yǐngdié

Pisces NOUN
双鱼座 Shuāngyú Zuò *(sign)*
□ I'm Pisces. 我是双鱼座。Wǒ shì Shuāngyúzuò.

pitch NOUN
▷ *see also* **pitch** VERB
球场 qiúchǎng [个 gè] *(field)*
□ a football pitch 足球场 zúqiúchǎng

to **pitch** VERB
▷ *see also* **pitch** NOUN
搭帐篷 dā zhàngpéng *(tent)*
□ We pitched our tent near the beach. 我们在海滩附近搭帐篷。Wǒmen zài hǎitānfùjìn dā zhàngpéng.

pity NOUN
▷ *see also* **pity** VERB
同情 tóngqíng *(compassion)*
■ **It is a pity that...** *(misfortune)* 真遗憾… Zhēn yíhàn...
■ **What a pity!** 真可惜！ Zhēn kěxī!

to **pity** VERB
▷ *see also* **pity** NOUN
同情 tóngqíng *(person)*

pizza NOUN
比萨饼 bǐsàbǐng [个 gè]

place NOUN
▷ *see also* **place** VERB
1 地方 dìfāng [个 gè] *(location)*
□ It's a quiet place. 那是个安静的地方。Nà shìgè ānjìngde dìfāng. □ There are a lot of interesting places to visit. 有很多有趣的地方可以参观。Yǒu hěnduō yǒuqùde dìfāng kěyǐ cānguān.
2 空位 kòngwèi [个 gè] *(space)*
□ a parking place 停车空位 tíngchē kòngwèi
3 座位 zuòwèi [个 gè] *(seat)*
■ **to change places** 换座位 huànzuòwèi
□ Hui, change places with Rong! 慧，跟蓉换座位。Huì,gēn Róng huànzuòwèi.

4 名额 míng'é [个 gè] *(at university, on course, in team)*
◻ a university place 上大学的名额 shàngdàxuéde míng'é

5 名次 míngcì [个 gè] *(in competition)*
■ **some place** (US) 某个地方 mǒugè dìfāng
■ **in places** 有几处 yǒu jǐchù
■ **to take somebody's place** 代替某人 dàitì mǒurén
■ **to take place** *(happen)* 发生 fāshēng
■ **at somebody's place** *(home)* 在某人的家里 zài mǒurén de jiālǐ ◻ Shall we meet at your place? 在你家见面吗？ Zài nǐjiā jiànmiàn ma?
■ **to my place** 来我家 láiwǒjiā ◻ Do you want to come round to my place? 你想来我家吗？ Nǐ xiǎng lái wǒjiā ma?

to **place** VERB
▷ *see also* **place** NOUN
放 fàng *(put)*
◻ He placed his hand on hers. 他把他的手放在了她手上。Tā bǎ tādeshǒu fàngzàile tāshǒushāng.

placement NOUN
安排 ānpāi
■ **to do a work placement** 做工作安排 zuò gōngzuò ānpái

plain ADJECTIVE
▷ *see also* **plain** NOUN

1 无图案花纹的 wú tú'àn huāwén de *(not patterned)*
◻ a plain carpet 无图案花纹的地毯 wútú'àn huāwéndedìtǎn

2 素雅 sùyǎ *(not fancy)*
◻ a plain white blouse 一件素雅的白衬衫 yíjiàn sùyǎde báichènshān

plain NOUN
▷ *see also* **plain** ADJECTIVE
平原 píngyuán [个 gè] *(area of land)*

plain chocolate NOUN
纯巧克力 chúnqiáokèli

plait NOUN
▷ *see also* **plait** VERB
辫子 biànzi [条 tiáo]
◻ She wears her hair in a plait. 她梳了条辫子。Tā shūle tiáo biàn zi.

to **plait** VERB
▷ *see also* **plait** NOUN
编 biān

plan NOUN
▷ *see also* **plan** VERB

1 计划 jìhuà [个 gè] *(scheme, project)*
◻ What are your plans for the holidays? 你假期计划是什么？ Nǐ jiǎqī jìhuà shì shénme? ◻ to make plans 定计划 dìngjìhuà ◻ Everything went according to plan. 一切都按计划进行。Yíqiè dōu ànjìhuà jìnxíng.

2 详图 xiángtú [张 zhāng] *(map, drawing)*
◻ a plan of the campsite 野营地的详图 yěyíngdì de xiángtú

to **plan** VERB
▷ *see also* **plan** NOUN

1 计划 jìhuà
◻ We're planning a trip to France. 我们正在计划去法国旅游。Wǒmén zhèngzài jìhuà qù fǎguó lǚyóu. ◻ Plan your revision carefully. 好好计划你的复习。Hǎohǎo jìhuà nǐde fùxí.

2 打算 dǎsuàn *(think ahead)*
■ **to plan to do something** 打算做某事 dǎsuàn zuò mǒushì ◻ I'm planning to get a job in the holidays. 我打算在假期找个工作。Wǒ dǎsuàn zài jiàqī zhǎo gè gōngzuò.

plane NOUN
飞机 fēijī [架 jià]
◻ by plane 坐飞机 zuòfēijī

planet NOUN
行星 xíngxīng [个 gè]

plant NOUN
▷ *see also* **plant** VERB

1 植物 zhíwù [株 zhū]
■ **to water the plants** 为植物浇水 wèizhíwù jiāoshuǐ

2 工厂 gōngchǎng [个 gè] *(factory, power station)*

to **plant** VERB
▷ *see also* **plant** NOUN
栽种 zāizhòng

plant pot NOUN
盆栽 pénzāi [个 gè]

plaque NOUN
匾额 ébiǎn [块 kuài] *(on wall)*

DID YOU KNOW...?
Many traditional businesses and tourist sites in China feature large wooden plaques inscribed with their names in treasured calligraphy and hung in places of prominence.

plaster NOUN

1 灰泥 huīní *(for wall)*

2 橡皮膏 xiàngpígāo [块 kuài] *(sticking plaster)*
◻ Have you got a plaster, by any chance? 你有橡皮膏吗？ Nǐ yǒu xiàngpígāo ma?
■ **in plaster** 打了石膏的 dǎle shígāo de
◻ Her leg's in plaster. 她的腿打了石膏。Tādetuǐ dǎle shígāo.

plastic NOUN
▷ *see also* **plastic** ADJECTIVE
塑料 sùliào [种 zhǒng]

□ It's made of plastic. 是由塑料作的。Shì yóu sùliào zuòde.

plastic ADJECTIVE
▷ *see also* **plastic** NOUN
塑料的 sùliào de *(bucket, chair, cup)*
■ **a plastic bag** 塑料袋 sùliàodài

plastic wrap NOUN (US)
保鲜膜 bǎoxiān mó [张 zhāng]

plate NOUN
碟 dié [个 gè]

platform NOUN
1 平台 píngtái [个 gè] *(stage)*
2 站台 zhàntái [个 gè] *(in station)*
□ The train leaves from platform 7. 火车从七号站台出发。Huǒchē cóng qīhào zhàntái chūfā.

play NOUN
▷ *see also* **play** VERB
戏剧 xìjù [出 chū]
□ a play by Shakespeare 莎士比亚的戏剧 Shāshìbǐyàde xìjù
■ **to put on a play** 演出 yǎnchū

to **play** VERB
▷ *see also* **play** NOUN
1 玩 wán *(game, chess)*
□ to play cards 玩纸牌 wán zhǐpái □ I play hockey. 我玩曲棍球。Wǒ wán qūgùnqiú. □ Can you play pool? 你玩台球吗？Nǐ wán táiqiú ma?
2 踢 tī *(football)*
3 打 dǎ *(cricket, tennis)*
4 同...比赛 tóng...bǐsài *(team, opponent)*
□ China will play France next month. 下个月中国同法国比赛。Xiàgèyuè Zhōngguó tóng Fǎguó bǐsài.
5 扮演 bànyǎn *(part, role, character)*
6 弹 tán *(instrument, piece of music, orchestra)*
□ I play the guitar. 我弹吉他。Wǒ tán jítā. □ What sort of music do they play? 他们弹什么类型的音乐？Tāmen tán shénme lèixíng de yīnyuè?
7 播放 bōfàng *(CD, record, tape)*
□ She's always playing that song. 她总播放那首歌。Tā zǒng bōfàng nàshǒugē.
8 玩耍 wánshuǎ *(children)*
□ He's playing with his friends. 他和他的朋友玩耍。Tā hé tāde péngyǒu wánshuǎ.

to **play back** VERB
回放 huífàng

player NOUN
1 选手 xuǎnshǒu [名 míng]
□ a football player 足球选手 zúqiúxuǎnshǒu
2 演奏者 yǎnzòuzhě [名 míng] *(of instrument)*
□ a trumpet player 一名小号演奏者 yìmíng xiǎohào yǎnzòuzhě □ a piano player 一名钢琴演奏者 yìmíng gāngqín yǎnzòuzhě

playful ADJECTIVE
嬉戏的 xīxìde

playground NOUN
1 运动场 yùndòng chǎng [个 gè] *(at school)*
2 游戏场 yóuxì chǎng [个 gè] *(in park)*

playing card NOUN
纸牌 zhǐpái [张 zhāng]

playing field NOUN
运动场 yùndòng chǎng [个 gè]

playtime NOUN
娱乐时间 yúlèshíjiān [段 duàn]

playwright NOUN
剧作家 jùzuòjiā [位 wèi]

pleasant ADJECTIVE
1 令人愉快的 lìngrén yúkuài de *(agreeable)*
2 友善的 yǒushàn de *(friendly)*

please EXCLAMATION
▷ *see also* **please** VERB
请 qǐng
□ Two coffees, please. 请来两杯咖啡。Qǐnglái liǎngbēi kāfēi. □ Please write back soon. 请尽快回信。Qǐng jìnkuài huíxìn.
■ **Yes, please.** 好的。Hǎode.

to **please** VERB
▷ *see also* **please** EXCLAMATION
使高兴 shǐ gāoxìng *(satisfy)*

pleased ADJECTIVE
开心的 kāixīn de
□ My mother's not going to be very pleased. 我母亲不会很开心的。Wǒmǔqīn búhuì hěnkāixīnde.
■ **pleased with something** 对某事满意 duì mǒushì mǎnyì □ It's beautiful: she'll be pleased with it. 很美：她会很满意的。Hěn měi: tā huì hěn mǎnyì de.
■ **Pleased to meet you!** 见到你很高兴！Jiàndào nǐ hěn gāoxìng!

pleasure NOUN
1 高兴 gāoxìng *(happiness, satisfaction)*
2 享乐 xiǎnglè *(fun)*
□ I read for pleasure. 我为享乐看书。Wǒ wèi xiǎnglè kànshū.
■ **It's a pleasure!** 乐意效劳 Lèyì xiàoláo

plenty NOUN, PRONOUN
1 很多 hěnduō *(lots)*
□ I've got plenty. 我有很多。Wǒ yǒu hěnduō.
2 足够 zúgòu *(sufficient)*
□ That's plenty, thanks. 足够了，谢谢。Zúgòule, xièxiè.
■ **plenty of** 很多 hěnduō □ We've got plenty of time. 我们有很多时间。Wǒmen yǒu hěnduō shíjiān.

LANGUAGE TIP You can also use 许多 xǔduō to translate **plenty of**.

□ I've got plenty of things to do. 我有许多事要做。Wǒ yǒu xǔduōshì yàozuò.

plot NOUN
▷ *see also* **plot** VERB
1 情节 qíngjié [个 gè] *(of story, play, film)*
2 地 dì [块 kuài] *(of land)*
□ a vegetable plot 菜地 càidì
3 阴谋 yīnmóu [个 gè] *(secret plan)*
□ a plot against the president 针对总统的阴谋 zhēnduì zǒngtǒngde yīnmóu
■ **a plot to do something** 一个做某事的阴谋 yígè zuò mǒushì de yīnmóu

to **plot** VERB
▷ *see also* **plot** NOUN
密谋 mìmóu *(conspire)*
■ **to plot to do something** 密谋做某事 mìmóu zuò mǒushì □ They were plotting to kill him. 他们密谋杀他。Tāmén mìmóu shātā.

plough NOUN
▷ *see also* **plough** VERB
耕地 gēngdì [块 kuài]

to **plough** VERB
▷ *see also* **plough** NOUN
耕地 gēngdì

plug NOUN
1 插头 chātóu [个 gè] *(on appliance)*
2 插座 chāzuò [个 gè] *(socket)*
3 塞子 sāizi [个 gè] *(in sink, bath)*

to **plug in** VERB
插上...的插头 chāshang...de chātóu
□ Is it plugged in? 插上了吗？ Chāshàng le ma?

plum NOUN
梅子 méizi [颗 kē] *(fruit)*

plumber NOUN
管子工 guǎnzi gōng [位 wèi]

plump ADJECTIVE
丰满的 fēngmǎnde

to **plunge** VERB
跳进 tiàojìn

plural ADJECTIVE
▷ *see also* **plural** NOUN
复数的 fùshù de

plural NOUN
▷ *see also* **plural** ADJECTIVE
复数 fùshù [个 gè]

plus PREPOSITION, ADVERB, ADJECTIVE, NOUN
1 加 jiā *(added to)*
□ 4 plus 3 equals 7. 四加三等于七。Sì jiā sān děngyú qī.
2 和 hé *(as well as)*
□ three children plus a dog 三个孩子和一条狗 sāngè háizi hé yìtiáo gǒu
3 附加 fùjiā *(additionally)*
■ **B plus** *(school mark)* B加 bìjiā
■ **It's a plus.** *(informal)* 这是个附加的好处。Zhè shì gè fùjiā de hǎochù.

PM NOUN *(= private message)*
▷ *see also* **PM** VERB
私信 sīxìn

to **PM** VERB *(= private message)*
▷ *see also* **PM** NOUN
私信 fā sīxìn

p.m. ABBREVIATION *(= post meridiem)*
下午 xiàwǔ
□ at 8 p.m. 下午八点 xiàwǔ bādiǎn

pneumonia NOUN
肺炎 fèiyán

poached ADJECTIVE
■ **a poached egg** 荷包蛋 hébāodàn

pocket NOUN
口袋 kǒudài [个 gè]
■ **pocket money** 零花钱 línghuāqián □ £8 a week pocket money 每周八镑零花钱 měizhōu bābàng línghuāqián

pocketbook NOUN (US)
1 皮夹 píjiā [个 gè] *(wallet)*
2 手提包 shǒutíbāo [个 gè] *(handbag)*

poem NOUN
诗 shī [首 shǒu]

poet NOUN
诗人 shīrén [位 wèi]

poetry NOUN
1 诗 shī *(poems)*
2 诗歌 shīgē *(form of literature)*

point NOUN
▷ *see also* **point** VERB
1 论点 lùndiǎn [个 gè] *(in report, lecture, interview)*
□ He made some interesting points. 他提出了一些有趣的论点。Tā tíchūle yìxiē yǒuqùde lùndiǎn.
2 观点 guāndiǎn [个 gè] *(of argument, discussion)*
□ That's a good point! 那是个好的观点！Nà shì gè hǎode guāndiǎn!
3 目的 mùdì *(purpose)*
4 位置 wèizhi [个 gè] *(place)*
□ a point on the horizon 地平线的一个位置 dìpíngxiànde yígè wèizhi
5 时刻 shíkè [个 gè] *(moment)*
□ At that point, we decided to leave. 在那个时刻，我们决定离开。Zài nàgè shíkè, wǒmen juédìng líkāi.
6 尖 jiān [个 gè] *(tip)*
□ a pencil with a sharp point 一只尖头铅笔 yìzhī jiāntóu qiānbǐ
7 分 fēn *(in score, competition, game, sport)*
□ They scored 5 points. 他们得了五分。Tāmén déle wǔfēn.
8 小数点 xiǎoshùdiǎn [个 gè] *(decimal point)*
■ **two point five** *(2.5)* 二点五 èrdiǎnwǔ

■ **There's no point.** 没有意义。Méiyǒu yìyì. □ There's no point in waiting. 等是没意义的。Děng shì méiyìyìde.
■ **What's the point?** 有什么意义？Yǒu shénme yìyì? □ What's the point of leaving so early? 早走有什么意义？Zǎozǒu yǒu shénme yìyì?
■ **a point of view** 观点 guāndiǎn
■ **to get the point** 明白 míngbai □ Sorry, I don't get the point. 对不起，我没明白。Duìbùqǐ, wǒ méi míngbai.

to **point** VERB
▷ *see also* **point** NOUN
指出 zhǐchū *(with finger, stick)*
□ Don't point! 不要指！ Búyào zhǐ!
■ **to point at somebody** 指着某人 zhǐzhe mǒurén □ She pointed at Anne. 他指着安娜。Tā zhǐzhe Ānnà.
■ **to point something at somebody** 把某物瞄准某人 bǎ mǒuwù miáozhǔn mǒurén □ He pointed a gun at them. 她把枪瞄准他们。Tā bǎ qiāng miáozhǔn tāmen.

to **point out** VERB
指出 zhǐchū
□ The guide pointed out the Forbidden City to us. 导游给我们指出故宫。Dǎoyóu gěi wǒmén zhǐchū gùgōng.
■ **to point out that...** *(mention)* 指出… zhǐchū... □ I should point out that... 我应该指出… Wǒ yīnggāi zhǐchū ...

pointless ADJECTIVE
无意义的 wú yìyì de
□ It's pointless to argue. 争论是无意义的。Zhēnglùn shì wúyìyìde.

poison NOUN
▷ *see also* **poison** VERB
毒药 dúyào [种 zhǒng]

to **poison** VERB
▷ *see also* **poison** NOUN
下毒 xiàdú

poisonous ADJECTIVE
有毒的 yǒudú de *(animal, plant, chemicals)*

poker NOUN
扑克牌 pūkèpái [副 fù]
□ I play poker. 我玩扑克牌。Wǒ wán pūkèpái.

> **DID YOU KNOW...?**
> Chinese poker has its own rules which vary from province to province.

Poland NOUN
波兰 Bōlán

polar bear NOUN
北极熊 běijíxióng [头 tóu]

Pole NOUN
波兰人 Bōlánrén [个 gè]

pole NOUN
1 杆 gān [根 gēn] *(post)*
□ a telegraph pole 电线杆 diànxiàngān □ a tent pole 一支帐篷杆 yìzhī zhàngpéng gān □ a ski pole 一支滑雪杆 yìzhī huáxuěgān
2 地极 dìjí [个 gè] *(north, south)*
■ **the North Pole** 北极 běijí

> **LANGUAGE TIP** Word for word, this means 'the northern extremity'.

■ **the South Pole** 南极 nánjí

> **LANGUAGE TIP** Word for word, this means 'the southern extremity'.

police PL NOUN
1 警察 jǐngchá *(organization)*
□ We called the police. 我们叫了警察。Wǒmén jiàole jǐngchá.
2 警察 jǐngchá *(members)*
■ **a police car** 警车 jǐngchē

policeman NOUN
男警察 nán jǐngchá [个 gè]
□ He's a policeman. 他是个男警察。Tā shì gè nánjǐngchá.

police station NOUN
警察局 jǐngchá jú [个 gè]

policewoman NOUN
女警察 nǔ jǐngchá [个 gè]
□ She's a policewoman. 她是个女警察。Tā shìgè nǔjǐngchá.

polio NOUN
脑灰质炎 nǎohuīzhìyán

Polish ADJECTIVE
▷ *see also* **Polish** NOUN
波兰的 Bōlán de

Polish NOUN
▷ *see also* **Polish** ADJECTIVE
波兰语 Bōlányǔ *(language)*

polish NOUN
▷ *see also* **polish** VERB
上光剂 shàngguāng jì [盒 hé]

to **polish** VERB
▷ *see also* **polish** NOUN
1 擦亮 cāliàng *(shoes)*
2 上光 shàngguāng *(furniture, floor)*

polite ADJECTIVE
有礼貌的 yǒu lǐmào de

politely ADVERB
有礼貌地 yǒulǐmàode

politeness NOUN
礼貌 lǐmào

political ADJECTIVE
政治的 zhèngzhì de

politician NOUN
政治家 zhèngzhì jiā [位 wèi]

politics NOUN
1 政治 zhèngzhì *(activity)*
2 政治学 zhèngzhìxué *(subject)*
□ I'm not interested in politics. 我对政治不

感兴趣。Wǒ duì zhèngzhì bù gǎnxìngqù.

poll NOUN

民意测验 mínyìcèyàn [次 cì]

□ A recent poll revealed that... 最近的一次民意测验显示… Zuìjìn de yícì mínyì cèyàn xiǎnshì....

pollen NOUN

花粉 huāfěn

to **pollute** VERB

污染 wūrǎn

polluted ADJECTIVE

被污染的 bèi wūrǎn de

pollution NOUN

1 污染 wūrǎn *(process)*

2 污染物 wūrǎn wù *(substances)*

polo shirt NOUN

运动体恤 yùndòng tīxù [件 jiàn]

polythene bag NOUN

聚乙烯塑料袋 jùyǐxī sùliàodài [个 gè]

pond NOUN

池塘 chítáng [个 gè]

□ We've got a pond in our garden. 我们的花园里有池塘。Wǒmende huāyuánlǐ yǒu chítáng.

pony NOUN

小马 xiǎomǎ [匹 pǐ]

ponytail NOUN

马尾辫 mǎwěibiàn [条 tiáo]

□ He's got a ponytail. 他梳了马尾辫。Tā shūle mǎwěibiàn.

poodle NOUN

狮子狗 shīzigǒu [只 zhī]

pool NOUN

1 水塘 shuǐtáng [个 gè] *(pond)*

2 游泳池 yóuyǒngchí [个 gè] *(swimming pool)*

3 美式台球 měishì táiqiú *(game)*

□ Shall we have a game of pool? 我们玩台球吧？ Wǒmen wán táiqiú ba?

poor ADJECTIVE

1 贫穷的 pínqióng de *(badly-off)*

□ a poor family 贫穷的家庭 pínqióngde jiātíng

■ **the poor** 穷人 qióngrén

2 贫困的 pínkùn de *(country, area)*

3 可怜的 kéliánde *(unfortunate)*

□ Poor old Bill! 可怜的老比尔 kélián de lǎo Bǐ'ěr □ Poor David, he's very unlucky! 可怜的大卫，他很不走运！ Kéliánde Dàwèi, tā hěn bùzǒuyùn.

4 低的 dī de *(bad)*

□ a poor mark 低分 dīfēn

5 差的 chà de *(wages, conditions, results, attendance)*

poorly ADJECTIVE

身体不舒服的 shēntǐ bùshūfude

□ She's poorly. 她身体不舒服。Tā shēntǐ bùshūfu.

pop NOUN

▷ *see also* **pop** ADJECTIVE

1 流行音乐 liúxíng yīnyuè *(music)*

2 爸爸 bàba [个 gè] (US: *father)*

pop ADJECTIVE

▷ *see also* **pop** NOUN

流行的 liúxíngde

□ pop music 流行音乐 liúxíng yīnyuè

□ a pop star 流行歌星 liúxíng gēxīng

□ a pop song 流行歌曲 liúxíng gēqǔ

to **pop in** VERB

顺便进来 shùnbiàn jìnlái

□ I just popped in to say hello. 我只是顺便进来打个招呼。Wǒ zhǐshì shùnbiàn jìnlái dǎ gè zhāohu.

to **pop out** VERB

跑去 pǎoqù

□ He's just popped out to the supermarket. 他刚跑到超市去了。Tā gāng pǎodào chāoshì qùle.

to **pop round** VERB

去一下 qùyíxià

□ I'm just popping round to John's. 我去一下约翰那里。Wǒ qùyíxià Yuēhàn nàlǐ.

popcorn NOUN

爆米花 bàomǐhuā [粒 lì]

pope NOUN

教皇 jiàohuáng [位 wèi]

poppy NOUN

罂粟 yīngsù

Popsicle® NOUN (US)

冰棒 bīngbàng [根 gēn]

popular ADJECTIVE

1 受欢迎的的 shòuhuānyíngde *(person, place, thing)*

□ She's a very popular girl. 她是个很受欢迎的女孩。Tā shì gè hěn shòuhuānyíngde nǚhái. □ This is a very popular style. 这是个很受欢迎的款式。Zhè shì gè hěn shòuhuānyíngde kuǎnshì.

2 时髦的 shímáo de *(name, activity)*

population NOUN

人口 rénkǒu [个 gè]

porch NOUN

门廊 ménláng [个 gè]

pork NOUN

猪肉 zhūròu

□ a pork chop 猪肉排骨 zhūròupáigǔ

□ I don't eat pork. 我不吃猪肉。Wǒ bùchī zhūròu.

porridge NOUN

粥 zhōu

English-Chinese

DID YOU KNOW...?
粥 zhōu usually refers to rice porridge, a staple of the traditional Chinese breakfast.

port NOUN
1 港口 gǎngkǒu [个 gè] *(harbour)*
2 港市 gǎngshì [座 zuò] *(town)*
■ **a glass of port** 一杯波特酒 yìbēibōtèjiǔ

portable ADJECTIVE
便携式的 biànxiéshì de
□ a portable TV 便携式电视 biànxiéshì diànshì

porter NOUN
1 门房 ménfáng [个 gè] *(doorkeeper)*
2 列车员 lièchēyuán [位 wèi] *(US: on train)*

portion NOUN
份 fèn
□ a large portion of chips 一大份薯条 yídàfèn shǔtiáo

portrait NOUN
画像 huàxiàng [幅 fú] *(picture)*

Portugal NOUN
葡萄牙 Pútáoyá

Portuguese ADJECTIVE
▷ *see also* **Portuguese** NOUN
葡萄牙的 Pútáoyá de

Portuguese NOUN
▷ *see also* **Portuguese** ADJECTIVE
1 葡萄牙人 Pútáoyárén [个 gè] *(person)*
2 葡萄牙语 Pútáoyáyǔ *(language)*

posh ADJECTIVE
豪华的 háohuá de *(informal)*
□ a posh hotel 一家豪华酒店 yìjiā háohuá jiǔdiàn

position NOUN
1 位置 wèizhi [个 gè] *(of house, person, thing)*
2 姿势 zīshì [种 zhǒng] *(of person's body)*
□ an uncomfortable position 一种不舒服的姿势 yìzhǒng bùshūfùde zīshì

positive ADJECTIVE
1 积极的 jījí de *(good)*
□ a positive attitude 积极的态度 jījíde tàidù
2 阳性的 yángxìng de *(test, result)*
3 确信的 quèxìnde *(sure)*
□ I'm positive. 我很确信。Wǒ hěn quèxìn.
■ **to be positive about something** 确信某事 quèxìn mǒushì

to **possess** VERB
拥有 yōngyǒu

possession NOUN
拥有 yōngyǒu
■ **possessions** *(things)* 财产 cáichǎn
□ Have you got all your possessions? 你带上你所有的财产了吗？ Nǐ dàishàng nǐ suǒyǒude cáichǎn le ma?

possibility NOUN
1 可能性 kěnéngxìng [种 zhǒng] *(might be true)*
□ It's a possibility. 这是一种可能。Zhè shì yìzhǒng kěnéng.
2 可能的事 kěnéng de shì [件 jiàn] *(might happen)*
3 可选性 kěxuǎnxìng [种 zhǒng] *(option)*

possible ADJECTIVE
1 可能的 kěnéng de *(event, reaction, effect, consequence)*
2 潜在的 qiánzài de *(risk, danger)*
3 可接受的 kě jiēshòu de *(answer, cause, solution)*
■ **It's possible that...** 可能… Kěnéng...
■ **if possible** 如有可能 rúyǒu kěnéng
■ **as soon as possible** 尽快 jǐnkuài

possibly ADVERB
大概 dàgài *(perhaps)*
□ Are you coming to the party? — Possibly. 你会来聚会吗？嗯— 大概。Nǐ huì lái jùhuì ma? — En, dàgài.
■ **...if you possibly can.** …如果你大概可以。...rúguǒ nǐ dàgài kěyǐ.
■ **I can't possibly come.** 我大概不能来。Wǒ dàgài bùnéng lái.

post NOUN
▷ *see also* **post** VERB
1 柱子 zhùzi [根 gēn] *(pole)*
□ The ball hit the post. 球打在柱子上了。Qiú dǎzài zhùzishàng le.
2 职位 zhíwèi [个 gè] *(job)*
■ **the post 1** *(service, system)* 邮政 yóuzhèng **2** *(letters, delivery)* 邮件 yóujiàn
□ Is there any post for me? 有我的邮件吗？Yǒu wǒde yóujiàn ma?
■ **by post** 以邮寄的方式 yǐ yóujì de fāngshì

to **post** VERB
▷ *see also* **post** NOUN
邮寄 yóujì *(letter)*
□ I've got some cards to post. 我有卡要邮寄。Wǒ yǒu kǎ yào yóujì.

postage NOUN
邮资 yóuzī

postbox NOUN
邮筒 yóutǒng [个 gè] *(in street)*

postcard NOUN
明信片 míngxìnpiàn [张 zhāng]

postcode NOUN
邮政编码 yóuzhèng biānmǎ [个 gè]

poster NOUN
海报 hǎibào [张 zhāng]
□ I've got posters on my bedroom walls. 我的卧室墙上有海报。Wǒde wòshì qiángshàng yǒu hǎibào.

P

postman NOUN
邮递员 yóudìyuán [位 wèi]
□ He's a postman. 他是位邮递员。Tā shì wèi yóudìyuán.

postmark NOUN
邮戳 yóuchuō [个 gè]

post office NOUN
邮局 yóujú [个 gè]
□ Where's the post office, please? 请问邮局在哪？ Qǐngwèn yóujú zàinǎ? □ She works for the post office. 她在邮局工作。Tā zài yóujú gōngzuò.

to **postpone** VERB
推迟 tuīchí
□ The match has been postponed. 比赛推迟了。Bǐsài tuīchí le.

postwoman NOUN
女邮递员 nǚ yóudìyuán [位 wèi]
□ She's a postwoman. 她是位女邮递员。Tā shì wèi nǚyóudìyuán.

pot NOUN
1 锅 guō [口 kǒu] *(for cooking)*
□ the pots and pans 锅锅罐罐 guōguōguànguàn
2 茶壶 cháhú [个 gè] *(teapot)*
3 咖啡壶 kāfēihú [个 gè] *(coffeepot)*
4 罐 guàn [个 gè] *(for paint, jam)*
5 花盆 huāpén [个 gè] *(flowerpot)*

potato NOUN
土豆 tǔdòu [个 gè]
□ potato salad 土豆沙拉 tǔdòu shālà
□ mashed potatoes 土豆泥 tǔdòu ní
□ boiled potatoes 煮土豆 zhǔ tǔdòu □ a baked potato 烤土豆 kǎotǔdòu

potato chips PL NOUN (US)
薯片 shǔpiàn [袋 dài]

potential NOUN
▷ *see also* **potential** ADJECTIVE
潜力 qiǎnlì
□ He has great potential. 他有很大的潜力。Tā yǒu hěndàde qiǎnlì.

potential ADJECTIVE
▷ *see also* **potential** NOUN
潜在的 qiǎnzàide
□ a potential problem 潜在的问题 qiǎnzàide wèntí

pottery NOUN
1 陶艺 táoyì *(work, hobby)*
2 制陶厂 zhìtáo chǎng [家 jiā] *(factory, workshop)*

pound NOUN
1 镑 bàng *(unit of money)*
□ How many yuan do you get for a pound? 一英镑可以兑换多少元？ Yìyīngbàng kěyǐ duìhuàn duōshǎo yuán?
■ **a pound coin** 一镑硬币 yíbàng yìngbì
■ **a five-pound note** 五镑纸币 wǔbàng zhǐbì
2 磅 bàng *(unit of weight)*
■ **half a pound of sugar** 半磅糖 bànbàngtáng

to **pour** VERB
■ **to pour something into something** 灌某物到某物里 guàn mǒuwù dào mǒuwù lǐ
□ She poured some water into the pan. 她往锅里灌了水。Tā wǎng guōlǐ guànle shuǐ.
■ **to pour somebody something** 给某人倒某物 gěi mǒurén dào mǒuwù □ She poured him a drink. 她给他倒了一杯饮料。Tā gěi tā dàole yìbēi yǐnliào. □ Shall I pour you a cup of tea? 给你倒杯咖啡好吗？ Gěi nǐ dào bēi kāfēi hǎoma?
■ **It's pouring.** 大雨如注。Dàyǔ rúzhù.

poverty NOUN
贫穷 pínqióng

powder NOUN
粉 fěn [袋 dài]

power NOUN
1 权力 quánlì *(over people, activities)*
□ to be in power 在权 zàiquán
2 电力 diànlì *(electricity)*
□ The power's off. 停电了。Tíngdiàn le.
■ **a power cut** 停电 tíngdiàn
■ **a power point** 电源插座 diànyuánchāzuò
■ **a power station** 电厂 diàn chǎng
3 能源 néngyuán *(energy)*
■ **nuclear power** 核能源 hénéngyuán
■ **solar power** 太阳能源 tàiyáng néngyuán

powerful ADJECTIVE
1 有影响力的 yǒu yǐngxiǎnglì de *(influential)*
2 强健的 qiángjiàn de *(physically strong)*
3 大功率的 dà gōnglǜ de *(engine, machine)*

practical ADJECTIVE
1 实践的 shíjiàn de *(difficulties, experience)*
2 切合实际的 qièhé shíjì de *(ideas, methods, advice, suggestions)*
3 有实际经验的 yǒu shíjì jīngyàn de *(person, mind)*
■ **She's very practical.** 她是个很实际的人。Tā shì gè hěn shíjì de rén.

practically ADVERB
几乎 jīhū
□ It's practically impossible. 几乎不可能。Jīhū bùkěnéng.

practice NOUN
1 练习 liànxí *(exercise, training)*
■ **football practice** 足球练习 zúqiú liànxí
■ **2 hours' piano practice** 二小时的练琴时间 liǎng xiǎoshí de liànqín shíjiān
2 实习 shíxí [次 cì] *(training session)*
■ **It's normal practice in our school.** 在我

们学校这是很常见的做法。Zài wǒmén xuéxiào zhè shì hěnchángjiàn de zuǒfǎ.
■ **in practice** *(in reality)* 实际上 shíjì shàng

to **practise** (US **practice**) VERB
练习 liànxí
□ I ought to practise more. 我应该多练习。Wǒ yīnggāi duō liànxí. □ I practise the flute every evening. 我每天晚上练习长笛。Wǒ měitiān wǎnshàng liànxí chángdí. □ I practised my French when we were on holiday. 度假时我练习法语。Dùjiàshí wǒ liànxí Fǎyǔ.

to **praise** VERB
称赞 chēngzàn
□ Everyone praises her cooking. 每个人都称赞她的厨艺。Měi gè rén dōu chēngzàn tāde chúyì. □ The teachers praised our work. 老师称赞了我们的工作。Lǎoshī chēngzànle wǒmende gōngzuò.

pram NOUN
婴儿车 yīng'érchē [辆 liàng]

prawn NOUN
虾 xiā [只 zhī]

to **pray** VERB
祷告 dǎogào
□ to pray for something 为某事祷告 wèi mǒushì dǎogào

prayer NOUN
祈祷文 qídǎowén [篇 piān] *(words)*

precaution NOUN
预防措施 yùfáng cuòshī [项 xiàng]
■ **to take precautions** 采取预防措施 cǎiqǔ yùfángcuòshī

preceding ADJECTIVE
前述的 qiánshùde

precinct NOUN
区域 qūyù [片 piàn]
□ a shopping precinct 商业区域 shāngyè qūyù

precious ADJECTIVE
1 宝贵的 bǎoguì de *(time, resource, memories)*
2 贵重的 guìzhòng de *(financially)*

precise ADJECTIVE
1 精确的 jīngquè de *(time, nature, position, circumstances)*
□ at that precise moment 在那个精确的时刻 zài nàgè jīngquède shíkè
2 准确的 zhǔnquè de *(figure, definition)*
3 清晰的 qīngxī de *(explanation)*
4 详尽的 xiángjìn de *(instructions, plans)*

precisely ADVERB
1 确实如此 quèshírúcǐ *(exactly)*
□ Precisely! 确实如此！ Quèshírúcǐ!
2 正好 zhènghǎo *(referring to time)*
□ at 10 a.m. precisely 正好上午十点 zhènghǎo shàngwǔ shídiǎn

to **predict** VERB
预言 yùyán

predictable ADJECTIVE
可预言的 kěyùyánde

prediction NOUN
预言 yùyán [种 zhǒng]

to **prefer** VERB
偏爱 piān'ài
□ Which would you prefer? 你偏爱哪个？Nǐ piān'ài nǎgè?
■ **I'd prefer to go by train.** 我宁愿坐火车去。Wǒ nìngyuàn zuò huǒchē qù.
■ **to prefer coffee to tea** 喜欢咖啡胜于茶 xǐhuan kāfēi shèngyú chá

preference NOUN
偏爱 piān'ài [种 zhǒng]

pregnant ADJECTIVE
怀孕的 huáiyùn de
■ **3 months pregnant** 怀孕三个月 huáiyùn sāngèyuè

prehistoric ADJECTIVE
史前的 shǐqiánde

prejudice NOUN
偏见 piānjiàn [种 zhǒng]

prejudiced ADJECTIVE
■ **to be prejudiced against somebody** 对某人抱有偏见 duìmǒurén bàoyǒu piānjiàn

premature ADJECTIVE
早产的 zǎochǎnde
□ a premature baby 早产儿 zǎochǎn'ér

Premier League NOUN
■ **the Premier League** 超级联赛 Chāojí Liánsài

premises PL NOUN
房屋 fángwū
□ They're moving to new premises. 他们正搬新房。Tāmen zhèngbān xīnfáng.

premonition NOUN
预感 yùgǎn [个 gè]

preoccupied ADJECTIVE
全神贯注的 quánshén guànzhùde

preparation NOUN
准备 zhǔnbèi
■ **in preparation for something** 为某事而准备的 wèi mǒushì ér zhǔnbèi de
■ **preparations for something** *(arrangements)* 为某事的准备工作 wèi mǒushì de zhǔnbèi gōngzuò

to **prepare** VERB
1 准备 zhǔnbèi
2 预备 yùbèi *(food, meal)*
□ She has to prepare lessons in the evening. 她晚上得备课。Tā wǎnshàng děibèikè.
■ **to prepare for something** 为某事做准备 wèi mǒushì zuò zhǔnbèi □ We're preparing for our skiing holiday. 我们正为滑

雪假期做准备。Wǒmen zhèngwèi huáxuě jiàqī zuòzhǔnbèi.

■ **to prepare to do something** *(get ready)* 准备好做某事 zhǔnbèi hǎo zuò mǒushì

prepared ADJECTIVE

■ **to be prepared to do something** *(willing)* 愿意做某事 yuànyì zuò mǒushì □ I'm prepared to help you. 我愿意帮你。Wǒ yuànyì bāngnǐ.

■ **prepared for something** *(ready)* 对某事有所准备的 duì mǒushì yǒu suǒ zhǔnbèi de

prep school NOUN

预备学校 yùbèi xuéxiào [所 suǒ]

to **prescribe** VERB

开 kāi

prescription NOUN

1 处方 chǔfāng [个 gè] *(slip of paper)* □ You can't get it without a prescription. 你没有处方就拿不到那个。Nǐméiyǒu chǔfāng jiù nábúdào nàge.

2 药方 yàofāng [个 gè] *(medicine)*

presence NOUN

存在 cúnzài

■ **presence of mind** 沉着冷静 chénzhuó lěngjìng

present ADJECTIVE

▷ *see also* **present** NOUN, VERB

1 现在的 xiànzài de *(current)* □ the present situation 现在的情况 xiànzàide qíngkuàng

2 在场的 zàichǎng de *(in attendance)*

■ **to be present at something** 出席某事 chūxí mǒushì □ He wasn't present at the meeting. 他没有出席会议。Tā méiyǒu chūxí huìyì.

■ **the present tense** 现在时 xiànzàishí

present NOUN

▷ *see also* **present** ADJECTIVE, VERB

礼物 lǐwù [件 jiàn] *(gift)* □ I'm going to buy presents. 我要去买礼物。Wǒ yào qùmǎi lǐwù.

■ **to give somebody a present** 给某人一件礼物 gěi mǒurén yíjiàn lǐwù

■ **the present 1** *(not past)* 目前 mùqián 2 *(present tense)* 现在时态 xiànzài shítài

■ **at present** 现在 xiànzài

■ **up to the present** 到现在 dào xiànzài

■ **for the present** 暂时 zànshí

to **present** VERB

▷ *see also* **present** ADJECTIVE, NOUN

■ **to present somebody with something** *(prize, medal)* 授予某人某物 shòuyǔ mǒurén mǒuwù

presenter NOUN

主持人 zhǔchírén [位 wèi] *(on TV)*

president NOUN

总统 zǒngtǒng [位 wèi]

press NOUN

▷ *see also* **press** VERB

■ **the press** 新闻界 xīnwén jiè

■ **a press conference** 记者招待会 jìzhě zhāodàihuì

to **press** VERB

▷ *see also* **press** NOUN

1 按 àn *(button, switch, bell)* □ He pressed the accelerator. 他按了加速器。Tā ànle jiāsùqì. □ Don't press too hard! 别太用力按！Bié tàiyònglì'àn!

2 熨平 yùnpíng *(iron)*

pressed ADJECTIVE

■ **to be pressed for time** 时间紧迫 shíjiān jǐnpò

press-up NOUN

■ **to do press-ups** 做俯卧撑 zuò fǔwòchēng □ I do twenty press-ups every morning. 我每天早晨做二十个俯卧撑。Wǒ měitiān zǎochén zuò èrshígè fǔwòchēng.

pressure NOUN

▷ *see also* **pressure** VERB

压力 yālì [种 zhǒng] □ He's under a lot of pressure at work. 他工作压力很大。Tā gōngzuòyālì hěndà.

■ **to put pressure on somebody to do something** 逼迫某人做某事 bīpò mǒurén zuò mǒushì

■ **a pressure group** 一个压力集团 yígè yālì jítuán

to **pressure** VERB

▷ *see also* **pressure** NOUN

施加压力 shījiā yālì □ My parents are pressuring me. 我父母对我施加压力。Wǒ fùmǔ duìwǒ shījiā yālì.

to **pressurize** VERB

逼迫 bīpò

■ **to pressurize somebody to do something** 逼迫某人做某事 bīpò mǒurén zuòmǒushì □ My parents are pressurizing me to stay on at school. 我父母逼迫我继续上学。Wǒ fùmǔ bīpòwǒ jìxù shàngxué.

prestige NOUN

声望 shēngwàng

prestigious ADJECTIVE

享有盛誉的 xiǎngyǒushèngyùde

presumably ADVERB

大概 dàgài

to **presume** VERB

认为 rènwéi □ I presume so. 我认为是这样。Wǒ rènwéi shìzhèyàng.

to **pretend** VERB

■ **to pretend to do something** 假装做某事

jiǎzhuāng zuò mǒushì □ He pretended to be asleep. 他假装睡着了。Tā jiǎzhuāng shuìzháole.

■ **to pretend that...** 假装… jiǎzhuāng...

pretty ADJECTIVE

▷ *see also* **pretty** ADVERB

漂亮的 piàoliang de

□ She's very pretty. 她非常漂亮。Tā fēicháng piàoliang.

pretty ADVERB

▷ *see also* **pretty** ADJECTIVE

相当 xiāngdāng *(quite)*

□ The weather was pretty awful. 天气相当糟糕。Tiānqì xiāngdāng zāogāo.

■ **It's pretty much the same.** 几乎是一样的。Jīhū shì yíyàngde.

to **prevent** VERB

1 阻止 zǔzhǐ *(war, disease, situation)*

2 防止 fángzhǐ *(accident, fire)*

■ **to prevent somebody from doing something** 阻止某人做某事 zǔzhǐ mǒurén zuò mǒushì □ They try to prevent us from smoking. 他们设法阻止我们吸烟。Tāmen shèfǎ zǔzhǐ wǒmen xīyān.

■ **to prevent something from happening** 防止某事发生 fángzhǐ mǒushì fāshēng

previous ADJECTIVE

1 前的 qián de *(marriage, relationship, experience, owner)*

2 以前的 yǐqián de *(chapter, week, day)*

previously ADVERB

以前 yǐqián

■ **10 days previously** 十天前 shí tiān qián

prey NOUN

捕食 bǔshí

□ a bird of prey 猛禽 měngqín

price NOUN

价格 jiàgé [种 zhǒng]

to **prick** VERB

刺 cì

□ I've pricked my finger. 我刺到了手指。Wǒ cìdàole shǒuzhǐ.

pride NOUN

自豪 zìháo [种 zhǒng]

■ **to take pride in something** 因某事而自豪 yīn mǒushì ér zìháo

priest NOUN

神职人员 shénzhí rényuán [位 wèi]

primarily ADVERB

主要地 zhǔyào de

primary ADJECTIVE

首先的 shǒuxiānde

primary school NOUN

小学 xiǎoxué [所 suǒ]

□ She's still at primary school. 她还在上小学。Tā háizài shàng xiǎoxué.

DID YOU KNOW...?
Primary school in China lasts for six years, from the ages of seven to thirteen.

prime minister NOUN

总理 zǒnglǐ [位 wèi]

primitive ADJECTIVE

原始的 yuánshǐde

prince NOUN

王子 wángzǐ [位 wèi]

■ **the Prince of Wales** 威尔士亲王 Wēiěrshì qīnwáng

princess NOUN

公主 gōngzhǔ [位 wèi]

□ Princess Anne 安妮公主 Ānní gōngzhǔ

principal ADJECTIVE

▷ *see also* **principal** NOUN

主要的 zhǔyào de

principal NOUN

▷ *see also* **principal** ADJECTIVE

校长 xiàozhǎng [位 wèi] *(of school, college)*

principle NOUN

准则 zhǔnzé [个 gè]

■ **in principle** *(in theory)* 原则上 yuánzé shàng

■ **on principle** 根据原则 gēnjù yuánzé

print NOUN

▷ *see also* **print** VERB

1 照片 zhàopiān [张 zhāng] *(photograph)*

□ colour prints 彩色照片 cǎisè zhàopiān

2 字体 zìtǐ [种 zhǒng] *(letters)*

□ in small print 用小号字体 yòng xiǎohào zìtǐ

3 指纹 zhǐwén [个 gè] *(fingerprint)*

to **print** VERB

▷ *see also* **print** NOUN

1 出版 chūbǎn *(story, article)*

2 印花 yìnhuā *(pattern)*

3 用印刷体写 yòng yìnshuātǐ xiě *(in block letters)*

4 打印 dǎyìn *(on computer)*

to **print out** VERB

打印出 dǎyìn chū

printer NOUN

打印机 dǎyìnjī [台 tái]

printout NOUN

打印输出 dǎyìn shūchū [次 cì]

priority NOUN

优先 yōuxiān [种 zhǒng]

■ **to give priority to something** 给某事以优先权 gěi mǒushì yǐ yōuxiān quán

■ **priorities** *(chief concerns)* 优先考虑的事 yōuxiān kǎolǜ de shì

prison NOUN

1 监狱 jiānyù [个 gè] *(institution)*

2 坐牢 zuòláo *(imprisonment)*

■ **in prison** 坐牢 zuòláo

prisoner NOUN
囚犯 qiúfàn [个 gè]
prison officer NOUN
狱警 yùjǐng [名 míng]
privacy NOUN
隐私 yǐnsī [个 gè]
private ADJECTIVE
1 私人的 sīrén de *(property, land, plane)*
□ a private bathroom 私人浴室 sīrén yùshì
■ **'private property'** "私有财产" "sīyǒu cáichǎn"
2 私有的 sīyǒu de *(education, housing, health care, industries)*
□ a private school 私立学校 sīlì xuéxiào
□ I have private lessons. 我有私人课程。Wǒ yǒu sīrén kèchéng.
3 秘密的 mìmì de *(confidential)*
■ **'private'** *(on envelope)* "私人信件" "sīrénxìnjiàn"
■ **in private** 私下 sīxià
to **privatize** VERB
私有化 sīyǒuhuà
privilege NOUN
特权 tèquán [项 xiàng]
prize NOUN
奖 jiǎng [个 gè]
□ to win a prize 获奖 huòjiǎng
prizewinner NOUN
获奖者 huòjiǎngzhě [位 wèi]
pro PREPOSITION
▷ *see also* **pro** NOUN
赞成 zànchéng *(in favour of)*
pro NOUN
▷ *see also* **pro** PREPOSITION
■ **the pros and cons** 赞成与反对的观点 zànchéng yǔ fǎnduì de guāndiǎn □ We weighed up the pros and cons. 我们权衡了赞成与反对的观点。Wǒmen quánhéngle zànchéng yǔ fǎnduì de guāndiǎn.
probability NOUN
可能性 kěnéngxìng [种 zhǒng]
probable ADJECTIVE
可能的 kěnéng de
probably ADVERB
可能 kěnéng
□ probably not 可能不是 kěnéng búshì
problem NOUN
问题 wèntí [个 gè]
□ What's the problem? 有什么问题吗? Yǒu shénme wèntí ma? □ I had no problem finding her. 我要找到她没问题。Wǒ yào zhǎodào tā méiwèntí.
■ **No problem!** 没问题! Méi wèntí!
process NOUN
▷ *see also* **process** VERB
过程 guòchéng [个 gè]
□ We're in the process of painting the kitchen. 我们正在粉刷厨房的过程中。Wǒmen zhèngzài fěnshuā chúfáng de guòchéngzhōng.
■ **the peace process** 和平进程 hépíng jìnchéng
to **process** VERB
▷ *see also* **process** NOUN
处理 chǔlǐ *(data)*
procession NOUN
列队行进 lièduì xíngjìn
to **produce** VERB
1 促成 cùchéng *(effect, result)*
2 生产 shēngchǎn *(goods, commodity)*
3 上演 shàngyǎn *(play, film, programme)*
producer NOUN
1 制片人 zhìpiànrén [位 wèi] *(of film, play, programme)*
2 产地 chǎndì [个 gè] *(of food, material: country)*
3 制造商 zhìzào shāng [个 gè] *(of goods: company)*
product NOUN
产品 chǎnpǐn [个 gè]
production NOUN
1 生产 shēngchǎn *(process)*
2 产量 chǎnliàng *(amount produced, amount grown)*
□ They're increasing production of luxury models. 他们正在提高豪华款的产量。Tāmen zhèngzài tígāo háohuákuǎn de chǎnliàng.
3 作品 zuòpǐn [部 bù] *(play, show)*
□ a dramatic production 一部戏剧作品 yíbù xìjù zuòpǐn
■ **a production of Hamlet** 一场哈姆雷特的演出 yìchǎng Hāmǔléitè de yǎnchū
profession NOUN
职业 zhíyè [种 zhǒng]
professional ADJECTIVE
▷ *see also* **professional** NOUN
1 职业的 zhíyè de *(photographer, musician, footballer)*
□ a professional musician 一位职业音乐家 yíwèi zhíyè yīnyuèjiā
2 专业的 zhuānyè de *(advice, help)*
3 专业水平的 zhuānyè shuǐpíng de *(skilful)*
□ a very professional piece of work 一部非常有专业水平的作品 yíbù fēicháng yǒu zhuānyè shuǐpíng de zuòpǐn
professional NOUN
▷ *see also* **professional** ADJECTIVE
专业人员 zhuānyè rényuán [位 wèi]
professionally ADVERB
专业地 zhuānyè de
□ She sings professionally. 她专业唱歌。Tā zhuānyè chànggē.

professor NOUN
1 教授 jiàoshòu [位 wèi] *(in Britain)*
□ He's the Chinese professor. 他是一位中文教授。Tā shì yíwèi Zhōngwén jiàoshòu.
2 教员 jiàoyuán [位 wèi] *(in US)*

profit NOUN
利润 lìrùn
■ **to make a profit** 赚取利润 zhuànqǔ lìrùn

profitable ADJECTIVE
有利润的 yǒu lìrùn de

program NOUN
▷ *see also* **program** VERB
程序 chéngxù [个 gè]
■ **a computer program** 一个电脑程序 yígè diànnǎo chéngxù
■ **a TV program** (US) 一个电视节目 yígè diànshì jiémù

to **program** VERB
▷ *see also* **program** NOUN
■ **to program something to do something** 为某物编程做某事 wèi mǒwù biānchéng zuò mǒushì

programme (US **program**) NOUN
▷ *see also* **programme** VERB
1 节目 jiémù [个 gè] *(on radio, TV)*
2 节目宣传册 jiémù xuānchuáncè [本 běn] *(for theatre, concert)*
3 节目单 jiémù dān [个 gè] *(of talks, events, performances)*

to **programme** VERB
▷ *see also* **programme** NOUN
■ **to programme something to do something** 设定某事做某事 shèdìng mǒushì zuò mǒushì

programmer NOUN
程序员 chéngxùyuán [位 wèi]

programming NOUN
编程 biānchéng

progress NOUN
1 进展 jìnzhǎn *(headway)*
2 进步 jìnbù *(advances)*

LANGUAGE TIP Word for word, this means 'forward step'.

■ **to make progress** 取得进步 qǔdé jìnbù
□ You're making progress! 你正在取得进步！Nǐ zhèngzài qǔdé jìnbù！

to **prohibit** VERB
禁止 jìnzhǐ
□ Smoking is prohibited. 禁止吸烟。Jìnzhǐ xīyān.

project NOUN
1 项目 xiàngmù [个 gè]
□ a development project 一个发展项目 yígè fāzhǎn xiàngmù
2 科研项目 kēyán xiàngmù [个 gè] *(research)*
□ I'm doing a project on education in China. 我正在做一个关于中国教育的科研项目。Wǒ zhèngzài zuò yígè guānyú Zhōngguó jiàoyù de kēyán xiàngmù.

projector NOUN
投影仪 tóuyǐngyí [台 tái]

promenade NOUN
散步 sànbù

promise NOUN
▷ *see also* **promise** VERB
承诺 chéngnuò [个 gè]
□ He made me a promise. 他对我许下一个承诺。Tā duìwǒ xǔxià yígè chéngnuò.
□ That's a promise! 那是承诺了！ Nà shì chéngnuò le.
■ **to break a promise to do something** 违背承诺去做某事 wéibèi chéngnuò qù zuò mǒushì
■ **to keep a promise** 遵守诺言 zūnshǒu nuòyán

to **promise** VERB
▷ *see also* **promise** NOUN
保证 bǎozhèng
□ I'll write, I promise! 我会写的，我保证。Wǒ huì xiěde, wǒbǎozhèng.
■ **to promise to do something** 保证做某事 bǎozhèng zuò mǒushì □ She promised to write. 她保证写。Tā bǎozhèngxiě.
■ **to promise somebody something** 向某人保证某事 xiàng mǒurén bǎozhèng mǒushì

promising ADJECTIVE
有前途的 yǒu qiántúde
■ **a promising player** 一个有前途的选手 yígè yǒuqiántúde xuǎnshǒu

to **promote** VERB
晋升 jìnshēng
■ **to be promoted** 获得晋升 huòdé jìnshēng □ She was promoted after six months. 她六个月后获得了晋升。Tā liùgèyuèhòu huòdéle jìnshēng.

promotion NOUN
晋级 jìnjí [次 cì]

prompt NOUN
▷ *see also* **prompt** ADJECTIVE, ADVERB
提示符 tíshì fú [个 gè] *(on screen)*

prompt ADJECTIVE, ADVERB
▷ *see also* **prompt** NOUN
1 准时的 zhǔnshí de *(on time)*
□ at 8 o'clock prompt 八点准时 bādiǎn zhǔnshí
2 迅速的 xùnsù de *(rapid: action, response)*
□ a prompt reply 一个迅速的答复 yígè xùnsùde dáfù

promptly ADVERB
准时地 zhǔnshí de
□ We left promptly at seven. 我们七点准时离开。Wǒmen qīdiǎn zhǔnshí líkāi.

pronoun NOUN
代词 dàicí [个 gè]

to **pronounce** VERB
发音 fāyīn
□ How do you pronounce that word? 这个单词怎么发音？Zhège dāncí zěnme fāyīn?

pronunciation NOUN
发音 fāyīn [个 gè]

proof NOUN
证据 zhèngjù [个 gè]

proper ADJECTIVE
1 恰当的 qiàdàng de *(procedure, place, word)*
□ You have to have the proper equipment. 你得有恰当的工具。Nǐ děi yǒu qiàdàngde gōngjù. □ If you had come at the proper time... 要是你来的时间恰当… Yàoshì nǐ láide shíjiān qiàdàng...
2 正经的 zhèngjingde *(real)*
□ We didn't have a proper lunch, just sandwiches. 我们没正经吃午饭，只吃了三明治。Wǒmen méi zhèngjing chīwǔfàn, zhǐ chīle sānmíngzhì. □ It's difficult to get a proper job. 很难找到一份正经工作。Hěnnán zhǎodào yífèn zhèngjing gōngzuò.

properly ADVERB
1 充分地 chōngfèn de *(eat, work, concentrate)*
2 体面地 tǐmiàn de *(behave)*
3 恰当地 qiàdàngde *(appropriately)*
□ Dress properly for your interview. 面试时要穿着恰当。Miànshìshí yào chuānzhuó qiàdàng. □ You're not doing it properly. 你做得不恰当。Nǐ zuòde búqiàdàng.

property NOUN
1 财产 cáichǎn *(possessions)*
□ stolen property 被盗的财产 bèidàode cáichǎn
2 地产 dìchǎn [处 chù] *(buildings and land)*
■ **'private property'** "私有财产" "sīyǒucáichǎn"

proportional ADJECTIVE
成比例的 chéngbǐlìde
□ proportional representation 比例代表制 bǐlì dàibiǎozhì

proposal NOUN
建议 jiànyì [条 tiáo] *(suggestion)*

to **propose** VERB
提议 tíyì
□ I propose a new plan. 我提议一个新计划。Wǒ tíyì yígè xīnjìhuà.
■ **to propose to do something** 提议做某事 tíyì zuò mǒushì □ What do you propose to do? 你提议做什么？ Nǐ tíyì zuò shénme?
■ **to propose to somebody** *(ask to marry)* 向某人求婚 xiàngmǒurén qiúhūn □ He proposed to her at the restaurant. 他在那家饭店向她求婚。Tā zài nàjiā fàndiàn xiàngtā qiúhūn.

to **prosecute** VERB
起诉 qǐsù
□ They were prosecuted for murder. 他们以谋杀罪受到起诉。Tāmen yǐ móushāzuì shòudào qǐsù.
■ **'Trespassers will be prosecuted'** "侵犯他人土地者将受到起诉" "Qīnfàntāréntǔdìzhě jiāng shòudào qǐsù"

prospect NOUN
前景 qiánjǐng [片 piàn]
□ It'll improve my career prospects. 它会改善我的事业前景。Tā huìgǎishàn wǒde shìyè qiánjǐng.

prostitute NOUN
妓女 jìnǚ [个 gè] *(female)*
■ **a male prostitute** 男妓 nánjì

to **protect** VERB
保护 bǎohù
■ **to protect somebody from something** 保护某人不受某物的伤害 bǎohù mǒurén bùshòu mǒuwù de shānghài

protection NOUN
保护 bǎohù [种 zhǒng]

protein NOUN
蛋白质 dànbáizhì [种 zhǒng]

protest NOUN
▷ *see also* **protest** VERB
抗议 kàngyì [个 gè]
□ He ignored their protests. 他不理睬他们的抗议。Tā bùlǐcǎi tāmende kàngyì.
■ **a protest march** 抗议游行 kàngyì yóuxíng

to **protest** VERB
▷ *see also* **protest** NOUN
示威 shìwēi *(voice opposition to)*
■ **to protest about something** 抗议某事 kàngyì mǒushì

Protestant NOUN
▷ *see also* **Protestant** ADJECTIVE
新教徒 Xīnjiàotú [个 gè]

Protestant ADJECTIVE
▷ *see also* **Protestant** NOUN
新教的 Xīnjiào de
□ a Protestant church 一座新教教堂 yízuò xīnjiào jiàotáng

protester NOUN
抗议者 kàngyìzhě [名 míng]

proud ADJECTIVE
1 自豪的 zìháo de *(parents, owner)*
■ **to be proud of somebody** 为某人感到自豪 wèi mǒurén gǎndào zìháo □ Her parents are proud of her. 她父母为她感到自豪。Tā fùmǔ wèitā gǎndào zìháo.
2 骄傲的 jiāo'ào de *(arrogant)*

to **prove** VERB
证明 zhèngmíng *(idea, theory)*

English-Chinese

P

□ The police couldn't prove it. 警方不能证明这个。Jǐngfāng bùnéng zhèngmíng zhège.
■ **to prove somebody right** 证明某人是对的 zhèngmíng mǒurén shì duìde
■ **to prove that...** **1** *(person)* 证明… zhèngmíng... **2** *(situation, experiment, calculations)* 显示… xiǎnshì...

proverb NOUN
谚语 yànyǔ [条 tiáo]

to **provide** VERB
1 供应 gōngyìng *(food, money, shelter)*
2 提供 tígōng *(answer, opportunity, details)*
■ **to provide somebody with something** 为某人提供某物 wèi mǒurén tígōng mǒuwù □ They provided us with maps. 他们为我们提供了地图。Tāmen wèi wǒmen tígōng le dìtú.

to **provide for** VERB
供养 gōngyǎng
□ He can't provide for his family any more. 他不能再供养家庭了。Tā bùnéng zài gōngyǎng jiātíng le.

provided CONJUNCTION
假如 jiǎrú

prune NOUN
梅干 méigān [枚 méi]

PS ABBREVIATION *(= postscript)*
附言 fùyán

psychiatrist NOUN
精神病医生 jīngshénbìng yīshēng [位 wèi]

psychoanalyst NOUN
心理分析学者 xīnlǐ fēnxī xuézhě [位 wèi]

psychological ADJECTIVE
心理的 xīnlǐ de

psychologist NOUN
心理学家 xīnlǐxué jiā [位 wèi]

psychology NOUN
心理学 xīnlǐxué

PTO ABBREVIATION *(= please turn over)*
请翻过来 qǐng fān guòlái

pub NOUN
酒吧 jiǔbā [个 gè]

public ADJECTIVE
▷ *see also* **public** NOUN
1 公众的 gōngzhòng de *(support, opinion, interest)*
2 公共的 gōnggòng de *(building, service, library)*
3 公开的 gōngkāi de *(announcement, meeting)*
■ **the public address system** 公共广播系统 gōnggòng guǎngbō xìtǒng

public NOUN
▷ *see also* **public** ADJECTIVE
■ **the public** 公众 gōngzhòng □ open to the public 对公众开放 duì gōngzhòng kāifàng
■ **in public** 当众 dāngzhòng

publican NOUN
酒馆老板 jiǔguǎn lǎobǎn [位 wèi]

public holiday NOUN
法定假期 fǎdìng jiàqī [个 gè]

publicity NOUN
1 宣传 xuānchuán *(information, advertising)*
2 关注 guānzhù *(attention)*

public school NOUN
1 私立中学 sīlì zhōngxué [所 suǒ] *(in Britain: private school)*
2 公立学校 gōnglì xuéxiào [所 suǒ] *(US: state school)*

public transport NOUN
公共交通 gōnggòng jiāotōng

to **publish** VERB
出版 chūbǎn *(book, magazine)*

publisher NOUN
出版社 chūbǎnshè [家 jiā] *(company)*

pudding NOUN
甜点 tiándiǎn [份 fèn] *(dessert)*
□ What's for pudding? 甜点是什么？Tiándiǎn shì shénme?
■ **black pudding** 血肠 xiěcháng

LANGUAGE TIP Another word for **pudding** is the phonetic loanword 布丁 bùdīng.

□ rice pudding 米饭布丁 mǐfàn bùdīng

puddle NOUN
水坑 shuǐkēng [个 gè]

puff pastry NOUN
松饼 sōngbǐng [个 gè]

to **pull** VERB
1 用力拉 yònglìlā *(without object in the sentence)*
□ Pull! 用力拉！Yònglìlā!
2 拖 tuō *(rope, hair)*
3 拉 lā *(handle, door, cart, carriage)*
4 扣 kòu *(trigger)*
□ He pulled the trigger. 他扣动了扳机。Tā kòudòngle bānjī.
■ **to pull a muscle** 扭伤肌肉 niǔshāng jīròu □ I pulled a muscle when I was training. 我训练时扭伤了肌肉。Wǒ xùnliànshí niǔshāngle jīròu.
■ **to pull somebody's leg** 开某人的玩笑 kāi mǒurén de wánxiào □ You're pulling my leg! 你拿我开玩笑！Nǐ náwǒ kāiwánxiào!

to **pull down** VERB
拆毁 chāihuǐ *(building)*

to **pull in** VERB
停靠 tíngkào *(at the kerb)*

to **pull out** VERB
1 开出 kāichū *(from kerb)*
2 进入超车道 jìnrù chāochēdào *(when overtaking)*

□ The car pulled out to overtake. 那辆车进入了超车道超车。Nàliàng chē jìnrù le chāochēdào chāochē.

3 退出 tuìchū *(from agreement, contest)*
□ She pulled out of the tournament. 她退出了比赛。Tā tuìchūle bǐsài.

to **pull through** VERB

1 恢复健康 huīfù jiànkāng *(from illness)*
□ They think he'll pull through. 他们认为他会恢复健康。Tāmen rènwéi tā huì huīfù jiànkāng.

2 渡过难关 dùguò nánguān *(from difficulties)*

to **pull up** VERB

1 拉起 lāqǐ *(socks, trousers)*

2 拔除 báchú *(plant, weed)*

3 停下 tíngxià *(stop)*
□ A black car pulled up beside me. 一辆黑车在我身边停了下来。Yíliàng hēichē zài wǒ shēnbiān tíngle xiàlái.

pull-off NOUN (US)
路侧停车处 lùcè tíngchēchù [个 gè]

pullover NOUN
套头衫 tàotóushān [件 jiàn]

pulse NOUN
脉搏 màibó [下 xià]
■ **to feel somebody's pulse** 给某人诊脉 gěi mǒurén zhěnmài □ The nurse felt his pulse. 护士给他诊脉。Hùshì gěitā zhěnmài.

pump NOUN
▹ *see also* **pump** VERB

1 泵 bèng [个 gè] *(for liquid, gas)*
□ petrol pump 油泵 yóubèng

2 抽水机 chōushuǐjī [台 tái] *(for getting water)*

3 打气筒 dǎqìtǒng [个 gè] *(for inflating)*
□ a bicycle pump 一个自行车打气筒 yígè zìxíngchē dǎqìtǒng

4 轻舞鞋 qīngwǔxié *(shoe)*

to **pump** VERB
▹ *see also* **pump** NOUN
抽 chōu

to **pump up** VERB
打气 dǎqì

pumpkin NOUN
南瓜 nánguā [个 gè]

punch NOUN
▹ *see also* **punch** VERB

1 拳打 quándǎ [顿 dùn]
□ He gave me a punch. 他给了我一拳。Tā gěile wǒ yìquán.

2 潘趣酒 pānqùjiǔ *(drink)*

to **punch** VERB
▹ *see also* **punch** NOUN

1 用拳打击 yòng quán dǎjī *(hit)*
□ He punched me! 他打我！ Tā dǎ wǒ!

2 敲击 qiāojī *(button, keyboard)*

3 在...上打孔 zài...shàng dǎkǒng *(ticket, paper)*
□ He forgot to punch my ticket. 他忘了在我的票上打孔。Tā wàngle zài wǒde piàoshàng dǎkǒng.

to **punch in** VERB
敲入 qiāorù

punch-up NOUN
斗殴 dòu'ōu [次 cì]

punctual ADJECTIVE
准时的 zhǔnshí de

punctuation NOUN
标点 biāodiǎn [个 gè]

puncture NOUN
▹ *see also* **puncture** VERB
刺孔 cìkǒng [个 gè]
□ I had to mend a puncture. 我得修理车胎上扎的一个孔。Wǒ děi xiūlǐ chētāishàng zhāde yígèkǒng.
■ **to have a puncture** 轮胎被扎破了 lúntāi bèi zhāpò le □ I had a puncture on the motorway. 我在公路上轮胎给扎破了。Wǒ zài gōnglùshàng gěi zhāpòle.

to **puncture** VERB
▹ *see also* **puncture** NOUN
戳破 chuōpò *(tyre, lung)*

to **punish** VERB
惩罚 chéngfá
■ **to punish somebody for something** 因某事而惩罚某人 yīn mǒushì ér chéngfá mǒurén

punishment NOUN

1 惩罚 chéngfá [种 zhǒng]

2 处罚 chǔfá [次 cì] *(penalty)*

punk NOUN
朋克 péngkè [个 gè] *(person)*
■ **a punk rock band** 一支朋克摇滚乐队 yìzhī péngkè yáogǔn yuèduì

pupil NOUN
学生 xuéshēng [名 míng]

puppet NOUN
木偶 mù'ǒu [个 gè]

puppy NOUN
小狗 xiǎogǒu [只 zhī]

to **purchase** VERB
购买 gòumǎi

pure ADJECTIVE

1 纯的 chún de *(silk, gold, wool)*

2 纯净的 chúnjìng de *(clean)*
□ pure orange juice 纯橙汁 chúnchéngzhī
□ He's doing pure maths. 他在做纯数学。Ta zài zuò chúnshùxué.

purple ADJECTIVE
▹ *see also* **purple** NOUN
紫色的 zǐsè de

purple NOUN
▹ *see also* **purple** ADJECTIVE
紫色 zǐsè [种 zhǒng]

purpose NOUN
1 目的 mùdì [个 gè] *(of person)*
□ his purpose in life 他的人生目的 tāde rénshēng mùdì
2 意义 yìyì [个 gè] *(of act, meeting, visit)*
□ What is the purpose of these changes? 这些变化有什么意义？ Zhèxiē biànhuà yǒu shénme yìyì?
■ **on purpose** 故意地 gùyì de □ He did it on purpose. 他故意这么做的。Tā gùyì zhème zuòde.

to **purr** VERB
咕噜咕噜叫 gūlūgūlūjiào

purse NOUN
1 钱包 qiánbāo [个 gè] *(for money)*
2 手袋 shǒudài [个 gè] (US: *handbag)*

to **pursue** VERB
追求 zhuīqiú

pursuit NOUN
追击 zhuījī
□ outdoor pursuits 户外追击 hùwài zhuījī

push NOUN
▷ *see also* **push** VERB
推 tuī [下 xià]
■ **to give somebody a push** 推某人一下 tuī mǒurén yíxià □ He gave me a push. 他推了我一下。Tā tuīle wǒ yíxià.
■ **at the push of a button** 只要按一下按钮 zhǐyào àn yīxià ànniǔ

to **push** VERB
▷ *see also* **push** NOUN
1 按 àn *(press)*
2 挤 jǐ *(shove)*
□ Don't push! 别挤！ Biéjǐ!
3 推 tuī *(car, door, person)*
■ **to push somebody out of the way** 把某人推开 bǎ mǒurén tuīkāi
■ **to push a door shut** 把门推上 bǎ mén tuīshàng
■ **to push one's way through the crowd** 挤过人群 jǐguò rénqún
■ **to push forward** 向前挤 xiàngqián jǐ
■ **to push somebody to do something** 逼迫某人做某事 bīpò mǒurén zuò mǒushì
□ My parents are pushing me to go to university. 我父母逼迫我上大学。Wǒ fùmǔ bīpò wǒ shàngdàxué.
■ **to be pushed for time** 赶时间 gǎn shíjiān

to **push in** VERB
插队 chāduì *(in queue)*

to **push over** VERB
推倒 tuīdǎo *(person, wall, furniture)*

to **push through** VERB
挤过 jǐguò
□ The ambulance men pushed through the crowd. 救护人员挤过人群。Jiùhù rényuán jǐguò rénqún. □ I pushed my way through. 我挤了过去。Wǒ jǐle guòqù.

to **push up** VERB
提高 tígāo *(total, prices)*

pushchair NOUN
幼儿车 yòu'érchē [辆 liàng]

push-up NOUN
■ **to do push-ups** 做俯卧撑 zuò fǔwòchēng

to **put** VERB
1 放 fàng *(thing)*
□ Where shall I put my things? 我把东西放哪儿？ Wǒ bǎ dōngxi fàngnǎr? □ She's putting the baby to bed. 她正把宝宝放到床上。Tā zhèngbǎ bǎobao fàngdào chuángshàng.
2 安置 ānzhì *(person: in institution)*
3 写 xiě *(write, type)*
□ Don't forget to put your name on the paper. 别忘了在答卷上写名字。Bié wàngle zài dájuànshàng xiěmíngzì.
■ **to put a lot of effort into something** 投入大量的努力于某事 tóurù dàliàng de nǔlì yú mǒushì
■ **How shall I put it?** 我该怎么说呢？ Wǒ gāi zěnme shuō ne?

to **put across** VERB
讲清 jiǎngqīng *(ideas, argument)*

to **put aside** VERB
保留 bǎoliú
□ Can you put this aside for me till tomorrow? 你能为我把这个保留到明天吗？ Nǐnéng wèiwǒ bǎ zhège bǎoliú dào míngtiān ma?

to **put away** VERB
把...收起来 bǎ...shōuqǐlái
□ Can you put away the dishes, please? 能请你把盘子收起来吗？ Néng qǐngnǐ bǎ pánzi shōuqǐlái ma?

to **put back** VERB
1 放回 fànghuí *(replace)*
□ Put it back when you've finished with it. 完了以后把它放回去。Wánle yǐhòu bǎtā fànghuíqù.
2 倒拨 dàobō *(watch, clock)*

to **put down** VERB
1 放下 fàngxià *(on floor, table)*
□ I'll put these bags down for a minute. 我要把这些袋子放下一会儿。Wǒ yào bǎ zhèxiē dàizi fàngxià yìhuìr.
2 写下 xiěxià *(in writing)*
□ I've put down a few ideas. 我已经写下了一些想法。Wǒ yǐjīng xiěxiàle yìxiē xiǎngfǎ.
■ **to have an animal put down** 让一只动物安乐死 ràng yìzhī dòngwù ānlèsǐ □ We had to have our old dog put down. 我们不得不让我们的老狗安乐死。Wǒmen bùdébù

ràngwǒmende lǎogǒu ānlèsǐ.

to **put forward** VERB

1 提出 tíchū *(ideas, proposal, name)*

▫ to put forward a suggestion 提出一项建议 tíchū yíxiàng jiànyì

2 拨快 bōkuài

▫ Don't forget to put the clocks forward. 别忘了把时钟拨快。Bié wàngle bǎ shízhōng bōkuài.

to **put in** VERB

1 提出 tíchū *(request, complaint, application)*

2 安装 ānzhuāng *(install)*

▫ We're going to get central heating put in. 我们要装中央暖气系统了。Wǒmen yào zhuāng zhōngyāng nuǎnqì xìtǒng le.

3 做 zuò *(do)*

▫ He has put in a lot of work on this project. 他在这个项目中做了很多工作。Tāzài zhège xiàngmùzhōng zuòle hěnduō gōngzuò.

to **put off** VERB

1 推迟 tuīchí *(delay)*

▫ I keep putting it off. 我总是推迟那件事。Wǒ zǒngshì tuīchí nàjiànshì.

■ **to put off doing something** 推迟做某事 tuīchí zuò mǒushì

2 使分心 shǐ fēnxīn *(distract)*

▫ Stop putting me off! 别再让我分心了！Biézài ràngwǒ fēnxīn le！

3 使气馁 shǐ qìněi *(discourage)*

▫ He's not easily put off. 他不容易气馁。Tā bùróngyì qìněi.

to **put on** VERB

1 穿戴 chuāndài *(clothes, make-up, glasses)*

▫ I'll put my coat on. 我要穿上外衣。Wǒ yào chuānshàng wàiyī.

2 开 kāi *(light, TV, radio, oven)*

▫ Shall I put the heater on? 要我开加热器吗？Yàowǒ kāi jiārèqì ma?

3 放 fàng *(CD, video)*

4 上演 shàngyǎn *(play, show)*

▫ We're putting on Bugsy Malone. 我们正在上演龙蛇小霸王。Wǒmen zhèngzài shàngyǎn Lóngshé Xiǎobàwáng.

5 开始烹饪 kāishǐ pēngrèn *(start cooking)*

▫ I'll put the potatoes on. 我要开始烹饪马铃薯。Wǒ yào kāishǐ pēngrèn mǎlíngshǔ.

■ **to put on weight** 增重 zēngzhòng

▫ He's put on a lot of weight. 他增重很多。Tā zēngzhòng hěnduō.

to **put out** VERB

1 熄灭 xīmiè *(candle, cigarette)*

2 扑灭 pūmiè *(fire, blaze)*

▫ It took them five hours to put out the fire. 他们用了五个小时才扑灭了大火。Tāmen yòngle wǔgè xiǎoshí cái pūmièle dàhuǒ.

3 关 guān *(switch off)*

to **put over** VERB

讲清 jiǎngqīng *(ideas, argument)*

to **put through** VERB

接通 jiētōng

▫ I'm putting you through. 正在为您接通。Zhèngzài wèinín jiētōng.

to **put up** VERB

1 建造 jiànzào *(fence, building, tent)*

▫ We put up our tent in a field. 我们把帐篷建在了一片空地上。Wǒmen bǎ zhàngpéng jiànzài le yípiàn kòngdìshàng.

2 张贴 zhāngtiē *(poster, sign)*

▫ I'll put the poster up on my wall. 我要把那张海报贴在我屋里的墙上。Wǒ yàobǎ nàzhāng hǎibào tiēzài wǒwūlǐde qiángshàng.

3 撑起 chēngqǐ *(umbrella, hood)*

4 提高 tígāo *(price, cost)*

▫ They've put up the price. 他们提高了价格。Tāmen tígāole jiàgé.

5 为…提供住宿 wèi…tígōng zhùsù *(accommodate)*

▫ My friend will put me up for the night. 我朋友晚上会为我提供住宿。Wǒ péngyǒu wǎnshàng huìwèiwǒ tígōng zhùsù.

■ **to put up one's hand** 举手 jǔshǒu

▫ If you have any questions, put up your hand. 有问题举手。Yǒuwèntí jǔshǒu.

to **put up with** VERB

容忍 róngrěn

▫ I'm not going to put up with it any longer. 我不再容忍了。Wǒ búzài róngrěnle.

puzzle NOUN

1 谜 mí [个 gè] *(riddle, conundrum)*

2 测智玩具 cèzhì wánjù [套 tào] *(toy)*

3 谜团 mítuán [个 gè] *(mystery)*

puzzled ADJECTIVE

茫然的 mángrán de

▫ You look puzzled! 你看起来很茫然！Nǐ kànqǐlái hěn mángrán!

puzzling ADJECTIVE

使人费解的 shǐrén fèijiěde

pyjamas (US **pajamas**) PL NOUN

睡衣裤 shuìyīkù

■ **a pair of pyjamas** 一套睡衣裤 yítào shuìyīkù

■ **a pyjama top** 一件睡衣 yíjiàn shuìyī

pylon NOUN

电缆塔 diànlǎn tǎ [个 gè]

pyramid NOUN

金字塔 jīnzì tǎ [座 zuò]

Pyrenees PL NOUN

比利牛斯山脉 Bǐlì niúsī shānmài

Qq

quaint ADJECTIVE
古雅的 gǔyǎ de *(house, village)*

qualification NOUN
学历资格 xuélìzīgé [个 gè]
■ **to leave school without any qualifications** 中途辍学没有任何学历 zhōngtú chuòxué méiyǒu rènhé xuélì

qualified ADJECTIVE
合格的 hégé de
□ a qualified driving instructor 一名合格的驾驶教练 yìmíng hégéde jiàshǐ jiàoliàn
■ **fully qualified** 完全合格的 wánquán hégé de

to **qualify** VERB
1 取得资格 qǔdé zīgé *(pass examinations)*
■ **to qualify as...** 取得…的资格 qǔdé...de zīgé □ She qualified as a teacher last year. 她去年取得了教师资格。Tā qùnián qǔdé le jiàoshī zīgé.
2 获得参赛资格 huòdé cānsài zīgé *(in competition)*
□ Our team didn't qualify. 我们的队伍没有获得参赛资格。Wǒmen de duìwǔ méiyǒu huòdé cānsài zīgé.

quality NOUN
1 质量 zhìliàng *(standard)*
□ good-quality ingredients 高质量的配料 gāozhìliàng de pèiliào
2 品质 pǐnzhì [种 zhǒng] *(characteristic)*
□ She's got lots of good qualities. 她具备很多优秀品质。Tā jùbèi hěnduō yōuxiù pǐnzhì.
■ **quality of life** 生活质量 shénghuó zhìliàng

quantity NOUN
1 数量 shùliàng *(amount)*
■ **a small quantity** 少量 shǎoliàng
2 容量 róngliàng *(volume)*

quarantine NOUN
检疫隔离 jiǎnyìgélí [次 cì]
■ **in quarantine** 被隔离 bèi gélí

quarrel NOUN
▷ *see also* **quarrel** VERB
吵架 chǎojià [次 cì]

to **quarrel** VERB
▷ *see also* **quarrel** NOUN
争吵 zhēngchǎo

quarry NOUN
采石场 cǎishí chǎng [座 zuò]

quarter NOUN
四分之一 sìfēnzhīyī
■ **to cut something into quarters** 把某物切成四份 bǎ mǒuwù qiēchéng sìfèn
■ **a quarter of an hour** 一刻钟 yíkèzhōng
□ three quarters of an hour 三刻钟 sānkèzhōng
■ **It's a quarter to three.** 现在是三点差一刻。Xiànzài shì sāndiǎn chà yíkè.
■ **It's a quarter of three.** (US) 现在是三点差一刻。Xiànzài shì sāndiǎn chà yíkè.
■ **It's a quarter past three.** 现在是三点一刻。Xiànzài shì sāndiǎn yíkè.
■ **It's a quarter after three.** (US) 现在是三点一刻。Xiànzài shì sāndiǎn yíkè.

quarter-final NOUN
四分之一决赛 sìfēnzhīyī juésài [场 chǎng]

quartet NOUN
四重奏 sìchóngzòu [首 shǒu]
□ a string quartet 一首弦乐四重奏 yìshǒu xiányuè sìchóngzòu

quay NOUN
码头 mǎtóu [个 gè]

queasy ADJECTIVE
令人作呕的 lìng rén zuòǒu de
■ **to feel queasy** 感到恶心想吐 gǎndào ěxīn xiǎngtù

queen NOUN
1 女王 nǚwáng [位 wèi] *(monarch)*
□ Queen Elizabeth 伊丽莎白女王 Yīlìshābái Nǚwáng
2 王后 wánghòu [位 wèi] *(king's wife)*
3 王后 wánghòu [张 zhāng] *(playing card)*
□ the queen of hearts 一张红心王后 yìzhāng hóngxīn wánghòu

query NOUN
▷ *see also* **query** VERB
疑问 yíwèn [个 gè]

to **query** VERB
▷ *see also* **query** NOUN
质疑 zhìyí *(figures, bill, expenses)*

□ No one queried my decision. 没人质疑我的决定。Méirén zhìyí wǒde juédìng.

question NOUN
▷ *see also* **question** VERB
1 问题 wèntí [个 gè] *(query)*
□ Can I ask a question? 我能提个问题吗？Wǒ néng tí gè wèntí ma?
■ **to ask somebody a question** 问某人一个问题 wèn mǒurén yígè wèntí
2 议题 yìtí [项 xiàng] *(issue)*
□ Three questions were discussed at the meeting. 会上讨论了三个议题。Huì shàng tǎolùn le sāngè yìtí.
3 试题 shìtí [道 dào] *(in written exam)*
■ **to be out of the question** 不可能的 bù kěnéng de

to **question** VERB
▷ *see also* **question** NOUN
审问 shěnwèn *(interrogate)*
□ He was questioned by the police. 他受到了警方的审问。Tā shòudàole jǐngfāngde shěnwèn.

question mark NOUN
问号 wènhào [个 gè]

questionnaire NOUN
问卷 wènjuàn [份 fèn]

queue NOUN
▷ *see also* **queue** VERB
队 duì [条 tiáo]

to **queue** VERB
▷ *see also* **queue** NOUN
排队 páiduì
□ We had to queue for tickets. 我们不得不排队买票。Wǒmen bùdébù páiduì mǎipiào.

quick ADJECTIVE
▷ *see also* **quick** ADVERB
1 快的 kuài de *(fast)*
□ She's a quick learner. 她学东西很快。Tā xué dōngxi hěnkuài. □ It's quicker by train. 坐火车更快点。Zuòhuǒchē gèng kuàidiǎn.
■ **Be quick!** 快点！ Kuàidiǎn!
2 快速的 kuàisù de *(look)*
3 简短的 jiǎnduǎn de *(visit)*
4 迅速的 xùnsùde *(reply, response, decision)*
□ a quick decision 一个迅速的决定 yígè xùnsùde juédìng

quick ADVERB
▷ *see also* **quick** ADJECTIVE
快地 kuài de
□ Quick, phone the police! 快给警察局打电话！ Kuài gěi jǐngchájú dǎ diànhuà!

quickly ADVERB
1 迅速地 xùnsù de *(walk, grow, speak, work)*
2 快地 kuài de *(realize, change, react, finish)*
□ It was all over very quickly. 很快就都结束了。Hěnkuài jiù dōu jiéshù le.

quiet ADJECTIVE
1 轻声的 qīngshēng de *(voice, music)*
2 平静的 píngjìng de *(place)*
□ a quiet little town 一座平静的小镇 yízuò píngjìng de xiǎozhèn □ a quiet weekend 一个平静的周末 yígè píngjìng de zhōumò
3 沉默的 chénmò de *(person)*
□ You're very quiet today. 你今天很沉默。Nǐ jīntiān hěn chénmò.
■ **to be quiet** *(silent)* 安静的 ānjìng de
□ Be quiet! 请安静！ Qǐng ānjìng!

quietly ADVERB
1 轻声地 qīngshēng de *(speak, play)*
□ "She's dead," he said quietly. "她死了，" 他轻声地说。"Tā sǐ le," tā qīngshēng de shuō.
2 默默地 mòmò de *(silently)*
□ He quietly opened the door. 他默默地打开了门。Tā mòmòde dǎkāile mén.

quilt NOUN
被子 bèizi [床 chuáng] *(duvet)*

to **quit** VERB
1 停止 tíngzhǐ *(stop)*
2 辞去 cíqù *(job)*
□ She's decided to quit her job. 她决定辞去工作。Tā juédìng cíqù gōngzuò.
3 辞职 cízhí *(resign)*
4 放弃 fàngqì *(give up)*
□ I quit! 我放弃！ Wǒ fàngqì!

quite ADVERB
1 很 hěn *(rather)*
□ quite good 很好 hěnhǎo □ It's quite warm today. 今天很暖和。Jīntiān hěn nuǎnhuo. □ I quite liked the film, but... 我很喜欢那部电影，但是… Wǒ hěn xǐhuān nà bù diànyǐng, dànshì...
2 十分 shífēn *(completely)*
□ I'm not quite sure. 我不是十分肯定。Wǒ búshì shífēn kěndìng. □ It's not quite finished. 像是还没结束。Xiàng shì hái méi jiéshù.
■ **I see them quite a lot.** 我常常见到他们。Wǒ chángcháng jiàndào tāmen.
■ **quite a lot of money** 很多钱 hěnduō qián
■ **It costs quite a lot to go abroad.** 出国要花很多钱。Chūguó yào huā hěnduō qián.
■ **quite a few** 相当多 xiāngdāng duō
■ **It's quite a long way.** 这段路很远。Zhè duàn lù hěn yuǎn.
■ **Quite!** 确实如此！ Quèshí rúcǐ!
■ **It was quite a sight.** 景象十分了得。Jǐngxiàng shífēn liǎodé.

quiz NOUN

猜谜游戏 cāimíyóuxì [个 gè] *(game)*

quota NOUN

配额 pèi'é [份 fèn]

quotation NOUN

1 引语 yǐnyǔ [句 jù]

□ a quotation from Shakespeare 一句引自莎士比亚的话 yíjù yǐnzì Shāshìbǐyà de huà

2 报价 bàojià [个 gè] *(estimate)*

to **quote** VERB

▷ *see also* **quote** NOUN

1 引用 yǐnyòng *(politician, author)*

□ He's always quoting Shakespeare. 他总是引用莎士比亚的话。Tā zǒngshì yǐnyòng Shāshìbǐyà de huà.

2 引述 yǐnshù *(line)*

quote NOUN

▷ *see also* **quote** VERB

名言 míngyán [句 jù]

□ a Shakespeare quote 一句莎士比亚的名言 yíjù Shāshìbǐyà de míngyán

■ **quotes** *(quotation marks)* 引号 yǐnhào

□ in quotes 在引号里 zài yǐnhào lǐ

Rr

rabbi NOUN
拉比 lābǐ [位 wèi]
rabbit NOUN
兔子 tùzi [只 zhī]
■ **a rabbit hutch** 一个兔笼子 yígè tù lóngzi
rabies NOUN
狂犬病 kuángquǎnbìng
□ a dog with rabies 一只患狂犬病的狗 yìzhī huàn kuángquǎnbìng de gǒu
race NOUN
▷ *see also* **race** VERB
1 竞赛 jìngsài [场 chǎng]
□ a cycle race 一场自行车竞赛 yìchǎng zìxíngchē jìngsài
■ **a race against time** 抢时间 qiǎng shíjiān
2 种族 zhǒngzú [个 gè] *(ethnic group)*
■ **race relations** 种族关系 zhǒngzú guānxì
■ **the human race** 人类 rénlèi
to **race** VERB
▷ *see also* **race** NOUN
1 参赛 cānsài *(have a race)*
2 疾走 jízǒu *(go fast)*
□ We raced to catch the bus. 我们疾走去搭巴士。Wǒmen jízǒu qù dā bāshì.
3 与...赛跑 yǔ...sàipǎo *(race against)*
□ I'll race you! 我将和你赛跑！ Wǒ jiāng hé nǐ sàipǎo!
racecourse NOUN
赛马场 sàimǎchǎng [个 gè]
racehorse NOUN
赛马 sàimǎ [匹 pǐ]
racetrack NOUN
1 赛道 sàidào [条 tiáo] *(for cars)*
2 赛马场 sàimǎchǎng [个 gè] *(US: for horses)*
racial ADJECTIVE
种族的 zhǒngzú de
□ racial discrimination 种族歧视 zhǒngzú qíshì [种 zhǒng]
racing driver NOUN
赛车手 sàichēshǒu [位 wèi]
racism NOUN
种族主义 zhǒngzú zhǔyì
racist ADJECTIVE
▷ *see also* **racist** NOUN
1 种族主义的 zhǒngzú zhǔyì de *(policy, attack, idea)*
2 有种族偏见的 yǒu zhǒngzú piānjiàn de *(person, organization)*
racist NOUN
▷ *see also* **racist** ADJECTIVE
种族主义者 zhǒngzú zhǔyìzhě [个 gè]
rack NOUN
1 行李架 xínglijià [个 gè] *(luggage rack)*
2 架 jià [个 gè] *(for hanging clothes, dishes)*
racket NOUN
1 球拍 qiúpāi [个 gè]
□ my tennis racket 我的网球拍 wǒde wǎngqiúpāi
2 噪音 zàoyīn [xiē] *(noise)*
□ They're making a terrible racket. 他们一直在制造噪音。Tāmen yìzhí zài zhìzào zàoyīn.
racquet NOUN
球拍 qiúpāi [副 fù]
radar NOUN
雷达 léidá [个 gè]
radiation NOUN
辐射 fúshè
radiator NOUN
暖气片 nuǎnqìpiàn [个 gè]
radio NOUN
1 收音机 shōuyīnjī [台 tái] *(receiver)*
2 广播 guǎngbō *(broadcasting)*
■ **on the radio** 广播中 guǎngbō zhōng
radioactive ADJECTIVE
放射性的 fàngshèxìng de
radio station NOUN
广播电台 guǎngbō diàntái [个 gè]
radish NOUN
水萝卜 shuǐ luóbo [个 gè]
RAF NOUN *(= Royal Air Force)*
■ **the RAF** 皇家空军 Huángjiā Kōngjūn
□ He's in the RAF. 他参加了皇家空军。Tā cānjiā le Huángjiā Kōngjūn.
raffle NOUN
抽奖 chōujiǎng [次 cì]
□ a raffle ticket 一张抽奖彩票 yìzhāng

chōujiǎng cǎipiào

raft NOUN
筏 fá [只 zhī]

rag NOUN
破布 pòbù [块 kuài]
□ a piece of rag 一块破布 yíkuài pòbù
■ **dressed in rags** 衣衫褴褛 yīshānlánlǚ

rage NOUN
怒 shèngnù [阵 zhèn]
□ mad with rage 气疯了 qìfēng le
■ **to be in a rage** 非常气愤 fēicháng qìfèn
□ She was in a rage. 她非常气愤。Tā fēicháng qìfèn.

to **raid** VERB
▷ *see also* **raid** NOUN
1 突袭 tūxí *(soldiers, police)*
□ The police raided the club. 警方突袭了那家俱乐部。Jǐngfāng tūxí le nàjiā jùlèbù.
2 袭击 xíjī *(criminal)*

raid NOUN
▷ *see also* **raid** VERB
1 盗窃 dàoqiè [次 cì] *(burglary)*
□ There was a bank raid near my house. 我家附近发生了一起银行盗窃案。Wǒjiā fùjìn fāshēng le yìqǐ yínháng dàoqiè àn.
2 突袭 tūxí [次 cì]
□ a police raid 一次警方突袭 yícì jǐngfāng tūxí

rail NOUN
1 扶手 fúshǒu [个 gè] *(for safety on stairs)*
2 横栏 hénglán [个 gè] *(on bridge, balcony)*
□ Don't lean over the rail! 不要伏身趴在横栏上！Búyào fǔshēn pāzài hénglán shàng!
3 横杆 hénggān [根 gēn] *(for hanging clothes)*
4 铁轨 tiěguǐ [条 tiáo] *(for trains)*
■ **by rail** 乘火车 chéng huǒchē

railcard NOUN
火车卡 huǒchēkǎ [张 zhāng]
□ a young person's railcard 一张青年火车卡 yìzhāng qīngnián huǒchēkǎ

railroad NOUN (US)
1 铁路 tiělù *(system)*
2 火车道 huǒchēdào [条 tiáo] *(line)*
■ **a railroad station** 一个火车站 yígè huǒchēzhàn

railway NOUN
1 铁路 tiělù *(system)*
□ the privatization of the railways 铁路私有化 tiělù sīyǒuhuà
2 铁道 tiědào [条 tiáo] *(line)*

railway line NOUN
铁路线 tiělùxiàn [条 tiáo]

railway station NOUN
火车站 huǒchēzhàn [个 gè]

rain NOUN
▷ *see also* **rain** VERB
雨 yǔ
■ **in the rain** 在雨中 zài yǔzhōng

to **rain** VERB
▷ *see also* **rain** NOUN
下雨 xiàyǔ
□ It's raining. 正在下雨。Zhèngzài xiàyǔ.
□ It rains a lot here. 这里经常下雨。Zhèlǐ jīngcháng xiàyǔ.

rainbow NOUN
彩虹 cǎihóng [道 dào]

raincoat NOUN
雨衣 yǔyī [件 jiàn]

rainforest NOUN
雨林 yǔlín [片 piàn]

rainy ADJECTIVE
多雨的 duōyǔ de

to **raise** VERB
▷ *see also* **raise** NOUN
1 举起 jǔqǐ *(lift a hand, a glass)*
□ He raised his hand. 他举起了手。Tā jǔqǐ le shǒu.
2 增加 zēngjiā *(increase a salary, a rate)*
3 提高 tígāo *(morale, standards)*
□ They want to raise standards in schools. 他们想提高学校里的标准。Tāmen xiǎng tígāo xuéxiào lǐ de biāozhǔn.
4 抚养 fǔyǎng *(child, family)*
■ **to raise money** 筹集经费 chóují jīngfèi
□ The school is raising money for a new gym. 学校正在为一个新运动馆筹集经费。Xuéxiào zhèngzài wèi yígè xīn yùndòngguǎn chóují jīngfèi.

raise NOUN (US)
▷ *see also* **raise** VERB
加薪 jiāxīn [次 cì] *(pay rise)*

raisin NOUN
葡萄干 pútáogān [袋 dài]

rake NOUN
耙子 pázi [个 gè]

rally NOUN
1 集会 jíhuì [次 cì] *(public meeting)*
2 拉力赛 lālìsài [场 chǎng] *(for cars)*

ram NOUN
▷ *see also* **ram** VERB
公羊 gōngyáng [只 zhī] *(sheep)*

to **ram** VERB
▷ *see also* **ram** NOUN
撞 zhuàng *(vehicle)*
□ The thieves rammed a police car. 那些贼撞上了一辆警车。Nàxiē zéi zhuàng shàng le yíliàng jǐngchē.

Ramadan NOUN
斋月 Zhāiyuè

rambler NOUN
漫步者 mànbùzhě [个 gè]

ramp NOUN
坡道 pōdào [条 tiáo]

ran VERB ▷ *see* **run**

ranch NOUN
大农场 dànóngchǎng [个 gè]

random ADJECTIVE
任意的 rènyì de
■ **a random selection** 一个任意的选择 yígè rènyì de xuǎnzé
■ **at random** 随意地 suíyì de ◻ We picked the number at random. 我们随意地选了这个数字。Wǒmen suíyì de xuǎn le zhègè shùzì.

rang VERB ▷ *see* **ring**

range NOUN
▷ *see also* **range** VERB
1 范围 fànwéi [个 gè] *(of ages, prices)*
■ **a wide range of colours** 多种颜色 duōzhǒng yánsè
2 系列 xìliè [个 gè] *(of subjects, possibilities)*
◻ We study a range of subjects. 我们学习一系列的科目。Wǒmen xuéxí yíxìliè de kēmù.
3 山脉 shānmài [个 gè] *(mountain range)*

to **range** VERB
▷ *see also* **range** NOUN
■ **to range from... to...** 在…到…之间 zài... dào...zhījiān ◻ Temperatures in summer range from 20 to 35 degrees. 夏天里气温在二十到三十五度之间。Xiàtiān lǐ qìwēn zài èrshí dào sānshíwǔ dù zhījiān.

rank NOUN
▷ *see also* **rank** VERB
■ **a taxi rank** 一个出租车站 yígè chūzūchē zhàn

to **rank** VERB
▷ *see also* **rank** NOUN
排名 páimíng
◻ He's ranked third in the United States. 他在美国排名第三。Tā zài Měiguó páimíng dìsān.

ransom NOUN
赎金 shújīn [次 cì]

rap NOUN
说唱音乐 shuōchàngyīnyuè [段 duàn] *(music)*

rape NOUN
▷ *see also* **rape** VERB
强奸 qiángjiān [次 cì]

to **rape** VERB
▷ *see also* **rape** NOUN
强奸 qiángjiān

rapids PL NOUN
湍流 tuānliú

rapist NOUN
强奸犯 qiángjiānfàn [个 gè]

rare ADJECTIVE
1 稀有的 xīyǒu de
◻ a rare plant 一种稀有植物 yìzhǒng xīyǒu zhíwù
2 半熟的 bànshóu de *(steak)*

rarely ADVERB
很少 hěnshǎo

rash NOUN
皮疹 pízhěn
◻ I've got a rash on my chest. 我胸上长了皮疹。Wǒ xiōngshàng zhǎng le pízhěn.

raspberry NOUN
山莓 shānméi [只 zhī]
◻ raspberry jam 山莓酱 shānméijiàng

rat NOUN
鼠 shǔ [只 zhī]

rate NOUN
▷ *see also* **rate** VERB
1 价格 jiàgé [种 zhǒng] *(price)*
◻ There are reduced rates for students. 针对学生有优惠价格。Zhēnduì xuéshēng yǒu yōuhuì jiàgé.
2 比率 bǐlǜ *(level)*
◻ the divorce rate 离婚率 líhūnlǜ ◻ a high rate of interest 一个高利息率 yígè gāo lìxīlǜ

to **rate** VERB
▷ *see also* **rate** NOUN
被评价 bèi píngjià
◻ He is rated the best. 他被评价为最好的。Tā bèi píngjià wéi zuì hǎo de.

rather ADVERB
相当 xiāngdāng
◻ I was rather disappointed. 我相当失望。Wǒ xiāngdāng shīwàng.
■ **rather a lot** 相当多 xiāngdāng duō
◻ £20! That's rather a lot! 二十英镑！那相当多啊！ Èrshí yīngbàng！ Nà xiāngdāng duō a! ◻ I've got rather a lot of homework to do. 我有相当多的作业要做。Wǒ yǒu xiāngdāng duō de zuòyè yào zuò.
■ **I would rather go than stay.** 我宁愿走而不愿留下来。Wǒ níngyuàn zǒu ér búyuàn liúxià lái.
■ **I'd rather have an apple than a banana.** 我宁愿要一个苹果而不是一个香蕉。Wǒ níngyuàn yào yīgè píngguǒ ér búshì yígè xiāngjiāo.
■ **I'd rather not say.** 我宁可不说。Wǒ nìngkě bùshuō.
■ **rather than** 而不是 érbúshì ◻ We decided to camp, rather than stay at a hotel. 我们决定了去露营，而不是住宾馆。Wǒmen juédìng le qù lùyíng, érbúshì zhù bīnguǎn.

rattle NOUN

发响玩具 fāxiǎng wánjù [件 jiàn] *(for baby)*

rattlesnake NOUN

响尾蛇 xiǎngwěishé [条 tiáo]

to **rave** VERB

热评 rèpíng *(in a positive sense)*

□ They raved about the film. 他们热评了这部电影。Tāmen rèpíng le zhèbù diànyǐng.

raven NOUN

乌鸦 wūyā [只 zhī]

ravenous ADJECTIVE

■ **to be ravenous** 饿极了的 è jíle de □ I'm ravenous! 我饿极了! Wǒ è jíle!

raw ADJECTIVE

生的 shēng de

raw materials PL NOUN

原材料 yuáncáiliào

razor NOUN

1 剃须刀 tìxūdāo [个 gè]

□ some disposable razors 一些一次性剃须刀 yìxiē yícìxìng tìxūdāo

2 电动剃须刀 diàndòng tìxūdāo [个 gè] *(electric razor)*

razor blade NOUN

剃须刀刀片 tìxūdāo dāopiàn [个 gè]

RE NOUN

宗教课 zōngjiàokè

to **reach** VERB

▷ *see also* **reach** NOUN

1 到达 dàodá *(place, destination)*

□ We reached the hotel at 7 p.m. 我们晚上七点到达了宾馆。Wǒmen wǎnshàng qīdiǎn dàdáo le bīnguǎn.

2 达成 dáchéng *(conclusion, agreement, decision)*

□ Eventually they reached a decision. 他们最终达成了一个决定。Tāmen zuìzhōng dáchéng le yígè juédìng.

3 进入 jìnrù *(stage, level, age)*

□ We hope to reach the final. 我们希望能进入决赛。Wǒmen xīwàng néng jìnrù juésài.

■ **He reached for his gun.** 他伸手够到他的枪。Tā shēnshǒu gòudào tāde qiāng.

reach NOUN

▷ *see also* **reach** VERB

■ **out of reach** 够不着 gòubùzháo □ The light switch was out of reach. 灯的开关够不着。Dēngde kāiguān gòubùzháo.

■ **within easy reach of...** 离…很近 lí... hěnjìn □ The hotel is within easy reach of the town centre. 宾馆离城中心很近。Bīnguǎn lí chéngzhōngxīn hěnjìn.

to **react** VERB

反应 fǎnyìng

reaction NOUN

反应 fǎnyìng [种 zhǒng]

reactor NOUN

反应器 fǎnyìngqì [个 gè]

□ a nuclear reactor 一个核反应器 yígè hé fǎnyìngqì

to **read** VERB

1 读 dú

□ Have you read Animal Farm? 你读过动物农场没有? Nǐ dúguò Dòngwù nóngchǎng méiyǒu? □ Read the text out loud. 大声读出正文。Dàshēng dúchū zhèngwén.

2 阅读 yuèdú *(spend time reading)*

□ I don't read much. 我不常阅读。Wǒ bùcháng yuèdú.

3 攻读 gōngdú *(study at university)*

to **read out** VERB

朗读 lǎngdú

□ He read out the article to me. 他朗读这篇文章给我听。Tā lǎngdú zhèpiān wénzhāng gěi wǒ tīng.

to **read through** VERB

1 浏览 liúlǎn *(quickly)*

2 仔细阅读 zǐxì yuèdú *(thoroughly)*

reader NOUN

读者 dúzhě [位 wèi] *(person)*

readily ADVERB

欣然地 xīnrán de

□ She readily agreed. 她欣然同意了。Tā xīnrán tóngyì le.

reading NOUN

阅读 yuèdú

□ Reading is one of my hobbies. 阅读是我的一个爱好。Yuèdú shì wǒde yígè àihào.

ready ADJECTIVE

做好准备的 zuòhǎo zhǔnbèi de

□ She's nearly ready. 她快做好准备了。Tā kuài zuòhǎo zhǔnbèi le.

■ **to get ready** 准备就绪 zhǔnbèi jiùxù □ She's getting ready to go out. 她正在准备就绪然后出去。Tā zhèngzài zhǔnbèi jiùxù ránhòu chūqù.

■ **to get something ready** 将某物准备就绪 jiāng mǒuwù zhǔnbèi jiùxù □ He's getting the dinner ready. 他正在准备晚饭。Tā zhèngzài zhǔnbèi wǎnfàn.

■ **to be ready to do something** 1 *(all set)* 准备做某事 zhǔnbèi zuò mǒushì 2 *(willing)* 愿意做某事 yuànyì zuò mǒushì □ He's always ready to help. 他总是愿意帮助别人。Tā zǒngshì yuànyì bāngzhù biérén.

■ **a ready meal** 一顿准备好的饭 yídùn zhǔnbèi hǎo de fàn

real ADJECTIVE

1 真正的 zhēnzhèng de *(leather, gold)*

2 真实的 zhēnshí de *(reason, interest, name)*

□ Her real name is Cordelia. 她的真实名字

叫做科德丽娅。Tāde zhēnshí míngzi jiàozuò Kēdélìyà.
3 现实的 xiànshí de *(life, feeling)*
□ in real life 在现实生活中 zài xiànshí shēnghuó zhōng
4 完全的 wánquán de *(absolute)*
□ It was a real nightmare. 那完全就是个噩梦。Nà wánquán jiùshi gè èmèng.

realistic ADJECTIVE
1 现实的 xiànshí de *(practical, sensible)*
2 逼真的 bīzhēn de *(book, film, portrayal)*

reality NOUN
现实 xiànshí *(real things)*
■ **in reality** 事实上 shìshí shàng

reality TV NOUN
真人电视节目 zhēnrén diànshì jiémù [个 gè]
□ a reality TV show 一个真人秀 yígè zhēnrénxiù

to **realize** VERB
意识到 yìshídào
■ **to realize that...** 意识到… yìshí dào...
□ We realized that something was wrong. 我们意识到有些东西不对劲。Wǒmen yìshídào yǒuxiē dōngxi búduìjìn.

really ADVERB
1 非常地 fēicháng de *(very)*
□ really good 非常好 fēichánghǎo
□ She's really nice. 她人非常好。Tā rén fēichánghǎo.
2 确实 quèshí *(genuinely)*
□ Do you really think so? 你确实这么想的吗？ Nǐ quèshí zhème xiǎngde mā?
3 确定地 quèdìng de *(after negative)*
□ Do you want to go? — Not really. 你想去吗？ — 并不确定。Nǐ xiǎng qù mā? — Bìng bù quèdìng.
■ **Really?** *(indicating surprise, interest)* 真的吗？ Zhēnde ma? □ I'm learning German. — Really? 我在学德语。— 真的吗？Wǒ zài xué Déyǔ. — Zhēnde mā?

realtor NOUN (US)
房地产商 fángdìchǎn shāng [个 gè]

rear NOUN
▷ *see also* **rear** VERB, ADJECTIVE
后面 hòumian *(back)*
■ **at the rear of the train** 在火车尾部 zài huǒchē wěibù

to **rear** VERB
▷ *see also* **rear** NOUN, ADJECTIVE
饲养 sìyǎng *(cattle, chickens)*

rear ADJECTIVE
▷ *see also* **rear** NOUN, VERB
后面的 hòumian de *(back)*
■ **a rear wheel** 一个后轮 yígè hòulún

reason NOUN
理由 lǐyóu [个 gè]
□ There's no reason to think that. 没有理由那样想。Méiyǒu lǐyóu nàyàng xiǎng.
□ for security reasons 出于安全考虑 chūyú ānquán kǎolǜ
■ **the reason for something** 某事的理由 mǒushì de lǐyóu □ That was the main reason I went. 那就是我去的主要理由。Nà jiùshì wǒ qù de zhǔyào lǐyóu.
■ **the reason why** …的理由 ...de lǐyóu

reasonable ADJECTIVE
1 理智的 lǐzhì de *(person, decision)*
□ Be reasonable! 理智些！ Lǐzhì xiē!
2 相当的 xiāngdāng de *(number, amount)*
3 合理的 hélǐ de *(price)*
4 凑合的 còuhe de *(not bad)*
□ He wrote a reasonable essay. 他完成了一篇还凑合的论文。Tā wánchéng le yìpiān hái còuhe de lùnwén.

reasonably ADVERB
相当地 xiāngdāng de *(moderately)*
□ The team played reasonably well. 这个队打得相当好。Zhègè duì dǎ dé xiāngdāng hǎo.

to **reassure** VERB
使安心 shǐ ānxīn

reassuring ADJECTIVE
令人安心的 lìngrén'ānxīn de

rebellious ADJECTIVE
谋反的 móufǎn de

receipt NOUN
收据 shōujù [张 zhāng]

to **receive** VERB
收到 shōudào

receiver NOUN
听筒 tīngtǒng [个 gè] *(of phone)*
■ **to pick up the receiver** 拿起听筒 náqǐ tīngtǒng

recent ADJECTIVE
最近的 zuìjìn de

recently ADVERB
最近 zuìjìn
□ I've been doing a lot of training recently. 我最近做很多练习。Wǒ zuìjìn zuò hěnduō liànxí.
■ **until recently** 直到最近 zhídào zuìjìn

reception NOUN
1 接待处 jiēdàichù *(in hotel, office)*
□ Please leave your key at reception. 请把你的钥匙留在接待处。Qǐng bǎ nǐde yàoshi liúzài jiēdàichù.
2 欢迎会 huānyínghuì [个 gè] *(party)*
□ The reception will be at a big hotel. 欢迎会将在一家大宾馆举行。Huānyínghuì jiāng zài yìjiā dà bīnguǎn jǔxíng.
3 反响 fǎnxiǎng [种 zhǒng] *(welcome)*

receptionist NOUN
接待员 jiēdàiyuán [位 wèi]

recipe NOUN
食谱 shípǔ [个 gè]

to **reckon** VERB
认为 rènwéi *(think)*
□ What do you reckon? 你怎么认为的？ Nǐ zěnme rènwéi de?

reclining ADJECTIVE
■ **a reclining seat** 一个靠背可调整的座位 yígè kàobèi kě tiáozhěng de zuòwèi

recognizable ADJECTIVE
可辨认的 kě biànrèn de

to **recognize** VERB
认出 rènchū
□ You'll recognize me by my red hair. 你会由我的红色头发认出我。Nǐ huì yóu wǒde hóngsè tóufa rènchū wǒ.

to **recommend** VERB
推荐 tuījiàn
□ What do you recommend? 你推荐什么？ Nǐ tuījiàn shénme?

record NOUN
▷ *see also* **record** VERB, ADJECTIVE
1 唱片 chàngpiàn [张 zhāng] *(sound-recording)*
□ my favourite record 我最喜欢的唱片 wǒ zuì xǐhuān de chàngpiān
2 纪录 jìlù [个 gè] *(unbeaten statistic)*
□ the world record 世界纪录 shìjiè jìlù
3 记录 jìlù [个 gè] *(note)*
□ There is no record of your booking. 这里没有你预订的记录。Zhèlǐ méiyǒu nǐ yùdìng de jìlù.
■ **to keep a record of something** 记录某事 jìlù mǒushì
■ **a criminal record** 一个犯罪记录 yígè fànzuì jìlù
■ **records** *(of police, hospital)* 记录 jìlù

to **record** VERB
▷ *see also* **record** NOUN, ADJECTIVE
录制 lùzhì *(make recording of)*
□ They've just recorded their new album. 他们刚刚录制了一张新唱片。Tāmen gānggāng lùzhì le yìzhāng xīn chàngpiān.

record ADJECTIVE
▷ *see also* **record** NOUN, VERB
创纪录的 chuàng jìlù de *(sales, profits, levels)*
■ **in record time** 破纪录地 pò jìlù de □ She finished the job in record time. 她破纪录地完成了这个工作。Tā pò jìlù de wánchéng le zhègè gōngzuò.

recorded delivery NOUN
挂号式邮寄 guàhàoshì yóujì
■ **to send something recorded delivery** 以挂号的方式寄某物 yǐ guàhào de fāngshì jì mǒuwù

recorder NOUN
1 录音机 lùyīnjī [台 tái] *(of sound)*
2 刻录机 kèlùjī [台 tái] *(video)*
■ **a DVD recorder** 一台DVD 刻录机 yìtái DVD kèlùjī

recording NOUN
录音 lùyīn [次 cì]

record player NOUN
留声机 liúshēngjī [台 tái]

to **recover** VERB
恢复 huīfù
□ He's recovering from a knee injury. 他正从膝盖伤中恢复过来。Tā zhèng cóng xīgàishāng zhōng huīfù guòlái.

recovery NOUN
康复 kāngfù
□ Best wishes for a speedy recovery! 祝你早日康复！ Zhù nǐ zǎorì kāngfù!

rectangle NOUN
长方形 chángfāngxíng [个 gè]

rectangular ADJECTIVE
长方形的 chángfāngxíng de

to **recycle** VERB
循环利用 xúnhuán lìyòng

recycling NOUN
循环利用 xúnhuán lìyòng

red ADJECTIVE
▷ *see also* **red** NOUN
1 红色的 hóngsè de
□ a red rose 一朵红玫瑰 yìduǒ hóng méiguī □ red meat 红肉 hóngròu
2 涨红的 zhànghóng de *(face, person)*
3 红褐色的 hónghèsè de *(hair)*
□ Sam's got red hair. 萨姆有一头红褐色头发。Sàmǔ yǒu yìtóu hónghèsè tóufa.
4 红的 hóng de *(wine)*
■ **a red light** *(traffic light)* 一个红灯 yígè hóngdēng □ to go through a red light 闯红灯 chuǎng hóngdēng

DID YOU KNOW...?
Red is the colour for good luck in China. A lot of people in China get married in a red wedding dress, because it is felt to be a happier colour than the white dress worn in the West. Traditionally in China, white was the colour for funerals.

red NOUN
▷ *see also* **red** ADJECTIVE
红色 hóngsè [种 zhǒng]

Red Cross NOUN
■ **the Red Cross** 红十字会 Hóngshízìhuì

redcurrant NOUN
红醋栗 hóng cùlì [颗 kè]

to **redecorate** VERB
重装饰 chóng zhuāngshì *(with wallpaper)*
red-haired ADJECTIVE
红棕色头发的 hóngzōngsè tóufa de
red-handed ADJECTIVE
▪ **to catch somebody red-handed** 抓住某人做错事 zhuāzhù mǒurén zuò cuòshi
□ He was caught red-handed. 他被抓住做了错事。Tā bèi zhuāzhù zuòle cuòshi.
redhead NOUN
红头发的人 hóng tóufà de rén *(person)* [个 gè]
to **redo** VERB
重做 chóngzuò
to **reduce** VERB
减少 jiǎnshǎo
▪ **to reduce something to...** 将某物减少到… jiāng mǒuwù jiǎnshǎo dào...
reduction NOUN
1 减少 jiǎnshǎo *(decrease)*
2 减价 jiǎnjià [次 cì] *(discount)*
□ a 5% reduction 减价百分之五 jiǎnjià bǎifēnzhī wǔ
redundancy NOUN
多余 duōyú
□ There were fifty redundancies. 有五十个多余的。Yǒu wǔshí gè duōyú de.
redundant ADJECTIVE
被裁员的 bèi cáiyuán de
▪ **to be made redundant** 被裁员 bèi cáiyuán □ He was made redundant yesterday. 他昨天被裁员了。Tā zuótiān bèi cáiyuán le.
red wine NOUN
红酒 hóngjiǔ
reed NOUN
芦苇 lúwěi [丛 cóng] *(plant)*
reel NOUN
线轴 xiànzhóu *(of thread)* [个 gè]
to **refer** VERB
▪ **to refer somebody to** *(authority, book)* 叫某人参看 jiào mǒurén cānkàn
▪ **to refer to** 指 zhǐ □ What are you referring to? 你指什么？ Nǐ zhǐ shénme?
referee NOUN
裁判员 cáipànyuán [位 wèi] *(in sport)*
reference NOUN
1 提到 tídào *(mention)*
□ He made no reference to the murder. 他没有提到那个谋杀案。Tā méiyǒu tídào nàgè móushā'àn.
2 推荐信 tuījiànxìn [封 fēng] *(for job application)*
□ Would you please give me a reference? 你能给我提供一封推荐信么？ Nǐ néng gěi wǒ tígōng yìfēng tuījiànxìn me?

to **refill** VERB
再装满 zàizhuāngmǎn
refinery NOUN
炼油厂 liànyóuchǎng [座 zuò]
to **reflect** VERB
1 映出 yìngchū *(image)*
2 反射 fǎnshè *(light, heat)*
reflection NOUN
1 影像 yǐngxiàng [个 gè] *(image)*
2 沉思 chénsī *(thought)*
reflex NOUN
反射 fǎnshè [种 zhǒng]
refresher course NOUN
进修课程 jìnxiū kèchéng [门 mén]
refreshing ADJECTIVE
提神的 tíshén de
refreshments PL NOUN
饮料及小吃 yǐnliào jí xiǎochī [套 tào]
refrigerator NOUN
冰箱 bīngxiāng [个 gè]
to **refuel** VERB
补给燃料 bǔjǐ ránliào
□ The plane stops in Boston to refuel. 飞机停在波士顿补给燃料。Fēijī tíngzài Bōshìdùn bǔjǐ ránliào.
refuge NOUN
避难所 bìnànsuǒ [个 gè]
refugee NOUN
难民 nànmín [个 gè]
refund NOUN
▷ *see also* **refund** VERB
退款 tuìkuǎn [笔 bǐ]
to **refund** VERB
▷ *see also* **refund** NOUN
偿还 chánghuán
refusal NOUN
拒绝 jùjué [次 cì]
to **refuse** VERB
▷ *see also* **refuse** NOUN
拒绝 jùjué
▪ **to refuse to do something** 拒绝做某事 jùjué zuò mǒushì
▪ **to refuse somebody permission** 不批准某人 bù pīzhǔn mǒurén
refuse NOUN
▷ *see also* **refuse** VERB
垃圾 lājī
▪ **refuse collection** 垃圾清理 lājī qīnglǐ
to **regard** VERB
▷ *see also* **regard** NOUN
认为 rènwéi *(consider, view)*
▪ **to regard something as** 将某物认为是 jiāng mǒuwù rènwéishì
regard NOUN
▷ *see also* **regard** VERB
▪ **to give one's regards to** 向…表示问候

xiàng...biǎoshì wènhòu □ Give my regards to Alice. 请向爱丽丝表示我的问候。Qǐng xiàng Àilìsī biǎoshì wǒde wènhòu.
■ **with kind regards** 表示诚挚的问候 biǎoshì chéngzhì de wènhòu

regarding PREPOSITION
关于 guānyú
□ the laws regarding the export of animals 关于出口动物的法律 guānyú chūkǒu dòngwù de fǎlǜ □ Regarding John,... 关于约翰，… Guānyú Yuēhàn,...

regardless ADVERB
不顾 búgù
■ **regardless of the consequences** 不顾后果 búgù hòuguǒ

region NOUN
区域 qūyù [个 gè]

regional ADJECTIVE
地区的 dìqū de

register NOUN
▷ *see also* **register** VERB
1 登记 dēngjì [个 gè] *(at hotel)*
2 注册 zhùcè [个 gè] *(in school)*

to **register** VERB
▷ *see also* **register** NOUN
注册 zhùcè *(at school, college)*

registered ADJECTIVE
挂号的 guàhào de

registration NOUN
登记 dēngjì [个 gè] *(of birth, death, students)*

to **regret** VERB
▷ *see also* **regret** NOUN
后悔 hòuhuǐ
□ Give me the money or you'll regret it! 给我钱，要不你会后悔的！ Gěi wǒ qián, yàobù nǐ huì hòuhuǐ de!
■ **to regret that...** 对…感到后悔 duì... gǎndào hòuhuǐ
■ **to regret doing something** 后悔做某事 hòuhuǐ zuò mǒushì □ I regret saying that. 我后悔说了那些。Wǒ hòuhuǐ shuōle nàxiē.

regret NOUN
▷ *see also* **regret** VERB
遗憾 yíhàn [个 gè]
■ **to have no regrets** 没有遗憾 méiyǒu yíhàn

regular ADJECTIVE
1 有规律的 yǒu guīlǜ de
□ at regular intervals 在有规律的时间间隔内 zài yǒu guīlǜ de shíjiān jiàngé nèi
2 经常的 jīngcháng de *(visitor)*
■ **a regular verb** 一个规则动词 yígè guīzéxìng dòngcí
■ **a regular portion of fries** 一包中包薯条 yìbāo zhōngbāo shǔtiáo
■ **to take regular exercise** 做规律性的练习 zuò guīlǜxìng de liànxí

regularly ADVERB
经常 jīngcháng

regulation NOUN
规章 guīzhāng [套 tào]

rehearsal NOUN
排练 páiliàn [次 cì]

to **rehearse** VERB
排练 páiliàn

reindeer NOUN
驯鹿 xùnlù [只 zhī]

to **reject** VERB
1 拒绝接受 jùjué jiēshòu
□ We rejected that idea straight away. 我们直截拒绝接受那个主意。Wǒmen zhíjié jùjué jiēshòu nàgè zhǔyì.
2 拒绝 jùjué *(applicant, admirer)*
■ **I applied but they rejected me.** 我申请了但是他们拒绝了我。Wǒ shēnqǐng le dànshì tāmen jùjué le wǒ.

related ADJECTIVE
有亲缘关系的 yǒu qīnyuán guānxì de *(people)*
□ We're related. 我们有亲缘关系。Wǒmen yǒu qīnyuán guānxì.

relation NOUN
1 亲戚 qīnqi [个 gè] *(relative)*
□ He's a distant relation. 他是一个远方亲戚。Tā shì yígè yuǎnfáng qīnqi. □ I've got relations in London. 我在伦敦有亲戚。Wǒ zài Lúndūn yǒu qīnqi.
2 关系 guānxì [种 zhǒng] *(connection)*
□ It has no relation to reality. 它和现实没有关系。Tā hé xiànshí méiyǒu guānxì.
■ **in relation to** 与…有关 yǔ...yǒuguān

relationship NOUN
1 联系 liánxì [个 gè] *(connection)*
2 关系 guānxì [种 zhǒng] *(rapport)*
■ **to have a good relationship** 关系亲密 guānxi qīnmì
3 恋爱关系 liàn'ài guānxì [种 zhǒng] *(affair)*
■ **to be in a relationship** 在谈恋爱 zài tán liàn'ài □ I'm not in a relationship at the moment. 我目前没有在谈恋爱。Wǒ mùqián méiyǒu zài tán liàn'ài.

relative NOUN
亲戚 qīnqi [个 gè]
□ my close relatives 我的近亲 wǒde jìnqīn

relatively ADVERB
相对 xiāngduì

to **relax** VERB
放松 fàngsōng
□ I relax listening to music. 我听音乐放松。Wǒ tīng yīnyuè fàngsōng. □ Relax! Everything's fine. 放松点！一切都

好。Fàngsōng diǎn！ Yíqiè dōu hǎo.

relaxation NOUN
消遣 xiāoqiǎn [种 zhǒng]

relaxed ADJECTIVE
1 放松的 fàngsōng de
2 轻松的 qīngsōng de *(discussion, atmosphere)*

relaxing ADJECTIVE
令人放松的 lìng rén fàngsōng de
■ **I find cooking relaxing.** 我发现烹饪令人放松。Wǒ fāxiàn pēngrèn lìng rén fàngsōng.

release NOUN
▷ *see also* **release** VERB
1 释放 shìfàng [次 cì]
□ the release of the prisoners 释放罪犯 shìfàng zuìfàn
2 发行 fāxíng
■ **the band's latest release** 这个乐队的最新专辑发行 zhègè yuèduì de zuìxīn zhuānjí fāxíng

to **release** VERB
▷ *see also* **release** NOUN
1 释放 shìfàng *(person)*
2 发行 fāxíng *(record, film)*

relevant ADJECTIVE
切题的 qiètí de
■ **That's not relevant.** 那是不切题的。Nà shì bú qiètí de.
■ **relevant to** 和…相关的 hé...xiāngguān de □ Education should be relevant to real life. 教育应该和现实生活相关。Jiàoyù yīnggāi hé xiànshí shénghuó xiāngguān.

reliable ADJECTIVE
1 可靠的 kěkào de
□ He's not very reliable. 他不是很可靠。Tā búshì hěn kěkào.
2 可信赖的 kěxìnlài de *(method, machine)*
□ a reliable car 一辆可信赖的车 yíliàng kěxìnlài de chē

relief NOUN
如释重负 rú shì zhòng fù
□ That's a relief! 真是如释重负啊！Zhēnshì rú shì zhòng fù a！

relieved ADJECTIVE
宽慰的 kuānwèi de
□ I was relieved to hear... 我听闻…感到宽慰 Wǒ tīngwén...gǎndào kuānwèi
■ **to be relieved that...** 对…感到放心 duì...gǎndào fàngxīn

religion NOUN
1 宗教信仰 zōngjiào xìnyǎng *(belief)*
□ What religion are you? 你的宗教信仰是什么？ Nǐde zōngjiào xìnyǎng shì shénme?
2 宗教 zōngjiào [种 zhǒng] *(set of beliefs)*

religious ADJECTIVE
1 宗教的 zōngjiào de *(activities, faith)*
□ my religious beliefs 我的宗教信仰 wǒde zōngjiàoxìnyǎng
2 笃信宗教的 dǔxìn zōngjiào de *(person)*
□ I'm not religious. 我不信宗教。Wǒ búxìn zōngjiào.

reluctant ADJECTIVE
不情愿的 bùqíngyuàn de
■ **to be reluctant to do something** 不愿做某事 bùyuàn zuò mǒushì

reluctantly ADVERB
不情愿地 bùqíngyuàn de

to **rely on** VERB
1 依赖 yīlài *(be dependent on)*
2 信赖 xìnlài *(trust)*
□ I'm relying on you. 我信赖你。Wǒ xìnlài nǐ.

to **remain** VERB
1 仍然是 réngrán shì *(continue to be)*
■ **to remain silent** 保持沉默 bǎochí chénmò
2 逗留 dòuliú *(stay)*

remaining ADJECTIVE
剩下的 shèngxià de
□ the remaining ingredients 剩下的成分 shèngxià de chéngfèn

remains PL NOUN
剩余物 shèngyúwù
□ the remains of the picnic 野餐剩余物 yěcān shèngyúwù □ human remains 人体残骸 réntǐ cánhái [堆 duī]
□ Roman remains 古罗马遗址 Gǔluómǎ yízhǐ

remark NOUN
评论 pínglùn [个 gè] *(comment)*

remarkable ADJECTIVE
不寻常的 bù xúncháng de

remarkably ADVERB
极其地 jíqí de

to **remarry** VERB
再婚 zàihūn
□ She remarried three years ago. 她三年前再婚了。Tā sānniánqián zàihūn le.

remedy NOUN
治疗法 zhìliáofǎ [种 zhǒng]
□ a good remedy for a sore throat 一种治疗喉咙痛的好方法 yìzhǒng zhìliáo hóulóngtòng de hǎo fāngfǎ

DID YOU KNOW...?
In discussing remedies, the Chinese often talk about the **symptom** 治标 zhìbiāo or the **root problem** 治根 zhìgēn. It's generally considered that Western medicine is better for quickly getting rid of symptoms, while Chinese medicine is better for curing root problems.

to **remember** VERB
1 记得 jìdé *(person, name, event)*
□ I can't remember his name. 我记不得他的名字了。Wǒ jìbúdé tāde míngzi le.
□ I don't remember. 我不记得了。Wǒ bú jìdé le.
2 回想起 huíxiǎngqǐ *(bring back to mind)*
3 牢记 láojì *(bear in mind)*
□ Remember your passport! 牢记带你的护照。Láojì dài nǐde hùzhào. □ Remember to write your name on the form. 牢记在表上填你的名字。Láojì zài biǎoshàng tián nǐde míngzì. □ She remembered to do it. 她记得要做某事。Tā jìdé yào zuò mǒushì.

to **remind** VERB
提醒 tíxǐng
□ I'll remind you tomorrow. 我明天会提醒你。Wǒ míngtiān huì tíxǐng nǐ.
■ **to remind somebody to do something** 提醒某人做某事 tíxǐng mǒurén zuò mǒushì □ Remind me to speak to Daniel. 提醒我去和丹尼尔谈话。Tíxǐng wǒ qù hé Dānní'ěr tánhuà.
■ **to remind somebody of something** 使某人想起某事 shǐ mǒurén xiǎngqǐ mǒushì □ It reminds me of Scotland. 它让我想起了苏格兰。Tā ràng wǒ xiǎngqǐ le Sūgélán.

remorse NOUN
悔恨 huǐhèn [种 zhǒng]
□ He showed no remorse. 他没有丝毫悔恨之意。Tā méiyǒu sīháo huǐhèn zhīyì.

remote ADJECTIVE
遥远的 yáoyuǎn de
□ a remote village 一个遥远的村庄 yígè yáoyuǎn de cūnzhuāng

remote control NOUN
遥控器 yáokòngqì [个 gè]

remotely ADVERB
■ **I'm not remotely interested.** 我并非不感兴趣。Wǒ bìngfēi bùgǎnxìngqù.
■ **Do you think it would be remotely possible?** 你觉得它可能性很小吗？Nǐ juédé tā kěnéngxìng hěnxiǎo mā?

removal NOUN
搬家 bānjiā *(from house)*
■ **a removal van** 一辆搬家的货车 yíliàng bānjiā de huòchē

to **remove** VERB
1 移走 yízǒu *(object, organ)*
□ Please remove your bag from my seat. 请把你的包从我的座位上移走。Qǐng bǎ nǐde bāo cóng wǒde zuòwèishàng yízǒu.
2 脱下 tuōxià *(clothing, bandage)*
3 清除 qīngchú *(stain)*
□ Did you remove the stain? 你把污渍清除了吗？ Nǐ bǎ wūzì qīngchú le mā?

rendezvous NOUN
约会 yuēhuì [次 cì]

to **renew** VERB
延长 yáncháng *(loan, contract)*

renewable ADJECTIVE
可更新的 kěgēngxīn de *(energy, resource)*

rent NOUN
▷ *see also* **rent** VERB
租金 zūjīn [笔 bǐ]

to **rent** VERB
▷ *see also* **rent** NOUN
1 租用 zūyòng *(car, house, room)*
□ We rented a car. 我们租用了一辆车。Wǒmen zūyòng le yíliàng chē.
2 出租 chūzū *(landlord: house, room)*

rental NOUN
租金 zūjīn [笔 bǐ]
□ Car rental is included in the price. 车的租金是包括在这个价格里的。Chē de zūjīn shì bāokuò zài zhègè jiàgé lǐ de.

rental car NOUN
用于租赁的车 yòngyú zūlìn de chē [辆 liàng]

to **reorganize** VERB
重组 chóngzǔ

rep NOUN
商品经销代理 shāngpǐn jīngxiāo dàilǐ [位 wèi]

repaid VERB ▷ *see* **repay**

repair NOUN
▷ *see also* **repair** VERB
修理 xiūlǐ [次 cì]

to **repair** VERB
▷ *see also* **repair** NOUN
1 修理 xiūlǐ
■ **to get something repaired** 修理某物 xiūlǐ mǒuwù □ I got the washing machine repaired. 我把洗衣机修理了。Wǒ bǎ xǐyījī xiūlǐ le.
2 维修 wéixiū *(damage)*

to **repay** VERB
偿还 chánghuán

repayment NOUN
偿还 chánghuán [次 cì]

to **repeat** VERB
▷ *see also* **repeat** NOUN
1 重复 chóngfù *(say again)*
2 重做 chóngzuò *(action, mistake)*

repeat NOUN
▷ *see also* **repeat** VERB
重复的内容 chóngfù de nèiróng [个 gè]
□ There are too many repeats on TV. 电视上有太多重复的内容了。Diànshì shàng yǒu tàiduō chóngfù de nèiróng le.

repeatedly ADVERB
反复地 fǎnfù de

repellent NOUN
■ **insect repellent** 驱虫剂 qūchóngjì [瓶 píng]

repetitive ADJECTIVE
重复的 chóngfù de *(movement, work)*

to **replace** VERB
1 将...放回 jiāng...fànghuí *(put back)*
2 代替 dàitì *(take the place of)*

replay NOUN
▷ *see also* **replay** VERB
重赛 chóngsài [场 chǎng] *(of match)*
□ There will be a replay on Friday. 星期五会有一场重赛。Xīngqīwǔ huì yǒu yìchǎng chóngsài.

to **replay** VERB
▷ *see also* **replay** NOUN
重新播放 chóngxīn bōfàng *(track, song)*
■ **to replay a match** 重新比赛 chóngxīn bǐsài

reply NOUN
▷ *see also* **reply** VERB
回答 huídá [个 gè]
□ There's no reply. 没有人回答。Méiyǒurén huídá.

to **reply** VERB
▷ *see also* **reply** NOUN
答复 dáfù

report NOUN
▷ *see also* **report** VERB
1 报告 bàogào [个 gè] *(account)*
□ a report in the paper 报纸上的一个报告 bàozhǐshàng de yígè bàogào
2 成绩单 chéngjìdān [份 fèn] *(at school)*
□ I got a good report this term. 我这学期拿到了一份不错的成绩单。Wǒ zhèxuéqī nádào le yífèn búcuò de chéngjìdān.

to **report** VERB
▷ *see also* **report** NOUN
1 报案 bào'àn *(theft, accident, death)*
□ I reported the theft to the police. 我向警方报了这个偷窃案。Wǒ xiàng jǐngfāng bàole zhègè tōuqiè'àn.
2 告发 gàofā *(person)*
■ **to report to** *(present oneself)* 告知 gàozhī
□ Report to reception when you arrive. 你到达后请告知接待处。Nǐ dàodá hòu qǐng gàozhī jiēdàichù.

report card NOUN (US)
学生成绩报告单 xuéshēng chéngjì bàogàodān [份 fèn]

reporter NOUN
记者 jìzhě [名 míng]
□ I'd like to be a reporter. 我想当一名记者。Wǒ xiǎng dāng yìmíng jìzhě.

to **represent** VERB
代表 dàibiǎo *(person, nation)*

representative NOUN
▷ *see also* **representative** ADJECTIVE
代表 dàibiǎo [个 gè]

representative ADJECTIVE
▷ *see also* **representative** NOUN
有代表性的 yǒu dàibiǎoxìng de

reptile NOUN
爬行动物 páxíngdòngwù [种 zhǒng]

republic NOUN
共和国 gònghéguó [个 gè]

reputation NOUN
名声 míngshēng [个 gè]

request NOUN
▷ *see also* **request** VERB
要求 yāoqiú [个 gè]

to **request** VERB
▷ *see also* **request** NOUN
要求 yāoqiú

to **require** VERB
需要 xūyào *(need)*
□ The job requires good computational skills. 这个工作需要有好的电脑技能。Zhègè gōngzuò xūyào yǒu hǎode diànnǎo jìnéng.
■ **to be required** 必须有 bìxū yǒu
□ What qualifications are required? 哪些条件是必须有的？Nǎxiē tiáojiàn shì bìxū yǒu de?

requirement NOUN
要求 yāoqiú [个 gè]
□ What are the requirements for the job? 这个工作的要求是什么？Zhègè gōngzuò de yāoqiú shì shénme?
■ **entry requirements** *(for university)* 入学要求 rùxué yāoqiú

rescue NOUN
▷ *see also* **rescue** VERB
营救 yíngjiù [次 cì]
□ a rescue operation 一次营救行动 yícì yíngjiù xíngdòng
■ **to come to somebody's rescue** 救助某人 jiùzhù mǒurén □ He came to my rescue. 他来救助我了。Tā lái jiùzhù wǒ le.

to **rescue** VERB
▷ *see also* **rescue** NOUN
解救 jiějiù

research NOUN
研究 yánjiū [个 gè]
■ **to do research** 做研究 zuò yánjiū □ He's doing research. 他正在做研究。Tā zhèngzài zuò yánjiū. □ She's doing some research in the library. 他正在图书馆里做研究。Tā zhèngzài túshūguǎn lǐ zuò yánjiū.

resemblance NOUN
相似 xiāngsì [种 zhǒng]

to **resent** VERB

讨厌 tǎoyàn
□ I really resented your criticism. 我真的讨厌你的批评。Wǒ zhēnde tǎoyàn nǐde pīpíng.

resentful ADJECTIVE
厌恶的 yànwù de
■ **to feel resentful towards somebody** 对某人感到厌恶 duì mǒurén gǎndào yànwù

reservation NOUN
预定 yùdìng [个 gè]
□ I've got a reservation for two nights. 我拿到了两个晚上的预定。Wǒ nádào le liǎnggè wǎnshàng de yùdìng.
■ **to make a reservation** *(in hotel, restaurant)* 预定 yùdìng □ I'd like to make a reservation for this evening. 我想为今晚做个预定。Wǒ xiǎng wèi jīnwǎn zuò gè yùdìng.

reservation desk NOUN (US)
预定台 yùdìngtái [个 gè]

to **reserve** VERB
▷ *see also* **reserve** NOUN
预定 yùdìng
□ I'd like to reserve a table for tomorrow evening. 我想为明晚预定一张桌子。Wǒ xiǎng wèi míngwǎn yùdìng yìzhāng zhuōzi.

reserve NOUN
▷ *see also* **reserve** VERB
1 保留区 bǎoliúqū [块 kuài] *(place)*
□ a nature reserve 一块自然保留区 yíkuài zìrán bǎoliúqū
2 后备队员 hòubèi duìyuán [名 míng] *(person)*
□ I was reserve in the game last Saturday. 在上周六的比赛中我是后备队员。Zài shàng zhōuliù de bǐsài zhōng wǒ shì hòubèi duìyuán.

reserved ADJECTIVE
1 已预定的 yǐ yùdìng de
□ a reserved seat 一个已预定的座位 yígè yǐ yùdìng de zuòwèi
2 矜持的 jīnchí de *(person)*
□ He's quite reserved. 他十分的矜持。Tā shífēn de jīnchí.

reservoir NOUN
水库 shuǐkù [座 zuò]

resident NOUN
居民 jūmín [位 wèi]

residential ADJECTIVE
住宅的 zhùzhái de
□ a residential area 一片住宅区 yípiàn zhùzháiqū

to **resign** VERB
辞职 cízhí

to **resist** VERB
克制 kèzhì *(temptation, urge)*

to **resit** VERB
补考 bǔkǎo
□ I'm resitting the exam in December. 我将在十二月时参加补考。Wǒ jiāng zài shí'èr yuè shí cānjiā bǔkǎo.

resolution NOUN
决心 juéxīn [个 gè]
■ **New Year's resolution** 新年决心 Xīnnián juéxīn □ Have you made any New Year's resolutions? 你下什么新年决心了没有？ Nǐ xià shénme Xīnnián juéxīn le méiyǒu?

resort NOUN
度假胜地 dùjià shèngdì [个 gè]
□ It's a resort on the Costa del Sol. 它是太阳海岸上的一个度假胜地。Tā shì Tàiyáng hǎi'àn shàng de yígè dùjià shèngdì.
■ **a ski resort** 一个冬季运动胜地 yígè dōngjì yùndòng shèngdì
■ **as a last resort** 作为最后手段 zuòwéi zuìhòu shǒuduàn

resources PL NOUN
1 资源 zīyuán *(coal, iron, oil)*
2 财力 cáilì *(money)*
■ **natural resources** 自然资源 zìrán zīyuán

respect NOUN
▷ *see also* **respect** VERB
尊敬 zūnjìng
■ **to have respect for somebody** 对某人心怀敬意 duì mǒurén xīnhuái jìngyì

to **respect** VERB
▷ *see also* **respect** NOUN
尊敬 zūnjìng

respectable ADJECTIVE
1 体面的 tǐmiàn de *(area, background)*
2 受人尊敬的 shòurén zūnjìng de *(person)*

responsibility NOUN
1 职责 zhízé [个 gè] *(duty)*
2 义务 yìwù [项 xiàng] *(obligation)*
■ **responsibilities** 责任 zérèn

responsible ADJECTIVE
1 负有责任的 fùyǒu zérèn de *(at fault)*
2 负责的 fùzé de *(in charge)*
■ **to be responsible for something** 负责某物 fùzé mǒuwù □ He's responsible for booking the tickets. 他负责订票。Tā fùzé dìngpiào.
3 有责任感的 yǒu zérèngǎn de *(sensible, trustworthy)*
□ You should be more responsible. 你应该更有责任感一些。Nǐ yīnggāi gèng yǒu zérèngǎn yìxiē.
■ **It's a responsible job.** 这是一个责任重大的工作。Zhè shì yígè zérèn zhòngdà de gōngzuò.

rest NOUN

▷*see also* **rest** VERB

1 休息 xiūxi [次 cì] *(relaxation, break)*

□ five minutes' rest 五分钟的休息 wǔ fēnzhōng de xiūxi

■ **to have a rest** 休息片刻 xiūxi piànkè

□ We stopped to have a rest. 我们停下来休息片刻。Wǒmen tíng xiàlái xiūxi piànkè.

2 剩余 shèngyú *(remainder)*

□ I'll do the rest. 我会把剩余的做完。Wǒ huì bǎ shèngyú de zuòwán. □ the rest of the money 余额 yú'é

■ **the rest of them** 其余的人 qíyú de rén

□ The rest of them went swimming. 其余的人去游泳了。Qíyú de rén qù yóuyǒng le.

to **rest** VERB

▷*see also* **rest** NOUN

1 休息 xiūxi *(relax)*

□ She's resting in her room. 她在她的房间休息。Tā zài tāde fángjiān xiūxi.

2 放松 fàngsōng *(not overstrain: eyes, legs, muscles)*

□ He has to rest his knee. 他得放松一下他的膝盖。Tā děi fàngsōng yíxià tāde xīgài.

■ **to rest something against something** 把某物靠在某物上 bǎ mǒuwù kàozài mǒuwù shàng □ I rested my bike against the window. 我把自行车靠在窗户旁。Wǒ bǎ zìxíngchē kào zài chuānghù páng.

rest area NOUN (US)

路边服务站 lùbiān fúwùzhàn [个 gè]

restaurant NOUN

餐馆 cānguǎn [家 jiā]

□ We don't often go to restaurants. 我们不常去餐馆吃饭。Wǒmen bù cháng qù cānguǎn chīfàn.

■ **a restaurant car** 一列餐车 yíliè cānchē

restless ADJECTIVE

坐立不安的 zuòlì bù'ān de *(fidgety)*

to **restore** VERB

修复 xiūfù

to **restrict** VERB

1 限制 xiànzhì *(growth, membership, privilege)*

2 约束 yuēshù *(activities)*

rest room NOUN (US)

洗手间 xǐshǒujiān [个 gè]

result NOUN

▷*see also* **result** VERB

1 后果 hòuguǒ [种 zhǒng] *(of event, action)*

2 结果 jiéguǒ [个 gè] *(of match, election, exam, competition)*

□ my exam results 我的考试结果 wǒde kǎoshì jiéguǒ □ What was the result? — One-nil. 结果怎么？— 一比零。Jiéguǒ zěnmeyàng? — Yī bǐ líng.

3 答案 dá'àn [个 gè] *(of calculation)*

■ **as a result of** 由于 yóuyú

to **result** VERB

▷*see also* **result** NOUN

产生 chǎnshēng

■ **to result in** 导致 dǎozhì □ Many road accidents result in head injuries. 很多车祸会导致头部损伤。Hěnduō chēhuò huì dǎozhì tóubù sǔnshāng.

■ **to result from** 因…而产生 yīn...ér chǎnshēng

résumé NOUN

简历 jiǎnlì [份 fèn] (US: *CV*)

to **retire** VERB

退休 tuìxiū

□ He retired last year. 他去年退休了。Tā qùnián tuìxiū le.

retired ADJECTIVE

退休的 tuìxiū de

□ She's retired. 她退休了。Tā tuìxiū le.

■ **a retired teacher** 一名退休教师 yìmíng tuìxiū jiàoshī

retiree NOUN (US)

领养老金的人 lǐng yǎnglǎojīn de rén [位 wèi]

retirement NOUN

退休 tuìxiū

to **return** VERB

▷*see also* **return** NOUN, ADJECTIVE

1 回来 huílái *(come back)*

□ I've just returned from holiday. 我刚度假回来。Wǒ gāng dùjià huílái.

■ **to return home** 回家 huíjiā

2 回去 huíqù *(go back)*

□ He returned to France the following year. 他第二年就回法国去了。Tā dì èr nián jiù huí Fǎguó qù le.

3 归还 guīhuán *(give back)*

□ She borrows my things and doesn't return them. 她常借我一些东西但从不归还。Tā cháng jiè wǒ yìxiē dōngxi dàn cóng bù guīhuán.

return NOUN

▷*see also* **return** VERB, ADJECTIVE

1 返回 fǎnhuí *(of person)*

□ after our return 我们返回以后 wǒmen fǎnhuí yǐhòu

2 归还 guīhuán *(of something borrowed or stolen)*

3 回车键 huíchējiàn *(computer key)*

4 往返票 wǎngfǎnpiào [张 zhāng] *(ticket)*

□ A return to London, please. 一张去伦敦的往返票。Yìzhāng qù Lúndūn de wǎngfǎnpiào.

■ **in return** 作为回报 zuòwéi huíbào □ ... and I help her in return. …然后我帮助她作为回报。...ránhòu wǒ bāngzhù tā zuòwéi

huíbào.
■ **in return for...** 作为… 的回报 zuòwéi... de huíbào
■ **Many happy returns!** 生日快乐！Shēngrì kuàilè!

return ADJECTIVE
▷ *see also* **return** VERB, NOUN
往返的 wǎngfǎn de *(journey, ticket)*
□ the return journey 往返的行程 wǎngfǎn de xíngchéng
■ **a return match** 一场重赛 yìchǎng chóngsài

to **retweet** VERB
转发 zhuǎn fā

reunion NOUN
团聚 tuánjù [次 cì]

to **reveal** VERB
透露 tòulù *(make known)*

revenge NOUN
复仇 fùchóu
■ **to take revenge** 报复 bàofù □ They planned to take revenge on him. 他们计划报复他。Tāmen jìhuà bàofù tā. □ in revenge 报复地 bàofù de

to **reverse** VERB
▷ *see also* **reverse** ADJECTIVE
倒车 dàochē *(car)*
□ He reversed without looking. 他看都没看就倒车了。Tā kàn dōu méi kàn jiù dàochē le.
■ **to reverse the charges** *(telephone)* 被呼叫方付款 bèi hūjiàofāng fùkuǎn

reverse ADJECTIVE
▷ *see also* **reverse** VERB
相反的 xiāngfǎn de
□ in reverse order 按相反的顺序 àn xiāngfǎn de shùnxù
■ **in reverse gear** 在倒车档 zài dàochēdǎng

review NOUN
评论 pínglùn [个 gè] *(of book, film)*
□ The book had good reviews. 这本书受到好的评论。Zhè běn shū shòudào hǎode pínglùn.

to **revise** VERB
1 复习 fùxí *(study)*
□ I haven't started revising yet. 我还没开始复习。Wǒ hái méi kāishǐ fùxí.
2 修正 xiūzhèng
■ **I've revised my opinion.** 我修正了我的意见。Wǒ xiūzhèng le wǒde yìjiàn.

revision NOUN
复习 fùxí [遍 biàn]
□ Have you done a lot of revision? 你已经复习很多了吗？Nǐ yǐjīng fùxí hěnduō le mā?

revolting ADJECTIVE
叛变的 pànbiàn de

revolution NOUN
1 革命 gémìng [场 chǎng] *(political)*

> DID YOU KNOW...?
> The 1966-1977 Great Proletarian Cultural Revolution, or 文化大革命 wénhuà dà gémìng, is the revolution you are most likely to hear referred to while in China.

2 变革 biàngé [场 chǎng] *(in industry, education)*

revolutionary ADJECTIVE
革命的 gémìng de

revolver NOUN
左轮手枪 zuǒlún shǒuqiāng [把 bǎ]

reward NOUN
▷ *see also* **reward** VERB
奖励 jiǎnglì [种 zhǒng]

to **reward** VERB
▷ *see also* **reward** NOUN
奖赏 jiǎngshǎng

rewarding ADJECTIVE
值得做的 zhídé zuò de
□ a rewarding job 一份值得做的工作 yífèn zhídé zuò de gōngzuò

to **rewind** VERB
倒带 dàodài

rhinoceros NOUN
犀牛 xīniú [头 tóu]

rhubarb NOUN
大黄 dàhuáng [株 zhū]
□ a rhubarb tart 一个大黄馅饼 yígè dàhuáng xiànbǐng

rhythm NOUN
节奏 jiézòu [个 gè]

rib NOUN
肋骨 lèigǔ [根 gēn]

ribbon NOUN
饰带 shìdài [条 tiáo]

rice NOUN
1 大米 dàmǐ [粒 lì] *(grain)*
2 米饭 mǐfàn [碗 wǎn] *(when cooked)*
■ **rice pudding** 大米布丁 dàmǐ bùdīng

> DID YOU KNOW...?
> Rice is a staple in Chinese cuisine but in a restaurant it may be difficult to get a bowl early in a meal. Traditionally, rice is filled up on at the end of the meal.

rich ADJECTIVE
富有的 fùyǒu de *(person, country)*
■ **the rich** 富人 fùrén

to **rid** VERB
■ **to get rid of something** 扔掉某物 rēngdiào mǒuwù □ I want to get rid of some old clothes. 我想扔掉一些旧衣服。Wǒ xiǎng rēngdiào yìxiē jiù yīfu.

ridden VERB ▷ *see* **ride**

ride NOUN
▷ *see also* **ride** VERB
1 兜风 dōufēng [次 cì] *(in car, on bicycle)*
2 乘坐 chéngzuò [次 cì] *(on horse, bus, train)*
□ It's a short bus ride to the town centre. 去城中心只需乘坐一小段巴士。Qù chéngzhōngxīn zhǐ xū chéngzuò yìxiǎoduàn bāshì.
■ **to go for a ride 1** *(on horse)* 去骑马 qù qímǎ **2** *(on bike)* 去骑车 qù qíchē
□ We went for a bike ride. 我们去骑车了。Wǒmen qù qíchē le.
■ **to give somebody a ride** (US: *in car*) 让某人搭顺风车 ràng mǒurén dā shùnfēngchē

to **ride** VERB
▷ *see also* **ride** NOUN
1 骑马 qímǎ *(on horseback)*
□ I'm learning to ride. 我正在学骑马。Wǒ zhèngzài xué qímǎ.
2 骑车 qíchē *(on bicycle)*
3 乘坐 chéngzuò *(in car)*
4 骑 qí *(horse, bicycle, motorcycle)*
■ **to ride a bike** 骑自行车 qí zìxíngchē
□ Can you ride a bike? 你会骑自行车吗？Nǐ huì qí zìxíngchē mā?
5 行进 xíngjìn *(distance)*

rider NOUN
1 骑马者 qímǎzhě *(on horse)*
□ She's a good rider. 她是一个优秀的骑马者。Tā shì yígè yōuxiù de qímǎzhě.
2 骑自行车的人 qí zìxíngchē de rén *(on bike)*

ridiculous ADJECTIVE
荒谬的 huāngmiù de
□ Don't be ridiculous! 不要太荒谬了！Búyào tài huāngmiù le!

rifle NOUN
步枪 bùqiāng [支 zhī]
□ a hunting rifle 一支狩猎步枪 yìzhī shòuliè bùqiāng

right ADJECTIVE, ADVERB, EXCLAMATION
▷ *see also* **right** NOUN
1 右边的 yòubiān de *(not left)*
□ my right hand 我的右手 wǒde yòushǒu
2 右边地 yòubiān de *(turn, look)*
□ Turn right at the traffic lights. 在交通灯处向右转。Zài jiāotōngdēng chù xiàng yòu zhuǎn.
3 正确的 zhèngquè de *(correct)*
□ the right answer 正确的答案 zhèngquè de dá'àn □ We're on the right train. 我们上了正确的火车。Wǒmen shàngle zhèngquè de huǒchē.
4 合适的 héshì de *(person, place, clothes)*
□ It isn't the right size. 这不是合适的尺码。Zhè búshì héshì de chǐmǎ.
5 准确的 zhǔnquè de *(decision, direction, time)*
□ Do you have the right time? 你有准确的时间吗？Nǐ yǒu zhǔnquè de shíjiān mā?
6 正确地 zhèngquè de *(correctly)*
□ Am I pronouncing it right? 我发音正确吗？Wǒ fāyīn zhèngquè mā?
7 道德上正确的 dàodéshàng zhèngquè de *(morally correct)*
□ It's not right to behave like that. 那样做是不正确的。Nàyàng zuò shì bú zhèngquè de. □ You did the right thing. 你做得对。Nǐ zuòde duì.
8 恰当 qiàdàng *(properly, fairly)*
□ You did right. 你做得很恰当。Nǐ zuòdé hěn qiàdàng.
■ **to be right 1** *(person)* 正确的 zhèngquè de □ You were right! 你是正确的！Nǐ shì zhèngquè de! **2** *(answer, fact)* 对的 duìde □ That's right! 那是对的！Nà shì duìde! **3** *(clock)* 准确的 zhǔnquè de
9 好的 hǎode *(exclamation)*
□ Right! Let's get started. 好的！让我们开始吧。Hǎode! Ràng wǒmen kāishì ba.
■ **right away** 立即 lìjí □ I'll do it right away. 我立即开始做。Wǒ lìjí kāishǐ zuò.

right NOUN
▷ *see also* **right** ADJECTIVE, ADVERB, EXCLAMATION
1 右边 yòubiān *(not left)*
■ **on the right** 在右侧 zài yòucè
□ Remember to drive on the right. 记得在右侧行驶。Jìdé zài yòucè xíngshǐ.
■ **to the right** *(move)* 向右 xiàngyòu
2 权利 quánlì [个 gè] *(entitlement)*
□ You've got no right to do that. 你没有权利那么做。Nǐ méiyǒu quánlì nàme zuò.
■ **right of way** 先行权 xiānxíngquán □ It was our right of way. 那是我们的先行权。Nà shì wǒmen de xiānxíngquán.

right-hand ADJECTIVE
■ **the right-hand side** 右侧 yòucè □ It's on the right-hand side. 它就在右侧。Tā jiù zài yòucè.

right-handed ADJECTIVE
惯用右手的 guànyòng yòushǒu de

rightly ADVERB
正确地 zhèngquè de
□ She rightly decided not to go. 她正确地做了决定不去。Tā zhèngquè de zuòle juédìng búqù.
■ **...if I remember rightly.** …如果我记对了的话。...rúguǒ wǒ jìduì le de huà.

ring NOUN
▷ *see also* **ring** VERB
1 戒指 jièzhi [枚 méi] *(on finger)*
□ a gold ring 一枚金戒指 yìméi jīn jièzhi
□ a diamond ring 一枚镶钻戒指 yìméi xiāngzuàn jièzhi

■ **a wedding ring** 一枚结婚戒指 yìméi jiéhūn jièzhi
2 圈 quān [个 gè] *(circle)*
□ to stand in a ring 站成一个圈 zhànchéng yígè quān
3 门铃声 ménlíngshēng [阵 zhèn] *(of bell)*
□ There was a ring at the door. 门口有门铃声。Ménkǒu yǒu ménlíngshēng.
■ **to give somebody a ring** 给某人打电话 gěi mǒurén dǎ diànhuà □ I'll give you a ring this evening. 我今天傍晚会给你打电话。Wǒ jīntiān bàngwǎn huì gěi nǐ dǎ diànhuà.

to **ring** VERB
▹ *see also* **ring** NOUN
1 鸣响 míngxiǎng *(bell)*
2 响 xiǎng *(telephone)*
□ The phone's ringing. 电话在响。Diànhuà zài xiǎng.
3 打电话 dǎ diànhuà *(call)*
□ Your mother rang this morning. 你母亲今天早上打过电话来。Nǐ mǔqīn jīntiān zǎoshàng dǎ guò diànhuà lái.
4 给...打电话 gěi...dǎ diànhuà *(contact by phone)*
□ I'll ring you tomorrow morning. 我明天早上会给你打电话。Wǒ míngtiān zǎoshàng huì gěi nǐ dǎ diànhuà.
■ **to ring the bell** 按门铃 àn ménlíng
□ I rang the bell three times. 我按了三次门铃。Wǒ ànle sāncì ménlíng.

to **ring back** VERB
回电 huí diàn
□ I'll ring back later. 我待会儿再回电。Wǒ dāihuì'r zài huídiàn.
■ **to ring somebody back** 回电话给某人 huídiànhuà gěi mǒurén

to **ring up** VERB
打电话 dǎ diànhuà *(on telephone)*
■ **to ring somebody up** 给某人打电话 gěi mǒurén dǎ diànhuà

ring binder NOUN
活页簿 huóyèbù [本 běn]

ringtone NOUN
手机铃声 shǒujī língshēng [种 zhǒng]

rink NOUN
溜冰场 liūbīngchǎng [个 gè] *(for ice-skating)*

to **rinse** VERB
漂洗 piǎoxǐ *(dishes, clothes)*

riot NOUN
▹ *see also* **riot** VERB
暴乱 bàoluàn [次 cì] *(disturbance)*

to **riot** VERB
▹ *see also* **riot** NOUN
闹事 nàoshì

ripe ADJECTIVE
成熟的 chéngshú de

rise NOUN
▹ *see also* **rise** VERB
1 加薪 jiāxīn [次 cì] *(salary increase)*
2 上升 shàngshēng [次 cì] *(in prices, temperature, crime rate)*
■ **a sudden rise in temperature** 一次气温猛升 yícì qìwēn měngshēng

to **rise** VERB
▹ *see also* **rise** NOUN
1 爬升 páshēng *(move upwards)*
2 上升 shàngshēng *(prices, numbers)*
□ Prices are rising. 价格在上升。Jiàgé zài shàngshēng.
3 升起 shēngqǐ *(sun, moon)*
□ The sun rises early in June. 六月时，太阳升起得早。Liùyuè shí, tàiyáng shēngqǐ dé zǎo.
4 起身 qǐshēn *(from chair)*

risk NOUN
▹ *see also* **risk** VERB
1 危险 wēixiǎn [个 gè] *(danger)*
2 风险 fēngxiǎn [种 zhǒng] *(possibility, chance)*
■ **to take a risk** 担风险 dān fēngxiǎn
■ **It's at your own risk.** 你得自己承担风险。Nǐ děi zìjǐ chéngdān fēngxiǎn.

to **risk** VERB
▹ *see also* **risk** NOUN
冒险做 màoxiǎn zuò *(take the chance of)*
□ You risk getting a fine. 你在冒被罚款的险。Nǐ zài mào bèi fákuǎn de xiǎn.
■ **to risk it** 冒险一试 màoxiǎn yíshì
□ I wouldn't risk it if I were you. 如果我是你的话，我不会冒险一试。Rúguǒ wǒ shì nǐ de huà, wǒ búhuì màoxiǎn yíshì.

risky ADJECTIVE
冒险的 màoxiǎn de

rival NOUN
▹ *see also* **rival** ADJECTIVE
竞争对手 jìngzhēng duìshǒu [个 gè]

rival ADJECTIVE
▹ *see also* **rival** NOUN
1 对立的 duìlì de *(teams, groups, supporters)*
□ a rival gang 一个对立的帮派 yīgè duìlì de bāngpài
2 有竞争力的 yǒu jìngzhēnglì de
□ a rival company 一家有竞争力的公司 yìjiā yǒu jìngzhēnglì de gōngsī

rivalry NOUN
竞争 jìngzhēng [种 zhǒng] *(between towns, schools)*

river NOUN
河 hé [条 tiáo]
□ The river runs alongside the canal. 这条河

顺着运河道流淌。Zhè tiáo hé shùnzhe yùnhédào liútǎng.

river bank NOUN
河岸 hé'àn [个 gè]

Riviera NOUN
里维埃拉 Lǐwéi'āilā

road NOUN
1 公路 gōnglù [条 tiáo] *(in country)*
□ There's a lot of traffic on the roads. 公路上车很多。Gōnglù shàng chē hěnduō.
□ It takes four hours by road. 要花四小时的车程。Yào huā sì xiǎoshí de chēchéng.
2 路 lù [条 tiáo] *(in town)*
□ They live across the road. 他们住在这条路的对面。Tāmen zhùzài zhètiáo lù de duìmiàn.

road map NOUN
道路图 dàolùtú [张 zhāng]

road rage NOUN
嚣张驾驶 xiāozhāng jiàshǐ [次 cì]

road sign NOUN
交通标志 jiāotōng biāozhì [个 gè]

roadworks PL NOUN
道路整修 dàolù zhěngxiū [次 cì]

to **roast** VERB
▷ *see also* **roast** ADJECTIVE
烤 kǎo

roast ADJECTIVE
▷ *see also* **roast** VERB
烤的 kǎo de
□ roast chicken 烤鸡肉 kǎo jīròu

to **rob** VERB
抢劫 qiǎngjié
□ I've been robbed. 我被抢劫了。Wǒ bèi qiǎngjié le.
■ **to rob somebody of something** 抢夺某人的某物 qiǎngduó mǒurén de mǒuwù
□ He was robbed of his wallet. 他被抢夺了钱包。Tā bèi qiǎngduó le qiánbāo.
■ **to rob a bank** 抢劫银行 qiǎngjié yínháng

robber NOUN
盗窃犯 dàoqièfàn [个 gè]
■ **a bank-robber** 一个银行盗窃犯 yígè yínháng dàoqièfàn

robbery NOUN
抢劫 qiǎngjié [次 cì]
■ **a bank robbery** 一次银行抢劫 yícì yínháng qiǎngjié
■ **armed robbery** 持枪抢劫 chíqiāng qiǎngjié

robin NOUN
知更鸟 zhīgēngniǎo [只 zhī]

robot NOUN
机器人 jīqìrén [个 gè]

rock NOUN
▷ *see also* **rock** VERB
1 巨石 jùshí [块 kuài] *(boulder)*
□ I sat on a rock. 我坐在一块巨石上。Wǒ zuòzài yíkuài jùshí shàng. □ They tunnelled through the rock. 他们从巨石中间凿了一条通道。Tāmen cóng jùshí zhōngjiān záole yìtiáo tōngdào.
2 小石子 xiǎoshízǐ [块 kuài] *(US: small stone)*
□ The crowd started to throw rocks. 人群开始掷小石子。Rénqún kāishǐ zhì xiǎoshízǐ.
3 摇滚乐 yáogǔnyuè *(music)*
□ a rock concert 一场摇滚音乐会 yìchǎng yáogǔn yīnyuèhuì □ He's a rock star. 他是个摇滚明星。Tā shì gè yáogǔn míngxīng.
4 硬糖 yìngtáng [块 kuài] *(sweet)*
□ a stick of rock 一个硬棒糖 yígè yìngbàngtáng
■ **rock and roll** 摇滚乐 yáogǔnyuè

to **rock** VERB
▷ *see also* **rock** NOUN
摇摆 yáobǎi

rockery NOUN
岩石 yánshí

rocket NOUN
1 火箭 huǒjiàn [支 zhī] *(spacecraft)*
2 火箭式礼花 huǒjiànshì lǐhuā [个 gè] *(firework)*

rocking chair NOUN
摇椅 yáoyǐ [把 bǎ]

rod NOUN
1 杆 gān [根 gēn] *(pole)*
2 钓鱼竿 diàoyúgān [根 gēn] *(for fishing)*

rode VERB ▷ *see* **ride**

role NOUN
1 作用 zuòyòng [个 gè] *(function)*
2 角色 juésè [个 gè] *(in play, film)*

roll NOUN
▷ *see also* **roll** VERB
1 一卷 yì juǎn [个 gè]
□ a roll of tape 一卷带子 yìjuǎn dàizi □ a toilet roll 一卷卫生纸 yìjuǎn wèishēngzhǐ
2 面包卷 miànbāojuǎn [个 gè] *(bread)*
□ a ham roll 火腿面包卷 huǒtuǐ miànbāojuǎn

to **roll** VERB
▷ *see also* **roll** NOUN
滚动 gǔndòng *(ball, stone)*
■ **to roll something** 使某物滚动 shǐ mǒuwù gǔndòng
■ **to roll out the pastry** 擀面皮 gǎnmiànpí

roll call NOUN
点名 diǎnmíng [次 cì]

roller NOUN
卷发器 juǎnfàqì [个 gè] *(for hair)*

Rollerblades® PL NOUN

直排轮溜冰鞋 zhípáilún liūbīngxié [双 shuāng]

rollercoaster NOUN
过山车 guòshānchē [辆 liàng] *(at funfair)*

roller skates PL NOUN
旱冰鞋 hànbīngxié [双 shuāng]

roller-skating NOUN
滑旱冰 huáhànbīng [次 cì]
■ **to go roller-skating** 去滑旱冰 qù huáhànbīng

rolling pin NOUN
擀面杖 gǎnmiànzhàng [根 gēn]

Roman ADJECTIVE
▷ *see also* **Roman** NOUN
1 古罗马的 gǔ Luómǎ de *(of ancient Rome)*
2 罗马的 Luómǎ de *(of modern Rome)*
□ a Roman villa 一栋罗马式别墅 yídòng luómǎshì biéshù □ the Roman empire 古罗马帝国 Gǔluómǎ dìguó

Roman NOUN
▷ *see also* **Roman** ADJECTIVE
古罗马人 gǔ Luómǎrén [个 gè] *(in ancient Rome)*

Roman Catholic ADJECTIVE
▷ *see also* **Roman Catholic** NOUN
天主教的 Tiānzhǔjiào de

Roman Catholic NOUN
▷ *see also* **Roman Catholic** ADJECTIVE
天主教教徒 Tiānzhǔjiào Jiàotú [个 gè]
□ He's a Roman Catholic. 他是一个天主教教徒。Tā shì yígè Tiānzhǔjiào Jiàotú.

romance NOUN
1 恋情 liànqíng [种 zhǒng] *(affair)*
□ a holiday romance 一段假期恋情 yíduàn jiàqī liànqíng
2 迷人之处 mírén zhī chù *(charm, excitement)*
□ the romance of Paris 巴黎的迷人之处 Bālí de mírén zhī chù
3 浪漫小说 làngmàn xiǎoshuō *(romantic fiction)*
□ I read a lot of romance. 我读了很多浪漫小说。Wǒ dúle hěnduō làngmàn xiǎoshuō.

Romania NOUN
罗马尼亚 Luómǎníyà
□ in Romania 在罗马尼亚 zài Luómǎníyà

Romanian ADJECTIVE
▷ *see also* **Romanian** NOUN
罗马尼亚的 Luómǎníyà de

Romanian NOUN
▷ *see also* **Romanian** ADJECTIVE
1 罗马尼亚人 Luómǎníyàrén [个 gè] *(person)*
2 罗马尼亚语 Luómǎníyàyǔ *(language)*

romantic ADJECTIVE
1 浪漫的 làngmàn de *(person, holiday, dinner)*
2 爱情的 àiqíng de *(film, story)*

roof NOUN
1 屋顶 wūdǐng [个 gè] *(of building)*
2 顶 dǐng [个 gè] *(of cave, mine, vehicle)*

room NOUN
1 房间 fángjiān [个 gè] *(in house)*
□ the biggest room in the house 房子里最大一个房间 fángzi lǐ zuìdà yígè fángjiān
■ **a single room** 一个单人间 yígè dānrén jiān
■ **a double room** 一个双人间 yígè shuāngrén jiān
2 卧室 wòshì [个 gè] *(bedroom)*
□ She's in her room. 她在她的卧室里。Tā zài tāde wòshì lǐ.
3 室 shì [个 gè] *(in school)*
□ the music room 音乐室 yīnyuèshì
4 空间 kōngjiān [个 gè] *(space)*
□ There's no room for that box. 没有多余的空间来放那个盒子了。Méiyǒu duōyú de kōngjiān lái fàng nàgè hézi le.

roommate NOUN
室友 shìyǒu [个 gè]

root NOUN
根 gēn [个 gè]

rope NOUN
绳子 shéngzi [根 gēn]

rose VERB ▷ *see* **rise**

rose NOUN
玫瑰 méigui [朵 duǒ] *(flower)*

to **rot** VERB
1 使腐坏 shǐ fǔhuài *(cause to decay)*
2 腐烂 fǔlàn *(suffer decay: teeth, wood, fruit)*

rotten ADJECTIVE
1 腐烂的 fǔlàn de *(decayed)*
□ a rotten apple 一个腐烂的苹果 yígè fǔlàn de píngguǒ
2 恶劣的 èliè de *(awful)*
□ rotten weather 恶劣的天气 èliè de tiānqì
□ That's a rotten thing to do. 做那种事是很恶劣的。Zuò nàzhǒngshì shì hěn èliè de.
■ **to feel rotten** 感觉不舒服 gǎnjué bùshūfu

rough ADJECTIVE
1 粗糙的 cūcāo de *(skin, surface, cloth)*
□ My hands are rough. 我的手很粗糙。Wǒde shǒu hěn cūcāo.
2 崎岖的 qíqū de *(terrain)*
3 波涛汹涌的 bōtāo xiōngyǒng de *(sea, crossing)*
□ The sea was rough. 海面波涛汹涌。Hǎimiàn bōtāo xiōngyǒng.
4 粗鲁的 cūlǔ de *(person)*
5 治安混乱的 zhì'ān hùnluàn de *(town, area)*
□ It's a rough area. 这是一个治安混乱的区域。Zhè shì yígè zhì'ān hùnluàn de qūyù.
6 粗略的 cūlüè de *(outline, plan, idea)*

□ I've got a rough idea. 我有了一个粗略的想法。Wǒ yǒule yígè cūlüè de xiǎngfǎ.

■ **to feel rough** 感觉不舒服 gǎnjué bùshūfu □ I feel rough. 我感觉不舒服。Wǒ gǎnjué bùshūfu.

roughly ADVERB

1 粗暴地 cūbào de *(violently)*

2 大约 dàyuē *(approximately)*

□ It weighs roughly 20 kilos. 它大约重二十千克。Tā dàyuē zhòng èrshí qiānkè.

■ **roughly speaking** 粗略地说 cūlüè de shuō

round NOUN

▷ *see also* **round** ADJECTIVE, ADVERB, PREPOSITION

1 一轮 yìlún *(in competition)*

2 一场 yíchǎng *(of golf)*

■ **a round of drinks** 一轮饮料 yìlún yǐnliào □ He bought a round of drinks. 他买了一轮饮料。Tā mǎi le yìlún yǐnliào.

■ **a round of applause** 掌声雷动 zhǎngshēng léidòng

round ADJECTIVE, ADVERB, PREPOSITION

▷ *see also* **round** NOUN

1 圆的 yuán de *(circular)*

□ a round table 一张圆桌 yìzhāng yuánzhuō

2 球形的 qiúxíng de *(spherical)*

3 不计尾数的 bù jì wěishù de *(figure, sum)*

4 围绕 wéirào *(surrounding)*

□ We were sitting round the table. 我们围坐在桌前。Wǒmen wéizuò zài zhuō qián.

■ **It's just round the corner.** *(very near)* 它就在拐角处。Tā jiùzài guǎijiǎochù.

■ **to go round to somebody's house** 造访某人 zàofǎng mǒurén □ I went round to my friend's house. 我造访了我朋友。Wǒ zàofǎng le wǒ péngyǒu.

■ **I'll be round at 6 o'clock.** 我会在六点钟到你家。Wǒ huì zài liùdiǎnzhōng dào nǐjiā.

■ **to have a look round** 四处看看 sìchù kànkan □ We're going to have a look round. 我们去四处看看。Wǒmen qù sìchù kànkan.

■ **to go round something** *(castle, museum)* 游览某处 yóulǎn mǒuchù

■ **to move round the room** 绕房间一周 rào fángjiān yìzhōu

■ **round here** 附近 fùjìn □ Is there a chemist's round here? 这附近有药房吗？Zhè fùjìn yǒu yàofáng ma?

■ **all round** 在…周围 zài...zhōuwéi □ There were mountains all round. 这周围都是山。Zhè zhōuwéi dōushì shān.

■ **all year round** 一年到头 yìnián dàotóu

■ **round the clock** 连续二十四小时 liánxù èrshísì xiǎoshí

■ **round about** *(approximately)* 大约 dàyuē □ It costs round about £100. 它大约要一百英镑。Tā dàyuē yào yìbǎi yīngbàng.

□ round about 8 o'clock 大约八点 dàyuē bādiǎn

to **round up** VERB

1 驱拢 qūlǒng *(cattle, sheep)*

2 围捕 wéibǔ *(people)*

3 把...调高为整数 bǎ...tiáogāo wéi zhěngshù *(price, figure)*

to **round off** VERB

圆满结束 yuánmǎn jiéshù *(meal, evening)*

□ They rounded off the meal with liqueurs. 他们用饭后甜酒收尾圆满结束了晚餐。Tāmen yòng fànhòu tiánjiǔ shōuwěi yuánmǎn jiēshù le wǎncān.

roundabout NOUN

环形交叉路 huánxíng jiāochālù [个 gè] *(for traffic)*

rounders NOUN

圆场棒球 yuánchǎng bàngqiú

□ Rounders is a bit like baseball. 圆场棒球有一点像棒球。Yuánchǎngbàngqiú yǒu yìdiǎn xiàng bàngqiú.

round trip NOUN (US)

往返旅行 wǎngfǎn lǚxíng [次 cì]

■ **a round-trip ticket** 一张往返票 yìzhāng wǎngfǎnpiào

route NOUN

1 路 lù [条 tiáo] *(path, journey)*

2 路线 lùxiàn [条 tiáo] *(of bus, train)*

□ We're planning our route. 我们正在计划我们的路线。Wǒmen zhèngzài jìhuà wǒmen de lùxiàn.

routine NOUN

例行公事 lìxíng gōngshì [次 cì]

■ **my daily routine** 我每天的例行公事 wǒ měitiān de lìxíng gōngshì

row NOUN

▷ *see also* **row** VERB

1 一排 yì pái *(of people, houses)*

□ a row of houses 一排房子 yìpái fángzi

2 排 pái *(of seats in theatre, cinema)*

□ Our seats are in the front row. 我们的座位在前排。Wǒmen de zuòwèi zài qiánpái.

■ **in a row** 连续 liánxù □ five times in a row 连续五次 liánxù wǔcì

3 吵闹声 chǎonàoshēng *(noise)*

□ What's that terrible row? 那糟糕的吵闹声是怎么回事？Nà zāogāo de chǎonàoshēng shì zěnme huíshì?

4 吵架 chǎojià [场 chǎng] *(noisy quarrel)*

■ **to have a row** 吵架 chǎojià □ They've had a row. 他们刚吵完一架。Tāmen gāng chǎo wán yíjià.

to **row** VERB

▷ *see also* **row** NOUN

1 划船 huáchuán *(in boat)*

□ We took turns to row. 我们轮流划船。Wǒmen lúnliú huáchuán.

2 划赛艇 huá sàitǐng *(as sport)*

■ **to row a boat** 划船 huáchuán

rowboat NOUN (US)

划艇 huátǐng [艘 sōu]

rowing NOUN

赛艇 sàitǐng

□ My hobby is rowing. 我的爱好是赛艇。Wǒde àihào shì sàitǐng.

rowing boat NOUN

划艇 huátǐng [艘 sōu]

royal ADJECTIVE

皇家的 huángjiā de

■ **the royal family** 皇室 huángshì

to **rub** VERB

1 揉 róu *(with hand, fingers)*

□ Don't rub your eyes! 不要揉你的眼睛！Búyào róu nǐde yǎnjīng!

2 擦 cā *(with cloth, substance)*

■ **to rub something out** 擦掉某物 cādiào mǒuwù

rubber NOUN

1 橡胶 xiàngjiāo *(substance)*

□ rubber soles 橡胶鞋底 xiàngjiāo xiédǐ

■ **a rubber band** 一个橡胶圈 yígè xiàngjiāoquān

2 橡皮擦 xiàngpícā [个 gè] *(eraser)*

□ Can I borrow your rubber? 我能借用你的橡皮擦吗？ Wǒ néng jièyòng nǐde xiàngpícā mā?

rubber boot NOUN (US)

橡胶长统靴 xiàngjiāo chángtǒngxuē [双 shuāng]

rubbish NOUN

▷ *see also* **rubbish** ADJECTIVE

1 垃圾 lājī *(refuse)*

□ When do they collect the rubbish? 他们什么时候来收垃圾？ Tāmen shénme shíhòu lái shōu lājī?

2 残品 cánpǐn *(inferior material)*

□ They sell a lot of rubbish at the market. 他们在市场上卖很多残品。Tāmen zài shìchǎng shàng mài hěnduō cánpǐn.

3 废话 fèihuà *(nonsense)*

□ Don't talk rubbish! 不要讲废话！ Búyào jiǎng fèihuà!

■ **rubbish!** 胡说！ Húshuō!

■ **That's a load of rubbish!** *(informal)* 废话！ Fèihuà!

■ **a rubbish dump** 一个垃圾堆 yígè lājīduī

rubbish ADJECTIVE

▷ *see also* **rubbish** NOUN

糟糕的 zāogāo de

■ **I'm rubbish at golf.** 我高尔夫球打得很糟糕。Wǒ gāo'ěrfūqiú dǎde hěn zāogāo.

□ They're a rubbish team! 他们是个糟糕的队！ Tāmen shì gè zāogāo de duì!

rubbish bin NOUN

垃圾箱 lājīxiāng [个 gè]

rucksack NOUN

背包 bèibāo [个 gè]

rude ADJECTIVE

1 无礼的 wúlǐ de

□ It's rude to interrupt. 打断别人是无礼的。Dǎduàn biérén shì wúlǐ de.

2 粗鄙的 cūbǐ de *(word, joke, noise)*

□ a rude word 一个粗鄙的词 yígè cūbǐ de cí

■ **to be rude to somebody** 对某人无礼 duì mǒurén wúlǐ □ He was very rude to me. 他对我很无礼。Tā duì wǒ hěn wúlǐ.

rug NOUN

1 小地毯 xiǎodìtǎn [块 kuài]

□ a Persian rug 一块波斯产的小地毯 yíkuài Bōsī chǎn de xiǎodìtǎn

2 毯子 tǎnzi *(blanket)*

□ a tartan rug 一张格子呢的毯子 yìzhāng gézíní de tǎnzi

rugby NOUN

英式橄榄球 yīngshì gǎnlǎnqiú

□ I play rugby. 我打英式橄榄球。Wǒ dǎ yīngshì gǎnlǎnqiú.

ruin NOUN

▷ *see also* **ruin** VERB

废墟 fèixū [片 piàn]

■ **ruins** *(of building, castle)* 废墟 fèixū

■ **to be in ruins** *(building, town)* 破败不堪 pòbài bùkān

to **ruin** VERB

▷ *see also* **ruin** NOUN

1 毁坏 huǐhuài *(clothes, carpet)*

□ You'll ruin your shoes. 你会毁坏你的鞋子的。Nǐ huì huǐhuài nǐ de xiézi de.

2 完全破坏 wánquán pòhuài *(plans, prospects)*

□ It ruined our holiday. 它完全破坏了我们的假期。Tā wánquán pòhuài le wǒmen de jiàqī.

3 使破产 shǐ pòchǎn *(financially)*

□ That one mistake ruined the business. 那个错误使生意破产了。Nàgè cuòwù shǐ shēngyì pòchǎn le.

rule NOUN

规则 guīzé [条 tiáo]

■ **It's against the rules.** 这是不合规定的。Zhèshì bùhé guīdìng de. □ the rules of grammar 语法规则 yǔfǎ guīzé

■ **as a rule** 通常 tōngcháng

to **rule out** VERB
排除 páichú *(possibility)*
□ I'm not ruling anything out. 我并不是要排除掉所有的。Wǒ bìng búshì yào páichú diào suǒyǒu de.

ruler NOUN
直尺 zhíchǐ [把 bǎ] *(for measuring)*
□ Can I borrow your ruler? 我能借用你的直尺吗？ Wǒ néng jièyòng nǐde zhíchǐ ma?

rum NOUN
朗姆酒 lǎngmǔjiǔ [瓶 píng]

rumour (US **rumor**) NOUN
谣言 yáoyán [个 gè]
□ It's just a rumour. 这仅仅是个谣言。Zhè jǐnjǐn shì gè yáoyán.

rump steak NOUN
后腿肉牛排 hòutuǐròu niúpái [块 kuài]

run NOUN
▷ *see also* **run** VERB
1 跑步 pǎobù [次 cì] *(as exercise, sport)*
□ I did a ten-kilometre run. 我完成了十千米跑。Wǒ wánchéng le shí qiānmǐ pǎo.
2 跑动得分 pǎodòng défēn [次 cì] *(in cricket, baseball)*
□ to score a run 跑动得分 pǎodòng défēn
■ **to go for a run** 跑步锻炼 pǎobù duànliàn
■ **on the run** 在逃的 zàitáo de □ The criminals are still on the run. 那些罪犯依然在逃。Nàxiē zuìfàn yīrán zàitáo.
■ **in the long run** 终究 zhōngjiū

to **run** VERB
▷ *see also* **run** NOUN
1 跑 pǎo *(race, distance)*
□ I ran five kilometres. 我跑了五千米。Wǒ pǎo le wǔ qiānmǐ.
■ **to run a marathon** 跑马拉松 pǎo mǎlāsōng
2 经营 jīngyíng *(operate: business, shop, country)*
□ He runs a large company. 他经营着一家大公司。Tā jīngyíng zhe yìjiā dà gōngsī.
3 组织 zǔzhī *(organize)*
□ They run music courses in the holidays. 他们在假期期间组织音乐课程。Tāmen zài jiàqī qījiān zǔzhī yīnyuè kèchéng.
4 进行 jìnxíng *(program, test)*
5 流 liú *(water)*
□ Don't leave the tap running. 不要让水龙头流水。Búyào ràng shuǐlóngtóu liúshuǐ.
■ **to run a bath** 放一盆洗澡水 fàng yìpén xǐzǎoshuǐ
6 开车 kāichē *(by car)*
□ I'll run you to the station. 我开车送你去车站。Wǒ kāichē sòng nǐ qù chēzhàn.

to **run after** VERB
追赶 zhuīgǎn *(chase)*

to **run away** VERB
逃 táo *(from home, situation)*
□ They ran away before the police came. 他们在警察来前逃跑了。Tāmen zài jǐngchá lái qián táopǎo le.

to **run into** VERB
1 偶然碰见 ǒurán pèngjiàn *(person)*
2 遭遇 zāoyù *(trouble, problems)*

to **run off** VERB
跑掉 pǎodiào *(flee)*

to **run out** VERB
1 用完 yòngwán *(time, money, luck)*
□ Time is running out. 时间快用完了。Shíjiān kuài yòng wán le.
2 到期 dàoqī *(lease, passport)*

to **run out of** VERB
耗尽 hàojìn
□ We ran out of money. 我们把钱耗尽了。Wǒmen bǎ qián hàojìn le.

to **run over** VERB
撞倒 zhuàngdǎo *(person)*
■ **to get run over** 被撞倒 bèi zhuàngdǎo
□ Be careful, or you'll get run over! 小心点，要不你会被撞倒的！ Xiǎoxīn diǎn, yàobù nǐ huì bèi zhuàngdǎo de!

rung VERB ▷ *see* **ring**

runner NOUN
赛跑者 sàipǎozhě [个 gè] *(in race)*

runner beans PL NOUN
红花菜豆 hónghuā càidòu

runner-up NOUN
亚军 yàjūn [个 gè]

running NOUN
跑步 pǎobù
□ Running is my favourite sport. 跑步是我最喜欢的运动。Pǎobù shì wǒ zuì xǐhuān de yùndòng.
■ **6 days running** 连续六天 liánxù liùtiān

run-up NOUN
前期 qiánqī *(time before)*
■ **in the run-up to Christmas** 在圣诞节前期 zài Shèngdànjié qiánqī

runway NOUN
跑道 pǎodào [条 tiáo]

rural ADJECTIVE
农村的 nóngcūn de

rush NOUN
▷ *see also* **rush** VERB
匆忙 cōngmáng *(hurry)*
■ **in a rush** 匆忙地 cōngmáng de

to **rush** VERB
▷ *see also* **rush** NOUN
1 急速前往 jísù qiánwǎng
□ Everyone rushed outside. 每个人都急速走出门外。Měigèrén dōu jísù zǒu chū ménwài.

2 匆忙 cōngmáng *(hurry)*
□ There's no need to rush. 没有必要匆忙。Méiyǒu bìyào cōngmáng.

rush hour NOUN
高峰时间 gāofēng shíjiān [段 duàn]
□ in the rush hour 在高峰时间期间 zài gāofēng shíjiān qījiān

Russia NOUN
俄罗斯 Éluósī
□ in Russia 在俄罗斯 zài Éluósī □ to Russia 去俄罗斯 qù Éluósī

Russian ADJECTIVE
▷ *see also* **Russian** NOUN
俄罗斯的 Éluósī de

Russian NOUN
▷ *see also* **Russian** ADJECTIVE
1 俄罗斯人 Éluósīrén [个 gè] *(person)*
2 俄语 Éyǔ *(language)*

rust NOUN
铁锈 tiěxiù

rusty ADJECTIVE
1 生锈的 shēngxiù de *(surface, object)*
□ a rusty bike 一辆生锈的自行车 yíliǎng shēngxiù de zìxíngchē
2 荒疏的 huāngshū de *(skill)*
□ My Chinese is very rusty. 我的中文很荒疏。Wǒde zhōngwén hěn huāngshū.

RV NOUN (US) *(= recreational vehicle)*
娱乐车 yúlèchē [辆 liǎng]

rye NOUN
黑麦 hēimài *(cereal)*
■ **rye bread** 黑麦面包 hēimài miànbāo

Ss

sack NOUN
▷ *see also* **sack** VERB
麻袋 mádài [个 gè]
■ **to get the sack** *(informal)* 被解雇 bèijiěgù

to **sack** VERB
▷ *see also* **sack** NOUN
■ **to sack somebody** 解雇某人 jiěgù mǒurén □ He was sacked. 他被解雇了。Tā bèijiěgù le.

sacred ADJECTIVE
神圣的 shénshèngde

sacrifice NOUN
牺牲 xīshēng [次 cì]

sad ADJECTIVE
1 伤心的 shāngxīn de
2 令人悲伤的 lìngrén bēishāng de *(distressing)*

saddle NOUN
1 马鞍 mǎ'ān [副 fù] *(for horse)*
2 车座 chēzuò [个 gè] *(on bike, motorbike)*

sadly ADVERB
1 伤心地 shāngxīndè
□ 'She's gone,' he said sadly. "她走了，"他伤心地说。"Tā zǒu le," tā shāngxīndè shuō.
2 不幸的是 búxìngdeshì *(unfortunately)*
□ Sadly, it was too late. 不幸的是，太晚了。Búxìngdeshì, tàiwǎnle.

safe ADJECTIVE
▷ *see also* **safe** NOUN
1 安全的 ānquán de
□ Don't worry, it's perfectly safe. 别担心，很安全。Biédānxīn, hěn ānquán. □ This car isn't safe. 这辆车不安全。Zhèliàngchē bù ānquán.
■ **Is it safe?** 安全吗？Ānquán ma?
2 脱险的 tuōxiǎn de *(out of danger)*
□ You're safe now. 你现在脱险了。Nǐ xiànzài tuōxiǎn le.
■ **to feel safe** 感到安全 gǎndào ānquán
■ **safe sex** 安全性较 ānquán xìngjiāo

safe NOUN
▷ *see also* **safe** ADJECTIVE
保险箱 bǎoxiǎnxiāng [个 gè]
□ She put the money in the safe. 她把钱放进了保险箱。Tā bǎqián fàngjìnle bǎoxiǎnxiāng.

safety NOUN
安全 ānquán
■ **a safety belt** 安全带 ānquándài
■ **a safety pin** 安全别针 ānquán biézhēn

Sagittarius NOUN
人马座 Rénmǎzuò
□ I'm Sagittarius. 我是人马座的。Wǒ shì Rénmǎzuòde.

Sahara NOUN
■ **the Sahara Desert** 撒哈拉沙漠 Sàhālāshāmò

said VERB ▷ *see* **say**

sail NOUN
▷ *see also* **sail** VERB
帆 fān [张 zhāng]

to **sail** VERB
▷ *see also* **sail** NOUN
1 航行 hángxíng *(ship)*
□ The boat sails at eight o'clock. 这船八点钟开始航行。Zhèchuán bādiǎnzhōng kāishǐ hángxíng.
2 乘船航行 chéngchuán hángxíng *(passenger)*

sailing NOUN
帆船运动 fānchuán yùndòng
□ His hobby is sailing. 他的爱好是帆船运动。Tāde àihào shì fānchuán yùndòng.
■ **to go sailing** 去航行 qù hángxíng
■ **a sailing boat** 帆船 fānchuán
■ **a sailing ship** 大帆船 dàfānchuán

sailor NOUN
水手 shuǐshǒu [位 wèi]
□ He's a sailor. 他是位水手。Tā shì wèi shuǐshǒu.

saint NOUN
圣徒 shèngtú [个 gè]

sake NOUN
■ **for the sake of** 为了 yìsōu

salad NOUN
沙拉 shālā [份 fèn]
■ **salad cream** 沙拉酱 shālàjiàng

■ **salad dressing** 沙拉调味汁 shālà tiáowèizhī

salami NOUN
意大利腊肠 Yìdàlìlàcháng [根 gēn]

salary NOUN
薪水 xīnshuǐ [份 fèn]

sale NOUN
打折 dǎzhé [次 cì]
□ There's a sale on at Harrods. 哈罗兹百货公司有打折活动。Hāluózī bǎihuògōngsī yǒu dǎzhéhuódòng.

DID YOU KNOW...?
Sales in China are advertised by how much of the original price remains, not how much is being deducted.

■ **to be on sale** 上市 shàngshì
■ **The factory's for sale.** 该工厂待售。Gāigōngchǎngdàishòu.
■ **for sale** 待售 dàishòu

sales PL NOUN
销售量 xiāoshòuliàng
□ Newspaper sales have fallen. 报纸的销售量下降了。Bàozhǐde xiāoshòuliàng xiàjiàng le.

sales assistant NOUN
售货员 shòuhuòyuán [位 wèi]
□ She's a sales assistant. 她是位售货员。Tā shì wèi shòuhuòyuán.

salesman NOUN
1 推销员 tuīxiāo yuán [位 wèi] *(sales rep)*
□ He's a salesman. 他是位推销员。Tā shì wèi tuīxiāo yuán.
■ **a double-glazing salesman** 双层玻璃推销员 shuāngcéng bōlí tuīxiāo yuán
2 售货员 shòuhuòyuán *(sales assistant)*

sales rep NOUN
销售代理 xiāoshòudàilǐ [位 wèi]

saleswoman NOUN
1 女推销员 nǚ tuīxiāoyuán *(sales rep)*
□ She's a saleswoman. 她是位女推销员。Tā shì wèi nǚ tuīxiāoyuán.
2 售货员 shòuhuòyuán *(sales assistant)*

salmon NOUN
大马哈鱼 dà mǎhā yú [条 tiáo]

LANGUAGE TIP Salmon is increasingly known as 三文鱼 sānwényú in China, which is a loan word from the English.

salon NOUN
美发廊 měifà láng [家 jiā]
■ **a hair salon** 一家美发廊 yìjiā měifàláng
■ **a beauty salon** 一家美容院 yìjiā měiróngyuàn

salt NOUN
盐 yán

salty ADJECTIVE
咸的 xián de

to **salute** VERB
敬礼 jìnglǐ

Salvation Army NOUN
救世军 jiùshìjūn

same ADJECTIVE
1 相同的 xiāngtóng de *(size, colour, age)*
□ the same model 相同的模型 xiāngtóng de móxíng
2 同一个的 tóngyīgè de *(place, person, time)*
□ at the same time 同时 tóngshí
■ **They're exactly the same.** 他们完全相同。Tāmen wánquán xiāngtóng.
■ **It's not the same.** 这不同。Zhè bùtóng.

sample NOUN
1 样品 yàngpǐn [件 jiàn]
2 采样 cǎiyàng [个 gè] *(of blood, urine)*

sand NOUN
沙子 shāzi

sandal NOUN
凉鞋 liángxié [双 shuāng]
□ a pair of sandals 一双凉鞋 yìshuāng liángxié

sand castle NOUN
沙堡 shābǎo [座 zuò]

sandwich NOUN
三明治 sānmíngzhì [份 fèn]
□ a cheese sandwich 一份奶酪三明治 yífèn nǎilào sānmíngzhì

sang VERB ▷ *see* **sing**

sanitary napkin NOUN (US)
卫生巾 wèishēng jīn [块 kuài]

sanitary towel NOUN
卫生巾 wèishēng jīn [块 kuài]

sank VERB ▷ *see* **sink**

Santa Claus NOUN
圣诞老人 Shèngdàn Lǎorén [位 wèi]

sarcastic ADJECTIVE
讽刺的 fěngcìde

sardine NOUN
沙丁鱼 shādīng yú [条 tiáo]

SARS NOUN *(= severe acute respiratory syndrome)*
非典型性肺炎 fēi diǎnxíngxìng fèiyán

SAT NOUN (US)
学业能力倾向测试 Xuéyè Nénglì Qīngxiàng Cèshì

sat VERB ▷ *see* **sit**

satchel NOUN
小背包 xiǎobēibāo [只 zhī]

satellite NOUN
人造卫星 rénzào wèixīng [颗 kē]
□ by satellite 通过人造卫星 tōngguò rénzào wèixīng
■ **a satellite dish** 卫星接收器 wèixīngjiēshōuqì

■ **satellite television** 卫星电视 wèixīng diànshì

satisfactory ADJECTIVE
令人满意的 lìngrén mǎnyì de

satisfied ADJECTIVE
满足的 mǎnzú de
■ **to be satisfied with something** 对某事满意 duì mǒushì mǎnyì

sat nav NOUN
卫星导航 wèixīngdǎoháng

Saturday NOUN
星期六 xīngqīliù [个 gè]
□ on Saturday 在星期六 zàixīngqīliù □ on Saturdays 在星期六 zàixīngqīliù □ every Saturday 每个星期六 měigè xīngqīliù □ last Saturday 上个星期六 shànggè xīngqīliù □ next Saturday 下个星期六 xiàgè xīngqīliù
■ **I've got a Saturday job.** 我有了一份星期六上班的工作。Wǒ yǒule yífèn xīngqīliù shàngbānde gōngzuò.

sauce NOUN
酱 jiàng [种 zhǒng]

saucepan NOUN
深平底锅 shēn píngdǐ guō [个 gè]

saucer NOUN
茶杯碟 chábēi dié [个 gè]

Saudi Arabia NOUN
沙特阿拉伯 Shātè Ālābó

sauna NOUN
桑那浴 sāngnáyù [次 cì]

sausage NOUN
香肠 xiāngcháng [根 gēn]
■ **a sausage roll** 香肠卷 xiāngchángjuǎn

to **save** VERB
1 积攒 jīzǎn
□ I've saved £50 already. 我已经积攒了五十英镑。Wǒ yǐjīng jīzǎnle wǔshí yīngbàng.
2 节省 jiéshěng *(spend less)*
□ I saved £20 by waiting for the sales. 等到打折才买帮我节省了二十英镑。Děngdào dǎzhé cáimǎi bāng wǒ jiéshěngle èrshí yīngbàng.
■ **to save time** 节省时间 jiéshěng shíjiān
□ We took a taxi to save time. 我们为了节省时间坐了计程车。Wǒmen wèile jiéshěng shíjiān zuòle jìchéngchē. □ It saved us time. 这为我们节省了时间。Zhè wèi wǒmen jiéshěngle shíjiān.
3 救 jiù
□ Luckily, all the passengers were saved. 幸运的是，所有的乘客都获救了。Xìngyùndeshì, suǒyǒude chéngkè dōu huòjiùle.
■ **to save somebody's life** 挽救某人的生命 wǎnjiù mǒurén de shēngmìng
4 存储 cúnchǔ *(on computer)*
□ Don't forget to save your work regularly. 别忘记经常存储你的文档。Bié wàngjì jīngcháng cúnchǔ nide wéndǎng.

to **save up** VERB
储蓄 chǔxù
□ I'm saving up for a new bike. 我为买一台新的自行车而储蓄。Wǒ wèimǎi yìtái xīnde zìxíngchē ér chǔxù.

savings PL NOUN
存款 cúnkuǎn [笔 bǐ]
□ She spent all her savings on a computer. 她把所有的存款都用在买电脑上了。Tā bǎ suǒyǒude cúnkuǎn dōu yòngzài mǎidiànnǎo shàngle.

savoury (US **savory**) ADJECTIVE
咸辣的 xiánlà de
□ Is it sweet or savoury? 是甜的还是咸辣的? Shì tiánde háishì xiánlàde?

saw VERB ▷ *see* **see**

saw NOUN
▷ *see also* **saw** VERB
锯子 jùzi [把 bǎ]

to **saw** VERB
▷ *see also* **saw** NOUN
锯 jù

sax NOUN
萨克斯 sàkèsī [根 gēn]
□ I play the sax. 我吹萨克斯。Wǒ chuī sàkèsī.

saxophone NOUN
萨克斯管 sàkèsī guǎn [根 gēn]
□ I play the saxophone. 我吹萨克斯管。Wǒ chuī sàkèsī guǎn.

to **say** VERB
1 说 shuō
□ What did he say? 他说什么了？Tā shuō shénmè le? □ Did you hear what she said? 你听到她所说的了吗？Nǐ tīngdào tā suǒshuōde le ma?
■ **to say something to somebody** 告诉某人某事 gàosù mǒurén mǒushì
■ **Could you say that again?** 你能再说一遍吗？Nǐ néng zàishuō yíbiàn ma?
■ **to say yes** 同意 tóngyì
■ **to say no** 不同意 bù tóngyì
■ **That goes without saying.** 不言而喻 Bùyánéryù.
2 显示 xiǎnshì *(clock, watch)*
□ The clock said four minutes past eleven. 表显示的是十一点零四分。Biǎo xiǎnshìde shì qīdiǎn língsì fēn.

saying NOUN
谚语 yànyǔ [个 gè]
□ It's just a saying. 只是个谚语。Zhǐshìgè yànyǔ.

English-Chinese

scale NOUN
1 比例 bǐlì
□ a large-scale map 大比例的地图 dà bǐlìde dìtú
2 规模 guīmó *(size, extent)*
□ a disaster on a massive scale 大规模的灾难 dàguīmóde zāinàn
3 音阶的升降 yīnjiēde shēngjiàng *(in music)*

scales PL NOUN
秤 chèng
■ **bathroom scales** 浴室的秤 yùshìde chèng

scampi PL NOUN
炸虾球 zhàxiāqiú

scandal NOUN
丑闻 chǒuwén [条 tiáo]
□ It caused a scandal. 它导致了丑闻。Tā dǎozhì le chǒuwén.

Scandinavia NOUN
斯堪的纳维亚 Sīkāndìnàwéiyà
■ **in Scandinavia** 在斯堪的纳维亚 zài Sīkāndìnàwéiyà

Scandinavian ADJECTIVE
斯堪的纳维亚的 Sīkāndìnàwéiyàde

scanner NOUN
扫描仪 sǎomiáo yí [台 tái] *(for computer)*

scar NOUN
伤疤 shāngbā [个 gè]

scarce ADJECTIVE
短缺的 duǎnquē de
□ Jobs are scarce these days. 最近工作很短缺。Zuìjìn gōngzuò hěn duǎnquē.

scarcely ADVERB
几乎不 jīhūbù
□ I scarcely knew him. 我几乎不认识他。Wǒ jīhūbù rènshi tā.

to **scare** VERB
让害怕 ràng hàipà
■ **to scare somebody** 让某人害怕 ràng mǒurén hàipà □ He scares me. 他让我害怕。Tā ràng wǒ hàipà.

S

scarecrow NOUN
稻草人 dàocǎorén [个 gè]

scared ADJECTIVE
■ **to be scared** 恐惧的 kǒngjùde □ I was scared stiff. 我恐惧的都僵硬了。Wǒ kǒngjùde dōu jiāngyìng le.
■ **to be scared of** 害怕 hàipà □ Are you scared of him? 你害怕他吗？Nǐ hàipà tā ma?

scarf NOUN
1 围巾 wéijīn [条 tiáo] *(long)*
2 头巾 tóujīn [块 kuài] *(square)*

scary ADJECTIVE
恐怖的 kǒngbùde
□ It was really scary. 那很恐怖。Nà hěn kǒngbù.

scene NOUN
1 现场 xiànchǎng [个 gè] *(place)*
□ The police were soon on the scene. 警察很快到了现场。Jǐngchá hěnkuài dàole xiànchǎng. □ the scene of the crime 犯罪现场 fànzuì xiànchǎng
2 场景 chángjǐng [个 gè] *(event, sight)*
□ It was an amazing scene. 那是很壮观的场景。Nà shì hěn zhuàngguānde chǎngjǐng.
■ **to make a scene** 大吵大闹 dàchǎodànào

scenery NOUN
风景 fēngjǐng [道 dào]

scent NOUN
香味 xiāngwèi [股 gǔ] *(perfume)*

schedule NOUN
1 日程安排 rìchéng ānpái [个 gè]
□ a busy schedule 紧张的日程安排 jǐnzhāngde rìchéngānpái
2 时间表 shíjiān biǎo [个 gè] (US: *of trains, buses)*
■ **on schedule** 准时 zhǔnshí
■ **to be behind schedule** 落后于计划 luòhòu yú jìhuà

scheduled flight NOUN
定期航班 dìngqīhángbān [次 cì]

scheme NOUN
1 方案 fāng'àn [个 gè] *(plan)*
□ a crazy scheme he dreamed up 他想出的疯狂方案 tā xiǎngchūde fēngkuáng fāngàn
2 计划 jìhuà [项 xiàng] *(project)*
□ a council road-widening scheme 市政府扩路计划 shìzhèngfǔ kuòlù jìhuà

scholarship NOUN
奖学金 jiǎngxué jīn [项 xiàng]

school NOUN
1 学校 xuéxiào [所 suǒ]
■ **to go to school** 上学 shàngxué
■ **to leave school** 毕业 bìyè
2 大学 dàxué [所 suǒ] (US: *university)*

schoolbag NOUN
书包 shūbāo [个 gè]

schoolbook NOUN
教科书 jiàokēshū [本 běn]

schoolboy NOUN
男生 nánshēng [个 gè]

schoolchildren PL NOUN
学童 xuétóng

schoolgirl NOUN
女生 nǚshēng [个 gè]

school uniform NOUN
校服 xiàofú [件 jiàn]

science NOUN
1 科学 kēxué *(scientific study)*
2 学科 xuékē [个 gè] *(school subject)*

science fiction NOUN
科幻小说 kēhuàn xiǎoshuō [部 bù]

scientific ADJECTIVE
科学的 kēxué de

scientist NOUN
科学家 kēxué jiā [位 wèi]
□ He trained as a scientist. 他培训成科学家。Tā péixùnchéng kēxuéjiā.

scissors PL NOUN
剪刀 jiǎndāo
□ a pair of scissors 一把剪刀 yìbǎ jiǎndāo

scooter NOUN
1 小型摩托车 xiǎoxíng mótuō chē [辆 liàng] *(motorcycle)*
2 踏板车 tàbǎnchē [辆 liàng] *(child's toy)*

score NOUN
▹ *see also* **score** VERB
比分 bǐfēn [个 gè]
□ The score was three nil. 比分是三比零。Bǐfēn shì sān bǐ líng.

to **score** VERB
▹ *see also* **score** NOUN
1 得 dé
■ **to score a goal** 射门得分 shèmén défēn
■ **to score 6 out of 10** 总分十分得了六分 zǒngfēn shífēn déle liùfēn
2 得分 défēn *(keep score)*
□ Who's going to score? 谁会得分? Shuí huì défēn?

Scorpio NOUN
天蝎座 Tiānxiēzuò
□ I'm Scorpio. 我是天蝎座。Wǒ shì tiānxiēzuò

Scot NOUN
苏格兰人 Sūgélánrén [位 wèi]
■ **the Scots** 苏格兰人 Sūgélánrén

Scotch tape® NOUN (US)
透明胶带 tòumíng jiāodài

Scotland NOUN
苏格兰 Sūgélán
■ **in Scotland** 在苏格兰 zài Sūgélán
■ **to Scotland** 到苏格兰 dào Sūgélán
■ **I'm from Scotland.** 我来自苏格兰。Wǒ láizì Sūgélán.

Scots ADJECTIVE
苏格兰的 Sūgélánde
□ a Scots accent 苏格兰的口音 Sūgélánde kǒuyin

Scotsman NOUN
苏格兰男人 Sūgélán nánrén [位 wèi]

Scotswoman NOUN
苏格兰女人 Sūgélán nǚrén [位 wèi]

Scottish ADJECTIVE
苏格兰的 Sūgélán de
□ a Scottish accent 苏格兰的口音 Sūgélánde kǒuyīn

scout NOUN
侦察 zhēnchá [次 cì]
■ **I'm in the Scouts.** 我是童子军。Wǒ shì tóngzǐjūn.

scrambled egg NOUN
炒鸡蛋 chǎo jīdàn [盘 pán]

to **scrap** VERB
▹ *see also* **scrap** NOUN
废弃 fèiqì
□ The idea was scrapped. 这个观点被废弃了。Zhègè guāndiǎn bèi fèiqì le.

scrap NOUN
▹ *see also* **scrap** VERB
1 小片 xiǎopiàn [块 kuài]
□ a scrap of paper 一块小片纸 yíkuài xiǎopiàn zhǐ
2 打架 dǎjià [次 cì] *(fight)*
■ **scrap iron** 铁屑 tiěxiè

scrapbook NOUN
剪贴簿 jiǎntiēbù [个 gè]

scratch NOUN
▹ *see also* **scratch** VERB
1 刮痕 guāhén [条 tiáo] *(on car, furniture)*
2 擦伤 cāshāng [处 chù] *(on skin)*
■ **to start from scratch** 从头开始 cóngtóukāishǐ

to **scratch** VERB
▹ *see also* **scratch** NOUN
1 挠 náo *(because of itch)*
□ Stop scratching! 不要挠了! Búyào náole!
2 划破 huápò *(cut)*
□ He scratched his arm on the bushes. 他被灌木丛划破了胳膊。Tā bèi guànmùcóng huápò le gēbo.
3 划破 huápò *(damage)*
□ You'll scratch the worktop with that knife. 那把刀会划破工作台的。Nà bǎ dāo huì huápò gōngzuòtáide.

to **scream** VERB
▹ *see also* **scream** NOUN
尖声喊叫 jiānshēng hǎnjiào

scream NOUN
▹ *see also* **scream** VERB
尖叫 jiānjiào [次 cì]

screen NOUN
1 银幕 yínmù [个 gè] *(at cinema)*
2 屏幕 píngmù [个 gè] *(of television, computer)*

screen-saver NOUN
屏保 píngbǎo [个 gè]

screw NOUN
螺丝 luósī [个 gè]

screwdriver NOUN
螺丝起子 lúosīqǐzi [把 bǎ]

to **scribble** VERB

乱写 luànxiě

to **scrub** VERB

擦洗 cāxǐ

■ **to scrub a pan** 擦洗锅 cāxǐguō

sculpture NOUN

雕塑 diāosù [座 zuò]

sea NOUN

海洋 hǎiyáng [个 gè]

seafood NOUN

海味 hǎiwèi [种 zhǒng]

□ I don't like seafood. 我不喜欢海味。Wǒ bùxǐhuan hǎiwèi.

seagull NOUN

海鸥 hǎi'ōu [只 zhī]

seal NOUN

海豹 hǎibào [只 zhī]

seaman NOUN

水手 shuǐshǒu [个 gè]

to **search** VERB

搜查 sōuchá

□ They searched the woods for her. 他们为了找她搜查了树林。Tāmén wèile zhǎotā sōuchá le shùlín.

■ **to search for something** 找某物 zhǎomǒuwù □ He searched for evidence. 他找证据。Tā zhǎo zhèngjù.

search engine NOUN

搜索引擎 sōusuǒyǐnqíng [个 gè]

DID YOU KNOW...?
The most popular internet search engine China is Baidu 百度 Bǎidù.

seashore NOUN

海岸 hǎi'àn [个 gè]

□ on the seashore 在海岸上 zàihǎi'ànshàng

seasick ADJECTIVE

晕船的 yūnchuán de

■ **to be seasick** 感到晕船恶心 gǎndào yūnchuán ěxīn

seaside NOUN

海边 hǎibiān

□ at the seaside 在海边 zàihǎibiān

season NOUN

季节 jìjié [个 gè]

□ What's your favourite season? 你最喜欢的季节是什么？ Nǐ zuìxǐhuande jìjié shì shénme?

■ **out of season** 淡季 dànjì □ It's cheaper to go there out of season. 淡季时去那里更便宜。Dànjìshí qù nàlǐ gèngpiányì.

■ **during the holiday season** 在度假季节 zàidùjiàjìjié

■ **a season ticket** 季票 jìpiào

seat NOUN

1 椅子 yǐzi [把 bǎ] *(chair)*

2 座位 zuòwèi [个 gè] *(in theatre, bus, train)*

□ Is this seat taken? 这个座位有人吗？ Zhègè zuòwèi yǒurén ma?

■ **to take a seat** 就座 jiùzuò

seat belt NOUN

安全带 ānquán dài [条 tiáo]

sea water NOUN

海水 hǎishuǐ

seaweed NOUN

海藻 hǎizǎo

second ADJECTIVE, ADVERB

▷ *see also* **second** NOUN

第二的 dì'èr de

□ on the second page 在第二页 zài dì'èryè

■ **the second of March** 三月二号 sānyuè èrhào

■ **to come second** *(in race)* 第二名 dì'èrmíng

second NOUN

▷ *see also* **second** ADJECTIVE, ADVERB

秒 miǎo

□ It'll only take a second. 一秒钟就够了。Yìmiǎozhōng jiùgòu le.

secondary school NOUN

中学 zhōngxué [所 suǒ]

second-class ADJECTIVE, ADVERB

1 二等 èrděng *(ticket, compartment)*

■ **to travel second class** 二等舱旅行 èrděngcāng lǚxíng

2 二类 èrlèi *(stamp, letter)*

■ **to send something second class** 按二类邮件邮某物 àn èrlèi yóujiàn yóu mǒuwù

second-hand ADJECTIVE

二手的 èrshǒu de

□ a second-hand car 一辆二手车 yíliàng èrshǒuchē

secondly ADVERB

其次 qícì

■ **firstly ... secondly ...** 首先…其次… shǒuxiān...qícì □ Firstly, it's too expensive. Secondly, it wouldn't work anyway. 首先，它太贵了。其次，它根本行不通。Shǒuxiān, tā tàiguìle. Qícì, tā gēnběn xíngbùtōng.

secret ADJECTIVE

▷ *see also* **secret** NOUN

秘密的 mìmì de

□ a secret mission 秘密任务 mìmì rènwu

secret NOUN

▷ *see also* **secret** ADJECTIVE

秘密 mìmì [个 gè]

□ It's a secret. 那是个秘密。Nàshìgè mìmì. □ Can you keep a secret? 你能保密吗？ Nǐnéng bǎomì ma?

■ **in secret** 秘密地 mìmìde

secretary NOUN

秘书 mìshū [位 wèi]

secretly ADVERB
秘密地 mìmìde

section NOUN
部分 bùfen [个 gè]

security NOUN
保安措施 bǎo'ān cuòshī
□ a campaign to improve airport security 提高机场保安措施的活动 tígāo jīchǎng bǎo'ān cuòshīde huódòng
■ **to have no job security** 没有工作的稳定性 méiyǒu gōngzuòde wěndìngxìng

security guard NOUN
保安 bǎo'ān [名 míng]

sedan NOUN (US)
轿车 jiàochē [辆 liàng]

to **see** VERB
1 看见 kànjiàn
□ I can't see. 我看不见。Wǒ kànbújiàn.
■ **to see somebody do something** 看见某人做某事 kànjiàn mǒurén zuò mǒushì
2 见 jiàn *(meet)*
□ I saw him yesterday. 我昨天看见他了。Wǒ zuótiān kànjiàn tā le.
■ **to go and see somebody** 去见某人 qùjiàn mǒurén
3 看 kàn *(film, play)*
■ **to see a doctor** 看医生 kàn yīshēng
■ **See you later!** 一会儿见！Yíhuìr jiàn!
■ **I see** *(understand)* 我明白 wǒ míngbai

seed NOUN
籽 zǐ [粒 lì]
□ sunflower seeds 向日葵籽 xiàngrìkuízǐ

to **seek** VERB
寻求 xúnqiú
■ **to seek help** 寻求帮助 xúnqiúbāngzhù

to **seem** VERB
似乎 sìhū
□ She seems tired. 她似乎累了。Tā sìhū lèile. □ That seems like a good idea. 那似乎是个好主意。Nà sìhū shìgè hǎozhúyì.
□ There seems to be a problem. 似乎有个问题。Sìhū yǒugè wèntí.
■ **It seems that...** 看来… Kànlái... □ It seems she's getting married. 看来她快结婚了。Kànlái tā kuài jiéhūn le.

seen VERB *▷ see* **see**

seldom ADVERB
不常 bùcháng

to **select** VERB
挑选 tiāoxuǎn

selection NOUN
供选择的范围 gōng xuǎnzéde fànwéi [个 gè] *(range)*

self-confidence NOUN
自信心 zìxìn xīn

self-conscious ADJECTIVE
■ **to be self-conscious 1** *(embarrassed)* 不好意思 bùhǎoyìsī □ She was really self-conscious at first. 开始她很不好意思。Kāishǐ tā hěn bùhǎo yìsī. **2** *(shy)* 害羞 hàixiū
□ He's always been rather self-conscious. 他一直就很害羞。Tā yìzhí jiù hěn hàixiū.

self-defence (US **self-defense**) NOUN
自卫 zìwèi
□ She killed him in self-defence. 她自卫杀了他。Tā zìwèi shāle tā.

self-discipline NOUN
自律 zìlǜ

self-employed ADJECTIVE
■ **to be self-employed** 自雇的 zìgùde

selfie NOUN
自拍照 zìpāi zhào
□ to take a selfie 自拍 zì pāi

selfish ADJECTIVE
自私的 zìsī de
□ Don't be so selfish. 别这么自私。Bié zhème zìsī.

self-service ADJECTIVE
自助的 zìzhù de *(café, shop)*
□ It's self-service. 是自助的。Shì zìzhùde.
■ **a self-service restaurant** 一家自助的餐厅 yìjiā zìzhùde cāntīng

to **sell** VERB
卖 mài
□ He sold it to me. 他把它卖给我。Tā bǎ tā màigěi wǒ.

> LANGUAGE TIP The words for **buy** 买 mǎi and **sell** 卖 mài are near identical in pronunciation, and the characters are closely related to each other as well, making them hard to tell apart.

to **sell off** VERB
廉价卖清 liánjiàmàiqīng

to **sell out** VERB
卖光 màiguāng
□ The tickets sold out in three hours. 票在三个小时之内就卖光了。Piào zài sāngèxiǎoshí zhīnèi jiù màiguāng le.
■ **The tickets are all sold out.** 票已经卖光了。Piào yǐjīng màiguāng le.

sell-by date NOUN
最迟销售日期 zuìchí xiāoshòurìqī [个 gè]

Sellotape® NOUN
透明胶带 tòumíng jiāodài [卷 juǎn]

semicircle NOUN
半圆形 bànyuánxíng [个 gè]

semicolon NOUN
分号 fēnhào [个 gè]

semi-detached house NOUN
半独立的房子 bàndúlìde fángzi [座 zuò]
□ We live in a semi-detached house. 我们住

在半独立的房子里。Wǒmen zhùzài bàndúlìde fángzilǐ.

semi-final NOUN
半决赛 bàn juésài [场 chǎng]

semi-skimmed milk NOUN
半脱脂牛奶 bàntuōzhīniúnǎi

to **send** VERB
1 邮寄 yóujì *(by post)*
□ She sent me a birthday card. 她给我寄了一张生日卡。Tā gěiwǒ jìle yìzhāng shēngrì kǎ.
2 派遣 pàiqiǎn *(person)*
□ He was sent to London. 他被派遣到伦敦。Tā bèi pàiqiǎn dào Lúndūn.

to **send back** VERB
退还 tuìhuán

to **send off** VERB
1 寄出 jìchū *(goods, letter)*
2 被罚下场 bèifáxiàchǎng *(in sports match)*
□ He was sent off. 他被罚下场了。Tā bèifáxiàchǎngle.

sender NOUN
寄件人 jìjiànrén [个 gè]

senior ADJECTIVE
高级的 gāojí de
■ **senior management** 高管 gāoguǎn
■ **senior school** 大龄儿童学校 dàlíng értóng xuéxiào

senior citizen NOUN
已届退休年龄的公民 yǐjiè tuìxiū niánlíng de gōngmín [位 wèi]

senior high (US **senior high school**) NOUN
高中 gāozhōng [所 suǒ]

sensational ADJECTIVE
非常好的 fēichánghǎode

sense NOUN
1 明智 míngzhì
□ Have a bit of sense! 明智点！ Míngzhì diǎn!
■ **common sense** 常识 chángshí
■ **It makes sense.** 很合理。Hěn hélǐ.
2 感觉官能 gǎnjué guānnéng [种 zhǒng]
□ the five senses 五官感觉 wǔguāngǎnjué
■ **the sense of touch** 触觉 chùjué
■ **the sense of smell** 嗅觉 xiùjué
■ **sense of humour** 幽默感 yōumògǎn
□ He's got no sense of humour. 他没有幽默感。Tā méiyǒu yōumògǎn.

senseless ADJECTIVE
无感觉的 wúgǎnjuéde

sensible ADJECTIVE
1 理智的 lǐzhìde
□ Be sensible! 理智点！ Lǐzhìdiǎn!
2 明智的 míngzhì de *(decision, suggestion)*

sensitive ADJECTIVE
敏感的 mǐngǎnde
□ She's very sensitive. 她很敏感。Tā hěn mǐngǎn.

sent VERB ▷ *see* **send**

sentence NOUN
▷ *see also* **sentence** VERB
1 句子 jùzi [个 gè]
□ What does this sentence mean? 这句话是什么意思？ Zhèjùhuà shì shénme yìsī?
2 判决 pànjué *(punishment)*
□ the death sentence 死刑判决 sǐxíngpànjué
■ **He got a life sentence.** 他被判终身监禁。Tā bèipàn zhōngshēnjiānjìn.

to **sentence** VERB
▷ *see also* **sentence** NOUN
判决 pànjué
■ **to sentence somebody to life imprisonment** 判决某人终身监禁 pànjué mǒurén zhōngshēnjiānjìn
■ **to sentence somebody to death** 判某人死刑 pàn mǒurén sǐxíng

sentimental ADJECTIVE
感伤的 gǎnshāngde

separate ADJECTIVE
▷ *see also* **separate** VERB
1 分开的 fēnkāi de
□ I wrote it on a separate sheet. 我在分开的纸上写。Wǒ zài fēnkāide zhǐshàngxiě.
2 单独的 dāndú de
□ The children have separate rooms. 孩子们有单独的房间。Háizimen yǒu dāndúde fángjiān.
■ **on separate occasions** 在不同的场合 zài bùtóngde chǎnghé

to **separate** VERB
▷ *see also* **separate** ADJECTIVE
1 分开 fēnkāi
□ The police tried to separate the two groups. 警察试着将两个人群分开。Jǐngchá shìzhe jiāng liǎnggèrénqún fēnkāi.
2 分居 fēnjū
□ My parents have separated. 我父母已经分居了。Wǒ fùmǔ yǐjīng fēnjū le.

separately ADVERB
单独地 dāndúde

separation NOUN
分开 fēnkāi

September NOUN
九月 jiǔyuè
□ in September 在九月 zàijiǔyuè □ the first of September 九月一日 jiǔyuè yīrì □ at the beginning of September 在九月初 zài jiǔyuè chū □ at the end of September 在九月末 zài jiǔyuè mò □ every September 每年九月 měinián jiǔyuè

sequel NOUN
续集 xùjí [部 bù] *(book, film)*
sergeant NOUN
1 军官 jūnguān [位 wèi] *(army)*
2 警官 jǐngguān [位 wèi] *(police)*
serial NOUN
1 连续剧 liánxùjù [部 bù] *(on TV, radio)*
DID YOU KNOW...?
Historical drama serials are extremely popular on Chinese television.
2 连载 liánzǎi [个 gè] *(in magazine)*
series NOUN
1 一系列 yíxìliè [个 gè]
2 系列节目 xìliè jiémù [个 gè]
□ a TV series 一部电视连续剧 yíbù diànshìliánxùjù
3 数列 shùliè [组 zǔ] *(of numbers)*
serious ADJECTIVE
1 严重的 yánzhòng de *(illness, mistake)*
2 严肃的 yánsù de
□ You look very serious. 你看起来很严肃。Nǐ kànqǐlái hěn yánsù.
■ **Are you serious?** 你是说真的吗？ Nǐ shì shuōzhēnde ma?
seriously ADVERB
说真的 shuōzhēnde
□ No, but seriously ... 不，但是说真的… Bù, dànshì shuōzhēnde...
■ **to take somebody seriously** 把某人认真对待 bǎmǒurén rènzhēnduìdài
■ **seriously injured** 严重受伤 yánzhòngshòushāng
■ **Seriously?** 说真的？Shuōzhēnde?
servant NOUN
仆人 púrén [名 míng]
to **serve** VERB
▷ *see also* **serve** NOUN
1 招待 zhāodài *(in shop, bar)*
□ Are you being served? 有人招待你吗？Yǒurén zhāodài nǐ ma?
2 端上 duānshàng
□ She served the meal at 7 o'clock. 她七点钟的时候端上饭的。Tā qīdiǎnzhōngde shíhòu duānshàngfànde. □ Dinner is served. 晚餐端上来了。Wǎncān duānshàng lái le.
3 发球 fāqiú *(tennis)*
□ It's Murray's turn to serve. 该莫丽发球了。Gāi Mòlì fāqiúle.
4 监禁 jiānjìn *(prison sentence)*
■ **to serve time** 服刑 fúxíng
■ **It serves you right.** 你活该。Nǐ huógāi.
serve NOUN
▷ *see also* **serve** VERB
发球 fāqiú [次 cì] *(tennis)*
■ **It's your serve.** 该你发球了。Gāi nǐ fāqiú le.
server NOUN
服务器 fúwùqì [个 gè] *(computing)*
service
▷ *see also* **service** VERB NOUN
1 服务 fúwù [项 xiàng]
□ service not included 不含服务费 bùhán fúwùfèi □ a bus service 公车服务 gōngchēfúwù
2 保养 bǎoyǎng *(of car)*
3 仪式 yíshì [个 gè] *(church service)*
■ **the Fire Service** 消防队 xiāofángduì
■ **the armed services** 武装部队 wǔzhuāng bùduì
to **service** VERB
▷ *see also* **service** NOUN
维修 wéixiū *(car, washing machine)*
service charge NOUN
服务费 fúwùfèi [笔 bǐ]
□ There's no service charge. 不收服务费。Bùshōu fúwùfèi.
serviceman NOUN
男军人 nánjūnrén [位 wèi]
service station NOUN
加油站 jiāyóu zhàn [座 zuò]
servicewoman NOUN
女军人 nǚjūnrén [位 wèi]
serviette NOUN
餐巾 cānjīn [张 zhāng]
session NOUN
会议 huìyì [次 cì]
set NOUN
▷ *see also* **set** ADJECTIVE, VERB
1 套 tào *(of cutlery, saucepans, books, keys)*
□ a set of keys 一套钥匙 yítào yàoshi
■ **a chess set** 一副国际象棋 yífù guójì xiàngqí
■ **a train set** 模型铁路 móxíngtiělù
2 一局 yìjú *(in tennis)*
set ADJECTIVE
▷ *see also* **set** NOUN, VERB
规定的 guīdìng de *(routine, time, price)*
to **set** VERB
▷ *see also* **set** NOUN, ADJECTIVE
1 设定 shèdìng
□ I set the alarm for 7 o'clock. 闹钟我定在七点。Nàozhōng wǒ dìngzài qīdiǎn.
2 创下 chuàngxià
□ The world record was set last year. 世界纪录是去年创下的。Shìjièjìlù shì qùnián chuàngxiàde.
3 确定 quèdìng *(time, price, rules)*
4 落山 luòshān
□ The sun was setting. 太阳落山了。Tàiyáng luòshānle.

■ **The film is set in Morocco.** 电影的场景是在摩洛哥。Diànyǐngde chǎngjǐng shì zài Móluògē.

■ **to set sail** 出海 chūhǎi

■ **to set the table** 摆桌子 bǎizhuōzi

to **set off** VERB
启程 qǐchéng
□ We set off for London at 9 o'clock. 我们九点启程去伦敦。Wǒmen jiǔdiǎn qǐchéng qù Lúndūn.

to **set out** VERB
出发 chūfā
□ We set out for London at 9 o'clock. 我们九点出发去伦敦。Wǒmen jiǔdiǎn chūfā qù Lúndūn.

settee NOUN
长沙发椅 cháng shāfāyǐ [个 gè]

to **settle** VERB
1 支付 zhīfù *(bill, account)*
2 解决 jiějué *(argument)*
■ **to settle on something** 决定某事 juédìng mǒushì

to **settle down** VERB *(calm down)*
冷静 lěngjìng
■ **Settle down!** 冷静一下！Lěngjìng yíxià!

to **settle in** VERB
迁入 qiānrù

seven NUMBER
七 qī
□ She's seven. 她七岁。Tā qīsuì.

seventeen NUMBER
十七 shíqī
□ He's seventeen. 他十七岁。Tā shíqīsuì.

seventeenth ADJECTIVE
第十七 dìshíqī
□ her seventeenth birthday 她十七岁的生日 tā shíqīsuìde shēngrì □ the seventeenth floor 十七层 shíqīcéng □ the seventeenth of August 八月十七号 bāyuèshíqīhào

seventh ADJECTIVE
第七 dìqī
□ the seventh floor 七层 qīcéng □ the seventh of August 八月七号 bāyuèqīhào

seventy NUMBER
七十 qīshí

several ADJECTIVE, PRONOUN
几个 jǐgè
□ several schools 几个学校 jǐgèxuéxiào
■ **several of them** 他们中的几个 tāmenzhōngde jǐgè □ I've seen several of them. 我见过他们中的几个。Wǒ jiànguò tāmenzhōngde jǐgè.

severe ADJECTIVE
1 严重的 yánzhòng de *(pain, damage, shortage)*
2 严厉的 yánlì de *(punishment, criticism)*

to **sew** VERB
缝 féng

sewing NOUN
缝纫 féngrèn
□ I like sewing. 我喜欢缝纫。Wǒ xǐhuan féngrèn.
■ **a sewing machine** 缝纫机 féngrènjī

to **sew up** VERB
缝 féng *(tear)*

sewn VERB ▷ *see* **sew**

sex NOUN
性别 xìngbié [种 zhǒng]
□ the opposite sex 相反的性别 xiāngfǎnde xìngbié
■ **to have sex with somebody** 和某人性交 hé mǒurén xìngjiāo
■ **sex education** 性教育 xìngjiàoyù

sexism NOUN
性别歧视 xìngbié qíshì

sexist ADJECTIVE
性别歧视的 xìngbié qíshì de

sexual ADJECTIVE
性的 xìng de
□ sexual discrimination 性别歧视 xìngbié qíshì □ sexual harassment 性骚扰 xìngsāorǎo

sexuality NOUN
性取向 xìngqǔxiàng

sexy ADJECTIVE
性感的 xìnggǎn de

shabby ADJECTIVE
破旧的 pòjiùde

shade NOUN
1 阴凉处 yīnliáng chù
■ **in the shade** 在阴凉处 zài yīnliángchù
□ It was 35 degrees in the shade. 阴凉处有三十五度。Yīnliáng chù yǒu sānshíwǔdù.
2 色度 sèdù [种 zhǒng] *(of colour)*

shadow NOUN
影子 yǐngzi [个 gè]

to **shake** VERB
1 摇晃 yáohuàng *(bottle, cocktail, medicine)*
□ 'Shake well before use' '使用前请摇晃好' 'Shǐyòngqián qǐng yáohuàng hǎo'
2 抖落 dǒuluò
□ She shook the rug. 她抖落了毯子。Tā dǒuluò le tǎnzi.
3 发抖 fādǒu *(tremble)*
□ He was shaking with cold. 他冷的发抖。Tā lěngde fādǒu.
■ **to shake one's head** *(in refusal)* 摇头拒绝 yáotóu jùjué
■ **to shake hands with somebody** 和某人握手 hé mǒurén wòshǒu □ They shook hands. 他们握了手。Tāmen wòle shǒu.

DID YOU KNOW...?
The handshake has become the commonly accepted greeting in modern China, replacing the traditional bow with clasped hands held at one's chest.

shaken ADJECTIVE
惊讶 jīngyà
□ I was feeling a bit shaken. 我感到有点惊讶。Wǒ gǎndào yǒudiǎn jīngyà.

shaky ADJECTIVE
颤抖的 chàndǒude *(hand, voice)*

shall VERB
■ **Shall I open the door?** 我把门打开好吗？ Wǒ bǎ mén dǎkāi hǎoma?

shallow ADJECTIVE
浅的 qiǎn de

shambles NOUN
混乱 hùnluàn
□ It's a complete shambles. 完全混乱的局面。Wánquán hùnluànde júmiàn.

shame NOUN
耻辱 chǐrǔ
□ The shame of it! 太耻辱了！ Tài chǐrǔ le!
■ **What a shame!** 太遗憾了！ Tài yíhàn le!
■ **It is a shame that...** …真遗憾 ...zhēn yíhàn □ It's a shame he isn't here. 他不在真遗憾。Tābúzài zhēn yíhàn.

shampoo NOUN
洗发液 xǐfàyè [瓶 píng]
□ a bottle of shampoo 一瓶洗发液 yìpíng xǐfàyè

shape NOUN
形状 xíngzhuàng [种 zhǒng]

share NOUN
▷ *see also* **share** VERB
1 一份 yífèn
□ Everybody pays their share. 每个人都自付各自的一份。Měigèrén dōu zìfù gèzìde yífèn.
2 股票 gǔpiào [支 zhī]
□ They've got shares in the company. 他们有公司的股票。Tāmen yǒu gōngsīde gǔpiào.

to **share** VERB
▷ *see also* **share** NOUN
1 合用 héyòng *(room, bed, taxi)*
2 分担 fēndān *(job, task)*

to **share out** VERB
平均分配 píngjūn fēnpèi
□ They shared the sweets out among the children. 他们把糖平均分给了孩子们。Tāmen bǎ táng píngjūn fēngěile háizimen.

shark NOUN
鲨鱼 shāyú [条 tiáo]

sharp ADJECTIVE
▷ *see also* **sharp** ADVERB
1 锋利的 fēnglì de *(knife, teeth)*
2 尖锐的 jiānruì de *(point, edge)*
3 急转的 jízhuǎn de *(curve, bend)*

sharp ADVERB
▷ *see also* **sharp** ADJECTIVE
■ **at 2 o'clock sharp** 两点整 liǎng diǎn zhěng

to **shave** VERB
剃 tì
■ **to shave one's legs** 剃腿毛 tìtuǐmáo

shaver NOUN
剃须刀 tìxūdāo [个 gè]
□ an electric shaver 电子剃须刀 diànzitìxūdāo

shaving cream NOUN
剃须膏 tìxūgāo [瓶 píng]

shaving foam NOUN
剃须泡沫 tìxūpàomò

she PRONOUN
她 tā
□ She's very nice. 她人很好。Tā rén hěnhǎo.

she'd = **she had, she would**

shed NOUN
小屋 xiǎowū [间 jiān]

sheep NOUN
绵羊 miányáng [只 zhī]

sheepdog NOUN
牧羊犬 mùyángquǎn [只 zhī]

sheer ADJECTIVE
纯粹的 chúncuìde
□ It's sheer greed. 纯粹是贪婪。Chúncuìshì tānlán.

sheet NOUN
床单 chuángdān [床 chuáng] *(on bed)*
■ **a sheet of paper** 一张纸 yìzhāngzhǐ

shelf NOUN
1 架子 jiàzi [个 gè] *(bookshelf)*
2 搁板 gēbǎn [块 kuài] *(in cupboard)*

shell NOUN
1 贝壳 bèiké [只 zhī] *(on beach)*
2 壳 ké [个 gè] *(of egg, nut, snail)*

she'll = **she will**

shellfish PL NOUN
贝类海鲜 bèilèi hǎixiān *(as food)*

shelter NOUN
▷ *see also* **shelter** VERB
遮蔽处 zhēbìchù [个 gè] *(building)*
■ **a bus shelter** 公车候车处 gōngchē hòuchēchù
■ **to take shelter** 躲避 dǒubì

to **shelter** VERB
▷ *see also* **shelter** NOUN
躲避 duǒbì

shelves PL NOUN ▷ *see* **shelf**

shepherd NOUN
牧羊人 mùyángrén [个 gè]

sheriff NOUN
州县治安长官 zhōuxiàn zhì'ān zhǎngguān [位 wèi]

sherry NOUN
雪梨酒 xuělíjiǔ

she's = **she is, she has**

Shetland NOUN
设得兰群岛 Shèdélánqúndǎo

to **shift** VERB
▷ *see also* **shift** NOUN
移动 yídòng
□ I couldn't shift the wardrobe on my own. 我自己没法移动衣柜。Wǒzìjǐ méifǎ yídòng yīguì.

shift NOUN
▷ *see also* **shift** VERB
倒班 dǎobān [个 gè]
□ His shift starts at 8 o'clock. 他八点开始倒班。Tā bādiǎn kāishǐ dǎobān. □ the night shift 夜班 yèbān
■ **to do shift work** 倒班 dǎobān

shifty ADJECTIVE
1 靠不住 kàobúzhù *(person)*
□ He looked shifty. 他看起来靠不住。Tā kànqǐlái kàobúzhù.
2 诡诈的眼神 guǐzhàdeyǎnshēn *(eyes)*

shin NOUN
胫部 jìngbù

to **shine** VERB
照耀 zhàoyào
□ The sun was shining. 太阳照耀。Tàiyáng zhàoyào.

shiny ADJECTIVE
闪耀的 shǎnyàode

ship NOUN
船 chuán [艘 sōu]

shipbuilding NOUN
造船 zàochuán

shipyard NOUN
造船厂 zàochuánchǎng [家 jiā]

shirt NOUN
衬衫 chènshān [件 jiàn]

to **shiver** VERB
发抖 fādǒu

shock NOUN
▷ *see also* **shock** VERB
1 震骇 zhènhài [个 gè]
□ The news came as a shock. 这条新闻是个震骇。Zhètiáo xīnwén shì gè zhènhài.
2 触电 chùdiàn [次 cì] *(electric)*
□ I got a shock when I touched the switch. 碰开关的时候我触电了。Pèng kāiguānde shíhòu wǒ chùdiànle.
■ **an electric shock** 电击 diànjī

to **shock** VERB
▷ *see also* **shock** NOUN
1 震惊 zhènjīng
□ They were shocked by the tragedy. 他们被这出悲剧震惊了。Tāmen bèi zhèchū bēijù zhènjīng le. □ He'll be shocked if you say that. 如果你这么说，他会很震惊的。Rúguǒ nǐ zhèmeshuō, tā huì hěn zhènjīngde.
2 使厌恶 shǐyànwù *(scandalize)*
□ I was rather shocked by her attitude. 她的态度让我很厌恶。Tāde tàidù ràng wǒ hěn yànwù.

shocking ADJECTIVE
令人震惊的 lìngrén zhènjīngde
□ It's shocking! 这很令人震惊！Zhè hěn lìngrén zhènjīng!
■ **a shocking waste** 令人震惊的浪费 lìngrén zhènjīngde làngfèi

shoe NOUN
鞋 xié [只 zhī]
□ a pair of shoes 一双鞋 yìshuāng xié

shoelace NOUN
鞋带 xiédài [根 gēn]

shoe polish NOUN
鞋油 xiéyóu [盒 hé]

shoe shop NOUN
鞋店 xiédiàn [家 jiā]

shone VERB ▷ *see* **shine**

shook VERB ▷ *see* **shake**

to **shoot** VERB
1 向...开枪 xiàng...kāiqiāng *(kill)*
□ He was shot by a sniper. 他被狙击手开枪击中。Tā bèi jūjīshǒu kāiqiāng jīzhòng.
2 枪决 qiángjué *(execute)*
□ He was shot at dawn. 他在凌晨被枪决。Tā zài língchén bèi qiāngjué.
3 开枪 kāiqiāng *(gun)*
□ Don't shoot! 别开枪！Bié kāiqiāng!
■ **to shoot at somebody** 朝某人射击 cháo mǒurén shèjī
■ **He shot himself with a revolver.** *(dead)* 他用左轮枪自杀了。Tā yòng zuǒlúnqiāng zìshā le.
■ **He was shot in the leg.** *(wounded)* 他的腿中弹了。Tade tuǐ zhòngdàn le.
■ **to shoot an arrow** 射箭 shèjiàn
4 拍电影 pāidiànyǐng *(film)*
□ The film was shot in Prague. 这部电影是在布拉格拍的。Zhèbù diànyǐng shì zài Bùlāgé pāide.
5 射门 shèmén *(in football)*

shooting NOUN
1 开枪 kāiqiāng
□ They heard shooting. 他们听到了开枪

声。Tāmen tīngdàole kāiqiāngshēng.

■ **a shooting** 枪战 qiāngzhàn □ a drive-by shooting 开车枪战 kāichē qiāngzhàn

2 打猎 dǎliè *(hunting)*

■ **to go shooting** 去打猎 qù dǎliè

shop NOUN

商店 shāngdiàn [家 jiā]

□ a sports shop 运动商店 yùndòng shāngdiàn

shop assistant NOUN

店员 diànyuán [位 wèi]

shopkeeper NOUN

店主 diànzhǔ [位 wèi]

shoplifting NOUN

商店行窃 shāngdiànxíngqiè

shopping NOUN

1 购物 gòuwù *(activity)*

□ I love shopping. 我喜欢购物。Wǒ xǐhuan gòuwù.

2 所购之物 suǒgòu zhī wù *(goods)*

□ Can you get the shopping from the car? 你能把所购之物从车上拿出来吗？Nǐ néng bǎ suǒgòuzhīwù cóng chēlǐ náchūlái ma?

■ **to go shopping** 1 *(for food)* 去买东西 qù mǎi dōngxi 2 *(for pleasure)* 逛街 guàngjiē

■ **a shopping bag** 购物袋 gòuwùdài

shopping centre (US **shopping center**) NOUN

购物中心 gòuwù zhōngxīn [个 gè]

shop window NOUN

商店橱窗 shāngdiàn chúchuāng [个 gè]

shore NOUN

岸 àn [个 gè]

■ **on shore** 在岸上 zài ànshàng

short ADJECTIVE

1 短的 duǎn de *(in length)*

□ a short skirt 短裙 duǎnqún □ short hair 短发 duǎnfà

2 短暂的 duǎnzàn de *(in time)*

□ a short break 短暂的休息 duǎnzànde xiūxi □ a short walk 短暂的散步 duǎnzànde sànbù

■ **too short** 太短暂了 tài duǎnzàn le □ It was a great holiday, but too short. 度假很愉快，但太短暂了。Dùjià hěn yúkuài, dàn tài duǎnzàn le.

3 矮的 ǎi de *(not tall)*

□ She's quite short. 她挺矮的。Tā tǐng ǎi de.

■ **to be short of something** 缺某物 quē mǒuwù □ I'm short of money. 我缺钱。Wǒ quē qián.

■ **at short notice** 在短时间内 zài duǎnshíjiān nèi

■ **In short, the answer's no.** 简而言之，不行。Jiǎněryánzhī, bùxíng.

shortage NOUN

短缺 duǎnquē [种 zhǒng]

□ a water shortage 缺水 quēshuǐ

short cut NOUN

近路 jìnlù [条 tiáo]

□ I took a short cut. 我抄了近路。Wǒ chāole jìnlù.

shortly ADVERB

马上 mǎshàng

> LANGUAGE TIP Word for word, this means 'on horseback'.

□ I'll be there shortly. 我马上就到。Wǒ mǎshàng jiùdào.

■ **She arrived shortly after midnight.** 在午夜后不久她到了。Zàiwǔyèhòu bùjiǔ tā dào le.

shorts PL NOUN

1 短裤 duǎnkù *(short trousers)*

□ a pair of shorts 一条短裤 yìtiáo duǎnkù

2 男用短衬裤 nányòng duǎnchènkù (US: *underpants*)

short-sighted ADJECTIVE

近视的 jìnshì de

shot VERB ▷ *see* **shoot**

shot NOUN

1 射击 shèjī [阵 zhèn]

□ He thought he heard a shot. 他好像听到了一阵射击声。Tā hǎoxiàng tīngdàole yízhèn shèjīshēng.

2 拍摄 pāishè

□ a shot of Edinburgh Castle 拍摄爱丁堡城堡 pāishè àidīngbǎo chéngbǎo

3 射门 shèmén [次 cì] *(in football)*

□ What a shot! 好棒的射门！Hǎobàngde shèmén!

4 皮下注射 píxià zhùshè [针 zhēn] *(injection)*

shotgun NOUN

鸟枪 niǎoqiāng [只 zhī]

should VERB

应该 yīnggāi *(ought to)*

□ I should go now. 我现在应该走了。Wǒ xiànzài yīnggāi zǒule. □ He should have arrived by now. 他现在应该到了。Tā xiànzài yīnggāi dàole.

> LANGUAGE TIP In informal speech, 应该 yīnggāi can be shortened to simply 该 gāi.

□ You should go. 你该走了。Nǐ gāi zǒu le

> LANGUAGE TIP When something was supposed to happen but didn't, use 本该 běngāi.

□ You should have been more careful. 你本该更加小心。Nǐ běngāi gèngjiā xiǎoxīn. □ I should have told you before. 我本该早告诉你。Wǒ běngāi zǎo gàosù nǐ.

LANGUAGE TIP When **should** has the meaning of **would**, use会 huì.

□ I should go if I were you. 如果我是你，我会去的。Rúguǒ wǒ shì nǐ, wǒ huì qùde.

LANGUAGE TIP To describe a likelihood or probability, use 该 gāi.

□ He should be there by now. 他现在该到那儿了。Tā xiànzài gāi dào nàrle. □ He should get there soon. 他该很快就到那儿了。Tā gāi hěnkuài jiù dào nàrle.

shoulder NOUN
肩膀 jiānbǎng [个 gè]
■ **a shoulder bag** 肩背包 jiānbēibāo

to **shout** VERB
喊叫 hǎnjiào
□ Don't shout! 不要喊叫！ Búyào hǎnjiào! □ 'Go away!' he shouted. '走开！', 他喊叫着。'Zǒukāi!', tā hǎnjiàozhe.
■ **to shout at somebody** 对某人喊叫 duì mǒurén hǎnjiào

shovel NOUN
铲子 chǎnzi [把 bǎ]

show NOUN
▷ *see also* **show** VERB
1 演出 yǎnchū *(on stage)*
2 节目 jiémù [个 gè] *(on TV, radio)*
3 展览 zhǎnlǎn [个 gè] *(exhibition)*

to **show** VERB
▷ *see also* **show** NOUN
1 给看 gěikàn
■ **to show somebody something** 给某人看某物 gěi mǒurén kàn mǒuwù □ Have I shown you my new trainers? 我给你看我的新运动鞋了吗？ Wǒ gěinǐ kàn wǒde xīnyùndòngxié le ma?
2 显示 xiǎnshì
□ She showed great courage. 她显示出巨大的勇气。Tā xiǎnshì chū jùdàde yǒngqì.
■ **to show somebody how to do something** 示范某人如何做某事 shìfàn mǒurén rúhé zuò mǒushì

to **show off** VERB
显耀 xiǎnyào *(brag)*

to **show up** VERB
出现 chūxiàn *(turn up)*
□ He showed up late as usual. 同平时一样他出现晚了。Tóng píngshí yíyàng tā chūxiàn wǎnle.

shower NOUN
1 淋浴 línyù [个 gè]
■ **to have a shower** 洗淋浴 xǐ línyù
2 阵雨 zhènyǔ [场 chǎng] *(of rain)*

shown VERB ▷ *see* **show**

shrank VERB ▷ *see* **shrink**

shrimp NOUN
1 小虾 xiǎoxiā [只 zhī] *(small)*
2 虾 xiā [只 zhī] *(us: bigger)*

to **shrink** VERB
缩水 suōshuǐ

Shrove Tuesday NOUN
忏悔星期二 Chànhuǐ xīngqī'èr

to **shrug** VERB
■ **to shrug one's shoulders** 耸肩 sǒngjiān

shrunk VERB ▷ *see* **shrink**

to **shudder** VERB
战栗 zhànlì

to **shuffle** VERB
■ **to shuffle the cards** 洗牌 xǐpái

to **shut** VERB
1 关上 guānshàng
□ He forgot to shut the door. 他忘记关门了。Tā wàngjì guānmen le.
2 打烊 dǎyàng
□ What time do the shops shut? 商店什么时候打烊? Shāngdiàn shénme shíhòu dǎyàng?
3 闭上 bìshàng *(mouth, eyes)*
■ **to shut one's eyes** 闭上眼睛 bìshàng yǎnjīng

to **shut down** VERB
关门 guānmén
□ The cinema shut down last year. 电影院去年关门了。Diànyǐngyuàn qùnián guānmén le.

to **shut up** VERB
1 关上 guānshàng *(close)*
2 住口 zhùkǒu *(be quiet)*
■ **Shut up!** 住口！ Zhùkǒu!

shuttle NOUN
1 穿梭班机 chuānsuō bānjī [架 jià] *(plane)*
2 班车 bānchē [辆 liàng] *(bus)*

shuttlecock NOUN
羽毛球 yǔmáoqiú [只 zhī] *(badminton)*

shy ADJECTIVE
害羞的 hàixiū de

sick ADJECTIVE
1 患病的 huànbìng de
□ She looks after her sick mother. 她照顾她患病的妈妈。Tā zhàogù tā huànbìngde māma.
2 变态的 biàntàide *(joke, humour)*
□ That's really sick! 那太变态了！ Nà tài biàntài le!
■ **to be sick** *(vomit)* 呕吐 ǒutù
■ **to feel sick** 感觉恶心 gǎnjué ěxīn
■ **to be sick of something** 讨厌某物 tǎoyàn mǒuwù □ I'm sick of your jokes. 我很讨厌你的笑话。Wǒ hěn tǎoyàn nǐde xiàohuà.

sickening ADJECTIVE
令人作呕 lìngrén zuò'ǒu

sick leave NOUN
病假 bìngjià [次 cì]

sickness NOUN
患病 huànbìng

sick note NOUN
1 病假条 bìngjiàtiáo [张 zhāng] *(from parents)*
2 有病诊断 yǒubìngzhěnduàn [份 fèn] *(from doctor)*

sick pay NOUN
病假工资 bìngjià gōngzī

side NOUN
1 边 biān [个 gè] *(of road, bed)*
□ He was driving on the wrong side of the road. 他把车开到了错的一边。Tā bǎ chē kāidàole cuòde yìbiān.
2 侧面 cèmiàn [个 gè] *(of building, vehicle)*
3 体侧 tǐcè [边 biān] *(of body)*
4 一面 yímiàn [个 gè] *(of paper, face, brain)*
5 坡 pō [个 gè] *(of hill, valley)*
6 队 duì [支 zhī] *(team)*
7 一方 yìfāng *(in conflict, contest)*
■ **He's on my side.** 1 *(on my team)* 他是我们组的。Tā shì wǒmenzǔde. 2 *(supporting me)* 他支持我。Tā zhīchí wǒ.
■ **side by side** 并肩 bìngjiān

LANGUAGE TIP Word for word, this means 'merging shoulders'.

■ **the side entrance** 侧门 cèmén
■ **to take sides** 偏袒 piāntǎn □ She always takes his side. 她总是偏袒他。Tā zǒngshì piāntǎn tā.

side-effect NOUN
副作用 fù zuòyòng [个 gè]

side street NOUN
边街 biānjiē [条 tiáo]

sidewalk NOUN (US)
人行道 rénxíngdào [条 tiáo]

sideways ADVERB
1 侧面 cèmiàn *(look, be facing)*
2 斜着 xiézhe *(move)*
■ **sideways on** 向一边 xiàngyìbiān

sieve NOUN
筛子 shāizi [个 gè]

to **sigh** VERB
▷ *see also* **sigh** NOUN
叹气 tànqì

sigh NOUN
▷ *see also* **sigh** VERB
叹息 tànxī [声 shēng]

sight NOUN
1 视力 shìlì
■ **to have poor sight** 视力不好 shìlì bùhǎo
■ **to know somebody by sight** 见过某人 jiànguòmǒurén
2 景象 jǐngxiàng [种 zhǒng] *(spectacle)*
□ It was an amazing sight. 很壮观的景象。Hěn zhuàngguānde jǐngxiàng.
■ **in sight** 看得见 kàndéjiàn
■ **out of sight** 看不见 kànbújiàn
■ **the sights** *(tourist spots)* 景点 jǐngdiǎn
■ **to see the sights of London** 看伦敦的景点 kàn Lúndūnde jǐngdiǎn

sightseeing NOUN
观光 guānguāng
■ **to go sightseeing** 观光游览 guānguāng yóulǎn

sign NOUN
▷ *see also* **sign** VERB
1 指示牌 zhǐshìpái [块 kuài]
□ There was a big sign saying 'private'. 有块大指示牌写着"闲人免入"。Yǒukuài dàzhǐshìpái xiězhe "xiánrénmiǎnrù".
2 路标 lùbiāo [个 gè]
■ **a road sign** 路标 lùbiāo
3 迹象 jìxiàng [种 zhǒng] *(gesture, indication)*
□ There's no sign of improvement. 没有变好的迹象。Méiyǒu biànhǎode jìxiàng.
■ **It's a good sign.** 这是个好兆头。Zhèshi gè hǎo zhàotou.
■ **What sign are you?** *(star sign)* 你是什么星座？ Nǐ shìshénme xīngzuò?

to **sign** VERB
▷ *see also* **sign** NOUN
签署 qiānshǔ

to **sign on** VERB
1 办理失业登记手续 bànlǐ shīyè dēngjì shǒuxù *(as unemployed)*
2 报名参加 bàomíng cānjiā *(for course)*

signal NOUN
▷ *see also* **signal** VERB
1 指令 zhǐlìng [个 gè] *(to do something)*
2 信号机 xìnhàojī [部 bù] *(for train)*
3 信号 xìnhào [个 gè] *(for mobile phone)*
□ I can't get a signal here. 我手机没有信号。Wǒ shǒujī méi xìnhào.

to **signal** VERB
▷ *see also* **signal** NOUN
■ **to signal to somebody** 向某人示意 xiàng mǒurén shìyì

signature NOUN
签名 qiānmíng [个 gè]

sign language NOUN
手语 shǒuyǔ [种 zhǒng]

signpost NOUN
路标 lùbiāo [个 gè]

silence NOUN
寂静 jìjìng [片 piàn]
■ **in silence** 鸦雀无声 yāquè wúshēng

silent ADJECTIVE
1 寂静的 jìjìngde *(place)*
2 沉默的 chénmò de *(person)*

English-Chinese

S

silk NOUN
▷ *see also* **silk** ADJECTIVE
丝绸 sīchóu [块 kuài]

DID YOU KNOW...?
The Silk Road 丝绸之路 sīchóu zhī lù was one of the world's oldest and most important trade routes connecting Asia with Africa and Europe.

silk ADJECTIVE
▷ *see also* **silk** NOUN
丝绸 sīchóu
□ a silk scarf 丝绸围巾 sīchóu wéijīn

silky ADJECTIVE
丝绸的 sīchóude

silly ADJECTIVE
1 愚蠢的 yúchǔn de
2 可笑的 kěxiào de *(idea, object)*

silver NOUN
银 yín
□ a silver medal 银牌 yínpái

SIM card NOUN
手机智能卡 shǒujī zhìnéngkǎ [张 zhāng]

LANGUAGE TIP Nowadays this is more commonly known among the younger generation as SIM卡 SIM kǎ.

similar ADJECTIVE
相似的 xiāngsì de
■ **to be similar to something** 和某事物类似 hé mǒu shìwù lèisì

simple ADJECTIVE
1 简单的 jiǎndān de *(easy)*
2 简朴的 jiǎnpǔ de *(meal, life, cottage)*
3 头脑简单 tóunǎojiǎndān *(simple-minded)*
□ He's a bit simple. 他有点头脑简单。Tā yǒudiǎn tóunǎojiǎndān.

simply ADVERB
完全 wánquán
□ It's simply not possible. 那完全不可能。Nà wánquán bù kěnéng.

simultaneous ADJECTIVE
同时的 tóngshíde

sin NOUN
▷ *see also* **sin** VERB
罪过 zuìguò [个 gè]

to **sin** VERB
▷ *see also* **sin** NOUN
有罪过 yǒuzuìguò

since PREPOSITION, ADVERB, CONJUNCTION
1 之后 zhīhòu
□ since Christmas 圣诞节之后 shèngdànjié zhīhòu □ since then 此后 cǐhòu □ I haven't seen him since. 此后我没见过他。Cǐhòu wǒ méi jiànguò tā.
■ **ever since** 从那时起 cóng nàshí qǐ
2 自从 zìcóng
□ I haven't seen her since she left. 自从她离开我再也没见过她。Zìcóng tā líkāi, wǒ zàiyě méi jiànguò tā.
3 因为 yīnwèi *(because)*
□ Since you're tired, let's stay at home. 因为你累了，我们还是呆在家里吧。Yīnwèi nǐ lèile, wǒmen háishì dāizài jiālǐ ba.

sincere ADJECTIVE
真诚的 zhēnchéng de

sincerely ADVERB
由衷地 yóuzhōng de
■ **Yours sincerely** 谨上 Jǐnshàng

to **sing** VERB
1 唱歌 chànggē *(person)*
□ He sang out of tune. 他唱歌跑调。Tā chànggē pǎodiào.
2 唱 chàng *(song)*
□ Have you ever sung this tune before? 你唱过这支歌吗？Nǐ chàngguò zhèzhī gē ma?
3 鸣 míng *(bird)*

Singapore NOUN
新加坡 Xīnjiāpō

singer NOUN
歌手 gēshǒu [位 wèi]

singing NOUN
唱歌 chànggē

single ADJECTIVE
▷ *see also* **single** NOUN
1 单身的 dānshēn de *(unmarried)*
2 单人 dānrén *(for one person)*
□ a single room 一间单人房 yìjiān dānrénfáng
■ **not a single thing** 不是一件事 búshì yíjiànshì

single NOUN
▷ *see also* **single** ADJECTIVE
单程票 dānchéngpiào [张 zhāng] *(ticket)*
□ A single to Shanghai, please. 一张去上海的单程票。Yìzhāng qù shànghǎide dānchéng piào.

DID YOU KNOW...?
It is only possible to buy single train tickets in China; return tickets are not available.

■ **a CD single** 唱片单曲 chàngpiàndānqǔ

single parent NOUN
单亲 dānqīn [个 gè]
□ She's a single parent. 她是单亲妈妈。Tā shì dānqīn māma. □ a single parent family 单亲家庭 dānqīn jiātíng

singles PL NOUN
单打 dāndǎ *(in tennis)*
□ the women's singles 女子单打 nǚzǐ dāndǎ

singular NOUN

单数 dānshù
□ in the singular 单数的 dānshùde
sinister ADJECTIVE
险恶的 xiǎn'ède
sink NOUN
▷ *see also* **sink** VERB
洗涤槽 xǐdí cáo [个 gè]
to **sink** VERB
▷ *see also* **sink** NOUN
沉没 chénmò
□ We sank the enemy's ship. 我们沉没了敌方的船。Wǒmen chénmò le dífāngde chuán. □ The boat was sinking fast. 这船沉得很快。Zhèchuán chénde hěn kuài.
sir NOUN
先生 xiānsheng
■ **Yes sir.** 是的，先生。Shìde, xiānsheng.
■ **Dear Sir** 亲爱的先生 Qīn'ài de Xiānsheng
■ **Dear Sir or Madam** 亲爱的先生或女士 Qīn'ài de xiānsheng huò nǚshì
siren NOUN
警报器 jǐngbàoqì [个 gè]
sister NOUN
1 姐姐 jiějie [个 gè] *(elder)*
2 妹妹 mèimei [个 gè] *(younger)*
■ **my brothers and sisters** 我的兄弟姐妹们 wǒde xiōngdì jiěmèi men
3 护士 hùshì [位 wèi] *(nurse)*
sister-in-law NOUN
1 姑子 gūzi [个 gè] *(husband's sister)*
2 姨子 yízi [个 gè] *(wife's sister)*
3 嫂子 sǎozi [位 wèi] *(older brother's wife)*
4 弟媳 dìxí [个 gè] *(younger brother's wife)*
to **sit** VERB
坐下 zuòxià
■ **to sit on something** 坐在某物上 zuòzài mǒuwù shàng □ She sat on the chair. 她坐在椅子上。Tā zuòzài yǐzi shàng.
■ **to be sitting** 坐着 zuòzhe
■ **to sit an exam** 参加考试 cānjiā kǎoshì
to **sit down** VERB
坐下 zuòxià
■ **to be sitting down** 就座 jiùzuò
sitcom NOUN
情景喜剧 qíngjǐng xǐjù [个 gè]
site NOUN
1 地点 dìdiǎn [个 gè]
□ the site of the accident 事故的地点 shìgùde dìdiǎn
2 露营地 lùyíngdì [个 gè] *(campsite)*
3 网址 wǎngzhǐ [个 gè] *(website)*
■ **an archaeological site** 考古现场 kǎogǔ xiànchǎng
■ **a building site** 工地 gōngdì
sitting room NOUN
起居室 qǐjūshì [间 jiān]
situated ADJECTIVE
位于 wèiyú
□ The village is situated on a hill. 村子位于山上。Cūnzi wèiyú shānshàng.
situation NOUN
情况 qíngkuàng [种 zhǒng]
six NUMBER
六 liù
□ He's six. 他六岁。Tā liùsuì.
sixteen NUMBER
十六 shíliù
□ He's sixteen. 他十六岁。Tā shíliùsuì.
sixteenth ADJECTIVE
第十六 dìshíliù
□ the sixteenth floor 十六层 shíliùcéng
■ **the sixteenth of August** 八月十六号 bāyuè shíliùhào
sixth ADJECTIVE
第六 dìliù
□ the sixth floor 六层 liùcéng
■ **the sixth of August** 八月六号 bāyuè liùhào
sixth form NOUN
六年级 liùniánjí
sixty NUMBER
六十 liùshí
size NOUN
1 大小 dàxiǎo [种 zhǒng] *(of object)*
□ plates of different sizes 大小不一的盘子 dàxiǎo bùyíde pánzi
2 规模 guīmó *(of area, building, task, loss)*
3 尺码 chǐmǎ [个 gè] *(of clothing, shoes)*
■ **I'm a size ten.** 我的尺码是十号。Wǒde chǐmǎ shì shíhào.
■ **What size shoes do you take?** 你穿几号的鞋？Nǐ chuān jǐhào de xié?
to **skate** VERB
1 溜冰 liūbīng *(ice-skate)*
2 溜旱冰 liūhànbīng *(roller-skate)*
skateboard NOUN
滑板 huábǎn [个 gè]
skateboarding NOUN
玩滑板 wánhuábǎn
■ **to go skateboarding** 去玩滑板 qùwán huábǎn
skates PL NOUN
溜冰鞋 liūbīngxié
skating NOUN
溜冰 liūbīng *(ice-skating)*
■ **to go skating** 去溜冰 qù liūbīng
■ **a skating rink** 溜冰场 liūbīngchǎng
skeleton NOUN
骨骼 gǔgé [副 fù]
sketch NOUN
素描 sùmiáo [张 zhāng] *(drawing)*

to **ski** VERB
▷ *see also* **ski** NOUN
滑雪 huáxuě
ski NOUN
▷ *see also* **ski** VERB
滑雪 huáxuě [次 cì]
■ **ski boots** 滑雪靴 huáxuěxuē
■ **a ski lift** 滑雪吊索设备 huáxuě diàosuǒ shèbèi
■ **ski pants** 滑雪裤 huáxuěkù
■ **a ski slope** 滑雪坡 huáxuěpō
■ **a ski suit** 滑雪服 huáxuěfú
skier NOUN
滑雪的人 huáxuěderén [位 wèi]
skiing NOUN
滑雪 huáxuě
■ **to go skiing** 去滑雪 qù huáxuě
■ **to go on a skiing holiday** 度假去滑雪 dùjià qù huáxuě
skilful (US **skillful**) ADJECTIVE
1 老练的 lǎoliàn de
2 技巧娴熟的 jìqiǎo xiánshú de *(use, choice, management)*
skill NOUN
1 技巧 jìqiǎo
□ He played with great skill. 他演奏的技巧很了不起。Tā yǎnzòu de jìqiǎo hěn liǎobùqǐ.
2 技能 jìnéng [项 xiàng]
□ She has many skills. 她有很多技能。Tā yǒu hěnduō jìnéng.
skilled ADJECTIVE
技巧娴熟的 jìqiǎo xiánshú de
□ a skilled worker 一位技巧娴熟的工人 yíwèi jìqiǎo xiánshú de gōngrén
skimmed milk NOUN
脱脂牛奶 tuōzhī niúnǎi
skin NOUN
1 皮肤 pífū
■ **skin cancer** 皮肤癌 pífūái
2 皮 pí [张 zhāng] *(of animal)*
skinny ADJECTIVE
瘦弱的 shòuruòde
to **skip** VERB
▷ *see also* **skip** NOUN
故意不做 gùyì bùzuò
■ **to skip school** 故意不上学 gùyì búshàngxué
skip NOUN
▷ *see also* **skip** VERB
废料桶 fèiliàotǒng [个 gè] *(container)*
skirt NOUN
裙子 qúnzi [条 tiáo]
skittles NOUN
九柱游戏 jiǔzhùyóuxì
■ **to play skittles** 玩九柱游戏 wán jiǔzhùyóuxì
to **skive off** VERB
逃避应该做的事 táobì yīnggāizuòde shì
■ **to skive off school** 逃学 táoxué
skull NOUN
颅骨 lúgǔ [个 gè]
sky NOUN
天空 tiānkōng [片 piàn]
Skype® NOUN
▷ *see also* **Skype** VERB
Skype网络电话 Skype wǎngluò diànhuà
to **Skype®** VERB
▷ *see also* **Skype** NOUN
用Skype进行网络通话 yòng Skype jìnxíng wǎngluò tōnghuà
skyscraper NOUN
摩天大厦 mótiān dàshà [座 zuò]
to **slam** VERB
砰的关上 pēngde guānshàng
□ The door slammed. 门砰的关上了。Mén pēngde guānshàng le. □ She slammed the door. 她砰的把门关上了。Tā pēngde bǎ mén guānshàng le.
slang NOUN
俚语 lǐyǔ [个 gè]
slap NOUN
▷ *see also* **slap** VERB
耳光 ěrguāng [个 gè]
to **slap** VERB
▷ *see also* **slap** NOUN
打耳光 dǎ'ěrguāng
□ to slap somebody 打某人耳光 dǎ mǒurén ěrguāng
sled NOUN (US)
雪橇 xuěqiāo [副 fù]
sledge NOUN
雪橇 xuěqiāo [副 fù]
sledging NOUN
乘雪橇 chéng xuěqiāo
■ **to go sledging** 乘雪橇 chéngxuěqiāo
sleep NOUN
▷ *see also* **sleep** VERB
1 睡眠 shuìmián
□ lack of sleep 缺少睡眠 quēshǎo shuìmián
2 睡觉 shuìjiào *(nap)*
■ **to go to sleep** 去睡觉 qù shuìjiào
to **sleep** VERB
▷ *see also* **sleep** NOUN
睡 shuì
□ Shh, he's sleeping. 嘘，他在睡觉。Xū,tā zài shuìjiào
■ **to sleep with somebody** 和某人一起睡 hémǒurén yìqǐ shuì
to **sleep in** VERB
1 睡过头 shuìguòtóu *(accidentally)*

□ I'm sorry I'm late, I slept in. 对不起，我来晚了，我睡过头了。Duìbùqǐ, wǒ láiwǎnle, wǒ shuìguòtóu le.

2 睡懒觉 shuìlǎnjiào *(on purpose)*

to **sleep together** VERB

一起睡 yìqǐshuì

sleeping bag NOUN

睡袋 shuìdài [个 gè]

sleeping car NOUN

卧车 wòchē [辆 liàng]

sleeping pill NOUN

安眠药 ānmiányào [片 piàn]

sleepy ADJECTIVE

困的 kùnde

■ **to feel sleepy** 感到困 gǎndào kùn

□ I was feeling sleepy. 我感到很困。Wǒ gǎndào hěn kùn.

■ **a sleepy little village** 寂静的小村庄 jìjìngde xiǎochūnzhuāng

sleet NOUN

雨夹雪 yǔjiāxuě

sleeve NOUN

袖子 xiùzi [个 gè]

□ long sleeves 长袖 chángxiù □ short sleeves 短袖 duǎnxiù

sleigh NOUN

雪橇 xuěqiāo [架 jià]

slept VERB ▷ *see* **sleep**

slice NOUN

▷ *see also* **slice** VERB

片 piàn

to **slice** VERB

▷ *see also* **slice** NOUN

切片 qiēpiàn

slick NOUN

漂浮物 piāofúwù

■ **an oil slick** 浮油 fúyóu

slide NOUN

1 滑梯 huátī [个 gè] *(in playground)*

2 幻灯片 huàndēngpiān [张 zhāng] *(photo)*

3 发夹 fàjiā [个 gè] *(hair slide)*

slight ADJECTIVE

微小的 wēixiǎo de

□ a slight problem 小问题 xiǎo wèntí □ a slight improvement 小的提高 xiǎode tígāo

slightly ADVERB

略微地 lüèwēi de

slim ADJECTIVE

▷ *see also* **slim** VERB

苗条的 miáotiáo de

to **slim** VERB

▷ *see also* **slim** ADJECTIVE

节食减肥 jiéshí jiǎnféi *(be on a diet)*

□ I'm slimming. 我正在节食减肥。Wǒ zhèngzài jiéshí jiǎnféi.

sling NOUN

悬带 xuándài [条 tiáo]

□ She had her arm in a sling. 她把她的胳膊套在悬带上。Tā bǎ tāde gēbò tàozài xuádàishàng.

slip NOUN

▷ *see also* **slip** VERB

1 差错 chācuò [个 gè] *(mistake)*

2 衬裙 chènqún [件 jiàn] *(underskirt)*

■ **a slip of paper** 一片纸 yípiànzhǐ

■ **a slip of the tongue** 说错 shuōcuò

to **slip** VERB

▷ *see also* **slip** NOUN

滑跤 huájiāo *(person)*

□ He slipped on the ice. 他在冰上滑跤了。Tā zài bīngshàng huájiāo le.

to **slip up** VERB

疏忽 shūhū *(make a mistake)*

slipper NOUN

拖鞋 tuōxié [只 zhī]

□ a pair of slippers 一双拖鞋 yìshuāngtuōxié

slippery ADJECTIVE

滑的 huá de

slope NOUN

斜坡 xiépō [个 gè]

sloppy ADJECTIVE

1 草率的 cǎoshuàide *(work)*

2 邋遢的 lātāde *(person, appearance)*

slot NOUN

投币口 tóubìkǒu [个 gè]

slot machine NOUN

1 投币机 tóubìjī [个 gè] *(vending machine)*

2 吃角子老虎机 chījiǎozi lǎohǔjī [部 bù] *(for gambling)*

slow ADJECTIVE, ADVERB

1 慢的 màn de

□ We were behind a very slow lorry. 我们在一个慢速卡车的后面。Wǒmen zài yígè mànsù kǎchē hòumiàn.

2 慢慢 mànmàn

■ **to go slow** *(person, car)* 慢慢走 mànmànzǒu □ Drive slower! 慢慢开！Mànmàn kāi!

■ **My watch is 20 minutes slow.** 我的表慢了二十分钟。Wǒde biǎo mànle èrshí fēnzhōng.

to **slow down** VERB

放松 fàngsōng

slowly ADVERB

慢慢地 mànmàn de

slug NOUN

蛞蝓 kuòyú [个 gè]

sly ADJECTIVE

狡猾的 jiǎohuáde *(person)*

■ **a sly smile** 狡猾的微笑 jiǎohuáde wēixiào

to **smack** VERB
■ **to smack somebody** 打某人 dǎ mǒurén

small ADJECTIVE
1 小的 xiǎo de
□ My house is quite small. 我的房子挺小的。Wǒde fángzi tǐngxiǎode.
2 年幼的 niányòu de *(young)*
□ two small children 两个年幼的孩子 liǎngge niányòude háizi
3 微不足道的 wēibùzúdào de *(mistake, problem, change)*

smart ADJECTIVE
1 时髦的 shímáo de
□ a smart suit 时髦的套装 shímáode tàozhuāng
2 聪明的 cōngmíng de *(clever)*
■ **a smart idea** 聪明的主意 cōngmíngde zhúyì

smart phone NOUN
智能手机 zhinéng shǒujī [部 bù]

to **smash** VERB
打碎 dǎsuì
□ I've smashed my watch. 我打碎了我的表。Wǒ dǎsuìle wǒdebiǎo.
□ The glass smashed into tiny pieces. 玻璃打碎了。Bōlí dǎsuì le.

smell NOUN
▷ *see also* **smell** VERB
气味 qìwèi [种 zhǒng]
■ **the sense of smell** 嗅觉 xiùjué

to **smell** VERB
▷ *see also* **smell** NOUN
1 发臭 fāchòu *(stink)*
■ **to smell nice** 很香 hěnxiāng
■ **to smell of something** 有某物的气味 yǒu mǒuwù de qìwèi □ It smells of petrol. 有汽油味。Yǒu qìyóuwèi.
2 闻到 wéndào *(detect)*
□ I can't smell anything. 我什么也闻不到。Wǒ shénme yě wénbúdào. □ I can smell gas. 我闻到汽油味。Wǒ wéndào qìyóuwèi.

smelly ADJECTIVE
臭的 chòude
□ He's got smelly feet. 他的脚很臭。Tāde jiǎo hěnchòu.

smelt VERB ▷ *see* **smell**

smile NOUN
▷ *see also* **smile** VERB
微笑 wēixiào [个 gè]

to **smile** VERB
▷ *see also* **smile** NOUN
微笑 wēixiào
■ **to smile at somebody** 对某人微笑 duì mǒurén wēixiào

smoke NOUN
▷ *see also* **smoke** VERB
烟 yān [股 gǔ]

to **smoke** VERB
▷ *see also* **smoke** NOUN
1 吸烟 xīyān *(person)*
□ I don't smoke. 我不吸烟。Wǒ bù xīyān.
2 抽 chōu *(cigarette, cigar, pipe)*
□ He smokes cigars. 他抽香烟。Tā chōu xiāngyān.

smoker NOUN
吸烟者 xīyānzhě [个 gè]

smoking NOUN
吸烟 xīyān
■ **to give up smoking** 戒烟 jièyān
■ **Smoking is bad for you.** 吸烟对你有害。Xīyān duìnǐ yǒuhài.
■ **'no smoking'** "禁止吸烟" "jìnzhǐ xīyān"

smooth ADJECTIVE
光滑的 guānghuá de *(not rough)*

to **smother** VERB
使窒息 shǐ zhìxī

SMS NOUN
短信息服务 duǎn xìnxī fúwù
□ Enter your number and we'll send an SMS to your phone. 输入你的号码，我们会给你发短信。Shūrù nǐde hàomǎ, wǒmen huì gěi nǐ fā duǎnxìn.

to **smuggle** VERB
走私 zǒusī
□ to smuggle cigarettes into a country 走私香烟到一个国家 zǒusī xiāngyān dào yígè guójiā
■ **They managed to smuggle him out of prison.** 他们悄悄把他弄出监狱。Tāmen qiāoqiāo bǎtā nòngchū jiānyù.

smuggler NOUN
走私犯 zǒusīfàn [名 míng]

smuggling NOUN
走私 zǒusī

snack NOUN
小吃 xiǎochī [份 fèn]
■ **to have a snack** 吃小吃 chīxiǎochī

snack bar NOUN
快餐柜 kuàicānguì [个 gè]

snail NOUN
蜗牛 wōniú [只 zhī]

snake NOUN
蛇 shé [条 tiáo]

to **snap** VERB
折断 zhéduàn *(break)*
□ The branch snapped. 树枝折断了。Shùzhī zhéduàn le.
■ **to snap one's fingers** 打响指 dǎxiǎngzhǐ

snapshot NOUN

快照 kuàizhào [张 zhāng]

to **snarl** VERB

咆哮 páoxiào *(animal)*

to **snatch** VERB

抢 qiǎng

□ He snatched the keys from my hand. 他从我手里抢走了钥匙。Tā cóng wǒshǒulǐ qiǎngzǒu le yàoshi. □ My bag was snatched. 我的包被抢了。Wǒde bāo bèi qiǎng le.

to **sneak** VERB

偷偷摸摸做 tōutōumōmō zuò

■ **to sneak in** 偷偷进入 tōutōu jìnrù

■ **to sneak out** 偷偷出来 tōutōuchūlái

■ **to sneak up on somebody** 悄悄出现吓某人 qiāoqiāo chūxiàn xiàmǒurén

sneakers PL NOUN (US)

胶底运动鞋 jiāodǐ yùndòngxié [双 shuāng]

to **sneeze** VERB

打喷嚏 dǎ pēntì

to **sniff** VERB

1 用鼻吸气 yòngbíxīqì

□ Stop sniffing! 别吸气了！ Bié xīqì le!

2 闻 wén

□ The dog sniffed my hand. 狗闻了我的手。Gǒu wénle wǒdeshǒu.

snob NOUN

势利小人 shìlì xiǎorén [个 gè]

snooker NOUN

英式台球 yīngshì táiqiú

LANGUAGE TIP The loan word 斯诺克 sīnuòkè is also used.

snooze NOUN

打盹 dǎdǔn [个 gè]

■ **to have a snooze** 打个盹 dǎgedǔn

to **snore** VERB

打鼾 dǎhān

snow NOUN

▷ *see also* **snow** VERB

雪 xuě

to **snow** VERB

▷ *see also* **snow** NOUN

下雪 xiàxuě

■ **It's snowing.** 下雪了。Xiàxuě le.

snowball NOUN

雪球 xuěqiú [个 gè]

snowflake NOUN

雪花 xuěhuā [朵 duǒ]

snowman NOUN

雪人 xuěrén [个 gè]

■ **to build a snowman** 做雪人 zuòxuěrén

so CONJUNCTION, ADVERB

1 因此 yīncǐ *(therefore)*

□ He didn't come, so I left. 他没来，因此我走了。Tā méilái, yīncǐ wǒ zǒule.

■ **So what?** 那又怎么样？ Nà yòu zěnme yàng?

2 为的是 wèi de shì *(so that)*

□ I brought it so you could see it. 我带过来为的是给你看。Wǒ dàiguò lái wèideshì gěi nǐ kàn.

3 如此 rúcǐ *(to such a degree)*

□ He was talking so fast I couldn't understand. 他说话如此快以至于我听不懂。Tā shuōhuà rúcǐkuài yǐzhìyú wǒ tīngbùdǒng.

■ **He's like his sister but not so clever.** 他像他的姐姐但没那么聪明。Tā xiàng tāde jiějie dàn méi nàme cōngmíng.

4 非常 fēicháng *(very)*

■ **I was so happy!** 我非常幸福！ Wǒ fēicháng xìngfú!

■ **It's not so heavy!** 它不是非常重！Tā búshì fēicháng zhòng!

■ **How's your father? — Not so good.** 你父亲好吗？ — 不是非常好。Nǐ fùqīn hǎo ma? — Búshì fēicháng hǎo.

■ **so much** 那么多 nàme duō □ I love you so much. 我那么爱你。Wǒ nàme àinǐ. □ I've got so much work. 我有那么多工作。Wǒ yǒu nàmeduō gōngzuò.

■ **so many** 那么多 nàme duō □ I've got so many things to do today. 我今天有那么多的工作要做。Wǒ jīntiān yǒu nàmeduōde gōngzuò yàozuò.

■ **so do I** 我也是。Wǒ yě shì. □ I love horses. — So do I. 我喜欢马。— 我也是。Wǒ xǐhuanmǎ. — Wǒ yě shì.

■ **so have we** 我们也是 Wǒmen yě shì □ I've been to France twice. — So have we. 我去过法国两次。— 我们也是。Wǒ qùguò Fǎguó liǎngcì. — Wǒmen yě shì.

■ **If you don't want to go, say so.** 如果你不想去，就说你不想去。Rúguǒ nǐ bùxiǎng qù, jiù shuō nǐ bùxiǎng qù.

■ **if so** 如果这样 rúguǒ zhèyàng

■ **That's not so.** 不是那样。Búshì nàyàng.

■ **I hope so.** 我希望如此。Wǒ xīwàng rúcǐ.

■ **I think so.** 我认为如此。Wǒ rènwéi rúcǐ.

■ **so far** 迄今为止 qìjīn wéizhǐ □ It's been easy so far. 迄今为止很简单。Qìjīn wéizhǐ hěnjiǎndān.

■ **so far so good** 到现在为止，一切顺利。Dào xiànzài wéizhǐ, yíqièshùnlì.

■ **and so on** 等等 děngděng

■ **ten or so people** 十个人左右 shígèrén zuǒyòu

■ **at five o'clock or so** 五点钟左右 wǔdiǎnzhōngzuǒyòu

to **soak** VERB

浸泡 jìnpào

soaked ADJECTIVE
湿透了 shītòule
□ By the time we got back we were soaked. 回去时我们都湿透了。Huíqùshí wǒmen dōu shītòu le.

soaking ADJECTIVE
1 湿透的 shītòu de *(person)*
□ By the time we got back we were soaking. 回去时我们都湿透了。Huíqùshí wǒmen dōu shītòu le.
2 湿淋淋的 shīlínlín de *(clothes)*
□ Your shoes are soaking. 你的鞋湿淋淋的。Nǐdexié shīlínlín de.

soap NOUN
肥皂 féizào [块 kuài]

soap opera NOUN
肥皂剧 féizào jù [部 bù]

to **sob** VERB
啜泣 chuòqì
□ She was sobbing. 她在啜泣。Tā zài chuòqì.

sober ADJECTIVE
未醉的 wèizuìde

to **sober up** VERB
清醒 qīngxǐng

soccer NOUN
足球 zúqiú
■ **to play soccer** 踢足球 tī zúqiú
■ **a soccer player** 足球运动员 zúqiúyùndòngyuán

social ADJECTIVE
社会的 shèhuì de
□ social problems 社会问题 shèhuì wèntí
■ **I have a good social life.** 我有很好的社交生活。Wǒ yǒu hěnhǎode shèjiāo shēnghuó.

socialism NOUN
社会主义 shèhuì zhǔyì

socialist ADJECTIVE
▷ *see also* **socialist** NOUN
社会主义的 shèhuì zhǔyì de

socialist NOUN
▷ *see also* **socialist** ADJECTIVE
社会主义者 shèhuì zhǔyìzhě [位 wèi]

social media NOUN
社交媒体 shèjiāo méitǐ

social security NOUN
1 社会保障金 shèhuì bǎozhàngjīn *(money)*
■ **to be on social security** 依靠社保金 yīkào shèbǎojīn
2 社会保障 shèhuì bǎozhàng *(organization)*

social worker NOUN
社会福利工作者 shèhuì fúlì gōngzuòzhě [位 wèi]

society NOUN
1 社会 shèhuì
□ We live in a multi-cultural society. 我们生活在多元化社会。Wǒmen shēnghuó zài duōyuánhuà shèhuì.
2 社团 shètuán
□ a drama society 戏剧社团 xìjùshètuán

sock NOUN
袜子 wàzi [双 shuāng]

socket NOUN
插座 chāzuò [个 gè]

soda NOUN
苏打 sūdá *(soda water)*

soda pop NOUN (US)
汽水 qìshuǐ

sofa NOUN
沙发 shāfā [个 gè]

soft ADJECTIVE
1 松软的 sōngruǎn de *(towel)*
2 柔软的 róuruǎn de *(skin)*
3 软和的 ruǎnhuode *(bed, paste)*
■ **to be soft on somebody** *(be kind to)* 善待某人 shàndài mǒurén
■ **a soft drink** 一瓶软性饮料 yìpíng ruǎnxìng yǐnliào
■ **soft drugs** 软毒品 ruǎndúpǐn

software NOUN
软件 ruǎnjiàn [个 gè]

soil NOUN
土壤 tǔrǎng [种 zhǒng]

solar power NOUN
太阳能 tàiyáng néng

sold VERB ▷ *see* **sell**

soldier NOUN
士兵 shìbīng [位 wèi]
□ He's a soldier. 他是位士兵。Tā shì wèi shìbīng.

sole NOUN
底 dǐ [个 gè]

solicitor NOUN
律师 lǜshī [位 wèi] *(for lawsuits)*

solid ADJECTIVE
1 坚实的 jiānshí de *(not soft)*
□ a solid wall 坚实的墙 jiánshíde qiáng
2 纯质的 chúnzhì de
□ solid gold 纯质的金子 chúnzhìde jīnzi.
■ **for three hours solid** 整整三个小时 zhěngzhěng sāngè xiǎoshí

solo NOUN
独奏曲 dúzòuqǔ [支 zhī]
□ a guitar solo 吉他独奏 jítādúzòu

solution NOUN
解决方案 jiějué fāng'àn [个 gè]

to **solve** VERB
1 破解 pòjiě *(mystery, case)*
2 解决 jiějué *(problem)*

some ADJECTIVE, PRONOUN
1 一些 yìxiē
□ some milk 一些牛奶 yìxiē niúnǎi □ some books 一些书 yìxiē shū □ Are these

mushrooms poisonous? — Only some. 这些蘑菇有毒吗？— 只是一些有毒。Zhèxiē mógù yǒudú ma? — Zhǐshì yìxiē yǒudú.

2 某些 mǒuxiē *(certain, in contrasts)*
□ Some people say that... 有些人说… Yǒuxiē rén shuō...
■ **some of them** 他们中的一些 tāmen zhōng de yìxiē □ I only sold some of them. 我只卖了它们的一些。Wǒ zhǐ màile tāmende yìxiē.
■ **I only took some of it.** 我只拿了一些。Wǒ zhǐ nále yìxiē.
■ **I'm going to buy some stamps. Do you want some too?** 我要去买一些邮票。你也要一些吗？ Wǒ yào qù mǎi yìxiē yóupiào. Nǐ yě yào yìxiē ma?
■ **Would you like some coffee? — No thanks, I've got some.** 你要点咖啡吗？— 不，谢谢，我已经有了。Nǐ yào diǎn kāfēi ma? — Bù, xièxie, wǒ yǐjīng yǒu le.
■ **There was some left.** 还剩下一些。Hái shèngxià yìxiē.

somebody PRONOUN
某人 mǒurén
□ I saw somebody in the garden. 我看见花园里有人。Wǒ kànjiàn huāyuán lǐ yǒurén.
■ **somebody else** 别人 biérén

somehow ADVERB
设法 shèfǎ
□ I'll do it somehow. 我明天会设法做的。Wǒ míngtiān huì shèfǎ zuòde.
■ **Somehow I don't think he believed me.** 不知怎么的我觉得他不信任我。Bùzhīzěnmede wojuéde tā bú xìnrèn wǒ.

someone PRONOUN
某人 mǒurén
□ I saw someone in the garden. 我看见花园里有人。Wǒ kànjiàn huāyuán lǐ yǒurén.
■ **someone else** 别人 biérén

someplace ADVERB (US) ▷ *see* **somewhere**

something PRONOUN
某事物 mǒushìwù
□ something special 特别的事物 tèbiéde shìwù □ Wear something warm. 穿点暖和点。Chuān nuǎnhuo diǎn. □ It cost £100, or something like that. 要一百英磅左右。Yào yìbǎi yīngbàng zuǒyòu. □ Would you like a sandwich or something? 你要来点三明治或其他什么东西吗？ Nǐ yào lái diǎn sānmíngzhì huò qítā shénme dōngxi ma?
■ **That's really something!** 那真了不起！Nà zhēnliǎobùqǐ!
■ **something else** 其他事情 qítā shìqing

sometime ADVERB
某个时候 mǒugè shíhòu
□ You must come and see us sometime. 你一定要在某个时候来见我们。Nǐ yídìng yàozài mǒugè shíhòu láijiàn wǒmen.
■ **sometime last month** 上个月的某个时候 shànggeyuède mǒugè shíhòu

sometimes ADVERB
有时 yǒushí
□ Sometimes I think she hates me. 有时我觉得她恨我。Yǒushí wǒ juéde tā hènwǒ.

somewhere (US **someplace**) ADVERB
某个地方 mǒugèdìfāng
□ I need somewhere to live. 我需要找个地方住。Wǒ xūyào zhǎogè dìfang zhù.
□ I must have lost it somewhere. 我一定把它丢在某个地方了。Wǒ yídìng bǎ tā diū zài mǒugè dìfāng le.
■ **Let's go somewhere quiet.** 我们去个安静的地方吧。Wǒmen qù gè ānjìng de dìfang ba.
■ **somewhere else** 别的地方 biéde dìfang

son NOUN
儿子 érzi [个 gè]

song NOUN
歌曲 gēqǔ [首 shǒu]

son-in-law NOUN
女婿 nǔxu [个 gè]

soon ADVERB
1 不久 bùjiǔ *(in a short time)*
□ I'm going on holiday soon. 不久我会去度假。Bùjiǔ wǒ huì qù dùjià.
2 很快 hěnkuài *(a short time later)*
□ He soon came back. 他很快就回来了。Tā hěnkuài jiù huílái le.
3 早 zǎo *(early)*
□ She came too soon and I wasn't ready. 她来的太早了，我还没准备好。Tā láide tàizǎo le, wǒ hái méi zhǔnbèi hǎo.
■ **soon afterwards** 不久后 bùjiǔ hòu
■ **as soon as possible** 尽快 jìnkuài
■ **quite soon** 很快 hěnkuài
■ **See you soon!** 再见！ Zàijiàn!

sooner ADVERB
更早 gèngzǎo
□ Can't you come a bit sooner? 你能来的更早一点吗？ Nǐ néng láide gèngzǎo yìdiǎn ma?
■ **sooner or later** 迟早 chízǎo
■ **the sooner the better** 越快越好 yuè kuài yuè hǎo

sophomore NOUN (US)
大二学生 dà'èr xuéshēng [个 gè]

sore ADJECTIVE
痛的 tòng de
□ My feet are sore. 我的脚痛。Wǒde jiǎo tòng. □ It's sore. 很痛。Hěn tòng.

■ **That's a sore point.** 那是痛点。Nàshì tòngdiǎn.

sorry ADJECTIVE
对不起 duìbùqǐ
□ I'm really sorry. 很对不起。Hěn duìbùqǐ. □ I'm sorry, I haven't got any change. 对不起，我没有零钱。Duìbùqǐ, wǒ méiyǒu língqián. □ I'm sorry I'm late. 对不起，我来晚了。Duìbùqǐ, wǒ láiwǎn le.
■ **sorry!** 对不起！ duìbùqǐ!
■ **sorry?** 请再讲一遍? qǐng zài jiǎng yíbiàn?
■ **I'm sorry about the noise.** 对于噪音我很抱歉。Duìyú zàoyīn wǒ hěn bàoqiàn.
■ **You'll be sorry!** 你会后悔的！ Nǐ huì hòuhuǐde!
■ **to feel sorry for somebody** 对某人表示同情 duì mǒurén biǎoshì tóngqíng

sort NOUN
▷ *see also* **sort** VERB
种 zhǒng
□ What sort of bike have you got? 你有哪种自行车？ Nǐ yǒu nǎzhǒng zìxíngchē?
■ **all sorts of** 各种不同的 gèzhǒng bùtóng de

to **sort** VERB
▷ *see also* **sort** NOUN
1 把...分类 bǎ...fēnlèi *(papers, mail, belongings)*
2 整理 zhěnglǐ

to **sort out** VERB
1 整理 zhěnglǐ *(objects)*
2 解决 jiějué *(problem)*

so-so ADVERB
一般的 yìbānde
□ How are you feeling? — So-so. 你感觉怎么样？ — 一般。Nǐ gǎnjué zěnme yàng? — Yìbān.

sought VERB ▷ *see* **to seek**

soul NOUN
灵魂 línghún *(spirit)*

sound NOUN
▷ *see also* **sound** VERB, ADJECTIVE, ADVERB
1 声音 shēngyīn [种 zhǒng]
□ the sound of footsteps 脚步声 jiǎobùshēng □ Don't make a sound! 别出声！ Bié chūshēng!
2 音量 yīnliàng
□ Can I turn the sound down? 我可以把音量降低吗？ Wǒ kěyǐ bǎ yīnliàng jiàngdī ma?

to **sound** VERB
▷ *see also* **sound** NOUN, ADJECTIVE, ADVERB
听起来 tīng qǐlái
□ That sounds like an explosion. 听起来像是爆炸声的。Tīngqǐlái xiàngshì bàozhàshēng de. □ That sounds like a great idea. 这主意听起来妙极了。Zhè zhǔyì tīngqǐlái miàojí le.
■ **It sounds as if...** 听起来似乎… Tīngqǐlái sìhū... □ It sounds as if she's doing well at school. 听起来似乎她在学校学得不错。 Tīngqǐlái sìhū tā zài xuéxiào xuéde búcuò.

sound ADJECTIVE, ADVERB
▷ *see also* **sound** NOUN, VERB
■ **That's sound advice.** 那是好的建议。Nàshì hǎode jiànyì.
■ **sound asleep** 熟睡 shúshuì

soundtrack NOUN
声道 shēngdào [条 tiáo]

soup NOUN
汤 tāng [份 fèn]
□ vegetable soup 蔬菜汤 shūcàitāng

sour ADJECTIVE
酸的 suān de

south NOUN
▷ *see also* **south** ADJECTIVE, ADVERB
南方 nánfāng
□ in the south 在南方 zàinánfāng
□ the South of China 中国南方 Zhōngguó nánfāng

south ADJECTIVE, ADVERB
▷ *see also* **south** NOUN, ADVERB
南部的 nánbù de
□ the south coast 南部海岸 nánbù hǎi'àn
□ We were travelling south. 我们去南方旅行。Wǒmen qù nánfāng lǚxíng.
■ **south of...** 在…以南 zài...yǐnán □ It's south of London. 在伦敦以南。Zài Lúndūn yǐnán.

South Africa NOUN
南非 Nánfēi

South America NOUN
南美洲 Nán měizhōu

South American NOUN
▷ *see also* **South American** ADJECTIVE
南美洲人 Nánměizhōurén [个 gè]

South American ADJECTIVE
▷ *see also* **South American** NOUN
南美洲的 Nánměizhōude

southbound ADJECTIVE
往南的 wǎngnánde
■ **The southbound carriageway is blocked.** 往南的路堵上了。Wǎngnánde lù dǔshàng le.
■ **We were going southbound on the M1.** 我们在一号高速公路上南行。Wǒmen zài yíhào gāosù gōnglùshàng nánxíng.

southeast NOUN
东南 dōngnán
□ southeast England 英格兰东南

Yīnggélán dōngnán

southern ADJECTIVE
南方的 nánfāng de
■ **the southern hemisphere** 南半球 nán bànqiú
■ **Southern England** 英格兰南部 Yīnggélán nánbù

South Korea NOUN
韩国 Hánguó

South Pole NOUN
■ **the South Pole** 南极 Nánjí

South Wales NOUN
南威尔士 Nán Wéi'ěrshì

southwest NOUN
西南 xīnán
□ southwest China 中国西南 Zhōngguó xīnán

souvenir NOUN
纪念品 jìniàn pǐn [件 jiàn]
■ **a souvenir shop** 纪念品店 jìniànpǐndiàn

Soviet ADJECTIVE
■ **the former Soviet Union** 前苏联 qián Sūlián

soya NOUN
黄豆 huángdòu [颗 kē]

soy sauce NOUN
酱油 jiàngyóu

space NOUN
1 空间 kōngjiān *(room)*
□ There isn't enough space. 没有足够的空间。Méiyǒu zúgòude kōngjiān.
2 地方 dìfāng [个 gè] *(place)*
■ **to clear a space for something** 为某物腾地方 wèi mǒuwù téng dìfang
■ **a parking space** 停车地方 tíngchē dìfāng
3 太空 tàikōng *(beyond Earth)*
■ **to go into space** 进入太空 jìnrù tàikōng
■ **a space shuttle** 太空穿梭机 tàikōng chuānsuōjī
4 空 kòng *(gap)*
□ Leave a space after your answer. 在答案后留个空。Zài dáàn hòu liúgè kòng.

spacecraft NOUN
太空船 tàikōngchuán [艘 sōu]

spade NOUN
锹 qiāo [把 bǎ]
■ **spades** *(in cards)* 黑桃 hēitáo □ the ace of spades 黑桃A hēitáo ēi

spaghetti NOUN
意大利面 yìdàlì miàn [份 fèn]

Spain NOUN
西班牙 Xībānyá

Spaniard NOUN
西班牙人 Xībānyárén [个 gè]

spaniel NOUN
拍马屁者 pāimǎpìzhě [个 gè]

Spanish ADJECTIVE
▷ *see also* **Spanish** NOUN
西班牙的 Xībānyá de
□ She's Spanish. 她是西班牙人。Tāshì Xībānyárén.

Spanish NOUN
▷ *see also* **Spanish** ADJECTIVE
西班牙语 Xībānyáyǔ *(language)*
■ **the Spanish** *(people)* 西班牙人 Xībānyárén

spanner NOUN
扳钳 bānqián [个 gè]

spare ADJECTIVE
▷ *see also* **spare** NOUN, VERB
1 多余的 duōyú de *(free)*
■ **spare time** 业余时间 yèyú shíjiān
□ What do you do in your spare time? 你在业余时间做什么？ Nǐ zài yèyúshíjiān zuò shénme?
2 备用的 bèiyòng de *(extra)*
□ spare batteries 备用电池 bèiyòngdiànchí
□ a spare part 一个备件 yígèbèijiàn
■ **a spare room** 一间备用房间 yìjiān bèiyòng fángjiān
■ **spare wheel** 备用轮胎 bèiyòng lúntāi

spare NOUN
▷ *see also* **spare** ADJECTIVE, VERB
■ **a spare** 多余的 duōyúde □ I've lost my key. — Have you got a spare? 我把钥匙丢了。— 你有多余的吗？ Wǒ bǎ yàoshi diūle. — Nǐ yǒu duōyúde ma?

to **spare** VERB
▷ *see also* **spare** ADJECTIVE, NOUN
■ **Can you spare a moment?** 你能抽出一点时间吗？Nǐ néng chōuchū yìdiǎn shíjiān ma?
■ **I can't spare the time.** 我抽不出时间。Wǒ chōubùchū shíjiān.
■ **There's no room to spare.** 没有空房间。Méiyǒu kòngfángjiān.
■ **We arrived with time to spare.** 我们早到所以有时间。Wǒmen zǎodào suǒyǐ yǒu shíjiān.

sparkling ADJECTIVE
有泡的 yǒupàode *(water)*
■ **sparkling wine** 汽酒 qìjiǔ

sparrow NOUN
麻雀 máquè [只 zhī]

spat VERB ▷ *see* **spit**

to **speak** VERB
1 讲 jiǎng
□ Do you speak English? 你讲英语吗？ Nǐ jiǎng Yīngyǔ ma?
2 讲话 jiǎnghuà *(talk)*

□ She was so nervous she could hardly speak. 她太紧张了都不能讲话了。Tā tài jǐnzhāng le dōu bùnéng jiǎnghuà le.
■ **to speak to somebody** 同某人讲话 tóng mǒurén jiǎnghuà □ Have you spoken to him? 你同他讲话了吗？ Nǐ tóng tā jiǎnghuà le ma? □ She spoke to him about her difficulty. 她同他谈了她的困难。Tā tóng tā tánle tādekùnnán.

to **speak up** VERB
大点声 dàdiǎnshēng
□ Speak up, we can't hear you. 大点声，我们听不清。Dàdiǎnshēng, wǒmen tīngbùqīng.

speaker NOUN
1 扬声器 yángshēngqì [只 zhī] *(loudspeaker)*
2 演讲人 yǎnjiǎngrén [个 gè] *(in debate)*

special ADJECTIVE
1 特别的 tèbié de *(important)*
■ **It's nothing special.** 没什么特别的。Méi shénme tèbié de.
2 专门的 zhuānmén de *(particular)*
□ We only use these plates on special occasions. 我们只在特别场合才用这些碟子。Wǒmen zhǐzài tèbié chǎnghé cái yòng zhèxiē diézi.

specialist NOUN
专家 zhuānjiā [位 wèi]

speciality (US **specialty**) NOUN
1 特制品 tèzhìpǐn [种 zhǒng] *(product)*
2 特产 tèchǎn [种 zhǒng] *(food)*

to **specialize** VERB
专攻 zhuāngōng
□ We specialize in skiing equipment. 我们专攻滑雪器材。Wǒmen zhuāngōng huáxuě qìcái.

specially ADVERB
1 专门地 zhuānmén de
□ It's specially designed for teenagers. 专门为青少年设计的。Zhuānmen wèi qīngshàonián shèjìde.
■ **not specially** 不是很 búshìhěn □ Do you like opera? — Not specially. 你喜欢歌剧吗？ — 不是很喜欢。Nǐ xǐhuān gējù ma? — Búshì hěnxǐhuān.
2 特别 tèbié
□ It can be very cold here, specially in winter. 这里可能会很冷，特别是冬天。Zhèlǐ kěnéng huì hěnlěng, tèbié shì dōngtiān.

specialty NOUN (US)
1 特制品 tèzhìpǐn [种 zhǒng] *(product)*
2 特产 tèchǎn [种 zhǒng] *(food)*

species NOUN
种 zhǒng [个 gè]

specific ADJECTIVE
1 特别的 tèbiéde *(particular)*
□ certain specific issues 一些具体的问题 yìxiējùtǐde wèntí
2 具体的 jùtǐ de *(exact)*
□ Could you be more specific? 你能具体一点吗？ Nǐ néng jùtǐ yìdiǎn ma?

specifically ADVERB
1 专门 zhuānmén
□ It's specifically designed for teenagers. 专门为青少年设计的。Zhuānmen wèi qīngshàonián shèjìde.
2 具体的 jùtǐde
□ in Britain, or more specifically in England 在英国，或者更具体的在英格兰。Zài Yīngguó, huòzhě gèngjùtǐde zài Yīnggélán.
■ **I specifically said that ...** 我明确地说… Wǒ míngquèdèshuō...

specs, spectacles PL NOUN
眼镜 yǎnjìng [副 fù]

spectacular ADJECTIVE
1 壮丽的 zhuànglìde *(view, scenery)*
2 惊人的 jīngrénde *(rise, growth)*
3 引人注目的 yǐnrén zhùmù de *(success, result)*

spectator NOUN
观众 guānzhòng [个 gè]

speech NOUN
演说 yǎnshuō [场 chǎng]
■ **to make a speech** 演说 yǎnshuō

speechless ADJECTIVE
说不出话 shuōbùchūhuà
□ speechless with admiration 崇拜得说不出话 chóngbàide shuōbùchūhuà

speed NOUN
速度 sùdù [种 zhǒng]
■ **at a speed of 70km/h** 以时速七十公里 yǐ shísù qīshí gōnglǐ

to **speed up** VERB
加快 jiākuài

speedboat NOUN
高速游艇 gāosùyóutǐng [艘 sōu]

speeding NOUN
超速 chāosù
□ He was fined for speeding. 他因超速被罚款。Tā yīn chāosù bèi fákuǎn.

speed limit NOUN
速度极限 sùdù jíxiàn [个 gè]
■ **to break the speed limit** 超速 chāosù

speedometer NOUN
速度计 sùdùjì [只 zhī]

to **spell** VERB
▷ *see also* **spell** NOUN

LANGUAGE TIP Chinese is not spelled, it is written, so the equivalent to the English **spell** would be **write**.

□ How do you spell that word? 那个字怎么写？ Nàge zì zěnme xiě?

■ **Can you spell that please?** *(out loud)* 你能拼出来吗？ Nǐ néng pīnchū lái ma?

■ **He can't spell.** 他不会拼写。Tā bùhuì pīnxiě.

spell NOUN

▷ *see also* **spell** VERB

魅力 mèilì

■ **to cast a spell on somebody** 对某人施魔法 duì mǒurén shīmófǎ

■ **to be under somebody's spell** 被某人的魅力迷住 bèi mǒurén de mèilì mízhù

spelling NOUN

LANGUAGE TIP Chinese is not spelled, it is written, so the equivalent to the English **spelling** would be **writing**.

□ a spelling mistake 一个拼写错误 yígè pīnxiě cuòwù

■ **My spelling is terrible.** *(ability to spell)* 我的拼写能力很差。Wǒde pīnxiě nénglì hěnchà.

spelt VERB ▷ *see* **spell**

to **spend** VERB

1 花费 huāfèi *(money)*

2 度过 dùguò *(time)*

□ He spent a month in France. 他在法国度过了一个月。Tā zài Fǎguó dùguò le yígèyuè.

spent VERB ▷ *see* **spend**

spice NOUN

香料 xiāngliào [种 zhǒng]

spicy ADJECTIVE

辛辣的 xīnlà de

spider NOUN

蜘蛛 zhīzhū [只 zhī]

to **spill** VERB

1 使溢出 shǐ yìchū

■ **He spilled his coffee over his trousers.** 他把咖啡洒在了裤子上。Tā bǎ kāfēi sǎzài le kùzishàng.

2 洒出 sǎchū *(get spilt)*

□ The soup spilled all over the table. 汤洒在桌子上到处都是。Tāng sǎzài zuōzishàng dàochùdōushì.

spinach NOUN

菠菜 bōcài [斤 jīn]

spine NOUN

脊柱 jǐzhù [根 gēn]

spirit NOUN

1 精神 jīngshen *(courage)*

■ **to be in good spirits** 兴高采烈 xìnggāocǎiliè

2 精力 jīnglì *(energy)*

spirits PL NOUN

烈酒 lièjiǔ

□ I don't drink spirits. 我不喝烈酒。Wǒ bùhē lièjiǔ.

spit NOUN

▷ *see also* **spit** VERB

唾液 tuòyè *(saliva)*

to **spit** VERB

▷ *see also* **spit** NOUN

吐唾液 tǔ tuòyè

■ **to spit something out** 把某物吐出 bǎ mǒuwù tǔchū

spite NOUN

恶意 èyì

■ **out of spite** 出于恶意 chūyú èyì

■ **in spite of** 尽管 jǐnguǎn

spiteful ADJECTIVE

1 恶意的 èyìde *(action)*

2 怀恨的 huáihènde *(person)*

to **splash** VERB

▷ *see also* **splash** NOUN

溅 jiàn

□ Careful! Don't splash me! 小心！别溅我一身！ Xiǎoxīn! Biéjiàn wǒ yìshēn!

splash NOUN

▷ *see also* **splash** VERB

泼洒 pōsǎ

□ I heard a splash. 我听到泼洒声。Wǒ tīngdào pōsǎshēng.

■ **a splash of colour** 颜色的飞溅 yánsède fēijiàn

splendid ADJECTIVE

极好的 jíhǎo de

splinter NOUN

碎片 suìpiàn [块 kuài]

to **split** VERB

1 把...划分 bǎ...huàfēn

□ He split the wood with an axe. 他用斧子把木头一分为二。Tā yòng fǔzi bǎ mùtóu yìfēnwéièr.

2 裂开 lièkāi

□ The ship hit a rock and split in two. 船撞上岩石裂开成了两半。Chuán zhuàngshàng yánshí lièkāi chéngle liǎngbàn.

3 平分 píngfēn *(divide up)*

□ They decided to split the profits. 他们决定平分利润。Tāmen juédìng píngfēn lìrùn.

to **split up** VERB

1 分手 fēnshǒu

□ My parents have split up. 我父母分手了。Wǒ fùmǔ fēnshǒu le.

2 分组 fēnzǔ *(group)*

to **spoil** VERB

1 损害 sǔnhài *(damage)*

2 溺爱 nì'ài *(child)*

spoiled ADJECTIVE

宠坏的 chǒnghuài de

□ a spoiled child 宠坏的孩子 chǒnghuàide háizi

spoilt VERB ▷ *see* **spoil**
spoilt ADJECTIVE
宠坏的 chǒnghuài de
□ a spoilt child 一个宠坏的孩子 yígè chǒnghuàide háizi
spoke VERB ▷ *see* **speak**
spoke NOUN
轮辐 lúnfú *(of wheel)*
spoken VERB ▷ *see* **speak**
spokesman NOUN
男发言人 nán fāyánrén [位 wèi]
spokeswoman NOUN
女发言人 nǚ fāyánrén [位 wèi]
sponge NOUN
海绵 hǎimián
■ **a sponge bag** 一只盥洗用具袋 yìzhī guànxǐ yòngjùdài
■ **a sponge cake** 一块松糕 yíkuài sōnggāo
sponsor NOUN
▷ *see also* **sponsor** VERB
主办方 zhǔbànfāng [个 gè]
to **sponsor** VERB
▷ *see also* **sponsor** NOUN
主办 zhǔbàn
□ The festival was sponsored by ... 该节是由…主办的。Gāijié shì yóu...zhǔbànde.
spontaneous ADJECTIVE
自发的 zìfāde
spooky ADJECTIVE
1 怪异的 guàiyìde *(eerie)*
□ a spooky story 一个怪异的故事 yígè guàiyìde gùshì
2 奇怪的 qíguàide *(strange)*
□ a spooky coincidence 一个奇怪的巧合 yígè qíguàide qiǎohé
spoon NOUN
匙 chí [把 bǎ]

DID YOU KNOW...?
If you struggle with chopsticks, the waiter may, out of politeness, offer you a spoon instead.

spoonful NOUN
一勺 yìsháo
□ two spoonfuls of sugar 两勺糖 liǎngsháotáng
sport NOUN
1 运动 yùndòng [项 xiàng] *(particular game)*
□ What's your favourite sport? 你最喜欢的运动是什么？ Nǐ zuìxǐhuande yùndòng shì shénme?
2 体育 tǐyù *(generally)*
□ Do you like sport? 你喜欢体育吗？ Nǐ xǐhuan tǐyù ma?
■ **a sports bag** 一个运动包 yígè yùndòngbāo
■ **a sports car** 一辆跑车 yíliàng pǎochē
■ **a sports jacket** 一件运动服 yíjiàn yùndòngfú
■ **Go on, be a sport!** 继续，够朋友一点！Jìxù, gòu péngyǒu yìdiǎn!
sportsman NOUN
运动员 yùndòngyuán [名 míng]
sportswear NOUN
运动服 yùndòngfú
sportswoman NOUN
女运动员 nǚyùndòngyuán [名 míng]
sporty ADJECTIVE
爱运动 àiyùndòng
□ I'm not very sporty. 我不是很爱运动。Wǒ búshì hěn ài yùndòng.
spot NOUN
▷ *see also* **spot** VERB
1 斑点 bāndiǎn [个 gè] *(mark)*
□ There's a spot on your shirt. 你的衬衫上有个斑点。Nǐde chènshānshàng yǒugè bāndiǎn.
2 点 diǎn [个 gè] *(dot)*
□ a red dress with white spots 带白点的红色裙子 dài báidiǎnde hóngsè qúnzi
3 疵点 cīdiǎn [个 gè] *(pimple)*
□ He's covered in spots. 他脸上有很多疵点。Tā liǎnshàng yǒu hěnduō cīdiǎn.
4 地方 dìfāng [个 gè] *(place)*
□ It's a lovely spot for a picnic. 那是个野餐的好地方。Nàshì gè yěcānde hǎodìfāng.
■ **on the spot 1** *(in that place)* 在现场 zài xiànchǎng □ Luckily they were able to mend the car on the spot. 幸运的是，他们可以现场修车。Xìngyùndeshì,tāmen kěyǐ xiànchǎng xiūchē. **2** *(immediately)* 当场 dāngchǎng □ They gave her the job on the spot. 他们当场就把工作给她了。Tāmen dāngchǎng jiù bǎ gōngzuò gěitā le.
to **spot** VERB
▷ *see also* **spot** NOUN
发现 fāxiàn
□ I spotted a mistake. 我发现了一个错误。Wǒ fāxiàn le yígè cuòwù.
spotless ADJECTIVE
没有污点的 méiyǒu wūdiǎnde
spotlight NOUN
聚光灯 jùguāngdēng [盏 zhǎn]
□ The universities have been in the spotlight recently. 最近大学总是在聚光灯下。Zuìjìn dàxué zǒngshì zài jùguāngdēngxià.
spotty ADJECTIVE
多粉刺的 duōfěncìde *(pimply)*
spouse NOUN
配偶 pèiǒu [个 gè]
to **sprain** VERB

■ **to sprain one's ankle** 扭伤脚踝 niǔshāng jiǎohuái

to **spray** VERB

▷ *see also* **spray** NOUN

1 喷 pēn

□ Somebody had sprayed graffiti on the wall. 有人在墙上喷了涂鸦。Yǒurén zài qiángshàng pēnle túyā.

2 向...喷杀虫剂 xiàng...pēn shāchóng jì *(crops)*

spray NOUN

▷ *see also* **spray** VERB

喷雾 pēnwù [瓶 píng] *(spray can)*

spread NOUN

▷ *see also* **spread** VERB

■ **cheese spread** 奶酪酱 nǎilàojiàng

■ **chocolate spread** 巧克力酱 qiǎokēlìjiàng

to **spread** VERB

▷ *see also* **spread** NOUN

1 涂 tú

□ to spread butter on a slice of bread 在一片面包上涂奶油 zài yípiàn miànbāoshàng tú nǎiyóu

2 传播 chuánbō *(disease, news)*

□ The disease spread rapidly. 疾病传播得很快。Jíbìng chuánbōde hěnkuài.

to **spread out** VERB

散开 sànkāi *(people)*

□ The soldiers spread out across the field. 士兵在田地里散开。Shìbīng zài tiándìlǐ sànkāi.

spreadsheet NOUN

电子表格 diànzǐ biǎogé [份 fèn]

spring NOUN

1 春季 chūnjì [个 gè] *(season)*

■ **in (the) spring** 在春季 zài chūnjì

2 弹簧 tánhuáng [个 gè] *(metal coil)*

3 泉水 quánshuǐ [眼 yǎn] *(water hole)*

springtime NOUN

春季 chūnjì

■ **in springtime** 在春季 zàichūnjì

sprouts PL NOUN

嫩芽 nènyá

■ **Brussels sprouts** 芽甘蓝 yágānlán

spy NOUN

▷ *see also* **spy** VERB

间谍 jiàndié [个 gè]

to **spy** VERB

▷ *see also* **spy** NOUN

■ **to spy on somebody** 监视某人 jiānshìmǒurén

spying NOUN

当间谍 dāng jiàndié

square NOUN

▷ *see also* **square** ADJECTIVE

1 正方形 zhèngfāng xíng [个 gè]

□ a square and a triangle 一个正方形和一个三角形 yígè zhèngfāngxíng hé yígè sānjiǎoxíng

2 广场 guǎngchǎng [个 gè]

□ the town square 市中心广场 shìzhōngxīn guǎngchǎng

DID YOU KNOW...?
The most famous town square in China is the 天安门广场 Tiān'ānmén guǎngchǎng **Tiananmen Square** in Beijing, which is the largest city centre square in the world.

square ADJECTIVE

▷ *see also* **square** NOUN

正方形的 zhèngfāng xíng de

■ **2 square metres** 二平方米 liǎng píngfāngmǐ

■ **It's 2 metres square.** 那是两米的正方形。Nàshì liǎngmǐde zhèngfāngxíng.

squash NOUN

▷ *see also* **squash** VERB

壁球 bìqiú *(sport)*

□ I play squash. 我打壁球。Wǒ dǎ bìqiú.

■ **a squash court** 一个壁球场 yígè bìqiúchǎng

■ **a squash racket** 一个壁球拍 yígè bìqiúpāi

■ **orange squash** 鲜橙汁 xiān chéngzhī

■ **lemon squash** 鲜柠檬汁 xiān níngméngzhī

to **squash** VERB

▷ *see also* **squash** NOUN

把...压碎 bǎ...yāsuì

□ You're squashing me. 你压死我了。Nǐ yāsǐ wǒ le.

to **squeak** VERB

1 尖叫 jiānjiào *(mouse, child)*

2 吱吱声 zhīzhishēng *(creak)*

to **squeeze** VERB

用力捏 yònglì niē

to **squeeze in** VERB

1 挤进 jǐjìn

□ It was a tiny car, but we managed to squeeze in. 车很小，但是我们还是都挤进去了。Chē hěnxiǎo, dànshì wǒmen háishì dōu jǐjìn qù le.

2 挤 jǐ *(for appointment)*

□ I can squeeze you in at two o'clock. 我可以把你挤进两点的时段。Wǒ kěyǐ bǎ nǐ jǐjìn liǎngdiǎnde shíduàn.

to **squint** VERB

斜视 xiéshì

squirrel NOUN

松鼠 sōngshǔ [只 zhī]

to **stab** VERB

刺 cì

stable ADJECTIVE
▷ *see also* **stable** NOUN
稳定的 wěndìng de
□ a stable relationship 一个稳定的关系 yígè wěndìngde guānxì

stable NOUN
▷ *see also* **stable** ADJECTIVE
马厩 mǎjiù [个 gè]

stack NOUN
堆 duī
□ a stack of books 一堆书 yìduīshū

stadium NOUN
体育场 tǐyùchǎng [个 gè]

staff NOUN
职员 zhíyuán [名 míng]

staffroom NOUN
员工室 yuángōngshì [间 jiān]

stage NOUN
1 舞台 wǔtái [个 gè] *(in theatre)*
2 讲台 jiǎngtái [个 gè] *(for speeches, lectures)*
■ **at this stage** 在这个阶段 zài zhègè jiēduàn □ At this stage, it's too early to comment. 在这个阶段作评论还为之过早。Zài zhègè jiēduàn zuòpínglùn hái wéizhīguòzǎo.
■ **to do something in stages** 按步骤做某事 àn bùzhòu zuò mǒushì

stain NOUN
▷ *see also* **stain** VERB
污迹 wūjì [处 chù]

to **stain** VERB
▷ *see also* **stain** NOUN
沾污 zhānwū

stainless steel NOUN
不锈钢 bùxiù gāng

stain remover NOUN
除锈剂 chúxiùjì [种 zhǒng]

stair NOUN
梯级 tījí [层 céng] *(step)*

staircase NOUN
楼梯 lóutī [个 gè]

stairs PL NOUN
楼梯 lóutī

stale ADJECTIVE
不新鲜的 bùxīnxiānde *(bread)*

stall NOUN
货摊 huòtān [个 gè]
□ He's got a market stall. 他有个市场货摊。Tā yǒugè shìchǎnghuòtān.
■ **the stalls** *(in cinema, theatre)* 正厅 zhèngtīng

stamina NOUN
毅力 yìlì

stammer NOUN
口吃 kǒuchī
■ **He's got a stammer.** 他口吃。Tā kǒuchī.

stamp NOUN
▷ *see also* **stamp** VERB
1 邮票 yóupiào [枚 méi] *(for letter)*
□ My hobby is stamp collecting. 我的爱好是收集邮票。Wǒde àihào shì shōujíyóupiào.
■ **a stamp album** 一个集邮册 yígè jíyóucè
2 章 zhāng [个 gè] *(in passport)*
3 橡皮图章 xiàngpítúzhāng [枚 méi] *(rubber stamp)*

to **stamp** VERB
▷ *see also* **stamp** NOUN
盖章于 gàizhāng yú *(passport, visa)*
■ **to stamp one's foot** 跺脚 duòjiǎo

stamped ADJECTIVE
贴了邮票的 tiēle yóupiào de
□ The letter wasn't stamped. 这封信没有贴邮票。Zhèfēng xìn méiyǒu tiē yóupiào.
■ **Enclose a stamped addressed envelope.** 请附上一个贴了邮票写好地址的信封。Qǐng fùshàng yígè tiēle yóupiào xiěhǎo dìzhǐde xìnfēng.

to **stand** VERB
1 站立 zhànlì
□ He was standing by the door. 他站在门边。Tā zhànzài ménbiān.
2 站起来 zhàn qǐlái *(stand up)*
□ They all stood when I came in. 我进去时他们都站起来了。Wǒ jìnqùshí tāmen dōu zhànqǐlái le.
3 容忍 róngrěn *(tolerate, withstand)*
□ I can't stand all this noise. 我没法容忍这些噪音。Wǒ méifǎ róngrěn zhèxiē zàoyīn.

to **stand for** VERB
1 代表 dàibiǎo *(be short for)*
□ 'BT' stands for 'British Telecom'. 'BT' 代表'英国电讯'。'BT' dàibiǎo 'Yīngguódiànxùn'.
2 容忍 róngrěn *(tolerate)*
□ I won't stand for it! 我不会容忍的！Wǒ búhuì róngrěnde!
■ **to stand in for somebody** 代替某人 dàitì mǒurén

to **stand out** VERB
醒目 xǐngmù
□ None of the candidates really stood out. 没有一个候选人很醒目。Méiyǒu yígè hòuxuǎnrén hěn xǐngmù.
■ **She really stands out in that orange coat.** 那件橘黄色的衣服使她看起来很醒目。Nàjiàn júhuángsède yīfú shǐtā kànqǐlái hěn xǐngmù.

to **stand up** VERB
起立 qǐlì *(get up)*

■ **to stand up for** 捍卫 hànwèi □ Stand up for your rights! 捍卫你的权利！ Hànwèi nǐde quánlì!

standard NOUN
▷ *see also* **standard** ADJECTIVE
标准 biāozhǔn [种 zhǒng]
□ The standard is very high. 标准很高。 Biāozhǔn hěn gāo.
■ **the standard of living** 生活标准 shēnghuóbiāozhǔn
■ **She's got high standards.** 她的标准很高。Tāde biāozhǔn hěn gāo.

standard ADJECTIVE
▷ *see also* **standard** NOUN
1 普通的 pǔtōng de *(size)*
2 标准的 biāozhǔn de *(procedure, practice)*
3 规范的 guīfàn de *(model, feature)*

stank VERB ▷ *see* **stink**

staple NOUN
▷ *see also* **staple** VERB
钉书钉 dìngshūdīng [枚 méi]

to **staple** VERB
▷ *see also* **staple** NOUN
分等级 fēnděngjí

stapler NOUN
钉书器 dìngshūqì [个 gè]

star NOUN
▷ *see also* **star** VERB
1 星 xīng [颗 kē] *(in sky)*
2 明星 míngxīng [个 gè] *(celebrity)*
LANGUAGE TIP Word for word, this means 'bright star'.
□ He's a TV star. 他是个电视明星。Tā shì gè diànshì míngxīng.
■ **the stars** *(horoscope)* 星宿 xīngxiù

to **star** VERB
▷ *see also* **star** NOUN
主演 zhǔyǎn
■ **to star in a film** 主演一部电影 zhǔyǎn yíbùdiànyǐng
■ **The film stars Glenda Jackson.** 该电影的主演是格伦达・杰克逊。 Gāi diànyǐngde zhǔyǎn shì Gélúndá Jiékèxùn.
■ **... starring Johnny Depp** …主演强尼・德普 ...zhǔyǎn Qiángní Dépǔ.

to **stare** VERB
■ **to stare at something** 盯着某物 dīngzhe mǒuwù

start NOUN
▷ *see also* **start** VERB
1 开始 kāishǐ [个 gè]
□ It's not much, but it's a start. 不多，但这只是一个开始。Bùduō,dàn zhè zhǐshì yígè kāishǐ.
■ **Shall we make a start on the washing-up?** 我们开始洗碗吧？ Wǒmen kāishǐ xǐwǎn ba?
2 起点 qǐdiǎn *(of race)*

to **start** VERB
▷ *see also* **start** NOUN
1 开始 kāishǐ *(begin)*
□ What time does it start? 什么时候开始？ Shénme shíhòu kāishǐ?
■ **to start doing something** 开始做某事 kāishǐ zuò mǒushì □ I started learning French three years ago. 我三年前开始学法语。Wǒ sānniánqián kāishǐ xué Fǎyǔ.
2 创建 chuàngjiàn *(organization)*
□ He wants to start his own business. 他希望创建自己的公司。Tā xīwàng chuàngjiàn zìjǐde gōngsī.
3 发起 fāqǐ *(campaign)*
□ She started a campaign against drugs. 她发起了一个反对毒品的运动。Tā fāqǐ le yígè fǎnduì dúpǐn de yùndòng.
4 启动 qǐdòng *(engine, car)*
□ He couldn't start the car. 他没法启动车。Tā méifǎ qǐdòngchē. □ The car wouldn't start. 车启动不了。Chē qǐdòng bùliǎo.

to **start off** VERB
开始 kāishǐ *(leave)*
□ We started off first thing in the morning. 早晨我们开始了第一件事。Zǎochén wǒmen kāishǐ le dìyījiànshì.

to **start on** VERB
开始 kāishǐ

to **start up** VERB
创办 chuàngbàn

starter NOUN
开胃菜 kāiwèi cài [道 dào]

to **starve** VERB
饿死 èsǐ *(die from hunger)*
■ **I'm starving!** *(very hungry)* 我饿极了！ Wǒ è jí le!

state NOUN
▷ *see also* **state** VERB
1 状态 zhuàngtài [种 zhǒng]
□ The house was in a poor state. 房子的状况很差。Fángzi de zhuàngkuàng hěnchà.
□ She was in a state of depression. 她很忧郁的状态。Tā hěn yōuyùde zhuàngtài.
2 国家 guójiā [个 gè] *(country)*
□ It's an independent state. 它是个独立的国家。Tā shì gè dúlìde guójiā.
■ **the state** *(government)* 政府 zhèngfǔ
■ **the States** *(USA)* 美国 Měiguó

to **state** VERB
▷ *see also* **state** NOUN
1 声明 shēngmíng *(say)*
□ He stated his intention to resign. 他声明

他打算辞职。Tā shēngmíng tā dǎsuàn cízhí.
2 提供 tígòng *(give)*
□ Please state your name and address. 请提供你的姓名和地址。Qǐng tígòng nǐde xìngmíng hé dìzhǐ.

statement NOUN
声明 shēngmíng [个 gè]

station NOUN
车站 chēzhàn [个 gè] *(railway)*
■ **the bus station** 公共汽车站 gōnggòngqìchēzhàn
■ **a police station** 一家警察局 yìjiā jǐngchájú
■ **a radio station** 一家电台 yìjiādiàntái

stationer's NOUN
文具店 wénjùdiàn [家 jiā]

station wagon NOUN (US)
旅行车 lǚxíngchē [辆 liàng]

statue NOUN
塑像 sùxiàng [尊 zūn]

stay NOUN
▷ *see also* **stay** VERB
逗留 dòuliú [次 cì]
□ my stay in China 我在中国逗留 wǒ zài Zhōngguó dòuliú

to **stay** VERB
▷ *see also* **stay** NOUN
1 呆 dāi *(in place, position)*
□ Stay here! 呆在这儿！ Dāi zàizhèr!
□ We stayed in Scotland for a few days. 我们在苏格兰呆了几天。Wǒmen zài Sūgélán dāile jǐtiān.
2 暂住 zànzhù *(in town, hotel, someone's house)*
■ **to stay with friends** 在朋友家暂住 zài péngyǒujiā zànzhù □ Where are you staying? 你住在哪儿？ Nǐ zhùzài nǎr?
■ **to stay the night** 过夜 guòyè

to **stay in** VERB
呆在家里 dāizài jiālǐ *(not go out)*

to **stay up** VERB
熬夜 áoyè
□ We stayed up till midnight. 我们熬夜到午夜。Wǒmen áoyè dào wǔyè.

steady ADJECTIVE
1 稳步的 wěnbùde
□ steady progress 稳步的进展 wěnbùde jìnzhǎn
2 固定的 gùdìng de
□ a steady job 一份固定的工作 yífèn gùdìngde gōngzuò
3 坚定的 jiāndìngde *(voice, hand)*
4 稳重的 wěnzhòngde *(person)*
■ **a steady boyfriend** 一个固定的男友 yígè gùdìngde nányǒu
■ **a steady girlfriend** 一个固定的女友 yígè gùdìngde nǚyǒu

steak NOUN
牛排 niúpái [份 fèn]
□ steak and chips 牛排和薯条 niúpái hé shǔtiáo

to **steal** VERB
1 偷窃 tōuqiè
■ **He stole it from me.** 他从我这里把它偷走了。Tā cóng wǒ zhèlǐ bǎ tā tōuzǒu le.
2 行窃 xíngqiè
□ It's wrong to steal. 行窃是错的。Xíngqiè shìcuòde.

steam NOUN
蒸汽 zhēngqì
□ a steam engine 一台蒸汽机 yìtái zhēngqìjī

steel NOUN
钢铁 gāngtiě
□ a steel door 一个钢铁门 yígè gāngtiěmén

steep ADJECTIVE
陡的 dǒu de

steering wheel NOUN
方向盘 fāngxiàng pán [个 gè]

step NOUN
▷ *see also* **step** VERB
1 步 bù *(pace)*
□ He took a step forward. 他向前走了一步。Tā xiàngqián zǒule yíbù.
2 梯级 tījí [层 céng] *(stair)*
□ She tripped over the step. 她被楼梯绊倒了。Tā bèi lóutī bàndǎo le.

to **step** VERB
▷ *see also* **step** NOUN
迈步 màibù
■ **to step aside** 避开 bìkāi
■ **to step back** 后退 hòutuì

stepbrother NOUN
1 异母兄弟 yìmǔ xiōngdì [个 gè] *(with shared father)*
2 异父兄弟 yìfù xiōngdì [个 gè] *(with shared mother)*

stepdaughter NOUN
继女 jìnǚ [个 gè]

stepfather NOUN
继父 jìfù [位 wèi]

stepladder NOUN
活梯 huótī [个 gè]

stepmother NOUN
继母 jìmǔ [位 wèi]

stepsister NOUN
1 异母姐妹 yìmǔ jiěmèi [个 gè] *(with shared father)*
2 异父姐妹 yìfù jiěmèi [个 gè] *(with shared mother)*

stepson NOUN
继子 jìzǐ [个 gè]
stereo NOUN
立体声装置 lìtǐ shēng zhuāngzhì [套 tào]
sterling ADJECTIVE
■ **one pound sterling** 一英镑 yì yīngbàng
stew NOUN
炖的食物 dùn de shíwù [种 zhǒng]
steward NOUN
乘务员 chéngwù yuán [位 wèi]
stewardess NOUN
女乘务员 nǚ chéngwù yuán [位 wèi]
stick NOUN
▷ *see also* **stick** VERB
1 棍子 gùnzi [根 gēn]
2 拐杖 guǎizhàng [根 gēn] *(walking stick)*
to **stick** VERB
▷ *see also* **stick** NOUN
粘 zhān
□ Stick the stamps on the envelope. 将邮票粘在信封上。Jiāng yóupiào zhānzài xìnfēngshàng.
to **stick out** VERB
伸出 shēnchū
□ A pen was sticking out of his pocket. 一只笔从他的口袋里伸出。Yìzhībǐ cóng tāde kǒudàilǐ shēnchū.
■ **Stick your tongue out and say 'ah'.** 伸出舌头说'啊'。Shēnchū shétóu shuō 'ā'.
sticker NOUN
不干胶标签 bù gānjiāo biāoqiān [个 gè]
sticky ADJECTIVE
1 黏的 nián de
■ **to have sticky hands** 手黏 shǒunián
2 黏性的 niánxìng de
□ a sticky label 黏标签 niánbiāoqiān
stiff ADJECTIVE, ADVERB
1 酸痛的 suāntòng de *(person)*
■ **to feel stiff** 感到酸痛 gǎndàosuāntòng
2 僵硬的 jiāngyìng de *(neck, arm)*
■ **to have a stiff neck** 脖子僵硬 bózi jiāngyìng
■ **to be bored stiff** 讨厌极了 tǎoyàn jíle
3 呆板的 dāibǎnde
■ **to be frozen stiff** 冻僵了 dòngjiāngle
■ **to be scared stiff** 吓死了 xiàsǐle
still ADJECTIVE
▷ *see also* **still** ADVERB
1 不动的 bùdòng de
■ **Keep still!** 别动！ Biédòng!
■ **Sit still!** 坐着别动！ Zuòzhe biédòng!
2 无气泡的 wú qìpào de *(not fizzy)*
□ Would you like sparkling water or still water? 你要有气的水还是无气的水？ Nǐ yào yǒuqìdeshuǐ háishì wúqìdeshuǐ?

still ADVERB
▷ *see also* **still** ADJECTIVE
1 仍然 réngrán
□ Are you still in bed? 你仍然在床上吗？ Nǐ réngrán zài chuángshàng ma? □ Do you still live in London? 你仍然住在伦敦吗？ Nǐ réngrán zhùzài Lúndūn ma?
2 还 hái
□ He still hasn't arrived. 他还没到。Tā hái méi dào.
3 尽管如此 jǐnguǎn rúcǐ *(nonetheless)*
□ She knows I don't like it, but she still does it. 她知道我不喜欢，尽管如此她还那样做。Tā zhīdào wǒ bùxǐhuan, jǐnguǎn rúcǐ tā hái nàyàng zuò.
4 毕竟 bìjìng *(after all)*
□ Still, it's the thought that counts. 毕竟，有心意就行了。Bìjìng, yǒuxīnyì jiù xíngle.
■ **better still** 更好的 gènghǎode
sting NOUN
▷ *see also* **sting** VERB
刺 cì [根 gēn]
□ a bee sting 蜜蜂刺 mìfēngcì
to **sting** VERB
▷ *see also* **sting** NOUN
叮 dīng
□ I've been stung. 我被叮了。Wǒ bèidīng le.
stingy ADJECTIVE
吝啬的 lìnsède
stink NOUN
▷ *see also* **stink** VERB
恶臭 èchòu [种 zhǒng]
□ the stink of garlic 臭蒜味 chòusuàn wèi
to **stink** VERB
▷ *see also* **stink** NOUN
发臭 fāchòu
□ It stinks! 那很臭！ Nà hěn chòu!
to **stir** VERB
搅动 jiǎodòng
stitch NOUN
1 针 zhēn *(in sewing)*
2 缝针 féngzhēn [枚 méi] *(in wound)*
□ I had five stitches. 我缝了五针。Wǒ féngle wǔzhēn.
stock NOUN
▷ *see also* **stock** VERB
1 供应物 gōngyìng wù [种 zhǒng]
■ **in stock** 有货 yǒuhuò
■ **out of stock** 没货 méihuò
2 汤料 tāngliào
□ chicken stock 鸡汤料 jītāngliào
3 股票 gǔpiào [支 zhī]
to **stock** VERB
▷ *see also* **stock** NOUN
有货 yǒuhuò *(have in stock)*

□ Do you stock camping stoves? 露营炉有货吗？ Lùyínglú yǒuhuò ma?

to **stock up** VERB

■ **to stock up with something** 储备某物 chǔbèi mǒuwù

stock cube NOUN

固体汤料 gùtǐtāngliào [个 gè]

stock exchange NOUN

股票交易所 gǔpiào jiāoyì suǒ [个 gè]

stocking NOUN

长统袜 chángtǒng wà [双 shuāng]

stole, stolen VERB ▷ *see* **steal**

stomach NOUN

胃 wèi [个 gè]

■ **to have an upset stomach** 胃不舒服 wèi bùshūfu

stomachache NOUN

■ **to have stomachache** 胃痛 wèitòng

stone NOUN

1 石头 shítou [块 kuài]

□ a stone wall 一堵石头墙 yìdǔ shítóuqiáng

2 石子 shízǐ [颗 kē] *(pebble)*

3 核 hú [个 gè] *(in fruit)*

□ a peach stone 一个桃核 yígètáohú

■ **I weigh eight stone.** 我重一百一十二磅。Wǒ zhòng yìbǎi yīshíèr bàng.

stood VERB ▷ *see* **stand**

stool NOUN

凳子 dèngzi [个 gè]

to **stop** VERB

▷ *see also* **stop** NOUN

1 停 tíng

□ The bus doesn't stop there. 公车不在这里停。Gōngchē bú zài zhèlǐ tíng.

2 停止 tíngzhǐ

□ The music stopped. 音乐停了。Yīnyuè tíngle. □ I think the rain's going to stop. 我想雨会停的。Wǒ xiǎng yǔ huì tíngde.

■ **to stop doing something** 停止做某事 tíngzhǐ zuò mǒushì □ He's stopped going to dance lessons. 他停止去上舞蹈课了。Tā tíngzhǐ qù shàng wǔdǎokè le.

■ **to stop smoking** 戒烟 jièyān

3 阻止 zǔzhǐ *(prevent)*

□ a campaign to stop whaling 一个为了阻止捕鲸的活动 yígè wèile zǔzhǐ bǔjīngde huódòng

■ **to stop somebody doing something** 阻止某人做某事 zǔzhǐ mǒurén zuò mǒushì □ She wants to stop us seeing each other. 她想阻止我们见面。Tā xiǎng zǔzhǐ wǒmen jiànmiàn.

■ **Stop crying!** 别哭了！ Biékū le!

■ **Stop it!** 住手！ Zhùshǒu!

■ **Stop!** 停止！ Tíngzhǐ!

stop NOUN

▷ *see also* **stop** VERB

车站 chēzhàn [个 gè]

□ a bus stop 一个公车站 yígè gōngchēzhàn □ This is my stop. 这是我下车的车站。Zhèshì wǒ xiàchēde chēzhàn.

stoplight NOUN (US)

交通信号灯 jiāotōng xìnhào dēng [个 gè] *(in road)*

stopwatch NOUN

秒表 miǎobiǎo [只 zhī]

store NOUN

▷ *see also* **store** VERB

1 大商店 dà shāngdiàn [家 jiā] *(large shop)*

□ a furniture store 一家家具店 yìjiā jiājùdiàn

2 店铺 diànpù [家 jiā] (US: *shop*)

3 储藏 chǔcáng *(stock, storeroom)*

to **store** VERB

▷ *see also* **store** NOUN

1 存放 cúnfàng

□ They store potatoes in the cellar. 他们把土豆存放在地窖里。Tāmen bǎ tǔdòu cúnfàngzài dìjiàolǐ.

2 存储 cúnchǔ *(information)*

storey (US **story**) NOUN

层 céng

□ a three-storey building 一栋三层的楼房 yídòng sāncéng de lóufáng

storm NOUN

暴风雨 bàofēngyǔ [场 chǎng]

stormy ADJECTIVE

有暴风雨的 yǒu bàofēngyǔ de

story NOUN

1 描述 miáoshù [种 zhǒng] *(account)*

2 故事 gùshì [个 gè] *(tale)*

3 报道 bàodào [条 tiáo] *(in newspaper)*

4 层 céng (US: *of building*)

stove NOUN

炉子 lúzi [个 gè]

straight ADJECTIVE, ADVERB

1 直的 zhí de

□ a straight line 一条直线 yìtiáo zhíxiàn

□ straight hair 直发 zhífà

2 异性恋 yìxìngliàn *(heterosexual)*

■ **straight away** 马上 mǎshàng

■ **straight on** 径直的 jìngzhíde

straightforward ADJECTIVE

简单的 jiǎndān de

strain NOUN

▷ *see also* **strain** VERB

心理负担 xīnlǐ fùdān [个 gè] *(pressure)*

□ It was a strain. 那是个心理负担。Nà shì gè xīnlǐ fùdān.

to **strain** VERB

▷ *see also* **strain** NOUN

扭伤 niǔshāng

□ I strained my back. 我扭伤了我的背。 Wǒ niǔshāng le wǒde bèi.

■ **to strain a muscle** 扭伤肌肉 niǔshāng jīròu

strained ADJECTIVE

扭伤的 niǔshāngde *(muscle)*

stranded ADJECTIVE

困住的 kùnzhùde

□ We were stranded. 我们被困住了。Wǒmen bèi kùnzhù le.

strange ADJECTIVE

1 奇怪的 qíguài de *(odd)*

□ That's strange! 那很奇怪！ Nà hěn qíguài!

2 陌生的 mòshēng de *(unfamiliar)*

stranger NOUN

陌生人 mòshēng rén [个 gè]

□ Don't talk to strangers. 别跟陌生人讲话。Biégēn mòshēngrén jiǎnghuà.

■ **I'm a stranger here.** 我在这儿是个陌生人。Wǒ zàizhèr shìge mòshēngrén.

to **strangle** VERB

勒死 lēisǐ

strap NOUN

带 dài [根 gēn] *(of watch, bag)*

straw NOUN

1 稻草 dàocǎo *(for animals)*

2 吸管 xīguǎn [根 gēn] *(for drinking)*

■ **That's the last straw!** 那是最后一击。Nàshì zuìhòu yìjī.

strawberry NOUN

草莓 cǎoméi [个 gè]

□ strawberry jam 草莓酱 cǎoméijiàng. □ a strawberry ice cream 一个草莓冰激凌 yígè cǎoméi bīngjīlíng

stray NOUN

走失 zǒushī

■ **a stray cat** 一只走丢的猫 yìzhī zǒudīude māo

stream NOUN

溪流 xīliú [条 tiáo]

street NOUN

街道 jiēdào [条 tiáo]

□ in the street 在街上 zàijiēshàng

streetcar NOUN (US)

有轨电车 yǒuguǐ diànchē [部 bù]

streetlamp NOUN

街灯 jiēdēng [个 gè]

street plan NOUN

街道计划 jiēdàojìhuà [个 gè]

strength NOUN

1 力气 lìqi

■ **with all his strength** 他的全力 tāde quánlì

2 强度 qiángdù *(of object, material)*

stress NOUN

▷ *see also* **stress** VERB

压力 yālì [个 gè]

to **stress** VERB

▷ *see also* **stress** NOUN

强调 qiángdiào

□ I would like to stress that ... 我想强调…。Wǒ xiǎng qiángdiào ....

stressful ADJECTIVE

紧张的 jǐnzhāng de

to **stretch** VERB

1 伸懒腰 shēn lǎnyāo

□ The dog woke up and stretched. 狗醒来伸懒腰。Gǒu xǐnglái shēnlǎnyāo.

2 变大 biàndà *(get bigger)*

□ My sweater stretched when I washed it. 洗毛衣时毛衣变大了。Xǐmáoyīshí máoyī biàndà le.

3 伸展 shēnzhǎn *(stretch out)*

□ They stretched a rope between two trees. 他们在两棵树之间伸展了一条绳子。Tāmen zài liǎngkeshù zhījiān shēnzhǎnle yìtiáo shéngzi.

■ **to stretch out one's arms** 伸胳膊 shēn gēbo

to **stretch out** VERB

伸出 shēnchū *(arm, leg)*

stretcher NOUN

担架 dānjià [个 gè]

stretchy ADJECTIVE

有弹性的 yǒutánxìngde

strict ADJECTIVE

1 严格的 yángé de *(rule, instruction)*

2 严厉的 yánlì de *(person)*

strike NOUN

▷ *see also* **strike** VERB

罢工 bàgōng [次 cì]

■ **to be on strike** 在罢工 zài bàgōng

■ **to go on strike** 进行罢工 jìnxíng bàgōng

to **strike** VERB

▷ *see also* **strike** NOUN

1 罢工 bàgōng *(go on strike)*

2 报时 bàoshí *(clock)*

□ The clock struck three. 钟报时三点。Zhōng bàoshí sāndiǎn.

3 打 dǎ *(hit)*

■ **to strike a match** 点燃火柴 diǎnrán huǒchái

striker NOUN

1 罢工者 bàgōng zhě [名 míng] *(person on strike)*

2 前锋 qiánfēng [个 gè] *(footballer)*

striking ADJECTIVE

1 罢工的 bàgōngde *(on strike)*

□ striking miners 罢工的矿工 bàgōngde kuànggōng

2 明显的 míngxiǎnde *(noticeable)*

□ a striking difference 一个明显的不同 yígè míngxiǎnde bùtóng

string NOUN

1 细绳 xìshéng [根 gēn]
□ a piece of string 一根细绳 yìgēn xìshéng

2 弦 xián [根 gēn] *(on guitar, violin)*

strip NOUN
▷ *see also* **strip** VERB
狭条 xiátiáo [条 tiáo] *(of paper, cloth)*
■ **a strip cartoon** 一个连环漫画 yígè liánhuánmànhuà

to **strip** VERB
▷ *see also* **strip** NOUN
脱光衣服 tuōguāng yīfu *(undress)*

stripe NOUN
条纹 tiáowén [个 gè]

striped ADJECTIVE
有条纹的 yǒu tiáowén de
□ a striped skirt 一条有条纹的裙子 yìtiáo yǒu tiáowénde qúnzi

stripper NOUN
脱衣舞者 tuōyīwǔzhě [个 gè]

stripy ADJECTIVE
有条纹的 yǒutiáowénde
□ a stripy shirt 一件有条纹的衬衫 yíjiàn yǒutiáowénde chènshān

stroke NOUN
▷ *see also* **stroke** VERB
中风 zhòngfēng [次 cì]
■ **to have a stroke** 中风 zhòngfēng

to **stroke** VERB
▷ *see also* **stroke** NOUN
抚摸 fǔmō

stroll NOUN
闲逛 xiánguàng
■ **to go for a stroll** 去闲逛 qù xiánguàng
LANGUAGE TIP Word for word, this means 'to go on leisurely steps'.

stroller NOUN (US)
婴儿小推车 yīng'ér xiǎo tuīchē [辆 liàng]

strong ADJECTIVE

1 有力的 yǒulì de *(person, arms, grip)*
□ She's very strong. 她很有力。Tā hěn yǒulì.

2 牢固的 láogù de *(object, material)*

3 强劲的 qiángjìng de *(wind, current)*

strongly ADVERB
强力地 qiánglìde
□ We recommend strongly that ... 我们强力推荐… Wǒmen qiánglì tuījiàn...
■ **He smelt strongly of tobacco.** 他身上的烟味很浓。Tā shēnshàngde yānwèi hěn nóng.

struck VERB ▷ *see* **strike**

to **struggle** VERB
▷ *see also* **struggle** NOUN
挣扎 zhēngzhá
□ He struggled, but he couldn't escape. 他挣扎着，但是没能逃脱。Tā zhēngzházhe, dànshì méinéng táotuō.
■ **to struggle to do something** 1 *(fight)* 尽力做某事 jìnlì zuò mǒushì □ He struggled to get custody of his daughter. 他尽力争取他女儿的监护权。Tā jìnlì zhēngqǔ tānǚérde jiānhùquán. 2 *(have difficulty)* 艰难做某事 jiānnán zuò mǒushì □ She struggled to get the door open. 她艰难地把门打开。Tā jiānnándè bǎmen dǎkāi.

struggle NOUN
▷ *see also* **struggle** VERB
斗争 dòuzhēng [次 cì] *(for independence, equality)*
■ **It was a struggle.** 那是个斗争。Nàshìgè dòuzhēng.

stubborn ADJECTIVE
倔强的 juèjiàng de

to **stub out** VERB
踩熄 cǎixī *(cigarette)*

stuck VERB ▷ *see* **stick**

stuck ADJECTIVE
卡住 qiǎzhù *(object)*
□ It's stuck. 卡住了。Qiǎzhùle.
■ **to get stuck** 困住 kùnzhù □ We got stuck in a traffic jam. 我们在交通堵塞中困住了。Wǒmen zài jiāotōng dǔsè zhōng kùnzhù le.

student NOUN

1 大学生 dà xuéshēng [名 míng] *(at university)*
□ a law student 一名法律学生 yìmíng fǎlǜ xuéshēng

2 中学生 zhōng xuéshēng [名 míng] *(at school)*

studio NOUN

1 演播室 yǎnbō shì [个 gè] *(TV, radio)*
□ a TV studio 一个电视演播室 yígè diànshìyǎnbōshì

2 画室 huàshì [个 gè] *(of artist)*
■ **a studio flat** 一套一居室公寓 yítàoyìjūshìgōngyù

study NOUN
▷ *see also* **study** VERB
书房 shūfáng [间 jiān] *(room)*

to **study** VERB
▷ *see also* **study** NOUN

1 攻读 gōngdú *(subject)*
□ I plan to study biology. 我计划攻读生物学。Wǒ jìhuà gōngdú shēngwùxué.

2 学习 xuéxí *(do homework)*
□ I've got to study tonight. 我今晚要学习。Wǒ jīnwǎn yào xuéxí.

stuff NOUN

1 物品 wùpǐn *(things)*

□ There's some stuff on the table for you. 桌上有些给你的物品。Zhuōshàng yǒuxiē gěinǐde wùpǐn.
2 东西 dōngxi *(possessions)*
□ Have you got all your stuff? 带上你所有的东西了吗？Dàishàng nǐ suǒyǒude dōngxī le ma?
3 东西 dōngxi *(substance)*
□ I need some stuff for hay fever. 我需要一些治花粉症的东西。Wǒ xūyào yìxiē zhì huāfěnzhèngde dōngxi.

stuffy ADJECTIVE
闷热的 mēnrè de
■ **It's really stuffy in here.** 这里很闷热。Zhèlǐ hěn mēnrè.

to **stumble** VERB
绊倒 bàndǎo

stung VERB ▷ *see* **sting**

stunk VERB ▷ *see* **stink**

stunned ADJECTIVE
震惊 zhènjīng *(amazed)*
□ I was stunned. 我很震惊。Wǒ hěn zhènjīng.

stunning ADJECTIVE
1 惊人的 jīngrén de *(impressive)*
2 极漂亮的 jí piàoliang de *(beautiful)*

stunt NOUN
特技 tèjì [个 gè] *(in film)*

stuntman NOUN
特技演员 tèjì yǎnyuán [个 gè]

stupid ADJECTIVE
1 笨的 bèn de
2 愚蠢的 yúchǔn de *(question, idea, mistake)*

to **stutter** VERB
▷ *see also* **stutter** NOUN
口吃 kǒuchī

stutter NOUN
▷ *see also* **stutter** VERB
口吃 kǒuchī
□ He's got a stutter. 他口吃。Tā kǒuchī.

style NOUN
1 风度 fēngdù *(elegance)*
2 风格 fēnggé *(way of doing things)*
□ That's not his style. 这不是他的风格。Zhè búshì tāde fēnggé.

subject NOUN
1 主题 zhǔtí [个 gè]
□ The subject of my project was the internet. 我项目的主题是因特网。Wǒ xiàngmùde zhǔtí shì yīntèwǎng.
2 科目 kēmù [个 gè] *(at school)*
□ What's your favourite subject? 你最喜欢的科目是什么？Nǐ zuìxǐhuānde kēmù shì shénme?

submarine NOUN
潜水艇 qiánshuǐtǐng [艘 sōu]

substance NOUN
物质 wùzhì [种 zhǒng]

substitute NOUN
▷ *see also* **substitute** VERB
1 代替者 dàitì zhě [位 wèi] *(person)*
2 代用品 dàiyòngpǐn [件 jiàn] *(thing)*

to **substitute** VERB
▷ *see also* **substitute** NOUN
代替 dàitì
□ to substitute A for B 用A代替B yòng A dài tì B

subtitled ADJECTIVE
有字幕的 yǒuzìmùde

subtitles PL NOUN
字幕 zìmù
□ a Chinese film with English subtitles 有英文字幕的中文电影 yǒu Yīngwénzìmùde Zhōngwéndiànyǐng

> **DID YOU KNOW...?**
> Because of the wide variety of regional languages and dialects in China, most television programmes are broadcast with subtitles by default, especially on state-controlled television channels.

subtle ADJECTIVE
微妙的 wēimiàode

to **subtract** VERB
减去 jiǎnqù
■ **to subtract 3 from 5** 五减三 wǔjiǎnsān

suburb NOUN
郊区 jiāoqū [个 gè]
□ a suburb of Beijing 北京的一个郊区 Běijīng de yígè jiāoqū
■ **the suburbs** 郊区 jiāoqū □ They live in the suburbs. 他们住在郊区。Tāmen zhùzài jiāoqū.

subway NOUN
1 地道 dìdào *(underpass)*
2 地铁 dìtiě [条 tiáo] (US: *underground railway*)

to **succeed** VERB
成功 chénggōng
■ **to succeed in doing something** 成功地做某事 chénggōng de zuò mǒushì

success NOUN
成功 chénggōng [个 gè]
□ The play was a great success. 这部剧很成功。Zhèbùjù hěn chénggōng.
■ **without success** 一无所成 yī wú suǒ chéng

successful ADJECTIVE
成功的 chénggōng de
□ He's a successful businessman. 他是位成功的商人。Tā shìwèi chénggōngde shāngrén. □ a successful attempt 一次成

功的尝试 yícì chénggōngde chángshì
■ **to be successful in doing something** 成功的做了某事 chénggōngde zuòle mǒushi

successfully ADVERB
成功地 chénggōng de

such ADJECTIVE, ADVERB
如此 rúcǐ
□ such nice people 如此好的人 rúcǐhǎoderén □ such a long journey 如此长的旅程 rúcǐchángde lǚchéng
■ **such a lot of** 那么多 nàme duō □ such a lot of work 那么多的工作 nàmeduōde gōngzuò
■ **such as** *(like)* 像 xiàng □ hot countries, such as India 炎热的国家，像印度 yánrèdeguójiā, xiàng Yìndù
■ **not as such** 本身不是 běnshēngbúshì
□ He's not an expert as such, but ... 他本身不是个专家，但是… Tā běnshēn búshì gè zhuānjiā, dànshì...
■ **There's no such thing.** 没这样的事。Méi zhèyàngde shì. □ There's no such thing as the yeti. 没有雪人这回事。Méiyǒu xuérén zhèhuíshì.

such-and-such ADJECTIVE
这样的 zhèyàngde
□ such-and-such a place 这样的一个地方 zhèyàngde yíge dìfang

to **suck** VERB
吮吸 shǔnxī
■ **to suck one's thumb** 吮吸拇指 shǔnxī mǔzhǐ

sudden ADJECTIVE
意外的 yìwài de
□ a sudden change 一个意外的变化 yígè yìwàide biànhuà
■ **all of a sudden** 突然 tūrán

suddenly ADVERB
突然 tūrán
□ Suddenly, the door opened. 突然间，门开了。Tūránjiān, ménkāile.

suede NOUN
软羔皮 ruǎngāopí
□ a suede jacket 一件软羔皮夹克 yíjiàn ruǎngāopí jiákè

to **suffer** VERB
受苦 shòukǔ
□ They suffered a lot during the war. 他们在战争中受了很多苦。Tāmen zài zhànzhēngzhōng shòule hěnduō kǔ.
■ **to suffer from a disease** 受病痛之苦 shòu bìngtòng zhīkǔ □ I suffer from hay fever. 我受花粉症之苦。Wǒ shòu huāfěnzhèng zhīkǔ.

to **suffocate** VERB
窒息 zhìxī

sugar NOUN
糖 táng [勺 sháo]

to **suggest** VERB
建议 jiànyì
□ I suggested they set off early. 我建议他们早点出发。Wǒ jiànyì tāmén zǎodiǎn chūfā.

suggestion NOUN
建议 jiànyì [条 tiáo]
■ **to make a suggestion** 提建议 tí jiànyì

suicide NOUN
自杀 zìshā
■ **to commit suicide** 自杀 zìshā

suicide bomber NOUN
人肉炸弹 rénròu zhàdàn [个 gè]

suit NOUN
▷ *see also* **suit** VERB
西装 xīzhuāng [套 tào]

to **suit** VERB
▷ *see also* **suit** NOUN
1 对...合适 duì...héshì *(be convenient for)*
□ What time would suit you? 什么时间对你合适？ Shénme shíjiān duì nǐ héshì?
□ That suits me fine. 那对我很合适。Nà duì wǒ hěn héshì.
2 适合 shìhé *(look good on)*
□ That dress really suits you. 那件衣服很适合你。Nàjiàn yīfú hěnshìhénǐ.
■ **Suit yourself!** 随你的便！ Suí nǐdebiàn!

suitable ADJECTIVE
1 合适的 héshì de
□ a suitable time 一个合适的时间 yígè héshìde shíjiān
2 适合的 shìhé de *(clothes)*
□ suitable clothing 适合的衣服 shìhéde yīfú

suitcase NOUN
手提箱 shǒutíxiāng [个 gè]

to **sulk** VERB
生气 shēngqì

sultana NOUN
无子葡萄 wúzǐ pútáo [串 chuàn]

sum NOUN
1 算术题 suànshù tí [道 dào] *(calculation)*
□ She's good at sums. 她擅长算术题。Tā shàncháng suànshù tí.
2 数额 shù'é [笔 bǐ] *(amount)*
■ **a sum of money** 一笔钱 yìbǐqián

to **sum up** VERB
总结 zǒngjié

to **summarize** VERB
概括 gàikuò

summary NOUN
摘要 zhāiyào [个 gè]

summer NOUN
夏季 xiàjì [个 gè]

■ **in summer** 在夏季 zài xiàjì
■ **summer clothes** 夏季衣服 xiàjì yīfú
■ **the summer holidays** 暑假 shǔjià
■ **a summer camp** (US) 夏令营 xiàlìngyíng

summertime NOUN
夏季 xiàjì
■ **in summertime** 在夏季 zàixiàjì

summit NOUN
峰会 fēnghuì [次 cì]

sun NOUN
1 太阳 tàiyáng [轮 lún] *(in the sky)*
2 阳光 yángguāng *(sunshine)*
□ in the sun 在阳光下 zàiyángguāngxià

to **sunbathe** VERB
晒日光浴 shài rìguāngyù

sun block NOUN
防晒霜 fángshàishuāng

sunburn NOUN
晒斑 shàibān

sunburnt ADJECTIVE
晒伤的 shàishāng de
□ I got sunburnt. 我被晒伤了。Wǒ bèi shàishāng le.

Sunday NOUN
星期天 xīngqītiān [个 gè]
□ on Sunday 在星期天 zàixīngqītiān □ on Sundays 在星期天 zàixīngqītiān □ every Sunday 每个星期天 měigè xīngqītiān □ last Sunday 上个星期天 shànggè xīngqītiān □ next Sunday 下个星期天 xiàgè xīngqītiān

Sunday school NOUN
主日学校 zhǔrì xuéxiào
■ **to go to Sunday school** 去主日学校 qù zhǔrì xuéxiào

sunflower NOUN
向日葵 xiàngrìkuí [棵 kē]
□ sunflower seeds 向日葵籽 xiàngrìkuízǐ

sung VERB ▷ *see* **sing**

sunglasses PL NOUN
墨镜 mòjìng

sunk VERB ▷ *see* **sink**

sunlight NOUN
日光 rìguāng

sunny ADJECTIVE
晴朗的 qínglǎng de
□ a sunny morning 一个晴朗的早晨 yígè qínglǎngde zǎochén □ a sunny day 一个晴朗的日子 yígè qínglǎngde rìzǐ
■ **It's sunny.** 天气晴朗。Tiānqì qínglǎng.

sunrise NOUN
拂晓 fúxiǎo

sunroof NOUN
凉棚 liángpéng [个 gè]

sunscreen NOUN
遮光剂 zhēguāng jì [个 gè]

sunset NOUN
日落 rìluò [次 cì]

sunshine NOUN
阳光 yángguāng

sunstroke NOUN
中暑 zhòngshǔ
■ **to get sunstroke** 中暑 zhòngshǔ

suntan NOUN
晒黑 shàihēi [处 chù]
■ **to get a suntan** 晒黑 shàihēi
■ **suntan lotion** 防晒液 fángshàiyè
■ **suntan oil** 防晒油 fángshàiyóu

super ADJECTIVE
极好的 jíhǎo de

superb ADJECTIVE
极好的 jíhǎo de

supermarket NOUN
超级市场 chāojí shìchǎng [个 gè]

supernatural ADJECTIVE
超自然的 chāozìránde

superstitious ADJECTIVE
迷信的 míxìnde

to **supervise** VERB
监督 jiāndū

supervisor NOUN
督管 dūguǎn [位 wèi] *(in factory)*

supper NOUN
1 晚餐 wǎncān [顿 dùn] *(early evening)*
2 夜宵 yèxiāo [顿 dùn] *(late evening)*

supplement NOUN
补充 bǔchōng [个 gè]

supplies PL NOUN
供应 gōngyìng *(food)*

to **supply** VERB
▷ *see also* **supply** NOUN
提供 tígòng
■ **to supply somebody with something** 为某人提供某物 wèimǒurén tígòng mǒuwù
□ The centre supplied us with all the equipment. 中心提供给我们所有的器材。Zhōngxīn tígònggěi wǒmen suǒyǒude qìcái.

supply NOUN
▷ *see also* **supply** VERB
供应量 gōngyìng liàng
□ a supply of paper 纸的供应量 zhǐde gōngyìng liàng
■ **the water supply** *(to town)* 供水 gōngshuǐ

to **support** VERB
1 支持 zhīchí
□ My mum has always supported me. 我妈妈一直支持我。Wǒmāma yìzhí zhīchíwǒ.
□ What team do you support? 你支持哪个队？Nǐ zhīchí nǎgè duì?
2 供养 gōngyǎng *(financially)*

□ She had to support five children on her own. 她必须供养五个孩子。Tā bìxū gōngyǎng wǔgè háizi.

supporter NOUN
支持者 zhīchí zhě [个 gè]
□ a Liverpool supporter 一个利物浦队的支持者 yígè Lìwùpǔduìde zhīchízhě □ a supporter of the Labour Party 一个工党的支持者 yígè gōngdǎngde zhīchízhě

to **suppose** VERB
1 想 xiǎng
□ I suppose he's late. 我想他晚了。Wǒ xiǎng tā wǎnle.
2 假设 jiǎshè
□ Suppose you won the lottery. 假设你中了彩票。Jiǎshè nǐ zhòngle cǎipiào.
■ **I suppose so.** 我看是。Wǒ kàn shì.
■ **to be supposed to do something** 应该做某事 yīnggāi zuò mǒushì □ You're supposed to show your passport. 你应该出示你的护照。Nǐ yīnggāi chūshì nǐde hùzhào.

supposing CONJUNCTION
假使 jiǎshǐ
□ Supposing you won the lottery... 假使你中了彩票… Jiǎshǐ nǐ zhòngle cǎipiào...

sure ADJECTIVE
有把握的 yǒu bǎwò de
□ Are you sure? 你有把握吗？ Nǐ yǒu bǎwò ma?
■ **Sure!** 当然了！ Dāngrán le!
■ **to make sure that...** *(check)* 确保… bǎozhèng... □ I'm going to make sure the door's locked. 我要确保门锁了。Wǒ yào quèbǎo mén suǒ le.

surely ADVERB
肯定 kěndìngde
□ Surely you've been to London? 你肯定去过伦敦吧？ Nǐ kěndìng qùguò Lúndūn ba?
□ The shops are closed on Sundays, surely? 商店肯定周日关门了吧？ Shāngdiàn kěndìng zhōurì guānmén le ba?

to **surf** VERB
冲浪 chōnglàng
■ **to surf the Net** 网上冲浪 wǎngshàng chōnglàng

surface NOUN
表面 biǎomiàn [个 gè]
■ **on the surface** 在表面上 zài biǎomiàn shàng

surfboard NOUN
冲浪板 chōnglàng bǎn [块 kuài]

surfing NOUN
冲浪 chōnglàng
■ **to go surfing** 去冲浪 qù chōnglàng

surgeon NOUN
外科医师 wàikē yīshī [位 wèi]

surgery NOUN
1 外科手术 wàikē shǒushù [次 cì] *(treatment)*
2 诊所 zhěnsuǒ [家 jiā] *(room)*

surname NOUN
姓 xìng [个 gè]

surprise NOUN
▷ *see also* **surprise** VERB
意想不到的事物 yìxiǎng búdào de shìwù [个 gè] *(unexpected event)*
■ **to my surprise** 使我惊奇的是 shǐ wǒ jīngqí de shì □ To my surprise she arrived on time. 使我惊奇的是她按时到了。Shǐ wǒ jīngqí de shì tā ànshí dàole.

to **surprise** VERB
▷ *see also* **surprise** NOUN
使感到意外 shǐ gǎndào yìwài

surprised ADJECTIVE
惊讶的 jīngyà de
□ I was surprised to see him. 看到他我很惊讶。Kàndào tā wǒ hěn jīngyà.

surprising ADJECTIVE
出人意外的 chūrén yìwài de

to **surrender** VERB
投降 tóuxiáng

to **surround** VERB
包围 bāowéi
□ The police surrounded the house. 警察包围了房子。Jǐngchá bāowéi fángzi.
□ You're surrounded! 你被包围了！ Nǐ bèi bāowéile!
■ **surrounded by** 环绕 huánrào □ The house is surrounded by trees. 房子由树环绕着。Fángzi yóu shù huánràozhe.

surroundings PL NOUN
环境 huánjìng
□ a hotel in beautiful surroundings 环境优美的一家酒店 huánjìng yōuměide yìjiā jiǔdiàn

survey NOUN
民意测验 mínyì cèyàn [项 xiàng]

surveyor NOUN
1 检察员 jiǎncháyuán [位 wèi] *(of buildings)*
2 测量员 cèliángyuán [位 wèi] *(of land)*

to **survive** VERB
幸存 xìngcún

survivor NOUN
幸存者 xìngcúnzhě [个 gè]
□ There were no survivors. 没有幸存者。Méiyǒu xìngcúnzhě.

suspect NOUN
▷ *see also* **suspect** VERB
嫌疑犯 xiányí fàn [个 gè]

to **suspect** VERB
▷ *see also* **suspect** NOUN

1 怀疑 huáiyí *(person)*
■ to suspect somebody of a crime 怀疑某人犯罪 huáiyí mǒurén fànzuì □ He's suspected of murder. 他被怀疑谋杀。Tā bèi huáiyí móushā.
2 怀疑 huáiyí *(think)*
■ to suspect that... 怀疑… huáiyí...

to **suspend** VERB
1 暂停 zàntíng *(from school, team)*
□ He's been suspended. 他被暂停。Tā bèi zàntíng.
2 停职 tíngzhí *(from job)*

suspenders PL NOUN (US)
吊带 diàodài *(braces)*

suspense NOUN
1 焦虑 jiāolǜ
□ The suspense was terrible. 焦虑太恐怖了。Jiāolǜ tài kǒngbù le.
2 悬念 xuánniàn *(in story)*
□ a film with lots of suspense 有很多悬念的电影 yǒu hěnduō xuánniànde diànyǐng

suspicious ADJECTIVE
可疑的 kěyí de
□ He died in suspicious circumstances. 他死的很可疑。Tā sǐde hěn kěyí. □ He was suspicious at first. 开始他很可疑。Kāishǐ tā hěn kěyí.

to **swallow** VERB
吞下 tūnxià

swam VERB ▷ *see* **swim**

swan NOUN
天鹅 tiān'é [只 zhī]

to **swap** VERB
交换 jiāohuàn
□ Do you want to swap? 你要交换吗？Nǐyào jiāohuàn ma?
■ to swap A for B 以A换B yǐ A huàn B
■ to swap places with somebody 与某人换位子 yǔ mǒurén huàn wèizi

to **swear** VERB
发誓 fāshì *(make an oath, curse)*

swear word NOUN
骂人的话 màrén de huà [句 jù]

to **sweat** VERB
▷ *see also* **sweat** NOUN
出汗 chūhàn

sweat NOUN
▷ *see also* **sweat** VERB
汗 hàn

sweater NOUN
毛衣 máoyī [件 jiàn]

sweatshirt NOUN
棉毛衫 miánmáoshān [件 jiàn]

sweaty ADJECTIVE
1 出汗 chūhàn *(person, face)*
□ I'm all sweaty. 我出了很多汗。Wǒ chūle hěnduō hàn.
2 爱出汗的 ài chūhànde *(hands)*

Swede NOUN
瑞典人 Ruìdiǎnrén [位 wèi] *(person)*

swede NOUN
甘蓝 gānlán [颗 kē] *(vegetable)*

Sweden NOUN
瑞典 Ruìdiǎn

Swedish NOUN
▷ *see also* **Swedish** ADJECTIVE
瑞典语 Ruìdiǎnyǔ *(language)*

Swedish ADJECTIVE
▷ *see also* **Swedish** NOUN
瑞典人 Ruìdiǎnrén
□ She's Swedish. 她是瑞典人。Tāshì Ruìdiǎnrén.

to **sweep** VERB
扫 sǎo
■ to sweep the floor 扫地 sǎodì

sweet NOUN
▷ *see also* **sweet** ADJECTIVE
1 糖果 tángguǒ [颗 kē]
□ a bag of sweets 一包糖 yìbāotáng
2 甜点 tiándiǎn [份 fèn] *(pudding)*
□ What sweet did you have? 你吃了什么甜点？ Nǐ chīle shénme tiándiǎn?

sweet ADJECTIVE
▷ *see also* **sweet** NOUN
1 甜的 tián de *(not savoury)*
2 好 hǎo
□ That was really sweet of you. 你太好了。Nǐ tàihǎo le.
3 可爱的 kě'ài *(cute)*
□ Isn't she sweet? 她很可爱吧？ Tā hěn kě'ài ba?
■ sweet and sour pork 糖醋猪肉 tángcù zhūròu

sweet corn NOUN
玉米 yùmǐ

swept VERB ▷ *see* **sweep**

to **swerve** VERB
突然转向 tūrán zhuǎnxiàng
□ He swerved to avoid the cyclist. 他突然转向回避骑车人。Tā tūrán zhuǎnxiàng huíbì qíchērén.

to **swim** VERB
▷ *see also* **swim** NOUN *(person, animal)*
1 游泳 yóuyǒng *(as sport)*
□ Can you swim? 你会游泳吗？ Nǐ huì yóuyǒng ma?
2 游 yóu *(distance)*
□ She swam across the river. 她游到了河对面。Tā yóudào le hé duìmiàn.

swim NOUN
▷ *see also* **swim** VERB
游泳 yóuyǒng

■ **to go for a swim** 去游泳 qù yóuyǒng

swimmer NOUN
游泳者 yóuyǒngzhě [位 wèi]
□ She's a good swimmer. 她擅长游泳。Tā shàncháng yóuyǒng.

swimming NOUN
游泳 yóuyǒng
□ Do you like swimming? 你喜欢游泳吗？Nǐ xǐhuan yóuyǒng ma?
■ **to go swimming** 去游泳 qù yóuyǒng
■ **a swimming cap** 一个游泳帽 yígè yóuyǒng mào
■ **a swimming costume** 一件游泳衣 yíjiàn yóuyǒngyī
■ **a swimming pool** 一个游泳池 yígè yóuyǒngchí
■ **swimming trunks** 泳裤 yǒngkù

swimsuit NOUN
游泳衣 yóuyǒng yī [套 tào]

swing NOUN
▷ *see also* **swing** VERB
秋千 qiūqiān [副 fù]

to **swing** VERB
▷ *see also* **swing** NOUN
1 荡秋千 dàngqiūqiān *(on a swing)*
2 晃动 huàngdòng
□ Her bag swung as she walked. 她在走路时她的包在晃动。Tā zài zǒulù shí tādebāo zài huàngdòng.
3 摆动 bǎidòng *(arms, legs)*
□ He sat on the table, swinging his legs back and forth. 他坐在桌子上，腿来回摆动。Tā zuòzài zhuōzishang, tuǐ láihuí bǎidòng.

Swiss ADJECTIVE, NOUN
瑞士人 Ruìshìrén
□ Sabine's Swiss. 萨宾是个瑞士人。Sàbīn shìgè Ruìshìrén.
■ **the Swiss** 瑞士人 Ruìshìrén

switch NOUN
▷ *see also* **switch** VERB
开关 kāiguān [个 gè]

to **switch** VERB
▷ *see also* **switch** NOUN
换 huàn
□ We switched partners. 我们换了搭档。Wǒmen huànle dādàng.

to **switch off** VERB
关掉 guāndiào *(light, engine, radio)*

to **switch on** VERB
开启 kāiqǐ *(light, engine, radio)*

Switzerland NOUN
瑞士 Ruìshì

swollen ADJECTIVE
肿胀的 zhǒngzhàng de

to **swop** VERB
交换 jiāohuàn
□ Do you want to swop? 你要交换吗？Nǐ yào jiāohuàn ma?
■ **to swop A for B** 用A换B yòng A huàn B
■ **to swop places with somebody** 与某人换位子 yǔ mǒurén huàn wèizi

sword NOUN
剑 jiàn [把 bǎ]

swore, sworn VERB ▷ *see* **swear**

swot NOUN
▷ *see also* **swot** VERB
苦读的人 kǔdúderén [个 gè]

to **swot** VERB
▷ *see also* **swot** NOUN
苦读 kǔdú
□ I'll have to swot for my maths exam. 我必须为我的数学考试而苦读。Wǒ bìxū wèi wǒde shùxué kǎoshì ér kǔdú.

swum VERB ▷ *see* **swim**

swung VERB ▷ *see* **swing**

syllabus NOUN
教学大纲 jiàoxué dàgāng [个 gè]

symbol NOUN
象征 xiàngzhēng [种 zhǒng] *(sign)*

sympathetic ADJECTIVE
有同情心的 yǒu tóngqíngxīn de

to **sympathize** VERB
同情 tóngqíng
■ **to sympathize with somebody** 同情某人 tóngqíngmǒurén

sympathy NOUN
同情心 tóngqíng xīn

symptom NOUN
症状 zhèngzhuàng [个 gè]

syringe NOUN
注射器 zhùshè qì [支 zhī]

system NOUN
方法 fāngfǎ [种 zhǒng] *(method)*

Tt

table NOUN
桌子 zhuōzi [张 zhāng]
■ **to lay the table** 摆餐桌 bǎi cānzhuō
tablecloth NOUN
桌布 zhuōbù [块 kuài]
tablespoon NOUN
餐匙 cānchí [把 bǎ]
□ two tablespoons of sugar 两匙糖 liǎng chí táng
tablet NOUN
1 药片 yàopiàn [片 piàn] *(medicine)*
2 平板电脑 píngbǎn diànnǎo *(computer)*
table tennis NOUN
乒乓球 pīngpāngqiú
■ **to play table tennis** 打乒乓球 dǎ pīngpāngqiú
tackle NOUN
▷ *see also* **tackle** VERB
1 铲球 chǎnqiú [次 cì] *(in football)*
2 擒抱 qínbào [次 cì] *(in rugby)*
■ **fishing tackle** 钓具 diàojù
to **tackle** VERB
▷ *see also* **tackle** NOUN
1 铲球 chǎnqiú *(in football)*
2 擒抱 qínbào *(in rugby)*
■ **to tackle a problem** 解决问题 jiějué wèntí
tact NOUN
机智 jīzhì
tactful ADJECTIVE
老练的 lǎoliàn de
tactics PL NOUN
策略 cèlüè
tactless ADJECTIVE
不圆滑的 bù yuánhuá de
□ He's so tactless. 他太不圆滑了。Tā tài bù yuánhuá le. □ a tactless remark 一句不圆滑的话 yíjù bù yuánhuá de huà
tadpole NOUN
蝌蚪 kēdǒu [只 zhī]
taffy NOUN (US)
太妃糖 tàifēitáng [块 kuài]
tag NOUN
标签 biāoqiān [个 gè] *(label)*
tail NOUN
尾巴 wěiba [条 tiáo]
■ **Heads or tails?** 正面还是背面？ Zhèngmiàn háishì bèimiàn?
tailor NOUN
裁缝 cáiféng [个 gè]
to **take** VERB

LANGUAGE TIP In many situations where the verb **take** is used in English, it is either omitted or a more specific verb is used in Chinese.

1 度 dù *(holiday, vacation)*
2 洗 xǐ *(shower, bath)*
3 拿 ná *(take hold of)*
4 偷走 tōuzǒu *(steal)*
5 送 sòng *(accompany)*
6 携带 xiédài *(carry, bring)*
7 带 dài *(person)*
□ When will you take me to London? 你什么时候带我去伦敦？ Nǐ shénme shíhòu dài wǒ qù Lúndūn?
8 走 zǒu *(road)*
9 乘坐 chéngzuò *(bus, train)*
10 穿 chuān *(size)*
11 花 huā *(time)*
□ It takes about an hour. 这大约要花一小时。Zhè dàyuē yào huā yìxiǎoshí.
12 参加 cānjiā *(exam, test)*
□ Have you taken your driving test yet? 你参加驾驶考试了没有？ Nǐ cānjiā jiàshǐ kǎoshìle méiyǒu?
13 服用 fúyòng *(drug, pill)*
14 要 yào *(effort, skill)*
□ That takes a lot of courage. 那要很大的勇气。Nà yào hěndà de yǒngqì.
15 忍受 rěnshòu *(tolerate)*
□ He can't take being criticized. 他不能忍受被批评。Tā bùnéng rěnshòu bèi pīpíng.
16 选修 xuǎnxiū *(subject)*
□ I decided to take French instead of German. 我决定选修法语而不是德语。Wǒ juédìng xuǎnxiū Fǎyǔ ér búshì Déyǔ.
■ **to take something somewhere** 带某物去某地 dài mǒuwù qù mǒudì
□ Don't forget to take your umbrella with you. 别忘了带雨伞。Bié wàngle dài yǔsǎn.

■ **It takes a lot of money to do that.** 那要花很多的钱。Nà yào huā hěnduō de qián.

to **take apart** VERB

■ **to take something apart** 拆开某物 chāikāi mǒuwù

to **take away** VERB

1 拿走 názǒu *(remove)*

□ They took away all his belongings. 他们拿走了他所有的财产。Tāmen názǒu le tā suǒyǒu de cáichǎn.

2 外卖 wàimài *(carry off)*

□ hot meals to take away 外卖的热饭食 wàimài de rèfànshí

to **take back** VERB

退回 tuìhuí

□ I took it back to the shop. 我把它退回给店里了。Wǒ bǎ tā tuìhuí gěi diàn lǐ le.

■ **I take it all back!** 我说的全部收回！Wǒ shuō de quánbù shōuhuí!

to **take down** VERB

记 jì

□ He took down the details in his notebook. 他在笔记本里记下细节。Tā zài bǐjìběn lǐ jìxià xìjié.

to **take in** VERB

理解 lǐjiě *(understand)*

□ I didn't really take it in. 我不太理解。Wǒ bútài lǐjiě.

to **take off** VERB

1 起飞 qǐfēi

□ The plane took off twenty minutes late. 飞机迟了二十分钟起飞。Fēijī chí le èrshí fēnzhōng qǐfēi.

2 脱 tuō *(clothes)*

□ Take your coat off. 把你的大衣脱掉。Bǎ nǐ de dàyī tuō diào.

to **take out** VERB

带 dài

□ He took her out to the theatre. 他带她去了剧院。Tā dài tā qù le jùyuàn.

to **take over** VERB

接管 jiēguǎn

□ I'll take over now. 现在由我来接管。Xiànzài yóu wǒ lái jiēguǎn.

■ **to take over from somebody** 由某人那里接管 yóu mǒurén nàlǐ jiēguǎn

to **take up** VERB

1 开始 kāishǐ

□ He took up golf when he retired. 他退休以后开始打高尔夫球了。Tā tuìxiū yǐhòu kāishǐ dǎ gāo'ěrfūqiú le.

2 占用 zhànyòng *(time, space)*

takeaway NOUN

1 外卖店 wàimàidiàn [家 jiā] *(shop, restaurant)*

2 外卖 wàimài [个 gè] *(food)*

taken VERB ▷ *see* **take**

takeoff NOUN

起飞 qǐfēi [次 cì]

takeout NOUN (US)

1 外卖店 wàimàidiàn [家 jiā] *(shop, restaurant)*

2 外卖 wàimài [个 gè] *(food)*

tale NOUN

故事 gùshì [个 gè]

talent NOUN

1 天份 tiānfèn

□ She's got lots of talent. 她很有天份。Tā hěn yǒu tiānfèn.

2 才能 cáinéng [种 zhǒng]

■ **to have a talent for something** 有某种才能 yǒu mǒuzhǒng cáinéng □ He's got a real talent for languages. 他很有语言才能。Tā hěnyǒu yǔyán cáinéng.

talented ADJECTIVE

有才华的 yǒu cáihuá de

□ She's a talented pianist. 她是个有才华的钢琴家。Tā shìge yǒucáihuá de gāngqínjiā.

talk NOUN

▷ *see also* **talk** VERB

1 讲话 jiǎnghuà [次 cì] *(speech)*

□ She gave a talk on rock climbing. 她就攀岩运动做了讲话。Tā jiù pānyán yùndòng zuò le jiǎnghuà.

2 谣传 yáochuán *(gossip)*

□ It's just talk. 这只是谣传。Zhè zhǐshì yáochuán.

3 交谈 jiāotán [次 cì] *(conversation)*

□ I had a talk with my Mum about it. 我和妈妈交谈了这件事。Wǒ hé māma jiāotán le zhèjiànshì.

to **talk** VERB

▷ *see also* **talk** NOUN

1 说话 shuōhuà *(speak)*

□ She talks too fast. 她说话太快了。Tā shuōhuà tài kuài le.

2 谈论 tánlùn *(chat)*

□ to talk about something 谈论某事 tánlùn mǒushì

■ **to talk to somebody** 跟某人谈话 gēn mǒurén tánhuà

■ **to talk about something** 谈论某事 tánlùn mǒushì

talkative ADJECTIVE

健谈的 jiàntán de

talk show NOUN (US)

脱口秀 tuōkǒuxiù [个 gè]

tall ADJECTIVE

高的 gāo de

□ He's 6 feet tall. 他六英尺高。Tā liù yīngchǐ gāo.

tame ADJECTIVE
驯服的 xùnfú de *(animal)*

tampon NOUN
月经棉栓 yuèjīng miánshuān [个 gè]

tan NOUN
晒黑的肤色 shàihēi de fūsè [种 zhǒng]

LANGUAGE TIP Word for word, this means 'sun-blackened skin colour'.

□ She's got an amazing tan. 她晒黑的肤色漂亮极了。Tā shàihēi de fūsè piàoliang jíle.

DID YOU KNOW...?
Being tanned was not traditionally seen as a mark of beauty in China.

tangerine NOUN
红橘 hóngjú [个 gè]

tank NOUN
1 坦克 tǎnkè [辆 liàng] *(military)*
2 箱 xiāng [个 gè] *(for petrol, water)*
■ **a fish tank** 一个鱼缸 yígè yúgāng

tanker NOUN
1 油轮 yóulún [艘 sōu] *(ship)*
■ **an oil tanker** 一艘油轮 yìsōu yóulún
2 油罐车 yóuguànchē [辆 liàng] *(truck)*
■ **a petrol tanker** 一辆汽油油罐车 yíliàng qìyóu yóuguànchē

tanned ADJECTIVE
晒黑的 shàihēi de

tap NOUN
1 龙头 lóngtóu [个 gè]
□ the hot tap 热水龙头 rèshuǐ lóngtóu
2 敲门声 qiāoménshēng [声 shēng]
□ I heard a tap on the door. 我听到一声敲门声。Wǒ tīngdào yìshēng qiāoménshēng.

tap-dancing NOUN
踢踏舞 tītàwǔ
□ I do tap-dancing. 我跳踢踏舞。Wǒ tiào tītàwǔ.

to **tape** VERB
▷ *see also* **tape** NOUN
录 lù
□ Did you tape that film last night? 你有把昨晚的电影录下来吗？Nǐ yǒu bǎ zuówǎn de diànyǐng lù xiàlái ma?

tape NOUN
▷ *see also* **tape** VERB
1 磁带 cídài [盘 pán] *(cassette)*
2 胶带 jiāodài [卷 juǎn] *(adhesive)*

tape measure NOUN
卷尺 juǎnchǐ [把 bǎ]

tape recorder NOUN
录音机 lùyīnjī [台 tái]

tar NOUN
沥青 lìqīng

target NOUN
目标 mùbiāo [个 gè]

tarmac NOUN
碎石沥青 suìshílìqīng *(on road)*

tart NOUN
馅饼 xiànbǐng [个 gè]
□ an apple tart 一个苹果馅饼 yígè píngguǒ xiànbǐng

tartan ADJECTIVE
苏格兰方格的 Sūgélán fānggé de
□ a tartan scarf 一条苏格兰方格围巾 yìtiáo Sūgélán fānggé wéijīn

task NOUN
任务 rènwù [项 xiàng]

taste NOUN
▷ *see also* **taste** VERB
1 味道 wèidao [种 zhǒng]
□ It's got a really strange taste. 这有种很奇怪的味道。Zhè yǒu zhǒng hěn qíguài de wèidào.
■ **Would you like a taste?** 你想尝一尝吗？Nǐ xiǎng chángyicháng ma?
2 品位 pǐnwèi
□ I don't share his taste in music. 我跟他对音乐的品位不同。Wǒ gēn tā duì yīnyuè de pǐnwèi bùtóng.
■ **a joke in bad taste** 一个低俗的玩笑 yígè dīsú de wánxiào

to **taste** VERB
▷ *see also* **taste** NOUN
尝 cháng
□ Would you like to taste it? 你想要尝下吗？Nǐ xiǎng yào chángxià ma?
■ **to taste of something** 像某物的味道 xiàng mǒuwù de wèidao □ It tastes of fish. 尝起来像鱼的味道。Cháng qǐlái xiàng yú de wèidào.
■ **You can taste the garlic in it.** 你能尝到里面有大蒜的味道。Nǐ néng chángdào lǐmiàn yǒu dàsuàn de wèidào.

tasteful ADJECTIVE
有品位的 yǒu pǐnwèi de

tasteless ADJECTIVE
1 无味的 wúwèi de *(food)*
2 粗俗的 cūsú de *(in bad taste)*
□ a tasteless remark 一句粗俗的话 yíjù cūsú de huà

tasty ADJECTIVE
味美的 wèiměi de

tattoo NOUN
纹身 wénshēn [个 gè]

taught VERB ▷ *see* **teach**

Taurus NOUN
金牛座 Jīnniúzuò
□ I'm Taurus. 我是金牛座的。Wǒ shì Jīnniúzuò de.

tax NOUN
税 shuì [种 zhǒng]

taxi NOUN
出租车 chūzūchē [辆 liàng]
■ **a taxi driver** 出租车司机 chūzūchē sījī
taxi rank NOUN
出租车候客站 chūzūchē hòukèzhàn [个 gè]
taxi stand NOUN (US)
出租车候客站 chūzūchē hòukèzhàn [个 gè]
TB NOUN
肺结核 fèijiéhé
tea NOUN
1 茶 chá [杯 bēi] *(drink)*
□ a cup of tea 一杯茶 yì bēi chá
2 茶叶 cháyè [片 piàn] *(dried leaves)*
3 下午茶 xiàwǔchá [次 cì] *(evening meal)*
□ We were having tea. 我们在喝下午茶。Wǒmen zài hē xiàwǔchá.
■ **a tea bag** 一个茶包 yígè chábāo
to **teach** VERB
1 教 jiāo
□ My sister taught me to swim. 我姐姐教会我游泳。Wǒ jiějie jiāo huì wǒ yóuyǒng.
2 书 jiāoshū *(in school)*
□ She teaches physics. 她教物理。Tā jiāo wùlǐ.
■ **That'll teach you!** 这下你可要学乖了！Zhè xià nǐ kě yào xué guāi le!
teacher NOUN
老师 lǎoshī [位 wèi]
□ a maths teacher 一位数学老师 yíwèi shùxué lǎoshī □ She's a teacher. 她是位老师。Tā shì wèi lǎoshī. □ a primary school teacher 一位小学老师 yíwèi xiǎoxué lǎoshī
team NOUN
队 duì [支 zhī]
□ a football team 一支足球队 yìzhī zúqiúduì
teapot NOUN
茶壶 cháhú [个 gè]
tear NOUN
▷ *see also* **tear** VERB
眼泪 yǎnlèi [滴 dī]
□ She was in tears. 她眼泪汪汪。Tā yǎnlèi wāngwāng.
■ **to burst into tears** 哭起来 kū qǐlái
to **tear** VERB
▷ *see also* **tear** NOUN
1 撕破 sīpò
□ Be careful or you'll tear the page. 小心点，不然你会把书页撕破的。Xiǎoxīndiǎn, bùrán nǐ huì bǎ shūyè sīpò de. □ He tore his jeans. 他把牛仔裤撕破了。Tā bǎ niúzǎikù sīpò le.
2 破 pò
□ It won't tear, it's very strong. 它不会撕破的，很结实。Tā búhuì sīpò de, hěn jiēshi.
to **tear up** VERB
撕毁 sīhuǐ
□ He tore up the letter. 他撕毁了那封信。Tā sīhuǐ le nà fēng xìn.
to **tease** VERB
1 欺负 qīfu
□ Stop teasing that poor animal! 不要再欺负那可怜的动物了！Búyào zài qīfu nà kělián de dòngwù le!
2 逗 dòu *(jokingly)*
□ He's teasing you. 他在逗你呢。Tā zài dòu nǐ ne.
teaspoon NOUN
茶匙 cháchí [把 bǎ]
□ two teaspoons of sugar 两茶匙糖 liǎng cháchí táng
teatime NOUN
茶点时间 chádiǎn shíjiān *(in evening)*
□ It was nearly teatime. 快到茶点时间了。Kuàidào chádiǎn shíjiān le.
■ **Teatime!** 吃晚饭了！Chī wǎnfàn le!
tea towel NOUN
擦拭杯碗的布 cāshì bēiwǎn de bù [块 kuài]
technical ADJECTIVE
1 技术的 jìshù de *(problems, advances)*
2 专业的 zhuānyè de *(terms, language)*
■ **a technical college** 一所技术学院 yìsuǒ jìshù xuéyuàn
technician NOUN
技师 jìshī [位 wèi]
technique NOUN
技巧 jìqiǎo [种 zhǒng]
techno NOUN
科技舞曲 kējì wǔqǔ *(music)*
technological ADJECTIVE
技术上的 jìshùshàng de
technology NOUN
技术 jìshù [种 zhǒng]
teddy bear NOUN
玩具熊 wánjùxióng [只 zhī]
teenage ADJECTIVE
青少年的 qīngshàonián de
□ a teenage magazine 一本青少年杂志 yìběn qīngshàonián zázhì □ She has two teenage daughters. 她有两个十几岁的女儿。Tā yǒu liǎngge shíjǐsuì de nǚ'ér.
teenager NOUN
青少年 qīngshàonián [个 gè]
tee-shirt NOUN
T恤衫 T xù shān [件 jiàn]
teeth PL NOUN ▷ *see* **tooth**
牙齿 yáchǐ
telecommunications PL NOUN
电信 diànxìn
telephone NOUN
电话 diànhuà [部 bù]

□ on the telephone 在打电话 zài dǎdiànhuà
■ **a telephone box** 一个电话亭 yígè diànhuàtíng
■ **a telephone call** 一个电话 yígè diànhuà
■ **the telephone directory** 电话号码簿 diànhuà hàomǎ bù
■ **a telephone number** 一个电话号码 yígè diànhuà hàomǎ

telesales PL NOUN
电话销售 diànhuà xiāoshòu
□ She works in telesales. 她从事电话销售。Tā cóngshì diànhuà xiāoshòu.

telescope NOUN
望远镜 wàngyuǎnjìng [架 jià]

television NOUN
1 电视机 diànshìjī [台 tái] *(set)*
2 电视 diànshì *(system)*
■ **on television** 在电视上 zài diànshì shàng
■ **a television licence** 一个电视许可证 yígè diànshì xǔkězhèng
■ **a television programme** 一个电视节目 yígè diànshì jiémù

to **tell** VERB
■ **to tell somebody something** 告诉某人某事 gàosù mǒurén mǒushì □ Did you tell your mother? 你告诉你妈妈了吗？ Nǐ gàosù nǐ māma le ma? □ I told him that I was going on holiday. 我告诉他我在度假。Wǒ gàosù tā wǒ zài dùjià.
■ **to tell somebody to do something** 让某人做某事 ràng mǒurén zuò mǒushì □ He told me to wait a moment. 他让我等一会儿。Tā ràng wǒ děngyíhuìr.
■ **to tell lies** 撒谎 sāhuǎng
■ **to tell a story** 讲故事 jiǎng gùshì
■ **I can't tell the difference between them.** 我看不出它们有什么区别。Wǒ kànbuchū tāmen yǒu shénme qūbié.

to **tell off** VERB
■ **to tell somebody off** 斥责某人 chìzé mǒurén

teller NOUN (US)
出纳员 chūnàyuán [个 gè] *(in bank)*

telly NOUN
电视 diànshì [台 tái]
□ to watch telly 看电视 kàn diànshì
■ **on telly** 在电视上 zài diànshì shàng

temper NOUN
脾气 píqi [种 zhǒng]
□ He's got a terrible temper. 他脾气坏得吓人。Tā píqi huài de xiàrén.
■ **to be in a temper** 在生气 zài shēngqì
■ **to lose one's temper** 发脾气 fāpíqi □ I lost my temper. 我发脾气了。Wǒ fā píqi le.

temperature NOUN
1 气温 qìwēn *(of place)*
□ The temperature was 30 degrees. 气温是三十度。Qìwēn shì sānshí dù.
2 体温 tǐwēn *(of person)*
■ **to have a temperature** 发烧 fāshāo

temple NOUN
庙宇 miàoyǔ [座 zuò]

temporary ADJECTIVE
临时的 línshí de

to **tempt** VERB
诱惑 yòuhuò
□ I'm very tempted! 我非常受诱惑！Wǒ fēicháng shòu yòuhuò!
■ **to tempt somebody to do something** 诱惑某人做某事 yòuhoù mǒurén zuò mǒushì

temptation NOUN
诱惑 yòuhuò [种 zhǒng]

tempting ADJECTIVE
诱人的 yòurén de

ten NUMBER
十 shí
□ She's ten. 她十岁。Tā shí suì.

tenant NOUN
房客 fáng kè [位 wèi]

to **tend** VERB
■ **to tend to do something** 通常做某事 tōngcháng zuò mǒushì □ He tends to arrive late. 他通常迟到。Tā tōngcháng chí dào.

tennis NOUN
网球运动 wǎngqiú yùndòng
□ Do you play tennis? 你打网球吗？ Nǐ dǎ wǎngqiú ma?
■ **a tennis ball** 一个网球 yígè wǎngqiú
■ **a tennis court** 一个网球场 yígè wǎngqiúchǎng
■ **a tennis racket** 一个网球拍 yígè wǎngqiúpāi

tennis player NOUN
网球选手 wǎngqiú xuǎnshǒu [位 wèi]
□ He's a tennis player. 他是位网球选手。Tā shì wèi wǎngqiú xuǎnshǒu.

tenor NOUN
男高音 nángāoyīn [位 wèi]

tenpin bowling NOUN
打保龄球 dǎ bǎolíngqiú
□ to go tenpin bowling 去打保龄球 qù dǎ bǎolíngqiú

tense ADJECTIVE
▷ *see also* **tense** NOUN
紧张的 jǐnzhāng de

tense NOUN
▷ *see also* **tense** ADJECTIVE
时态 shítài [种 zhǒng]
■ **the present tense** 现在时 xiànzàishí

■ **the future tense** 将来时 jiāngláishí

tension NOUN
1 紧张的局势 jǐnzhāng de júshì [个 gè] *(of situation)*
2 焦虑 jiāolǜ *(of person)*

tent NOUN
帐篷 zhàngpeng [顶 dǐng]

tenth ADJECTIVE
第十的 dìshíde
□ the tenth floor 第十一层 dìshíyī céng
■ **the tenth of August** 八月十号 bāyuè shíhào

term NOUN
学期 xuéqī [个 gè] *(at school)*
■ **in the short term** 短期 duǎnqī
■ **to be on good terms with somebody** 与某人关系好 yǔ mǒurén guānxì hǎo
■ **to come to terms with something** 设法忍受某事 shèfǎ rěnshòu mǒushì

terminal ADJECTIVE
▷ *see also* **terminal** NOUN
晚期的 wǎnqī de

terminal NOUN
▷ *see also* **terminal** ADJECTIVE
1 终端 zhōngduān [个 gè] *(of computer)*
2 航站楼 hángzhànlóu [座 zuò] *(at airport)*

terminally ADVERB
■ **to be terminally ill** 病入膏肓的 bìngrùgāohuāng de

terrace NOUN
1 成排的房屋 chéngpái de fángwū [排 pái] *(row of houses)*
2 平台 píngtái [个 gè] *(patio)*
■ **the terraces** *(at stadium)* 观众席 guānzhòngxí [个 gè]

terraced ADJECTIVE
■ **a terraced house** 一间排屋 yìjiān páiwū

terrible ADJECTIVE
1 可怕的 kěpà de *(accident)*
2 糟糕的 zāogāo de *(very poor)*
□ My Chinese is terrible. 我的中文很糟糕。 Wǒ de zhōngwén hěn zāogāo.

terribly ADVERB
1 非常 fēicháng *(very)*
□ I'm terribly sorry. 我非常抱歉。 Wǒ fēicháng bàoqiàn.
2 极 jí *(very badly)*
□ He suffered terribly. 他遭受了极大的伤害。 Tā zāoshòu le jídà de shānghài.

terrific ADJECTIVE
极好的 jíhǎode
□ That's terrific! 那好极了！ Nà hǎojí le!
■ **You look terrific!** 你看上去好极了！ Nǐ kànshàngqù hǎojí le!

terrified ADJECTIVE
吓坏的 xiàhuài de
□ I was terrified! 我被吓坏了！ Wǒ bèi xiàhuài le!

terror NOUN
恐惧 kǒngjù

terrorism NOUN
恐怖主义 kǒngbù zhǔyì

terrorist NOUN
恐怖分子 kǒngbù fènzǐ [个 gè]
■ **a terrorist attack** 一次恐怖袭击 yícì kǒngbù xíjī

test NOUN
▷ *see also* **test** VERB
1 测验 cèyàn [个 gè] *(at school)*
□ I've got a test tomorrow. 我明天有个测验。 Wǒ míngtiān yǒuge cèyàn.
2 试验 shìyàn [次 cì] *(trial, check)*
□ nuclear tests 核试验 hé shìyàn
3 检查 jiǎnchá [次 cì] *(medical)*
□ a blood test 一次血液检查 yícì xuěyè jiǎnchá □ They're going to do some more tests. 他们打算做更多的检查。 Tāmen dǎsuàn zuò gèngduō de jiǎnchá.
■ **driving test** 驾驶考试 jiàshǐ kǎoshì
□ He's got his driving test tomorrow. 他明天有驾驶考试。 Tā míngtiān yǒu jiàshǐ kaǒshì.

to **test** VERB
▷ *see also* **test** NOUN
1 试验 shìyàn *(try out)*
■ **to test something out** 试验某物 shìyàn mǒuwù
2 测试 cèshì *(at school)*
□ He tested us on the vocabulary. 他测试了我们的词汇。 Tā cèshì le wǒmen de cíhuì.
■ **She was tested for drugs.** 她做了毒品测试。 Tā zuò le dúpǐn cèshì.

test tube NOUN
试管 shìguǎn [根 gēn]

tetanus NOUN
破伤风 pòshāngfēng
□ a tetanus injection 一次破伤风疫苗注射 yícì pòshāngfēng yìmiáo zhùshè

text NOUN
▷ *see also* **text** VERB
手机短信 shǒujī duǎnxìn [条 tiáo] *(on mobile phone)*
LANGUAGE TIP This is often shortened to 短信 duǎnxìn.
□ I just got your text. 我刚收到你的短信。 Wǒ gāng shōudào nǐde duǎnxìn.

to **text** VERB
▷ *see also* **text** NOUN
■ **to text someone** 给某人发短信 gěi mǒurén fā duǎnxìn

textbook NOUN
课本 kèběn [本 běn]

□ a Chinese textbook 一本汉语课本 yìběn Hànyǔ kèběn

text message NOUN
短信 duǎnxìn [条 tiáo]

than CONJUNCTION
比 bǐ
□ She's taller than me. 她比我高。Tā bǐ wǒ gāo. □ I've got more books than him. 我的书比他多。Wǒ de shū bǐ tā duō.
■ **more than ten years** 十年以上 shínián yǐshàng
■ **more than once** 不止一次 bùzhǐ yícì

to **thank** VERB
感谢 gǎnxiè
□ Don't forget to write and thank them. 别忘了写信感谢他们。Bié wàng le xiěxìn gǎnxiè tāmen.
■ **thank you** 谢谢你 xièxie nǐ
■ **no, thank you** 不，谢谢 bù, xièxie
■ **thank you very much** 非常感谢你 fēicháng gǎnxiè nǐ
■ **to thank somebody for something** 感谢某人某事 gǎnxiè mǒurén mǒushì

thanks EXCLAMATION
谢谢 xièxie
■ **no, thanks** 不，谢谢 bù, xièxie
■ **thanks a lot** 多谢 duōxiè
■ **thanks to** 多亏 duōkuī □ Thanks to him, everything went OK. 多亏了他，一切顺利。Duōkuī le tā, yíqiè shùnlì.

Thanksgiving Day NOUN (US)
感恩节 Gǎn'ēnjié [个 gè]

that ADJECTIVE, PRONOUN, CONJUNCTION
那个 nàge
□ that man 那个男人 nàge nánrén □ that woman 那个女人 nàge nǚrén □ This man? — No, that one. 这个男人？— 不，那个。Zhège nánrén? — Bù, nàge. □ You see that? 你看见那个了吗？Nǐ kànjiàn nàge le ma?
■ **What's that?** 那是什么？Nàshì shénme?
■ **Who's that?** 那是谁？Nàshì shuí?
■ **Is that you?** 是你吗？Shì nǐ ma?
■ **That's...** 那是… nàshì... □ That's my house. 那是我的房子。Nàshì wǒde fángzi. □ That's what he said. 那是他说的话。Nàshì tā shuō de huà.

LANGUAGE TIP When used to introduce a clause, **that** is generally not translated.

□ He thought that I was ill. 他以为我病了。Tā yǐwéi wǒ bìngle. □ I know that she likes chocolate. 我知道她喜欢巧克力。Wǒ zhīdào tā xǐhuan qiǎokèlì.
■ **It was that big.** 有那么大。Yǒu nàme dà.
■ **It's not that difficult.** 不是那么难。Búshì nàme nán.

the ARTICLE

LANGUAGE TIP The definite article **the** is generally not translated in Chinese.

□ the man 男人 nánrén □ the girl 女孩 nǚhái □ the house 房子 fángzi □ the men 男人 nánrén □ the women 女人 nǚrén

LANGUAGE TIP When used before seasons, directions, dates, etc, **the** is not translated.

□ the fifth of March 三月五日 sānyuè wǔrì
□ the nineties 九十年代 jiǔshí niándài

theatre (US **theater**) NOUN
1 剧院 jùyuàn [座 zuò] *(for plays)*
2 手术室 shǒushùshì [间 jiān] *(operating theatre)*

theft NOUN
盗窃 dàoqiè [次 cì]

their ADJECTIVE
1 他们的 tāmen de *(of men, boys, mixed group)*
□ their house 他们的房子 tāmen de fángzi
2 她们的 tāmen de *(of women, girls)*
□ their parents 她们的父母 tāmen de fùmǔ
3 它们的 tāmen de *(of things, animals)*

theirs PRONOUN
1 他们的 tāmen de *(of men, boys, mixed group)*
□ This car is theirs. 这辆车是他们的。Zhè liàng chē shì tāmen de. □ It's not our car, it's theirs. 这不是我们的车，是他们的。Zhè búshì wǒmen de chē, shì tāmen de.
2 她们的 tāmen de *(of women, girls)*
□ They're not our ideas, they're theirs. 这些不是我们的主意，是她们的。Zhèxiē búshì wǒmen de zhǔyì, shì tāmen de.
3 它们的 tāmen de *(of animals)*
■ **Is this theirs?** 1 *(masculine owners)* 这是他们的吗？Zhè shì tāmen de ma?
2 *(feminine owners)* 这是她们的吗？Zhè shì tāmen de ma?

them PRONOUN
1 他们 tāmen *(referring to men, boys, mixed group)*
□ I didn't see them. 我没有见到他们。Wǒ méiyǒu jiàn dào tāmen.
2 她们 tāmen *(referring to women, girls)*
□ I told them the truth. 我告诉了她们真相。Wǒ gàosù le tāmen zhēnxiàng.
3 它们 tāmen *(referring to things and animals)*

theme park NOUN
主题公园 zhǔtí gōngyuán [座 zuò]

themselves PRONOUN
1 他们自己 tāmen zìjǐ *(referring to men, boys, mixed group)*
□ They talked mainly about themselves. 他们只谈自己的事。Tāmen zhǐ tán zìjǐ de shì.

2 她们自己 tāmen zìjǐ *(referring to girls, women)*
□ Did they hurt themselves? 她们伤到自己了吗？ Tāmen shāng dào zìjǐ le ma?
3 它们自己 tāmen zìjǐ *(referring to animals)*
4 他们本人 tāmen běnrén *(emphatic: referring to men, boys, mixed group)*
5 她们本人 tāmen běnrén *(emphatic: referring to women, girls)*
■ **by themselves** **1** *(unaided)* 他们独立地 tāmen dúlì de **2** *(alone)* 他们独自地 tāmen dúzì de

then ADVERB, CONJUNCTION
1 之后 zhīhòu *(after that)*
□ I get dressed. Then I have breakfast. 我穿好衣服，之后吃早饭。Wǒ chuān hǎo yīfu, zhīhòu chī zǎofàn.
2 那时 nàshí *(at that time: past)*
□ There was no electricity then. 那时没有电。Nàshí méiyǒu diàn.
3 那时 nàshí *(at that time: future)*
4 那么 nàme *(in that case)*
□ My pen's run out. — Use a pencil then! 我的笔没水了。— 那么就用铅笔！ Wǒ de bǐ méi shuǐ le. — Nàme jiù yòng qiānbǐ!
■ **now and then** 时不时 shíbùshí □ Do you play chess? — Now and then. 你们下棋吗？— 时不时。Nǐmen xià qí ma? — Shíbùshí.
■ **By then it was too late.** 到那时就太迟了。Dào nàshí jiù tài chí le.

therapy NOUN
疗法 liáofǎ [种 zhǒng]

there ADVERB
那儿 nà'r
□ They've lived there for 30 years. 他们在那儿住了三十年。Tāmen zài nàr zhùle sánshí nián. □ Put it there, on the table. 把它放在那儿，桌子上。Bǎ tā fàng zài nàr, zhuōzi shàng. □ He went there on Friday. 他星期五去了那儿。Tā xīngqīwǔ qù le nàr. □ Beijing? I've never been there. 北京？我从来没去过那儿。Běijīng? Wǒ cónglái méi qù guò nàr.
■ **It's over there!** 在那边！ Zài nàbiān!
■ **There he is!** 他在那儿呐！ Tā zài nàr na!
■ **Is Shirley there please?** *(on telephone)* 请问雪莉在吗？ Qǐngwèn Xuělì zàima?
■ **There you are.** *(offering something)* 给你 Gěinǐ.
■ **There is ...** 有… Yǒu... □ There's a factory near my house. 我家附近有座工厂。Wǒ jiā fùjìn yoǔ zuò gōngchǎng.
■ **There are ...** 有… Yǒu... □ There are five people in my family. 我家有五口人。Wǒ jiā yǒu wǔ kǒu rén.
■ **There has been an accident.** 发生了一个事故。Fāshēng le yígè shìgù.
■ **Will there be a buffet?** 会有自助餐吗？ Huì yǒu zìzhùcān ma?

therefore ADVERB
因此 yīncǐ

there's = **there is, there has**

thermometer NOUN
温度计 wēndùjì [个 gè]

Thermos® NOUN
保温瓶 bǎowēn píng [个 gè]

these ADJECTIVE, PRONOUN
这些 zhèxiē
□ these shoes 这些鞋子 zhèxiē xiézi □ I want these! 我要这些！ Wǒ yào zhèxiē!

they PRONOUN
1 他们 tāmen *(referring to men, boys, mixed group)*
□ You're looking for the boys? They went out. 你要找男孩子们？他们出去了。Nǐ yào zhǎo nánháizimen? Tāmen chūqù le.
2 她们 tāmen *(referring to women, girls)*
□ I spoke to my sisters. They agree with me. 我和姐妹们谈过了。她们都赞同我。Wǒ hé jiěmèimen tán guò le. Tāmen dōu zàntóng wǒ.
3 它们 tāmen *(referring to animals, things)*
□ Are there any tickets left? — No, they're all sold. 还有票吗？— 没有了，它们都卖光了。Hái yǒu piào ma? — Méi yǒu le, tāmen dōu mài guāng le.
4 人们 rénmen *(in generalizations)*
□ They say that the house is haunted. 人们说那房子闹鬼。Rénmen shuō nà fángzi nàoguǐ.

they'd = **they had, they would**

they'll = **they shall, they will**

they're = **they are**

they've = **they have**

thick ADJECTIVE
1 厚的 hòu de *(slice, line, book, clothes)*
2 浓的 nóng de *(sauce, mud, fog)*
■ **It's 20 cm thick.** 有二十厘米厚。Yǒu èrshí límǐ hòu.
3 迟钝的 chídùn de *(stupid)*

thief NOUN
贼 zéi [个 gè]

thigh NOUN
大腿 dàtuǐ [条 tiáo]

thin ADJECTIVE
1 薄的 báo de *(slice, line, book, material)*
2 瘦的 shòu de *(person, animal)*

thing NOUN
东西 dōngxi
□ What's that thing called? 那个东西叫什么？ Nàge dōngxi jiào shénme?

◻ beautiful things 美丽的东西 měilì de dōngxi

■ **my things** *(belongings)* 我的东西 wǒ de dōngxi

■ **She had lots of things to do.** 她有很多事要做。Tā yǒu hěn duō shì yào zuò.

■ **You poor thing!** 你真可怜！Nǐ zhēn kělián!

■ **A strange thing happened.** 发生了一件奇怪的事。Fāshēng le yījiàn qíguài de shì.

■ **How are things going?** 情形如何？Qíngxíng rúhé?

to **think** VERB

1 认为 rènwéi *(be of the opinion)*
◻ I think you're wrong. 我认为你错了。Wǒ rènwéi nǐ cuò le. ◻ What do you think about the war? 你认为战争如何？Nǐ rènwéi zhànzhēng rúhé?

2 考虑 kǎolǜ *(spend time thinking)*
◻ Think carefully before you reply. 回复前仔细考虑下。Huífù qián zǐxì kǎolǜ xià. ◻ I'll think about it. 我会考虑的。Wǒ huì kǎolǜ de.

■ **What are you thinking about?** 你在想什么？Nǐ zài xiǎng shénme?

3 想象 xiǎngxiàng *(imagine)*
◻ Think what life would be like without cars. 想象一下没有车生活会是怎样。Xiǎngxiàng yíxià méiyǒu chē shēnghuó huì shì zěnyàng.

■ **I think so.** 我想是的。Wǒ xiǎng shì de.

■ **I don't think so.** 我想不是的。Wǒ xiǎng búshì de.

■ **I'll think it over.** 我会仔细考虑下。Wǒ huì zǐxì kǎolǜ xià.

third ADJECTIVE

▷ *see also* **third** NOUN

第三 dì sān
◻ the third day 第三天 dì sān tiān ◻ the third time 第三次 dì sān cì ◻ I came third. 我是第三个。Wǒ shì dì sān gè.

■ **the third of March** 三月三号 sān yuè sān hào

third NOUN

▷ *see also* **third** ADJECTIVE

三份 sānfèn
◻ a third of the population 三分之一的人口 sān fēn zhī yī de rénkǒu

thirdly ADVERB

第三 dì sān

Third World NOUN

■ **the Third World** 第三世界 Dì Sān Shìjiè

thirst NOUN

口渴 kǒukě [阵 zhèn]

thirsty ADJECTIVE

渴的 kě de
◻ I'm thirsty. 我口渴。Wǒ kǒu kě.

thirteen NUMBER

十三 shísān
◻ I'm thirteen. 我十三岁。Wǒ shísān suì.

thirteenth ADJECTIVE

第十三的 dì shísān de
◻ her thirteenth birthday 她的十三岁生日 tā de shí sān suì shēng rì ◻ the thirteenth floor 第十四层 dì shísì céng

■ **the thirteenth of August** 八月十三号 bā yuè shí sān hào

thirty NUMBER

三十 sānshí

this ADJECTIVE, PRONOUN

1 这 zhè
◻ this man 这个男人 zhègè nánrén ◻ this house 这座房子 zhèzuò fángzi

■ **this one** 这 zhè ◻ Pass me that pen. — This one? 递给我那支笔。— 这支？Dì gěi wǒ nà zhī bǐ. — Zhè zhī? ◻ This one is better than that one. 这个比那个好。Zhège bǐ nàge hǎo.

■ **this morning** 今天早上 jīntiān zǎoshang

■ **this afternoon** 今天下午 jīntiān xiàwǔ

2 这个 zhège
◻ You see this? 你看到这个了？Nǐ kàn dào zhège le?

■ **What's this?** 这是什么？Zhèshì shénme?

■ **This is my mother.** *(introduction)* 这是我妈妈。Zhè shì wǒ māma.

■ **This is Susan speaking.** *(on the phone)* 我是苏珊。Wǒ shì Sūshān.

thorough ADJECTIVE

1 彻底的 chèdǐ de
◻ a thorough check 一次彻底的检查 yícì chèdǐ de jiǎnchá

2 细致的 xìzhì de
◻ She's very thorough. 她很细致。Tā hěn xìzhì.

thoroughly ADVERB

彻底地 chèdǐ de *(examine)*

those ADJECTIVE, PRONOUN

那些 nàxiē
◻ those shoes 那些鞋 nà xiē xié ◻ I want those! 我要那些！Wǒ yào nàxiē! ◻ I'm looking for some sandals. Can I try those? 我想买双凉鞋。能试下那双吗？Wǒ xiǎng mǎi shuāng liángxié. Néng shì xià nà shuāng ma? ◻ Are those yours? 那些是你的吗？Nàxiē shì nǐde ma?

though CONJUNCTION, ADVERB

尽管 jǐnguǎn

□ Though she was tired, she stayed up late. 尽管她很累，还是很晚才睡。Jǐnguǎn tā hěn lèi, hái shì hěn wǎn cái shuì.
■ **He's a nice person, though he's not very clever.** 他人很好，尽管不是很聪明。Tā rén hěn hǎo, jǐnguǎn búshì hěn cōngmíng.
■ **even though** 尽管 jǐnguǎn

thought VERB ▷ *see* **think**

thought NOUN
想法 xiǎngfǎ [个 gè]
□ I've just had a thought. 我刚有个想法。Wǒ gāng yǒuge xiǎngfǎ.
■ **It was a nice thought, thank you.** 是个好想法，谢谢你。Shìge hǎo xiǎngfǎ, xièxie nǐ.

thoughtful ADJECTIVE
1 若有所思的 ruò yǒu suǒ sī de *(deep in thought)*
□ You look thoughtful. 你看起来若有所思。Nǐ kànqǐlái ruò yǒu suǒ sī.
2 体贴的 tǐtiē de *(considerate)*
□ She's very thoughtful. 她非常体贴。Tā fēicháng tǐtiē.

thoughtless ADJECTIVE
不体贴的 bù tǐtiē de *(behaviour, person)*
■ **He's completely thoughtless.** 他一点都不体贴。Tā yìdiǎn dōu bù tǐtiē.

thousand NUMBER
千 qiān
□ a thousand yuan 一千元 yìqiān yuán
■ **£2000** 两千镑 liǎngqiān bàng
■ **thousands of people** 许许多多的人 xǔxǔduōduō de rén

thousandth ADJECTIVE, NOUN
第一千的 dì yìqiān de

thread NOUN
线 xiàn [根 gēn]

threat NOUN
威胁 wēixié [个 gè]

to **threaten** VERB
威胁 wēixié
□ He threatened me. 他威胁了我。Tā wēixié le wǒ.
■ **to threaten to do something** 威胁做某事 wēixié zuò mǒushì

three NUMBER
三 sān
□ She's three. 她三岁。Tā sān suì.

threw VERB ▷ *see* **throw**

thrifty ADJECTIVE
节俭的 jiéjiǎn de

thrilled ADJECTIVE
激动的 jīdòng de *(pleased)*
■ **I was thrilled.** 我很激动。Wǒ hěn jīdòng.

thriller NOUN
惊险 jīngxiǎn [场 chǎng]

thrilling ADJECTIVE
令人兴奋的 lìng rén xīngfèn de

throat NOUN
咽喉 yānhóu [个 gè]
■ **to have a sore throat** 嗓子疼 sǎngzi téng

to **throb** VERB
■ **a throbbing pain** 一跳一跳的疼 yítiàoyítiào de téng
■ **My arm's throbbing.** 我胳膊一跳一跳的。Wǒ gēbo yítiàoyítiào de.

throne NOUN
王位 wángwèi [个 gè]

through (US **thru**) PREPOSITION, ADJECTIVE, ADVERB
1 穿过 chuānguò
□ to go through a tunnel 穿过一条隧道 chuānguò yìtiáo suìdào □ The thief got in through the window. 小偷从窗户进来。Xiǎo tōu cóng chuānghu jìnlái. □ I saw him through the crowd. 我穿过人群看到了他。Wǒ chuānguò rénqún kàndào le tā. □ The window was dirty and I couldn't see through. 窗户太脏我看不清楚。Chuānghu tài zāng wǒ kànbuqīngchǔ.
2 整个 zhěnggè
□ all through the night 整个晚上 zhěng gè wǎnshàng □ from May through to December 整个五月到十二月 zhěnggè wǔyuè dào shíèryuè
3 通过 tōngguò
□ I know her through my sister. 我通过姐姐认识了她。Wǒ tōngguò jiějie rènshí le tā.
■ **a through train** 一列直达列车 yíliè zhídá lièchē
■ **'no through road'** "此路不通" "cǐ lù bù tōng"

throughout PREPOSITION
1 遍及 biànjí *(place)*
□ throughout Britain 遍及英国 biànjí Yīngguó
2 贯穿 guànchuān *(time)*
□ throughout the year 贯穿全年 guànchuān quánnián

to **throw** VERB
丢 diū
□ He threw the ball to me. 他把球丢给我。Tā bǎ qiú diū gěi wǒ.
■ **to throw a party** 举行聚会 jǔxíng jùhuì
■ **That really threw him.** 那真是让他慌乱了。Nà zhēnshì ràng tā huāngluàn le.

to **throw away** VERB
1 扔掉 rēngdiào *(rubbish)*
2 错过 cuòguò *(opportunity)*

to **throw out** VERB
1 扔掉 rēngdiào *(rubbish)*
2 赶走 gǎnzǒu *(person)*
□ I threw him out. 我把他赶走了。Wǒ bǎ tā gǎnzǒu le.

to **throw up** VERB
呕吐 ǒutù

thru PREPOSITION, ADJECTIVE, ADVERB (US)
▷ *see* **through**

thug NOUN
恶棍 ègùn [个 gè]

thumb NOUN
大拇指 dàmǔzhǐ [个 gè]

thumbtack NOUN (US)
图钉 túdīng [颗 kē]

to **thump** VERB
■ **to thump somebody** 重打某人 zhòngdǎ mǒurén

thunder NOUN
雷 léi

thunderstorm NOUN
雷雨 léiyǔ [阵 zhèn]

thundery ADJECTIVE
要打雷的 yào dǎléi de

Thursday NOUN
星期四 xīngqīsì [个 gè]
□ on Thursday 在星期四 zài xīngqīsì
□ on Thursdays 在每个星期四 zài měigè xīngqīsì □ every Thursday 每个星期四 měigè xīngqīsì □ last Thursday 上个星期四 shàngge xīngqīsì □ next Thursday 下个星期四 xiàge xīngqīsì

tick NOUN
▷ *see also* **tick** VERB
1 勾号 gōuhào [个 gè] *(mark)*
2 滴答声 dīdāshēng *(of clock)*
■ **I'll be back in a tick.** 我马上就回来。Wǒ mǎshàng jiù huílaí.

to **tick** VERB
▷ *see also* **tick** NOUN
1 打勾 dǎgōu
□ Tick the appropriate box. 在恰当的框上打勾。Zài qiàdàng de kuāng shàng dǎgōu.
2 嘀嗒作响 dīdā zuòxiǎng *(clock, watch)*

to **tick off** VERB
打勾 dǎgōu
□ He ticked off our names on the list. 他在名单上勾了我们的名字。Tā zài míngdān shàng gōu le wǒmen de míngzi.

ticket NOUN
票 piào [张 zhāng] *(for public transport, theatre, raffle)*
□ an underground ticket 一张地铁票 yìzhāng dìtiě piào
■ **a parking ticket** 一张违章停车罚单 yìzhāng wéizhāng tíngchē fádān

ticket inspector NOUN
查票员 chápiàoyuán [位 wèi]

ticket office NOUN
售票处 shòupiàochù [个 gè]

to **tickle** VERB
挠 náo

tide NOUN
潮汐 cháoxī

> **DID YOU KNOW...?**
> The tidal bore on the Qiantang river, 钱塘江涌潮 qiántángjiāng yǒngcháo, in picturesque Hangzhou, is famous across China.

■ **high tide** 涨潮 zhǎng cháo
■ **low tide** 落潮 luò cháo

tidy ADJECTIVE
▷ *see also* **tidy** VERB
整洁的 zhěngjié de
□ Your room's very tidy. 你的房间非常整洁。Nǐde fángjiān fēicháng zhěngjié.
□ She's very tidy. 她非常整洁。Tā fēicháng zhěngjié.

to **tidy** VERB
▷ *see also* **tidy** ADJECTIVE
整理 zhěnglǐ
□ Go and tidy your room. 去整理你房间。Qù zhěnglǐ nǐ fángjiān.

to **tidy up** VERB
整理 zhěnglǐ
□ Don't forget to tidy up afterwards. 别忘了之后要整理。Bié wàng le zhīhòu yào zhěnglǐ.

tie NOUN
▷ *see also* **tie** VERB
1 领带 lǐngdài [条 tiáo] *(necktie)*
2 平局 píngjú [个 gè] *(in sport)*

to **tie** VERB
▷ *see also* **tie** NOUN
1 捆 kǔn *(parcel)*
2 系 jì *(knot)*
■ **to tie a knot in something** 给某物系个结 gěi mǒuwù jìge jié
■ **to tie one's shoelaces** 系鞋带 jì xiédài
3 打平 dǎpíng *(in sport)*
□ They tied three all. 他们三比三打平。Tāmen sān bǐ sān dǎpíng.

to **tie up** VERB
1 捆绑 kǔnbǎng *(parcel, person)*
2 拴 shuān *(dog)*

tiger NOUN
老虎 lǎohǔ [只 zhī]

tight ADJECTIVE
1 紧身的 jǐnshēn de *(shoes, clothes)*
2 紧张的 jǐnzhāng de *(budget, schedule)*
3 严格的 yángé de *(security, controls)*

to **tighten** VERB

1 系紧 jìjǐn *(rope)*
2 拧紧 nǐngjǐn *(screw)*

tightly ADVERB
紧紧地 jǐnjǐn de

tights PL NOUN
连裤袜 liánkùwà

tile NOUN
1 瓦 wǎ [片 piàn] *(on roof)*
2 砖 zhuān [块 kuài] *(on floor, wall)*

tiled ADJECTIVE
1 铺瓦的 pūwǎ de *(roof)*
2 镶瓷砖的 xiāng cízhuān de *(wall, floor, room)*

till NOUN
▷ *see also* **till** PREPOSITION, CONJUNCTION
收音机 shōuyínjī [个 gè]

till PREPOSITION, CONJUNCTION
▷ *see also* **till** NOUN
1 直到…时 zhídào…shí
□ I waited till ten o'clock. 我一直等到十点钟。Wǒ yìzhí děng dào shídiǎnzhōng.
2 直到…才 zhídào…cái
□ It won't be ready till next week. 要到下周才能好。Yào dào xiàzhōu cáinéng hǎo.
□ We stayed there till the doctor came. 我们一直待到医生来才离开。Wǒmen yìzhí dāi dào yīshēng lái cái líkāi.
■ **till now** 直到现在 zhídào xiànzài □ It's never been a problem till now. 直到现在才成了问题。Zhí dào xiànzài cái chéngle wèntí.
■ **till then** 直到那时为止 zhídào nàshí wéizhǐ □ Till then I'd never been to France. 直到那时为止我从没去过法国。Zhídào nàshí wéizhǐ wǒ cóng méi qùguò Fǎguó.

timber NOUN
木料 mùliào

time NOUN
1 时候 shíhòu *(on clock)*
□ What time do you get up? 你什么时候起床？Nǐ shénme shíhòu qǐchuáng?
■ **What time is it?** 几点了？Jǐdiǎn le?
■ **on time** 准时 zhǔnshí □ He never arrives on time. 他从不准时到。Tā cóng bù zhǔnshí dào.
■ **at the same time** 同时 tóngshí
2 时间 shíjiān
□ I'm sorry, I haven't got time. 对不起，我没有时间。Duìbùqǐ, wǒ méiyǒu shíjiān.
■ **to spend one's time doing something** 花时间做某事 huā shíjiān zuò mǒushì
■ **from time to time** 时不时 shíbushí
■ **in time** 正好赶上 zhènghǎo gǎnshàng □ We arrived in time for lunch. 我们正好赶上午饭。Wǒmen zhènghǎo gǎnshàng wǔfàn.
■ **all the time** 总是 zǒngshì
■ **in no time** 立刻 lìkè □ It was ready in no time. 立刻就准备好了。Lìkè jiù zhǔnbèi hǎo le.
■ **It's time to go.** 该走了。Gāi zǒu le.
■ **a long time** 很久 hěnjiǔ □ Have you lived here for a long time? 你住在这儿很久了吗？Nǐ zhù zài zhèr hěn jiǔ le ma?
3 时机 shíjī *(moment)*
□ This isn't a good time to ask him. 这可不是问他的好时机。Zhè kě búshì wèn tā de hǎo shíjī.
■ **for the time being** 暂时 zànshí
4 次 cì *(occasion)*
□ this time 这次 zhècì □ next time 下次 xiàcì □ three times a day 一日三次 yìrì sāncì □ two at a time 一次两个 yícì liǎng gè
■ **How many times?** 多少次？Duōshǎo cì?
■ **at times** 有时 yǒushí
■ **in a week's time** 一周以后 yìzhōu yǐhòu □ I'll come back in a month's time. 我一个月以后回来。Wǒ yígè yuè yǐhòu huílái.
■ **Come and see us any time.** 随时可以来看我们。Suíshí kěyǐ lái kàn wǒmen.
■ **to have a good time** 玩得开心 wán de kāixīn □ Did you have a good time? 你玩得开心吗？Nǐ wán de kāixīn ma?
■ **2 times 2 is 4** 二乘二等于四 èr chéng èr děngyú sì

time off NOUN
休假 xiūjià

timetable NOUN
1 时刻表 shíkèbiǎo [个 gè] *(for train, bus)*
2 课程表 kèchéngbiǎo [个 gè] *(at school)*

time zone NOUN
时区 shíqū [个 gè]

tin NOUN
1 罐 guàn [个 gè] *(can)*
□ a tin of soup 一罐汤 yí guàn tāng
2 听 tīng *(container: for biscuits, tobacco)*
□ a biscuit tin 一个饼干听子 yígè bǐnggān tīngzi
3 锡 xī *(metal)*

tinned ADJECTIVE
罐头的 guàntóu de *(food)*
□ tinned peaches 罐头桃子 guàntóu táozi

tin opener NOUN
开罐器 kāiguànqì [个 gè]

tinsel NOUN
闪亮的金属装饰 shǎnliàng de jīnshǔ zhuāngshì

tiny ADJECTIVE
极小的 jíxiǎo de

tip NOUN

▷ *see also* **tip** VERB

1 小费 xiǎofèi [笔 bǐ] *(to waiter)*

□ Shall I give him a tip? 我该给他小费吗？ Wǒ gāi gěi tā xiǎofèi ma?

DID YOU KNOW...?
Tipping is not generally expected in mainland China, although it is becoming more common.

2 提示 tíshì [个 gè] *(advice)*

□ a useful tip 一个有用的提示 yígè yǒuyòng de tíshì

3 尖 jiān [个 gè] *(end)*

□ It's on the tip of my tongue. 它在我的舌尖上。Tā zài wǒ de shé jiān shàng.

■ **a rubbish tip** 弃置场 qìzhìchǎng

■ **This place is a complete tip!** 这地方简直就是个垃圾场！ Zhè dìfāng jiǎnzhí jiùshì gè lājīchǎng!

to **tip** VERB

▷ *see also* **tip** NOUN

1 给...小费 gěi...xiǎofèi

□ Don't forget to tip the taxi driver. 别忘了给出租车司机小费。Bié wàng le gěi chūzūchē sījī xiǎofèi.

2 倒出 dàochū *(pour)*

tipsy ADJECTIVE

微醉的 wēizuì de

to **tiptoe** VERB

▷ *see also* **tiptoe** NOUN

踮着脚走 diǎnzhe jiǎo zǒu

tiptoe NOUN

▷ *see also* **tiptoe** VERB

■ **on tiptoe** 踮着脚走 diǎnzhe jiǎo zǒu

tire NOUN (US)

轮胎 lúntāi [个 gè]

tired ADJECTIVE

累的 lèi de

□ I'm tired. 我累了。Wǒ lèi le.

■ **to be tired of something** 厌倦于某事 yànjuàn yú mǒushì

tiring ADJECTIVE

令人疲劳的 lìng rén píláo de

tissue NOUN

纸巾 zhǐjīn [张 zhāng] *(paper handkerchief)*

title NOUN

标题 biāotí [个 gè] *(of book, play)*

to PREPOSITION

LANGUAGE TIP When **to** is used after the verb **to go**, it is not translated.

□ to go to Paris 去巴黎 qù Bālí □ to go to school 去上学 qù shàngxué □ to go to the theatre 去剧院 qù jùyuàn □ to go to the doctor's 去看医生 qù kàn yīshēng □ Let's go to Anne's house. 我们去安妮家吧。Wǒmen qù Ānní jiā ba.

LANGUAGE TIP When **to** is used to describe doing something to somebody, it is translated with 对 duì.

□ to talk to somebody 对某人说 duì mǒurén shuō □ We said goodbye to the neighbours. 我们对邻居说再见。Wǒmen duì línjū shuō zàijiàn.

LANGUAGE TIP When used to indicate giving and receiving, **to** is not translated.

□ a letter to his wife 给他妻子的一封信 gěi tā qīzi de yìfēng xìn □ the answer to the question 问题的答案 wèntí de dá'àn

LANGUAGE TIP When **to** is used as an infinitive, it is usually not translated.

□ ready to go 准备走 zhǔnbèi zǒu □ It's easy to do. 这很容易做。Zhè hěn róngyì zuò.

■ **from... to...** 从…到… cóng...dào...

□ from here to London 从这儿到伦敦 cóng zhèr dào Lúndūn □ from May to September 从五月到九月 cóng wǔyuè dào jiǔyuè

■ **to give something to somebody** 给某人某物 gěi mǒurén mǒuwù

■ **to count to ten** 从一数到十 cóng yī shǔ dào shí

■ **I did it to help you.** 我这么做是为了帮你。Wǒ zhème zuò shì wèile bāngnǐ.

toad NOUN

蟾蜍 chánchú [只 zhī]

toast NOUN

1 烤面包 kǎomiànbāo *(bread)*

□ a piece of toast 一片烤面包 yípiàn kǎo miànbāo

2 祝酒 zhùjiǔ [次 cì]

■ **to drink a toast to somebody** 向某人祝酒 xiàng mǒurén zhùjiǔ

toaster NOUN

烤面包机 kǎo miànbāo jī [台 tái]

tobacco NOUN

烟草 yāncǎo

tobacconist's NOUN

烟草店 yāncǎodiàn [家 jiā]

today ADVERB

今天 jīntiān

□ What did you do today? 今天你做了什么？ Jīntiān nǐ zuòle shénme?

toddler NOUN

学步的小孩 xuébù de xiǎohái [个 gè]

toe NOUN

脚趾 jiǎozhǐ [个 gè]

toffee NOUN

1 太妃糖 tàifēitáng *(substance)*

2 太妃糖果 tàifēi tángguǒ [颗 kē] *(sweet)*

together ADVERB

1 一起 yìqǐ
□ Are they still together? 他们还在一起吗？ Tāmen hái zài yìqǐ ma?
2 同时 tóngshí *(at the same time)*
□ Don't all speak together! 别同时说话！ Bié tóngshí shuōhuà!
■ **together with** 连同 liántóng

toilet NOUN
厕所 cèsuǒ [间 jiān]
■ **to go to the toilet** 上厕所 shàng cèsuǒ

toilet paper NOUN
卫生纸 wèishēngzhǐ [卷 juǎn]

toiletries PL NOUN
卫生用品 wèishēng yòngpǐn

toilet roll NOUN
卫生卷纸 wèishēng juǎnzhǐ [卷 juǎn]

token NOUN
代金券 dàijīnquàn [张 zhāng]
■ **a gift token** 一张礼券 yìzhāng lǐquàn

told VERB ▷ *see* **tell**

tolerant ADJECTIVE
宽容的 kuānróng de

toll NOUN
通行费 tōngxíngfèi [笔 bǐ] *(on road, bridge)*

tomato NOUN
番茄 fānqié [个 gè]
□ tomato sauce 番茄酱 fānqié jiàng
□ tomato soup 番茄汤 fānqié tāng

tomorrow ADVERB
明天 míngtiān
□ tomorrow morning 明天早晨 míngtiān zǎochén □ tomorrow night 明天晚上 míngtiān wǎnshang
■ **the day after tomorrow** 后天 hòutiān

ton NOUN
吨 dūn
□ a ton of coal 一吨煤炭 yìdūn méitàn

tongue NOUN
舌头 shétou [个 gè]

tonic NOUN
奎宁水 kuíníngshuǐ *(tonic water)*
■ **a gin and tonic** 一杯金汤尼鸡尾酒 yìbēi jīntāngní jīwěijiǔ

tonight ADVERB
今晚 jīnwǎn
□ Are you going out tonight? 你今晚出去吗？ Nǐ jīnwǎn chūqù ma? □ I'll sleep well tonight. 我今晚可以睡好了。Wǒ jīnwǎn kěyǐ shuìhǎo le.

tonsillitis NOUN
扁桃腺炎 biǎntáoxiànyán

tonsils PL NOUN
扁桃腺 biǎntáoxiàn

too ADVERB
1 也 yě *(as well)*
□ My sister came too. 我姐姐也来了。Wǒ jiějie yě lái le.
2 太 tài *(excessively)*
□ The water's too hot. 水太烫了。Shuǐ tài tàng le. □ We arrived too late. 我们到得太晚了。Wǒmen dào de tài wǎn le.
■ **too much** *(with noun)* 太 tài □ too much noise 太吵 tài chǎo □ At Christmas we always eat too much. 圣诞节我们总是吃太多。Shèngdànjié wǒmen zǒngshì chī tài duō. □ Fifty euros? That's too much. 五十欧元？太贵了。Wǔshí ōuyuán? Tài guì le.
■ **too many** 太多 tàiduō □ too many hamburgers 太多汉堡 tàiduō hànbǎo
■ **Too bad!** 太糟了！ Tài zāo le!

took VERB ▷ *see* **take**

tool NOUN
用具 yòngjù [种 zhǒng]
■ **a tool box** 一个工具箱 yígè gōngjùxiāng

tooth NOUN
牙齿 yáchǐ [颗 kē]

toothache NOUN
牙痛 yátòng [阵 zhèn]
□ to have toothache 牙痛 yátòng

toothbrush NOUN
牙刷 yáshuā [把 bǎ]

toothpaste
牙膏 yágāo [管 guǎn]

top NOUN
▷ *see also* **top** ADJECTIVE
1 顶部 dǐngbù [个 gè] *(of mountain, building, tree, stairs)*
□ at the top of the stairs 在楼梯顶部 zài lóutī dǐngbù
2 顶端 dǐngduān [个 gè] *(of page)*
□ at the top of the page 在这页顶端 zài zhè yè dǐngduān
3 上面 shàngmiàn *(of surface, table)*
□ on top of the fridge 在冰箱上面 zài bīngxiāng shàngmiàn
4 盖子 gàizi [个 gè] *(of box, jar, bottle)*
5 上衣 shàngyī [件 jiàn] *(blouse)*
■ **There's a surcharge on top of that.** 除那之外还有附加费。Chú nà zhīwài háiyǒu fùjiāfèi.
■ **from top to bottom** 从头到脚 cóng tóu dào jiǎo □ I searched the house from top to bottom. 我把家里从头到脚搜了个遍。Wǒ bǎ jiālǐ cóng tóu dào jiǎo sōu le ge biàn.

top ADJECTIVE
▷ *see also* **top** NOUN
1 最高的 zuìgāo de *(shelf, step, storey, marks)*
□ He always gets top marks in French. 他法语总是得到最高分。Tā Fǎyǔ zǒngshì dédào zuìgāo fēn.
■ **the top floor** 顶楼 dǐnglóu □ on the top floor 在顶楼 zài dǐnglóu

2 顶级的 dǐngjí de
□ a top surgeon 顶级的外科医生 dǐngjí de wàikē yīshēng □ a top model 一位顶级模特 yíwèi dǐngjí mótè

topic NOUN
话题 huàtí [个 gè]
□ The essay can be on any topic. 论文可以写任何话题。Lùnwén kěyǐ xiě rènhé huàtí.

top-secret ADJECTIVE
最高机密的 zuìgāo jīmì de
□ top-secret documents 最高机密文件 zuìgāo jīmì wénjiàn

torch NOUN
手电筒 shǒudiàntǒng [个 gè]

tore, torn VERB ▷ *see* **tear**

tortoise NOUN
乌龟 wūguī [只 zhī]

torture NOUN
▷ *see also* **torture** VERB
酷刑 kùxíng
□ It was pure torture. 这纯粹是种酷刑。Zhè chúncuì shì zhǒng kùxíng.

to **torture** VERB
▷ *see also* **torture** NOUN
折磨 zhémó
□ Stop torturing that poor animal! 停止折磨那可怜的动物！Tíngzhǐ zhémó nà kělián de dòngwù!

Tory ADJECTIVE
▷ *see also* **Tory** NOUN
保守党的 bǎoshǒudǎng de
□ the Tory government 保守党政府 bǎoshǒudǎng zhèngfǔ

Tory NOUN
▷ *see also* **Tory** ADJECTIVE
保守党成员 bǎoshǒudǎng chéngyuán [个 gè]
■ **the Tories** 保守党 bǎoshǒudǎng

to **toss** VERB
抛 pāo
□ to toss pancakes 抛薄煎饼 pāo báojiānbǐng □ Shall we toss for it? 我们要不要抛硬币来决定？Wǒmen yàobuyào pāo yìngbì lái juédìng?

total ADJECTIVE
▷ *see also* **total** NOUN
总的 zǒng de
□ the total amount 总量 zǒngliàng

total NOUN
▷ *see also* **total** ADJECTIVE
总数 zǒngshù [个 gè]
□ the grand total 总计 zǒngjì
■ **in total** 总共 zǒnggòng

totally ADVERB
1 完全地 wánquán de *(agree, destroy)*
2 绝对地 juéduì de *(different, new)*

touch NOUN
▷ *see also* **touch** VERB
接触 jiēchù [次 cì] *(contact)*
■ **to get in touch with somebody** 与某人联系 yǔ mǒurén liánxì
■ **to keep in touch with somebody** 与某人保持联系 yǔ mǒurén bǎochí liánxì
■ **Keep in touch!** 多联系！Duō liánxì!
■ **to lose touch** 失去联系 shīqù liánxì
■ **to lose touch with somebody** 与某人失去联系 yǔ mǒurén shīqù liánxì

to **touch** VERB
▷ *see also* **touch** NOUN
碰 pèng *(with hand, foot)*
□ Don't touch that! 别碰那个！Bié pèng nàge!

touched ADJECTIVE
被感动的 bèi gǎndòng de
□ I was really touched. 我真的被感动了。Wǒ zhēnde bèi gǎndòng le.

touching ADJECTIVE
感人的 gǎnrén de

tough ADJECTIVE
1 坚韧的 jiānrèn de
2 嚼不动的 jiáobúdòng de
□ The meat's tough. 肉嚼不动。Ròu jiáobúdòng.
3 艰难的 jiānnán de *(physically)*
□ It was tough, but I managed OK. 很艰难，但是我努力度过了。Hěn jiānnán, dànshì wǒ nǔlì dùguò le. □ It's a tough job. 这工作很难。Zhè gōng zuò hěn nán.
4 坚强的 jiānqiáng de
□ She's tough. She can take it. 她很坚强。她能承受得了。Tā hěn jiānqiáng. Tā néng chéngshòu de liǎo.
5 强壮的 qiángzhuàng de
□ He thinks he's a tough guy. 他以为自己是个壮汉。Tā yǐwéi zìjǐ shìgè zhuànghàn.
■ **Tough luck!** 真不走运！Zhēn bù zǒuyùn!

tour NOUN
▷ *see also* **tour** VERB
1 旅行 lǚxíng [次 cì] *(journey)*
□ Her parents are going on a tour of China. 她父母要去中国旅行了。Tā fùmǔ yào qù Zhōngguó lǚxíng le.
■ **a package tour** 一次包办旅行 yícì bāobàn lǚxíng
2 观光 guānguāng [次 cì] *(of town, factory, museum)*
□ We went on a tour of the city. 我们去了那城市观光。Wǒmen qù le nà chéngshì guānguāng.
3 巡回表演 xúnhuí biǎoyǎn [个 gè] *(by*

English-Chinese

t

singer, group)
□ on tour 巡回表演中 xúnhuí biǎoyǎn zhōng
■ **to go on tour** 去做巡回表演 qù zuò xúnhuí biǎoyǎn

to **tour** VERB
▷ *see also* **tour** NOUN
巡回表演 xúnhuí biǎoyǎn
□ The band is touring Europe. 乐队在欧洲巡回表演。Yuèduì zài Ōuzhōu xúnhuí biǎoyǎn.

tour guide NOUN
导游 dǎoyóu [位 wèi]

tourism NOUN
旅游业 lǚyóuyè

tourist NOUN
游客 yóukè [位 wèi]
■ **tourist information office** 旅游咨询局 lǚyóu zīxún jú

tournament NOUN
锦标赛 jǐnbiāosài [次 cì]

tour operator NOUN
包价旅游承包商 bāojià lǚyóu chéngbāoshāng [个 gè]

to **tow** VERB
拖 tuō *(vehicle, trailer)*

to **tow away** VERB
拖走 tuōzǒu *(vehicle)*

towards PREPOSITION
1 朝着 cháozhe *(in direction of)*
□ He came towards me. 他朝我走来。Tā cháo wǒ zǒu lái.
2 对 duì *(with regard to)*
□ my feelings towards him 我对他的感觉 wǒ duì tā de gǎnjué

towel NOUN
毛巾 máojīn [条 tiáo]

tower NOUN
塔 tǎ [座 zuò]

tower block NOUN
高楼大厦 gāolóu dàshà [座 zuò]

town NOUN
城镇 chéngzhèn [个 gè]
■ **the town centre** 市中心 shìzhōngxīn
■ **the town hall** 市政厅 shìzhèngtīng

tow truck NOUN (US)
拖车 tuōchē [部 bù]

toy NOUN
玩具 wánjù [个 gè]
LANGUAGE TIP Word for word, this means 'play utensil'.
■ **a toy shop** 一间玩具店 yìjiān wánjùdiàn

trace NOUN
▷ *see also* **trace** VERB
1 踪迹 zōngjì [个 gè] *(of person)*
□ There was no trace of the robbers. 没有任何抢劫犯的踪迹。Méiyǒu rènhé qiǎngjiéfàn de zōngjì.
2 痕迹 hénjì [个 gè] *(of substance)*

to **trace** VERB
▷ *see also* **trace** NOUN
描绘 miáohuì *(draw)*

track NOUN
1 小径 xiǎojìng [条 tiáo] *(path)*
2 轨道 guǐdào [条 tiáo] *(railway line)*
3 赛道 sàidào
□ two laps of the track 绕赛道两圈 rào sàidào liǎngquān
4 曲目 qǔmù [个 gè] *(song)*
□ This is my favourite track. 这是我最喜欢的曲目。Zhè shì wǒ zuì xǐhuan de qǔmù.
5 足迹 zújì *(trail)*
□ They followed the tracks for miles. 他们跟着足迹追了数英里。Tāmen gēnzhe zújì zhuī le shù yīnglǐ.

to **track down** VERB
■ **to track somebody down** 追踪某人 zhuīzōng mǒurén □ The police never tracked down the killer. 警方一直没有追踪到杀人凶手。Jǐngfāng yìzhí méiyǒu zhuīzōng dào shārén xiōngshǒu.

tracksuit NOUN
运动服 yùndòngfú [套 tào]

tractor NOUN
拖拉机 tuōlājī [部 bù]

trade NOUN
手艺 shǒuyì [门 mén] *(skill, job)*
■ **to learn a trade** 学一门手艺 xué yìmén shǒuyì

trade union NOUN
工会 gōnghuì [个 gè]

tradition NOUN
传统 chuántǒng [个 gè]

traditional ADJECTIVE
传统的 chuántǒng de

traffic NOUN
交通 jiāotōng
□ The traffic was terrible. 交通遭透了。Jiāotōng zāo tòu le.

traffic circle NOUN (US)
转盘 zhuànpán [个 gè]

traffic jam NOUN
交通阻塞 jiāotōng zǔsè [阵 zhèn]

traffic lights PL NOUN
红绿灯 hónglǜdēng

traffic warden NOUN
交通管理员 jiāotōng guǎnlǐyuán [位 wèi]

tragedy NOUN
极大的不幸 jídà de bùxìng [个 gè] *(disaster)*

tragic ADJECTIVE
悲惨的 bēicǎn de

trailer NOUN

1 拖车 tuōchē [部 bù] *(vehicle)*
2 房式拖车 fángshì tuōchē [辆 liàng] *(US: caravan)*

train NOUN
▷ *see also* **train** VERB
1 火车 huǒchē [辆 liàng]
■ **a train set** 一套火车组合玩具 yítào huǒchē zǔhé wánjù
2 地铁 dìtiě *(on underground)*

to **train** VERB
▷ *see also* **train** NOUN
1 培训 péixùn *(teach skills to)*
2 受培训 shòu péixùn *(learn a skill)*
■ **to train as a teacher** 受教师培训 shòu jiàoshī péixùn
3 训练 xùnliàn *(sport)*
□ to train for a race 为赛跑而训练 wèi sàipǎo ér xùnliàn
■ **to train an animal to do something** 训练动物做某事 xùnliàn dòngwù zuò mǒushì

trained ADJECTIVE
经专门训练的 jīng zhuānmén xùnliàn de
□ She's a trained nurse. 她是个受过专门训练的护士。Tā shìgè shòu guò zhuānmén xùnliàn de hùshi.

trainee NOUN
1 受训者 shòuxùnzhě [位 wèi] *(apprentice)*
□ a trainee plumber 一个受训水管工 yígè shòuxùn shuǐguǎngōng
2 实习生 shíxíshēng [个 gè] *(in office, management job)*
□ She's a trainee. 她是个实习生。Tā shìgè shíxíshēng.

trainer NOUN
1 教练 jiàoliàn [位 wèi] *(sports coach)*
2 运动鞋 yùndòngxié [只 zhī] *(shoe)*
□ a pair of trainers 一双运动鞋 yì shuāng yùndòngxié

training NOUN
1 培训 péixùn
□ a training course 一个培训课程 yígè péixùn kèchéng
2 训练 xùnliàn *(sport)*

tram NOUN
有轨电车 yǒuguǐ diànchē [辆 liàng]

tramp NOUN
流浪者 liúlàngzhě [个 gè]

trampoline NOUN
蹦床 bèngchuáng [个 gè]

tranquillizer NOUN
镇定剂 zhèndìngjì [种 zhǒng]
□ She's on tranquillizers. 她用了镇定剂。Tā yòng le zhèndìngjì.

transfer NOUN
转移 zhuǎnyí [次 cì] *(of money, documents)*

transfusion NOUN
输血 shūxuě [次 cì]

to **translate** VERB
翻译 fānyì
□ to translate something into English 把某物翻译成英语 bǎ mǒuwù fānyì chéng Yīngyǔ

translation NOUN
1 译文 yìwén [篇 piān] *(text)*
2 翻译 fānyì *(act of translating)*

translator NOUN
翻译 fānyì [个 gè]
□ Anita's a translator. 阿妮塔是个翻译。Ānítǎ shìgè fānyì.

transparent ADJECTIVE
透明的 tòumíng de

transplant NOUN
移植 yízhí [次 cì]
□ a heart transplant 一次心脏移植 yícì xīnzàng yízhí

transport NOUN
▷ *see also* **transport** VERB
交通工具 jiāotōng gōngjù [种 zhǒng]
□ public transport 公共交通 gōnggòng jiāotōng

to **transport** VERB
▷ *see also* **transport** NOUN
运送 yùnsòng

transportation NOUN
运输 yùnshū *(US: transport)*

trap NOUN
▷ *see also* **trap** VERB
陷阱 xiànjǐng [个 gè]

to **trap** VERB
▷ *see also* **trap** NOUN
诱捕 yòubǔ *(animal)*

trash NOUN (US)
垃圾 lājī
■ **the trash can** 垃圾桶 lājītǒng

trashy ADJECTIVE
垃圾的 lājī de
□ a really trashy film 一部垃圾的电影 yíbù lājī de diànyǐng

traumatic ADJECTIVE
痛苦的 tòngkǔ de
□ It was a traumatic experience. 这是一段痛苦的经历。Zhè shì yíduàn tòngkǔ de jīnglì.

travel NOUN
▷ *see also* **travel** VERB
旅行 lǚxíng *(travelling)*

to **travel** VERB
▷ *see also* **travel** NOUN
1 旅行 qiánwǎng
□ I prefer to travel by train. 我更愿意做火车旅行。Wǒ gèng yuànyì zuò huǒchē

English-Chinese

t

lǚxíng. □ I'd like to travel round the world. 我想要周游世界。Wǒ xiǎngyào zhōuyóu shìjiè.
2 走过 zǒuguò
□ We travelled over 800 kilometres. 我们走了超过八百公里。Wǒmen zǒu le chāoguò bābǎi gōnglǐ.
■ **News travels fast!** 消息传千里！Xiāoxi chuán qiānlǐ!

travel agency NOUN
旅行社 lǚxíngshè [个 gè]

travel agent NOUN
1 旅行代理人 lǚxíng dàilǐrén [个 gè]
□ She's a travel agent. 她是个旅行代理人。Tā shìgè lǚxíng dàilǐrén.
2 旅行中介 lǚxíng zhōngjiè [个 gè] *(shop, office)*

traveller (US **traveler**) NOUN
旅行者 lǚxíngzhě [位 wèi]

traveller's cheque (US **traveler's check**) NOUN
旅行支票 lǚxíng zhīpiào [张 zhāng]

travelling (US **traveling**) NOUN
旅行 lǚxíng
□ I love travelling. 我爱旅行。Wǒ ài lǚxíng.

travel sickness NOUN
1 晕车 yūnchē *(in car)*
2 晕船 yūnchuán *(on boat)*
3 晕机 yūnjī *(on plane)*

tray NOUN
托盘 tuōpán [个 gè]

to **tread** VERB
踏 tà
□ to tread on something 踏在某物上 tà zài mǒuwù shàng

treasure NOUN
宝藏 bǎozàng [个 gè]

to **treat** VERB
▷ *see also* **treat** NOUN
1 对待 duìdài
□ She treats him really badly. 她对待他糟透了。Tā duìdài tā zāo tòu le.
2 医治 yīzhì *(patient, illness)*
■ **to treat somebody to something** 请某人吃某物 qǐng mǒurén chī mǒuwù □ He treated us to an ice cream. 他请我们吃冰淇淋。Tā qǐng wǒmen chī bīngqílín.

treat NOUN
▷ *see also* **treat** VERB
1 礼物 lǐwù *(present)*
2 款待 kuǎndài *(food)*
■ **to give somebody a treat** 款待某人 kuǎndài mǒurén

treatment NOUN
治疗 zhìliáo [次 cì] *(medical)*

to **treble** VERB
增至三倍 zēng zhì sānbèi
□ The cost of living there has trebled. 那里的生活开销增加到三倍。Nàlǐ de shēnghuó kāixiāo zēngjiādào sānbèi.

tree NOUN
树 shù [棵 kē]

to **tremble** VERB
战栗 zhànlì

trend NOUN
1 趋势 qūshì [种 zhǒng]
□ There's a trend towards part-time employment. 就业趋势倾向于兼职。Jiùyè qūshì qīngxiàngyú jiānzhí.
2 潮流 cháoliú [个 gè] *(fashion)*
□ the latest trend 最新的潮流 zuìxīn de cháoliú

trendy ADJECTIVE
时髦的 shímáo de

trial NOUN
审理 shěnlǐ [次 cì] *(in court)*

triangle NOUN
三角 sānjiǎo [个 gè]

tribe NOUN
部落 bùluò [个 gè]

trick NOUN
▷ *see also* **trick** VERB
1 恶作剧 èzuòjù [个 gè]
□ to play a trick on somebody 对某人玩恶作剧 duì mǒurén wán èzuòjù
2 戏法 xìfǎ [个 gè] *(by conjuror)*

to **trick** VERB
▷ *see also* **trick** NOUN
欺骗 qīpiàn
■ **to trick somebody** 欺骗某人 qīpiàn mǒurén

tricky ADJECTIVE
棘手的 jíshǒu de

tricycle NOUN
三轮车 sānlúnchē [辆 liàng]

to **trim** VERB
▷ *see also* **trim** NOUN
1 修剪 xiūjiǎn *(hair)*
2 修整 xiūzhěng *(grass)*

trim NOUN
▷ *see also* **trim** VERB
理发 lǐfà [次 cì] *(haircut)*
□ to have a trim 去理发 qù lǐfà

trip NOUN
▷ *see also* **trip** VERB
出行 chūxíng [次 cì]
■ **to go on a trip** 外出旅行 wàichū lǚxíng
□ Have a good trip! 旅行愉快！Lǚxíng yúkuài!
■ **a day trip** 一次一日游 yícì yírìyóu

to **trip** VERB
▷ *see also* **trip** NOUN

绊倒 bàndǎo

triple ADJECTIVE
三倍的 sānbèide

triplets PL NOUN
三胞胎 sānbāotāi

triumph NOUN
巨大的成功 jùdà de chénggōng [个 gè]

trivial ADJECTIVE
琐碎的 suǒsuì de

trod, trodden VERB ▷ *see* **tread**

trolley NOUN
1 手推车 shǒutuīchē [辆 liàng] *(for shopping)*
2 电车 diànchē [辆 liàng] *(US: vehicle)*

trombone NOUN
长号 chánghào [只 zhī]
□ I play the trombone. 我吹长号。Wǒ chuī chánghào.

troops PL NOUN
部队 bùduì [支 zhī]
□ British troops 英国部队 Yīngguó bùduì

trophy NOUN
奖品 jiǎngpǐn [个 gè]
■ **to win a trophy** 赢得一个奖品 yíngdé yígè jiǎngpǐn

tropical ADJECTIVE
热带的 rèdài de

trouble NOUN
1 麻烦 máfan [个 gè] *(difficulties, bother, effort)*
■ **to be in trouble** *(with police, authorities)* 惹上麻烦 rěshàng máfan
■ **Don't worry, it's no trouble.** 别担心，这不麻烦。Bié dānxīn, zhè bù máfan.
■ **to take a lot of trouble over something** 费很大麻烦做某事 fèi hěndà máfan zuò mǒushì
2 问题 wèntí
□ The trouble is, it's too expensive. 问题是，它太贵了。Wèntíshì, tā tài guì le.
■ **What's the trouble?** 有什么问题？Yǒu shénme wèntí?
■ **stomach trouble** 胃部毛病 wèibù máobìng

troublemaker NOUN
惹是生非的人 rěshìshēngfēi de rén [个 gè]

trousers PL NOUN
裤子 kùzi [条 tiáo]
□ a pair of trousers 一条裤子 yìtiáo kùzi

trout NOUN
鳟鱼 zūnyú [条 tiáo]

truant NOUN
■ **to play truant** 旷课 kuàngkè

truck NOUN
卡车 kǎchē [辆 liàng]
■ **a truck driver** 卡车司机 kǎchē sījī
□ He's a truck driver. 他是位卡车司机。Tā shì wèi kǎchē sījī.

true ADJECTIVE
真的 zhēnde
■ **That's true.** 那是真的。Nà shì zhēnde.
■ **to come true** 成真 chéngzhēn □ I hope my dream will come true. 我希望我的梦能成真。Wǒ xīwàng wǒ de mèng néng chéngzhēn.
■ **true love** 真爱 zhēn'ài

truly ADVERB
确实地 quèshí de
□ It was a truly remarkable victory. 那确实是非凡的胜利。Nà quèshí shì fēifán de shènglì.
■ **Yours truly** 您忠诚的 Nín zhōngchéng de

trumpet NOUN
小号 xiǎohào [把 bǎ]
□ She plays the trumpet. 她吹小号。Tā chuī xiǎohào.

trunk NOUN
1 树干 shùgàn [个 gè] *(of tree)*
2 象鼻 xiàngbí [个 gè] *(of elephant)*
3 后备箱 hòubèixiāng [个 gè] *(US: of car)*

trunks PL NOUN
游泳裤 yóuyǒngkù *(for swimming)*
■ **a pair of trunks** 一条游泳裤 yìtiáo yóuyǒngkù

to **trust** VERB
▷ *see also* **trust** NOUN
相信 xiāngxìn
■ **to trust somebody** 相信某人 xiāngxìn mǒurén □ Don't you trust me? 难道你不相信我？Nándào nǐ bùxiāngxìn wǒ? □ Trust me! 相信我！Xiāngxìn wǒ!

trust NOUN
▷ *see also* **trust** VERB
信任 xìnrèn
■ **to have trust in somebody** 信任某人 xìnrèn mǒurén

trusting ADJECTIVE
信任的 xìnrèn de

truth NOUN
事实 shìshí

truthful ADJECTIVE
诚实的 chéngshí de
□ She's a very truthful person. 她是个非常诚实的人。Tā shìgè fēicháng chéngshí de rén.

try NOUN
▷ *see also* **try** VERB
尝试 chángshì [个 gè]
□ his third try 他的第三次尝试 tā de dìsāncì chángshì
■ **to have a try** 试一试 shìyishì
■ **It's worth a try.** 值得一试。Zhídé yíshì.
■ **to give something a try** 试试某事 shìshi mǒushì

to **try** VERB
▷ *see also* **try** NOUN
1 试图 shìtú
■ **to try to do something** 试图做某事 shìtú zuò mǒushì
2 试 shì
□ I'll try. 我会试试。Wǒ huì shìshi.
■ **to try again** 再试试 zài shìshi
3 尝 cháng *(taste)*
□ Would you like to try some? 你想尝点吗？ Nǐ xiǎng cháng diǎn ma?

to **try on** VERB
试穿 shìchuān *(clothes)*

to **try out** VERB
试验 shìyàn

T-shirt NOUN
T恤衫 T xù shān [件 jiàn]

tub NOUN
1 缸 gāng [个 gè] *(container)*
2 浴缸 yùgāng [个 gè] *(US: bath)*

tube NOUN
管子 guǎnzi [根 gēn]
■ **the Tube** *(underground)* 地铁 dìtiě

tuberculosis NOUN
肺结核 fèijiéhé

Tuesday NOUN
星期二 xīngqī'èr [个 gè]
□ on Tuesday 在星期二 zài xīngqī'èr □ on Tuesdays 每个星期二 měigè xīngqī'èr
□ every Tuesday 每逢星期二 měiféng xīngqī'èr
■ **last Tuesday** 上个星期二 shànggè xīngqī'èr
■ **next Tuesday** 下个星期二 xiàgè xīngqī'èr

tuition NOUN
教学 jiàoxué
■ **private tuition** 私人教学 sīrén jiàoxué

tulip NOUN
郁金香 yùjīnxiāng [朵 duǒ]

tumble dryer NOUN
滚筒干衣机 gǔntǒng gānyījī [台 tái]

tummy NOUN
肚子 dùzi [个 gè]

tuna NOUN
金枪鱼 jīnqiāngyú [条 tiáo]

tune NOUN
曲调 qǔdiào [个 gè] *(melody)*
□ to play in tune 合着曲调演奏 hézhe qǔdiào yǎnzòu
■ **to sing out of tune** 唱歌跑调 chànggē pǎodiào

Tunisia NOUN
突尼斯 Tūnísī

tunnel NOUN
隧道 suìdào [条 tiáo]
■ **the Channel Tunnel** 英吉利海峡隧道 Yīngjílì hǎixiá suìdào

Turk NOUN
土耳其人 Tǔ'ěrqírén [个 gè]

Turkey NOUN
土耳其 Tǔ'ěrqí

turkey NOUN
1 火鸡 huǒjī [只 zhī] *(bird)*
2 火鸡肉 huǒjī ròu [块 kuài] *(meat)*

Turkish ADJECTIVE
▷ *see also* **Turkish** NOUN
土耳其的 Tǔ'ěrqí de

Turkish NOUN
▷ *see also* **Turkish** ADJECTIVE
土耳其语 Tǔ'ěrqíyǔ *(language)*

turn NOUN
▷ *see also* **turn** VERB
轮流 lúnliú [个 gè]
□ It's my turn! 轮到我了！ Lúndào wǒ le!
■ **to take turns** 轮流 lúnliú

to **turn** VERB
▷ *see also* **turn** NOUN
1 旋转 xuánzhuǎn *(object, wheel)*
□ The wheel turned round and round. 车轮一圈圈旋转。Chēlún yìquānquān xuánzhuàn.
2 转身 zhuǎnshēn *(person)*
□ She turned to face him. 她转身面对他。Tā zhuǎnshēn miànduì tā.
3 转 zhuǎn *(part of body)*
□ He had to turn his head to see. 他必须转过头才能看见。Tā bìxū zhuǎn guò tóu cái néng kànjiàn.
4 转向 zhuǎnxiàng *(vehicle)*
□ Turn right at the lights. 在红绿灯处向右转。Zài hónglǜdēng chù xiàng yòu zhuǎn.
5 调转 diàozhuǎn *(object)*
6 转动 zhuǎndòng *(handle, key)*
■ **Turn the page.** 翻页。Fānyè.
7 转 zhuǎn *(become)*
□ to turn red 转红 zhuǎn hóng
■ **to turn into something** 变成某物 biàn chéng mǒuwù □ The frog turned into a prince. 青蛙变成了一位王子。Qīngwā biànchéng le yíwèi wángzǐ.

to **turn back** VERB
往回走 wǎnghuí zǒu
□ We turned back. 我们往回走。Wǒmen wǎng huí zǒu.

to **turn down** VERB
1 回绝 huíjué
□ He turned down the offer. 他回绝了那提议。Tā huíjué le nà tíyì.
2 调低 tiáodī *(heat, sound)*
□ Shall I turn the heating down? 我应该把暖气调低吗？ Wǒ yīnggāi bǎ nuǎnqì tiáodī ma?

to **turn off** VERB
1 关 guān *(light, radio, tap)*
2 关掉 guāndiào *(engine)*

to **turn on** VERB
1 打开 dǎkāi *(light, radio, tap)*
2 关闭 guānbì *(engine)*

to **turn out** VERB
关掉 guāndiào *(light, gas)*
■ **It turned out to be a mistake.** 这原来是个错误。Zhè yuánlái shì gè cuòwu.
■ **It turned out that she was right.** 她原来是对的。Tā yuánlái shì duìde.

to **turn round, turn around** VERB
调转 diàozhuǎn *(person, vehicle)*

to **turn up** VERB
1 露面 lòumiàn *(person)*
2 出现 chūxiàn *(lost object)*
3 调高 tiáogāo *(radiator, heater)*
□ Could you turn up the radio? 你能把收音机音量调高吗？Nǐ néng bǎ shōuyīnjī yīnliàng tiáo gāo ma?

turning NOUN
拐弯 guǎiwān [个 gè] *(in road)*
□ It's the third turning on the left. 是左边的第三个拐弯处。Shì zuǒbiān de dìsānge guǎiwānchù. □ We took the wrong turning. 我们拐错弯了。Wǒmen guǎi cuò wān le.

turnip NOUN
芜菁 wújìng [个 gè]

turn signal NOUN (US)
转弯灯 zhuǎnwāndēng [个 gè]

turquoise ADJECTIVE
青绿色的 qīnglǜsè de *(colour)*

turtle NOUN
龟 guī [只 zhī]

tutor NOUN
家庭教师 jiātíng jiàoshī [位 wèi]

tuxedo NOUN (US)
男式晚礼服 nánshì wǎnlǐfú [件 jiàn]

TV NOUN
电视 diànshì

tweet NOUN
▷ *see also* **tweet** VERB
推文 tuīwén *(on Twitter)*

to **tweet** VERB
▷ *see also* **tweet** NOUN
推文 fā tuīwén *(on Twitter)*

tweezers PL NOUN
镊子 nièzi
■ **a pair of tweezers** 一把镊子 yìbǎ nièzi

twelfth ADJECTIVE
第十二的 dìshí'èr de
□ the twelfth floor 第十三层 dì shísān céng □ the twelfth of August 八月十二号 bāyuè shí'èr hào

twelve NUMBER
十二 shí'èr
□ She's twelve. 她十二岁。Tā shí'èr suì.
■ **at twelve (o'clock)** 1 *(midday)* 中午十二点 zhōngwǔ shí'èr diǎn 2 *(midnight)* 凌晨零点 língchén língdiǎn

twentieth ADJECTIVE
第二十的 dì èrshí de
□ the twentieth time 第二十次 dì èrshí cì
□ the twentieth of May 五月二十号 wǔyuè èrshí hào

twenty NUMBER
二十 èrshí
□ He's twenty. 他二十岁。Tā èrshí suì.

twice ADVERB
两次 liǎngcì
■ **twice as much** 两倍 liǎngbèi □ He gets twice as much pocket money as me. 他的零用钱是我的两倍。Tāde língyòngqián shì wǒde liǎngbèi.

twin NOUN
双胞胎 shuāngbāotāi [对 duì]
□ my twin brother 我的双胞胎兄弟 wǒ de shuāngbāotāi xiōngdì □ her twin sister 她的双胞胎姐妹 tā de shuāngbāotāi jiěmèi
■ **identical twins** 同卵双胞胎 tóngluǎn shuāngbāotāi
■ **a twin room** 一间双人房 yìjiān shuāngrénfáng

to **twist** VERB
1 拧 nǐng *(turn)*
2 扭伤 niǔshāng
□ I've twisted my ankle. 我扭伤了脚踝。Wǒ nǐu shāng le jiǎohuái.

Twitter® NOUN
推特 Tuītè

two NUMBER
二 èr
■ **She's two.** 她两岁。Tā liǎng suì.

two-percent milk NOUN (US)
半脱脂奶 bàn tuōzhīnǎi

type NOUN
▷ *see also* **type** VERB
类型 lèixíng [种 zhǒng]
□ What type of camera have you got? 你用的是哪种照相机？Nǐ yòng de shì nǎ zhǒng zhàoxiàngjī?

to **type** VERB
▷ *see also* **type** NOUN
打字 dǎzì
■ **to type a letter** 打一封信 dǎ yìfēng xìn

typewriter NOUN
打字机 dǎzìjī [台 tái]

typical ADJECTIVE
典型的 diǎnxíng de

tyre (US **tire**) NOUN
轮胎 lúntāi [个 gè]
■ **the tyre pressure** 轮胎气压 lúntāi qìyā

Uu

UFO NOUN
不明飞行物 bùmíng fēixíngwù [个 gè]
ugh EXCLAMATION
呃 è
ugly ADJECTIVE
丑陋的 chǒulòu de
UK NOUN
■ **the UK** 大不列颠及北爱尔兰联合王国 Dàbúlièdiān jí Běi'ài'ěrlán Liánhéwángguó
■ **from the UK** 从英国 cóng Yīngguó
■ **in the UK** 在英国 zài Yīngguó
■ **to the UK** 去英国 qù Yīngguó
ulcer NOUN
溃疡 kuìyáng [处 chù]
■ **a mouth ulcer** 一处嘴上的溃疡 yí chù zuǐshàngde kuìyáng
Ulster NOUN
乌尔斯特 Wūěrsītè
ultimate ADJECTIVE
终极的 zhōngjíde
□ the ultimate challenge 终极挑战 zhōngjí tiǎozhàn
ultimately ADVERB
最终 zuìzhōng
□ Ultimately, it's your decision. 最终，是你的决定。Zuìzhōng, shì nǐ de juédìng.
umbrella NOUN
1 雨伞 yǔsǎn
2 遮阳伞 zhēyángsǎn *(for sun)*
LANGUAGE TIP 伞 sǎn can also be used by itself for both meanings.
umpire NOUN
裁判员 cáipànyuán [位 wèi]
UN NOUN
■ **the UN** 联合国 Liánhéguó
unable ADJECTIVE
■ **to be unable to do something** 不能做某事 bùnéng zuò mǒushì □ I was unable to come. 我没能来。Wǒ méinéng lái.
unacceptable ADJECTIVE
不可接受的 bùkějiēshòu de
unanimous ADJECTIVE
一致同意的 yízhì tóngyì de
□ a unanimous decision 一个一致同意的决定 yígè yízhì tóngyì de juédìng
unattended ADJECTIVE
无人照顾的 wúrénzhàogù de
■ **Do not leave your luggage unattended.** 请保管好您的行李。Qǐng bǎoguǎnhǎo nín de xínglǐ.
unavoidable ADJECTIVE
不可避免的 bùkě bìmiǎn de
unaware ADJECTIVE
■ **to be unaware 1** *(not know about)* 不知道 bù zhīdào □ I was unaware of the regulations. 我不知道这些规章制度。Wǒ bù zhīdào zhèxiē guīzhāng zhìdù. **2** *(not notice)* 没有意识到的 méiyǒu yìshi dào de □ She was unaware that she was being filmed. 她没有意识到自己被拍摄下来了。Tā méiyǒu yìshi dào zìjǐ bèipāi xià lái le.
unbearable ADJECTIVE
难以忍受的 nányǐ rěnshòu de
unbeatable ADJECTIVE
不可战胜的 bùkězhànshèng de
unbelievable ADJECTIVE
不可思议的 bùkěsīyì de
unborn ADJECTIVE
未出生的 wèi chūshēng de
■ **the unborn child** 未出生的孩子 wèi chūshēng de háizi
unbreakable ADJECTIVE
不可破坏的 bù kě pòhuài de
uncertain ADJECTIVE
不确定的 bú quèdìng de
□ The future is uncertain. 未来是不确定的。Wèilái shì búquèdìng de.
■ **to be uncertain about something** 对某事不确定 duì mǒushì búquèdìng
uncivilized ADJECTIVE
不文明的 bù wénmíng de
uncle NOUN
1 伯父 bófù [位 wèi] *(father's older brother)*
2 叔父 shūfù [位 wèi] *(father's younger brother)*
3 姑父 gūfù [位 wèi] *(father's sister's husband)*
4 舅父 jiùfù [位 wèi] *(mother's brother)*
5 姨父 jífù [位 wèi] *(mother's sister's husband)*
uncomfortable ADJECTIVE

1 不舒服的 bù shūfu de *(person)*
2 不舒适的 bù shūshì de *(chair, journey)*

unconscious ADJECTIVE
失去知觉的 shīqù zhījué de

uncontrollable ADJECTIVE
不可控制的 bù kě kòngzhì de

unconventional ADJECTIVE
非传统的 fēi chuántǒng de

under PREPOSITION
1 在…下面 zài…xiàmian
□ The cat's under the table. 猫在桌子下面。Māo zaì zhuōzi xiàmiàn.
2 不到 búdào *(less than)*
□ under 20 people 不到二十人 búdào èrshí rén
3 以下 yǐxià *(in age, price)*
□ children under 10 十岁以下的儿童 shí suì yǐxià de értóng
■ **under there** 在那下面 zài nà xiàmiàn
□ What's under there? 什么在那下面？Shénme zài nà xiàmiàn?

underage ADJECTIVE
未成年的 wèi chéngnián de
■ **He's underage.** 他未成年。Tā wèi chéngnián.

undercover ADJECTIVE, ADVERB
秘密的 mìmì de
□ undercover investigation 秘密的调查 mìmi de diàochá
■ **She was working undercover.** 她曾经做秘密工作。Tā céngjīng zuò mìmì gōngzuò.

to **underestimate** VERB
低估 dīgū
□ I underestimated her. 我低估了她。Wǒ dīgūle tā.

to **undergo** VERB
经受 jīngshòu
■ **undergo an ordeal** 经受考验 jīngshòu kǎoyàn

underground NOUN
▷ *see also* **underground** ADJECTIVE, ADVERB
地铁 dìtiě
□ Is there an underground in Beijing? 北京有地铁吗？Běijīng yǒu dìtiě ma?

underground ADJECTIVE
▷ *see also* **underground** NOUN, ADVERB
地下的 dìxià de
□ an underground car park 地下停车场 dìxià tíngchē chǎng

underground ADVERB
▷ *see also* **underground** NOUN, ADJECTIVE
在地下 zài dìxià
□ Moles live underground. 鼹鼠生活在地下。Yànshǔ shēnghuó zài dìxià.

to **underline** VERB
在…下面划线 zài…xiàmian huàxiàn

underneath PREPOSITION, ADVERB
在…下面 zài…xiàmiàn
□ underneath the carpet 在地毯下面 zài dìtǎn xiàmian □ I got out of the car and looked underneath. 我下了车往下面看。Wǒ xià le chē wǎng xiàmiàn kàn.

underpaid ADJECTIVE
报酬过低的 bàochóu guòdī de
□ Teachers are underpaid. 老师的报酬过低。Lǎoshī de bàochóu guòdī.

underpants PL NOUN
内裤 nèikù [条 tiáo]

underpass NOUN
地下通道 dìxià tōngdào [条 tiáo]

undershirt NOUN (US)
贴身内衣 tiēshēn nèiyī [件 jiàn]

underskirt NOUN
内衣 nèiyī [件 jiàn]

to **understand** VERB
1 明白 míngbai
□ Do you understand? 你明白了吗？Nǐ míngbai le ma?
2 懂 dǒng *(to apprehend clearly the character/ nature of)*
□ I don't understand this word. 我不懂这个词。Wǒ bùdǒng zhège cí. □ She doesn't understand Chinese. 她不懂汉语。Tā bùdǒng Hànyǔ. □ Is that understood? 懂了吗？Dǒng le ma? □ I don't understand why he did it. 我不懂他为什么做了这件事。Wǒ bùdǒng tā wèishénme zuòle zhèjiànshì.

understanding ADJECTIVE
通情达理的 tōngqíng dálǐ de
□ She's very understanding. 她非常通情达理。Tā fēicháng tōngqíng dálǐ.

understood VERB ▷ *see* **understand**

undertaker NOUN
丧事承办人 sāngshì chéngbàn rén [个 gè]

underwater ADVERB
在水下 zài shuǐxià
□ This sequence was filmed underwater. 这分段是在水下拍摄的。Zhè fēnduàn shì zài shuǐxià pāishè de.

underwear NOUN
内衣 nèiyī [件 jiàn]

underwent VERB ▷ *see* **undergo**

to **undo** VERB
1 解开 jiěkāi *(button, knot)*
2 拆开 chāikāi *(parcel)*

to **undress** VERB
脱衣服 tuō yīfu
□ The doctor told me to undress. 医生让我脱衣服。Yīshēng ràng wǒ tuō yīfu.

unemployed ADJECTIVE
失业的 shīyè de

□ He's been unemployed for a year. 他失业一年了。Tā shīyè yìnián le.
■ **the unemployed** 失业者 shīyèzhě

unemployment NOUN
失业 shīyè

unexpected ADJECTIVE
意外的 yìwài de
□ an unexpected visitor 意外的访客 yìwài de fǎngkè

unexpectedly ADVERB
意外地 yìwài de
□ They arrived unexpectedly. 他们意外地到达了。Tāmen yìwài de dàodá le.

unfair ADJECTIVE
不公平的 bù gōngpíng de
□ This law is unfair to women. 这部法律对女性不公平。Zhèbù fǎlǜ duì nǚxìng bù gōngpíng.

unfamiliar ADJECTIVE
陌生的 mòshēng de
□ I heard an unfamiliar voice. 我听到了一个陌生的声音。Wǒ tīngdào le yígè mòshēng de shēngyīn.

unfashionable ADJECTIVE
过时的 guòshí de

unfit ADJECTIVE
不太健康的 bú tài jiànkāng de
■ **I'm rather unfit.** 我非常不健康。Wǒ fēicháng bú jiànkāng.

to **unfold** VERB
展开 zhǎnkāi
□ She unfolded the map. 她展开了地图。Tā zhǎnkāi le dìtú.

unforgettable ADJECTIVE
难忘的 nánwàng de

unfortunately ADVERB
可惜 kěxī
□ Unfortunately, I arrived late. 很可惜，我迟到了。Hěn kěxī, wǒ chídào le.

unfriendly ADJECTIVE
不友善的 bù yǒushàn de
□ The waiters are a bit unfriendly. 这些服务员不太友善。Zhèxiē fúwùyuán bú tài yǒushàn.

ungrateful ADJECTIVE
忘恩负义的 wàng'ēnfùyìde

unhappy ADJECTIVE
不快乐的 bú kuàilè de
□ He was very unhappy as a child. 他小时候不快乐。Tā xiǎoshíhòu bù kuàilè.
■ **to look unhappy** 看起来不快乐 kànqǐlái bù kuàilè

unhealthy ADJECTIVE
1 身体不佳的 shēntǐ bùjiā de *(person)*
2 不利于健康的 bú lìyú jiànkāng de *(place, diet)*

uni NOUN
大学 dàxué [所 suǒ] *(university)*
□ to go to uni 上大学 shàng dàxué

uniform NOUN
制服 zhìfú [套 tào]
□ my school uniform 我学校的制服 wǒ xuéxiào de zhìfú

uninhabited ADJECTIVE
无人居住的 wúrén jūzhù de

union NOUN
工会 gōnghuì [个 gè] *(trade union)*

Union Jack NOUN
英国国旗 Yīngguó guóqí [面 miàn]

unique ADJECTIVE
罕有的 hǎnyǒu de

unit NOUN
1 单位 dānwèi [个 gè]
□ a unit of measurement 一个测量单位 yígè cèliáng dānwèi
2 组合 zǔhé [套 tào] *(piece of furniture)*
□ a kitchen unit 一套厨房家具组合 yítào chúfáng jiājù zǔhé

United Kingdom NOUN
■ **the United Kingdom** 大不列颠及北爱尔兰联合王国 Dàbùlièdiān Jí Běi'àiěr'lán Liánhéwángguó

United Nations NOUN
■ **the United Nations** 联合国 Liánhéguó

United States NOUN
■ **the United States** 美国 Měiguó

universe NOUN
宇宙 yǔzhòu [个 gè]

university NOUN
大学 dàxué [所 suǒ]
□ She's at university. 她在上大学。Tā zài shàng dàxué. □ Edinburgh University 爱丁堡大学 Àidīngbǎo Dàxué
■ **to go to university** 上大学 shàng dàxué

unkind ADJECTIVE
刻薄的 kèbó de

unleaded petrol NOUN
无铅汽油 wúqiān qìyóu

unless CONJUNCTION
除非 chúfēi
□ I won't come unless you phone me. 我不会来，除非你打电话给我。Wǒ búhuìlái, chúfēi nǐ dǎ diànhuà gěi wǒ.

unlike PREPOSITION
不像 búxiàng
□ Unlike him, I really enjoy flying. 不像他，我很喜欢飞行。Búxiàng tā, wǒ hěn xǐhuan fēixíng.

unlikely ADJECTIVE
不太可能的 bú tài kěnéng de
□ He is unlikely to win. 他不太可能获胜。Tā bú tài kěnéng huòshèng.

unlisted ADJECTIVE (US)
未登记的 wèi dēngjì de
■ **an unlisted number** 一个未登记的号码 yígè wèi dēngjì de hàomǎ

to **unload** VERB
卸 xiè
□ We unloaded the furniture. 我们卸下了家具。Wǒmen xièxià le jiājù. □ The lorries go there to unload. 货车去那里卸货。Huòchē qù nàlǐ xièhuò.

to **unlock** VERB
开 kāi
□ He unlocked the door of the car. 他打开了车门锁。Tā dǎkāi le chēmén suǒ.

unlucky ADJECTIVE
■ **to be unlucky 1** *(person)* 不幸运的 bù xìngyùn de □ Did you win? — No, I was unlucky yesterday. 你赢了吗？ — 没有，我昨天不幸运。Nǐ yíng le ma? — Méiyǒu, wǒ zuótiān bù xìngyùn. **2** *(number, object)* 不吉利的 bù jílì de □ They say thirteen is an unlucky number. 他们说十三是个不吉利的数字。Tāmen shuō shísān shì gè bùjílì de shùzì.

unmarried ADJECTIVE
未婚的 wèihūn de
□ an unmarried couple 一对未婚情侣 yíduì wèihūn qínglǚ

unnatural ADJECTIVE
反常的 fǎncháng de

unnecessary ADJECTIVE
不必要的 bú bìyào de

unofficial ADJECTIVE
1 非正式的 fēi zhèngshì de *(meeting, leader)*
2 未经许可的 wèi jīng xǔkě de *(strike)*

to **unpack** VERB
1 打开行李 dǎkāi xínglǐ
□ I went to my room to unpack. 我去房间打开行李。Wǒ qù fángjiān dǎkāi xínglǐ.
2 打开…取出东西 dǎkāi...qǔchū dōngxi *(suitcase, bag)*
□ I unpacked my suitcase. 我打开了行李箱取出东西。Wǒ dǎkāi le xínglǐxiāng qǔchū dōngxi.

unpleasant ADJECTIVE
1 使人不愉快的 shǐ rén bù yúkuài de *(person)*
2 令人讨厌的 lìng rén tǎoyàn de *(person, manner)*

to **unplug** VERB
拔去…的插头 báqù...de chātóu

unpopular ADJECTIVE
不受欢迎的 bú shòu huānyíng de

unpredictable ADJECTIVE
不可预知的 bù kě yùzhī de

unreal ADJECTIVE
不可思议的 bùkěsīyìde *(incredible)*
□ It was unreal! 真是不可思议！Zhēnshì bùkěsīyì!

unrealistic ADJECTIVE
不切实际的 bú qiè shíjì de

unreasonable ADJECTIVE
无理的 wúlǐ de
□ Her attitude was completely unreasonable. 她太无理了。Tā tài wúlǐ le.

unreliable ADJECTIVE
1 不可信赖的 bù kě xìnlài de *(person, firm)*
□ He's completely unreliable. 他完全不可信赖。Tā wánquán bù kě xìnlài.
2 不可靠的 bù kěkào de *(machine, method, person)*
□ It's a nice car, but a bit unreliable. 这是辆不错的车，就是不太可靠。Zhèshì liàng búcuò de chē, jiùshì bú tài kěkào.

to **unroll** VERB
展开 zhǎnkāi

unsatisfactory ADJECTIVE
不满意的 bù mǎnyì de

to **unscrew** VERB
旋开 xuánkāi
□ She unscrewed the top of the bottle. 她旋开了瓶盖。Tā xuánkāi le pínggài.

unshaven ADJECTIVE
未剃须的 wèi tìxū de

unstable ADJECTIVE
不稳定的 bù wěndìng de

unsteady ADJECTIVE
不稳 bù wěn *(walk, voice)*
■ **He was unsteady on his feet.** 他站不稳。Tā zhàn bù wěn.

unsuccessful ADJECTIVE
1 失败的 shībài de
2 不成功的 bù chénggōng de
■ **to be unsuccessful in doing something** 做某事不成功 zuò mǒushì bù chénggōng

unsuitable ADJECTIVE
1 不适宜的 bú shìyí de *(place, time, clothes)*
2 不合适的 bù héshì de *(candidate, applicant)*

untidy ADJECTIVE
1 不整洁的 bù zhěngjié de
□ My bedroom's always untidy. 我的卧室经常不整洁。Wǒ de wòshì jīngcháng bù zhěngjié.
2 邋遢的 lātā de *(person, appearance)*
□ He's always untidy. 他经常邋遢。Tā jīngcháng lātā.
3 懒散的 lǎnsǎn de *(in character)*
□ He's a very untidy person. 他很懒散。Tā hěn lǎnsǎn.

to **untie** VERB
1 解开 jiěkāi *(knot, parcel)*
2 放生 fàngshēng *(animal)*

DID YOU KNOW...? 放生 fàngshēng is the Buddhist ritual of releasing animals. Many Buddhist temples will house vendors selling fish or birds, which can be bought and subsequently released.

until PREPOSITION, CONJUNCTION

1 直到...点 zhídào...diǎn
□ I waited until ten o'clock. 我一直等到十点。Wǒ yìzhí děngdào shí diǎn.
■ **until now** 直到现在 zhídào xiànzài
□ It's never been a problem until now. 这直到现在都不是个问题。Zhè zhídào xiànzài dōu bú shì gè wèntí.
■ **until then** 到那个时候 dào nàge shíhòu
□ Until then I'd never been to France. 到那时，我还没有去过法国。Dào nàshí, wǒ hái méiyǒu qùguò Fǎguó.

2 到...为止 dào...wéizhǐ
□ We stayed there until the doctor came. 我们在那里直到医生来了为止。Wǒmen zài nàlǐ zhídào yīshēng lái le wéizhǐ.

unusual ADJECTIVE
不寻常的 bù xúncháng de
□ an unusual shape 不寻常的形状 bù xúncháng de xíngzhuàng □ It's unusual to get snow at this time of year. 一年的这个时间下雪很不寻常。Yìnián de zhègè shíjiān xiàxuě hěnbù xúncháng.

unwilling ADJECTIVE
■ **to be unwilling to do something** 不愿做某事 búyuàn zuò mǒushì □ He was unwilling to help me. 他不愿帮我。Tā búyuàn bāng wǒ.

to **unwind** VERB
放松 fàngsōng *(relax)*

unwise ADJECTIVE
不明智的 bù míngzhì de *(person)*
□ That was rather unwise of you. 你那么做不太明智。Nǐ nàme zuò bù tài míngzhì.

unwound VERB ▷ *see* **unwind**

to **unwrap** VERB
打开...的包装 dǎkāi...de bāozhuāng
□ After the meal we unwrapped the presents. 吃了饭，我们打开了礼物的包装。Chīlefàn, wǒmen dǎkāi le lǐwù de bāozhuāng.

up PREPOSITION, ADVERB

LANGUAGE TIP For other expressions with **up**, see the verbs **go**, **come**, **put**, **turn** etc.

在...上 zài...shàng *(at higher point on)*
□ up on the hill 在山上 zài shānshàng
■ **up here** 这上面 zhè shàngmiàn
■ **up there** 那上面 nà shàngmiàn
■ **to be up** *(out of bed)* 起床 qǐchuáng
□ We were up at 6. 我们六点起床。Wǒmen liùdiǎn qǐchuáng. □ He's not up yet. 他还没起床。Tā hái méi qǐchuáng.
■ **What's up?** 怎么样了？ Zěnmeyàng le?
□ What's up with her? 她怎么样了？ Tā zěnmeyàng le?
■ **to get up** *(in the morning)* 起床 qǐchuáng
□ What time do you get up? 你几点起床？ Nǐ jǐdiǎn qǐchuáng?
■ **to go up** 往上走 wǎng shàng zǒu □ The bus went up the hill. 公共汽车往山上走。Gōnggòng qìchē wǎng shānshàng zǒu.
■ **up to now** 直到现在 zhídào xiànzài
■ **She came up to me.** 她朝我走来。Tā cháo wǒ zǒu lái.
■ **It's up to you.** 随便你。Suíbiàn nǐ.

upbringing NOUN
抚养 fǔyǎng

uphill ADVERB
往坡上 wǎng pōshàng
■ **to go uphill** 去爬山 qù páshān

upper ADJECTIVE
上面的 shàng miàn de
□ on the upper floor 上面一层 shàngmiàn yìcéng

upper sixth NOUN
■ **the upper sixth** 六年制高年级 liùnián zhì gāo niánjí □ She's in the upper sixth. 她是六年制的高年级学生。Tā shì liùnián zhì gāo niánjí xúesheng.

upright ADVERB
挺直地 tǐngzhí de
□ to stand upright 挺直站 tǐngzhí zhàn

to **upset** VERB
▷ *see also* **upset** ADJECTIVE
使苦恼 shǐ kǔnǎo
■ **to upset somebody** 使某人苦恼 shǐ mǒurén kǔnǎo

upset ADJECTIVE
▷ *see also* **upset** VERB
心烦意乱的 xīnfán yìluàn de
□ She's still a bit upset. 她还是心烦意乱。Tā háishì xīnfányìluàn.
■ **to be upset about something** 为某事感到烦恼 wèi mǒushì gǎndào fánnǎo
■ **I had an upset stomach.** 我胃不舒服。Wǒ wèi bù shūfu.

upside down ADVERB
上下颠倒地 shàngxià diāndǎo de
□ That painting is upside down. 这幅画上下颠倒了。Zhè fú huà shàngxià diāndǎo le.

upstairs ADVERB

1 在楼上 zài lóushàng *(be)*
□ Where's your coat? — It's upstairs. 你的衣服呢？ — 在楼上。Nǐ de yīfu ne? — Zài lóushàng.

2 往楼上 wǎng lóushàng *(go)*
□ He went upstairs to bed. 他上楼睡觉了。Tā shànglóu shuìjiào le.

uptight ADJECTIVE
焦虑的 jiāolǜ de
□ She's really uptight. 她非常焦虑。Tā fēicháng jiāolǜ.

up-to-date ADJECTIVE
最新的 zuìxīn de
□ an up-to-date timetable 最近的时间表 zuìxīn de shíjiānbiǎo
■ **to bring something up to date** 更新某物 gèngxīn mǒuwù

upwards ADVERB
向上 xiàngshàng
□ to look upwards 向上看 xiàngshàng kàn

urgent ADJECTIVE
紧急的 jǐnjí de
□ Is it urgent? 这个紧急吗？ Zhège jǐnjí ma?

urine NOUN
尿液 niàoyè

US NOUN
■ **the US** 美国 Měiguó

us PRONOUN
我们 wǒmen
□ They helped us. 他们帮助了我们。Tāmen bāngzhù le wǒmen. □ They gave us a map. 他们给我们一张地图。Tāmen gěi wǒmen yìzhāng dìtú.

USA NOUN
■ **the USA** 美国 Měiguó

use NOUN
▷ *see also* **use** VERB
用处 yòngchù [种 zhǒng]
■ **It's no use.** 没用的。Méiyòng de.
□ It's no use shouting, she's deaf. 喊是没用的，她耳聋。Hǎn shì méiyòng de, tā ěrlóng.
■ **It's no use, I can't do it.** 这没用，我做不了。Zhè méiyòng, wǒ zuò bùliǎo.
■ **to make use of something** 利用某物 lìyòng mǒuwù

to **use** VERB
▷ *see also* **use** NOUN
使用 shǐyòng
□ Can we use a dictionary in the exam? 考试中可以使用字典吗？ Kǎoshì zhōng kěyǐ shǐyòng zìdiǎn ma? □ Can I use your phone? 我可以用你的手机吗？ Wǒ kěyǐ yòng nǐ de shǒujī ma?
■ **to use the toilet** 用厕所 yòngcèsuǒ
■ **I used to live in London.** 我曾经住在伦敦。Wǒ céngjīng zhùzài Lúndūn.
■ **I used not to like maths, but now I love it.** 我过去不喜欢数学，现在非常喜欢。Wǒ guòqù bù xǐhuan shùxué, xiànzài fēicháng xǐhuan.
■ **to be used to something** 习惯于某事 xíguàn yú mǒushì □ He wasn't used to driving on the right. 他不习惯在右边开车。Tā bù xíguàn zài yòubiān kāichē.
■ **to get used to something** 习惯于某事 xíguàn yú mǒushì □ I am getting used to getting up early. 我开始习惯于早起。Wǒ kāishǐ xíguàn yú zǎoqǐ.
■ **a used car** 旧车 jiùchē

to **use up** VERB
用完 yòngwán
□ We've used up all the paint. 我们已经用完了所有的油漆。Wǒmen yǐjīng yòngwán le suǒyǒu de yóuqī.

useful ADJECTIVE
有用的 yǒuyòng de

useless ADJECTIVE
1 没用的 méiyòng de
□ a piece of useless information 一条没用的消息 yì tiáo méiyòng de xiāoxī □ This map is just useless. 这张地图一点用处都没有。Zhè zhāng dìtú yìdiǎn yòngchu dōu méiyǒu. □ You're useless! 你真没用！ Nǐ zhēn méiyòng!
2 徒劳的 túláo de *(pointless)*
□ It's useless asking her! 问她是徒劳的！Wèn tā shì túláo de!

user NOUN
使用者 shǐyòngzhě [位 wèi]

user-friendly ADJECTIVE
易于使用的 yìyú shǐyòng de

usual ADJECTIVE
平常的 píngcháng de
■ **as usual** 像往常一样 xiàng wǎngcháng yíyàng
■ **warmer than usual** 比平常暖和 bǐ píngcháng nuǎnhuo

usually ADVERB
通常地 tōngcháng de
□ I usually get to school at about half past eight. 我通常在八点半到学校。Wǒ tōngcháng zài bādiǎn bàn dào xuéxiào.

utility room NOUN
储物室 chǔwùshì [个 gè]

U-turn NOUN
一百八十度转弯 yìbǎi bāshí dù zhuǎnwān [个 gè]
□ The car made a U-turn on the road. 那辆车在路上来了个一百八十度大转弯。Nà liàng chē zài lùshang lái le ge yìbǎi bāshí dù dà zhuǎnwān.

vacancy NOUN
1 空缺 kòngquē [个 gè] *(job)*
2 空房 kòngfáng [间 jiān] *(hotel room)*
■ **'no vacancies'** *(on sign)* "客满" "kèmǎn"

vacant ADJECTIVE
空着的 kòngzhe de

vacation NOUN (US)
休假 xiūjià [次 cì]
■ **to take a vacation** 休假 xiūjià
■ **to be on vacation** 在度假 zài dùjià
■ **to go on vacation** 去度假 qù dùjià

to **vaccinate** VERB
■ **to vaccinate somebody against something** 给某人接种疫苗预防某疾病 gěi mǒurén jiēzhòng yìmiáo yùfáng mǒu jíbìng

to **vacuum** VERB
用吸尘器打扫 yòng xīchénqì dǎsǎo
■ **to vacuum the hall** 用吸尘器打扫大厅 yòng xīchénqì dǎsǎo dàtīng

vacuum cleaner NOUN
真空吸尘器 zhēnkōng xīchénqì [台 tái]

vague ADJECTIVE
不清楚的 bù qīngchǔ de

vain ADJECTIVE
自负的 zìfù de *(person)*
□ He's so vain! 他太自负了！ Tā tài zìfù le!
■ **in vain** 徒劳 túláo

Valentine card NOUN
情人节贺卡 Qíngrénjié hèkǎ [张 zhāng]

Valentine's Day NOUN
情人节 Qíngrénjié [个 gè]

DID YOU KNOW...?
Although Valentine's day is celebrated in China on 14 February, the traditional lunar calendar has a similar festival for lovers, 七夕 qīxī, which takes place on the seventh day of the seventh lunar month.

valid ADJECTIVE
有效的 yǒuxiào de
□ This ticket is valid for three months. 这张票三个月内有效。Zhè zhāng piào sāngè yuè nèi yǒuxiào.

valley NOUN
山谷 shāngǔ [个 gè]

valuable ADJECTIVE
宝贵的 bǎoguì de
□ a valuable picture 一张宝贵的照片 yì zhāng bǎoguì de zhàopiān

valuables PL NOUN
贵重物品 guìzhòng wùpǐn [件 jiàn]
□ Don't take any valuables with you. 不要随身带贵重物品。Bú yào suíshēn dài guìzhòng wùpǐn.

value NOUN
1 价值 jiàzhí [种 zhǒng] *(financial worth)*
2 价格 jiàgé *(worth in relation to price)*
■ **It's good value for money.** 这很合算。Zhè hěn hésuàn.

van NOUN
厢式运货车 xiāngshì yùnhuòchē [辆 liàng]

vandalism NOUN
蓄意破坏 xùyì pòhuài

to **vandalize** VERB
肆意毁坏 sìyì huǐhuài

vanilla NOUN
香草 xiāngcǎo
□ vanilla ice cream 香草冰激淋 xiāngcǎo bīngjīlín

to **vanish** VERB
消失 xiāoshī

varied ADJECTIVE
各种各样的 gèzhǒng gèyàng de

variety NOUN
1 多样性 duōyàngxìng *(diversity)*
2 种类 zhǒnglèi *(range: of objects)*

various ADJECTIVE
不同的 bùtóng de
□ We visited various villages in the area. 我们参观了该地区不同的村庄。Wǒmen cānguān le gāi dìqū bùtóng de cūnzhuāng.

to **vary** VERB
1 改变 gǎibiàn *(make changes to)*
2 使多样化 shǐ duōyàng huà *(be different)*

vase NOUN
花瓶 huāpíng [个 gè]

VAT NOUN *(= value added tax)*
增值税 zēngzhíshuì

VCR NOUN *(= video cassette recorder)*
录像机 lùxiàngjī [台 tái]

VDT NOUN (US) *(= visual display terminal)*
视频显示终端 shìpín xiǎnshì zhōngduān

VDU NOUN *(= visual display unit)*
视频显示装置 shìpín xiǎnshì zhuāngzhì

veal NOUN
小牛肉 xiǎoniúròu [克 kè]

vegan NOUN
纯素食主义者 chún sùshí zhǔyìzhě [个 gè]
▫ I'm a vegan. 我是个纯素质主义者。Wǒ shìgè chún sùshí zhǔyìzhě.

vegetable NOUN
蔬菜 shūcài [种 zhǒng]
▫ vegetable soup 蔬菜汤 shūcài tāng

vegetarian NOUN
▹ *see also* **vegetarian** ADJECTIVE
素食者 sùshízhě [个 gè]
▫ I'm a vegetarian. 我是个素食者。Wǒ shìgè sùshízhě.

vegetarian ADJECTIVE
▹ *see also* **vegetarian** NOUN
的 sù de *(diet, restaurant etc)*
▫ Is there anything vegetarian on the menu? 菜单上有什么素菜吗？ Càidān shàng yǒu shénme sùcài ma?

vehicle NOUN
载运工具 zàiyùn gōngjù [辆 liàng]

vein NOUN
静脉 jìngmài [条 tiáo]

velvet NOUN
天鹅绒 tiān'éróng [块 kuài]

vending machine NOUN
自动售货机 zìdòng shòuhuòjī [部 bù]

verb NOUN
动词 dòngcí [个 gè]

verdict NOUN
判决 pànjué [个 gè]

versus PREPOSITION
对 duì

vertical ADJECTIVE
垂直的 chuízhí de

vertigo NOUN
眩晕 xuànyūn
▫ I get vertigo. 我会感到眩晕。Wǒ huì gǎn dào xuànyūn.

very ADVERB
很 hěn
▫ very tall 很高 hěn gāo ▫ not very interesting 不是很有趣 búshì hěn yǒuqù
▪ **the very beginning** 一开始 yì kāishǐ
▪ **the very end** 最终 zuìzhōng
▪ **very much so** 确实如此 quèshí rúcǐ
▪ **very little** 极少的 jíshǎo de
▪ **there isn't very much of...** …不太多了… bùtài duōle

vest NOUN
1 汗衫 hànshān [件 jiàn] *(underwear)*
2 马甲 mǎjiǎ [件 jiàn] (US: *waistcoat)*

vet NOUN
兽医 shòuyī [个 gè] *(veterinary surgeon)*

veterinarian NOUN (US)
兽医 shòuyī [个 gè]

via PREPOSITION
经由 jīngyóu
▫ We went to Paris via Boulogne. 我们经由布洛涅到巴黎。Wǒmen jīngyóu Bùluònìe dào Bālí.

vicar NOUN
教区牧师 jiàoqū mùshī [位 wèi]

vice versa ADVERB
反之亦然 fǎn zhī yì rán

vicious ADJECTIVE
1 凶狠的 xiōnghěn de *(attack, blow)*
▫ a vicious attack 一次凶狠的攻击 yícì xiōnghěn de gōngjī
2 凶残的 xiōngcán de *(person, dog)*
▪ **a vicious circle** 一种恶性循环 yìzhǒng èxìng xúnhuán

victim NOUN
受害者 shòuhàizhě [个 gè]
▪ **to be the victim of** 成为…的受害者 chéngwéi...de shòuhàizhě ▫ He was the victim of a mugging. 他是行凶抢劫的受害者。Tā shì xíngxiōng qiǎngjié de shòuhàizhě.

victory NOUN
胜利 shènglì [次 cì]

video NOUN
▹ *see also* **video** VERB
1 录像 lùxiàng [段 duàn] *(film)*
▫ a video of my family on holiday 一段我全家度假时的录像 yíduàn wǒ quánjiā dùjià shí de lùxiàng
2 录像带 lùxiàngdài [盘 pán] *(cassette)*
▫ She lent me a video. 她借我一盘录像带。Tā jiè wǒ yìpán lùxiàngdài.
3 录像机 lùxiàngjī [台 tái] *(machine)*
▪ **a video shop** 一家录像带租赁店 yì jiā lùxiàngdài zūlìn diàn

to **video** VERB
▹ *see also* **video** NOUN
录 lù

video camera NOUN
摄像机 shèxiàngjī [台 tái]

video game NOUN
电子游戏 diànzǐ yóuxì [个 gè]
▫ He likes playing video games. 他喜欢玩电子游戏。Tā xǐhuan wán diànzǐ yóuxì.

videophone NOUN
可视电话 kěshì diànhuà [部 bù]

video recorder NOUN

录像机 lùxiàngjī [台 tái]

Vietnam NOUN
越南 Yuènán

Vietnamese ADJECTIVE
▷ *see also* **Vietnamese** NOUN
越南的 Yuènán de

Vietnamese NOUN
▷ *see also* **Vietnamese** ADJECTIVE
1 越南人 Yuènánrén [个 gè] *(person)*
2 越南语 Yuènányǔ *(language)*

view NOUN
1 风景 fēngjǐng [道 dào]
□ There's an amazing view. 这里风景真迷人。Zhèlǐ fēngjǐng zhēn mírén.
2 看法 kànfǎ [种 zhǒng] *(opinion)*
■ **in my view** 在我看来 zài wǒ kàn lái

viewpoint NOUN
观点 guāndiǎn [个 gè]

vile ADJECTIVE
恶心的 ěxīn de *(smell, food)*

villa NOUN
别墅 biéshù [座 zuò]

village NOUN
村庄 cūnzhuāng [个 gè]

villain NOUN
1 恶棍 ègùn [个 gè] *(criminal)*
2 坏人 huàirén [个 gè] *(in film)*

vine NOUN
葡萄藤 pútáoténg [条 tiáo]

vinegar NOUN
醋 cù [瓶 píng]

vineyard NOUN
葡萄园 pútáoyuán [座 zuò]

violence NOUN
暴力 bàolì [种 zhǒng]

violent ADJECTIVE
暴力的 bàolì de

violin NOUN
小提琴 xiǎotíqín [把 bǎ]
□ I play the violin. 我拉小提琴。Wǒ lā xiǎotíqín.

violinist NOUN
小提琴手 xiǎotíqínshǒu [个 gè]

viral ADJECTIVE
热门的 rèmén de
□ to go viral 成为热门话题 chéngwéi rèmén huàtí

virgin NOUN
处女 chǔnǚ [个 gè]

Virgo NOUN
处女座 Chǔnǚ Zuò *(sign)*
□ I'm Virgo. 我是处女座的。Wǒ shì Chǔnǚ Zuò de.

virtual reality NOUN
虚拟现实 xūnǐ xiànshí

virus NOUN
病毒 bìngdú [种 zhǒng] *(in medicine, computing)*

visa NOUN
签证 qiānzhèng [个 gè]

visible ADJECTIVE
看得见的 kàndéjiàn de

visit NOUN
▷ *see also* **visit** VERB
1 拜访 bàifǎng [次 cì] *(to person)*
■ **my last visit to my grandmother** 我上次对祖母的拜访 wǒ shàngcì duì zǔmǔ de bàifǎng
2 旅行 lǚxíng [次 cì] *(to place)*
□ Did you enjoy your visit to France? 你的法国之旅开心吗？ Nǐ de Fǎguó zhī lǚ kāixīn ma?

to **visit** VERB
▷ *see also* **visit** NOUN
1 拜访 bàifǎng *(person)*
□ to visit somebody 拜访某人 bàifǎng mǒurén
2 游览 yóulǎn *(place)*
□ We'd like to visit the castle. 我们想去游览城堡。Wǒmen xiǎng qù yóulǎn chéngbǎo.

to **visit with** VERB (US)
拜访 bàifǎng

visitor NOUN
1 游客 yóukè [位 wèi] *(to city, country)*
2 访客 fǎngkè [位 wèi] *(to person, house)*
■ **to have a visitor** 有客到访 yǒu kè dàofǎng

visual ADJECTIVE
视觉的 shìjué de

to **visualize** VERB
设想 shèxiǎng

vital ADJECTIVE
至关重要的 zhìguān zhòngyào de

vitamin NOUN
维生素 wéishēngsù [种 zhǒng]

vivid ADJECTIVE
1 生动的 shēngdòng de
■ **to have a vivid imagination** 具有生动的想象力 jùyǒu shēngdòng de xiǎngxiànglì
2 鲜艳的 xiānyàn de *(colour, light)*

vocabulary NOUN
1 词汇量 cíhuìliàng *(of person)*
2 词汇 cíhuì [个 gè] *(of language)*

vocational ADJECTIVE
职业的 zhíyè de
■ **a vocational course** 一个职业课程 yígè zhíyè kèchéng

vodka NOUN
伏特加酒 fútèjiā jiǔ [瓶 píng]

voice NOUN
声音 shēngyīn [种 zhǒng]

voice mail NOUN
语音留言 yǔyīn liúyán [个 gè]
volcano NOUN
火山 huǒshān [座 zuò]
volleyball NOUN
排球 páiqiú
□ to play volleyball 打排球 dǎ páiqiú
volume NOUN
音量 yīnliàng *(of TV, radio, stereo)*
■ **volume two** *(of book)* 第二册 dì'èrcè
voluntary ADJECTIVE
1 自愿的 zìyuàn de *(not compulsory)*
2 志愿的 zhìyuàn de *(work, worker)*
■ **to do voluntary work** 做志愿工作 zuò zhìyuàn gōngzuò
volunteer NOUN
▷ *see also* **volunteer** VERB
志愿者 zhìyuànzhě [个 gè] *(unpaid worker)*
to **volunteer** VERB
▷ *see also* **volunteer** NOUN
■ **to volunteer to do something** 志愿做某事 zhìyuàn zuò mǒushì
vomit NOUN
▷ *see also* **vomit** VERB
呕吐物 ǒutùwù
to **vomit** VERB
▷ *see also* **vomit** NOUN
1 吐 tù *(food)*
2 呕吐 ǒutù
□ I vomited this morning. 我今天早晨呕吐了。Wǒ jīntiān zǎochén ǒutù le.
vote NOUN
▷ *see also* **vote** VERB
选票 xuǎnpiào [张 zhāng]
to **vote** VERB
▷ *see also* **vote** NOUN
投票 tóupiào
■ **to take a vote on something** 就某事进行投票 jiù mǒushì jìnxíng tóupiào
■ **to vote for somebody** 投某人票 tóu mǒurén piào
■ **to vote against something** 投票反对某事 tóupiào fǎnduì mǒushì
voucher NOUN
代金券 dàijīnquàn [张 zhāng]
□ a gift voucher 一张代金卷 yìzhāng dàijīnjuàn
vowel NOUN
元音 yuányīn [个 gè]
vulgar ADJECTIVE
粗俗的 cūsú de

Ww

wafer NOUN
威化饼 wēihuà bǐng [个 gè]

wage NOUN
工资 gōngzī [份 fèn]
▫ He collected his wages. 他领了他的工资。Tā lǐngle tāde gōngzī.

waist NOUN
1 腰 yāo
2 腰身 yāoshēn [个 gè] *(of clothing)*

waistcoat NOUN
马甲 mǎjiǎ [件 jiàn]

to **wait** VERB
等待 děngdài
▫ to wait for something 等待某物 děngdài mǒuwù ▫ to wait for somebody 等待某人 děngdài mǒurén ▫ I'll wait for you. 我会等你。Wǒ huì děng nǐ.
▪ **Wait for me!** 等我！ Děng wǒ!
▪ **Wait a minute!** 等一下！ Děng yixià!
▪ **to keep somebody waiting** 让某人等 ràng mǒurén děng ▫ They kept us waiting for hours. 他们让我们等了几个小时。Tāmen ràng wǒmen děngle jǐgèxiǎoshí.
▪ **I can't wait for the holidays.** 我很期待假期。Wǒ hěn qīdài jiàqī.
▪ **I can't wait to see him again.** 我很期待再见到他。Wǒ hěn qīdài zàijiàndào tā.

to **wait up** VERB
不睡觉等待 búshuìjiào děngdài
▫ My mum always waits up till I get in. 我妈总是不睡觉等我回来。Wǒmā zǒngshì búshuìjiào děngwǒ huílài.

waiter NOUN
男服务员 nán fúwùyuán [位 wèi]
▪ **Waiter!** 服务员！ Fúwùyuán!

waiting list NOUN
等候者名单 děnghòuzhě míngdān [个 gè]

waiting room NOUN
等候室 děnghòushì [间 jiān]

waitress NOUN
女服务员 nǔ fúwùyuán [位 wèi]

to **wake** VERB
醒来 xǐnglái

to **wake up** VERB
醒来 xǐnglái
▫ I woke up at six o'clock. 我在六点钟醒来。Wǒ zài liùdiǎnzhōng xǐnglái.
▪ **to wake somebody up** 唤醒某人 huànxǐng mǒurén ▫ Please would you wake me up at seven o'clock? 你能在七点钟的时候唤醒我吗？ Nǐ néng zài qīdiǎnzhōngde shíhòu huànxǐng wǒ ma?

Wales NOUN
威尔士 Wēi'ěrshì
▪ **the Prince of Wales** 威尔士王子 Wēi'ěrshì Wángzǐ
▪ **I'm from Wales.** 我来自威尔士。Wǒ láizi Wēi'ěrshì.

walk NOUN
▹ *see also* **walk** VERB
散步 sànbù [次 cì]
▪ **to go for a walk** 去散步 qù sànbù
▪ **It's 10 minutes' walk from here.** 从这儿就十分钟的路程。Cóng zhèr jiù shífēnzhōngde lùchéng.

to **walk** VERB
▹ *see also* **walk** NOUN
走 zǒu
▫ He walks fast. 他走的快。Tā zǒude kuài. ▫ We walked 10 kilometres. 我们走了十公里。Wǒmen zǒule shígōnglǐ. ▫ Are you walking or going by bus? 你是走路还是坐公车？ Nǐ shì zǒulù háishì zuògōngchē?
▪ **to walk the dog** 遛狗 liùgǒu

walking NOUN
徒步旅行 túbù lǚxín
▫ I did some walking in the Himalayas last summer. 去年夏天我在喜马拉雅山徒步旅行。Qùnián xiàtiān wǒ zài Xǐ'mǎlāyàshāng túbù lǚxíng.

wall NOUN
1 墙 qiáng [堵 dǔ] *(of building, room)*
2 围墙 wéiqiáng [圈 quān] *(around garden, field)*

wallet NOUN
钱包 qiánbāo [个 gè]

wallpaper NOUN
墙纸 qiángzhǐ [张 zhāng]

walnut NOUN
核桃 hétao [个 gè]

to **wander** VERB
漫游 mànyóu
■ **to wander around** 漫游 mànyóu
□ I just wandered around for a while. 我只是漫游了一会儿。Wǒ zhǐshì mànyóule yíhuìr.

to **want** VERB
1 想要 xiǎngyào *(wish for)*
□ Do you want some cake? 你想要些蛋糕吗？ Nǐ xiǎngyào xiē dàngāo ma?
■ **to want to do something** 想要做某事 xiǎngyào zuò mǒushì □ I want to go to the cinema. 我想去电影院。Wǒ xiǎngqù diànyǐngyuàn. □ What do you want to do tomorrow? 你明天想做什么？ Nǐ míngtiān xiǎngzuò shénme?
■ **to want somebody to do something** 希望某人做某事 xīwàng mǒurén zuò mǒushì
2 需要 xūyào *(need)*
□ We have all we want. 我们有了我们所需要的。Wǒmen yǒule wǒmen suǒ xūyàode.

war NOUN
战争 zhànzhēng [场 chǎng]

ward NOUN
病房 bìngfáng [间 jiān] *(in hospital)*

wardrobe NOUN
衣橱 yīchú [个 gè]

warehouse NOUN
仓库 cāngkù [间 jiān]

warm ADJECTIVE
▷ *see also* **warm** VERB
1 温热的 wēnrè de *(meal, soup, water)*
□ warm water 温水 wēnshuǐ
2 暖和的 nuǎnhuo de *(day, weather)*
□ It's warm in here. 天很暖和。Tiān hěn nuǎnhuo. □ Are you warm enough? 你觉得够暖和吗？ Nǐ juéde gòu nuǎnhuo ma? □ I'm too warm. 我太暖和了。Wǒ tài nuǎnhuo le.
3 保暖的 bǎonuǎn de *(clothes, blankets)*
4 热情的 rèqíng de *(applause, welcome)*
□ a warm welcome 一次热情的欢迎 yícì rèqíngde huānyíng

to **warm** VERB
▷ *see also* **warm** ADJECTIVE
加热 jiārè *(food)*

to **warm up** VERB
1 热身 rèshēn *(athlete, pianist)*
2 加热 jiārè
□ I'll warm up some noodles for you. 我给你加热点面条。Wǒ gěi nǐ jiārè diǎn miàntiáo.

to **warn** VERB
■ **to warn somebody that...** 警告某人··· jǐnggào mǒurén... □ Well, I warned you! 好，我警告过你了！ Hǎo, wǒ jǐnggào guò nǐ le!
■ **to warn somebody not to do something** 告诫某人不要做某事 gàojiè mǒurén búyào zuò mǒushì

warning NOUN
1 警告 jǐnggào [个 gè] *(action, words, sign)*
2 预兆 yùzhào [个 gè] *(notice)*

was VERB ▷ *see* **be**

wash NOUN
▷ *see also* **wash** VERB
洗 xǐ [下 xià]
■ **to have a wash** 洗一下 xǐyíxià □ I had a wash. 我洗了一下。Wǒ xǐle yíxià.
■ **to give something a wash** 洗某物 xǐ mǒuwù □ He gave the car a wash. 他洗了车。Tā xǐle chē.

to **wash** VERB
▷ *see also* **wash** NOUN
洗 xǐ
□ to wash something 洗某物 xǐ mǒuwù
□ Every morning I get up, wash and get dressed. 每天早上我起床，洗一下，穿好衣服。Měitiānzǎoshàng wǒ qǐchuáng, xǐyíxià, chuānhǎo yīfu.
■ **to wash one's hands** 洗手 xǐshǒu
■ **to wash one's hair** 洗头 xǐtóu

to **wash up** VERB
1 洗餐具 xǐ cānjù
□ I'll wash up and you dry. 我洗餐具你把它们擦干。Wǒ xǐ cānjù nǐ bǎ tāmen cāgān.
2 洗 xǐ (US: *have a wash*)
□ Go and wash up before dinner. 晚饭前去洗一下。Wǎnfànqián qù xǐ yixià.

washbasin NOUN
脸盆 liǎnpén [个 gè]

washcloth NOUN (US)
毛巾 máojīn [条 tiáo]

washing NOUN
1 待洗衣物 dàixǐ yīwù *(dirty clothes)*
□ Have you got any washing? 你有待洗衣物吗？ Nǐ yǒu dàixǐ yīwù ma?
2 洗好的衣物 xǐhǎo de yīwù *(clean clothes)*
■ **to do the washing** 洗衣服 xǐ yīfu

washing machine NOUN
洗衣机 xǐyījī [台 tái]

washing powder NOUN
洗衣粉 xǐyīfěn [袋 dài]

washing-up NOUN
要洗的碗 yàoxǐ de wǎn
■ **to do the washing-up** 洗碗 xǐwǎn

washing-up liquid NOUN
洗碗剂 xǐwǎnjì

wasn't = **was not**

wasp NOUN
黄蜂 huángfēng [只 zhī]

waste NOUN
▷ *see also* **waste** VERB
1 浪费 làngfèi *(of resources, food, money)*
□ It's such a waste! 真浪费！ Zhēn làngfèi!
■ **It's a waste of time.** 这是浪费时间。 Zhè shì làngfèi shíjiān.
2 废料 fèiliào *(rubbish)*
■ **nuclear waste** 核废料 héfèiliào

to **waste** VERB
▷ *see also* **waste** NOUN
1 浪费 làngfèi *(money, energy, time)*
□ I don't like wasting money. 我不喜欢浪费钱。 Wǒ bùxǐhuan làngfèiqián.
■ **to waste time** 浪费时间 làngfèi shíjiān
□ There's no time to waste. 没时间浪费。 Méishíjiān làngfèi.
2 失去 shīqù *(opportunity)*

wastepaper basket NOUN
废纸篓 fèizhǐlǒu [个 gè]

watch NOUN
▷ *see also* **watch** VERB
手表 shǒubiǎo [块 kuài]

to **watch** VERB
▷ *see also* **watch** NOUN
1 仔细看 zǐxìkàn *(look at)*
□ Watch me! 仔细看着我！ Zǐxì kànzhe wǒ!
■ **to watch somebody do something** 看着某人做某事 kànzhe mǒurén zuò mǒushì
2 看 kàn *(match, programme, TV)*
□ I like to watch television. 我喜欢看电视。 Wǒ xǐhuan kàndiànshì.
3 关注 guānzhù *(pay attention to)*
4 监视 jiānshì *(keep a watch on)*
□ The police were watching the house. 警察在监视这座房子。 Jǐngchá zài jiānshì zhèzuòfángzi.

to **watch out** VERB
小心 xiǎoxīn
■ **Watch out!** *(informal)* 小心！ Xiǎoxīn!

water NOUN
▷ *see also* **water** VERB
水 shuǐ
■ **a drink of water** 一杯水 yìbēishuǐ

to **water** VERB
▷ *see also* **water** NOUN
给…浇水 gěi…jiāoshuǐ *(plant)*
□ He was watering his tulips. 他给他的郁金香浇水。 Tā gěi tāde yùjīnxiāng jiāoshuǐ.

waterfall NOUN
瀑布 pùbù [条 tiáo]

watering can NOUN
喷壶 pēnhú [只 zhī]

watermelon NOUN
西瓜 xīguā [个 gè]

waterproof ADJECTIVE
防水的 fángshuǐ de
□ Is this jacket waterproof? 这上衣是防水的吗？ Zhèshàngyī shì fángshuǐde ma? □ a waterproof watch 一块防水表 yíkuài fángshuǐbiǎo

water-skiing NOUN
滑水 huáshuǐ
■ **to go water-skiing** 去滑水 qùhuáshuǐ

wave NOUN
▷ *see also* **wave** VERB
1 挥动 huīdòng [下 xià] *(of hand)*
■ **We gave him a wave.** 我们向他挥手。 Wǒmen xiàngtā huīshǒu.
2 波浪 bōlàng [个 gè] *(sea)*

to **wave** VERB
▷ *see also* **wave** NOUN
挥手示意 huīshǒu shìyì
□ to wave at somebody 向某人挥手示意 xiàngmǒurén huīshǒu shìyì
■ **to wave somebody goodbye** 向某人挥手告别 xiàng mǒurén huīshǒu gàobié
□ I waved her goodbye. 我向她挥手告别。 Wǒ xiàngtā huīshǒu gàobié.

wavy ADJECTIVE
波状的 bōzhuàngde
□ wavy hair 波状头发 bōzhuàng tóufà

wax NOUN
蜡 là

way NOUN
1 路 lù [条 tiáo] *(route)*
■ **to lose one's way** 迷路 mílù
■ **the way back** 回去的路 huíqù de lù
■ **on the way** 在路上 zài lùshàng □ We stopped on the way. 我们在路上停下了。 Wǒmen zài lùshàng tíngxià le.
2 距离 jùlí *(distance)*
□ Hong Kong is a long way from Shanghai. 香港离上海的距离很远。 Xiānggǎng lí Shànghǎi de jùlí hěn yuǎn.
■ **It's a long way away.** 离这儿很远。 Lí zhèr hěnyuǎn.
3 方向 fāngxiàng [个 gè] *(direction)*
□ I don't know the way. 我不知道路的方向。 Wǒ bùzhīdào lùde fāngxiàng.
□ Which way is it? 往哪边？ Wǎng nǎbiān?
□ The supermarket is this way. 超市在这边。 Chāoshì zài zhèbiān. □ Do you know the way to the station? 你知道火车站的方向吗？ Nǐ zhīdào huǒchēzhànde fāngxiàng ma?
4 方式 fāngshì [种 zhǒng] *(manner)*
□ She looked at me in a strange way. 她以一种奇怪的方式看着我。 Tā yǐ yìzhǒng qíguài de fāngshì kànzhe wǒ.
5 方法 fāngfǎ [个 gè] *(method)*
□ This book tells you the right way to do it.

这本书告诉你正确的方法。Zhèběnshū gàosù nǐ zhèngquède fāngfǎ. □ You're doing it the wrong way. 你做的方法不对。Nǐ zuòde fāngfǎ búduì.
■ **a way of life** 生活方式 shēnghuó fāngshì
■ **to give way** *(break, collapse)* 倒塌 dǎotā
■ **the wrong way round** 刚好相反 gānghǎo xiāngfǎn
■ **'way in'** "入口" "rùkǒu"
■ **'way out'** "出口" "chūkoǔ"
■ **in a way...** 在某种程度上… zài mǒuzhǒng chéngdùshàng...
■ **by the way...** 顺便说一下… shùnbiàn shuōyixià...

ways PL NOUN
习俗 xísú *(habits)*

we PRONOUN
我们 wǒmen
□ We're staying here for a week. 我们在这儿住一个月。Wǒmen zài zhèr zhù yígèyuè.

weak ADJECTIVE
1 虚弱的 xūruò de
2 淡的 dàn de *(tea or coffee)*

wealthy ADJECTIVE
富有的 fùyǒu de

weapon NOUN
武器 wǔqì [种 zhǒng]

to **wear** VERB
1 穿着 chuānzhe
□ She was wearing black. 她穿着黑色的衣服。Tā chuānzhe hēisède yīfu.
■ **I can't decide what to wear.** 我拿不定主意该穿什么。Wǒ nábúdìng zhǔyi gāi chuān shénme.
2 戴着 dàizhe *(spectacles, jewellery, hat)*
□ She was wearing a hat. 她戴着帽子。Tā dàizhe màozi.

to **wear out** VERB
耗尽 hàojìn

weather NOUN
天气 tiānqì
□ The weather was lovely. 天气很好。Tiānqì hěnhǎo.
■ **What's the weather like?** 天气怎么样？Tiānqì zěnmeyàng?

weather forecast NOUN
天气预报 tiānqì yùbào [个 gè]

web NOUN
■ **the Web** 互联网 hùliánwǎng
■ **on the Web** 在互联网上 zài hùliánwǎng shàng

web address NOUN
网络地址 wǎngluòdìzhǐ [个 gè]

web browser NOUN
网络浏览器 wǎngluò liúlǎnqì [个 gè]

webcam NOUN
网络摄影器 wǎngluò shèyǐngqì [个 gè]

webmaster NOUN
网站管理员 wǎngzhàn guǎnlǐyuán [位 wèi]

web page NOUN
网页 wǎngyè [个 gè]

website NOUN
网址 wǎngzhǐ [个 gè]

we'd = **we had, we would**

wedding NOUN
婚礼 hūnlǐ [场 chǎng]
■ **our wedding anniversary** 我们的结婚纪念日 wǒmende jiéhūnjìniànrì
■ **a wedding dress** 一件婚纱 yíjiàn hūnshā

Wednesday NOUN
星期三 xīngqīsān [个 gè]
□ on Wednesday 在星期三 zài xīngqīsān
□ on Wednesdays 在星期三 zài xīngqīsān
□ every Wednesday 每个星期三 měigè xīngqīsān □ last Wednesday 上个星期三 shànggè xīngqīsān □ next Wednesday 下个星期三 xiàgè xīngqīsān

weed NOUN
杂草 zácǎo [丛 cóng]
□ The garden's full of weeds. 花园长满了杂草。Huāyuán zhǎngmǎnle zácǎo.

week NOUN
星期 xīngqī [个 gè]
■ **this week** 这个星期 zhègè xīngqī
■ **once a week** 一周一次 yìzhōu yícì
■ **last week** 上周 shàngzhōu
■ **every week** 每周 měizhōu
■ **next week** 下周 xiàzhōu
■ **in a week's time** 在一周之后 zài yìzhōu zhīhòu
■ **a week on Friday** 下个周五 xiàgè zhōuwǔ

weekday NOUN
工作日 gōngzuòrì [个 gè]
LANGUAGE TIP Word for word, this means 'work day'.
■ **on weekdays** 在工作日 zài gōngzuòrì

weekend NOUN
周末 zhōumò [个 gè]
□ at the weekend 在周末 zài zhōumò
□ this weekend 这个周末 zhègè zhōumò
□ at weekends 在周末 zài zhōumò □ last weekend 上个周末 shànggè zhōumò
□ next weekend 下个周末 xiàgè zhōumò

to **weigh** VERB
称…的重量 chēng...de zhòngliàng
□ First, weigh the flour. 首先，称面粉。Shǒuxiān, chēng miànfěn.

■ **How much do you weigh?** 你有多重？Nǐ yǒu duōzhòng?
■ **She weighs 50kg.** 她的体重为五十公斤。Tāde tǐzhòng wéi wǔshí gōngjīn.
■ **to weigh oneself** 称自己 chēngzìjǐ

weight NOUN
重量 zhòngliàng
■ **to lose weight** 减重 jiǎnzhòng
■ **to put on weight** 增重 zēngzhòng

weights PL NOUN
举重器械 jǔzhòng qìxiè *(in gym)*

weird ADJECTIVE
奇怪的 qíguàide

welcome NOUN
▷ *see also* **welcome** VERB
欢迎 huānyíng
□ They gave her a warm welcome. 他们对她热烈欢迎。Tāmen duì tā rèliè huānyíng.
■ **Welcome!** 欢迎！ Huānyíng!
□ Welcome to Beijing! 欢迎到北京来！Huānyíng dào Běijīng lái!

to **welcome** VERB
▷ *see also* **welcome** NOUN
欢迎 huānyíng
■ **to welcome somebody** 欢迎某人 huānyíng mǒurén
■ **Thank you! — You're welcome!** 谢谢你。— 别客气！ Xièxie nǐ. — Bié kèqi!

well ADVERB
▷ *see also* **well** ADJECTIVE, EXCLAMATION, NOUN
1 好 hǎo *(to a high standard)*
■ **to do well** 做得好 zuòde hǎo □ She's doing really well at school. 她在学校表现很好。Tā zài xuéxiào biǎoxiàn hěnhǎo.
□ You did that really well. 你做的很好。Nǐ zuòde hěnhǎo.
2 充分地 chōngfèn de *(completely)*
■ **as well** *(in addition)* 也 yě □ I decided to have dessert as well. 我决定也吃甜点。Wǒ juédìng yě chī tiándiǎn. □ We went to Hong Kong as well as Shanghai. 我们不仅去了上海，还去了香港。Wǒmen bùjǐn qùle Shànghǎi, hái qùle Xiānggǎng.
■ **Well done!** 做得好！ Zuò de hǎo!

well ADJECTIVE
▷ *see also* **well** ADVERB, EXCLAMATION, NOUN
身体好的 shēntǐ hǎo de *(healthy)*
■ **to be well** 身体好的 shēntǐ hǎo de □ I'm not very well at the moment. 我现在身体不太好。Wǒ xiànzài shēntǐ bútàihǎo.
■ **I don't feel well.** 我觉得不舒服。Wǒ juéde bù shūfu.
■ **Get well soon!** 早日康复！ Zǎorì kāngfù!

well EXCLAMATION
▷ *see also* **well** ADVERB, ADJECTIVE, NOUN
嗯 ǹg
□ It's enormous! Well, quite big anyway. 太大了！嗯，反正比较大。Tàidà le! Ǹg, fǎnzhèng bǐjiào dà.
■ **Well, as I was saying...** 那么，像我刚才所说的… Nàme, xiàng wǒ gāngcái suǒshuō de...

well NOUN
▷ *see also* **well** ADVERB, ADJECTIVE, EXCLAMATION
井 jǐng [口 kǒu]

we'll = **we will, we shall**

well-behaved ADJECTIVE
行为端正 xíngwéi duānzhèng

well-dressed ADJECTIVE
衣着入时 yīzhúo rùshí

wellingtons PL NOUN
高筒靴 gāotǒngxuē

well-known ADJECTIVE
1 有名的 yǒumíng de *(person)*
□ a well-known film star 有名的电影明星 yǒumíngde diànyǐng míngxīng
2 众所周知的 zhòng suǒ zhōu zhī de *(fact, brand)*

well-off ADJECTIVE
富裕的 fùyù de

Welsh ADJECTIVE
▷ *see also* **Welsh** NOUN
威尔士的 Wēi'ěrshì de
■ **Welsh people** 威尔士人 Wēi'ěrshìrén

Welsh NOUN
▷ *see also* **Welsh** ADJECTIVE
威尔士语 Wēi'ěrshìyǔ *(language)*

Welshman NOUN
威尔士男人 Wēi'ěrshì nánrén [个 gè]

Welshwoman NOUN
威尔士女人 Wēi'ěrshì nǚrén [个 gè]

went VERB ▷ *see* **go**

were VERB ▷ *see* **be**

we're = **we are**

weren't = **were not**

west NOUN
▷ *see also* **west** ADJECTIVE, ADVERB
西方 xīfāng *(direction)*
□ in the west 在西方 zàixīfāng
■ **the West** *(politics)* 西方国家 xīfāng guójiā

west ADJECTIVE
▷ *see also* **west** NOUN, ADVERB
西部的 xībù de
□ the west coast 西海岸 xīhǎiàn

west ADVERB
▷ *see also* **west** NOUN, ADJECTIVE
向西 xiàng xī
□ We were travelling west. 我们向西方旅行。Wǒmen xiàng xīfāng lǚxíng.
■ **west of** …以西 ...yǐxī □ Stroud is west of Oxford. 斯特劳在牛津的西边。Sītèláo zài

Niújīnde xībiān.

westbound ADJECTIVE
向西的 xiàngxī de
■ **The truck was westbound on the M5.** 卡车在五号公路上西行。Kǎchē zài wǔhào gōnglùshàng xīxíng.
■ **Westbound traffic is moving very slowly.** 西行的车很缓慢。Xīxíngde chē hěn huǎnmàn.

western ADJECTIVE
▷ *see also* **western** NOUN
西部的 xībù de *(geography)*
□ the western part of the island 岛的西部 dǎode xībù
■ **Western Europe** 西欧 Xī'Ōu

western NOUN
▷ *see also* **western** ADJECTIVE
西部片 xībùpiān [部 bù] *(film)*

West Indian ADJECTIVE
▷ *see also* **West Indian** NOUN
西印度群岛的 Xīyìndù Qúndǎo de
□ She's West Indian. 她是西印度群岛人。Tā shì xīyìndùrén.

West Indian NOUN
▷ *see also* **West Indian** ADJECTIVE
西印度群岛人 Xīyìndù Qúndǎorén [个 gè]

West Indies PL NOUN
■ **the West Indies** 西印度群岛 Xīyìndù Qúndǎo

wet ADJECTIVE
1 湿的 shī de
□ wet clothes 湿衣服 shīyīfu
■ **to get wet** 弄湿 nòngshī
2 未干的 wèigān de *(paint, cement, glue)*
3 多雨的 duōyǔ de *(rainy)*
□ It was wet all week. 整周多雨。Zhěngzhōu duōyǔ.
■ **wet weather** 多雨天气 duōyǔ tiānqì

wetsuit NOUN
湿式潜水服 shīshì qiǎnshuǐfú [件 jiàn]

we've = **we have**

whale NOUN
鲸 jīng [头 tóu]

what PRONOUN, ADJECTIVE, EXCLAMATION
1 什么 shénme
□ What is it? 那是什么？ Nàshì shénme?
□ What are you doing? 你在干什么？ Nǐ zài gànshénme? □ What did you say? 你说什么？ Níshuō shénme? □ What colour is it? 是什么颜色？ Shì shénme yánsè?
□ What's the matter? 什么事？ Shénme shì?
■ **What time is it?** 几点了？ Jǐdiǎn le?

LANGUAGE TIP 什么 shénme is also used in indirect questions or relative phrases.

□ Do you know what's happening? 你知道发生了什么事吗？ Nǐ zhīdào fāshēng le shénme shì ma? □ Tell me what you did. 告诉我你做了什么。Gàosù wǒ nǐ zuòle shénme. □ I heard what he said. 我听到他说的了。Wǒ tīngdào tā shuōde le.

LANGUAGE TIP 什么 shénme is also used in exclamations.

□ What, no coffee! 什么，没咖啡了！ Shénme, méi kāfēi le!
■ **What a mess!** 真是一团糟！ Zhēnshì yìtuán zāo!
2 所...的 suǒ...de
□ What you say is wrong. 你所说的不对。Nǐ suǒshuōde búduì.
3 多么 duōme *(in exclamations)*
□ What a lovely day! 多么好的天气啊！ Duōme hǎo de tiānqì a!

whatever ADVERB, PRONOUN
任何 rènhé *(whatsoever)*
■ **Do whatever is necessary.** 做任何必要的事情。Zuò rènhé bìyào de shìqing.

wheat NOUN
小麦 xiǎomài [株 zhū]

wheel NOUN
轮 lún [个 gè]
■ **the steering wheel** 方向盘 fāngxiàngpán

wheelchair NOUN
轮椅 lúnyǐ [部 bù]

when ADVERB, CONJUNCTION, PRONOUN
1 什么时候 shénme shíhou *(in question)*
□ When did it happen? 什么时候发生的？ Shénme shíhou fāshēng de? □ When did he go? 他什么时候走的？ Tā shénme shíhòu zǒude?
■ **the day when...** 当…的那一天 dāng...de nà yì tiān
2 当...时 dāng...shí

LANGUAGE TIP 当…时 dāng...shí is used when **when** is used as a conjunction.

□ She was reading when I came in. 当我进来时她正在阅读。Dāng wǒ jìnlái shí tā zhèngzài yuèdú.
■ **Be careful when you cross the road.** 过马路时要当心。Guò mǎlù shí yào dāngxīn.
■ **I know when it happened.** 我知道什么时候发生的。Wǒ zhīdào shénme shíhou fāshēng de.

where ADVERB, CONJUNCTION
1 在哪里 zài nǎli
□ Where's Emma today? 爱玛今天在哪？ Àimǎ jīntiān zàinǎ? □ Where do you live? 你住在哪？ Nǐ zhùzài nǎ? □ Where are you

going? 你去哪？ Nǐ qù nǎ?

2 哪里 nǎli

□ Where are you from? 你是哪里人？ Nǐ shì nǎlǐ rén?

LANGUAGE TIP When **where** is used as a conjunction, it is not translated.

□ a shop where you can buy noodles 可以买面条的商店 kěyǐ mǎi miàntiáode shāngdiàn

whether CONJUNCTION

是否 shìfǒu

□ I don't know whether to accept or not. 我不知道是接受还是不接受。Wǒ bù zhīdào shì jiēshòu háishì bù jiēshòu. □ I don't know whether to go or not. 我不知道是否该去。Wǒ bùzhīdào shìfǒu gāiqù.

which ADJECTIVE, PRONOUN

1 哪个 nǎgè

LANGUAGE TIP 哪个 nǎgè is used to translate **which** in direct and indirect questions in the singular.

□ Which one? 哪个？ Nǎgè? □ Which of these are yours? 这些中的哪个是你的？Zhèxiē zhōng de nǎgè shì nǐde? □ He asked which book I wanted. 他问我要哪本书。Tā wènwǒ yào nǎběn shū.

2 哪些 nǎxiē

LANGUAGE TIP 哪些 nǎxiē is used to translate **which** in direct and indirect questions in the plural.

□ Which ones? 哪些？ Nǎxiē? □ Which books are yours? 哪些书是你的？Nǎxiēshū shì nǐde? □ He told me which ones I could take. 他告诉我哪些我可以拿。Tā gàosù wǒ nǎxiē wǒ kěyǐ ná.

3 …的那个… ...de nàge...

LANGUAGE TIP Use …的那个… ...de nàge... when **which** is used in a relative clause, as an object or subject.

□ the CD which is playing now 正在播放的那个CD zhèngzài bōfàng de nàge CD □ the CD which I bought today 我今天买的那个CD wǒ jīntiān mǎide nàge CD

while NOUN, CONJUNCTION

1 一会儿 yíhuìr

□ after a while 一会儿 yíhuìr

■ **a while ago** 一会儿前 yíhuìr qián

□ He was here a while ago. 他一会儿前还在。Tā yíhuìr qián háizài.

■ **for a while** 有一会儿 yǒu yíhuìr □ I lived in London for a while. 我住在伦敦有一会儿了。Wǒ zhùzài Lúndūn yǒu yíhuìr le.

■ **quite a while** 一阵子 yízhènzi □ I haven't seen him for quite a while. 我有一阵子没见到他了。Wǒ yǒu yízhènzi méijiàndào tā le.

2 虽然 suīrán *(although)*

□ While I'm very fond of him, I don't actually want to marry him. 虽然我很喜欢他，但我真的不想嫁给他。Suīrán wǒ hěn xǐhuan tā, dàn wǒ zhēnde bùxiǎng jiàgěi tā.

□ You hold the torch while I look inside. 我向里看的时候你举着手电筒。Wǒ xiànglǐ kàndeshíhòu nǐ jǔzhe shǒudiàntǒng.

□ Isobel is very dynamic, while Kay is more laid-back. 伊莎贝儿很有活力，而凯很懒散。Yīshābèiěr hěnyǒu huólì, ér Kǎi hěn lǎnsǎn.

whipped cream NOUN

生奶油 shēngnǎiyóu

whisk NOUN

搅拌器 jiǎobànqì [个 gè]

whiskers PL NOUN

胡须 húxū

whisky (US **whiskey**) NOUN

威士忌酒 wēishìjì jiǔ [瓶 píng]

to **whisper** VERB

低语 dīyǔ

to **whistle** VERB

▷ *see also* **whistle** NOUN

吹口哨 chuī kǒushào

whistle NOUN

▷ *see also* **whistle** VERB

1 哨子 shàozi [个 gè] *(device)*

2 口哨声 kǒushàoshēng [声 shēng] *(sound)*

white ADJECTIVE

▷ *see also* **white** NOUN

1 白的 bái de

□ He's got white hair. 他有白头发。Tā yǒu báitóufà.

■ **white bread** 白面包 báimiànbāo

■ **white wine** 白葡萄酒 báipútáojiǔ

2 白种人的 báizhǒngrén de *(person)*

■ **a white man** 一位白种男人 yíwèi báizhǒng nánrén

■ **a white woman** 一位白种女人 yíwèi báizhǒng nǚrén

■ **white people** 白人 báirén

■ **white coffee** 牛奶咖啡 niúnǎikāfēi

white NOUN

▷ *see also* **white** ADJECTIVE

白色 báisè *(colour)*

who PRONOUN

谁 shéi

□ Who is it? 是谁？ Shì shéi? □ Who did you discuss it with? 你和谁讨论了？ Nǐ hé shéi tǎolùn le?

LANGUAGE TIP 谁 shéi is also used in indirect speech.

□ I told her who I was. 我告诉了她我是谁。Wǒ gàosù le tā wǒ shì shéi. □ I don't know who he gave it to. 我不知道他把它给了谁。 Wǒ bù zhīdào tā bǎ tā gěile shéi.

LANGUAGE TIP 的那个 de nàgè is used for a relative subject or object.

□ the girl who came in 进来的那个女孩 jìnlai de nàgè nǚhái □ the man who we met in Sydney 我们在悉尼遇到的那个男子 wǒmen zài Xīní yùdào de nàgè nánzǐ

whole ADJECTIVE

▷ *see also* **whole** NOUN

整个的 zhěnggè de

□ the whole class 整个班级 zhěnggè bānjí □ the whole afternoon 整个下午 zhěnggè xiàwǔ □ the whole world 整个世界 zhěnggè shìjiè

whole NOUN

▷ *see also* **whole** ADJECTIVE

整体 zhěngtǐ [个 gè] *(entirety)*

■ **the whole of something** 整个某物 zhěnggè mǒuwù □ The whole of Japan was affected. 整个日本都受了影响。Zhěnggè Rìběn dōushòu le yǐngxiǎng.

■ **the whole of the time** 所有的时间 suǒyǒu de shíjiān

■ **on the whole** 大体上 dàtǐ shàng

wholemeal ADJECTIVE

全麦的 quánmàide

■ **wholemeal bread** 全麦面包 quánmài miànbāo

wholewheat ADJECTIVE (US)

全麦的 quánmàide

whom PRONOUN

1 谁 shéi *(in question)*

□ Whom did you see? 你看见谁了？ Nǐ kànjiàn shéile?

2 所...的那个... suǒ...de nàge... *(relative)*

□ the man whom I saw 我见过的那个男的 wǒ jiànguò de nàge nánzi

whose ADJECTIVE, PRONOUN

谁的 shéi de

□ Whose is this? 这是谁的？ Zhè shì shéi de? □ Whose book is this? 这本书是谁的？ Zhèběnshū shì shéide?

LANGUAGE TIP 的 de is used to translate **whose** in relative clauses.

□ the woman whose car was stolen 汽车给偷走的那个女的 qìchē gěi tōuzǒu de nàgè nǚde

why CONJUNCTION, ADVERB

为什么 wèishénme

□ Why is he always late? 为什么他总是迟到？ Wèishénme tā zǒngshì chídào? □ I don't know why. 我不知道为什么。 Wǒ bù zhīdào wèishénme. □ I wonder why he said that. 我想知道他为什么那么说。 Wǒxiǎng zhīdào tā wèishénme nàme shuō.

■ **Why not?** 为什么不呢？ Wèishénme bù ne? □ I've never been to China. — Why not? 我从来没去过中国。— 为什么没呢？ Wǒ cónglái méiqùguò Zhōngguó. — Wèishénme méi ne?

■ **the reason why he did it** 他那么做的原因 tā nàme zuò de yuányīn

wicked ADJECTIVE

1 邪恶的 xié'è de *(evil: person)*

2 罪恶的 zuì'è de *(act, crime)*

wide ADJECTIVE

▷ *see also* **wide** ADVERB

1 宽的 kuān de

□ a wide road 一条宽的路 yìtiáo kuānde lù

2 广泛的 guǎngfàn de *(range, variety, publicity, choice)*

wide ADVERB

▷ *see also* **wide** ADJECTIVE

□ to open something wide 张大某物 zhāngdà mǒuwù

■ **wide open** 敞开 chǎngkāide

■ **wide awake** 醒着 xǐngzhe

widow NOUN

寡妇 guǎfù [个 gè]

widower NOUN

鳏夫 guānfū [个 gè]

width NOUN

宽度 kuāndù [个 gè]

wife NOUN

妻子 qīzi [个 gè]

wig NOUN

假发 jiǎfà [个 gè]

wild ADJECTIVE

1 野生的 yěshēng de

□ a wild animal 一只野生动物 yìzhī yěshēng dòngwù

2 狂野的 kuángyě de *(person, behaviour)*

□ She's a bit wild. 她有点狂野。Tā yǒudiǎn kuángyě.

wildlife NOUN

野生动物 yěshēng dòngwù [种 zhǒng]

will VERB

▷ *see also* **will** NOUN

LANGUAGE TIP Chinese has no future tense, as verb forms do not change according to tense. Context is generally used to work out the tense. However, modal markers 会 huì, 将 jiāng or 要 yào can be used to indicate the future tense.

□ I will call you tonight. 我今晚会给你打电话的。Wǒ jīnwǎn huì gěi nǐ dǎ diànhuà de. □ I'll show you your room. 我将带你参观你的房间。Wǒ jiāng dài nǐ cānguān nǐde fángjiān. □ What will you do next?

下面你要做什么？ Xiàmiàn nǐ yào zuò shénme?
■ **He'll be there by now.** 他现在该到了。Tā xiànzài gāidào le.
■ **Will you be quiet!** 你安静点！ Nǐ ānjìng diǎn!

will NOUN
▷ *see also* **will** VERB
1 意志 yìzhì
■ **against his will** 违背他的意愿 wéibèi tāde yìyuàn
2 遗嘱 yízhǔ [个 gè] *(testament)*
□ to make a will 立遗嘱 lì yízhǔ

willing ADJECTIVE
■ **to be willing to do something** 愿意做某事 yuànyì zuò mǒushì

to **win** VERB
▷ *see also* **win** NOUN
1 赢 yíng
□ Did you win? 赢了吗? Yíng le ma?
2 在…中获胜 zài…zhōng huòshèng *(game, fight)*
3 赢得 yíngdé *(prize, medal)*

win NOUN
▷ *see also* **win** VERB
胜利 shènglì [个 gè]

wind NOUN
风 fēng [阵 zhèn]
□ There was a strong wind. 一阵强风。Yízhèn qiángfēng.
■ **a wind instrument** 管弦乐器 guǎnxuán yuèqì
■ **wind power** 风力 fēnglì

windmill NOUN
风车 fēngchē [架 jià]

window NOUN
1 窗户 chuānghu [扇 shàn]
□ a broken window 一扇破窗 yíshàn pòchuāng
2 橱窗 chúchuāng [个 gè] *(in shop)*
3 车窗 chēchuāng [个 gè] *(in car, train)*
4 视窗 shìchuāng [个 gè] *(computing)*
□ You have too many windows open on your screen. 你打开了太多的视窗。Nǐ dǎkāi le tàiduō de shìchuāng.

windscreen NOUN
挡风玻璃 dǎngfēng bōlí [块 kuài]

windscreen wiper NOUN
挡风玻璃刷 dǎngfēng bōlíshuā [只 zhī]

windshield NOUN (US)
挡风玻璃 dǎngfēng bōlí [块 kuài]

windshield wiper NOUN (US)
挡风玻璃刷 dǎngfēng bōlíshuā [只 zhī]

windsurfing NOUN
帆板运动 fānbǎn yùndòng

windy ADJECTIVE
有风的 yǒufēng de *(weather, day)*
■ **It's windy.** 今天风很大。Jīntiān fēng hěndà.

wine NOUN
葡萄酒 pútáojiǔ [瓶 píng]
□ a bottle of wine 一瓶葡萄酒 yìpíng pútáojiǔ □ a glass of wine 一杯葡萄酒 yìbēi pútáojiǔ
■ **white wine** 白葡萄酒 báipútáojiǔ
■ **red wine** 红葡萄酒 hóngpútáojiǔ
■ **a wine bar** 一家葡萄酒馆 yìjiā pútáojiǔguǎn
■ **a wine glass** 玻璃酒杯 bōlí jiǔbēi
■ **the wine list** 葡萄酒单 pútáojiǔdān

wing NOUN
1 翅膀 chìbǎng [个 gè]
2 机翼 jīyì [个 gè] *(of aeroplane)*
3 侧楼 cèlóu [座 zuò] *(of building)*

to **wink** VERB
眨眼 zhǎyǎn *(person)*
□ to wink at somebody 向某人眨了眨眼 xiàng mǒurén zhǎlezhǎ yǎn □ He winked at me. 他向我眨了眨眼。Tā xiàng wǒ zhǎlezhǎ yǎn.

winner NOUN
获胜者 huòshèngzhě [位 wèi]

winter NOUN
冬季 dōngjì [个 gè]
■ **in winter** 在冬季 zài dōngjì

to **wipe** VERB
擦 cā *(dry, clean)*
■ **to wipe one's nose** 擦鼻子 cā bízi
■ **to wipe one's feet** 擦脚 cājiǎo □ Wipe your feet! 擦脚！ Cājiǎo!

to **wipe up** VERB
把…擦干净 bǎ…cā gānjìng

wire NOUN
电线 diànxiàn [根 gēn] *(electrical)*

wisdom tooth NOUN
智齿 zhìchǐ [颗 kē]

wise ADJECTIVE
睿智的 ruìzhì de

wish NOUN
▷ *see also* **wish** VERB
愿望 yuànwàng [个 gè]
□ to make a wish 许愿望 xǔ yuànwàng
■ **Give her my best wishes.** 代我向她致意。Dài wǒ xiàng tā zhìyì.
■ **Best wishes** *(on greetings card)* 美好的祝愿 Měihǎo de zhùyuàn
■ **With best wishes, Kathy.** 祝好，凯西。Zhùhǎo, Kǎixī.

to **wish** VERB
▷ *see also* **wish** NOUN
想要 xiǎngyào
■ **to wish to do something** 想要做某事

xiǎngyào zuò mǒushì
■ to wish for something 想要某物 xiǎngyào mǒuwù □ What more could you wish for? 你还想要什么？ Nǐ hāi xiǎngyào shénme? □ I wish to make a complaint. 我要投诉。Wǒ yào tóusù. □ I wish you were here! 我希望当时你在！ Wǒ xīwàng dāngshí nǐ zài! □ I wish you'd told me! 我希望你早点告诉我！Wǒ xīwàng nǐ zǎodiǎn gàosù wǒ.

with PREPOSITION
1 和...在一起 hé...zài yìqǐ
□ I was with him. 我和他在一起。Wǒ hé tā zài yìqǐ. □ We stayed with friends. 我们和朋友们呆在一起。Wǒmen hé péngyǒumen dāizài yìqǐ. □ I'll be with you in a minute. 请稍等。Qǐng shāoděng.
2 有 yǒu
□ the man with blue eyes 有蓝眼睛的男人 yǒu lán yǎnjīng de nánrén
3 用 yòng *(by means of)*
□ You can open the door with this key. 你可以用这把钥匙打开门。Nǐ kěyǐ yòng zhèbǎ yàoshi dǎkāi mén.
■ to walk with a stick 拄着拐杖走 zhǔzhe guǎizhàng zǒu
■ to fill something with water 在某物里装满水 zài mǒuwù lǐ zhuāngmǎn shuǐ
■ red with anger 气得涨红了脸 qìde zhànghóngle liǎn

without PREPOSITION
没有 méiyǒu
□ without a coat 没穿外套 méichuān wàitào □ without speaking 没有说话 méiyǒu shuōhuà

witness NOUN
目击者 mùjīzhě [位 wèi] *(law)*
□ There were no witnesses. 没有目击者。Méiyǒu mùjīzhě.

witty ADJECTIVE
诙谐的 huīxié de

wives PL NOUN ▷ *see* **wife**

woke VERB ▷ *see* **wake**

woken VERB ▷ *see* **wake**

wolf NOUN
狼 láng [条 tiáo]

woman NOUN
妇女 fùnǚ [位 wèi]
□ a woman doctor 一位女大夫 yíwèi nǚ dàifū

won VERB ▷ *see* **win**

to **wonder** VERB
想知道 xiǎngzhīdào
□ to wonder whether 想知道是否 xiǎng zhīdào shìfǒu
■ to wonder why 想知道为什么 xiǎng zhīdào wèishénme □ I wonder why she said that. 我想知道为什么她那么说。Wǒ xiǎng zhīdào wèishénme tā nàmeshuō. □ I wonder what that means. 我想知道那是什么意思。Wǒ xiǎng zhīdào nàshì shénme yìsī. □ I wonder where Caroline is. 我想知道凯洛林在哪。Wǒ xiǎng zhīdào Kǎiluòlín zài nǎ.

wonderful ADJECTIVE
绝妙的 juémiào de

won't = **will not**

wood NOUN
1 木材 mùcái
□ It's made of wood. 是木材做的。Shì mùcái zuòde.
2 树林 shùlín [棵 kē] *(forest)*
□ We went for a walk in the wood. 我们去了树林散步。Wǒmen qùle shùlín sànbù.

wooden ADJECTIVE
木制的 mùzhìde
□ a wooden chair 一只木制的椅子 yìzhī mùzhìde yǐzi

wool NOUN
羊毛 yángmáo
□ It's made of wool. 是羊毛的。Shì yángmáode.

word NOUN
1 词 cí [个 gè]
□ a difficult word 一个难词 yígè náncí
□ What's the word for 'pen' in Chinese? "Pen" 这个单词在汉语里怎么说？"Pen" zhègè dāncí zài Hànyǔ lǐ zěnme shuō?
■ in other words 换句话说 huàn jù huà shuō
■ the words *(lyrics)* 歌词 gēcí □ I really like the words of this song. 我很喜欢这首歌的歌词。Wǒ hěn xǐhuan zhèshǒugēde gēcí.
2 诺言 nuòyán *(promise)*

word processing NOUN
文字处理 wénzì chǔlǐ

word processor NOUN
文字处理器 wénzì chǔlǐqì [个 gè]

wore VERB ▷ *see* **wear**

work NOUN
▷ *see also* **work** VERB
1 工作 gōngzuò *(job)*
□ She's looking for work. 她在找工作。Tā zài zhǎogōngzuò. □ He's at work at the moment. 他在工作。Tā zài gōngzuò.
■ to be off work *(sick)* 休病假 xiū bìngjià
□ He's been off work for a week. 他已经休了一周病假。Tā yǐjīng xiūle yìzhōu bìngjià.
■ He's out of work. 他失业了。Tā shīyè le.
2 事情 shìqing *(tasks, duties)*

■ **It's hard work.** 很难的事情。Hěn nánde shìqíng.

to **work** VERB

▷ *see also* **work** NOUN

1 工作 gōngzuò *(have a job, do tasks)*
□ She works in a shop. 她在商店工作。Tā zài shāngdiàn gōngzuò.
■ **to go to work** 去上班 qù shàngbān
■ **to be out of work** 失业 shīyè
■ **to work hard** 努力工作 nǔlì gōngzuò

2 运行 yùnxíng *(function)*
□ The heating isn't working. 供热没有正常运行。Gōngrè méiyǒu zhèngcháng yùnxíng.

3 起作用 qǐ zuòyong *(be successful)*
□ My plan worked perfectly. 我的计划完美地起了作用。Wǒde jìhuà wánměi de qǐle zuòyòng.

to **work out** VERB

1 锻炼 duànliàn *(exercise)*
□ I work out twice a week. 我一周锻炼两次。Wǒ yìzhōu duànliàn liǎngcì.

2 弄明白 nòngmíánbái *(answer, solution)*
□ I just couldn't work it out. 我弄不明白。Wǒ nòng bùmíngbái.

3 进行 jìnxíng *(plan, details)*
□ In the end it worked out really well. 最后它进行得很好。Zuìhòu tā jìnxíng de hěnhǎo.

worker NOUN

工人 gōngrén [位 wèi]
□ He's a factory worker. 他是位工人。Tā shì wèi gōngrén. □ She's a good worker. 她是个好工人。Tā shì gè hǎo gōngrén.
■ **a hard worker** 工作努力的人 gōngzuò nǔlì de rén

work experience NOUN

工作经验 gōngzuò jīngyàn [种 zhǒng]
□ I'm going to do work experience in a factory. 我打算去工厂积累工作经验。Wǒ dǎsuàn qù gōngchǎng jīlěi gōngzuò jīngyàn.

working-class ADJECTIVE

工人阶级的 gōngrénjiējí de
□ a working-class family 一个工人阶级家庭 yígè gōngrén jiējí jiātíng

worksheet NOUN

工作表 gōongzuòbiǎo [个 gè]

workstation NOUN

1 工作台 gōngzuòtái [个 gè] *(desk)*

2 工作站 gōngzuòzhàn [个 gè] *(computer)*

world NOUN

■ **the world** 世界 shìjiè □ He's the world champion. 他是世界冠军。Tā shì shìjiè guànjūn.
■ **all over the world** 全世界 quán shìjiè

World Wide Web NOUN

■ **the World Wide Web** 万维网 Wànwéiwǎng

worm NOUN

虫 chóng [只 zhī]

worn VERB ▷ *see* **wear**

worn ADJECTIVE

旧 jiù
□ The carpet is a bit worn. 地毯有点旧。Dìtǎn yǒudiǎn jiù.
■ **worn out** *(tired)* 疲劳 píláo

worried ADJECTIVE

担心的 dānxīn de
□ She's very worried. 她很担心。Tā hěn dānxīn.
■ **to be worried about something** 担心某事 dānxīn mǒushì □ I'm worried about the exams. 我担心考试。Wǒ dānxīn kǎoshì.
■ **to look worried** 看起来很担心 kànqǐlái hěn dānxīn □ She looks a bit worried. 她看起来有点担心。Tā kànqǐlāi yǒudiǎn dānxīn.

worry NOUN

▷ *see also* **worry** VERB

1 忧虑 yōulǜ *(feeling of anxiety)*

2 担心 dānxīn [种 zhǒng] *(cause of anxiety)*

to **worry** VERB

▷ *see also* **worry** NOUN

担心 dānxīn
■ **Don't worry!** 别担心！Bié dānxīn.

worse ADJECTIVE

更坏的 gènghuài de
□ It was even worse than that. 比那更坏。Bǐ nà gènghuài. □ My results were bad, but his were even worse. 我的结果不好，他的更坏。Wǒde jiéguǒ bùhǎo, tāde gènghuài.
■ **to get worse** 逐渐恶化 zhújiàn èhuà □ I'm feeling worse. 我感觉更坏。Wǒ gǎnjué gènghuài.

to **worship** VERB

崇拜 chóngbài *(God)*
■ **He really worships her.** 他很崇拜她。Tā hěn chóngbài tā.

worst ADJECTIVE

▷ *see also* **worst** NOUN

最差的 zuìchà de
□ the worst student in the class 班里最差的学生 bānlǐ zuìchāde xuéshēng □ He got the worst mark in the whole class. 他的成绩是班里最差的。Tāde chéngji shì bānlǐ zuìchàde. □ my worst enemy 我最大的敌人 wǒzuìdàde dírén
■ **Maths is my worst subject.** 数学是我最差的学科。Shùxué shì wǒ zuìchà de xuékē.

worst NOUN
▷ *see also* **worst** ADJECTIVE
最坏的事 zuì huài de shì
■ **at worst** 在最坏的情况下 zài zuìhuài de qíngkuàng xià ◻ The worst of it is that... 最坏的是… Zuìhuàide shì...
■ **if the worst comes to the worst** 万一出现最坏的情况 wànyī chūxiàn zuìhuàide qíngkuàng

worth ADJECTIVE
▷ *see also* **worth** NOUN
值 zhí
■ **to be worth £50** 值五十英镑 zhí wǔshí yīngbàng
■ **400 dollars' worth of damage** 价值四百美元的损失 jiàzhí sìbǎi měiyuán de sǔnshī
■ **It's worth it.** 这是值得的。Zhèshì zhídé de.
■ **It's not worth it.** 不值得。Bùzhíde.
■ **it would be worth doing...** 值得做… zhídé zuò...
■ **How much is it worth?** 值多少钱？ Zhí duōshǎoqián?

worth NOUN
▷ *see also* **worth** ADJECTIVE
价值 jiàzhí

would VERB
LANGUAGE TIP Although there is no direct translation for **would**, and it is often left untranslated, it can sometimes be equated with the modal particle 会 huì.
◻ I would love to go to Italy. 我很愿意去意大利。Wǒ hěn yuànyì qù Yìdàlì. ◻ I'm sure he wouldn't do that. 我确定他不会那么做的。Wǒ quèdìng tā búhuì nàme zuòde.
LANGUAGE TIP **would** can be used in offers, invitations, requests.
◻ Would you like a biscuit? 你要来块饼干吗？ Nǐ yào lái kuàn bǐnggān ma?
◻ Would you like to go and see a film? 你想去看电影吗？ Nǐ xiǎng qù kàndiànyǐng ma? ◻ Would you ask him to come in? 你要叫他进来吗？ Nǐ yào jiàotā jìnlái ma?
■ **I'd like...** 我要… Wǒ yào...
LANGUAGE TIP **would** can also mean **be willing to**.
◻ She wouldn't help me. 她不愿意帮助我。Tā bú yuànyì bāngzhù wǒ.
LANGUAGE TIP **would** can be used in indirect speech.
◻ He said he would be at home later. 他说他晚点儿会在家的。Tā shuō tā wǎndiǎnr huì zàijiā de.

wouldn't = **would not**

wound NOUN
伤口 shāngkǒu [个 gè]

to **wrap** VERB
包 bāo *(cover)*
◻ She's wrapping her Christmas presents. 她在包圣诞节礼物。Tā zài bāo shèngdànjié lǐwù.
■ **Can you wrap it for me please?** *(in shop)* 可以包一下吗？ Kěyǐ bāo yixià ma?

to **wrap up** VERB
包起来 bāo qǐlái *(pack)*

wrapping paper NOUN
包装纸 bāozhuāngzhǐ [张 zhāng] *(gift wrap)*

wreck NOUN
▷ *see also* **wreck** VERB
1 残骸 cánhái [个 gè] *(wreckage)*
2 事故 shìgù [次 cì] (US: *accident)*

to **wreck** VERB
▷ *see also* **wreck** NOUN
1 摧毁 cuīhuǐ *(car, building)*
◻ The explosion wrecked the whole house. 爆炸摧毁了整座房子。Bàozhà cuīhuǐle zhěngzuò fángzi.
2 毁掉 huǐdiào *(plan, holiday)*
◻ The trip was wrecked by bad weather. 这次旅行被坏天气毁了。Zhècì lǚxíng bèi huàitiānqì huǐle.

wrestler NOUN
摔跤选手 shuāijiāo xuǎnshǒu [位 wèi]

wrestling NOUN
摔跤 shuāijiāo

wrinkled ADJECTIVE
布满皱纹的 bùmǎn zhòuwén de

wrist NOUN
手腕 shǒuwàn [个 gè]

to **write** VERB
1 写下 xiěxià *(address, number)*
2 写 xiě *(letter, note)*
◻ I wrote a letter. 我写了一封信。Wǒ xiěle yìfēngxìn.
■ **to write to somebody** 写信给某人 xiěxìn gěi mǒurén ◻ I'm going to write to her in Chinese. 我会用中文给她写信。Wǒ huì yòng Zhōngwén gěitā xiěxìn.
3 创作 chuàngzuò *(novel, music)*
4 开 kāi *(cheque, receipt, prescription)*

to **write down** VERB
记下 jìxià
◻ I wrote down the address. 我记下了地址。Wǒ jìxiàle dìzhǐ. ◻ Can you write it down for me, please? 你能给我写下来吗？ Nǐ néng gěi wǒ xiěxiàlái ma?

writer NOUN
作家 zuòjiā [位 wèi]

writing NOUN

1 文字 wénzì *(something written)*
2 笔迹 bǐjì *(handwriting)*
□ I can't read your writing. 我没法辨认你的笔迹。Wǒ méifǎ biànrèn nǐde bǐjì.
■ **in writing** 以书面形式 yǐ shūmiàn xíngshì

written VERB ▷ *see* **write**

wrong ADJECTIVE
▷ *see also* **wrong** ADVERB
1 不合适的 bù héshì de *(person, equipment, kind, job)*
2 错误的 cuòwù de *(answer, information, report)*
□ The information they gave us was wrong. 他们给我们的信息是错的。Tāmen gěi wǒmende xìnxī shì cuòde.
■ **the wrong answer** 错的答案 cuòde dá'àn
3 不道德的 bú dàodé de *(morally bad)*
□ I think hunting is wrong. 我认为打猎是不道德的。Wǒ rènwéi dǎliè shì búdàodéde.
□ You've got the wrong number. 你打错了。Nǐ dǎ cuòle.
■ **to be wrong 1** *(answer)* 是错的 shì cuòde **2** *(person)* 弄错的 nòng cuò de
□ You're wrong about that. 你弄错了。Nǐ nòngcuòle.
■ **What's wrong?** 出了什么事？ Chūle shénme shì?
■ **What's wrong with you?** 你怎么了？Nǐ zěnme le?

wrong ADVERB
▷ *see also* **wrong** ADJECTIVE
错误地 cuòwù de *(incorrectly)*
■ **to go wrong 1** *(plan)* 失败 shībài
□ The robbery went wrong and they got caught. 抢劫失败，他们被捕了。Qiǎngjié shībài, tāmen bèibǔle. **2** *(machine)* 发生故障 fāshēng gùzhàng
■ **to do something wrong** 做错某事 zuòcuò mǒushì □ You've done it wrong. 你已经做错了。Nǐ yǐjīng zuòcuò le.

wrote VERB ▷ *see* **write**

WWW NOUN *(= World Wide Web)*
万维网 Wànwéiwǎng

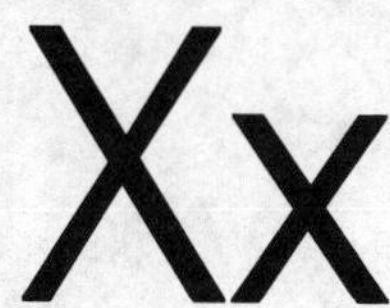

Xerox® NOUN (US)
复印机 fùyìnji [台 tái]

to **xerox** VERB (US)
复印 fùyìn

XL ABBREVIATION *(= extra large)*
特大号 tèdàhào

Xmas NOUN *(= Christmas)*
圣诞节 Shèngdànjié

X-ray NOUN
▹*see also* **X-ray** VERB
X光检查 X guāng jiǎnchá [张 zhāng] *(photo)*
▪ **to have an X-ray** 做一次X光检查 zuò yícì X guāng jiǎnchá

to **X-ray** VERB
▹*see also* **X-ray** NOUN
用X光检查 yòng X guāng jiǎnchá
▪ **to X-ray something** 用X光检查某物 yòng X guāng jiǎnchá mǒuwù ▫ They X-rayed my arm. 他们用X光检查了我的胳膊。Tāmen yòng X guāng jiǎnchále wǒde gēbo.

xylophone NOUN
木琴 mùqín [台 tái]

Yy

yacht NOUN
1 帆船 fānchuán [艘 sōu] *(sailing boat)*
2 游艇 yóutǐng [艘 sōu] *(luxury boat)*

yard NOUN
庭院 tíngyuàn [座 zuò] (US: *garden*)
▫ in the yard 在庭院里 zàitíngyuànlǐ

to **yawn** VERB
▹ *see also* **yawn** NOUN
打呵欠 dǎ hēqiàn

yawn NOUN
▹ *see also* **yawn** VERB
呵欠 hēqiàn [个 gè]

year NOUN
1 年 nián
▫ We lived there for years. 我们住在那儿有好多年了。Wǒmen zhùzài nàr yǒu hǎoduō nián le.
▪ **to be 15 years old** 十五岁 shíwǔsuì
▪ **an eight-year-old child** 一个八岁的孩子 yígè bāsuìde háizi
▪ **every year** 每年 měinián
▪ **this year** 今年 jīnnián
▪ **last year** 去年 qùnián
▪ **next year** 明年 míngnián
▪ **per year** 每年 měinián
2 学年 xuénián [个 gè] *(school)*
▫ year 7 七年级 qīniánjí ▫ year 8 八年级 bāniánjí ▫ year 9 九年级 jiǔniánjí ▫ year 10 十年级 shíniánjí ▫ year 11 十一年级 shíyī niánjí ▫ She's in year 11. 她上十一年级。Tā shàng shíyī niánjí. ▫ He's a first-year. 他上一年级。Tā shàng yī niánjí.

to **yell** VERB
大叫 dàjiào

yellow ADJECTIVE
▹ *see also* **yellow** NOUN
黄色的 huángsè de

yellow NOUN
▹ *see also* **yellow** ADJECTIVE
黄色 huángsè [种 zhǒng]

yes ADVERB
▹ *see also* **yes** NOUN
是的 shìde
▫ Do you like it? — Yes. 你喜欢吗？ — 是的。Nǐ xǐhuan ma? — Shìde. ▫ Would you like a cup of tea? — Yes please. 要喝杯茶吗？ — 是的，谢谢。Yào hē bēichá ma? — Shìde, xièxiè. ▫ You're not Thai, are you? — Yes I am! 你不是泰国人，对吗？ — 不，我是。Nǐ búshì Tàiguórén, duìma? — Bù, wǒshì.

yes NOUN
▹ *see also* **yes** ADVERB
是 shì *(answer)*

yesterday ADVERB
▹ *see also* **yesterday** NOUN
昨天 zuótiān
▫ yesterday morning 昨天早晨 zuótiān zǎochén ▫ yesterday afternoon 昨天下午 zuótiān xiàwǔ ▫ yesterday evening 昨天晚上 zuótiān wǎnshàng ▫ all day yesterday 昨天一整天 zuótiān yìzhěngtiān

yesterday NOUN
▹ *see also* **yesterday** ADVERB
昨天 zuótiān
▫ the day before yesterday 前天 qiántiān

yet ADVERB
▹ *see also* **yet** CONJUNCTION
1 还 hái *(up to now, used with negative)*
▫ They haven't finished yet. 他们还没完工。Tāmen hái méi wángōng.
2 已经 yǐjīng *(in questions)*
▫ Have you finished yet? 已经做完了吗？Yǐjīng zuòwán le ma?

yet CONJUNCTION
▹ *see also* **yet** ADVERB
然而 rán'ér
▪ **not yet** 还未 háiwèi
▪ **not as yet** 尚未 shàngwèi ▫ There's no news as yet. 尚未有任何新闻。Shàngwèi yǒu rènhé xīnwén.
▪ **yet again** 又一次 yòu yícì

to **yield** VERB (US)
让行 ràngxíng *(on road sign)*

yob NOUN
小流氓 xiǎoliúmáng [个 gè]

yoghurt NOUN
酸奶 suānnǎi [瓶 píng]

yolk NOUN
蛋黄 dànhuáng [个 gè]

you PRONOUN
1 你 nǐ *(singular)*
□ Do you like football? 你喜欢足球吗? Nǐ xǐhuan zúqiú ma? □ Can I help you? 我能帮你吗? Wǒ néng bāng nǐ ma? □ It's for you. 给你的。Gěi nǐde. □ She's younger than you. 她比你年轻。Tā bǐnǐ niánqīng.
2 你们 nǐmen *(plural)*
□ Do you like football? 你们喜欢足球吗? Nǐmen xǐhuan zúqiú ma? □ I saw you. 我看到你们了。Wǒ kàndào nǐmen le. □ I'll come with you. 我会跟你们去。Wǒ huì gēn nǐmen qù.
3 任何人 rènhérén *(one)*
□ You must look both ways when crossing the road. 任何人在过马路时都要看路的两边。Rènhérén zài guòmǎlùshí dōuyào kànlùde liǎngbiān.
■ **You never know.** 谁知道。Shuí zhīdào.

young ADJECTIVE
年轻的 niánqīng de
■ **young people** 年轻人 niánqīngrén

younger ADJECTIVE
更年轻 gèngniánqīng
□ He's younger than me. 他比我更年轻。Tā bǐ wǒ gèngniánqīng. □ my younger brother 我弟弟 wǒdìdi □ my younger sister 我妹妹 wǒmèimei

youngest ADJECTIVE
最小的 zuìxiǎode
□ my youngest brother 我最小的弟弟 wǒ zuìxiǎode dìdi. □ She's the youngest. 她是最小的。Tā shì zuìxiǎode.

your ADJECTIVE
1 你的 nǐ de *(of one person)*
□ your brother 你的兄弟 nǐde xiōngdì □ your sister 你的姐妹 nǐde jiěmèi □ your parents 你的父母 nǐde fùmǔ □ Would you like to wash your hands? 你要洗手吗? Nǐ yào xǐshǒu ma? □ your friend *(male)* 你的朋友 nǐde péngyǒu
2 你们的 nǐmen de *(of more than one person)*
□ your house 你们的房子 nǐmende fángzi □ your seats 你们的座位 nǐmende zuòwèi

yours PRONOUN
1 你的 nǐ de *(of one person)*
□ Is this yours? 这是你的吗? Zhèshì nǐ de ma? □ I've lost my pen. Can I use yours? 我的笔丢了。我可以用你的吗? Wǒdebǐ diūle. Wǒ kěyǐ yòng nǐde ma?
2 你们的 nǐmen de *(of more than one person)*
□ I like that car. Is it yours? 我喜欢那辆车。是你们的吗? Wǒ xǐhuan nàliàngchē. Shìnǐmende ma? □ my parents and yours 我的父母和你们的 wǒde fùmǔ hé nǐmende
■ **Yours sincerely...** 你真挚的 Nǐ zhēnzhì de
■ **Yours faithfully...** 你忠实的 Nǐzhōngshíde

yourself PRONOUN
1 你自己 nǐzìjǐ
□ Have you hurt yourself? 你伤了你自己吗? Nǐ shāngle nǐzìjǐ ma? □ Tell me about yourself! 告诉我关于你自己的事情! Gàosù wǒ guānyú nǐzìjǐde shìqíng! □ Do it yourself! 你自己做! Nǐzìjǐ zuò!
2 你 nǐ *(you)*
□ an intelligent person like yourself 像你一样聪明的人 xiàng nǐ yíyàng cōngmíngde rén
■ **by yourself 1** *(unaided)* 独立地 dúlì de
□ Did you do your homework by yourself? 你的家庭作业是你独立作的吗? Nǐde jiātíngzuòyè shì nǐ dúlì zuòde ma?
2 *(alone)* 独自地 dúzì de
□ Do you live by yourself? 你独自住吗? Nǐ dúzì zhù ma?

yourselves PRONOUN
1 你们自己 nǐmen zìjǐ
□ Did you enjoy yourselves? 你们玩得开心吗? Nǐmen wánde kāixīn ma? □ Did you make it yourselves? 是你们自己做的吗? Shì nǐmenzìjǐ zuòde ma?
2 你们 nǐmen *(you)*
■ **by yourselves 1** *(unaided)* 独力地 dúlì de **2** *(alone)* 独自地 dúzì de

youth club NOUN
青年俱乐部 qīngnián jùlèbù [个 gè]

youth hostel NOUN
青年招待所 qīngnián zhāodàisuǒ [个 gè]

Yugoslavia NOUN
南斯拉夫 Nánsīlāfū
□ in the former Yugoslavia 在前南斯拉夫 zài qián Nánsīlāfū

English-Chinese

y

Zz

zany ADJECTIVE
滑稽的 huájìde
zebra NOUN
斑马 bānmǎ [匹 pǐ]
zebra crossing NOUN
斑马线 bānmǎxiàn [条 tiáo]
zero NOUN
1 零 líng [个 gè] *(number)*
□ 5 degrees below zero 零下五度 língxià wǔdù
2 没有 méiyǒu *(nothing)*
Zimbabwe NOUN
津巴布韦 Jīnbābùwéi
■ **in Zimbabwe** 在津巴布韦 zài Jīnbābùwéi
Zimmer frame® NOUN
齐默式助行架 qímòshìzhùxíngjià
zip NOUN
▷ *see also* **zip** VERB
拉链 lāliàn [条 tiáo]
to **zip** VERB
▷ *see also* **zip** NOUN
1 拉拉链 lālāliàn *(a coat)*
2 压缩 yāsuō *(a file)*
zip code NOUN (US)
邮政编码 yóuzhèng biānmǎ [个 gè]
zipper NOUN (US)
拉链 lāliàn [条 tiáo]
zit NOUN
青春痘 qīngchūn dòu
zodiac NOUN
十二宫图 shíèrgōngtú
LANGUAGE TIP Word for word, this means **twelve palace pictures**. **Palace** here refers to the celestial houses of the horoscope.
□ the signs of the zodiac 黄道十二宫 huángdào shíèrgōng
zone NOUN
地带 dìdài [个 gè] *(area)*
zoo NOUN
动物园 dòngwùyuán [个 gè]
zoom lens NOUN
变焦透镜 biànjiāotòujìng [块 kuài]
zucchini NOUN (US)
绿皮密生西葫芦 lǜpí mìshēng xīhúlu [个 gè]